THE POLITICS OF CULTURE
IN
SOVIET-OCCUPIED
GERMANY, 1945-1949

David Pike

THE POLITICS OF CULTURE IN SOVIET-OCCUPIED GERMANY, 1945-1949

STANFORD UNIVERSITY PRESS
STANFORD, CALIFORNIA

Stanford University Press

Stanford, California

© 1992 by the Board of Trustees of the

Leland Stanford Junior University

Printed in the United States of America

CIP data appear at the end of the book

For Jane and the girls

CONTENTS

PREFACE

This book was nearly finished when the wall that divided East from West Berlin, and one Germany from the other, fell; and in retrospect, I cannot escape the feeling that the decade or so that I spent writing it paralleled the final agony of the East German regime. When I arrived in the country for a six-month stay in January 1979, Erich Honecker was at the height of his power, and the party that he headed did not relish the presence of American scholars who hoped to use East Germany's exchange agreement with the United States to examine archival material related to the history of the German Communist or Socialist Unity party. In 1979, I was at work on an earlier book, *German Writers in Soviet Exile, 1933-1945* (which I already assumed would develop into this one); and to this day, I consider my success in gaining access to unpublished materials held in the archives of the Akademie der Künste, limited as it was, to be miraculous. Granted, the miracle was made possible in part by several archivists who took the risk of allowing me a glimpse at the files—certain in their own minds, I am sure, that change in East Germany had to begin with a candid reassessment of party history and the country's own past. Still, I was shown only portions of the holdings, and some of these archivists have spent their time since the fall of the wall making the most of recently "discovered" materials, there all along, the existence of which they earlier denied in conversations with me. But I saw nothing then in the former Zentrales Staatsarchiv in Potsdam, which remained closed to me, nor in the Zentrales Parteiarchiv within the Institut für Marxismus-Leninismus. When I returned to the country in winter 1984, again as an exchange scholar and again trying to use ostensibly binding agreements to gain admission to those repositories, I encountered further obstacles that included persistent efforts to keep me out of East Germany altogether. What I did not know, and found out only during my third stay in winter 1989, was that my efforts to work in the Institute of Marxism-Leninism in 1979 backfired. According to instructions drawn up within the East German interior ministry, I was to be denied permanently admission to *any* state archive.

In 1984, and again in 1989, following five intervening years in which the authorities managed to block my return to the country altogether, I took it for granted that the publication of *German Writers in Soviet Exile* in 1981 was the cause of the hostility. After all, while in East Germany three years later, I found myself branded in *Die Weltbühne* as a "producer of imperialist ideology" who had written a book that misused "objective contradictions in developments of the past," as well as individual "subjective misinterpretations of the situation," to disqualify Communist strategy and tactics in the nineteen thirties altogether.* The subject of my book then was the fate of German Communist politicians and intellectuals who fled to the Soviet Union after 1933 and perished, in horrifying numbers, in Stalin's camps. These matters were rarely ever alluded to in East Germany. In fact, the party daily, *Neues Deutschland*, published a commemorative article on the occasion of Stalin's one hundredth birthday in 1979 that barely managed a reference to his "theoretical and practical mistakes."† But Stalin's decimation of German Communists, most of whom hallowed the ground that he walked on, always seemed to me to belong at the center of any discussion of the history of German communism through the war's end. I also took it for granted that the unique experience of the survivors, scarred for life by what J. R. Becher later called the "jungle-like atmosphere" of those years in Soviet exile,‡ provided the best context for a fuller understanding of the thinking of those who returned home sadly unreconstructed—still unable to envision a Germany uncorrupted by the political, ideological, and cultural malevolence of Stalinism. Becher may have understood this after Stalin had been denounced by Khrushchev at the twentieth party congress of the Soviet Communist party in 1956. Feeling the pangs of a guilty conscience, Becher confessed the following in a poem that remained unpublished until the German Democratic Republic had effectively ceased to exist:

> He who has had his backbone broken once
> Can scarcely be persuaded
> To be upright in his conduct
> Because memories
> Of the broken back
> Frightened him—
>
> Even
> After the fracture has long since healed
> And there no longer exists any reason
> To break one's own back.§

---

*See Hiebel, "Weiskopf in Prag," *Die Weltbühne* 11 (1984): 341-45.
†Teschner, "Zum 100. Geburtstag J. W. Stalins," *Neues Deutschland*, 21 December 1979.
‡See Müller, *Die Säuberung. Moscow 1936: Stenogramm einer geschlossenen Parteiversammlung*, p. 50.
§"Wem einmal das Rückgrat gebrochen wurde, / Der ist kaum dazu zu bewegen, / Eine aufrechte Haltung einzunehmen, / Denn die Erinnerung / An das gebrochene Rückgrat / Schreckte ihn. / Auch dann noch, / Wenn die Bruchstelle längst verheilt is / Und keinerlei Anlaß mehr gegeben ist, / Sich das Rückgrat zu brechen." Becher, "Gedichte" ["Gebranntes Kind"], *Sinn und Form* 2 (1990): 344.

Reflecting now upon my ten years of work on this book, I think that I was probably fortunate, in a strange way, to have been denied access to the archives in the eighties. The unavailability of unpublished materials forced me to engage first in a far more meticulous study of what I might otherwise have underestimated as mostly extraneous information—the enormous public record of the Communist or Socialist Unity party itself and all of its affiliated organizations. I remember thinking in the beginning that there would likely be only a few scattered facts, previously unknown, worth establishing on the basis of these materials; and if the doors to the archives had swung open at that moment, I might well have focused my attention upon this kind of more "authentic" information, neglecting to scrutinize available materials with the necessary care out of a feeling that published commentaries and public statements had been largely successful in hiding the true nature of events. As a consequence, I fear that I would have been guilty of what Sergej Tjulpanov characterized, in private conversation with top German Communists, as their "underestimation of ideology as a means of control."* Or, to put the matter in Stalin's own words, I would probably not have tried first to trace the tiniest fluctuations and nuances of the ideologically "correct line," the effective implementation of which, according to Stalin, then hinged upon organizational work that focused upon the "right selection of people," upon "supervising adherence to the resolutions of the regulatory organs."† As it was, having already constructed my book around an exhaustive examination of ideological rhetoric, which yielded surprising results and included an analysis of cultural corollaries, I found myself in a unique position to consider just such discussions of executive strategies when a wealth of unpublished matter suddenly became accessible after 1989. This material then fit remarkably well into my previous treatment of available information, corroborating and confirming earlier suppositions, but also allowed for an inquiry into additional undertakings, such as the development of censorship, about which next to nothing was known.

Wherever extant materials permitted it, I have also discussed the dealings of the Soviet military administration (SMAD) with German Communists and with organizations run openly or surreptitiously by them. This is not a study of the SMAD itself, however;‡ though ultimately indispensable to a definitive treatment of politics and culture in Soviet-occupied Germany, such an

---

* Tulpanow Bericht. Bericht über innerparteiliche Lage im letzten Halbjahr I u. II 47. Zentrales Parteiarchiv, NL 36/734/300.

†Stalin, "Rechenschaftsbericht an den XVII. Parteitag," *Fragen des Leninismus*, pp. 577-79.

‡I refer the reader to the best of what is currently available on the subject: Foitzik, "Sowjetische Militäradministration," *SBZ-Handbuch*, pp. 7-69, and Strunk, "Die Sowjetische Militäradministration in Deutschland (SMAD) und ihr politischer Kontrollapparat," *Sowjetisches Modell und nationale Prägung*, pp. 143-176. Tjulpanow's memoirs, *Deutschland nach dem Kriege (1945-1949)*, can also be read profitably if certain allowances are made for his efforts to avoid the real issues.

examination is impossible until the records of the occupation regime are accessible, without restriction, to outside scholars. These materials may or may not alter the facts and findings presented in my book, though they will surely augment them. Nor can my necessarily peripheral discussion of Soviet policy and Stalin's objectives in occupied Germany replace an exhaustive investigation into the thinking within Stalin's own entourage, his secretariat, the party apparatus, state agencies, and of instructions given to top officers and diplomats of the occupation administration in Germany. This kind of reconstruction, provided that more or less complete records have even survived, is central to a final verdict on the nature of Soviet objectives in occupied Germany and requires further research. The lingering mysteries surrounding the personality of Stalin himself also stand in the way of definitive conclusions; though Soviet archives will no doubt shed light on some of these, important questions pertaining to the state of his mind may never be answered, and it is entirely possible that Stalin's intentions at any given moment can never be established.

I could not have written this book without the unusually generous support and constant encouragement of the Alexander von Humboldt-Stiftung. I am especially grateful to the president of the foundation, Heinrich Pfeiffer, and to Thomas Berberich, whose interest in the project never slackened. My three extended visits to East Germany were made possible by the International Research and Exchanges Board (IREX) and contributed to a general understanding of the German Democratic Republic that would have been far less complete had I been compelled to form opinions about the country from a distance. Ursula Heukenkamp, who served as my liaison to the Humboldt University during my stay in 1989, deserves a special word of thanks for an association with me that was not without some risk. I also received a fellowship from the American Council of Learned Societies (ACLS) in the spring of 1991 that enabled me, late in the game, to spend the necessary time in the archives. Finally, I benefited immensely during years of research and writing from the friendship of Wolfgang and Hildegard Holl, Berlin, and Ernst and Carola Paulsen, Bonn. My memories of work on this book will forever be connected in my mind with fond recollections of the time spent with them and of their continual inspiration. The debt of gratitude that I owe three other companions has been expressed on an earlier page.

David Pike
October 1992

PART ONE:

DOCTRINAL ADJUSTMENTS AND CULTURAL COROLLARIES (1945-1949)

CHAPTER ONE

Sovietization or Democracy?

The leaders of the German Communist party (KPD) left the Soviet Union in spring 1945 anxious to take advantage of opportunities at home. The Red Army now occupied part of Germany, and the Communists fully expected to benefit from their close relationship with the Russians. On 4 June 1945, for instance, Walter Ulbricht, Anton Ackermann, and Gustav Sobottka rejoined Wilhelm Pieck in Moscow for consultations with Stalin, Zhdanov, and Molotov. During these talks, Stalin said that he expected "two Germanies" to emerge in the aftermath of the war, but he also talked about the need to secure German unity through a "unified KPD, a unified C[entral] C[ommittee], a unified party of working Germans, a unified party at the center."[1] Because neither assessment lent itself to public acknowledgment, however, the discussions must have concentrated on those phrases in the party's impending "proclamation" that professed a desire for cooperation with other "antifascist democratic" parties and future "mass organizations" at the expense of the KPD's traditional ambitions.[2] But coming from a party notorious for its commitment to revolution and dictatorship, the sudden interest in democracy had a hollow ring to it, though revolution and dictatorship were what the Communists ruled out after alluding to the fact that in years past they had indeed considered a "Soviet system" best for Germany. Without such an admission, their new promise of democracy made no sense; with it, the Communists could logically conclude that "forcing the Soviet system upon Germany" would be mistaken because such an approach conflicted with "current circumstances." The better way "in the present situation" called for an antifascist-democratic regime that offered its citizens the assurance of traditional rights and liberties.[3]

The trouble with phrases like "under current circumstances" or "in the present situation" was that they paved the way for the abandonment of a

---

[1]Bericht - Walter, Ackermann, Sobottka am 4. 6. 1945 um 6 Uhr bei Stal[in], Mol[otov], Shdan-[ov]. Zentrales Parteiarchiv, NL 36/629/62-4.
[2]According to Paul Wandel, who was still in Moscow at the time, Georgij Dimitrov, Palmiro Togliatti, and Dmitrij Manuilskij also helped formulate the document that first presented the KPD's new political program to the postwar public. (In conversation with the author in 1989.)
[3]"Aufruf der Kommunistischen Partei Deutschlands," *Deutsche Volkszeitung*, 13 June 1945.

promise without requiring it to be formally broken; and their presence suggests that the authors of the document had their reasons for including them in it. After the discussions in Moscow were over, developments then unfolded in rapid succession. The Soviet military administration or SMAD came into being on the basis of its own order no. 1 on 9 June; the SMAD issued its second decree on the 10th, permitting political parties and "mass organizations";[4] the KPD delegation returned to Germany the same day; the party formally reconstituted itself on the 11th; and the proclamation, also dated the 11th, appeared in the inaugural issue of the party newspaper on 13 June. This kind of methodical reorganization had acquired particular urgency because Stalin seems to have used the discussions in Moscow to tell the Germans that he would permit organized political activity in the first place; whereas, before the talks, they thought that no plans existed for the reestablishment of any political parties, theirs included.[5] The prospect of rival organizations now, whose existence was intended to foster the impression of a developing democracy, then generated the need for creative tactics in pursuit of the kind of party dominance alluded to by Stalin in the discussions recorded by Pieck. On the one hand, the earliest known postwar plans for the reorganization of the KPD, prepared in Moscow and dated 9 June 1945, called for a campaign in support of the party's platform and the "bloc of antifascist parties," as well as the creation of "free trade unions"; but on the other hand, they provided for party branches at the local level, the publication of official newspapers, and the formulation of ideas related to work in "all" areas of activity. These plans also assigned responsibility for the formation of a Kulturbund or cultural league to Wilhelm Pieck—weeks before it was set up as an organization with no acknowledged party affiliation. The plans provided additionally for a provisional central committee comprised of the sixteen Communists whose signatures appeared on the appeal, thirteen émigrés from the Soviet Union; as well as for a five-man secretariat whose first three members were Ulbricht, Ackermann, and Pieck.[6]

But Pieck's impressions of the conversation with Stalin remain the best indication of Soviet intentions toward occupied Germany right after the war and, possibly, of Stalin's doubts about the reliability of the German Communists. For instance, if Pieck's notes reflect Stalin's remarks correctly, and if Stalin had any intention of acting upon them, then the idea that national

---

[4]See "Befehl Nr. 1. Über die Organisation der Militärverwaltung zur Verwaltung der sowjetischen Besatzungszone in Deutschland [9 June 1945]"; and "Befehl Nr. 2 [10 June 1945]," in *Befehle des Obersten Chefs der Sowjetischen Militärverwaltung in Deutschland*, pp. 9-10.

[5]As late as 30 May 1945, Ulbricht apparently had no idea that he would soon be beckoned to Moscow; and it appears that the SMAD only recently allowed KPD functionaries and "comrades" to schedule meetings. See Ulbricht's letter to Pieck, in Ulbricht, *Zur Geschichte der deutschen Arbeiterbewegung*, vol. II, 1933-1946, Zusatzband, p. 207.

[6]Nächste zentrale Aufgaben der Parteiführung auf Grund des Aufrufes des ZK der KPD. 9 June 1945. Zentrales Parteiarchiv. NL 36/734/34-35.

unity hinged upon the preeminence of the Communist party prefigured the development of two Germanies—whether Stalin realized it in spring 1945 or not. For in the absence of a willingness to subject the KPD to the whims of real democracy, party dominance required a degree of SMAD favoritism that made a mockery of bloc politics and dramatically reduced prospects for reunification. In this respect, the simple fact that Stalin "consulted" with the German Communists in June 1945 at all, perfectly normal to those involved and a practice that continued, augured ill for the future of the nation as a whole; and the same can be said of the fact that party leaders referred to SMAD officers privately as "comrades."[7] Indeed, Stalin's references to "two Germanies" *and* German unity already captured a sense of the later division because unification occurred to him and the officers of the SMAD who carried out his orders only in connection with broadening the party's influence. The KPD's perception of its right to rule and the relentless pursuit of practical measures calculated to ensure it worsened prospects for unification immensely; and if Stalin failed to foresee the consequences in June 1945, he must have grasped the fact soon after. Otherwise the need for interim politics defined as "very elastic" would not have been a subject of discussions between the Communists and officers and diplomats of the SMAD.[8] But "elasticity" was a tactical, not practical consideration; and one searches in vein for any private hint of concern about the divisive consequences of local policies in discussions between party leaders and SMAD representatives whose opinions must have reflected impressions of their own talks with Stalin. Even early conversations in "Karlshorst," the headquarters of the SMAD, disclose an inflexibility that developed only gradually into an integral part of the party's public rhetoric. Lieutenant General Bokov, a leading member of the SMAD's military council, told Pieck in September 1945 that Germany's prospects for "strong growth" required the country to "draw near to the USSR"; spoke of the "road to democratization" and the "authority of the C[ommunists]" as if they were parallel objectives; complained of the defamatory "filth" flung at Communists, mostly by Social Democrats; apparently criticized the KPD for being too timid about "reaction"; and contrasted the "consistent" democratization in Soviet-occupied Germany with conditions in other zones.[9]

But if Stalin ever suspected that the local Communists would be powerless to extend their influence nationally based on the popular appeal of their political program, and that the allies would not allow them to achieve it through the use of methods possible in the Soviet zone, then he probably realized or came to realize that ensuring the dominance of the KPD risked

[7]See Pieck's early list of "responsible SMAD comrades," ibid., NL 36/734/10.
[8]See Pieck's notes of a talk with Vladimir Semjonov in late August 1945, ibid., NL 36/754/119.
[9]Gespräch mit Bockow am 25. 9. 1945 um 10 Uhr in Karlshorst. Zentrales Parteiarchiv. NL 36/734/129-33.

establishing full control in one zone at the price of diminished prospects for much influence outside of it. Later developments certainly proved that the one objective conflicted with the other, and it is not at all clear that any change in allied policy toward occupied Germany short of an acceptance of Soviet demands could have resolved the contradiction. Moreover, if the German Communists themselves sensed the implications, they must have been content to barter away national unity in return for Stalin's assurance of vast political influence. That offer is implicit in Pieck's record of discussions with Stalin; and if the Germans overlooked its disunifying implications, they may have missed the point because Stalin dazzled them with the one promise that he was unable to keep—political dominance *and* national unity. In fact, over the next several years the German Communists deluded themselves with the same rhetoric; and it is virtually impossible to know how many of them actually believed that both goals were attainable. As for Stalin, who almost certainly knew better, but trusted no one, it is entirely possible that he had other reasons for couching the argument in national terms. He could scarcely have ruled out the possibility that the Communists, once the consequences of the policy became obvious, might develop second thoughts and force him to pursue his objectives in Germany without their assistance. If so, his worries were unfounded; but whatever his intentions, Stalin needed the German Communists, maybe even as much as they needed him; and he perhaps figured that they were less likely to bolt if they believed in the sincerity of his commitment to German unity.

But Stalin's public support of German nationalism and the party's own posturing served additional purposes. These were related to the general uncertainties of the situation right after the war, the need to keep or appear to keep a variety of local and international options open, and the party's own reputation. After all, its past behavior and the history of international communism suggested that the initial display of multi-party democracy hid something less enduring than an honest commitment to sharing power. The KPD had rarely collaborated with rivals in the past for any reason other than to dispose of the need for cooperation, and these sporadic displays of moderation tended to materialize whenever the party's customary extremism pushed it to the fringe of German politics. This was especially true of the party's dealings with Social Democracy; and the coercion soon used to compel the SPD to "merge" with the KPD to form the Socialist Unity party (SED) in spring 1946 was a sure sign of things to come. Still, whether the prewar pattern of party conduct would hold completely this time around hinged on a variety of factors. Some of these resembled earlier cycles of moderation and extremism, others differed considerably or were, in 1945, still unknown. In spite of the fact that a reversion to the classic ideological mainstays of Marxism-Leninism and the Soviet-zone equivalent of one-party politics finally occurred, much of what was responsible for setting both the pace and direction of the German Communist party, primarily the shape of Soviet foreign policy, crystallized only with the passage of time. Even in light of Stalin's early reference to "two Germanies," the eventual outcome should not necessarily be regarded as a foregone conclusion, though it may have been; nor should it be seen rigidly as a conscious objective from the start. But it is true that skepticism about the future of the Soviet zone obstructed the party's pursuit of its more immediate goals in 1945 and 1946; that measures needed to be taken to stop the spread of apprehension about the party's ulterior motives; and that the manner in which the KPD's rhetoricians went about their job—making and breaking promises, bending the rhetoric to rationalize every assurance given and subsequently broken—reveals much about the party's takeover of power.

These circumstances created political and ideological challenges that the Communists had never encountered before. Given the nature of Soviet occupation, it must have been hard for them to think in terms of their own weakness and to see any reason for pretending that their differences with Social Democrats and everyone else was over. But the top party leaders had at least some sense of the fact that the restraint expected of them now was dictated by tactics, not weakness; and there was certainly nothing about their normal political inclinations to mark them as timid. If it sometimes seemed as if the top officers of the SMAD needed to prod the Germans periodically, the impression is misleading because the Russians just as frequently had to restrain them. In both politics and culture, what sometimes resembled hesitation during the first few years after the war resulted either from an assessment of tactical necessity or from uncertainty caused by the peculiar tactic, practiced by the SMAD in its dealings with the Communists, of building two emphases into a strategy with one favored objective. This allowed the SMAD officers or diplomats, whom Stalin probably kept in a similar position of uncertainty, to fault the Germans whenever they pleased by shifting the emphasis from one aspect of the tactics to the other. Vladimir Semjonov often voiced dissatisfaction with the performance of party leaders who followed his directives; it was a way of absolving himself of any responsibility for the insufficiencies of an approach generally and those arising out of circumstances beyond his control. Moreover, it was perfectly understandable that no Soviet diplomat or occupation officer accustomed to dealing with Stalin relished the thought of being faulted for the shortcomings of his policies; and they often appear to have blamed problems on the local Communists instead.[10] The records of internal discussions convey the impression that SMAD officers and diplomats regarded the behavior of their local counterparts alternately as overly hesitant or excessively zealous. But the tension caused by

[10]See Pieck's notes of a discussion with Semjonov on 28 August 1945. Zentrales Parteiarchiv. NL 36/734/121.

fluctuations between both poles was built into the strategy; the problems of a specific undertaking could always be attributed to the inability of party functionaries to strike the proper balance between inordinate zeal and insufficient resolve; whereas there was no such thing as a proper balance when dealing with doctrinal principles, only the pretense of one that was supposedly capable of reconciling the inherent contradiction between consensus democracy and single-party rule.

Nor is there any reason to believe that party leaders talked back to the representatives of the SMAD or the Soviet government, much less to Stalin himself, when criticized unfairly. There was frequent negotiation over day-to-day issues of administration and tactics, but these kinds of discussions were a far cry from disagreements over policy decisions made at higher levels. None of this, however, was related to a natural reluctance on the part of the top Communists themselves; if the Russians had been prepared to take the risk internationally in 1945 or 1946, there is no indication that party leaders would have balked at doing then what they did later, but only in one third of Germany. As it was, the party's democratic gestures in 1945 and 1946 derived from the blend of its own strength in one zone and the hope of improving the much dimmer prospects for influencing events in the other. The party's self-restraint was the result of Stalin's sense of the necessity of abiding, or appearing to abide, by the policies of all four occupying powers. This posture delayed the complete seizure of power in one part of the country until opportunities for acquiring influence throughout the remainder, including reparations, had been exhausted.

The party's rhetoric itself indicates that the leaders had few doubts about their own ultimate objectives, only questions pertaining to the pace and problems devising language capable of concealing old proclivities. Self-restraint was ordinarily so alien to the reflexes of German Stalinists, the more so when presented with tantalizing opportunities, that most probably regarded the show of moderation instinctively as tactical. Tolerance toward rivals who fit the description of antifascist and democratic could never have been perceived as an end in itself for the simple reason that the entire concept was a synonym for Marxist-Leninist. In theory, this ought to have meant that the existence of more than one party was pointless; the thrust of the KPD's "unity" rhetoric suggested as much; and those parties that nonetheless defied the consensus because of its fraudulence were then vilified as antidemocratic opponents of a united antifascist Germany. But the Communists did so without indulging themselves quite yet in abuse derived from basic Marxist-Leninist notions of class warfare. Even if antifascist-democratic and Marxist-Leninist were considered synonymous political commitments, the Communists were initially cautious about saying so and, in fact, routinely denied it right after the war out of an awareness that none of the other political parties would be foolish enough to join in a voluntary "bloc" with the KPD on the basis of its orthodoxy. Even so, as part of the tactical process of differentiating publicly between antifascist-democratic and Marxist, but also because the Communists could never admit to a break with their own doctrine, they still needed to explain why their new democratic stance was still inherently compatible with Marxism-Leninism without being identical to it. As a consequence, the Communists rationalized what amounted to a radical change in tactics as the purest expression of their own convictions while clinging to the pillars of an orthodoxy whose past failures generated the need for a new approach to begin with. When the experiment ended ingloriously a few years later, they promptly justified the shift back to their original tenets by denouncing what they had just considered to be doctrinally definitive as a flagrant departure from sacrosanct principles. This is not to contend that the process unfolded as a result of intricate advanced planning, either Soviet or German Communist, only that this is what ultimately happened and that it evolved as an outgrowth of furtive policy-making on a day-to-day basis, designed to suit specific occasions and then altered with little regard for previous public assurances. But the manner in which this took place can only be understood by being mindful of the persistent adjustments in the larger context of developing Soviet foreign policy and the attempts to define, refine, and implement it in Soviet-occupied Germany. Suffice it to say that in 1945, without knowing exactly what was to come during the next few years, the upper echelon of party leaders would still have been right to assume that their prospects had never been brighter, if only in part of Germany and not necessarily immediately; and that they never heard otherwise in conversations with Soviet military officers responsible for the implementation of policy in occupied Germany or from Stalin himself.

Still, contingent upon the measured articulation of Soviet objectives in occupied Germany, the process developed slowly; and it was by no means understood at all times and in its many stages by the very personalities who carried it out. Those local Communists who wished for a road to power in greater conformity with basic doctrinal suppositions probably felt that prime opportunities had been squandered. Others, Communists who lived in the American and English zones while attempting to operate in Berlin, were even angrier. According to information obtained by the Soviet NKVD General Serov, these people argued that the SED needed to break with its "reformist pseudo-internationalism" because Soviet-Russian methods could not be transferred "mechanically" to the specific conditions of other countries. The second half of this assessment sounded just like official party arguments; but the thinking behind it derived from entirely different considerations. One of the oppositionists summed up the views of his group by explaining that "most SED leaders" were émigrés from the Soviet Union who represented the foreign policy of the USSR; fully implemented, their actions would benefit the "imperialist goals" of the Soviet Union, not the German working class.[11] Such groups may have posed no real threat to the SED in its own zone, but the ideas themselves and their implications for the party's nationalist posture were always dangerous. To refute them the party developed rhetoric designed to convey the impression that its older tactics represented outmoded practices of the past. This required the abbreviation of intrinsic ideological postulates to the point that only initiated insiders and knowledgeable outsiders could discern the original concepts; and the Communists then enveloped them in an expedient new language of democracy. Finally, they focused this rhetoric on the issue of national unity in an attempt to popularize party policies in the Western regions of the country by contrasting their national solutions with allied plans for "dismemberment."

Antifascism and Democracy

But from the beginning, the KPD's new devotion to democracy was widely regarded as just a passing relaxation of the party's natural inclinations; and things worsened considerably when the Communists forced the Social Democratic party into an unwanted merger in early 1946. Still, the Communists denied harboring any interest in a "single-party system,"[12] disputed the notion that the KPD or SED took orders from the Russians, and continued to extol their idea of a new democracy as the only national guarantee for the German people.[13] The Communists insisted accordingly that their conversion to democracy broke completely with the party's previous posture; but they also maintained that they had been democrats all along. In fact, the Communists insisted that the KPD spent the last twenty-seven years pursuing a *"unified basic line"* and that Marxism was to thank for the party's unblemished history of accomplishments. Because no rival organization benefited in a similar fashion from what was now called tactfully or tactically "consistent Marxism," as opposed to Marxism-Leninism, no party had had a chance of equaling the KPD's struggle against fascism in favor of democracy; and this flawless scientific doctrine placed the KPD far ahead of all other parties in its ability to deliver the nation from its current predicament now.[14] But the common assumption that the KPD's former radical conduct was built upon doctrinal premises still incompatible with democracy was the reason why the Communists restructured their new politics around the promise of antifas-

---

[11]Mitteilungen von Serow am 7. 8. 1946 über Arbeit oppos. Gruppen aus der alten KPD in Berlin gegen die Politik der SED [Pieck's notes], ibid., NL 36/723/197-99.

[12]See "Manifest an das deutsche Volk," *Dokumente der Sozialistischen Einheitspartei Deutschlands* [21 April 1946], p. 25.

[13]See Ackermann, "Um Sein oder Nichtsein unseres Volkes," *Deutsche Volkszeitung*, 13 January 1946.

[14]See *Der Spartakusbund und die Gründung der KPD*, p. 27.

cism *and* democracy. This twofold commitment contained the tacit admission that the KPD had always been antifascist, but not necessarily amply democratic. The slogan "antifascist-democratic" was supposed to provide the reassurance that the party would retain its opposition to fascism while moderating the rigid side of its policies with a more emphatic commitment to democracy. But these assurances also meant that the Communists failed to regard visions of democracy contrary to theirs as "consistently" antifascist; far worse, the same pair of concepts lent themselves to the old argument that "bourgeois democracies" used democratic superstructures to conceal a class dictatorship with an underlying fascist basis.

The Communists thus managed to build two sets of political and ideological options into their promise of antifascism and democracy without the need to opt yet in favor of one or the other. The more moderate possibility suggested greater programmatic flexibility through the party's disavowal of dictatorship and assurance of democracy, whereas the line of reasoning used to explain why rival perceptions of democracy were intrinsically dictatorial—and a certain kind of dictatorship utterly democratic—remained intact. The Communists naturally shied away from dissecting their early rhetoric like this because a close look at the implications of their devotion to both antifascism and democracy in 1945 would have focused attention less on what was new about the old than on the old in the new. But this in turn confronted the KPD with a dilemma. The Communists desperately needed to inspire confidence in their conversion to democracy; doing so required that they deal critically with their own past; and yet any admission of failure prior to 1933 or after Hitler's accession to power discredited the party's use of its own antifascism as the prime excuse for exercising its political prerogatives now. Without the antifascist nimbus, the KPD would have lost its key ideological advantage and been compelled to choose more forcefully between competing democratically with other parties or taking open advantage of its special relationship with the Russians.

Even with it, however, the Communists had to ignore key aspects of the party's past record because the KPD's adherence to Marxism-Leninism was chiefly responsible ideologically for its inability to respond effectively to fascism prior to 1933; and none of its doctrinal obsessions created quite as many problems for the KPD as the notion of fascism as the ultimate manifestation of monopoly capitalism. In particular, the deductions associated with this argument caused the Communists to spend twelve years anticipating the outbreak of a popular rebellion under Hitler. Starting in 1933, the party leadership thought that "dissatisfaction and indignation" was growing everywhere.[15] Five years later there was still no trace of a rebellion, but the party's exiled leadership imagined that the dimensions of the basic contra-

[15]Pieck, *We are fighting for a Soviet Germany*, p. 25.

diction between the ruled and the rulers had continued to grow.[16] This discontentedness never amounted to anything either; but the Communists dismissed the idea that the persistent absence of unrest bore witness to a broad consensus in support of Hitler as slander. They deluded themselves instead into thinking that fascism and the will of working Germans were incompatible, and once the war broke out the Communists assumed that the Nazis were even more vulnerable. By fall 1942, "growing misery, hunger, and depravation" had supposedly combined with Gestapo terror at home and casualties at the front to exacerbate contradictions between the masses and the "fascist-plutocratic upper stratum."[17] Finally, less than six months before the war's end, party leaders felt that fascism might continue to terrorize the people into submission for a while longer, but the inevitable rebellion would break out all the more suddenly.[18] The Communists clung to these illusions until spring 1945 and then shifted to a radically different theory of collective guilt without ever having speculated about the cause of the earlier thinking along the lines of "two Germanies." But then Soviet and Comintern illusions about German resistance to Hitler had easily matched the KPD's; just weeks after the German invasion, Stalin still felt confident that the Soviet Union would find allies not just in the peoples of Europe and America but also among Germans, who had been "enslaved" by the fascists;[19] and the Communists hailed his remarks as an expression of profound confidence in the German people.[20] Stalin's later statement that "the Hitlers come and go, but the German people, the German nation, remains,"[21] then survived the war and was repeated in Soviet-occupied Germany for many years to come.

The remark appears to contradict the argument that the concept of "two Germanies" had shifted to national or collective guilt, even though little was left of the earlier notion by spring 1945. True, as late as April 1945, Stalin sponsored an attack upon the Soviet writer and journalist Ilja Ehrenburg for writing articles that grouped ordinary Germans and Nazis, as Georgij Alexandrov said in *Pravda*, into a single "colossal band," whereas Alexandrov made it clear that no one had any intention of "exterminating" the German people along with the fascists;[22] and when the Russians new Soviet zone

[16]See Ulbricht, "Das Gebot der Stunde" and "Zur Lage in Deutschland," in Ulbricht, *Zur Geschichte der deutschen Arbeiterbewegung*, vol. II, 1933-1946, pp. 109 and 208-9.
[17]Ulbricht, "Die zunehmende Erschöpfung Deutschlands und die 'neue Phase' der deutschen Wirtschaft," ibid., pp. 276-78.
[18]Pieck, "Die KPD—ihr Aufbau und ihre organisationspolitischen Probleme [14 December 1944]," *Gesammelte Reden und Schriften*, vol. 6, p. 324.
[19]Stalin, "Vystuplenie po radio," *O velikoj otechestvennoj vojne*, p. 12.
[20]Pieck, "Im Sieg der Roten Armee liegt die Rettung des deutschen Volkes [7 July 1941]," Pieck, *Gesammelte Reden und Schriften*, vol. 6, p. 80.
[21]Stalin, "Prikaz narodnogo komissara oborony [23 February 1942]," *O velikoj otechestvennoj vojne*, p. 46.
[22]Alexandrov, "Genosse Ehrenburg vereinfacht!" *Tägliche Rundschau*, 16 May 1945.

daily featured the German translation of Alexandrov's article a month later, it appeared to breath new life into the idea of two Germanies. Stalin's earlier talk of the Hitlers who "come and go" was also compatible with it. But in the meantime, that celebrated remark had experienced a subtle shift in meaning. Useless as an expression of confidence in the existence of two Germanies under Hitler, the phrase served now as a gesture of reconciliation toward the local population—if they would just acknowledge their guilt. The retention of the slogan certainly made sense from this angle, except that contradictions developed when the increasing frequency of concurrent references to the blanket guilt of the German people interfered with the message of reconciliation with the German nation. In fact, the day before Alexandrov's article appeared in German, the *Tägliche Rundschau* reprinted Stalin's older remarks to the effect that Germans would prove to be loyal allies in the struggle against fascism. In one of the rare instances in which a Soviet newspaper denied Stalin the qualities of a prophet, the article added that his prediction had not come true.[23]

Few traces of the notion of two Germanies still lingered by the time the Communist party reorganized in the Soviet zone on 11 June 1945; and in its opening proclamation the KPD now declared that "millions and millions" of Germans had succumbed to Nazi ideology after all.[24] Because responsibility for the catastrophe fell upon "the entire German people," every single person had to atone for having done nothing to correct the impression that Hitler acted with their undiminished support.[25] The workers were included for the simple reason, the argument ran, that no regime based on violence and terror could have entrenched itself in power without the acquiescence of labor.[26] Of course, the Communists had claimed for over twelve years that Gestapo terror accounted for the absence of mass unrest, but the assumption that Hitler waged war only by means of the "most cruel terror against his own people" was brushed aside. "Imperialist, militarist ideology" had extended its roots deeply into the people,[27] and the Communists now belittled talk of repression as a cowardly excuse used to blame "the fateful passivity and the culpability of the German people" exclusively on Nazi terror;[28] even the Gestapo would have been "helpless and impotent" had Nazi ideology not taken hold of the masses.[29] Moreover, however true it was that countless numbers

[23]"Die Zeitung der Roten Armee in Berlin," *Tägliche Rundschau*, 15 May 1945.
[24]"Aufruf der Kommunistischen Partei Deutschlands," *Deutsche Volkszeitung*, 13 June 1945.
[25]See "Kundgebung der KPD," *Tägliche Rundschau*, 10 July 1945; and Pieck, "Antifaschistische Einheitsfront der demokratischen Parteien," *Deutsche Volkszeitung*, 17 July 1945.
[26]"Hitler—der Mörder der deutschen Arbeiterschaft," *Tägliche Rundschau*, 1 June, 1945; and "Großkundgebung der KPD," *Deutsche Volkszeitung*, 20 September 1945.
[27]See Ulbricht, "Erste Funktionärskonferenz der KPD Groß-Berlins," *Einheitsfront der antifaschistisch-demokratischen Parteien*, p. 15.
[28]"Die Mitschuld des deutschen Volkes," *Deutsche Volkszeitung*, 10 July 1945.
[29]Ibid.; "War illegaler Kampf möglich?" *Deutsche Volkszeitung*, 17 July 1945.

had been sacrificed in the struggle waged by labor's "antifascist avant-garde," the workers' interests were poorly served by equating "the avant-garde with the working class as a whole."[30] Much the same was said of Germans generally—without an acknowledgment of guilt, the people would never move in the direction of a "new democratic Germany."[31]

Within weeks of the war's end, the Communists had started talking about a broad antifascist-democratic consensus; and it soon became routine for them to speak in terms of a "mass movement" to argue that considerable segments of the population favored the KPD's policies.[32] As early as June 1945, an editorial in the party daily spoke of the assumption among working people that the Germans would have been spared the horrors of the war had they heeded the party's warnings.[33] A few days later, the paper even claimed that "millions" looked upon the Communists as the representatives of that party whose entire activity was calculated to save Germany from ruin. Having been "right in the past," broad segments of the people listened to what the Communists had to say about the future now.[34] But unless one assumes that masses of Germans had quickly recovered what the Communists so recently called their lost "sense of justice and decency,"[35] the notion of an antifascist ground swell squared poorly with the idea of collective guilt. Because they served equally useful rhetorical purposes, however, the Communists began equivocating on the subject of collective guilt within days of introducing it. Whenever ordinary Germans balked at the policies of the KPD, they were excoriated for exhibiting political irresponsibility typical of their behavior during the years of fascism and for refusing to embrace the ideals of a new democracy. But at the same time, the Communists cultivated the impression of a popular ground swell by speaking in the name of the people, and they often used this fiction as the justification for policies to which, turning the argument around yet again, the people were expected to conform if they wished to atone for the past. Besides, it stood to reason that Germans would respond better to "greater differentiation," as SMAD officers suggested to Ulbricht, in the matter of "war guilt."[36]

The key idea to emerge from the notion of a ground swell, however, was the KPD's insistence on the need for unity in the struggle to eradicate fas-

---

[30]"Großkundgebung der KPD," *Deutsche Volkszeitung*, 20 September 1945.
[31]Ulbricht, "Erste Funktionärskonferenz der KPD Groß-Berlin," *Einheitsfront der antifaschistisch-demokratischen Parteien*, pp. 17-18; Pieck, "Der Weg zum Wiederaufbau Deutschlands," *Deutsche Volkszeitung*, 21 July 1945.
[32]See Oelßner, "Freund und Führer des Volkes," *Wilhelm Pieck. Dem Vorkämpfer für ein neues Deutschland zum 70. Geburtstag*, pp. 80-81.
[33]"Partei des schaffenden Volkes," *Deutsche Volkszeitung*, 27 June 1945.
[34]"Die Bewährungsprobe," *Deutsche Volkszeitung*, 3 July 1945.
[35]"Aufruf der Kommunistischen Partei Deutschlands," *Deutsche Volkszeitung*, 13 June 1945.
[36]Information von Walter Ulbricht über ein Gespräch mit Bockow, Tulpanow, Wolkow am 22. 12. 1945. Zentrales Parteiarchiv. NL 36/734/144.

cism and establish democracy. The proclamation that remarked upon the millions of Germans who succumbed to Nazi ideology also talked about the growing awareness of the extent of the recent catastrophe to which past rifts within German politics had contributed; and this recognition supposedly caused the "impulse toward unity" to burst forth "more and more powerfully."[37] The Communists also used arguments in favor of unity to justify the exercise of what they took to be their natural prerogatives. They argued that Germany's only hope as a nation lay in national unity and attributed the "particularism" of the past to the unwillingness of various political parties to work together for the good of the nation.[38] The Communists thus used what they derided as party "squabbling" to brand differences of opinion as harmful to the cause of democracy and conducive to the restoration of fascism. They reasoned similarly in an attempt to influence the implementation of the "unity of action" agreement entered into by the Communists and Social Democrats as the first step leading toward a "single, unified party."[39] But none of the rhetoric was ever couched in zonal terms; the Communists argued that the consensus on vital national issues called for by their program would spread to all portions of Germany to produce the only kind of unanimity capable of barring the return of fascism and safeguarding democracy. Reverting to the idea of collective guilt, however, they also contended that this political framework could be used to help the German people atone for their guilt, develop a "genuine democratic consciousness," and find the way to a future free of reaction and fascism.[40] Unity alone assured victory, and to all those who wished to work toward these ends the Communists offered their cooperation in order "to turn this united front of four antifascist-democratic parties into a united front comprised of the German people and all other democratic and peace-loving peoples."[41] It was imperative, therefore, that all special interests be subordinated to the goal of a unified democratic Germany in conformity with what Pieck called the importance of putting "das Vaterland über alles";[42] indeed, he said in summer 1945, Germans frowned upon "those elements who consider party bickering to be more important."[43]

This was the kind of rhetoric used to question the effectiveness of multiparty systems even as the Communists tried to establish their own democra-

[37]"Aufruf der Kommunistischen Partei Deutschlands," *Deutsche Volkszeitung*, 13 June 1945.
[38]See Roerig, "Politisch unreif? Politisch unfähig?" *Tägliche Rundschau*, 28 March 1946.
[39]See "Die antifaschistisch-demokratische Einheit ist da [14 July 1945]" and "Vereinbarung des Zentralkomitees der Kommunistischen und des Zentralausschusses der Sozialdemokratischen Partei Deutschlands [19 June 1945]," *Einheitsfront der antifaschistisch-demokratischen Parteien*, pp. 42-45.
[40]"Die Einheit garantiert den Sieg," *Deutsche Volkszeitung*, 14 August 1945.
[41]"Das Wollen der antifaschistischen Einheitsfront," *Tägliche Rundschau*, 14 August 1945.
[42]Pieck, "Um die Einheit der deutschen Nation," *Deutsche Volkszeitung*, 1 February 1946.
[43]Pieck, "Feste Einheit der demokratischen Kräfte," *Einheitsfront der antifaschistisch-demokratischen Parteien*, p. 12.

tic credentials by championing a four-party alliance. The concept of "unity" implied a willingness to cooperate with other parties in the interest of a common cause; but it also functioned rhetorically to pressure them into adapting to the policies of the only party claiming to be in the privileged possession of consistently antifascist-democratic attributes. In other words, the notion of "unity," in the form of a mass movement or as a popular ground swell, used less doctrinally offensive language to restate old arguments pertaining to the leading role of the Communist party. Worse, phrases like "das Vaterland über alles," to say nothing of concepts like "German movement," as well as the party's habit of calling competition among parties divisive political bickering, were transparent attempts to use popular attitudes formed under Hitler to the party's advantage. Rhetoric first favoring, then opposing the merger of KPD and SPD in a single Socialist Unity party relied upon similar manipulation. For various reasons, in summer 1945 the Social Democrats advocated unification of the two parties. The Communists rejected the overtures, Ulbricht's reason being that a "new type of unified party of working-class people" required absolute clarity regarding socialism in the Soviet Union and "Marxism-Leninism." This was true, but Ulbricht resorted to the idea of collective guilt to make the point. Because fascism had so devastated class consciousness, the workers lagged behind the advances of the "science of Marxism and Leninism";[44] and until "ideological questions" had been resolved, talk of merging the two parties was premature.

By the time the Communists reconsidered in fall 1945, however, the Social Democrats had reversed themselves and now resisted pressure to merge; whereupon the Communists grew all the more insistent that the popular unity of antifascist-democratic elements nationwide was the only way of advancing the interests of national unity. Moreover, the organizational expression of the existing consensus was the bloc of antifascist-democratic parties, and the success of this coalition was in turn said to hinge upon the stability possible only through unification of the labor movement. The merger had become an "urgent national necessity" because every step in the direction of labor unity promised to strengthen national unity.[45] Finally, the Communists capped their rhetoric with apocalyptic contrasts between the likely "destruction" or "enslavement" of the German people in the absence of steps toward complete democratization and the party's millenarian vision of the "dawning of a new age."[46] The problem was that the Communists insisted upon playing the "leading role in the antifascist-democratic movement," leading critics to predict that "unity" meant "the death of democracy."[47] Ulbricht's guess

[44]Ulbricht, "Erste Funktionärskonferenz der KPD Groß-Berlins," ibid., p. 26.
[45]"Die zweite Phase der Einheit," *Tägliche Rundschau*, 27 December 1945.
[46]Pieck, *Probleme der Vereinigung von KPD und SPD* [2-3 March 1946], p. 7; "Die zweite Phase der Einheit," *Tägliche Rundschau*, 27 December 1945.
[47]Pieck, in *Probleme der Vereinigung von KPD und SPD*, pp. 9 and 15.

that Social Democrats who wondered whether the Communists went "far enough in their espousal of consequent democracy" would change their minds if they competed with the KPD "in the struggle for the democratic construction" was empty rhetoric.[48] The more insistently the party pushed for the "democratization of our national existence" while claiming exclusivity,[49] the greater the suspicion that transplanting the Soviet system to Germany remained the real issue. The theory of collective guilt figured prominently here, too; the Communists argued that their ideas regarding the "new democratic Germany" coincided with the needs of the nation, and these reflected the necessity of completing the "democratic renewal begun in 1848." Because the majority of the people had so recently tied their destiny to "such a reactionary and uncontrollable imperialist regime," "forcing the Soviet system upon Germany would be wrong and end in an utter fiasco."[50]

These arguments seldom occurred in the absence of efforts to impugn the motives of anyone mistrustful of this underlying promise. Prior to the war's end, the Communists said, the Soviet government had declared that it would leave the social systems in nations occupied by the Red Army alone. Though the Nazis had always dismissed this declaration as camouflage for "violent world-revolutionary plans," Hitler's defeat and the triumph of the Red Army had not produced the prompt "bolshevization of Germany." But talk of this prospect still influenced broad segments of the people in spite of the party's assurances that its advocacy of an antifascist-democratic regime was "no underhanded tactic, diplomacy, or camouflage."[51] None of these assurances persuaded Social Democrats of the wisdom of merger. Some may have gone along, but many concluded that unification was no more than a way of rejuvenating the Communist party through the use of Social-Democratic "blood donors." In response the Communists referred to the notion that they intended to "start" with Social Democracy before devouring the Christian and Liberal Democrats, leaving only a single party, as "scandalous nonsense."[52] Moreover, Ulbricht assured Social Democrats that the unity party would not be run internally like a "dictatorship"; the Communists were not in the business of "dictating" to others;[53] whereas Pieck professed bewilderment at the worries of Social Democrats that they might not be able to hold their own after unification, asking, "Hold their own against whom?" The idea was

[48]Ulbricht, "Offene Antwort an sozialdemokratische Genossen," *Deutsche Volkszeitung,* 16 February 1946.
[49]See Ackermann, "Wohin soll der Weg gehen?" *Einheitsfront der antifaschistisch-demokratischen Parteien,* pp. 34-37.
[50]Ibid., p. 35.
[51]The above quotations are from ibid., pp. 34-35.
[52]Pieck, "Einheit sichert den Aufstieg unseres Volkes," *Deutsche Volkszeitung,* 12 March 1946.
[53]Ulbricht, "Offene Antwort an sozialdemokratische Genossen," *Deutsche Volkszeitung,* 16 January 1946; "Die Aufgaben der KPD im Kampf um die Herstellung der Einheit der Arbeiterklasse," *Zur Geschichte der deutschen Arbeiterbewegung,* Zusatzband, pp. 328-29.

"absolutely unproductive," considering that the Communists only wished to join forces with Social Democrats in fighting reaction;[54] and the necessity of doing so made resistance to unity "incomprehensible."[55]

Pieck's remark reflected the attitude that opposition to the unity of SPD and KPD had to come from "enemies of the nation";[56] and equally harsh assessments were delivered in private. In consultations with the SMAD, Pieck apparently argued in favor of a more vigorous approach to the merger; "enemies of democracy," he told Bokov, no longer qualified as anything akin to a loyal "opposition."[57] Bokov agreed, too; he noted that "reaction" was at work, spoke of "terrorist acts" the closer that unification came, and apparently planned "decisive measures" in April because the "enemy" could not be won over through persuasion. He instructed the KPD to be more aggressive, saying that acting meekly encouraged opposition.[58] Not that there was much doubt now about the outcome of the merger; on 23 January 1946, Bokov informed Pieck of Stalin's wish that the pace of unification be accelerated and spoke of the desirability of completing the process in time to stage a celebration in connection with May day.[59] This decision reflected a change in tactics. One month before, Ulbricht seems to have been told that merger in "four months" would be too soon and that the entire process needed to make less commotion because of the allies.[60] It was also decided then that the matter of the new party's political program, centering on the issue of democracy and the "transition" to socialism, had to be settled in Moscow."[61]

During talks with Ulbricht in February 1946, Stalin appears to have approved measures leading up to formation of the SED and set 27, 28, and 29 April as the dates for it (later moved forward to 21 and 22 April). The party's platform was also discussed in terms of its "minimum" program, focusing on the unity of Germany, and a "maximum" program that Stalin characterized by contrasting Russia's "quickest path" to the rule of the working class and socialism with what he called a democratic way to worker power that was "not dictatorship."[62] Moreover, the name Socialist Unity party was probably decided upon in Moscow, too; Ulbricht's report of his conversations leaves that impression.[63] During a meeting of the KPD's secretariat the

[54]Pieck, *Probleme der Vereinigung von KPD und SPD*, p. 12.
[55]Pieck, "Einheit sichert den Aufstieg unseres Volkes," *Deutsche Volkszeitung*, 12 March 1946.
[56]See Ulbricht, "Die Einheit der Arbeiterklasse ist die Grundfrage für die Zukunft der Nation [11 January 1946]," *Zur Geschichte der deutschen Arbeiterbewegung*, Zusatzband II, p. 404.
[57]Besprechung bei Bockow am 4. 2. 1946. Zentrales Parteiarchiv. NL 36/734/164-66.
[58]Besprechung abends 9 Uhr [18 March 1946] bei Bockow, ibid., NL 36/734/175.
[59]Besprechung am 23. 1. 1946 in Karlshorst bei Marsch. Bockow, ibid., NL 36/734/148.
[60]Information von Walter Ulbricht über ein Gespräch mit Bockow, Tulpanow, Wolkow am 22. 12. 1945, ibid., NL 36/734/143-44.
[61]Besprechung am 23. 1. 1946 in Karlshorst bei Marsch. Bockow, ibid., NL 36/734/151.
[62]Bericht von Walter Ulbricht am 6. 2. 1946 um 9 Uhr abends, ibid., NL 36/631/33.
[63]See Pieck's notes of Ulbricht's report ("Change the name KPD to Social. Un. party"). Ibid.

day before his departure for Moscow, questions for Ulbricht's discussions were prepared and a decision made to recast the "draft program for the Socialist Workers' party" in the form of "a declaration regarding the principles of the Socialist Workers' party."[64] The change in name to Socialist Unity party, evidently at Stalin's suggestion, reflected the SED's early definition of itself as an organization more accessible to all Germans than a workers' party. It certainly corresponded generally to Stalin's linkage of national unity to the internal cohesion and preeminence of a broadly conceived "unified workers' party" back in June 1945—aided now by the removal of Social Democracy, renamed because of intervening developments, and presented to the public with an ostensibly broadened base. At the KPD's last congress on 19 and 20 April, both the old KPD and the future SED were described as parties that concentrated on the "construction of a new state" in accordance with the overall interests of the German people *and* its working-class segments.[65] Ackermann's remark that "our broad national policy will allow us to become the decisive force of all the people" and that, as a party of millions, the SED would "take over the lead at the head of the entire nation" fits the same description. Ackermann even disclosed that the leadership had made a conscious decision to exclude the phrase "workers' party" from its new name and explained the reasons why.[66] But in light of the SED's determination to define itself as "the truly national party of the German people" that fought as an "independent party in *its* country for the true national interests of *its* people,"[67] Ackermann keep quiet about Stalin's participation in the choice of names.

Stalin may have made other suggestions for alterations to the party's draft program during consultations with Ulbricht in early February. At a meeting of the KPD secretariat on 23 February, it was decided to accept the "new draft" of the SED's principles and goals, its *Grundsätze und Ziele*, worked out by Ackermann and Helmut Lehmann and to add the sentence, "This goal, solving the national and social questions of our people's existence, can only be achieved through socialism."[68] Indeed, the language used in this document was chosen just as carefully as that in the KPD's original proclamation; and the party leadership went to considerable lengths to prevent it from being tampered with in discussions with Social Democrats prior to the merger. During talks with Bokov on 18 March, it was decided "not to

---

[64]Protokoll Nr. 8/65 der Sitzung des Sekretariats am 27. Januar 1946, ibid., I 2/5/51/24.

[65]Dahlem, "Die Organisationspolitik der Partei," *Bericht äber die Verhandlungen des 15. Parteitages der Kommunistischen Partei Deutschlands*, p. 65.

[66]Ackermann, "Der ideologische Kampf der Partei," ibid., pp. 111 and 116.

[67]"Grundsätze und Ziele der Sozialistischen Einheitspartei Deutschlands [21 April 1946]" and "Manifest an das deutsche Volk [21 April 1946]," *Dokumente der Sozialistischen Einheitspartei Deutschlands*, pp. 10 and 26.

[68]Protokoll Nr. 14/71 der Sitzung des Sekretariats am 23. Februar 1946. Zentrales Parteiarchiv, I 2/5/51/40.

allow a discussion of the statutes" at an upcoming district party discussion because the "majority will be opposed to unity."[69] For obvious reasons, these considerations were kept from the Social Democrats; and the Communists continued to insist that there was nothing underhanded about the merger. If certain Social Democrats remained agitated, their misgivings sprang from memories of pre-1933 quarrels or resulted from "instances of tactlessness" on the part of lower-level KPD functionaries.[70] Those who persisted in questioning the honesty of the Communists merely displayed their ignorance about "the development of our party."[71]

It was certainly true that the party leadership had assumed some of the responsibility for Hitler in its proclamation of June 1945; but the self-critical remarks were carefully crafted to enhance the Communists' own reputation by evoking the blood of their martyrs, reducing party accountability for Hitler to an abstraction, and contending that Social Democrats were chiefly at fault for the KPD's errors prior to 1933 anyway. This had been the first of the party's expressions of self-criticism, and some of the later statements actually went further than anything like them before. One internal document blamed the "unintelligible language of the Comintern," a too narrowly defined "class standpoint," and errors in united-front tactics for "complicating" the formation of working-class unity and for the KPD's "false assessment" of the situation. This led the Communists to underestimate fascism and caused the KPD to direct its "main fire" against the Weimar Republic when it ought to have joined with other forces in the defense of democratic liberties.[72] But for one, this confession was printed in an internal document; and for another, there is no trace of an admission that the party's sectarian policies had resulted from a "scientific world view" of fascism as the natural byproduct of capitalism or that the Communists regarded revolution and dictatorship as the sole solution to fascism. Besides, the statement implied that the party's policies never eliminated the possibility of a united front altogether, meaning that Social Democracy had no reason to reject the KPD's united-front overtures during the years leading up to Hitler's takeover of power; and none of this ever altered the conviction that "the Communist party was the only party to have waged a courageous and resolute struggle against the Hitler dictatorship, tactical errors notwithstanding."[73] But it was well understood that the party needed to be cautious about criticizing itself for the sake of facilitating a merger with Social Democracy; questioning its

---

[69]Besprechung bei Bockow in Wendenschloß. Ulbricht-Pieck / Grotewohl, Fechner, Lehmann, ibid., NL 36/734/175.
[70]Pieck, *Probleme der Vereinigung von KPD und SPD*, p. 14.
[71]Pieck, "Einheit sichert den Aufstieg unseres Volkes," *Deutsche Volkszeitung*, 12 March 1946.
[72]*Der Sieg des Faschismus in Deutschland und seine Lehren für unseren gegenwärtigen Kampf*, pp. 5-10.
[73]Ibid.

own past practices reflected poorly upon the policies of both Stalin and the Comintern; and analyses of that sort made the SMAD uneasy. Semjonov advised members of the KPD's secretariat against too much *"criticism of the past"* because it complicated "our position."[74]

These rounds of self-criticism demonstrated the need to alleviate doubts about the party's conversion to democracy without challenging its right to govern the country. Virtually every such utterance intimated that the Communists had been provoked into errors of judgment and that these were historically insignificant when compared with the actions of Social Democrats who seized upon the Communists' tactical excesses as an excuse to shun cooperation. Besides, older Social Democrats knew the Communist party only from "the pre-Hitler years when, as we have stated ourselves, we committed many mistakes"; these had now been corrected "unreservedly." In fact, the Communists said, the result of the party's process of self-examination begun as early as 1935 was nothing less than a "genuine realignment" of the KPD's entire approach to politics. Consequently, there was no conceivable reason to mistrust its assurances of democratic change now; where resistance to the merger of KPD and SPD persisted, it reflected the refusal of Social Democrats to deal with their own past as critically as the Communists had dealt with theirs.[75] The Communists never admitted that the SPD had any reason to be leery about the KPD's united-front overtures prior to 1933 or any excuse whatsoever after 1935, making it all the easier to contend that skepticism about its intentions in 1945 or 1946 was unjustifiable. But the skepticism deepened, and the cause of it was that the KPD's daily conduct failed to elicit any real confidence in its understanding of "unity." The Communists then responded by phrasing their vague admissions of "sectarianism" in ways calculated to blunt the charge that its extremism was not a tactical lapse but the essence of party doctrine. The Communists thus accepted a limited measure of responsibility for Hitler even as they placed the burden of guilt upon the SPD for its "fateful policy of coalition" with the bourgeois parties in the Weimar Republic.[76] Ulbricht spoke of "profound sectarian hindrances" and the first revision of the party's tactics in 1935; but he argued concurrently that the KPD had conducted itself during the Hitler era in conformity with its historical obligations.[77] Pieck struck a similarly tenuous balance; the Communists had corrected their earlier mistakes; but these never caused them to lead workers into a state of passivity or impotence in the face

---

[74]Mitglieder des Zentralsekretariats zur Besprechung bei Bockow [20 February or March 1946]. Zentrales Parteiarchiv, NL 36/734/211.

[75]See Pieck, "Einheit sichert den Aufstieg unseres Volkes," *Deutsche Volkszeitung*, 12 March 1946.

[76]Ibid.

[77]Ulbricht, "Die Politik der Partei," *Bericht über die Verhandlungen des 15. Parteitages der Kommunistischen Partei Deutschlands*, p. 37.

of reaction. The party simply outpaced the development of the labor movement in general and allowed itself to be side-tracked by the reactionary policies of the Social Democratic leadership.[78]

These remarks lacked the slightest hint of an admission that the entire program of revolution and dictatorship had failed and that the blame lay with Stalin and those German Communists who never challenged his authority. In fact, by 1948 at the latest the Communists were actively engaged in the celebration of Stalin's personality and had, even before that, begun ritualizing the practice of exalting their own leaders. However, because most of the men responsible for the party's "mistakes" were basking in the glow of their antifascist past, a special effort was necessary to acquit them of any responsibility for the very mistakes for which the party halfheartedly apologized. It now turned out that these personalities were not the converted leaders of an erstwhile antidemocratic party at all; they had been passionate advocates of democracy all along. It was thus natural that the Communists exalted Wilhelm Pieck as the "pioneer of a unified labor party" and as the "great unifier of the people."[79] The highlight of his seventieth birthday celebration in February 1946 was an "oath in support of unity," during which Ulbricht characterized Pieck as the guarantor that the "future of the nation" would be saved by way of the "unity of the working class" and the consolidation of all antifascist-democratic forces.[80] It was argued accordingly that Pieck had proven himself in the struggle against fascism at a time when the KPD's "sectarian errors" had diverted many impulses leading toward working-class unity. Together with Ernst Thälmann, he had approached the SPD with "sincere proposals" to unite against fascism, and Pieck was not to blame if the rejection of these proposals allowed Hitler to triumph.[81]

This assessment brazenly ignored Pieck's actual performance. In his address to the KPD's conference in October 1935, Pieck called for the "complete eradication" of the sectarianism that had hindered the party in its struggle against Hitler; but only to insist that the fight to free working people from "capitalist servitude" under Hitler must end in a "proletarian revolution, the establishment of the dictatorship of the proletariat, and formation of a free socialist Soviet Germany."[82] It is hardly surprising that the reprint of Pieck's speech, the party's resolutions, and its manifesto, which stated that the Communists desired the "triumph of Soviet power" in Germany, failed to come out in Soviet-occupied Germany until 1947. Even if Pieck express-

---

[78]Quoted in "Großkundgebung der KPD," *Deutsche Volkszeitung*, 20 September 1945.

[79]See *Wilhelm Pieck. Dem Vorkämpfer für ein neues Deutschland zum 70. Geburtstag*, pp. 36-46 and 62-76.

[80]See *Gelöbnis zur Einheit*, p. 8 and passim; Ulbricht, "Wilhelm Pieck, der Vorkämpfer für eine einheitliche Arbeiterpartei," *Wilhelm Pieck. Dem Vorkämpfer für ein neues Deutschland*, p. 46.

[81]"Wilhelm Pieck—ein großer Deutscher," *Deutsche Volkszeitung*, 3 January 1946.

[82]Pieck, *Der neue Weg zum gemeinsamen Kampfe für den Sturz der Hitlerdiktatur*, pp. 138-39.

ed his hope in spring 1946 that the protocol would be republished soon as proof of the party's outlook, his remarks were incompatible with the KPD's representations about its commitment to democracy.[83] Whatever tactical errors might have been made by the Communists were therefore divorced from ideological postulates about fascism that were as valid in 1945 as they had been in 1933; and the Communists never backed away from their claim that they had been the first to isolate the reasons for fascism's victory in the "rift within the progressive democratic forces of our people."[84] They never admitted that the exclusivity of their own doctrine helped cause it; and they certainly saw no reason to apologize for the split in the German labor movement; rather, they turned the schism that resulted in formation of the KPD in 1918 into a consequent "struggle for the only platform suitable for preserving and solidifying unity." Their right-wing opponents within the party had been the ones to leave the "granite footing of Marxism," with rupture being the natural consequence.[85] When it came to essentials, the party had always been right; "we Communists said just where things had to end if the German people followed the Nazi demagogues and war mongers," they claimed, but downplayed the importance of their insistence upon dictatorship as the sole solution to Germany's political ills. Even so, they now bemoaned the fact that all their warnings about fascism had fallen on deaf ears.[86] "What would have become of Germany had the people taken *the other road in 1932*, the one pointed out by the antifascist forces and especially by the Communist party!" Germany would be "*a paradise today!*"[87]

Other discussions held that the revolution in November 1918 was the real turning point; the absence of a "united Marxist workers' party with resolute leaders at its head" made it difficult for the Germans to take the "road of the Russian revolution," and the Weimar Republic culminated "in the fascist dictatorship of monopoly capital."[88] For this reason, the Communists defined the unity party proposed by them now as the kind missing in 1918, even as they insisted that true democracy, not the Soviet system, was appropriate for Germany under present conditions. It was just that this democracy must never be the "impotent" form characteristic of Weimar because Weimar culminated in fascism.[89] Not that democracy in itself contained "organic weaknesses"; Weimar foundered because "pseudodemocratic parties" spent their

[83]See Pieck, "Einheit sichert den Aufstieg unseres Volkes," *Deutsche Volkszeitung*, 12 March 1946.
[84]Oelßner, "Über die historische Verantwortung der Kommunisten," *Deutsche Volkszeitung*, 28 October 1945.
[85]"Wilhelm Pieck—ein großer Deutscher," *Deutsche Volkszeitung*, 3 January 1946.
[86]Ackermann, "Mut zu neuem Leben," *Deutsche Volkszeitung*, 23 June 1945.
[87]Behrens, *Der geistige Arbeiter im Kampf um ein neues Deutschland*, pp. 7-8.
[88]Dahlem, "Keine Wiederholung der Fehler von 1918," *Deutsche Volkszeitung*, 9 November 1945.
[89]Pieck, "Der Weg zum Wiederaufbau Deutschlands," *Deutsche Volkszeitung*, 21 July 1945.

time "bickering" among themselves while the voice of the true defenders of the popular interest went unheeded by "those in the service of big capital."[90] As for their policies, the Communists had "always supported democracy" anyway, but the kind that safeguarded "the rights and liberties of the working people."[91]

The Russians' Party

Every problem caused by the KPD's reputation as the "Russians' party" carried over to the SED as well; and both before and after the merger, the Communists tried to improve upon it by insisting that they had never allied themselves with the Soviet Union for the sake of pursuing policies contrary to the national interest. Rather, the KPD had always focused on national concerns, the most conclusive evidence of which was the fact that the Communists were not thinking in terms of socialism patterned after the Soviet Union now either. But when they varied the theme of collective guilt to explain why not, the reason again involved the manipulation of rhetoric that left the shape of the future subject to doubt—the people had to free themselves first from the reactionary ideology of their own past.[92] By rights, this argument ought to have undercut the party program because it implied that the Germans would be ready for an unwanted Soviet system as soon as they acknowledged the error of their ways. But for the time being, disavowing the "Soviet system" in favor of democracy remained the party's principal promise to the German people, and it continued after formation of the SED. The Communists insisted upon it even though the disavowal catered to the very feelings of hostility toward anything Soviet that the party's rhetoricians otherwise denounced. Regardless, the political immaturity of the people and the military occupation were said to comprise special conditions mitigating against the immediate realization of socialism; and for those reasons it was considered a mistake to force the Soviet system upon Germany.

Nonetheless, the rhetoric always had a way of suggesting that the objectives disavowed by the Communists in public were the ones uppermost in their minds. Though their official goals centered on antifascism, democracy, and national unity, the party's policies really served the interests of no more than the first. Still, the Communists developed their program in 1945 starting with collective guilt and proceeding by way of antifascism and democracy to

[90]See "Die demokratischen Parteien Deutschlands," *Tägliche Rundschau*, 14 August 1945; and "Die demokratischen Parteien und die Zukunft Deutschlands," *Tägliche Rundschau*, 1 November 1945.

[91]Dahlem, "Die Einheit und die Aufgabe der Arbeiterklasse," *Deutsche Volkszeitung*, 26 October 1945.

[92]See Pieck, "Der Weg zum Wiederaufbau Deutschlands," *Deutsche Volkszeitung*, 21 July 1945.

national unity. Ulbricht argued that the ideological devastation extending deep into the working class made the rapid realization of socialism unthinkable, the more so due to the absence of a "unified party of the working people"; a road matched to Germany's specific conditions was more appropriate.[93] Forcing the Soviet system upon Germany was considered pointless, then, because the minds of the Germans were so corrupted by fascist ideas; and under these conditions, attempting to impose the Soviet system would be doomed to failure.[94] Even referring to socialism now was denounced as an "aberration or deception" in light of the fact that the people were too immature; they had to be "educated" toward a Soviet system first. The Communists even said that they opposed "sovietization by force"; instead, they wanted a democracy "unencumbered by all the errors of democracy in the years 1918-33." Most importantly, the Communists insisted that they had national reasons for their opposition to "sovietization"; they pursued policies appropriate not just to "the sector occupied by the Red Army but for *all* of Germany" as a means of safeguarding the interests of "our entire country, our entire people." They had no intention of taking advantage of the opportunities in the Soviet zone to engage in partisan politics "leading toward sovietization"; the party's strategic goal remained formation of a "real, genuine, honest democracy in Germany."[95]

This assessment was especially revealing because it betrayed such an awareness of the fact that "sovietization," which ordinary Germans considered synonymous with Communist party dominance, was incompatible with national unity. Party leaders certainly suffered from few illusions about its implications now and for that reason concentrated so heavily on inventing misleading ways of characterizing their policies. The blunt phrase "sovietization by force" vanished soon after it was first uttered in June 1945; but countless other variations reappeared over the next few years. Ulbricht argued that Communists and Social Democrats had to locate together the road of the *"antifascist struggle"* in accordance with the special conditions in Germany, but this road could not be "a schematic transfer of the Soviet development to Germany."[96] Thus it was that an "antifascist-democratic parliamentary republic" became the party's "minimum" objective, though the Communists made no secret of the fact that their "maximum" or long-term goal remained the "realization of socialism by way of exercising the political dominion of the working class in the sense of the leadership of the doctrine

[93]Ulbricht, "Erste Funktionärskonferenz der KPD Groß-Berlins," *Einheitsfront der antifaschistisch-demokratischen Parteien*, pp. 24-25.
[94]See Oelßner, "Zum 28. Jahrestag der Großen Sozialistischen Oktoberrevolution," *Deutsche Volkszeitung*, 4 November 1945.
[95]Selbmann, *Aufbruch des Geistes*, pp. 6-10.
[96]Ulbricht, "Das Aktionsprogram der KPD in Durchführung," *Deutsche Volkszeitung*, 14 October 1945.

of consistent Marxism."[97] By February 1946, the party was ready to summarize its thinking on the subject of a "special German road to socialism," and Anton Ackermann drew up the definitive statement that remained officially valid until he was compelled to retract in late 1948 what he had been instructed to write in 1946. Ackermann's article may well have developed out of Ulbricht's discussions with Stalin in February;[98] Ackermann was the main author of the SED's "principles and goals" that recast the arguments used in his article; and he was capable of better circumlocutions than Ulbricht. But not even Ackermann's article avoided the principal issue. The Communists favored a parliamentary republic, he said, but argued that such a republic would provide the "socialist labor movement" with a prime opportunity to attain "all power in the state"; and Ackermann made it just as clear that the realization of socialism hinged ultimately on the acquisition of state power—"'the revolutionary dictatorship of the proletariat.'"[99] By his own admission, then, the special road to socialism amounted to nothing more than a transitional phase that left ultimate objectives unchanged; and the use of the same word in Ulbricht's conversations with Stalin, transition, underscores the fact that the concept centered upon the question of a peaceful and democratic versus violent non-democratic passage to dictatorship. When Stalin referred to a Western parliamentary tradition and a "democr. road to worker power," as opposed to a dictatorship, the distinction applied only to the "question of transition."[100] Russia's was "shortest," elsewhere the process would take longer, both roads culminated in dictatorship.

In other words, "democracy" was the most expedient means to an end still understood to be dictatorship, even if Ackermann was one of the few Communists to utter the word out loud prior to 1948, and even he said it only once. In spring 1946, the theoretical issue boiled down to the question of whether the transition from a democratic republic to a "workers' state" could occur by means of a parliamentary republic or only through the "revolutionary use of force"; and the Communists answered that there was indeed a "possibility" of avoiding violence. But everything hung in the balance until the two labor parties merged. If the new democracy turned back into a reactionary vehicle of repression, bloody confrontations were unavoidable;

[97]"Die zweite Phase der Einheit," *Tägliche Rundschau*, 17 December 1945.
[98]This is not reflected directly in the decisions taken by the KPD's secretariat; in fact, Leonhard writes that Ackermann was at work on the article in November 1945 (Leonhard, *Die Revolution entläßt ihre Kinder*, p. 346). Still, final plans for the dissemination of the first issue of *Einheit*, apparently ready for printing and with Ackermann's article in it, were made after Ulbricht's return from Moscow. See Protokoll Nr. 9/66 der Sitzung des Sekretariats am 7. Februar 1946 and Protokoll Nr. 12/69 am 12. Februar 1946 (I 2/5/51/29 and 33). At the time, the secretariat was meeting almost daily on 7, 8, 9, and 12 February.
[99]Ackermann, "Gibt es einen besonderen deutschen Weg zum Sozialismus?" *Einheit* 1 (1946): 23.
[100]Bericht von Walter Ulbricht: am 6. 2. 1946. Zentrales Parteiarchiv. NL 36/631/33.

whereas there would be no institutional means for violence to express itself if the antifascist-democratic republic stood its ground in the interests of all working Germans; and ultimately the pace of Germany's strides toward socialism, the definitive guarantee of peace and social tranquillity, depended upon the speed with which "the unity party is realized now!" No one hoped as earnestly than the Communists, Ackermann said, that "renewed bloodshed" could be avoided.[101]

But these assurances failed to lessen the impression that the impending merger marked the beginning of the end of democracy, even if the new party quickly issued a "manifesto" in April 1946 that made no mention of dictatorship. The manifesto stressed the SED's desire to cooperate with the other antifascist-democratic parties; and these had every right to their own world view. The SED was not in favor of a *"single-party system,"* it simply desired an end to the *"rupture of the labor movement and strengthening of the antifascist-democratic bloc."*[102] The party still aspired to socialism, but the road to it remained embedded in the promise of democracy, and democracy was defined as a nonviolent transition. Even then, the party leaders failed to rid their rhetoric of indications that they considered violence to be inevitable. Ulbricht intimated that violence was the only guarantee of non-violence; he professed again that the Communists wished to "travel consistently the democratic road in accordance with the special conditions in Germany" and that they wanted to "follow the road to its end"; but the principal assurance of democracy remained the unification of KPD and SPD because a democratic road to socialism was not possible if the two parties failed to merge. Even after such a merger, Ulbricht warned that, if any "elements hostile to the people" contemplated resistance, the united working class would "respond with all the means at its command."[103] Then there were other aspects of a democracy that hinted already at the suspension of democratic principles for the sake of their protection. Though they focused much of their attention upon the contrast between "sovietization" and democracy, the Communists also spoke glowingly of "Soviet democracy." They may have concentrated less on this issue right after the war than on their own promises for Germany, but scattered efforts still took place to define a preliminary context within which democracy and dictatorship could coincide. The party daily *Neues Deutschland* suggested that, with the sole exception of a fascist dictatorship, the "mechanistic dichotomy of *democracy* and *dictatorship*" was false.[104]

---

[101]Ackermann, "Gibt es einen besonderen deutschen Weg zum Sozialismus?" *Einheit* 1 (1946): 31.

[102]"Manifest an das deutsche Volk [21 April 1946]," *Dokumente der Sozialistischen Einheitspartei Deutschlands*, p. 25.

[103]Ulbricht, quoted in "Das Tor zur Einheit geöffnet," Deutsche Volkszeitung, 12 February 1946.

[104]G. B., "Was ist Demokratie?" *Neues Deutschland*, 30 April 1946.

"Soviet democracy" then served as the classic illustration of a dialectical synthesis as "the most perfect form of democracy in the world"—"incomparably superior to any other type of democracy."[105]

The advantages of extolling Soviet democracy become clearer in light of statements to the effect that the Soviet people "stood shoulder to shoulder" during the war and that Soviet democracy now marched "at the head of world democracy."[106] The purpose of establishing such connections in Soviet-occupied Germany was to take the concept of "unity" far beyond the transition from collective guilt to national consensus and reconcile dictatorship with the fledgling idea of an antifascist-democratic regime. The irony of this argument is that the Stalinist myth of the moral-political unity of the people underscored the compatibility of "democracy" and dictatorship in the USSR; whereas in Soviet-occupied Germany, the idea emerged first as the key component of an argument based upon their incompatibility. Either way, the concept of the "moral-political unity of the people" was geared to making dictatorship seem less frightening by reconciling it with the will of the people. Nor would the practice of defining antinomies in terms of equivalence have been unknown to ordinary Germans who had just gone through twelve years in which dictatorship merged with the idea of a classless *Volksgemeinschaft*. Stalin's "political-moral unity of the people" had much in common conceptually with the notion of *"ein Reich, ein Volk, ein Führer."* In this sense, Stalinist mythology tied in with the KPD's departure from thinking along the lines of collective guilt and coalesced with its earliest variations on the theme of unanimity built around an antifascist-democratic consensus with one party, to quote Stalin, "at the center." But the point of departure remained the USSR. Ulbricht explained that the revolution of 1917 had allowed the Soviet people to create a democracy capable of saving civilization from fascism because it provided for the "unity and unanimity" of people and state—incontrovertible evidence that the Soviet Union was "politically, economically, and militarily the most progressive state."[107] True, Soviet democracy owed its strength to Marxism; but even then, talk about the "dictatorship of the Communist party of the USSR" was considered irresponsible because Marxism was the "most consistent doctrine for the democratic self-consciousness of the people" and thus for democracy.[108]

This is how the advocates of a single-party system transformed dictatorship into democracy, or consummate democracy into a beneficent dictator-

---

[105]See the headlines and articles in *Deutsche Volkszeitung*, 7 November 1945 and, "Verfassung der UdSSR," *Tägliche Rundschau*, 5 December 1945.

[106]"Die Sowjetdemokratie—die vollendetste Demokratie der Welt," *Deutsche Volkszeitung*, 7 November 1945.

[107]Ulbricht, "Erste Funktionärskonferenz der KPD Groß-Berlins," *Einheitsfront der antifaschistisch-demokratischen Parteien*, pp. 16-17.

[108]Schemjakin, "Reaktionäre vom 'Tagesspiegel' außer Rand und Band," *Tägliche Rundschau*, 30 November 1945.

ship, and back again; and the reasoning allows the deeper meaning of the party's transition from collective guilt to a broad antifascist-democratic consensus to reveal itself. The point of it all was to transform the non-Marxian or even anti-Marxist expedient of collective guilt into a Marxist-Leninist version of the will of the people. The ideological dilemma sprang from the fact that these statements tended to underscore the inherent identity of what the German Communists were otherwise compelled to contrast. To make matters worse, they tried to buttress their arguments by reverting to the idea of collective guilt when it served another purpose. The Communists gradually began stressing the importance of lasting friendship with a country whose social order was depicted as the highest plateau of democracy, even though its immediate *imposition* upon Germany infringed upon basic principles of the same. The German invasion of the USSR had been the "greatest crime" against Germany herself, they said; and "the way of peace and friendship with the Soviet Union" was now a "national imperative."[109]

This rhetoric exacerbated the very problems that the Communists went to such lengths to resolve because the party's prime obstacle remained the visceral fear that "sovietization" underlay Soviet and German Communist policy. Words in the newspaper to the effect that in "this period of development" the people living in regions occupied by the Red Army selected the form of government desired by them probably changed few minds.[110] Worse, many of the statements surely aggravated matters, such as the one that spoke of the Red Army's "discipline" and insisted that its soldiers and officers regularly exhibited a "high political niveau and humanity."[111] The scars left upon German civilians by their first encounter with Red Army soldiers simply could not be healed by the contention that Germans were eyewitnesses to the "chivalrous behavior of the Red Army toward the peaceful population of the vanquished country."[112] Boasting about the moral superiority of Soviet society simply squared too poorly with local impressions; and the KPD's insistence upon friendship with the Soviet Union then decreased its popularity. In the eyes of the public, it remained a party, the Russians', that answered to the SMAD and was disliked with equal intensity. There were a few official attempts to say something about the Red-Army rapes, but these consisted of

---

[109]Ulbricht, "Die Politik der Partei," *Bericht über die Verhandlungen des 15. Parteitages der KPD* [19-20 April 1946], pp. 45-46; and Pieck, "Enge Freundschaft mit der Sowjetunion," *Deutsche Volkszeitung*, 7 November 1945.

[110]Schemjakin, "Ruhm der heldenhaften Roten Armee!" *Tägliche Rundschau*, 23 February 1946.

[111]"Die Zeitung der Roten Armee in Berlin," *Tägliche Rundschau*, 15 May 1945.

[112]"Ein Monat nach der Kapitulation," *Tägliche Rundschau*, 8 June 1945. The subject came up repeatedly in Pieck's discussions with SMAD officers, and some thought was given to commenting publicly upon the "rumors about supposed plundering and rapes." See Pieck's notes of talks with Marshal Zhukov on 11 July 1945 and with Bokov on 23 January 1946 (Zentrales Parteiarchiv. NL 36/734/116-17, 149).

little more than vague allusions to the "behavior of the occupation troops"; and even then, it was considered infinitely more important to remember that Hitler's army had caused immeasurable suffering to the inhabitants of other countries.[113] Ulbricht charged flatly that much of the outrage over the "transgressions" against civilians were fascist provocations or came from people trying to discredit the KPD by holding the party responsible for unspecified acts of arbitrariness. These attempts to benefit from the "unpleasantries connected here and there with the occupation," Ulbricht said, were filthy maneuvers that the German working class and all healthy segments of the population condemned. *"Our people desire that a different road be taken once and for all."*[114]

The labeling of undesirable outlooks as residues of fascist attitudes in one breath while referring to the will of the people in another was a practice that continued throughout 1945 and 1946. The theory of collective guilt predominated in certain contexts; whereas in others the Communists embellished their proposals with talk of the yearnings of the masses. In August 1945 Pieck had already attributed progress toward formation of an "antifascist-democratic united front" to the will toward unity "very substantially present in the masses of the German people."[115] The move toward cooperation taken by the four parties was not "a decision reached under coercion"; rather, *"the united front of the antifascist parties sprang forth"* from the masses almost by itself due to their "instinctive" realization that any rift in the political consensus would immediately jeopardize the Germans' last chance for an existence as a nation.[116] There was even talk of "healthy common sense"—a growing maturity that had manifested itself increasingly in "profound confidence in the KPD."[117] The habit of tying Germany's future as a nation to unconditional acceptance of the Communist party's political program and presenting it as a direct response to the political demands of the masses then spilled over into other areas. The most bizarre was the flamboyant birth of a new personality cult in the form of a seventieth birthday celebration for Wilhelm Pieck. This ceremony, in honor of the "true *Führer* of the German people" who represented the "overriding national interests" of them all and was therefore uniquely qualified to "mobilize" the masses,[118] grew into a "large-

[113]Pieck, "Der Weg zum Wiederaufbau Deutschlands," *Deutsche Volkszeitung*, 21 July 1945.

[114]Ulbricht, "Das Aktionsprogram der KPD in Durchführung," *Deutsche Volkszeitung*, 14 October 1945.

[115]"Das Wollen der antifaschistischen Einheitsfront," *Tägliche Rundschau*, 14 August 1945.

[116]See "Einheitsfront ist Voraussetzung für Deutschlands Aufbau," *Tägliche Rundschau*, 1 November 1945; and Sch., "Lehren der Geschichte," *Tägliche Rundschau*, 16 November 1945.

[117]Oelßner, "Über die historische Verantwortung der Kommunisten" and, Dahlem, "Deutschland braucht eine starke kommunistische Partei," *Deutsche Volkszeitung*, 28 October and 2 November 1945.

[118]Oelßner, "Freund und Führer des Volkes," *Wilhelm Pieck, dem Vorkämpfer für ein neues Deutschland*, pp. 86 and 89.

scale *demonstration in support of the unity of the working people and the entire German people.*" Those fortunate enough to participate in the festivities had witnessed "the desire and will of the German people in its clearest expression." This celebration confirmed the "passionate impulse favoring unity" and was unmistakable proof of "the rapid maturation of our people." After twelve years of "dictated 'celebrations' in ordered cadences," the people had gathered together in a spontaneous "joyful celebration of its love"; all segments of the population—men and women, workers, farmers, intellectuals—had "joined hands to celebrate in Pieck the unity of antifascist Germany."[119] Lest any concern be expressed about Pieck's ideological leanings, the planners freely acknowledged that he was a "consequent advocate of the struggle for proletarian dictatorship"; but as a Marxist-Leninist he knew that such a struggle was not always appropriate. Pieck had recognized "years ago" that the immediate task of the German working class could not be the violent formation of "Soviet power," and his commitment to democracy was said to be identical to the party's promise that the "Soviet system" would not be imposed upon Germany.[120]

The gathering momentum toward the merger of KPD and SPD was seen as a similar expression of popular unity and unanimity. Though Social Democrats in the West expressed their concern that unification was being "dictated," Ulbricht insisted that this contention had no basis in fact.[121] The desire for a single party of the working class was growing at the grass-roots level and pressuring the leadership of the two parties to respond accordingly. "Some ask," Ulbricht said, "whether the unification of the two working-class parties is not occurring under pressure"; it was, he answered, "under the pressure of the Thuringians and the Saxons," who were urging unification without asking their party headquarters for permission first. He was seconded by Pieck, who talked of the "movement for unity."[122] Members of both parties were now said to be asking why discussions about unification could not be terminated in favor of simply bringing it about.[123]

Finally, as the campaign neared its end, plans were prepared for the organization of a "spontaneous" demonstration of popular support for the SED—just as Stalin had apparently suggested to Ulbricht in early February. Everything was to be done, said Pieck several weeks before the event, "to

[119]"Die wuchtige Demonstration für die Einheit," *Deutsche Volkszeitung*, 6 January 1946; "Wilhelm Pieck—der Vertrauensmann des Volkes," *Deutsche Volkszeitung*, 4 January 1946.
[120]Oelßner, "Freund und Führer des Volkes," *Wilhelm Pieck, dem Vorkämpfer für ein neues Deutschland*, pp. 88-89.
[121]Ulbricht, "Offene Antwort an sozialdemokratische Genossen," *Deutsche Volkszeitung*, 16 January 1946.
[122]Ulbricht, "Das Tor zur Einheit geöffnet," *Deutsche Volkszeitung*, 12 February 1946; "Resolution für die Parteikonferenz der KPD am 2. und 3. März 1946," *Deutsche Volkszeitung*, 16 February 1946.
[123]Pieck, *Probleme der Vereinigung von KPD und SPD*, p. 11.

ensure that plans for the May-day demonstration are carefully set in the eight days following the merger and leading up to 1 May; and so that the world-wide holiday in honor of labor can be kept for the first time in Germany under the leadership of the Socialist Unity party."[124] The rhetoric of spontaneity then culminated in the May-day march that marked the preliminary end to the transition from collective guilt to antifascist-democratic consensus. The parade was said to have been a clear manifestation of the "spiritual awakening of the masses";[125] Berlin, the capital, had joined the march in celebration of the Socialist Unity party; and the SED responded to talk of "pressure" and accusations of totalitarianism by exclaiming, "what a feeling of joy, but also of political reassurance and significance that the idea of the unity of all working people has fallen on such fertile soil!" Though the SED had existed a scant few days, the masses marched for hours in "free, joyful self-determination"; and those who experienced it could say that a profound spiritual process was unfolding—the spirit of *"moral restitution."* There were neither posed pictures here, nor cries of Sieg heil; rather, the animation of the processions, the plastic diversity of the banners and flags, the happy spring-time laughter of the people—it was "a magnificent picture of the masses," in a word, "the *entire people!*"[126] Still, Otto Grotewohl felt compelled to issue a warning; if the new freedom had to be defended by force of arms, those who were vile enough to raise their hand against the true interests of the people would be responsible for the violence, not the party.[127]

Peaceful Development

These conceptions of collective guilt *and* grass-roots antifascism accentuated the meaninglessness of such conflicting views of the German people; and the Communists had no choice but to shuffle the components of their rhetoric in an effort to locate the doctrinal mix best able to justify the widening rift between program and practice. The more intricate workings of this rift may not always be easy to trace; much of what the Communists were up to at any given time was clandestine in nature, generally denied in public, and constantly shifting as the shape of international politics slowly emerged. But the artificiality of the ideology highlights its quality as a cover for the objectives of Soviet policy toward Germany and certainly reveals much about the ambitions of the local Communists who endorsed them. Soviet policy was, after all, carried out by Germans who surely pondered the implications of

[124]Ibid., p. 17. See also, in connection with the "mass demonstrations on 1 May," Protokoll Nr. 12/69 der Sitzung des Sekretariats am 12. February 1946. Zentrales Parteiarchiv. I 2/5/51/33.
[125]"Der neue Tag," *Neues Deutschland*, 4 May 1946.
[126]"Mai-Erkenntnisse," *Neues Deutschland*, 3 May 1946.
[127]See "Unter dem Banner der Arbeiterschaft," *Neues Deutschland*, 3 May 1946.

their actions; indeed, many must have arrived at conclusions that either troubled them little or that they kept to themselves because airing them, even internally, was impossible without identifying contradictions few felt safe in acknowledging. But it would still be misleading to assume that there was a uniform awareness of a cynical rift between ideology and politics within the KPD or to infer that leading German Communists were necessarily or routinely underhanded in doctoring the ideology to cloak their determination to take advantage of unprecedented opportunities. They were all inherently arrogant; and this conceit often explains the deviousness with which they designed strategy as much as deliberate demagogy. Besides, when it came to the pursuit of key objectives, the basic attitudes coincided anyway until the shape of Soviet policy had sufficiently crystallized to eliminate much of the need to be devious in the first place.

By late 1948, few residues of the party's earlier democratic gestures remained; and if one rejects the contention that the earlier "moderate" episode was meticulously planned from the beginning, there was certainly a natural impulse to design a public program that retained old ideological postulates for possible use later. In addition, it can probably be argued that the local Communists rarely needed to know the exact complexion of Soviet objectives in order to be effectively used by the Russians. This had been true in years past, and the reasons why, having to do with the workings of an adjustable but binding dogma, still existed in 1945. For all those accustomed to thinking in ideological terms and, at the same time, long since inured to precipitous reversals, the rhetoric invariably turned on the kind of logic impossible to refute without infringing upon the doctrine as it presented itself at any given time. Moreover, the very idea that anything like a normal rift between power and its legitimization might characterize the relationship between Marxism-Leninism and the policies derived from it would never have occurred to the more idealistically minded Communists; and for the cynical who surmised that it may have, such considerations were hardly worth a second thought. To these Communists, questions of intrinsic ideological validity were immaterial because ideology and power were self-certifying patterns of thought. Ideology rationalized an elemental political prerogative, and it could not serve any other purpose without impinging upon the basic prerogatives of power. Once attained, though seldom by force of persuasion, power then kept the orthodoxy from atrophying because it was infused with artificial life by people whose unscrupulousness in doing so resulted from their claim to be answering a historical calling.

Whatever the patterns of private thought, the party was charged with implementing policies that served Soviet interests even as the Communists rejected accusations that their party was "dependent" upon Moscow.[128] Be-

---

[128]See Pieck, *Probleme der Vereinigung von KPD und SPD*, p. 13.

cause "lumping the German Communists together with the Russian Bolsheviks" had been a keynote of Nazi propaganda, derogatory allusions to "the
Russians' party" or suggestions that its policies were non-German were considered direct evidence of opposition to plans for a Socialist Unity party and
denounced as a lingering effect of Goebbels' propaganda.[129] Whether top
Communists ever believed that their party led an independent existence or
whether the absolute identity of interests, outlooks, and policies was viewed
as part of the historical process, matters little in the end. Contorting logic
and sublimating possible private reservations to the necessity of deriving an
ideological rationale for measures based only marginally on doctrinal principles was a long-standing practice, and by 1945 it must have been largely
reflexive, especially for those who returned from Soviet exile. Ultimately it
was a question of locating the most effective doctrinal legitimization for policies that few Communists ever dreamt of questioning anyway because the
premise that truth emanated from Moscow, or rather from Stalin, remained
unimpugnable. This had been drummed into them all over a period of many
years, or they had drummed it into themselves, often under circumstances in
which their lives were threatened by the very object of their ideological
affections; and these perverse circumstances doubtless conditioned intellectual reflexes. To what precise extent this was the case is always hard to tell;
but combining the reflex to synchronize ideology and power with a natural
reluctance to question the line usually meant that tampering with theoretical
rationalizations was the sole means of resolving contradictions. Convincing
themselves afterwards that their contrivances reflected a theoretical reality
with greater validity for ordinary people than empirical reality was likely the
second step. Of course, other Communists understood fully how best to use
an ideology with a shifting profile for their own purposes, but those adept at
regulating the doctrine to mask personal ambition fall into a separate category.

Either way, the nature of the contradictions still suggests that leading
Communists were either possessed of a remarkable capacity to overlook the
implications of their own policies or bent upon pursuing them regardless.
Alternating between sweeping accusations of collective guilt and celebrations of a German mass movement, the party's public posture then acquired
another dimension. Loath to concede the right of anyone to object to policies
that they defined as the exclusive expression of the national interest, the
Communists developed the habit of treating all impulses in favor of pluralism either as the obvious symptom of a lingering fascist malignancy or as a
telltale sign of the reemerging virus of "reaction." These otherwise crude
allusions to "enemies" had a veneer of theoretical subtlety. The Communists
used the idea to strike a precarious balance between the polar extremes of

---

[129]See Ackermann, *Fragen und Antworten*, p. 4.

collective guilt and common consensus, but only as a justification for hardening policies. Adhering to their latest premise that overwhelming numbers of Germans were caught up in the spontaneous process of renewal, the Communists could always contend that this was nevertheless not universally true or, outside the Soviet zone, true at all. "Enemies" of an antifascist democracy still abounded—comprised of fascists and reactionaries, average Germans, and politically indifferent intellectuals who all refused to atone for the past by confessing the error of their ways and embracing the ideals of antifascism and democracy.

But incongruities developed immediately because the presence of "enemies" clashed with the party's assertions about the "possibility" of a peaceful road to socialism. However much the Communists explained the new policy now as a reflection of the "revolutionary teachings of Marx, Engels, Lenin, and Stalin,"[130] the concept of such a transition flew in the face of doctrine. In order to sustain the promise of a peaceful road to socialism, notions like Lenin's that "decisive questions in the lives of the peoples are only solved through violence" had to be suspended, and so did the axiom that the "genuinely revolutionary class" had to place "the call for dictatorship on the agenda" the moment reactionaries resorted to violence.[131] The implications of such notions in a divided Germany, the Western half said to be economically and politically unreconstructed and the Eastern half fervently hopeful of a nonviolent road to socialism, yet equally committed to the use of force in its own defense, are fairly apparent. Stalin's theoretical pronouncements, like Lenin's also in print in the zone by 1946, similarly reaffirmed the assumption that "the basic question of the revolution is the question of power" and that, once there, maintaining the working class in power was the task of the "dictatorship of the proletariat."[132] The correct ideological inference, the one drawn internally, was that the party's policies would inevitably end in dictatorship; nor was there any real likelihood of peaceful development up to that point. Party spokesmen made it perfectly clear that a violent response required no additional justification in the event of a challenge to democracy and added that the specter of its restoration and the general menace of "reaction" lingered regardless of the defeat of fascism. The Communists believed that reactionary powers always responded to the growth of democratic forces by availing themselves of an "open dictatorial regime of violence,"[133] but they used that argument to develop yet another. Whether the road to so-

[130]See Pieck, *Probleme der Vereinigung von KPD und SPD*, p. 20, and Ulbricht, "Erste Funktionärskonferenz der KPD Groß-Berlins," *Einheitsfront der antifaschistisch-demokratischen Parteien*, p. 25.
[131]Lenin, *Zwei Taktiken der Sozialdemokratie in der demokratischen Revolution*, p. 110.
[132]Stalin, *Über die Grundlagen des Leninismus*, pp. 27-28.
[133]Leonhard, "Über den deutschen Weg zum Sozialismus," *Deutsche Volkszeitung*, 24 March 1946.

cialism would be democratic or marked by bloodshed hinged upon the "consistent implementation of democratic renewal" because reaction would then be unable to use "violence and civil war" to obstruct the final liberation of the working class, thereby relieving the party of the need to respond with "new mass sacrifices." A delay in the formation of a unified party would only permit "reaction" to reentrench itself in order to stifle democratic renewal and block the road to socialism with open violence.[134]

But the Communists insisted that reaction was mustering its forces in order to sabotage democratic reconstruction in Germany even after formation of the SED. The only difference then was that the SED and the united front of the four antifascist parties constituted a formidable opponent—"the closed ranks of working people."[135] The outspoken guarantee that the unity party could be counted upon to employ "revolutionary means" if the so-called capitalist class left "the soil of democracy" remained, however, at the center of the definition of a democratic road to socialism.[136] The SED thus favored the use of force, the overriding characteristic of dictatorship in the first place, as the necessary means of defending a democracy that persisted in distinguishing itself from dictatorship. When critics of the merger pointed out that the rift in the working class continued after creation of the SED because the Communists yearned for dictatorship, whereas Social Democrats strove for the "realization of socialism with democratic means," party spokesmen countered with lectures on the meaning of true democracy. The SED aspired to *this* kind of "real democracy," a democracy not for capitalist reaction but for working people—"a democracy for democrats." Moreover, because realizing socialism "without aspiring to the construction of such a democracy" was impossible, no difference of opinion between the SED and "real" socialists existed.[137] But behind these arguments hid the same implicit assurance of violent confrontations between real and bogus democrats characteristic of the Communist attitude toward democracy in the Weimar era, and for that radical past the party permitted itself no more than shifty apologies. Ulbricht praised the party's break with its own "sectarianism," claimed that the resolutions passed at the Brussels conference in 1935 made a democratic republic the party's strategic goal,[138] but neglected to mention Pieck's call for a "free, socialist Soviet Germany" by way of revolution and dictatorship. Instead, Ulbricht praised the KPD's advocacy of a single working-class party by citing the very passage in the resolutions calling for such a party as the

[134]Ibid.
[135]Walden, "Das deutsche Volk auf dem Wege zur Demokratie," *Tägliche Rundschau*, 9 May 1946.
[136]G. B., "Was ist Demokratie?" *Neues Deutschland*, 30 April 1946.
[137]Ibid.
[138]See Ulbricht, "Die Politik der Partei," *Bericht über die Verhandlungen des 15. Parteitages der KPD*, p. 36.

sole means of toppling fascism, only to omit the next sentence: "Such a mass party will only fulfill its obligations . . . if it accepts the necessity of a revolutionary ouster of the bourgeoisie and the creation of a dictatorship of the proletariat in the form of Soviets."[139]

Part of the broader problem now was that calls for a Soviet Germany in 1932, 1933, or even 1935 all sprang from the Leninist theory of imperialism and the Stalinist theory of fascism engendered by it, which branded bourgeois democracy in its pre-1933 hidden or post-1933 unmasked form as a dictatorship; and in 1945, the Communists still considered it axiomatic that fascism was the "open, terroristic dictatorship of the most reactionary, chauvinistic, and imperialist elements of the ruling bourgeois class."[140] The party's dilemma now was that the core dogmas pertaining to monopoly capitalism and fascism could not be discarded because the Communists based their right to power on claims of infallibility that ruled out an admission of critical shortcomings in their response to fascism. The impression that the Communists had not espoused democracy in the Weimar era, they said, was mistaken. But all things considered, there were then few assurances in the Communist program that the party would not revert to some or eventually all of the goals considered historically necessary prior to 1933 once their policies encountered opposition; in fact, the Communists routinely evoked the specter of bloodshed and warned of "enemies." Ulbricht insisted that "only he who favors unification of the working class is a consequent democrat,"[141] and the SED's principles and goals added that preventing the restoration of reaction now required "the unity of the labor movement and the bloc of all antifascist democratic parties." The collapse of the reactionary state apparatus and the construction of a democratic state on a new economic foundation thus created the opportunity for a peaceful road to socialism; and the SED said that it preferred a democratic path. But its pledge to "reach for revolutionary means if the capitalist class leaves the soil of democracy,"[142] the single most important sentence in the party's principles and goals, anchored the promise of dictatorship in a program publicly committed to a democratic transition to socialism. Force was synonymous with dictatorship; and dictatorship was indistinguishable from a "Soviet system." On the one hand, talk of resistance to democracy served as the perennial justification for political, economic, and cultural initiatives that came about independent of local opposition; in fact, the reverse was true; the change caused the opposition,

---

[139]Ibid., pp. 36-40; Pieck, "Schlußbemerkung" and "Resolution der Brüsseler Parteikonferenz der KPD vom Oktober 1935," *Der neue Weg zum gemeinsamen Kampf für den Sturz der Hitlerdiktatur*, pp. 139 and 170-71.

[140]Behrens, *Der geistige Arbeiter im Kampf um ein neues Deutschland,* p. 21.

[141]Ulbricht, "Unsere Stärke liegt in unserer Einheit [21 and 22 April 1946]," in Ulbricht, *Zur Geschichte der deutschen Arbeiterbewegung*, vol. III, p. 11.

[142]"Grundsätze und Ziele der Sozialistischen Einheitspartei Deutschlands," *Dokumente der Sozialistischen Einheitspartei Deutschlands*, pp. 5 and 9.

even if the two processes, action and reaction, soon merged into one irretrievable situation; whereas, on the other hand, the promise to respond in a "revolutionary" fashion to capitalist misconduct provided the Communists with an alibi for pursuing separate policies in their own zone—always in response to the restoration of reaction in the West.

Only rarely did the Communists acknowledge that the "possibility" of nonviolent change derived from a military occupation. Pieck referred to it just once, though he presented the situation as a symbiosis that resulted from the coincidence of military occupation, arising out of the fact of the Germans' collective guilt, and the spontaneous formation of a mass movement in favor of antifascism and democracy. Even then, Pieck still managed to twist the argument to rationalize the party's previous policy. Because the old state apparatus had remained intact, and the working class failed to overcome its disunity, it would have been impossible to topple capitalism in earlier years and carry out the transition to socialism without revolutionary violence. Nowadays, Germany, or part of it, benefited from "special conditions"—the military occupation. Through the consistent implementation of the Potsdam accords in Soviet-occupied Germany, the reactionary state apparatus had been crushed and a new state and economic apparatus created, or was being created, upon a democratic foundation. Consequently, reaction had been deprived of the power to wield violence against the working class. The questions involved were entirely unrelated to any doctrinal "principle," let alone its abandonment for the sake of "crass opportunism"; rather, they pertained to tactics in the sense of practical politics: whether the reactionary forces would be shorn of their power base under the occupation and whether unification of the KPD and SPD would guarantee "that the working people, not reaction, will determine the course of future development." Pieck went on to say that the Communist promise not to "impose" a Soviet system was not a tactical ploy calculated to "pacify anxious minds, but rather corresponded and corresponds precisely to the specific conditions of the situation in Germany." Nevertheless, in the same context Pieck made the first alteration to the usual comment regarding the possibility of a peaceful transition to socialism. "We speak of the possibility of such a road, that is to say under the special conditions of the situation in Germany"; and these promised the chance "of growth into socialism that is peaceful *to a certain extent.*"[143]

Consequent Marxism

Soviet policy-makers in Moscow and the occupation officers in the zone felt from the outset that their early goals had the best chance of success if they

---

[143]Pieck, *Probleme der Vereinigung von KPD und SPD*, pp. 19-21, 23. My italics.

were couched in the language of democracy. It made little difference what the local party called itself or whether its program in any way infringed upon the "consequent Marxism." The overriding consideration was the party's capacity to act as an appendage of Soviet policy, if possible in all four zones; and in 1945 and 1946 the decision to avoid brute force sprang in part from the hope that a convincing display of democracy might make the effort to extend Soviet influence into those portions of Germany not occupied by the Russians more successful. This is one of the reasons why the Communists needed to pretend that "the KPD of today is no longer that of 1920 or 1932" and that the Socialist Unity party would be a "new kind of party," neither the old SPD nor the old KPD.[144] Problems arose because of the answer that the Communists supplied to what they themselves acknowledged to be "the most significant question of all"[145]—the "programmatic" or ideological basis for unification. Without a reasonably convincing answer to that question, any hope of impressing Social Democrats, much less ordinary Germans, with the distinction between democracy and "sovietization" dwindled considerably; and in December 1945, the Communists considered the new party's "maximum" program to be "the realization of socialism through the political hegemony of the working class in accordance with the doctrine of consequent Marxism."[146] The term "consequent Marxism" was, in fact, fairly routine; but the diction was deceptive. The Communists chose it to convey a relaxed attitude toward Leninist notions of revolution and dictatorship when the phrase meant orthodox Marxism-Leninism. As early as summer 1945, Ulbricht already linked democracy to the "profound insights taught us by Marx, Engels, Lenin, and Stalin" and said that the party's fight for democracy did not take place out of "momentary considerations of expedience."[147]

Actually, that linkage made any other theoretical distinction largely irrelevant. The argument that the SED would rid itself of the "opportunism of the old SPD" and the "dogmatism of the old KPD" may have seemed like an equal apportioning of responsibility for past failings; the stress on a "Marxist" merger, "finding the way back to Marxism,"[148] suggested that both KPD and SPD had fallen short of being "truly" Marxist. But these comments never squared with the party's concurrent claims of ideological consistency; and no sooner had the final obstacles to the merger been cleared away then the phrase "consequent Marxism" began to be replaced with remarks to the effect that the new party would rest "upon consequent Marxism-Leninism,

---

[144]Ackermann, *Fragen und Antworten*, pp. 27 and 28. Ackermann's phase was "Partei neuer Art."
[145]See Ackermann, "Gibt es einen besonderen deutschen Weg zum Sozialismus?" *Einheit* 1 (1946): 22.
[146]"Die zweite Phase der Einheit," *Tägliche Rundschau*, 27 December 1945.
[147]Ulbricht, "Erste Funktionärskonferenz der KPD Groß-Berlins," *Einheitsfront der antifaschistischen Parteien*, p. 25.
[148]The citations are from Ackermann, *Fragen und Antworten*, pp. 18, 25-26.

which has to be the granite foundation of the party."[149] Moreover, well in advance of the merger, the Communists had an agreement with Social Democrats stipulating that the SED's "maximum program" would rest on the "consequent Marxism" of the *Communist Manifesto* as well as Marx' critique of the Gotha program. Even if the "maximum" was a future prospect, the "minimum" goal being a "new democratic Germany in the sense of a *parliamentary-democratic Republic*,"[150] according to Marx' *Kritik des Gothaer Programms* the revolutionary transformation of a capitalist into a Communist society included a transitional period during which the "state can be nothing other than the revolutionary dictatorship of the proletariat."[151] It is equally revealing that Marx' *Kritik des Gothaer Programms*, the publication of which Ulbricht had demanded since late 1945,[152] was also used to applaud Marx' rejection of "opportunistic mistakes" made by the leaders of Social Democracy and his "sharp criticism" of dogmas associated with the "illusion of a 'peaceful evolution' into socialism."[153]

Nor was Marx' *Kritik des Gothaer Programms* the only "classic" used to argue implicitly in favor of eventual dictatorship; various treatises by Lenin, Stalin's *Problems of Leninism*, and, importantly, the *History of the Communist Party of the Soviet Union (Bolsheviki)* came out during the first half of 1946, the latter publication a book that Ulbricht said should be studied "in close connection with the questions that we have to solve today."[154] But Ulbricht made those remarks to a private audience; and in internal discussions, there was an acute awareness of the risks involved when the SED identified itself too closely with the Soviet Communist party. The *Short Course History* of the USSR was scheduled for release in December 1945, but then delayed out of a belated recognition of the need to change the publisher's imprint from Verlag Neuer Weg, an SED publishing house, to that of the Soviet military administration; and there appears to have been an additional dispute over the use of the phrase "Proletarians of the world, unite!" on the title page.[155] Recognizing the potential for harmful associations with Soviet-occupied Germany in discussions of "a party of a new type, a Marxist-

---

[149]Pieck, *Probleme der Vereinigung von KPD und SPD*, p. 24.

[150]Ackermann, "Wohin soll der Weg gehen?" *Einheitsfront der antifaschistischen Parteien*, p. 34.

[151]Quoted from "Zur Neuausgabe von Karl Marx Kritik des Gothaer Programms," *Neuer Weg* 1 (1946): 34-35.

[152]See "Die Aufgaben der KPD im Kampf um die Herstellung der *Einheit der Arbeiterklasse* [8-9 January 1946]," *Zur Geschichte der deutschen Arbeiterbewegung*, Zusatzband, p. 335.

[153]"Zur Neuausgabe von Karl Marx Kritik des Gothaer Programms," *Neuer Weg* 1 (1946): 34-35.

[154]Ulbricht, "Über die nächsten Aufgaben der Kommunisten zur Entwicklung antifaschistisch-demokratischer Verhältnisse in der sowjetischen Besatzungszone [early December 1945]," *Zur Geschichte der deutschen Arbeiterbewegung*, vol. II, 1933-1946, 2. Zusatzband, p. 356.

[155]See Besprechung am 23. 1. 1946 bei Marsch. Bockow. Zentrales Parteiarchiv. NL 36/734/153.

Leninist party, a party of social revolution" capable of organizing the proletarian revolution and establishing the dictatorship of the proletariat,[156] Fred Oelßner tried to strike a balance. He referred to the *Short Course History* as the "textbook of living Marxism," as a "primer of Leninism, the Marxism in the age of imperialism,"[157] but softened the remark by adding that the book contained no ready-made prescriptions.

Prior to the merger and then for some time afterwards, references to "consequent Marxism" still outnumbered calls for Marxism-Leninism proper, in addition to which the Communists emphasized that the SED's principles and goals were not "Communist."[158] But a scant year later, Ulbricht re-echoed the Stalinist characterization of a Marxist-Leninist "new type of party" codified in the *Short Course History*. He noted that the SED was the continuation neither of the old SPD or old KPD, but rather *"a new type of party"*[159]—a definition built around two contradictory assessments. Either the SED was "a new type of party" in the old Stalinist sense and, latently, no different from the KPD; or it was no longer the old KPD, in which case it could not be "a new type of party" in the real meaning of a phrase known to every leading German Communist. Ulbricht's characterization of the SED as the kind of party described in the *Short Course History* was thus an early anticipation of the open crusade that began in late 1948 to transform the SED into a Marxist-Leninist "new type of party." But the same phrase had also shown up much earlier; in June 1945, an article in the *Deutsche Volkszeitung* said that only "narrow-minded sectarians for whom living Marxism-Leninism and the teachings of Stalin concerning the new type of party" would think of arguing in favor of restricting party membership to workers.[160] Now ordinarily, Stalin's rigid definition of a "new type of party" denoted an elite cadre party, not a mass organization. But expedience in summer 1945 required that the KPD increase its depleted membership if it wished to compete with the larger SPD at a stage when prolonged competition seemed quite likely; and it apparently caused the Communists to try to broaden their appeal while clinging to old characterizations. Nor should it be assumed that the phrase "party of new type" made it into print accidentally. The *Deutsche Volkszeitung* was the only newspaper in the zone not then subject to SMAD censorship, and Paul Wandel was its editor; he approved every word published in it, staying up until early in the morning to finish the job.[161] Besides, two days earlier, and a full two months before the Communists spoke out in

[156]*Geschichte der Kommunistischen Partei der Sowjetunion (Bolschewiki) Kurzer Lehrgang*, pp. 427 and 429.

[157]Oelßner, "Das Lehrbuch des lebendigen Marxismus," *Neuer Weg* Heft 1 (1946): 33-34.

[158]See Ulbricht, "Einheit der Arbeiterklasse—Gebot der Stunde [26 March 1946]," *Zur Geschichte der deutschen Arbeiterbewegung*, 2. Zusatzband, p. 431.

[159]Ulbricht, "Die geschichtliche Rolle der SED," *Neuer Weg* 3/4 (1947): 4-5.

[160]"Partei des schaffenden Volkes," *Deutsche Volkszeitung*, 27 June 1945.

[161]As he told me in 1989.

favor of merger, Ulbricht uttered the same phrase; he argued that a "new type of unified party of the working people" presupposed a "scientific understanding" of socialism in the Soviet Union and the world view of Marxism and Leninism by the most progressive segments of the working class.[162]

This was the crux of the matter; no such consensus existed in summer 1945, and there could be no Marxist-Leninist party in its absence. But by fall, the KPD had reversed its opposition to merger, and Ulbricht promptly defined the proposed party using the old definition of a "new type of party." In November 1945, he explained that cooperation between Communists and Social Democrats was designed to help clarify all ideological issues within the German labor movement as a first step toward creation of "*a new type of unified party of the German working class.*" Because no such party had existed in 1918, the opportunities present then due to the collapse of German imperialism had been lost; and "formation of a new type of united party of the German working class as a precondition for the unity of the working class" was the top priority now. Ulbricht ended by calling upon "comrades of both working-class parties" to heed the lesson taught by the history of the German labor movement and forge "a unified party of the working class, a new type of party."[163]

Even though the description "new type of party" applied only to Marxist-Leninist cadre parties, Ulbricht now chose to characterize one as the outcome of a merger with Social Democracy—a senseless undertaking doctrinally because the designation had more aptly defined a splinter party. But Ulbricht utilized a term that denoted a political schism to signify its opposite. Later, the Communists categorically denied that unification had produced a "party of a new type,"[164] and transforming the SED back into a Leninist-Stalinist "party of a new type" in 1948 then restored the KPD's old orthodoxy with the added benefit that Soviet-zone Social Democracy no longer existed. Even so, none of these incongruities kept Ulbricht from his early use of old Stalinist phrases to describe an ostensibly new party. Communists and Social Democrats, he said in late 1945, needed to realize "that the united party of the working class as a new type of party, a party guided by the scientific teachings of Marxism-Leninism, must be forged."[165] During one of Ulbricht's closed speeches to the leadership of the KPD's regional

---

[162]Ulbricht, "Erste Funktionärskonferenz der KPD Groß-Berlins," *Einheitsfront der antifaschistisch-demokratischen Parteien*, p. 26. Ulbricht's phrase was "einheitliche Partei des werktätigen Volkes neuen Typus"—distinctly reminiscent of the phrase "einheitliche Partei der Werktätigen" apparently used by Stalin in his discussions with the Germans barely three weeks earlier.

[163]Ulbricht, "9. November 1918 in Deutschland," *Deutsche Volkszeitung*, 9 November 1945.

[164]See, for instance, "Wie schaffen wir eine Partei neuen Typus," *Sozialistische Bildungshefte* 9 (1948): 3.

[165]"Hallesche Sozialdemokraten und Kommunisten für die Einheit der Arbeiterklasse," *Deutsche Volkszeitung*, 11 November 1945. See also Ulbricht, "Die nächsten Aufgaben der KPD [19 October 1945]," *Zur Geschichte der deutschen Arbeiterbewegung*, Zusatzband, p. 279.

branch in Thuringia, he actually made remarks that effectively coupled Stalin's reference to a "unified party" in June 1945 with the notion of ideological exclusivity characteristic of the old KPD. The "unity of the working class," Ulbricht reportedly said, should be linked to the "essence of the party of a new type."[166] Nor were Ulbricht's early statements isolated; some of his others fell partly into the category of appeals for a "new type of party" in the deceptive sense of a "reformed" KPD and SPD bent upon continuing "all the good traditions of the socialist labor movement and still drawing self-critically upon the lessons from mistakes of the past."[167] But Ulbricht also made use of the term "new type of party" to refer to the arch-Stalinist KPD. On one occasion, he noted that the absence of a consequent struggle against "the imperialist rulers" during the first world war or after the November revolution in Germany had "made formation of the Communist party as a party of a new type necessary, one resting on the solid footing of the teachings of Marx and Engels and continuing the best traditions of Social Democracy during the early phase of the labor movement." He then praised Pieck, at his seventieth birthday party, by explaining that Pieck had expended all his energies down through the years in order to "make the Communist party into a workers' party of a new type and to bring about an antifascist united front."[168] This remark was calculated to create the impression that ideological integrity and the party's devotion to a "united front" were the two sides, then and now, of an identical political commitment based on genuine cooperation.

The problem with Ulbricht's appeals for a "new type of party" was that they clashed with the idea of a democratic transition to socialism because the concept had never been separable from the bedrock principles of dictatorship. Not that these contradictions in any way mirrored a clash of opinions between the men most prominent in stating them, Ulbricht and Ackermann; rather, policies sanctioned by Stalin were involved, and these had little to do with the preferences of those selected to articulate them. Besides, both men made public utterances that summed up each other's position. Ackermann spoke on at least one occasion of a "party of a new kind"; whereas Ulbricht noted periodically that the "Soviet order" would not be "imposed from the outside"—the Soviet government had said as much.[169] In addition, the very existence of the Social Democratic party and the bourgeois parties offered

---

[166]"Aufzeichnung über eine Besprechung Walter Ulbrichts mit der Bezirksleitung der KPD in Weimar [13 December 1945]," *Zur Geschichte der deutschen Arbeiterbewegung,* vol. II, 2. Zusatzband, p. 379.

[167]Ulbricht, "Die geschichtliche Rolle der SED," *Neuer Weg* 3/4 (1947): 4-5.

[168]Ulbricht, "Wilhelm Pieck der Vorkämpfer für eine einheitliche Arbeiterpartei," *Wilhelm Pieck. Dem Vorkämpfer für ein neues Deutschland zum 70. Geburtstag,* pp. 43 and 46.

[169]Ackermann, *Fragen und Antworten,* p. 27; and Ulbricht, "Die Einheit der Arbeiterklasse ist die Grundfrage für die Zukunft der Nation [11 January 1946]," *Zur Geschichte der deutschen Arbeiterbewegung,* vol. II, 2. Zusatzband, p. 408.

conclusive evidence that "the Soviet government is not imposing the Soviet system upon the German people,"[170] and Marshal Zhukov had repeated the assurance; the Soviet Union did not intend "somehow to force the Soviet order upon the German people." Ulbricht then contrasted a "Soviet system" with democracy by adding that Zhukov's comment warranted an important conclusion—in Soviet-occupied Germany a "democratic development was possible."[171]

Ulbricht's fondness for variations on the theme of a "new type of party," even as he disavowed the Soviet system for Germany and insisted that the nation would develop in accord with "its own circumstances,"[172] hinted at the possibility of a more rapid form of "sovietization" than the one actually occurring; and it may also have divulged his personal distaste for relinquishing notions of revolutionary development in favor of the less definite tactics. His stand on the question of a "new type of party" could easily have reflected a natural predisposition to abide by old concepts, alter them just enough to eliminate the toughest revolutionary rhetoric, describe the policies as new, and then couple them to a variety of other assumptions that retained their old meaning. That approach permitted flexibility in the implementation of tactical policies that might be continued or abandoned on a moment's notice. As for Ackermann, he may or may not have thought of the nonviolent road to socialism as something more than an expedient to be abandoned as soon as circumstances permitted; but neither his nor anyone else's motives had too much to do with the thinking behind Soviet sponsorship of the idea. Each approach was a tactical variant of Soviet policy toward Germany in general, and Ackermann's theses never precluded the kind of development that later turned the SED openly into a Stalinist "new type of party." Ackermann's promise of revolutionary "bloodshed" if the democratic road to socialism encountered any resistance addressed the issue squarely. It is certainly true that the disavowal of the German and other national roads to socialism might have occurred later than 1948 had it served Soviet interests to maintain the appearance of democracy or popular democracy a bit longer, just as Ulbricht's more immediate call for a Marxist-Leninist party could have been pushed more vigorously prior to 1948 had the imperatives of Soviet foreign policy made it expedient. But it is hard to ignore the fact that the recourse to revolutionary measures leading to the quicker realization of "socialism" had been a distinct possibility allowed for by the Communists from the outset. This is the key idea conjoining both concepts; the clear threat of violence made its way into the SED's principles and goals right after the merger, and,

---

[170]Ulbricht, "Offene Antwort an sozialdemokratische Genossen," *Deutsche Volkszeitung*, 16 January 1946.
[171]Ulbricht, *Der Plan des demokratischen Neuaufbaus*, pp. 15-16.
[172]Ulbricht, "Erste Funktionärskonferenz der KPD Groß-Berlin," *Einheitsfront der antifaschistisch-demokratischen Parteien*, p. 25.

indeed, the threat of coercion, as well as its use, figured centrally in the tactics employed to force the merger to begin with. In early 1946, Pieck criticized those who suggested that unification was unfolding "under force and pressure by the Soviet occupation authorities," asking what difference it made. There was "no sense regretting it if, as a result, unification of the working class is achieved so that we have things firmly under control with regard to reaction." Naturally the Communists opposed "overzealous" occupation officers attempting to accelerate unification by exerting pressure, but only because such practices were "absolutely superfluous."[173]

That remark was hollow talk given the thinking of those for whom the idea of "voluntary" cooperation was perfectly compatible with the use of force to encourage it. Besides, "progress" in the Soviet zone could be expected to provoke reaction into an intensification of violence, and a Soviet-zone equivalent of Stalin's theoretical rationale for the use of terror in the Soviet Union developed soon enough: "The more marvelous and effective the victories won by the forces of democracy, the stauncher the resistance put up by reaction and the vestiges of fascism, the meaner and craftier the methods of struggle employed by enemies of human progress, the more active their attempts to retard the advance of democracy."[174] The need to resort to violence out of self-defense was therefore as predictable as the "resistance" used by the Communists as an excuse to modify their commitment to democracy. Persons who opposed the need for democracy to defend itself were said to desire a political regime that merely masqueraded as democracy because they were bent upon granting enemies of the people the opportunity to exploit the "rules of democracy" to their own advantage.[175] By early 1946, then, the Communists began to speak increasingly of Western violations of the Potsdam accords, and a short time later, the traditional Communist two-camps dichotomy reappeared. Stalin's speech in February 1946 signaled the transition and provided the necessary encouragement for related arguments in Soviet-occupied Germany. Stalin contrasted the internal contradictions of capitalism with the superiority of the Soviet system; reintroduced the notion of the incompatibility of the two social systems; underscored the unavoidability of future military conflict; and insinuated that, as an outgrowth of capitalism, the West was responsible for fascism. When Churchill denounced the Soviet Union for violating the Yalta agreements two months later in his iron-curtain speech, Stalin charged the West with war-mongering.[176]

Correspondingly, Ackermann warned in March 1946 that reaction had just begun "crawling out of its hidden nooks again." "Cautiously in the be-

---

[173]Quoted from Weber, "Zum Transformationsprozeß des Parteiensystems in der SBZ/DDR," *Parteiensystem zwischen Demokratie und Volksdemokratie*, p. 33.
[174]See Rosen, "Die Demokratie marschiert," *Tägliche Rundschau*, 6 February 1946.
[175]G.B. "Was ist Demokratie," *Neues Deutschland*, 30 April 1946.
[176]See *Ein Interview J.W. Stalins durch den Korrespondenten der "Prawda,"* p. 5.

ginning," it extended its feelers, "venturing here and there an impertinent assault before giving ground again the moment it encounters serious resistance, only to gather its forces anew and continue its sinister maneuvers using a different approach." Prompt unification of SPD and KPD was alone capable of dealing with the menace; indeed, in the event that the rift in the working class continued, a new triumph of reaction would be inevitable, "and our people will stride toward a dark, hopeless future."[177] This was the threat invoked by the German Communists; what makes Ackermann's lurid language worth quoting is that, in most other contexts, the promise of nonviolence in traveling the road to socialism had been based on the advantageous circumstances in part of Germany. It now developed that there was still an abundance of enemies; worse, reaction mounted its opposition "from within the ranks of the German labor movement," stirring up confusion by means of its "agents within the working class" and hindering efforts leading toward organizational unity of both workers' parties.[178] Ulbricht's show of anger at the disruption of the "comradely relationship" between the KPD and the other antifascist-democratic parties taking place "from outside, through agents of all sorts," was an example of this rhetoric,[179] and Pieck advanced similar arguments. He pointed out that reaction began marshaling its forces because the decision to move ahead with formation of a unity party "mobilized both friends and enemies of working-class unity;"[180] whereas Ulbricht talked of the fight between the "progressive-democratic" and the "fascist-reactionary forces" taking place throughout all of Germany. This struggle was reflected most clearly in the question of working-class unity, he said, because the fascist-reactionary forces were bent upon salvaging as much as possible from German imperialism and Prussian militarism. They exerted tremendous pressure upon the workers in order to create yet another rift, hindering unification. Ulbricht called this "an entirely normal development."[181]

But that normalcy did not prevent the Communists from feigning surprise at the intensity of the response to their actions. Whereas the decision to merge had predictably filled the "hearts of the workers with enthusiasm," the Communists claimed that the unpredictable effect upon the "circles of German reaction" caught them off guard.[182] The Communists then blamed opposition within the Soviet zone on Western interference anyway in a clear restatement of the typical Stalinist notion of capitalist encirclement—reaction

[177]Ackermann, *Fragen und Antworten*, pp. 11-12.
[178]Ulbricht, "Die Einheit der Arbeiterklasse ist die Grundfrage für die Zukunft der Nation [11 January 1946]," *Zur Geschichte der deutschen Arbeiterbewegung*, vol. II, Zusatzband, p. 411; and Pieck, *Probleme der Vereinigung von KPD und SPD*, p. 8.
[179]Ulbricht, *Der Plan des demokratischen Neuaufbaus*, p. 41.
[180]Pieck, *Probleme der Vereinigung von KPD und SPD*, p. 9.
[181]Ulbricht, "Die Aufgaben der KPD im Kampf um die Herstellung der Einheit der Arbeiterklasse [9 January 1946]," *Zur Geschichte der deutschen Arbeiterbewegung*, Zusatzband, p. 327.
[182]"Vor der Vereinigung," *Neuer Weg* 1 (1946): 1.

introduced alien ideas and ideologies as the only means of confounding efforts leading to democracy. As a consequence, promises of peaceful development were always highly conditional. "If we provide [the forces of democracy] with firm leadership through formation of the Socialist Unity party," said Pieck, "this certainly opens up the possibility of carrying out the transition to socialism by traveling this democratic road." Even then, however, such a development could not exclude the possibility "that the working class might be constrained by acts of sabotage engaged in by the factory owners and by their assault upon democracy to proceed against them with revolutionary means, answering violence with violence."[183]

By early 1946, Ulbricht insisted that a tenacious struggle was underway between the "old fascist and reactionary forces and the progressive, democratic forces," and he even claimed that paramilitary groups, camouflaged "democratically," operated in Soviet-occupied Germany. To the cry from his audience, "Give the police weapons," Ulbricht responded that they would soon have them.[184] In his plea for the means to protect democracy, Ulbricht then focused on accusations that the party's brand of democracy reeked of dictatorship. But what was meant by "dictatorship"? For the first time in German history, he answered, the "representatives" of working people were deciding things in a large portion of Germany, leading others to conclude that "dictatorial methods" were used in the process. To this he retorted: "When certain people speak of 'dictatorship,' I tell them: behind [such talk] lurk those circles who wish to use democratic slogans to reorganize reactionary, fascist forces, and when one puts a stop to their activity they speak of 'dictatorship.' Well, they can call it by whatever name they want, but working people must not allow reaction to reorganize."[185] By March 1946, Ulbricht hinted that the party had every intention of pushing ahead with its policies. The hope of rebuilding the nation in all of Germany had not turned into reality; but for that reason the Communists were going to great lengths to provide "the best possible example" for the other zones. If policies implemented locally caused a rift with the other zones, responsibility for it lay with the Western allies because they had failed to adhere to the Potsdam accords; and the "most characteristic feature" of the current situation consisted of the fact that an "embittered battle is being fought between the democratic forces, who wish to build Germany anew, and the old fascist and reactionary forces."[186] As tensions worsened internationally, a new note crept into party rhetoric and infused what had earlier passed as German national politics with

[183]Pieck, *Probleme der Vereinigung von KPD und SPD*, p. 22.
[184]Ulbricht, "Die Einheit der Arbeiterklasse ist die Grundfrage für die Zukunft der Nation [11 January 1946]," *Zur Geschichte der deutschen Arbeiterbewegung*, vol. II, 2. Zusatzband, pp. 404-7.
[185]Ulbricht, "Einheit der Arbeiterklasse—Gebot der Stunde [26 March 1946]," ibid., p. 437.
[186]Ulbricht, *Der Plan des demokratischen Neuaufbaus*, pp. 5 and 45.

a broader dimension. True, Ulbricht said, a battle was being waged in Germany between those who had learned from the catastrophe of two wars and the forces of reaction; but the battle was complicated "due to the fact that foreign elements are at work, strengthening the forces of reaction in the western territories." Churchill's iron-curtain speech, Ulbricht added, showed just what was at stake in Germany.[187]

For the duration of the year, the Communists continued to emphasize their commitment to policies that they considered appropriate for the entire nation; but they made it equally plain that those policies would not be compromised locally for the sake of rapid reunification. The forces behind fascism retained much of their power; these forces sought to "turn back the wheel of history" by retarding democratic development in Germany; and for the party to back away from its obligations just for the sake of national unity would be tantamount to allowing the reactionaries to salvage much from German imperialism.[188] In private consultations with the SMAD, the commitment to Soviet-zone policies appeared even clearer by July 1946. Sounding like Stalin the year before, Bokov brought up the "question of government" and apparently discussed it with both Pieck and Grotewohl in the same general context as the SED's *"perspectives."* These he characterized as the party's "considerable power," "leading role," and "great responsibility." Among other things, Bokov pressed for a sharper struggle against "sectarians, reformists, Trotskyists" in order to strengthen what he called the "party's effectiveness"; and in this connection, he emphasized the need for the SED to "become a state power." Bokov's remarks captured the essence of Stalin's earlier correlation of national unity with the existence of a "unified party at the center"; and further comments made during the discussion between Pieck, Grotewohl, and Bokov on 27 July 1946 were similarly reminiscent of Stalin's talk of "two Germanies" in the same context as the need to secure national unity through a powerful Communist party. Bokov told the Germans that the English and the Americans had taken steps toward a "new state order"; and he stressed the importance of keeping the initiative "in our hands" by developing guidelines for a "future state order" that Bokov characterized as a democratic republic. He also remarked upon the need to accelerate demands for a "unif.[ied] German government" and a constitution in connection with a future peace conference.[189]

Aside from the points that Bokov's remarks shared with Stalin's older comments, his conversation with the Germans in Karlshorst was just as important in the context of the speech delivered by Molotov a few weeks be-

[187]Ulbricht, "Der Plan des demokratischen Neuaufbaus und seine Gegner [15 March 1946]," *Zur Geschichte der deutschen Arbeiterbewegung*, vol. II, 2. Zusatzband, p. 421.
[188]Ulbricht, *Der Plan des demokratischen Neuafbaus*, p. 5.
[189]See Besprechung bei Bockow am 26. 7. 1946 / Grotewohl und ich; and Besprechung am 26. 7. 1946 in Karlshorst um 9 Uhr abends. Zentrales Parteiarchiv. NL 35/734/187 and 190-91.

fore at the foreign ministers' conference in Paris. Molotov's pronouncements attracted so much attention because the Russians had previously said little about Germany's future as a nation—in stark contrast to the elaborate outlines of the program advocated by the German Communists. Molotov broke the silence when he announced that the time had come to discuss the shape of postwar Germany and a peace treaty. He began by repeating the contention that the Soviet Union was not bent upon revenge; there was a difference between Hitler and the German people. But nor could the Germans ignore their responsibility, and any future government had to guarantee the eradication of all "vestiges of fascism in Germany."[190] Of course, the German Communists and their Soviet advisors felt that only one party demonstrated the requisite commitment to eradicating fascism; and this hubris, especially in connection with the necessity of turning the SED into a "state power," was reflected in the discussions on 27 June 1946 in Karlshorst. Molotov, however, shied away from the subject in public; he limited himself to phrases from the Potsdam accords concerning the "liquidation" of fascism, accused the Americans of having reneged on these commitments, and noted that the Soviet Union considered the fulfillment of such obligations as an "indispensable condition for the reconstruction of the German state on a democratic foundation." Molotov did stress that this goal required *the active support by our side for the democratic forces in Germany*," but he referred only in passing to "serious democratic elements" in the Soviet zone that had attained a "certain measure of success" in their efforts to reconstruct Germany democratically." He also insisted that Germany remain an industrialized nation, as opposed to its being reduced to an agrarian land punished by the allies through the deprivation of its industry.

Most importantly, Molotov couched each of his constructive and conciliatory arguments addressed to the German people in language implying that the British and Americans preferred to punish them. Unlike the Soviet Union, the allies were driven by revenge, and their advocacy of dismemberment through "federalism" clashed with the Soviet support of German unity. The USSR naturally intended to respect the wishes of the people in the event that they actually favored federalism, Molotov hastened to add, but there was only a scant likelihood of that because the Western allies were the ones who advocated federalism; whereas their preferences and *the genuine wish of the German people, or at least the German people in this or that portion of Germany, are two different things.*" With this line of reasoning, Molotov took the more common assumption that the Soviet Union intended to impose its system of government upon the Germans and directed the accusation back at the allies. Such contempt for the wishes of the local population con-

---

[190]See "Um das Schicksal Deutschlands. Voller Wortlaut der zweiten Rede Molotows auf der Sitzung der Außenministerkonferenz in Paris vom 10. Juli," *Neues Deutschland*, 12 July 1946.

trasted vividly with the Soviet determination not to "force upon the Germans this or that resolution of the question."[191] But there was nothing in Molotov's remarks to indicate any willingness to compromise on the subject of "democratization" nationwide; instead, it was taken for granted that unity without prior democratization in all zones jeopardized the progress made in Soviet-occupied Germany. In response to Western calls for economic ties between the four zones, Stalin insisted that "the political unity of Germany" had to be reestablished first.[192]

Marx, Engels, Lenin, Stalin

The SED's determination to become a "state power" was immediately reflected in the party's rhetoric. The SED would see to it that the working masses "broadened" their powerful influence in the eastern zone; and any effort undertaken by reactionary elements to "turn back the wheel of history, casting the labor movement into the same reversionary and lamentable circumstances as those still existing today in Germany's western territories," would be rebuffed.[193] Those remarks mimicked Molotov in implying that national unity must occur on terms set in the East. An article published later in the year was better yet at applying Molotov's remarks to Soviet-occupied Germany:

> Although socialism, which could transform Germany into a flourishing land, has unfortunately not yet been able to be realized, we can nevertheless go forward step by step if this time we take the *German* road of our *natural development* prescribed by the conditions of our entire existence. What does this consist of? In taking power away from the nobility, the large land owners, the monopolists, the militarists, and the active Nazis—*in all of Germany* following the example of the eastern zone; in the planned organization of our economy and increasing production through the active involvement of the working class and the farmers in reconstruction—*throughout all of Germany* in line with the example set by the eastern zone; in renouncing chauvinism in favor of the unity of our nation and peace between our people with all peoples—*throughout the whole of Germany* following the example of the eastern zone; in the demilitarization and total democratization of *all* of Germany following the example of the eastern zone; in turning away once and for all from the more or less *constant* hostile German policy toward the Soviet Union

[191]"Molotow über Deutschlands Schicksal," *Neues Deutschland*, 11 July 1946.
[192]"Stalin gegen das Gerede von einem 'neuen Krieg,'" *Neues Deutschland*, 25 September 1946; "Stalin zur Sicherung des Weltfriedens," *Neues Deutschland*, 30 October 1946.
[193]Dahlem, "Vom Wesen und von den Aufgaben der SED," *Neuer Weg* 6 (1946): 1-2.

—throughout all of Germany in keeping with the example set by the eastern zone.

This had nothing to do with socialism, even less with "sovietization, and was utterly unrelated to any so-called eastern influences." Rather, these were imperatives that emerged "from *our* circumstances" and pointed toward the way "*of Germany's natural development*."[194] It was especially important in fall 1946 that the Communists repeat their disavowal of "sovietization" because communal, state, and Berlin elections were approaching. But following Molotov's speech in Paris, the argument nonetheless supported Soviet foreign policy and, for that reason alone, risked pointing back at "sovietization" unless it was denied that Soviet objectives in occupied Germany and the advocacy of dictatorship coincided. Commentary in the local press set out to prove accordingly that the Soviet Union sided with Germany's national interest. An article in the SED's *Einheit* called Molotov's comments the "decisive and sensational high point" of the Paris conference because they established the "sole possible basis" on which Germany's political and economic reconstruction could go forward. True, Molotov had referred only briefly to the measured success of indigenous "democratic elements" in Germany, and *Einheit* followed suit by omitting any reference to the SED. But Molotov's speech had still called steps taken in the Eastern zone "exemplary" for the West as well.[195] Also echoing Molotov, Alexander Abusch linked democratization along antifascist lines directly to the coming elections. Hope for the future lay in the Germans' own efforts toward democratization, he said, the question being whether the people were capable of redoubling their efforts to prove to the world that they were ready for self-government. Abusch then proceeded to an attack upon the Western zones and called attention to the present danger posed by those who favored "separatism and federalism" as a substitution for real national unity. Molotov's Paris speech, by contrast, contained "the most well-reasoned program thus far, prepossessing in its antifascist consistency, striking in its democratic generosity, and absent any feelings of revenge."[196]

Western proposals, by contrast, were denounced as a bid to dismember the country through schemes of separation, particularism, and federalization. "All those forces opposing progress, democracy, and peace," wrote Grotewohl, "have joined together in western Germany"; left up to them, the country would have "thirteen fatherlands," rather than a single, unified one.[197] Ulbricht also brought up the "dismemberment of Germany into separate, au-

---

[194]Ende, "Vergleichende November-Betrachtungen," *Neues Deutschland*, 7 November 1946.
[195]"Die Bedeutung der Molotow-Rede," *Einheit* 3 (August) 1946: 186-87.
[196]Abusch, "Paris—und die Wahlen," *Die Weltbühne* 4 (1946): 100-1.
[197]"Grotewohl fordert Volksentscheid über die Einheit Deutschlands," *Neues Deutschland*, 13 September 1946.

tonomous states." Whereas Molotov had expressed the Soviet Union's unequivocal opposition to federalism and insisted that the "true desires of the German people" must be taken into consideration, the American secretary of state answered Molotov by calling for just such a federal system. Worse, the Western allies were going ahead with plans to unite the English and American zones—measures serving only to prevent "Germany's unity and further her dismemberment."[198] Echoing Stalin, the SED also editorialized that economic without political unity worked to the advantage of those who, wielding economic power and influence, would persist in using it to the disadvantage of the people"; whereas Stalin revealed the road to democratization and thus to resolution of the German problem.[199] But given the implications of these assessments, remarks made by Ulbricht just days after Molotov's speech actually confirmed his awareness of the fact that the SED's policies widened the rift between the two Germanies. "If we were to go one step further in implementing our democratic politics in the Soviet zone of occupation," he said, "this would create the danger of tearing Germany apart. . . . We do not want to give the reactionary elements in the other zones any pretext to persist in their federalist policies." All measures taken in support of democratic construction and the democratization of the economy had to be calculated so as to make it possible for them to be realized throughout the whole of Germany; "it must be possible," he concluded, "to win the majority of the people for this policy."[200] When that failed to happen, however, and when the party accelerated the pace of "democratization" anyway, it was easy to fall back on the argument that policy-making in the West had become the preserve of local and foreign reactionaries and that unification under those conditions would spell a quick end to democratic gains made in the East. Moreover, the reactionaries much preferred "a dismembered, federalized Germany" because it offered them the best opportunity to go on spinning their "dark intrigues against progress and peace."[201] The reestablishment of Germany's unity was thus quite naturally "a question of democratization in all parts of the country," Ulbricht said in an effort to explain why neither East nor West wanted reunification under current conditions. But he did so in a manner designed to convey the impression that his party was nonetheless blameless. In accord with the "will of the majority of our people," he concluded, "we declare resolutely that neither a bizonal system, a federal state system, nor any other federalist or even separatist resolution will meet with the approval of our people. *Our people want a united, democratic Germany.*"[202]

[198]Ulbricht, "Um die Zukunft Deutschlands," *Neues Deutschland*, 12 September 1946.
[199]"Stalin und Deutschland," *Neues Deutschland*, 30 October 1946.
[200]Ulbricht, *Demokratischer Wirtschaftsaufbau*, pp. 18-19.
[201]"Der neue Tag," *Neues Deutschland*, 13 July 1946.
[202]Ulbricht, "Das Zweizonen-Abkommen," *Neues Deutschland*, 5 December 1946.

In discussions connected with the fall elections, the Communists redoubled their efforts to rid the SED of its reputation as the "Russians' party" by trying to persuade the public that it fought for Germany's national interests. The Communists hit hard on the themes of antifascism, democracy, and national unity; explicit mention of Marxism-Leninism, to say nothing of "sovietization" or dictatorship, tended to be avoided in favor of appropriate euphemisms. But the Communists still had to contend with critics who persisted in accusing the party of being guided by the very objective that it publicly renounced, "sovietization," and who then related that objective to the recent past. These accusations took the party's own habit of slurring its critics by impugning their antifascism and turned it into a campaign issue against the party itself. The SED's "leading personalities," as an editorial in the party daily put it, were shamelessly accused of harboring the same intentions against which they had just spent thirteen years battling: "single-party system, authoritarianism, repression of the individual." This "witches' dance" of accusations contrasted graphically with the party's categorical disavowal of a single-party system in favor of an antifascist, democratic republic.[203] Nonetheless, the party was still accused of aspiring to a dictatorship by employing methods actually comparable to those used by the Nazis, and the Communists denounced these attacks as an affront to their integrity that qualified as latent fascism themselves. When the two labor parties resolved to merge after years of division, ran one of the SED's counterarguments, self-styled advocates of democracy bandied about concepts like "dictatorship, yearnings towards totality, centralism, and so on—in a word, something akin to the reintroduction of a kind of fascism." Such enemies of democracy warned of a new form of "state tutelage and regimentation of the individual," which the people promptly associated with "dictatorship, ostensibly the antithesis of democracy, freedom, and self-determination." Even if thinking people knew enough to ask the real question, dictatorship by whom, over whom, and to what end, "the enemy" employed the concept in full awareness of the fact that the masses understood "dictatorship" to be nothing more than a government exercised by extremists who relied upon "terror."[204]

The nature of this disavowal suggested that the SED's public opposition to single-party systems only served to hide its own leanings toward one. But whatever prospects existed for the party to acquire support among the population rested on the ability of its spokesmen to establish the SED's democratic credentials in the eyes of the public, and this involved belittling the "ridiculous reproach" that the SED was a "'totalitarian' party" out to absorb all others and establish a one-party system or its equivalent.[205] Proof that this

[203]"Gruselpropaganda," *Neues Deutschland*, 6 August 1946.
[204]Weinert, "Cui bono?" *Die Weltbühne* 2 (1946): 33-34.
[205]"Totalitäre Partei?" *Neues Deutschland*, 10 October 1946. See also Grotewohl, "Die Grundrechte des deutschen Volkes und der Weg zur Einheit Deutschlands," *Einheit* 6 (1946): 331.

was not so, read the commentary just referred to, lay in the very existence of other parties in the Soviet zone that enjoyed complete freedom of activity and ample opportunity to win the confidence of the population. Even the SED's enemies had to admit that elections in Soviet-occupied Germany were free and democratic; and the SED had no way of dissolving the other parties even if it secretly aspired to "totality." Nor did whispers about the role of the "occupation authorities" mean anything; the Russians were the ones who permitted the formation of four different antifascist parties to begin with.[206] Nonetheless, concern lingered about an understanding of democracy that branded the SED's critics as fascist and reactionary. Who exactly qualified as a reactionary? Anyone who stood in the way of a complete eradication of fascism, thwarted policies designed to transform Germany into a genuinely democratic nation, subscribed to its dismemberment through federalization, paid lip service to democratizing the economy while opposing the nationalization of the factories, and campaigned chauvinistically against other peoples and against the Soviet Union. Additionally, anyone who chose to impugn the Communists' commitment to democracy was said to reveal complete ignorance of "scientific socialism" because mechanical juxtapositions of dictatorship and democracy were so nefariously undialectical. Fascist dictatorship aside, the elements of democracy and dictatorship were always tightly intertwined; the question came down to "*who* possesses democratic freedoms and *who* is limited or denied access to them." A system in which political power was exercised by the people, who curtailed or suspended democratic rights and liberties available to "reactionary enemies of the people," was under no circumstances a "dictatorship pure and simple." Those who disputed the qualities of "real democracy" by denouncing it as a dictatorship merely demonstrated that they desired neither democracy nor socialism; they were reactionaries.[207] The Communists also denied that they "invented" reaction as a ruse to stigmatize their opponents. The SED merely wished to end monopoly capitalism as the only way of exterminating fascism and preventing new imperialist wars, as a result of which reaction denied that the SED was independent and democratic, slurred it as a vehicle of the Russians, and slandered it further by charging that the party was the old KPD "under a new name."[208]

The Communists engaged in a new round of self-criticism in response, as if disavowing their past misconduct made up for present behavior or offered any guarantees for the future. Pieck voiced cautious criticism of the KPD for having advocated a dictatorship of the proletariat in the years leading up to Hitler's accession to power when it ought to have placed a higher premium upon the defense of democracy; the strategical error lay in the party's pre-

[206]"Totalitäre Partei?" *Neues Deutschland*, 10 October 1946.
[207]"Wer sind die Reaktionäre?" *Neues Deutschland*, 10 November 1946.
[208]Oelßner, "Was heißt heute Reaktion?" *Neues Deutschland*, 28 September 1946.

mature goal of a revolution and dictatorship and in the tactical error of failing to discriminate between the Nazis and Social Democracy.[209] Not surprisingly, the self-criticism omitted any reference to the original source of policies pursued by the KPD—its membership in the Comintern and utter subservience to the Soviet Communist party and to Stalin. This irony was all the greater because the Communists criticized themselves, by implication, for having copied the Russians and for seeking to apply Soviet standards and solutions to Germany's problems in the past while engaging in a concurrent line of reasoning that established certain Soviet principles as a model for Germany. Anton Ackermann argued in late 1946 that one could not be a "proponent of scientific socialism" at all without acknowledging the socialist character of the Russian revolution. Nowadays this meant that "our united Marxist party must aspire to a new, higher plateau with respect to the Russian October revolution and the USSR than the SPD and KPD managed to do in the Weimar republic." The SPD had wanted nothing to do with the Soviet Union in the past, he said, whereas the KPD correctly assessed the character of the revolution and adopted a "positive stance" toward the USSR; it had merely erred in its bid to transfer "*schematically* the forms and appearances of the movement in Russia to wholly different German conditions." That lesson had been learned, and the SED, as a "consistently Marxist party," was now confronted with the task of linking "the positive attitude toward the USSR that is self-evident for all Marxists to a self-evident attitude as an independent German Marxist party."[210]

This was the clearest description yet of the dilemma facing the German Communists and the necessity of splitting doctrinal hairs to solve it. What exactly was the nature of relations between the Socialist Unity and Soviet Communist party? Discussions of the question had always risked complicating matters for the SED, but by fall 1946, with the elections over, the party began comparing the two parties favorably. Franz Dahlem called for supplying the SED with a body of "functionaries of a new type" because in the current phase of Germany's development Stalin's sage advice that "*the cadres make all the difference*" was the answer to the tasks confronting the party.[211] Other comments were more systematic in the articulation of arguments that appeared to contradict notions of a democratic road to socialism. A graphic illustration was the growing emphasis upon lessons taught by the *Short Course* history of the Soviet Communist party. The SED was not a mere fusion of two parties that overcame this or that previous direction of the divided labor movement, an ideologist by the name of Hoffmann wrote in *Ein-*

[209]Pieck, "Leitfaden zur Geschichte der KPD. Vortrag, gehalten von Wilhelm Pieck im Dezember 1943," *Neuer Weg* 2 (1946): 19.

[210]Ackermann, "29. Jahrestag der Großen Sozialistischen Oktober-Revolution," *Neues Deutschland*, 7 November 1946.

[211]Dahlem, "Der neue Typus des Funktionärs der SED," *Einheit* 4 (1946): 198-99.

heit; the SED was "*a new party* of the German working class" that would infuse new meaning into the "Marxist German labor movement" even as it maintained a tradition as old as Marxism itself: the "living dialectical link of theory and practice."[212] These remarks were a roundabout way of claiming that Marxism would be adapted to suit German needs not as a "dogma," but as a guide to action in accordance with "present conditions and possibilities." Because the struggle for formation of a Russian labor party provided an example of just such a dialectical view of Marxism, the *Short Course* history was considered a fount of practical wisdom. This led straight to the matter of the "party of a new type." So much was owed to Lenin and Stalin because they had devoted their efforts to investigating the "new conditions of imperialism with Marxist consistency," the result of their endeavors being the "*Leninist* doctrine of the party of the new type." Lenin developed the organizational and ideological basis for the party of a new type; whereas Stalin systematized these characteristics. Lenin first and then Stalin had taken Marxism a step beyond Marx, enriching it with the insights of Leninism so that Leninism could be considered Marxism in the era of imperialism.

The hybrid, Marxism-Leninism, was therefore the dialectical application of classic Marxism to conditions prevailing in Soviet Russia during the era of imperialism; and Bolsheviks could rightly call themselves Marxist-Leninists. Hoffmann went on to develop a chain of arguments leading to a gradual reconciliation of the practical application in Germany of policies customarily identified with Lenin and Stalin with the avoidance of "sovietization." The critical passage stated that the SED had the historic obligation to end the division within the working class and point the way to a new road to the future. "This road cannot be identical with the Russian, English, or American way; it must, it can be only a German road in accordance with conditions in our country and in line with the interests of our people." It could be based "solely on the foundations of Marxism as Marxism was grounded in the classical writings of *Marx, Engels, Lenin, and Stalin* and in the course of the practical struggle."[213] With those words, Hoffmann managed to combine Leninist-Stalinist definitions of the Marxist-Leninist party with the notion of a democratic road to socialism geared to local conditions and led by an "independent" German party. The primary purpose of his remarks was to emphasize the importance of every critical ideological principle with the exception of the one, dictatorship, upon which all others hinged and which so flagrantly contradicted the promise of a democratic transition to socialism. These issues caused problems precisely because its democratic gestures prevented the party from subscribing publicly to doctrinal principles that it could never categorically renounce either.

[212]Hoffmann, "Lehren des 7. November," *Einheit* 7 (1946): 357.
[213]Ibid., pp. 358-60.

The leadership certainly understood the volatility of the issue and sought to resolve the contradiction in late October 1946. At a meeting of the SED's executive board, the Parteivorstand, comprised of eighty members (roughly half of whom were former Social Democrats), Anton Ackermann reaffirmed the party's commitment to its "principles and goals" accepted in April 1946. He focused particularly on the words "political rule of the working class as the precondition of socialism" in order to emphasize that the phrase was not a synonym "for something else." Ackermann agreed with Paul Wandel that the "political power of the working class" involved the necessary use of some force against the bourgeoisie; for it was a utopian notion to think that the bourgeoisie would suffer the loss of its power without putting up any resistance. In fact, the inevitability of resistance was the alpha and omega of Marxism, and breaking it required the political might of the working class.[214] But Ackermann's arguments were based on deception, and not just because of what he and others had said previously about a peaceful transition. The "principles and goals" that he now reemphasized because they outlined possibilities other than dictatorship had contained the promise of a democratic road to socialism *contingent* upon the existence of a precondition now categorically denied. The SED desired a democratic road, the document read, but guaranteed a violent response *if* the "capitalist class" itself behaved undemocratically by engaging in resistance. But if resistance was as inevitable as the party's use of force to subdue it, as Ackermann now argued, then the possibility of a democratic road to socialism had never existed doctrinally; the original claim to the contrary, the essence of the party's endorsement of democracy over dictatorship, was based on a lie. The problem with drawing any of these conclusions at this point was that a program built upon dictatorship would have violated the Potsdam accords, which called for democratization, contradicted Molotov's comments in Paris, and devastated prospects for national unity.

Of course, there were parallel attempts to reconcile "true" democracy or consistent democratization with dictatorship, but these occurred in somewhat separate contexts until the two lines of reasoning converged. That came later; in October 1946 Ackermann tried to persuade the former Social Democrats sitting in his audience of the continuing validity of the SED's commitment to democracy and prevent radical Communists also present from owning up publicly to much different proclivities. The real question, Ackermann argued, was whether the political rule of the working class absolutely must take the same form as in Russia; and "we say, no." But his reasons were tactical, not ideological, and thus departed from the theoretical basis given as the reason for the discussion in the first place. Use of the words "dictatorship

[214]Referat und Schlußwort Anton Ackermanns auf der 6. Tagung des Parteivorstandes der SED. 24./25. Oktober 1946. Zentrales Parteiarchiv, NL 109/14/297-9.

of the working class" reminded everyone of the Soviet Union; this was why "we have abandoned use of the concept." This explanation was true, though Ackermann also contended that the approach was "scientifically" sound as well. But he sidestepped another important issue. He linked the "political power of the working class," the only means of breaking the inevitable resistance of the bourgeoisie, to the issue of *transition*. Ackermann focused his attention on the road to socialism, what the Communists called their "minimum" goal, and not on the "maximum" ultimate objective always understood to be dictatorship. When Ackermann emphasized the continuing validity of the SED's "principles and goals" in order to reaffirm the party's commitment to objectives that were not "synonymous" with dictatorship, he was then compelled to continue an earlier ruse. In declaring his support for the "principles and goals" in October 1946, with some slight alterations Ackermann used the exact language contained in the original programmatic document formally accepted in April 1946. But the words at issue here, which Ackermann *contrasted* with dictatorship, were virtually identical to the language chosen by him in his article dealing with the German road to socialism published in February 1946, except for one addition. In February, Ackermann called the acquisition of "all" power by the working class the precondition of socialism; but, quoting Marx, he added that these circumstances constituted the "revolutionary dictatorship of the proletariat."

In February 1946, Ackermann must have had the end result in mind; if so, the original program amounted to no more than the promise of a "democratic" path to dictatorship. Nonetheless, he made no discernible attempt the following April or October to distinguish between transitional forms and ultimate outcomes; and his language was substantially identical in every instance. This suggests that later use of the same general phrase at issue here, but without the apposition "revolutionary dictatorship of the proletariat," was a deliberate omission. Any reference to the political power of the working class as the fundamental precondition of socialism was thus logically synonymous with "something else"—dictatorship. In contrasting Ackermann's three statements, there was at most the slightest trace of a distinction between "all" power in the hands of the working class as the "fundamental prerequisite for the realization of socialism"; and the acquisition of political power by the working class, "allied with other working people," as the fundamental prerequisite for the establishment of a socialist society. But for one, the terms "realization" and "acquisition" both describe processes as much as aftermaths; and for another, even if Ackermann intended such analogous phrases to convey a distinction along the lines of a temporary minimum and permanent maximum objective, the lack of clarity still served a political purpose in confusing the issue. Besides, any contrast between "all" power and power exercised in alliance with "other working people" implied that the party looked forward to the time when it could rid itself of allies needed during the transition or convert them to the cause. Either way, "all" power was unshared power.

During the discussion in October 1946, Ackermann then further misrepresented his earlier arguments by claiming to have stated in February 1946 that developments in Germany might unfold differently than in the Soviet Union "even after the takeover of power by the proletariat." He based his conclusion on the argument that "we have, in particular, the possibility of establishing the unity of the working class in all of Germany." These remarks had vast implications. Establishing the unity of the working class in all of Germany came down to the SED's acquisition of the same power and influence that it enjoyed locally; and yet, as Ackermann implied, attaining the party's objectives was tantamount to a "takeover of power by the proletariat" that mysteriously fell short of dictatorship. There was no other way for him to emphasize national unity, retain the essence of old postulates, and still promise "no sovietization." His analysis of the situation in October 1946 was actually reminiscent of Stalin's reference in June 1945 to securing German unity through the centrality of a unified party of the working class. Nor was there any discrepancy between Ackermann's discussion of the problem as it pertained to the SED and Molotov's more general assessment of the basis for reunification in July 1946. But one last conclusion followed. The "form of political rule in Germany" would be fundamentally different from Russia's, Ackermann said, *if* the SED established working-class unity nationwide. His remark echoed Stalin's again, except that Ackermann used this contingency to explain why there must be no talk within the party or outside of it about the "dictatorship of the proletariat." Ackermann knew that the direct threat of dictatorship as a political program was incompatible with the promise of national unity and needed to be ignored for that reason. Thus, he concluded, the emphasis should continue to be on the "political power of the working class" with the additional stress on the "possibility that this power can be wielded through the use of democratic means." Here again the statements made a distinction that the combination of the two discounted. If the phrase "political power of the working class" was *not* synonymous with dictatorship, then limiting the democratic exercise of that power to a distant possibility rendered the distinction meaningless. Nonetheless, Ackermann finished by stating that the party had "no need of a discussion about dictatorship"; sloganeering about "Lenin or Stalin" was unnecessary; the SED should derive its doctrinal requirements from Marx, Engels, Plechanov, Kautsky, Liebknecht, Hilferding, and only "up to a certain point Lenin and Stalin." They had not spoken of Marx and Lenin, Ackermann ended, but of consequent Marxism; yet they knew "that it must undergo a further development that corresponds to our party and our German necessities."[215]

[215]Ibid.

None of this suggests that the Communists were confounded by the intricacies of their own rhetoric; in most cases they knew exactly what they were saying and understood the implications perfectly well. But their efforts often rendered them incapable of masking private preferences. The many allusions to an avant-garde Marxist-Leninist party, which by definition existed to defend the interests of a single class, failed to stop them from engaging in parallel definitions that characterized the SED as a "party of the people."[216] Indeed, some of these definitions pointed in the direction of a general linkage of the two notions. Franz Dahlem praised the merger for having created a "mass party of a higher, progressive character" and also described the SED as the party of "state reconstruction"—as opposed, presumably, to a violently revolutionary party—whose policies served the "overall interests of the German people"; and he rounded out that description by lauding the party's internal structure as an "organization of a new type."[217] Obviously, the characterization stressing the party's "millions," comprised of working people from all segments of the population, fit in better with the SED's aspirations toward a "popular democracy," *Volksdemokratie*, than the notion of a Marxist-Leninist new type of party. Moreover, in fall 1946 the Communists engaged in further discussions of the "essence of a progressive-democratic order" in Germany that revealed as much about their private thoughts on the subject of government as their attempts to clarify the specific role of their own party in it. The new democracy would certainly not be a "formal democracy" akin to Weimar, Ulbricht said, but he pledged that it would not be a German imitation of the Soviet system either; the coming democracy would be a "popular democracy"; and Ulbricht insisted that the leader in the "struggle for a popular-democratic order" was the working class or, more specifically, the SED.[218]

Mechanical Transfers

The question of popular democracy in Soviet-occupied Germany caused the SED as many problems as its conflicting self-definitions because the party's critics were able to draw such vast conclusions from developments in Poland, Hungary, and Czechoslovakia. Like eastern Germany, these countries were occupied by the Red Army and dominated by the policies of local Communists who employed tactics similar to those characteristic of Soviet-occupied Germany. For that reason, the Communists often relied upon arguments designed to minimize the harm done by their sporadic use of the term

---

[216]Dahlem, "Vom Wesen und von den Aufgaben der SED," *Neuer Weg* 6 (1946): 2.
[217]Dahlem, "Der neue Typus des Funktionärs der SED," *Einheit* 4 (1946): 193 and, "Die Organisationspolitik der Partei," *Bericht über die Verhandlungen des 15. Parteitag der KPD*, p. 65.
[218]Ulbricht, "Strategie und Taktik der SED," *Einheit* 5 (1946): 262-64.

"popular democracy." In certain contexts, they denied that developments in different parts of central Europe were identical; in Soviet-occupied Germany, the idea of a nonviolent transformation leading along a democratic path to socialism was built around the notion of collective guilt—the people were too immature for a "Soviet system" after twelve years of fascism. The "minimal" objective, therefore, was an antifascist-democratic transformation that would complete the bourgeois revolution of 1848 and bring about "real democracy." In eastern Europe, the theory of collective guilt did not apply to the populations of countries occupied by the Nazis. There, new forms of democracies, popular democracies, were being established to meet the national needs of those specific countries. What eastern Europe and Soviet-occupied Germany had in common, however, was the idea that growth toward socialism would occur when democracy developed into "higher forms" as a part of the process of breaking the resistance of reaction and educating the people in a genuinely democratic spirit.[219]

Ulbricht had called early on for a popular-democratic order in the Soviet zone; and prior to formation of the SED he added the phrase "democratic peoples' Germany," tying its realization to the existence of the "antifascist-democratic united front" and to formation of a single working-class party.[220] Ulbricht's first references to a popular democracy were picked up and developed further in late summer and fall 1946. The new regime in Czechoslovakia was applauded because it went beyond "mere formal parliamentary democracy" to institute the *"rule of a genuine popular democracy"* comprised of "democratic popular institutions of a new type." This "revolution" in Czechoslovakia was national, antifascist, and democratic.[221] Several weeks later, popular democracy cropped up again in an article by Alexander Abusch, who sought to silence critics scornful of the word by stating categorically that "we will have such a democracy or none at all."[222] Of course, designating the "revolution" in Czechoslovakia as national and democratic was simply a way of contrasting it with Soviet democracy; indeed, the entire idea of a popular or "peoples' democracy" countered suggestions that these democracies were imitations of the Soviet system and constituted dictatorships. Fall 1946 accordingly brought a flurry of assurances that Soviet democracy was not the model for democracy everywhere; democracy was not a tree that could be transplanted without considering local conditions. This was particularly the case in Germany because of the lingering effects of fascism; the form of government exercised by the Soviet people could scarcely be appropriate for a people who, as a consequence of a totalitarian dictator-

[219]G. B. "Was ist Demokratie?" *Neues Deutschland*, 30 April 1946.

[220]See Ulbricht's remarks in *Deutsche Volkszeitung*, 4 January 1946; the complete version is in Ulbricht, "Das Volk will die Einheit," *Gelöbnis zur Einheit*, pp. 14-15.

[221]Appelt, "Volksdemokratie in der Tschechoslowakei," *Einheit* 2 (1946): 83-85.

[222]Abusch, "Bruderkampf oder Zusammenarbeit," *Die Weltbühne* 6 (1946): 168.

ship, were entirely unaccustomed to "their own democratic road."[223]

But the most authoritative linkage of references to the inappropriateness of the Soviet system, Germany's own democratic road to socialism, and a popular democracy occurred in an anonymous article in September 1946. Translated from the Russian,[224] it was intended to stamp Ackermann's article of early 1946 with the impress of authority and repeated many of his basic points. But with "popular democracy," the same article added a new dimension to the argument. There existed, the analysis began, a form of democracy midway between bourgeois and socialist democracy, such as the popular republics in Czechoslovakia, Poland, Bulgaria, Rumania, and Yugoslavia. These in-between forms were more progressive than bourgeois democracy and were doing away with imperialist monopolies, implementing land reform, dealing with urgent economic and cultural problems, "liquidating" the vestiges of fascism and political reaction throughout the land, and laying the foundation for the construction of socialism. This type of democracy was also the "most acceptable form for the current stage of Germany's development" because the SED was opposed to a "mechanical transfer of the Soviet system, just as it opposes a mechanical transfer of the English, American, or French system to German conditions." The SED fought instead "for the formation of a unified popular-democratic state in Germany"—a middle-road form of democracy.[225]

There were ostensibly three different kinds of democracy; the bourgeois-capitalist and Soviet-socialist brands were two of them; the third was democracy "of a new type, so-called popular democracy." Socialist democracy, such as it existed in the Soviet Union, was clearly out of the question for eastern Europe because it presupposed the existence of socialism, which had yet to be established. Developments in the territories formerly occupied by the Nazis thus fell into a different category. "This new type of democracy is neither bourgeois-capitalist . . . nor socialist. . . . Rather, it differs from these two forms and stands midway between them."[226] True, such democracy upset representatives of English and American imperialism, such as Churchill, who chose to twist the expression of a popular will into the "'repression' of the people through a 'single-party system' representing nothing other than the 'dictatorship' of the Communist party"; and such people willfully likened events in those countries to the replacement of one "'totalitarian regime'" with another by hinting darkly that the new system represented the "'sovietization'" of these nations. But talk of a "single-party system" was a conscious fabrication; several political parties existed in each eastern European country, revealing the absurdity of any suggestion that political life in the popular

[223]Grotewohl, "Im Kampfe um unsere Zukunft," *Einheit* 4 (1946): 199-200.
[224]See Leonhard, *Die Revolution entläßt ihre Kinder*, pp. 364-65.
[225]"Was ist Demokratie?" *Einheit* 4 (September) 1946: 221-22.
[226]Appelt, "Ein neuer Typus der Demokratie," *Einheit* 6 (1946): 339-40.

democracies had been "brought into line." Which form of democracy, then, should the German people select—the bourgeois-parliamentary kind, patterned after Weimar, or a progressive popular democracy? If the Germans decided in favor of the latter, bearing in mind that a "popular democracy in Germany must be adjusted to the special German development," things would unfold in the direction of socialism. Indeed, since the liberation from fascism a series of measures had been implemented in Soviet-occupied Germany that "already transcend the bounds of a formal parliamentary democracy and reveal the essential traits of democracy of a new type." The point now was to extend these "progressive accomplishments in the Soviet zone throughout all of Germany."[227]

Linking developments in the direction of a popular democracy with the Socialist Unity party then occurred several months after the elections when Ulbricht determined that the SED had created "*the foundations of a popular-democratic order* in one third of Germany" by establishing a variety of "pillars of popular democracy"; and the SED was clearly a "new type of party" because of its sponsorship of those measures. More importantly, Ulbricht argued that party members would have a compass in hand to guide them in their activity only once they recognized the "essence of a popular-democratic order"; only when the scientific theory of Marx, Engels, and Lenin guided the party could it wage a struggle "for the annihilation of reaction in all of Germany."[228] With these final admonitions, Ulbricht acknowledged that popular democracy and Marxism-Leninism were synonymous.

Undistorted Marxism

The fall elections tested these arguments, and when the votes were counted the outcome was anything but an unqualified success for the SED. In many areas, an absolute majority eluded the party; and in greater Berlin, where it had competed with the still-existing SPD on a much fairer footing, the party garnered less than 20 percent of the vote. In fact, despite its many organizational advantages throughout the zone, the SED actually campaigned under unfavorable circumstances. The need to set itself apart from its competitors required the use of the very rhetoric responsible for causing the greatest concern about its actual political ambitions. A party that considered the programs of all others to be a mere "instrument of propaganda" and insisted that its program alone showed the people the "way and the goal";[229] a party, moreover, that laid exclusive claim to the qualities of democracy and

[227]Ibid., pp. 341-42, 352. The phrase is "Gleichschaltung."
[228]Ulbricht, "Die geschichtliche Rolle der SED," *Neuer Weg* 3/4 (1947): 4.
[229]"Zu den nächsten Aufgaben," *Neuer Weg* 3 (1946): 1.

antifascism, lauded itself as the "only inwardly unified party with a program based on scientific doctrines," and branded the Christian and the Liberal Democrats as parties whose commitment to antifascism and democracy was incompatible with the influence within them of "large capitalist circles, as well as Western monopoly capital,"[230] distinguished itself by defaming all other parties as inherently reactionary. These tactics then reflected poorly upon the SED's own commitment to democracy by compelling the Communists to state openly what they had believed about their antifascist-democratic partners all along. The truth was that the bourgeois parties had never shown themselves capable of answering the existential questions of the German people; nowadays only the SED could "lead our people out of the catastrophe of Hitler"; only the Communists were consistent defenders of national unity." Moreover, the cardinal questions in the elections amounted to a simple choice between "democracy or fascism"; and this particular commentary drew the clear conclusion that antifascism and democracy translated into far more definite ideological objectives: "The SED has a clear socialist goal; the SED is the party of undistorted Marxism."[231] It followed logically that "every vote not cast in its favor constitutes a building block for reaction."[232]

In response, one Social Democrat in Berlin argued that the SED would be well-advised to reflect more deeply upon the meaning of democracy as it applied to governmental and administrative practices and avoid the imitation of "Soviet-Russian administrative methods."[233] Everyone then agreed, including Alexander Abusch, that the atmosphere of the elections had been poisoned by polemics comparing this or that party's tactics with those of the Nazis; but Abusch nonetheless accused the Christian Democratic and Liberal Democratic parties of having served as a "shield of Nazi and militaristic circles" during the campaign. Abusch also brought up the subject of the SED's usage of slogans that reminded some Germans of the recent past, to which he responded by explaining that, when the SED cried out, "'The people with us and with us victory!' or put on popular festivals," these things had nothing in common with Nazi propaganda; and the socialist marching song, "with its appeal to close ranks and let the red banner wave," a restatement of the opening line of the Horst Wessel song, had existed since Bismarck. In any case, Abusch insisted that the "new German democracy" did not result from a recipe borrowed from a foreign country; those who thought that it did mistook a "German necessity, the elementary precondition of German democracy," for the "imitation of a Russian model."[234]

[230]Ulbricht, "Strategie und Taktik der SED," *Einheit* 5 (1946): 267.
[231]Oelßner, "Die SED und die anderen Parteien," *Neues Deutschland*, 14 September 1946.
[232]Weinert, "'Die Kunst dem Volk,'" *Berliner Zeitung*, 20 October 1946.
[233]"Für Entgiftung des politischen Kampfes," *Die Weltbühne* 6 (1946): 163 and 165.
[234]"Für Entgiftung des politischen Kampfes," ibid., pp. 166-69.

A combination of factors worked to the party's disadvantage in the context of the elections; but central among them were the Communists' efforts to set themselves apart from the Russians even as they extolled the virtues of the Soviet Union in a fashion that could only be construed as favoring the emulation of the essential characteristics of its state and party system. There was thus a concerted effort in fall 1946 to clarify "misunderstandings" about the Soviet Union. People who advocated bourgeois democracy reproached the USSR because only one party existed there, read one such attempt; but these people forgot that different parties were the "advance party" of different social classes; multiple parties existed only where "antagonistic contradictions" between classes still prevailed.[235] But that argument had nettlesome implications. In particular, the unrelenting pursuit of "unity" pointed most directly to the arch-Stalinist idea of the moral-political unity of the people and, again, echoed Stalin's comments in July 1945 regarding the necessity of securing national unity through a "unified party at the center." As Pieck put it, "without a unified leadership, that is, in the absence of a unification of both labor parties, there can be no unified working class; without a unified working class there can be no real democracy, lacking democracy, no economic reconstruction, no peace, no national unity for Germany. Thus these elements hang together like the links on a chain. He who fails to grasp that and acts to contravene it, becomes, regardless of his intentions and whether he is aware of it or not, a vermin harmful to our people and a servant of reaction."[236]

Not that the notions of a collectivist consensus were absolutely identical with or yet coupled directly to Stalin's moral-political unity of the people; but the similarities cannot be overlooked either. A prime opportunity to hint at them was seized upon in connection with the tenth anniversary of the "Stalin constitution" in December 1946 and the related celebration of "Soviet democracy." One of Stalin's chief spokesmen introduced the question by asking which form of democracy had proven itself the strongest during the war and which nation fought today with "*unsurpassed consistency* for a general, lasting, just, and truly *democratic* peace?" The Soviet state was the answer; according to Georgij Alexandrov, "one of Soviet democracy's great achievements . . . is its brilliant resolution of the question of building a morally and politically unified socialist society cast from a single mold." The creation of the political unity of Soviet society was "*the greatest attainment of Soviet democracy and the most important result of the entire political development in the world.*"[237] In their commentary, the German Communists concluded similarly that class contradictions and antagonisms had disappear-

---

[235]"Was ist Demokratie?" *Einheit* 4 (1946): 221.
[236]Pieck, "Die Sicherung der Einheit Deutschlands—eine Lebensfrage unseres Volkes," *Einheit Deutschlands und Gemeindewahlen*, pp. 9-10.
[237]Alexandrov, "Über die Sowjetdemokratie," *Tägliche Rundschau*, 24 December 1946.

ed in the Soviet Union because the entire people entertained one and the same ultimate objective; and this popular unity meant that the Soviet people, being of one mind, recognized only one party, the Bolshevik party.[238] Wilhelm Pieck then launched into his own praise of the Stalin constitution and applied similar reasoning to the SED. The Soviet constitution was a source of moral support for those who carried on the struggle against fascist barbarity, he said, and went on to claim that the German people had concluded from the struggle for socialism in the Soviet Union that there could be no democratic and peaceful development in Germany in the absence of a complete annihilation of the power of the Junkers and capitalists. To that end, the "democratic, antifascist forces" in Germany needed to fight together with a single, unified political leadership leading the way.[239]

But by the end of 1946, the SED was ready to take the risk that its warnings about "antibolshevism," which dominated discussions throughout 1947, would be taken as advocacy of the Soviet system for Germany. The Soviet constitution offered conclusive evidence, read one discussion, that the accusations leveled against the USSR by "world reaction," such as "brutal arbitrary rule and servitude," were groundless fabrications.[240] Similar statements praised the constitution because it guaranteed freedom of speech, freedom of the press, freedom of assembly, freedom to demonstrate, freedom to organize in social organizations of all kinds, and protection against "arrest without a court order."[241] Indeed, said Wolfgang Harich, anyone worried about human rights and liberties in the Soviet Union need only take the trouble to read the "Stalin Constitution of 1936."[242] Most importantly, the Communists charged that it had again become the custom in certain German circles to regard the Soviet Union with hostility and that these critics had learned nothing from Germany's recent experience with anti-Sovietism. For these various "hostile attitudes" toward the USSR were expressions of the same old anti-Bolshevist mind-set produced by Hitlerism. If the SED warned against a renewal of antibolshevism, this was no indication that the "perfidious insinuations" used against the party during the election and still continuing had any validity. "We reject antibolshevism because it is political insanity."[243]

A few weeks after those remarks were published, Pieck met once more with representatives of the SMAD. During these discussions, on 23 December 1946, the Russians told him that the Western allies intended to enslave the country economically and that the Soviet Union would stand beside Germany. He was given to understand that "big capitalist bankers" were "buy-

---

[238]Stern, "Die Sowjetdemokratie," *Neues Deutschland*, 7 November 1946.
[239]"Zehn Jahre Stalinsche Verfassung," *Neues Deutschland*, 5 December 1946.
[240]Ibid.
[241]Stern, "Die Sowjetdemokratie," *Neues Deutschland*, 7 November 1946.
[242]Harich, "Roepke, Pechel und der 'Totalitarismus.'" *Tägliche Rundschau*, 23 August 1946.
[243]"Zehn Jahre Stalinsche Verfassung," *Neues Deutschland*, 5 December 1946.

ing up the econ.[omy]" in the British zone; whereas the policies of the Soviet Union conformed with the Postdam accords. Even such damaging Soviet practices as the dismantling of industrial equipment and complexes had been much less extensive "than anticipated"; and reparations, too, fell far short of what the USSR had every right to expect. Moreover, Pieck's notes of the discussion suggest that these arguments were all put in terms of the Soviet interest in a "later indepen.[dent] state"; the English and the Americans were, by contrast, bent upon the *"destruction* of Germany" through its *"dismemberment"* and *"enslavement."* The continuing occupation of Germany by Soviet troops was then justified with the argument that their presence was needed "until a *democ.*[ratic] state" was formed and in order to *"thwart a fut.*[ure] *war."*[244] These remarks echoed Molotov's; they hinted just as strongly at a Soviet decision to step up the pace of "democratization" in Soviet-occupied Germany in spite of damage to prospects for reunification; and this decision was presented to Pieck in the same national context of the economic and political threat to the country posed by the Western allies. On 21 January 1947, apparently in conversations with Zhukov's replacement, Marshal Sokolovskij, a number of subjects then came up that touched on what Bokov had called the "question of government" the previous summer. In Pieck's notes, these covered issues like *"unity* or *federalism,"* a central administration versus a central government, American influence in Europe along with British submission to it, matters pertaining to a peace treaty, and perhaps a general "analysis of the constellation of power."[245]

But more importantly, plans were now set for the party leaders to consult with Stalin again; as Pieck seems to have been told, decisions would then be made in Moscow about what was to follow.[246] Pieck, Grotewohl, Ulbricht, Max Fechner, and Fred Oelßner left Berlin the morning of 30 January 1947; and the five of them held a three-hour discussion with Stalin from 9 to midnight on the 31st, apparently attended by Mikhail Suslov,[247] Volkov, and Semjonov. The delegation met with Semjonov on 2 February for additional consultations and had one last discussion with Suslov on 4 February.[248] According to Pieck's record of the late-night discussion, the points made by Stalin fit the same dichotomies emphasized by Molotov the previous sum-

---

[244]Besprechung am 23. 12. 1946 um 12 Uhr in Karlshorst. Zentrales Parteiarchiv. NL 36/734/244-47. Interestingly, in July 1946 Bokov indicated to Pieck that the "period of occupation" might be concluded quickly because the British and Americans could not bear the financial burden. See Besprechung am 26. 7. 1946 in Karlshorst um 9 Uhr abends, ibid., NL 36/734/192.
[245]Besprechung mit Marschall am 21. 1. 1947 um 4.30 Uhr, ibid., NL 36/734/282-83.
[246]Ibid.
[247]Suslov seems to have been assigned responsibility "for Germany" within the central Soviet party apparatus. See Pieck's notes of discussions in Karlshorst. 19. 9. 1946 abends 1/2 9 Uhr in Karlshorst / Tulpanow, Panuschkin, Korotkewitsch, ibid., NL 36/734/204.
[248]Aus Kalender und Chronik. Ablauf der Reise nach Moskau (Pieck, Grotewohl, Ulbricht, Fechner, Fred Oelßner), ibid., NL 36/694/1.

mer; and, much like Molotov, Stalin appears to have advocated the rigorous pursuit of Soviet policies in occupied Germany without acknowledging that these policies were bound to be restricted to one zone and thus culminate in two Germanies. Instead, Stalin accused the allies of obstructing what he favored—national unity. He expressed his approval of the SED's position on the subject, for instance, explaining that the British, Americans, and French preferred federalism because it "weakened" Germany. A weak Germany, Stalin argued, was to be prevented from influencing world economic markets and developing its foreign trade; and this was why the Western allies opposed a "central government" or a "central administration." The Soviet "concept," he said, was diametrically opposed. Germany and Japan needed access to the world market because the attendant lowering of prices and improvement in commodities would redound to the "benefit of mankind"; whereas the rule of America promised high prices and poor goods.[249] Such was the substance of Stalin's remarks as reflected in Pieck's notes; and the shallowness of his arguments may well have stemmed from the attempt to persuade his listeners that he was indeed "Germany's best friend," as the Communists declared publicly two years later. Human progress demanded that Germany again have access to the world market, he continued; seventy million Germans could not be written out of world history; nor could they be kept in a state of impoverishment. Subjugation and isolation nourished thoughts of revenge and pointed toward the likelihood of a new war; and besides, Stalin told the Germans, "we are comrades; it pains us that German workers suffer"; the German proletariat deserved a higher standard of living.

Stalin then turned to the administrative implications of his remarks. The Americans spoke of "economic unity" while opposing a unified government, he said; in the absence of political unity, economic unification denoted *"unification of the occupiers"*; whereas the quicker Germany's unity and the more rapid the establishment of a German government, the swifter the economic upswing. Stalin then went on to discuss his ideas about a central Soviet-zone administration—in essence, a provisional government that, under the circumstances, amounted to plans for the formation of a separate German state. Stalin expected the Americans, as he put it, to resist formation of a government; and for that reason he proposed a *"German central administration* as a temporary situation." It was not clear from Pieck's notes whether Stalin distinguished any further between a central administration set up to coordinate economic matters nationwide or defined it in terms of Soviet-occupied Germany; but his opposition to "economic" in advance of "political unity" points to an awareness that such a central administration amounted to formation of a separate provisional government. True, two days later Sem-

---

[249]Besprechung Freitag, 31. 1. 1947, in Moskau, 9-12 Uhr abends / Stalin, Marschall [?] Suslov, Semjonov, Wolkow - Pieck, Grotewohl, Ulbricht, Fechner, Oelßner. Ibid., NL 36/694/3.

jonov told the German delegation that the signing of a peace treaty and formation of a government would be delayed and, because of it, a "unified central administration for all of Germany" needed to be established until a permanent government could be formed.[250] When the German Communists then embarked upon a zone-wide expansion of the authority and jurisdiction of the various central administrations already operating in Soviet-occupied Germany,[251] they essentially followed Semjonov's advice to use these administrations as an "immediate *platform*, as a stage" leading toward formation of a government. The implications of these measures for the future of a reunited Germany were just as clear as Suslov's discussion of party structure and privilege generally. The "*basic principle*," he told the Germans, was that the Communists were "responsible for everything" and that their influence needed to cover "all areas."[252]

[250]Besprechung Semjonow Sonntag 2. 2. abends 7 Uhr, ibid., NL 36/734/694/7.
[251]See Chapter Two.
[252]4. 2. 1947 Information Suslow, abends 8 Uhr, ibid., NL 36/734/694/8.

CHAPTER TWO

Organization and Bureaucracy

Politics in Soviet-occupied Germany developed out of strategies devised by the Communist International and the German Communist party in the mid thirties. But a political program reminiscent of an earlier era now benefited from political "blocs" and cultural "alliances" dominated by the Communists who worked within them and in close consultation with the SMAD. This advantage fostered the illusion of vitality in a program of democracy whose sponsors actually felt no obligation to subject their ideas, political or cultural, to genuine competition. In the thirties, by comparison, cooperation between the KPD and SPD, as well as the grand alliance with other organizations and intellectuals known as the popular front, collapsed because participation had been voluntary. Political figures and cultural personalities who joined in these organizations did so on condition that the Communist party adhere to traditional notions of democracy while working within them; and when the Communists subverted cooperation, among other things, by demanding definitions of democracy and antifascism based upon their ideological assumptions, the coalitions quickly unraveled. The KPD simply lacked the means to compel anyone to remain part of associations in which members were denied the right to criticize Stalin, object to the Moscow show trials, or differ with the Communists on principles of democracy.

All this changed when the end of the war left part of Germany under Soviet occupation; it was difficult from the outset there, and soon impossible, to engage in political or cultural pursuits outside the confines of tightly controlled "antifascist-democratic" parties, coalitions, and mass organizations set up by the Communists as a means of subordinating their activity to the interests of their own party. But this was not always apparent to those caught up in the process, especially in the beginning; indeed, the original necessity of hiding that fact helps explain the deliberate deception characteristic of the party's rhetoric; and other participants who understood or came to understand the situation often continued to work within the various organizations out of a reluctance to abandon the hope of a turn for the better. Once they had, by the late forties or early fifties, they generally had to chose between accommodation, passivity, or flight to the West. Those with fewer scruples or grander illusions, both politicians and members of what the Communists called a "new democratic intelligentsia," were quick to take their place. Unlike the popular front, then, the "antifascist-democratic" bloc held together, though seldom for reasons related to the persuasive logic of the politics behind it. Nonetheless, the Communist party acted as if its program had been an immense success all along and that Germans generally and intellectuals particularly were appropriately impressed with the ideals. Privately, the leadership knew better; the notion of collective guilt, never abandoned, suggests as much; animosity toward the party continued to cause problems; and the Communists tried everything to improve the situation short of altering their policies. By 1949, the SED was all but indistinguishable ideologically from the old KPD; and the other parties, along with the network of subsidiary or subservient mass organizations, existed only as part of a grand coalition that went by the misnomer of a national front—dominated by the SED, as Stalin had said in June 1945, "at the center."

Not that the Communists had anticipated these difficulties and returned from Soviet exile with advanced plans for forcing their policies upon a sullen and uncooperative population; for one, the Communists were initially constrained by the necessity of keeping the international consequences of their policies in mind until these gradually receded in importance in 1947 and 1948; and for another, many in the party honestly believed that their brand of politics served the interests of the people best and were the purest expression of a broad consensus—whether it actually existed yet or not. It was merely a matter of convincing the people that their future and the future of the nation rested in the hands of the only party qualified to lead the country along the road to national deliverance. The Communists were thus anxious in the beginning to try to convince the people that the KPD, and by mid-1946, the SED had all the answers; but they never hesitated to take unfair advantage of a political opportunity any time one presented itself, always ready to claim a resounding popular success for their policies when none existed; and, if necessary, to generate an antifascist-democratic "consensus" by intimidating anyone who defied it. But by the same token, their political and cultural reputation suffered immeasurably from developments in Soviet-occupied Germany that heightened fears of "sovietization"; worse, few developments pointed in any other direction, and rhetoric designed to soften the impression tended to confirm it. The more systematic the party's subversion of democratic principles, the more tortured the logic used to explain why the abolition of democracy was real democracy in action, and the flimsier the party's recurrent promise not to impose the "Soviet system" on Germany. Nonetheless, efforts to influence the public never ceased just because of their general ineffectiveness; and the Communists continued to think in terms of using prominent intellectuals and artists, those who belonged to the party and those who did not, to help popularize their policies. But the success of the strategy hinged particularly upon the party's ability to repudiate accusations that it controlled "nonpartisan" organizations like the Kulturbund or budding administrative bureaucracies like the Deutsche Verwaltung für Volksbildung (DVV); and doing so required additionally that party intellectuals and administrators who ran these kinds of undertakings be persuasive when disclaiming their own close ties to it and the SMAD.

Cultural Alliances and Intellectual Renewal

None of this is the same as saying that the party's cultural-political policy was rigidly in place by mid-1945, much less that events through 1949 unfolded smoothly or in perfect conformity with prearranged plans. But there was an indisputable consistency regardless of the early need to adapt policy tactically to local circumstances. Continual adjustments also occurred in response to the evolution of Soviet foreign and domestic policy and associated shifts in international politics; but the modifications and variations, always tactical and combined with the retention of key principles, actually testify to the basic cohesiveness. The most significant immediate alteration concerned the official role of the Communist party in cultural affairs, and this first tactical shift in summer 1945, as well as the next reversal scarcely a year later, helps explain the nature of the party's cultural policy in the very beginning. At issue was the political "nonpartisanship" of organized cultural pursuits generally and the necessity of managing these affairs surreptitiously until the party was ready to claim its cultural prerogatives openly. In a proposal prepared for the party by Johannes R. Becher in fall 1944, he developed the idea of the "reeducation of the German people toward freedom";[1] and this same idea, based on early notions of collective guilt, figured just as centrally after the capitulation. But specific remarks made by Becher in 1944, and again in early 1945, were absent from otherwise identical comments made during the first year after his return to Soviet-occupied Germany—only to reappear, this time for good, in late summer 1946. In 1944, Becher wrote that reeducation had to be carried out in what he called the *"ideological-moral sphere"* and added that the Communist party was destined to distinguish itself in this struggle because of its doctrine of objective truth. The intellectual standards and values derived from it, all based on Marxism, expressed themselves politically then through the activities of a "new type of party." Becher developed these ideas further a few months later and not long before he returned to Germany in the company of Ulbricht, Ackermann, Sobottka, Wandel, and Max Keilson on 10 June 1945.[2] Again Becher's argu-

---

[1]Becher, "Bemerkungen zu unserer Kulturaufgabe," *Publizistik,* vol. II, p. 362.

[2]The first three had just finished their consultations with Stalin; according to what Wandel told me in 1989, those conversations included the Soviet "suggestion" that the party publish a daily newspaper. Though it had earlier been decided that Wilhelm Pieck would return to Germany,

ments revolved around notions of collective guilt; but he now voiced his conviction that "millions" of Germans would be anxious because of it to work toward evolving "antiimperialist trains of thought." The situation thus presented the Communists with an opportunity to exceed the limitations of what Becher called superficial antifascism by channeling it in the direction of "conscious antiimperialism"; and the quickest route to this goal, he argued, ran by way of a "universal policy of alliances." Just such a grand coalition, based on "creative Marxism," would be able to rally all segments of the German people. But Becher also reiterated that the driving "spiritual and organizational" force behind what he called "political-ideological unity" was the Communist party; "of all the possible or even thinkable party organizations for Germany," he concluded, "the [Communist] party, a new type of party," was the only one to combine "the cognitive means of recognizing objective truth and the organizational ability to implement it as an agent of historical necessity."[3]

Becher's analysis of collective guilt and the role of the Communist party corresponded with the KPD's political assessment right after the war; and the cultural-political dimension of his remarks just as accurately reflected internal thinking on the subject of the party's direct involvement in cultural affairs. But after his return to Germany, Becher and others routinely omitted any mention of the KPD while working toward the formation of "alliances" built intellectually around the notion of collective guilt as the precondition of cultural renewal. The basic problem now, wrote Heinz Willmann, was that the fact of Germany's "spiritual" collapse had not yet been widely accepted because any acknowledgment of a moral catastrophe of equal proportion to the material and political devastation was tantamount to an admission of universal guilt, which too few Germans willingly accepted.[4] Indeed, those who

---

with Wandel remaining behind for six months as the party's main representative in Moscow (unlike Pieck, Wandel spoke Russian), during these discussions Ulbricht proposed Wandel for the job of chief editor of the *Deutsche Volkszeitung*, and Wandel left for Germany with the rest of the party delegation "two days later." His sudden new assignment may also explain why Pieck, instead of Wandel, remained in Moscow until 1 July 1945. On 2 July, the KPD formally set up its "Sekretariat" (the 2nd is, in fact, listed as the day on which the secretariat held its first meeting [Auszug aus den Notizkalendern von Wilhelm Pieck. Zentrales Parteiarchiv, NL 36/631/1]). Curiously enough, Wandel, under his party pseudonym Paul Klaßner, was listed in the party's initial organizational plans as "Chefredakteur"; but "Chef" was crossed out and replaced, in Pieck's handwriting, by "verantwortlich" or responsible—probably a better definition of Wandel's political assignment. Apart from Keilson, the main editors included Fritz Erpenbeck, who had returned with Ulbricht originally in early April. See Nächste zentrale Aufgaben der Parteiführung auf Grund des Aufrufes des ZK der KPD, 9 June 1945, ibid., NL 36/734/34.
[3]Becher, "Zur Frage der politisch-moralischen Vernichtung des Faschismus," *Publizistik*, vol. II, pp. 405-6, 430, 433-35.
[4]Willmann, "Ansprache des Generalsekretärs," *Um Deutschlands neue Kultur*. Aufruf und Ansprachen gehalten bei der Gründungs-Kundgebung des Kulturbundes zur demokratischen Erneuerung Deutschlands für die Provinz Sachsen am 14. Oktober 1945 in Halle (Saale), p. 8.

avoided the issue hampered reconstruction and consciously or unconsciously prepared the way for new intellectual aberrations.[5] These kinds of sweeping condemnations bolstered the KPD's definition of its own program as the only solution to the enormous range of cultural and intellectual problems associated with the guilt of the German people; but for the time being, these direct linkages remained unacknowledged because of the deliberate omission now of that critical component which had to do with Becher's earlier understanding of the party's leading *cultural* role. It vanished entirely in favor of professions of nonpartisanship, at least until it resurfaced in 1946; whereas in politics, the Communists tried to combine approaches. They maintained that it would be presumptuous for any single party to claim an exclusive right to lead the German people; the tasks confronting the nation could only be solved through the *"closest cooperation of all antifascist-democratic forces* within the parties and trade unions."[6] But they remained persistent in their assertions that one party, theirs, had a natural right to unique political privileges. Critics spotted the contradiction and took it as ample proof that the party's rhetoric had little in common with its actual objectives. Similar suspicions existed in cultural affairs, too, increasing the need to combat the impression that the "renewal movement," quoting Becher's mass-movement rhetoric,[7] was covertly coupled to the KPD. The Communists thus promoted solutions to Germany's cultural predicament that, until February 1946, they never located publicly within the context of the party's parallel political objectives and certainly never identified as being in any way Communist.

A flurry of articles published first in the *Tägliche Rundschau* in late summer 1945 concerning the priority of the "moral rebirth of our people" over "material" reconstruction illustrated the importance of the argument.[8] Bernhard Kellermann, a novelist who had remained in Germany during the Hitler years, published an article called "What should we do?" and made the mistake of reversing the priorities. His talk of the "dark masters of the 'Third Reich'" who threw millions of unemployed into the armaments industry, turned Germany into a single armed camp, and set out to conquer wantonly was fine as far as it went; but he expressed bewilderment at the fact that thousands of high state dignitaries and diplomats, hundreds of generals, and representatives of heavy industry knew of the plan and backed it anyway.[9] The Communists were not similarly perplexed; and in any event, Kellermann was corrected by a variety of intellectuals who labored under none of

[5]Selbmann, *Aufbruch des Geistes*, pp. 2-4.
[6]Pieck, "Die Lehren der deutschen Novemberrevolution 1918 und die Ergebnisse der Großen Sozialistischen Oktoberrevolution 1917," *Deutsche Volkszeitung*, 10 November 1945.
[7]Becher, "Rede an München," *Deutsches Bekenntnis*, p. 70.
[8]Becher's phrase comes from his "Rede an München," *Deutsches Bekenntnis*, p. 71.
[9]Kellermann, *Was sollen wir tun?* p. 19.

his illusions. Theodor Plievier, the author of *Stalingrad* who had spent years in Soviet exile, demanded that "the question of guilt" be acknowledged as the first step toward national recovery.[10] Such opinions were by no means exclusive to members of the Communist party, and within a few years Plievier had fled to the West. But his remarks contributed to the general prevalence of thinking along the lines of collective guilt and served a useful political purpose for that reason. Some of the other contributors to the discussion pursued the subject of collective guilt even more vigorously. All efforts to turn the country around materially, wrote one, would amount to nothing without a "*radical and irreversible recognition*" by Germans themselves.[11] Worse still, said another, without a spiritual reversal, the old nemesis of German chauvinism would continue to poison the fruit of reconstruction, and endanger the "fate of our people once and for all." But that apocalyptic vision contrasted with the prospects for a genuinely new Germany, a "democracy of a new type," which would be ushered in by a truly "progressive-democratic renewal of the German people."[12] Finally, a man by the name of Bernhard Bechler, a former member of the Moscow-based national committee for a free Germany, shifted the argument from collective guilt to grassroots antifascism when he applauded land reform as a spontaneous act of antifascist-democratic restitution that represented the first step on the way to "our new, militant popular democracy"—*Volksdemokratie*. Bechler felt confident that the masses of the German people had learned from the experience of the war and would continue to travel the path leading by way of the "new militant popular democracy" to the freedom of the German people.[13]

But Johannes R. Becher, in other contexts and on countless occasions, was best at couching doctrinal principles in language that appeared to be ideologically noncommittal; and his arguments invariably revolved around the familiar issues of guilt and atonement. Indeed, what he had to say differed little in substance from remarks made by the party's main rhetoricians, but the ideological context was far less readily apparent. Becher argued that the historical road traveled by the German people and the German nation, especially during the last twelve years, led toward "damnation" and the "hell of hopelessness"; but he used words taken from Shakespeare's *The Tempest* as an effective reminder that out of hopelessness came hope:

> O, out of that no hope,
> What great hope have you! no hope, that way, is
> Another way so high an hope . . .[14]

[10]Plievier, ibid., p. 24.
[11]Th. Lieser, ibid., pp. 27 and 30.
[12]Adam Scharrer, ibid., pp. 32-35.
[13]Bechler, ibid., pp. 36-38.
[14]Becher, "Auf andere Art so große Hoffnung," *Deutsches Bekenntnis*, p. 108.

Or, "auf andere Art so große Hoffnung." The "hope" that Becher had in mind sprang from the presence of what he considered an inherently different course of intellectual development down through the nation's history, one distinct from the often parallel but separate currents that culminated in fascism; and this other "way," epitomized by such towering figures as Goethe and Schiller, had simply never achieved political expression in Germany. Now, however, it represented the only chance for the "resurrection" of the nation.[15] Even so, the opportunity could only be seized once the Germans began "rehabilitating" themselves through a "process of politicization."[16] Some of the Communists who had recently emerged from Nazi dungeons and concentration camps said much the same thing about politicizing outlooks and attitudes, and the entire notion of "politicization," which Becher and others tried so hard to reconcile with "nonpartisanship" during the coming months and years, became the dominant consideration in all Soviet-zone discussions devoted to cultural affairs. Fritz Selbmann, a party member since 1922 who spent twelve years in prison under the Nazis, insisted that politics were nothing less than the supreme manifestation of art and the highest incarnation of the intellect. These kinds of sentiments led to the conclusion that those who "work with their minds" must never again turn a deaf ear to the voice of politics because past indifference to politics had blinded the intellectuals to fascism.[17] The obvious problem was that intellectuals in Soviet-occupied Germany were urged to take a passionate interest in politics at a time when only one brand was permitted and then excoriated for their political abstinence if they either spurned this request or had the effrontery to honor someone else's.

These demands only increased with time and soon grew far more specific. But the general parallels with political conceptions based both on collective guilt and national atonement existed from the beginning. In cultural politics, the idea of an emerging antifascist ground swell matched the party's early claims of a popular consensus in support of its policies, but appeared somewhat altered in the form of a "German" cultural movement embodying what Becher called the principle of "the tie that binds, in questions of ideology as well of public, political life, and in the question of the nation and the life of the peoples." He stressed that, "whenever we draw a dividing line and sever our ties [to others], our struggle and our objectives are constantly influenced by our desire to achieve a higher harmonious unity by transcending that which clashes and conflicts." Referring specifically to "our movement," he also explained that "we not only believe in the truth; we know for a fact that truth exists, too, even if we are not yet able to recognize it in its separate

---

[15]Ibid.

[16]See "Für die demokratische Kunst," *Tägliche Rundschau*, 20 June 1945; and Becher, "Auf andere Art so große Hoffnung," *Deutsches Bekenntnis*, p. 85.

[17]Selbmann, *Aufbruch des Geistes*, p. 5.

parts or in its overall totality. We say 'yes'; we give enthusiastic approval to everything that is good and beautiful, true and freedom-loving; and when we say 'no' to something pernicious and injurious, this 'no' incorporates a resounding, eloquent 'yes' to all that is noble and consummate."[18] Becher never spoke of Marxism-Leninism in this context, but his abstractions convey at least a hint of his earlier emphasis upon the need to transform "superficial antifascism" into "conscious antiimperialism," to say nothing of the distant echoes in his remarks of class warfare; and under the circumstances, the mass movement supposedly behind the process of cultural renewal embodied the Stalinist ideal of "moral-political unity." Becher's remarks captured the essence of Marxism-Leninism as effectively as the sharper pronouncements of the party's mainline politicians, only better tailored, and deliberately so, to the non-Communist audience that Becher was courting. By negating the bad, said Becher, "we approve of the good and endeavor to remove it from the influence of the bad." This brought him back to "the tie that binds" and to the subject of unity in all its forms—"the unity of man, the unity of a people, the unity of all mankind."[19]

But behind Becher's pathos lay pure dogma. His early appeals contained the same stress on historical truth present in his 1944 and 1945 draft proposals written in Soviet exile, except that unalloyed nationalism had replaced the doctrine without changing Becher's mind about the nature of historical necessity. Not that these considerations were immediately discernible in his remarks; searching for the truth today, he said instead, meant to go in quest of that which Germany truly needed; recognizing the truth today entailed "*a profession of faith in Germany*"; and fighting for the truth meant fighting "for Germany" in a struggle inseparable from Germany's national unity. There could be no "spiritual renewal" and no subsequent material improvement if the nation's best failed to join together "in an *inviolable antifascist unity*" because such unity was "synonymous today with Germany's unity."[20] Becher's emotional plea for antifascist unity thus derived, like so many of his other comments, from an understanding of truth identical to key passages in his 1944 draft linked directly to the Communist party. But these earlier remarks disappeared from his later comments because Becher and the party knew that the intellectuals could not be mobilized on the strength of purified Marxism-Leninism; a German nationalism imbued with the principles of antifascism and democracy, by contrast, offered promising possibilities. Even so, the rhetoric was accompanied from the outset by laments that, for unfathomable reasons, not all the intellectuals would join the movement. One early unsigned editorial published in the party daily noted approvingly that there were certain "stirrings" among the intellectuals; but reconstruction remained

[18]Becher, "Rede an München," *Deutsches Bekenntnis*, pp. 78, 81-82.
[19]Ibid., p. 82.
[20]Becher, "An die Kulturschaffenden," *Deutsche Volkszeitung*, 5 July 1945.

an eminently political undertaking that required an acknowledgment of personal and collective guilt based on a proper awareness of the causes of the catastrophe. Moreover, ordinary Germans themselves supposedly demanded that artists and intellectuals legitimize themselves in the eyes of the people by proving that they wanted to pull together with those whose manual labor provided the material basis for intellectual endeavors. Unfortunately, some of the artists still entertained the illusion of "slipping comfortably" from one regime into the other and demonstrated their passivity by retreating into the "ivory tower with a smug, clear conscience"; whereas they had a sacred obligation to work toward a *"conscious spiritual reorientation"* and then create "a new *democratic culture"* that required a "consistently antifascist orientation."[21]

Arguing along the same lines, Fritz Erpenbeck hailed what he called the growing unity among intellectuals especially because "it had nothing in common with the uniformity and pseudo-unity associated with Nazi lies about a *Volksgemeinschaft";* this unity, one of "diversity," imposed limitations on the individual only to the extent that constraints happened to be dictated by a "recognition of necessity." Necessity, as Erpenbeck defined it, was "antifascist democracy"; and he went on to extol the "compelling language" of such a democracy in connection with early discussions involving the Kulturbund. Moreover, this consensus emerged because no one told lies and because the necessity of the goal was so universally recognized; the consensus itself, he said, eliminated any need for "tactical maneuvers" or "administrative tricks"—as if tricks and maneuvers were legitimate otherwise in response to the absence of real agreement or justified in any effort to achieve it. Erpenbeck hastened to add only that historical and dialectical materialism were by no means unimportant to Communists; it was just that this "conflict in the area of world views" had now been openly acknowledged, making unity possible in spite of differences of opinion. For this reason, Erpenbeck could not imagine why any intellectual would refuse to join the movement; "the healing of our fatherland and each individual's personal share of atonement for his own and the general German guilt" obliged them to join the movement.[22] In spite of it all, however, certain intellectuals failed to take their obligations as seriously as Erpenbeck wished out of fear that the Communists planned on using the organized "movement" to extend their control over culture as well as politics. The party's responses to these concerns fell into two categories over the next few years; one turned on insinuations derived from the general notion of collective guilt and shaded into sinister remarks regarding the alleged conduct of currently uncooperative intellectuals under Hitler; the other called for additional assurances that the Communists

[21]"Neuorientierung der geistig Schaffenden," *Deutsche Volkszeitung,* 21 June 1945.
[22]Erpenbeck, "Einheit der geistig und künstlerisch Schaffenden," *Deutsche Volkszeitung,* 4 July 1945.

had no intention of decreeing an end to ideological and religious views or trying to settle them violently. The Communists championed the causes of freedom of religion, belief, and of world view, period, "not as a maneuver, not as a tactic, but for the simple reason that we cannot allow ourselves to waste even a *single* source of free creative strength in the years to come."[23]

But unable to abstain from commenting generally on cultural affairs, the Communists undercut their own efforts to hide the existence of a party policy right after the war by making vast statements, like the above, that resulted in damaging assumptions about their ulterior motives. For instance, the party's calls for a politicization of culture sparked unwelcome comparisons between the Nazis and the Communists that proved impossible to ignore, and the Communists responded by claiming that their motives, unlike the Nazis', were pure. They fully recognized that nothing had more dire consequences than the "shackling" of creativity caused by "forcing things into prearranged schemes"; and nothing was worse than this "regimentation of the intellect" in the form of an "enforced uniformity." Taking off the brown strait jacket and slipping into a red one now was no solution to the problems caused by the recent past; the only hope for the future lay in an acknowledgment of the "principle of free expression and the development of all the creative forces of the people."[24] Equation "red" and "brown" methods of regimenting the intellect, and its renunciation in favor of a democratic culture, conveyed two impressions: that the Communists differed in every respect from the Nazis and that sovietization never entered their minds either. The latter assurance apparently came up in cultural affairs, too, even if it was rarely given as directly as the party's political equivalent. But on one occasion in particular, a Soviet occupation officer publicly disavowed the Soviet system as unsuitable for Germany in connection with the same promise for culture. Major General Vassilij Sharov explained that the Soviet Union had no desire to "force its system upon the German people; the development of their political and cultural life is in their own hands," he said, while adding that the creative intelligentsia could count upon the help and support of the Red Army.[25]

Otherwise, the promise that the Soviet system would not be forced on Germany figured in the cultural rhetoric only by inference. After all, "no sovietization" was a very public stance taken by the leaders of the KPD; on the lips of the party's cultural figures active in "nonpartisan" organizations, the assurance would have called unwanted attention to their real political allegiance and place them in the awkward position of endorsing a widely disbelieved political promise. Rather then enhance the credibility of such organizations, the explicit promise would have diminished it. The party itself

[23]Selbmann, *Aufbruch des Geistes*, pp. 15-16.
[24]Ibid.
[25]"Die neue Humanität," *Das Volk*, 3 April 1946.

had little to lose by making such pledges; in the short run, they might actually change a few minds, whereas any later disavowals would presumably occur in connection with a decision to ignore public opinion anyway. But in either instance, the party's dominant role in Soviet-zone politics remained unaffected. For the cultural organizations, echoes of the Communist party's most hollow promise within nonpartisanship organizations would have lent credence to the suggestion that these functioned as the party's cultural-political branches and took their orders from it. Cultural functionaries who claimed to be acting autonomously in spite of their party membership could ill afford to mimic its flimsiest promises without fostering the impression that they spoke on behalf of the party or in favor of its policies.

The Kulturbund

The tighter the party's grip on politics in Soviet-occupied Germany, the more the Communists raised the pitch of their rhetoric in favor of nonpartisanship and unity as the only conscientious attitude toward the national challenge that faced all political parties. Because they considered it self-evident that their own program was the only undefiled expression of both antifascism and democracy, the twin pillars of national unity, the Communists were just as confident that the universality of their proposals made them uniquely suited to rally all antifascist-democratic forces in Germany and to avoid the political rifts responsible for fascism in the past; whereas the reality of political life in Soviet-occupied Germany was that nonpartisanship for persons, parties, and all other political or cultural organizations inside the Soviet zone amounted to a compulsory commitment to a wide range of objectives designed to benefit one party acting on behalf of one occupying power. With the strength of the SMAD behind it, the organized antifascist "movement" improvised a show of dynamics that no other public endeavor had the political strength to resist; and as time went on, whatever chance that any of these other undertakings may have had of pursuing policies and programs independent of the KPD or SED vanished. This was equally true of cultural processes and of what Becher was so fond of calling "a German movement" of cultural renewal that spread out from the Kulturbund. Unity rapidly came to mean the kind of unanimity that replaced any real consensus with tight restrictions on unrehearsed discussions of central issues like antifascism and democracy; because spontaneity was incompatible with this process, the Communists engaged in intricate acts of organization calculated both to prevent the development of unregulated forms of political and cultural activity and to foster the opposite impression of an antifascist democratic ground swell governed by its own internal dynamic.

The Kulturbund was the best example of a cultural organization publicly geared to the principles of nonpartisanship, though it actually came into existence after a professional organization called the Kammer der Kulturschaffenden, limited to Berlin, began work on or around 20 June 1945. Fritz Erpenbeck was the top Communist on its executive board; the actor Paul Wegener served as the "unanimously" elected president and head of a board comprised of Erpenbeck, Erich Otto, Michael Bohnen, and Eduard von Winterstein. Different sections were placed in charge of literature, music, the graphic arts, film, crafts, and dance; each branch had its own representatives, and these then elected independent working committees that voted upon all matters concerning the individual sections.[26] The extent of Becher's involvement in the Kammer der Kulturschaffenden is not known; his name was missing in all the early announcements, though he delivered the keynote address at the organization's first rally.[27] Nor is there any apparent explanation for the early emergence of two similar organizations in Berlin; and, in any case, the Kulturbund rapidly surpassed the Kammer der Kulturschaffenden in importance. Within a year, the latter organization existed no more. In any case, Becher's formal request to the Soviet military commander of the city of Berlin, applying for permission to create an organization called the Kulturbund, designed to gather together "the broadest strata" of the intelligentsia for the sake of purging the nation of fascism and reacquiring the respect of other peoples, "especially that of the peoples of the Soviet Union," as dated 27 June 1945.[28] Several weeks more then passed before the SMAD's military council permitted the Kulturbund's activity throughout the entire zone on 31 July 1945.[29]

Even so, concrete plans for a "nonpartisan" organization called the Kulturbund, upon which Becher was hard at work throughout the month of June, existed well before either of the above dates; these plans went back to the discussions held in Moscow the beginning of June and almost certainly came up in connection with Stalin's decision to permit the activities of political parties and mass organizations in Soviet-occupied Germany. As early as 6 June 1945, Wilhelm Pieck drew up a document outlining initial ideas for a "Kulturbund für demokratische Erneuerung" charged with working toward the "intellectual and moral destruction of nazism in the area of literature, science, and art" and assisting in the "intellectual rebirth of the German people in conformity with democracy and progress." The names of six personalities, only two of them Communists, Becher and Otto Winzer, were listed as members of a presidium; but "we reserve the right to make addi-

[26]According to the article "Für die demokratische Kunst," *Tägliche Rundschau*, 20 June 1945.
[27]See "Die für geistige Freiheit litten und starben," *Tägliche Rundschau*, 21 August 1945.
[28]See the photograph of that letter, dated 27 June 1945 and addressed to the military commander of the city of Berlin in *Um die Erneuerung der deutschen Kultur. Dokumente*, p. 64.
[29]See Schulmeister, *Auf dem Wege zu einer neuen Kultur*, p. 55.

tions and undertake a reorganization," wrote Pieck, "as soon as prominent writers and scientists come back from abroad." Pieck also proposed an executive board comprised of 20-25 members; and in this particular document listed himself and Walter Ulbricht as prime candidates.[30] Neither ultimately served on it, the job of representing the party officially having been entrusted to Anton Ackermann. Indeed, the KPD's organizational plans drawn up in Moscow, dated 9 June 1945, and apparently reflecting general ideas developed in the conversations with Stalin, assigned responsibility for "propaganda," "party schools," "publishing," "information," the party's "central organ," and "cultural work" to Ackermann; and over the next several years, he remained the man in charge of most cultural matters, including the Kulturbund, within the top party leadership.[31] The document drawn up on 9 June nonetheless included "organization of the 'Kulturbund' in Berlin" as one of Pieck's chief responsibilities, but that apparently changed with the decision to keep him in Moscow for a while and send Paul Wandel to Germany instead. After all, Ackermann and Becher were home on 10 June, and Becher appears to have begun working on the formation of a Kulturbund immediately. Pieck's return was delayed until 1 July 1945.

Problems with the Kulturbund arose immediately; they developed out of skepticism with regard to its ceaseless assertions of nonpartisanship, and reservations about the organization's actual allegiances continued until few if any illusions about it remained. By then, the earlier tactics had exhausted their usefulness; in addition, times had changed; the Kulturbund's political loyalties were taken for granted, and, along with every other "mass organization," the Kulturbund aligned itself openly with the party that had overseen its activities from the outset. But difficulties threatened it all along the way, and virtually every one of them resulted from the original deception governing its operation. The first crisis actually endangered early cooperation between the SPD and KPD. When the SPD's executive board got wind of an imminent "charter meeting" for a cultural league, the Social Democrats concluded that the Communist party's involvement in it was disturbingly reminiscent of the KPD's conspiratorial conduct during the pre-Hitler years. It seems that the Communists had neglected to mention the Kulturbund at meetings of the joint committee set up by both parties just days earlier to discuss their ideological differences, and in that sneakiness, the Social Democrats saw a repeat of the "same old Communist tactics." Otto Grotewohl argued that the SPD should demand an immediate stop to such behavior if the Communists had indeed kept quiet about the Kulturbund; the SPD then dispatched a letter to the Communists protesting the "flagrant violation" of

[30]Schaffung eines "Kulturbundes für demokratische Erneuerung." Zentrales Parteiarchiv, NL 36/734/32-33. See also the scattered papers in Ulbricht's files (NL 182/931/2 and 4).
[31]Nächste zentrale Aufgaben der Parteiführung auf Grund des Aufrufes des ZK der KPD, ibid., NL 36/734/134-5.

the ground rules agreed upon for cooperation and threatening to terminate the agreement. The KPD then sent Ackermann to SPD headquarters to patch things up; he maintained that the KPD's secretariat had been caught off guard itself by the zealousness of its own comrades involved in the Kulturbund and that the party had said nothing because of its reluctance to interfere in non-party business.[32] This particular incident anticipated countless others like it and illustrates the nature of the problems inherent to party strategy in all areas of its activity. Whether in bloc politics, cultural alliances, or other mass organizations, real grass-roots activities in the form of independent undertakings were best prevented through the prior creation of organizations that resulted from the party's own swift initiative. But the men and women who ran these organizations for the party faced the constant challenge of pursuing objectives without conceding that their own political affiliation diminished their commitment to nonpartisanship or in any untoward way affected the activities of the organization itself.

Privately, the failure of the policy was acknowledged almost immediately, though this recognition never led to the adoption of a different approach. For the next several years, the Communists adhered to a strategy riddled by contradictions inherent in their attempt to reconcile "nonpartisanship" with the ruthless politicization of mass organizations along the lines of Marxism-Leninism. In fact, without Becher and his unique ability to discuss Marxism-Leninism in terms of "objective truth," the Kulturbund would likely have been far less successful and probably abandoned its pretense of nonpartisanship much earlier; and yet Becher helped cause the very problems that his rhetoric attempted to solve because he was elected president. Following the first public Kulturbund rally on 3 July 1945, the organization's charter committee met on 8 August in the Kulturbund's designated building in Berlin-Charlottenburg, the former headquarters of the Nazi Reichsschriftumskammer and Reichsfilmkammer, to elect an executive board.[33] Becher chaired the meeting and nominated the novelist Bernhard Kellermann for president, arguing that Kellermann was better for the job because he had spent the last twelve years in Germany, besides which, said Becher, he knew the limits of his own endurance and, in nominating Kellermann, only acted "out of cultural-political expedience."[34] Thus far, perhaps, things had developed roughly according to plan. But the "earnest" arguments made by others in Becher's favor won him over, and his unanimous election followed.[35] None of the vice presidents, Kellermann, the painter Karl Hofer, Johannes Stroux, and Ferdinand Friedensburg, belonged to the party. Paul Wiegler, Herbert Ihe-

---

[32]See Gniffke's account of the affair in, *Jahre mit Ulbricht*, pp. 55-57.
[33]The address was Schlüterstraße 45. See ibid., p. 51 and, Willmann, *Steine klopft man mit dem Kopf*, p. 319.
[34]See Schulmeister, *Auf dem Wege zu einer neuen Kultur*, p. 51.
[35]See "Wende und Wiedergeburt der deutschen Kultur," *Tägliche Rundschau*, 18 August 1945.

ring, Paul Wegener, Eduard von Winterstein, Karl-Heinz Martin, Ernst Legal, and Renée Sintenis served on the board, joined by Ernst Lemmer (CDU), Gustav Dahrendorf (SPD), and Ackermann. Heinz Willmann, a Communist also just back from Soviet exile, assumed the job of general secretary. But within a matter of weeks, Lieutenant General Bokov told Wilhelm Pieck that Becher as president was a "mistake"; the Kulturbund needed to engage in "elastic tactics," and a Communist at the head of it was imprudent. Bokov went on to say that Kellermann would have been a better choice because now the English and Americans "used Becher against us" by calling the Kulturbund a "bolsh.[evist] Moscow org.[anization]." Bokov seems to have held Ackermann, who "slept through the first three months," responsible for the error in permitting Becher's election to take place.[36]

But "elastic" or not, tactics were the issue; the Kulturbund was created to offer the party and the SMAD indirect organizational and programmatic advantages in the pursuit of cultural objectives; and the problems of achieving these without Becher as president, Bokov's attitude notwithstanding, would have been considerable. Still, in early 1946, complaints about Becher and the Kulturbund, a "bad mistake," were voiced again in discussions with Bokov; and toward the end of the year, some thought may have been given to his resignation.[37] But none of these considerations alter the singularity of his contribution to the success of the Kulturbund measured in terms of the organization's usefulness to the party. None of the SED's political functionaries, such as Ackermann, could have hoped to replace him. Their politics were utterly unambiguous, whereas Becher's reputation as writer enabled him to claim that his obligations as artist and intellectual somehow outweighed his membership in the party or were unaffected by it when he engaged in the work of the Kulturbund. None of the party's other cultural figures shared any of Becher's qualities and few of his abilities; whereas an outsider like Kellermann, or even Heinrich Mann,[38] would have been far less useful despite Kellermann's sense of a general affinity with party policies.

The Kulturbund's manifesto and its programmatic guidelines were written entirely by Becher and represent the best early example of a concealed party cultural program. The manifesto began by accusing German intellec-

---

[36]Gespräch mit Bockow am 25. 9. 1945. Zentrales Parteiarchiv, NL 36/734/133.

[37]Mitglieder des Zentralsekretariats zur Besprechung bei Bockow, 20 February or 20 March 1946; and Besprechungen 12. 11. 1946 10 Uhr in Karlshorst. Zentrales Parteiarchiv, NL 36/734/210 and 231. The references are vague: "Kulturbund schwerer Fehler/Becher"; and "Becher—Kulturbund demissioniert." The latter remark may have reflected Pieck's own desire to replace Becher as president; the subject apparently came up because Pieck put it on the agenda. (Fragen für Besprechungen, 11 November 1946, ibid., NL 36/734/237).

[38]The name of Heinrich Mann came up in Pieck's discussions with Tjulpanov, Panushkin, and Georgij Korotkevich; Mann had apparently indicated that he would settle in the Soviet zone if he were asked by "writers a.[nd] Kulturbund" to return to Germany. See 19. 9. 1946 abends 1/2 9 Uhr in Karlshorst Tulpanow, Panuschkin, Korotkewitsch, ibid., NL 36/734/205.

tuals of having failed the test of history and called upon them to admit it if they wished to have a collective say in the future of the people. Referring to the Kulturbund specifically as the nucleus of a "German movement of renewal," an agency for reawakening the conscience of the nation, the unsigned manifesto went on to claim that the Kulturbund nonetheless had no partisan agenda; "we aspire to a new, free, democratic world view"; "we call for the education of the German people in the spirit of the truth, in the spirit of militant democratism." There was no way of knowing at the time that the manifesto was punctuated throughout by verbatim passages lifted from the draft manuscripts drawn up by Becher in Soviet exile. The phrase regarding the urgent necessity of a national act of liberation and reconstruction in the ideological and moral sphere came straight from Becher's 1944 proposal, with the now familiar deletion. Whereas Becher had originally followed his call for ideological and moral reconstruction by extolling the "new type" of party, the Communist party, he excised that reference now and put his comments instead in a deceptively nonpartisan context by talking about the "sacred knowledge that we have a truly national obligation to fulfill in wrestling for the German soul."[39] The Kulturbund's guidelines called specifically for 1) formation of a nationwide united front of German intellectuals, strengthened by an inviolable unity of the intelligentsia and the people; 2) rebirth of the German intellect imbued with a "militant democratic world view"; 3) reevaluation of the historical development of the German people that would sift through the positive and negative forces influential in German intellectual life; and 4) dissemination of truth based on the reacquisition of "objective standards and values."[40] Though the manifesto expressed the Kulturbund's desire to acquaint the German people with the cultural attainments of all nations, "above all with those of the Soviet Union," the guidelines steered clear of a potentially disunifying issue and called only for "incorporating the intellectual accomplishments of other peoples into cultural reconstruction in Germany." The guidelines then went on to stress the "noble political mission" of art in substituting "new, genuine values" for Nazi pseudo-values and in exposing fascist ideologies that had been converted into political power by mercenaries acting in the interests of a "small group of enemies of the people." The point of art was to educate the masses, and the Kulturbund had a tremendous pedagogical task before it; but the nature of the organization marked a break with the practices of the fascists inasmuch as it had no intention of "forcing ideologies upon people."[41]

This latter remark was a distant echo of the party's promise not to impose the "Soviet system" upon Germany; but Becher went no further. True,

[39]"Manifest zur Gründung des 'Kulturbundes,'" *Deutsche Volkszeitung*, 4 July 1945.
[40]"Leitsätze des Kulturbundes zur demokratischen Erneuerung Deutschlands," *Um die Erneuerung der deutschen Kultur. Dokumente*, pp. 68-70.
[41]"Manifest zur Gründung des 'Kulturbundes,'" *Deutsche Volkszeitung*, 4 July 1945.

in his speech to the opening meeting of the Kulturbund in July 1945, he talked of the historical opportunity missed by the German people to avoid war altogether or to end it promptly and also called for a fundamental renunciation of "imperialist methods." Clearer still was his rejection of any definition of fascism that refused to label it German monopoly capital as effective preparation for "a new world war."[42] But in these early months, Becher always avoided the logical inferences of his remarks and invoked instead the spirit of nonalignment by stressing the Kulturbund's "commitment to objective, independent, responsible thinking." "We acknowledge completely valid, effective truths present in both nature and society," he explained; "we demand firm standards and values; we demand logical thinking, thinking in context."[43] But Becher had modified these phrases, too, employing a sentence taken word for word from the 1945 proposal drafted in Moscow, only to eliminate the claim that its doctrine of objective truth distinguished the KPD "ideologically" as the party of German intellectual renewal. What remained was Becher's assurance that the Kulturbund stood "in the service of neither the one nor the other occupying power"; it was oriented neither to the east nor to the west; rather, the Kulturbund represented "a German movement"—*eine deutsche Bewegung*. "Our gaze is fixed upon Germany," he said, "our concern lies with Germany's renewal."[44]

These remarks also promised, furtively, that the Kulturbund would not be used as a vehicle of cultural sovietization, much as the Communist party had sworn that it would not impose the Soviet system upon Germany; and to dispel any lingering doubt about the Kulturbund's liaison with a party suspected of such ambitions, Becher insisted that the organization stood "in the service of neither the one nor the other party"; the Kulturbund served all parties, though only to the extent, he added, that they were "seriously devoted to the realization of democracy."[45] In place of ideology and consciousness, then, Becher substituted the pathos of collective conversion and even strained to bring Martin Luther, whose four-hundredth birthday occurred in 1946, into the argument. Explaining the need for a "philosophy of resurrection, a German doctrine of renewal, an ideology of reconstruction" capable of guiding the people out of the "deepest pit of its history," Becher went on to add that "we cry out for such a conversion, for such a transformation, for such an act of reformation." For Germany would be a free, democratic country or it would be a "historical no man's land."[46] But Becher retained his public confidence in the people; in the name of all true Germans, he said, himself emulating Luther, "in the profound hour of our people's need, I ven-

[42]"Johannes R. Becher an die Kulturschaffenden," *Deutsche Volkszeitung*, 5 July 1945.
[43]Ibid.
[44]Becher, "Auf andere Art so große Hoffnung," *Deutsches Bekenntnis*, pp. 82-83.
[45]Ibid., p. 86.
[46]"Johannes R. Becher an die Kulturschaffenden," *Deutsche Volkszeitung*, 5 July 1945.

ture to utter the words of profession: Here I stand, I cannot help myself. I believe in the German people. I believe in my home, in my fatherland. I believe in Germany."[47] Other aspects of the Kulturbund's objectives came out elsewhere. In his address to the rally on 3 July, Bernhard Kellermann referred to the Kulturbund as the "intellectual and cultural parliament of our country"; this parliament would be duty bound to defend the inviolable rights of the people, specifically "freedom of speech and writing, freedom of the arts and sciences."[48] An editorial published in the *Deutsche Volkszeitung* added more polish. Following the disgrace of the Nazi era, "our people must learn that there once was a truly German culture"; but first a new Germany had to arise, the paper said, quoting Stalin's words to the effect that the German people remained long after the Hitlers were gone; and today it was "the most sacred task of the German people to pull out by the roots everything pernicious, cultivate everything good in its tradition, and achieve a Germany of culture, progress, and peace."[49]

However eloquent the rhetoric, by early 1946 the Kulturbund had nonetheless encountered resistance stiff enough to warrant mention in the press. In February, Heinz Willmann deplored the "occasional lack of understanding" regarding the Kulturbund's goals. Repeating the stock assurance that the league was "not a side organization of a party or a group of parties," he insisted that it was political nevertheless and assailed those who made a virtue of their disinterest in politics. Critics responded by wondering publicly whether the party's drive to politicize every aspect of society really set the Communists apart from the Nazis at all; and Willmann answered that, following the disaster of fascism, it was imperative that "all progressively minded elements" stand shoulder to shoulder. Here the Kulturbund figured prominently because it emphasized the *"indivisible unity of all Germans,"* political and cultural. But Willmann also issued a warning. *"In all efforts calculated to confound German unity we see a bid to perpetuate the selfishness of the Hitler years, giving up the totality for the sake of material advantages in the hope therefore of escaping responsibility for the past."* In one form or another such efforts also existed in the Kulturbund, Willmann went on, because much that occurred in its name still had little in common with the goals and tasks as set down by the central board. The very fact that "one reactionary vied with the other" in some Kulturbund meetings offered convincing evidence of his assertion.[50] Similar comments by others reaffirmed the desire of the Kulturbund to unite all creative intellectuals "who are of goodwill," but added that good will meant those "who wish to work in concert toward the democratic renewal of our fatherland." By no means, was the

[47]"'Die für geistige Freiheit litten und starben,'" *Tägliche Rundschau*, 21 August 1945.
[48]"Der Geistesschaffende wird zum Kämpfer," *Deutsche Volkszeitung*, 6 July 1945.
[49]"Deutschlands Kultur am neuen Anfang," *Deutsche Volkszeitung*, 15 August 1945.
[50]Willmann, "Das hohe Ziel des Kulturbundes," *Tägliche Rundschau*, 19 February 1946.

Kulturbund a "nonpolitical organization," but it refused to "serve *a single political party*"; for reasons of its own nonpartisanship, the Kulturbund could work congenially with "all *democratic* parties and organizations," but remain subordinate to no other authority and independent in its decisions.[51]

The Deutsche Verwaltung für Volksbildung

The Deutsche Verwaltung für Volksbildung (DVV) was a much different organization that operated within a broader political context and with far more comprehensive powers; its impact upon cultural development in Soviet-occupied Germany was correspondingly vaster, too, and longer-lasting. The Kulturbund lost its significance in the early fifties, replaced by newly created associations like the writers' union that worked on the basis of more specific mandates; whereas, the divisions of the DVV responsible for culture generally and the arts specifically branched off into a separate ministry of culture with enormous power and influence. The Verwaltung für Volksbildung began, however, as just one of the original "central administrations" whose creation was decreed by an unpublished SMAD order dated 27 July 1945 that required the formation of twelve such agencies, most of them concerned with economic matters, by 10 August; that order came just a few weeks after the SMAD approved regional German administrations set up as quasi-governments at the state or provincial level in Saxony, Saxony-Anhalt, Brandenburg, Thuringia, and Mecklenburg-Vorpommern.[52] For the duration of their existence, the activities of the central administrations raised sensitive political questions because the agencies were conceived as precursors of a national government; whereas the Potsdam accords stipulated that there would be no such central German administration "for the foreseeable future." The accords called instead for the organization of five central administrative divisions for all of occupied Germany and the establishment of a German administrative apparatus to help in running the economy. When the French vetoed their creation, and no substitute agreement was reached, early Soviet steps in the direction of central administrations smacked of an effort to create a German apparatus dominated by local Communists, based in Berlin, answerable to the SMAD, and with claims on the entire country.

Once those ambitions were stymied outside of Soviet-occupied Germany, the central agencies still appeared to square with the SED's public commitment to a national German state that contrasted with Western schemes of

---

[51]*Unser Weg*. Veröffentlichung der Landesleitung des Kulturbundes . . . anläßlich der ersten Wiederkehr des Gründungstages des Kulturbundes, p. 23.

[52]See "Befehl Nr. 17 der SMAD über die Bildung von deutschen Zentralverwaltungen in der sowjetischen Besatzungszone Deutschlands [27 July 1945]," in *Geschichte des Staates und des Rechts der DDR*, pp. 69-70.

"dismemberment" through federalism; and the reputation of a military administration that supposedly trusted the local population enough to let Germans run their own affairs was thought to benefit from them as well. But the existence of the agencies, especially when questions of their authority over regional administrations arose, conflicted with provisions of the Potsdam accords calling for the "administration of Germany . . . in the direction of a decentralization of the political structure and the development of local responsibility." These were critical issues for the Russians and the German Communists in 1945 and remained so until formation of a separate government, which turned the central administrations into ministries, ended the controversy in October 1949.

But in 1945, the establishment of a central administrative apparatus suggested "sovietization" just by itself; and the party's domination of these agencies by way of key functionaries who held influential positions in them made the impression that much harder to avoid. Of course, the full extent of the party's control over the administrations in Berlin was scarcely common knowledge, at least not in the beginning, and party leaders needed little encouragement, as Bokov advised Pieck in September 1945, to "assist" Communists working within them.[53] The public knew even less about the extent of the SMAD's supervision of the activity of each agency; it assigned individual officers to work with division heads and office chiefs who, at least in the case of the DVV, were expected to keep the Russians abreast of every initiative and usually developed these plans in the first place only after consulting with Soviet officers in charge of specific branches. Oftentimes, particularly in instances that involved undertakings with important political or ideological implications, plans could not be carried out formally in the absence of an official, through generally unpublished,[54] SMAD order bearing the signature of some top officer or of the supreme commander himself.

Most SMAD orders were treated confidentially, and few seem to have been routinely available to lower-level German administrators who, follow-

---

[53]Gespräch mit Bockow am 25. 9. 1945 um 10 Uhr in Karlshorst. Zentrales Parteiarchiv, NL 36/734/132. The emphasis nonetheless remained on the "tactics" of their work and the way in which the Communist administrators ought to "conduct themselves." See also the instructions regarding "cooperation with party comrades in the central administrations" drawn up at a meeting of the SED's central secretariat in December 1946 (Protokoll der Sitzung des Zentralsekretariats am 24. 12. 1946, ibid., IV 2/2.1/55). Weber, *Geschichte der DDR*, pp. 96-110, as well as Welsh and Zank, "Zentralverwaltungen," *SBZ-Handbuch*, 201-6, offer additional general information on these various agencies and details regarding the party affiliation of the top administrators. A formal decision reached by the KPD's central secretariat at a meeting in spring 1946, which discussed matters pertaining to the central administrations, illustrates the imperiousness of its tactical decisions. With respect to the administration in charge of agriculture and forestry, it was decided that "the president . . . shall be a Communist" (Protokoll Nr. 19/76 der Sitzung am 30. März 1946. Zentrales Parteiarchiv, I 2/5/51/63).
[54]See Foitzik, "Sowjetische Militäradministration in Deutschland (SMAD)," *SBZ-Handbuch*, pp. 40-44.

ing the general instructions of their immediate superiors, were charged with their implementation. These sensitivities also influenced the announcement of the decision to authorize the establishment of the first twelve central administrations.[55] Apart from naming them, SMAD order 17, dated 27 July 1945, decreed that the "president" of each agency should prepare a budget and submit it to the SMAD by 1 August 1945; and a report on compliance with the order was expected in occupation headquarters by 10 August.[56] But no public announcement was made until 13 September and then only in the form of a truncated version of the original order that omitted any mention of earlier deadlines. Moreover, the public notification referred only to administrations, whereas the order called them *central* administrations. But then the official announcement, as if to emphasize that Germans had not been put in charge of governmental organizations, also stated that the agencies exercised their activity in accordance with the "directives" of corresponding offices within the SMAD and under their "direct control."[57] A few days after the announcement, Anton Ackermann also characterized the organizations as central administrations, but insisted that their creation was important for "our entire German fatherland." He contended that they allowed for a standardization of administration throughout the five German provinces not yet practicable, unfortunately, nationwide; but followed up those comments with an attempt to strike the proper balance with respect to the issue of jurisdiction. He asserted that the five state-level administrations would welcome the creation of central agencies as a "healthy synthesis between centralization and local administration" because they assured the states of the "necessary latitude for the development of their own creative initiative"; and he denied that Zhukov's order provided for a government in regions of Germany occupied by the Red Army. There was no administration in charge of internal affairs (for the time being), nor any single agency assigned to oversee the work of all twelve central administrations; the executive emphasis remained in the hands of the state and provincial administrations.[58]

In private, there was far less local enthusiasm than Ackermann implied; and that mistrust existed because the agencies in Berlin moved so relentlessly in the direction of centralized authority. At an early meeting between the five presidents of the regional administrations, the vice-presidents and presidents of the central administrations, top Soviet officers, and Marshal Zhukov, the points raised underscored the conflict. Asked about his relation-

[55]At the time, there were Zentralverwaltungen in charge of Verkehrswesen, Nachrichtenwesen, Brennstoffindustrie, Handel und Versorgung, Industrie, Landwirtschaft, Finanzen, Arbeit und Sozialfürsorge, Gesundheitswesen, Volksbildung, and Justiz.

[56]*Geschichte des Staates und des Rechtes der DDR*, pp. 69-70

[57]"Errichtung von deutschen Verwaltungen in der sowjetischen Okkupationszone," *Befehle des Obersten Chefs der Sowjetischen Militärverwaltung in Deutschland*, pp. 34-35.

[58]Ackermann, "Was wir von den Zentralverwaltungen erwarten," *Deutsche Volkszeitung*, 19 September 1945.

ship with the agencies in Berlin, the Thuringian president Rudolf Paul, who fled to the West in fall 1947, told the Russians that his administration had initially welcomed their formation, but went on to complain that they had not limited themselves to a general coordination of efforts; they interfered directly—and "unacceptably"—in provincial business. Paul said that he could not allow the agencies to meddle everywhere in his administration or to engage in hirings and firings without his knowledge; and he argued that no law should be passed without consulting with the provincial administration first. Finally, he asked Zhukov for a clear description of the responsibilities of the central agencies versus those of provincial administration.[59] He failed to get one, and, in the course of the discussion, the presidents of the Berlin administrations whose remarks were recorded came out in favor of central authority. Even a non-Communist like Ferdinand Friedensburg called the idea of central administrations "healthy" and argued that a precise separation of power was virtually impossible. Moreover, Friedensburg asked Zhukov to provide the central agencies with the right to issue mandatory "instructions" to the provinces. But Zhukov failed to comply with Friedensburg's request either, and the president of Saxony, Rudolf Friedrichs, later sided with Paul in agreeing that the central administrations interfered too heavily in the affairs of the provinces. They should pass laws in matters pertaining to affairs applicable throughout the zone; but actual administration belonged in the hands of the states and provinces; and Friedrichs concluded that "we will complicate matters later, when things are standardized in all of Germany, if we overly centralize the central administrations."[60]

Organizational Matters

This discussion ended with no resolution of the problem of jurisdiction; and the issue proved nettlesome in efforts that fall to define the statutory authority of the DVV. The actual SMAD order was devoid of detail about it, alluding solely to the DVV's responsibility for "schools" and "educational institutions." The order even failed to name the president of the organization, though Paul Wandel had already been appointed. Wilhelm Pieck apparently informed him on 24 July that he had been put in charge of the DVV and would take over the next day.[61] The order itself was evidently read to Wandel in Karlshorst a day or so before the date, 27 July, listed on the actual

[59]Bericht über die Beratung der Präsidenten der Provinzial- und Landesverwaltungen, der Vize-Präsidenten und der Präsidenten der Zentralverwaltung mit den Chefs der sowjetischen Militär-Administration und Marschall Schukow, 13 November 1945. Zentrales Parteiarchiv, NL 36/734/101.
[60]Ibid., NL 36/734/105-111.
[61]Wandel, "Die Partei der Arbeiterklasse war vorbereitet," . . . *einer neuen Zeit Beginn*, p. 546.

document;[62] and he heard for the first time that the SMAD expected a preliminary budget by 1 August.[63] Whether the Russians themselves had a clear idea of the organization at this time is unlikely. According to Wandel's account,[64] the document read to him in Karlshorst added the supervision of artistic, cultural, and scientific institutions to the DVV's duties. The public announcement made on 13 September then expanded the agency's duties to include, apart from schools, the supervision of artistic activities, museums, theaters, movie houses, and scientific and cultural institutions engaged in "enlightenment."[65] These broader responsibilities appear to have coincided with the original structure of the SMAD's Abteilung für Volksbildung, run by P. V. Solotuchin,[66] though the DVV dealt just as often with the office of information, run by Sergej Tjulpanov, and its cultural division, headed by Alexander Dymschitz. This branch of the SMAD began work shortly after the Abteilung für Volksbildung, on 18 August 1945; and in 1946, responsibility for cultural affairs generally was completely reassigned to it and its more than 150 officers.[67]

But there must have been a more specific sense of the kinds of duties to be assumed by the DVV, expanded to include cultural affairs, in advance of the announcement on 13 September, though few Germans associated with the developing agency other than Wandel, who dealt most directly with the SMAD,[68] were likely well acquainted with the original ideas. If no such plans had existed at all, however, the SMAD could not have drafted an order as early as 4 September, numbered 51, that governed the "recommencement and activity of art institutions" while relying heavily upon the DVV for enforcement. At the time, no DVV division had yet been set up to deal with

---

[62]As Wandel told me in March 1989.

[63]Wandel, "Die Partei der Arbeiterklasse war vorbereitet," p. 546.

[64]See ibid.

[65]See "Errichtung von deutschen Verwaltungen in der sowjetischen Okkupationszone," *Befehle des Obersten Chefs der Sowjetischen Militärverwaltung in Deutschland*, pp. 34-35.

[66]Solotukhin, a Lieutenant General who had previously headed the Leningrad edition of *Pravda*, then Leningrad University, before becoming the assistant minister of culture and education in the Russian Federated Republic, had arrived in Berlin on 6 July 1945; by early August, the SMAD's Abteilung für Volksbildung had fifty-five employees (including translators). See *Errichtung des Arbeiter und Bauernstaates der DDR*, p. 195. Wandel also told me that the various offices of the SMAD's Abteilung für Volksbildung, comprised of five sections placed in charge of schools, universities, cultural "enlightenment," art, and museums, were already set up at the time of his discussion in Karlshort a day or two before 27 July.

[67]See Foitzik, "Sowjetische Militäradministration in Deutschland (SMAD)," pp. 23-24.

[68]Little information about Wandel's own dealings with the SMAD is available; either records of his discussions were not kept, which is doubtful, or these documents remained separate from other DVV files later deposited in the archives. Wandel's talks with the SMAD in Karlshorst appear to have been plentiful; one letter sent by Wandel's office staff to the SMAD indicated that he visited Karlshorst on 24, 25, 27, 28, and 29 May; and was apparently expected at meetings on 1 and 3 June 1946 as well (see the letter dated 12 June 1946, Bundesarchiv, Abt. Potsdam, R-2/6269/77).

these kinds of issues; the earliest suggestion for the creation of an office responsible for the oversight of theaters and art exhibitions goes no further back than 17 September;[69] in fact, the impetus behind it surely developed out of the need to comply with the broader assignment of responsibilities to the DVV first alluded to in the public announcement on 13 September; and much like order 17 behind that announcement, no. 51, pertaining to the activities of "art institutions," was not released until 25 September, though only in an abridged version that revealed much less about its censorial aspects. The public announcement talked of "confirmation procedures" to be followed in the approval of theater repertories and art exhibitions, whereas the order itself used the actual word "banning." Indeed, its provisions are the best early illustration of the DVV's future role as an executive arm of the occupation administration and contained the first references to obligations associated explicitly with censorship.

Order 51 called for the liberation of art from Nazi, racist, military, and "other reactionary ideas and tendencies" and insisted upon the "active utilization of artistic means in the struggle against fascism and for the reeducation of the German people in the sense of a consequent democracy." All stage, opera, and operetta theaters, all symphony orchestras and bands in the Soviet sector of Berlin had to be registered with the SMAD's Abteilung für Volksbildung upon recommendation by the DVV. The same kind of theaters in other cities, along with all varieté and popular music stages, cabarets and their repertoires were to be registered by the SMAD in the provinces, states, counties, and by the Soviet military commander in the cities and localities. All administrative and artistic directors of theater and music institutions likewise had to be registered with the SMAD at all administrative levels of the zone; and the same went for the composition of acting troupes and musical groups "upon recommendation by the organs of the local German administrative offices." All art societies and associations that had existed prior to the end of the war were now retroactively dissolved, as of 9 May 1945, and the formation of new ones permitted only after approval by the SMAD's Abteilung für Volksbildung "upon recommendation by the Zentralverwaltung für Volksbildung or its local offices." Art exhibits in the Soviet zone and sector of Berlin were banned without the prior knowledge and approval of the Zentralverwaltung or its local offices. In addition, the precise makeup of all exhibitions in the Soviet sector of Berlin and the provincial and state capitals had to be confirmed in advance following the same procedure. As president, Wandel was personally ordered to provide additionally a register listing all persons active in the Soviet zone in the area of theater, music, dance, film, and the graphic arts; to supply the SMAD's Abteilung für Volksbildung with

[69]Entwurf. Den Herren Abteilungsleitern vorzulegen. Gez. Wandel, 17 September 1945 [Zusatz für Herrn Volkmann], ibid., R-2/805/1-2. See below for further details.

suggested names for the administrative and artistic directorships of all theaters and musical groups active in the Soviet sector of Berlin; and to submit for approval the repertory plans of all such theaters and music groups as well as all art exhibition plans. Solotuchin was charged with the overall implementation of order 51, and the local city and county military commanders were ordered to supervise all stage activity and exhibitions. No performance was allowed without approval by the relevant SMAD authorities.[70]

Censorship soon developed into one of the DVV's prime responsibilities, even though the SMAD never granted the organization specifically or German agencies generally complete control of publishing; and the same is true of stage censorship. All such activities came under the initial purview of the SMAD's own "section for propaganda and censorship" attached to the political division of the occupation administration on the basis of order 29, dated 18 August 1945. This order was the same one that created the office assigned to Sergej Tjulpanov, later renamed "information"; and from the beginning, the DVV's burgeoning bureaucracy was used to assist the SMAD in all matters pertaining to censorship. For this reason alone, putting Tjulpanov's office in charge of culture and "enlightenment" and making the DVV accountable to it in those matters, rather than to Solotuchin's division, made perfect sense. But for now, SMAD order 29 omitted any reference to the DVV, whose own responsibilities were still being defined, and said nothing about general cultural issues either. The order concentrated upon setting up departments of censorship within the central SMAD administration in Berlin and as part of all state, regional, and city branches of the SMAD. Specifically, the section or division of propaganda and censorship controlled all forms of printed matter, "newspapers, books, brochures, posters, leaflets, etc.," throughout Soviet-occupied Germany and in Berlin; all printing presses fell under its jurisdiction and were prohibited from producing printed matter of any kind in the absence of permission granted by it or its censors; all material intended for radio broadcast likewise required prior censorship; no films could be shown without advance screening by Soviet censors; and control over the work of theaters and cabarets, whose productions were subject to approval by the censors, was to be "assumed."[71] Order 51 outlined the procedures involved in the implementation of those responsibilities and conveyed a sense of the need for a German bureaucracy to assist in what soon developed into a massive undertaking.

[70]See "Wiedererrichtung und Tätigkeit der Kunstinstitutionen. Befehl Nr. 51 des Obersten Chefs der Sowjetischen Militäradministration in Deutschland," *Um die Erneuerung der deutschen Kultur. Dokumente*, p. 85. See the published version, "Über die Wiedererrichtung und die Tätigkeit der Kunstinstitutionen in der sowjetischen Besatzungszone Deutschlands," *Tägliche Rundschau*, 25 September 1945.

[71]Befehl des Obersten Chefs der Sowj. Militärischen Administration in Deutschland. Nr. 29, 18. August 1945. Inhalt: Über die Tätigkeit der Sektion für Propaganda und Zensur der Pol. Abteilung der Sowj. Mil. Adm. in Deutschland. Bundesarchiv, Abt. Postdam, X-1.

But getting organized took time; in fall 1945, most of the attention was paid to early definitions of the DVV's responsibilities and to setting up the agency accordingly. These initial efforts included attempts to clarify the extent of its authority, and here confusion reigned—almost certainly because the Russians themselves wanted a centralized administrative apparatus, but worried about the international consequences if they were too obvious about creating one. Early planning may have reflected the vacillation caused by these conflicting ambitions. The Zentralverwaltung für Volksbildung, read a tentative set of organizational statutes drafted in November 1945, was charged with the supervision of educational, scientific, artistic, and cultural institutions; and it received additional authorization through orders issued by the SMAD. But such authority was confined to supervision and oversight, general planning, and the development of administrative regulations uniform throughout Soviet-occupied Germany, rather than law-making as such. Nor was the DVV empowered to enact "legal ordinances" binding upon state and provincial administrations; these bodies enjoyed their own legislative authority, whereas the DVV was limited to the issuance of administrative ordinances like organizational and institutional instructions. Moreover, the DVV did not qualify as an "organ of self-administration"; it answered to the corresponding department of the SMAD and operated in accordance with its directives.[72]

Another attempt to provide the agency with executive powers in the form of a "law," apparently prepared for submission to the SMAD as one of its documents, might have clarified matters, but was certainly never accepted. This document referred to the DVV as an "independent administration" that governed the affairs of science, art and literature, research and educational instruction; otherwise "sovereign" in its duties, it nonetheless operated according to SMAD guidelines, but passed its own directives and regulations. The draft law even referred to the DVV as a "newly created central agency with the rights and authority of a ministry."[73] But in spite of one other characterization of the DVV as the "embryo" of a central agency or *Reichsbehörde*, the state and provincial administrations remained unimpressed. In fact, the statutes just mentioned reflected the agency's original sense of its limited mandate as well as its natural impulse to centralize. While being as obliging as possible toward state and provincial agencies, the document said, the DVV would try to foster understanding at the local level for the necessity of a "central authority" and seek to gain recognition as such an agency. Its legal means were "negotiation, compromise, and, if the public interest makes intervention seem urgently necessary, an appeal to the SMAD."[74] The

[72]Organisationsstatut, ibid., R-2/6250/24.
[73]Gesetz über die Einrichtung einer Deutschen Zentralverwaltung für Volksbildung, ibid., R-2/6250/18. The document was dated, by hand, 20 November 1945.
[74]Ibid.

problem of jurisdiction changed over the course of several months, and the subject comes up again later; but in fall 1945, the DVV's top administrators spent their time developing the organization's own internal structure, assigning responsibilities to its specific divisions, and filling the positions with employees regarded as "truly reliable, democratic elements."[75]

The earliest of these *Geschäftsverteilungspläne* was probably one referred to as the "Kurasov plan." It provided for 115 employees working within seven major divisions (not counting the office of the president): schools, institutions of higher education and science, art affairs (with two subdivisions, one in charge of the pictorial arts, the other, theaters, movie houses, and music), cultural institutions and publishing houses, a personnel office, an office of finance, and general administration.[76] This document was undated, but likely originated in late August or early September. It amounted to nothing more than a plain structural plan with an assignment of responsibilities and a budget based on the monthly salaries of the unnamed employees. But its original proposals were adhered to; the basic organizational scheme remained roughly intact, and through March 1946 the SMAD never approved more than 125 administrators and employees.[77] The first formal structural and organizational proposal, which, like the Kurasov plan, probably dated back to late August, then reflected more than those that followed it the initial intention of staffing the DVV by appointing "antifascist-democratic elements in consideration of the unity of the labor movement (parity) and bloc politics to responsible positions and technical-administrative areas of responsibility."[78] On 18 August 1945, the SPD's executive board made some suggestions, two of which were initially accepted.[79] The ensuing proposal provided for five "major offices" or *Hauptämter*: general administration, science and research, schools, art and literature (the earliest inclusion of literature among the agency's responsibilities), and what was then called general cultural education or *Allgemeine Volksbildung*. At this stage, the office of personnel was attached to the office of the president dominated by members of the KPD. The two vice presidents, Erwin Marquardt and Menke-Glückert, belonged to other parties (the SPD and LDP); and the plan reflected the initial concern with political "parity." The head of general administration, Reichwaldt, belonged to the SPD, and so did Erwin Redslob, nominat-

[75]See the personnel files, most of which date back to August, September, and October 1945, in ibid., R-2/928-936. Wandel included the characterization in instructions to the head of his agency's personnel office, Ernst Hoffmann, on 3 January 1946 (ibid., R-2/629/75).

[76]Kurasow-Plan! Stellenplan der SMA für die ZV. für Volksbildung, ibid., R-2/6250/28-29.

[77]See Betr.: Grundsätzliche Erwägungen zur Begründung der 252 Personalplanstellen seitens der DVV, 8 February 1946; Tätigkeitsbericht der Personalabteilung von 1945 bis 1948; and Tätigkeitsbericht von 1945-1948, 9 August 1948, ibid., R-2/911/65-68; R-2/925-6/1-7 and 9-18.

[78]See Tätigkeitsbericht der Personalabteilung, ibid., R-2/925/9.

[79]Sozialdemokratische Partei Deutschland. Zentralausschuß. Sachbearbeiter-Vorschläge für die zentrale Verwaltung Volksbildung, 18 August 1945, ibid., R-2/1291/71.

ed by his party to head art and literature; Dr. Theodor Brugsch, in charge of science and research, was unaffiliated, whereas Ernst Hadermann (schools) and Wolfgang Heise (cultural education) were Communists. A scattering of Liberal and Christian Democrats, as well as an assortment of other Communists and Social Democrats, occupied lower-level posts.[80]

The basic structure suggested in this plan must have been approved in principle, though some of the original staff recommendations soon changed. By 17 September 1945, the division chiefs had been appointed, and, as part of the development of the DVV's first formal organizational and personnel plan, Wandel asked them for their own proposals regarding the further structuring of their offices. Herbert Volkmann,[81] a Communist who became head of art and literature instead of Redslob and developed into one of the DVV's most important bureaucrats, was encouraged to set up subdivisions in charge of the pictorial arts and museums and to oversee theater, film, music, and crafts; whereas Heise's division of cultural education included offices or *Referate* for publishing houses and the press, lay culture, adult education, and youth and women's affairs.[82] Another plan followed the beginning of October; it indicated that the vice presidents had been assigned individually to oversee the major divisions; Menke-Glückert would have supervised cultural education, Marquardt, the school system, and a third vice president, Johannes R. Becher, art and literature. Becher never played any role in the DVV and was replaced as third vice president by Erich Weinert in February 1946.[83] Otherwise, there were few alterations; in addition to art and literature, Volkmann also ran the office of literature within it. No office head was yet listed for pictorial arts and museums; and the Social Democrat Siegfried Nestriepke, one of the SPD's original nominees, appeared with responsibility for the office of theater, film, music, and crafts. Cultural education, like art and literature, also took Wandel's advice of 17 September; and, as in the

---

[80]Zentralverwaltung für die Volksbildung innerhalb der Besatzungszone der UdSSR. Organisations- und Verteilungsvorschlag, ibid., R-2/1007/24-27.

[81]See Volkmann's "Personal-Fragebogen," which refers to 10 September 1945 as the date of his appointment as head of art and literature within the DVV, ibid., R-2/936/30. This file (38) also contains Wandel's papers; he responded to the question about his party membership in years past by answering "CPSU 1933-45."

[82]Entwurf. Den Herren Abteilungsleiter vorzulegen, 17 September 1945. Gez. Wandel (Zusatz für Herrn Volkmann. Zusatz für Herrn Heise), ibid., R-2/805/1-2.

[83]See Sowjetische Militäradministration. Propagandaverwaltung, 21 February 1946. Tjulpanov to Wandel (ibid., R-2/911/215), approving Weinert as the DVV vice president in charge of the divisions of art and literature and cultural enlightenment. In 16 February Wandel had "nominated" Weinert in a letter to Bokov, in whose name Tjulpanov responded. See also Präsidialkanzlei an die Herren Abteilungsleiter, 8 March 1946. Gez. Wandel (R-2/1007/36). Actually, Weinert joined the DVV as Wandel's deputy when Wandel fell sick; and was given the assignment in the form of a decision rendered by the KPD secretariat (See Protokoll Nr. 8/65 der Sitzung des Sekretariats am 27. Januar 1946. Zentrales Parteiarchiv, I 2/5/51/24-25). Presumably, the secretariat's decision then went to the SMAD in the form of a request that the Russians approved.

first "organizational proposal" drawn up a few weeks earlier, Lothar von Balluseck, a Communist, appeared as head of the office, "publishing houses and the press," out of which literary censorship, the infamous Kultureller Beirat, soon developed. The other posts remained unfilled.[84]

The next "tentative" plan followed on 10 November 1945 and included the first job descriptions. Gerhart Strauß had now been appointed head of pictorial arts within the division of art and literature. Some of its more important responsibilities included "exhibits and other exhibition matters," art-historical institutes, art education, art associations and organizations, art publishing houses, artists and unions, cultivating world art and "promoting understanding for Russian art," as well as "popularizing artistic work and incorporating it into antifascist-democratic education." Other offices, like film or even music, also had duties rife with political implications; the theater office was in charge of the "screening" of theater, orchestra, and small-stage personnel "in an artistic as well as political respect"; and had responsibility for "exerting influence over the repertories of the stage theaters, especially over their antifascist orientation." The screening of performances was listed separately. The duties of literature, run by Volkmann, remained vague.[85] The plan also provided details about cultural education, now headed by Wilhelm Girnus a Communist who had spent time in a Nazi concentration camp. Soon renamed cultural enlightenment or Kulturelle Aufklärung, its office of publishing, press, and now radio was still run by von Balluseck, and Alfred Frommhold, also a Communist, was assigned responsibility for the initial screening of license applications submitted by publishing houses, the scrutiny of publishing plans, the preliminary examination of license applications for journals and other periodicals; and Alfred Weiland was charged with examining applications for new newspapers as well as "registering and watching over the press." Matters related to broadcasting were not taken up until several weeks later.[86] The more precise duties of the other offices set up within cultural education were also defined, including youth affairs assigned to Erich Honecker.[87] Another plan followed on 24 November 1945 that differed little from the previous one dated 10 November and could be the final "tentative" version approved by the Russians;[88] in fact, this plan may well

[84]DVV. Stand: Anfang Oktober 1945. Bundesarchiv, Abt. Potsdam, R-2/1007/28- 29.

[85]Vorläufiger Entwurf eines Geschäftsverteilungsplans, 10 November 1945, Geschäftsverteilungsplan der Abteilung für Kunst und Literatur, ibid., R-2/807 /8 and 27-35.

[86]The SMAD assigned the DVV responsibility for the Soviet-zone broadcasting system on 21 December 1945. See Propagandaabteilung an Paul Wandel, 21 December 1945, ibid., R-2/1090/1.

[87]Geschäftsverteilungsplan für die Abteilung "Allgemeine Volksbildung," ibid., R-2/807/39.

[88]Vorläufiger Entwurf eines Geschäftsverteilungsplans, 24 November 1945, ibid., R-2/1007/7-23. The plan covered six divisions (Kunst und Literatur; Allgemeine Volksbildung; Personal- und Wirtschaftsabteilung; Allgemeine Verwaltungs- und Finanzangelegenheiten; Wissenschaft und Forschung; and Schulwesen).

have been adhered to through the following summer when, on 28 August 1946, Reichwaldt informed the separate DVV divisions that the "tentative draft of the assignment of responsibilities" was soon to be replaced with a definitive version.[89]

The DVV's top administrators soon discovered, in early 1946, that the organization's expanding responsibilities had outpaced staffing restrictions set by the SMAD. In February, it was argued that the original approval of 115 employees would not suffice to enable the agency to discharge its duties effectively in the implementation of educational reform and in cultural-political areas like broadcasting, the press, publishing houses, pictorial arts, theater, film, literature, and both youth and women's affairs. Even though all central administrations were temporarily limited to merely "advisory" work and oversight, the DVV's responsibilities were said to differ markedly from those of other administrations and combined with anticipated changes in the "economic and social structure of the Soviet Russian occupation zone" to create the need for a considerably larger staff. The DVV planned on asking the SMAD to approve a total of 252 positions, and the Russians had probably promised a favorable response beforehand.[90] The DVV's first complete set of budgetary, personnel, and organizational plans for 1946, which called for 202 employees and was authorized by SMAD order 68 dated 5 March 1946, then took shape in March and April 1946. The KPD was provided with a list of the DVV's top administrators drawn from these plans on 27 March; and the same structural, staff, and budget plans received the necessary approval of the Soviet-zone central finance administration on 17 April 1946.[91] Just how rapidly the DVV expanded is apparent upon comparison with its overall expenses for the first four months of its existence from 1 September through 31 December 1945, 800,000 marks, with the almost 56 million marks approved for 1946.[92] In December 1946, then, the DVV asked the SMAD for permission to expand the organization by well over a third, increasing its authorized staff level to 376; the Russians refused, and the DVV had to content itself with the previous 210.[93] On 11 February 1947, the

[89]Betrifft: Aufstellung eines endgültigen Geschäftsverteilungsplans. Gez. Reichwaldt, 28 August 1946, ibid., R-2/806/22.

[90]Betr.: Grundsätzliche Erwägungen zur Begründung der 252 Personalplanstellen, 8 February 1946, ibid., R-2/911/65-66. Wandel referred internally to the anticipated hiring of a number of new employees as early as 3 January 1946 (Wandel to Hoffman [Personalabteilung], R-2/629/75).

[91]See Aufstellung der leitenden Personen. 27 March 1946 [written in hand: "an ZK"], ibid., R-2/1291/22. See also Organisations- und Stellenplan . . . gemäß Schreiben der Deutschen Zentralfinanzverwaltung vom 17. 4. 46 (R-2/1007/77-84).

[92]See the Kurzer Abriß über das Material zum ersten Jahresbericht, 10 July 1946, ibid., R-2/806/41; and Festgestellter Haushalt für das Rechnungsjahr 1946 (1. Januar bis zum 31. Dezember 1946), 17 April 1946 (R-2/810/1-13).

[93]See Material: Vorschlag zur Besprechung am 18. XII 46 i. Karlshorst, K.[ader]-Abt.; and Material: Ergebnis nach der Sitzung am 18. XII. 46 in Karlshorst, K.-Abt., ibid., R-2/941/1-35.

SMAD's Abteilung für Volksbildung formally approved these positions.[94] In 1948, the DVV expanded to 271 (not counting an additional sixteen temporaries); this came close to being the largest number of employees ever, and the organization ended the year with total expenditures of well over 100 million marks.[95]

These figures convey a sense of the size of the developing bureaucracy, and a few additional details round out the organizational and structural picture through 1949. New summaries were drawn up in 1948 and 1949,[96] the first based generally on 271,[97] the second on staff reductions back to approximately 220 employees due to a combination of financial exigencies and political considerations. Underfunding chronically hampered the work of the DVV, and some of its more vexing problems arose simply because of the lack of money necessary to meet obligations assigned the organization by the SMAD to begin with. As early as summer 1946, for instance, the occupation administration's office of revenue asked the DVV to prepare a report covering the first year of its activity in order to demonstrate how successfully the organization made use of financing in considerable excess of earlier outlays; the request was made along with the point that the easy availability of funds was now over.[98] But financial shortfalls were by no means unique

[94]See Übersicht über die Gliederung und den Personalbestand, which was sent to the SMAD's Savanjuk, its finance division, and the Soviet-zone central revenue finance administration (ibid., R-2/804/20-32 and 6; and Abteilung für Volksbildung der Sowjetischen Militäradministration (I. Artjukhin), 11 February 1947, to Paul Wandel, ibid., R-2/804/38. See also Namentliches Verzeichnis . . . entsprechend des mit Schreiben der SMA-Nr. 27/39 vom 11. 2. 1947 genehmigten Stellenplanes 1947 (R-2/2950/221); and Stellenplan. Gültig vom 1. Januar 1947. Bestätigt gemäß dem Schreiben der UdSSR, Abteilung für Volksbildung der SMA / 11. 2. 1947 Nr. 27/39 (R-2/1007/101).
[95]See Tätigkeitsbericht der Personalabteilung der Deutschen Verwaltung für Volksbildung vom 1945 bis 1948 (ibid., R-2/925/16); and 1948 Jahreshaushalt (R-2/2072/11).
[96]See Struktur- und Stellenplan für das Rechnungsjahr 1948, 22 March 1948; and An die Sowjetische Militäradministration—Zivile Verwaltung—z. Hdn. von Herrn Oberstleutnant Wallejew, 8. September 1949. Planstellen ... mit dem Stand vom 1. 9. 1949 (ibid., R-2/918/23-36 and R-2/911/41) This latter plan referred to 222 employees actually working (out of 247 approved positions). See also the diagram of the DVV and its various subsidiary agencies prepared by the office of the president (Strukturplan der Deutschen Verwaltung für Volksbildung. January 1949), the similar diagram (listing 229 employees out of 245 approved positions) dated September 1949, the graph describing personnel fluctuations from 1945-1948 (R-2/1007/85), and the set of illustrations of the DVV's structure as it expanded from the original six divisions in 1945 to seven in 1946, and nine from 1947 to 1949 (R-2/944/1-13). By then these included the following divisions: Präsidialabteilung (Pr.) Personalabteilung (PA), Abteilung für Allgemeine Verwaltung, Finanzen und Statistik (Z), Abteilung für Wissenschaft und Hochschulen (W), Abteilung für Schulwesen (Sch), Zentralbild- und Lehrmittelstelle (Bi), Zentral-Jugendamt (Ju), Abteilung für Kunst und Literatur (K), and Abteilung für Kulturelle Aufklärung (V).
[97]See the precise listing, complete with names, birthdates, and specific assignments drawn up by the DVV's personnel division. Personalliste, 30 August 1948, ibid., R-2/911/120-28.
[98]Abteilung Allgemeine Verwaltung an Herrn Präsidenten der Zentralverwaltung für Volksbildung, 22 July 1946, gez. Boeltz (reporting on discussions in Karlshorst), ibid., R-2/809/18.

to the DVV, and the problems apparently worsened when the economy deteriorated in 1947. In February 1948, the SMAD issued an order that set up a personnel commission within the Soviet-zone office of finance to audit all central administrations and reduce the "superfluous body of administrators" within them.[99] The DVV was the first administration audited for the sake of "reducing employees to a minimum." Curiously, the board of examiners approved the figure of 271, though it also turned down a number of specific projects and criticized the DVV for its profligacy.[100]

In this connection apparently, but for additional reasons having to do with political considerations unique to the time, the size of the bureaucracy shrunk in 1948 and early 1949. In December 1948, the DVV's personnel manager, Willi Lehmann, told the SED that the agency currently employed 294 persons (including the semiautonomous office of censorship, the Kultureller Beirat, as well as technical help not listed in the budget). According to Lehmann's statistics, the DVV was assigned 253 positions in 1948, but only 224 for 1949 after examination "by the Malz commission."[101] Asked by the party for his assessment of the strength of the "group of reactionary administrative employees who, a), consciously work for the return of past conditions and who, b), remain unenthusiastic," Lehmann answered that these "elements" had been discharged during the agency's reorganization—an apparent reference to dismissals carried out under the guise of budgetary constraints.[102] Either way, these reductions had taken such a toll that the DVV was compelled to appeal to the SED's own cultural division in March 1949 to support its request for the retention, minimally, of the organization's approved 224 positions; the DVV requested a decision by the party's highest-level "Kleines Sekretariat."[103]

[99]Befehl des Obersten Chefs der Sowjetischen Militäradministration des Oberbefehlshabers der Gruppe der Sowjetischen Besatzungstruppen in Deutschland. Nr. 23. 6 February 1948. Inhalt: Über die Regelung des Aufbaus, des Personalbestandes und der Besoldungssätze der deutschen Verwaltungen der sowjetischen Okkupationszone Deutschlands, ibid., R-2/2168/1-2.

[100]See Abt. Z an die Präsidialabteilung, 10 February 1948; and Personalbestandskommission bei der Deutschen Zentralfinanzverwaltung in der sowjetischen Besatzungszone an die Deutsche Verwaltung für Volksbildung. Betr.: Prüfung des Struktur- und Stellenplanes der DVV gemäß Befehl Nr. 23 vom 6. February 1948, 24 February 1948, ibid., R-2/2168/7 and 15.

[101]The "Malz commission" must have been an investigating committee, so called after a man named Malz working within the administration of internal affairs and charged with screening the personnel of other central administrations in line with a specific political assignment.

[102]Personalabteilung. Willi Lehmann. An die Sozialistische Einheitspartei Deutschlands. Zentralsekretariat. Z. Hdn. Gen. Plenekowski, 11 December 1948, ibid., R-2/911/115.

[103]Präsidialkanzlei an die Kulturabteilung der SED. Genossen Stefan Heymann, 14 March 1949. Betr.: Dringende Planstellenanforderung unserer Verwaltung, ibid., R-2/1007/48.

Cadre Politics

The DVV's personnel office, headed first by Ernst Hoffmann, then by Lehmann,[104] was a division with unique responsibilities and vast authority both within the organization and outside of it. Prospective employees and administrators all required the approval of the personnel office before they could be offered a position in any of the DVV divisions; and personnel was the only section to which corresponding offices within the equivalent branch of the state administrations answered directly. Moreover, this responsibility extended to hirings and firings in areas outside the administrative apparatus proper—such as the developing school and university system—that fell under the general classification of *Volksbildung*. The DVV's personnel office, or "PA," discharged its external responsibilities initially in compliance with directive no. 24, issued by the allied control council on 26 January 1946, which called for a purge of Nazis from administrative and other influential posts. This was particularly the case in steps taken to replace Nazi party members in all educational institutions and to prevent the wrong people from getting jobs within the system. But denazification quickly developed into what the party and the Russians considered "cadre politics"—the appointment to the most sensitive administrative positions of persons regarded as politically reliable.[105] In the process, schools, too, were packed with instructional personnel who belonged to the SED or joined it to get the jobs.

Within the DVV itself, however, tactics influenced some early personnel decisions because of the initial need to appear "nonpartisan"—at least in the case of more visible higher-level administrators. But the political composition of the administration reveals that "cadre politics" still took precedence. The application process began with the completion of questionnaires filed with the personnel office by all prospective employees; these papers and other materials, along with recommendations for further action, then went to the SMAD's office of cadres within the Abteilung für Volksbildung for final approval; and these files contained the relevant information about an applicant's political background. Considering the circumstances, gathering information about party membership or political activity prior to 1945 or even be-

[104]See Wandel's "ideological" characterization of Lehmann: "Active party worker who came out of the old Marxist-Leninist labor movement (participation in democratic org.). Absolutely reliable pillar of the party and friend of the Soviet Union" (Vertraulich. Betr. Fachliches und weltanschauliches Gutachten über Willi Lehmann, geb. 15. 7. 1900. Gez. Wandel, ibid., R-2/1347/30).

[105]In August 1947, for instance, there was an internal reference made to the need for "our comrade personnel managers to make sure that the 'sum' of employees in individual divisions and institutions be systematically filled with politically clear-thinking comrades." Unsere personalpolitischen Aufgaben! 23 August 1947. W. Fischer, ibid., R-2/942/4-8.

fore 1933 needed little justification; the critical distinction is that the identical inquiry was also made about current party membership. This information allowed the DVV and the SMAD, which expected to be kept informed, never hesitated about asking for more information, and reacted testily when procedures were not followed,[106] to keep track of the entire administrative apparatus. One of the earlier sets of statistics, dated 25 May 1946, already listed 120 members of the SED out of a total of 210 employees; 69 of the rest were unaffiliated, but, of these, 54 held the lowliest positions (secretaries, janitors, messengers, etc.). At the level of division head (Abteilungsleiter) or office chief (Referent), the statistics were still more revealing; 11 of 14 division heads and their deputies, 17 of 22 office heads, and 33 out of 54 office-level administrators belonged to the SED. Of the remaining 21 from the last category, there were 11 unaffiliated, 5 Christian Democrats, 2 Liberal Democrats, and 2 "enemies of unity"—apparently, personnel's confidential designation for Social Democrats who preferred not to join the SED after the merger. Six others were characterized in this fashion, too, though in later compilations they appear to have been listed again as "SPD." These persons also tended to hold the lowest positions and presumably lived in the Western sectors of Berlin.[107] By December 1948, there were only 3 Social Democrats left in the entire organization; they joined 6 Christian and 6 Liberal Democrats. At the same time, 158 out of 294 employees belonged to the SED; but, again, fully 121 of the rest were unaffiliated and worked mostly in positions of technical or clerical assistance.[108]

The kind of work engaged in by the DVV's PA office was invariably confidential; and the record of its activities are more fragmentary because of it than the extant files of other divisions. The office began work earlier than other divisions, too, though its responsibilities were limited for the time being to the initial organization of the separate DVV divisions;[109] otherwise, the PA supervised 125 DVV employees in 1945, "screened" 245 prospective employees, and completed 210 of what it called "registered" tasks. For "understandable reasons," the PA later said, it restricted its activities in 1945 to

[106]See UdSSR. Abteilung Volksbildung der SMAD. Solotukhin to Wandel. 14 November 1946; and Artjuchin (Solotukhin's later replacement) to Wandel, 26 September 1947, ibid., R-2/1911/150-51.

[107]See Übersicht über die Zusammensetzung sämtlicher Mitarbeiter. 25 May 1946, ibid., R-2/1291/29. See the other sets of statistics for June, July, August, and September 1946 (R-2/1291/26-27). The SED's dominance is just as apparent in the list of 98 top-level administrators compiled in March 1947 (Namensliste der leitenden Angestellten. Stand: 10.3.1947, R-2/918/43-50).

[108]Personalabteilung. Willi Lehmann. An die SED. Zentralsekretariat, 11 December 1948, ibid., R-2/911/115. Other such documents, of which there is an abundance, tell the same story. See the many compilations, drawn up periodically, in R-2/999.

[109]See Geschäftsverteilungsplan für die Personal- und Wirtschaftsabteilung [24 November 1945], ibid., R-2/1007/9-10. One of the office's tasks was characterized here as "verifying the purge of members of the former Nazi party from all jobs belonging to the area of responsibility assigned to the DVV."

Berlin. Now, by themselves these figures reveal little, but the extent of the office's work becomes more apparent when the numbers are likened to statistics for 1946, 1947, and 1948. In 1946, the personnel office shifted from improvisation to "systematic administrative management," extending its authority to other institutions like the Charité hospital, the university and its clinics, the film agency DEFA, and the Volk und Wissen publishing house with a total of 3,200 employees (compared with 125 in 1945). There were 800 so-called screenings and 2,185 individual assignments completed in 1946. The following year, personnel doubled its responsibility; it oversaw 6,500 employees, registered 4,758 operations, and finished 1,310 screenings. During the first half of 1948, the office managed 7,500 employees, undertook 900 screenings, and finished 4,900 tasks.[110]

These activities served purposes directly related to the creation of a centralized governmental apparatus throughout Soviet-occupied Germany staffed by reliable administrators and employees. Much of this work focused on the acquisition of power over and extension of authority to state and local administrations and needs to be reexamined later in connection with jurisdictional considerations. But it helps to understand now that one of the PA's earliest initiatives outside the DVV involved instructions passed along to the state and provincial administrations mandating the creation of the post of personnel manager within their own agencies or, after the elections in fall 1946, ministries of culture and education. Lehmann underscored the injunction by telling the states that he was following specific orders given him by the SMAD's Abteilung für Volksbildung.[111] The establishment of local PA's thus became a binding "recommendation," and the request could not be ignored in the same way that local administrations frequently balked at other instructions issued by the DVV without the explicit backing of the SMAD. More information followed a few months later when Lehmann asked the division of culture and education within the state administration of Mecklenburg-Vorpommern, run by Gottfried Grünberg (a Communist and former Soviet exile), whether a personnel office had been set up yet and who headed it. The choice was critical because that PA would be expected to "guarantee" the reliability of all staff working in culture and education and be responsible for the implementation of school reform. The PA within the division of cultural education was expected to report both to the main personnel office set up within the state administration, but also to the DVV in Berlin.[112] A month later, Lehmann was in Karlshorst to talk with the Abteilung für Volksbildung, office of cadres, about methods of "screening" to be used in

[110]Tätigkeitsbericht der Personalabteilung von 1945 bis 1948, ibid., R-2/941-46/18-27.
[111]An die Provinzialverwaltung Mark Brandenburg. Betr.: Statutenentwurf, 11 January 1946, ibid., R-2/969/176.
[112]An die Landesverwaltung Mecklenburg-Vorpommern—Abteilung Volksbildung—z. Hd. Herrn Vizepräsident Grünberg. Betrifft: Personalabateilung, 6 May 1946, ibid., R-2/961/5.

examining teachers at universities and institutes; and he was saddled with a deadline of 15 June 1946 for working out a network of PA's throughout the states and provinces. Lehmann came away from the meeting with the understanding that the SMAD wished to strengthen "cadre politics and to work systematically throughout the zone according to unified directives." Butov, the SMAD officer, told Lehmann that state and provincial PA's within culture and education were subordinate to the DVV's corresponding division in Berlin.[113]

In late summer 1946, the personnel office looked back upon its accomplishments after a year of activity and considered its future priorities. The office now set its sights on screening the "antifascist elements" currently at work in culture and education, hired hastily right after the war, for the sake of a better assessment of their abilities and in order to "develop qualified cadres as quickly as possible"; the successful reconstruction of "our fatherland in the interests of the working people," it was argued, hinged upon that question. The prime objectives of PA's within divisions of culture and education throughout Soviet-occupied Germany now included "screening, regulating, hiring, firing, and salary-setting" as these duties pertained to all employees working in the state or provincial divisions of cultural education and associated institutions. It was emphasized yet again that the fulfillment of these and other obligations required recognition of the special status of the PA's—if necessary, by calling upon the SMAD for enforcement—and that personnel matters involving questions of culture and education fell under the jurisdiction of these special offices, rather than the main personnel office working within the regional administrations. Finally, the DVV characterized itself as the "central agency" in this regard; while promising due consideration of local laws and the needs reflected by them, the DVV expected to take the lead in issuing zone-wide instructions because all persons who worked in culture and education needed to be screened and registered in accordance with standard guidelines.[114]

In December 1946, the state and provincial PA managers met with their counterparts from the DVV to discuss the standardization of their efforts; and the regional heads were called upon to improve their cooperation with Berlin in order to enhance the "centralization of work." Guidelines issued in Berlin needed to be followed clearly, and the DVV insisted that the PA's keep the central agency up to date about managerial-level employees, school superintendents, and the directors of a variety of other institutions such as libraries and museums.[115] Just a few months later, the DVV began scheduling

[113]Aktennotiz [z.d.A. SMA Kaderabt.] Betrifft: Unterredung am 30. 5. 46 mit Herrn Butoff in der Abteilung Volksbildung, Kaderabteilung, Karlshorst, 4 June 1946, ibid., R-2/911/195.
[114]Aufgaben und Stellung der Personalabteilung in der Zone [ca. July 1946], ibid., R-2/1068/10-12.
[115]Protokoll der ersten Tagung der Personalabteilung in den Abteilungen Volksbildung der Pro-

courses for their own and regional employees in an attempt to improve the "quality" of cadres. Planned lectures included talks on Germany's "national catastrophe" by Walter Ulbricht and the "decline of German culture and problems of its reestablishment" by Anton Ackermann.[116] There was nothing new about the idea of "schooling," however; as early as October 1945, the head of the KPD's division of cadres, Franz Dahlem, asked Wandel whether there were any plans within the DVV to use special courses to develop "leading cadres" for work within the administration; and in December 1945, the question came up again during a meeting between representatives from the central administrations who belonged to the KPD and members of the central-committee apparatus. The agencies were told of the need to prepare young administrators, "not just party members," for greater responsibilities and to develop a corps of new employees. Assigning "politically schooled" and competent workers to the provinces created problems enough; and it would be more difficult when work had to be done all around the country—*im Reichsmaßstab*. The central administrations were then asked to submit course plans in connection with the need to train new administrators,[117] though the courses failed to materialize until April 1947, possibly because it took that long to resolve certain jurisdictional matters with the state governments. Even then, whether the idea of courses was an initiative of the DVV's personnel office or had been insisted upon recently by the SMAD was unclear. Either way, the DVV's various divisions provided Lehmann with course topics relevant to their areas of responsibility in May 1947;[118] and in June he sent the Russians his draft of an official order that, once signed, would fund short courses for administrators working in various areas of culture and education—"at the request of the SMAD."[119]

"Schooling" became a special concern in 1947 because the work of the central administrations and state governments had undergone a shift in emphasis. On 16 August 1947, the SMAD issued an order, numbered 201, that marked the last phase of denazification in Soviet-occupied Germany. Order 201 made "nominal" members of the Nazi party eligible for jobs denied

---

vinzial- und Landesverwaltungen am 4. und 5. 12. 1946, 12 December 1946, ibid., R-2/993/1.

[116]Entwurf zur Einrichtung von Kurzkursen für die Mitarbeiter der ZVV und der Volksbildungsministerien der Länder, 26 April 1947, ibid., R-2/968/1-2.

[117]Dahlem to Wandel, 25 October 1945, ibid., R-2/1291/70; and Bericht der Sitzung im Z.K. der Z.V. am 5. 12. 1945, ibid., R-2/1291/40.

[118]See the list submitted by Volkmann, Abteilung Kunst und Literatur, on 7 May 1947; and suggestions made by Hans Mahle, Kulturelle Aufklärung, on 22 May 1947 (ibid., R-2/968/6-12).

[119]An den Chef der Abteilung Volksbildung der Sowjetischen Militärverwaltung. Herrn Minister Solotukhin. Betr.: Schulung der Referenten der Deutschen Verwaltung für Volksbildung und der Volksbildungsministerien der Länder der Sowjetischen Besatzungszone. June 1947; and Befehl der Oberkommandierenden der Sowjetischen Militärverwaltung—des Oberbefehlshabers der Gruppe der Sowjetischen Besatzungstruppen—in Deutschland. Nr....., June 1947, ibid., R-2/968/42-43.

them before; and for personnel offices in agencies like the DVV, which had been set up originally to rid the administrative apparatus of Nazis, the approaching completion of denazification raised questions about the nature of the organization's future work. Personnel management discovered quickly enough that it still had a critical role to play—the office needed to balance the requirements of order 201 in such a way as to contribute to "our flourishing democracy," that is, by including broader segments of the population in its construction, but without damaging that democracy by treating nominal Nazis with excessive generosity and thus creating a "reactionary danger within administration." In particular, a counterweight had to be developed by putting "our comrades" in appropriate functions within administration.[120]

But entirely new responsibilities also beckoned. For the first time, the DVV's personnel office declared its intention of compiling lists of and files on "all creative artists";[121] in 1947, the office divided these activities into four specific departments in charge of 1) "personnel matters" within the DVV, 2) the school system, 3) institutions of higher education, and 4) "art, culture, and cultural enlightenment." When personnel first began work in the latter area, however, it quickly discovered how little the DVV's respective divisions of art and literature and cultural enlightenment had done. Apparently, work had to start from scratch; but by the end of the year, personnel reported that it had made headway in putting together its first "files" on 170 singers and instrumentalists, 120 actors and dancers, 55 conductors and band leaders, 40 authors and writers, 35 composers, and 30 stage producers and directors. In addition, reference materials had been prepared for all schools of art in Soviet-occupied Germany and Berlin, all theaters and theater halls, and all movie houses and libraries. Finally, 270 "inquiries, evaluations, and characterizations" had been compiled on intellectuals active in cultural areas and for scientists. The following year, that figure rose to 320 and was complemented by no less than 1,200 general index files on cultural intellectuals.[122]

Finally, in December 1947, the state personnel managers met once again with their counterparts from the DVV for a two-day discussion. Lehmann began the meeting by talking about the "ideological foundation" for future work. They all faced new tasks, he explained, that now transcended the first phase of initial "screenings" and the hiring of antifascist-democratic employees. Specifically, he told the personnel managers that in Soviet-occupied Germany a democratic order had replaced the previous capitalist, imperialist system; but further defined conditions as "popular-democratic," not socialist, before going on to characterize the administrative apparatus as an "instrument of rule in the hands of the progressive, democratic majority." The task

---

[120]Unsere personalpolitischen Aufgaben! 23 August 1947. W. Fischer, ibid., R-2/942/4-8.
[121]Ibid.
[122]Tätigkeitsbericht der Personalabteilung von 1945 bis 1948, ibid., R-2/941-46/23-24.

of this apparatus now was to develop and educate new democratic elements as well as to search out and destroy "enemies of democracy" and their "agents." Though Lehmann put it differently, the issuance of SMAD order 201 had effectively prompted the DVV's personnel office to redirect its attention to the broader category of "enemies of democracy," rather than to focus on persons who could no longer be legally disadvantaged because of their membership in the Nazi party. The interest in creative intellectuals, along with "screenings" of cultural institutions like theaters and their personnel, evidently developed within this context. In addition, Lehmann called upon the personnel managers to assist in the organization of all state ministries of cultural education along the lines of the DVV's nine divisions; and he encouraged them to structure their own personnel offices like the administration's in Berlin. His recommendation called accordingly for a section in charge specifically of personnel matters in "art and literature"; and following presentations on other issues, the DVV's Willi Fischer explored that subject in greater detail. A conscious decision had been taken, he explained, to concentrate the office's skills acquired in other areas on both art and literature and cultural enlightenment; and the DVV expected the ministries to follow suit. A "very critical attitude" needed to be taken toward all creative intellectuals; and regional PA's should assist their ministry's own divisions of art and literature in acquiring greater influence. It was especially important, Fischer went on, that cultural political establishments be directed by "unambiguously, democratically, and progressively thinking and acting persons"; and working toward this objective required the systematic registration of, 1) all art and theater schools; 2) all radio stations, theaters, film studios, and concert halls; and 3) all creative intellectuals, grouped according to the nature of their activity. Files should be prepared on them all.[123] Fischer gave the states until 15 January 1948 to submit their reports on the first two categories; and he requested the submission of material to the DVV that fell into the third on an ongoing basis.

Jurisdictional Disputes

These documents indicate that efforts to direct the activities of personnel offices working out of the culture and education divisions of state or provincial administrations, which became state ministries of cultural education in the five regional governments after the elections in fall 1946, had yet to achieve anything resembling effective coordination. The fact that these operations unfolded in Soviet-occupied Germany with the blessing of the Russians was

[123]Protokoll über die Tagung der Leiter der Personalabteilung der Volksbildungsministerien am 5. und 6. 11. 1947, 3 December 1947, ibid., R-2/945/1-12.

insufficient in itself to overcome an assortment of technical and administrative problems resulting from untrained or politically unreliable personnel, poor communications, and transportation difficulties. The politically sensitive nature of the central administrations in Berlin made matters worse because the Russians remained reluctant to issue instructions that actually ordered the state governments to comply with regulations passed in Berlin. What occurred instead can best be described as an attempt by DVV administrators, with the connivance of the SMAD, to accomplish the same objective in areas other than personnel management without acknowledging their intentions; and, though it did not guarantee success, the policy benefited from the fact that the Communists had placed party members in most of the directorial or ministerial positions within the regional offices of cultural education. The DVV began to extend its influence by establishing contact with the regional administrations as early as 19 October 1945. The DVV's personnel office asked the Brandenburg administration on that date for organizational plans covering its division of cultural education and for copies of questionnaires filled out by employees, particularly upper-level managers and administrators, holding positions within the division. The DVV also provided Brandenburg with a supply of new questionnaire forms that had been drawn up by the office of cadres of the SMAD's Abteilung für Volksbildung.[124] Still, the DVV remained cautious about issuing direct orders. In late November 1945, Wandel was asked by one of his administrators, Paul Reichwaldt, to draft instructions calling upon the regional administrations to submit organizational and personnel plans for their divisions of cultural education. Such plans had not been requested before, said Reichwaldt, because in recent negotiations local representatives had protested emphatically against any interference in their affairs; and they justified their stance by pointing out that their administrations enjoyed legislative privileges, whereas the DVV did not. Reichwaldt advised accordingly against any attempt to "prescribe" standardized guidelines to these local offices.[125]

The same concern did not prevent the DVV from issuing more requests for initial information, however; messages must have gone to the regional administrations on 5 December 1945 because the province of Saxony responded to such a request by submitting its plans. These showed a division of cultural education organized around several offices that included a so-called Kammer der Kunstschaffenden; this office was broken down further into divisions in charge of literature, the performing arts, the pictorial arts,

[124]Personalabteilung (O.[skar] H.[offmann]) an den Präsidenten der Provinzialverwaltung für die Provinz Brandenburg. The DVV received the information a month later (ibid., R-2/917/1-3). See also the list of names of administrators working in the Brandenburg and Saxon divisions of cultural education sent to the SMAD along with their questionnaires (Personalabteilung an die Russische Militäradministration—Abteilung Volksbildung, 21 December 1945. R-2/911/211).
[125]Reichwaldt to Wandel, 29 November 1945, ibid., R-2/807/41.

and music; as well as a general cultural office responsible for libraries, publishing houses, and book stores. The Kammer der Kunstschaffenden characterized its obligations generally as "screening all areas of art," "sifting out the politically compromised," and working toward the "fundamental orientation of art and artists on a democratic basis."[126] The DVV's next initiative tried to go much further, and it probably took place in connection with the preparation of an internal draft of statutes intended to formalize the DVV's responsibilities and to define the exact nature of its jurisdiction over the regional administrations. The DVV's draft statutes, which the SMAD probably asked for, but definitely failed to approve, had no date on them. They were likely drawn up in early 1946, however, and would have coincided with the preparation of a corresponding set of draft statutes that the DVV sent the regional administrations in January 1946.[127]

Those administrations must have rejected the statutes, however, and would have been well within their rights to do so because of jurisdictional provisions that the SMAD declined to approve when the same ones appeared in the DVV's own proposal. This document characterized the agency as the "supreme organ of German administration in the area of cultural education" or *Volksbildung*; and assigned to it responsibility for all cultural and educational institutions operating under the regional administrations. These institutions, the statutes read, were subordinate to the DVV; moreover, the states and provinces were bound by all guidelines, ordinances, and injunctions prepared by the DVV in implementation of orders issued by the SMAD and subject only to approval by its own Abteilung für Volksbildung.[128] These passages were unacceptable to the SMAD, though it is hard to believe that the DVV's personnel office, which drew up the document, had not consulted with the Russians first. There is a greater likelihood that the draft statutes, as well as other documents drawn up in early fall 1945, reflected original SMAD objectives abandoned in spring 1946 out of political considerations connected with the idea of central administrations. The statutes otherwise contained a description of the DVV's eight divisions and some of the responsibilities assigned to each of them at the time.[129]

---

[126]Geschäftsverteilungsplan der Abteilung Volksbildung der Provinz Sachsen, and Stellenplan der Abteilung Volksbildung der Provinz Sachsen, ibid., R-2/916/1-6.
[127]See Tätigkeitsbericht der Deutschen Verwaltung für Volksbildung von 1945-1948, 9 August 1948 and Tätigkeitsbericht der Personalabteilung von 1945 bis 1948 (ibid., R-2/925/5 and R-2/941-46/19).
[128]Statut der DVV in der sowjetischen Besatzungszone Deutschlands, ibid., R-2/1033/21-25.
[129]See below for further detail. The divisions then included the following: Schulabteilung (schools), Abteilung für Hochschulen und Wissenschaft (higher education and science), Abteilung für Kulturelle Aufklärung (cultural enlightenment), Abteilung für Kunst und Literatur (art and literature), Personalabteilung (personnel), Allgemeine Verwaltung- und Finanzabteiliung (general administration and revenue), and the Präsidialsekretariat (office of the president). Ibid.

On 3 January 1946, then, the agency's personnel office sent the regional administrations documents that recommended a structural plan much like the DVV's; and a meeting was scheduled for 9 and 10 January 1946 between Paul Wandel and representatives from each of the regional divisions of cultural education. They would be expected to suggest changes there, if they so desired, but it was also made clear to them that a uniform plan had to result from the discussions and that the DVV had prepared the proposal in the first place at the direct request of the SMAD. Finally, the regional administrations were told that the SMAD intended to issue an order making the plan mandatory.[130] Several days later, "draft statutes" followed with the request that the administrations needed to respond to them as well. Though the cover letter did not indicate that the statutes themselves had the blessing of the SMAD, the document called for the creation of a personnel office, and the accompanying letter stated that that provision was the result of "explicit instructions" issued by the SMAD's Abteilung für Volksbildung.[131] The statutes sent to the regional administrations were substantially identical and corresponded roughly to those prepared for the DVV. In the matter of jurisdiction, too, the statutes indicated that the division of cultural education "operated under the leadership" of the DVV and "adhered to its regulations and guidelines." These were issued by the DVV on the basis of SMAD orders. The regional statutes promised halfheartedly, however, that consideration would be given now and then to "essential characteristics" of the states and provinces. The heads of these divisions would be named by the regional Soviet commander upon recommendation by the administrations "in accord" with the DVV; final confirmation came from the SMAD's supreme commander in Karlshorst. Like the DVV's statutes, these likewise established the structure of the regional divisions, and that structure corresponded generally to the central administration's in Berlin.[132]

These documents appear to have settled little; even if organizational standardization served a potential political purpose and was mandated by an SMAD order, the existence of parallel structures could not compare in importance with the critical issue of jurisdiction. But then centralization, if approved, was certainly thought to hinge on such standardization; and within a short time, the DVV began working closely with the SMAD to establish offices of cultural education throughout Soviet-occupied Germany at a variety of levels below that of state or provincial administration. The DVV elicited

[130]Personalabteilung an die Provinzialverwaltung Sachsen. Abteilung Volksbildung. Betrifft: Vorschlag für die Struktur Ihrer Abteilung, 3 January 1946, ibid., R-2/916/14.
[131]Personalabteilung an die Provinzialverwaltung Mark Brandenburg. Betr.: Statutenentwurf, 11 January 1946, ibid., R-2/969/176.
[132]See Statutenentwurf für die Abteilung Volksbildung in den Landes- und Provinzialverwaltungen (ibid., R-2/1033/27-30); and Statuten-Entwurf für die Abteilung Volksbildung der Provinz Brandenburg (R-2/969/174-5).

cooperation in the venture with references to specific SMAD orders that authorized the undertaking. Organizational plans and typical budgets were then prepared for these local agencies;[133] and these budgets, as well as the structural plans and budget proposals for the divisions of cultural education in the regional administrations, were discussed with SMAD officers representing its Abteilung für Volksbildung, office of cadres, and its finance division on 7 March 1946. The DVV administrators came away with the unmistakable impression that the SMAD planned on keeping regional administrations understaffed and underfunded as a way of creating "dependency." The Soviet officers indicated that, "in cases in which it cannot prevail over the provincial administrations, the central administration should compensate for its temporary absence of legislative powers by availing itself of the authority of the SMAD in Karlshorst to issue orders."[134] In any case, structural and budgetary plans for the regional administrations were approved at this meeting; the DVV was given until 19 March 1946 to develop model budgets for offices of cultural education located in regions (Bezirke), counties (Kreise), and cities; and the DVV's own structural and budgetary plans were approved by the SMAD at roughly the same time.[135]

In spring 1946, however, the DVV suddenly developed enough of a concern about creating too strong an impression of centralized authority—or possibly just found out that the SMAD had decided against accepting the draft statutes—to tell its division chiefs that their communications with the regional administrations must contain no instructions or regulations without the prior approval of the SMAD; this measure was designed to prevent the states from objecting to these ordinances in the first place.[136] In July, Wandel repeated his instructions, adding that all such regulations had to be shown to him personally first or result directly from SMAD orders. DVV administrators were also told that their communications with the SMAD had to refer to the organization now "only as the 'Deutsche Verwaltung für Volksbildung,' *not* as the *Zentral*verwaltung."[137] In all likelihood, this sudden sensitivity

[133]See Reichwaldt an die Budjetabteilung der SMA, z.H. von Herrn Rutkowski, 6 March 1946 (curiously, the reference here to divisions of cultural education, or Volksbildung, was to "otdel 'iskusstva i literatury'" or art and literature); Abteilung Kunst und Literatur and die Abteilung Z. Betrifft: Struktur- und Stellenpläne für Kunst und Literatur in Kreisen und Städten, March 1946; Ferngespräch an den Herrn Leiter der Volksbildungsabteilung bei der Landesverwaltung in Dresden, 9 March 1946, ibid., R-2/4807/234, 88, 60.

[134]Aktennotiz. Betrifft: Etatbesprechung bei der Budgetabteilung der SMA in Karlshorst, 8 March 1946, ibid., R-2/4807/115.

[135]See above. See also ibid. and Abteilung für Finanzen und Statistik an die Budget-Abteilung der SMAD. Z.Hd. von Herrn Dr. Rutkowski. An die Kadersektion der SMAD. Z.Hd. von Herrn Dr. Sawanuk, 9 March 1946, ibid., R-2/4807/117.

[136]Präsidialkanzlei. Rundschreiben Pr. 21/46, 1 April 1946, ibid., R-2/629/40.

[137]Geschäftsanweisung, 6 July 1946, ibid., R-2/1046/4-9. In a related vein, the division heads were told one month later that, in the future, they needed to use special letter-head stationery referring to the agency as the Deutsche Verwaltung in all correspondence with the SMAD (R-2/

sprang from the desire to avoid controversy in connection with the Paris foreign ministers' conference and probably continued on into the fall out of concern over the outcome of state and local elections. In one instance, DVV business and personnel administrators tried to "audit" the division of cultural education within the Brandenburg provincial administration and were actually turned away by local authorities who referred to their own "sovereignty." The auditors received authorization from Karlshorst the next day; but they were still refused cooperation in Potsdam until, "relying upon the influence of the SMA Potsdam," they began work.[138] Even so, the DVV proceeded cautiously; in late October, Wandel told his division heads that office chiefs had been active in the states and provinces repeatedly without having informed the regional administrations of their arrival and their purpose. DVV inspectors and officials were told or reminded that they could not issue binding instructions, only impart advice.[139]

Things began changing gradually later that fall with the development of a new approach probably necessitated by the formation of state and provincial governments in the aftermath of the elections. These governments represented a potential threat to the overall authority of the SED, and ways needed to be found to limit their independence by influencing the legislative process in the parliaments, though without relying upon measures that would destroy the appearance of both decentralized government and constitutional democracy. In October, Wandel sent out invitations to the heads of the five regional ministries of cultural education to attend their first conference in Berlin;[140] and a proposed agenda, prepared by each of the DVV's own internal divisions, was enclosed. The items for the division of art and literature called for discussion of the "screening" of personnel working within the corresponding office of the state ministry; the formation of local "advisory art committees"; the submission of guidelines; the announcement of openings for artistic personnel in theaters and art schools; the issuance of food-rationing certificates for artists; and the supervision of art exhibits. The DVV's division of cultural enlightenment proposed a discussion of issues related to broadcasting in the states and provinces, publishing houses, individual licenses for newspapers and books granted by local Soviet occupation administrations, and the Kultureller Beirat—the office of censorship.[141] As plans for the conference

---

808/68).

[138]Bericht über die Überprüfung der Volksbildungsabteilung bei der Provinzialverwaltung in Potsdam und beim Oberlandrat in Brandenburg, 24 September 1946, ibid., R-2/823/95-99.

[139]Der Präsident an alle Abteilungsleiter, 22 October 1946, ibid., R-2/808/92.

[140]Actually, there had been a lengthy discussion among DVV administrators and state and provincial division heads with the SMAD in June 1946, but it concentrated almost exclusively on school issues. See Tagung bei der SMA, Abt. Volksbildung, in Karlshorst am 24. und 25. Juni 1946, ibid., R-2/1332/1-205.

[141]Präsidialkanzlei an die Leiter der Volksbildungsabteilungen der Länder und Provinzen der sowjetischen Besatzungszone [Fritz Rücker, Potsdam; Gottfried Grünberg, Schwerin; Herbert

developed, Wandel insisted that the SMAD officers in charge of the DVV's internal divisions be kept fully apprised of preparations; and he ordered his division chiefs, who had apparently been remiss in doing so, to supply the SMAD well beforehand both with copies of materials drawn up for final approval at the meeting and with the DVV's position on specific issues.[142] The conference, with three representatives from the SMAD in attendance, then took place on 18 and 19 December; and the decisions taken there, none of which were of overweening importance, will be discussed in other contexts.[143]

The next ministers' conference took place one month later, concentrating on issues related to a second round of denazification in the schools;[144] and the third followed—after a one-month delay caused apparently by the foreign-ministers' meeting in Moscow and the usual concern about political implications inherent to the activities of central administrations—on 18 and 19 March 1947.[145] Indeed, complaints about the DVV and its interference in state government had sharpened in January; but there was just as much frustration within the central administrations over their inability to work effectively, and the presidents of these agencies soon appealed to the SMAD for a change in policy. Private discussions between party leaders and SMAD representatives in December 1946 and January 1947 certainly indicate that the subject of centralization was uppermost in their minds; and, during his consultations with the German Communists on 31 January, Stalin also remarked frequently upon the issue of central administration. In fact, a few weeks in advance of the meeting with Stalin, the party leadership prepared plans for the creation of an agency, called a Deutsches Amt für Wirtschaftsplanung (DAW), that would have coordinated the work of all Soviet-zone central administrations with responsibility for one or the other branch of the economy; but more importantly, the draft proposal spoke of the DAW's recommended authority to pass economic decrees and injunctions binding in all of Soviet-occupied Germany and added that the central administrations, which

---

Gute, Dresden; Ernst Schneller, Dresden; Otto Halle, Halle; Linke, Halle; Walter Wolf, Weimar), 29 October 1946, ibid., R-2/808/96-97.

[142]Der Präsident an alle Abteilungsleiter, 11 December 1946, ibid., R-2/808/104.

[143]See Konferenz der Minister für Volksbildung aus den Ländern und Provinzen der Sowjetischen Besatzungszone Deutschlands am 18. und 19. Dezember 1946. Beschluß-Protokoll vom 18. Dezember 1946, ibid., R-2/51/9. There was a passing reference to a particular decision reached by the ministers at a "November conference," but this must have been some kind of ad hoc meeting.

[144]See the fragmentary materials Konferenz der Minister für Volksbildung aus den Ländern und Provinzen am 13. und 14. Januar 1947. Beschluß-Protokoll vom 13. und 14. Januar 1947; and Beratung der Minister für Volksbildung, ibid., R-2/52.

[145]The February conference had been called off suddenly, only two days in advance of its meeting on 26 and 27 February 1947, due to otherwise unspecified "special circumstances." See Präsidialabteilung. Rundschreiben, 24 February 1947, ibid., R-2/53/151.

would then operate on the basis of instructions developed by the DAW, should have the right to issue mandatory instructions to the states and provinces.[146] This proposal was actually approved by the SED's secretariat at a meeting, held on 18 January 1947, that finalized preparations for the consultation with Stalin.[147] But Pieck must have mentioned it as early as 23 December 1946 in Karlshorst, jotting down the apparent response, "centr. economic planning / see no usefulness yet"—a cryptic remark followed immediately by the note, "*zonal government / 1947* proposal / untouched text."[148]

The matter of central administrations then came up in the discussions held in Karlshorst on 9 and 21 January; and again when the Germans sat down with Stalin on 31 January.[149] It is impossible to tell from Pieck's notes whether the SED delegation actually raised the subject of a central economic agency with Stalin, though the idea remained under discussion during spring 1947 and eventually culminated in SMAD order 138, dated 4 June, setting up the Deutsche Wirtschaftskommission (DWK). The SMAD failed to grant the DWK full authority to issue binding instructions to the states, however, until February 1948. But these developments affected the work of the DVV in winter 1947 because the problem of its exact authority could scarcely be addressed without some kind of broader agreement defining the relations of all central administrations to state government. The pace of discussions picked up when Saxony-Anhalt complained to Wandel on 16 January 1947 that a number of central-administration presidents had recently issued legal ordinances of a "normative nature" for all of Soviet-occupied Germany; in the past, the provincial administration had taken the steps necessary to legalize these regulations in Saxony-Anhalt; but Wandel was told that the state constitutions no longer permitted the acceptance of such ordinances because legislative authority resided exclusively with regional government. Saxony-Anhalt understood fully that the SMAD retained the right to implement its orders acting through the central administrations; and no agency of provincial government would refuse to comply. But the province doubted that the administrations in Berlin were empowered to issue legal ordinances, with the force of law, based solely on the general authorization or approval of the SMAD. Saxony-Anhalt suggested that the central-administration presidents discuss their draft ordinances first with the appropriate ministries within the state or provincial governments before passing these proposals along to the

[146]Strukturplan. Vorschlag für die Organisation der deutschen wirtschaftlichen Verwaltungen in der sowjetischen Besatzungszone [in Pieck's handwriting: 1. Entwurf. Gen. Pieck. Streng vertraulich (Top secret)]. Zentrales Parteiarchiv, NL 36/734/221-26
[147]See Protokoll Nr. 66 der Sitzung des Zentralsekretariats am 18. 1. 1947, ibid., IV 2/2.1/59.
[148]Besprechung am 23. 12. 1946 um 12 Uhr in Karlshorst, ibid., NL 36/734/247.
[149]Besprechung am: 9. 1. 1947 mit Makarow, Tulpanow, Kurotschkin und Marschall; Besprechung mit Marschall am 21. 1. 1947 (ibid., NL 36/734/254-58 and 282-83); Besprechung Freitag, 31. 1. 1947, in Moskau, 9-12 Uhr abends. Stalin, Marschall (?) Suslov, Semjonow, Wolkow—Pieck, Grotewohl, Ulbricht, Fechner, Oelßner, ibid., NL 36/694/3-7.

regional parliaments for final disposition; and until the matter was settled, Saxony-Anhalt refused to formalize any further ordinances sent by central administrations in Berlin.[150]

Events then followed in rapid succession; the central-administration presidents or their representatives met two days later to discuss the nature of agencies, like theirs, that existed "between self-administration and military government." Apparently, Saxony-Anhalt had not been the only regional government to refuse further cooperation; the Brandenburg president, Carl Steinhoff, had actually issued an injunction prohibiting interference in his government in the absence of specific SMAD orders. Gustav Sobottka, one of the central-administration presidents, reported that the SMAD wished to be informed whenever the regional governments balked. But it was considered imperative nonetheless that "Karlshorst" define the exact nature of the authority invested in the central administrations despite the fact that no one expected a resolution of the matter from Karlshorst "prior to the [foreign ministers'] negotiations in Moscow."[151]

Within a week, the presidents of the central administrations or their vice-presidents met with Konstantin Koval, deputy supreme commander of the SMAD, to discuss matters further. He said plainly that the state governments existed to end discussions, as he put it, on the subject of "interrelations between state government and c[entral] a[dministration]"; and his further remarks suggested strongly that the SMAD still preferred some kind of compromise solution capable of sustaining the appearance of local autonomy while allowing for central oversight. Following Koval's noncommittal remarks, Leo Skrzypczynski insisted bluntly that the positions of the central administrations and the "limits of their responsibility" should be clearly defined; in particular, Skrzypczynski asked for "statutes" that would establish once and for all the relation between state government and central administration. Koval was unenthusiastic; "we don't like it when Skrzypczynski says that we want to *settle here* the question of relationship," he said, telling the Germans that they needed to resolve the matter with the states and provinces themselves; it was merely a question of "coordination," Koval insisted, but proceeded to describe a cooperative relationship that had failed. He then indicated that the SMAD would approve an understanding between the central administrations and the states if it were mutually agreed upon. Sobottka was unimpressed and spoke in detail of "problems of coordination" and simple ill will on the part of the governments; but Koval again declined to commit the SMAD to concrete measures and put his finger on the real issue;

---

[150]Provinzialregierung Sachsen-Anhalt an die DVV. Betr.: Gesetzgebungskompetenz der deutschen Verwaltungen für die Sowjetische Besatzungszone. Bundesarchiv. Abt. Potsdam, R-2/2128/7.

[151]Der Erste Vizepräsident. Betr.: Präsidentenbesprechung am 18. 1. 1947, 24 January 1947, ibid., R-2/2128/5.

"there is no provisional government in existence," he said; "I cannot decide with you the question of a provisional government. That's not up for discussion." Another SMAD officer backed Koval fully; "*we consider the argument strange that things hinge upon statutes,*" he said, and echoed Koval in issuing vague advice about cooperation and coordination. Wilhelm Fitzner then repeated the demand for legal authority; "if we do not get it," he said, "we will continue to swing back and forth," whereupon Koval relented and authorized the central administrations to prepare statutes. But he cautioned the Germans that Western inquiries had been made about the central administrations in terms of "statutes and the nature of their work"; and he warned them about circulating any internal material without permission. He concluded that "we shall see who works better and which form is right" in the competition developing between zones, adding, "the desire that we have for our work to be better is not dictated by ulterior motives. Every supreme commander of a zone wants things to work well in his zone. . . . For ours, I want a strong German apparatus capable of mastering its tasks."[152]

The DVV expected a discussion of the agreement regulating its affairs with the states at the ministers' conference set for 26 and 27 February;[153] and on 5 February, Wandel informed the government of Saxony-Anhalt, which had written to him three weeks earlier, that the SMAD would probably establish clear guidelines defining the nature of the authority invested in each of the central administrations. In the meantime, Wandel agreed generally with the issues raised in the letter from Saxony-Anhalt, but pointed out that the DVV already operated in accord with those principles. In monthly meetings with the state or provincial ministers of culture and education, all matters of sufficient importance to require final dispensation in the form of a law or ordinance had been discussed; and, if need be, the ministers intended to present these matters at the cabinet level and within the state parliament for approval. This procedure was designed to achieve the fullest possible agreement and standardization in administrative agencies operating in Soviet-occupied Germany.[154] The February conference was the one postponed; but when it met on 18 and 19 March, with Mitropolskij and two other unidentified men from the SMAD in attendance, Wandel quickly introduced two draft documents for discussion. The first, which established procedures

---

[152]Konferenz Koval—ZV-Präsidenten bzw. Vizepräsidenten, 24 January 1947. Zentrales Parteiarchiv, NL 36/734/285-92.
[153]See Tagesordnung der Ministerkonferenz am 26. und 27. Februar 1947, 13 February 1947. Bundesarchiv. Abt. Potsdam, R-2/53/8-9.
[154]Der Präsident an die Provinzialregierung Sachsen-Anhalt. Betr.: Gesetzgebungskompetenz der deutschen Verwaltungen für die sowjetische Besatzungszone, 5 February 1947, ibid., R-2/2128/3-4. The first draft of Wandel's letter included a paragraph, now crossed out, taken verbatim from the conference of central-administration presidents and vice-presidents on 18 January. The portion eliminated indicated, among other things, that the conference intended to work for SMAD guidelines in which "the obligation to cooperate is explicitly prescribed."

for the monthly ministers' conferences and was approved with little debate, merely formalized the order in which business would be conducted. For instance, decisions agreed upon at the conferences were to be considered binding in the sense that the ministers would present them in their own states for final approval at the cabinet level or in parliament. The document also provided for parallel meetings between the DVV's division heads and their counterparts from the state or provincial ministries. The corresponding SMAD representatives had to be invited to each conference, and the occupation administration would be informed of all formal decisions. Finally, the DVV was not authorized to lodge any objection to the decisions of state government unless these contradicted SMAD orders.[155]

But there was a discussion of certain phrases contained in the proposed agreement intended to formalize the relationship between the DVV and the regional ministries of culture and education. It began when two of the ministers indicated that their governments would never approve the document. In fact, Wandel introduced the subject in the first place with extraordinary caution, asking the ministers merely to accept the document in principle, discuss it within their respective governments, and then make suggestions for changes that could be debated at the next ministers' conference. For now, the concern focused mostly upon passages considered too blunt or aggressive in defining DVV prerogatives connected with its oversight of the regional ministries. Fritz Rücker said that there was no hope of getting one of them in particular through parliament. In response, Wandel insisted that the DVV did not aspire to "control"; the agency merely wanted the opportunity to express its opinion about measures and initiatives under discussion locally; but he said that the agreement would never be presented to the regional parliaments for approval in the first place if he and the assembled ministers failed to convince the state or provincial presidents first.[156] The language of the draft was then changed to reflect the concerns raised by the ministers at the March meeting; and they voted their approval of it during the next conference on 22 and 23 April 1947.[157] The document itself went

[155]See Entwurf einer Geschäftsordnung für die Ministerkonferenzen, ibid., R-2/53/214. See also the definitive version dated 12 March 1947 (R-2/53/267).

[156]See the discussion in Ministerbesprechung am 18. und 19. März 1947, ibid., R-2/53/13-16.

[157]The document itself existed in various drafts. The first was evidently prepared by Wandel's office (Vereinbarung über die gegenseitige Zuständigkeit zwischen der DVV und den Ministern für Volksbildung bzw. den Regierungen in den Ländern und Provinzen der sowjetischen Besatzungszone [ibid., R-2/53/104]). Another, referred to as the "Mecklenburg agreement," had apparently been drafted outside of the DVV and was probably intended to serve as a model for all central-administration agreements with the ministries of state or provincial government. This draft contained the language considered most objectionable (see Entwurf. R-2/53/105-6); once eliminated or replaced with phrases taken from the DVV draft, it became the version accepted by the ministers (see Entwurf, with certain passages crossed out and dated 8 April; and "Vereinbarung über die Zusammenarbeit zwischen der Deutschen Verwaltung für Volksbildung und den Landes- und Provinzialregierungen," dated 23 April 1947 [R-2/53/21 and 268]).

into considerable detail in defining the relationship, and probably eliminated enough of the ambiguity to forestall major misunderstandings in the future; but the fact remains that the DVV had still not been invested with the power to issue mandatory instructions to the regional governments or to pass binding legislation with the exception of measures taken in compliance with specific SMAD orders. Now as before, however, nothing prevented the DVV from circumventing that restriction by developing important initiatives, preparing a corresponding SMAD draft order that sanctioned the measure, acquiring the support of the appropriate SMAD officer or office, obtaining final approval in Karlshorst, and proceeding from there.

Art and Literature

Initiatives developed by the divisions of art and literature and cultural enlightenment are the best examples of the role played by the DVV in the implementation of cultural policy in Soviet-occupied Germany, though these two divisions spent a fair amount of their time through early 1947 just getting organized. Still, a number of activities date back to the first phase of each division's work and prepared the way for much of what followed. Early actions taken by art and literature fit two descriptions. The first focused on ideas designed to engage creative intellectuals in the "construction of a democratic Germany" and accounts for the DVV's interest in organizing various groups or advisory councils distinct from the Kulturbund. The other initiative concentrated on the "administration or oversight of the administration of cultural institutions" such as theaters, art schools, museums, and such.[158] These broad responsibilities meant that art and literature faced a tremendous challenge in fall 1945, and yet the division was one of the DVV's smallest. It began operating with a staff of only fourteen working in four offices or *Referate* that remained mostly intact through 1949—pictorial arts and museums; theaters, amateur art, and music; film; and literature.[159] There was little turnover among the chief administrators either.[160] Erwin Reiche replaced Siegfried Nestriepke as head of theaters, amateur art, and music in early 1947; and Carola Gärtner-Scholle, the official responsible for art affairs within the office of arts and museums, was fired in mid-1947. Otherwise, Herbert Volkmann headed the division, as well as its office of literature, and worked for the DVV through 1949. So did Volkmann's deputy, Gerhart Strauß.

[158]Arbeitsbericht der Abteilung Kunst und Literatur für das Jahr 1945/46, ibid., R-2/629-30/1.
[159]Vorläufiger Entwurf eines Geschäftsverteilungsplans, 24 November 1945, ibid., R-2/1007/7, 18-21).
[160]See Aufstellung sämtlicher Angestellten der DVV, 8 May 1946 (ibid., R-2/911/201); and Geschäftsverteilungsplan der Abteilung Kunst und Literatur, March 1947 (R-2/2950/200-3).

Strauß, Gärtner's boss within arts and museums, ran that office from the beginning, and his staff probably faced a greater initial challenge than any of the other offices attached to art and literature. SMAD order 51 put the DVV in charge of all art exhibitions in Soviet-occupied Germany on 4 September 1945, before Strauß's office even existed, and instructed Wandel to register all persons active in the performing and pictorial arts by 1 October 1945. These instructions were virtually impossible to comply with, much less by 1 October 1945. When the DVV's personnel office began compiling files on creative intellectuals in mid-1947, the complaints about the laxness of art and literature in taking on the task earlier confirms that systematic registration in the context of denazification had been considered part of the division's earliest duties and that little had yet been done about it. In fact, regional authorities took the initiative first in response to order 51, probably at the behest of branch offices of the SMAD. In late September 1945, the province of Saxony passed an ordinance intended to regulate the activity of all persons professionally involved in any activity classified as cultural; such persons had to be in possession of an *Unbedenklichkeitskarte*, a certificate of clearance issued by the provincial office of cultural education then known as the Kammer der Kunstschaffenden. This "certificate of clearance valid for their particular profession" was mandatory for all entrepreneurs, exhibitors, and other enterprises of a cultural nature. All "public artistic activity" was banned without it and subject to criminal prosecution under occupation law. Artists for the purposes of the ordinance were actors, singers, dancers, and all other members of the stage; musicians, conductors, agents, and music teachers; artists, performers, entrepreneurs, sponsors, stage directors, stage teachers and agents; acting, dance, song, and music schools; and painters, sculptors, architects, craftsmen, stage designers, graphic artists, art publishers, and art dealers. Writers, creative and otherwise, were also required to register. Enforcement of the ordinance was up to the local offices of cultural education that were expected to "provide notification" whenever "publicly active artists and sponsors" lacked the certificate of clearance.[161]

The DVV's Gerhart Strauß heard of these operations in detail when he visited both Sachsen and Thuringia in December 1945 and January 1946. Upon his return to Berlin, he reported that Thuringia had also developed a program of "registration" as part of an effort to combine "political screening" with a crackdown on the proliferation of phony artists and artistic enterprises run by people intent upon avoiding real work. Those applicants who passed muster politically and artistically received an identification card that classified them as artists and automatically permitted them to exhibit their work. (The matter of licensing specific exhibitions and the individual works shown in them, however, was a separate issue.) Strauß was in basic

---

[161]"Die Unbedenklichkeitskarte," *Deutsche Volkszeitung*, 21 September 1945.

agreement with this approach, though he had recommended that Saxony provide for occasional exhibitions of works by artists not "officially recognized" as a way to take advantage of "every halfway usable painter"; and he recommended that the FDGB organize such exhibitions. In fact, Thuringia intended to work through the union to screen artists, but Strauß advised against that solution because it would have forced union membership upon artists—a measure considered ill-advised at the time.[162]

The subject of registration then came up much later during discussions among the state ministers of cultural education. On 19 March 1947, Volkmann told the assembled ministers that he considered the idea of a "recognition card" more trouble than it was worth; he saw no point in setting up a system resembling the one developed by the Nazis. Besides, he said, "we have a variety of institutions through which we can control at least a portion of the artists." Volkmann was particularly troubled by the prospect of having to license artists whom the DVV found objectionable, but whose names could not legitimately be placed on an index. Apparently, if licensing took place at all, the SMAD leaned in favor of granting licenses to everyone engaged in artistic activity; and Volkmann must have concluded that questionable artists could be more effectively controlled without requiring recognition cards difficult to withhold in the absence of compelling reasons. After the SMAD issued order 201, which banned discrimination against "nominal" members of the Nazi party, the DVV would have been forced to license such artists. It was apparently self-evident to those present that these persons could actually be better controlled without licensing because the DVV, or corresponding local agencies, could simply decline to include their work in approved exhibitions. The ministers then voted in favor of reviewing the problem once more at their next meeting, but also asked Volkmann to convey their opposition to recognition cards to the SMAD.[163] At a meeting of the heads of art and literature within the state ministers of cultural education on 15 and 17 May 1947, the subject of certificates of clearance, *Unbedenklichkeitsbescheinigungen*, then came up again. Herbert Gute, the Saxon minister, proposed that such certificates be issued in cooperation with the SMAD; this was the way things had been done, in part, in Saxony. But Volkmann opposed the idea; the military administration should only be involved, he said, if the Russians took the initiative first. With that remark, the subject was apparently dropped, though the DVV's personnel office most likely developed its own interest in registering creative artists, if not licensing them, along with screening entire institutions, out of these earlier discussions;[164]

---

[162]Referat Bildende Kunst. Dr. Strauß. Betrifft: Förderung moderner Kunst, Gestaltungsprobleme moderner Kunst, Organisation der Künstler, Ausstellungswesen, 11 January 1946. Bundesarchiv, Abt. Potsdam, R-2/629-30/93-94.

[163]Ministerbesprechung am 18. und 19. März 1947, ibid., R-2/53/57-58.

[164]Protokoll über die Besprechung der Leiter der Abteilung Kunst und Literatur bei den Volks-

and in a related vein, the compilation of politically motivated cultural statistics continued. The DVV's division of theater and music prepared a survey on 3 January 1947 of seventy-six theaters in Soviet-occupied Germany according to the party membership of their directors. The survey, not including Berlin, revealed that 39 directors belonged to the SED. Of the remainder, 35 were unaffiliated, but a mere 2 belonged to the LDPD, and there was only one single member of the CDU.[165]

Regulating art exhibitions in compliance with SMAD order 51 must have been a less formidable administrative challenge for the DVV, though procedures needed to be established and standardized. As late as November 1945, Wandel, Volkmann, and Strauß concluded that the order itself was largely unknown in Soviet-occupied Germany; and they planned on informing offices in outlying areas that "wildcat exhibitions" were impermissible. But the DVV intended to transfer its authority to license exhibitions to state, provincial, and city administrations. Even then, the DVV still expected the regional agencies to provide detailed information about exhibitions held and scheduled in their areas because of the need to supply the SMAD with this data.[166] It was only natural that the subject of artistic preferences also surfaced in connection with these discussions of art exhibitions. The issue of those preferred artistic styles, as well as the ones frowned upon, quickly began dominating public discussions as well, especially in connection with the first major Soviet-zone exhibit staged in May 1946 in Berlin; and the predisposition for certain styles, along with the opening condemnations of "decadence" and "formalism," were the chief topic of discussion during the Dresden art exhibition in fall 1946. But it was on the minds of the party's cultural functionaries earlier, even if their true feelings were still tempered by political tactics. Gerhard Strauß told his regional counterparts in December 1945 and January 1946, for instance, that there should be no "coercion exerted in the direction of a certain stylistic orientation"; some artists needed to experiment. But he made it abundantly clear that the authorities expected to back those artists who had a keen sense of social problems and daily life and engaged in such activities as visits to factories. "Experimenters" would generally have to fend for themselves.[167] Nor was Strauß thinking only of moral support; in 1946, the DVV had 300,000 marks to spend on—among other

---

bildungsministerien der Länder und Provinzen am 15. und 17. Mai 1947, ibid., R-2/1035/12.
[165]Referat Theater und Musik. Dr. Reiche, 3 January 1947. Vermerk. Betr.: Statistische Feststellung, ibid., R-2/1091/157.
[166]An die Abteilung Volksbildung. Z. Hd. von Herrn Girnus. Betreff: I) Überwachung von Kunstausstellungen, II) Erfassung von Ausstellungsräumen, III) Kunstvereine, Denkmalpflege, 29 November 1945, ibid., R-2/629-30/45-47.
[167]Referat Bildende Kunst. Dr. Strauß. Betrifft: Förderung moderner Kunst, Gestaltungsprobleme moderner Kunst, Organisation der Künstler, Ausstellungswesen, 11 January 1946. Bundesarchiv, Abt. Potsdam, R-2/629-30/93-94.

things—stipends for "worthy" artists and for the "popularization of pictorial arts, especially for the reeducation of the German people in terms of world art and the art of the Soviet people."[168]

But officials said little in public about Soviet art until the Dresden exhibition in fall 1946. Meanwhile, private discussions of problems related to the organization of artists in formal groups overseen by DVV administrators or other officials who answered to the SED preceded major public discussions of "theoretical issues." The solution hit upon, organizing creative intellectuals in several "divisions" within one of eighteen subordinate branches of the only authorized union, the *Freier Deutscher Gewerkschaftsbund (FDGB)*, was one of the most complex and poorly planned initiatives undertaken in Soviet-zone cultural politics. The Gewerkschaft Kunst und Schrifttum, the seventeenth of eighteen unions set up under the umbrella of the FDGB and subject to its statutes, began work in earnest in December 1946 and needs to be examined in greater detail later. For now it is sufficient to understand how the Schutzverband Bildender Künstler (SBK) and a matching writers' association called the Schutzverband Deutscher Autoren (SDA) came about. The SDA organized first, though details are sparse. The initiative behind its formation in late 1945 may in fact have had little to do initially with the SMAD or KPD and might also have been only loosely related to the formation of the Gewerkschaft für Kunst und Schrifttum. According to one report, the suggestion for a Schutzverband Deutscher Autoren came from the Kammer der Kulturschaffenden,[169] and the original idea behind it probably developed out of the need to protect authors from the unscrupulous use of their work by publishers, newspapers, journals, and the like during the chaotic months following the end of the war. But quick steps were taken to link the writers' association to the FDGB by way of the Gewerkschaft für Kunst und Schrifttum; and the result was to tie a potentially independent writers' association to a larger organization heavily influenced by the KPD.

The first public meeting held to discuss formation of a writers' association gathered on 29 October 1945, which suggests that the earliest steps taken to organize the SDA came after the start of talks related to creation of the Gewerkschaft für Kunst und Schrifttum. But Fritz Erpenbeck had written about a writers' association even earlier, on 9 October, and already took an adamant stand on what proved to be the controversial question of tying it to the FDGB. Again, details are sparse, but some of the inferences suggested by the manner in which Erpenbeck couched his arguments point in unmistakable directions. Erpenbeck argued—in the KPD's daily—that a writers' association could only exist on a union basis before resorting to some abstruse logic to suggest that the reason why should be plainly evident to any-

---

[168]See Festgestellter Haushalt für das Rechnungsjahr 1946 (1. Januar bis zum 31. Dezember 1946). Förderung der bildenden Kunst, ibid., R-2//810/6.
[169]Schendell, "Der neue Schutzverband," *Der Autor* 1 (1947): 6.

one not still suffering from "vestiges of Nazi . . . notions."[170] It seems safe to assume, then, that the party had an early interest in seeing to it that any writers' association be coupled to an overall organizational apparatus already in place and under the substantial influence, if not yet complete control, of the party. But tying any such association to the FDGB, should the FDGB prove unpopular or be widely regarded as a party undertaking, also ran the risk of limiting the association's membership. As Gerhart Strauß said a few weeks later in opposition to the Thuringian plan of using the union to screen creative intellectuals, no one could be forced to join. Erpenbeck thus tried to pressure writers into becoming members of a still non-existent organization, denying that anyone dreamt of using coercion, but also hinting that the formation of a writers' association under the yoke of the FDGB may not have been met with widespread enthusiasm:

> There are writers—most of them are not among the strongest personalities—who desire to make up for their lack of intellectual potency by putting on a display of "individualism" and eccentricity. Forget about them; people who fear losing their "personality" in a voluntary organization count for little as personalities, and no such thing as an organizational *compulsion* exists in democratic Germany, nor will it ever exist again. It is a question of those who *want* to integrate themselves in order to work creatively that much better and with fewer worries. What we need . . . is a professional affiliation that is *recognized* by the occupation powers. Any organization permitted by just one of the occupying powers would be a form of cliquishness and legally meaningless in the "zones."

Erpenbeck went on to add that just such an organization already existed for journalists, who had rightly recognized that a "German cause" was at issue here for creative intellectuals, not something designed for a single zone. His argument was that the journalists had formed an independent professional union under the aegis of the more general category created for those involved in cultural pursuits, the Gewerkschaft für Kunst und Schrifttum within the FDGB; and Erpenbeck characterized the FDGB as the only "democratic union organization" recognized by "all the occupation regimes." Only within this organization did the opportunity present itself for an effective representation of the writers and their needs—"independent of their individual political and ideological outlook, provided only that it be democratic and antifascist." It was up to the writers to grasp that opportunity before they lost time in "senseless debates and futile organizational experiments."[171] On 31 October 1945, the party daily published a brief announcement to the

[170]fr. "Schriftstellersorgen," *Deutsche Volkszeitung*, 7 October 1945.
[171]Ibid.

effect that a gathering of writers had resolved to form a "professional organization" under the aegis of the FDGB.[172] A few other facts emerged later; the SDA had been created at a meeting held on 9 November 1945 and elected a board comprised of some twenty-three writers; it included only three prominent Communists, Becher, Friedrich Wolf, and Hedda Zinner (none ever played any role in it). At this meeting, "the overwhelming majority" of those present decided in favor of union affiliation.[173]The Schutzverband Bildender Künstler emerged several months later. On 28 March 1946, Carola Gärtner or Gärtner-Scholle sent Herbert Volkmann and Paul Wandel a memorandum alerting them to the fact that twenty of Berlin's best-known artists had met on 22 March to discuss formation of an appropriate association and that, in her opinion, their urge to organize needed to be channeled in the right direction. She had managed to block plans for a large organizational rally, she said, but was unable to prevent the artists from creating a committee to look into matters further. Gärtner strongly recommended that steps be taken to integrate the group into the FDGB and that, prior to a definitive resolution of the question, the association be approved by the SMAD and "watched by us in a regulatory fashion."[174] Many of the personalities involved, said Gärtner a few days later, had been impressed by comments made at a reception for creative intellectuals given by General Sokolovskij on 1 February; though many of the artists now involved in discussions resided in the British sector of Berlin and used to be disinterested in politics, Gärtner said that they had still submitted willingly to "the soft touch of our leadership" and were ready to move in a different political direction—even if the decision had more to do with "material than materialistic" considerations.[175]

Shortly after, Volkmann informed Wandel that the matter of an artists' organization had been "under our supervision for some time now," but had repeatedly failed to materialize because of the FDGB's reluctance to allow artists to organize as union members. As a consequence, some of them had moved forward on their own, and the DVV now risked "temporarily losing influence over the development." In the meantime, Volkmann had discovered that opinions within the FDGB were actually divided; two top functionaries, Bernhard Göring and Hans Jendretzky, advocated the organization of creative intellectuals within the union; two others, Karl Fugger and Roman Chwalek, wanted it limited to "employees" in the traditional sense of the word. Volkmann had also been told that the SMAD, too, rejected the notion

---

172"Was du ererbt von deinen Vätern," *Deutsche Volkszeitung*, 31 October 1945.
173Schendell, "Der neue Schutzverband," *Der Autor* 1 (1947): 6-7.
174Referat Bildende Kunst. Frau Gärtner. Herrn Volkmann zur Kenntnis mit der Bitte um Weiterleitung an die S.M.A, 28 March 1946. Bundesarchiv. Abt. Potsdam, R-2/1038/51-52.
175Referat Bildende Kunst. Frau Gärtner. Betr.: Organisation der Bildenden Künstler, 30 March 1946, ibid., R-2/1038/46-48.

of an "artists' association within the FDGB," but when asked about it, Dymschitz told Volkmann that he had no such reservations and promised to bring up the matter with officers in charge of union affairs. Volkmann was assured of a positive decision in a few days and made recommendations in anticipation of it: 1) setting up a "representative organization of artists" around Karl Hofer, Heinrich Ehmsen, and Otto Nagel; 2) forming the group as an "independent" association within the FDGB's Gewerkschaft 17; 3) substituting the designation "Kunst und Schrifttum" for the previous "stage, film, music"; and 4) working to make the Schutzverband Deutscher Autoren, "which was also organized with our involvement and has been trying for weeks to affiliate with the FDGB," part of the union along with the artists' association and every other group representing the interests of creative artists. Volkmann considered union affiliation for artists desirable because "we otherwise have only the Kulturbund as an organization, which is apparently not yet established at the moment in all provinces and states and unable to carry out its responsibilities satisfactorily."[176] Volkmann's recommendations must have been accepted by the SMAD because negotiations with the FDGB concluded in early June and ended in the acceptance of his proposals. The SDA and SBK were designated as branches of the Gewerkschaft 17 within the FDGB. Things thus turned out, Volkmann told Wandel, "the way we wanted."[177]

With some of these organizational matters tentatively settled, stylistic concerns moved to the forefront in questions of art and immediately became entangled in political tactics. Late in the year, Gerhart Strauß detailed the concerns that governed the work of his office in a report apparently passed along to the party leadership. Like "every other kind of political activity," he said, his office faced three sets of issues: 1) society was not unified; 2) "no revolutionary situation exists"; and 3) the SED was not the only party. These various factors precluded the existence of a "uniform art" and ruled out the use of "revolutionary methods." The "*obvious* favorization" of SED artists by the DVV, which was not a political party, would only spawn accusations of partisanship and interfere with the attempt to win the backing of those artists whose attitude was still distant or even those who sympathized "with us." Strauß then outlined a strategy geared toward winning the political support of a broad spectrum of artists and lifting their "class consciousness"; acquiring the backing of talented and sympathetic artists by using their connection with the DVV to create political trust, thereby opening the road "to us politically"; and acting in such a way as to demonstrate that the interests of art and science were best represented "by us."[178] Problems developed be-

176Abteilung Kunst und Literatur. Volkmann. Herrn Präsidenten Wandel. Betrifft: Bildung einer Organisation der Bildenden Künstler, 3 April 1946, ibid., R-2/1038/50.
177Abteilung Kunst und Literatur. Herrn Präsidenten Wandel. Gez. Volkmann, 3 June 1946, ibid., R-2/1038/49.
178Referat Bildende Kunst. Dr. Strauss. Aktennotiz. Betreff: Richtlinien der Kunstpolitik, 11

cause the DVV needed to concentrate its efforts on artists who sympathized, rather than on those who already belonged to the party, and this approach was not greatly appreciated by the latter category. But Strauß considered it critically important to use discussions of art as the basis for creating mutual trust and as a foundation for the awakening of "new political insights." Repetition of old tactics involving harsher methods had to be avoided at all cost because "political opponents and the allies" kept a watchful eye on developments and seized upon mistakes as evidence for use "against the officially expressed intentions of the SED." The DVV could ill afford to back the work of comrades, who considered themselves artists, just because they belonged to the party; instead, the Soviet-zone solution needed to be seen as proof of the fact that hostility toward culture—as the fascists said of the USSR and reactionaries claimed about the SED—was untrue.[179]

Strauß then characterized the otherwise favorable situation in terms of cadre politics. "Comrades" ran the offices of cultural education in the state administrations of Saxony and Mecklenburg and in the provincial administrations of Saxony and Brandenburg, he said; and "comrades" also held the top position in corresponding offices in Dresden, Potsdam, and Schwerin. Moreover, he had discussed matters generally with the SMAD's Dymschitz and Captain Barski, both of whom were in complete agreement with assessments of party artists along the lines of three distinctions: "good comrade, bad artist"; "good comrade, passable artist"; and "good artist, good comrade." Only the latter category could be "recognized artistically." It was imperative to understand that the DVV could only afford to further artists whose work enhanced its image and the reputation of the SED. This basic policy was difficult for "some comrades" to understand; but it resulted from an "overarching political necessity." The best solution, which Strauß also applied to the Kulturbund, was to utilize only members of the SED whose qualities as artists enabled them to prevail with their political opinions and would lead others to make "decisions as we wish them." Strauß argued along similar tactical lines when discussing stylistic matters; even though he endorsed realism, he understood the need for stylistic leeway; but he also believed that art generally, as one form of activity capable of leading to "human truth," would contribute to the discovery of such verities and end in "valid political decisions." Combined with sufficiently rigorous thinking, the regularities of the historical process themselves guaranteed that such decisions would turn out "as we wish them."[180]

Volkmann's office of literature had fewer initial responsibilities than did Strauß's pictorial arts. Censoring writers required procedures much different

---

November 1946. Zentrales Parteiarchiv, IV 2/906/170/1-14.

[179]Ibid.

[180]Ibid.

from those needed to control the work of artists, and the agency responsible for literary censorship, the Kultureller Beirat, actually developed out of cultural enlightenment. Not that the office of literature stood idly by; it carried out an early survey of writers that corresponded roughly to registration efforts undertaken by the regional administrations.[181] Every person who had listed himself as a writer, presumably in documents filed with employment offices, was sent a questionnaire and asked to provide writing samples. Volkmann considered most of the work submitted to be unspeakably bad; some 200 writers were "thoroughly" screened and those considered artistically deficient or politically compromised "temporarily set aside." The result by mid-1946 was a card-index of writers expanded constantly with supplementary information about newspaper and publishing-house employees. Separate files were kept on "personalities" who had worked as writers, cartoonists, and the like during the Third Reich. Volkmann's office also developed plans for a secluded retreat for recognized writers, the Wiepersdorf palace in Brandenburg (the former residence of Bettina and Achim von Arnhem), expected to open its doors on 1 October 1946.[182]

But the most interesting of the early initiatives never panned out. In mid-November 1946, Volkmann asked Tjulpanov to approve the creation of a council on art and literature. This was an important request, he told Tjulpanov, because his office was simply too small now to handle the chores that had developed since its general completion of the earliest round of technical and administrative work in the area of art and literature; besides which there was the added advantage that such a council would enable the DVV to bring in leading personalities and provide them with "cultural-political direction." Volkmann recommended that the council be comprised of representatives of the FDGB (particularly delegates who belonged to the individual sections of the Gewerkschaft 17), the Kulturbund, the directors of art and music schools, the heads of regional and local offices of cultural education, the presidents of art academies and art associations, representatives of women's committees and youth affairs, and "prominent personalities in the area of art and literature." Volkmann suggested a total of fifty persons, to be named by Paul Wandel, and recommended that half of the positions be comprised of members of the above institutions and half reserved for personalities whose inclusion guaranteed the "progressive character" of the council. Volkmann

---

[181]In fact, art and literature was first set up with an internal section, run by a man named Walter Gerull-Kardas, in charge of a "literature card-index." Cuno Wojczewski headed another section responsible for "modern literature" and "organizational questions pertaining to literature." See Geschäftsverteilungsplan der Abteilung für Kunst und Literatur; and Abteilung Kunst und Literatur. Bundesarchiv. Abt. Potsdam, R-2/807/74-85.
[182]Arbeitsbericht der Abteilung Kunst und Literatur für das Jahr 1945/46, ibid., R-2/629-30/8-9. See also the file on Wiepersdorf (R-2/1369).

specifically proposed that the council advise the DVV in all questions of art and literature, recommend persons for important managerial or directorial positions, screen the curricular plans of art schools, and oversee and evaluate exhibition plans and stage repertories.[183] Nothing further came of the project, which Volkmann undertook to develop in conjunction with other "advisory councils" working within the DVV's divisions of schools and higher education. The whole idea may actually have come from the SMAD, which had its own reasons for failing to pursue this one, let another be developed, and resurrected plans for a third much later.[184] In early 1949, the SMAD instructed Wandel to form an advisory council of scholars that had been among the three originally proposed in late 1946.[185] The council on art and literature, however, whose proposed responsibilities were later assumed by other organizations and institutions anyway, died before birth.

Cultural Enlightenment

The division of cultural enlightenment, taken over by Wilhelm Girnus on 5 November 1945 while still called general cultural education, was a much larger operation than art and literature and oversaw other kinds of activities. The division was split into a number of offices that initially included adult education, amateur art, both youth and women's affairs, and something called *Volksaufkärung* further divided into areas in charge of the press, periodicals, broadcasting, books and brochures, and "visual propaganda." Generally speaking, cultural enlightenment was taken to be the supervision of "measures that serve education of the masses in the spirit of democracy and their ideological purification of all fascist, militarist, and other kinds of reactionary influences"; and it also included the control of all activity in the private sector, such as "publishing houses," associated with these general responsibilities.[186] In accordance with the broader range of obligations, cultural enlightenment had a larger staff at its disposal than art and literature, too; early plans, dated 24 November 1945, referred to forty-six employees, and forty-eight appeared on a list five months later.[187] Though there may have been

---

[183]Volkmann an die Oberste Sowjetische Militäradministration. Propagandaleitung. Z. Hd. Herrn Tjulpanow. Betriff: Bildung eines Rates für Kunst und Literatur, 15 November 1946, ibid., R-2/1091/25-28.

[184]See the materials pertaining to formation of the Pädagogischer Beirat in ibid., R-2/2143.

[185]Kabanow, Stellvertretender des Obersten Chefs der SMAD in Deutschland für Ziviladministration, an Paul Wandel [early 1949], ibid., R-2/4699/12.

[186]Abt. Allgemeine Volksbildung. Bericht, 17 November 1945, ibid., R-2/629-30/105.

[187]See Vorläufiger Entwurf eines Geschäftsverteilungsplans. 24 November 1945 and Aufstellung sämtlicher Angestellten der DVV, 8 May 1946, ibid., R-2/1007/7-9 and 22-26 and 911/195-205.

some early pressure to reduce those numbers, on 5 April 1946 the DVV asked the Soviet-zone finance office for approval of more positions due to the fact that the substantially expanded work of the office in charge of the publishing and book trade required a complete reorganization of the overall division and more employees. The finance office appears to have approved only forty-six positions, and the same figure reappeared in October 1946. Then, in December 1946, the DVV attempted to persuade the Russians to authorize an increase in the size of the entire administration from just over 200 employees to 376, with cultural enlightenment jumping from 46 to 121. But the SMAD must have scaled the figure of 46 all the way back to the 31 positions that the Russians authorized on 11 February 1947.[188] Later, in 1948, there was an attempt to overhaul the division of cultural enlightenment and turn it into a massive propaganda administration; this initiative, undertaken with the knowledge of the SED, was unsuccessful then, though in late 1949 and 1950, the East-German information agency or Amt für Information evolved out of the DVV's original division of cultural enlightenment and was conceived of as just such a propaganda ministry.

The early activities of cultural enlightenment are particularly important as they pertain to the development of a system responsible for controlling publishing generally and, specifically, regulating the plans of approved publishing operations. This latter aspect of the office of publishing or Verlagswesen automatically turned into the censorship of submitted manuscripts, soon became a separately designated agency called the Kultureller Beirat, and in early 1947 acquired a measure of independence from the DVV on the strength of a secret SMAD order that considerably expanded its responsibilities. Verlagswesen thus started work in two closely related areas of activity—screening publishers who had run businesses prior to 1945 and recommending to the SMAD that firms be permitted to operate again if they had not compromised themselves during the Hitler years; and inspecting the plans of licensed publishers who were obliged to submit both general reports and individual manuscripts to the Kultureller Beirat for its blessing. The earliest reference in extant documents to a so-called "kultureller Beirat" occurred no sooner than 4 April 1946.[189] It is highly unlikely that steps to set up the agency took place much before then because the need for it arose to

---

[188]See An die Deutsche Zentralfinanzverwaltung. Betr.: Erweiterung des Stellenplans für die Hauptabteilung Kulturelle Aufklärung. 5 April 1946 (ibid., R-2/624/4); Organisations- und Stellenplan gemäß Schreiben der Deutschen Zentralfinanzverwaltung vom 17. 4. 46 (R-2/1007/82); Übersicht über den Besoldungsaufwand im Oktober 1946 (R-2/805/8); Vorschlag zur Besprechung am 18. XII 46 i. Karlshorst, K.[ader]-Abt (R-2/941/1-2, and 7-16); Ergebnis nach der Sitzung am 18. XII. 46 in Karlshorst, K.-Abt. (R-2/941/28-34); and Stellenplan. Bestätigt gemäß dem Schreiben der UdSSR, Abteilung für Volksbildung der SMA in Deutschland 11. 2. 1947 Nr. 27/39 (R-2/2950/217).

[189]Verlagswesen. Arbeitsplan, 4 April 1946. Bundesarchiv. Abt. Potsdam, R-2/896/65.

begin with in connection with the SMAD's decision to license a handful of publishing firms; and the Russians reached that decision, belatedly, only when confronted with the likelihood that established companies located in Soviet-occupied Germany would transfer their operations to the Western zones if the SMAD continued to withhold licenses.

The subject of rekindling publishing activity, as well as dealing with a range of regulatory problems, surfaced early enough; it was uppermost in the mind of Lothar von Balluseck in mid-October 1945 when he reported that proposals for a "restructuring of the publishing business" were under consideration. At the time, the SMAD allowed no publishing whatsoever with the exception of a few privileged presses like the Aufbau Verlag.[190] Within days, Balluseck warned that the absence of any "central control" threatened to cause complications because of haphazard undertakings approved in the states and provinces. Central regulation was urgently required, Balluseck said, and enclosed proposals for both press and publishing.[191] These certainly resembled and may well have been identical to suggestions made by Balluseck on 1 November 1945. He argued in favor of permitting each state or province to allow approximately two firms specializing in creative literature to do business. In order to avoid the "problematic formalism" of lists of banned authors, the publishing programs scrutinized by both regional administrations and by Wojczewski's office within Volkmann's division should result in classifications according to "urgency," *Dringlichkeitsstufung*; and the plans prepared by the few already licensed presses ought to be "sensibly coordinated."[192] Censorship developed out of these ideas, derived from the real necessity of conserving raw materials like paper through the avoidance of duplication and by ranking manuscripts according to "need"; and these earliest proposals also established the justification for all subsequent denials that the Kultureller Beirat actually censored. Two weeks later, the SMAD had yet to approve Balluseck's proposals, though he expected word presently;[193] and the general modalities of regulation were clearly understood within the overall division of cultural enlightenment. Books were considered to be an important means of conveying a "consistently democratic world view, based upon a scientific foundation," to ordinary Germans; but meeting that need required a complete restructuring of publishing operations. Verlagswesen now looked forward to "standardizing the publishing trade in terms of its

[190]Referat Presse und Verlagswesen. Tätigkeitsbericht, 11 October 1945, ibid., R-2/896/198.

[191]Betrifft: Die allgemeine Lage im Presse- und Verlagswesen, 18 October 1945, ibid., R-2/896/196-97.

[192]Aufgaben der Abteilung "Presse- und Verlagswesen," Lothar von Balluseck, 1 November 1945, ibid., R-2/896/190. Balluseck also discussed regulatory matters pertaining to the book trade, the periodical and daily press, and broadcasting (R-2/896/191-94).

[193]Abt. Presse- u. Verlagswesen. Bericht. Verlagswesen und technische Erleichterungen für die Buch- und Zeitungsproduktion, 16 November 1945, ibid., R-2/896/189.

new, educational responsibility; screening license applications and setting the levels of "urgency"; preparing an overall plan for restructuring the system; and controlling its development.[194]

Major problems cropped up immediately because the Russians remained so reluctant to allow *any* private publishing house to operate on their territory; in fact, the establishment of the Kultureller Beirat, though still with limited authority, was surely part of the high price paid for a general commencement of publishing in Soviet-occupied Germany, though none of the personalities involved in setting it up had any apparent reservations about the idea. As of mid-January 1946, the office of publishing expected that the SMAD would actually agree to license only five private presses, but also came up with an imaginative way of controlling other previously independent publishers, even those firms whose owners had emigrated as political opponents of German fascism, such as Wieland Herzfelde's Malik-Verlag; they would be "fused" with authorized operations.[195] By then, the DVV was fully aware of the fact that urgent measures were needed in the case of internationally known firms whose owners never compromised with the Nazis; otherwise, "a further departure of these businesses to the Western zones will take place." The situation had become so bad that consideration was given to banning any such departure by prohibiting the transfer of a publisher's previous agreements with authors.[196] Matters appear to have worsened considerably, however, before the Russians awakened to the seriousness of the problem. In early February 1946, Verlagswesen prepared a list of about a dozen firms that it urgently recommended licensing (including Insel, Fischer, Kiepenheuer, and Malik); ranked another fifteen at the next level of priority; named still more that could be bunched together or formed under the aegis of Volk und Wissen; and provided an additional register of companies once owned by the Nazi party or clearly fascist.[197]

The SMAD signaled its intention of approving this kind of approach following discussions between Wandel, Major Davidenko, Heinrich Becker,

[194]Abt. Allgemeine Volksbildung. Bericht, 17 November 1945, ibid., R-2/629-30/106.

[195]The idea generally came up as early as December 1945. See Balluseck an die Sowjetische Militärverwaltung. Betr. [In hand:] Das Deutsche Verlagswesen in der sowjetischen Besatzungszone. [Crossed out: Interessengemeinschaft der deutschen Verleger in der sowjetischen Besatzungszone.] 13 December 1945, ibid., R-2/893-94/9-11.

[196]See Abteilung Verlagswesen. Betrifft: Wiederingangsetzung des Verlagswesens, 7 January 1946; and Verlagsabteilung. Aktennotiz. Betr.: Fusionisierung nicht zugelassener Verlage mit dem Verlag Volk und Wissen. Gez. Frommhold, 14 January 1946, ibid., R-2/896/161 and 155-57.

[197]Verlagswesen. Liste der vordringlich zu genehmigenden Verlage; Liste von Verlagen deren Zulassung in zweiter Linie zu erwägen ist; List von Verlage, die zu Gruppen zusammenzuschließen oder mit Volk und Welt zu vereinigen sind; Liste von Verlagen, die nicht wieder zugelassen werden dürfen, da sie im Besitz der NSDAP oder eindeutig faschistisch festgelegt waren, 9 February 1946, ibid., R-2/896/118-29.

and Wilhelm Girnus around 19 February.[198] Nonetheless, Girnus still filed a report with Walter Ulbricht on 20 February 1946 outlining the problems caused by the SMAD's procrastination in dealing with critical areas of responsibility assigned to the DVV's division of cultural enlightenment. Marshal Zhukov had placed cultural enlightenment in charge of the entire Soviet-zone broadcasting system on 20 December 1945, for instance, but only after "protracted struggles" with the SMAD had the Russians approved a budget of 20 million marks. Similar difficulties plagued the division in its attempt to regulate the press. Girnus complained that statutes "approved by the SMAD" assigned responsibility for the press to his division;[199] but the SMAD had yet to approve the office's personnel proposals; and, even after several discussions between himself, Wandel, and Fred Oelßner, its actual duties remained hazy. Girnus told Ulbricht that the party secretariat needed to render a formal decision that could serve as a clear guideline for work in this area. But Girnus saved his strongest warning for last. The SMAD's long delay in coming to a decision about publishing in Soviet-occupied Germany threatened to develop into a full-blown catastrophe, Girnus said, because American and British occupation authorities had promised licenses to publishers in Soviet-occupied Germany if they moved to the Western zones. Some business were already long gone, together with their authors' rights. The remaining publishers, nervous about the situation, besieged the DVV constantly with requests for licenses and clarification. The SMAD itself, Girnus went on, had not adopted a unified position; in conversations with Major Davidenko, at which Paul Wandel was also present, the Soviet officer indicated that private publishers were, in principle, *not* going to be licensed in the future. But the SMAD had evidently been prevailed upon to reconsider the licensing of well-known firms like Insel, Reclam, and Kiepenheuer that would then exist along with a number of other operations organized in groups. Girnus told Ulbricht that certain private publishing firms, in which the DVV, the states, or the Kulturbund retained some involvement, were necessary to prevent the complete elimination in Soviet-occupied Germany of private initiative and to keep "an instrument in hand for use in exerting influence throughout the other zones."[200]

[198]Verlagswesen. Aktennotiz. Gez. Frommhold, 19 February 1946, ibid., R-2/896/114.
[199]Girnus referred to the DVV's statutes as having been approved by the SMAD; if this is true, then the SMAD must have thought better of the decision soon after and withdrawn its approval. Curiously enough, at a meeting of his division's office heads in July 1946, Girnus told them that the DVV would be granted "executive power" on the first anniversary of its organization. Protokoll der Besprechung innerhalb der Abtlg. Kulturelle Aufklärung am 29. 7. 1946, ibid., R-2/629-30/30. The passage was crossed out by hand.
[200]Abt. Kulturelle Aufklärung. An das ZK der KPD. Z. Hd. Genossen Ulbricht. Bericht über die Abt. Kulturelle Aufklärung. Abt. Leiter: Genosse Wilhelm Girnus, 20 February 1946, ibid., R-2/629-30/35-42. As a matter of fact, Reclam soon signed a contract with the Kulturbund that

Fourteen publishing firms were ultimately licensed by the SMAD between 15 March and 4 April 1946 and, in connection with the issuance of these licenses as well as in anticipation of "a substantial increase in publishing activity in the Soviet occupation zone," the Kultureller Beirat was established to regulate their activities.[201] Von Balluseck remained in charge overall of the DVV's office of publishing, but expected to concentrate on running the Kultureller Beirat (Frommhold stayed in charge of screening license applications submitted by other potential publishers and sent recommendations to the SMAD for final dispensation). Specifically, von Balluseck would work closely with the SMAD, the Kulturbund, the state and provincial administrations, the KPD's central committee, unions, the rest of the DVV's main divisions, and other central administrations; and he was supposed to chair the meetings of the Kultureller Beirat while also negotiating with publishers and publishing groups. Because each book of scientific or creative literature required the approval of the SMAD, publishers were required to submit their manuscripts to the DVV's office of publishing together with accurate information regarding author, print-run, design, and size. An evaluation would then be prepared by that office and, if favorable, permission to publish requested of the SMAD. Once granted, the publisher could begin work; but prior to printing, each manuscript still needed the approval of Soviet censors operating out of whichever local branch of the SMAD happened to be based in the same area as the publisher.

The exact relationship between the DVV's office of publishing and the Kultureller Beirat had not yet been finalized,[202] but Balluseck soon submitted more specific plans that called for an advisory board comprised of 19 members. Seven were affiliated with the DVV, two represented other central administrations, one the FDGB, and there were eight other writers and artists (Becher, Günter Weisenborn, Friedrich Wolf, Paul Wiegler, Dieter Bassermann, Karl Hofer, Hilde Körber, and Hedda Zinner). Further plans called for meetings weekly, during which the nominal president of the Kultureller Beirat, Erich Weinert, would present information prepared by the office of publishing and send "suggestions" back to it. All manuscripts intended for

---

granted the organization a virtual veto over its publishing plans if these were at odds with the Kulturbund's "goals and interests." See Verlagswesen. Besprechung am 22. February 1946 anläßlich der geplanten Lizensierung des Verlages Philipp Reclam und Ventilierung einer Verknüpfung des Verlages Reclam mit dem Kulturbund. Gez. Balluseck, 23 February 1946; and the contract (ibid., R-2/896/198 and 199). Reclam was licensed by the SMAD on 15 March, together with Insel and Volk und Welt, the day after the contract was signed on 14 March 1946 (see Verlagswesen an die Präsidialkanzlei. Betrifft: Philipp Reclam. Gez. Balluseck, 18 March 1946. R-2/896/92).

[201]Bericht. Gez. Girnus. Undated, ibid., R-2/6299-30/44-45.

[202]Verlagswesen. Arbeitsplan, 4 April 1946, ibid., R-2/896/65-68. Further information was then compiled about the proposed members of the board and manuscript readers (Verlagswesen. Kultureller Beirat, 6 May 1946. R-2/896/49-51).

submission to the SMAD for licenses were thus required to pass the scrutiny of the Kultureller Beirat first, whose deliberations focused on the matter of "urgency" or need; and the entire undertaking intended to concentrate its efforts on the publication of books designed to develop the "cultural niveau" of the German population after the years of fascism.[203] The SMAD approved formation of the board on or around 24 May, and the Kultureller Beirat held its first meeting on 3 June 1946.[204]

[203]Aufgaben des Kulturellen Beirats. [In hand:] Entwurf! 12 April 1946, ibid., R-2/896/59-61.
[204]Verlagswesen. Aktennotz. Betr.: Kultureller Beirat. [In hand: Girnus], 24 May 1946; Verlagswesen. Arbeitsplan für Juni 1946, 4 June 1946, ibid., R-2/896/45-46.

CHAPTER THREE

Seizing the Initiative

These kinds of developments, along with the general organization of an administrative bureaucracy such as the DVV, occurred within the context of a party policy that began concentrating more intently on cultural-political objectives in early 1946. But this policy immediately exacerbated the problems that it was intended to solve because the KPD claimed *publicly*, for the first time ever, the right to define cultural-political priorities. Nor was this decision made on the spur of the moment by the German Communists alone; there is ample evidence that the SMAD encouraged the initiative and was equally responsible for its underlying contradiction. In late December 1945, Ulbricht conferred with the SMAD's Bokov, Tjulpanov, and Volkov and appeared to have been advised to sharpen the party's focus on cultural issues, but the instructions had the effect of setting two incompatible objectives. The Russians told Ulbricht that "we Communists" needed to take a broader approach to cultural issues, meaning that the Germans would be wise to present themselves "as representatives of German culture." Mid-January was then mentioned as some kind of significant date, and at a meeting of the secretariat on 14 January 1946, a cultural conference was scheduled for 4 and 5 February.[1] Not that party leaders had neglected cultural issues before; in fact, the stenographic record of the proceedings that took place as scheduled the beginning of February contained the fitting remark, written in hand, that "months of strenuous work in cultural-political areas already lie behind us."[2] In one way or another, that work centered on masking the consolidation of power through ceaseless allusions to a nonexistent antifascist-democratic consensus; and this general strategy, trying to reconcile the notion of a "broader" approach with proprietary claims on German cultural ideals and traditions, made ample allowance for party initiatives in those areas.

The difference now was that, starting in February 1946, some of these became public. Not always, however; the KPD's attitude toward the "non-

[1]Information von Walter Ulbricht über ein Gespräch mit Bockow, Tulpanow, Wolkow am 22. 12. 1945; Protokoll Nr. 4/61 der Sitzung des Sekretariats am 14. Januar 1946. Zentrales Parteiarchiv. NL 36/734/143-44 and I 2/5/51/13-15.
[2]Um die Erneuerung der deutschen Kultur. Erste Zentrale Kulturtagung der KPD vom 3. bis 5. Februar 1946 zu Berlin (Stenographische Niederschrift), ibid., I 2/2/26/177.

partisan" Kulturbund is a prime example of the contradiction embedded in both the private and public approaches. The very notion of a genuine non-partisan organization sponsored and overseen by a Marxist-Leninist party, an idea hatched in Moscow as early as June 1945, following consultations with Stalin, was patently absurd; it made sense only as a ploy, and internal discussions show that the Communists were not the least bit shy about using such an organization to their own advantage. No time was wasted reflecting upon the inherent dishonesty of talk about the Kulturbund's fictitious non-partisanship because manipulating it seemed like the natural thing to do. But by the same token, the party faced a chronic dilemma because of the Kultur-bund's inherent contradictions. In January 1946, difficulties with the organization came up for discussion at a meeting of the KPD's secretariat attended by various cultural functionaries, Becher and Willmann from the Kulturbund and Hans Mahle and Paul Wandel from the DVV, and by secretariat regulars like Pieck, Ulbricht, Dahlem, Ackermann, and Oelßner.[3] The discussion that followed the report by Willmann on 18 January was not recorded, only the decision that Ackermann, Becher, and Willmann were told to write a final summation for acceptance at a later meeting of the secretariat.[4]

That report was a classic example of inner-party thinking on the subject of "nonpartisanship." The secretariat generally endorsed the "work of the Kulturbund and the line represented by our comrades"; the organization could boast of some considerable successes and had extended its influence over intellectuals, particularly over writers and artists. The problem was that the relatively low number of Communists in comparison with other members had thus far prevented the Kulturbund from concentrating on a variety of critically important cultural-political issues. The report then called for a shift in emphasis with far-reaching consequences—along with its efforts to eradicate Nazi ideology, the Kulturbund should now direct its attention more to the struggle against "reactionary influences and tendencies." Issues of internal leadership were understandably important in this context, and the KPD's own division of cadres was instructed to suggest a "comrade" especially well-qualified to run the Berlin chapter of the Kulturbund as well as to place a number of other party members in important positions within its central organization. Doing so was apparently no particular challenge, and other problems associated with personnel decisions needed solving elsewhere. In Saxony, the "comrade" charged with overseeing the work of the Kulturbund had allowed a "pernicious tendency" to develop that favored turning the organization, "autonomous and independent," into an appendage of the local bloc of antifascist-democratic parties. That particular approach created difficulties because the principle of political parity, something akin to equal par-

---

[3]Protokoll Nr. 4/61 der Sitzung des Sekretariats am 14. Januar 1946, ibid., I 2/5/51/13-15.
[4]Protokoll Nr. 5/62 der Sitzung des Sekretariats am 18. Januar 1946, ibid., I 2/5/51/16.

ty representation on the Kulturbund's board in Dresden, then governed its composition rather than "cultural-political considerations." The KPD's secretariat ordered its own branch organization in Saxony to "correct the mistake immediately." Both the analysis of the problem and its recommended solution leaves little else to say about the nature of the Kulturbund's nonpartisanship; the related recommendation in Thuringia that the local party branch replace "Comrade Lindemann" with a "prominent nonparty intellectual or artist" and to broaden the Kulturbund's regional board so as to make it more representative is an exception that merely confirms the rule. In conformity with the SMAD's instructions to Ulbricht in December 1945, the "Communists within the Kulturbund" were to concentrate much more on emphasizing the freedom-loving and progressive traditions in German history and culture.[5]

But the party obviously understood these objectives only in a tactical context; and no amount of "broadening" altered the fact that the Kulturbund was designed to work for the KPD. Besides, by the time the report was formally accepted on 14 February 1946, the party had already held its cultural conference and presented its public vision of what Pieck called "our cultural ideal."[6] This was the conference first scheduled at the secretariat meeting on 14 January, and it must have been the initiative already referred to in general terms during Ulbricht's discussion with the SMAD in late December 1945. Indeed, there are ample indications that a coordinated approach had been developed between the party and the SMAD calling for a greater concentration on cultural affairs; and the remarks made at the KPD's cultural conference from 3 to 5 February 1946 should be kept in mind when considering virtually every other cultural-political development that occurred between December 1945 and early 1947. It is also worth recalling that Ulbricht met with Stalin on 2 February 1946 to discuss tactical issues pertaining to the imminent formation of a Socialist Unity, rather than Socialist Workers' party; and received additional instructions emphasizing "transitional" considerations such as democracy instead of dictatorship. For these and other reasons, it is justifiable to suggest that the cultural-political initiative, based on an ostensible "broadening" of the party's public posture, was motivated in part by the need to compensate for the rigor with which the KPD and SMAD intended to force the issue of an unpopular merger with Social Democracy. The timing of the reception given for German artists and creative intellectuals on 1 February 1946 by the SMAD's top officer, Sokolovskij, Zhukov's replacement, was hardly coincidental either and represents a further indication that

[5]Beschluß des Sekretariats vom 18. Januar 1946 zur Arbeit des Kulturbunds. Bestätigt in der Sitzung des Sekretariats am 14.2. 1946. Protokoll Nr. 13/70 der Sitzung des Sekretariats am 14. Februar 1946, ibid., I 2/5/51/36.
[6]Pieck, "Um die Erneuerung der deutschen Kultur," *Erste Zentrale Kulturtagung der Kommunistischen Partei Deutschlands vom 3. bis 5. Februar*, p. 21.

the new initiative was a coordinated effort. If so, it may also mean that the SMAD had deliberately slowed the development of the DVV in late 1945 and early 1946. The DVV's first organizational, personnel, and budgetary plans were not formally approved by the SMAD until early March 1946; and the disappearance of certain obstructions, such as those blocking licenses for Soviet-zone publishers, might easily have resulted from the Russians' decision now to move forward with cultural undertakings. But these new initiatives, which placed cultural affairs under the tighter control of the party and administrative agencies like the DVV, still needed to be presented to the public in ways that discouraged further accusations of "sovietization."

This must have been the sense of the advice given Ulbricht in Karlshorst on 23 December 1945 to "broaden" the party's approach to culture; and the Russians hardly looked on passively as events unfolded. As the DVV's Carola Gärtner reported, Sokolovskij's remarks apparently impressed many of those who attended his reception in Karlshorst on 1 February 1946.[7] Certain Germans made remarks there, too, that fit the description of "broadening." Bernhard Kellermann, for instance, argued in favor of a "new culture with intimate ties to the people." But the fact that top party cultural functionaries and personalities also had a great deal to say is additional proof of the coordinated nature of the overall undertaking. Becher voiced his usual opinions; Klaus Gysi called for the creation of a "progressive intelligentsia"; and Gerhart Strauß promised that the DVV would do everything in its power to further the art of a new Germany. But "*all* [cultural] *endeavors must culminate in serving the cause of the unity of people and state,*" he said; and pleaded with the creative intellectuals to "end your isolation; acknowledging a standpoint does not imply dogmatic constriction."[8] The Russians echoed Strauß in lauding the participants for having focused upon the "oneness of the German people"; this was an important breakthrough because, according to the *Deutsche Volkszeitung*, "only a people that acts as one to create its culture is a genuine people." The responsibility of creating "their *German* culture" thus lay with the people themselves and not just with the "current activists of cultural and intellectual life."[9] Sokolovskij had spoken in the same vein, telling the assembled that they must play an inspirational role in directing the "democratic and cultural education of the German intelligentsia and the entire people."[10] By way of a final assurance he added that the development toward a golden age of German cultural and intellectual life remained a "*matter for*

---

[7]Referat Bildende Kunst. Betr.: Organisation der Bildenden Künstler. Gez. Gärtner, 30 March 1946. Bundesarchiv, Abt. Potsdam, R-2/1038/46-48.

[8]See Leuteritz, "Für die geistige Wiedergeburt des deutschen Volkes," *Tägliche Rundschau*, 1 February 1946.

[9]"Um Deutschlands kulturelle Neugeburt," *Deutsche Volkszeitung*, 1 February 1946.

[10]Leuteritz, "Für die geistige Wiedergeburt des deutschen Volkes," *Tägliche Rundschau*, 1 February 1946.

the Germans" themselves; he, Sokolovskij, could only offer advice and remove obstacles.[11]

The *Tägliche Rundschau* capped the event a few days later, with an editorial that took stock of cultural developments in Soviet-occupied Germany since the war's end and situated the "creation of a new, democratic culture" squarely within a familiar political context. Shemjakin, head of the paper's cultural section, insisted that hatred of the fascist past was the precondition of love for a democratic future; for such hatred resembled a "purifying flame" capable of forging the steel of the new culture in a "peaceful and democratic Germany." But it quickly transpired that Shemjakin was less concerned with hatred toward the fascist past than with fostering an awareness of the present danger posed by "reactionaries of all colors" who criticized "modern German democracy" for doing everything backwards. He then delved into the relationships that governed democratic principles and cultural affairs, explaining that true democracy would always aspire to involve the people in ascending the heights of culture; democracy would be unfailing in its appreciation of its own traditions, but respect for the culture of other peoples was inseparable from the development of one's own. Finally, Shemjakin referred to Sokolovskij's remarks about the Kulturbund on 31 January, the thrust of which was identical to the resolution discussed by the KPD's secretariat at its meeting on the 18th of the month and accepted on 14 February 1946—fourteen days after Sokolovskij's reception. "The Kulturbund, as a mass organization of politically unaffiliated intellectuals, has to be more active in reaching out to the people in order to overcome the isolation of intellectuals . . . from the broad segments of the population. Doing so will further the democratization of the intelligentsia, instill it with optimism, reveal its prospects for the future, and, by the same token, inspire large segments of the population to participate in cultural life."[12]

Similar rhetoric dominated a series of other meetings in spring 1946; but this language also figured prominently in the keynote speeches delivered by Pieck and Ackermann at the party's cultural conference in early February. The difference was that the Communists made no secret of their intention to "seize the initiative in the area of culture, for the purpose of renewing German culture, much as we have already done politically and economically in order to build the economy, develop a truly militant democracy, safeguard peace and German national unity, and, above all else, establish the basis for the united action of all progressive democratic elements and for the unification of both working parties into a single socialist workers' party."[13] Moreover, the Communists acknowledged openly that they viewed the conference

[11]Quoted from Schulmeister, *Auf dem Wege zu einer neuen Kultur*, p. 80.
[12]Schemjakin, "Die neue Kultur Deutschlands," *Tägliche Rundschau*, 5 February 1946.
[13]Pieck, "Um die Erneuerung der deutschen Kultur," *Erste Zentrale Kulturtagung der Kommunistischen Partei Deutschlands*, pp. 11-12.

as a watershed and accurately characterized their efforts during the period preceding it. The KPD had been working "concentratedly for nine months in the area of cultural-political rebuilding," but now considered it time to "summarize its position with respect to the most important questions of German cultural life and heed the judgment of the democratic public."[14] Even if the party had been active in this area all along, however, establishing the principle that the Communists were entitled to intervene in cultural affairs was critically important at this juncture because it began the more open process of systematizing the party's arguments in favor of a far greater intrusion into the realm of culture in the future.

These objectives, however "broadly" stated, had never before been put so unequivocally; and one of the reasons why the KPD decided to take the risk now was surely because doing so no longer jeopardized the imminent formation of the SED. But the process was also encouraged by growing tensions internationally. Stalin delivered his tough "campaign speech" in February 1946, which adumbrated the return to dichotomous two-camps thinking not made completely official until eighteen months later; and Churchill delivered his famous Iron-Curtain comments a few weeks after that, followed by lurid Soviet accusations of Western war-mongering. Even so, the remarks made at the cultural conference began with the older ideas of guilt and restitution. Pieck indicted the intellectuals for having gone along with the prostitution, desecration, and barbarization of art and science under the Nazis because the overwhelming majority of them had declined to recognize the antifascist "progressive forces" located in the midst of the working class and join in forming a common alliance against preparations for war. This "failure of the German intellectuals," Pieck charged, stemmed from their uncertainty about the "superior scientific theories" used by the working class as a weapon against fascism and out of fear of the "bold, practical conclusions and demands derived from these theories." Upon the heels of this general argument about the past failures of the intellectuals to align themselves with "the working class" and its "scientific theory" followed Pieck's practical and predictable assessment of the present situation. The renewal of German cultural life could only be carried out now on the basis of unity between the intellectuals and working people. But Pieck insisted that the creative intelligentsia be fired with enthusiasm for "our cultural ideal"—"our" clearly signifying the Communist party in its historical role as the embodiment of all working-class aspirations. Not that the conference brought a shift in the party's objectives, only the beginning of the institutionalization of these objectives as they came openly under the administrative and ideological purview of one party. In dropping the pretense of impartiality, however, the Communists risked kindling or rekindling fears that they planned on some kind of

---

[14]Quoted from the introduction to the published record, ibid., p. 7.

"sovietization" of German culture; and because the party's reputation was so tainted, Pieck sensed the need to mingle his call for a militant democracy based on the unification of all antifascist forces with the plea that "pressure" be avoided in pursuit of the KPD's cultural ideal.[15]

Ackermann provided the same kind of assurance when he said that the Communists had no intention of degrading art to the status of a "handmaiden of the powers-that-be."[16] But he openly advocated party leadership in cultural revitalization, even if he undertook at the same time to allay fears associated with the party's "seizure" of the initiative. Ackermann contended that the KPD's cultural activity had never desired partisan advantage; rather, the cultural-political proposals made by the Communists now were designed "to unite all genuinely national forces in a common act" for the immediate goal of renewing German culture. This comment was the conciliatory side of the argument; the other side followed in his blistering accusation that anyone who threatened that unity by attacking the antifascist-democratic bloc or by obstructing efforts leading toward state unity committed "a crime against our people." But Ackermann concentrated most of his attention on the issue of "sovietization." He never mentioned it outrightly, but his emphasis on the national essence of German culture accomplished the same thing; and in so doing, Ackermann applied the political promise made by him and the party in the February issue of *Einheit* to cultural policy—the road forward, political and cultural, would correspond to conditions in Germany, rather than duplicate the Soviet system. Culture always manifested itself in a national form and could only evolve in those forms now; all culture past and present was thus an expression of its national attributes; and cultural renewal could only unfold "in the national forms that accord with our unique German characteristics." Moreover, because the German people constituted the "German nation" by dint of a common language, shared territory, and a mutual economic life, Ackermann considered it self-evident that the development of culture hinged upon the "fate of our people" in the entire country.[17]

This remark was the same as saying that "non-German" influences in cultural matters would rend the country in two culturally and could thus not be considered a viable solution to Germany's economic, political, or cultural ills; and yet the inclusion of the Communist party in cultural revitalization at this precise time led to the same result and had no more of a beneficial effect upon the prospects for unifying the zones than the attempt to use coalition politics and the SED as the nucleus for an antifascist-democratic movement in all of Germany. Ackermann's additional comments make this clear. He asked what forces were uniquely qualified today to "master the fate of the

[15]Pieck, "Um die Erneuerung der deutschen Kultur." *Erste Zentrale Kulturkonferenz der KPD*, pp. 15-16, 21.
[16]Ackermann, "Unsere kulturpolitische Sendung," ibid., p. 17.
[17]Ibid., pp. 35, 40-41. The German is *gesamtnationales Schicksal*.

nation" and lend cultural development a "new impulse"; and he answered his own question by insisting that "only the champions of Marxism" had consistently stood for "progress and the interests of the nation." Every other party had either vacillated or opposed "Marxism"; and in Ackermann's mind this conduct had rendered direct assistance to reaction and fascism. Only the "socialist labor movement" represented the "genuinely patriotic movement of Germany" and now constituted the driving force behind German democratic renewal and cultural revitalization.[18] One of the problems associated with this new nationalism, of course, was that the party staunchly advocating it had been traditionally linked to a foreign country; and besides, glaring contradictions remained between the party's nationalist program and common assumptions about Marxism generally. Some critics considered the shift from the traditional Marxist-Leninist emphasis on internationalism to local politics to be doctrinally erratic and thus little more than a cheap trick; whereas others drew unflattering parallels between the Marxist-Leninist nationalism in vogue now and the fetid nationalism of the last twelve years. But during the February conference, Paul Wandel considered it entirely appropriate for the Communists to emphasize "our national obligations," in spite of the fact that Germany had just been lifted from the "swamp of chauvinism and racist insanity"; it was proper because a clear recognition of that national obligation had to be at the forefront of "our cultural work." Moreover, Wandel insisted that the party's national orientation by no means contradicted "our socialist outlook" because the stress on antifascism as the basis for a national consensus formed an integral component of the party's desire for a democratic road to socialism. The fact was, he said, that the Communists served the interests of humanity best in their capacity as defenders of the national interests of their people; and the time had come for the "banner of true national interests to fall into the hands of those who alone can claim it, in the firm grasp of the people, the working class, our party."[19]

This was the essence of the KPD's "broader" approach to culture, and it marked the start of a concerted effort, as the Russians had recommended to Ulbricht in December 1945, to establish the Communists as the true representatives of German culture.[20] Naturally, the conspicuous fact that a single political party sponsored its own cultural rally in the first place raised a welter of questions; but the KPD sought to allay fear about its bid to outmaneuver the other parties in cultural affairs by insisting that the program was not its private prerogative; like every other activity engaged in by the party, it

[18]Ibid., pp. 41-42.
[19]Wandel, "Zwei Probleme: die nationale Frage und unser Verhalten zur Intelligenz," *Erste Zentrale Kulturtagung der KPD*, pp. 119 and 121.
[20]The KPD's secretariat talked about the cultural conference on 7 February 1946 (Protokoll Nr. 9/66 der Sitzung des Sekretariats am 7. Februar 1946. Zentrales Parteiarchiv, I 2/5/51/29).

was quintessentially nonpartisan because the principles associated with that program represented the universal "goals of democratic cultural politics," making the party's cultural policy valid for all. This marked a break with the past because such a cultural gathering today was no longer just the business of that party, "as it would have been in earlier political epochs"; it was an undertaking "designed to serve the nationwide interest"; the conference had, after all, been attended by *representatives of all the parties*," including the intelligentsia, many of whom had no party affiliation. The cultural goal proclaimed by the KPD therefore offered a "sweeping solution to today's problems" and ought to be at the forefront of thinking by "*all progressive Germans*," regardless of party allegiance.[21] The commentators rounded out their arguments with the standard promise that culture was not being "commanded or decreed here, after the customary fashion of the Goebbels-Rosenberg era"; rather, there was an "honest *wrestling* with the fundamental problems and the essential questions of German life," followed by "complete unanimity in all basic questions regarding Germany's cultural renewal, complete agreement with the main demands elaborated upon, no essential differences."[22]

The Communist party's cultural conference truly began a new era, but in a much different sense than the one alluded to above. Though the KPD's claim to exercise a historical prerogative in cultural affairs was the natural extension of the historical sanction that it claimed for its policies in general, the last barrier to a qualitatively new dimension had been removed and the door thrown open to the public articulation of a specifically Communist cultural policy. Within a month of the conference, Ulbricht listed the creation of a "new, democratic culture" as one of three principal prerequisites to his and the party's program of reconstruction.[23] Immediately after the conference, and just a few weeks before the creation of the SED, some of the KPD's other cultural functionaries expanded upon the major points, always working in line with the hierarchy of what Wandel had called "the people, the working class, our party." Fred Oelßner contended that the "working class" was the driving force in the battle to eradicate reaction and militarism in politics and economics, but it acted likewise as the "motor for purging our public life of nazism and militarism" in the cultural-political sphere.[24] The German working class could thus be expected to exert a steadying influence upon the intellectuals as they set out to overcome the decline of German culture, except that these intellectuals first needed to acknowledge that workers had a legitimate say in cultural matters. Oelßner went on to argue that the working class had its own "cultural-political sending" and defined it once

[21]Ltz., "Das Ziel demokratischer Kulturpolitik," *Tägliche Rundschau*, 8 February 1946.
[22]Ltz., "Demokratische Kultur auf breiter Basis," *Tägliche Rundschau*, 17 March 1946.
[23]Ulbricht, *Der Plan des demokratischen Neuaufbaus*, p. 13.
[24]Oelßner, "Kulturelle Einheit—nationale Einheit," *Deutsche Volkszeitung*, 19 March 1946.

again in national terms as part of the party's effort to suggest that these arguments did not herald the imminent "sovietization" of German culture. He thus echoed Ackermann in explaining that culture always cloaked itself in "national raiments" and that this shared bond constituted one of the decisive characteristics defining the German people as a unified nation. Just as national unity was a cause furthered through cultural politics, maintaining it remained one of the essential preconditions for the reconstruction of the nation's culture. Oelßner concluded by saying that the working class represented the strongest force in the struggle to maintain Germany's national unity; and it was also "the most important guarantee that the national foundation of our culture will be maintained and fortified."[25]

Attempts were made to get the message across at other cultural gatherings in winter and spring 1946 organized by the DVV.[26] The first, for sculptors and painters, met in late January amidst appeals to involve art in the problems of the day. Herbert Volkmann provided the usual assurance that artistic issues must not be resolved "on a doctrinaire basis"; while Herbert Gute insisted that artists needed to overcome their fear of politics. "We certainly do not wish to make the same mistake as the fascists and decree art," he said, "the point is to give the artist the experience of democracy and let him realize that a militant democracy is not a parliamentary form, but an attitude of life." The SMAD was also represented; and Dymschitz used the opportunity to expound upon the principles of socialist realism. Neither an aesthetic law, nor a dogma, much less a decree, socialist realism was simply a creative "method" opposed only to boring art.[27] Another important rally took place on 4 March 1946. The Communist speakers again dwelled on the historical failure of Germans and their intellectuals, did so in a self-serving fashion by broaching the subject of collective guilt, and excoriated the people for not having taken advantage of "a great historical opportunity . . . as a means of accelerating events through a genuine uprising, shaking off the burden of the past, and reaching the banks of new shores." To judge by the account of the rally given in the Communist press, an attempt to introduce arguments that amounted to an indirect endorsement of what many recognized now as the party's cultural policy must have been made; and it appears that these arguments met with disapproval. The commentary in the paper ran, "Just as in political life in general the struggle for a German democracy and its fortification against all attacks by reaction has entered a decisive stage, the rally likewise . . . reflected this situation in the intellectual and artistic sphere." For it was clear to all those wrestling for progress that "we are in the midst of a battle" and that the "intellectual confusion" of the last

---

[25]Ibid; Oelßner, "Kultur und Arbeiterklasse," *Deutsche Volkszeitung*, 2 March 1946.
[26]See the references in Arbeitsbericht der Abteilung Kunst und Literatur für das Jahr 1945/46. Bundesarchiv. Abt. Potsdam, R-2/629-30/1.
[27]Leuteritz, "Wohin, moderne Kunst?" *Tägliche Rundschau*, 1 February 1946.

twelve years had by no means been overcome.[28]

There is little information about this rally other than a few press reports, but these suffice to suggest that a heated debate took place. The *Tägliche Rundschau* concluded that the question of whether "we shall ever reach the banks of new shores" came out clearly—even if that perhaps meant "that the framework of such a rally threatens to break down." Still, in 1946 it was still fairly common for party functionaries to soften the impact of their hardening rhetoric with soothing assurances. Wandel pledged that there would be "no state art after the fashion of the past" and that the "real artist" would not have to contend with the state; but he linked "real" artists to the people in the standard argument used as the prelude to identifying the people with the party that would eventually constitute the state. "Nowadays artists have one obligation," said Wandel; that was to take a stand where the people stood in demanding their historical right to reap the benefits of culture. "The freedom of the personality, of which the artists speak particularly, is guaranteed, limited only by [the artist's] obligation with respect to the people." Erich Weinert elaborated upon that obligation in a speech characterized officially as the high point of the rally. Weinert attempted to distinguish between narrowly tendentious political writers whose artistic abilities were insufficient to allow them to go beyond the interpretation of political programs; and those poets who encompassed the ideals and aspirations of ordinary people. His point was that such artists could influence the people in ways unavailable to a political party. The problem now was caused not by inconsequential writers but by talented ones "who, through their own indolent posture, have contributed more to the benightedness of the people than to their enlightenment."[29]

The account of the rally published in the CDU's daily *Neue Zeit*, which still enjoyed some independence, sheds a little more light on the discussion. The commentary was necessarily circumspect, but the article managed to stress that art and culture could not have new life infused into it as a "consequence of congresses, conferences, and resolutions." Art could only result from the "spiritual readiness of the entire people, that is to say concretely, from the readiness of each individual." Writing mostly between the lines, the commentator then succeeded in arguing against the collectivist approach to art and culture dominating discussions in Soviet-occupied Germany. As for Wandel's assurances, the *Neue Zeit* responded with an argument, brimming with sarcasm, that embraced his promise that there would be "no officially oriented art" in the future and that no one thought of "regimenting art through bureaucrats and regulations." In closing, the paper even dared to question the wisdom of pretending that a new culture could be talked into existence through lofty rhetoric, the declaration of noble principles, and tes-

---

[28]"Zu neuen Ufern," *Deutsche Volkszeitung*, 6 March 1946.
[29]Ibid. The *Tägliche Rundschau* carried the complete speech in its 6 March issue.

timonials to past sins and shortcomings. Art and literature could never be a collective process, a guided and managed enterprise; the eternal strains of Mozart and Gluck that opened and closed the rally served as a "living admonition to all artists not to fall back upon words and resolutions but to produce deeds."[30] The DVV organized one other conference in late May, for writers and publishers, that corresponded roughly with the formation of the Kultureller Beirat. The SMAD's *Tägliche Rundschau* wrote a glowing report about the consensus of opinion; but Volkmann's office reported that the publishers in attendance sat passively during the entire meeting.[31]

Internal Affairs

One of the sentences in the stenographic record of the KPD's cultural conference in February 1946, crossed out prior to publication of the proceedings, promised that "we Communists" regarded the meeting not as an end, but a beginning;[32] and there was surely a growing awareness that success in "seizing the initiative" hinged upon better organization within the party's own executive apparatus. In fact, representatives of the SPD, KPD, and FDGB met on 23 January 1946 to form a "joint cultural committee of worker organizations"; Fred Oelßner and Josef Naas (KPD), Richard Weimann and Max Nierich (SPD), Karl Fugger and Walter Maschke (FDGB) made up the committee,[33] and its first act was to announce a "week of culture" scheduled for "all of Germany" in late March. This series of programs, supporting "German culture as the basis of German unity," was intended to demonstrate the "unified national character of German culture" and underscore its ties with the working class. Echoing the language used at the conference in February, the announcement of the slate of events stressed the need to show the masses that "our culture is not Prussian, not Bavarian, not Saxon, not Swabian, but rather *German* culture; and that maintaining national unity is not only the imperative of our cultural heritage but the prerequisite of our cultural renewal." By seizing the initiative in sponsoring the week of culture, the labor organizations witnessed to the "profound cultural mission" of the German worker.[34] Little else about this week of culture was said in papers published in the Soviet sector of Berlin, perhaps because the former capital

---

[30]—ert., "Kultur," *Neue Zeit*, 6 March 1946.

[31]Livius, "Aufgaben einer neuen deutschen Literatur," *Tägliche Rundschau*, 26 May 1946; and Referat Literatur. Wojcewski. Aktennotiz zur Konferenz der Autoren und Verleger am 24. 5. 46, 28 May 1946. Bundesarchiv, Abt. Potsdam, R-2/1038/70.

[32]Erste Zentrale Kulturtagung der Kommunistischen Partei Deutschlands vom 3. bis 5. Februar 1946 zu Berlin (Stenographische Niederschrift), ibid., I 2/2/26/177.

[33]"Einig vorwärts im Kulturaufbau," *Deutsche Volkszeitung*, 25 January 1946.

[34]"Kulturausschuß der KPD, SPD und des FDGB. Kulturwoche vom 24. bis 31. März," *Deutsche Volkszeitung*, 21 February 1946.

itself was excluded from the schedule of events.[35] Regardless, that kind of activity amounted to a meaningless stunt when compared with other organizational measures underway. For instance, an office of culture and education, Kultur und Erziehung, existed within the KPD's central apparatus as early as January 1946.[36]

Josef Naas was in charge of it, assisted by Erich Paterna; and Oelßner also played a role, though Ackermann continued as the head man within the central secretariat responsible for cultural affairs. This division, still called Kultur und Erziehung, was then listed along with nineteen others scheduled to be set up within the secretariat of the united party's executive board in accordance with plans made by the KPD's secretariat on 23 February—two months before the SED was formally established.[37] Whether the Communists had bothered to consult with Social Democrats first is unclear; none were listed as present at this meeting. Roughly the same number of central-secretariat divisions also appeared on a later document; Richard Weimann and Josef Naas were in charge jointly of Kultur und Erziehung and its internal offices assigned responsibility for schools; institutions of higher education; adult or continuing education; stage, film, and music; pictorial arts; literature; sports; and church affairs. Their work was overseen from within the SED's secretariat by Ackermann and the former Social Democrat Otto Meier. Ackermann's personal assistant, Karl Raab, replaced Naas in January 1947.[38] The personnel division within the secretariat should also be mentioned here because one of its seven offices concerned itself with the SED's "stock of functionaries" in the unions, mass organizations, and "cultural undertakings."[39] Kultur und Erziehung remained intact through 1949, though it merged with a division called "Parteischulung" in October 1947; Oelßner, who had previously headed that division, retained his old responsibilities, as did Weimann. The reorganization called only for the "coordination" of both areas, though some restructuring also took place.[40] In January 1949, Weimann left the division and was replaced by Stefan Heymann.[41]

Reconstructing the activities of Kultur und Eziehung is not especially easy because so few of its files exist. Its most important undertakings tended

[35]See Richard Weimann's comments in *40. Parteitag der Sozialdemokratischen Partei Deutschlands* [19-20 April 1946], p. 55.

[36]Protokoll Nr. 4/61 der Sitzung des Zentralsekretariats am 14. Januar 1946. Anlage zum Protokoll der Sekretariats-Sitzung am 14. 1.1946. Zentrales Parteiarchiv, I 2/5/51/13-16.

[37]Protokoll Nr. 14/71 der Sitzung des Sekretariats am 23. Februar 1946, ibid., I 2/5/51/40.

[38]Protokoll [der Sitzung des Zentralen Kulturausschusses am 17. 1. 1947], ibid., IV 2/906/4/47.

[39]Abteilungen beim Zentralsekretariat des Parteivorstandes, ibid., IV 2/906/9/5-8.

[40]Protokoll Nr. 3 (II) der Sitzung des Zentralsekretariats am 1. 10. 47, ibid., IV 2/2.1/135; see the plans passed at a meeting of the central secretariat on 6 October 1947 (Protokoll Nr. 5 [II] der Sitzung des Zentralsekretariats am 6. 10. 47; and Anlage Nr. 4 zum Protokoll Nr. 5 vom 6. 10. 47. Aufbau der Parteischulung, Kultur und Erziehung, ibid., IV 2/2.1/137).

[41]Protokoll Nr. 144 (II) der Sitzung des Zentralsekretariats am 17. 1. 1949; and Protokoll Nr. 145 (II) der Sitzung des Zentralsekretariats am 23. 1. 1949, ibid., IV 2/2.1/262 and 263.

to occur in later years anyway; in August 1949, for example, the division expected to turn the Schutzverband Deutscher Autoren into a writers' union;[42] this proposal was possibly the earliest mention of an East-German writers' union that was not actually established until a few years later. The important issue here is simply that the idea was developed by the party in the first place—an initiative hardly given a second thought by 1949. Action taken in 1946 was more limited in scope. In May, Kultur und Erziehung drew up a tentative list of duties that included preparation of general guidelines governing the party's cultural politics as well as providing the secretariat with proposals that that body would formally pass upon. The more specific responsibilities called for working with the intellectuals; engaging in cultural-political work in the countryside; dealing with matters connected with cultural institutions, "such as the Kulturbund"; drafting a cultural manifesto; and cooperating with certain party agencies active in cultural areas. The division's several offices were also expected to begin work on a "file index" that listed intellectuals in Germany, develop suggestions with regard to "political work among creative intellectuals," and make proposals related to the "party's politics" in the area of the stage, film, literature, and the pictorial arts.[43] In June, Kultur und Erziehung held a four-day meeting together with the divisions of Werbung und Schulung and Presse, Rundfunk, Information; this meeting was also attended by the corresponding division or office heads of the party's regional branches and by representatives of the DVV—eighty participants in all. Ackermann spoke to them of "our objectives in the ideological struggle," Wandel talked about school reform, Otto Meier went into matters related to "winning the intelligentsia," Oelßner discussed schooling within the party, and Weimann spoke of the renewal of German culture.[44]

These early organizational efforts included the drafting of guidelines governing the creation of similar party cultural divisions at the state, provincial, regional, and county level. The branch divisions were expected to "organize the totality of cultural work, control the implementation of tasks assigned them, and report regularly to the central [*die Zentrale*] on the development of cultural work." The guidelines stressed that the precondition of "our work" was the "*cooperation between the localities, counties, regions, and states or provinces with the central,*" for no such close association from "top to bottom and from the bottom up" yet existed. The party asked for a complete list of the addresses of both the cultural divisions at all local levels as well as a register of all "comrades" working full-time in them to include

[42]Vorschlag zum Arbeitsplan der Abteilung Kultur und Erziehung für August und September. Gez. Kaufmann, 17 August 1949, ibid., IV 2/906/10/62.
[43]Arbeitsplan für die Abteilung Kultur und Erziehung, 9 May 1946, ibid., IV 2/906/10.
[44]Zentrale Arbeitstagung der Abteilungen "Werbung und Schulung", "Kultur und Erziehung", "Presse, Rundfunk, Information" am 5., 6., 7. und 8. Juni 1946, ibid., IV 2/906/9.

their special areas of responsibility and "earlier party affiliation since ? (SPD or KPD)." The local offices were also instructed to provide the central with regular monthly reports on the activity of their cultural divisions and to keep SED headquarters in Berlin up to date on all *"especially important cultural matters*, conferences, programs, theater premieres, art exhibitions, and so on." In matters of general significance, the approval of the so-called central was required. The local SED cultural divisions were likewise told to cooperate closely with the Kulturbund and with the various sections of the FDGB in charge of film or art, and the central expected regular reports on this cooperation. All material, instructions, circulars, publications, programs, and so on issued at the local level of party organization were to be sent to party headquarters in Berlin; the same went for planning materials for the various areas of work, announcements of programs, school curricula, and book catalogues. The guidelines also asked for information on all existing *"public cultural offices"* in the states, counties, and localities, along with the names, addresses, and party affiliation of those working in them. At the same time, the regional and local party organizations were expected to keep in touch with the cultural agencies and offices at the community, regional, state, and provincial level; "to represent the cultural interests of the broad, popular masses vis-à-vis these agencies"; encourage their work in accordance with "our cultural demands"; and to "make our influence sufficiently felt." Of considerable importance, too, was close cooperation with the "SED comrades" working in public cultural and educational agencies.[45]

Other early organizational efforts concentrated on the establishment of an additional committee, called the Zentraler Kulturausschuß, to advise the cultural division of the secretariat; and on 27 June 1946, letters went out from Kultur und Erziehung announcing that the SED planned on organizing such a committee. Prospective members were invited to attend the first meeting on 4 July.[46] Weimann and Naas, who headed Kultur und Erziehung anyway, were elected co-chairmen; and Weimann explained the purpose of the new committee to the thirty-seven persons in attendance. The Kulturausschuß, he said, was intended to be a focal point for the party's cultural work "internally and externally"; and for that reason, the SED had placed on it persons representing the unions, organized youth, the Kulturbund, the DVV, and the broadcasting system. The committee would be regarded as an "advisory body" and answer to the SED's secretariat and executive board. Because Kultur und Erziehung was structured around seven offices, including

[45]"Aufbau und nächste Aufgaben der Abteilungen Kultur und Erziehung beim Zentralsekretariat, bei den Landes- (Provinzial-), Bezirks- und Kreisvorständen der SED. Richtlinien des Zentralsekretariats der SED (Juli 1946)," *Um die Erneuerung der deutschen Kultur. Dokumente,* pp. 167-69. See also Zentrales Parteiarchiv, IV 2/906/9.

[46]Zentralsekretariat der SED. Abt. Kultur und Erziehung. Gez. Weimann and Naas, 27 June 1946. Zentrales Parteiarchiv, IV 2/906/4/3.

one in charge of art and literature and another responsible for stage and film, Weimann envisioned the formation of corresponding "expert commissions" or Fachkommissionen; and he also announced their initial composition. Art and literature would be headed by Max Grabowski, who ran the matching office within Kultur und Erziehung; and Hans Klering was put in charge of stage and film. As one of the committee's immediate objectives, Weimann listed the further formation of "working groups" of all intellectuals and creative artists who belonged to the party. These specialized groups would advise it on cultural matters relevant to their area of expertise; and they were expected to engage in "systematic propaganda" within associated circles of intellectuals with the goal of identifying interests that the party was willing to support. Weimann reported that one such "working group," comprised of party artists, was already in the process of organization.[47]

That particular "working group" caused the party nothing but trouble. In mid-June, the division of Kultur und Erziehung must have begun drawing up guidelines for its specific offices because Grabowski, already in charge of pictorial arts within it, prepared a list of its recommended responsibilities. These included the preparation of a file-index encompassing all painters, sculptors, persons working in applied arts, architects, critics, art historians, gallery and museum directors, and top administrators in art-related agencies and organizations. Apart from standard information, these indexes were to include an assessment of each person's "political attitudes." In addition, Grabowski expected to use the office as a means of expanding the party's influence through support given to artists active "in a progressive way" and to fight against "all reactionary endeavors in the area of art." Other objectives included winning over the artists for the "goals of the party" through the use of propaganda tailored to their mentality; and Grabowski made a point of insisting that the party must acquire "decisive influence" over the Schutzverband Bildender Künstler within the FDGB, as well as over the Kulturbund. He indicated further that Kultur und Erziehung would work closely with such organizations and particularly with "comrades active in the same in order to coordinate initiatives in the area of art and to influence them in a progressive sense." But Grabowski also listed his office's intention of establishing contact with artists who belonged to the SED as a means of keeping up-to-date about undertakings in artistic affairs.[48] This was his first allusion to the formation of a "working group" of artists who belonged to the SED. Within a few weeks, though just a day after creation of the Kul-

---

[47]Protokoll über die am 4. 7. 46 abgehaltene erste Sitzung des Zentralkulturausschusses der SED, ibid., IV 2/906/4/6. The list of persons belonging to the Kulturausschuß included forty-six names; virtually all of the DVV's top administrators were on it along with Anton Ackermann and Otto Meier from the SED's secretariat (see Kulturausschuß der SED, IV 2/906/4/1-2.).
[48]Richtlinien für die Arbeit der Kulturabteilung der Bezirke der Partei in den Sektoren Bildende Kunst betreffend, 15 June 1946, ibid., IV 2/906/172/1-3.

turausschuß and Weimann's reference to such a "working group," Grabowski convened a gathering of "SED artists" in order to organize them.

There were twenty-two "SED artists" in attendance at the meeting sponsored by the division of pictorial arts within Kultur und Erziehung; present, too, were Weimann, Grabowski, Ernst Niekisch from the Kulturbund, and a man named Alex Vogel. Vogel represented the Schutzverband Bildender Künstler as a division of the Gewerkschaft 17 within the FDGB. But the discussions, which otherwise revolved around broad issues like "the party's policies in the area of pictorial arts," signaled trouble because the artists used the occasion to demand special treatment. For instance, they voiced their displeasure with criticism of their work published in "our press" for being insufficiently positive. The real problems, however, resulted from dissatisfaction with the formation of the Schutzverband Bildender Künstler; members of the SED, the party artists complained, had been inadequately involved in the initial talks or passed over altogether in favor of other colleagues with "highly questionable" attitudes. Vogel rejected the criticism and promised that "the influence of the SED was assured through the adequate involvement of our colleagues."[49] But problems quickly surfaced anyway because the party had backed the formation of two competing groups with what proved to be conflicting priorities and was initially ineffectual in controlling either. For the time being, however, the artists complied gladly with the suggestion that they form a "working group" run by an "expert commission" or "Fachkommission 'Bildende Kunst'" in accordance with tactics announced at the first meeting of the Kulturausschuß the day before. Accordingly, they had every reason to believe that setting cultural-political policy in art affairs would then fall under their purview. The party artists also stressed the need for an art monthly and demanded that one be published. This was a need that others had already recognized, and within a few days Grabowski wrote Ackermann and Meier to request that the secretariat approve such a journal. After numerous delays, the first issue of *Bildende Kunst* appeared in April 1947.[50]

But the problems that later crippled it and ultimately led to the journal's demise existed well in advance of its publication. Grabowski argued that the journal should "inform and educate all circles interested in art in terms of the goals of our party"; and those objectives proved just as illusive here as anywhere else because the idea behind *Bildende Kunst*, influencing non-party artists, required that it be simultaneously open- and closed-minded. Nonetheless, Grabowski argued that the journal include an informational bulletin is-

[49]Bericht über die Konferenz der bildenden Künstler der SED am 5. 7. 1946, ibid., IV 2/906/4/ 158-60.
[50]Zentralsekretariat der SED. Abt. Kultur und Erziehung. Referat: Bildende Kunst. An das Zentralsekretariat der SED. Z.Hd. d. Gen. Anton Ackermann und Otto Meier. Gez. Grabowski, 12 July 1946, ibid., IV 2/906/171.

sued by the Schutzverband Bildender Künstler, but recommended strongly against allowing the SBK to actually edit it. Matters were then further complicated because the "Fachkommission Bildender Künstler der SED" naturally wished to participate in the journal and expected the party to "assure itself of decisive, direct influence" over it. At the time, at least in the eyes of the party artists, those two objectives were identical; and for the same reason, the group also rejected the idea of having the Kulturbund edit the publication because they feared that certain artists active in the organization would influence it "unfavorably." Indeed, Grabowski went on to argue that the head editor—he suggested the Soviet exile Max Keilson—needed to be a "politically unambiguous" person.[51] But early negotiations led nowhere; at a meeting of the Kulturausschuß in August 1946, it was reported that initial talks ended in a stalemate. The opinions of "artists close to us" and a segment of the others diverged so substantially that each group wished to publish its own journal. Efforts to bridge the gap with a single monthly, one that united all important currents, would continue.[52]

An agreement of sorts was eventually reached; Keilson sat on the board, but never edited *Bildende Kunst*; the co-editors were Karl Hofer and Oskar Nerlinger. Nerlinger belonged to the party and followed instructions, whereas Hofer's views conflicted dramatically with the SED's and, naturally, the SMAD's. When the party began to insist generally that artists adhere to specific political principles in their work, the resulting controversy quickly carried over into the journal. But problems connected with the existence of two rival artists' organizations, the party's tactical decision to favor only one, and the angry reaction of the other group preceded those difficulties. On 2 October 1946, the "artists in the SED" met to talk about the general situation and air their grievances. The gathering was addressed by Carola Gärtner, who probably felt that she struck the proper balance between aggressive political partisanship and a cooperative attitude toward non-party artists; but, having sided with the party artists against those active in the Schutzverband Bildender Künstler, she had now become one of the chief zealots. She referred to the "ruling role" that party artists should play in all areas of theoretical and practical activity; characterized that role further as a "right to lead" or *Führungsanspruch*, advocated the organization of corresponding bands of party artists throughout Soviet-occupied Germany; and insisted that "parity" needed to be reestablished within the SBK—the positions of leadership and the organization's orientation could no longer be left *"in the hands of persons"* whose pasts justified the fear that the SBK would support politically regressive undertakings.[53] The discussion that followed, though replete with

[51]Ibid.
[52]Protokoll über die am 22. 8. 46 abgehaltene Sitzung des Zentralen Kulturausschusses, ibid., IV 2/906/4/22.
[53]Referat: "Die Aufgaben der Bildenden Kunst u. der Bildenden Künstler im Rahmen des kultu-

talk of democracy, then focused on further complaints about the SBK, the party's insufficient appreciation of its own artists, and their manifold discontents. The meeting finished with the passage of a series of resolutions that included one calling for an appeal to the SED's secretariat, the SMAD, the DVV, and the Berlin office of art. The appeal should demand that the "SED artists" be involved in the cultural reconstruction of the nation.[54]

The letter discussed these grievances in detail and announced challengingly that the party artists would no longer wait upon the SED or the administrative agencies; the group intended to join together instead to lend a sense of urgency to its demand to be recognized and utilized. The appeal expressed the group's full acceptance of the goal of influencing "bourgeois intellectuals"; but in the context of its general political outlook and nonnegotiable demands, that commitment was meaningless. Among other things, the SED artists insisted upon a complete reorganization of art exhibitions because the "dictatorship of a small clique" of persons responsible for mounting these exhibitions made a practice of excluding certain pictures—theirs. The letter was signed by several artists, including Horst Strempel and Fritz Duda.[55] Thereafter the situation rapidly deteriorated. On 5 November 1946, Gärtner complained bitterly about the "mistaken policy on art pursued by us, railed at the Schutzverband Bildender Künstler; emphasized the importance of her efforts to organize party artists for "fractional" activity within the union; and requested a meeting with the cultural division of "Karlshorst."[56] Angry memoranda then followed in quick succession. A few weeks after the meeting on 2 October 1946, the SED's cultural division had evidently asked the head of the Gewerkschaft 17, Amandus Prietzel, to propose names of artists qualified to work within the party's cultural commissions of experts, whereupon the "SED artists" promptly informed Prietzel that such a Fachkommission had been formed long ago at the meeting of party artists back in July 1946. That commission, comprised of the painters Schulze-Liebisch, Duda, Nerlinger, Strempel, and Hölter, had since waited expectantly for the party to call upon them—only to discover now, in mid-November, that a new commission had just been formed with a membership of fifty. None of

rellen Aufbaus. Gehalten 2. 10. 46 SED-Haus. Gez. Gärtner, ibid., IV 2/906/170 and Bundesarchiv, Abt. Potsdam, R-2/1353/9-13.
[54]Protokoll Versammlung Bild. Künstler. Parteihaus Behrenstr. 2. 10. 46. Zentrales Parteiarchiv, IV 2/906/170. The letter to the SMAD was later considered by Gärtner to be one of the reasons used to justify actions leading to her dismissal from the DVV (see Bericht der Genossin Gärtner-Scholle, betrifft Bildende Kunst Groß-Berlin, zu Händen Gen. A. Ackermann, 24 December 1946. Bundesarchiv, Abt. Potsdam, R-2/1353/14 and 41-7).
[55]An die Oberste Sowjetische Militär-Administration; die Deutsche Zentralverwaltung; das General-Sekretariat [sic] der SED in Berlin, Kulturabteilung; den Landesverband der SED; das Kunstamt im Magistrat der Stadt Berlin. Zentrales Parteiarchiv, IV 2/906/170.
[56]Betr. Schutzverband der bildenden Künstler. Gez. Gärtner, 5 November 1946. Bundesarchiv, Abt. Potsdam, R-2/1353/43-47.

the SED artists were included.[57] On the same day, Duda told the Schutzverband Bildender Künstler that the SED artists considered its first attempt at self-definition, especially the remark that the SBK pursued "neither political nor religious goals," incompatible with the FDGB's statutes.[58]

On 20 November 1946, Duda then wrote Weimann on behalf of many of the same SED artists to complain bitterly about the DVV and its policy on art. The artists objected to arguments advanced by Gerhart Strauß during a meeting held on 19 November within the central secretariat and reacted vehemently to Strauß's and Nerlinger's constant talk about the poor quality of work done by artists organized in the SED. Duda went so far as to complain that "our younger comrades" were developing an inferiority complex because of the arguments used to justify an "errant policy on art"; and he insisted that the cause of the problem resided in Strauß's denial that a revolutionary situation existed in Soviet-occupied Germany. Duda insisted angrily that "they want to brand us old party functionaries as sectarians! They want to silence us as a forward-marching revolutionary force so as to allow the opportunists to continue in their opportunism. They want to disguise the fact that, while we waged an illegal struggle against fascism and war, and for a socialist Germany, they participated in the privileges of the oppressors."[59] This latter remark alluded to aspersions cast by the same group upon Nerlinger that soon resulted in countless letters to the party secretariat alleging improper conduct during the Nazi years. These accusations were apparently based on records obtained by Gärtner, acting in her capacity as a DVV official, from the archive of the former Nazi Kunstkammer.[60]

To make a long story short, in late December 1946 Gärtner complained to Ackermann that she had been refused admission to a meeting of the Fachkommission within the SED's cultural division; Weimann told her that pursuing one's own brand of politics was unacceptable. She followed that letter with a further complaint about Strauß, Grabowski, Weimann, Nerlinger, Alice Lex-Nerlinger, and others who had become the targets of her enmity.[61]

[57]An das Zentralsekretariat der SED. Z.Hd. des Gen. Weimann, 15 November 1946, ibid., R-2/1353/38.
[58]An den Schutzverband Bildender Künstler, 15 November 1946, ibid., R-2/1353/3940. See the copy of the SBK's description of itself (R-2/1353/52); typed in by those who objected to its content was the remark that the leaflet had been printed and disseminated with the approval of Nerlinger; the SED artists dispatched "agents" to collect the copies before they became widely available.
[59]Duda an das Zentralsekretariat der SED. Kulturabteilung. Betr.: Sitzung der Fachkommission bildender Künstler am 19. 11. 46, 20 November 1946, ibid., IV 2/906/170. Strauß's presentation must have been identical to his written report dated 11 November 1946 and discussed in Chapter Two in connection with the activities of the DVV.
[60]See Gärtner-Scholle an die Kulturpolitische Abteilung im Central-Sekretariat der SED. Z. Hd. Genossen Raab. Betr.: Angelegenheit Nerlinger! 15 July 1947, ibid., IV 2/906/170/225. The stack of denunciations are also preserved in this file (226-71).
[61]Bericht der Genossin Gärtner-Scholle, betrifft Bildende Kunst Gross-Berlin, zu Hd. Gen.

Finally, in May 1947 steps were taken to remove her from her position within the DVV's division of art and literature. The SED artists protested the decision, charging that their demand for an investigation of Nerlinger's past had precipitated her firing. Soon after, however, several of these artists were also prevented from attending meetings of the Fachkommission Bildende Kunst. They objected strenuously to the violation of democracy, but to no avail.[62]

All this wrangling is important only because of what it reveals about the SED's early determination to treat non-party intellectuals and artists as solicitously as possible. In fact, Nerlinger's own summation of the damage done by Gärtner conveys a sense of the tactical significance attached to the party's cultural-political priorities. Not only had Gärtner's conduct been falsely identified with the policies of the DVV, along with her supporters she had appeared at meetings of the Schutzverband Bildender Künstler as an "ultraradical group" that discredited both the overall band of SED artists *and* the party itself. Her behavior subsequently resulted in a crushing defeat for the SED during the election of a new SBK board. As a further consequence, the SBK had since developed into a *l'art pour l'art* group of bourgeois artists with a pronounced animosity toward the Gewerkschaft 17 and the FDGB. Finally, Gärtner and her followers instigated a party investigation of his own conduct during the Hitler years in an attempt to intimidate him; and his concluding recommendation, to Pieck and Grotewohl, was that the SED artists be prevented from appearing in public as a group, at least for the time being. Nerlinger did, however, argue in favor of permitting them to work as originally planned, *parteintern*, with the eventual goal of reappearing in public once their attitudes had changed.[63]

Ironically, attitudes had already started shifting in fall 1946, but back toward radical positions in connection with the issuance of harsh new Soviet central-committee edicts on art and literature; and the eventual repercussions locally were immense.[64] But within the party's developing cultural apparatus, the year came to a close with a series of meetings convened by the SED's Kulturausschuß in the aftermath of the fall elections.[65] The result had

---

Ackermann. 24 December 1946; and Betr. Dr. Str. Gez. Gärtner-Scholle, 2 January 1947, ibid., R-2/1353/14 and 41-7.

[62]Arbeitsgemeinschaft der in der SED organisierten bildenden Künstler. An den Vorstand der SED, z. Hd. der Genossen Pieck und Grotewohl. 21 May 1947; Arbeitsgemeinschaft der in der S.E.D. organisierten bild. Künstler. An das Zentralsekretariat Abtlg. Kulturpolitik. 4 August 1947. Zentrales Parteiarchiv, IV 2/906/170.

[63]Nerlinger an die Vorsitzenden des Zentralvorstandes der SED. Genossen Pieck und Grotewohl, ibid., IV 2/906/170/286.

[64]See Chapter Five.

[65]See Zentraler Kulturausschuß am 7. 11. 1946; Fortsetzung der Sitzung des zentralen Kulturausschusses vom 7. 11. 46 am 21. 11. 46; Fortsetzung der Sitzung des zentralen Kulturausschusses vom 7. 11. am 25. 11. 46. Zentrales Parteiarchiv. IV 2/906/4/25-36.

been sobering, and cultural functionaries who spoke up at the gathering knew it. Alfred Lindemann, for instance, attributed the disastrous outcome of the Berlin elections on 20 October 1946 to the last eighteen months of the party's contradictory politics. "The unity of Germany? Fine, but only by way of socialism. Peace in the world? Fine, but only by way of socialism. Then we say that socialism is not currently up for discussion." Paul Wandel concurred, but apparently only in the sense of the party's "disavowal of socialism." Wandel acknowledged that the party had failed to raise the majority of Germans to a new level of awareness; they had remained remarkably immature in their practical attitude toward socialism. But in these and earlier utterances, Wandel clearly endorsed the idea of a more aggressive brand of politics. He argued that "reaction" had succeeded in gathering its forces during the preceding eighteen months, though it was more important to realize that the "major offensive" mounted by reaction developed because "we have taken over extraordinarily important positions in critical areas." Wandel noted that the theater was "solidly in our hands"; film, cabaret, the Kulturbund—these were all "strong positions, not in the hands of reaction," from which "we are able not just to defend, but to attack." The Kulturbund particularly was a location within which "our standpoint must be clearly expressed"; and Wandel finished his remarks with one last point. Though some people believed otherwise, the presence of the Red Army had been anything but an impairment because "in postwar Germany we would have chaos" in its absence; and he concluded by answering his own question: "Where have we assumed our positions? Wherever the Red Army stands."

CHAPTER FOUR

Theory and Practice

Marxism-Leninism was unique in its capacity for stimulating the leaders of the parties that advocated it to explain their actions and intentions in elaborate ideological or programmatic terms. This was true from the start, having begun with Lenin. But the urge to rationalize publicly became all the more compulsive in the Soviet Union during the Stalin years because the widening gap between the regime's theoretical postulates and its actual practices enhanced the need for efficient obfuscation; these reflexes carried over into the Communist International and were ingrained in the German Communist party long before the war ended. As part of this process, party intellectuals became schooled rhetoricians who were by nature professional and proficient obscurantists. The full extent to which veteran Stalinists understood that they were caught up in such a process is largely unknowable; for some, the more idealistic, deception had become instinctive; for others it involved a more conscious and deliberate kind of cynicism colored by lingering residues of idealism; for still others it went hand in hand with the simple enhancement of personal power and influence. But the very fact that such a system of obscurantism existed means that there is a chance of deciphering it in hopes of gaining a better understanding of the actual objectives concealed behind public programs, either by comparing rhetoric with actual circumstances or by spotting in the rhetoric the earliest anticipation of actions that took firmer shape later as concrete policies. This kind of analysis is particularly feasible when circumstances conspired to force a Communist party not yet in complete power to mask its intentions. For parties like the KPD, in all of Eastern Europe, adapted their programs from dogma; without it, nothing set them apart from rival political parties, and nothing could have excused them then from the obligation of competing for power democratically other than their own talk of historical necessity. Historical necessity, however, and party prerogatives derived from it, merely placed dogma back at the center of the discussion. By its very nature, the doctrine defied revision because revision was deviation—unless the leadership itself engaged in it. Doing so then made reforms appear possible, but promptly suspect in the eyes of outside observers. Either the Communist party had converted to democracy and was no longer a Communist party; or, if it continued to behave like a Communist party in its dealings with other political parties, then the conversion was spurious, temporary, and only meant to mask its overweening ambitions. The nature of the orthodoxy was also such that, however much the Communists refined and redefined it as democracy, they could no more argue persuasively that the dogma had ceased to exist than they could exist programmatically without it. Dogma was perpetually present in the minds of the Communists, and little of the rhetoric managed to hide that fact very effectively.

The Errant Way of a Nation

The same was true of the party's cultural politics. The identical mixture of local and foreign circumstances responsible for their political posturing caused the German Communists to develop matching rhetoric for cultural-political use; and this process generally revolved around familiar definitions of "true" democracy. Perhaps the best example was the attempt to refashion antonyms like politicization and nonpartisanship into synonyms designed to bolster the SED's seizure of the cultural-political "initiative." But the more apparent the party's readiness to claim its right to regulate culture, the less willing many intellectuals were to comply, and the greater the resistance to arguments that fashioned the party's cultural "ideal" out of its expedient definition of antifascist democracy. When intellectuals and artists declined to join the "movement," such as one sculptor who reportedly answered "plaster and to be left alone" when asked what he needed for his work,[1] the party press responded with increasingly harsh recriminations. But the developing backlash against their policies then forced the Communists to go further than they might have wished to distinguish their demands for the politicization of cultural life from the habits of two other political parties, one recent and indigenous, the other in power and foreign, that many Germans now rejected with varying degrees of intensity.

The Communists thus spent their time in late 1945 and 1946 partly explaining how their understanding of political serviceability differed from the Nazis misuse of culture, partly denying any intention of conspiring with the Russians to impose Soviet norms upon German art (and politics), and partly struggling to locate their ideas somewhere safely between those two extremes. The Communists hoped to alleviate these two main concerns by assigning their concept of art a prominent place within the overall "movement" officially characterized not just as antifascist but as German, democratic, and nonpartisan as well. One of the most effective methods in the broad struggle against the "vestiges of fascism" and for "the democratization of Germany,"

[1]"Keine Flucht ins Unverbindliche!" *Tägliche Rundschau*, 14 April 1946.

they said, was art, asking, "What should it be like?" In order for art to be antifascist, they answered, it stood to reason that its creators had to be clear in their own minds about the nature of fascism, especially considering the culpability of the intellectuals over the past twelve years. The new art could only participate in the *"education of the German people in the spirit of a consequent democracy"* provided that the consciousness of many artists be cleansed first of fascist, militaristic, and "other reactionary ideas and tendencies."[2]

Derived from the theory of collective guilt, this line of reasoning insinuated that the intellectuals had no excuse for denying support to the only party in Soviet-occupied Germany allowed to set and enforce the rules governing antifascist and democratic conduct in the first place. But if they ever hoped to win the voluntary backing of the creative intelligentsia for cultural policies that functioned as an adjunct to the party's general program of reconstruction, the Communists still had to establish themselves as the only proponents of true democracy. They attempted to do so in part by means of a deterministic analysis of Germany's history, arguing that the "working class" enjoyed a lawful claim to political power and that the Communist party was the organizational embodiment of the historical elect. However, venerable and venerated postulates such as the one that "the history of mankind is the history of class struggle" no longer figured centrally. The Communists stressed instead a less abrasive reading of history focusing on the more broadly defined struggle between human progress and the various forms of reaction down through the centuries. Once they were prepared to follow through with the inherent logic, the Communists could draw upon what began as an outlook less fraught with the mentality of class warfare and internecine bloodshed associated with the old KPD to place the "labor movement," that is the Communist party, at the culmination point of all democratic trends in German history. The Communists then fit their concept of art and literature into this mold. "True democratic art" had always aided human progress, and in the present predicament Germany's artists could follow in the footsteps of past great humanists by assisting in the "rehabilitation" of the Germans[3]—provided, of course, that the intellectuals "rehabilitated" themselves first.

These basic ideas were not new; most had shown up in the tactics of Marxism-Leninism during the popular-front era. But they all resurfaced in 1945, for instance in the statutes written for the Kulturbund. These called for "a reevaluation of the entire historical development of the German people" based on scrutiny of the "positive and negative forces influential in German intellectual life."[4] In the context of the times, branding fascism as the ex-

---

[2]"Antifaschistische demokratische Kunst," *Tägliche Rundschau*, 22 September 1945.
[3]Ibid.
[4]"Leitsätze des Kulturbundes [3 July 1945]," *Um die Erneuerung der deutschen Kultur*, p. 69.

pression of all that was negative in German history seemed reasonable, and the prospects for gaining widespread acceptance ought to have improved in the early absence of an indiscriminately divisive ideological dimension. Pitting the German people, for all their historical shortcomings, against the forces of reaction down through the centuries was in fact a shrewd way of reintroducing a refurbished theory of two Germanies. But then again the Communists could always fall back upon the obverse of the theory, declaring the "working class" and, by implication, the Communist party to be the contemporary reification of all that was good in Germans. Besides, the entire idea of sifting through Germany's history actually reflected a rigid belief in straightforward basis-superstructure relations between the social-economic order prevailing at any given time and the culture that grew out of it. Alexander Abusch's book *Der Irrweg einer Nation*, first published in Soviet-occupied Germany in 1946, systematized the basic dichotomies that reduced German history to an enduring struggle between reaction and progress. Abusch's book showed how centuries-old developments subsumed under the rubric "reaction" culminated in Hitlerism, defined by Abusch in a slight variation of superannuated Comintern language as "the most poisonous flower growing out of the soil of an economically moribund, politically unscrupulous, morally corrupt monopoly capitalism." For all the historical and ideological factors shaping the development of the German people, however, Abusch insisted that Hitlerism was not foreordained to triumph over the "democratic popular forces" likewise present in German history; but a fuller understanding of Germany's necessary direction now hinged upon the exposure of "all reactionary elements in German history, literature, and philosophy that prepared the way for Hitler" and involved close scrutiny of the "entire botched history of the German nation."[5]

Certain writings by Georg Lukács then picked up where Abusch's book left off. Indeed, Lukács had already constructed an elaborate system of historical, philosophical, and artistic dichotomies; during the twelve years that he spent in Soviet exile, he had devised detailed patterns for distinguishing between progress and reaction (or rationalism and irrationalism) in German philosophy, constrained by his own stringent determinism to declare virtually all thinkers who fell into the wrong category to be forerunners of fascism. Lukács combined his philosophical studies in a huge book, *Die Zerstörung der Vernunft*, that he finished while in Soviet exile but failed to publish until 1953. His theory of literature fit much the same mold; he labeled a wide variety of writers as either forerunners of fascism or heralds of what he styled revolutionary democracy. During the popular-front era, Lukács' theory of literature came to represent the cultural-political accompaniment to the Comintern's substitution of democracy for proletarian dictatorship and conform-

---

[5]See Abusch, *Der Irrweg einer Nation*, pp. 6, 226-27, 236-37.

ed with its efforts to enlist the aid of non-Communist intellectuals and writers in the worldwide crusade against fascism. There was, however, a thoroughly dogmatic side to Lukács' theory of literature with considerable implications for Soviet-occupied Germany. Using his notion of the objectivity of art forms, Lukács had always posited a direct correlation between "forms" of writing and specific historical periods. The dimension of Lukács' theory that stressed the "triumph of realism" on the part of past classics like Goethe or Tolstoy, whose style permitted them to transcend instinctively the bounds of their natural class bias, allowed the Communists to claim the classics as forerunners of the party's brand of democracy. During the popular front, the theory also allowed for cooperation with contemporary writers whose intuitive realism made them potential allies because they supposedly depicted the world in basic if not yet perfect harmony with historical truth. But Lukács dogmatized his theory through his obsession with historically "objective" literary forms; as a result, he stigmatized everything that he considered naturalistic, modernistic, experimental, or avant-garde as the decadent by-product of dying capitalism. The writer's political sympathies were immaterial; Communist or sympathizer, no artist who utilized an improper form could ever write realistic literature.

In the atmosphere of 1945 to 1947, these ideas, present in pamphlets like *Fortschritt und Reaktion in der deutschen Literatur* and *Deutsche Literatur während des Imperialismus*,[6] helped elicit appropriate answers to the question, "What should art be like?" Because the Germans faced ruin as a result of their own failures, wrote Lukács, literature had to assist them in coming to terms with the consequences of their guilt.[7] But of course, as long as the writers and intellectuals themselves remained helpless because of their own incomprehension of fascism, literature could scarcely be used to assist in reeducating the people. Here Lukács reverted to his own obsession with formalistic considerations by setting up a register of forms that he found either objectively progressive, able to contribute to the reeducation of the German people, or that he felt represented the historical expression of moribund capitalism regardless of the author's intentions. Some aspects of Lukács' theory were thus tailor-made for the post-war years, whereas others created momentarily inopportune tensions. Lukács' old objections to schematic working-class literature, for instance, provided a theoretical framework useful to the party in dealing with overzealous Communist writers now out of tactical step with the policy of apparent moderation. Apart from the artistic poverty of such writing in the past, Lukács explained, a certain wishful thinking on the part of these writers had contributed to a distorted view of reality because they focused single-mindedly upon the imminent collapse of capitalist

---

[6]Published in Berlin by the Aufbau Verlag in 1946 and 1947. Both booklets were written during the last year of the war.
[7]Lukács, *Deutsche Literatur während des Imperialismus*, p. 4.

society by means of revolution. Having lived for years outside of Germany and with no personal knowledge of events inside the country, other writers continued to regard the fascists as a small clique ruling over an entire people whose majority yearned for the overthrow of the tyranny. By no means limited to literature, these misconceptions had been devastatingly repudiated by the experience of the war.[8] For obvious reasons, Lukács chose not to dwell on the real cause of the ill-conceived notions of two Germanies responsible for producing all the "artistically pernicious effects" that he now deplored—the party's own theory of fascism. But because the idea of collective guilt played a central role in the party's program now, Lukács' repudiation of the notion of broad popular opposition to Hitler met a number of immediate needs. In particular, it denied legitimacy to the more radically minded Communist writers who now hoped to revitalize the proletarian literature of the twenties and early thirties; and it cautiously restated party arguments disapproving of revolution and dictatorship. The other dimensions of Lukács' theory were the ones causing problems because Lukács made any preference for the "wrong" kind of literary form akin to an indictable political offense. Here his bias against Brecht reappeared, whom Lukács criticized for his belief in a "'radically new' art requiring completely different kinds of means of expression."[9] Now in Brecht's case, Lukács' objections coincided generally with the party's; but in other cases, Gerhart Hauptmann's especially, they clashed with the party's cultural-political objectives. In 1932, Lukács had assailed Hauptmann for going along with cultural decline in the age of imperialism, "thereby prostituting and passing sentence upon himself as a poet."[10] Lukács' latest comments then added insult to injury when he charged that Hauptmann had "drifted weakly back and forth between the most varying political directions" until his "undignified" capitulation to Hitler. Lukács' remarks were ill-timed in 1946, and he was asked "to be more careful with such categorical judgments"; Hauptmann's writing never "consciously rendered assistance to any kind of intellectual fascism."[11]

Non-art

Issues related to matters of progress and reaction throughout German history, along with their latter-day corollaries, thus came up for frequent discussion. The Communists reiterated that past great cultural achievements had always been coupled with advances toward democracy; by learning how to

[8]Ibid., pp. 55, 63-66.
[9]Ibid., p. 57.
[10]Lukács, "Gerhart Hauptmann," *Die Linkskurve* 10 (1932): 12.
[11]Leuteritz, "Die deutsche Literatur und der Imperialismus," *Tägliche Rundschau*, 16 October 1945.

differentiate between "regressive and progressive cultural tendencies" in their own history, the Germans could apply these lessons to the construction of "a new, progressive culture." More specifically, their newly acquired understanding of culture would permit the people to spot the link with its contemporary "progressive motive force" or, put more vividly, "only when Germans . . . cease to vacillate wildly between the two spirits inhabiting Faust's breast, turning instead with good will in the direction of the constructive spirit, then and only then will Germany acquire a culture and enjoy the respect of the world."[12] This particular editorial had an obvious metaphysical dimension and corresponded to Abusch's characterization of nazism as the "avaricious heir of everything iniquitous in Germany's past," the "incarnation of everything evil, the negation of all that was good in Germany's history," the "empire of bestiality," and so on. But Abusch always capped his arguments with remarks that equated the demonic with "morally corrupt monopoly capitalism," the "most modern form of counterrevolution,"[13] and the above editorial did likewise. Other analyses also used incorporeal rhetoric to explain the fate of culture under nazism—the "rebellion of all wild, uncontrolled, animal instincts" that reason had held in check for over two thousand years—but combined it with a variety of economistic points that complemented the party's political strategy. Nazism was the "product of the decaying process of a moribund reactionary society, a blood-and-iron culture of monopoly capitalism that would have doomed genuine culture if there had not been segments of the German people powerful enough to stave off the catastrophe." The backbone of these segments was the working class.[14]

In this manner, the Communists established the bounds for distinguishing between their plans for politicizing culture and the perversions characteristic of the Nazis talking about the past superstructural dependency of art and literature upon its monopoly-capitalist basis. The Communists thus ridiculed the "degradation of literature to the status of an unprincipled instrument of unprincipled politics," but pleaded in the same breath for the politicization of literature now so that it might evolve "freely."[15] The dilemma derived from the obvious problem of reconciling cultural politicization with pleas for creative freedom, and the Communists attempted to solve it in part through the deterrent example of those writers, historians, and philosophers who helped popularize the goals of a fascist regime. Whose work, after all, achieved notoriety? "The drum-beaters, the graphomaniacs, those lacking any trace of real talent and working with extravagant superlatives in singing the praises of Hitler's Reich." Their "trash" ought to be burned.[16]

[12]Livius, "Vom fortschrittlichen Geiste der Kultur," *Tägliche Rundschau*, 14 May 1946.
[13]Abusch, *Der Irrweg einer Nation*, pp. 224-31.
[14]Aunius, "Zurück zu den ewigen Quellen," *Tägliche Rundschau*, 21 March 1946.
[15]Zwetting, "Literatur unter der Naziherrschaft," *Tägliche Rundschau*, 26 June 1945.
[16]Leuteritz, "Klare Scheidung der Geister." *Tägliche Rundschau*, 8 September 1945.

What had changed? Plainly the Nazi "art dictatorship" had collapsed and the artists could again create freely;[17] but which artistic legacies provided examples worth emulating now? Obviously not those of the past twelve years; and how in fact was literature and art supposed to be (re-)politicized without again becoming the handmaid of a single party? This question and others arose because the Communists' discussion of the recent experience with state or party art constrained them to explain how their brand of politicization, however much they talked of nonpartisanship, would produce something other than state art or make it plausible to argue that the future of German culture was inextricably bound up with the success of their party's politics throughout the entire nation. The latter argument, the national one, indeed supplied the principal impetus to cultural politics in the zone. But the success of those policies hinged upon a delicate balance because there were not many serviceable "legacies" available to the Communists in 1945. The chief heritage, Soviet art and literature, was unavailable because of the party's general repudiation of any "schematic transferal of the Soviet system to Germany"—socialist realism, at least under its real name, was out of the question for the time being. Nor did Weimar culture fit the need. In politics, Weimar paved the way for fascism and offered only negative instruction in the mores of democracy now, the related argument in the area of art and literature being that "we must not pick up where we had to leave off in 1933."[18] There were many reasons why; some were given, others—such as this one—withheld for now: any practice openly identified as a continuation of the German proletarian-revolutionary literary movement would have created insurmountable obstacles because of its links to the accompanying political program of revolution and dictatorship. Besides, everyone knew that the League of Proletarian Revolutionary Writers was a creation of the Communist party, and functionaries like Becher spent the first months following the war's end denying that cultural politics in Soviet-occupied Germany or organizations such as the Kulturbund were affiliated with any single party or any one occupation power. But many of the Leninist-Stalinist literary theories that men like Lukács and Becher helped to dominance in the late twenties and thirties were the exact ones being reintroduced in the Soviet zone; the difference was that this occurred cautiously, enabling the Communists to suggest that they had also broken with their past radical practices in culture. But upon closer examination, the theories monopolizing cultural life in the zone show themselves to be slightly thinned extracts of dogmas articulated and implemented during the thirties; and these were little more than the norms associated with socialist realism in the Soviet Union during the same decade.

---

[17]Keilson, "Was gibt uns die heutige bildende Kunst?" *Deutsche Volkszeitung,* 9 August 1945.
[18]"Zu neuer künstlerischer Tat," *Tägliche Rundschau,* 26 August 1945.

The Communists could ill afford to point this out—anymore than they dared call attention to theoretical and tactical dominants in their advocacy of democracy identical in substance to postulates related to revolution and dictatorship. But these dominants were present, built into both political and cultural-political strategy from the outset so that they could easily be called by name when and if the time came. Interfering with it now, however, were all the other rival trends that had distinguished Weimar culture while proletarian-revolutionary literature and incipient socialist realism languished in obscurity. As a means of steering the "new art" in the right direction, the Communists argued against the continuation of styles characteristic of the Weimar republic; and the usual target was literary and artistic expressionism or whatever else the Communists dismissed as "modern." One article criticized prominent German artists for the pacifistic nature of their past attacks upon militarism; because "expressionism lacked . . . a deep-reaching analysis and clear ideological perspective," it was no wonder that it had been effortlessly shouted down. The kind of art and literature that dominated the scene during Weimar played into the hands of the fascists, and "such conditions must not be allowed to repeat themselves." Freed of the schemes and clichés dictated by the Nazis, the artists could now set out in quest of new themes and forms; but "attempts to galvanize expressionism, which are showing up now, especially in painting, are out of step with the realistic world view of the new democracy."[19]

In their attempt to prevent a resurrection of styles and forms that might inherently resist their kind of politicization, the Communists encountered the same problem that plagued them in their political rhetoric. Their opposition to Weimar bore an embarrassing resemblance to that of the Nazis. In art history, this took the shape of hostility toward modern abstract art, which the Nazis had likewise traduced as decadent. As a consequence, the Communists had to repudiate these forms of art as circumspectly as possible. They knew full well, read one analysis, that much of artistic value in form and content originated in 1923 along side hundreds of worthless products. But only the cultural politics of the Nazis had defamed that period and its artists by lumping them all together. As far as the Communists were concerned, there was "no such thing as a *degenerate* art," only "*non-art*.[20] That distinction allowed the party's literary authorities to criticize abstract art and unwelcome literary styles of the Weimar republic without resorting to the same vulgar terms employed by the Nazis, at least for the time being. "Non-art," it turned out, referred only to Nazi art; whereas other forms represented a natural byproduct of the age, definitely inappropriate now but not to be denounced in the same terms. But why was such art inappropriate under present circum-

[19]Ditz, "Krieg und Kunst," *Tägliche Rundschau*, 1 August 1945.
[20]Keilson, "'Ismus' oder Kunst?" *Deutsche Volkszeitung*, 11 October 1945.

stances? The answer was that their lack of a "political upbringing" had rendered the problems of society impenetrable to those Weimar artists who created it and caused them to react to the socio-economic conditions around them solely through *"formal solutions."* In other words, their art was formalist. As such, it lacked an association with daily life, though "the absence of a political perspective," not just the formal abstraction, was ultimately responsible for the alienation between art and the people; and that absence, in turn, was the fault of the lack of *"real democracy"* in Weimar. The logic of such arguments was that the transformation of Weimar into a true democracy—in accordance with the natural laws governing basis-superstructure relationships—would have generated a different type of art by having redirected the paths of artists in tune with their times. As it was, the "din" made by the abstract artists drowned out the sound of "profound changes and enormous possibilities"; unable to defend themselves later, these artists became "wax in Goebbels' hand." What worried the Communists now was that art seemed preoccupied with "reestablishing the connection with *earlier* times."[21]

Inherent in the entire polemic against Weimar culture, or in political life for that matter, was the assumption that the KPD had presented viable democratic alternatives in either area. Though the opposite was true, the Communists now promised that they had no desire to "repeat the mistakes of the fascists and decree art"; they wished merely to allow "the artist to partake of democracy so that he will regard a militant democracy not as a parliamentary form but as a way of life."[22] Within months of the capitulation, then, the Communists were issuing warnings about "strange ideas regarding intellectual renewal" and trying, while keeping the role of the party itself out of the discussions, to push their own notion of "democratic art" as the only workable solution.[23] But the key question still centered on the appropriate legacy. Though the Communists used every opportunity to stress appreciation of Germany's cultural heritage, they also required contemporary models whom writers and artists could be urged to emulate. Their own literary theories of the late twenties and early thirties, falling into the category of proletarian-revolutionary art, were ruled out in no small measure due to the likelihood that their open advocacy now would have generated unwanted associations with the party's disreputable past. Both as a means of calming those worries and tempering radical outlooks in their own ranks, the Communists rejected proletarian art, even though any superstructure-basis approach to culture suggested that a state in which the working class or "working people" exerted the dominant influence would automatically breed some kind of proletarian culture. For instance, Fred Oelßner cautioned that, though the "cultural-political sending" of the working class called for an end to its long-standing ex-

[21]Ibid.
[22]Leuteritz, "Wohin, moderne Kunst?" *Tägliche Rundschau*, 1 February 1946.
[23]Enno Kind, "Index," *Deutsche Volkszeitung*, 4 October 1945.

clusion from culture, past culture should not be renounced in favor of a "proletcult." Oelßner's next assertion that the heritage of "Schiller and Goethe, Lessing and Herder, Bach and Beethoven" rightfully belonged to the German worker then restated the party's indirect claim to everything worthy in German history, tacitly repudiating jaundiced suggestions that the Communists opposed past art as the cultural superstructure of ruling-class societies. The argument concurrently undercut the position of unduly or inopportunely radical Communists criticized for believing that the time was right for a "'socialist school,' for 'revolutionary film,' or otherwise for an "'entirely new,' so-called "'proletarian art.'"[24] Such statements had the added advantage of appearing to rule out the idea of an impending "sovietization" of German culture even as unnamed Soviet aesthetic norms actually underlay all conceptions of "democratic art."

None of these constraints meant that the Communists refrained in the beginning from defining Soviet culture in indirect terms suggesting that it was exemplary for the new democratic German art, anymore so than they shied away from general praise of Soviet democracy that implied its worthiness as the only true model for German democracy. Still, for several months the two sets of arguments flowed along separate but parallel channels before eventually merging. That is, the Communists were reticent at first to round out their discussions of the irreproachable characteristics of Soviet society and culture with an appeal to the Germans to emulate such qualities, though such pleas grew more common by spring 1946 and routine in the course of 1947. Even earlier, though, there was a discernible tendency to stigmatize an inadequate understanding or appreciation of the Soviet Union as a residue of fascism or, worse, as proof that the people and the intellectuals had not yet embarked upon their own "rehabilitation." One of the main preconceptions regarding the Soviet Union, ran one argument, was the notion that the state-run houses published only those writers actively engaged in "political propaganda," a false assumption redolent of fascist thinking because people could not get it into their heads that, in a genuine democracy, people and state were one. "No 'political commissar,' no censor, but the *reader*" determined the size of a print run.[25]

Behind these early statements on the subject of Soviet art was the repudiation of popular preconceptions regarding sponsored art and literature in the USSR generally and socialist realism in particular. In aesthetic or formal terms, the counterarguments usually translated into the contention that Soviet art enjoyed great formal refinement in addition to its "profound richness of ideas,"[26] a formulation that tried to reconcile political commitment with incontestable artistry. But at the same time, the Communists developed other

[24]Oelßner, "Kultur und Arbeiterklasse," *Deutsche Volkszeitung*, 2 March 1946.
[25]Erpenbeck, "Schrifttum in der Sowjetunion," *Deutsche Volkszeitung*, 7 November 1945.
[26]"Die Sowjetkunst blüht auf," *Tägliche Rundschau*, 3 June 1945.

arguments acknowledging the likelihood of short-term artistic imperfection as a consequence of politicization because the ideal of an art indissolubly bound up with the people, an ideal that had become reality in the Soviet Union, remained only a distant possibility in Germany. Nevertheless, the Communists used the notion of a mature German reading audience, utterly incompatible with the concurrent idea of collective guilt, to prod the writers. One early example was an editorial decrying the corruption of intellectuals under Hitler and insisting that they now steep themselves in democracy. After all, ordinary Germans "expected" their writers, artists, composers, and actors to help in the process of cleansing the people "from the fascist infection" and to "depict the great ideals of democracy in an artistically perfect form"[27]—aberrant logic considering the stridency of simultaneous rhetoric centering on collective guilt. These arguments nonetheless revolved around calls for a solid bond between the working class and the intellectuals; this would lead to the eventual unity of people and state, an outcome predicated upon a broad process of politicization, though the direct injection of politics into the creative process was the cause of concern about freedom in the choice of form and content to begin with.

Here again, Soviet literature served by implication as the example. The "new realism" in Russia was said to exhibit "a limitless array of the most varying styles and manners of depiction," thereby granting writers the widest possible latitude. All kinds of styles thrived in Soviet literature due to its "complete realism" and because it followed the example of Russian literature in its close association with the vital interests of the people.[28] Thus it was that Russian classical literature, the bearer of progressive democratic ideals, heralded ideas that "predetermined" those of the Russian revolution, traditions continued by Soviet literature. Though the connection was not made outrightly, the lesson was easily applied to German literature by declaring the heritage of German classical culture to be the rightful legacy of working people generally and the working class in particular, making the Communist party by implication the sole trustee of that inheritance. But for now, in 1945 and 1946, these direct links were omitted, and most attention in discussions of "Soviet realism" focused upon its essence—a broad representational range of styles that afforded the greatest freedom to the creative quest of the writer.[29] The key to all definitions of creative freedom, however, lay in the need to establish first the existence of an overarching unity of people and state. Soviet society was thus said to be comprised of three social groups—the worker, the peasant, and the intelligentsia; these were forged together "in a single indivisible whole by a common idea and common thoughts" possible only because the Soviet intelligentsia was a "special in-

[27]"Antifaschistische demokratische Kunst," *Tägliche Rundschau*, 22 September 1945.
[28]"Die freie Kunst der freien Völker," *Tägliche Rundschau*, 7 November 1945.
[29]Sabara, "Zeitgenössische Literatur," *Tägliche Rundschau*, 5 December 1946.

telligentsia"; in a word, Soviet intellectuals constituted a "new type of intelligentsia" never before known to humankind.[30] These arguments all had a direct if, for the time being, unstated bearing upon circumstances in Germany; and in one form or another contained the tacit reassurance that Soviet culture had never been forced upon the Soviet or any other people (nor would they be transferred, "schematically" or otherwise, to Germany). After all, the Stalin constitution guaranteed the freedom of cultures within the USSR; "'socialist in content, national in form'—thus reads the classic formulation in the Soviet Union"; the notion of a "hodgepodge of conformity" was just as preposterous as the idea of an "artistic rape by the larger nation."[31]

Socialist in Content, Realistic in Form

Read in conjunction with articles dealing with plans for the revitalization of German culture, the early discussions of Soviet art bring the process of cultural politicization into sharper focus; but the fact remains that neither the Soviet nor the German Communist party figured in any of the major deductions prior to February 1946. Whereas the previous articles dealt routinely with questions of a politicized art, arguing that politicization actually presupposed rather than precluded creative freedom, cultural affairs had yet to be declared the domain of a single party. By early 1946, this began changing conspicuously in selected articles and speeches, but most dramatically at the KPD's cultural conference held that February. This was a dramatic public change, though it had much less of an effect upon the underlying reality of cultural affairs that had been governed all along by the political objectives of one party. Nor did the previous arguments undergo a radical revision; for the most part they were just tightened up. Now as before, the guarantee of *"unconditional freedom for scientific research and artistic endeavor"* figured prominently, though the Communists usually limited their promise of freedom by making it contingent upon *"a single, self-evident condition"*: those who enjoyed the freedom must never abuse it "in a way pernicious to our people" and end up "sabotaging democracy." Indeed, those people thinking of misusing creative freedom were warned by Pieck that they ran the risk of being stripped categorically of the "right to be . . . active in German cultural life." It followed that the party must create all the "preconditions and guarantees" necessary to prevent cultural life from slipping back into the "reactionary and chauvinistic hollows where it will degenerate and decay in the

[30]"Die Sowjetintelligenz," *Tägliche Rundschau*, 14 December 1945; *Geschichte der Kommunistischen Partei der Sowjetunion (Bolschewiki)*, p. 416.
[31]Erpenbeck, "Sowjet-Nationalitäten im Spiegel der Kunst," *Tägliche Rundschau*, 5 December 1945. The German is *Einheitsbrei*.

suffocating air of a newly emergent fascism."[32]

Like Pieck, Ackermann also sought to legitimize the curtailment of creative freedom in the name of antifascism and democracy by hinging it upon the "single precondition" that it never again be misused to strangle freedom; no institution and no party would have the right to interfere as long as artistic concerns were involved, and this promise of no interference extended to the artist's freedom to select the form that he regarded "as the solely artistic one." This argument clearly meant to alleviate concern that the Communist party would insist upon having the dominant voice in determining appropriate content and acceptable forms in compliance with the imperatives of a political art. Ackermann tried to confront this particular issue, but only succeeded in providing an early indication that the Communists indeed had socialist realism in the back of their minds when talking about democratic art. "We see our ideal in an art that is socialist in content and realistic in form," Ackermann said; but using an adroit modification of the party's renunciation of the Soviet system for Germany "under current conditions," he implied that socialist realism was not predestined to become the norm. Right now everything was in too great a state of flux for a judgment to be made one way or the other, and many wrong turns would still be taken before the art best suited to depict "our present and future" emerged.[33]

Ackermann's rhetoric was a shrewd way of implying that socialist realism would result from a process of trial and error flowing spontaneously from the establishment of a new democratic socio-economic and political basis; without it, there could be no cultural and literary corollary. But for this to happen, freedom of art and the opportunity to experiment remained an "unconditional necessity," Ackermann concluded, only to undercut his own assurances. A quick visit to certain art exhibits sufficed for one "to reach the regrettable conclusion that isms are sometimes being chosen that were already tried out after world war one and are evidently unable today to improve upon their accomplishments back then. There is no need for such pseudo-art to think that it will benefit from any particular material support made available by our impoverished people."[34] Behind the contradictions in Ackermann's remarks lay the incompatibility of political control and creative freedom. The Communists insisted that both were possible; they wanted an art suitable for influencing the people politically, but they had been saying all along that they did not "want to make the same mistake committed during the past twelve years and, just turning things around, degrade art to a handmaid of the powers-that-be."[35] But every conclusion reached by them

---

[32]Pieck, "Um die Erneuerung der deutschen Kultur," *Erste Zentrale Kulturtagung der KPD der KPD*, pp. 21-22.
[33]Ackermann, "Unsere kulturpolitische Sendung," ibid., pp. 51-52.
[34]Ibid.
[35]Selbmann, *Aufbruch des Geistes*, pp. 17, 19-20.

connoted political interference: "The artist who fails to understand that he has a mission to fulfill is not worth giving the chance to show his face. He ought to go shovel dirt, and that's just what we'll let him do."[36] Because they perceived no antinomies in their approach to art and culture, or because they discerned them clearly and still hoped to hide their existence, the Communists continued to state their opposition to "hindering scientists, artists, and teachers by means of any dogma, any aesthetic or methodological regulation"; and yet these promises invariably contained an important caveat: "We have every right to demand that the freedoms granted so abundantly not be misused in an antidemocratic manner."[37]

By early spring 1946, deductions inherent in standard superstructure-basis considerations permitting cultural processes and general artistic theory to be wedded to the "ideal" of a single party became the rule rather than the exception; and late in the year what had begun as a more moderate approach to the cultural heritage reverted more and more to the rigidly dichotomous "two-camps" attitude reminiscent of the twenties and early thirties. Even so, for most of 1946 the Communists tended to utilize implied basis-superstructure arguments more with an eye to integrating, however restrictively, than ostracizing unnecessarily, and they made abundant use of these arguments to present themselves as the only true nationalists. In 1945 and early 1946, this thinking acted to soften the primitive side of basis-superstructure arguments by allowing the Communists to identify with progressive culture at any point in German history up to and including the present day; but because the approach could at any time revert to two-camp, two-world, who-whom notions, it likewise contained the germ of a dialectical-materialist rationalization of the growing political, cultural, and geographical division of the nation. Indeed, by spring 1946 and in the aftermath of the February cultural conference, the party's positions were shifting with growing momentum, though not in every context and certainly not with a complete abandonment of the earlier tactical forbearance. The changing line was apparent in comments made at a cultural gathering in March sponsored by the KPD, where the relative obscurity of the event may have encouraged greater openness. A man by the name of Franz Lepinski, a Social Democrat who later fled to the West, still emphasized moderation, insisting just a few weeks before formation of the SED that the unity socialists bore the responsibility of resurrecting the culture of "the other, the *genuine Germany*."[38] But how, he asked, did this square with the assumption that medieval or bourgeois culture of-

---

[36]Ibid.

[37]*Die Erneuerung der deutschen Kultur*, Vortragsdisposition Nr. 9, p. 15.

[38]Lepinski, "Die Arbeiterbewegung als die Erbin der großen deutschen Literatur," *Deutsche Kultur und Arbeiterbewegung*, p. 6. Further page references, as well as those following the first footnoted reference to remarks made by Walter Wolf and Maxim Vallentin below, are included in the text.

fered little of value to the working class and might only diminish class consciousness? In answering his question, Lepinski pointed out that changes in economic life brought shifts in the ideological and cultural superstructure, affecting the "minds of thinkers, writers, and artists," but never "mechanically." This explanation toned down the harshness of a phrase still much too strident in early 1946, "class warfare," by defining the labor movement as the continuation of the universal "struggle of mankind" waged by anyone who ever fought for cultural renewal (9).

This way class warfare came across not as civil war waged in the name of an ideology perceived to be alien, Soviet; rather, the party's backing of everything progressive in German history represented the consummate expression of true nationalism. By relating the issues of culture and nation, Lepinski voiced national arguments presumed to be attractive to ordinary Germans on two levels. Every utterance tinged with nationalism pleaded for state unity and against policies favoring decentralization or, worse, dismemberment in the form of "federalism" or "particularism"; and these arguments incorporated the tacit assurance that the Communists rejected "sovietization." But how did their nationalism differ from that of the Nazis? Whereas the German nation had always represented a "cultural community of the ruling class" in the past, nowadays the reconstruction of German culture would be carried out by other social forces; "this reordering of our fatherland will not be dictated from above, either by a dictator or a clique of political power-holders," but, fought out on the soil of democracy, would work its way up "from below" (11). Lepinski's argument contrasted the tainted notion of a *Volksgemeinschaft* with what he called a *Kulturgemeinschaft*, a community bound together by culture. Freed from coercion, fear, and deprivation, creative intellectuals could combine forces with the people to construct a culture infused with new values "contrary to the old ones" of the bourgeoisie. Bridging the gap that separated German nationalism from the internationalism of Marxism-Leninism, Lepinski explained that the new culture, while evolving "on the soil of a nation," would transcend the bounds of national constraints because it mirrored human life in general; great cultures brought the peoples of the world together, and it was natural that the names of Marx and Engels could be seen along side those of Lenin and Stalin on the red banners of the Russian occupation regime (11-15).

Lepinski's comments bolstered the efforts of the party to shed its radical image by tempering the rhetoric of class warfare, allowing the party's program to come across as the sole means of national deliverance for all Germans. The Communists still stuck by their position that the "Marxist party" was a workers' party, and Ackermann acknowledged in April 1946 that historical circumstances had earlier constrained the KPD to emphasize class divisions; but more lofty tasks confronted it today, namely "the struggle for the leadership of the entire people, the battle to take the destiny of the entire nation in hand." The Marxist party had thus become the party of "all segments of the working people," by which Ackermann meant "workers as well as the employees, above all the farmers and the small businessmen, and especially the intelligentsia in all their constituent parts: the scientists, teachers, doctors, engineers, agriculturists, and, last but not least, the artists." Therefore, the Marxist party was "the party of all genuinely progressive and freedom-loving forces within the people"; and every worker, farmer, middle-class citizen, and intellectual could regard the SED as "his" party.[39]

In concluding his remarks at the March gathering, Lepinski argued in much the same vein that the working class was the legitimate heir of German culture and that culture would forge an "indivisible unity" extending across zonal boundaries to nullify the destructive efforts of those bent upon dividing the nation (15). Walter Wolf, a Communist, took these general arguments closer to an endorsement of one party's politics. He began by noting that the future of German culture hinged on the building of "a new democratic social order" because such an order alone would generate a democratic art in harmony with the true interests of the people. Moreover, by cooperating with each other in every sphere of cultural activity Germans living throughout four different occupied territories could contribute to that national unity, now endangered, which would serve as the necessary basis for a "new, democratic national culture."[40] But Wolf then reverted to rigid basis-superstructure arguments, proving that the reductionist approach could just as easily stamp unwanted cultural or literary-theoretical preferences with the label "reactionary" as bestow upon related or different ideas the quality of being "progressive." Wolf posited a more immediate relationship between ideological or cultural superstructure and political or socio-economic basis than Lepinski had done, and he did so as a way of establishing a direct link between the new culture and partisan political change in Germany. *"The dominant culture of an age is always the culture of the ruling class"* (25), he said, a statement that singled out the more dogmatic side of the theory for emphasis. He then gave it its democratic twist by insisting that culture must be borne by the entire people before making this circumstance contingent upon the eradication first of the antagonism inherent to class society. Thus it was that "creation of a new, a democratic art and science hinges upon changes in the economic basis of society"; in other words, a new democratic culture was unthinkable without first smashing monopoly capitalism (26).

What little ambiguity remained in that remark vanished in the next when Wolf argued that it would be the job of the "socialist unity party of all working people" to discern, organize, and implement cultural tasks. "We will

---

[39]Ackermann, "Der ideologische Kampf der Partei," *Bericht über die Verhandlungen des 15. Parteitages der Kommunistischen Partei Deutschlands*, pp. 116-19.
[40]Wolf, "Nationale Einheit und neue demokratische Kultur," *Deutsche Kultur und Arbeiterbewegung*, p. 19. (Additional page references to Wolf's comments are provided in the text.)

build a new democratic culture," he said, and this culture would help the working class to attain the economic, political, scientific, and artistic significance that it had coming to it (28). Even then, none of this amounted to a workers' culture; and Wolf drew on those dimensions of the basis-superstructure rationale allowing for "dissynchronous" change to dismiss the idea. To do otherwise would have constrained him to make the new culture contingent upon the immediate realization of socialism; and he extricated himself from the impasse by arguing that giving art to the broad masses was a political question whose resolution had to await the economic liberation of the working class. Still, the dialectically many-layered transition to socialism could already "reveal as yet modest beginnings of a transformation of the ideological superstructure" (29).

Lest anyone conclude that such stirrings allowed for experimental styles of writing, however, Wolf added that contriving "new art forms" was out of the question; the objective was *"to depict the democratic content of our day in familiar, proven forms."* Form and content being a dialectical unity, the new content presupposed novel forms, not the other way around, because working out new forms before effecting a basic ideological transformation was "historically nonsensical" (37). The "idea content" of art had to be reformed first, which was simply Wolf's demand for the politicization of art and literature in accordance with prevailing political currents. But if they wished to incorporate progressive ideas into the new art, the artists could not be divorced from politics" (38); for only when progressive Germans became champions of progressive ideas, establishing a perfect unity of economic basis and ideological superstructure, would the cultural and democratic unity of the German people be guaranteed. Consequently, "our new German culture—national in form as German culture and in content democratic—must eventually become socialist if it is to guarantee the unity of the nation once and for all" (41). What constituted progress in art? The answer was obviously the depiction of socio-political change in line with the party's definition of democracy, but the content still required the proper form. *"All genuine art has to be realism"* (39).

Maxim Vallentin, a Communist stage producer who spent the preceding twelve years in Soviet exile, defined "realism" even more precisely, invoking the authority of Lukács as the greatest expert on the subject of "our concept of democratic art" and coming closer still to naming socialist realism as the only acceptable manner of writing. Applauding Lukács' *Deutsche Literatur während des Imperialismus*, Vallentin focused on the key ingredient in Lukács' theory, "realism in artistic praxis"; and realism, said Vallentin, stood for "the fanatical will to attain the highest degree, the most total comprehension and representation of objective truth," to hold a mirror up to the world as a means of helping to improve it. In a word, realism was no less than the yardstick of any "genuine democratic understanding of art and criticism." But contemporary artists still needed to perceive of realism as more than just form and content, seeing it above all as "the profound 'quo vadis'"; and this "quo vadis," the goal, was "the reorganization of a social order . . . in harmony with our age"—or socialism.[41] At this juncture, Vallentin again established the connection that the Communists had avoided until spring 1946, linking writers to the party. Subjective intentions notwithstanding, he argued, the "bourgeois humanism" of most German writers had culminated in the fascist liquidation of humanity. Not that a reversal of the processes originally leading in the direction of that outcome had been impossible; the example set by the Russian intelligentsia proved as much. But then the Russian intellectuals benefited from a source of strength and guidance not available to the German intellectuals—"a working class with a consistently Marxist leadership." The problems of the German intelligentsia were thus caused by the "ideological and political weakness of the German working class," that is, its disunity (51-52); and it followed logically that such working-class unity represented the prerequisite now for a "new German democratic culture." Vallentin went on to express his hope that the soon-to-be united German working class would not only learn the lesson of its own past but make the experiences of the Russian proletariat its own, going on to form a "genuinely Marxist party of a new type" to lead the German nation. Only then would the Germans witness the rebirth of their literature, acquire a "constructive" creative intelligentsia, and become a "people of political, people-oriented poets and thinkers" (53).

But this marriage of politics and art remained a dubious proposition to anyone who feared that the politicization of culture translated into a mandated literature; and many intellectuals continued to regard cultural politicization as a way of placing art and literature at the disposal of a single party whose program they declined to consider an exclusive set of remedies for Germany's political and cultural ills. The party's bellicose reaction to the hesitancy of these intellectuals to involve themselves in processes that channeled their activities in preset directions then revealed as much about the actual attitudes and underlying objectives as the program itself. Artists with real character, the Communists lectured, had never chosen to ignore the "basic, existential problems of the people," and no intellectual ought now to be seen fleeing "into the realm of the non-committal." Indeed, the polemic continued, it was hard to imagine that not all creative intellectuals felt compelled to express the profound political and intellectual shift now in progress. Even worse, significant currents existed within the artistic community favoring a "*certain non-committal aestheticism*," and some circles even chose to equate artistic quality with apoliticality, hiding their own "reactionary disposition" behind a professed inclination toward "inwardness." But by avoiding

[41]Vallentin, "Abweg und Ausweg der neuen deutschen Literatur," ibid., pp. 45 and 48.

politics, these people adopted a posture antagonistic to democracy by absolving themselves of any moral obligation to get involved; they thus transacted the business of reaction.[42]

Inner Emigration vs. Exile

A few days after those comments appeared and just a day or so before the official formation of the Socialist Unity party, Wilhelm Pieck drew some practical conclusions. Following twelve years of fascism, intellectuals could once again "work freely, answerable to no one but their own conscience"; but this liberty by no means meant that they had the right to "withdraw from politics in order to weave this or that cerebral fantasy." The genuine artist and true scientist would always seek the proximity of the popular masses and realize that the survivability and strength of democracy was an existential question for science and art; and for these very reasons the intellectual belonged "in the forefront of the working people"; his political home was the "party of these people—the Socialist Unity party."[43] Ironically, Pieck had just scoffed at the notion that coercion went hand in hand with the drive to fuse his party with Social Democracy; and he declared it equally absurd to insinuate that the KPD planned to stamp out democracy by "swallowing" the SPD before devouring the other parties. For all the hysterical screaming about a lurid "rape of the rank and file," the only pressure applied was that which their own consciences exerted upon the advocates of unity, compelling them to take the single step able to block a restoration of the conditions responsible for fascism.[44]

The Communists used a recognizable variant of the same rhetoric in their efforts to fashion unity among the intellectuals. They continually denied that the Kulturbund answered to any political party or occupying power and insisted that it was "a German movement of renewal" open to all intellectuals regardless of their political orientation; beyond that, its activities had to be designed to attract the participation of "all the people," for democratic renewal, the Kulturbund's sole objection, encompassed the German people in their entirety.[45] These arguments were the cultural-political pendant to the KPD-SED's insistence that it did not aspire to a "single-party system," represented the broadest popular interest, and was the "genuinely national party of the German people."[46] Still, during the first few years, there was a differ-

[42]"Keine Flucht ins Unverbindliche!" *Tägliche Rundschau*, 14 April 1946.
[43]Pieck, "Die Einheit des schaffenden Volkes." *Bericht über die Verhandlungen des 15. Parteitages der KPD*, pp. 214-15.
[44]Ibid., pp. 189 and 203-5.
[45]"Kulturbund für jedermann," *Berliner Zeitung*, 6 February 1946.
[46]"Manifest an das deutsche Volk [21 April 1946]," *Dokumente der Sozialistischen Einheitspar-*

ence between the patterns of political and cultural-political transformation in the zone. The Communists generally had to steer clear of the ceaseless badgering and outright coercion that were characteristic of their behavior in bloc politics, relying more on persuasion to prevail in discussions with intellectuals. Nonetheless, just prior to formation of the Socialist Unity party, Pieck declared it "foolish" to imagine that socialism could be achieved other than through "bitter class warfare"; the impending creation of the SED had been greeted by "howls of rage emanating from the reactionary mob" that sensed the threat to it posed by unity. "Let them howl and rage," Pieck said, these "bosses of monopoly capitalism and reaction; we have every intention of providing them with all the more cause!"[47]

That kind of blood-curdling rhetoric, the undeviating assurance of "a sanguinary civil war" in case "certain possibilities inherent in the current situation" were not grasped, accompanied by the solemn promise that the Communists did not aspire, yet, to a dictatorship,[48] was still largely absent in cultural affairs. But the national argument was much the same; the principal means of nudging the intellectuals into support of the overall antifascist "movement" was the contention that this democratic ground swell broke completely with those lines of historical continuity culminating in fascism and reestablished the reign of progressive cultural traditions whose roots were sunk deep in the German past. The aggregate of arguments connected with the division of the nation's history into reactionary and progressive lines of development relieved the Communists of the burden of speaking like internationalists committed to internecine warfare and allowed them to pose instead as unmitigated champions of the German cultural heritage. Concurrently, by presenting their program as the sole means by which the German people might avoid the civil war that they, the Communists, promised to wage otherwise, the party transformed the notion of a peaceful and democratic road to socialism into a synonym for the promise of no revolution and no dictatorship—"no sovietization." Moreover, by declaring themselves the rightful heirs of the cultural heritage, the Communists hoped to strengthen their rhetorical hand further, contriving additional arguments to refute any contention that their ultimate objective was the importation of Soviet cultural norms into Germany. As Ackermann put it, when Marxist-Leninists set out to eradicate everything "reactionary, despicable, and pernicious" from the German tradition and furthered all that was "progressive" and "noble," they stood up for the genuine "greatness of our fatherland."[49]

---

tei Deutschlands, pp. 25-26.

[47]Pieck, "Die Einheit des schaffenden Volkes," *Bericht über die Verhandlungen des 15. Parteitages der KPD* [19-20 April 1946], pp. 213 and 221.

[48]Ibid., pp. 207-9.

[49]Ackermann, "Unsere kulturpolitische Sendung," *Erste Zentrale Kulturtagung der KPD*, p. 48.

By sheer coincidence, the KPD's cultural conference in February 1946 also marked the four-hundredth anniversary of Martin Luther's death and posed a problem. To which of the two traditions just referred to by Ackermann should Luther be assigned to now or was there no choice but to play both ends against the middle? In the past, the Communists had always regarded Thomas Münzer, not Luther, as the national hero. But commemorating Luther's death by expressing disgust with his actions and ideas during the peasant revolts would scarcely have polished the national image that the Communists were determined to project culturally since Ulbricht's visit to Karlshorst in December 1945. Under the circumstances, striking a precarious balance by situating Luther's legacy within the context of the party's program of national unity, even as the general framework for his "rehabilitation" remained the conflict between progress and reaction down through German history, appears to have been the only answer to the problem. This battle was occasionally fought in the form of "two souls" vying with each other within the breast of a single Faustian German, read one commentary, and a "regressive and a progressive phase" could often be discerned in the lives of German geniuses.[50] These were the two tendencies in need of reconciliation in Luther's case. An article written for the *Deutsche Volkszeitung* tried to mediate between them by explaining that Luther had indeed sided with the "enemies of the people" when the peasants rose up against their oppressors; but his creation of a single German language nonetheless paved the way for national unity by providing a weapon against "particularism and separatism," precisely that legacy which now needed to be defended against today's "obscurantists."[51] Another article published the same day in the SMAD's *Tägliche Rundschau* conveyed similar sentiments, but with greater understanding for the historical context. Though Luther had been unable to fathom the nature of change in Germany, it was senseless to reproach him for it four hundred years after the fact; and besides, he had been a "pioneer of German unity."[52] The *Berliner Zeitung* drew comparably strained parallels with current events—"What was at stake back then was in part only realized in recent days through land reform"—and criticized Luther for siding against the peasants. The paper balanced its assessment by characterizing his "personality as the crystallization point for those forward-moving elements that broke through at the beginning of the sixteenth century," but still noted that Luther had not been the *Volksführer* able to lead them to victory.[53]

All other evaluations of Luther oscillated between these poles. Some slipped into historiographical vulgarities in an attempt to give a topical slant

[50]Livius, "Vom fortschrittlichen Geiste der Kultur," *Tägliche Rundschau*, 14 May 1946.
[51]Lange, "Martin Luther. Zu seinem 400. Todestage," *Deutsche Volkszeitung*, 19 February 1946
[52]Reinhold, "Luther, der deutsche Kämpfer an der Schwelle der Neuzeit," *Tägliche Rundschau*, 19 February 1946.
[53]Horn, "Dr. Martin Luther. Zu seinem 400. Todestag," *Berliner Zeitung*, 17 February 1946.

to events over four centuries old. One of these said that the road to Hitler began with the inadequacies of the German people during the peasant uprisings of 1525; the omissions of Luther's reformation thus bore a major share of the responsibility for that eventual outcome. Luther had admittedly joined forces with the "humanistic lower nobility," the urban bourgeoisie, and the revolutionary peasants in fighting for independence from Rome; unified, this "front" would have been unbeatable because Germany would have acquired its national unity, thus sparing the nation the four-hundred-year ordeal ending in Hitler. But Luther threw in with the local princes instead and contributed to the fact that "we still have to wrestle for Germany's *political* unity today." All this notwithstanding, through his translation of the Bible Luther accomplished much with respect to the "*cultural* unity of Germany." The lessons for the present accordingly fit into two categories; one, the reformation failed because of Luther's leanings toward the "federalist aspirations" of the local princes; and, two, Luther's contribution to national unity in the area of culture was not "devoid of significance." Thanks in no small measure to Luther, the federalists in southern and western Germany could properly be lectured today on the existence of "a single *German* culture."[54]

There were a few half-hearted objections to what one critic, Paul Merker, called the "mechanical historiography" of arguing that Hitler's accession to power was the ineluctable consequence of the failed peasant uprising and the ill-fated revolution of 1848-49; but Merker himself bunched Luther together with Friedrich the Great, Bismarck, Wilhelm II, and then Hitler, all of whom he contrasted with such figures as Hutten, Münzer, Lessing, Herder, Schiller, Hölderlin, Goethe, Heine, Marx, Engels, and the Liebknechts, ending with Ernst Thälmann and "the heroes of the German underground." Worse, Merker's rejection of one form of historical teleology for a more serviceable kind came in a review of Abusch's *Der Irrweg einer Nation*, a book that Merker welcomed because it bucked the determinist trend.[55] But this was strange praise considering that Abusch had not minced any words when he called Luther the "grave digger" of the peasant rebellion and likened this "social betrayal" to a "betrayal of the nation."[56] Abusch's remark that Luther's Bible translation helped "intellectually" to pave the way for a unified Germany scarcely redressed the balance. Regardless, in June 1946 a series of events honoring Luther were scheduled for the Wartburg on 31 August and 1 September and Theodor Plievier was put in charge of the preparations.[57] But the commemoration appears to have been postponed until October, perhaps because the Communists hoped that their sponsorship of a "Martin Luther Memorial Week," with an opening speech by Pieck, might

[54]Lenzer, "Luther und die Einheit Deutschlands," *Neues Deutschland*, 3 October 1946.
[55]Merker, "Der Irrweg einer Nation," *Neues Deutschland*, 7 September 1946.
[56]Abusch, *Der Irrweg einer Nation*, pp. 22-25.
[57]See "Luther auf der Wartburg," *Neues Deutschland*, 25 June 1946.

enhance their prospects in the state and provincial elections set for then. *Neues Deutschland* reported the event, however, by publishing the article least sympathetic to Luther.[58]

The events surrounding Luther's four-hundredth anniversary and the differences of emphasis in discussions devoted to his legacy have two possible explanations; first, on controversial issues like this one the Communists tended to straddle the fence; unable for tactical reasons to be as categorical in their views as they once were or would have preferred to be, they softened them when necessary, but either failed to hide the underlying rigidity or saw no reason to do so; and, two, what appears to be hedging in early 1946 may not always have been deliberate. That is, the coordination of cultural politics in Soviet-occupied Germany still had a ways to go. Indeed, there are sporadic indications that tactical disagreements between the SMAD, whose leading cultural-political officers were more savvy than the more inflexible of the German Communists, also help explain the differing nuances, and disputes among the local Communists themselves almost certainly entered in. Even so, these inconsistencies should not be exaggerated; everyone involved used Luther and a similar brand of teleology to make a number of virtually identical points, and the two positions converged anyway when it came time to work out the historical validation for the party's national program.

Similar fluctuations characterized opinions toward other cultural figures, still alive at the time, whose past some Communists considered checkered; the dramatist Gerhart Hauptmann serves as the best example. But these divergent attitudes make sense only in a much broader context that has its own importance for what it reveals about the party's cultural policies. First of all, no matter what they said publicly, the Communists plainly had misgivings about ordinary intellectuals who had remained in Germany after 1933. However often they parroted Stalin's remark about the Hitlers who came and went, their public rhetoric could hardly have altered the real emotions of the local Communists who had endured long years of exile, confinement in prisons and concentration camps, or both. Indeed, considering that the Communists had clung tenaciously to their belief in the existence of "two Germanies" prior to 1945, being forced to admit to themselves right after the war that they could not have been more mistaken probably deepened their feelings of resentment. Besides, the "failure of the intellectuals," which the Communists considered to be the natural outcome of too half-hearted a commitment to antifascism, was a feeling embedded far too deeply in the KPD's theory of collective guilt to be easily set aside; and when it was, indications are that the same expedience responsible for the party's fluctuation between undiscriminating accusations of guilt and spontaneous antifascism tended to be the reason why. These circumstances soon led to disagreements over the

[58]See Note 54 (Pieck's speech appears not to have published).

question of the respective merits of the "external" versus the "inner" emigration, though the controversy broke out in the western zones first when "inner émigrés" Walter von Molo and Frank Thieß lashed out at Thomas Mann for remarks to the effect that books published in Germany from 1933 to 1945 ought to be pulped and for acknowledging his disinterest in returning home.[59] For their part, von Molo and Thieß took pride in the existence of an "inner emigration," supposedly snubbed by the exiles, and retorted that the latter had enjoyed the luxury of watching the German tragedy play out from the "theater boxes and orchestra seats of foreign countries."[60] In response to this exchange of open letters, Johannes R. Becher tried to mediate between both sides of the dispute, though he did so with the clear intention of tailoring it to fit the cultural-political needs of his party's policies.[61]

The controversy over the inner versus the external emigration raged in both western and eastern zones, then, but with important differences. In the West, the polemics mirrored the hostility toward exiles who still lived abroad and delivered long-distance lectures about the depths of Germany's collective depravity; whereas many exiles, mostly Communists, had already returned to that part of Germany occupied by the Soviet Union and seized the pulpit preaching much the same thing. Their moralizing would have sufficed by itself to exacerbate tensions locally, and yet the bad impression made by the Communists anyway was worsened by the fact that they identified so completely with an unpopular party and with the Soviet military administration. The conflict between the exiles and those who had remained at home consequently acquired its own peculiar dimension in the Soviet zone because relatively few ordinary Germans could think of anything commendable about the KPD. The outside perception of its past record of antifascism simply focused too intently on the simultaneous advocacy of dictatorship, and the definite sense that this contradiction lingered on plagued the party now. But the Communists had little choice but to cleave to their antifascism as the only potentially credible source of legitimization, even though doing so surrounded their dealings with everyone else with an air of patronization and, in certain contexts, marked them as hypocrites. The limits to the effectiveness of the related lessons in democracy and national unity then narrowed further because they were delivered by people who answered to the Russians, hardly democrats themselves, and were burdened by loyalties that rendered their national orientation indeterminate at best.

But in line with Becher's vision of a "universal policy of alliances" and his party's approach to coalition politics, the Communists showered their affections upon the same intellectuals whose past "failures" they brought up,

[59]The letter, dated 12 October 1945, is included in the collection dealing with the entire controversy, *Die große Kontroverse*, p. 31.
[60]Letter dated 18 August 1945, ibid., p. 24.
[61]See Becher's letter to Thieß dated 26 January 1946, ibid., p. 99.

connecting them with their present transgressions, whenever cajolery failed. At a meeting sponsored by the Kammer der Kulturschaffenden in August 1945, the memory of several Germans who had died during the preceding twelve years, both exiles and "inner émigrés," was honored. Though the list included many who had had nothing in common with the Communists, this did not prevent Becher from laying claim to their personal and artistic legacy as martyrs of "intellectual freedom." Representatives of a "literature true to reality," "blood witnesses" to the omnipotence of human reason who lived and died for a *humane Reich of the German nation*," these artists had begun a new epoch of German literature whose overriding characteristics would be its humanity, realism, and genuine nationalism—"all traits marking a demo-cratic literature, a people's literature." Becher then ended his comments with a different twist; for all the reasons just given, these writers had been *"political"* in the genuine meaning of the word; and "as executors of their spiritual testament, we stand here in the glow of the light emanating from them."[62] This was Becher at his eloquent and disingenuous best, the voice that he projected whenever he chose to forego comments regarding the fail-ure of the intellectuals in favor of statements more in tune with his related idea of "a German movement" of intellectual renewal. Indeed, Becher's rhe-torical shifts generally derived from his modulations of the inherent opti-mism expressed by the Shakespearian "Another way so high an hope." He even went so far as to say that "those who remained within Germany" en-dured banishment just as much as the ones forced to leave; and besides, the exiles never claimed to be the only true representatives of German culture anyway. But the intellectuals who stayed behind did not have the right either to think that exile represented "the comfortable way out." In any case, it would be irresponsible to erect artificial barriers between the exiles and the inner émigrés, and this was why the Kulturbund had issued an appeal to exiles still abroad to return home and help rebuild:

> You should know that your homeland has not forgotten you and that we . . . are preparing the day of your return by creating a new, freedom-loving Germany. Just as you always knew that intellectual forces had remained in Germany to wrestle with the powers of ruination under cir-cumstances of profound distress, . . . those who stayed at home thought of you continually in thankful recognition, you who endeavored to hold high the honor of Germany while enduring the hardship and spiritual an-guish of banishment and whose works and deeds bore public witness to all people that the genuine, freedom-loving spirit of Germany still lived and worked actively for certain victory. You listened and gave voice to the "eloquent" silence and the "cum tacent, clamant" of those awaiting

[62]Becher, "'Die für geistige Freiheit litten und starben,'" *Tägliche Rundschau*, 21 August 1945.

liberation within Germany. . . . The years of emigration are over, both within Germany and beyond its frontiers.[63]

As for the overtures to those who had stayed in Germany, there were apparently significant numbers of intellectuals who continued to respond to the blandishments hesitantly. To a considerable extent this was because so many identified organizations like the Kulturbund with the Communist party and because, try as they might, the Communists could never bring themselves to regard non-Communists as being or having ever been inherently antifascist. To a limited extent, there was an understandable context for this hubris. The Communists were antifascist in different ways—commendable in their opposition to fascism, less laudable in what they hoped to replace it with. The trouble was that they never separated the two and persisted in holding intellectuals who had remained in Germany to stringent standards hardly met by the leadership of the German Communist party itself. True, those Communists who stayed behind in Germany, putting their lives on the line daily and often losing them, fit a different category than the ones who threw themselves into antifascist activities from abroad. But the latter group, the repatriated, now had the loudest voices and the most influential positions. They may well have been thoroughly "antifascist" in a doctrinal sense, too, and this was just as true of those who settled in the Soviet Union; moreover, the lives of the latter group were likely just as much at risk by the mid-thirties as the lives of their counterparts in Germany. For that very reason, however, the former Soviet exiles had the least excuse for reacting so contemptuously to suggestions that a margin of intellectual and political compromise might have been necessary as the price of simple survival in Nazi Germany. But then Becher's "Another way" just happened to be a political expedient that thrived especially within the undifferentiated context of mass culpability. It is all the more ironic, then, that the Communists who sought refuge in the Soviet Union acted as if they had the clearest consciences; in fact, many probably convinced themselves that they had paid a particularly high price for being antifascists because, however perversely, their commitment to political principles had meant risking their lives in the Soviet Union as much as or more than if they had stayed at home. That the political circumstances under which they would have perished differed radically from Nazi Germany need not have altered the idea of the perilous risks involved in being a Communist and an antifascist. Strange as it may sound, these risks were then blamed on Hitler, not Stalin. Still, there was something painfully dishonest about the omission from the list of "martyrs" mentioned at the rally sponsored by the Kammer der Kulturschaffenden of any German writer whose

---

[63]"Ruf an die Emigranten!" *Tägliche Rundschau*, 22 November 1945. See also Leuteritz, "Die geschichtliche Rolle der Literatur in der Zeitwende," *Tägliche Rundschau*, 24 November 1945.

life ended in a Stalinist prison camp. True, other than the Soviet exiles, few of those in attendance at the commemoration would have noticed their absence; but men like Becher knew, kept silent, and adopted an intellectual posture that appears to have been impervious to much self-examination.

The arrogance was especially apparent in public disputes over the inner and external emigration. For instance, a writer by the name of Hans Franck was careless enough to speak of the "numerically significant number of German writers who, though they stayed at home and renounced the hopeless struggle within the Reich, more or less quickly dissociated themselves spiritually from national socialism . . . and went into internal emigration." His conclusion, which may admittedly have gone too far, was that a considerable number of writers eschewed fascism even if they became party members as a consequence of direct threats to their lives. This, Franck added, constituted a "sham-relationship" entered into for the sake of their work, writing naturally produced for the desk drawer.[64] Franck's remarks were quickly disqualified, probably by Willi Bredel. Just as some of the exiles left Germany to ensure their own creature comforts, his rebuttal went, the departure of others constituted the sole means of continuing the antifascist struggle; and in much the same way, some of those who remained in Germany used every opportunity to resist, whereas others distanced themselves from fascism in a meaningless manner discernible only to themselves. But Bredel's rhetoric then turned expedient; neither those who left to save their skins nor those who stayed behind only to "crawl back into their snail's shell of a highly private isolation or climb the ivory tower of timeless aestheticism" had the right to stand next to active antifascists of any kind. For "we," he said, had "the right to demand that Germany's cultural and creative intellectuals arrive themselves at a state of complete *clarity regarding values and concepts* before they insist upon being recognized by the German people as the guardians of spiritual values and as the interpreters of our times."[65]

The Communists displayed a more forgiving spirit when it came to *prominent* literary and cultural figures who never left Germany and whose pasts could not be considered entirely spotless. One of the best examples was the spirited defense of the conductor Wilhelm Furtwängler when he appeared before the allied denazification commission.[66] *Neues Deutschland* defended him vigorously, and the *Berliner Zeitung* insisted that Furtwängler made no "deals" with the Nazis.[67] The writer Hans Fallada benefited from

---

[64]Franck, "Bekenntnis eines Schriftstellers," *Demokratische Erneuerung* 3 (1946): 8.

[65]"'Innere Emigration.' Eine notwendige Klarstellung," *Demokratische Erneuerung* 4 (1946): 3.

[66]See Wilhelm Girnus' account, "Musik im großen Spiel der Welt," . . . *einer neuen Zeit Beginn*, pp. 174-79 and Jäger, "Literatur und Kulturpolitik in der Entstehungsphase der DDR (1945-1952)," in "Aus Politik und Zeitgeschichte," *Das Parlament*, 5 October 1985, pp. 35-37.

[67]*Neues Deutschland* for 16 June as well as 14 and 18 December 1946; see also "Ein Beitrag zur Diskussion um Furtwängler" and "Volle Rechtfertigung Furtwänglers," in the *Berliner Zeitung*, 16 November 1945 and 18 December 1946.

similar treatment, even though, according to the *Tägliche Rundschau*, he had scarcely taken an "open stand on politics." Nonetheless, the Communists expressed their understanding of the fact that he had retreated into isolation as a way of waiting for more favorable times and again writing about the *"truth of social circumstances."*[68] Easily the most prominent case, however, was Hauptmann's; and from Johannes R. Becher came the comforting sounds of moderation. He was not unmindful of the fact, Becher said, that Hauptmann's early socially critical writing yielded later to "quieter, contemplative, occasionally dubious sounds of reverie." Precisely when Hauptmann ought to have issued "storm warnings," he fell silent and often showed that his genius was unpolitical and neutral. In much of what he did and failed to do against fascism, then, Hauptmann's road to humanity had often grown difficult to discern. Nonetheless, "the bell that seemed buried soon sounded again and surprised us with a new, vibrant ring."[69] Becher's article, coincidentally or not, appeared in the *Tägliche Rundschau*, the official organ of the SMAD, and so did some others that likewise stressed Hauptmann's essential antifascism. One in particular noted that Nazi efforts to win him for their cause failed "with very few [sic!] exceptions";[70] and though some had mistakenly regarded him as a mystic, Hauptmann was "a great realist who never shut his eyes to the facts of history."[71]

But certain other Communists who had followed Hauptmann's career could scarcely bring themselves to accept that kind of statement, least of all Georg Lukács, who saw in Hauptmann a writer whose naturalist style made his later flirtations with fascism inevitable. In fact, not long after the articles came out in the *Tägliche Rundschau*, *Neues Deutschland* marked what would have been Hauptmann's eighty-fourth birthday by excerpting unfavorable passages drawn from Lukács' *Deutsche Literatur im Zeitalter des Imperialismus*. Whether it no longer mattered because Hauptmann had died six months before or whether the attacks pointed to differences among the Communists themselves, or between some of them and the SMAD, is impossible to say. Regardless, according to Lukács, Hauptmann's "fate" shed light on an entire literary movement and revealed a general tendency that influenced many writers belonging to his generation. Lukács' discourse on the intrinsic inadequacies of naturalism (as well as impressionism, expressionism, and symbolism) followed.[72] The categorical rejection of Hauptmann's writing at the same time that Becher and others laid judicious claim to his legacy, then, combined with the eagerness to excuse his dalliances with national socialism to underscore the contradictions inherent in the coordination

[68]Gulitz, "Gespräch mit Hans Fallada," *Tägliche Rundschau*, 25 October 1945.
[69]Becher, "Versunkene Glocke," *Tägliche Rundschau*, 11 October 1945.
[70]"Gerhart Hauptmann und unsere Zeit," *Tägliche Rundschau*, 11 October 1945.
[71]Leuteritz, "Gespräch mit Gerhart Hauptmann," *Tägliche Rundschau*, 11 October 1945.
[72]Lukács, "Gerhart Hauptmann und der Naturalismus," *Neues Deutschland*, 16 November 1946.

of cultural-political strategy. The unkindest assessment of Hauptmann came from two other Communists, Walter Wolf and Maxim Vallentin. Both echoed Lukács' comment that Hauptmann's development was characteristic of a certain kind of German intellectual who had proven receptive to Nazi ideology.[73] Hauptmann's experience in particular was tantamount to "the declaration of bankruptcy of the vacillating—I am tempted to say morally destitute—German intellect of 1945." This plunge into Nazi barbarity contrasted with the different "historical intellectual development" of the Russian intelligentsia. Whereas Russian intellectuals overcame their waverings to maintain their ties to the working class, being won over for the cause of socialism, German bourgeois humanism culminated in the "fascist chaos of the nihilistic liquidation of humankind."[74]

There was simply no way to square that kind of vituperation with an acceptance of non-Communist writers as equals in their antifascism. It may be that some of the Communists overstepped their rhetorical bounds, but, if so, the radicals did no more than voice openly what others thought privately. Indeed, some of the party's writers emerging from fascist dungeons objected bitterly to the flirtations with non-Communist personalities. One complained to Becher in late 1945 that "Mr. Fallada is already back, Mr. Heinrich Mann . . . , Mr. Hauptmann, and all the rest, whatever the names they go by." But Becher warned against creating circumstances in which the Communists might again isolate themselves in the "venerable proletcultist fashion" so that a minuscule group of chemically pure writers would end up facing overwhelming numbers of reactionaries. Becher's principal task had been first to commit to "us" all those who had vacillated before and could again fall into enemy hands overnight, this "we" not meaning "us" in the narrowest sense of communism. In the process, those who could be unconditionally relied upon, the Communist writers, had regrettably been assigned a second level of priority. However acute the bitterness felt by some, it ought to be tempered by a degree of objectivity.[75] As for the "chance" given the non-Communists, it had always been coupled to conditions; and scarcely had that chance been granted than the terms tightened. In early 1947, Erich Weinert noted that the Communists had perhaps been too indulgent toward writers like Fallada and Hauptmann. In any case, he declared, "we are not going to obscure the boundary lines separating us from those with whom we no longer wish to be associated. Let them be thankful if nothing more happens to them than that they be granted the privilege of probation."[76]

---

[73]See Wolf, "Nationale Einheit und neue demokratische Kultur," *Deutsche Kultur und Arbeiterbewegung*, p. 30.
[74]See Vallentin, "Abweg und Ausweg der neuen deutschen Literatur," ibid., pp. 30, 50-51.
[75]Quoted from *Weimarer Beiträge* 5 (1985): 730-31, 740.
[76]Weinert, "Kulturarbeit nach der Befreiung [17 May 1947]." Quoted from *Neue Deutsche Literatur* 4 (1980): 23-24.

Food First, Then Morality

Considering the conditions attached to their probation, the intellectuals and artists were bound to violate them; indeed, sporadic discussions of what was considered irresponsible began appearing in the Soviet-zone press within a few months of the war's end. The first rebukes came in the shape of objections to small art exhibits that showed works whose formal characteristics the Communists condemned. The criticism of one exhibit in particular, in a western sector of Berlin, fit the pattern of past party polemics in disputes over art and literature at the same time that the complaint foreshadowed the crackdown of 1948 and 1949, during which artists like Picasso and Klee were bunched together as "formalists." The review of the Berlin showing published in the *Tägliche Rundschau* assailed the exhibited paintings for their "mixture of inexpressive naturalism and lifeless formalism," "crass expressionism," absence of "individuality," "distorted naturalism," and "inexpressive formalism." Just as regrettably, the works revealed not a "trace of understanding for liberated Germany's awakening from nazism to true humanity and democracy"; rather, the artists chose to pass over the problems of the day in favor of formal trumps, behind whose loud colors and senseless confusion of line hid sheer artistic incompetence. In the face of this affront, the commentary went on, "we have to demand all the more categorically from those who wish to be called artists, not bunglers, that they also express their ideas in a clear, understandable form." The critique ended by lamenting, "one should be ashamed that the likes of that is possible today."[77] Another commentary argued similarly; to judge by exhibits currently being shown, the artists had little to offer to those of their fellow citizens who were looking for a "new beginning"; the works failed to settle accounts with the past and exhibited no visible optimism with regard to the future.[78] The author of this criticism, Max Keilson, also complained that the new art resembled the same kind of "game-playing or speculation" engaged in following World War One, meaning chiefly the flowering of German expressionism, and added that the new art could not be rebuilt "beginning with the form or on the strength of hypertrophied musings; no, we can do just fine without a repeat of abstract art exhibits. We have no use for surrealism or any other kind of ism; we need an art representing life in a fashion that renders all its hidden interconnections more profoundly and in a thoroughly understandable fashion to the viewer, not less so or entirely incomprehensible."[79]

[77]—Seng. "Ausstellung junger Kunst," *Tägliche Rundschau*, 21 August 1945.
[78]Keilson, "Was gibt uns die heutige bildende Kunst?" *Deutsche Volkszeitung*, 9 August 1945.
[79]Keilson, "'Ismus' oder Kunst?" *Deutsche Volkszeitung*, 11 October 1945.

Unlike the discussions of Luther or Hauptmann, which hinted at differences of opinion between local Communists and the SMAD, these two reviews and others published in the Soviet-zone press suggest that there was a greater consensus behind the criticism of "abstract" art. When the architect Hermann Henselmann voiced his objections to all the new salons reminiscent of the years prior to 1933 (nothing new, just stagnation), a Lieutenant Kochetov from the SMAD agreed. Kochetov complained that recently exhibited art works disclosed no understanding for Germany's current predicament, a disinterested attitude that contrasted starkly with the work of Soviet artists. But it was Alexander Dymschitz who said that the basic principle of Soviet art was socialist realism, even if he added that this "method" was neither a dogma, a law of aesthetics, nor a decree.[80] From the outset, public criticism bore many of the marks of the aesthetic norms that the Communists, German and Soviet, had worked out during the last decade and a half; but for the time being, these were still restricted to an antifascist and democratic context and not linked directly to socialist realism. Socialist realism, after all, was a concept whose tenets could scarcely have been given as the answer to the question, "What should the new art be like?" as long as the party continued to stress the need for national solutions to German problems. This soon began to change, toward the end of 1946 at the latest; and in light of the growing rift between East and West, along with the onset of cultural zhdanovism within the Soviet Union the summer before, it is hard to imagine how the incorporation of socialist realism might have been prevented in the zone and by whom. The Communists tempered the harsher side of the aesthetic canon for a time as part of the process of courting the intellectuals; but considering the evolving dynamic of Soviet occupation and foreign policy, the driving force behind Communist behavior in both coalition and cultural politics, major complications seem destined to arise out of the contradictions caused by asking a question like "What should the new art be like?" when most of the answers already existed.

An early expression of such complications came in August 1945 when the Hebbel Theater staged Bertolt Brecht's *Dreigroschenoper*, though this controversy was no more the exclusive outgrowth of postwar paradoxes than any of the other early disputes. Those who were responsible for defining the party's view of aesthetics had maintained for years that Brecht's writing violated the imperatives of (socialist) realism, and these old habits of mind, which formed in the very early thirties and culminated in the notorious realism debates a few years later, resurfaced in Soviet-occupied Germany barely four months after the war's end. It is not certain whether Brecht knew of the attack upon the *Dreigroschenoper* (he was still in the United States), though he seems to have known of the play's performance in Berlin and later sent

[80]Leuteritz, "Wohin, moderne Kunst?" *Tägliche Rundschau*, 1 February 1946.

the Hebbel Theater new poems to be used in the performance.[81] At the very least, he had spotted the reappearance of perennial problems by fall 1947, having gotten hold of a book just published by Ottofritz Gaillard and Maxim Vallentin dealing with Stanislavskij.[82] The criticism of the *Dreigroschenoper* began with an article by Hans Jendretzky, who charged that it was inappropriate to stage a play that illustrated the motto "Feed them first, then talk morality" (*Erst kommt das Fressen, dann die Moral*) in front of people for whom the order of priorities needed to be reversed.[83] Jendretzky's central point clearly sprang from the party's concern with the consistency of its current message of collective guilt. But there was considerably more to it than just uneasiness over the possible effect of Brecht's slogan upon the demands for political and moral atonement. Fritz Erpenbeck, a man hopelessly antagonistic toward Brecht, joined in the discussion just one day after Jendretzky's article appeared, making it fairly certain that the attack on Brecht had been coordinated.[84] Erpenbeck pointed out that the phrase "Feed them first, then talk morality" was originally intended to express the essence of the Marxian "existence determines consciousness" and to ridicule the hypocrisy of the bourgeoisie in lecturing the hungry on the subject of morality. But this was precisely the political problem, or at least an important side to it. Erpenbeck and others in the party were apparently worried that, as he put it, "all of the plays written by our friend Bertolt Brecht, including the *Dreigroschenoper*, are generally labeled either by idiots (out of ignorance) or in reactionary quarters (out of demagogy) as 'Communist learning plays.'"[85] But, at least in a crude sense, some of Brecht's plays were just that; and his reputation may have caused important people in the party to worry in 1945 that the *Dreigroschenoper* might militate against the KPD's show of moderation toward non-Communist segments of society.

These were some of the contradictory concerns involved in this early dispute, and they resulted from the fact that the Communists were aware of the need for a new political and cultural image. The trouble was that their older reflexes had a habit of reasserting themselves at inopportune times; and

[81]See "'Dreigroschenoper'—Zeitgenuß," *Berliner Zeitung*, 21 May 1946. In conversation with the author in 1992, Wolfgang Harich claimed that Brecht was opposed to the performance and that the SMAD had been against it too.

[82]Gaillard, *Das deutsche Stanislawski-Buch*. By 1945, Vallentin was already the head of the theater division of the Weimar academy of music, and this particular booklet was presented as the result of work by Vallentin, Gaillard, and Otto Long centering around the ideas of Stanislavski and educating a new generation for a "new German stage." Referring to the ideas in the booklet as "Stanislavskijism," Brecht complained, among other things, that the arguments lacked a single example drawn from the "class struggle." See Brecht, *Arbeitsjournal* [15 September 1947 and 4 January 1948], pp. 784 and 810.

[83]Jendretzky, "Brief an den Intendanten," *Deutsche Volkszeitung*, 18 August 1945.

[84]Heinz Brandt recalled, in conversations with the author in 1985, that the attacks on Brecht were a chief topic of conversation in the upper echelons of the KPD's Berlin organization.

[85]Erpenbeck, "'Die Moral von der Geschicht,'" *Deutsche Volkszeitung*, 19 August 1945.

these controversies then suggested that the party's democratic attitudes were still a world apart from a genuine conversion. The Communists wanted to use art with a political message to mold the minds of the people; but in the case of Brecht, they were perfectly prepared to shun his kind of political art if it either interfered with the party's democratic gestures, undercut the message of collective guilt, or simply infringed upon an inviolate aesthetic canon. True, Erpenbeck couched his argument somewhat more subtly, but not enough to hide the real nature of his objections. When the play was first staged in 1930, he said, during a profound economic crisis, broad segments of the working and lower-middle class had already fallen into a lumpenproletarian existence. But this was still a far cry, Erpenbeck implied, from the debasement that resulted from twelve years of fascism. In 1930, the "ethical consciousness" of the people had simply not yet degenerated to such a degree that they might have made the "morality of the underworld" depicted by Brecht their own. Indeed, the play had a positive impact back then because people tended to shudder at the potential menace to morality shown on stage. Circumstances had changed; twelve years of moral deformation lay behind the Germans, making the effect of Brecht's play an entirely different one.[86] Other critics concurred, noting that the "*ideological and moral reeducation* of our people" was a principal means of eradicating fascism. Whereas Brecht's line about the precedence of hunger over morality spoke to the masses prior to 1933 because morality was still more or less intact, the year 1945 was different. Without a new morality, the chaos left by fascism would not be "liquidated," and it was wrong to assume that Brecht's name alone guaranteed the correctness in 1945 of what was "perhaps" acceptable in 1929 or 1933.[87] One of the producers responsible for the performance, Günther Weisenborn, responded by conceding that the meaning of the play had indeed changed; but it was appropriate to perform it as a way of reestablishing the link with Berlin's pre-Nazi theatrical life—precisely the argument rejected by the Communists out of a desire for what they called "a new democratic art." But Weisenborn was not part of the party's cultural strategy, and what mattered to him was that tens of thousands of young people had never seen the play. In his opinion, Brecht's dialectic blew up the rubble cluttering these minds; and the overall effect benefited reconstruction.[88]

This ended the controversy to the extent that it involved Brecht by name in summer 1945; indirectly the quarrel continued after its first outbreak in August 1945 and never really ceased until after his death in 1956. But had he been blackballed in the Soviet sector of Berlin as early as summer 1945? The fact that the Hebbel Theater put on the *Dreigroschenoper* was probably

---

[86]Ibid.
[87]Erxleben, "Bedeutungswandel," *Deutsche Volkszeitung*, 22 August 1945.
[88]Weisenborn, "Das Hebbel-Theater antwortet Hans Jendretzky," *Deutsche Volkszeitung*, 23 August 1945.

not coincidental; the theater was located in the Western sector of the city, and its repertory could not have been subject to the SMAD order no. 51 presumably in effect and governing the stage throughout the Soviet zone and in Soviet-occupied Berlin. True, the former capital was run by the Magistrat, which answered to the allied control council; and the Magistrat, whose own Amt für Volksbildung was in the hands of a Communist and former Soviet exile, Otto Winzer, had passed an ordinance prior to the arrival of the western allies that required the licensing of all theaters.[89] But this general oversight was not unusual; the British and the Americans also supervised repertories when they occupied their sectors on 3 July 1945.[90] In any case, it seems unlikely that Winzer could have used the Magistrat's Amt für Volksbildung to influence the choice of plays being performed in western Berlin in August 1945. How the scheduling of plays by Brecht in Soviet-occupied Berlin might have been affected, however, is hard to say. The Deutsches Theater, located in East Berlin and run by still another Soviet exile, Gustav von Wangenheim, announced plans to stage Brecht's *Galileo Galilei*,[91] but for unknown reasons never followed through with them. There was a performance on 16 May 1946 of Brecht's *Die Gewehre der Frau Carrer* and *Der Jasager*, but again in the Hebbel Theater. The *Tägliche Rundschau* and *Neues Deutschland* appear to have ignored the play; Paul Rilla, writing for the *Berliner Zeitung*, reviewed it fairly.[92]

No doubt the reemergence of hostility toward Brecht at the highest levels of the Communist party was at least partially involved here, a dislike and antagonism born of a mix of personal animosity, doctrinal objections to his experimental stage theories, and a keen awareness of the fact that Brecht had always been a controversial personality in the Soviet Union as well. But then again, in 1945 men like Tjulpanov and Dymschitz probably had a better sense of when theoretical disagreements over aesthetic issues needed to be set aside;[93] and these two figures were among the chief architects of cultural policy. They understood the importance of enhancing the credibility of the political and cultural-political processes occurring in the zone in 1945 and 1946 through the involvement of prominent artistic personalities, as opposed to scaring them away by hastily mandating socialist realism. The *Tägliche Rundschau* expressed no reservations about the performance of the *Dreigroschenoper*, for instance, going so far as to note that the Hebbel Theater had done much for the "popular orientation of antifascist art" with its pro-

[89]"Genehmigung von Theatern und Theaterunternehmungen. Verordnung des Magistrats der Stadt Berlin [11 June 1945]," *Um die Erneuerung der deutschen Kultur. Dokumente*, p. 55.
[90]See Chamberlin, *Kultur auf Trümmern*, passim.
[91]"Kunstnotizen," *Berliner Zeitung*, 13 February 1946.
[92]"Kunstnotizen" and Rilla, "Schuloper und Lehrstück," *Berliner Zeitung*, 14 and 18 May 1946.
[93]Indeed, two days before Jendretzky's article came out, the *Tägliche Rundschau* (16 August 1946) called Brecht a man whose art had torn the "mask from the mug of fascism."

ductions, among them Brecht's play.[94] For now, then, in summer 1945, open criticism of Brecht stopped. But indirect objections in the form of normative theater criticism was a different matter, the best example being the unspoken but clear contrast drawn between Brecht's writing and the plays of Julius Hay. If the criticism of Brecht smacked of orchestration, the same can be said of articles published just weeks later extolling the virtues of Hay. Calling him "maybe the most talented contemporary playwright," Erpenbeck argued that Hay's writing was not "antifascist tendentiousness" because he depicted human beings not as representatives of particular tendencies and in "artificially contrived" situations, but gave them flesh and blood. Hay's play *Damm an der Theiss*, for instance, dealt with the Hungarian liberation struggle of 1848; yet it could easily have been staged as a German contemporary play at a time in which it was urgently necessary to create a bourgeois democracy and a bloc of antifascist forces in Germany. Because Hay thought in historical terms as an artist, "fascism, its roots, its origin, its annihilation" became the axis for his entire body of work.[95]

The critics saved more specific praise for a staging of Hay's *Der Gerichtstag* in the Deutsches Theater, and they lavished it upon him in terms that also suggested criticism of Brecht. The fact that Gustav von Wangenheim was in charge of the theater makes it apparent that politics determined the choice of Lessing's *Nathan der Weise*, the first play performed in the Deutsches Theater; and they governed the selection of Hay's *Der Gerichtstag* as well. The appropriateness of *Nathan* within the context of the KPD's program of tolerance and against the backdrop of the Holocaust is obvious, but likewise, though for different reasons, the choice of *Der Gerichtstag* or *Judgment Day*. Unlike the *Dreigroschenoper*, Hay's play dealt directly with collective guilt; but also unlike Brecht, Hay used aesthetic methods acceptable to critics like Erpenbeck. *Der Gerichtstag*, wrote Hedda Zinner, portrayed historical movement, not the static conditions depicted in so-called topical plays or *Zeitstücke*, which Erpenbeck and Zinner associated with Brecht. Nor did Hay use the stage to lecture on history; rather, he was a disciple of the "realistic style of acting," whose zenith had been attained by Stanislavskij and Reinhardt, and an opponent of "every kind of formalistic, pseudo-revolutionary stage experiment." The clash of human passions on the stage as opposed to the confrontation of theoretical principles, action set in dialogue, rather than intellectualized discussions—that was true dramaturgy.[96] One additional commentary stressed the capacity of the play for confronting the Germans with their own historical inadequacies;[97] and another breathed a sigh of relief that a play daring to deal with the "problems of our existence"

[94]"Antifaschistische demokratische Kunst," *Tägliche Rundschau*, 22 September 1945.
[95]Fr. "Julius Hay," *Deutsche Volkszeitung*, 15 September 1945.
[96]Zinner, "Der Dramatiker Julius Hay," *Tägliche Rundschau*, 19 September 1945.
[97]Jung, "'Gerichtstag'—Dokument unserer Zeit," *Tägliche Rundschau*, 21 September 1945.

had found its way onto the stage.[98] But Erpenbeck issued the definitive verdict; to him the sight of "profoundly shaken" people leaving the theater was a mark of the play's effectiveness; here was a real poet at work, not a "writer of so-called topical plays." For in contrast to the likes of those, Hay's play was "historical" because it represented social connections, "our historical failure, our mistakes and weaknesses beginning in 1918, the consequences of which, gathering momentum like an avalanche, from 1933 on, perhaps for decades, swept away our individual and national happiness." *Der Gerichtstag* marked a turning point in the German tragedy that would decide whether Germany was capable of atoning for her guilt and making a new beginning.[99]

What might Brecht have done differently? The fact is that he could never have satisfied Erpenbeck's or anyone else's Lukácsian or Stalinist aesthetics; otherwise, in 1945 the *Dreigroschenoper* supplied a Marxian explanation for human behavior that was just as susceptible to a useful antifascist twist, the reversal of the priorities of food and morality notwithstanding. But these were times when psychological renditions of life under Hitler would have complicated the simplicities of the party's theory of collective guilt. The Communists were just not interested in understanding how human inadequacies made the masses easy victims of political demagogy unless those accounts dovetailed with political expedience. Food over morality did not, at least not in summer 1945. Hay's play, by contrast, reestablished the priority of collective guilt, and Erpenbeck made it clear that the audience had better draw the proper conclusions. No one had the right to act as if *Der Gerichtstag* lacked perspective, he said; anyone who did essentially insisted that he had a more developed sense of perspective than Hay. "Tell me," Erpenbeck asked, addressing the imaginary theater-going critic who had been unreceptive to Hay's message of collective guilt, "just how much perspective did you have prior to May 1945 with regard to recent events, perspective granting you the right to spot its absence in the work of a poet who wrote a play as early as 1943-44 that revealed such an astonishingly high degree of perspective that he was capable . . . of analyzing the predicament of our entire people clearly enough . . . to get a little 'too deeply' under your skin and prophetically foretelling the end of the tragedy—even as you, peerless art lover, may well have regarded a more bearable pretend-end as thinkable?"[100]

Even so, in spite of the praise lavished on *Der Gerichtstag* for its message of collective guilt, there had been private concerns about the political risks involved in being overly domineering when dealing with the subject. Wangenheim and several important German Communists held private dis-

[98]Liebig, "Zuschrift eines Lesers," *Deutsche Volkszeitung*, 22 September 1945.
[99]Erpenbeck, "Gerichtstag. Zur deutschen Uraufführung von Julius Hays Tragödie," *Deutsche Volkszeitung*, 22 September 1945.
[100]Ibid.

cussions with representatives of the "Russian office of censorship" attached to the Berlin Magistrat on 13 September 1945, following the first dress rehearsal.[101] In attendance, in addition to the Russian officers Rosanov, Levin, and Filipov, were Otto Winzer, Arthur Pieck, Ernst Erich Legal (the director of the Berlin opera house), the actor Heinrich Greif, and Elli Schmidt, Anton Ackermann's wife. Winzer was the first to voice a potential "political" or, rather, tactical concern. The most "despicable figure" in Hay's play was the SPD man Hessler; in contrast to him, "the representative of one of the four parties working together today," even the Nazi made a more positive impression. Greif, an actor who had belonged to the KPD for many years, was less concerned; he insisted that Hessler was the type who had existed in the SPD but that today's SPD was different. He felt sure that Social Democrats would not see in him an attack on the SPD. The other major problem, according to Winzer, was the Russians' concern that the play show an "honest and upright, positive German" along side "broken" figures. Following these exchanges, approval was granted to advertise the play, though the final decision on the play's performance was taken only after an additional debate on 17 September, again in the presence of the Russians, members of the Berlin Magistrat, and, according to the transcript of the discussion, "representatives of the parties." But this was hardly an accurate description of those in attendance; the only politicians there, Pieck and Oelßner, were Communists. Like Greif, Pieck worried that Social Democrats might be "irritated" by the play. Wangenheim tried to assure him that this was not the case by calling Pieck's attention to comments in it regarding the KPD's "shortcomings and mistakes." Filipov then authorized the performance, but said, "The play must show the Germans in the audience that there is a road other than the one taken by Germany up till now."

Progressive Art

Many of the considerations involved in discussions of stage performances were plainly coupled to the design of political strategy, though they also involved much more. Behind the elaborate discussions hid the gradual canonization of stage practices that had been elevated to prominence in the Soviet Union after 1935 under the mantle of socialist realism. That Stanislavskij's name cropped up everywhere as the only model worthy of emulation, combined with derogatory references to Meyerhold, also pointed to the steady encroachment of normative standards against which playwrights would be measured. What augured ill was that the Soviet exiles defined the new canon

---

[101]The following comments are drawn from the unpublished stage manuscript of *Der Gerichtstag*.

in a nonchalant fashion steeped in the mentality of Stalin's purges. Meyerhold did not die a natural death. Regardless, Wangenheim contended that the Soviet stage derived its humanism and inspiration directly from the people and that the "organized expression" of this "original populism" was what he called the "solicitude of party and government." The age of experiments had passed; "Stanislavskij's style, averse to all extremes, prevailed over the style practiced by formalists of all sizes and shapes." Various kinds of theaters, those run by different producers and exhibiting different styles, had "disappeared, replaced by a uniform theatrical frame of mind."[102] These were just some of the views working their way to the surface in Soviet-occupied Germany, many of them the patterned reflex of the many years that their spokesmen spent in Soviet exile; and all the talk about a new democratic art cannot obscure the fact that a brand of unidentified socialist realism, reflecting the theoretical basis for some of the worst practices of Stalinism, was being advocated in the Soviet zone of Germany within six months of the war's end.

Erpenbeck's comment that Stanislavskij's scenic realism "won out" on the Soviet stage vied with Wangenheim's remarks in its cynicism,[103] yet paled in comparison with essays by Julius Hay and Maxim Vallentin first published in 1938 in the USSR and reissued in Soviet-occupied Germany in late 1945. Vallentin pointed out that in 1938, "on the basis of the rejection of formalism in art by the masses of the Soviet people, certain views regarding the theater were theoretically and practically liquidated following several years of experiments and thorough discussion." Freed from various restrictions and irritations, those involved with the Soviet stage "flocked in unison around the imposing figure" of Stanislavskij even as the "formalistic currents dried up."[104] Whereas formalistic outlooks, including the urge to experiment for the sake of experimentation, had earlier forced their way to the forefront, in the long run "expressionism" did not meet with the approval of the people. "The Soviet Union ended this state of affairs; as a genuine people's state it responded to the clearly articulated will of the people and declared the rule of 'socialist realism' in art," the preeminent representative in the area of the stage being Stanislavskij.[105] Vallentin went on to say that in Germany there had been similar tendencies prior to 1933 among progressive theater people, leading to the isolation of the "modern theater" from the popular masses. But these tendencies had ended fruitlessly, and for that reason the discussion of the Soviet theater was intended now as "first aid for our antifascist theater people" in their search for a new beginning point.[106] Other

---

[102]Wangenheim, "Aus dem Werdegang des Sowjettheaters," *Deutsche Volkszeitung*, 8 November 1945.
[103]Erpenbeck, "Schrifttum in der Sowjetunion," *Deutsche Volkszeitung*, 7 November 1945.
[104]*Aus den Erfahrungen des Sowjet-Theaters*, p. 3.
[105]Quoted from the review published in the *Tägliche Rundschau*, 22 November 1945.
[106]*Aus den Erfahrungen des Sowjet-Theaters*, p. 3.

comments had much the same application to current circumstances in Soviet-occupied Germany; the more theoretical slant of Vallentin's remarks in *Aus den Erfahrungen des Sowjet-Theaters* and related articles may appear relatively harmless, for instance, in his discussion of production techniques; he merely emphasized the subordinate role of the producer. But he added that "all freedom-loving stage people" in Germany now needed to understand this particular idea as the first step in a process of curing "views still abundantly influenced by decadence"; a proper understanding of the producer's responsibility would ensure that "an array of grievous mistakes" would be impossible in the future by preventing producers from hindering the work of the actors and impressing upon them that they had also been responsible in the past for the "degeneration of dramatic art."[107] Still, Vallentin spoke too plainly when he wrote that "the renewed flowering of German theatrical culture" was thinkable only if it drew directly upon the results of the Soviet stage and upon the practices of Stanislavskij. Though this was the thrust of criticism being published in the local press, it was premature to say so quite so openly. Vallentin and Hay were rebuked in the *Tägliche Rundschau*, the chief argument used against them being that "the German stage must evolve freely in accord with its own laws"—a discernible variant of the promise that Germany would be allowed to develop in harmony with her own non-Soviet circumstances. Vallentin and Hay, by contrast, granted "validity" to socialist realism alone; this constituted an impermissible "constriction," and, though the brochure contained some worthwhile insights with respect to the Soviet stage, "its practical application to the German stage ought not to be automatically accepted."[108] Still, the brochure was republished in 1946.

Erpenbeck, on the other hand, in his articles and reviews written for the *Deutsche Volkszeitung*, managed to make many of the same prescriptive points as Vallentin, but without going too far tactically. At about the same time that he was attacking Brecht, Erpenbeck praised Carl Zuckmayer's *Der fröhliche Weinberg* because its realism contrasted with the "formalism" and the "pseudo-revolutionary experiment" that ruled the stage prior to 1933.[109] For Erpenbeck, what he called the purpose play, the *Tendenzstück*, was writing in which the ideological or political element failed to spring "*organically*" from its human and social material; the purpose play was really a "concoction with a *glued-on* slant." Such works lacked artistic merit because they put contrived figures on the stage in order to get across a direct message.[110]

---

[107]Vallentin, "Stanislawski und seine theatralische Sendung," *Tägliche Rundschau*, 30 September 1945. This article was adapted from the chapter "'Regie' und Regie," pp. 17-21, in *Aus den Erfahrungen des Sowjet-Theaters*, but was now applied to the post-war German stage.
[108]"Aus den Erfahrungen des Sowjet-Theaters," *Tägliche Rundschau*, 22 November 1945.
[109]Erpenbeck, "Ach, was hätte mer Heidelbeern . . ," *Deutsche Volkszeitung*, 24 August 1945.
[110]Erpenbeck, "Tendenzloses Theater," *Berliner Zeitung*, 20 February 1946.

These elaborations applied also to the classics. The staging of a classic in a given theater was tantamount to an expression of confidence in a certain form of "cultural politics."[111] With a play like *Hamlet*, just produced for the Deutsches Theater by Wangenheim, past stagings had often involved misconceived notions of topicality, an expression ultimately of formalism, reducing the entire question to one of "realism or formalism." Whereas *Hamlet* had a definite bearing upon current circumstances, "formalist experiments" were not the way to make that evident.[112] Wangenheim had managed to strike a balance, Erpenbeck concluded, preventing the depiction of Hamlet from "sliding into the decadent expressionism of the pre-1914 era."[113] Weisenborn's play *Die Illegalen,* by contrast, which portrayed the German underground, posed other difficulties. Content determined form, Erpenbeck began, the question being whether or not the illegal activity of a resistance group was a subject whose complexity lent itself to the art form of the drama. For various reasons, Erpenbeck concluded that it did not and that the subject matter, the content, led straight to "(undramatic) substitute forms, to formalism." Rhetoric replaced dialogue infused with human tensions; commentaries on contemporary events dominated by cabaret-like "inlays" worked in artificially to shed light on the social background. In a word, this particular content could not be adapted to the dramatic form; if an author chose it regardless, a "learning play," a *Lehrstück*, would result.[114] Whether other factors entered into Erpenbeck's criticism of Weisenborn's play, perhaps the feeling that a piece dealing with collective guilt, like Hay's, was more important than accounts of the German underground (one, moreover, in which Communists did not necessarily predominate), is hard to say. But there is no doubt about the nature of Erpenbeck's dramaturgical index—it hued to the tenets of socialist realism developed over the past several years. In many respects, things ultimately came down to the injunction that true stage criticism, as Erpenbeck understood it, meant "the rejection of a reactionary or irrelevant work even when it is presented with consummate artistry; and it means furthering a progressive play even if weaknesses show up in its artistic structure."[115]

Erpenbeck punctuated his other reviews with points highly charged with political implications that shed further light on early attitudes in Soviet-occupied Germany and make it easier to see how these paved the way for later constrictions. "We ought not to fall back into the same mistakes that we recognized or perceived as errors prior to 1933," he said; the cultural-political

111Erpenbeck, "Zeitnaher Hamlet," *Deutsche Volkszeitung*, 14 December 1945.
112Incidentally, one critic in West Berlin accused the performance of having a distinct "land-reform slant." See "Jugend kämpft um ihren Dichter," *Berliner Zeitung*, 16 April 1946.
113Erpenbeck, "Zeitnaher Hamlet," *Deutsche Volkszeitung*, 14 December 1945.
114Erpenbeck, "'Die Illegalen.'" *Deutsche Volkszeitung*, 4 March 1946.
115"Kunst und Kritik. Auftakt zur Thüringer Theaterschau," *Neues Deutschland*, 12 May 1946.

imperative of the day should be that "all progressive-thinking artists arrive at a meeting of the minds . . . at the very least with respect to that which is *not* progressive in art"—"not progressive," Erpenbeck concluded, being a "synonym for the nonartistic" or leading in that direction.[116]

One practical application of such theatrical-political sentiments worth mentioning in conclusion was a decree passed in May 1946 by the Saxon state administration. It governed "approval procedures for theaters and related undertakings" designed to end the activities both of "*unscrupulous jobbers*" who exploited the population with "performances of hopelessly low quality" and to get a handle on the rest of the "third-rate enterprises." The decree was accompanied by the paradoxical comment that the "problems of the stage" could not be solved by "administrative measures" but that its "organic development" had to be guaranteed; "unqualified and shady elements must be eradicated," the commentary read, and it went on to demand the exclusive use of "*people anxious to rebuild* in the sense of a democratic view of the state" in putting together stage ensembles. In the future, anything "politically or artistically questionable" had to "disappear from the boards of our stages"; those shameless enough to show up in public with "performances that are foolish and untimely" in essence continued the act of destruction engaged in by the Nazis and forfeited the right to participate in cultural reconstruction. The commentary closed by denying that it was "our intention to patronize art"; but limitations had to be imposed upon "arbitrariness" if the German stage was to become "the popularly backed educator of society in its entirety."[117] The implied threat and the potential for exploiting art to serve the immediate needs of a single party comes across clearly in these comments. Indeed, given the growing deterioration in East-West relations and in view of the increasing ideological and political rigidity of the German Communists by summer 1946, the following remark appears especially menacing: "Never again must the misuse of free art be allowed for the propagation of militaristic and imperialist tendencies. Here, too, the resolute cultural will of the German working class will keep a watchful vigil. If anywhere cultural institutions should emerge that either fail to recognize or consciously contravene this task, they shall forfeit their right to exist."[118]

116Erpenbeck, "'Macbeth' im Hebbel-Theater," *Deutsche Volkszeitung*, 5 October 1945.
117Gress, "Gegen das Geschäft mit der Kunst. Zur neuen Theaterverordnung der Landesverwaltung Sachsen," *Tägliche Rundschau*, 26 May 1946.
118Leuteritz, "Die Kunst und das werktätige Volk," *Tägliche Rundschau*, 28 November 1945.

CHAPTER FIVE

The Origins of Socialist Realism

In spring 1946, Anton Ackermann lectured for the last time on the subject of the mistakes made by the old KPD. He called the party's failure to discern the possibility of different transitions to socialism inherent in the Marxist-Leninist "theory of the state" its cardinal error and charged that the Communists came by their reputation as "anti-democrats," "advocates of a dictatorship of the minority," because of the party's overemphasis upon a "direct" route instead. Ackermann even acknowledged that they had often behaved like "enemies of democracy," whereas the Communists were actually the "most consistent democrats"; and it would be a grievous mistake now, one that risked "shipwreck," if the party applied "schematically" each and every one of the sentences uttered by Lenin and Stalin in response to the particularities of their country to the entirely different situation in Germany. But Ackermann punctuated his remarks with other comments that coupled his democratic gestures to older ideological presuppositions. He noted first that the "spiritual legacy of Marx and Engels shall always be sacred to us," but added that the party also needed to appropriate the teachings of the "great Marxist leaders and theoreticians of our epoch in order to apply this teaching to our own special circumstances, using our own reasoning and our own judgment." In this sense, the doctrines of Lenin and Stalin, as "living Marxism," were valid in all countries. Though the German Communists believed "fervently in the fundamental works of the theoretical leaders of our epoch, the works of Lenin and Stalin," misconstruing from this attitude anything akin to a dependency upon Soviet politics was absurd.[1]

Ackermann's emphasis on the party's national commitment was clearly intended to deflect attention away from the SED's underlying ideological allegiances. *"How does the Marxist stand on the question of the nation,"* was his formulation of the one issue; *"the Marxist party is the party of all segments of working people"* was his commitment to the other. These utterances then led to Ackermann's conclusion: "As Germans, we are *one* people, *one* nation, and for that reason we reject federalism." Through the party's commitment to the national interest, barriers had fallen that kept broad segments

[1]Ackermann, "Der ideologische Kampf der Partei," *Bericht über die Verhandlungen des 15. Parteitages der KPD* [19-21 April 1946], pp. 101-10 and 115-16.

of the people from joining the socialist movement in the past. Nor was there any contradiction between "patriotism" and the idea of "proletarian internationalism"; the party's national struggle against reaction and imperialism, Ackermann said, was proletarian internationalism in action. Still, his assertions all relied upon one of the party's frankest definitions yet of "consequent" Marxism; "without the teachings of Marx and Engels, Lenin and Stalin, we would stumble in darkness"; only by appropriating the entire richness of Marxist theory was there any possibility of recognizing "the present accurately, looking toward the future with foresight, designing our politics, propaganda, and agitation correctly, winning the masses, and leading the people to victory over all their enemies."[2]

Though the references to Lenin and Stalin had not previously dominated public discussions, with the merger certain, hesitation about mentioning the two names in connection with "consistent Marxism" lessened until the elections in fall 1946 served as a reminder of the continuing importance of political discretion over ideological acknowledgments. But in February 1946, at the party's cultural conference, Ackermann had already insisted that the "liquidation" of Nazism required a "tenacious *ideological struggle*" involving more than an obliteration of the spirit of Nazism; "a different spirit, a different ideology must inhabit the minds of the people," said Ackermann, concluding that no ideology was as contrary to Nazism as "scientific socialism"—the teachings of Marx, Engels, Lenin, and Stalin.[3] The SED's doctrinal presuppositions were growing clearer well before creation of the party in April; and it was a sign of the changing times that Ackermann adapted his remarks from the *Short Course* history of the Soviet Communist party.[4] Worse, the "short biography" of Stalin first published in 1939 in Moscow rolled off the presses in 1946 and took the deduction that Leninism was the Marxism of today a step further: "Stalin—he is the Lenin of today."[5] Portraying these assumptions as the ultimate guarantee of democracy and "no sovietization" now produced rhetorical inconsistencies at a prodigious rate. The merger of SPD and KPD made it "*the major force in politics, economics, and the cultural life of this part of Germany*"; as the "*leading state party*," the SED bore full responsibility for both the people's well-being and "*for the entire democratic reconstruction of the country*."[6]

---

[2]Ibid., pp. 100, 108, 111-12, 117.
[3]Ackermann, "Schlußwort," *Erste Zentrale Kulturtagung der KPD*, pp. 155-56.
[4]Compare his comments with the remarks in *Geschichte der Kommunistischen Partei der Sowjetunion*, pp. 427-39, especially p. 429.
[5]Stalin, *Kurze Lebensbeschreibung*, p. 71.
[6]Ulbricht, "Worum geht es bei den Berliner Gemeindewahen," *Neuer Weg* (1946): 4; and Dahlem, "Die Organisationspolitik der Partei," *Bericht über die Verhandlungen vom 15. Parteitag der KPD*, pp. 64-71.

Antibolshevism

A similar pattern developed in cultural-political affairs in the sense that the Communists set out to acquire control over cultural processes in Soviet-occupied Germany while praising their own efforts as democratic and antifascist objectives suitable for the rest of the country. In fact, using ideas derived from Soviet-zone cultural policies to proselytize in the West may actually have appeared more promising than prospects for popularizing the SED itself in the Western zones. Even then, however, due to the impending crackdown on Soviet culture and the eventual introduction of socialist realism throughout Eastern Europe, the notion was probably as illusory in the forties and fifties as the hope of polishing the image of the SED in West Germany had ever been. But at the time, it must have seemed like an idea with some likelihood of success; besides, trying to use cultural issues to influence public opinion in the Western zones risked little anyway. As one commentary put it, the failure to reach an agreement on German economic and political unity at the Paris foreign ministers' conference in summer 1946 and the fact that the Germans had been denied any real say in these affairs did not eliminate certain other ways, like cultural affairs, of influencing things nationwide.[7] This statement hinted at the realization that the opportunities to alter the course of events in the Western zones might be confined to the sphere of cultural politics. Even as the SED tightened its grip on Soviet-zone cultural life and further narrowed its definitions of "democratic" art, then, the party apparently convinced itself that the much-publicized program of democratic and antifascist cultural renewal had a chance to inspire influential intellectuals in the other zones. If the idea worked, the SED's cultural politics could conceivably help popularize in the Western regions of the country cultural initiatives linked to a specific political orientation and play more than a negligible role in making "popular democracy" appealing to West German public opinion.

But the paradox remained that arguments designed to depict the zone as a political and cultural-political model for all of Germany coincided with the general process of rigidification responsible for widening the gap between the zones. The toughening posture in cultural affairs associated with this overall hardening took a variety of shapes in late 1946, and Johannes R. Becher's reversion to old rhetoric was one of them. These inflections reestablished the preeminence of a Marxist-Leninist party and went much further in extolling the virtues of the Soviet Union when, in fall 1946, Becher's earlier avoidance of pure doctrine yielded to an openly ideological stance. His

[7] "Kulturaustausch—Kultureinheit," *Sonntag*, 28 July 1946.

proposals for the renewal of German culture drafted originally in Moscow in 1944 and early 1945, the ones that he had first edited for use in the zone by eliminating all references to the Communist "new type of party," were now recast to include a candid espousal of Marxism and an open endorsement of a Communist party. Becher's point of departure was the same as before—his emphasis upon the existence of "objective" or "historical" truth, which he established by combining collective guilt with the plea for a radical revision of German culture capable of reaffirming "objective standards and values."[8] But after repeating more phrases taken from his earliest post-war speeches and essays, Becher began to expand the ideological content of his arguments by modifying an unattributed quotation by Engels. Freedom, he said, entailed "recognized necessity" and could be attained only in harmony with the "historical requirements" of the times (64-67). Becher then followed up his allusions to Engels with a motif from Lenin, left unattributed, when he concluded that "the truth must become power; it must evolve into a material force" (123).

The "material force" was the party, and within the context of Becher's arguments there was little to prevent him from inquiring now about an "intellectual authority" qualified to establish the proper order of things, raising the issue of Marxism as objective truth, and exploring the organizational implications of it all. Having arranged the first part of the argument, Becher proceeded to define Marxism as the very antithesis of fascism and determined from there that a "genuine Marxist party" was anything but one among many others (*eine Partei unter Parteien*); it was "a new type of political organization" (124). Moreover, because the Communists had always viewed fascism itself as a manifestation of historical laws, it was easy for him to make the additional point that Marxism was the crowning of all "objective systems of thought" and, through the incarnation of historical truth in a single political party, the natural target of fascism (cf. 124-28). Returning to the kind of claims that he had first made in the old 1944-45 draft proposals, Becher then repeated many of his assumptions—such a party eliminated the dualism between insight and conduct, intellect and action, world view and world change because a Marxist party was "both a cognitive organ of objective truth and an executive organ of the historical necessities arising from this objective determination of truth" (64-67, 124-25). Becher's logic led him straight to serious warnings about a resurgence of antibolshevism because Germany's "national act of liberation and reconstruction in the ideological-moral sphere" required that the nation rid itself of anti-Soviet obsessions and replace them with a "new, realistic perception based on reason and truth." Doing so, he said, actually constituted an act of German nationalism; and in a related vein, Becher characterized the war against Russia as "Ger-

[8]Becher, *Erziehung zur Freiheit*, pp. 11-19, 54-55. All further citations are provided in the text.

many's war against Germany." In particular, he described an "unparalleled intellectual process of degeneration" that had robbed individuals of their last vestiges of reason and "thrust the German people in their entirety into a psychotic condition (131-32)." Finally, he talked about the "degree of imbecility in the ruling circles and the intelligentsia" generated by a "panicky fear of a new inner order" in Germany (131).

But the "panicky fear" that Becher made light of was, by 1946, the dread of dictatorship prompted by a shifting combination of fresh memories of the fascist past and more than a vague premonition of what a Stalinist future entailed. Not that Becher now favored patterning the new Germany after the Soviet system; the promise of a German road to socialism lingered for a few more years. But many of his statements narrowed the remaining gap between notions of a new democratic Germany and Soviet democracy. He argued that Russia's victory over Hitler's Germany testified to the "unbroken power" of the Soviet Union, unbroken in a national sense as the logical consequence of its "indivisible national unity" brought about by the policies of Lenin and Stalin (137-38).The lesson was obvious; but for now, Becher noted only that Germany required both national unity and a "genuine Marxist party" if it wished to prevent the reemergence of those forces responsible for fascism. Otherwise, he confined himself to extolling the existence in the USSR of something akin to a moral-political unity that served as the implied model of a German national consensus. Because of the "liquidation of class rule and the absence of class contradictions," he explained, the Soviet Union constituted an indivisible social unity. This "unity" was embodied in each individual Soviet man, as a result of which "fatherland" became a synonym for personal and national destiny—the destiny of all mankind. "A people in whose spirit such an identity, such a Trinity prevails," was immortal and unvanquishable (137). Becher maintained accordingly that Germany's spiritual renewal could not occur entirely from within her own cultural tradition, but needed to benefit from the "intellectual and cultural accomplishments of other peoples," giving a "certain precedence" to the Soviet Union. It was perfectly clear that Germans had the best of national reasons for reordering their relationship to the Soviet Union; and such a "reordering" had to receive top priority in a "German movement of renewal such as the Kulturbund."[9]

Western "Democracy" vs. Eastern "Dictatorship"

Becher's appeals were only marginally successful. Many of the intellectuals balked outrightly at political involvement or, at least, at involvement with

[9]Becher, "Das Reformationswerk deutscher Erneuerung," *Demokratische Erneuerung* 6 (1946): 5-8.

such limited possibilities for influencing the nature of the arrangement; and in summer 1946, the party reacted by hurling recriminations. These ranged from the general charge of apoliticality to that of irresponsible disinterest in forging a new German democracy. Such nonchalance, the critics charged, betrayed the lingering effects of fascism and verged on antisovietism. One of the attacks faulted the intellectuals for seeking to preserve the comfort and convenience of their own "splendid isolation" even while disparaging colleagues who were determined to rebuild; and this "escape into irresponsibility" made sense only as the consequence of profound ignorance with respect to the importance of politics.[10] Other commentary echoed these remarks, railing at intellectuals for shying away from any kind of political power, be it "of God or the devil," only to surrender to it the moment the power of politics deceived them into believing that it guaranteed them "success and pleasure." This allusion to the acquiescence of intellectuals while Hitler was in power then led to the next disparagement. Nowadays, one constantly encountered artists and writers "who distance themselves from politics and pretend that they are concerned with art alone," claiming first that politics were incompatible with a life devoted to art and then withdrawing into their ivory tower with denunciations of what this particular commentary said "ought to constitute politics" in the first place: personal involvement in and responsibility for shared goals and objectives.[11]

Of course, the crux of the matter was that politics in Soviet-occupied Germany partook of far more than "shared goals and objectives," unless one interprets this benign phrase to mean the voluntary endorsement of those pursued by a single party. The SED required compliance because it needed intellectually and culturally influential subordinates, willing ones if at all possible; and when too many intellectuals responded reluctantly, the Communists reacted with vituperation. Political apathy supposedly fit two categories of "intellectual betrayal"; the first was committed when the intellectuals acquiesced during the Third Reich, the second in their refusal to engage in politics now.[12] Neither offense was trivial by 1946, whereas actually linking past "acquiescence" under Hitler to present misgivings about the future of Soviet-occupied Germany amounted to a denunciation of the intellectuals for moral-political delinquency. The criticism grew increasingly strident as the elections approached in fall 1946. Any German who refused to "pitch in and help the German people create a new economic, political, and moral existence following the bankruptcy of the Hitler system *betrays his own people*"—exactly what many German intellectuals were doing.[13] This particular attack, one of a pair published in the *Tägliche Rundschau* under the pseudo-

[10]"Vom unpolitischen Menschen," *Sonntag*, 7 July 1946.
[11]Theunissen, "Der deutsche Intellektuelle und die Politik," *Die Weltbühne* 2 (1946): 42 and 44.
[12]Ibid.
[13]Walden, "Deutscher Geist 1946," *Tägliche Rundschau*, 18 August 1946.

nym "Walden," charged intellectuals who fired back at their critics with accusations of "intolerance" and an "undemocratic outlook" with dredging up the idea of the "Western cultural heritage."[14] Walden's use of this phrase criminalized opposition to Soviet-zone politics as a residual expression of fascism by establishing a connection between guilt incurred by way of passive consent during the Hitler years and political apprehension now. The problem was that fear of an importation of Soviet culture remained widespread; the more stubborn these fears, the more frequent the party's countercharge that hesitant intellectuals followed in the footsteps of Hitler and Goebbels, focusing upon the need to defend Western culture and using it as a pretext for attacking the Soviet Union. Indeed, nowadays "powerful, internationally allied forces of reaction"—Churchill's name surfaced—disseminated the same slogan. Walden continued in the same vein:

> For twelve years Hitler sought to use all the means of a diabolical rhetoric to persuade the world that an unbridgeable chasm existed between "West and East," an abyss that never existed in reality. For twelve years he called for a "crusade against Moscow." For twelve years many German intellectuals backed him in his efforts until he began his marauding expedition to the East, in the course of which all human values accumulated over three millennia of occidental culture were tossed overboard as waste . . . in the name of the "occidental culture of the German nation." *And now something shocking and grotesque is happening.* No sooner have the German people escaped the total annihilation intended for them by a doomed Hitler . . . , scarcely have the Germans again lifted their heads above the waters of a deluge that they brought upon themselves by allowing Hitler to demolish every protective barrier, *than a segment of the intellectuals come out and begin initial preparations for a new deluge, apparently again willing to commit the same mistakes that produced Germany's last misfortune.*

These were grievous accusations; but the diction suggested that opposition to the policies of the SED was at issue, not a willingness "to commit the same mistakes that produced Germany's last misfortune." Most of the intellectuals, Walden explained, contented themselves with a refusal to participate in the "practical tasks of real democracy and thus in the actual task of reconstruction itself, doing so in the name of 'true democracy' and concocting an entirely fictitious contradiction between Western 'democracy' and Eastern 'dictatorship.'" Whether such intellectuals were conscious of the import of their actions was immaterial, though it was true that "conscious saboteurs" were more easily dealt with than this kind of saboteur. Even so, the

[14]Ibid.

boundary of tolerance needed to be drawn here, for some people who had just "tolerated" Hitler's barbaric intolerance now responded to developments in Soviet-occupied Germany by asking, "Is that tolerance?" The real "occidental legacy" worthy of protection was the one extending from Athenian democracy by way of the French revolution to modern Soviet democracy. This was the heritage of the Occident attacked and defiled by Hitler. "Let us hope that, in the future, the German intellectuals will no longer stand in the *enemy* camp . . . , but defend these bastions standing shoulder to shoulder with working people."[15] The plain fact, said Walden in the other of his two commentaries, was that white-collar workers, writers, artists, teachers, scientists, doctors, engineers, and technicians failed to acknowledge the dimensions of Germany's national bankruptcy. Instead, the majority of the intellectuals had recently given dramatic evidence of "*le trahison des clercs*," shirking their responsibility and disclosing the "devastating moral results of the retreat of the intellect from the realm of politics." Therein lay the guilt of the intellectuals; but whether they possessed any awareness of it and were prepared to draw the consequences from earlier errors was "still *doubtful* today."[16] The party, too, came in for some criticism. Pleading for formation of a "new intelligentsia," an article in the *Tägliche Rundschau* pointed out that this task tied in directly with the democratic transformation of Germany's social structure;[17] and learning from the past meant that the Communists also needed "to learn from our own mistakes and weaknesses." To be equal to the tasks confronting it, the Socialist Unity party had to become an organization for all working people; "the scholar and the artist must feel just as at home in the SED as the industrial worker; the former have to be able to say with the same self-evident pride as the latter that the SED is my party."[18]

Nonpartisanship vs. Aimlessness

The effort made in fall 1946 to persuade the intellectuals to draw that conclusion coincided with the elections, and the necessity of running a hard-hitting campaign generally caused the party to succumb to the temptation of disparaging its rivals in language that further damaged its reputation. The pattern repeated itself when the SED persisted in reviling the intellectuals as part of the attempt to win their support and benefit from it electorally. The more the party derided the intellectuals, assailing them for passivity in the face of fascism, sluggish indifference to democracy now, and for "again" in-

---

[15]Ibid.
[16]Walden. "Wo stehen die deutschen Intellektuellen?" *Tägliche Rundschau*, 16 August 1946.
[17]Meusel, "Deutschlands neue Intelligenz," *Tägliche Rundschau*, 8 September 1946.
[18]Meusel, "Der deutsche Intellektuelle und die Arbeiterbewegung," *Tägliche Rundschau*, 17 October 1946.

dulging in fascistic manifestations of antibolshevism, the deeper the misgivings about the KPD-SED. When Walden insisted that the intellectuals atone for their guilt by altering their behavior,[19] which meant endorsing policies advocated by the SED, he and others like him never took account of the fact that the party had not satisfied the concerns of the very intellectuals who remained impervious to party lectures on the subject of political morality now. These same intellectuals were nonetheless expected to accept the proposition that real democratic cooperation denoted individual willingness to "accede to a larger collective by placing one's personal talents and energies at the disposal of the whole." In any case, the argument continued, the outcome of the elections would demonstrate the extent to which the "creative workers" had recognized the sign of the times by making a clear choice in favor of peace and for the German people; for only by "accompanying the masses of working people along the road to democracy" could the perennial rift between the masses and the intellectuals be closed.[20]

The intellectuals were thus given to understand that a vote in favor of the SED was expected of them; and the party looked for every opportunity to influence their thinking. The leadership of the Kulturbund took it for granted that it had a role to play, but, as an organization that claimed to favor no single party, involving itself in the campaign risked creating a rift within the organization. Indeed, the Kulturbund's first attempt to help determine the outcome of a vote, the plebiscite in Saxony on 30 June 1946 regarding the confiscation of property owned by war criminals,[21] turned out poorly. In this particular instance, there had been considerable concern that the SMAD and the SED intended to use the expropriation of Nazis guilty of war crimes, a measure to which none of the three Soviet-zone parties objected, as a pretext to camouflage "a general alteration of the socio-economic structure," even if the introduction of "revolutionary changes" in one part of Germany widened the rift between it and the other zones.[22] Because everyone knew that the idea of a plebiscite originated within the SED, the Kulturbund's involvement in popularizing the law amounted to its backing of the party. When the organization went to work in Saxony, it discovered that a "portion of the creative intelligentsia and the artists" were unenthusiastic, seeing in the measure the first step toward the nationalization of the entire private sector and eventual socialism.[23]

[19]Walden. "Die grosse Kluft," *Tägliche Rundschau*, 1 September 1946.
[20]Ibid.
[21]See Staritz, *Die Gründung der DDR*, pp. 108-12. See also the discussions within the coalition in June in Suckut, *Blockpolitik in der SBZ/DDR*, pp. 144-54.
[22]See "[Die CDU zum Volksentscheid in Sachsen. Beschluß des Hauptvorstandes vom 5. Juni 1946]," ibid., p. 145.
[23]According to an internal Kulturbund report mentioned by Schulmeister, *Auf dem Wege zu einer neuen Kultur*, p. 116 (and generally pp. 113-19).

There was apparently just as much debate about the Kulturbund's involvement in the communal and provincial elections. Whereas the plebiscite had not involved direct competition between the three parties, the fall elections pitted the SED against the CDU and the LDP. The possibilities for a rupture within the Kulturbund were rife because election campaigning generated friction between members who belonged to different parties. But it was evidently felt that the Kulturbund's Communist leadership should nonetheless not sit idly by, and disagreements on election tactics then developed immediately. As early as July 1946, the Kulturbund's executive board called a meeting of state-level local chairmen and top administrative personnel to discuss the question of nominating the organization's own candidates. That conference ended with a decision to refrain from running any for two reasons. First, there was a fear that many of the organization's members would pass over Kulturbund candidates in favor of their own party's nominees, in which case the resulting low vote would represent the Kulturbund's actual strength; and second, nominating its own representatives or favoring those of "certain parties" would threaten disintegration once the slate of Kulturbund candidates got elected to the local parliaments and were forced individually to side with one or the other party. In addition, there was evidently some doubt as to whether the election regulations even permitted such participation.[24] More discussion of these issues followed when the Kulturbund leadership met again on 30 July. At that meeting, J. R. Becher informed those in attendance that, other considerations aside, the Kulturbund had the legal right to participate in the election.[25]

Just a few days earlier, a private meeting had taken place between members of the SED's state-level organizations who ran their respective cultural divisions, Anton Ackermann from the party's central secretariat, and Kulturbund representatives who held important positions "centrally and also regionally." Twenty-two persons attended, without exception "comrades," and they talked mostly about the Kulturbund's involvement in the upcoming campaign. Befitting his position, Ackermann dominated the meeting and expressed his authoritative views on the subject of the Kulturbund's participation. He stressed the SED's determination to campaign, as he put it, against fascism and reaction, not against the other parties; but he voiced his expectation that the other parties would nonetheless attempt to win the "race" themselves and in this context suggested that the Kulturbund plan for certain activities. True, he argued that the organization was committed to nonpartisanship and, for that reason, had no intention of putting the names of its own members on the ballot.[26] But Ackermann's sense of the Kulturbund's non-

---

[24]Those conclusions were passed along to the state-level Kulturbund boards in a letter dated 9 July 1946, quoted in ibid., pp. 120-21.

[25]Ibid., p. 122.

[26]Protokoll über die am 26. 7. 46 abgehaltene Besprechung über Kulturfragen mit Vertretern des

partisanship failed to prevent him from speaking on its behalf now and, it seems, announcing a decision made for it by the party leadership. He would be content, he suggested, if the Kulturbund merely contributed to a large voter turnout; and added that the organization ought to work toward stimulating discussions generally with a strong emphasis on Germany's cultural renewal. Ackermann considered it particularly important, then, that the Kulturbund place cultural issues in the forefront of public attention and added that the organization could sponsor a variety of open meetings. He concluded that the Kulturbund should then pick those representatives to speak on its behalf who were "members of the SED"; and the discussion that followed brought general agreement from Kulturbund representatives in attendance with the notable exception of Becher.

Becher was either less enamored of the general principle of party members pretending that they were Kulturbund officials, more impressed with the importance of tactics, or simply preferred to devise the organization's strategy with less heavy-handed interference from Ackermann. The Kulturbund must not allow itself to become an organization of the SED, he said, by which he probably meant the capacity of politicians like Ackermann to meddle in its affairs, rather than substantive independence; the SED, he complained, had not always demonstrated "sufficient understanding for the Kulturbund"; and he added that it would be difficult to have the organization's representatives speak on behalf of the SED in the party's own election assemblies. According to the records of the meeting, Ackermann had actually suggested something quite different—SED members masquerading as Kulturbund representatives addressing audiences at Kulturbund gatherings. That was bad enough; but either way, the fact that this conspiratorial meeting took place at all says everything about the organization's nonpartisanship; and Ackermann's final remarks left even less to the imagination. The upcoming elections were critically important, he concluded, and the Kulturbund would surely find a "tactful way" of making its services available. "By treating important cultural issues at the center of public presentations, the Kulturbund's speaker at any given event would have the chance of referring to the goals and plans of the SED." In any case, Ackermann concluded, the result had to be success; "we know our job, our responsibility; we must and we shall prevail!"[27]

What followed this meeting was confusion. According to a report delivered by a Kulturbund official by the name of Kleinschmidt, he had been scheduled to address a group of intellectuals attending a Kulturbund rally and arrived to find the hall decorated with the SED's campaign slogans. The

Kulturbundes zur demokratischen Erneuerung Deutschlands, im Sitzungssaal der SED. Zentrales Parteiarchiv, IV 2/906/4/12.
[27]Ibid., IV 2/906/4/13.

Kulturbund's reputation as a nonpartisan organization, he said, had been "rather compromised." Worse, during the discussion that followed Kleinschmidt's talk, some party secretary in attendance chose to thank him for his remarks by indicating that, as everyone could plainly see, these comments characterized the SED. The man then enjoined the members of the audience to vote appropriately—for the party. Such instances of "tactlessness" complicated the work of the Kulturbund tremendously, said Kleinschmidt.[28] In any case, the general consensus had not changed prior to the elections; the Kulturbund should refrain from nominating candidates and content itself with a manifesto. At what appears to have been yet another gathering, this time of the Kulturbund presidium, the issue was nonetheless debated again. Some of those attending flatly rejected the idea of direct participation, whereas others—possibly those unfamiliar with the party position or even unaware that the SED was one—favored it; but a "unanimous resolution" then opted not to nominate candidates. As for the manifesto, it called upon all Germans to vote, reaffirmed the Kulturbund's commitment to Germany's intellectual renewal and to a unified Germany, and ended with a condemnation of "any attempt, under this or that pretext, to tear Germany apart." Members and friends of the organization were enjoined to cast their vote for "those men and women who offered the guarantee through their consistently democratic posture that they represent the goals" of the Kulturbund.[29] Similar manifestos appeared at the local level; one published by the Brandenburg branch explained that the Kulturbund had the right to come out with its own list of candidates, but voluntarily deferred because "members and supporters of all antifascist parties are working for the implementation of a progressive democratic cultural policy." Even so, the local population was encouraged to vote for men and women "who do more than pay lip service to democracy."[30]

Statements favoring candidates who were "consistent" antifascists and democrats were, of course, implicit endorsements of one party. Other calls to vote varied the same phrases, but were even less hesitant. Some were addressed to the general population: "all Germans with a sense of responsibility, who love our people and aspire to a happy future, must vote for those on 15 September who fought most resolutely for democratic land reform"; moreover, the voters needed to be aware of the urgent need to reestablish national unity, for both economic and political as well as cultural reasons, and to be mindful that "enemies of the people" willing to dismember the nation often "cloak themselves as me-too democrats." It was imperative that re-

[28]Stenographische Niederschrift über die SED-Kulturkonferenz am 28. / 29. Januar 1947, ibid., IV 2/906/59/71.
[29]"Der Kulturbund zur demokratischen Erneuerung Deutschlands anläßlich der bevorstehenden Wahl," *Neues Deutschland*, 1 August 1946.
[30]"Der Kulturbund und die Wahlen," *Die Aussprache* 2 (1946): 7-8.

sponsible Germans cast their vote for those who "consistently reject separatist and federalist projects and fight resolutely for the unity and indivisibility of Germany."[31] Prominent intellectuals also lent their voice to the campaign. Theodor Plievier, whose flight to the West was now only a year away, endorsed the election of those persons to local parliaments who guaranteed Germany's spiritual rebirth and demonstrated through their actions that they possessed the will to reconstruction.[32] The official reaction to the first round of communal elections, even if the outcome was styled a "triumph of democracy,"[33] indicates that the Kulturbund's campaigning made virtually no difference. In Western Germany, read one editorial, there were still forces and in the East "elements" working hard to block the road to a brighter future. In particular, part of the "garnished hood" of reaction was the "coat died in the colors of 'democracy,'" and such reactionaries made use of slogans that sounded democratic to hit at real democracy. In so doing, they took over the "favorite shibboleth of certain anti-Soviet circles, the famous 'iron curtain,' and lied systematically about the Soviet zone and the Soviet Union."[34]

As for the Kulturbund's electioneering, it turned out that some local chapters had run candidates anyway,[35] though it is unclear whether this had ever had the approval of the Berlin executive. In Jena, the local branch nominated candidates, notified Berlin, and settled upon twenty-two names, among them members of the SED, LDPD, and some unaffiliated. But the Kulturbund list received a disappointing 952 votes and a solitary seat on the city council.[36] In Leipzig, nineteen persons belonging to the Kulturbund ran, a total of two were elected as city councilmen.[37] Apparently, the Kulturbund's involvement in the elections in Jena and Leipzig had in fact been backed by the local Soviet commanding officers, the executive boards of the SED, and the Kulturbund directorate in Berlin. But the showing turned out to be so dismal that Becher and Klaus Gysi traveled to Dresden in late September to discuss the Kulturbund's nomination of candidates for the provincial elections on 20 October. There the decision was taken to nominate twenty-two Kulturbund candidates, eleven of whom belonged to the SED, the LDP, and the CDU; the other half was unaffiliated. This "nonpartisan" Kulturbund list, as it was called, was then accepted by the three-party coalition over the objections of local CDU and LDP headquarters as well as individual Kulturbund groups, who still had trouble reconciling direct campaigning

[31]"Zu den Wahlen am 15. September," *Demokratische Erneuerung* 5 (1946): 3-4.
[32]Plievier, "Die Tat entscheidet," *Neues Deutschland*, 7 September 1946.
[33]See Walden, "Schatten der Vergangenheit," *Tägliche Rundschau*, 8 September 1946.
[34]Ibid.
[35]See Schulmeister, *Auf dem Wege zu einer neuen Kultur*, p. 126.
[36]Ibid., p. 127.
[37]The "mass organizations," in Leipzig the Kulturbund and the women's committees, together received 2.5% of the vote. See *Parteiensystem zwischen Demokratie und Volksdemokratie*, p. 560.

with the organization's unaligned status. Speaking for the LDP, one critic noted that the Kulturbund could not yet claim to be constructed "from the ground up on a democratic foundation," an obvious allusion to the preponderance of SED members in leading positions; and he added that, if at all, only the politically unaffiliated ought to run. Otherwise, the LDP would expect that Kulturbund members belonging to their own party be nominated also and on the basis of absolute parity. In any case, the Kulturbund presidium backed the decision to run candidates in Saxony, even though it meant a break with the previous decision not to do so during the communal elections, a decision that that body had been unable to enforce.[38]

More controversy erupted at the local level in response to that decision. Kulturbund chapters in small localities canceled meetings because they opposed participation, and at a county conference in Zittau-Löbau the parties, including the SED, rejected participation altogether. In other towns, the dissemination of Kulturbund posters and leaflets was obstructed, and in Bad Schandau both the organization's board and the city mayor refused to participate. The locals then canceled a meeting scheduled for 18 October by the state board and informed the higher-ups that "we will not pick up the election materials intended for our chapter" and that "this decision is not going to be changed by more telegrams."[39] Throughout Saxony the Kulturbund candidates received a grand total of 19,148 votes out of 3,518,108 cast, one-half a percentage point.[40] Nor was it entirely clear just who had favored Kulturbund involvement, though in Mecklenburg-Vorpommern discussions took place that provide a few clues. The Kulturbund's "nonpartisanship" had always tried the patience of more hard-line Communists who in general fretted little about revealing the organization's support of the SED and could muster no particular sympathy for an unduly tactical approach to the elections. There may thus have been an attempt to nudge the Kulturbund back in the other direction by using it to influence the vote in favor of the SED. Whatever that attempt accomplished or failed to accomplish, it brought the political allegiances of certain Communist Kulturbund officials out into the open. The effort is interesting because it points to the existence within the local-level Communist or Communist-influenced leadership of sentiment against decisions reached in Berlin. At meetings called by the state chapter in Schwerin for the heads of the local branches on 5-6 October, a discussion ensued during which expectations were raised regarding the Kulturbund. These were summed up by Willi Bredel, the head of the state board, with respect to "certain plans for the participation of the Kulturbund in the county and provincial elections." Guidelines were then worked out for "all local groups at the state level to avoid splintering or aimlessness, such as occurred

[38]According to Becher, ibid., p. 129.
[39]Ibid., p. 133.
[40]See ibid., p. 134; and *Parteiensystem zwischen Demokratie und Volksdemokratie*, p. 553.

during the communal elections."[41]

But Bredel's rhetoric was a classic illustration of the fact that the opposite of "aimlessness" was the kind of uniformity and coordination certain to cause divisiveness because the party determined the acceptability of public attitudes toward controversial issues. "We German democrats ought not to be asking whether we orient ourselves toward the East or toward the West," he said; "rather, for us there can be only a single orientation: towards Germany!" Thus, "a schematic imitation of democratic institutions patterned after the American, English, or Soviet example" needed to be avoided for the sake of building "a *German democracy*," one growing on "German soil, resulting from German circumstances, and in accordance with the mentality of our German people." Even so, he added, a democratic rebirth of the German fatherland presupposed the attainment in "our intellectual, economic and political outlook" of the level reached by the most progressive nations. From there, a tacit allusion to the Soviet Union, Bredel proceeded to state that "the leading men of the Socialist Unity party" had just formulated a document concerning the "basic rights of the German people"; and the fact that the Kulturbund was a "nonpartisan organization" by no means suggested its lack of what he called a political orientation. "The serious efforts of the responsible leaders of the SED to establish the basic democratic rights of our people" ought to be welcomed, Bredel concluded, and the Kulturbund should lead a public discussion of the SED manifesto.[42]

The SED document to which Bredel referred, the "basic rights of the German people," came out a few days after the communal elections, and the party may have hoped that its various democratic promises—including a paragraph on the inviolability of art and science to be cultivated by the "power of the state" and protected from "all misuse"[43]—would aid in the next round of elections in October. This manifesto, drawn up by "the largest party in Germany," established that the country should be considered "an indivisible democratic republic" and prepared the way for the SED's draft proposal of a constitution for a German "people's republic," a "German Democratic Republic," published in mid-November 1946.[44] Both documents had a powerful national emphasis that was all the more urgent because the SED had been hurt by its position in the matter of Germany's eastern frontier. Party leaders had insisted that a final resolution of the "border question" was still outstanding and that the SED would oppose any "diminution" of German territory.[45] These discussions then produced an SED resolution, is-

[41]"Die Grundlinien der Arbeit im Kulturbund," *Demokratische Erneuerung* 7 (1946): 2.
[42]Bredel, "Überparteilichkeit heißt nicht richtungslos!" Ibid., p. 11.
[43]"Die Grundrechte des deutschen Volkes," *Neues Deutschland*, 22 September 1946.
[44]"Entwurf einer Verfassung für die Deutsche Demokratische Republik [14 November 1946]," *Dokumente der Sozialistischen Einheitspartei Deutschlands*, pp. 108-29.
[45]See "Klarheit in der Ostfrage!" *Neues Deutschland*, 14 September 1946.

sued the same day as its "basic-rights" document, charging that reactionary circles were exploiting the Oder-Neiße issue in a "new nationalistic-chauvinistic campaign" and that "disguised fascist and reactionary elements, who have burrowed into the bourgeois-democratic organizations," had refurbished the old Nazi notion of *Lebensraum* to obscure "federalist and separatist efforts" leading to the loss of territories in the West.[46] But those discussions came to an abrupt and embarrassing end for the SED six weeks later when Stalin answered "yes" to the question, "Does Russia regard Poland's western frontier as permanent?"[47]

These were the major national issues contested during the election campaign; the SED charged that "reactionary forces" had gained a toehold in the other parties and in "bourgeois-democratic" organizations, insisted that these elements advocated "subversive federalism," and concluded that, the stronger the party of "consistent democracy," the SED, the greater the success of its "national German policy."[48] The influential leaders of the Kulturbund adopted clear positions on the issues, even though its membership was comprised in part of intellectuals who belonged to these "reactionary" parties and honestly believed in their programs. The militant rhetoric of Bredel and Kleinschmidt in Mecklenburg-Vorpommern revealed just how divisive the election had become. Bredel brought up the subject of national unity, a question that he felt "no longer needs to be discussed within our Kulturbund" because the issue was a "self-evident and absolutely binding prerequisite" to membership. If the plans of the reactionary politicians became reality, Germany would be threatened with a fate similar to the situation centuries before because the "roots of the present national calamity" extended back to the seventeenth century. The eventual result was an "especially bestial subspecies of an imperialist-fascist dictatorship."[49] As Bredel saw it, the absence of German nationalism, not nationalism itself, gave birth to fascism; but it is important to note that he advanced arguments contrary to the cultural policies set in Berlin. Just weeks before, Becher had spoken at a Kulturbund meeting in Mecklenburg-Vorpommern on the subject of German renewal as an act of "reformation," making a positive reference to Luther's theses and adding that "our movement represents a new type of intellectual coming-together and pooling of resources."[50] When Bredel stated six weeks later in the same monthly, *Demokratische Erneuerung*, that Luther had become a "servile subject of the princes," contributing to their local power and,

[46]"Die SED zur Grenzfrage," *Neues Deutschland*, 21 September 1946.

[47]"Stalin zur Sicherung des Weltfriedens," *Neues Deutschland*, 30 October 1946.

[48]"Die Grundrechte des deutschen Volkes," *Neues Deutschland*, 22 September 1946; "Wahlaufruf der SED [7 October 1946]," *Dokumente der Sozialistischen Einheitspartei Deutschlands*, p. 95.

[49]Bredel, "Überparteilichkeit heißt nicht richtungslos!" pp. 11-12.

[50]Becher, "Das Reformationswerk deutscher Erneuerung," *Demokratische Erneuerung* 6 (1946): 6. Becher's phrase was "die Millionensehnsucht nach einem Anderswerden."

through his "fruitless theological disputations," pandering to currents leading to national division,[51] his remarks came close to an act of defiance.

Moreover, Becher had had an early premonition that trouble was afoot in Mecklenburg when he heard of plans back in October 1945 to publish a journal in Schwerin, *Demokratische Erneuerung*, as the voice of the Kulturbund there. He immediately wrote Paul Wandel, in his capacity as president of the Deutsche Verwaltung für Volksbildung, and insisted that the publication be shut down. Repeated requests had been made to permit the appearance of other periodicals, aside from the Kulturbund's monthly *Aufbau*; and these had all been rejected with the argument that the Kulturbund was a "unified undertaking" and possessed only one journal—*Aufbau*. With the appearance of additional publications, Becher said, "we would lose all control, creating the danger that the Kulturbund would fall apart ideologically." In addition, Bredel had been told explicitly in the presence of Anton Ackermann, and been acquainted with the relevant political considerations, that the publication of a journal competing with *Aufbau* was unwanted. On his own authority, Bredel had nonetheless gone ahead with plans for *Demokratische Erneuerung* anyway; and Becher now implored Wandel, unsuccessfully, to put an "immediate stop" to the journal.[52] Bredel's remarks now, in fall 1946, indicate that Becher's concern had been entirely justified. As Bredel saw it, even the most progressive German intellects had always "shied away from decisive political deeds and from an acknowledgment of their consequences." Klopstock and Schiller had cheered the French revolution until the Jacobins began "to get serious about the eradication of the aristocracy, which was conspiring against its own people, and several hundred heads belonging to these aristocratic regional and national traitors rolled in the sand, whereupon not only Klopstock and Schiller, but many more of the best Germans of the times turned away from the revolutionary events in France with outrage." Bredel vented his spleen on Schiller especially for a sentence in *Don Carlos* like, "Sire, grant us freedom of thought." It evidently never occurred to Schiller that freedom of thought could be seized from the "ruling reactionary regime and that he, Schiller, might have encouraged the people to battle from below what he was beseeching the monarch to grant from above." As for Schiller's *Wilhelm Tell*, he was a "typical German rebel" who did not cut down the tyrant because it served the interests of his people but because his family was being harassed and threatened. Bredel's

---

[51]Bredel, "Überparteilichkeit heißt nicht richtungslos!" p. 12.
[52]Becher to Wandel, 29 October 1945. Bundesarchiv. Abt. Potsdam, R-2/1146/1. Two years later, Wandel wrote the Mecklenburg state authorities to inform them that *Demokratische Erneuerung* came out with the "approval" of the SMA in Schwerin and that, due to new regulations, the state now needed to apply to the local SMA for a formal publication license. Wandel expressed "no political reservations" about Bredel. Wandel an die Landesregierung Mecklenburg/Vorpommern, Ministerium für Volksbildung, Abt. Allgemeine Volkskultur, 10 October 1947, ibid., R-2/1149/89.

arguments were generally relevant to the Kulturbund's involvement in the elections because he took them as proof that "genuine democrats are still a rare commodity in our land."[53]

Bredel's comments raised the pitch of Kulturbund rhetoric, and so did an article by Kleinschmidt published at the same time. Kleinschmidt's remarks actually went further than Bredel's and disclosed even more of the thinking behind efforts in Mecklenburg to involve the Kulturbund in the provincial elections. There was no doubt that the Kulturbund's electioneering threatened its internal cohesion, Kleinschmidt acknowledged; the vital question was whether there existed a "political *unity*" among Kulturbund members regardless of individual divergencies in political attitudes.[54] How, in fact, did one go about reconciling the organization's nonpartisanship with its keen interest not merely in cultural but in political and economic development? Kleinschmidt answered by noting that all Kulturbund members who participated in the recently concluded round of city and county elections had declared themselves—regardless of party affiliation—in favor of "Germany's inner *unity* and external *indivisibility*, a consequent *peace policy*, *land reform*, and democratic *school reform*." Kleinschmidt concluded that the "political unity of the Kulturbund" was not an expression of a propagandistic influence exerted over it by any "party-political program, to say nothing of an organizational dependency upon a political party"; rather, that unity was the result of like-minded thinking.[55] But the policies of the SED were involved, of course; and Kleinschmidt's further elaborations amounted to a bid to influence the other parties through Kulturbund members who belonged to them; or, failing that, to drive a wedge between the party leadership and these individual members as a means of inducing them to embrace the objectives of the SED. Having just concluded that Kulturbund members thought similarly, Kleinschmidt asked whether these members were always in complete accord with their own parties and insisted:

> The Kulturbund is politically independent. There is no authority in any position to impart political instructions to it or exert influence over its political objectives. It is a matter of complete indifference to the Kulturbund whether the SED, CDU or LDPD likewise works for the political demands that the Kulturbund embraces as a consequence of its own inner essence. Which parties do *not* do so, on the other hand, is a matter of concern to the Kulturbund. . . . One can say that the interest of the parties in the special objectives of the Kulturbund is in general still relatively underdeveloped, but—at least thus far—that the Socialist Unity party alone has tried hard for relations with the Kulturbund. . . . Now, the

[53]Bredel, "Überparteilichkeit heißt nicht richtungslos!" pp. 13-14.
[54]Kleinschmidt, "Nach und vor den Wahlen," *Demokratische Erneuerung* 7 (1946): 3.
[55]Ibid.

lesser interest of the two other political parties may originate in the Kulturbund's energetic pursuit of the above political demands, but that will not induce the organization to drop those demands or to push them any less energetically. It could cause the Kulturbund to ask just why there is disapproval of its advocacy of these demands. If this disapproval derives from an insufficient recognition of the national necessity of these demands, then the Kulturbund must strengthen and intensify its cultural-political educational work; but should it derive from the fact that these demands run counter to any kind of reactionary *interests*, then the Kulturbund must insist upon a choice. One cannot concurrently be a member of the Kulturbund for *democratic* renewal and an opponent of democracy—opposed to essential democratic prerequisites or opposed to principles and demands necessarily resulting from a commitment to democracy.[56]

Kleinschmidt's argument offered a clear rationale for the eventual repression of members who declined to stay in step with the organization's "unanimously agreed upon principles," even if that included an end to their affiliation with some other party. For the time being, however, he restricted himself to the insistence that Kulturbund members had the "moral obligation" to work within their own parties for adherence to the Kulturbund's principles and demands. Granted, he said, any election threatened overall unity by emphasizing differences; but because the divergent understanding within the parties on the subject of the appropriate "constitutional structure of the new democratic Germany" increased the threat to unity, the organization would underscore aggressively the threat of Germany's dismemberment and name those out to benefit from it. The Kulturbund had every right to push economic and political policies whose realization constituted the prerequisite for Germany's national unity and bona fide renewal. Democracy, Kleinschmidt concluded, had enemies who could not be persuaded to change their minds for the simple reason that their "antidemocratic *interest*" outweighed the best democratic argument. These people had to be subdued in a battle that was democratic only in the sense that it would be waged in the interest of the overwhelming majority.[57]

Totalitarianism

Though Kleinschmidt's remarks came as close as any within the Kulturbund to an open endorsement of the SED, other editorialists writing about culture

[56]Ibid., pp. 3-4.
[57]Ibid., p. 4.

in general minced even fewer words by late 1946. "Present times demand clear decisions in the political as well as moral, in the intellectual and artistic sphere," read one, which went on to criticize those who reproached "the new democracy for taking off its velvet gloves this time around and for expecting clear political decisions from both artist and intellectual."[58] Other commentaries varied the argument. Alexander Abusch, who had just been appointed head of a newly created "ideological-cultural division" of the Kulturbund,[59] went after reactionary publications for their notion of "pure democracy" and for discrediting the proponents of "real democratic reconstruction" in the process. When genuine antifascists in Germany were again slandered as "totalitarian," it served the direct cause of "the truly totalitarian, antidemocratic, antihumanistic, antisocialist, antibolshevist factory lords out to prevent their lasting removal from the life of the nation." If these reactionary circles prevailed, the freedom of art and science and the freedom of the individual, period, would be vassalized just as it had been before. It was therefore time now for Germany's intellectuals to show the world that they had learned something from the hellish years of Hitler.[60] Other Communist intellectuals, Friedrich Wolf for instance, said bluntly, "Today the SED is the party that effectively and seriously works to put an end to the war mongers in our country";[61] and Abusch, writing directly for *Neues Deutschland*, likewise endorsed the SED as the only party continuing the work of Germany's best past "freedom fighters." It only stood to reason, he said, that reaction today dressed up its lies about the SED with talk of democracy, much as it had reviled "all genuine democrats and socialists" in years gone by. These lies came from the "most venerable of arsenals" and were spread for the sole purpose of frightening people. But reaction and fear were twins, as Abusch explained it; and the SED brought the German people true freedom from fear after twelve years of coercion. Whereas Goebbels had declared open season on the intellectuals, the SED was the only antifascist party to guarantee the freedom of science and artistic creativity, as well as the freedom of religious faith and every other conviction.[62] The logical conclusion drawn elsewhere in the same paper, by Max Grabowski, was that "the artist's place is in the ranks of those elements seriously and purposefully working to rebuild our nation." The SED was not only the party that assured successful reconstruction; the party also had at its disposal a theory whose realization guaranteed a "bright future" for the economic and cultural rise of the German people. "The artist who is serious about our people and our fatherland, about art and culture, belongs therefore in the ranks of the Socialist Unity

[58]Leuteritz, "Der Kulturpessimismus und seine Folgen," *Tägliche Rundschau*, 18 October 1946.
[59]"Wir stellen vor: Alexander Abusch," *Die Aussprache* 3 (1946): 11.
[60]Abusch, "Humanismus der Gegenwart," *Sonntag*, 20 October 1946.
[61]Wolf, "Partei und Persönlichkeit," *Neues Deutschland*, 20 October 1946.
[62]Abusch, "Befreiung von Furcht und Reaktion," *Neues Deutschland*, 19 October 1946.

party of Germany."[63]

The SED actually fared worse in the October elections than in the September round, and the Kulturbund's involvement in the election provoked something of a backlash. But this can only be inferred from statements that claimed the contrary. Bernhard Bennedik, a music professor and member of the Kulturbund's presidium, contended that neither the outcome of the Berlin elections—which brought the SED a scant 20% of the vote—nor the "discrepancy" between the results in Berlin and throughout the rest of Soviet-occupied Germany necessitated any change in the activity of the Kulturbund. He then contended that most of the members of the Kulturbund presidium neither knew anything nor cared about the party affiliation of each individual member;[64] Ferdinand Friedensburg, another member of the presidium and later mayor of Berlin who was expelled from the Kulturbund for "antisovietism" during the Berlin blockade a scant two years later,[65] argued similarly. "Some leading personalities from the different political parties" sat on the board of the Kulturbund, he said, "more or less coincidentally"; but no one gave it a second thought; and in most cases "we have no idea whether they belong to a party at all."[66] Nonetheless, a sufficient number of other non-Communists apparently worried enough about the party affiliation of individual Kulturbund officials to do exactly what Friedensburg said occurred to no one—use the elections to argue in favor of "some kind of contrived parity in allocating our leading offices."[67] This bid to democratize the Kulturbund by replacing some of the Communists on its executive boards, using the party's showing in the Berlin elections as an appropriate justification, presumably reflected a growing resentment of the SED's dominance of the organization. Becher then lashed out at critics for their own ostensibly totalitarian aspirations:

> Some people just have to have their fun in calling for constituting the Kulturbund's boards according to the results of the elections, but this kind of wild idea could only originate in the mind of an incurable doctrinaire, an unscrupulous enforcer and idolater of the totalitarian concept, no matter how purposefully he poses as the exact opposite. Any such demand means that every Kulturbund organization would have to adjust itself proportionally after each election to that particular outcome, whether or not the membership of the affected organizations happens to be identical with the election results. Everyone can understand that culture cannot be forced into party formulas and that the weight of an intellectual per-

[63]Grabowski, "Bildende Künstler und Wahlen," *Neues Deutschland*, 19 October 1946.
[64]Bennedik, "Das Gesicht des Kulturbundes," *Sonntag*, 17 November 1946.
[65]See Friedensburg, *Es ging um Deutschlands Einheit*, pp. 58-59.
[66]Friedensburg, "Der Kulturbund und die Parteipolitik," *Sonntag*, 24 November 1946.
[67]Ibid.

sonality is not solely and exclusively determined by the person's belonging to a party and which one specifically. Such an impulse toward a totalitarian treatment of party life is absurd. . . . Such inconceivable demands unmask the ones making them as the unprincipled tongue-waggers they are, people who come out against the supposed totalitarian pretensions, the doctrinaire attitudes, and the lust to bring things into line attributed to others only because they see the totalitarian claims of their own clique in jeopardy.[68]

Despite Becher's dismay at tendencies within the Kulturbund designed to "bring it into line" with the outcome of the election, Becher himself knew perfectly well that his actions and the activities of the entire organization harmonized with the objectives of the SED; whether or not he bridled at direct intervention by the party is irrelevant; the Kulturbund existed for no other reason than to meet the needs of the SED, and whenever Becher suggested otherwise, he pretended in accordance with the lingering necessity of acting as if the Kulturbund was actually nonpartisan. But by late 1946, the party itself was considerably less reticent than before about claiming its cultural prerogatives. Pieck talked then of the party's natural "claim to leadership" in the matter of Germany's future political and economic development;[69] and Ulbricht applied the same argument to culture. With the foundation of a peaceful order laid, he said, the working class now had to stand up as "the bearer of a progressive democratic cultural development in Germany." Intelligentsia could see for themselves that the "future of German culture hinges upon close and congenial cooperation between the working class and the intelligentsia."[70] As always, the term "working class" connoted the SED, and the rest of Ulbricht's remarks amounted to a further exhortation that the intellectuals subscribe to the party's policies, if not join it outrightly. These sentiments had been reinforced at another of the SED's cultural conferences held just before the elections, on 15 and 16 August 1946. The account of the conference published in the SED's journal *Neuer Weg* noted that the party had an "excellent compass," Marxism-Leninism, to aid it in its cultural work. This realization was necessary in order to assess correctly the cultural factor in the reconstruction of "the new democracy" because German culture constituted a powerful impulse in the fight for the "unity of the Reich"; a culture, "democratic in content, national in form," strengthened the sense of togetherness and knew nothing of concepts like particularism or federalism. The conclusion:

---

[68]Becher, *Wir, Volk der Deutschen.* Rede auf der 1. Bundeskonferenz des Kulturbundes zur demokratischen Erneuerung Deutschlands [21 May 1947], pp. 68-69. The word throughout is "totalitär" or "Totalität," which was meant to be a synonym of "Totalitarismus."
[69]Pieck, "Unsere Partei nach den Wahlen," *Neuer Weg* 8 (1946): 3.
[70]Ulbricht, "Strategie und Taktik der SED," *Neuer Weg* 5 (1946): 265.

We want a democratic, peace-loving, united Germany. The SED is the most active champion of democratic reconstruction; no doubt the SED is the precondition for reconstruction. But that means that the SED has to cultivate a friendly, healthy relationship with the intelligentsia—those who work with the language, those who create culture and are concerned about it. This means that the SED must also become the party of the intelligentsia. However, the SED is not yet such a party, and the fault does not lie solely with the intellectuals, but with the party. The SED is the only force able to create a new, democratic intelligentsia; a proper relationship between the SED and the intelligentsia is thus the key to productive democratic cultural work and to the renewal of German intellectual life.

Unfortunately, certain comrades exhibited a "Marxist arrogance" toward the intellectuals that caused further errors. Functionaries and party members of this sort contrived contradictions between manual and intellectual work, refused to cooperate with the intellectuals, and held them responsible for the German catastrophe.[71] But considering the statements published in the party press so bitterly critical of the intellectuals, the SED had only itself to blame for radicalism in its own ranks; and besides, the problem was not one of insufficient sweet talk. The SED believed that the "excellent compass" of Marxism-Leninism aided it in its cultural work, but could not conceive of the reason why intellectuals distrusted the party's expressions of devotion to democracy; and when some of them voiced their disagreement, the SED responded with more innuendo. The conference referred to above determined that, "in the area of culture, honest artists and sincere democrats anxious to aid in reconstruction are running across sinister elements who, as a consequence of the setback dealt to the Nazis once worshipped by them, had been thrown out of their previous orbit and their earlier posts and now wanted to involve themselves in 'making culture.'" These people, posing as "free-lance artists" and passing themselves off as enthusiastic defenders of freedom, grabbed for their pens to write about "coercion and terror whenever anyone took a close look at their 'art' to determine its true value." The party's cultural functionaries needed to bear these factors in mind and pursue "a cultural policy separate from narrow-minded, egotistical considerations."[72] A growing domination of cultural matters and debates by the SED emerged during the second half of 1946 and into early 1947, then, and this domination was combined with brazen denials that organizations like the Kulturbund pursued anything other than an independent course. Becher actually

---

[71]K.K., "Zur Kulturtagung der SED," *Neuer Weg* 6 (1946): 17-18.
[72]Ibid.

called it "a simple act of self-assertion when we defend ourselves with the utmost resolution against interference by any party"; and he went on to insist that "we grant no party the right to lay exclusive claim to the intellectual and cultural renewal of Germany. . . . We oppose monopolies of any kind, even those in the sphere of culture and world view."[73]

Socialist Realism

Five weeks after Molotov's speech in Paris on 9 July 1946, the central-committee of the Soviet Communist party issued the first of four harsh decrees that cracked down on Soviet art and literature and helped set the direction of cultural politics in Soviet-occupied and East Germany for years to come. Looking back at the first three resolutions just after their announcement, Andrej Zhdanov explained the reasoning behind the decrees. It was "vitally necessary," he said, that the Soviet system never slacken its efforts to raise the political and cultural niveau of the population because an appropriate "socialist consciousness" enhanced the power of Soviet society. With the war on, the party had simply not been in a position to do justice to the ideological and cultural needs of the people, and in the meantime these had risen of their own accord to a still higher plateau. This fact alone meant that Soviet intellectuals shouldered a tremendous responsibility in meeting "the needs of the people and the state in public education, culture, and art." But at this critical juncture it had become apparent, Zhdanov went on to say, that the intellectuals themselves suffered from various ideological afflictions; most of these were related to their "unpolitical outlook," and the arts could not live up to their educative responsibilities until these maladies had been remedied. Fortunately, the party was fully cognizant of the source of the problem. It derived from the lingering "vestiges of capitalism in the consciousness" of those involved, and these residues had to be "surmounted and eradicated." The central-committee resolutions aimed therefore at the "intensification of Bolshevist single-mindedness with regard to ideological distortions of every kind" and were designed to elevate the level of socialist culture in the press, propaganda and agitation, science, literature, and art.[74]

The first decree, dated 14 August, concerned the monthlies *Zvezda* and *Leningrad*; the second, issued on 26 August, dealt with Soviet theaters; the third, published in early September 1946, discussed cinematography;[75] and capping them all was Zhdanov's choleric denunciation of *Zvezda* and *Leningrad* a few days later. All this had swift repercussions in Soviet-occupied

---

[73]Becher, *Wir, Volk der Deutschen*, pp. 65-67.
[74]Zhdanov, "Friedliche sozialistische Entwicklung," *Neues Deutschland*, 8 November 1946.
[75]The fourth and last, related to Soviet music, came out in 1948 and will be discussed later.

Germany, even though the actual text of the decrees was not published there until 1952. These edicts were so ruthless, their tone so arrogant and their rhetoric so censorial, that the SMAD must have decided to withhold them from publication in the zone until some later date. The announcement of the decrees had, after all, coincided with the election campaign and predated by just a few days the SED's proclamation of its "basic rights" document on 19 September. Neither the guarantee of the freedom of art contained in it, nor the SED's campaign rhetoric generally, had anything to gain from an uncut publication of the resolutions. Just how much damage knowledge of the edicts might have inflicted upon the SED's cultural-political reputation at this critical juncture is fairly apparent from their crude language The two literary journals *Zvezda* and *Leningrad* were taken to task for publishing such "dregs of society" as Mikhail Zoshchenko and the poetess Anna Akhmatova, the latter said to be notorious for composing "ideologically empty poetry alien to her own people." The work of these two writers, riddled with "bourgeois aristocratic aestheticism" and marred by the notion of "art for art's sake," simply would not be tolerated. Apart from Zoshchenko and Akhmatova, many other works had been published that exhibited a similar "servility towards the current bourgeois culture of the West," works imbued with "melancholy, pessimism, and disappointment in life." The sad fact was that the journals saw fit to allow the "penetration of ideologically alien works" into their pages, even though Soviet periodicals, as "powerful weapons in the education of the Soviet people," could not afford to be "apolitical"; indeed, the power of Soviet literature consisted of the fact that it was a "literature which neither has nor ever can have any interest besides the interest of its people and its state." Apolitical literature, "art for art's sake," was alien because it harmed those collective interests.[76]

Many of the same considerations, with some new ones added, showed up in the second decree devoted to the Soviet stage. The main problem with the repertory of Soviet theaters was the absence of plays by Soviet writers dealing with topical themes; and given the significance of the stage in the "Communist education of the people," the central committee pledged to concentrate its attention on the creation of a "contemporary Soviet repertory." Playwrights were enjoined to compose artistically distinctive works dealing with the life of Soviet society and with Soviet people, whose "best character traits" were to be depicted—optimism, joy of life, devotion to the homeland, and faith in the "victory of our cause." The sick preoccupation with "inferior and banal plays from abroad" needed to end immediately; for performing these foreign plays was tantamount to opening the Soviet stage to the dissemination of "reactionary bourgeois ideology and morality." They poisoned

[76]"Über die Zeitschriften 'Swesda' und 'Leningrad'. Aus dem Beschluß des ZK der KPdSU (B) vom 14. August 1946," *Beschlüsse des Zentralkomitees der KPdSU (B) zu Fragen der Literatur und Kunst (1946-1948)*, pp. 3-8.

the consciousness of Soviet people by presenting a world view that was wholly antagonistic to Soviet society and by rejuvenating the residues of capitalist preoccupations in the lives and minds of the people.[77] With a slight change here or there, much of this criticism could already have been leveled at creative intellectuals in the Soviet-zone and was in fact just beginning to find its way into the pages of the newspapers on a more frequent basis. But even then, the pace of that process could not be quickened too rapidly in late summer 1946 without endangering efforts to win the support of local intellectuals during the coming elections. Certainly, just about every admonishment contained in the decrees already had fairly direct equivalents in the Soviet zone, but the rhetoric there still took the form of less developed versions of Zhdanovist arguments. Complete publication of the edicts in Soviet-occupied Germany was thus probably regarded as imprudent at this critical juncture because bringing them out in their entirety would have rounded out arguments that the SED still preferred to truncate. An unambiguous endorsement of the decrees, along with their unabridged publication, would have pointed too clearly in the direction of the party's likely cultural-political objectives, cultural "sovietization," and the same is true of Zhdanov's speech in late September. Considering the disturbing similarities between his choice of words and the scarcely veiled threats against Soviet-zone intellectuals typical of the party's general rhetoric by early fall 1946, Zhdanov's torrent of formulas, cant, and denunciation would hardly have built confidence in the SED's cultural-political intentions.

Zhdanov savaged writers who created non-"party-minded" literature that was devoid of "ideas." Such defective literary works exhibited "great gaps and failings . . . on the ideological front" and "lagged behind" development generally. Indeed, some writers went so far as to suggest that a work of artistic value ought to be published regardless of any "rotten passages."[78] This "estrangement from contemporary Soviet themes" in the work of Soviet writers and the adoption of a "servile and reverent tone towards petit bourgeois foreign literature" then prompted Zhdanov to ask whether such servility was "becoming to us, Soviet patriots, we who have built the Soviet regime, which is a hundred times better and higher than any bourgeois regime?" Was it "becoming to our progressive literature . . . to grovel before the limited petit bourgeois literature of the West?" If someone like Zoshchenko did not approve of Soviet life, Zhdanov said, it was not for Soviet society to accommodate itself to him but for him to change or "clear out of Soviet literature." As for Akhmatova, a representative of "reactionary obscurantism" and part of an "empty reactionary bog," she filled her poetry

[77]"Über das Repertoire der Schauspielhäuser und Maßnahmen zu seiner Verbesserung. Beschluß des ZK der KPdSU (B) vom 26. August 1946," ibid., pp. 9-17.
[78]Quoted from Zhdanov's speech reprinted in *The Central Committee Resolutions and Zhdanov's Speech on the Journals Zvezda and Leningrad*, pp. 47-72.

with "mystical emotions mixed with eroticism" and made of herself "neither a nun nor a fornicator, but really both, mixing fornication with prayer." Her poetry and Osip Mandelshtam's, whose death in a Soviet camp Zhdanov declined to mention, had nothing in common with the interests of the Soviet people and the Soviet state.[79]

Such phrases would have dismayed Soviet-zone artists and intellectuals who already had grave misgivings about the politicization of culture there; and within days, the central-committee decrees had indeed impinged upon cultural politics in Soviet-occupied Germany. Even though they were not actually published, the SMAD's cultural officers had intimate knowledge of the decrees, which had appeared promptly in the Soviet press; and at the very least, the German Communists had also been briefed.[80] Moreover, men like Tjulpanov, Dymschitz, and certainly Semjonov may well have taken it for granted that these decrees, like any other important Soviet political development, would carry over into Soviet foreign policy and from there influence the direction of cultural politics in the zone. Once this was clear, every other consideration related to the use of the decrees in Soviet-occupied Germany was merely a matter of tactics. The importance of these encyclicals on the subject of socialist realism in the Soviet Union may have made it inevitable that the overall process of rigidification underway since early 1946 and accelerated by Molotov's speech in July would be further influenced by them; indeed, the decrees ended up shaping Soviet-zone cultural politics not just through the remainder of the year, but well beyond. In late summer 1946, however, continued assurances still had to be made that the Communists had no hidden agenda and no plans for some kind of transplantation of Soviet politics and political culture or cultural politics to occupied Germany. The various socialist-realist principles canonized in the central-committee decrees thus presented a unique challenge to the Soviet cultural officers because their announcement in the USSR came just as the local Communists were trying to influence the electorate by disavowing dictatorships and presenting the SED as the only genuinely national party in Germany. These reasons alone explain why the SMAD would have thought it wise to limit its commentary to a watered-down rendition of the decrees that took the form of seven articles by Alexander Dymschitz in the *Tägliche Rundschau*. These pieces touched on most of the essentials of socialist realism, but avoided the invective of the original decrees or of Zhdanov's rantings.

The first four, in which Dymschitz dealt with what he called the "characteristics of a new art," actually began just one day before the public an-

[79]Ibid., pp. 52-56.
[80]In March 1989, I asked Paul Wandel whether there had been a high-level party discussion of the edicts and whether a decision was made to withhold them from publication. He confirmed the first part of the question, but responded to the second with an expression of mistrust in the questioner.

nouncement of the first edict, and none of these four articles, the last published on 17 August, mentioned the decrees. Still, it is reasonable to assume that a decision had been made to hasten the introduction of the basic principles of socialist realism in Soviet-occupied Germany beginning in early fall 1946 and just as legitimate to see this move as part of the SED's intention of following up on its announcement several months previously to "seize the initiative" in the area of culture. Finally, that this intention coincided with the hardening Soviet policy toward occupied Germany presaged by Molotov the following summer only underscores the likelihood that none of these developments were the result of happenstance. Coincidental or not, any decision to press ahead with the introduction of socialist realism in fall 1946 was bound to precipitate cries of "sovietization" just as Germans who lived in the Soviet zone were deciding whether to cast their vote for the SED. In this context, Dymschitz' attempt to dampen the rhetoric of the resolutions makes sense. His initial series of four articles may thus have been motivated by the hope of mollifying those Soviet-zone intellectuals who were doubtful about the SED's cultural policy generally, feared "sovietization" in the form of socialist realism specifically, and were not about to support the party in the election as long as those doubts lingered.

Dymschitz began his first article by conceding that there had been much debate on the subject of socialist realism in Germany during the past year, though he must have been thinking mostly of discussions that went unreported in the press because the concept itself showed up only rarely in print prior to fall 1946, and it was mentioned even less often in terms of its applicability to German art and letters. But it was important to him now to suggest that no artist had anything to fear from socialist realism anyway; accordingly, the main purpose of Dymschitz' article was to scoff at the notion that socialist realism was a dogma; quite the contrary, he said, it was entirely open-minded with respect to any subject matter and any artistic form. Nor was socialist realism a "canonized concept," a school of thinking that either forced "everything into narrow norms" or was itself based upon "normative principles." Dymschitz then introduced an important caveat. Socialist realism did not favor "experiments"; rather, it constituted a new "artistic posture that represents and depicts life in its totality without prejudice." Soviet writers drew sustenance, he said, from a scientifically grounded world view that provided them with "transparently clear ideas and goals" and a "positive social program." Paraphrasing Marx, Dymschitz said that the Soviet writer desired not merely to interpret the world, but to change it, psychologically forming the new man in accordance with Stalin's apt description of such writers as "engineers of the human soul."[81] The positive attitude of these writers generated an art that bore "chiefly *affirmative characteristics*," with

[81]Dymschitz, "Züge einer neuen Kunst," *Tägliche Rundschau*, 13 August 1946.

the goal of looking to create a positive ideal in the shape of a "new type of human being."[82]

Because no definition of socialist realism was complete without a distinction between realism and its "half-brother" naturalism, Dymschitz went on to explain that realism "always wrestled for *social and psychological truth*," one of its main tasks being the "*representation of typical characters under typical circumstances*," that which was "typical" connoting the progressive essence of an era; whereas naturalism confined itself to the "purely empirical."[83] Dymschitz then proceeded to the next trait—"revolutionary romanticism." Revolutionary romanticism had been that blend of ostensible historical truth with a revolutionary pathos leading toward the depiction not of what was, but of what would be; but as Dymschitz explained it, there was no conflict with a realistic view of the world because revolutionary romanticism produced an understanding that included a forecast of further developments. Thus, "in socialist realism, eternal contradictions between both types of world views and various artistic methods are definitively surmounted."[84] In one way or the other, all socialist-realist norms and principles rested on the simple proposition that writers only needed to write the truth; this being the case, Dymschitz went on to explain that the politicization of art by placing it in the service of the state constituted no cause for alarm because the "tendentiousness" of a work of art failed to cancel out its truthfulness. This particular question, the presence of a "bias" or a "tendency" in art, was particularly acute because "true art" was biased in the best sense of the word; if art struggled for a new life, it could never be "unbiased"; and in this sense all works created by great artists had been biased in their unveiling of new paths of development. This kind of "true" bias contrasted with the false and mendacious kind "imposed upon art" and alien both to the genuine essence of man and, for that reason, to art as well.[85] In his concluding article, Dymschitz related his arguments to Germany. "Precisely in German circles there often exists the misguided opinion that socialist realism is an artistic dogma regulated by the state, that is, a norm forced upon the artist by the state and one that subjugates all other artistic forms." But the Soviet artist was a "free man"; to him socialism represented the "acknowledged necessity of a new, sensible world order." Service in support of this cause was therefore voluntary; and in the Soviet Union there was no such thing as a "forbidden topic"; to the contrary, all artistic forms were permitted. There was thus no conceivable reason why the experience of socialist realism was not similarly "important and instructive for Germany," for even though the relics of facist ideology needed to be dealt with mercilessly in intellectual life, this could

[82]Dymschitz, "Züge einer neuen Kunst," *Tägliche Rundschau*, 14 August 1946.
[83]Ibid.
[84]Dymschitz, "Züge einer neuen Kunst," *Tägliche Rundschau*, 15 August 1946.
[85]Ibid.

not be accomplished in the absence of positive ideals. Along with realistic depictions of the calamity, the artists also needed to direct their "romantic gaze" toward the future.[86]

These were all established principles of Soviet art and literature and had been since the mid thirties. In fact, Dymschitz' assertion that the doctrine of socialist realism was not a dogma had its own ideological parallels in Marxism-Leninism. Lenin's phrase about the omnipotence of Marx' teaching that derived from its underlying truth may have been more at home in political discussions than cultural debates (truth could never be dogma if the dogma was truth);[87] but in both instances the notion emphasized the basic argument that historical truth underlay the doctrine. Dymschitz' next series of articles appeared during the week leading up to the state and provincial elections. Unlike the first four, these last three dealt specifically with the central-committee decrees. Dymschitz began by complaining that a number of newspapers in Berlin's western sectors and in the western zones had published "impertinent lies" about these three resolutions.[88]

But instead of straightening out the misunderstandings by republishing the edicts and letting them speak for themselves, Dymschitz embarked upon an elaborate commentary that took up more printed space than the actual resolutions. Soviet artists, he argued, had recognized the central-committee pronouncements for what they were—a "defense and further development of the principles of socialist realism" necessitated by the threatening presence of literature "devoid of ideas." Both the decree concerning literature and Zhdanov's subsequent speech had made it abundantly clear that Soviet readers rejected Zoshchenko and Akhmatova as "profoundly backward and mindless literati" who were out of step with their own people. The work of these writers provided no source of "fruitful optimism" for the young generation of Soviet citizens raised in peace and in the spirit of humanism. Dymschitz likewise professed unhappiness with reporting in the West German press on that decree which dealt with the Soviet stage repertory. Contrary to Western insinuations, he said, there had been no ban on foreign plays; but just as Shaw, Priestley, Dreiser, Sinclair, Aragon, or Malraux struggled in their homeland against manifestations of "bourgeois decadence and Philistine superficiality in art," in much the same way the Soviet creative intelligentsia had made it clear that it would not tolerate the implantation of this "reactionary, mindless, amoral literature" into the Soviet theater. Specifical-

---

[86]Dymschitz, "Züge einer neuen Kunst," *Tägliche Rundschau*, 17 August 1946.

[87]See, for instance, Ackermann, "Der ideologische Kampf der Partei." *Bericht über die Verhandlungen des 15. Parteitages der KPD*, p. 100. Ackermann's comments are variations on identical claims in the *Short Course* history of the Soviet Communist party, namely that "one must not take Marxist-Leninist theory as a collection of dogmas, as a catechism, as an article of faith. . . . Marxist-Leninist theory is no dogma, but a guide to action!" *Geschichte der Kommunistischen Partei der Sowjetunion*, pp. 430-31.

[88]Dymschitz, "Probleme der heutigen Sowjetkunst," *Tägliche Rundschau*, 11 October 1946.

ly, Dymschitz mentioned plays by Morrison, Maugham, Kauffmann, and Hart, along with the works of any other "scribbler of plays" or reactionary writers whose works had been characterized by the resolution as undesirable.[89] This was why the edict had called upon Soviet playwrights to create powerful works dealing with "contemporary topics." Quoting Zhdanov, Dymschitz added that "'the people, the state, and the party object to the estrangement of literature from the present; they desire instead that literature delve actively into all areas of Soviet life.'"[90]

Following similar remarks about the third resolution on Soviet film-making, which included criticism of Eisenstein's *Ivan the Terrible* for belittling Ivan's "progressive role" in Russian history, Dymschitz concluded his second series of articles by explaining that the basis of the decrees was the "consequent struggle for the art of socialist realism." Not withstanding the charges printed in certain Berlin newspapers, he said, the decrees were by no means intended as an "attack" upon individual artists and writers, as the "liquidation" of foreign plays from the Soviet stage, or as "strictures" directed at outstanding filmmakers. The resolutions were designed to assure the further flourishing of Soviet culture. This culture, Dymschitz concluded, need not fear exposure in the international arena and refused to "hide behind an 'iron curtain.'"[91] Unlike the first articles in praise of socialist realism, however, this time Dymschitz made no mention of its applicability to German literature, a reluctance perhaps related to the fact that provincial elections were only five days away by now.

Theater Criticism

The central-committee resolutions had the quickest effect upon theater in the Soviet zone. Not that the various points discussed in the edict on the repertory of Soviet theaters showed up explicitly in criticism of specific productions or even general public debates about theaters in Berlin. Of course, related and identical points—the need for an optimistic outlook, the educational function of the stage, laments regarding the absence of plays dealing with contemporary themes—had been present in all criticism beginning with the attack upon Brecht in August 1945 and in the various treatments of Stanislavskij. Indeed, in many ways theater criticism and stage theory, as well as the criticism of various art exhibits, revealed the earliest incursion of a still unnamed form of socialist realism into Soviet-occupied Germany. Nor is there anything surprising about this; the stage offered more immediate

---

[89]Ibid.
[90]Dymschitz, "Probleme der heutigen Sowjetkunst," *Tägliche Rundschau*, 13 October 1946.
[91]Dymschitz, "Probleme der heutigen Sowjetkunst," *Tägliche Rundschau*, 15 October 1946.

possibilities for influencing the local population than prose writing. Fritz Erpenbeck developed the Schillerian idea of the theater as a "moral institution" and explained that theatrical art served to educate through its moral impact (or encouraged immorality if such art was "worthless"). But its moral impetus derived from specific means inherent to this particular form of art. Art was "represented life," he said, a depiction of life shorn of everything in non-conformity "with natural laws," and this lawful conformity represented simple truth. The theater-goer learned and morality was inculcated into him when he recognized or sensed this truth; but the truth aspired to by any art was "social truth," Erpenbeck said, and his main point was that "we cannot pick up where we left off in 1933" because the German theater had arrived at a dead end. It was pointless for the heads of theaters to go around "indiscriminately digging up and performing" plays that had been banned during the Hitler years; if the stage wished to be involved in the "reeducation of our people," it must first reeducate itself.[92]

Nothing in Erpenbeck's comments differed from his previous attitudes as a critic;[93] his insistence that the stage was not a "school," or the playwright a "lecturer,"[94] merely continued his campaign against a more unabashedly political art such as the kind practiced by Brecht. Nor did Erpenbeck's article betray any discernible traces of the Soviet resolutions or by itself point toward a worsening atmosphere with regard to stage productions. But in the context of a generally hardening cultural-political line, Erpenbeck's rigid focus on "social truth" was bound to have a direct effect given the growing predominance of a party that laid direct claim to it. Not that uniformity in stage criticism was the rule yet in the zone; other voices were raised in 1946 in specific defense of Brecht, for instance Herbert Ihering's, at the same conference attended by Erpenbeck in August and then again later in the year.[95] In December Ihering, who had been one of Brecht's earliest advocates in the twenties, wrote that a copy of Brecht's *Schweyk* had just reached him from the United States, and he used the manuscript as an occasion to discuss Brecht, praising him for the realistic truth of the depicted situations, the political clarity of his specific slant, and a well-rounded form.[96]

Erpenbeck would hardly have agreed with any of those points, and Ihering's added contention that *Die heilige Johanna der Schlachthöfe* and *Arturo Ui* would "sweep people's minds free of the last vestiges of fascism" and that it was time to put on plays like *Mutter Courage, Der gute Mensch*

---

[92]Erpenbeck, "Kunst ist gestaltetes Leben," *Tägliche Rundschau*, 20 August 1946.
[93]Erpenbeck was the first editor of the monthly of stage news and criticism *Theater der Zeit*, which began appearing in July 1946; and he introduced each number of the journal with his own editorial comments on various theoretical problems related to the stage.
[94]Erpenbeck, "Kunst ist gestaltetes Leben," *Tägliche Rundschau*, 20 August 1946.
[95]See Ihering, "Theater der Völker. Rede, gehalten auf der Theatertagung in Weimar," *Aufbau* 8 (1946): 795-804, especially pp. 800-801.
[96]Ihering, "Der neue Schweyk," *Die Weltbühne* 11 (1946): 339-41.

von Sezuan, and *Galileo Galilei*, as well as to publish Brecht's complete works, could scarcely have met with his approval either. Not that Brecht again became the center of controversy; nothing like the debate of a year earlier reoccurred for some time to come. The discussions focused instead on plays by a number of other playwrights, and it so happened that these productions again took place on the stage of the Hebbel Theater in West Berlin. Unlike Erpenbeck's more general comments, this round of criticism revealed unmistakable traces of the central-committee resolutions combined with previous criteria like the demand for plays dealing with contemporary topics. Thornton Wilder's *By the Skin of our Teeth* came in for sharp criticism, and Wolfgang Harich responded with something of a defense. According to Harich, Wilder's play had been accused of "rotting in the destructive pessimism of a lethargic, skeptical, decrepit bourgeoisie; taking a flippant attitude toward those recent catastrophes that might very well have been overcome through the radical application of reason; denying and ridiculing the progress of mankind; and showing itself to be more reactionary than the teaching of Spengler or representing the resigned irrationalism of a decadent, sickly, and hopeless philosophy."[97] Harich was not yet ready to concede those points, and neither was Ihering.[98] The last act of Wilder's play, said Harich, had yet to be written; for one, in view of the recently concluded round of genocide there was no reason to regard progress as inevitable (besides, Wilder had not ruled out the possibility of progress altogether); and for another, any proof that this task could be mastered was still outstanding, so that a playwright like Wilder ought not to be excoriated for failing to provide his play with a tidy ending.[99]

The articles by Harich and Ihering, published respectively in *Weltbühne* and *Aufbau*, predated by several days the central-committee resolutions and Dymschitz' opening discussion of socialist realism in mid-August. None of the criticism that came out afterwards in *Neues Deutschland* or the *Tägliche Rundschau*, however, found anything at all praiseworthy in Wilder's play and objected just as strenuously to a number of other performances of "foreign" plays. *Neues Deutschland* inveighed against the production of Paul Osborn's *Stay of Execution* in the Hebbel Theater and noted that other plays and films reaching Germany from Western Europe and America exhibited the same "spirit." If such products indeed reflected "the intellectual outlook of America" or had gained the upper hand there, a variety of fears were justified. These products propagated a cheap brand of romanticism disturbingly redolent of the shadowy spirit of that epoch which "we have just overcome

---

[97]Harich, "Thornton Wilder," *Die Weltbühne* 4 (1946): 119.
[98]See his general defense of Wilder as well as of other playwrights who soon came under intense fire, Osborn, Sartre, Giraudoux, and Anouilh, for instance, in "Theater der Völker," *Aufbau* 8 (1946): 795-804.
[99]Harich, "Thornton Wilder," *Die Weltbühne* 4 (1946): 120.

following a great deal of suffering and death and which we wish to keep behind us." Those in charge of the theaters needed to be told that they either acted negligently when offering the public plays the likes of *Stay of Execution* or that they were evidently incapable of spotting such dangers.[100] Other commentary fit the same pattern. The staging of Wilder's play, wrote an officer of the SMAD, marked a turning point in the post-war development of Berlin theaters, signaling the start of an indisputable "regression."[101]

Not that all plays by foreigners had been bad; there were productions of Priestley and Shaw lacking the "one-sided nihilistic criticism that performed the last rites for all mankind." These plays were infused with the desire to help humanity surmount the maladies of modern society, and in this sense their authors were "genuine humanists," whereas Wilder's play was bathed in an "antihumanistic tendency." Unfortunately this antihumanistic slant, so characteristic of "decadent art," had recently reached epidemic proportions in Berlin. Major objections then followed to both Osborn and the "decadent repertory" of Jean Anouilh, for "one had every right to mention Anouilh's name in the same breath as his countryman's, Jean-Paul Sartre, the founder of so-called existentialism, a French philosophy that is currently becoming extremely popular in reactionary European circles." This philosophy represented a mere variation of a German forerunner that contributed mightily to the "ideological preparation of fascism"; and there was no sense talking about a democratization of art in Germany as long as anyone believed that the stage was "enriched by such imports."[102] This particular article then took critics to task for defending the staging of such plays "for the sake of the experiment," Ihering, for instance,[103] who supposedly forgot about the general public in the process. The average German was in no position to draw strength and encouragement from these plays and left the theater weakened "from an encounter with foreign art." Above all, the present repertory lacked a contemporary social play born of the age, able to seize hold of the theatergoer and force him to make choices, not a "leading editorial in dialogue."[104]

None of these critical articles mentioned socialist realism outrightly or referred to the central-committee resolution on the Soviet stage. Two other articles late in the year, however, went further. Hedda Zinner, Erpenbeck's wife, commemorated the Russian revolution by again singing the praises of Stanislavskij, though she skirted the problem of "sovietization" by beginning with an indirect disclaimer. The cultural influence of one land upon another never involved the "simple exportation or importation" of artistic and scientific achievements; rather, a complicated historical process was involved that

---

[100]Kind, "Zurück zur Barbarei?" *Neues Deutschland*, 5 December 1946.
[101]Bergelson, "Theater auf bedenklichem Wege," *Tägliche Rundschau*, 31 December 1946.
[102]Ibid.
[103]See "Repertoirebildung," in *Theater der Zeit* 4 (1946).
[104]Bergelson, "Theater auf bedenklichem Wege," *Tägliche Rundschau*, 31 December 1946.

took an indirect path during "most of its phases." Zinner's discussion of Stanislavskij followed. With the generous support of the Soviet state, he had pushed forward toward "scenic realism," whereas the "expressionist and other avant-garde experiments of the great formalists Tairov, Vachtangov, and Meyerhold tried a different way." Nowadays Stanislavskij's work benefited progressive theater everywhere, not least of all in Germany, the lesson being that the Soviet state by no means negated, repressed, or eradicated the existing progressive elements of bourgeois culture but allowed them to evolve into something entirely new. Zinner, who surely knew as well as her husband that the "Soviet state" had indeed engaged in a pattern of negation, repression, and eradication in the case of the three names mentioned by her, concluded with the practical application to Germany. After having been hermetically sealed off from all the progressive insights and aspirations achieved outside of their own country, the Germans were slowly—though with "predominantly astonished admiration"—learning of the involvement of the Soviet Union in that world culture which had been unfettered by the Great Socialist October revolution.[105] One additional commentary late in December, written by the SMAD's Bergelson, finally mentioned the Soviet resolutions outrightly in a report on the Soviet conference of theater people that had been scheduled in the aftermath of the three edicts and Zhdanov's speech; and Bergelson noted that German spectators were often confronted with plays exhibiting a "pernicious, pessimistic slant or without any ideas whatsoever."[106]

These few examples of stage criticism published in Soviet-occupied Germany in late 1946 suffice to show that the Communists were serious about employing the theater as a "moral institution" for use in influencing the people politically, the more so considering that "morality," as Erpenbeck defined it a short time later, was seen as the "demand for democratic-humanistic feelings, thoughts, and desires applied to the absolutely concrete existence of life in Germany."[107] This naturally increased the need for plays dealing with specific contemporary topics with the appropriate political slant, for playwrights who could write them, and for ways of diminishing the influence of dramatic productions that interfered with "democratic-humanistic feelings, thoughts, and desires." This need had become particularly acute at roughly the same time as the Soviet central committee issued an edict designed to take care of a similar problem at home. By now, however, it had become fairly apparent that there was not going to be a rush of compliance with the emerging cultural norms of Soviet-occupied Germany. Of course, the difference in comparison with the Soviet Union was that zhdanovism there had teeth from the outset and an experienced Stalinist apparatus to en-

[105]Zinner, "Sowjetkultur und die Kultur der Welt," *Tägliche Rundschau*, 14 November 1946.
[106]See Bergelson, "Probleme des modernen Theaters," *Tägliche Rundschau*, 15 December 1946.
[107]Erpenbeck, "Krise des Theaters," *Einheit* 3 (1947): 312.

force the edicts; whereas any comparable crackdown by party or SMAD authorities, either to tighten the correspondence between the SED's political and its cultural-political policy or to bring both into absolute conformity with their Soviet counterparts, would have made a complete mockery of the party's display of broadmindedness.

All these factors figured into the local criticism of foreign plays. Not only did these performances undercut the thinking that the few approved plays available for staging in late 1946 tried to get across, these "contemporary" dramas in the Soviet sector of Berlin, *Zeitstücke*, evidently attracted far less enthusiastic audiences than the "imports" appearing on the West Berlin stage. In fact, in March 1947 Erpenbeck acknowledged that plays with what he regarded as considerable cultural-political value performed to "half-empty houses."[108] Apparently the plays that met with his specific and the party's general approval bored an apathetic public or, as Erpenbeck explained it, were disliked because Germans hesitated at having "feelings of guilt" about Hitler awakened within them. Not that Erpenbeck's point was groundless, but the problem was surely compounded by the public's disinclination to subject themselves to political morality plays that struck them as advertisements for one party's politics. The fact was that foreign plays intrigued theater-goers after twelve years of fascism—but only foreign in the sense of Western, not Soviet. Zinner deceived herself when she referred to the "predominantly astonished admiration" with which Germans learned of Soviet culture; and the regular insinuation that these American or French plays actually even smacked of the spirit of fascism illustrated how indiscriminately the Stalinists chose to bandy about that word.

Pseudo-Artistic Manifestations

A similar pattern emerged in the pictorial arts, but with a strange twist. In this area, public attitudes often coincided with Stalinist hostility toward "decadent" art, but for all the wrong reasons. The embarrassing fact was that the Nazis had disliked "degenerate" or "decadent" art, specifically German expressionism or, broadly speaking, modern abstract art, just as much as the Communists; and the public taste remained heavily influenced by twelve years of fascism. Complicating matters further was the additional fact that at least some of the general public, and certainly connoisseurs, wished to make up their own mind about works regarded by both Nazis and Communists as "degenerate"; and this interest surfaced just as the Communists began insisting that a rejuvenation of things as they had been "prior to 1933" was no answer to the cultural-political problems now facing the nation. Nonetheless,

[108]Ibid.

galleries and museums were exhibiting German expressionism along side western European abstract, surrealist, and other modern art (Picasso, Chagall, Dali, Braque, Matisse, and so on); and this art likewise appeared in West Berlin galleries together with the work of young German artists who preferred to imitate the style of modern art, rather than embrace techniques advocated in discussions in the Soviet zone. The Communists had to contend with these rival new practices while trying to steer clear of criticism that either sounded too much like Hitler's denunciation of "decadence" or hinted too strongly at the party's urge to mandate the direction of art.

The sporadic complaints about exhibits of apolitical art that appeared during the latter half of 1945 thus continued through spring 1946; one in particular objected to the absence in individual works of any treatment of the recent calamities and the preponderance of sentimental, lyrical themes lacking in depth.[109] But that criticism was relatively harmless when compared with remarks made by Carola Gärtner at the opening of another exhibition in late March 1946. Gärtner began with a categorical denial that her views led in the direction of "tendentious art"; artists in a democratic Germany, she promised, could create freely; no slant whatsoever was expected and no instructions of any kind given on matters of style. The artist would be allowed to create however he or she pleased, and no agency or institution "in the new democracy intended to dictate to him." Then came prescriptions in the form of Gärtner's talk of a new factor that made demands upon the artists—the viewing public, on whose behalf Gärtner passed along opinions sounding suspiciously like the very regimentation that she had just disavowed. "You may no longer stand off to the side and retreat into the ivory tower," she told the artists, "isolating yourself from the world and its sufferings!" If among "our artists" the aloof kind lingered for awhile, persuaded of their right to create solely for initiated "aesthetes," but powerless to prevent their work from deteriorating into "problems of form" whose dalliances succumbed to nervous prostration, such artists should go right ahead and ignore the needs of the people. They should continue producing for a few snobs, and the indifference paid them would be their full reward; all the while, real artists, "prototypes of the people," would create reflections of humanity absent any artificial slant.[110] In planning the DVV's first big art exhibit in May 1946,[111]

---

[109]Melis, "Moderne Berliner Malerei," *Neues Deutschland*, 18 May 1946. See also, "Ausstellung in Koepenick," *Neue Zeit*, 23 May 1946.

[110]H. C. Gärtner-Scholle. Ansprache bei der Eröffnung der Kunstausstellung in Hoppegarten am 24. März 1946. Bundesarchiv, Abt. Potsdam, R-2/1090/31-34.

[111]See her discussion of the technical difficulties encountered in setting up the exhibit, as well as her notorious inclination to attribute problems of every imaginable kind to "sabotage of democratic reconstruction" (Gärtner-Scholle to Herbert Volkmann ["mit der Bitte um Kenntnisgabe an die Oberste Sowjetische Militäradministration und Herrn Präsident Wandel"], 26 April 1946. Ibid., R-2/1038/58-61). See also her interim report on the organization of the exhibit (Referat Bildende Kunst. Gärtner. Betr. Kunstausstellung im Zeughaus. Zwischenbericht. 28. 4.

Gärtner proceeded from the same assumptions, but moderated them out of tactical considerations. As she told Erich Weinert, the exhibit was not organized around a specific theme whose "propaganda purposes" was identical with the objects shown; rather, "we wish primarily to demonstrate with this exhibition that artistic activity is coming to life in our sector and that we have not made any small-minded evaluations or appraisals of tendency." Thus, the works of certain artists whose interests remained "purely aesthetic" would naturally have to be displayed; and it would require persistent and unobtrusive "direction by us" to bring such artists to the point of occupying themselves with themes that "we find more acccptable." Finally, she explained that she had gone ahead and included a few good examples of abstract painting in order to dispense with the suspicion that "we insist upon a commissioned slant."[112]

Reactions in the Soviet-zone press hinted at the exact same tactical considerations. *Neues Deutschland* said that this "first German art exhibition" answered to no particular "programmatic demand"; rather, it served as an expression of an age that had clear political goals, but was still wrestling to find "new forms and new content." The exhibit prompted "our artists" to ask what direction their work should take now. "We arc endeavoring to fight our way through to a reordering of social and state organization," read the conclusion; those artists who spurned "ends in themselves" needed to recognize the necessity of a new art to go along with this reordering and to use their artistic creativity to depict the events of the day.[113] In the *Tägliche Rundschau*, Gärtner argued much as she had privately, but with greater self-restraint. Without "hindering" any particular direction, she said, the organizers had nonetheless sought to achieve a "harmonic overall impression," permitting the wealth of diversity to lead to a consciousness of the rich possibilities available to German culture. Now was the time to survey what was useful for the future, Gärtner added, in particular because persistent demands that the artists depict the "urgent questions of the present day" had appeared regularly in the press and in public forums during the past months.[114]

1946. Ibid., R-2/1038/56-57). This latter document illustrates the nature of the problems created by the need to obtain permission from the Russians for the tiniest of details. Gärtner complained of all the time lost in her repeated visits to SMAD offices and asked that she be granted a permanent pass as one means of preventing delays. She then went on to report that the exhibit poster was ready and awaited SMAD approval. The special postal imprint had also arrived at her office and would be passed along to the Russians for their consent. The exhibit catalog had posed particular problems because Gärtner had been forced to obtain an allotment of paper from the Verlag "Volk und Wissen" after the Russians turned her request down. Finally, the procurement of advertisements, presumably to help pay for the catalog, was almost complete and would likewise be sent along to the Russians for their blessing.
[112]Gärtner to Weinert, 2 May 1946, ibid., R-2/1090/30.
[113]Kind, "Erste Deutsche Kunst-Ausstellung," *Neues Deutschland*, 22 May 1946.
[114]Gärtner-Scholle, "Abbild deutschen Kunstschaffens," *Tägliche Rundschau*, 22 May 1946.

These comments point to the inescapable conclusion that the exhibition in May was intended to foster the impression of cultural diversity in Soviet-occupied Germany while creating the opportunity to pressure the artists into an endorsement of politically useful forms of art. The same was surely true of the full-scale Allgemeine Deutsche Kunstausstellung in Dresden that opened at a time, right before the elections, when the bestowal of a public blessing upon socialist-realist norms in Soviet-occupied Germany would scarcely have reinforced the party's calls for cultural unity on a national scale. There is thus ample reason to suggest that the Allgemeine Deutsche Kunstausstellung was mounted, at least in part, with an eye to helping refurbish the local and national reputation of the Socialist Unity party following the forced merger with the SPD and on the eve of the elections. Not that the SED participated publicly in the Dresden exhibition; it worked through its cultural functionaries within the DVV and the Kulturbund, which had also gotten into the act as one of the official sponsors.[115] Indeed, the public purpose of the exhibit was to take steps toward "transcending" the zones that divided Germany.[116] According to the published reports, works of art from all of Germany had been submitted "at the invitation of the organizers"—the Saxon state administration, the Dresden city council, and the Kulturbund. A total of 2,400 works were apparently sent in, and a jury comprised of the famous artists Karl Hofer and Max Pechstein and sculptors Richard Scheibe and Herbert Volwahsen, together with ten other "prominent personalities," picked five hundred for showing.[117] Among them were works by Erich Heckel, Karl Schmidt-Rottluff, Ernst Ludwig Kirchner, Max Beckmann, Oskar Kokoschka, Max Pechstein, Otto Dix, Paul Klee, Lyonel Feininger, Wilhelm Lehmbruck, Conrad Felixmüller, Ernst Barlach, and Käthe Kollwitz—all artists discountenanced by the Nazis as "degenerate." This point was made explicitly by Volwahsen; it was significant that the exhibit was held in Dresden because the showing of "degenerate art" used to "ostracize and defile German modern art" was opened there by Hitler twelve years before.[118]

More importantly, the works appeared to offer evidence that there was no official animosity toward expressionist art in Soviet-occupied Germany; "every direction from the naturalist via the abstract artist to the surrealist" had been granted the opportunity to exhibit works,[119] as *Neues Deutschland*

---

[115]Wandel declined an invitation by the head of his own office in charge of planning to deliver an address at the opening of the exhibition (Dr. Strauss to the Präsidialkanzlei, 10 August 1946. Bundesarchiv, Abt. Potsdam, R-2/1038/43).

[116]Schwerdfeger, "Allgemeine Deutsche Kunstausstellung," *Berliner Zeitung*, 30 August 1946.

[117]See the list in the exhibition catalog, *Allgemeine Deutsche Kunstausstellung Dresden 1946* [no date; no place of publication]; the catalogue reproduced ninety-six of the exhibited works.

[118]Schwerdfeger, "Die Kunst in Dresden," *Berliner Zeitung*, 28 August 1946.

[119]"Allgemeine Deutsche Kunstausstellung 1946 in Dresden eröffnet," *Neues Deutschland*, 28 August 1946.

made a point of mentioning. Moreover, Alexander Dymschitz expressed his hope at the opening that the show would serve as a form of "intellectual and cultural bridge-building" spanning all zonal borders to link every segment of Germany and the entire world; and he was seconded by the SMAD's Major General Dudorov, who noted that the exhibit "symbolized the unity of Germany."[120] But those comments already contrasted with the more detailed reporting in *Neues Deutschland*. The young generation of artists faced the task of using the exhibit to "divide the stylistic elements handed down to us into those pointing towards the future and those that proved unfruitful." This particular article ended by calling the Dresden exhibit a "separating line" in the sense that it showed the "controversial works of the twenties once more while permitting an early but clear recognition of the direction taken by a new road that must be pursued in full awareness of the profound responsibility borne today by our creators of art."[121] It was to be hoped, added Dudorov, that German artists would come to regard themselves one day as spokesmen for the "progressive impulses of the German people," just as Soviet artists were bonded together with their people.[122]

Though these comments disclosed traces of the thinking behind the exhibit, and coincided generally with remarks made privately by Gärtner in connection with the earlier Berlin exhibit, the discussions held during the Saxon cultural congress that marked the close of the show contained some of the sharpest rhetoric yet heard in Soviet-occupied Germany; and it was uttered by the two SMAD personalities chiefly responsible for overseeing cultural developments in the Soviet zone. Both Tjulpanov and Dymschitz delivered belligerent addresses that indicated the absence of any indulgence toward present-day "formalist" or expressionistic art and made explicit references to the central-committee resolutions. Tjulpanov began by stressing that art must educate through its "ideological content, expressed by way of a form organically bound up with the content." Because every genuine artist needed to fix his gaze on the future, German artists "must use their creative work" to show the German people the road leading to it.

Tjulpanov then proceeded to build an argument that culminated in the establishment of Soviet art as a model worth emulating by the "German democratic artist."[123] Ironically enough, however, Tjulpanov's opening deduction actually undercut the normal insistence upon close ties between the artists and the people (and demolished the basis of Gärtner's attempt to threaten individualist artists with public contempt). Circumstances forced Tjulpanov

[120]Schwerdfeger, "Die Kunst in Dresden," *Berliner Zeitung*, 28 August 1946.
[121]Uhlig, "Allgemeine Deutsche Kunstausstellung in Dresden," *Neues Deutschland*, 27 August 1946.
[122]"Freie Deutsche Kunst," *Sonntag*, 1 September 1946.
[123]Leuteritz, "Für Demokratie und Fortschritt. Oberst Tulpanow auf dem Sächsischen Kulturkongress in Dresden," *Tägliche Rundschau*, 29 October 1946.

to argue that artists could not "orient" themselves exclusively according to the taste of ordinary Germans, who had, after all, been exposed to the subversive effects of fascism. For that reason, he explained, the classical heritage of German culture took on added importance, though it was "impossible to create today" exclusively on the basis of the past either.[124] In other words, contemporary models were required, and the mere fact that the Nazis had denounced modern German art as degenerate by no means rendered it suitable for the present. Tjulpanov declined to say so outrightly, but this attitude underlay his argument and paralleled Erpenbeck's remark that plays ought not to be "indiscriminately dug up and performed" just because they had been banned or declared undesirable during the Hitler years.[125] Instead, Tjulpanov enjoined German artists to look to the Soviet Union for guidance, "acquainting themselves with the artistic experience" of the USSR and with the "accomplishments of our Soviet artists."[126] But the announcement of the central-committee decrees had combined with skepticism about Soviet art and culture generally to block the effectiveness of Tjulpanov's advice. He offered the following reassurance:

> I know that reactionary elements in the German press are very upset about the growing interest evinced by progressive German artists in Soviet art and that these elements have recently been spreading provocative rumors to the effect that there is supposedly no free creative activity in the Soviet Union and that state regimentation of art takes place in the USSR. Because the individual substandard and, in part, immoral works of several writers have recently been severely criticized in the Soviet Union, these reactionaries have raised a hue and cry in the newspapers. They accuse us Soviet people, as it were, of state interference in artistic affairs. I wish to expose this slander right now by telling you that in the Soviet Union, where art enjoys the love of the entire people and where the people care for it, criticism of anti-artistic manifestations is not regarded as intrusion into the area of art but as protection of art from the attempt by these insipid, vile, pseudo-artistic manifestations to intrude themselves into this exalted sphere.[127]

Tjulpanov's use of the words "protection" and "misuse" happened to correspond to that paragraph in the SED's "basic rights" which combined the promise of artistic freedom with the state's intention of protecting art from "misuse."[128] But it is more important to note that Tjulpanov's language

---

[124]Ibid.
[125]Erpenbeck, "Kunst ist gestaltetes Leben," *Tägliche Rundschau*, 20 August 1946.
[126]Leuteritz, "Für Demokratie und Fortschritt," *Tägliche Rundschau*, 29 October 1946.
[127]Ibid.
[128]"Entwurf einer Verfassung für die Deutsche Demokratische Republik," *Dokumente der Sozi-*

at the congress in Saxony came even closer to the cutting rhetoric of the original central-committee resolutions than Dymschitz' had just two weeks earlier. It is unclear, however, whether Tjulpanov's willingness to engage in it reflected the specific intent of sharpening cultural-political and literary-theoretical positions in the zone or indicated that certain restraints had been removed simply because, with the elections over, the SED had little to lose. Either way, the older democratic disclaimers still lingered. Tjulpanov defended state involvement in artistic matters with the usual distinction between "consequent" versus "verbal" democracy that allowed reaction to run unchecked; for that reason, the SMAD was troubled by the fact that, in those localities where his administration had no opportunity to "protect democracy entirely from its misuse," such as in parts of Berlin, reaction got away with all manner of "anti-Soviet provocations" and with the kind of incendiary chauvinistic propaganda that had cost the German people dearly twice this century. Speaking directly to the artists, Tjulpanov expressed his certainty that they had no desire to see the mistakes of the past repeated; and he promised that the SMAD would continue to support all measures in the area of art serving the "democratization of Germany and progress."[129] Heibert Gute, the Communist in charge of cultural affairs in Saxony, evidently felt the need to add that "we do not want a state art," for art could not be decreed; but he reiterated that each artist must be capable of individual self-criticism and able to "protect art from all misuse."[130]

Tjulpanov's speech opened the congress, Dymschitz' closed it and contrasted every bit as much as Tjulpanov's comments with the sense of broad-mindedness that the Dresden exhibit had been designed to convey. Dymschitz began with his own retrospective. In all matters pertaining to art, he had encountered an "organizational and intellectual chaos" upon arriving in Germany right after the war. Certain reactionary elements—"one-quarter, one-eighth, and one-half fascists"—had shown up immediately, threatening to cloud the "clear paths of the new art" by salvaging as much as possible from fascist ideology. Not at all "disposed to rebuilding in the cultural-ideological sphere," this group contrasted with another category of people who were "willing, but in practical terms incapable of reconstruction" because ideologically they "lagged behind, going back to the years of the Weimar republic." To Dymschitz this meant that half of that group wished to "rewarm bourgeois liberalism," whereas the other half—apparently hard-line Communists—remained mired in "anarchic radicalism." But in neither instance did these categories of intellectuals manage to develop a proper attitude toward problems common to the people in their entirety. Yet another group,

---

alistischen Einheitspartei, p. 110.
[129]Leuteritz, "Für Demokratie und Fortschritt," *Tägliche Rundschau*, 29 October 1946.
[130]Ibid.

however, had proven themselves to be genuine democrats, "independent of age, social position, or party affiliation"; and they deserved the thanks of the SMAD's cultural division, which bore the "responsibility for the democratization of German art." Dymschitz then took the Dresden art exhibit as an example of democratization, adducing as proof the fact that "different directions" in art had been represented there. But his conclusion suggested something different. "At this exhibition one senses the contrast between a genuine realistic art . . . as opposed to a formal abstraction that is lacking in ideas and therefore without any future."[131]

This statement alone indicates that the very exhibition mounted as a means of displaying artistic diversity was used at the first opportunity following the elections to illustrate the practical uselessness of much of the exhibited art. The attacks upon Picasso, or even more so upon Paul Klee and Schmidt-Rottluff published a few years later and spurred on by Dymschitz, represented a consistent if not absolutely inevitable development. But even without the specific criticisms of late 1948, Dymschitz' concluding remarks belied talk of tolerance. German art would have to "expand its ideological horizon" in order to continue along its new road, Dymschitz said; whereas German artists and writers had received a mere "sampling of Soviet art" over the past months, in the future they were to become acquainted "to a far greater extent and systematically with Soviet art," the point being that, first, German artists and intellectuals would come to recognize that Soviet art was intimately connected with Marxism and, second, no contemporary scientist or artist could regard himself as being "sufficiently oriented" before studying "Marx, Engels, Lenin, and Stalin." As for the "intellectual chaos" mentioned by Dymschitz early in his speech, the versions of the discussions held

[131]Dymschitz, "Rückblick und Ausblick. Rede auf der Schlußsitzung des 1. Künstlerkongresses gehalten am 30. Oktober 1946 in Dresden," *Sonntag*, 10 November 1946. It should come as no surprise that the "SED artists" latched on to the remarks made about "realism" by both Tjulpanov and Dymschitz in Dresden as prove of the political correctness of their own positions. Fritz Duda, in a letter sent to the SED's division of Kultur und Erziehung, quoted both of the Russians back to the party's secretariat and specifically cited the comments by Dymschitz footnoted here (see Duda an das Zentralsekretariat der SED. Kulturabteilung. Z.Hd. d. Gen. Weimann. Betr.: Sitzung der Fachkommission bildender Künstler am 19. 11. 46. 20 November 1946. Bundesarchiv. Abt. Potsdam, R-2/1353/56). See also an unsigned statement, presumably drawn up by the same group, that summed up its positions by, among other things, calling Karl Hofer "senile" in his creativity and complaining that "our functionaries" occasionally acted as if they were ashamed to belong to the SED when dealing with bourgeois intellectuals. The statement, intensely critical of the party's policy on art, was said to be the result of the articles published by Dymschitz in the *Tägliche Rundschau* and comments made in Dresden by Tjulpanov, Fradkin, and Dymschitz. These were taken to mean that the SMAD would be receptive to such criticism of the party (see Zur Berliner Kunstpolitik! 20 November 1946, ibid., R-2/1353/58-63). Carola Gärtner was not at all unjustified in arguing later, in connection with her dismissal from the DVV, that for one-and-a-half years she had done little more than what the papers demanded daily (Referat Bildende Kunst. Gärtner. Präsidialabteilung. Herrn Lehmann, Personalabteilung, Betriebsrat. 7 June 1947, ibid., R-2/1353/16-17).

during the congress published in the press seem designed to help clear up that kind of confusion through increasingly specific definitions of the new realism. One writer stated outrightly that the "lever" employed in the East to bring about social change was nothing other than the legacy of classical German philosophy, in other words Marxism, though this writer was apparently unable to discern any contradiction in his concurrent promise that the DVV would "never go about things dictatorially or bureaucratically" and would endeavor to "coordinate the ideological with the material realm." Another speaker went a step further, calling for "a new aesthetic theory,"[132] and, according to *Neues Deutschland*, the "basic demand for a new form of representation—whether in pictorial art, sculpture or graphic art, whether in dramaturgy, the art of acting, or in music—rang out in every speech and in all the discussions." German art had reached the point where only through a "means of expression valid for the contemporary age" would it again be able to justify its right to exist.[133]

The retrospectives published after the congress then summed up many of the developments underway since early 1946 and indicated that a far greater prescriptiveness now marred the official cultural "ideal" first described embryonically and with cautious restraint at the KPD's cultural conference in early 1946. The report on the congress published in the SMAD's *Tägliche Rundschau* repeated the common argument that "all the previously repressed currents of art" had surfaced with the defeat of fascism; much of this "driftwood," antiquated and superseded forms of art, pretended to point toward the future just because it found no home in Nazism. But the time had come to distinguish between a "genuinely progressive, realistic German art, which engaged in conscious political resistance and was banned for it, and those artistic counterfeiters who accidentally fell under the wheels." Though the debates about art at the congress ought to have produced "new, objective standards," separating the wheat from the chaff in order to establish the basis for a new aesthetic, most of the discussions degenerated into petty quarrels over style, and certain circles of German artists often forgot that the "quickest possible stabilization of political and economic conditions in Germany" represented the simplest basic preconditions for their work. There existed general agreement, the editorial explained, that one could not continue the "old artistic jog-trot" of the pre-1933 years; but confusion resulted the moment that certain of the conference speakers hinted at the direction of the coming art. The Dresden congress confirmed, "less in the speeches, to be sure, than during the discussion," just how much "intellectual uncertainty" still prevailed with respect to a determination of artistic goals.[134] This final comment appears to indicate that the speeches, and not just those by Dym-

[132]Ibid.
[133]W.K. "Kunst auf neuen Wegen," *Neues Deutschland*, 9 November 1946.
[134]Leuteritz, "Deutsche Kunstdiskussion 1946," *Tägliche Rundschau*, 14 November 1946.

schitz and Tjulpanov, had indeed been couched in purposeful terms, but that the ensuing discussions were not marked by universal accord and that Dymschitz' speech may not have elicited the "stormy approval" referred to in the press either.[135]

Four days after Dymschitz delivered his closing address to the artists' congress, the Kulturbund's weekly *Sonntag* followed up on the events in Dresden by publishing an article by a Soviet author declaring that Lenin and Stalin were authorities on art as well as on the science of Marxism.[136] That kind of remark had never been heard before in Soviet-occupied Germany and combined with the comments by Tjulpanov and Dymschitz in Dresden to shift the direction of cultural-political debates. The discussions of late fall 1946 staked out new theoretical territory, and fresh administrative and organizational measures soon followed. Though earlier commentary on the subject of Lenin's opposition to proletcult had appeared in print before, along with periodic references to Stalin's dictum that writers were "engineers of the soul," the article in *Sonntag* had gone on to characterize Lenin and Stalin as "enemies of any kind of formalist art that is incomprehensible to the masses and that distorts reality"; and it ended by noting that Stalin had proclaimed "socialist realism to be the basic method of Soviet art and literature." These comments went further than Ackermann's speech in February, Dymschitz' essays in mid-October, or even his and Tjulpanov's remarks to the artists' congress in Dresden. Of course, socialist realism was also defined as the "truthful replication of life," so that the aesthetic dogma, no less than Marxism itself, still came across as an expression of historically sanctioned truth, rather than as merely one of countless possible competing ideologies derived from purely political considerations.[137]

But the harsh reality behind the rhetoric remained unaffected by such subtleties. The autumn of 1946 brought some of the frankest arguments yet in opposition to pluralism in art, with hopes being expressed toward the end of the year that the various directions in realistic art developed over the last few decades would converge into a "single universally valid and binding representation." Anything but a "crude process of uniformization of the arts and a dictatorship over the artists," the liberty borne of apocalyptic darkness and unspeakable sacrifice needed to be "sheltered and guarded, shaped and revealed." Such an art would have to open the portals to a new reality if it wished to claim the right to exist; artists who declined to flee reality but held their ground against it properly bore the name of "realists," whereas those who succumbed to reality were simple naturalists; indeed, "most artists today still wander about blindly, lost between abstraction and naturalism be-

[135]Leuteritz, "Ausblick auf die Kunstwende," *Tägliche Rundschau*, 2 November 1946.
[136]Karpotschin, "Lenin und Stalin über Literatur und Kunst," *Sonntag*, 3 November 1946.
[137]Ibid.

cause of their inability to master reality."[138] As plain as the language spoken in fall 1946 had become, the full picture emerges only through a comparison of utterances made in a variety of contexts. The following commentary, for instance, published by *Neues Deutschland* as early as October, had already anticipated remarks made at the post-election artists' congress in Dresden, but comes into sharper focus when read together with the kinds of statements more common late in the year. Artists ought never to be subjected to such demands as "art should" or "art must" because "prescriptions alien to art" constricted the absolute freedom of development vital to all art, read the opening caveat. But it was quickly brushed aside in additional remarks to the effect that the social order of the future would be socialist; art, therefore, would be socialist as well. Moreover, the socialist world "will be realistic, that is, it will be firmly grounded in life and in reality and will affirm both life and reality. For that reason the coming art will also be realistic." Speaking truth required real words, however, not the inarticulate stuttering of abstractions; and the paper concluded by stating that in life and in art socialism spelled realism.[139]

---

[138]Theunissen, "Die höchste Aufgabe der Kunst," *Tägliche Rundschau*, 22 December 1946.
[139]"Zur Kunst des Volkes," *Neues Deutschland*, 4 October 1946.

PART TWO:

TWO CAMPS (1947)

CHAPTER SIX

Ideological Offensives

The German Communists sided with the Soviet Union on all major foreign and domestic issues in 1947, but never lowered the pitch of their national rhetoric or withdrew the related promise of an indigenous road to socialism. In light of the fact that the SED's strong endorsement of Soviet policies by late in the year even eclipsed the party's identification with Soviet positions in summer 1946, the continuation of a hollow promise like the German road to socialism only deepened doubts that the slogan had originally been designed to dispel. But the SED clung to the idea of "no sovietiz[ation] for the time being (!),"[1] even if it avoided phrases like "violent sovietization" in stating its opposition publicly. By 1947, however, there were other reasons for reemphasizing the party's commitment to national unity. The pledge of a peaceful or "non-Soviet" road to socialism had first been intended for all zones as the only perceived means of broadening support for a party not known for its devotion to democracy, though the KPD relied heavily upon the slogan to help set up the system of bloc politics locally and compel the SPD into a merger. After formation of the SED, the idea led an increasingly barren existence—refuted by the political realities of Soviet-occupied Germany. Nevertheless, it remained in effect even after the SED had largely consolidated its power and in spite of the growing Soviet readiness to settle for dominance in one third of Germany because of the lingering hope of using the party to influence the shape of political and economic developments in the western zones. If the SED were to be of any use to the Soviet Union beyond the one zone already controlled by it, that distant hope hinged on the party's success at selling its national-democratic objectives to Germans living in the West. Attempting to do so, the SED cast itself in the role of a self-sacrificial organization guided only by the national interest. Even though its adherence to the science of Marxism guaranteed its superiority over all other parties, endowing it with inalienable rights as the leading political force in all of Germany, the SED had "temporarily deferred" its initiative to better prospects for national unity. Slander to the contrary, none of

---

[1] "Agitprop-Mitteilungen der KPD-UBL. Leipzig. 1. Jg., Nr. 1, 30. 7. 1945," *DDR. Dokumente zur Geschichte der Deutschen Demokratischen Republik 1945-1985*, p. 46.

these actions resulted from dependence "upon the Soviet occupation authorities," though the SED admitted "great satisfaction" over the fact that the occupation regime backed the party in its national aspirations.[2]

Bastions of American Imperialism

The difficulty of reconciling these claims with the party's hardening stance only grew with the unsuccessful end of the foreign-ministers' conference in Moscow that spring, the start of the Marshall plan, and, more toward the end of the year, the creation of the Communist Information Bureau or Cominform. Not that the process of transition to a political order only marginally distinguishable from the Soviet system was finished by late 1947; a few major steps remained to be taken in 1948, chief among them the abandonment of all notions associated with national roads to socialism. But compared with the distance traveled through late 1947, a year that ended with constant imprecations against the West and its plans to wage atomic warfare against the USSR, developments in 1948 tended more to finalize changes fundamentally complete the year before. Nevertheless, the hostility toward the West in general and political circumstances in Western Germany in particular led to a strange intensification of the unity rhetoric; the more pronounced the impulse to consolidate power in Soviet-occupied Germany, the greater the effort expended in hopes of enhancing the reputation of the SED and the Soviet Union as champions of German unity. The Communists thus found themselves confronted with the need to cultivate ideological and programmatic rhetoric capable of rationalizing rigidity in one zone while appearing moderate enough to serve as a basis for influencing public opinion in the others. In effect, this amounted to a revolutionary offensive dressed up as a democratic initiative in order to achieve results in the Western zones identical to those already arrived at in the East. This approach then functioned as an adjunct to the Soviet position staked out at the meetings of foreign ministers in Moscow and again, late in the year, in London. In every respect, 1947 turned out just as *Neues Deutschland* predicted—as a "Year of Decision." "Give us in the West, too," the paper had pled, "the democratic right and legal basis for disposing once and for all of war criminals, revanchists, and saboteurs; *then let us be the masters of our own house!*"[3]

The paper strongly advocated an end to thinking in terms of zonal limitations by warning that hoisting the flag of federalism, rather than assisting in

[2]See "Die Grundsätze der Organisation unserer Partei," *Sozialistische Bildungshefte* 10 (1947): 4; Pieck, "Bericht des Parteivorstandes," *Protokoll der Verhandlungen des 2. Parteitages der SED* [20-24 September 1947], p. 78; "Jakob Kaisers Verleugnung," *Neues Deutschland*, 19 November 1947; "Ein Jahr SED," *Sozialistische Bildungshefte* 7 (1947): 7.
[3]"Jahr der Entscheidung," *Neues Deutschland*, 1 January 1947.

the breakthrough of historical progress in "all of Germany," would be tantamount to accomplishing in two years what Hitler fell short of achieving in
twelve—dragging the nation into the abyss. Renouncing "party demagogy or
propaganda tricks," the editorial associated "anti-unity" thinking with the
natural opposition of all reactionaries, home-grown and foreign, to cooperation between "democrats and socialists." For partitions of any kind, whether
into classes or parties, prevented Germans from forming the broad consensus necessary for the coordinated defense of their own national interests
against the threat posed by the "reactionary bourgeoisie," well on the way
again to dominance in western Germany after the defeats of 1918 and 1945
and about to auction the country off to the highest bidder.[4] Besides, as Ulbricht said several months later, the struggle between the progressive and reactionary forces in Germany was being complicated by *"Western monopoly
capital, which helps out the German authoritarian elements."*[5] Indeed, as
Neues Deutschland explained it, the only hope of stopping the reactionaries
from enslaving all working Germans, joining a western bloc designed to
split up "our fatherland," and turning the nation into different colonies resided in unity; Germans needed to adopt a unified position and speak in one
language, the paper concluded in reaffirming the preeminent role of the SED
in guaranteeing Germany's national future: "For the democratic unity of the
labor movement; for the democratic unity of our people; for the democratic
unity of Germany."[6] On the eve of the opening round of discussions in Moscow, then, the SED raised the pitch of its national rhetoric, but did so in a
fashion that prescribed the Soviet-zone solution to those regions occupied by
the Western allies. In Soviet-occupied Germany, the party said, the success
of democracy was assured; developments there would lead to the threshold
of socialism and create the preconditions for the socialist transformation of
the entire society, whereas in West Germany constrictions had been imposed
upon democracy, and developments threatened to lead to the reestablishment
of monopolistic capitalism rife with the urge to wage war.[7]

These pronouncements soon reflected the related understandings passed
along to the German Communists during their consultations with Stalin the
end of January. Indeed, the contours of SED rhetoric emerged clearly right
after that discussion in a speech delivered by Ulbricht. His comments contained the usual stark contrast between progress made in the Eastern and
Western zones, but he used conditions in Soviet-occupied Germany as a basis for arguing that national unification would present an opportunity for
what he called "a unified democratic development in all regions." Ulbricht's

---

[4]Ibid.
[5]Ulbricht, "Zur Vorbereitung des zweiten Parteitages der SED," *Neuer Weg* 7 (1947): 2.
[6]"Jahr der Entscheidung," *Neues Deutschland*, 1 January 1947.
[7]"Deutschland vor der Moskauer Konferenz [23 January 1947]," *Dokumente der Sozialistischen
Einheitspartei Deutschlands*, pp. 142 and 145.

remark also happened to reformulate the comment in *Neues Deutschland* on New Year's Day that "Germany is identical for us with the new German democracy," though the paper went a step further and added that the struggle "for a democratic order and for the unity of Germany can only be waged successfully if the SED expands its influence in all parts of Germany." Once the structural economic changes already complete in the East had been implemented, including the "liquidation" of cartels, big banks, and large estates, then the same possibility would exist in the West for a "democratic road to socialism . . . in accord with the current special conditions of the struggle in Germany."[8] As usual, the promise of a democratic transition was an implied repudiation of "sovietization," and yet these policies endorsed the Soviet position set forward by Molotov in Moscow during the foreign-ministers' conference in spring 1947. His demands there mostly restated those made by him the summer before in Paris, based on the accusation that the West had failed to demilitarize, denazify, and democratize its zones. By failing to follow through with the changes agreed upon at Potsdam and as a consequence of their insistence upon federalization, the allies pursued policies that jeopardized German unity; and Molotov repeated accusations made in Paris to the effect that plans existed for putting an end to Germany as a state unto itself. The Soviet Union, he said, would have none of it because the USSR had no desire to "destroy" Germany as a nation. Projects aimed at "dismantling" Germany through federalization or by severing West Germany from other parts of the country were incompatible with the task of democratization and posed a direct threat to the peace of the world.[9]

There was little new in this assessment except for the shriller insistence upon finding a resolution of the German problem in order to safeguard worldwide peace; and Molotov also contended now that democratization could only occur in all of Germany if "political parties" and "anti-Nazi organizations" were allowed to establish themselves in all zones. For in spite of the success achieved by democratic parties and trade unions "in Germany," as Molotov put it, the refusal to allow them to join together nationwide constituted a serious obstacle to their further development.[10] Of course, when Molotov referred to the success of these organizations "in Germany," he had only that portion occupied by the Russians in mind; and approval of parties nationwide also meant permission for the SED to work in the West along with those mass organizations, such as the Kulturbund or the FDGB, con-

[8]Ulbricht, "Die Lage in Deutschland und die Aufgaben der SED in Berlin. Referat auf der Landesvorstandssitzung der SED Groß-Berlin [21 February 1947]," *Zur Geschichte der deutschen Arbeiterbewegung,* vol. III, Zusatzband, pp. 174-76, 185.
[9]Molotov, "Über die zeitweise politische Organisation Deutschlands [22 March 1947]," *Fragen der Außenpolitik,* p. 424.
[10]Molotov, "Erklärung über die Entnazifizierung und Demokratisierung Deutschlands [13 March 1947]," ibid., pp. 383-84.

trolled by it. But the allies made permission for the SED to organize in the West contingent upon the reorganization of the SPD in the East; and that never happened, essentially ending the matter, though there had been some thought given by the Russians to just such drastic action.[11] In all likelihood, the emphasis on establishing the SED in the Western zones reflected the understanding that if the Russians proceeded to develop theirs separately, with the allies doing the same, the presence of parties and organizations masquerading as democratic and controlled by the East might prove to be the only possibility of influencing politics and public opinion in the West. For now, Molotov argued that the limitations imposed upon the activity of what he called democratic organizations and the interference in their internal affairs constituted a "fundamental distortion" of the Potsdam commitment to democratic development in Germany, preventing formulation of a "coordinated policy valid in all the zones."[12] Moving from the general to the specific, Molotov then called upon the allied control council to consult with the "democratic parties, free trade unions, and other anti-Nazi organizations" in preparing a temporary German constitution and advocated creation of a German advisory organ, comprised not only of representatives from the German states and provinces but also including members of all "democratic parties," unions, as well as "other anti-Nazi organizations, three of which, the Kulturbund among them, he mentioned by name.[13] In close consultation with this advisory body, the allied control council could begin preparing a temporary constitution, followed by elections to a German-wide parliament just prior to formation of a provisional government.

The Moscow conference in March and April 1947 ended with no agreement, and the SED attributed the unsuccessful outcome to the "considerable differences" among the former allies caused by dissimilarities in the social structure of the countries involved in the negotiations, the contrariety of the circles ruling there, the divergencies in state interests, and variations in the degree of closeness to Germany "in the past and in the future."[14] Whereas the commentator merely hinted now that the disinclination to demilitarize, denazify, and democratize the Western zones reflected the allies' congeniality toward an economic infrastructure that thrived after 1933 and still remained "completely untouched," by year's end the German Communists ea-

---

[11]The question of allowing the SPD to reorganize came up during Pieck's consultations in Karlshorst on 23 December 1946 ([Besprechung am 23. 12. 1946]. Zentrales Parteiarchiv, NL 36/734/245); and was also one of the points discussed with Stalin on 31 January 1947 (according to Pieck's notes, "*Permitting the SPD* in Sov.[iet] o[ccupation zone], whether SED afraid of SPD—needs to be defeated politically" [NL 36/694/5]).
[12]Molotov, "Erklärung über die Entnazifizierung und Demokratisierung Deutschlands [13 March 1947]," ibid., pp. 383-84.
[13]See "Über die zeitweise politische Organisation Deutschlands [22 March 1947]," and "Über den Staatsaufbau Deutschlands [2 April 1947]," ibid., pp. 429, 447, and 450.
[14]Zweiling, "Deutschland und die Moskauer Konferenz," *Einheit* 5 (1947): 417.

gerly linked negligent economic policies in the Western zones to an overall scheme that they characterized as imperialism or restored fascism; and considering the quality of conditions in the East, where labor unity allowed the working people to take over the "political leadership," there was simply no room in this assessment for any solution other than the transplantation of the Soviet-zone model to the Western regions. This same commentary then confronted the question of the party's identification with what were, after all, Soviet proposals. Time and again, Molotov had stood up to his Western counterparts in favor of "German political unity, approval nationwide of all antifascist organizations, a democratic central German government to assume responsibility and to be heard at the peace conference, of involving the parties in working out the new constitution, its confirmation through a plebiscite, and strengthening democracy in every other respect." There was not one genuine interest of the German people that went unmentioned; and because of that happy coincidence, the SED's endorsement of these positions caused its leaders to be denigrated as "agents of the Soviet Union." By the same aberrant logic, Molotov could be called an "agent of the German people," whereas his backing of a democratic development in Germany was merely the other side of his defense not only of Soviet interests but those of "all peace-loving people of the world." The same could not be said of the other nations participating in the negotiations; reactionary groups of monopolists in these capitalist countries were concerned with their own selfish interests, not those of their people.[15]

Other statements confirmed the "correctness" of the policies carried out in the Soviet zone, complaining about insufficient democratization in the West and demanding the approval of political parties in "all of Germany."[16] The SED called continually for a nationwide referendum on the subject of a "unified state under an autonomous, democratic administration" and castigated the "federalist" approach. These were the standard synonyms for Soviet as opposed to Western proposals for solving the German question, and the party attempted to create a sense of the presence in the West of a corresponding mass movement in support of the national policies of the SED.[17] Behind it all lay the demand for creation of a Socialist Unity party in the West that could act to diminish the influence of Social Democracy and enable working people to confront "their enemies" with a unified phalanx. For labor unity alone, the Communists argued, created the conditions for bloc politics with the bourgeois-democratic parties and could compel the SPD in the West to cease its cooperation with restorative elements there. Germany's

[15]The above quotations are all from ibid., pp. 422 and 427-29.

[16]"Zu dem Ergebnis von Moskau. Stellungnahme des Zentralsekretariats [6 May 1947]," *Dokumente der Sozialistischen Einheitspartei Deutschlands*, pp. 187-89.

[17]See "Volksentscheid für die Einheit Deutschlands [1 March 1947]," *Dokumente der Sozialistische Einheitspartei Deutschlands*, pp. 153-57.

future hinged, therefore, upon the mobilization of all democratic forces anxious to rebuild the nation and upon the unification of all working people in the Socialist Unity party.[18] The SED insisted during the following months that the allied refusal to allow the party to organize nationwide fit a pattern of Western violations of the Potsdam accords. Other notable contraventions were the obstruction of German unification, demilitarization, denazification, democratization, and the refusal to permit the Soviet Union to extract reparations from the Western zones. The reason for such conduct was that the "reactionary circles of monopoly capitalism" had expanded their influence in the West and were bent upon dismembering Germany as a means of extending their influence there. Just days after the foreign ministers began deliberations in Moscow, the United States announced the Truman Doctrine and was accused of justifying it with arguments "from the arsenal of the Hitler-Mussolini anti-Comintern pact." In response, the SED insisted that the German people take a hand in their own affairs, preparing themselves for the next round of negotiations scheduled for fall 1947, because the unity of all anti-fascist-democratic forces "throughout Germany" was more important than ever in the aftermath of the Moscow conference. Specifically, formation of the SED in the Western zones would "expand our struggle" and allow it to unfold uniformly throughout the entire country.[19]

Behind the national rhetoric now lay a strategy designed to gain acceptance of the SED in West Germany—perhaps even at the price of allowing the SPD to reorganize in Soviet-occupied Germany—as the first step in creating the matching appearance there of a popular movement; as the party put it, refashioning Germany's future hinged upon "the mobilization of all democratic elements of working people eager to rebuild and the concentration of the working class in the great Socialist Unity party of Germany."[20] Using bloc politics outside the Soviet zone to marshal opinion against Western policies labeled as anti-German and crypto-fascist might work to pressure the allies into concessions at the conference table; and in the event that they balked, the presence of a well-organized political force outside Soviet-occupied Germany still promised to assure some long-range influence in the West. But both hopes rested upon the party's ability to paint the bleakest imaginable picture of developments in the Western zones while using the rosiest hues for Soviet-occupied German—in spite of Pieck's later comment that the SED had no intention of painting things in "black and white."[21]

[18]Dahlem, "Der Kampf um die Zukunft Deutschlands. Zur Moskauer Konferenz," *Neuer Weg* 3/4 (1947): 3.
[19]"Nach der Moskauer Konferenz," *Sozialistische Bildungshefte* 13 (1947): 2-5, 12-13.
[20]The quotations are from "Volksentscheid für die Einheit Deutschlands," *Dokumente der Sozialistischen Einheitspartei Deutschlands*, pp. 156-57.
[21]Pieck, "Bericht des Parteivorstandes," *Protokoll der Verhandlungen des 2. Parteitages*, p. 101.

Particularly in response to the Marshall Plan announced in May 1947, Soviet-zone propaganda began concentrating not just upon Western monopoly capitalism, but upon parallels with fascism. American imperialism hoped to stave off the impending economic crisis by opening up new markets through the granting of state credits, tying local economies and the politics of other countries to the interests of American capital. According to the SED, this had been attempted before; following the First World War, American credits stifled socialist impulses in the German working force and enhanced the power of heavy industry. "This loan policy ended in crisis, fascism, and war." Much the same thing was happening now; Germany's industrial West was being integrated into a Western bloc that endangered peace by creating a new locus for "reactionary and war-mongering elements."[22] This was the thrust of all SED rhetoric directed at Western foreign policy and the Marshall Plan; and by fall 1947, the comparison with fascism had never been more stark. The SED disqualified all Western solutions to the German question by attributing to them an economic motive suggestive of affinities with fascism. Party spokesmen held monopoly capitalism and "its Hitler regime" accountable for the war and accused "foreign finance capital" of opposing German national unity now as a means of protecting itself from competition on the world market and subordinating the nation to the capitalist economy of the West.[23] Stalin told the German Communists exactly that in January 1947; and much of the rhetoric through the remainder of the year revolved around these key determinations. In September, Ulbricht insisted that the crisis of 1929 followed upon the heels of the dollar credits issued after the First World War; then came the reinforcement of monopoly capital, along with it the strengthening of fascism, and eventual catastrophe. "The Marshall plan . . . amounts to a repetition of this path."[24] Analyses published after Zhdanov's two-camps speech in September then fit the Marshall Plan into a grand strategy designed to isolate the USSR as the only force capable of impeding the expansionism of American monopolists, alter the course of developments in Eastern Europe by restoring capitalism, and erect a "cordon sanitaire" around the Soviet Union. Germany's role consisted in formation of a center for the Western bloc that presupposed creation of an "independent West-German federal republic." A political, economic, and military strong point would emerge in a West Germany transformed into a "bastion of American imperialism in Europe directed against the East." This was the aim of the American monopolies and the politics designated as the Truman Doctrine and Marshall Plan.[25]

[22]"Der Marshall-Plan und Deutschland [23 July 1947]," *Dokumente der Sozialistischen Einheitspartei Deutschlands*, p. 197.
[23]"Volksentscheid für die Einheit Deutschlands," ibid., pp. 153 and 157.
[24]Ulbricht, "Schlußwort," *Protokoll der Verhandlungen des 2. Parteitages*, p. 484.
[25]Albin, "Ursachen und Wirkungen des Marshall-Planes," *Einheit* 10 (1947): 901-3.

Claims of Totality

The SED's response to international developments and the division of the world into two hostile sides followed the pattern of the party's unqualified backing of Soviet foreign policy; rabid denunciation of the Western democracies was part of the same reflex. But both responses required explanations that hinged upon a reciprocal hardening of doctrine within the SED itself. The challenge was to alter the ideology in a way capable of legitimizing a toughening policy in the East while depicting the process as the model democracy for Western Germany as well. The first anniversary of the SED created a prime opportunity for redefining its political and doctrinal singularity, redoubling the party's public commitment to democracy, and, as subtly as possible, shifting these definitions toward greater rigidity. In the process, however, the Communists faced the same challenge that had earlier hampered the legitimization of the SED in its own zone. They had to deny constantly that the party was "dependent upon the Soviet occupation regime" and that it was neither a refurbished KPD nor SPD, but "a new party" committed to the national interests of its own people.[26] In a related vein, the Communists also needed to reconcile the SED's sense of its own exclusivity with support for a multi-party system in which political organizations ostensibly competed among themselves for the support of the electorate. Ulbricht made a feeble attempt to meld some of these elements by likening the SED's struggle for the unity of all democratic forces with the "election agitation" of other parties that contributed to the dispersion of Germans from all walks of life; and he painted an equally stark contrast between the other parties, as "mainly elected organizations," and the SED, a "genuine people's party,"[27] that, to his way of thinking, must have enjoyed a mandate free of any obligation to compete for support in an election.

The SED then concluded that the party set an "example for all of Germany";[28] and, pursuing the goal of organization in the western regions of the country, claimed in mid-February to have formed a so-called study group with representatives of the old rump KPD from the Western zones to work toward formation of a "unified socialist party throughout all of Germany." The rationale was identical to the one given in the Soviet zone; new circumstances required a refashioned program such as the one established by the SED's "principles and goals" and evidenced by the party's own politics.[29] In

[26]"Ein Jahr SED," *Sozialistische Bildungshefte* 7 (1947): 7.
[27]Ulbricht, "Die geschichtliche Rolle der SED," *Neuer Weg* 3/4 (1947): 4.
[28]"Ein Jahr SED," *Sozialistische Bildungshefte*, pp. 10 and 12.
[29]"Bildung einer soziaistischen Arbeitsgemeinschaft [14 February 1947]," *Dokumente der Sozialistischen Einheitspartei Deutschlands*, pp. 149-50.

this national context, the SED reemphasized its nature as "a new kind of party" that resembled neither SPD or KPD, but routinely blurred the distinction between a "new party" and a "party of a new type." Sometimes the phrases were uttered as synonyms; on other occasions, words that once characterized a Marxist-Leninist cadre party now alluded to mass membership in ways intended to imply a departure from past sectarianism. Ulbricht came right out and called the SED "a party of a type," a *Partei neuen Typus*; but he contradicted the real meaning of his remark by adding that the SED constituted "neither the continuation of the old KPD nor the old SPD."[30] The tone of the argument grew especially strident when the SED tried again to make national unity contingent upon labor unity and working-class unity synonymous with organization of the SED in the West. The special irony now was that the very Soviet-zone "successes" to which the SED referred as examples worthy of Western emulation were those made possible through the local expansion of the party's power at the expense of rival organizations. The SED insisted nonetheless that the success of progressive and democratic forces everywhere depended upon formation of an SED in West Germany; after all, it would have been impossible to defeat the "enemies of working people, set up and strengthen the underpinnings of democracy, and substantially alleviate the economic misery of our people" without the SED in the East. The only obstacle blocking those achievements in the West was the absence of organized labor there, which allowed "reaction" to expand its old positions of power and permitted Nazis to "sabotage all measures designed to advance the cause of democratic reconstruction."[31]

That kind of hubris combined with Western perceptions of the party as "a camouflaged KPD" to complicate matters tremendously;[32] and the concurrent hardening of its ideological claims only worsened the negative impressions. The assertion that the SED was naturally elevated "above all other parties," for instance, inspired little confidence in its commitment to democracy.[33] But the Communists had to fall back upon national and democratic rhetoric anyway in hopes of selling their political program to ordinary Germans and intellectuals in the West, even though these arguments withered outside of an ideological context that heightened the contradiction between claims of "scientific" exclusivity and respect for a multi-party "democracy." Ulbricht's pronouncements illustrated the difficulty of feigning moderation while expressing an ideological determination that ruled out anything akin to political pluralism. He argued that the SED had developed a program tai-

---

[30]Ulbricht, "Die geschichtliche Rolle der SED," *Neuer Weg* 3/4 (1947): 4.

[31]"Ein Jahr SED," *Sozialistische Bildungshefte*, p. 13; and Pieck, "Ein Jahr Sozialistische Einheitspartei," *Einheit* 4 (1947): 321-22, 329.

[32]See Oelßner, "Ein Jahr SED," *Neues Deutschland*, 27 March 1947.

[33]See "Die Grundsätze der Organisation unserer Partei," *Sozialistische Bildungshefte* 10 (1947): 4.

lored to the "new historical conditions in Germany" and thus echoed older disavowals of a "Soviet system"; but his remarks were prefaced by the contention that the program rested on the foundations of teachings developed by "Marx, Engels, and Lenin."[34] Other commentators soft-peddled the ideological legitimization in one breath and reinforced it in the next. Pieck insisted that the SED never forced any "claim of totality" or *Totalitätsanspruch* upon other parties; but a difference between them existed anyway, he said, because the SED had seized the initiative to deprive those responsible for war of their power base and worked to counteract all plans to split up the nation. Moreover, he added, Marxism was that characteristic which set the SED apart from all other parties, Social Democracy included. Bourgeois parties that worried about the SED could best alleviate their concerns by engaging in direct competition with it in defense of the interests of the German people. As for critics who shunned such competition because they considered the SED to be a "Russian state party," Pieck likened their opinions to "enemy agitation in the service of reaction."[35]

These assumptions were virtually impossible to reconcile with notions of a peaceful road to socialism, and yet the promise of democracy remained a critical element in the SED's rhetoric in large part because of the faint hope that it would resonate in the Western zones. The assurances were then linked to additional characterizations of the SED as a new kind of party. Socialism might well be realized democratically, ran one argument, but for that reason the old "organizational forms" of SPD and KPD could not be transferred schematically to the SED; the new party required forms that corresponded to the current situation. Still, the SED reintroduced that element of its "principles and goals" which, in the context of the times, effectively excluded the possibility of nonviolent evolution under any terms other than unconditional acceptance of Eastern solutions. The party would resort to "revolutionary measures" if the capitalist class left the soil of democracy; and the SED thus needed to be designed as an "*instrument of weaponry*," ready at all times to mobilize working people to assist in the implementation of "progressive politics."[36] In the end, the party's efforts to organize in the Western zones failed because of its inability to overcome the unsavory reputation acquired when it forced the SPD out of existence in its own zone. The allies made permission for the SED to operate in West Germany contingent upon the existence of a Soviet-zone SPD; and, though the Russians toyed throughout the spring with the idea of allowing the Social Democrats to reorganize, events overtook them. No such decision was ever made.[37]

[34]Ulbricht, "Zur Vorbereitung des zweiten Parteitages der SED," *Neuer Weg* 6 (1947): 4.
[35]Pieck, "Die Bedeutung des 2. Parteitages der SED," *Einheit* 9 (1947): 802 and 804.
[36]"Der organisatorische Aufbau der SED," *Sozialistische Bildungshefte* 11 (1947): 2.
[37]Speaking at the SED's first anniversary celebration, Tjulpanov referred to the SED's efforts to work nationwide; various other "democratic organizations" were doing likewise, and Tjulpanov

None of this lessened the party's stress on that passage in its principles and goals which promised a nonviolent road to socialism.[38] Anton Ackermann even buttressed the idea by insisting that Lenin developed the original concept. Arguing along these lines allowed Ackermann to reactivate the stagnating promise of nonviolence even as he invoked the names of those otherwise associated with concepts broadly thought to be incompatible with democracy—violent revolution and dictatorship. It suddenly transpired that Leninism was not prone to political violence at all. Ackermann explained that, in his "April theses," Lenin discussed the transition to socialism under the "special conditions that existed in Russia at the time"; and his analysis focused "upon a peaceful development of the revolution." Lenin believed strongly in the possibility of peaceful post-revolutionary development—a basic orientation to which he adhered "as long as its preconditions existed." Only when the bourgeoisie violated democratic legality by waging civil war did Lenin himself cease to abide by the norms of democracy and resort to revolutionary policies. Prospects for a democratic transition, which Lenin "fervently" longed for, were ultimately beyond his control; and the violence that he hoped to avoid was forced upon him by "capitalist reaction." Still, Ackermann concluded, this failed to alter the fact that "socialists" would stick to a democratic road whenever conditions allowed; and the same was true of German Marxists. It was just that that road presupposed the victory of the "new democracy throughout all of Germany."[39]

This argument shared certain characteristics with the rest of the party's rhetoric in 1947; it relied upon rationalizations that pressured competing parties and the general population to accept the SED's solutions or else; and in the context of the party's nationwide offensive, the guarantee of sure violence in the absence of full acceptance of the Soviet-zone brand of democracy took on menacing implications. All the assurances of peaceful development thus availed the SED little because the party could not shake its reputation as an arm of the Russians now reaching out toward the West; and the more the party's positions buttressed Soviet foreign policy and embraced Soviet history, the less credence was given to its constant talk of "true democracy." Late in the year, Otto Grotewohl tried to reconcile these contradictions in an article that commemorated the Russian revolution.[40] He called

---

added that "we have no reason" to hamper the development of "any democratic organization"—an allusion to the possibility of allowing the SPD to reorganize in the East ("Die SED ist eine bedeutende Kraft geworden," *Neues Deutschland*, 23 April 1947). Perhaps the last reference to "permitting the SPD in the Eastern zone" occurred in notes recorded by Pieck during a report delivered by Tjulpanov on 11 July 1947 (Tulpanow Bericht. 11. 7. 1947. Bericht über innerparteiliche Lage im letzten Halbjahr I u. II 47. Zentrales Parteiarchiv, NL 36/734/300).
[38]Lichtenstein, "Die Fahne der SED in ganz Deutschland," *Neuer Weg* 5 (1947): 1.
[39]Ackermann, "Der friedliche Weg zum Sozialismus," *Neues Deutschland*, 22 April 1947.
[40]Though it appears that Grotewohl merely read a transcript prepared for him by Communist instructors who taught at the SED's party school. See Gniffke, *Jahre mit Ulbricht*, pp. 265-66.

upon the German working class to overcome the decades of antibolshevism and to acquaint itself with real conditions in the Soviet Union because Russia would play a decisive role both in German reconstruction and in the "formation of a new perception of the world." Friendship with Russia, however, by no means denoted animosity toward any other country; and anyone who called the SED the Russians' hired hand acted just as mindlessly as those foolish enough to berate Molotov as a servant of the Germans when he stood up in favor of the interests of German democracy. Grotewohl went on to say that it made no sense for the SED to have bad relations with any of the occupying powers, and if the party's relations with them were not uniformly good, responsibility for that state of affairs lay with those occupation regimes who caused the friction by denying the SED, "a German party," the right to operate in its own country. As a positive example of the party's desire to get along with the occupying powers, Grotewohl even spoke of the "good relationship" that the SED enjoyed in those regions of the country where its operations were legal. So was it good or bad, he asked, to get along with the occupying power? The obvious answer proved how ridiculous it was to claim that the SED "transacts the business" of the Russians; and it was just as slanderous to suggest that they wished to force a Soviet "state form" upon Germany; statesmen like Molotov and Stalin had refuted that contention. The SED perceived the precondition of socialism to be the achievement of political power by the working class, and the party battled for "this new state within the parameters of a democratic republic."[41]

His characterizations of political rhetoric were all accurate enough, but the specific passage from the SED's "principles and goals" to which Grotewohl referred was that familiar phrase which wedded the promise of democracy to the guarantee of a "revolutionary" response if the capitalists conducted themselves undemocratically; and it is perhaps more significant that the party's official resolution passed at its second congress in September 1947 spoke of the validity of the original principles and goals with no explicit restatement of the promise of a democratic road.[42] As a matter of fact, Grotewohl's careful disavowal of a plan to impose the Soviet system upon Germany in September was one of the infrequent repetitions of that promise in 1947. Though the talk of democratic development continued to function as a euphemism for rejection of the Soviet way, leading party spokesmen had largely ceased issuing the more jarring assurance of no Soviet system for Germany. Little incentive to do so remained; after all, the achievement of political power by the working class, a phrase repeated by Grotewohl, was

---

[41]Grotewohl, "30. Jahrestag der Großen Sozialistischen Oktoberrevolution. Rede auf der Tagung des Parteivorstandes am 15./16. Oktober 1947," Sonderausgabe des *Neuen Deutschland*, im Oktober, pp. 7, 14, 15.

[42]See "Entschließung zur politischen Lage," *Protokoll der Verhandlungen des 2. Parteitages*, p. 545. The statutes would retain their relevancy "until a party program has been worked out."

doctrinally synonymous with dictatorship anyway; and much of Grotewohl's reasoning paralleled Ackermann's in this regard. Grotewohl made it clear that the SED considered the basic precondition of socialism to be the acquisition of all political power by the working class; but he steered clear of any further discussion of the meaning of "complete power." However, nothing prevented him from explaining that "democracy, which had been exterminated in numerous so-called democratic states, found a new home in a country that has supposedly placed all its hope in a dictatorship"—the Soviet Union. This point was lost upon those who regarded fascism and communism as two equally menacing forms of dictatorship. The standard arguments to the effect that proletarian dictatorship was temporary, the means to an end, the only kind of dictatorship whose sole purpose lay in self-abolition, and so forth, followed.[43]

The point of his remarks was to stress the fact that the SED preferred the democratic road to socialism (if circumstances only permitted it). Within the context of his arguments, this was an understandable aspiration that Ackermann had gone so far as to ascribe to a peace-loving Lenin; but in both cases, Ackermann's and Grotewohl's, it still turned on the assumption that nothing was wrong about the desire for complete political power and that opposition to one party's sense of its exclusive historical prerogatives fully warranted a violent response synonymous, by its very definition, with dictatorship. Grotewohl, or whoever authored his remarks, also used the occasion to hint at the inevitability of a state system patterned after the Soviet experience in other countries. These comments effectively discarded all previous arguments contrasting democracy and "sovietization;" and they did so by replacing what would have counted as world-revolutionary rhetoric two decades earlier with the forecast of a historical process whose inexorability transformed it into inherent democracy. The key sentence in a passage referring to "Lenin's work" read as follows: "As relentlessly as the sun follows its lawful path from the East to the West, so will the social events that derive from the work of Marx and Lenin follow its relentless path around the entire world."[44]

Ideological Unanimity

The SED's sense of its own exclusivity meant that it habitually claimed all of the credit for the considerable "successes" of Soviet-zone democracy. Granted, from time to time it would attribute the various advances made to the cooperation of "all antifascist-democratic forces"; but even then, organizing and coordinating these forces was said to have been the work of the

[43]Grotewohl, "30. Jahrestag der Grossen Sozialistischen Oktoberrevolution," p. 2.
[44]Ibid., p. 16.

SED.[45] Seeking to extend this system of "bloc politics" to the West, the SED had then broadened its national offensive by going beyond calls for creation of the party in the West and, echoing Molotov's suggestions at the Moscow conference, coupled that demand with proposals for expanding the entire bloc system of parties and mass organizations. After all, the argument went, the exercise in democracy characteristic of the Soviet zone derived its success from this unified political structure. In the West, by contrast, there had been no purge of fascists, no land reform, and no formation of a Socialist Unity party, even though prospects for fundamental change throughout all of Germany hinged upon a "broad popular movement comprised of all progressive men and women" set in motion through the initiative and cooperation of the labor parties. For that reason, the SED worked to develop a program *"for all of Germany,"* which contrasted starkly with the Western policy of dismembering the nation into an Eastern and Western segment and incorporating a truncated Germany into a Western bloc that contained the danger of new war preparations.[46] This kind of outlook makes it easy to see why the SED, using its own language, considered itself "the only democratic party still . . . prohibited in the West"; and as long as the ban continued, the SED recommended that those in the West who were sympathetic to the SED collect signatures, hold rallies, proselytize in the factories, and influence the unions in support of labor unity until it became possible "to create this mass movement in the West, too, with an organizational locus provided on the basis of recognition of the SED."[47]

The prohibition of the SED cast a corresponding shadow on the formation of Western branches of Soviet-zone mass organizations because they were looked upon as Communist fronts; and the party's ceaseless references to its "cooperation" with such organizations as evidence both of their political neutrality and its disinterest in hegemony never lessened the suspicions. Nonetheless, the SED stuck to its argument that German reconstruction hinged upon a broad effort, though it just as consistently undercut its position by adding that the "prerequisite" to antifascist bloc politics was the cooperation and eventual unification of the labor parties.[48] The sophistry was obvious and even more apparent in the distinctions drawn between "bourgeois coalition politics" ascribed to political parties in the West, especially the SPD, and "antifascist bloc politics." The SED defined the former as an alliance of several parties in a common government "led by the bourgeoisie" and under the direct influence of "reactionary forces," whereas the latter required that the "united labor movement assume the leading role in a demo-

[45]See "Zur Politik unserer Partei. Diskussionsgrundlage zur Vorbereitung des 2. Parteitages," *Einheit* 8 (1947): 706.

[46]Ibid., pp. 708-10, 715.

[47]See Fechner, "Der Kampf um die Einheit Deutschlands geht weiter!" *Neuer Weg* 8 (1947): 2.

[48]W. B. "Blockpolitik—Theorie und Praxis," *Neuer Weg* 6 (1947): 1.

cratic development and thus guarantee the construction of a real democracy."[49] Though the system of bloc politics in Soviet-occupied Germany had probably outlived its original usefulness by 1947, which had consisted of setting up a network of organizational constraints on unregulated activity, it continued to serve a purpose in connection with the necessity of making a developing dictatorship appear democratic. Whether anyone was still deceived, however, is another matter. In the West, it was considered self-evident that the mass organizations played an assigned role within a broader strategy aimed at establishing an SED base of operations outside Soviet-occupied Germany; and in the East, there was a growing tendency within the party to scoff at "cooperation" with non-Communists as an outmoded tactic. But the party leadership still thought in terms of appearances, both national and democratic, and insisted upon maintaining a façade threatened from two directions. The primary danger was said to be the widespread feeling within the SED that compelling reasons for cooperation with other parties and mass organizations no longer existed; the other was that bloc politics might be taken "too far" and lead to the abandonment of the SED's "fundamental principles." Bloc politics could not be allowed to degenerate into horse-trading with bourgeois parties because the SED was a "socialist party; thus, all of our measures must serve to bring us closer to our ultimate socialist goal."[50]

But that goal, the attainment of "all power" in the state, still faced a bit of an obstacle in political parties that retained a limited capacity to take their own existence seriously. In response, the Communists came up with an interesting new argument; the SED should strengthen its cooperation with these parties for the sake of "publicly exposing reactionary intrigues" within them and helping the bourgeois-democratic elements deflect the encroachment of reactionary influences.[51] There was even official criticism of "comrades" who refused to cooperate with the CDU and the LDP by claiming that they were "nothing more than reactionary parties in which fascist elements have entrenched themselves."[52] But the irony in all the appeals favoring bloc politics now, including the calls for establishing a matching system of cooperating parties in the West, was that the year neared its end with vicious attacks upon all competing politicians, the SPD's Schumacher in the West and Jakob Kaiser of the Christian Democratic party in the East, and concluded with the SMAD's dismissal from the leadership of the CDU of both Kaiser and Ernst Lemmer. Schumacher, a former concentration-camp inmate, was likened to Goebbels for slandering the Soviet Union and to Hitler in his "method of pogromist speeches." He was further accused of wishing to cede West Germany to the dictatorship of monopoly capital in connection with

---

[49]"Das Wesen der Blockpolitik," *Sozialistische Bildungshefte* 15 (1947): 9-10, 16.
[50]Ibid., p. 13.
[51]W.B. "Blockpolitik—Theorie und Praxis," *Neuer Weg* 6 (1947): 2.
[52]Ibid.

the American intention of using its "wartime 'enemies,'" German monopoly capital, as a friend against its "allies of yesterday." This particular polemic concluded with the remark that American monopoly capital was out to "atomize our fatherland," whereas the Soviet Union wished to maintain German national unity and sovereignty through establishment of a central government.[53] Kaiser fared no better; he was taken to task for directing his criticism at the SED and "against the East," giving voice to the opinions of the CDU's reactionary wing and backing politics, like Schumacher's, calculated to dismember Germany. What followed was worse:

> Without this Eastern zone, there would be no sense speaking anymore of a new Germany because the bizone is already in the hands of the old powers. What exists there is no more than a pasted-on "democracy." . . . Dr. Schumacher is the representative of Germany's dismemberment; he is pursuing the unequivocal goals of American monopoly capital. These are intended to transform a portion of Germany into a colony, play the West off against the East, and carry out dangerous plans. The Socialist Unity party of Germany provided an early warning of these dangers.... To put it crassly, the East stands for peace and the development of genuine civil liberties; the West stands for war and the suppression of civil liberties.[54]

Nor did the SED restrict its ideological offensive to rival parties in its own zone and its chief antagonist in the West, the SPD. Leading Communists now began to discuss the need for a purge of their own party. Pieck, for instance, referred to "unclean elements" that had snuck into the SED. The party needed to rid itself of them, prevent any further activity of this sort, and maintain the level of sharp political "vigilance."[55]

The problem was caused by the fact that the Communists had earlier skirted key ideological issues for the sake of merger; these reasserted themselves with a vengeance now and created tensions late in the year that threatened the party's viability. Given the growing radicalism of policies pursued by the Communists within the party, a purge of the recalcitrant was virtually inevitable and soon undertaken. Of course, there had been acts of repression against Social Democrats prior to the merger; to a considerable extent a successful outcome to the unity campaign had hinged upon the overt and covert pressure directed at those Social Democrats reluctant to merge. These actions went on throughout 1946, but increased dramatically in 1947;[56] and the internal transformation of the SED through the neutralization or elimination

[53]"Quisling Dr. Schumacher," *Neues Deutschland*, 15 November 1947.
[54]"Jakob Kaisers Verleugnung," *Neues Deutschland*, 19 November 1947.
[55]Pieck, "Die Bedeutung des 2. Parteitages der SED," *Einheit* 9 (1947): 807-8
[56]See Stößel, *Positionen und Strömungen in der KPD/SED 1945-1954*, pp. 190-96.

of one-time Social Democrats was supplied with a doctrinal rationale that corresponded to the overall process of ideological retrenchment. Not that ideology had played no role prior to the party's formation; but the creation of the SED was predicated upon assumptions and assurances that soon demanded clarification. In mid-May 1946, for instance, the SED had passed a resolution calling for educational evening courses, using the bi-monthly *Sozialistische Bildungshefte* as the basic text, to meet every two weeks. In addition, the party organized an elaborate schooling system at local levels and set up an advanced party institution bearing the name of Marx for the development of "qualified cadres."[57] In late October 1946, the SED followed up with another resolution criticizing the insufficient attention paid to the May resolution and explaining that the success of democratic reconstruction and "eventually the socialist transformation" of Germany depended heavily upon outfitting the party's millions of members with the requisite "Marxist armor." The party called for a greater emphasis upon the implementation of the earlier resolution as a means of helping make every party member "a convinced socialist."[58]

The problems alluded to in these documents resulted from the transformation of a Marxist-Leninist cadre party in whose top leadership the rituals of Stalinism were solidly embedded, the KPD, into a temporarily less controllable "mass party," the SED, and back again. As it toughened its stance in open advocacy of Soviet foreign policy, the SED then reacted naturally to Western criticism of Russian behavior throughout Eastern Europe with a declaration of ideological war against "reaction." Not unexpectedly, the party charged that reaction began its own "ideological offensive" first; but by explaining the Western refusal to "cooperate" with the Soviet Union in terms of those kinds of motives, the SED supplied itself with the necessary pretext for placing its own actions within an ideological context. The more emphatic the West's pursuit of ideologically defined objectives, the more rigid the SED's doctrinal self-defense in rationalizing the need for radical politics; and, along with it all, the more vexing the problems caused by Social-Democratic resistance within the SED to this overall process of rigidification. In January 1947, the party issued a third and tougher call for "ideological clarity and unanimity" on a variety of issues, among them the significance of consequent Marxism in battling for democracy and socialism, the need for a nationwide struggle against imperialist reaction, the nature of the new democracy and the preconditions of socialism, the essence of "the Marxist party," and so on.[59]

---

[57]See "Der Aufbau des Schulungssystems in der Sozialistischen Einheitspartei Deutschlands [14 May 1946]," *Dokumente der Sozialistischen Einheitspartei Deutschlands*, pp. 39-41.
[58]"Die Bildungsarbeit der SED [25 October 1946]," ibid., pp. 106-7.
[59]"Die Schulungs- und Bildungsarbeit der Sozialistischen Einheitspartei Deutschlands [23 January 1947]," *Dokumente der Sozialistischen Einheitspartei Deutschlands*, pp. 147-48.

The Internationale

The German Communists discussed these matters with the Russians intensely during the weeks leading up to the party congress in September 1947; and, public rhetoric to the contrary, the private documents available actually depict a party seriously endangered by its own internal contradictions. Paul Wandel's characterization of the second congress as an "offensive against reaction,"[60] for instance, was just one reflection of the growing realization that the SED needed to resolve those contradictions once and for all. The party had to forge ahead in the direction of a Stalinist "new type of party," reverting to ideological positions and practical conduct typical of the old KPD, or prepare to contend with crippling insufficiencies caused by internal dissension over the fundamental nature of its policies. Sergej Tjulpanov raised a number of these issues in private comments made on 11 July 1947 and devoted to the "inner-party situation" during the first half of the year. Judging by Pieck's notes, the only known record, Tjulpanov indulged in the SMAD's usual practice of chastising the party for the intrinsic shortcomings of policies either sanctioned by the Russians or devised by them to begin with. Tjulpanov attributed a wide range of inadequacies to "weaknesses in ideological work" that had generated "contradictions a.[nd] deviations" at various levels of the party leadership; he described these difficulties generally in terms of the penetration of "Schumacher ideology" into the party and categorized the problems further as a combination of opportunism and sectarianism. Attitudes evidently existed within the party that actually regarded "federalism" as preferable to a division of Germany into two halves; and the desire to see the SED take over power had apparently diminished out of concern over the "consequences." Some thought had even been given to distancing the SED from the SMAD and reorienting the party toward "Western democracy." Tjulpanov then intimated that the very notion of national unity, though "properly" advocated by the SED, threatened to develop into what he called bourgeois nationalism (he even objected to an excessively nationalistic speech given by Johannes R. Becher in May 1947);[61] and he proceeded to emphasize the importance of attitudes toward the Soviet Union as the sole "guarantor of democ.[racy] and peace"—the only counterweight, evidently, to excessive nationalism awakened by the party's own staunch advocacy of German unity. In much the same vein, Tjulpanov also criticized the SED for underestimating "ideology as a means of control" and focused on the party's

---

[60]Wandel, "Fortsetzung der Diskussion," *Protokoll der Verhandlungen des 2. Parteitages,* p. 448.
[61]See Chapter Eight.

failure to convey the right understanding of Soviet economic and political life.[62]

Tjulpanov voiced a variety of additional complaints; the party avoided the "most urgent questions," dealt with issues too "abstractly," failed to establish the right relation between "theory and practice," published articles in *Einheit* that exhibited an insufficiently "militant character"; and he faulted the party for its failure, of all things, to engage in "complete criticism of the earlier mistakes of the politics practiced by the KPD a.[nd] the SPD" that were responsible, Tjulpanov said, for easing Hitler's accession to power. A few details followed, but they only highlighted the hypocrisy of assailing the former leaders of the KPD for committing errors inherent in policies ordered by Stalin and the Comintern. Tjulpanov then proceeded to repeat the same pattern now by shifting the blame for the consequences of radical politics mandated or encouraged by the SMAD onto the shoulders of the local Communists, as if the party's faulty implementation of prudent policies was the source of the problem. Tjulpanov even objected to the SED's current criticism of oppositional Communists like "Thalheimer, Brandler, Trotskyists," instead of the Social Democrat Schumacher. The problems themselves were real, however; Tjulpanov alluded to "discord" between the party's executive board and the "masses" who failed to fight in support of the SED;[63] and other SMAD officers, in possession of precise information about inner-party dissension throughout Soviet-occupied Germany and unhappy with the party's preparations for the upcoming congress, painted a far bleaker picture. On 26 July 1947, one of the SMAD's political officers by the name of Nassarov stopped by party headquarters unannounced to warn Pieck that the membership continued to concern itself predominately with matters pertaining to the deteriorating economy at gatherings organized for the express purpose of discussing the political issues raised in the SED's draft resolution intended for formal acceptance at the fall congress.[64]

A memorandum dealing with the same general subject, probably reflecting SMAD concerns and quite likely written in late July, indicated that Tjulpanov had not imagined things when he spoke of a developing rift between party leaders and the rank-and-file. There was apparently dangerously little enthusiasm for the party's policies generally or its draft resolution specifically; and far worse than apathy were the powerful expressions of outright hostility attributed to "Schumacher people." During meetings called to discuss the resolution, for example, the greater interest in numerous localities throughout the zone was to debate the proposition that the unification of KPD and SPD had failed; that attempts to influence the Western zones

[62]Tulpanow Bericht. 11. 7. 1947 um 2 Uhr. Bericht über innerparteiliche Lage im letzten Halbjahr I u. II 47]. Zentrales Parteiarchiv, NL 36/734/299-303.
[63]Ibid.
[64]Gyptner to Pieck, 26 July 1947, ibid., NL 36/734/307.

would be futile; that the SED was internally disunited; and that the Communists were responsible for the state of affairs. Other discussions attempted to focus on "anti-Soviet propaganda" by characterizing the USSR as an "imperialist, expansionist state," sworn to state capitalism; and tried to establish the fact that nothing distinguished Soviet occupation politics from the corresponding practices of the capitalist countries. One party meeting held in Thuringia passed a formal resolution in favor of dissolving the local branch organization of the SED and forcing the occupying powers to alter their policies toward Germany. In other areas, substantial numbers of defectors, apparently all former Social Democrats, had been registered in connection with opposition to the party's policy of battling against "Schumacher people." References to an actual "Schumacher agency within the party" followed along with charges that its members used official meetings to inveigh against the central leadership. Equally harsh criticism was directed at party members who shied away from a "sharp ideological battle against this Schumacher propaganda." In fact, in Erfurt, during a meeting on 21 July, those in attendance agreed to send a revised version of the draft resolution back to the party executive in Berlin with the explanation that the original had not deviated from "old tactics" and that the "old tactics of making promises is discredited." In Mecklenburg, a former Social Democrat got up at a meeting to denounce the rumor that the United States favored the division of Germany; it was the other way around. The United States backed unification of the zones; resistance came from the East. His remarks were followed by a round of applause, and the board promptly elevated the man into the ranks of the branch leadership. In Rostock, another party member just released from an allied POW camp praised "true democracy in America" and said that it did not exist in Soviet-occupied Germany. Just as vexatious were objections raised by radical Communists to the party's "cooperation" with bourgeois parties; many of them apparently favored "forming a Soviet republic out of the Soviet occupation zone as a means of raising the population's standard of living." One line in the party's draft resolution generated particular controversy: "Hunger and cold can only be overcome through the reestablishment of German unity." The critics evidently took this nonsense to mean that those problems would linger interminably in the event that Germany failed to reunite.[65]

Other discussions with the SMAD took place at the highest level in an attempt to solve the problems in time for the party congress because, as one Russian officer said, the "ideological and organizational consolidation of the Socialist Unity party" was enormously important; and, apart from "genuine successes and achievements, this fraternal party exhibits many weaknesses and difficulties." The SMAD found fault specifically with the size of the

[65][No title; no date], ibid., NL 36/734/308-10.

party, now numbering some two million members. It was understandable that "ideological growth" needed to take precedence and that the leadership required "considerable assistance"; the SMAD remained committed to such assistance, and it ought not to be confused with the "petty condescension that has periodically occurred despite the strict orders" of the supreme command. This report spoke in considerable detail of "diversionaries," "other agencies of British and American secret services," "sabotage" and "saboteurs," "pernicious activity," "vermin" and "racketeers" inside the German administrative apparatus; explained the need to "purge the apparatus of hostile antidemocratic elements"; and discussed the damage caused by them within the context of a deteriorating economy. Apparently sensitive to the doubts expressed about the seriousness of the commitment to national unity, the speaker concluded that "we have fallen short of explaining to our German comrades in the SED in Germany the principles of our policy in Germany." The Soviet Union represented the interests of working Germans; "we want no division of Germany, no weakening of Germany as an economic power in Europe. We are intensely interested in genuine democratization of this land and seek to assist working Germans in the struggle against reaction." The English and Americans, by contrast, were bent upon enslaving the country, splitting it in two, blocking its access to free trade on the world market, and "liquidating the German state." The report also discussed the nature of changes in Soviet-occupied Germany generally and characterized it as a "new form of democratic order similar to the kind established in Hungary, Romania, Poland, Bulgaria."[66]

But with the congress rapidly approaching, the party leadership was apparently still plagued by uncertainty and repeatedly sought clarification. In late August, Pieck talked with Marshal Sokolovskij about the party's "thorough" preparations for the congress. The two men apparently discussed the possibility of introducing an additional formal document, dealing with ways of increasing productivity by improving discipline in the workplace; and Pieck raised the question of possible consultations in Moscow prior to the congress.[67] Just a few weeks later, Pieck conferred with another top officer, Makarov, and the two men apparently talked of the need for a "sharper" ideological struggle against the CDU and against Schumacher. Pieck's notes of the discussion also refer to "org.[anizational] measures against Schumacher people in the party" and to "vigilance toward enemies."[68] But doubt about their next step evidently still lingered in the minds of party leaders because they approached Stalin directly with a request for advice. The undated letter characterized the situation in Germany as "critical" and acknowledged that the resolution intended for passage at the upcoming congress had brought

[66][No date; no heading. Written in hand, "SMA" and "Gen. Pieck"], ibid., NL 36/734/347-63.
[67]Besprechung beim Marschall am 28. 8. 1947 um 8 Uhr, ibid., NL 36/734/327-29.
[68]Besprechung mit Makarow am 8. 9. 1947 um 8 Uhr, ibid., NL 36/734/364-66.

"all of the unresolved political issues present in the party and all of the short-comings of our work" out into the open. The rapid growth of the SED, which now suffered from the presence of poorly schooled members, had combined with the "economic difficulties" to cause serious deviations within the SED; these manifested themselves in the form of "pseudoradical, sectarian tendencies," on the one hand, and, on the other, "opportunistic views" with a right-wing orientation. Particular complaints about Social-Democratic agitation against the SED followed, and Stalin was provided with a copy of a defamatory party brochure published about Schumacher.[69] Even this, however, was considered to be a defensive measure; whereas the party really needed to take the "offensive against reaction," focusing upon American monopoly-capitalist intentions that were at the heart of the Marshall Plan and geared toward the domination of Germany. In this connection, the party leadership emphasized the importance of immediate action to improve the living standard of the local population and enclosed plans designed to increase production by improving discipline at work. (These materials were not actually introduced at the party congress, however; the economic plan was made public in the newspapers on 10 October as SMAD order 234.)[70] The letter to Stalin ended with a closing characterization of the party's current predicament as "serious" and concluded that even "comrades who hold responsible positions are being influenced by these difficulties and giving in to substantive deviations in the confidence placed by them in the power of our party." The leadership would have preferred to discuss these matters with Stalin prior to the congress, but no time remained, and Stalin was asked to make "one or two comrades" available for talks instead.[71]

Judging by remarks made during the SED's second congress, which met from 20 through 24 September, and by provocative demonstrations that occurred during the meeting, the party must have received all the necessary assurances that the Soviet Union was in complete accord with the beginning of an internal transformation of the SED into a "party of a new type" and an external "offensive against reaction." Sergej Tjulpanov opened the congress with a blistering invective against the Western allies and an unqualified endorsement of the policies pursued by the SED; and there is even one otherwise unsubstantiated report that, in private conversation with leading Communists in the SED, Tjulpanov hinted for the first time at the abandonment of the "special German road to socialism" that was not actually undertaken

[69]Presumably, Winzer, *Sozialistische Politik? Eine kritische Stellungnahme zu Reden und Aufsätzen von Dr. Kurt Schumacher.*

[70]See Chapter Eight for a discussion of order 234 in connection with its cultural-political repercussions.

[71]The letter, undated, contains neither an address nor any salutation. See Zentrales Parteiarchiv, NL 36/734/332-35.

for another year.[72] This report is indirectly confirmed by the nature of private discussions held between the party leadership and the SMAD; and in the letter to Stalin. The concern expressed by the Russians about excessive manifestations of nationalism, particularly in combination with criticism of the party's insufficient popularization of the Soviet Union, accords entirely with growing skepticism about outdated promises. The fact that the Russians considered serious misgivings about their commitment to German unity to be "nationalistic" sentiment, and then mislabeled it "anti-Soviet propaganda,"[73] merely emphasizes the irreconcilable contradiction of abandoning the earlier assurance of a "German road to socialism," coupling Soviet-occupied Germany to the USSR politically, ideologically, and economically, and still insisting that national unity remained the top priority of Soviet foreign policy. In fact, the hollowness of the argument probably helps explain why Soviet and local propaganda tried to focus attention upon Western plans to "colonize" or "enslave" the country and "liquidate the German state."[74] Within a matter of weeks, both categories of deductions, those professing Soviet respect for the national aspirations of all countries and those in staunch opposition to the objectives of imperialism worldwide, were firmly anchored in Zhdanov's two-camps speech delivered at a secret conference held in Poland to organize the Cominform.

This basic message was already clear in Tjulpanov's opening address to the party congress. He determined that two Germanies existed already, split along ideological lines; one backed friendship with the Soviet Union; the other, with the support of foreign and American capital, wished to drive the German people into the imperialist war now being prepared by monopoly capital. These latter intentions, said Tjulpanov, necessitated an "ideological and political campaign against Marxism, socialism, and bolshevism" distinctly reminiscent of the anti-Comintern pact and its crusade against the Soviet Union. Tjulpanov then spoke about the SED; he called it "the party of Marxists in Germany;" claimed that "the theory of Marx, Engels, Lenin, and Stalin is the sole key to the correct solutions to and understanding of the current situation"; and, without ever mentioning the previous promise of a German road to socialism directly or the disavowal of a Soviet system for Germany, delivered himself of a remark that could be taken to mean two entirely different things: "Marxism never passes over the experiences of . . . the socialist movement in other countries; quite the contrary, Marxism demands that these experiences be considered and critically processed. For that reason the experiences of the triumphant October revolution . . . must not be mechanically transferred to other countries."[75]

[72]See Leonhard, *Die Revolution entläßt ihre Kinder*, p. 385.
[73]Quoting Tjulpanov (Tulpanow Bericht. 11. 7. 1947). Zentrales Parteiarchiv, NL 36/734/299-303.
[74][No date; no heading. Written in hand, "SMA" and "Gen. Pieck"], ibid., NL 36/734/347-63.
[75]"Ansprache Oberst Tjulpanow," *Protokoll der Verhandlungen des 2. Parteitages*, pp. 16-20.

Max Fechner, a former Social Democrat, was the first major speaker after Tjulpanov, and his remarks were less aggressive. Fechner called the SED a "socialist party of a new type," but at least he linked its newness to the eradication of sectarianism and went on to speak of development toward socialism within a "real democracy" through the SED's creative synthesis of revolutionary élan and an eye for the possibilities existing within certain historical givens.[76] But Fechner's comments were much more interesting in comparison with opinions voiced by him several weeks earlier and missing now. Fechner failed to repeat that admonition in his address to the congress. Wilhelm Pieck followed him to the rostrum and said nothing about the German road to socialism either. Instead, he tried to counter charges that the SED had ulterior motives deriving from its "supposed dependency on a foreign power, this means the Soviet Union"; but argued nonetheless that the party could achieve its goals only by adhering consistently to Marxism-Leninism, not through "restraint or rotten compromises." The SED derived its right to lead the "large democratic mass movement" precisely from this doctrinal legitimization; and without the "reliable compass" of Marxism-Leninism, the party would become politically disoriented, losing sight of the goal, socialism, toward which it needed to direct its struggle.[77] Pieck steered clear of the phrase "party of a new type," but, a day or two later, Ulbricht contended that "we are on the way to becoming a party of a new type."[78] The official congress resolution went a step further and concluded categorically that the merger of SPD with KPD had created a "party of new type"—a phrase missing altogether in the more moderate draft version of the resolution that had been circulating at all levels of the party since 1 July and generating such controversy already.[79] Erich Gniffke, another Social Democrat, spoke after Pieck and was almost wistful in arguing that a "socialist mass party" needed to be infused with a basic democratic spirit; "we do not acknowledge a party dictatorship," he said, "we have none and never shall."[80] Gniffke's understanding of internal party democracy meshed poorly with Pieck's description of the SED as "a solid, inwardly closed, unified force";[81] and within a year, Gniffke had fled the zone.

[76]Fechner, "Eröffnungsansprache," ibid., pp. 49, 53-55.
[77]Pieck, "Bericht des Parteivorstandes," ibid., pp. 67 and 79, 93-94.
[78]Ulbricht, "Schlußwort," ibid., p. 479.
[79]See "Entschließung zur politischen Lage," ibid., p. 534; and "Zur Politik unserer Partei. Diskussionsgrundlage zur Vorbereitung des 2. Parteitages," Einheit 8 (August 1947): 705-15. Incidentally, Fechner's disavowal of a solution "schematically" borrowed from the Soviet Union appeared in this same issue of *Einheit*; and it is entirely possible that these kinds of discrepancies testify to a decision made at the highest levels of the Soviet government in late August or early September to begin the process of radicalizing the SED and isolating former Social Democrats within it.
[80]Gniffke, "Organisatorischer Bericht," *Protokoll der Verhandlungen des 2. Parteitages*, pp. 103-5, 112-13.
[81]Pieck, "Bericht des Parteivorstandes," ibid., p. 94.

There was far less confusion about which side Grotewohl, the other former Social Democrat, was on. He insisted that the achievement of socialism required the direction provided by Marxist doctrine and went on to speak plainly of its "further development." Grotewohl took "further development" to mean that the SED acknowledged the continuation and application of Marxism "by Lenin and Stalin" and wished now to extract from it that which was new and useful for German conditions. Grotewohl finished his speech by saying, "We wish, we must acquire precise knowledge of the achievements of Leninism in order to appropriate that which fits Germany. . . . Naturally, this does not mean that we may transfer schematically the Russian experiences and the insights of Russian theory to Germany."[82] In earlier passages, however, Grotewohl had already warned of the threat to world peace posed by the growing strength of the monopolies in the United States and added that "atomic diplomacy is intended to foster an anxiety psychosis with respect to the power of American monopoly capital." Because the Soviet Union waged a consistent struggle against a new war, it was only natural that the "monopolists" slandered the USSR and Soviet-occupied Germany by charging that freedom was denied altogether in the zone just because none existed for "monopolists, war mongers, and fascists."[83] Such comments left little room for doubt about whether the SED had chosen sides internationally; it had done so well before the party congress, but aligned itself even more tightly there when Pieck asked that the allies come to an agreement during the negotiations in London based on the "position advocated by the Soviet Union."[84] The interests of the German people corresponded with Molotov's demands at the international conferences, said another Communist, and this proved that "the peace-loving German people have a large and powerful friend, the Soviet Union," which stood at their side in the pursuit of those objectives.[85]

Further talk of Marxism-Leninism, especially together with allusions to a "new type of party," merely reflected the SED's organizational prerequisites to the pursuit of policies directly coupled to Soviet foreign policy. As Ulbricht put it, "our comrades must be so profoundly persuaded by the doctrine of Marxism-Leninism that they are capable of fighting successfully all reactionary ideologies brought in . . . from the outside."[86] Every expression of ideological commitment, such as Ulbricht's, tied the SED to a foreign power and undercut the credibility of its devotion to national politics. Nor is it easily argued that top Communists overlooked the broader implications of their

[82]Grotewohl, "Der Kampf um die nationale Einheit und um die Demokrataisierung Deutschlands," ibid., pp. 289 and 292.
[83]Ibid., pp. 244 and 252.
[84]Pieck, "Bericht des Parteivorstandes," ibid., pp. 67 and 79.
[85]Dahlem, "Diskussion zu den Referaten Grotewohl und Pieck," ibid., pp. 349-50.
[86]Ulbricht, "Schlußwort," ibid., p. 479.

own rhetoric. Fred Oelßner asked whether national unity was possible at all in light of the fact that "developments in the separate parts of Germany have taken such different directions." He answered himself by citing the emancipation of American slaves as proof that reunification was possible in spite of major differences; but his point was hardly reassuring. "Unity, Comrades, triumphed in America" only after four years of civil war; and German unity was similarly coupled, he added, with national liberation from various forms of capitalist exploitation. "Today we may say together with Abraham Lincoln that we do not believe our Germany can long exist bound over half to the slavery of the monopolies and half to liberty. We do not expect that the house will come tumbling down, but we expect that it will cease to be divided." With their reconstruction of the Soviet zone, then, the SED was not complicating reunification at all but rather creating the very preconditions for unity "because unity is impossible on the basis of the slavery practiced by the monopolies."[87] Shortly after the congress, both Pieck and Ulbricht made additional remarks about party priorities that shed light on the SED's understanding of national unity. Pieck noted that party schooling had been unable to keep up with the rapid pace of the SED's growth into an organization of two million members; whereas its capacity to meet the political demands placed upon it could only be acquired through the "teachings of *Marx-Engels-Lenin-Stalin.*"[88] Ulbricht, celebrating the thirtieth anniversary of the Russian revolution in November 1947, agreed and swore to develop the SED into a nationwide party that *"considers itself closely allied with socialist parties in all countries, above all with the great master, the Communist party of the Soviet Union."*[89]

Ulbricht's remarks built upon the thunderous ovation given Mikhail Suslov at the congress when he read aloud the greetings from the Soviet Communist party that wished the SED success in constructing a "united, democratic, and peace-loving Germany." The audience then broke out in a rousing rendition of the *Internationale,* a song that did double duty until 1944 and the dissolution of the Communist International as the Soviet national anthem. Suslov responded to the cheers by crying out, "Long live the Socialist Unity party," and Hermann Matern, presiding over the congress, answered with a salute to the Communist party of the Soviet Union, its central committee, and "their *Führer* Stalin."

[87]Oelßner, Fortsetzung der Diskussion," ibid., pp. 433-36.
[88]Pieck, "Die Bedeutung des 2. Parteitages der SED," *Einheit* 9 (1947): 806-7.
[89]"Ulbricht, "Die große Lehre," *Einheit* 11 (1947): 1075.

Two Camps

Small wonder that a debate broke out later at a meeting of the SED's central secretariat. But in the meantime, events had taken place elsewhere that established the broader context for the party's expressions of what Pieck had called "international solidarity" before ending the congress with the remark, "The Internationale shall be all mankind," and leading the audience in second round of the former Soviet national anthem.[90] In late September, "the representatives of several Communist parties," the Yugoslav, Bulgarian, Romanian, Hungarian, Polish, French, Czechoslovak, Italian, and Soviet, set up the Communist Information Bureau and reintroduced the idea of "two camps." The ideological points were plain enough; "essential changes" had occurred in the international situation since the war's end. Two camps had formed—"the imperialist and antidemocratic camp, whose main objective consists in establishing the world domination of American capital and the annihilation of democracy; and the antiimperialist and democratic camp, whose main objective remains the fortification of democracy and the liquidation of the vestiges of fascism." The latter camp now needed to join forces to develop an "action program" capable of meeting the challenge of worldwide imperialism, an attainable goal because of the gap between the imperialists' wish to unleash a new war and its actual capability to organize one.[91]

Andrej Zhdanov then provided additional detail. He determined that the USSR, "the bulwark of antiimperialist and antifascist policies, blocked the path in the American pursuit of world domination," and along side the Soviet Union stood the nations "of a new democracy." In all this, Germany often found itself at the center because the Soviet Union backed formation of a "unified, peaceful, demilitarized, democratic Germany," whereas the recent meeting of foreign ministers in Moscow had demonstrated that the United States, England, and France were prepared not only to "sabotage the democratization and demilitarization of Germany but even to liquidate Germany as a unified nation, splitting it up and resolving the peace issue separately." Zhdanov then went somewhat beyond the political argument to focus on the ideological motives that governed Western aggression. He likened American foreign policy to the conduct of German fascism and indicated that, "much like the Nazis . . . , the ruling circles in the USA today camouflage their policy of expansionism with pseudo-defensive anti-Communist goals." The ideological side to American political strategy called for the dissemination of lies and slander about the aggressiveness of the Soviet Union and the new

[90]Pieck, "Schlußwort," *Protokoll der Verhandlungen des 2. Parteitages*, p. 524.
[91]"Deklaration," *Für Frieden und Volksdemokratie*, pp. 5-7.

democracies so as to portray the Anglo-Saxon bloc in a defensive, democratic pose; and for the vilification of the USSR as an anti-democratic, totalitarian power. "The backbone of this propagandistic swindle is the claim that the presence of several parties, along with an organized minority in the opposition, supposedly constitutes a hallmark of genuine democracy."[92]

That latter comment defended the Soviet Union implicitly against the common charge that it could scarcely promote multi-party democracies in Eastern Europe or Soviet-occupied Germany itself, given the nature of its own political system, while also counteracting the impression caused by conspiratorial meetings of various national Communist parties discussing plans for Eastern Europe with a foreign country—in effect, re-creating the Communist International. The SED was in a different position; party leaders did not attend the meeting and could not have, really, because the SED continued to avow that it was not a Communist party at all. But by now, there was little plausibility left to the suggestion that the SED had not chosen sides; it only remained to outfit the political alignment with the appropriate ideological shell. This called for a two-pronged approach that included eloquent rehearsals in defense of Soviet democracy along with lurid warnings about the antibolshevism behind which hid the military intentions of Western capitalism. The German Communists quickly addressed themselves to what Zhdanov had called a "propagandistic swindle" and came out in defense of the single-party dictatorship in the Soviet Union. A second party in a socialist country like the USSR would simply serve to reestablish capitalism; besides, the highest form of democracy was Soviet democracy anyway.[93] Political parties came into existence, developed, and "perished" in the course of the class struggle, ran a related argument by Paul Merker, though at times they did not battle each other openly. For instance, during the war a united front of nations had formed against Germany, a kind of "cease-fire" that could end when the conditions creating it were present no longer; and in some European countries and in Soviet-occupied Germany, in which a "new kind of democracy" had developed, a similar united front came into being to surmount the difficulties caused by fascism.[94]

In contrast to the single-party system in the Soviet Union, read a similar commentary in the *Tägliche Rundschau*, bourgeois democracy merely cloaked the political structure of imperialism, imperialism produced war, and war turned the blood of millions of its victims into hard cash for the plutocrats and imperialists. Moreover, Germany, too, was "haunted by the obscure phantoms of those instigating a new war"; for these agents, paid with foreign money, sewed the seeds of hatred everywhere against the Soviet Union.[95]

[92]Zhdanov, "Über die internationale Lage," ibid., pp. 14, 18-19, 21.
[93]"30 Jahre Sowjetunion," *Sozialistische Bildungshefte* 18 (1947): 12-14.
[94]Merker, "Über die Sowjetdemokratie," *Einheit* 11 (1947): 1041-43.
[95]"Die Maske herunter!" *Tägliche Rundschau*, 3 October 1947.

The two main arguments, for the Soviet system and against Western imperialism, then merged when the Communists complained about those who likened dictatorship and the existence of a single party in the Soviet Union to the single-party dictatorship in fascist Germany. The former had nothing in common with the latter; whereas the only difference between German imperialism, which set up a fascist dictatorship as a better way of implementing its aggressive plans, and American imperialism was that it shrouded its triumphs in democratic phraseology. The new claimants to world domination were simply more adept in their methods than fascist dictatorships.[96] But at one point or another, the arguments all warned of the perils of antibolshevism and contended that its latest manifestation ignored the lessons of the last. In announcing the Truman doctrine, said one, the "freshly baked transatlantic prophets raised the tattered banner of anticommunism," and the peoples who had just seen the same banner in the blood-stained hands of the Hitlers and Mussolinis quickly spotted the wolf's teeth under the lamb's wool of these pseudo-democrats.[97] Anton Ackermann put things even more clearly. Hitler could not have come to power without an anti-Bolshevist smear campaign. Slanders and lies about the USSR had inundated Germany ever since 1917, and the people paid for antibolshevism with an ocean of blood and tears. The same alternatives now presented themselves again; "loud cries of war resound around the globe, and again it is the venerable pied-piper melody of antibolshevism used to provide the accompanying music. Wherever the large American trusts extend their greedy paws . . . , wherever dollar imperialism battles for the bridgeheads of a third world war, the transactions are all neatly wrapped up in antibolshevism." But nowadays, opposite the imperialist camp of warmongers, stood the peoples and nations fighting for a lasting peace and a better future.[98]

This obsession with antibolshevism served purposes directly related to the doctrine of two camps. Though the argument was ostensibly ideological, it undertook to sway public opinion worldwide in two directions for reasons clearly coupled to foreign-policy goals. The Soviet Union emerged as the embodiment of antifascism, peace, and democracy, whereas the West menaced these ideals. The SED's endorsement of Soviet foreign policy generally and Soviet society specifically then came across not as servility to an alien power that verged on a betrayal of national interests, but as a moral commitment that required no further justification. The more emphatic the ideologization of political and geopolitical issues, the fewer the reasons not to emulate the Soviet Union. The thirtieth anniversary of the Russian revolution coincided with the official separation of the world into two camps and provid-

[96]See Orlow, "Imperialismus und Aggression," *Tägliche Rundschau*, 1 August 1947.
[97]"Antikommunismus—der Rauchvorhang der Reaktion," *Tägliche Rundschau*, 2 October 1947.
[98]Ackermann, "Die historische Lehre für Deutschland," *Tägliche Rundschau*, 7 November 1947.

ed the German Communists with a prime opportunity to toughen their ideological posture further. Ulbricht did so with the clearest definition yet of the SED as a Marxist-Leninist-Stalinist party "of a new type." After a slight acknowledgment that conditions in Russia differed from those in Germany, Ulbricht said that the idea of "the party of a new type" had dominated the international labor movement since the beginning of the century, though such a party emerged in Russia alone because Lenin had worked out the theories pertaining to the party and the road to power; and he cemented the argument by stating that the recent congress had shown the SED "well on the way to becoming a party of a new type, a militant party of working people guided by the scientific theory of *Marx, Engels, Lenin, and Stalin.*"[99] Nor was Ulbricht alone in his ringing endorsement of Leninism-Stalinism. Pieck characterized the history of the Bolshevist party as "the history of a merciless fight against every attempt to move the party toward the relinquishment of the principles of Marxism." Lenin had been no dogmatist in this, said Pieck, and added:

> His genius revealed itself in the further development of the teaching of Marx and Engels in the epoch of the socialist revolution and the construction of socialism. What Lenin began, his best pupil and comrade-in-arms, Stalin, continued. Stalin embodies the rich knowledge and the experience of the labor movement in all countries, the ingenious application of these insights to new situations. . . . Stalin's great strength as leader of the party and the peoples of the Soviet Union resides in the profound conviction that the working class and its allies can only carry out their tasks when they allow themselves to be guided by Marxist-Leninist theory. . . . That is the secret behind the victory of Russian workers and peasants in 1917, and that is the explanation for the monumental success of socialist construction, the triumph of socialism over fascism.[100]

Grotewohl rounded out the argument by calling upon all those who loved peace to resist the "pernicious smear campaign" against the Soviet Union; in Germany especially the people needed to understand that Soviet Russia constituted a natural bastion of peace in the current worldwide power alignment, whereas "capitalism spells imperialism, imperialism signals expansion, expansion means war."[101] In light of these kinds of statements, it is difficult to imagine that further ideological reversions were possible, and yet the official abandonment of the German road to socialism and the full transformation of the SED into a Stalinist "party of a new type" was still a year away. For

[99]Ulbricht, "Die große Lehre," *Einheit* 11 (1947): 1070-75.
[100]Pieck, "Die siegreiche Partei," *Tägliche Rundschau,* 6 November 1947.
[101]Grotewohl, "Die Sowjetunion als Garant des Friedens," *Einheit. Sondernummer zum 30. Jahrestag der Oktoberrevolution* 11 (1947): 1011.

now, Pieck kept the promise of a democratic transition alive, barely, by referring to the development of a "democratic state power" as the top priority, though his remark that Stalin embodied the knowledge and experience of the labor movement of *all* countries, coupled with the reference to his ingenious application of these insights "to new situations," was clearly intended to suggest the compatibility of a non-Soviet path to socialism in Germany using Stalinist solutions.[102]

One day after the party's congress ended, the SED's executive board met for a preliminary assessment of the results. By formal decision of the secretariat, which met two hours before, a full discussion of the congress was pushed forward a month to the next board meeting in mid-October;[103] and Grotewohl, who addressed the board on behalf of the secretariat on 25 September, confined himself mostly to remarks that contrasted the party's "critical condition" going into the congress with the success of its "consolidation" internally and "offensive" positioning externally. Grotewohl went on to explain that the question of German unity remained the "cardinal problem" of the party's policies, along with issues of war or peace connected with the Marshall Plan and with monopoly capitalism, because Germany's political predicament resulted from this international situation. But Grotewohl considered the Soviet Union blameless and argued that the question of "peace propaganda" needed to be addressed more intensively as the key to Germany's relationship to the USSR. Even so, Grotewohl made a modest attempt to warn against awakening certain "illusions prematurely"; and he cautioned that Pieck's reference to the "beginnings of the International" should not generate talk within the party about a "newly emerging" body of that name. "We are not the ones authorized to form the International," he added, "but rather to participate in it once it develops again." Otherwise, Grotewohl concluded, he was at a loss to locate any negative economic, political or organizational aspects of the congress that would have caused anyone to leave the congress "dissatisfied."[104]

It seems that few of Grotewohl's former Social-Democratic colleagues shared his sentiments because they voiced considerable unhappiness at a secretariat meeting on 13 October.[105] Otto Meier captured the feelings of

[102]Pieck, "Zwei Revolutionen—zwei Wege," ibid., p. 1004.
[103]See Grotewohl's remarks (Stenographische Niederschrift über die 1. Sitzung des Parteivorstandes der Sozialistischen Einheitspartei Deutschlands am 25. September 1947. Zentrales Parteiarchiv, IV 2/1/14/11); Pieck's notes taken during the preceding meeting of the secretariat reveal very little (Zentralsekretariatssitzung am 25. 9. 1947, 10 Uhr, ibid., NL 36/656/189-90).
[104]Stenographische Niederschrift über die 1. Sitzung des Parteivorstandes der Sozialistischen Einheitspartei Deutschlands am 25. September 1947, ibid., IV 2/1/14/16-22.
[105]According to Pieck's notes of this meeting. Two sets exist; though both appear to apply to the discussion on 13 October, one set includes that date (Zentralsecr[etariatssitzung] 13. 10. [1947], 10 Uhr, ibid., NL 36/656/192-97); the other set carries the—incorrect?—notation "PV 25. 9. 1947" on the second of a three-page document. The first page, "[1. Sitzung des] PV am 25. 9.

former Social Democrats in remarks to the effect that they had not pictured things in this way; they felt "run over" and believed that the Communists had them exactly where they wanted; "now all we are is the Comm. party." The SPD had once been so powerful, compared with an "insignificant" KPD that owed its importance solely to the occupation administration. Another Social Democrat, Karl Litke, complained more specifically of the bad impression made by having Tjulpanov speak to the congress first, criticized the emphasis on the Soviet delegation as its high point, and objected to Matern's salute to the Soviet Communist party and its "Führer" Stalin. Käthe Kern also alluded to displeasure with the characterization of Stalin as "Führer"; and Litke apparently argued that the entire undertaking had focused too intently upon the Soviet Union. The congress did not reflect the attitudes of the masses within the party, and there was considerable mistrust of the East in connection with the feeling that "we aren't serious about the unity" of Germany. Helmut Lehmann seemed to agree in principle; the party's dilemma was that its attitude toward the Soviet Union happened to be correct; but that attitude raised a host of other questions. Ackermann, for instance, acknowledged that the foreign "delegations a.[nd] ovations" had been "too much of a good thing"; the problem, as he saw it, was that the Americans had embarked upon a cold war against the Soviet Union. The party could scarcely stand off to the side, though doing otherwise admittedly led to perceptions of the SED as a "Russ. party." In many respects, Gniffke was then correct in concluding that "we have lost the struggle"; after two-and-a-half years, "our propaganda methods are insufficient." But even Fechner insisted that "our position corresponds with Russ. politics"; and Hermann Matern charged that the "campaign against the East is preparation for the division of G[ermany]."[106]

The nature of the exchanges at the board meeting two days later demonstrated just how serious the Communist leadership was about "consolidating" the party internally. Pieck defended the raucous display of enthusiasm for the Soviet delegation and explained that the ovations, as well as the approval of Tjulpanov's remarks, resulted from an understanding of "mutual interests." Instead of confirming accusations that the SED was a Russian party and that the congress manifested a "unilateral Communist character," the gathering proved that the SED pursued an "entirely independent German policy" further characterized by Pieck as "new."[107] These comments set the tone for the rigid reaction of the top leadership to the concerns then voiced by a pair of former Social Democrats. Paul Szillat stressed again that Social

1947, 12 Uhr," with the signature NL 36/656/1, apparently does not belong with the second two.
[106]These remarks are all drawn from the two documents listed in the preceding footnote.
[107]Pieck, "Die dringendsten Aufgaben der Partei nach dem Parteitag," Stenographische Niederschrift über die 2. Tagung des Parteivorstandes der Sozialistischen Einheitspartei Deutschlands am 15./16. Oktober 1947, ibid., IV 2/1/15/8. Further citations are given in the text.

Democrats felt as if they had been "run over" and complained about "our dependence upon the occupation power." He characterized the rhetoric employed at the recent congress as "the biased language of a party of the past"; objected to the "stage management" that governed the public remarks and fostered the impression of a certain group determined to "drive back" another; and criticized the "declamatory" nature of schematic speeches. Szillat acknowledged the limits imposed upon the party by the military occupation, which he blamed on those Germans who started the war; but he argued that there was a world of difference between the sense of an internal accord with the "Russian people, the Russian party, and the occupation power" and a pronounced external political manifestation that could hamper the SED's struggle for German unity. However praiseworthy his remarks may have seemed to a socialist, Tjulpanov's speech served to confirm the "marching in step" that occurred during the congress and hardened impressions of dependency. Simple political prudence dictated a measure of restraint in order to avoid "endangering the struggle for the unity of Germany because of a one-sided affiliation and the accusation that we are not representing our own interests, but the interests of the occupying power." According to Szillat, malicious interpretations attached to the congress developed out of the "demonstration for Comrade Stalin" (42-47).

A West German board member by the name of Karl Hauser agreed generally with the assessment of tactical errors; but neither he nor Szillat said anything out loud that went beyond an expression of tactical concerns. "We should spread the word about the Marxism advocated together with Russia consistently and, if possible, implement it practically," said Hauser; but defending "sovereign Russian politics" was nonetheless highly problematical; and the Warsaw declaration that established the Communist Information Bureau ought not to be "ogled" (112-17).

That remark provided Ulbricht and Pieck with the chance to emphasize the party's "new" priorities. Ulbricht denied categorically that the congress had been one-sided or that the predominant views expressed there were reminiscent of an "old direction"; he insisted that "our own German peace policy and our German plan of reconstruction" dominated, not questions having to do with the relationship with the Communist party of the Soviet Union. But Ulbricht qualified his remarks by pointing out that the USSR, and those Eastern European countries in which "popular-democratic rule" had been set up, was the most powerful force in the world favoring peace; "we will not advance one step," he said, "without a battle against Soviet baiting," and that fight could not be fought from a defensive position. Ulbricht then praised the Warsaw declaration and its "exact analysis" of the worldwide situation; the document told antifascist-democratic forces around the world just who needed to join forces and against whom. "In this respect," Ulbricht said, "our political line, accepted at the party congress, conforms perfectly with the contents of the Warsaw document." These circumstances also made it clear that "those of us in Germany, too, have to carry out offensive propaganda in the matter of the Soviet Union and the new order in the popular-democratic countries"; and Ulbricht added that the Soviet Union was the first country to create a party of a new type. Those who felt "run over" could only utter that complaint in the first place because they stood still, whereas the party had embarked upon an "absolutely new road." As for the salute to Stalin, Ulbricht considered it time for an internal party discussion of the historical accomplishments of Lenin and Stalin—precisely because the SED was a German party and needed to know "who the international forces are that wish to help us and have previously shown the right way" (122-28).

Pieck concurred; there was nothing in the Warsaw document that could not be found in "our political resolution, even if the words were different"; and the Warsaw conference itself corresponded with the "large-scale demonstration of international solidarity that developed [at the congress] due to the presence of the foreign delegates." Pieck went on to call Szillat's talk of a favorization of Communists "dangerous," dismissed the notion of "stage management," and likened these opinions to views routinely expressed by Schumacher. (Szillat was just one of some two hundred thousand former Social Democrats and "deviationists" kicked out of the party by 1950.)[108] Pieck found particular fault with the suggestion that German unity might be jeopardized by the emphasis on "our relations with the Soviet Union." Tjulpanov's remarks corresponded entirely with "our views" and ought never to be taken to mean that "we might be dependent upon the Soviet Union or the occupying power in our political decisions"; the party was entirely independent in its political views and decisions and received instructions from no one. Pieck concluded that the SED had every reason to "intensify our policies in the closest cooperation with the Soviet occupation power in order, concurrently, to develop elements for us to pass along to the Western occupation zones and use in establishing contact, internationally too, with peaceloving elements around the world" (139-46).

At the end of the party's second congress and looking toward the next foreign-ministers' conference, the SED noted that Germany would become a prime source of danger to the world if agreement were not soon reached; and an important prerequisite to any such agreement was the "clear manifestation of the German people's desire for their own unity."[109] The "Volkskongreß," convened in December, was meant to offer the German people the opportunity to raise their voices in unison—in the form of "all antifascist-democratic parties, unions, and other mass organizations," along with representatives of science and art from "all of Germany." The SED called upon

[108]Müller, "Sozialistische Einheitspartei Deutschlands (SED)," *SBZ-Handbuch*, p. 500.
[109]"Entschließung zur politischen Lage," *Protokoll der Verhandlungen des 2. Parteitages*, p. 529.

the parties and organizations to prepare to send representatives to the Volks-kongreß for the purpose of electing a delegation to speak on behalf of the German people at the foreign-ministers' conference in London.[110] The Volks-kongreß was the culmination of the SED's attempt to cultivate the impression of a mass movement in support of its narrow objectives. Naturally, it was characterized as a nonpartisan "popular movement," rather than a "party-political organization";[111] but the SED planned the entire operation, most observers assumed as much, and the Communists spent a good deal of their time at the congress insisting that attempts to portray it as the equivalent of an SED party congress would fail, as Pieck said, because it represented a "broad movement" comprised of delegates from all regions of Germany. Pieck's efforts to blunt suggestions that the SED's support of unity and democracy throughout Germany represented a "political maneuver" fell largely on deaf ears, however, and the standard denials that the SED neither aspired to hegemonic goals nor served the interests of a foreign power became no more credible through repetition.[112] The congress nonetheless ended with the request that the "will of the German people," as expressed by a delegation elected at the Volkskongreß, be heard in London. Molotov repeated the request once the negotiations were underway, but the allies were not interested, and the conference soon ended, as Molotov said, "in a fiasco."[113]

---

[110]"Aufruf zu einem deutschen Volkskongress für Einheit und gerechten Frieden," *Dokumente der Sozialistischen Einheitspartei Deutschlands*, pp. 247-48.
[111]Külz, "Zum Geleit," *Protokoll des 1. Deutschen Volkskongresses für Einheit und gerechten Frieden am 6. und 7. Dezember 1947*, pp. 5-6.
[112]Pieck, "Eröffnungsansprache," ibid., pp. 15-18.
[113]Entschließung. Der Deutsche Volkskongress für Einheit und gerechten Frieden an die Londoner Außenministerkonferenz," ibid., pp. 103-4; Molotov, "Über die Ergebnisse der Londoner Außenministerberatung," *Fragen der Außenpolitik*, p. 600.

CHAPTER SEVEN

SED and Intelligentsia

The new year began with clear indications that the SED planned to continue a public policy of coupling the intellectuals more closely to the party and using them to popularize its plan of national reconstruction—in accordance with Pieck's declaration at the conference one year earlier to "seize the initiative . . . in the area of culture just as we have done in economic and political matters."[1] There had been some hesitation since then, probably caused by doubt about the outcome of the elections; considerations related to Soviet foreign policy also figured in, and seizing the initiative still coincided with the conflicting idea that "we Communists" needed to broaden the approach to cultural affairs by acting "as representatives of German culture."[2] But an editorial written by the cultural editor of the *Tägliche Rundschau*, Shemjakin, now reemphasized the necessity of seizing the initiative. Shemjakin boasted that reactionaries no longer dared to oppose political democracy in Soviet-occupied Germany openly; but they were much bolder about resisting cultural democracy and could play on certain prejudices that still festered in the minds of Germans because of twelve years of fascism.[3] Shemjakin stopped short of naming the prejudices that hindered advances in cultural democracy comparable to the political transformation of the zone; but just a few months earlier, both Sergej Tjulpanov and Alexander Dymschitz argued that the German intellectuals had an obligation to acquaint themselves with Soviet culture. Combined with the party's growing tendency to use the terms fascist and anti-Bolshevist interchangeably when reviling intellectuals who seemed either disinterested in Soviet culture or suspicious about the importation of its norms, it was abundantly clear that Shemjakin advocated alterations in cultural life possible only through the elimination of *anti-Soviet* "prejudices." One way of dealing with troublesome intellectuals, then, was by attributing these biases all the more aggressively to the lingering influence of fascism. This permitted the Communists to label opposition to their own poli-

[1]Pieck, "Um die Erneuerung der deutschen Kultur," *Erste Zentrale Kulturtagung der KPD*, pp. 11-12.
[2]Information von Walter Ulbricht über ein Gespräch mit Bockow, Tulpanow, Wolkow am 22. 12. 1945. Zentrales Parteiarchiv, NL 36/734/143-44.
[3]Schemjakin, "Demokratie und Volksbildung," *Tägliche Rundschau*, 7 January 1947.

cies as fascist and to pressure intellectuals into acknowledging the true nature of their own proclivities.

In late January 1947, the SED's division of Kultur und Erziehung called the party's various cultural functionaries together for a general discussion of strategy, and selected representatives of "nonpartisan" outfits and agencies like the DVV, FDJ, FDGB, and the Kulturbund attended, too. This gathering received far less publicity than the conference in February 1946,[4] however, and the deliberations took place behind closed doors—understandably so in light of the bluntness of the language used and the confusion that arose over the nature of the relationship between "seizing the initiative" and "broadening" the party's handling of cultural issues. The disagreement between the two principal speakers, Josef Naas from Kultur und Erziehung and Anton Ackermann from the SED's central secretariat, may not have been voiced in those terms; but it seems fairly apparent that the party's less experienced functionaries, such as Naas, could never match the abilities of dialecticians like Ackermann when it came to combining hardline policies with deceptively moderate rhetoric. Not everyone benefited from the doctrinal experience of years in Soviet exile, and those functionaries without it were more prone to err in the direction of one extreme or the other. Ackermann addressed the conference first and spent his time making ideological observations based mostly on the argument, months before creation of the Cominform, that "two camps" existed in Germany—one regressive and reactionary, the other progressive and bent upon changing the intellectual outlook of the German people.[5] But Ackermann, who called his presentation "The Intellectual Situation of the Present Day," softened the sound of class warfare by shifting his focus away from Marxism-Leninism to "scientific socialism"; as the quintessence of all science, he explained, socialism stood for more than the ideological platform of a Marxist-Leninist party because workers could not emancipate themselves without concurrently liberating all mankind, intellectuals included. This was how scientific socialism mastered its linkage of politics, economics, and cultural life, said Ackermann, mimicking the Stalinist axiom that socialism had nothing in common with lifeless principles and dead dogmas (6-7).

These were the kinds of syllogisms used to resolve the contradiction between a "seizure" of the initiative and a "broader" view of cultural-political objectives, and the same was true of Ackermann's conclusion that the party had talked "very little or not at all about socialism" because the requisite political maturity could only be acquired in the course of the "struggle for the

[4]See "Die geistige Situation. Beginn der großen Kulturtagung der SED"; "Die Kulturtagung der SED vom 28. bis 30. Januar 1947"; and "Dreiklang: Arbeiter, Bauer, Intelligenz. Die nächsten Aufgaben unserer Kulturarbeit," *Neues Deutschland*, 29, 30 January and 2 February 1947.
[5]Stenographische Niederschrift über die SED-Kulturkonferenz am 28./29. Januar 1947. Zentrales Parteiarchiv, IV 2/1.01/33/5. Additional page citations are provided in the text.

democratization of Germany." But rhetorical moderation had its limits, and Ackermann closed his remarks by claiming that the party had chosen a road leading to the "victory of democracy today and tomorrow to the triumph of socialism" (30-31). True, he did not link socialism to dictatorship, yet; by ignoring the crux of the matter, dictatorship, it was easier to wed cultural activities and the intellectuals to the political objectives of a single party that considered its policies nonpartisan just by declaring the doctrine behind its actions universal. Josef Naas, however, had the unenviable task of speaking more concretely on the subject of "SED and Intelligentsia" and, in Ackermann's opinion, missed the point altogether.[6] The problem was fairly simple; the party had not managed to acquire the political or cultural support of the intellectuals and, internally, at conferences such as this one, had no reason to pretend otherwise. Klaus Gysi provided the most optimistic view of things when he argued that the majority of intellectuals had adopted a wait-and-see attitude—not emphatically reactionary, not militantly hostile, by no means "positive" either, but laying low with an inherited reactionary streak.[7] The party's cultural functionaries needed to figure out how to win them over and exuded confidence that much could be accomplished through persuasion. Paul Wandel spoke of the widespread enthusiasm for a "new road to socialism that is not as terrible as the Russian road," though he characterized that path as the "least bloody" of any yet traveled; only to conclude that the Bolshevist party won millions of workers for its ideas by acquainting them with "elemental truths" (48).

By contrast, Naas got himself into trouble by considering the possibility that some of the German intellectuals would nonetheless refuse to listen. In many respects, Naas was no more dogmatic than Ackermann. The SED aspired to the "rule of the working class and the formation of a socialist society" via democratization and parliamentarism, he said; and there was no disputing the fact that working toward socialism presupposed an affiliation with the "party of the workers." Potential new party members, whether they came originally from the bourgeoisie, the peasantry, or the intelligentsia, had to be unfailing in their endorsement of the goal of "consequent socialism." Naas went on to explain further that the SED struggled for political power on behalf of the working class, not for itself; this altruism distinguished it from all other German parties and testified to the "unparalleled democratic character" of the SED. But Naas still wondered aloud how a consistently socialist or working-class party could ever appeal to the intellectuals. He never answered that key question satisfactorily and resorted to ultimatums instead. The intellectuals needed to be convinced of the inevitability of socialism because socialism was "coming with or without today's intellectuals," who were faced

[6]See the abridged version in Naas, "SED und Intelligenz," *Neues Deutschland*, 2 February 1947. [7]Stenographische Niederschrift über die SED-Kulturkonferenz am 28./29. Januar 1947. Zentrales Parteiarchiv, IV 2/1.01/33/161-62. Page citations are included in the text.

with the choice of deciding in favor of alliance with the working class or being outflanked by the next generation of intellectuals. Not that the party was entirely blameless; a "man like Major Dymschitz practically does his work in isolation and on his own." Still, Naas placed most of the blame on the intellectuals themselves, and he considered it time to start speaking to them in a "clear, unmistakable, firm language," replacing the previous solicitude with an unyielding attitude (112-25).

Ackermann objected to these remarks. He endorsed the notion that "seizing the political power of the working class" was the precondition for socialism; but, without yet identifying this phrase with the parenthetical "revolutionary dictatorship of the proletariat" (included in his seminal article on the German road to socialism), Ackermann went on to argue that the power of the working class was unthinkable in the absence of an alliance with other segments of the population—including the intellectuals. He did explain that the class rule of the bourgeoisie amounted to a dictatorship of the minority over the majority, though only to make the contrasting point that the "political rule of the working class" represented the "rule of the overwhelming majority of the people in the interest of the entire people and the interest of the nation." Ackermann could still have gone on from there, doctrinally, to explain that proletarian dictatorship was nothing more than the rule of just such a majority and thus consummate democracy. But he concentrated instead on the contention that the "political rule" of the working class was unthinkable without an alliance especially with the intelligentsia. Besides, intellectuals were not among those segments of the population destined to lose anything through socialism; they had, to the contrary, everything to gain—the "chance of a genuinely free development of science and art" together with the opportunity to place their creativity in the service of the people and the higher development of mankind. The irony of Ackermann's remarks resided, however, in the fact that he considered socialism and dictatorship to be identical, if not necessarily in terms of the road leading to them, then certainly in the final analysis; so that Ackermann effectively insisted upon policies and rhetoric designed to enlist the support of creative intellectuals in shortening the way to dictatorship. He ended his comments with a few additional points. He stressed again that there was no way for the party to achieve its objectives other than by establishing "solid and broad positions" among the peasantry, the middle class, and the intelligentsia. In answer to Naas' argument that socialism would develop "with or against the intelligentsia" (Naas actually said "with or without"), Ackermann expressed his agreement in principle. It was certainly possible that socialism might have to develop in opposition to the intellectuals; but the more important question was whether "we won't arrive at socialism faster and easier if we succeed in rallying major segments of the intelligentsia to our side." Ackermann also insisted that Naas was wrong to play the "new intelligentsia" off against the "old"; if the

SED had no more to offer the older generation than the promise of being supplanted by younger intellectuals, the first group would be right to "turn its back on us." Besides, Ackermann denied that he was discouraged about the current situation; "we don't yet have the entire intelligentsia behind us, but we have a considerable portion" (129-36).

The Gewerkschaft 17 für Kunst und Schrifttum beim FDGB

The Gewerkschaft 17, already referred to in the context of early efforts to unionize writers and artists,[8] was another of the organizations that endeavored to broaden support for party policies without acknowledging that the SED had its hands in the operation. In private, there was no sense pretending otherwise, but good reason to proceed cautiously. During the discussions in January 1947, Amandus Prietzel who headed the Gewerkschaft 17, warned of the danger of having "our bread buttered with the accusation: you just want to get us into the SED, you're only after a single party, and we've had enough of conditions like those under Hitler that allow one party to dominate art!" It was especially important to avoid that impression because "we want to try to build an organization for creative intellectuals in all of Germany patterned after the Gewerkschaft 17."[9] But those grand plans, along with the union's local ambitions, were effectively scuttled by problems that developed out of dissatisfaction with the organizational key to using it as an arm of the party to begin with. Though many actors, writers, musicians, artists, and the like had belonged to professional associations prior to 1933, neither the Russians nor the local Communists relished the prospect of their reorganization in 1945 as independent entities capable of rivaling monopolies like the Kulturbund. Consequently, the associations came back to life as subsidiaries of a new bureaucracy created specifically to coordinate and police their activities. Later, the Gewerkschaft 17 acknowledged that the old groups were resurrected under their original names in order to improve the attractiveness of the larger organization in the eyes of "members of artistic and cultural professions not yet enamored of the idea of unions."[10] But the idea backfired when using the names of associations with proud traditions for newly emasculated union "divisions" only deepened the resentment toward involuntary affiliations. One of the main reasons why was that creative artists tended to regard unions as a way of furthering their professional interests, whereas political objectives were uppermost in the minds of the organ-

[8]See Chapter Two.
[9]Stenographische Niederschrift über die SED-Kulturkonferenz am 28./29. Januar 1947. Zentrales Parteiarchiv, IV 2/1.01/33/165-67.
[10]See "Richtlinien für die Tätigkeit der Sparten in der Gewerkschaft Kunst und Schrifttum," *Kunst und Schrifttum* 3 (1948): 11.

izers. For example, at the conference in January, Prietzel welcomed suggestions that the SED pay more attention to the Gewerkschaft 17 in order to revitalize the union; but he stressed the need for the party to be judicious in its efforts because most union members had little interest in "socialist ideas."[11] By then, internal disagreements had crippled the organization anyway, and one man, Erich Otto, managed to cause most of them by refusing to submit to the authority of the central board. Otto, the last president of the Genossenschaft Deutscher Bühnenangehörigen (GDBA or actors' guild) prior to Hitler's assumption of power, was chosen to head the Berlin local of the Gewerkschaft 17 on 9 July 1946;[12] and at a conference in Weimar from 29 July to 2 August 1946, which coincided with the GDBA's seventy-fifth anniversary, Otto got his old job back as well. The influence that went with those two positions allowed him to obstruct key jurisdictional and programmatic decisions handed down by the board.

The idea of union representation for intellectuals actually dated as far back as May 1945, however, when representatives of actors, musicians, stage performers, and technical or administrative theater personnel met to form a group called the Verband Bühne-Film-Musik out of four professional associations that had existed for decades.[13] Before the end of the year, none other than Erich Otto, who initially favored the idea of a unified organization, undertook to convince writers and artists that they should also join the group. Ironically, the principal obstruction for a time was the FDGB itself. No unions or union-like organizations had a chance of being approved by the SMAD other than as federation branches, and the idea of organizing professionally independent creative intellectuals under the aegis of an industrial union structured around the principle of shop councils, "Betriebsräte," was resisted by its leadership. But FDGB officials changed their minds in early 1946, possibly encouraged to do so by the SMAD,[14] and "adjusted" the federation's proposed statutes to include intellectuals or "geistig Schaffende."[15]

---

[11]See Stenographische Niederschrift über die SED-Kulturkonferenz am 28./29. Januar 1947. Zentrales Parteiarchiv, IV 2/1.01/33/165-67.

[12]See *1. Geschäftsbericht des Freien Deutschen Gewerkschaftsbundes Groß-Berlin* 1946, p. 201.

[13]See Memorandum zur Gewerkschaft 17 Kunst und Schrifttum. [Ca. July 1948.] Archiv der Gewerkschaftsbewegung, Sig. 1480. The Genossenschaft Deutscher Bühnenangehörigen, the internationale Artisten-Loge, the Deutscher Musiker-Verband, and Technik und Verwaltung were the associations that represented, correspondingly, actors, performing artists, musicians, and stage personnel.

[14]See the discussion in Chapter Two concerning the Schutzverband Deutscher Autoren and the Schutzverband Bildender Künstler.

[15]See the comments in Gewerkschaft 17. Kunst und Schrifttum. Zentralvorstand. Bühnengenossenschaft und Gerwerkschaft. 27 January 1948 [Prietzel]. Archiv der Gewerkschaftsbewegung, Sig. 1480. Actually, the FDGB's provisional statutes, passed in early 1946 but probably revised throughout the spring, made no mention of "geistig Schaffende" or creative intellectuals and referred only to the unionization of "workers and employees." The statutes did, however, list the

In late April 1946, the FDGB's executive board formalized the decision to establish eighteen branches under the roof of the federation and to change the name of the Verband Bühne-Film-Musik to the Gewerkschaft 17, Kunst, Schrifttum und freie Berufe structured according to seven specialized divisions. The original four, the Genossenschaft Deutscher Bühnenangehörigen, Internationale Artisten-Loge, Deutscher Musiker-Verband, and Technik und Verwaltung, were now joined by three others—the Schutzverband Deutscher Autoren, Verband Deutscher Presse, and Schutzverband Bildender Künstler.[16]

Having approved the idea of a union branch for creative intellectuals, the FDGB now recommended that the Gewerkschaft 17 focus on the organizational activities of its subsidiaries and the selection of their governing bodies. Divisional delegates could then meet to set up regional offices of the Gewerkschaft 17 and elect the union's first official executive board. At this point, the FDGB also promised the divisions "organizational independence within the framework of the union," but it was already clear that they would be shackled by the statutes of the Gewerkschaft 17, which, in turn, answered directly to the federation.[17] In May 1946, an "organizational committee" of three, Prietzel, Hermann Fischer, and Maximilian Larsen, was chosen at a meeting in Halle and scheduled the union's first conference, attended by 106 delegates, for 17 and 18 June 1946 in Berlin. In his remarks to the delegates, Bernhard Göring, representing the FDGB, then defined union obligations in terms of "conscious political work" designed to prevail upon the state, economy, and society "in a socialist sense." Still at issue, however, were the modalities. Göring himself said only that the "intellectual occupations" needed to focus on cultural life in much the same way as the unions worked through political parties and "shop councils" to influence the economy. But other speakers were far more specific about the union's basic organizational principle and in their understanding of its cultural-political mandate. The problem was that certain divisions already chafed under the arrangement; some, like the GDBA, then began agitating for complete administrative and finan-

---

Gewerkschaft für Kunst und Schrifttum as the seventeenth of eighteen constituent affiliations governed by the official provisions of the central FDGB. (Only three of the eighteen, employees, teachers and educators, and Kunst und Schrifttum, failed to qualify as "industrial unions.") See "Vorläufige Satzung des Freien Deutschen Gewerkschaftsbundes," *Geschäftsbericht des Freien Deutschen Gewerkschaftsbundes 1946*, pp. 68-78. The FDGB's permanent statutes, passed in 1947, then added the phrase "creative intellectuals" to the earlier reference to "workers and employees" (see "Satzung des Freien Deutschen Gewerkschaftsbundes," *Parteiensystem zwischen Demokratie und Volksdemokratie*, p. 363).

[16]In August 1946, the SMAD granted the request to drop the designation "und freie Berufe" from the title. See Jendretzky and Goering to Prietzel, 5 August 1946. Archiv der Gewerkschaftsbewegung, Sig. 278.

[17]See Freier Deutscher Gewerkschaftsbund. Verband für Bühne, Film, Musik. 2 May 1946. Jendretzky. Göring, ibid., Sig. 1.

cial autonomy; and the stock assurances of "substantial independence" within the Gewerkschaft 17 fell on deaf ears.

As head of the union, Prietzel refused to budge; he declared that the organization's "program, statutes, membership card, and dues" were obligatory for *all* members and for *all* divisions of the Gewerkschaft 17 and that more than "lip service" had to be paid to the FDGB's program. If the divisions failed to coordinate their activities, the Gewerkschaft 17 would fall far short of its cultural-political objectives. Prietzel now identified these as turning most artistic undertakings like theaters over to the public and establishing the principle of union "codetermination" in the rest. He also insisted that acquiring the same kind of influence within public agencies charged with the oversight of cultural affairs, such as local and regional offices of culture and education (*Volksbildungsämter*), should also be considered part of the union's responsibilities.[18] Those principles, which mirrored the FDGB's own provisional statutes and their insistence upon the "uncontested right of codetermination" exercised via shop councils, were then written into the draft statutes of the Gewerkschaft 17. Under discussion as early as June 1946, the statutes established two related principles. First, the union aspired to a dominant position of influence within all administrative agencies responsible for the organization or regulation of cultural activities on the basis of the same "uncontested right of codetermination";[19] and, second, the Gewerkschaft 17 aimed to organize its members within individual operations. Though the statutes themselves were vague about it, this general provision was used to sanction the involvement of union councils in the *artistic* management of theaters.

By approving the statutes,[20] the SMAD also appeared to endorse the union's interpretation of them, though the ongoing controversy over both organizational and programmatic matters probably explains why all governing documents remained under internal discussion until February 1948. At the conference in June 1946, however, the sentiment of the board majority was clear. There should be one union for all creative intellectuals; and that union demanded the right to participate in decisions made—"in artistic matters as well"—within cultural administrative agencies and theaters. Otto representing actors who recoiled at the thought of stage-hands running their affairs, was staunchly opposed and now rejected the entire concept of a single organization like the Gewerkschaft 17. He uttered the ultimate insult by likening it to cultural-political practices characteristic of the Nazis and argued in favor of

[18]See Bericht über die Zonenkonferenz der Gewerkschaft 17 für Kunst, Schrifttum und freie Berufe am 17. und 18. Juni 1946, ibid.
[19]Freier Deutscher Gewerkschaftsbund. Gewerkschaft 17 Kunst und Schrifttum. Satzungsentwurf, ibid., Sig. 278.
[20]See Kunst, Schrifttum u. Freie Berufe an den Vorstand des FDGB über den Organisationsausschuß, 12 November 1946, Gez. Prietzel, ibid.

divisional autonomy. He was not initially opposed to a direct affiliation with the FDGB, but remained staunchly opposed to union participation in repertory decisions and in the hiring and firing of actors. Those matters belonged in the hands of the director, Otto said, and warned that a radical understanding of codetermination heralded the "collapse of German theater culture everywhere."[21] In spite of his protest, the June conference ended with the election of a union board packed with advocates of codetermination (the "Leipzig" faction) and with the endorsement of statutes that could be read as a mandate for codetermination. Otto, who represented the "Berlin faction," was also elected to the board, barely, but predicted that the views of the majority would prove "ruinous" and refused to join it.[22]

Concern that the GDBA now intended to enact policies at its upcoming meeting in Weimar at odds with the provisional statutes of the Gewerkschaft 17 surfaced one month later when the new board met on 16 July 1946. Prietzel again argued that the shop councils set up within the theaters needed to be heard in repertory and other *Regiefragen*, rather than restricting themselves to administrative matters; and virtually every other speaker concurred. One said that the GDBA had to subordinate itself to the Gewerkschaft 17.[23] The pressing problem now was that the association had invited representatives from the Western zones to attend the meeting in Weimar; and if resolutions that conflicted with the statutes of the Gewerkschaft 17 or the FDGB happened to be passed, especially with Westerners looking on, the challenge to central union authority would make a bad impression. The Weimar meeting, said a hardline board member by the name of Lenz, enjoyed "complete freedom" as long as voting delegates operated according to union statutes. The GDBA, he added, must not be permitted to withdraw from the Gewerkschaft 17 and affiliate itself directly with the FDGB. Another speaker worried similarly about "attempts to divide" the union and indicated that he had been asked by the local Soviet occupation administration to produce a list of colleagues who planned on attending the meeting in Weimar. Not that anyone objected in principle to a conference open to delegates from the West, but the danger that it might turn "reactionary" needed to be countered through the presence of a "progressive union man." The board members seemed to be especially irritated at the FDGB for sanctioning the meeting without consulting the board and complained further that representatives of the Gewerkschaft 17 had yet to receive an invitation. Prietzel expressed his general support of interzonal conferences organized by any one of the union's seven divisions, but in the future these should take place only when the Gewerkschaft 17 knew about them in advance. Another board member then

---

[21] Ibid.

[22] See Otto's letter to Prietzel, in ibid., Sig. 3.

[23] 1. Sitzung des Zentral-(Haupt)-Vorstandes der Gewerkschaft 17 für Kunst, Schrifttum und freie Berufe am 16. Juli 1946, ibid., Sig. 3.

intimated that "Karlshorst" actually looked favorably upon the conference as an opportunity to show off Soviet-zone reconstruction to representatives from the West; and Bernhard Göring made it clear that the FDGB also backed the Weimar meeting wholeheartedly. The federation saw this first interzonal conference as part of its national aspirations. Göring went on to express particular regret over Otto's withdrawal from the union board and conveyed his interest in seeing that tensions between the "Leipzig and the Berlin orientation" be overcome. Even so, the FDGB intended to prevent any development in Weimar that conflicted with what Göring called "the general direction and outlook in union affairs."[24]

While the board welcomed those assurances, further concern was expressed that the SMAD might use the Weimar conference to "remonstrate with the Gewerkschaft 17."[25] Why exactly is unclear; perhaps the board feared being held accountable for the outcome of a conference that it had never favored and could not control; or perhaps the Russians were unhappy that the board's tactless handling of the issue of codetermination might have provoked Otto into considering a break with the Gewerkschaft 17. The SMAD must have supported the concept in principle, but keeping the union together was evidently considered more important than codetermination. The SMAD seems to have helped finance the Weimar conference and engaged in direct discussions with Otto—all in what proved to be a futile effort to keep the Gewerkschaft 17 from splintering. Göring also declared his intention of trying to persuade Otto to rejoin the board.[26] But these efforts at accommodation with Otto never meant that the Gewerkschaft 17 lacked the general support of the FDGB or the SMAD in 1946 and 1947. The fact remains that the Gewerkschaft 17 never softened its position on the right of union councils to influence theater repertories and approve personnel decisions involving artists; and it is hard to understand how the SED-dominated board could have remained so consistently adamant about those issues in the absence of party approval. Moreover, as Prietzel never tired of pointing out, the SMAD had also endorsed the union's statutes. Those provisions may have been missing any specific mention of codetermination in artistic matters within theaters, and the lingering dispute probably prevented the statutes from being widely disseminated once they had been passed.[27] But there is still no proof that the

[24]Ibid.
[25]Ibid.
[26]See Aktennotiz. Betr. Tagung der Bühnengenossenschaft in Weimar, 22 July 1946, Gez. Jendretzky and Göring, ibid., Sig. 278.
[27]Both the statutes and the accompanying "guidelines" governing the activities of the divisions came up at the union's second central delegates' conference in November 1947, but final dispensation was delayed until a meeting of the newly elected board (see "Zweite Zentral-Delegiertenkonferenz," Kunst und Schrifttum 12 (1947): 2). That meeting took place on 17 December 1947, but again the decision was postponed ("Erste Sitzung des neugewählten Zentralvorstandes," Kunst und Schrifttum 1 (1948): 3). The smaller executive board or Geschäftsführender

SMAD opposed the idea of codetermination in theaters, only indirect suggestions that the Russians were reluctant to allow the union to split because of it. Besides, like all other "mass organizations," the Gewerkschaft 17 was expected to work for the enactment of measures beneficial to the consolidation of cultural-political power by the SED; and establishing union bodies authorized to participate in discussions of repertories was tantamount to placing censors in theaters around the country who answered to a central union that the party itself dominated. That must have been an appealing prospect to the party leadership, at least prior to the establishment of better mechanisms for controlling the performance plans of Soviet-zone theaters; and there is little doubt either that the SMAD was keen on finding a solution to the problem of theater regulation and censorship.[28]

That search actually lasted well into 1949 and beyond. Meanwhile, board sentiment in favor of union participation in artistic decisions never lessened. At a meeting in September 1946, several voices were raised in support of it,[29] though Prietzel seemed to realize that solving the dispute with the actors administratively was fraught with risks. The situation could have been avoided, he wrote Jendretzky and Göring, if only the FDGB had come out against stirrings of independence within the divisions; now the opportunity for a "radical" change in policy was lost, and a compromise needed to be found instead.[30] But Prietzel still stuck to the board's position on codetermination within theaters. On 20 September 1946, he told Jendretzky that his colleagues remained strongly in favor of the principle and repeated the argument that the concept should cover the hiring and firing of actors and rep-

---

Vorstand then met in mid-February 1948 and settled upon the "definitive formulation" of both statutes and "guidelines." The guidelines were subsequently published, though the board decided that the statutes themselves would only be sent or "at least" sent to union functionaries (see "Sitzung des Geschäftsführenden Vorstandes" and "Richtlinien für die Tätigkeit der Sparten in der Gewerkschaft Kunst und Schrifttum," *Kunst und Schrifttum* 3 (1948): 10-11). Interestingly, the new guidelines differed from the version first published fourteen months earlier ("Richtlinien für die Tätigkeit der Sparten innerhalb der Gewerkschaft für Kunst und Schrifttum im FDGB," *Kunst und Schrifttum* 1 (1947): 2). The old guidelines referred to the "complete independence" of the divisions within the context of the union's overall statutory provisions, which were not allowed to conflict with those of the Gewerkschaft 17; whereas the final version likewise banned decisions by any of the divisional boards that failed to correspond to the statutes either of the Gewerkschaft 17 or the FDGB. But the phrase "complete independence," even within that limited context, was missing. Both statutes and the guidelines were then printed after all, but in an edition that appears to have been intended for internal use only. See "Satzung des Gewerkschafts Kunst und Schrifttum; Richtlinien für die Tätigkeit der Sparten in der Gewerkschaft Kunst und Schrifttum," hg. vom Zentralvorstand der Industriegewerkschaft Kunst und Schrifttum im Freien Deutschen Gewerkschaftbund für die sowjetisch besetzte Zone [no date; probably 1948].

[28]See Chapters Eight and Fourteen for further discussion of stage censorship.

[29]See Bericht über die erweiterte Vorstandssitzung der IG. 17 (Kunst u. Schrifttum) am 3. September 46 in Leipzig, 9 September 1946. Archiv der Gewerkschaftsbewegung, Sig. 3.

[30]Prietzel to Jendretzky and Göring, 14 September 1946, ibid., Sig. 278.

ertory planning.[31] At the same time, an FDGB official, Hermann Schlimme, cautioned that most of the divisions advocated "total independence" as it had existed prior to 1933; complained that the application materials for membership in the GDBA made no mention of the FDGB; and demanded an end to those shenanigans.[32] An attempt to resolve the impasse then occurred at a meeting on 23 September between FDGB officials Jendretzky, Göring, and Schlimme and representatives of the Gewerkschaft 17. With Otto present, the participants passed a resolution that obligated the divisions to follow the instructions of the central board, as well as the FDGB, and declared the "strong authority of the union board of organization 17 to be the only road to a solution to the serious problems of unity in the area of art and science."[33] A few days later, however, the GDBA's own board threatened to "reexamine the organizational structure" of its division if changes were not made that guaranteed its ability to represent the interests of actors. "Now as before," the letter to the FDGB stated, "we consider the Gewerkschaft 17 to be an artificial, rather than organically developed construction that has all the makings of a contrived solution with the danger of failure built into it." Most actors, the letter added, demanded that the GDBA be granted total independence.[34]

Inge von Wangenheim, a member of the GDBA's Berlin board, also complained about the "complete incapacitation" of the Gewerkschaft 17, its state of paralysis, and the "irresponsible insistence upon experimentation." Like Otto, though for different political reasons, she advocated an end to the arrangement and argued in favor of affiliating the divisions directly with the FDGB.[35] Yet another attempt was made by union officials to reach an understanding with Otto that would keep the GDBA in the Gewerkschaft 17,[36] but functionaries like Prietzel also continued their defense of the "organizational form" of the Gewerkschaft 17, anchored in union statutes approved by Soviet "censors," and proposed no more than meaningless structural alterations.[37] Worse, Prietzel refused to alter the board's stance in the matter of codeter-

[31]Prietzel to Jedretzky, 20 September 1946, ibid.
[32]Für die Vorstandssitzung, 13 September 1946, gez. Schlimme, Ibid.
[33]Vorstand des FDGB. 2. Vorsitzender. Betr.: Ergebnis der Besprechung mit Vertretern der Vorstände der Gewerkschaft 17 "Kunst und Schrifttum" am 23. September 1946, 24 September 1946, gez. Göring, ibid., Sig. 278.
[34]Der Verwaltungsrat der Genossenschaft Deutscher Bühnenangehörigen in der Gewerkschaft Kunst und Schrifttum an den Vorstand des Freien Deutschen Gewerkschaftsbundes (Zone und Groß-Berlin), 1 November 1946, ibid.
[35]Inge v. Wangenheim (Mitglied des Vorstandes der Gewerkschaft 17 - Groß-Berlin) an den Bundesvorstand des FDGB. Z. H. des Kollegen H. Jendretzki. Vorschlag zur Reorganisierung der Gewerkschaft für Kunst und Schrifttum und damit zur tatsächlichen Erfüllung der ihr vom FDGB gestellten kulturpolitischen Aufgaben, ca. late November 1946, ibid.
[36]Aktennotiz. Betrifft: Bühnengenossenschaft. Gez. Schlimme, 23 November 1946, ibid.
[37]An den Bundnesvorstand des F.D.G.B. zu Hd. d. Koll. Jendretzky. Gegenäußerung zu dem Vorschlag der Kollegin I. v. Wangenheim zur Reorganisierung der Gewerkschaft 17, 25 November 1946, gez. Prietzel, ibid.

mination within Soviet-zone theaters, basing his position on the general principle included in the union's statutes and insisting that his interpretation of the document reflected the board's understanding.[38] That position was reaffirmed at the board meeting in December 1946 in spite of the fact that Jendretzky, trying to avoid a rift, made an attempt to weaken it. No one's mind was changed, and the opinions expressed by other speakers determined to use shop councils to influence repertories made a confrontation with the GDBA inevitable. Nor did board members indicate any interest in compromising on matters of divisional autonomy.[39]

Meanwhile, another way of influencing cultural developments in Soviet-occupied Germany was under consideration. The idea of "advisory art commissions" attached to outlying administrative agencies in charge of cultural affairs developed out of the same paragraph calling for codetermination included in the union's statutes and surfaced first at a board meeting on 3 September 1946. There was talk there of establishing "cultural-political commissions" based in offices of culture and education throughout Soviet-occupied Germany; but doing so required the cooperation of the DVV, which had its own regulatory claims on the state and local agencies.[40] Nonetheless, the DVV quickly endorsed the concept and in late October scheduled the proposal for further discussion at an upcoming meeting of the ministers of the state and provincial divisions of culture and education.[41] Guidelines governing the formation of these art commissions were drawn up at a meeting in November, possibly in the form of an "ordinance" dated 11 November,[42] and Herbert Volkmann raised the subject again at the ministers' conference in December 1946.[43] In the meantime, the DVV sent its guidelines to state and provincial administrations, urging them, apparently once "again," to form art commissions that were to be consulted in all matters pertaining to art and literature.[44] The opinion of the advisory commissions, broken down into five separate subdivisions of theater, music, entertainment, visual arts, and litera-

[38]An den Vorstand des F.D.G.B. Kollege Jendretzky. Mitbestimmungsrecht der Betriebsräte an den deutschen Theatern, 27 November 1946, gez. Prietzel, ibid.

[39]See Tagung des geschäftsführenden Vorstandes am 4. Dezember 1946; and Erweiterte Vorstandssitzung der Gewerkschaft 17 f. Kunst und Schrifttum am 5. Dezember 1946, ibid., Sig. 3.

[40]Bericht über die erweiterte Vorstandssitzung der IG. 17 am 3. September 46, ibid.

[41]Präsidialkanzlei an die Leiter der Volksbildungsabteilungen der Länder und Provinzen der sowjetischen Besatzungszone, 29 October 1946, Bundesarchiv. Abt. Potsdam, R-2/808/96-7.

[42]See Protokoll. Tagung der Sparte Genossenschaft Deutscher Bühnenangehöriger der Gewerkschaft 17 - Kunst und Schrifttum - im Freien Deutschen Gewerkschaftsbund in Weimar am 3. und 4. Juli 1947. Archiv der Gewerkschaftschaftsbewegung, Sig. 0809.

[43]See Konferenz der Minister für Volksbildung aus den Ländern und Provinzen am 18. und 19. 12. 1946. Vorläufige Tagesordnung; and Beschluß-Protokoll vom 18. Dezember 1946 (Zu 1 a. Bildung von beratenden Kunstausschüsse). Bundesarchiv. Abt. Potsdam, R-2/51/1 and 9.

[44]"Beratende Kunstausschüsse in der sowjetischen Besatzungszone," *Kunst und Schrifttum* 1 (1947): 4.

ture, was to be solicited by the state and provincial administrations in questions related to the development of young artists, the naming of prominent personalities to head art institutes of every kind, the licensing or franchising of artistic undertakings, the screening of theater and exhibition plans, and so on. These art commissions were conceived as a joint effort comprised of "progressive-democratic elements" represented by the divisions of the Gewerkschaft 17, the Kulturbund, directors of music and art schools, directors and conductors of leading theaters and orchestras, as well as by personalities known for their distinguished cultural achievements. The state and provincial branches of the Gewerkschaft 17 were to assume the responsibility for naming "suitable representatives" to the commissions, and similar such organizations were to be set up locally as well, at least in the larger cities.[45]

Further details came out at the union's board meeting on 4 and 5 December 1946, and Prietzel's reference there to the formation of an "art commission" attached to the DVV itself, operating as the "final authority,"[46] suggests that the idea of corresponding commissions in administrative agencies scattered throughout Soviet-occupied Germany developed in conjunction with the DVV's abortive plan to set up its own "council for art and literature." Volkmann's letter to Tjulpanov just four days after passage of the DVV's "ordinance," on 15 November 1946, was clear about the council's membership; it would be comprised of FDGB functionaries with cultural responsibilities, delegates from the Gewerkschaft 17, representatives of the union's seven divisions, state and provincial administrators in charge of culture and education, and an assortment of other officials. According to Volkmann, the council's duties needed to include "the supervision and evaluation of exhibition and repertory plans"[47]—another indication that different ways of controlling stage repertories by German agencies were under consideration. In fact, Jendretzky's opposition to union shop councils with a guaranteed say in the setting of theater repertories may well have reflected a growing awareness by FDGB and party officials that there was no point in splitting the union over the issue as long as other possibilities for repertory control existed. Besides, blinded by their own ambition, union officials and other administrators seemed to forget that repertory censorship still rested in the hands of the local Soviet military administrations. As Jendretzky put it, "We are unable to consider the involvement of shop councils in discussions about repertory management. Repertories are discussed with the occupation authorities; our council members really have nothing to do with artistic arrangements."[48]

[45]Ibid.

[46]Tagung des gewerkschaftsführenden Vorstandes am 4. Dezember 46. Archiv der Gewerkschaftsbewegung, Sig. 3. See also Prietzel's undated circular (late 1946), Sig. 278.

[47]An die Oberste Sowjetische Militäradministration. Propagandaleitung. Herrn Oberst Tjulpanow. Gez. Volkmann, 15 November 1946, Bundesarchiv. Abt. Potsdam, R-2/1091/25-28.

[48]Erweiterte Vorstandssitzung der Gewerkschaft 17 f. Kunst und Schrifttum am 5. Dezember

In the matter of art commissions attached to local and regional administrations, however, there appears to have been a general consensus. At the meeting on 4 December, Prietzel indicated that the union's corresponding state boards needed to send out instructions to cities, counties, and districts regarding the formation of art commissions; and Lenz returned to the idea the next day. He called these commissions the union's "central demand," but identified its other preoccupation as the issue of codetermination through shop councils in artistic matters. In fact, Lenz suggested that the Gewerkschaft 17 place "good artists" who might be councilmen already on the commissions organized by the DVV; if "criticism" of performance plans proved impossible by way of the councils set up within the theaters, then "we can perhaps achieve the same thing through the art commissions." Prietzel also mentioned those bodies during the discussion on 5 December and indicated that they had to be established by 1 January 1947—the identical date set by Volkmann for a progress report at the next ministers' conference.[49] The commissions were still being considered in May, June, and July 1947,[50] but little ever came of the idea. The likely reason was that the SED's successful use of "cadre politics" to take over administrative agencies and regulatory organs from within, as well as the party's general consolidation of power, eliminated the need for them; and the same can be said of union "codetermination" in other settings.

Nonetheless, the board of the Gewerkschaft 17 continued throughout 1947 and well into 1948 trying to develop plans for using codetermination as a way of exerting "a dominant art- and cultural-political influence in favor of democratic renewal and progressive thinking in all administrations and other agencies."[51] But simple union organization caused major problems as well. In May 1947, the Gewerkschaft 17 acknowledged that "many colleagues" had still not joined the union. Appeals to potential members to help make it the "reservoir of all progressive-thinking elements practicing artistic and cultural professions" followed,[52] to relatively little avail, and several months later the leadership was still trying to sell the concept, "new in the un-

1946. Archiv der Gewerkschaftsbewegung, Sig. 3.

[49]Ibid; and Beschlußprotokoll, 18 December 1946. Bundesarchiv, Abt. Potsdam, R-2/51/9

[50]Sitzung des Gesamtvorstandes der Gewerkschaft 17 - Kunst und Schrifttum - Zone am 29. u. 30 Mai 1947; and Tagung der Sparte Genossenschaft Deutscher Bühnenangehöriger am 2. und 4. Juli 1947. Archiv der Gewerkschaftsbewegung, Sig. 3 and Sig. 0809. See also the specific complaint in June 1947 that the opportunity available to the union through the establishment of the advisory art commissions to exert influence in artistic and cultural-political questions had not been fully exploited ("Tagung des Zentralvorstandes," *Kunst und Schrifttum* 6 [1947]: 1).

[51]"Unsere Spartentagungen. Sparte: Autoren. Schutzverband Deutscher Autoren," *Kunst und Schrifttum* 7-8 (1947): 7.

[52]"Zur Werbekampagne" and "Aufruf. An alle Schaffenden in den künstlerischen Betrieben und an die Angehörigen der künstlerischen und kulturellen Betriebe," *Kunst und Schrifttum* 6 (1947): 5.

ion movement,"[53] to independent or self-employed professionals. In one of Prietzel's articles aimed at acquiring the support of creative intellectuals, freelancers as well, he said that the Gewerkschaft 17 hoped to become the "most powerful democratic organization" exerting a powerful influence over both legislation and public administration in every imaginable area, including cultural politics.[54] In order to do so, the Gewerkschaft 17 had to develop into the "organizational catch-basin for broad circles of creative intellectuals—artists, writers, journalists, but also workers and employees to the extent that they have jobs in enterprises belonging to the sphere of the Gewerkschaft 17 (theaters, radio stations, movie houses, film industry)."[55] Still, Prietzel was keenly aware of the fact that the unionization of creative intellectuals, especially those who worked independently, posed special difficulties and warned that consideration had to be given to the attitudes peculiar to this group. A "wooden hammer" was not the proper tool for use in a process of intellectual reeducation, he said, the less so "in a country that may have to reckon with many more years of, at the least, a semi-capitalist economic and social order."[56]

But the main objection remained unchanged; creative intellectuals bridled at the affiliation with the FDGB and its Gewerkschaft 17. Adding insult to injury, the union warned repeatedly that the divisions were not "permitted" as autonomous organizations under occupation law.[57] Internally, Prietzel cautioned that the divisions needed to be explicit about their membership in the Gewerkschaft 17 and the FDGB when issuing public announcements or risk having their activities, possibly even the division itself, banned by the SMAD.[58] Acceptance as a member of an association to which individual artists or professionals had often belonged prior to 1933 thus meant automatic inclusion in the FDGB; and "membership in the Gewerkschaft für Kunst und Schrifttum and the FDGB," it was plainly stated, "is governed by the statutes of the FDGB and the Gewerkschaft für Kunst und Schrifttum."[59] As a unanimous resolution passed by the board in mid-1947 put it, "the union comes first; the division . . . takes second place"; and this order of priorities required the "absolute acknowledgment" of the principles and statutes of both the

[53]Prietzel, "Planmäßige Organisationsarbeit," *Kunst und Schrifttum* 2 (1948): 5.

[54]Prietzel, "Die gewerkschaftliche Erfassung der 'geistig Schaffenden,'" *Kunst und Schrifttum* 9 (1947): 3-4

[55]Ibid.; and "Freiberuflich Tätige—geistig Schaffende," *Kunst und Schrifttum* 4 (1947): 3, for Prietzel's discussion of the distinction between intellectuals engaged in cultural pursuits generally linked to a specific job or institution and those who worked on a freelance basis.

[56]Prietzel, "Die gewerkschaftliche Erfassung der 'geistig Schaffenden,'" *Kunst und Schrifttum* 9 (1947): 3-4

[57]Prietzel, "Planmäßige Organisationsarbeit," *Kunst und Schrifttum* 2 (1948): 5.

[58]Sitzung des Gesamtvorstandes der Gewerkschaft 17 - Kunst und Schrifttum - Zone am 29. u. 30. Mai 1947. Archiv der Gewerkschaftsbewegung, Sig. 3.

[59]"Richtlinien für die Tätigkeit der Sparten in der Gewerkschaft Kunst und Schrifttum," *Kunst und Schrifttum* 3 (1948): 11.

FDGB and the Gewerkschaft 17, as an "indivisible part of the federation"; as well as the unqualified acceptance of the jurisdiction of the central board in all common economic, social, and cultural questions.[60] Resolutions passed by division boards, the Spartenleitungen, were specifically prohibited from contradicting the statutes of the Gewerkschaft 17 (or the FDGB). If any did, the central board had the right of veto; and if doubt arose, the ultimate decision rested with the executive board of the entire Soviet-zone FDGB.[61]

Moreover, the boards of all local, state, and provincial offices of the Gewerkschaft 17 were expected to prepare written plans at least three months in advance; reports were then to be filed by the local and district offices with the state or provincial union leadership, which in turn reported to central headquarters.[62] These procedures became even more constricting with the passage of definitive guidelines governing the activities of the divisions and other regulations concerned with administrative oversight. The state boards of the Gewerkschaft 17 were required to file periodic reports with the central board covering, apart from business details, social and cultural-political matters.[63] Moreover, that board had the responsibility for setting up and implementing broader working plans; establishing the areas of responsibility assigned to the union's major internal departments as well as to the management of the seven divisions; and settling all economic, social, or cultural-political questions with a bearing on the union's general membership.[64] The divisions were also obliged to inform the union in writing of all "important matters";[65] and additional regulation took place at the state or provincial level. Among the duties of the union offices in the states and provinces were the "supervision of division activities and securing regular reports" from the divisions.[66]

This kind of regulatory authority could have assisted the central leadership tremendously in its efforts to realize the union's ambitions. As Prietzel imagined things in May 1947, "There ought not to be a single artistic or cultural event of any significance held, either locally or in the larger areas of regions, states, and provinces, in which the Gewerkschaft 17 has not been represented by its functionaries in the process of planning and implementation."[67] Indeed, the Gewerkschaft 17 was probably conceived of with ambitions something like those in mind; with proper organization, it might well

[60]"Tagung des Zentralvorstandes," *Kunst und Schrifttum* 6 (1947): 2.
[61]"Richtlinien für die Tätigkeit der Sparten," *Kunst und Schrifttum* 3 (1948): 11.
[62]"Arbeitspläne und Berichte," *Kunst und Schrifttum* 1 (1947): 4.
[63]"Arbeitspläne," *Kunst und Schrifttum* 3 (1948): 12.
[64]"Geschäftsordnung für den Zentralvorstand der Gewerkschaft 17 'Kunst und Schrifttum,'" *Kunst und Schrifttum* 5 (1948): 22.
[65]"Richtlinien für die Tätigkeit der Sparten in der Gewerkschaft Kunst und Schrifttum," *Kunst und Schrifttum* 3 (1948): 11.
[66]"Arbeitspläne," *Kunst und Schrifttum* 3 (1948): 12.
[67]Prietzel, "Von den Aufgaben unserer Funktionäre," *Kunst und Schrifttum* 5 (1947): 3.

have worked effectively toward them. But things developed so rapidly in the zone, and the international situation deteriorated so quickly, that much of the top-level thinking behind formation of the Gewerkschaft 17 probably shifted long before the union had a chance of amounting to anything. That irony makes the frenetic organizational activity of the Gewerkschaft 17 no less striking. Much of this work would have been normal for any union; as Prietzel put it as part of his announcement that the Gewerkschaft 17 numbered 44,000 by late 1946, "the stronger the organization, the greater its capacity for effective representation of the economic, social, and cultural claims and rights of its members."[68] But strength in numbers lost its significance against the backdrop of the SED's consolidation of power; the need to agitate in favor of occupational or professional interests dissolved when the representation of these and all other conceivable interests became the exclusive domain of the SED itself. It is important to understand, however, that these developments could not have been fully anticipated in 1945, and they were not entirely apparent in 1947 either. As a result, the Gewerkschaft 17 forged ahead with organizational activities in a tight race with political processes leading to its own superfluousness. The initiatives undertaken in Berlin and throughout Soviet-occupied Germany in 1947 generated a maze of executive meetings, delegates' conventions, division delegates' conventions, and conventions of delegates meeting separately to discuss the affairs of the divisions. These gatherings were broken down further according to state, province, city (Greater Berlin, as well as each of its twenty different districts), or zone; and designed to place the Gewerkschaft 17 in the organizational position necessary to pursue objectives developed as part of its original purpose.

A glance at the schedule of meetings and conventions in 1947 conveys the best sense of the importance that must have been attached to an extension of the union's structures throughout the towns and countryside of Soviet-occupied Germany. Following the formation of the union and its establishment in the regional capitals of Dresden (Saxony), Erfurt (Thuringia), Halle (province of Saxony), Schwerin (province of Mecklenburg-Vorpommern), and Potsdam (province of Brandenburg), and after the elections of the Soviet-zone executive board in July 1946 and the representatives of the seven divisions a few weeks later, the following months were spent getting the union set up locally, selecting their individual boards, and planning for separate delegates' meetings at the state and provincial level. As it happened, these never took place; the union's central board contented itself instead with planning equivalent meetings of each division at the level of its zonal organization—the "zentrale Spartentagungen im Zonenmaßstabe."[69] Before all of these meetings convened, however, the Berlin branch of the Gewerk-

[68]Ibid.
[69]See "Industrie Gewerkschaft—17—für Kunst und Schrifttum," *Gewerkschaftsbericht des FDGB 1946*, pp. 373-75; and "Spartenkonferenzen," *Kunst und Schrifttum* 3 (1947): 1.

schaft 17 held its first set of conferences in each of the city's twenty districts, apparently on 23 March 1947; at them, a total of eighty-eight delegates were elected to attend the citywide delegates' conference that met three days later.[70] Finally, just to give a sense of the pattern of organization, the Berlin district conferences had already elected eight delegates to attend the FDGB's citywide second delegates' conference on 29 and 30 March 1947, attended by that organization's various branches.[71] The FDGB's zone-wide second congress followed on 17-19 April; the Gewerkschaft 17 was represented by eleven delegates.[72]

In late May, the union's central board met again and bemoaned the fact that the division delegates' conferences or zentrale Spartentagungen had still not been held and set the dates: music (Deutscher Musiker-Verband), 19-20 June in Leipzig; journalists (Verband der deutschen Presse), 21-22 June in Altenburg or Weimar; Technik und Verwaltung, 2-3 July in Halle; visual arts (Schutzverband Bildender Künstler), 4-5 July in Leipzig; writers (Schutzverband Deutscher Autoren), 8-9 July in Berlin; and Genossenschaft Deutscher Bühnenangehörigen (GDBA), 26-27 June in Weimar.[73] The seventh division, the organization of performing artists or Internationale Artisten-Loge, had already met on 20-21 March.[74] After another change in scheduling, the conferences then took place roughly according to plan.[75] Scarcely had these meetings occurred than the anticipated dates for both the regional and central meetings of the Gewerkschaft 17 were scheduled and postponed. The new schedule, set by the central board, called for regional meetings or Landeskonferenzen in Mecklenburg on 1-2, Sachsen on 8-9, Sachsen-Anhalt on 14-15, Brandenburg on 16-17, and Thuringia on 21-22 October 1947. The central delegates' conference or Zentral-Delegierten-Konferenz was set tentatively for 5-6 November, to be attended by one delegate for every five hundred of the now 51,000 members of the Gewerkschaft 17.[76] This conference was unable to meet on time either; the new dates were 26-27 November 1947, and they were kept.[77]

[70]See "Delegierten Tagung der Gewerkschaft 17, Groß-Berlin," *Kunst und Schrifttum* 4 (1947): 1; "Delegierten-Konferenzen," *Kunst und Schrifttum* (Groß-Berlin) 3 (1947); Schlichting, "Die Delegierten-Konferenzen," *Kunst und Schrifttum* (Groß-Berlin) 4 (1947): 1.

[71]Prietzel, "Zweite Delegiertentagung des FDGB Groß-Berlin," *Kunst und Schrifttum* 4 (1947): 1.

[72]Prietzel, "Zweiter Zonen-FDGB-Kongreß," *Kunst und Schrifttum* 5 (1947): 1-2.

[73]See Prietzel, "Tagung des Zentralvorstandes. Organisations- und Finanzfragen, Zonen-Spartentagungen, Delegierten-Konferenz," *Kunst und Schrifttum* 6 (1947): 1-3.

[74]"Zweite- Zonenkonferenz der Internationalen Artisten-Loge," *Kunst und Schrifttum* 4 (1947): 1-3.

[75]"Unsere Spartentagungen," *Kunst und Schrifttum* 7/8 (1947): 1-8.

[76]"Termingverlegung," ibid., p. 1; "Die Wahlen in unserer Gewerkschaft," *Kunst und Schrifttum* 9 (1947): 1.

[77]"Verlegung der Zentral-Delegiertenkonferenz" and "Zweite Zentral-Delegiertenkonferenz," *Kunst und Schrifttum* 11 (1947): 1 and 12 (1947): 1-2.

These meetings were all used to work out policies related to the administrative structure of the union and schedule activities for both the central organization, as well as its seven divisions; and to establish hierarchical relationships between these central bodies and their regional counterparts. The conferences and congresses also addressed programmatic policies and became the major forum for public debates about the various controversial issues referred to above. Many of the recently unionized members of the organization, Prietzel lamented, were still unable to "get into the mood of the new labor-union movement."[78] But that assessment characterized attitudes that now began to generate much harsher commentary. When Prietzel cautioned in fall 1947 against "tearing a hole in union organization" by permitting "independent professional associations," he acknowledged that the idea of unionizing creative intellectuals had produced a "powerful wave of opposition both inside and outside of Germany." Resistance had even manifested itself within the ranks of the creative intellectuals, he said, though Prietzel insisted that there was no excuse for conscientious intellectuals to be uncomfortable with union organization within the FDGB. He attributed the general dissatisfaction instead to the "influence of reactionary forces who aspire to weaken the development of union power by propagating the notion of . . . autonomous professional associations independent of the union."[79]

The usual pejorative for these attitudes was "divisional egotism"[80]—the phrase used to characterize the desire of individual divisions to free themselves from the FDGB and the Gewerkschaft 17 by returning to their pre-1933 status as independent entities.[81] The divisions' unrelenting "aspirations for autonomy" resulted in no end of efforts by the union's top management to justify the original organizational idea behind the Gewerkschaft 17, and these efforts carried over into the FDGB as well.[82] At its second zonal congress in April 1947, for example, with Sergej Tjulpanov in prominent attendance, the "unity of the union movement based on nonpartisanship" was again hailed generally, along with the specific prerogative of the Gewerkschaft 17 to participate directly in all matters pertaining to the interests of "workers, employees, and creative intellectuals"—but with no "linkage to a political party." Organizationally, the congress strongly opposed the idea of ever again "permitting" the existence of "independent professional associations"; the insufficiencies of that organizational form, it was stated, had already been recognized prior to 1933.[83] The same subject came up again soon

---

[78]Prietzel, "Planmäßige Organisationsarbeit," *Kunst und Schrifttum* 2 (1948): 5.
[79]See Prietzel, "Die gewerkschaftliche Erfassung der 'geistig Schaffenden,'" *Kunst und Schrifttum* 9 (1947): 4.
[80]See "Unsere Spartentagungen," *Kunst und Schrifttum* 7/8 (1947): 1.
[81]See also Schwarz, "Spartenegoismus," *Kunst und Schrifttum* (Groß-Berlin) 1 (1948): 1.
[82]"Unsere Spartentagungen," *Kunst und Schrifttum* 7/8 (1947): 1.
[83]"Zweiter Zonen-FDGB-Kongreß," *Kunst und Schrifttum* 5 (1947): 1.

after when the board of the Gewerkschaft 17 met in late May 1947; but at this meeting, it was apparent that the "desire of certain individual union divisions for total independence" continued to cause problems and unpleasantries, though the hope was expressed that these difficulties would iron themselves out once the organization of the divisions had been completed "in accordance with the guidelines passed by the executive board" of the Gewerkschaft 17.[84] The opposite was the case, however, for in spite of the confidence expressed by union management after the meetings of the seven divisions,[85] the updated statutes and guidelines passed at the conference in November 1947 and formally accepted by the union's executive committee in February 1948 only intensified feelings of unhappiness.

Art and Estrangement

Complaints about German art expressed during the controversies of 1947 differed little in substance from earlier objections. An article published in *Neues Deutschland* on New Year's Day, for instance, charged that many of the exhibitions mounted in the Western sectors of Berlin showed art devoid of hope for the future; and in the Eastern sector, galleries hung apolitical works that ignored the recent past.[86] But the criticism soon grew harsher, while certain cardinal tenets of art favored openly by Tjulpanov and Dymschitz in remarks made in the wake of the Dresden exhibit in fall 1946 acquired a much stronger resemblance to acknowledged descriptions of socialist realism. The emergence of obligatory new standards, enhanced by deepening antagonism toward "formalism" and "decadence," then paralleled the general cultural crackdown underway in the Soviet Union since the release of the central-committee edicts the summer before. In Soviet-occupied Germany, earlier concerns now evolved into specific apprehension over the growing influence of modern and "abstract" art; and as the year progressed, the papers resorted to treating it as the cultural counterpart of alien ideologies—overall, a *pendant* to the party's obsession with the infiltration of subversive doctrines. Critics refused to concede that modern art had any commendable features, dismissed it as an expression of the existentialist philosophy dominating discussions in France, and defined existentialism as philosophical fascism. A rare opportunity to challenge some of these accusations arose, however, because of the mistake made in setting up an art journal originally intended to nurture the impression of open debate in Soviet-occupied Germany. *Bildende Kunst* developed out of disputes between

---

[84]"Tagung des Zentralvorstandes," *Kunst und Schrifttum* 6 (1947): 1.
[85]"Unsere Spartentagungen," *Kunst und Schrifttum* 7/8 (1947): 1.
[86]Vogt, "Die Kunst im vergangenen Jahr," *Neues Deutschland*, 1 January 1947.

"SED artists" bitter because of the party's inattentive attitude toward them and artists organized in the Schutzverband Bildender Künstler. The journal was supposed to provide each group with a forum, prevent either from dominating discussions, and establish the party's preferences by mediating between the two. *Bildende Kunst*, as Max Grabowski put it, needed to influence and educate the public "in accordance with the aims of our party."[87]

The goal of making the journal *appear* representative then required that the Communists place editors on the board whose differing positions reflected influential currents in art; but, at the same time, "the elements that agree with our political and cultural goals" still had to have the final word.[88] Karl Hofer was probably selected to be one of the two chief editors right away, but he lacked the political credentials, and the search for a coeditor took time. In fact, the SMAD licensed the proposed journal in November 1946, following the Dresden exhibition,[89] though the DVV, which acted on behalf of the party, had trouble finding the right person to offset Hofer's influence. Finally, in late January 1947, the DVV's Carola Gärtner informed Paul Wandel that she had been severely chastised by Dymschitz because of the delays; "political consideration for collaborators who officially sympathize with us," Dymschitz told her, had alone prevented him from canceling the license altogether; and he insisted that Gärtner locate an editor quickly who was capable of "balancing the scales" of what he called Hofer's editorial intentions.[90] Oskar Nerlinger was the logical choice, but the "SED artists" disliked him intensely; as a matter of fact, their accusations about Nerlinger's past may explain why his appointment took so long. Toward the end of the year, the internal party investigation undertaken as a result of those accusations confirmed the substance of some of them when it turned out that Nerlinger had sent an incriminating letter to the Nazi Reichskulturkammer. The SED's central secretariat considered it "unworthy" of an antifascist artist, provided the SMAD's office of information with a copy, but stopped short of taking what it called "organizational measures" against Nerlinger because of his postwar record of "attitude and activity."[91]

In the meantime, Wandel must have acted quickly on Gärtner's report of her conversation with Dymschitz because the SED's secretariat voted on the

[87]Zentralsekretariat der SED. Abt. Kultur und Erziehung. Referat: Bildende Kunst. an das Zentralsekretariat der SED z. Hd. d. Gen. Anton Ackermann und Otto Meier, 12 July 1946, gez. Grabowski. Zentrales Parteiarchiv, IV 2/906/171.

[88]Jahresbericht [1947] des Referats "Bildende Kunst," ibid., IV 2/906/169.

[89]See ibid and Halbjahresschrift über das Erscheinen unserer Zeitschrift, 5 November 1947, ibid., IV 2/906/171.

[90]Vermerk. Herrn Präsidenten Wandel. Herrn Vizepräsidenten Weinert zur Kenntnis. Betr.: Besprechung zwischen Major Dymschitz und Frau Gärtner am 24. Januar, 27 January 1947, gez. Gärtner. Bundesarchiv. Abt. Potsdam, R-2/1091/23.

[91]See Protokoll Nr. 22 (II) der Sitzung des Zentralsekretariats am 1. 12. 1947, and Protokoll Nr. 41 (II) am 26. 1. 48. Zentrales Parteiarchiv, IV2/2.1/151 and 168.

matter at its meeting two days later. Nerlinger and Grabowski were given 7,000 marks each of party money to help finance *Bildende Kunst* and appointed secretly to act as the SED's "trustees." Evidently, Hofer had already assented to providing the final third of the money out of his own pocket (probably without knowing the source of the rest), and the journal was set to be published by a newly created press operating on the basis of that start-up capital.[92] Nerlinger's work was definitely cut out for him, though, because Hofer exercised editorial prerogatives that immensely complicated the task of using the monthly to influence the public "in accordance with the goals of our party" and, in 1949, after some bitter experiences, the SED shut it down. In his remarks published on the first page of the inaugural issue of *Bildende Kunst* in April 1947, for instance, Hofer insisted that the journal would not take sides in debates over art.[93] But he also voiced a more specific opinion that clashed with the party's point of view and that Nerlinger quickly refuted. Ordinary Germans, Hofer, wrote, lacked the prerequisite for any appreciation of art. The conclusion was perfectly compatible with the party's ongoing emphasis on collective guilt; but it contradicted the concurrent assertion that popular attitudes in matters of politics and culture were fundamentally improved and that artists needed to heed the admonitions of the people. Writing on the very next page of the opening issue, Nerlinger appeared to side with Hofer when he referred to the "alienation" that existed between art and the public. But his allusion to the search for "new forms of artistic representation" assigned the blame to the artists, not the people; and by arguing that the establishment of a bond between artists and their public required the participation of creative intellectuals in "cultural construction," Nerlinger linked the party's politicization of art to the need for formal preferences directly associated with principles of socialist realism.[94]

Nerlinger's remarks were followed a page later by a further discussion of the same issues. In his belated assessment of the Dresden exhibition, Carl-Ernst Matthias backed up his own opinions with extensive references to authoritative comments made by Tjulpanov and Dymschitz in November 1946. Though Tjulpanov's utterances seemed to strike a balance by characterizing the artist as "servant and leader of the people," his remarks were studded with phrases that could have come straight from the edicts issued by the Soviet central committee. Among other things, he said that the function of art was to "acquaint the people with the progressive ideas of mankind through an appropriate manner of representation"; that a genuinely new art owed "its newness to the new ideology on which it is based"; or, applied to Soviet-occupied Germany, that raising their work to a progressive level required German artists to "take in" the creative experience of other democratic peoples,

[92]Protokoll Nr. 70 der Sitzung des Zentralsekretariats am 29. 1. 1947, ibid., IV 2/2.1/62.
[93]Hofer, "Zum Geleit," *Bildende Kunst* 1 (1947): 1.
[94]Nerlinger, "Was will die 'Bildende Kunst,'" *Bildende Kunst* 1 (1947): 2.

especially the creative experience of the Soviet Union. Tjulpanov's comments acquired additional importance now because of their republication in a fledgling journal presented to the public as nonpartisan. Matthias even quoted Tjulpanov's routine denial that the Soviet Union engaged in "state interference in the affairs of art," but also included a bizarre comment that anticipated major disagreements. Tjulpanov appeared to flatter the artists in attendance by noting that their best work had nothing in common with "Nazi degeneration and decadent abstraction."[95] But, apart from the fact that the opposite of "abstraction" applied to it, denouncing fascist art in those terms must have struck Tjulpanov's listeners as sheer nonsense. The Nazis themselves invented those pejoratives to stigmatize the "degenerate art" despised by them and, as everyone knew, had staged infamous derisive exhibitions of such works. Tjulpanov's rhetoric was not flattery at all, then, but a ungainly attempt to dissuade local artists from dabbling themselves in "abstract" art by calling it both decadent and fascist. In fact, Matthias then undercut his and Tjulpanov's argument by quoting statistical information relating to the opinions of ordinary Germans who attended the Dresden exhibit. Still heavily influenced by a taste in art cultivated by the Nazis, fully 65.7 percent of the questionnaires filled out by visitors leaving the exhibition found it objectionable mostly because of the "expressionistic and abstract art" included. That disclosure underscored the accuracy of Hofer's assessment and also established the embarrassing fact that Soviet and German Communist preferences coincided with fascist predilections for representational art. Adding to the confusion was Dymschitz' reference to the "advertisement-naturalism" of Nazi art, which scarcely defined it as abstract; and Matthias' added remark, using Zhdanovist language, that different works shown in Dresden contrasted "genuine realistic art" with "formalist abstractions devoid of ideas and, thus, without a future."[96]

Other commentaries supported Hofer's appraisal of popular attitudes by referring to especially crude remarks made by visitors to the exhibit. Art shown there failed to qualify as art at all, read one; it smacked of the "Weimar system" and compared poorly with the quality of work shown by the Nazis in Munich in opposition to decadent art. Another visitor declared that the Germans had missed nothing by having such art withheld from them.[97] These reactions were simply a reflection of the hostility toward modern art nurtured by twelve years of nazism. The commentary written by Communists proved to be just as primitive, however; Gustav Leuteritz published a critique of an exhibition in the Soviet sector of Berlin, sponsored by the French occupation administration, in which French impressionism predominated. Leuteritz called it the swan song of the wealthy, decaying bourgeoisie

[95]Matthias, "Künstlerkongress in Dresden," *Bildende Kunst* 1 (1947): 4-5
[96]Ibid., p. 9.
[97]Linfert, "Erinnerungen an die Dresdner Ausstellung," *Bildende Kunst* 1 (1947): 13.

because it mirrored a preoccupation with color and surface impressions, rather than a concern with the essence of things. The stark contrast between the opulent inside of the exhibition hall and the outside ruins especially offended his sensibilities. But, considering that this exhibition featured paintings by Rousseau and Cézanne, Renoir and Manet, Gauguin and van Gogh, the vulgarity of critical standards developing in Soviet-occupied Germany becomes painfully obvious. Leuteritz found the violin-playing Easter rabbit with wings (actually a donkey) and the upside-down figure in a painting by Chagall to be a mark of the limitations of the French symbolists.[98]

Leuteritz' remarks were followed in the next issue of *Bildende Kunst* by a vividly colored oil by Matisse on the back cover that seemed to serve as an answering "editorial"; and the following number featured both an "abstract" portrait of a women by Picasso and the first of two major articles by Hofer. Noting that Germans were confused, amazed, outraged, and disgusted when confronted with art from which they had been hermetically shut off for twelve years, Hofer argued again that they lacked any basis for its comprehension. He then went into a detailed analysis of the development of art down through the centuries, leading to the conclusion that abstraction in art had always been present; and only critics who acknowledged the role of abstraction had any right to criticize it on the basis of well-founded art-historical reasons. As for surrealism, Hofer discussed the nature of form in art generally and the manner in which form became dominant in surrealism before noting that some of the same general representational principles held true for all valid works of art, including those being created today.[99] In his second article, Hofer challenged the notion of "progress" in art altogether; he then conceded that there were people who considered a picture to be good merely because it was abstract or surrealist, but considered such "harmless" fools no better than those who asked, "What's that supposed to be?"[100] Heinz Lüdecke answered Hofer later in the year by expressing his unwillingness to condone surrealism under any circumstances. These frontal attacks on reason and logic constituted the last morbid aberrations of European cultural nihilism, said Lüdecke, and ended by claiming that existentialism, the philosophical correlate of surrealism, masqueraded as a philosophy or as aesthetics; whereas it actually amounted to nothing more than a dying class using its

---

[98]Leuteriz, "Französische Malerei in Berlin," *Bildende Kunst* 1 (1947): 16-19. Late in the year *Bildende Kunst* published an article on Chagall's "psychic formalism" (H. L., Marc Chagall und der 'psychische Formalismus,'" ibid., 8 [1847]: 11). The author, Heinz Lüdecke, said that Chagall's brand of formalism came dangerously close to the arbitrary psychic automatism of radical surrealists. Devoid of rational control, such "boundless individualism" did what it pleased with reality. As a one-of-a-kind artist, Lüdecke was prepared to concede that a painter like Chagall, might be "acceptable"; but his creative principle ultimately spelled the end of art because art required contact with a "controllable reality" to keep from developing into a playful pasttime.
[99]Hofer, "Wege der Kunst," *Bildende Kunst* 3 (1947): 4-14.
[100]Hofer, "Wege der Kunst II," *Bildende Kunst* 4/5 (1947): 25-30.

mystic formulas in a bid to avert the shadows of the oblivion to which history had consigned it.[101]

The *Tägliche Rundschau* generally set the standards in campaigning against modern art in 1947, though it began the new year publishing criticism considerably less abusive than the vitriol that soon stained its pages. One article referred to the darkening shadow of confusion associated with the nature of abstract art;[102] and in a later essay the same critic added that young artists, particularly those banned under the Nazis, created art that they derived from expressionism or that developed along non-representational lines. It was important to understand, however, that French painters like Matisse, Braque, and Picasso, the ones being imitated, had long since overcome their earlier tendencies and returned to the portrayal of figures and objects. For this and other reasons there was no sense defending young artists who had chosen to start work again by picking up the threads of expressionist and non-representational art.[103] The suggestion that painters like Picasso, had put their "abstract" past behind them was patently absurd, of course, though someone on the editorial board of *Bildende Kunst* may have tried to foster that impression in summer 1947 by reproducing Picasso's much older portrait of Gertrud Stein.[104] Or perhaps its publication was intended to prove to skeptical critics of abstract art that even Picasso, knew how to draw. Indeed, *Bildende Kunst* reproduced a number of abstract Picassos along with other paintings by Matisse, and Braque;, and the journal also ran a passage from an article by Ilja Ehrenburg published in the *Literaturnaja gazeta* full of favorable comments on the political postures of Picasso and Matisse.[105] Ehrenburg's remarks helped restrain local critics who were overly zealous in associating modern artists politically with decadence art. In Picasso's case, there were political sensitivities worth observing because of his depiction of fascist atrocities during the Spanish civil war—in the "abstract" or "surrealistic" painting of Guernica—and his membership in the French Communist party.

Even the comparatively moderate critics, however, were moving steadily toward a categorical renunciation of modern art. One of the articles in the *Tägliche Rundschau* suggested that artists who looked back at 1933 for inspiration ought to stick to their experiments within the walls of their private ateliers and stop presenting their work to the public as the latest in modern art.[106] Max Grabowski, who ran the SED's internal office of pictorial arts, was more specific still. He insisted that the artistic means of expression employed in the majority of works shown in Soviet-zone exhibits did not speak

[101]Lüdecke, "Die Bezüglichkeit des Beziehungslosen," *Bildende Kunst* 7 (1947): 9-13.
[102]See Theunissen, "Einsicht in die Welt," *Tägliche Rundschau*, 26 January 1947.
[103]Theunissen, "Wandlung zur Gestalt," *Tägliche Rundschau*, 18 July 1947.
[104]See *Bildende Kunst* 7/8 (1947): 47.
[105]"Ilja Ehrenburg über Matisse und Picasso," ibid.
[106]Theunissen, "Wandlung zur Gestalt," *Tägliche Rundschau*, 18 July 1947.

the language of the times because it was not as "realistic" as the prevalent attitude to all other aspects of German life.[107] The difficulty with Grabowski's accompanying argument that art "belonged to the people" or the related accusation that modern art alienated ordinary Germans, however, was its incompatibility with the party's own lingering theory of collective guilt. Contending that art had to be easily comprehended in order to reeducate average citizens politically, only to suggest that the same Germans were conscious enough to feel alienated by modern art because it failed to employ the realistic "language" common to political or other modes of discourse, made little sense. But the party's perception of the German people was largely an abstraction itself, an expedient, which allowed it to speak concurrently of collective guilt and popular consensus in the first place. Still, an entirely different consideration rendered the argument acutely embarrassing. Surveys taken at the Dresden exhibition revealed that the majority of Germans who saw it rejected most of the art shown there,[108] but for all the wrong reasons. Though it would otherwise have served the party's purposes to call attention to the displeasure felt by average Germans for the same works frowned upon by the SED or SMAD, this art had been banned under the Nazis, and visitors to the exhibition disliked it largely because their taste remained one conditioned by the experience of the preceding twelve years. The Communists then found themselves having to reject the same kind of work banned by the fascists while ignoring the real reasons for what Grabowski referred to as the people's sense of estrangement.

The irony of the situation was that socialist realism actually matched the "formal" taste of ordinary Germans far better than modern German art; but pictorially, Soviet art had virtually no chance of popular acceptance because of its obvious exaltation of all things "Bolshevist." As a consequence, the crackdown of 1947 manifested itself less in a broad effort to popularize Soviet painting than in the generally unacknowledged, though accelerated importation of its normative "aesthetic" and political premises. For now, then, the process of patterning local art after socialist realism occurred more in the context of what passed as a national or semi-national debate over the fate of German culture, rather than in a corresponding cultural act of "forcing the Soviet system" upon Germany. The first exhibition of Soviet art was not organized until mid-1947, for instance, and included no more than a few graphics and oils by a grand total of three artists.[109] Even in fall 1947, when the thirtieth anniversary of the Russian revolution provided a prime opportunity to extol Soviet art and establish its relevance for Germany, no attempt was made to take advantage of it. An article in *Bildende Kunst*, published to mark the occasion, reproduced only a few works entitled collective farm wo-

---

[107]Grabowski, "Die Volksentfremdung der Kunst," *Tägliche Rundschau*, 18 February 1947.
[108]See Trinks, "Die Spannung zwischen Kunst und Volk," *Aufbau* 7 (1947): 9.
[109]See CEM, "Erste sowjetische Kunstausstellung," *Bildende Kunst* 3 (1947): 31.

men on the way to work, industrial complex in the mountains, and so on.[110] Otherwise, however, with the exception of problems caused by an overemphasis on sound popular attitudes incompatible with notions of collective guilt, the fundamental principles of socialist realism fit official descriptions of the situation in Soviet-occupied Germany better with each passing day. In the article celebrating three decades of Soviet art, the author indicated that socialist realism still needed to prevail over formalist and naturalist tendencies, thereby offering a line of defense against the encroachment of a bourgeois reactionary art devoid of ideas.[111]

These same principles were rapidly emerging in Soviet-occupied Germany. In February, when Grabowski argued in favor of an art close to reality and with necessary ties to the people as the only way to overcome the formalistic snobbery in new German art,[112] he repeated certain postulates typical of socialist realism and parroted Zhdanov. But he shied away from mentioning socialist realism by name and never addressed the question of how the notion of "estrangement" squared with collective guilt. A few months later, he repeated the same arguments in the pages of *Bildende Kunst* by distinguishing between pseudo- and genuine or regressive versus progressive art. He defined the latter as a validation of the (unattributed) Feuerbach principle of the need to change, rather than merely interpret the world; and characterized the former as individualistic art that failed to develop in a historically determined direction and thus distanced itself from society. Unfortunately, he continued, nowadays the broad masses found themselves baffled by the majority of the new art works because, having isolated itself from the life of the people, art had fallen out of step with an age in which the people demanded to participate in all aspects of public life. The question came down to whether art would ever become a matter for the entire people and what ways might be found to accomplish the task. Without going into additional detail, Grabowski said that this required the free development of art—free, that is, from what Grabowski called the yoke of an aesthetisizing view and evaluation of art that emphasized form over content.[113] Grabowski still ignored the fact that popular taste remained considerably influenced by the preceding twelve years. Over two-thirds of the male students who filled out the questionnaire in Dresden rejected the entire show; more than half of the university students disapproved, and three-quarters of the workers were, to put it mildly, unimpressed. The author of the commentary published in the Kulturbund's *Aufbau* almost a year later had little doubt that the Nazi experience was the overriding cause of the rejection.[114] *Bildende Kunst* published

---

[110]Schnittke, "Dreißig Jahre sowjetische Malerei," *Bildende Kunst* 7 (1947): 6
[111]Ibid.
[112]Grabowski, "Die Volksentfremdung der Kunst," *Tägliche Rundschau*, 18 February 1947.
[113]Grabowski, "Kunst im Leben des Volkes," *Bildende Kunst* 3 (1947): 15-16.
[114]Trinks, "Die Spannung zwischen Kunst und Volk," *Aufbau* 7 (1947): 9-12.

a number of letters to the editor in late 1947 that also disclosed the nature of popular disgust. One letter to the editor used fascist slurs to suggest renaming the journal *Kunstschund Zeitschrift* or *Journal of Art-Trash* and characterized the works reproduced in its pages as manure; another said that the pictures struck him as the work of the mentally insane; a third thought the qualities of art could best be established by comparing the work reproduced in *Bildende Kunst* with the excellent paintings of Nazi artists; a fourth contended that the pictures offended good taste, if not humanity itself, etc.[115]

In fall 1947, Grabowski published still another article, this one in the SED's monthly *Einheit*, and delivered himself there of the toughest pronouncement on modern art yet. For the first time, he raised the question of the party's role in the development of art and, ironically, undertook to bring its political priorities in line with the radical demands more characteristic of the "SED artists" whose unruly behavior had only recently been considered such an impediment. Grabowski restated his stock argument that the works of art shown at various exhibitions baffled the working masses and went on from there to inquire specifically into the party's attitude toward modern art. As he saw it, the issue was whether modern art ought to be taken as a serious threat or merely dismissed as a reactionary reflection of a bourgeois-capitalist frame of mind that need not command the party's attention. The experience of the last twelve years answered his question clearly, he said, revealing his belief in the existence of parallels between Nazi art and the political role that he assumed present-day socio-political establishments had assigned to modern art in the national or international context of class warfare. Grabowski argued that the SED needed to understand contemporary artistic utterances if it wished to spot those endeavors in harmony with the party's political objectives and those in conflict. Moreover, by its very definition progressive art took a position on current problems; but it was important to understand that this involved more than a choice of subject matter. An artist had to be progressive in his understanding of the times, but equally so in his or her discernment of artistic forms that corresponded with the times. Grabowski concluded that new art would begin to emerge once the people endorsed a new social order as the guarantee of a bright future. A progressive work of art required the kind of formal structure that allowed it to speak in the language of the times; and the principal feature of art in a coming socialist world would be realism, not surrealism.[116]

Carola Gärtner, dismissed from the DVV for her opposition to the party's way of dealing with "sympathizing" artists and discriminating against the politically committed, took the arguments further in an article published in *Einheit* just a few months after Grabowski's. Gärtner, too, was unhappy

---

[115]"Das Publikum sagt seine Meinung," *Bildende Kunst* 6 (1947): 29.
[116]Grabowski, "Zur bildenden Kunst der Gegenwart," *Einheit* 10 (1947): 983-86.

with the level of discussion about the pictorial arts; unlike those related to literature and the stage, which had produced clear demands, sheer confusion reigned. This chaos had been caused in part by the fact that criticism remained largely the preserve of bourgeois critics who posed an even greater threat when they postured as democrats. Gärtner proposed to redress the balance with direct party intervention. Things had reached the stage, she complained, where surrealist painters might actually be granted teaching posts at Soviet-zone schools of art; and she now considered it imperative that the party keep its "veto power" in mind. In particular, Gärtner insisted that the SED get on with the business of meeting its obligations. The party's own theoreticians needed to abandon their studied indifference to the pictorial arts and pursue dialectical analyses that followed the lines suggested by her. A dialectical discussion of modern art, Gärtner insisted, should treat it as any other segment of the class struggle. This meant considering issues like the political-economic situation in post-war Germany, the cultural anarchy left behind by the Nazis, the role of cultural unity in the bitter struggle for national unity against the divisive efforts of the victorious capitalist powers and of deluded or reactionary segments of the population. It also included their cultural activities, including those pertaining to the visual arts, for here especially the efforts of the reactionaries crossed purposes with the progressive forces. Gärtner went on to advocate a categorization of artists into reactionary and progressive groups and paraphrased Marx to suggest that artists, or the benighted among them, were in dire need of a rough education at the hands of the people.[117]

These remarks suffered from the same contradiction as Grabowski's. The party wished to use art to influence ordinary Germans politically, and doing so presupposed winning artists for the party's cause first. But the argument turned on itself when the SED, or its self-anointed and appointed spokesmen, tried to pressure artists into producing work with an acceptable political slant through allusions to popular "demands." This approach derived from two contradictory but equally expedient theories of collective guilt. The party rationalized the need for a politicized art by speaking of its broad educational responsibilities with respect to the polluted minds of average Germans; but when confronted with the political inadequacies and idiosyncrasies of modern art, as well as its appeal to the younger generation, the party resorted to talk of the political failings of artists in years gone by and buttressed its opinions with the claim that ordinary citizens felt "estranged." Gärtner suggested. for instance, that considerable numbers of artists shared responsibility for the greatest fiasco in German history; and nowadays many refused to make up their minds politically. These artists needed to be taught about the essence of imperialist power politics and about the dubious quality

[117]Gärtner-Scholle, "Stiefkind bildende Kunst," *Einheit* 1 (1948): 65-73.

of certain democratic systems, she said, for only then could they decide either in favor of the new imperialism from the West, plutocratic democracy, or endorse the fresh insights coming out of the USSR. Gärtner argued that the first step should be to employ the most progressive artists in the recruitment and assimilation of their colleagues; and she repeated her older objections to the fact that, on the one hand, the party had inadequately promoted the works of the progressive artists and, on the other hand, failed to assist them in their effort to raise the consciousness of their fellow artists. Gärtner even contrasted the SED's attitude with the "patience" shown by the SMAD in working toward what she called the maturation of German artists, though little of what Tjulpanov and Dymschitz told them in Dresden the preceding fall, she added, had sunk in; and she rounded out this side of her argument by urging party functionaries to begin assessing and administering the visual arts according to the rules of historical materialism. This was all the more important and in the interests of all German artists in order to avoid regulations telling them what an artist could incorporate into his own work from other periods of time and what would not be permitted. Such prescriptions limited the freedom of artistic creation in a dictatorial way. It was far better to derive the hopes and expectations of a new art understandable by the people and achievable without giving orders in matters of "style and content" from the certainty of "new understandings" about the coming society. "The sun of a new conviction," Gärtner finished, "emanating from the first socialist state, casts its rays around the world." It was "the light of a sun that can never set again in the consciousness of any nation of culture today."[118] This was the kind of voluntary realization, not the unending quest for something "new" in art, that Gärtner saw as the key to opening unheard-of vistas of creativity and artistic accomplishment.

Studying Soviet Culture

Even if party spokesmen shied away from using Soviet art itself as a standard of comparison in 1947, in other areas the call for an end to certain "prejudices" issued by Shemjakin on 7 January 1947 was taken to heart in a new emphasis on the illustrious achievements of Soviet culture generally. But the very nature of the "prejudices" alluded to required that these discussions shift away from the reliance upon popular attitudes common in complaints about the abstract proclivities of modern art and fall back on notions of collective guilt. In March, for instance, the *Tägliche Rundschau* announced the opening of a house of Soviet culture and said that it was intended to help overcome the fear of all things Soviet used by the Nazis to establish the

[118]Ibid.

ideological preconditions for war against the USSR.[119] This line of reasoning marked the start of a campaign to popularize Soviet culture and to emphasize its model qualities for Germany; but the arguments in praise of Soviet cultural practices also went hand in hand with references to lingering fascist attitudes on the part of Germans whose only real transgression now was their skepticism. By ruling out the possibility that an attitude critical of the USSR could be anything but a residue of the recent past, the new campaign labeled concern over an accelerating process of "sovietization" as unwittingly or avowedly fascist. Moreover, because this anxiety matched similar worries in other regions of Germany and among the Western allies, the SED used it to smear opposition to local developments as a reactionary offensive launched from outside of the zone or of alien ideologies working seditiously within it. A further twist of logic implied that such opposition also violated the Potsdam accords. If the house of Soviet culture hastened democratization in Germany by tightening the bonds between Soviet and German intellectuals, then any objection to the undertaking breached the common policy of democratization favored by the allies in an agreement to which they had willingly affixed their signatures.[120]

But there was growing concern about the "prejudices" of ordinary Germans because their attitude toward the USSR mirrored the extent of their unhappiness with the SED. The problem had been around since the end of the war, but with nearly three full years having elapsed, the situation now reflected poorly upon the public appeal of the Communist party. In 1947, both SED and SMAD responded by blaming cultural ignorance for the stubborn refusal of ordinary citizens and local intellectuals to embrace the party's policies. Germans had known virtually nothing about the cultural development of the Soviet Union upon the arrival of allied troops in spring 1945, said Sergej Tjulpanov, and the first Soviet citizens to set foot on German territory were soldiers whose immediate preoccupation left them understandably little time to think about shaving or looking friendly. Tjulpanov's remark was a cryptic allusion to the behavior of Red Army soldiers that served as a backhanded apology of and for their conduct; and he used the context to launch into a discussion of the reasons why German divisions had been so easily mobilized for war against the USSR. His answer then provided Tjulpanov with a further opportunity to focus on the responsibility of the German people for atrocities committed on Soviet soil and to explain why feelings of hostility toward the Soviet Union took root in the first place. The Germans had been cut off culturally from the USSR, he explained, as a result of which the measures taken to acquaint them with the socialist culture of the Soviet Union now required little explanation—they served the cause of peace and

[119]"Die Kultur der UdSSR," *Tägliche Rundschau*, 1 March 1947.
[120]"Im Geiste kultureller Verständigung. Festliche Weihe des 'Hauses der sowjetischen Kultur' in Berlin," *Tägliche Rundschau*, 1 March 1947.

strengthened the forces of democracy in Germany itself.[121] But Tjulpanov went beyond generalities in beginning a gradual modification of the disavowal of a Soviet system for Germany. The SMAD wished, he said, to familiarize Germans with what stood at the gate of social and political developments in many other countries and what was reality in the USSR already. Though this statement may have stopped short of an open abandonment of the principle of "no sovietization," it certainly lessened the distance between that original assurance and party or SMAD rhetoric. Nor was the substance of Tjulpanov's remark diminished by his additional comment that "we do not take it upon ourselves to produce utilitarian imitations; we want understanding." This sounded reasonable, and Tjulpanov added further assurances; the Russians did not expect a general endorsement of their culture, neither in the form of their dialectical-materialist world view, the principle of society's control of free artistic creativity, nor in any other of its manifestations. There was just something ridiculous about rejecting Soviet culture in the absence of any knowledge of it.[122]

Similar commentary followed in response to the next development. In July 1947, a society for the study of the culture of the Soviet Union set up operations and was designed, like the house of Soviet culture, to deal with the distortions of Russian life said to be characteristic of Nazi propaganda.[123] But the new society, formed after the failure of the Moscow foreign-ministers' conference, proselytized far more aggressively and quickly acquired all the earmarks of another "mass organization." Jürgen Kuczynski, its first chairman, called it a democratic mass movement that offered the German people a welcome opportunity to acquaint themselves with Soviet culture;[124] and it resembled other mass organizations in the sense that it hoped to blanket the zone with subsidiaries required to report to the "central" in Berlin. It also professed to having the usual national aspirations.[125] But, echoing Tjulpanov, Kuczynski also characterized Germans as active participants in the crusade against the Soviet Union, used the reference as an allusion to collective guilt, and remarked that remedying this "absence of culture" was among the society's principal aims. "He who hates and despises human progress as it is manifested in the Soviet Union" said Kuczynski, "is himself odious and contemptible because he proves that he . . . has no sense of culture." In fact, Kuczynski conceded, the "overwhelming majority" of the German people remained ill-disposed toward the Soviet Union; and even in the Soviet zone,

[121]S.T. "Auftakt zu geistiger Verständigung. Gedanken eines russischen Offiziers zur Eröffnung des 'Hauses der Kultur der Sowjetunion' in Berlin," *Tägliche Rundschau*, 4 March 1947.
[122]Ibid.
[123]See "Ziel und Zweck der Gesellschaft zum Studium der Kultur der Sowjetunion," *Tägliche Rundschau*, 26 June 1947.
[124]Kuczynski, "Über einen Weg des Aufbaus deutscher Kultur," *Neue Welt* 15 (1947): 66.
[125]Kuczynski, "Zweck und Inhalt der Verständigung," *Tägliche Rundschau*, 2 July 1947.

many still labored under the influence of reaction. It was all the more imperative, then, that those Soviet cultural values useful to the German people in the construction of Germany's own society be "appropriated."[126] Kuczynski's rhetoric inched closer than Tjulpanov's to an endorsement of Soviet cultural norms for German application. By August, Kuczynski considered it "in need of no further explanation . . . that all progressive people must devote themselves to the study of Soviet culture"; for Soviet culture was "an entirely concrete, practical set of directions and collection of experiences for all of us in other countries who have challenged the decaying system of monopoly capitalism and imperialism." It was clear, he concluded, that the most progressive elements of the German people studied Soviet culture in seeking to discern the direction in which progress lay, and they could count on the "energetic backing" of the occupation authorities. But such support never took the form of "directives."[127]

In spring 1945, the KPD pledged not to impose the Soviet system upon Germany under current conditions, and the SED's slight variation of the same assurance in dismissing the idea of "schematic transferals" fostered the impression that conditions had not changed. Even so, though the early promises never ruled out "studying" the USSR, much less learning from its culture, the fact that doing so was largely obligatory now led to certain conclusions. People worried about the meaning of the word "appropriation," for instance, and the sound of the Soviet central-committee's cultural decrees provided little reassurance. Spokesmen like Dymschitz then intensified their efforts to present the crackdown in the Soviet Union as a defense of artistic freedom against Western threats and misconceptions. In Germany, he argued, socialist realism was the victim of a "certain bias" encouraged by "malicious anti-Soviet propaganda" disseminated by unscrupulous journalists. These people bemoaned the "suppression of artistic freedom" and the "imposition of prescribed ideological paradigms" in order to blacken the image of Soviet intellectual life.[128] When Ehrenburg's pamphlet *In America* came in for criticism in the West,[129] Dymschitz charged that "imperialist reaction" was incapable of answering criticism other than by "slanders supplied by venal and arrogant journalists."[130] The principal issue, though, was Dymschitz' assertion that socialist realism did not constitute "a dogma, a canon, an aesthetic norm," and that its development had nothing to do with "decrees."[131] But the arguments designed to extol the merits of socialist realism supplied much of

[126]Ibid.
[127]Kuczynski, "Über einen Weg des Aufbaus deutscher Kultur," *Neue Welt* 15 (1947): 63-64, 66; Kuczynski, "Zweck und Inhalt der Verständigung," *Tägliche Rundschau*, 2 July 1947.
[128]Dymschitz, "Das geistige Schaffen in der Sowjetunion," *Tägliche Rundschau*, 5 June 1947.
[129]The Russians quickly published it in German (*In Amerika*).
[130]Dymschitz, "Verleumdungen—made in New York," *Tägliche Rundschau*, 31 July 1947.
[131]See Dymschitz, "Das geistige Schaffen in der Sowjetunion," *Tägliche Rundschau*, 5 June 1947.

the rhetorical evidence to the contrary because the campaign focused so intently upon Western "decadent" art as an integral component of "alien ideologies." Dymschitz made no secret of the fact that socialist realism included a fight against "antirealistic currents in art flowing from the ground of bourgeois decadence"; and among such currents he counted "the formalists, the subjectivists, the abstractionists, the supporters of 'art' in its pure form, and the admirers of experimentation as an end in itself."[132] Not that socialist realism precluded the "aesthetic experiment"; socialist realism *was* a daring artistic experiment. But it forced norms upon no one and committed the writer solely to the search for truth and to "service to the ideals of democracy and socialism." If socialist realism opposed formalism, it did so not to constrict, but to challenge artistic forms "devoid of content and ideas."[133]

These remarks alleviated few of the prevalent concerns because those who endorsed the principles of socialist realism make it clear that these applied outside of the Soviet Union as well. The depth to which Zoshchenko and Akhmatova had descended, for instance, was blamed upon the harmful tendencies of "modern bourgeois art" in the West, under whose influence the pair had fallen and against which the Soviet Communist party acted in a conscientious effort to fight the putrefaction and intellectual impoverishment of art. Its actions were accordingly aimed at preserving "genuine art" at home *and* abroad.[134] After all, not all Western art qualified as decadent, said Dymschitz, and the Soviet Union was by no means comprised of "isolationists"; the USSR favored a "democratic world literature" and got along fine with modern bourgeois culture as long as it was "genuine culture." But "we take a dim view of a degenerate pseudo-culture," Dymschitz added, and mentioned two offenders by name—Jean-Paul Sartre and the "collaborationist" André Gide.[135] End-of-the-world attitudes expressed in much Western art influenced by existentialism no longer possessed any "right to live" in the USSR, which was the reason why the aesthetic obsessions of French art could not be taken seriously in the Soviet Union.[136] None of these considerations, however, were regarded as an infringement or impingement upon creative freedom. Late in the year, Kuczynski contrasted the plight of a writer in the United States with the favored status of artists in the USSR and reduced matters to the following dichotomy: "Freedom of progress and repression of reaction" on the one side contrasted with "freedom of reaction and repression of progress" on the other.[137]

---

[132]Ibid.
[133]Dymschitz, "Einfaltspinselei mit erschwerenden Umständen," *Tägliche Rundschau,* 31 October 1947.
[134]Altermann, "Über wirkliche and scheinbare Freiheit," *Tägliche Rundschau*, 14 December 1947.
[135]Dymschitz, "Sowjetische and bürgerliche Kunst," *Tägliche Rundschau,*4 December 1947.
[136]"Die Deutschen und die Sowjetkultur," *Sonntag*, 10 August 1947.
[137]Kuczynski, "Über die Freiheit des Schriftstellers," *Tägliche Rundschau*, 21 December 1947.

The Touchstone of Honesty

The Kulturbund began the new year embroiled in controversy that developed out of the elections the previous fall; and virtually all of it stemmed from doubts about its nonpartisanship. Was the Kulturbund a "Moscow affair" or was it really unaffiliated?[138] The rhetoric used by the leadership to deny its political loyalties varied in comparison with the discourse employed by other mass organizations, but the substance of the denials was the same. When Kuczynski declared that the "energetic support" provided his group by the SMAD never took the form of directives and that the Germans in charge of the society answered only to their fellow countrymen,[139] he defined the society as "nonpartisan" without resorting to the Kulturbund's choice self-characterization. But it all came down to the contention that none of these organizations acted on behalf of the SED and SMAD. That was certainly never true of the Kulturbund. In connection with the selection of its Berlin board in February, there was an effort made by members who belonged to other parties to use the SED's defeat in the elections to insist upon broader representation. The Kulturbund's weekly assailed the idea as a bid to carry "party squabbling" into the work of the organization;[140] whereas *Neues Deutschland* saw nothing wrong with having a representative from the SED's secretariat speak to Kulturbund delegates who belonged to the SED during a meeting in Potsdam. They were told to work hard at persuading the "progressive" members of other parties that the SED had better answers and given to understand that this task was "nonpartisan."[141]

These issues resurfaced at the Kulturbund's first central conference on 20 and 21 May 1947, and J. R. Becher raised most of them in his keynote address. Afterwards some of the delegates even praised Becher's remarks as discourse that avoided "dogmatically constrictive party language."[142] There was a kernel of truth to that characterization, too, but only in the sense that Becher again demonstrated his skill at couching doctrinal arguments in broadly moralistic and national terms. He began with a passionate defense of the organization's nonaligned status, defining it as an "independent and nonpartisan movement" created for that purpose alone.[143] This explained its resolute opposition to "any interference by a party"; the Kulturbund would

[138]See "Erneuerung des Kulturbundes," *Sonntag*, 9 February 1947.
[139]Kuczynski, "Zweck und Inhalt der Verständigung," *Tägliche Rundschau*, 2 July 1947.
[140]See "Notizen" and "Erneuerung des Kulturbundes," *Sonntag*, 2 and 9 February 1947.
[141]tr. "Kulturtagung in Potsdam," *Neues Deutschland*, 4 March 1947.
[142]For instance, Heinrich Mertens, in *Der erste Bundeskongress des Kulturbundes zur demokratischen Erneuerung Deutschlands am 20. und 21. Mai 1947*, p. 68.
[143]Becher, *Vom Willen zum Frieden*, p. 69. Further page citations are provided in the text.

cease to exist if the "movement" ever became a hotbed where political parties flexed their respective muscles (70;72). Becher's pronouncements may have sounded reassuring, but his remark that "we grant no party the right to stake an exclusive claim to the spiritual and cultural renewal of Germany" would have placed him and the Kulturbund at complete odds with the SED had he ever meant it; and the same goes for his comment that "we oppose monopolies of any kind, including those in the area of culture and world view" (71). Becher's utterances served other purposes, however; in line with efforts to extend the Kulturbund's activities to the Western zones, it was imperative to reassert strongly that the organization was nonaligned. Otherwise, it had little chance of obtaining Western permission to operate outside Soviet-occupied Germany. Moreover, such assertions provided the rhetorical context locally for deflecting efforts to restructure the Kulturbund's executive board according to the percentages of the Berlin elections. The SED's domination of the Kulturbund by way of its party proxies thus continued to expand, even as the rhetoric that denied the obvious grew increasingly caustic. Becher decried the lack of a "dispassionate, human tone" in intellectual disputes (59-64), but only to charge his and the Kulturbund's critics with resorting to a brand of polemics reminiscent of the Nazi press. Becher specifically smeared Kulturbund advocates of party parity within the organization, who tried to use the elections as an argument against SED domination, as practitioners of fascist tactics; they objected to the ostensible hegemonistic cravings of the other side, Becher said, because of the imminent threat to their own aspirations. Because these people were disturbed by the preponderance of Communists in the Kulturbund, and by the fact that Becher was also one, he charged that such circles regarded only those people who engaged in an "unconscionable anti-Bolshevist smear campaign" and who toyed with the idea of a new war as beyond reproach (74).

Nonetheless, Becher went on to say that the Kulturbund would not respond in kind to name-calling; instead, the "movement" sought to continue the antifascist tradition that had earlier united people in their struggle regardless of party affiliation (75). But in a different context, Becher defined fascism along lines that determined the corresponding definition of genuine antifascism. Capitalism became imperialism at the turn of the century, he said, and those who attempted to understand fascism without acknowledging that fact would lose their way in a "fog of irrationalism or mysticism" (39-40). Becher could not have made a more partisan remark; it was pure doctrine that allowed for an assortment of additional inferences. The most common one used this kind of definition of fascism to establish the Soviet Union as its antithesis. But Becher otherwise exercised restraint in his discussion of the USSR, and this surely had something to do with certain exigencies related specifically to the Kulturbund. The Kulturbund was not or not yet the equivalent of a society for the study of Soviet culture; for Becher to force the issue now, in early 1947, would have caused more problems than it solved; besides, Kuczynski's society was likely created in part to take up some of the slack caused by the Kulturbund's greater need to sustain the appearance of nonpartisanship. Becher thus proselytized for the USSR, relying upon references to Goethe, Hegel, Hölderlin, and Thomas Mann, more in connection with his general plea for the appropriation of worldwide cultural values. Within this broader setting, he then explained that fundamental changes in Germany's relationship with the Soviet Union took precedence. He offered various reasons why, but none of these departed meaningfully from comments that Becher had made in earlier speeches; and he ended his discussion of the subject by denying that any of this constituted "Soviet propaganda" (64-69).

Becher's plea for a "restructuring" of Germany's relationship with the Soviet Union and his definition of fascism went hand in hand with unflattering remarks about intellectual life in the West. He reduced it largely to the "fashionable philosophical disease of existentialism" (33), against which he warned because existentialism viewed history as senseless; the ensuing historical vacuum then allowed for the reintroduction of notorious fascist concepts like "providence" and "fate." By using existentialist considerations to expand the German crisis caused by fascism into one of all humanity, he said, Germany's particular plight, along with notions of guilt and atonement, ceased to be an issue (31-32). In spite of his declared opposition to "monopolies of any kind, even in the area of culture and world view," Becher then put the Kulturbund on record as espousing the only historical outlook commensurate with Germany's predicament and alone capable of contributing to its national deliverance; and he warned apocalyptically of what would happen if the German people ignored the lessons of the immediate past. The criticism of existentialism invariably regarded existentialism as the philosophical off-spring of fascism; and this argument engendered a host of others that discredited forms of artistic creativity regarded as violations of socialist realism to be props of a dying but dangerous class—whether in the form of French surrealism, abstract art, the writings of Sartre, Camus, Anouilh, Wilder, or even early modern Russian writers Sologub, Hippius, Mereshkovskij, or Akhmatova. One commentary echoed the Soviet central-committee edicts and redirected them at the West by insisting that this literature was suffused with a "sick eroticism" and that the creative writings of contemporary existentialists exuded the air of "pornography." Nor was there anything coincidental about the situation; the "reactionary bourgeoisie" backed Sartre because they saw in him a useful ideological tool. With the annihilation of fascism, France's "ruling financial aristocracy" shed its earlier ideological armor and donned a new suit; the fact that Sartre participated in the French resistance during the war only provided him with a certain democratic nimbus enabling him to combine "philosophical nihilism with democratic phraseology."[144] "Scientific materialist thinking" endangered the class interests of the German and French bourgeoisie, who approved of anything that could be used as a dam against it.[145] There were numerous similar treatments of the subject in the Soviet-zone press during the year;[146] but the above give a sense of the political motivation behind the opposition to existentialism in all of its manifestations, to illustrate its niche in the SED's obsession with intrusive "ideologies," and to locate Becher's equally adamant but rhetorically more restrained rejection of it at the Kulturbund conference.

To judge by the published record, Becher's remarks, and the comments of others who thought that they were echoing his sentiments, provoked some controversy during the proceedings. A man by the name of Mertens frowned upon the dismissal of existentialism as the "philosophical musical accompaniment" to the social dissolution of the bourgeoisie; for one, it needed to be discussed within its own conceptual coordinates; for another, the younger generation would not be won over by confronting them with "a nicely rounded world view that claims, within a closely knit conceptual system, to offer answers to every conceivable question." Contrasting national socialism with other "party-approved" world views and seeking to hammer these in with the same or similar methods of mass propaganda would only cause young people to plug their ears. Nonetheless, Mertens said that Becher's speech illustrated the right approach, and he concluded his remarks with a plea for nonpartisanship.[147] Alexander Abusch, who headed the Kulturbund's "department for ideology," spotted the criticism of Becher in Merten's comments, intended or not, and sought to set the record straight. There was no intention of outfitting the participants of the conference with a "formulaic conception of existentialist philosophy," Abusch said; Becher merely called attention to the different roles played by philosophies in countries like Germany and those with a "much deeper democratic development," indicating the especially dangerous significance of existentialism under Germany's current conditions (99). Abusch also sided with Becher in the dispute over the nature of fascism and, in so doing, drew inferences that Becher avoided. The deputy mayor of Berlin, Ferdinand Friedensburg, had reacted to Becher's speech by cautioning against explaining Germany's predicament exclu-

---

[144]D. S. "Philosophie des Verfalls. Sartre und die Existentialisten," *Tägliche Rundschau*, 2 February 1947.

[145]Stern, "Existentialismus. Bemerkungen zur neuesten philosophischen Modeschöpfung," *Neues Deutschland*, 4 July 1947.

[146]See, e.g., Niekisch, "Der Existentialismus. Eine neofaschistische Nachkriegsmode," *Tägliche Rundschau*, 10 January 1947; Hoecker, "Existentialismus—und was danach?" *Neues Deutschland*, 4 May 1947; "Die 'innere Emigration' als Weltanschauung," *Tägliche Rundschau*, 14 September 1947; Dultz, "Der Existentialismus als Ausdruck der bürgerlichen Intelligenzkrise," *Einheit* 6 (1947): 564-70; and Dymschitz, "Reise ans Ende der Nacht," *Tägliche Rundschau*, 21 December 1947.

[147]*Der erste Bundeskongreß*, pp. 69-70; further citations are provided in the text.

sively as the consequence of the transformation of monopoly capital into imperialism. Such narrow interpretations not only oversimplified the matter; if that kind of view came to be seen "as the position of the Kulturbund, then we ought not to be surprised when people outside the zone say that the Kulturbund appears to follow a certain narrow party-political line" (81). Abusch objected; working out certain "German particularities" and deriving certain "sociological insights" had nothing to do with party politics; rather, these merely underscored "the necessities resulting from German history." Moreover, when the subject of antibolshevism and its origin came up, Germans who belonged to the Kulturbund needed to understand that the smear campaign had been organized not only to combat the Soviet Union but to resist "German democratic reforms that of necessity arise out of our own German history" (100-101).

Abusch thus turned any criticism of the Soviet Union, or of "sovietization" inside the Soviet zone, into an attack upon local democracy with fascistic overtones; and, vice versa, objections to political developments in the Soviet zone were seen as an immediate condemnation of the Soviet Union that no German had the right to engage in. Abusch's insistence upon the interconnections between antibolshevism, fascism, and antifascism, and his bid to make the linkage part of the Kulturbund's program, was anything but nonpartisan; and other important Kulturbund leaders took much the same position. Being antifascist did not suffice by itself, said Bernhard Bennedik; fascism was a mere symptom, the culmination of a development whose roots extended into imperialism and militarism. Still, none of this went to prove that the Kulturbund was "Communist"; those who persisted in identifying the organization with party politics slandered it; "and we will not allow ourselves to be slandered defenselessly." Indeed, Bennedik went on to say that he had recently spent a few days in West Germany, "an intellectual house of poverty"; there he discovered what real antibolshevism was, and one could easily see the distortion of facts inherent in denigrating the Kulturbund as Communist merely because it refused to be antibolshevist (72-74). The comments of Bennedik, Abusch, and Becher may have made some of the conference delegates uneasy; and whether to calm their worries or simply as part of the general denial of the Kulturbund's political affiliation, Bennedik's derogatory reference to the West generated prompt expressions of official displeasure, regardless of the fact that his remarks differed little in substance from Abusch's or Becher's.

Becher called Bennedik's utterance a "stupid slip of the tongue" (113); and a delegate from the West, Günther Rebenstorf, pleaded for "more psychology" in criticizing circumstances in the Western zones. But Rebenstorf also attempted to explain the anti-Soviet, "anti-Eastern zone attitudes" prevalent in the West with oblique allusions to the conduct of the Soviet military administration. The worry in the West, he said cryptically, was that "certain things" were not being handled with an adequate understanding of the psychological prerequisites. Exactly what he meant by that was unclear, and he probably avoided spelling things out because of the risk of finding fault with either the SMAD or the SED at a conference in the Soviet-sector of Berlin. Rebenstorf confined himself to the comment that he and other delegates from the West had encountered no difficulty in getting inter-zonal passports to attend the meeting; whereas SMAD documents permitting Soviet-zone Germans to visit the West were apparently not so easily obtained. Unfortunately, he said, those people who showed up in the West with such coveted papers in their pockets were often "very dubious elements." His suggestion was that "decent people," not just the important politicians who tended to arrive with "fixed opinions" and whose visits provoked prejudice, be allowed to visit the Western zones (103).

Unfortunately, there is no way of knowing how the various delegates reacted privately to the positions staked out by speakers like Becher or Abusch or how many in the audience got there in the first place because their approval was certain. A tremendous amount of prior planning went into these conferences in order to keep them well-managed once they began; and, in fact, there appears to have been some effort to ensure that the discussion following Becher's remarks remained under tight control. It is unclear, for instance, how certain respondents were selected from among those wishing to speak, only that insufficient time was allotted for a full discussion because relatively few of the delegates who had raised their hands got to comment. Nevertheless, plenty of time was available for Abusch and another top Kulturbund Communist, Klaus Gysi, to go into detail refuting the suggestion that concepts like antifascism and democracy were "schematic" (110-11); and theirs was the last word on the subject. After the discussion Becher delivered his closing remarks, and these convey the clear impression that some concern over issues with recognizable doctrinal underpinnings still lingered. Becher began by pleading that Christianity, democracy, and socialism be reconciled in the idea of humanism; given that solid foundation, he said, the "role of monopoly capitalism" became far too unimportant to cause dissension capable of destroying the common foundation. After expressing his hope that his overall comments had not been mistaken as "any kind of an attempt at a doctrinaire impact," Becher finished by turning around outside objections raised against the preeminent role that he, as a Communist, a "revolutionary," or a "Bolshevist" played in an organization based on the public principle of nonpartisanship. Yes, he was a "revolutionary"; but if the term was used to designate someone who advocated forcing upon Germany a form of government under which other peoples lived, be they Russian, American, English, or French, and who attempted to copy patterns of democracy unusable under Germany's specific circumstances, then the designation was entirely inappropriate. Rather, a "revolutionary" supported the national sovereignty of German politics and opposed the introduction of foreign-policy conflicts into local political life. Their "mechanical transferal" seriously endangered the "independent self-determination of our people" (114).

Following his speech, Becher was reelected president of the Kulturbund as part of the selection of a new presidium that, if not rigged, was certainly irregular. Thirty positions on the presidium needed to be filled, with the chairmen of the Kulturbund's state-level organizations and the Berlin directorate joining it automatically. In order to choose the thirty, explained Karl Kleinschmidt, head of the election committee, the conference delegates were to be given a ballot containing the names of forty-five candidates; these names had already been selected by the previous presidium and approved, after certain "changes and additions," by the state-level directorates. Thus, strangely enough, Kleinschmidt said that the "election proposal" was not the work of any one particular group within the Kulturbund or even of the previous presidium. The delegates were now to see the list for the first time and be given sixty minutes to discuss additions. Apparently no names could be deleted, only new ones added if five delegates agreed; and from that list the thirty members were to be chosen. Evidently, the ballots were then handed out, but Kleinschmidt was alerted to the fact that the list contained only thirty names for the thirty positions, to which he responded lamely that "some group or other" had tried to doctor the outcome. But there seems to have been no attempt made by him or anyone else to ask who might have been in a position to tamper with the ballot or to investigate the matter; the original ballot with forty-five names must then have been located, or re-printed, an additional five names added by the delegates, and from that list thirty presidium members selected.[148] Then followed the election of the president, an easy task because Becher ran unopposed. Indeed, he was chosen with no abstentions and no votes against him; whether the result had anything to do with the fact that the vote was by show of hands, a procedure whose approval Kleinschmidt sought publicly from the delegates and to which no one dared object to publicly, is difficult to say (155-56).

The last major item on the agenda was an address by Sergej Tjulpanov. He challenged the Kulturbund with respect to its attitude toward the Soviet Union and, in the process, very nearly renounced the idea that the Soviet system was inappropriate for Germany because it did not suit its current national circumstances. His exact words were that "for Germany and the entire world the touchstone of honesty and the judge of a true democrat, to say nothing of those calling themselves socialists, is his relationship to the So-

---

[148]See pp. 180-81; the important Communists among them were Klaus Gysi, Anna Seghers, Alexander Abusch, Heinz Willmann, Robert Havemann, Willi Bredel, Paul Wandel, Anton Ackermann, Alfred Meusel, Wolfgang Langhoff, Victor Klemperer, Josef Naas, and Wolf Düwel.

viet Union." More importantly, he added that "many countries aspire to re-structure their economic, political, and cultural life in line with the experiences of the Soviet Union." Tjulpanov also spelled out a new program for the Kulturbund that would soon transform it into another mass organization for the "study of Soviet culture." The SMAD had done everything in its power to back the Kulturbund, he said; but the time had come for even closer and more intensive cooperation, the realization of which depended first and foremost upon the Kulturbund itself. For in spite of the organization's considerable success, much remained to be done because its previous achievements merely fulfilled the initial prerequisites for the "democratization of German culture." Tjulpanov then discussed the Kulturbund's proper place in the ranks of those fighting for "a lasting peace, a just social order, and against the war mongers" who misused the ideals of democracy in order to incite hatred against "other peoples"; and he coupled this political argument to an unambiguous cultural position. He spoke of the profound crisis of European bourgeois culture and blamed it on those of its cultural representatives who aspired to save the "bourgeois imperialist order" instead of working with the progressive elements of the times. Tjulpanov then called upon those at work building the new German culture to attack "decadent ideas" and echoed comments made by Shemjakin at the beginning of the year; the democratic intelligentsia needed to struggle harder toward the complete eradication of "prejudices regarding the Soviet Union, which remain widely disseminated among the German people."[149]

The discussion of substantive issues, which the Kulturbund's weekly called a "moving manifestation . . . of German unity,"[150] ended with a ringing endorsement of Soviet foreign policy that quickly crowded out the organization's official principles. Tjulpanov's approval of countries that aspired to "restructure" themselves in line with the Soviet experience, for instance, seriously undercut Becher's disavowal of any German attempt to "copy" unusable kinds of democracy, Western or Soviet. Now it may be that Becher consciously de-emphasized the use of force in any German "restructuring" in order to champion the process itself, but then the KPD's original promise did much the same thing. The rhetoric never stated that national sovereignty ruled out the adaptation of a "Soviet system" to German circumstances through time immemorial; circumstances could change, especially once the German people had atoned for the past, and the entire political process could well result as an act of national self-determination rather than a "mechanical transferal." Nor had Tjulpanov indicated that developments in other countries enamored of the Soviet experience unfolded in violation of democracy; such developments represented the consummate expression of it.

[149]Tjulpanov, "'Prüfstein der Ehrlichkeit,'" *Tägliche Rundschau*, 22 May 1947.
[150]Ihering, "Die Bundestagung," *Aufbau* 5 (1947): 459.

But considering the anti-Western rhetoric of Tjulpanov's speech, or of Becher's, for that matter, the statement in *Aufbau* that East and West Germany had never been closer to each other than in the Kulturbund's unanimous disapproval of Bennedik's slip of the tongue was profoundly misleading,[151] and the various exercises in the semantics of democracy ultimately offered little consolation to those Germans wary about "sovietization." Under the circumstances, they probably took it for granted that the democratic "restructuring" alluded to would scarcely happen if the German people were to arrive at a decision favoring it democratically; so tampering with the KPD's original promise, whether massive in Tjulpanov's comments or more tentative in Becher's, probably struck many as a clear signal of ulterior motives completely divorced from traditional concepts of democracy.

The Kulturbund's reaction when its critics declined to celebrate the organization's nonpartisanship as enthusiastically as its spokesman was to persist in its denials of the obvious. The conference had been devoid of "dogma and doctrine," read one commentary; it was equally free of "one-sided party-political ties," other than in the minds of those critics who considered the Kulturbund's resolute antifascism itself as dogmatism and who regarded it as a "club of dangerous revolutionaries" because of its militant posture in cultural-political questions.[152] Tjulpanov's speech belied such arguments, and the local press picked its words carefully in responding to his remarks and other utterances regarding the Soviet Union. *Sonntag* acted as if the speakers had called for nothing more than a "good relationship" with the Soviet Union, did not comment at all upon Tjulpanov's approval of those countries restructuring themselves "in line with the Soviet experience," and said explicitly that good relations with the USSR included ties with the "progressive elements of the West."[153] However, the rabid criticism of Western intellectual life clearly violated the spirit, if only the spirit, of the Kulturbund's assurance that it felt equally at one with the peoples of the East and West. For the rhetoric was carefully chosen to convey the sense that the Kulturbund was not unduly Soviet-oriented while leaving plenty of room for distinguishing between the democratically minded peoples of the West and the reactionary political establishment. It was scarcely coincidental that Abusch altered the standard phrase a bit when he called for a balanced outlook with respect to the "peoples of the East and the young democratic forces of the West."[154] His diction allowed the Kulturbund to toughen its rhetoric against Western reaction without contradicting its original principle. Another editorial in *Sonntag* used still more explicit rhetoric in assailing the enemies of democratic renewal. Repeating the pledge that the Kulturbund

[151]See Ihering, "Die Bundestagung," *Aufbau* 6 (1947): 459.
[152]Joho, "Das geistige Gesicht der Konferenz," *Sonntag*, 1 June 1947.
[153]Ibid.
[154]"Kein geistiges Vakuum," *Sonntag*, 8 June 1947.

sponsored an orientation with equal emphasis toward East and West, the editorial railed against critics who objected to its democratic elections and used "imported methods" to defame Kulturbund personalities, whose antifascism qualified themselves for positions of leadership, as Communists. It characterized these critics as practitioners of the anti-Bolshevist instigation perfected by Goebbels who, masking themselves as democratic opponents of totalitarianism, insisted upon bringing things "into line" in accordance with the Berlin elections and thus emerged as apostles of a new Nazi-style regimentation. Employing tactics scarcely discernible from those used by Goebbels, they practiced methods that prepared the way for a "new reactionary dictatorship."[155]

The Kulturbund defended itself against the accusation that it was Communist-run both by defining its leadership as immaculately antifascist and by berating those troubled by the organization's direction either as outright fascists or as criminally negligent. Using this logic, it made perfect sense to sidestep the real issue by explaining objections to the Kulturbund's partisanship in terms of a confrontation between fascism and antifascism. Gysi called the "smear campaign against antifascism" the most dangerous, contemporary manifestation of fascism; but he explained that the campaigners, in order to avoid the self-incrimination likely to result from any outburst against antifascism itself, resorted to character assassination instead; they slandered prominent personalities, proven antifascists, as the most convenient way of "mobilizing base instincts" among the people.[156] In another article, Gysi tried a slightly different approach. Ignoring the fact of the Kulturbund's nonpartisanship, he said, was tantamount to advocating a struggle within the organization against the influence of the "leftist elements of Marxism" because they supposedly used it to infiltrate their own ideas. All such charges were based on the ridiculous assumption that the "struggle against the left" overrode the urgency of combating the danger of nazism and disposed of the need for an organization open to antifascist intellectuals of varying political persuasion. Gysi added that the menace of fascism was by no means diminished, so that the defamation of "any of the intellectual currents" cooperating in the Kulturbund threatened to cause a rift among democrats working within it. Any such rift would return the German people to the very road responsible for the current catastrophe.[157]

Though the attempts to reconcile the Kulturbund's political posture with its claims of nonpartisanship continued unabated,[158] the organization's credibility dwindled steadily because the meaning of the principle had been completely corrupted. By late spring 1947, the concept of "nonpartisanship" was

[155]"Die demokratische Erneuerung und ihre Feinde," *Sonntag*, 1 June 1947.

[156]Gysi, "Vertrauen oder Mißtrauen," *Sonntag*, 7 September 1947.

[157]Gysi, "Überparteilichkeit und Diskussion," *Aufbau* 6 (1947): 460-61.

[158]See, Kleinschmidt, "Überparteilichkeit und politische Haltung," *Sonntag*, 22 June 1947.

comprised of a set of arguments that effectively muzzled Soviet-zone critics who were unwilling to risk being labeled fascist because of their "antibolshevism" and, no less vociferously, branded Western opponents as the legatees of Goebbels. With the passage of time, that dimension of Kulturbund nonpartisanship which Tjulpanov was the first to feature when he called the Soviet Union the "touchstone" of democracy became its dominant aspect. Afterwards, antifascism and nonpartisanship melted into unstinting fidelity to the Soviet Union.

CHAPTER EIGHT

Censorship and Controversy

The Kulturbund had developed steadily since its conception in spring 1945, if not always smoothly, and its rhetoric grew correspondingly sharper with the passage of time. But the basic idea of organizing intellectuals in support of causes that furthered the SED's political objectives never changed. Not that Ulbricht returned to Germany on 30 April 1945 with creation of a cultural organization uppermost in his mind. But once there, he was quick to spot the importance of "work among the intellectuals" and telegraphed Dimitrov in Moscow a scant ten days after his arrival with the first of several requests that Johannes R. Becher return to Germany to begin it.[1] Ulbricht sent Pieck and Dimitrov further reports on 17 May to the effect that he and his band of émigrés were in touch with "circles of intellectuals" in Berlin; but he indicated that plans for working with antifascists generally had run into problems caused by the "errant views" of local Communists who talked of "Soviet power" and winked at each other over the party's new approach to politics. In Berlin alone, the "party organization" counted some 5,000 members who had belonged to the KPD before 1933, many of whom failed to understand now why the party was "not yet able to conduct its work out in the open" and remained transfixed by the notion of Soviet power. Finally, Ulbricht spoke of the establishment of a "committee of scientists and artists" that could be expanded "into an association of friends of the Soviet Union";[2] and these remarks, along with his reference to a "popular league for democratic renewal," reveal the Kulturbund at the earliest point of its conceptualization. They also allude to the tactical considerations that governed its initial work and allow for other inferences that suggest why an undertaking dedicated to studying Soviet culture had to await a more opportune moment.

But the need to organize intellectuals was understood right away, and in developing the idea of a cultural association with the appearance of nonpar-

---

[1] Rekonstruktion eines Telegramms des Genossen Walter Ulbricht vom 10. Mai an den Gen. Dimitroff. Zentrales Parteiarchiv, NL 36/629/1.

[2] "Aus einem Brief an Genossen Wilhelm Pieck [17 May 1945]," Ulbricht, *Zur Geschichte der deutschen Arbeiterbewegung*, vol. II, Zusatzband, pp. 204-6; and Rekonstruierte Notizen aus einem Bericht des Gen. Walter Ulbricht an Gen. Dimitroff vom 17. Mai 1945. Zentrales Parteiarchiv, NL 36/629/9-11.

tisanship, there were certain strategies to fall back on. Becher's essay on the "political-moral annihilation of fascism," dated back to early 1945; and on 22 May, Pieck sent seventy-five copies of the manuscript, in which Becher discussed the need for a "universal policy of alliances" *and* praised the KPD as a "party of a new type," to Ulbricht in Berlin.[3] Organizational strategies for using party writers to assist in influencing intellectuals were slower to emerge, however; many of these men and women were waiting in Moscow for the opportunity to return to Germany, and, judging by letters written by Pieck to Ulbricht on 22 and 26 May, there had been remarkably little advance planning that included them.[4] This now began changing; though Dimitrov had decided by 22 May to send Becher home,[5] he was still in Moscow when Ulbricht, Ackermann, and Sobottka arrived for talks with Stalin on 4 June. In light of the fact that the first concrete plans for the Kulturbund developed out of these talks,[6] then, Becher's return to Germany with Ulbricht and others on 10 June establishes a connection between the KPD's opening manifesto and the role of an organization for intellectuals operating within the context of that appeal. The report of a Soviet Lieutenant Colonel Selesnov, back from Berlin and delivered orally to Pieck in Moscow on 26 June, must have further confirmed the urgency of appealing to intellectuals. Selesnov said that "workers and bourgeois elements" in Germany were critical of the KPD for having failed in 1933 and now expected more "civil war and chaos" from it. The KPD was considered capable of "crude methods of mass agitation" only and had "no intellectuals" who supported it.

At a later meeting of the KPD's secretariat and its agitprop functionaries in September, Fred Oelßner admitted that the party had repeatedly underestimated the importance of the intellectuals in the past and blocked "one of the most important channels for influencing public opinion." So it was a top priority now to "interest the intellectuals in the party, incorporate the best elements into the party, and make use of this channel (teachers, editors, etc.) for influencing the popular masses to our advantage." Because it was a "broad mass organization," however, the party opposed setting up Kulturbund branches anywhere "under a clearly Communist signboard." As Oelßner put it, "this does not benefit us in the least," and Ackermann echoed his remarks. The KPD would have a difficult time meeting its obligations without the intellectuals "on our side and even in the party," Ackermann said; thus, the KPD had to "fight for every prominent creative intellectual, educator, and artist"; and the existence of the Kulturbund by no means relieved the party of its own responsibilities. Rather, KPD and Kulturbund complemented each other. Officially, however, the Kulturbund had "nothing directly in

---

[3]See Pieck to Ulbricht, 22 May 1945. Zentrales Parteiarchiv, NL 36/629/12-15 and 18-41.
[4]See ibid and Pieck to Ulbricht, 26 May 1945, ibid., NL 36/629/58.
[5]See Pieck to Ulbricht, 22 May 1945, ibid., NL 36/629/12-15.
[6]See Chapters One and Two.

common with the Commparty," and it was regrettable when mistakes were made that allowed the Kulturbund to be discredited as Communist; that was "exactly what we must avoid."[7]

By September 1945, definitions of the Kulturbund as an organization for intellectuals of all kinds had then shifted away from the earliest considerations in July 1945 that it might work best as an "elite organization" open only to the prominent; and the organization boasted 93,000 members by May 1947. At the same time, Heinz Willmann confirmed that the Kulturbund had decided almost from the start to seek the support of a broad spectrum of culturally minded people by appealing to everyone capable of exerting an "intellectual influence" over Germans in general.[8] Even so, there was still a distinction made when it came to the cultural education of manual laborers; in the beginning, that task fell mostly to organizations like the FDGB (as opposed to the Gewerkschaft 17 within it), which had its own office in charge of "mass" cultural work. That office claimed to have set up cultural commissions in 10,000 out of 44,000 Soviet-zone factories by early 1947 and to have sponsored 3,000 events with over two-million participants.[9] Those were areas in which the Kulturbund was not really equipped to work, and the problem emerging now was that changes made in Soviet-occupied Germany since 1945 threatened the organization with irrelevance if it failed to adapt to a more politicized environment while still maintaining a nonpartisan façade. Tjulpanov's comment in May to the effect that the Kulturbund had not lived up to its potential, together with Willmann's remark that the organization often lacked the requisite "ties with life,"[10] were both allusions to problems caused by a lingering adherence to its original assignment and tension created by the transition to a new one.

Repertory Management

The growing limitations of the Kulturbund help explain why the Communists created additional organizations in 1947. The society for the study of Soviet culture was one, people's theaters, Volksbühnen, another. Not that these undertakings were always separate from the older ones; the Kulturbund and the FDGB, with the SED and SMAD behind the scenes, were offi-

[7]Stenographische Niederschrift über die Sekretariats- und Agitprop-Leiter-Sitzung am . . . 28. Sept. 1945, ibid., I 2/5/40/1-93.
[8]Willmann gave the following breakdown for the Kulturbund's Berlin organization: 23% were writers, publicists, journalists, or composers; painters, sculptors, or architects comprised 10.5%; 14% were teachers or professors; 9% were involved in either the film or the stage; the remainder qualified generally as "culturally interested," Willmann, "Tätigkeitsericht." *Der Bundeskongreß*, pp. 128-29.
[9]See "Kulturarbeit in den Betrieben," ibid., pp. 182-83.
[10]Willmann, "Tätigkeitsbericht," ibid., p. 137.

cial sponsors of the "people's theater movement," and Willmann insisted that the Bund Deutscher Volksbühnen or association of people's theaters, formed in May, would enable the Kulturbund to engage in "mass work" without neglecting its original responsibilities.[11] But the creation of people's theaters was also related to general dissatisfaction with the state of cultural affairs evident in the debate over modern art. The fact was that the party's efforts to use culture to win over the public had yielded disappointing results; and in the case of Soviet-zone and Berlin theaters, the discontent was deepened by the impact of the Soviet central-committee resolutions.

Fritz Erpenbeck lamented the absence of a "conscious progressive line" in stage repertories; few contemporary plays appeared on stage, and good performances of the classics were rare. By contrast, there was a "flood" of surrealistic plays, though Erpenbeck hoped that the emergence of a "powerful, promising people's theater movement" would solve "most of the problems."[12] He returned to these subjects repeatedly over the next few weeks, bemoaning "philosophical stagnation" and the tendency to give ground to the "forces of reaction" evident in repertory planning. Echoing the central-committee edicts, Erpenbeck objected to the preponderance of foreign plays because these fell mostly into the category of surrealism, which served to obscure the avoidance of critical philosophical problems in a cloud of formal experimentation.[13] For Erpenbeck, the problem was again one of intrusive "alien ideologies"; that is, the difficulties arose because young playwrights imitated foreign products. Erpenbeck charged them with yielding to the urge to distort contemporary events formalistically or to depict daily life naturalistically. Either way, they failed to comprehend the historical meaning of Germany's liberation from Hitlerism, and this deficient perspective clouded their view of both present and future.[14] Late in the year, an article in *Neues Deutschland* then situated the entire discussion of Soviet-zone and Western stage practices within the context of existentialism. The paper contended that the repertories of Western-zone theaters suffered under the influence of the decadent bourgeoisie; existentialism dominated the stage with performances of plays by Anouilh, Giraudoux, Thornton Wilder; and the reason for it was the intention of eliminating the theater as a vehicle of progress by using existentialist philosophy like a narcotic to lull audiences into a stupor. *Neues Deutschland* saw nothing coincidental in the prevalence of these tendencies and voiced its suspicion that a "conscious inculcation of nihilistic ideas" explained them; nor could there be any doubt about the forces behind the popularization of existentialism; the capitalist entertainment industry intended to use it to combat socialism. Indeed, the performances of such "political

[11]Ibid., p. 138.
[12]Erpenbeck, "Berliner Theaterleben," *Neues Deutschland*, 1 January 1947.
[13]Erpenbeck, "Krise des Theaters?" *Einheit* 3 (1947): 312-14.
[14]Erpenbeck, "Neues Theater im neuen Deutschland," *Neues Deutschland*, 22 April 1947.

box-office draws" threatened to split Germany into progressive and reactionary halves.[15]

The problems in the Soviet zone were twofold; first, young playwrights needed to be found and influenced; and two, useful plays had to reach ordinary Germans throughout the zone. Neither was thought to be happening, though at least one of the critics, Herbert Ihering, attributed the disinterest to simple apathy that dampened enthusiasm for cultural experiences of any kind, including "radical foreign plays."[16] Erpenbeck saw things differently and alluded to the problems in Berlin that were complicated by additional factors—the SMAD lacked any basis for influencing the repertory of Berlin theaters outside the Soviet sector. But Erpenbeck tacitly acknowledged that the wrong kinds of productions played in Berlin's Western sectors to receptive audiences, despite warnings published in the Soviet-zone press; whereas the plays dealing with contemporary issues, presumably staged in Soviet-sector theaters, soon performed to half-empty houses no matter how much the same press plugged them.[17] Under those circumstances, using the Deutsches Theater to stage a performance of Simonov's anti-American *Die russische Frage*—a play whose opening coincided roughly with the Kulturbund conference in May and in which the hero, much like Tjulpanov, called the "Russian question" the touchstone used to gauge the decency and honesty of people around the world[18]—accomplished nothing if spectators stayed home. Besides, theatergoers were mainly intellectuals themselves, whereas in 1947 the party was desperately in need of ways to influence the masses. In mid-1947, the SED's division of Kultur und Erziehung informed the corresponding divisions within the party's state-level organizations that it would provide them regularly with information on specific plays; these local boards were then to work with other "progressive organizations" to get the plays performed. In addition, the party requested that the boards file reports on all important theatrical events with Kultur und Erziehung in Berlin and, after informing it of openings for theater directors and producers, hear what the party thought about personalities suggested to fill the vacancies.[19]

The SED also hoped to solve the problems afflicting the theater in Soviet-occupied Germany by working behind the scenes to create a new network

[15]"Bizonale Theaterspielpläne. Die Seuche des Existentialismus grassiert," *Neues Deutschland*, 27 September 1947.
[16]Ihering, "Nach zwei Jahren," *Aufbau* 4 (1947): 329-34.
[17]See Erpenbeck, "Krise des Theaters," *Einheit* 3 (1947): 312.
[18]See Harich, "Mut zur Wahrheit, aktuellste Tugend. 'Die russische Frage' von Konstantin Simonow im Deutschen Theater"; "Auf der Bühne und hinter den Kulissen. 'Die russische Frage'—ein Prüfstein," *Tägliche Rundschau*, 4 and 11 May; 29 June 1947; Harich, "'Die russische Frage' neu gesehen," *Tägliche Rundschau*, 29 June 1947.
[19]"Unterstützung des Zeittheaters. Schreiben der Abteilung Kultur und Erziehung beim Zentralsekretariat der SED an alle Landesvorstände der SED [19 June 1947]," *Um die Erneuerung der deutschen Kultur. Dokumente*, pp. 191-92.

of organizations, called Volksbühnen, and to coordinate their activities by way of a central regulatory agency located in Berlin. Needless to say, the party's involvement was kept secret. Though a provisional Volksbühne attached to the Hebbel Theater already existed, headed by Karl-Heinz Martin, in mid-December 1946 the *Tägliche Rundschau* published a call for creation of new people's theaters in Berlin and throughout the zone; existing ones based on previous such establishments had not managed to become a "decisive factor" in the intellectual renewal of the German people because their doors were closed to the general public due to high ticket prices. The idea of the Volksbühne, which had a long and distinguished history up to 1933, now needed to be reawakened as a means of influencing the theater arts in the Soviet zone. The appeal added that the job of reorganizing and developing people's theaters should be taken up by "nonpartisan mass organizations" like the FDGB and the Kulturbund;[20] and, at least publicly, this is what happened. The FDGB's division of schooling and education discussed the "cultural situation" at a meeting in December 1946 and concluded that a return to earlier practices, such as "workers' culture organizations" or "proletcult," was undesirable. Instead, something called "people's culture organizations," to encompass all segments of the population, would combine with people's theaters as a specific part of that broader undertaking to create a more effective way of educating the masses culturally. Moreover, the people's theaters should aim toward the "conscious elevation of the cultural niveau" of the masses, rather than restricting themselves to making tickets available at a reduced price. The FDGB then instructed its state-level functionaries to lay the groundwork for people's theaters in all Soviet-zone states; and by early April 1947, these either existed or were on the verge of formation in the five regions of the country. Attention could then turn to the matter of an association of German people's theaters based in Berlin.[21] The FDGB meeting thus resulted in union advocacy of a "people's culture organization" in the form of people's theaters throughout the zone. Considered "nonpartisan," these were to be coordinated centrally; and because the FDGB was the "largest nonpartisan organization of working people," it regarded itself as the logical choice to join forces with the Kulturbund and other "nonpartisan organizations with cultural interests," grasp the initiative, and begin organizing the theaters.[22]

But much had already transpired behind the scenes. A Social-Democratic city councilman by the name of Siegfried Nestriepke had apparently been the first to broach the subject of reconstructing Berlin's Volksbühne, and he

[20]"Schafft neue Volksbühnen!" *Tägliche Rundschau*, 13 December 1946.

[21]"Kulturarbeit in den Gewerkschaften," *Geschäftsbericht des Freien Deutschen Gewerkschaftsbundes 1946*, p. 184.

[22]"Schaffung einer Volkskulturorganisation. Aufruf des Bundesvorstandes des FDGB [30 January 1947]," *Um die Erneuerung der deutschen Kultur. Dokumente*, pp. 178-79.

subsequently managed to block the efforts of the SED and SMAD to reestablish a people's theater licensed for all sectors of the old capital *and* controlled by them through its attachment to the FDGB.[23] Nestriepke is said to have contacted the Russians as early as May 1945, when his proposals for restructuring Berlin theaters came to the attention of the Soviet commander, Bersarin, and Nestriepke presumably discussed the matter with him. In late June, the Communist city councilman Otto Winzer then formed a commission to study the organization of a people's theater and asked Nestriepke to prepare a second proposal. Soon after, however, Winzer informed everyone that the plans had to be tabled, evidently because Nestriepke's suggestions did not allow for the direct participation of organizations like the FDGB and the Kulturbund in creating and supervising the people's theater. Following that decision, Nestriepke, whose title at the time was "Theaterreferent" in the Berlin Magistrat, continued his efforts to reestablish the people's theater. Next came the announcement in the *Tägliche Rundschau* on 13 December 1946, referred to above, calling for creation of people's theaters and insisting that it was the job of "nonpartisan" organizations like the unions, the Kulturbund, and the youth and women's leagues to take the initiative. Nestriepke, who had become the councilman in charge of cultural affairs after the fall elections, reacted by calling his own commission to plan for reconstituting the people's theater. This group was comprised of a sampling of all factions (including Communists);[24] it began meeting on 20 December 1946, and, apparently with the support of the majority of commission members, Nestriepke continued to develop plans for a people's theater that would not be under the auspices of the FDGB or the Kulturbund. In addition, he seems to have called upon an SPD committee to draw up a new proposal for a people's theater, and presumably did so because the Social Democrats had won the Berlin elections, represented the majority party in the Magistrat, and were empowered to act accordingly.

These activities stimulated a private response by the FDGB on 24 December 1946, complaining that attempts were underway to transform the people's theater into a Social-Democratic party affair. The FDGB's resolution of 30 January 1947, also referred to above, followed But prior to the issuance of this document, Nestriepke had again made it plain that a people's theater must develop independently of political parties, which also meant freedom from organizations dominated by any single party. On 15 January 1947, the SMAD answered Nestriepke by issuing a license to Karl-Heinz Martin, Heinz Litten, and Alfred Lindemann to "reconstruct the people's theater movement."[25] This intensified the struggle because the SMAD li-

---

[23]See Braulich, *Die Volksbühne. Theater und Politik der deutschen Volksbühnenbewegung*, pp. 173-89.
[24]See the list in ibid., p. 175.
[25]"Start der neuen Volksbühne in Berlin," *Tägliche Rundschau*, 16 January 1947.

cense was not recognized in the Western sectors. Even so, *Neues Deutsch-land* announced a few weeks later that guidelines had been prepared to help in organizing the theaters and to ensure that the people's culture organizations worked "systematically."[26] What the newspaper did not reveal was that these guidelines were the work of the SED's division of Kultur und Erziehung and that they had been under development for quite a while. Unpublished at the time, the document made it clear that the party viewed the people's theaters as part of an overall "people's culture organization"; by no means restricted to the staging of preferred plays, a people's culture organization would allow the party to coordinate cultural activity at all levels of society and to centralize its oversight of the entire network. The guidelines explained that this would occur through the establishment of an organizational hierarchy; each of these local people's theater circles were to be run by a collective comprised of persons who represented the FDGB, the FDJ, the Kulturbund, and individual artists; the committees answered to a board with jurisdiction for the entire state; these boards, whose members came from the same group of organizations, but with the addition of a representative from the state ministry of education, would then be consolidated in a people's theater association in Berlin. Its task was to unify and manage the organizations throughout the zone, providing them with standardized material and establishing "central facilities" designed to benefit the network.[27]

More of these details were worked out at the meeting convened to form the association of German people's theaters in May; but it is most important to understand that the SED and SMAD were behind plans for "people's theaters" from the beginning and that these plans were related to the growing need for some kind of apparatus capable of regulating stage repertories in Berlin, or half of it, and throughout the zone. The guidelines developed by the SED's division of Kultur und Erziehung and its advisory body, the Zentraler Kulturausschuß, were not accepted by the party's secretariat until 3 March 1947 but they came up for discussion internally at a meeting of the Kulturausschuß as early as 17 January 1947, during which the FDGB's Karl Fugger, who ran the union's office of schooling and education, gave his account of the problems caused by Nestriepke. According to Fugger, Nestriepke refused to guarantee the FDGB any say in the affairs of the Volksbühne organization in Berlin. In fact, Fugger, charged that the SPD in general was out to acquire control over the organization and warned that the emergence in Berlin of two such theaters had to be avoided at all cost. Another union official responsible for its cultural endeavors, Walter Maschke, then reported briefly on the guidelines developed by the SED's division of Kultur und Er-

---

[26]"Sozialistische Kulturpolitik," *Neues Deutschland*, 12 February 1947.
[27]"Aufbau von Volksbühnenvereinen (Volkskulturorganisation). Richtlinien der Abteilung Kultur und Erziehung beim Zentralsekretariat und des zentralen Kulturausschusses der SED [January 1947]," *Um die Erneuerung der deutschen Kultur. Dokumente*, pp. 174-77.

ziehung and warned likewise of the need to prevent "divisive tendencies"; whereas Robert Weimann, who headed Kultur und Erziehung, regretted the premature issuance of a license to Martin, Litten, and Lindemann and complained that the three men failed to inform the party beforehand. Weimann insisted that the Volksbühne needed to be nonpartisan, rather than a "family affair of the SED," but also insisted that the FDGB and the Kulturbund had the right to demand a voice in the organization. Lindemann defended himself by claiming that "the party" *had* been informed and that immediate action was necessary because Nestriepke was on the verge of expanding the Volksbühne organization in the English sector of Berlin. In the absence of peremptory measures, the British would have established for themselves a "dominant influence in repertory management." Lindemann assured the group, however, that the licensees had every intention of forming a joint committee along with the FDGB and the Kulturbund to run the Volksbühne and planned on approaching the allied Kommandantur for a license valid citywide. But he warned about trusting the SPD in matters related to the Volksbühne because its leadership wanted to "run us over."[28]

Further complaints about the issuance of a license were voiced by Heinz Willmann; he predicted "serious political consequences." But considering Lindemann's claim that he had indeed informed "the party," along with the simple fact that the SMAD granted a license, it seems reasonable to assume that the Russians had their reasons for taking action destined to split Berlin culturally; that it did so because other measures would have caused more serious problems; and that top party functionaries like Ackermann knew about it. But it must have been considered risky to keep bodies like the Kulturausschuß, which had numerous former Social Democrats on it, too well informed. In fact, certain committee members came to Nestriepke's defense at the meeting on 17 January; some even insisted that the SPD had a better chance of setting up a Volksbühne because the Social Democrats enjoyed broader support in Berlin.[29] Regardless, the draft guidelines governing the structure and activity of Volksbühne organizations were presented to the SED's cultural conference several days later, on 28 and 29 January 1947, in the form of a motion. Weimann introduced them by stressing again the importance of the FDGB and the Kulturbund as Volksbühne sponsors; explained the structure of the organization, which was scheduled to be set up in the form of local associations and state "centrals"; and went into greater detail about the creation of a "central for Volksbühne associations" charged with the systematic regulation of the entire "movement." Weimann said that "we are far enough along with our work" to be able to set up "the Volksbühne central" presently; and he made it clear that the undertaking would go far

[28]Protokoll [Sitzung des Zentralen Kulturausschusses], 17 January 1947, ibid., IV 2/906/4/47-50.
[29]Ibid.

beyond the establishment of an organization for the distribution of discounted theater tickets. Weimann hoped instead that the formation of Volksbühne organizations would lead to a complete "revitalization and restructuring" of the overall system of theaters by helping overcome the current lack of direction. "Developing out of the progressive spirit of the party, we hope to give theater life a goal and a direction in the sense of linking theater and art more tightly to the overall endeavors of our times."[30]

Meanwhile, most public discussion in early 1947 concentrated on the reorganization of the Berlin Volksbühne, which in years past had performed in a now bombed-out building on Karl-Liebknecht-Platz. Given the city's traditions, it was important there to distinguish between the pioneer organization and the new theater; the latter was to have much "broader tasks" than its predecessor.[31] Ihering explained that the new Volksbühne had to draw upon the experiences of the old one, but adapt its work to the "cultural-political needs" of the day; indeed, the Volksbühne should become a theater "for everyone," which suggested that the idea might ultimately render itself obsolete because, "if every theater were really conscious of its current sending," they would all pursue similar objectives.[32] At the time, this was still far from being a realistic prospect; according to the DVV's statistics, seventy-six theaters operated on the territory of Soviet-occupied Germany as of 1 December 1946; of these, thirty-nine were run by directors who belonged to the SED; but thirty-five had no political affiliation at all, and three belonged to other parties. Figures were unavailable for the twelve theaters located in the Soviet sector of Berlin.[33] The breakdown, which in one respect illustrates the party's cultural-political progress, in other ways underscores its failure. For instance, there is no way of knowing how many of the party's directors were former Social Democrats and, possibly, unreliable. Half of the other theaters presumably remained outside the sphere of the party's direct influence altogether, so that the possibilities for controlling repertories generally were still limited in 1947. These problems also pertained to the reorganization of the Berlin Volksbühne; the "movement" was geared to bringing the new theater under the influence of the party or its representatives, the difficulty being that entrusting known Communists with responsibility for the reorganization ran the risk of discrediting the undertaking as a party affair.

These issues surfaced in an editorial published under the pseudonym G. Berg, probably Bergelson, in the SMAD's *Tägliche Rundschau*, which had

[30]Stenographische Niederschrift über die SED-Kulturkonferenz am 28./29. Januar 1947, ibid., IV 2/1.01/33/184-85.
[31]Weimann, "Um die geistige Erneuerung Deutschlands," *Neues Deutschland*, 4 January 1947.
[32]Ihering, "Theater für alle. Einige Worte zur neuen Volksbühne," *Tägliche Rundschau*, 15 January 1947.
[33]Deutsche Verwaltung für Volksbildung. Referat Theater und Musik. Vermerk. Betr.: Statistische Feststellung, 3 January 1947, gez. Reiche. Bundesarchiv, Abt. Potsdam, R-2/1091/157.

printed the original call for new people's theaters. Berg complained that things had been entirely too slow to develop in Berlin, where "superfluous differences of opinion and discussions" had confused the issues. Berg said that the question of low ticket prices was naturally critical; but this did not justify the attempt to define the new people's theater in terms of its affordability—to the exclusion of repertory considerations, artistic methods, style, management, and ticket distribution. Indeed, said Berg, some of those involved with the new undertaking, like Nestriepke (who had worked from 1920 to 1933 in the old Volksbühne), ignored "ideological questions"; Nestriepke saw no practical way of influencing the repertory.[34] Remarks like these make it virtually certain that the hope of manipulating the selection of plays, to say nothing of determining the use of approved production, staging, and acting techniques, was one of the prime reasons why both SMAD and SED backed formation of a new theater or theater "organization." It was just as understandable why Berg was appalled at Nestriepke's intention of "tearing the Volksbühne away from the political life of the country and, particularly, to making it independent of the various democratic institutions—the parties, the unions, the Kulturbund, the women's committees, and the FDJ." This kind of tendency violated the "spirit of the people's theater movement" by seeking to separate it from the very organizations that served the interests of the people. But Berg's criticism suggests that the rush to reorganize the Volksbühne along lines substantially different from those governing the organization prior to 1933 had been spotted as a Communist-party and SMAD operation. Nestriepke was an obvious target of criticism because of the Magistrat's involvement in matters pertaining to the city of Berlin and probably, too, because of the need to have the Magistrat's endorsement if the new Volksbühne were to be regarded citywide as the sole legitimate successor to the old theater.

This never happened; one week after Berg's article appeared, the *Tägliche Rundschau* announced that the SMAD had responded to the appeal of 12 December 1946 by licensing pre-1933 Volksbühne personalities Martin, Litten, and Lindemann to "rebuild the people's theater movement" and begin preparations for reconstructing the building on Karl-Liebknecht-Platz.[35] A short time later, responding in part to what some saw as SMAD action in a matter not under its sole jurisdiction, Alexander Dymschitz explained that the SMAD had licensed the Volksbühne because the old house was located in the Soviet sector of Berlin and expressed his hope that the "other occupation powers" would understand the decision.[36] But after much behind-the-scenes maneuvering, the "other occupation powers" declined to approve the

[34]Berg, "Die Volksbühne," *Tägliche Rundschau*, 8 January 1947.
[35]"Start der neuen Volksbühne in Berlin," *Tägliche Rundschau*, 16 January 1947.
[36]"Theater aller Werktätigen. Der Aufbau der neuen Berliner Volksbühne," *Tägliche Rundschau*, 26 January 1947.

statutes proposed for the Berlin Volksbühne because of the organization's attachment to the FDGB.[37] In the interim, discussions over the establishment of the people's theater had continued in subsequent meetings of the Nestriepke commission. The FDGB representative, Fugger, insisted that his organization be regarded as the sponsor of the theater, and Nestriepke and his supporters refused to accept those conditions. Following a private discussion between Nestriepke, Fugger,, Lindemann, and one of the two CDU representatives on the commission, Tiburtius, with Dymschitz on 25 January 1947, the SMAD then tried to throw Nestriepke off his own commission. This only confirmed the suspicion that the SMAD and SED were determined to bring the Volksbühne under their control, an assumption unaffected by the assurance that, as Dymschitz put it, the Volksbühne must "absolutely" be kept free of any organizational link to "the political parties." Nor did Dymschitz' account of the affair appear especially persuasive; by criticizing the SMAD for licensing Martin, Lindemann, and Litten, Nestriepke violated the control council's ordinance outlawing criticism of the allies. In the future, Dymschitz told Nestriepke, the SMAD would work with him in matters related to the Volksbühne only if he apologized. He refused and was asked to leave the meeting.[38]

Supported by Social-Democratic members of the Berlin Magistrat and by the allies, Nestriepke apparently remained on the commission and continued to hold meetings that were nonetheless plagued by efforts to stack it with those who supported the idea of attaching the theater to the FDGB.[39] Finally, the allies dissolved the commission and proposed a new one to be comprised of four members from each sector—not necessarily a better solution from the perspective of the SMAD. In any case, a new organizational committee was formed under the chairmanship of Edwin Redslob, but at the first meetings, the old proposal to couple the people's theater to the FDGB and to the Kulturbund, originally submitted by Fugger, reappeared as the chief bone of contention. Whether this proposal was ever voted upon by the Redslob commission or was simply accepted soon after by the SMAD, perhaps in response to another call that August for creation of a people's theater in the Soviet-sector of Berlin,[40] is unclear. This time, however, Karl-Heinz Martin objected to the latest call for a Soviet-sector theater and turned in the license granted him by the SMAD months before. At roughly the same time, the Redslob commission dissolved itself, followed on 19 August 1947 by yet another commission—this time a Soviet-sector affair. Rapid progress was now made; a twenty-five member administrative council was chosen, and it elected a board comprised of the two older licensees, Litten and Lindemann,

[37]Braulich, *Die Volksbühne*, p. 178.
[38]"Theater aller Werktätigen," *Tägliche Rundschau*, 26 January 1947.
[39]See Braulich's account of these discussions in ibid., p. 235.
[40]Ibid., p. 179.

two representatives of the FDGB, one from the Kulturbund, and one from the Schutzverband Deutscher Autoren as a constituent organization of the FDGB by way of the Gewerkschaft 17.

Parallel to these developments, better progress had been made in the creation of what the FDGB representative in charge of the overall "movement," Maschke, characterized as a "consolidated people's theater organization" designed to coordinate the work of the local organizations, all of which were said to have been formed as a way of minimizing the "danger of a fragmentation of those persons interested in establishing cultural associations."[41] From 16 to 18 May, following prior approval by the SED's secretariat, meetings were held that concluded with the official formation of the association of German people's theaters.[42] The SED was the sole political party in attendance (represented by Pieck); the only other politicians there were the deputy mayor of Berlin, Ferdinand Friedensburg, along with Wandel from the DVV and Gustav Brack from the central administration for labor and social welfare. The meeting ended with the "appointment" of three chairmen to head the association, Martin (whose resignation several weeks later in the matter of the Berlin people's theater was apparently a separate development), Maschke, and Inge Wangenheim—the three names already approved by the SED. The main governing body also included top Communists like Friedrich Wolf, Alexander Abusch, and Wolfgang Langhoff.[43] At the meeting itself, Maschke, justified the need for a central association by alluding to the danger of allowing theater activity to develop "uninhibitedly." Of course, there would be criticism that the undertaking had not developed "organically," but from top to bottom; however, Maschke explained that the development of cultural organizations was too important to be left entirely to chance or permitted to emerge completely out of grassroots impulses from "below" (12). Dymschitz then spelled out the objectives of the association. The task of the people's theaters was the "democratization of German culture and the German stage"; these theaters would contribute to that objective by making it possible to acquaint German working people with the best writing of Germany "and the world," to wage a battle against the "pernicious influence" of reactionary and Nazi elements, as well as against "banality and benightedness" in art, and to involve the broadest segments of the population in active support of a democratic culture (16).

Addresses by Wolf, Erwin Reiche (the DVV's man in charge of theater affairs), and the new association's business manager Paul Bartolain followed

[41]"Wie wird die Volksbühne spielen?" *Neues Deutschland*, 25 February 1947.
[42]See Protokoll Nr. 94 der Sitzung des Zentralsekretariats am 3. 5. 1947; and Protokoll Nr. 95 der Sitzung des Zentralsekretariats vom 6. 5. 47. Zentrales Parteiarchiv, IV 2/2.1/ 84 and 85. The latter decision approved the composition of the central's executive board.
[43]See *Die deutsche Volksbühne. Protokoll des Bundes Deutscher Volksbühnen, Berlin, 16. bis 18. Mai 1947*, pp. 101-10. Further citations are given in the text.

these comments. Wolf denounced Western playwrights such as Anouilh for their "nihilism" before insisting that the people's theater organization find ways of using the stage against reaction and for a progressive world view, though not for "partisan politics." He then launched into a scurrilous attack upon critics worried about the politicization of the Volksbühne by likening the "masses of politically aloof brown and semi-brown fellow travelers" partly responsible for plunging Germany into the last catastrophe to those Germans who now talked of political neutrality. The fact was that a "cultural and political struggle" had again broken out, and neither the millions of today's concealed Nazis nor the "semi-Nazi political and cultural reactionaries of widely varying hues" had ceased their attack; it was just that they engaged in the "most hypocritically reactionary, the most sinister politics" under the guise of political disinterest. Wolf insisted that there be no weakening of opposition to the "familiar swarm of camouflaged hypocrites who claim art-political neutrality," and in a related vein he demanded that people's theater representatives keep their eyes glued on the management of other artistic undertakings. There could be "no mistaken compromises, no weak knees, no neglectfulness, no intellectual indolence"; and the Volksbühne had to make sure that "pure art" not be used as a pretext for political neutrality. In this struggle, the people's theaters had tremendous opportunities, and the plays performed by them or under their influence would be the ultimate measure of their success (41). Reiche's speech differed markedly in tone; and perhaps because of the belligerence of Wolf's comments, Reiche may have considered it prudent to insist that the theater in Soviet-occupied Germany was not "managed or given orders by the Soviets," only encouraged with expert advice and practical action; indeed, he said, under Soviet occupation the theater arts had flourished, with ninety-three theaters currently in operation. Still, not all was well; Reiche explained that the stages had yet to become genuine people's theaters because insufficient numbers of ordinary Germans attended performances. Despite his less abrasive tone, however, Reiche echoed Wolf's general sentiments, and those of virtually every other speaker at the meeting, when he stressed the need to influence the choice of plays performed. This would be accomplished in two ways; once the people's theater organizations moved into their own houses, the problem would be solved through the establishment of new troupes. In the meantime, most of the "organizations" would work as a circle of advocates within existing theaters whose repertories, whenever things had been left to the initiative of these houses, customarily failed to display "an intellectual and cultural-political line." Working as "guests," the organizations could pressure the management to meet specific repertory needs whenever the resident director failed to do so on his own volition (54).

The discussion that followed largely reemphasized or expanded upon the points already made, including the need to create an organization eventually capable of encompassing the Western zones. Bartolain explained that the people's theaters would serve the needs of working people, whose outlook was "socialist and democratic" and who aspired to a socialist community in a country free of fascism (84); whereas another participant expected the organization to work both for the general population and against the directors of theaters who for years, guided by financial considerations, had corrupted the public with their choice of plays (61-63). Otherwise, much of the discussion was taken up with a one-sided debate about organizational centralization—one-sided because, to judge by the published protocol, few if any participants voiced objections to it openly. But critics of the "movement," in attendance or not, were clearly worried about the implications of a proclamation that called for theaters for working people in the city and countryside, a central association in the Soviet zone, and one for a united Germany (58). During the discussion, various attempts were made to blunt general objections to this complex of ideas, even if no one actually articulated them at the conference. One such rebuttal employed the rhetoric of national unity to rationalize the need for an administrative and regulatory hierarchy; just as progressive-minded Germans advocated economic and political unity, so, too, did those active in cultural pursuits favor a "unified cultural organization, a German Volksbühne and a German association of people's theaters" (76). But the argument alleviated little of the apprehension; indeed, the general absence of representatives from Berlin theaters angered Wolf. To judge by the list of conference participants, none of the theaters located in the Western sectors answered the invitation to send representatives with the exception of Martin and Litten, both from the Volksbühne attached to the Hebbel Theater. Reiche complained also that theater people were poorly represented at the conference (89), and another speaker admitted that many artists "opposed" the idea, even though everything possible had been done to persuade them to join the "movement" (91).

The recurrent complaints about the poor attendance hint at something akin to a boycott of the conference, and it seems safe to assume that concern over the implications of the undertaking, its hostility toward established theaters, its Soviet-zone base of operations, its association with the FDGB, and the obvious organizational hierarchy, was widespread. If not, there would have been fewer strained attempts at the meeting to transform the idea of centralized control into the consummate expression of democracy. Centralization did not portend a lessening of independence but its strengthening (57), read one; another argued that the organizational and artistic efficiency of the theaters would only be enhanced by consolidating the regional people's theaters into statewide associations. Besides, the independence of these organizations remained unaffected by formation of the "central" headquartered in Berlin; indeed, their presence on that board ensured that no one would get carried away with centralism (83). The existence of local people's theaters and the state associations was thus a "democratic foregone conclusion." Comments such as, "that's come from above, not from below," were unwarranted because the operation evolved organically, though the initiative had to come from somewhere, and the beginnings of a "centralizing organization" of the movement had in fact originated from below (90). But centralization and "unity," at least in Berlin, were incompatible objectives. There had clearly been dissatisfaction with the Volksbühne set up as part of the Hebbel Theater under the direction of Karl-Heinz Martin, and one reference made at the conference in May confirmed it (63). Many of the plays performed in the Hebbel Theater and its people's theater troupe had fallen into what was now regarded as Western decadence, and neither the SMAD nor the SED had the jurisdiction to do anything about it. In fact, it may be that the choice of Martin and Litten to head the new Volksbühne in the Soviet sector was a calculated attempt to involve them in an undertaking whose administrative structure would channel their activity along more appropriate lines. Whether Martin's illness had anything to do with it (he died a year later), his appointment as chairman of the new "central," along with the SMAD license granted him to oversee reorganization of the Berlin Volksbühne on Karl-Liebknecht-Platz, had failed to produce the desired results. Indeed, in July 1947, Wolfgang Harich denounced him in the *Tägliche Rundschau*, accusing Martin of staging plays that ignored the problem of fascism. Worse, the Hebbel Theater performed foreign plays characteristic of "bourgeois decadence" without mounting counter-productions to combat the "threat of infection." Harich concluded by arguing that Martin had presumably tired of the Volksbühne even before its own house could be reconstructed.[44] There were no further attacks upon Martin, but by fall 1947 an entirely new situation existed in Berlin; two people's theaters, one in the East and its rival in the West were in the final stages of organization, leading to a call by Ihering for their (re-)"unification."[45] The weekly *Sonntag* argued similarly in October, but by then pleas for a merger of the two theaters occurred as part of scathing two-camps rhetoric that made the Soviet-zone appeals for cultural unity distinctly less persuasive.[46]

The regulation of Soviet-zone stages went back to the SMAD's order 51, dated 4 September 1945, which required the registration of institutions for the performing arts in Berlin and confirmation of their repertories by the SMAD's Abteilung für Volksbildung upon recommendation by the DVV. Similar procedures applied to theaters throughout the zone, except that registration took place at the level of the local or regional branches of the occupation administration. But there is little evidence to suggest that the DVV was systematically involved; and various indications, such as the controversy

---

[44]Harich, "Berliner Theaterbilanz," *Tägliche Rundschau*, 27 July 1947.
[45]Ihering, "Volksbühne 1947," *Sonntag*, 28 September 1947.
[46]See "Erkenntnis und Entscheidung," *Sonntag*, 19 October 1947.

over "shop councils" empowered by the Gewerkschaft 17 to influence repertory planning in theaters, that other solutions were being explored. The Volksbühne may then have been the first sustained initiative aimed at acquiring control of what was euphemistically called "repertory management" or *Spielplangestaltung* in Soviet-occupied Germany. After all, the idea behind the Volksbühne focused on ways of influencing the repertories of other theaters, even if the eventual goal remained the establishment of troupes with their own theaters. But Volksbühne organizations ran into immediate problems after creation of the central association in spring 1947; and some of these difficulties developed because any such coordinating office impinged upon the formal right of the states to run their own affairs.[47] Those responsible for drawing up the statutes of the "central," introduced at the May conference, were aware of the problem and tried to foster the impression that pursuit of the organization's objectives was up to the state and regional Volksbühnen.[48] But the SED's unpublished guidelines regarding the authority of the central stressed the need for "uniformity";[49] and the DVV's corresponding document called likewise for an organization structured to ensure a "unified approach" to the movement.[50]

As things transpired, however, the Volksbühne organizations proved unable to meet the expectations set in connection with repertory management. Further development of the Volksbühne "movement" thus unfolded in 1947 together with plans for additional measures designed to coordinate the activities of all Soviet-zone stages, beginning with the basic licensing or relicensing of their operations and ending with greater control over their repertories. By December 1946, there were repeated references in DVV memoranda to an imminent new "theater order" being prepared by the SMAD to govern the approval of stage repertories and the appointment of theater directors. Herbert Volkmann had intended to introduce the new order at the first ministers' conference in late December 1946 before deciding against it. He doubted, he wrote Wandel, that the SMAD still planned on issuing the decree in its current form because of what he called an "expected shift" in the way the DVV conducted its business—presumably, a reference to the changing relationship between state governments and central administrations. Though he had not discussed the matter "with Karlshorst," Volkmann thought that the setting of regulations concerning individual theaters was

---

[47]See the references to complaints about the "beginnings of centralizing organization of our Volksbühne movement," Braulich, *Die Volksbühne*, p. 90; as well as a general discussion of states' rights in Chapter Two.

[48]Ibid., p. 107.

[49]"Aufbau von Volksbühnenvereinen (Volkskulturorganisation). Richtlinien der Abteilung Kultur und Erziehung beim Zentralsekretariat und des zentralen Kulturausschusses der SED [January 1947]," *Um die Erneuerung der deutschen Kultur. Dokumente*, pp. 174-77.

[50]Richtlinien der Volksbühne [Ministerkonferenz am 22.-23. April 1947]. Bundesarchiv. Abt. Potsdam, R-2/54/34-35.

likely to remain with the regional governments, and the DVV would restrict itself to the issuance of basic guidelines.[51]

Just what the SMAD order stipulated is unclear; the Russians may have been pondering ways of improving centralized control as a result of the formation of semi-independent governments that followed the outcome of elections considered unfavorable to the SED; and then, to avoid the impression that they intended to set up central agencies, chose to back off in connection with the upcoming foreign ministers' conference in Moscow. This speculation seem warranted because confusion about the relationship between the central administrations and the outlying governments had never been greater than it was right now; and matters pertaining to the oversight of Soviet-zone theaters were discussed at the minister's conferences along with a variety of other measures that fit the general description of expanding centralization. Public mention of plans to create a main Volksbühne association occurred first in the FDGB's proclamation dated 30 January 1947, which followed the SED's formulation of guidelines two weeks before; and the prime motivation behind these and developing plans for what came to be called internally a "reorganization" of the entire theater system, as well as passage of a standardized "theater law" for all of Soviet-occupied Germany, definitely qualified as central regulation. These questions were then intermingled in closed discussions that took place over the next few years. The state ministers had already agreed in December 1946 to have Herbert Gute prepare proposals regarding the licensing of theaters for the next ministers' conference; these proposals, based on regulations in Saxony, were to address political, artistic, and economic considerations (in that order).[52] Whether the new regulations had anything to do with what Volkmann referred to just a day earlier as an SMAD "theater order" is uncertain; it is conceivable that the two proposals were identical because the enactment of central ordinances often required an SMAD order to back them up. This cannot be known for sure, but it is worth considering that no further reference to any SMAD "theater order" occurs in the DVV's extant files; moreover, new licensing regulations did not come up for discussion again until May 1947, by which time the foreign ministers' conference in Moscow was no longer cause for concern; and from here on out, the regulations themselves were referred to explicitly as a "theater law." After May 1947, however, these matters were impossible to disentangle from internal consultations related to the Volksbühne and its many difficulties. In fact, some of the solutions proposed later as a remedy for problems endemic to all Soviet-zone theaters may have been designed originally to

---

[51]Betrifft: Ministerbesprechung. Volkmann (Abteilung Kunst und Literatur) to Paul Wandel and Erich Weinert, 17 December 1946. Bundesarchiv. Abt. Potsdam, R-2/51/7.
[52]Konferenz der Minister für Volksbildung aus den Ländern und Provinzen der Sowjetischen Besatzungszone Deutschlands am 18. und 19. Dezember 1946. Beschluß-Protokoll vom 18. Dezember 1946 5. Lizenzierung von Theatern, ibid., R-2/51/9-10.

correct the congenital deficiencies of the Volksbühne. If so, these solutions were then applied to the "reorganization" of all theaters when it became clear that the Volksbühne "idea" had worked poorly when it came to influencing the repertorial and managerial decisions of other theaters. In this respect, both the "theater law" and the emergence months later of a supervisory agency in matters of program planning, a central "artistic council" decided upon in January 1948,[53] were the early precursors of a system of censorship of all Soviet-zone and East-German theaters.

The earliest discussions, however, focused on the modalities of control of the stage through the Volksbühnen. At their conference in March 1947, the ministers of culture and education spent a considerable amount of time discussing the draft statutes governing the activities of Volksbühnen through the zone;[54] this proposal must have been based on the SED's guidelines, formally accepted on 3 March; the DVV had a copy on file, though the ministers asked that the version discussed by them in March be reworked and voted upon at the next conference.[55] Otherwise, perhaps to avoid the appearance of coordination, Volkmann stressed the need to construct the Volksbühne organizations from the ground up, rather than creating the body responsible for "holding the undertaking together" first; and he emphasized the importance of locating the right people to work within it. "Genuinely progressive elements" needed to be brought into the management of the Volksbühne, and the state ministries of culture and education, working with their theater chiefs, could exert a broad influence in this regard. Wandel added that the "formation of this undertaking must occur in a way calculated to guarantee our influence," but suggested a need to act as if the process itself had preceded the guidelines designed to govern the activities of the organization. Volkmann then announced his intention of asking state officials to provide his office with information regarding the status of the outlying Volksbühne organizations as well as with copies of their statutes; but he was not optimistic about the response. The inquiries that his office sent out to the states and provinces, he complained, tended to be answered unsatisfactorily, as a result of which he was constrained to inform the SMAD that it could not be provided with requested information. Finally, Volkmann spoke of plans for the meeting in May 1947 to establish the central Volksbühne association; the invitations were to be issued by the FDGB, the Kulturbund, and other mass organizations "responsible" for the Volksbühne.[56] These invitations,

---

[53]See Abteilung Kunst und Literatur. Referat Theater. Vorlage für die Ministerkonferenz. Betrifft: Künstlerischer Rat für das Theaterwesen, 24 January 1948, ibid., R-2/72/44.

[54]See Entwurf eines Rahmenstatuts der Volksbühne [written in hand: "Lt. Ministerbeschluß v. 18./19. 3. 47: angenommen"], ibid., R-2/57/50.

[55]Beschlußprotokoll für die Ministerkonferenz vom 18. und 19. März 1947. 1. Volksbühne, 3 April 1947, ibid., R-2/53/120.

[56]Ministerbesprechung am 18. und 19. März 1947, ibid., R-2/5350-54.

with references to the need for "interregional cooperation" and a "central agency," went out under the signatures of Maschke and Willmann a month later.[57]

Before it met, however, the definitive version of the overall Volksbühne statutes was voted upon at the ministers' conference on 22 and 23 April—a full six weeks after their passage by the SED's central secretariat. These particular guidelines were almost identical to the SED's version, and both re-emerged in the slightly altered form of the Volksbühne statutes passed at the May conference and published. But SED and DVV documents were not absolutely identical; the language of the SED guidelines was a bit more direct. The Volksbühne would be expected to secure the means of influencing the "theaters in the sense of furthering progressive-democratic ideas," read one line; this goal could be achieved through the selection of "suitable antifascist personalities as directors of the organizations and theaters to which [the organizations] are attached" and "by influencing the development of the repertory." Like the SED's guidelines, the DVV's version called similarly for creation of "artistic advisory boards," *künstlerische Beiräte*; the SED advocated establishment of such boards in all larger localities for the purpose of setting up theater programs in consultation with the central executive committee charged with overseeing the activities of the local Volksbühne organizations; and the DVV guidelines called for both an administrative council as a means of "supervising" the executive committee and artistic advisory boards, separate from the executive, responsible for setting up theater programs.[58] This early call for the establishment of "artistic advisory boards," which tellingly failed to appear in the statutes passed at the conference in May 1947, must have led to the idea behind creation of a central "artistic council" in January 1948 to oversee local "artistic advisory boards."

The next development, discussion of provisions to be included in the new "theater law," was oddly interwoven with the constituent assembly of the Volksbühne association in Berlin. The proposal to pass a theater law, modeled after ordinances already in effect in Thuringia and Saxony, but valid for the entire zone and justified in terms of the need for a "unified system of licensing and supervision of theaters" in all of Soviet-occupied Germany,[59] was introduced first at a meeting of the department heads of art and literature on 15 and 17 May; whereas the Volksbühne conference met in between and after on 16 and 18 May. At the preliminary discussion of depart-

---

[57]FDGB. Hauptabteilung 8. Schulung und Bildung. Betrifft: Gründung eines Bundes der Volksbühnen" 19 April 1947, ibid., R-2/57/52.
[58]Zentralsekretariat der SED. Abteilung Kultur und Erziehung. Zentraler Kulturausschuß. Richtlinien für den Aufbau von Volksbühnen-Vereinen (Volkskulturorganisationen), ibid., R-2/1080/92; Richtlinien der Volksbühne (Ministerkonferenz am 22.-23. April 1947), ibid., R-2/54/34-35.
[59]See Abteilung Kunst und Literatur. Betrifft: Ministerkonferenz 3./4.6.47. Entwurf eines Theatergesetztes, 13 May 1947, ibid., R-2/55/24.

ment heads, it was decided to develop "guidelines" for the zone based on the "fifth version" of the Thuringian draft and the theater ordinance passed in Saxony, presumably at the instigation of Herbert Gute, on 14 February. The anticipated law stipulated that decisions regarding the issuance of a license for any theater organization would be made by the state ministries of culture and education. The department heads then agreed to work out a specific draft for final approval at the next ministers' conference.[60] This draft, dated 27 May 1947, called for the licensing of all professional theater and stage organizations by the state or provincial ministries of culture and education; licenses would be granted only in accordance with conditions that included, 1) "recognition of the public need"; 2) "personal and political reliability, suitability, and economic efficiency of the applicant and his deputy"; 3) "composition of the ensemble and all other personnel from elements supportive of reconstruction in terms of a democratic view of the state"; and 4) "shaping of the repertory in accordance with democratic renewal, the elimination of kitsch, as well as anything politically and artistically questionable." This latter provision did not outline any particular method of influencing or censoring program planning; it allowed only for the withholding of a license in the event that a theater's repertory failed to win the approval of the local authorities—in this case, the state or provincial ministries of culture and education—in line with the above political criteria. Be that as it may, permission to perform in one state or province, once granted, was valid elsewhere with the provision that the other ministries of culture and education retained the right to reexamine the question of public need. Finally, all earlier licenses would automatically expire and require reapplication and reassessment of the "public need" in consonance with the stipulated criteria within three months of the effective date of the new law.[61] The proposal came up for final discussion at the ministers' conference on 3 and 4 June and was accepted, in an apparently revised version dated 3 June, subject to objections or suggested changes from the state governments.[62]

Meanwhile, the Volksbühne organizations had developed a variety of ailments to go along with modest successes. In Dresden, the FDGB had failed to provide the organization with enough money, and the Volksbühne had apparently managed to influence the repertories of local theaters only marginally. In Mecklenburg, there were similar complaints about the FDGB; all theaters were suffering financially; and the cities had as little money as the state. "The FDGB refuses to shoulder the start-up risk for the Volksbühne

[60]Protokoll über die Besprechung der Leiter der Abteilung Kunst und Literatur bei den Volksbildungsministerien der Länder und Provinzen am 15. und 17. Mai 1947, ibid., R-2/1035/12.
[61]Entwurf eines Theatergesetzes der Länder und Provinzen der sowjetischen Besatzungszone Deutschlands, Fassung vom 27. 5. 47, ibid., R-2/1035/39
[62]Beschlußprotokoll der Ministerkonferenz am 3. und 4. Juni 1947, 9 June 1947, ibid., R-2/55/10.

and erects obstacles wherever it can." For the creation of the statewide organization, the union had provided a grand total of 500 marks. In Brandenburg, by contrast, the Volksbühne had no problems with the unions; and in Saxony-Anhalt, the Kulturbund and the FDGB had provided 50,000 marks for the Volksbühne. In Halle, the union made 200,000 marks available for a resident theater, whereas in Thuringia there was "nothing positive to report." Volkmann then summed up the situation by recommending that the head of the Soviet-zone FDGB be approached personally whenever problems with local FDGB officials or offices persisted; and if financial difficulties continued, the DVV could perhaps make funds available. But an SMAD order would likely be necessary before that action could be taken.[63] Several weeks later, Volkmann wrote Dymschitz with a request that the SMAD help set up a fund in the amount of four-million marks to further the organization of the Volksbühne as well as the creation of its own theaters and ensembles. Volkmann justified his request with a reference to the importance of the Volksbühne in connection with the "re-formation of the entire theater system in a political and cultural respect."[64] It is unclear whether the SMAD actually approved the request. Several weeks later, the SED's secretariat contributed 100,000 marks to a "fund" designated to help set up the Volksbühne,[65] but that amount was a pittance compared with the money needed.

Nor were the financial problems the only difficulty. In July, the ministers were informed of others in a proposal prepared by Volkmann. Though there were some successes to report, according to Volkmann the danger for the further development of the Volksbühne "movement" resided in the lack of awareness, even among leading personalities involved in the movement, that the idea behind the undertaking required adherence to a "progressive artistic and cultural basic line"; the Volksbühne movement had never been conceived simply as a means of providing for inexpensive tickets; rather, the Volksbühne acquired importance only by following a cultural-political and artistic line in repertory plans. Though every Volksbühne retained the objective of acquiring its own house, until that happened the organization needed to concentrate on "improving" the quality of the local ensembles and repertories in the theaters in which they were currently based.[66] At the June meeting, the ministers also agreed to ask FDGB and Volksbühne officials to testify at an upcoming conference and to provide the states with an opportunity to voice their reservations about "certain developmental tendencies" within the

[63]Protokoll über die Besprechung der Leiter der Abteilung Kunst und Literatur bei den Volksbildungsministerien der Länder und Provinzen am 15. und 17. Mai 1947, ibid., R-2/1035/12-14.
[64]An die Sowjetische Militäradministration. Informationsverwaltung. Abteilung Kultur. Herrn Major Dymschitz. Betrifft: Volksbühne, 28 July 1947, gez. Volkmann, ibid., R-2/ 1091/5.
[65]Protokoll Nr. 136 der Sitzung des Zentralsekretariats am 5. 9. 1947. Zentrales Parteiarchiv, IV 2/2.1/123/5.
[66]Zur Vorlage bei der Ministerkonferenz vom 15. bis 18. Juli 1947. Betreff: Bericht über die Volksbühnenbewegung, 28 June 1947. Bundesarchiv, Abt. Potsdam, R-2/57/42

Volksbühne movement. Finally, the records of the July meeting made the first reference to an overall "reorganization of the theater system in the zone in organizational matters and with respect to the planning of repertories."[67] Other materials also stressed the importance of the Volksbühne in the design of repertories. The SED's division of Kultur und Erziehung expressed its intention privately of using the Volksbühne association as a way of exerting a "stronger influence over theater life in its entirety by working systematically to affect repertory plans."[68] In a semi-public report on its activities, the party's same cultural apparatus spoke again of its support for the Volksbühne, but revealed ideas of its own. Kultur und Erziehung had informed its corresponding branches at the regional level, the Landes-Kulturabteilung, of their responsibility for "influencing repertory planning"; and assisted them by formulating an official opinion on all new productions based on discussions held by the theater commission within the Kulturausschuß. The "results" of these discussions were then passed along to the regional branches of Kultur und Erziehung.[69] How this worked in practice is hard to tell, but the interest in repertory planning no doubt existed at the highest levels of the party. In late 1947, the central secretariat instructed Kultur und Erziehung to work with the DVV in devoting "particular attention to questions related to the design of the theater plan for Berlin theaters"; and Ackermann himself was asked to prepare a summary for the two party chairman, Pieck and Grotewohl, that could serve as the basis for an upcoming "discussion" with the SMAD.[70]

"Reorganization of the theater system," along with related issues linked to the development of the Volksbühne, came up again at the DVV meeting of the regional heads of art and literature in late October 1947, along with complaints about the problem of influencing theater programming and the inadequacies of Volksbühne managers. Where the managers failed, the entire organization foundered; and if it was necessary to relieve them, said Volkmann, they should be replaced in part by capable personalities who had returned from exile. Volkmann also indicated that subsidies now appeared likely for the Volksbühne organizations and that the SMAD had no objec-

---

[67]Präsidialabteilung. Vorläufiges Beschlußprotokoll der Ministerkonferenz vom 16. bis 19. Juli 1947, 19 July 1947, ibid., R-2/57/12.

[68]Arbeitsplan der Abteilung Kultur und Erziehung. Zentrales Parteiarchiv, IV 2/906/10/ 46.

[69]*Sozialistische Kulturarbeit. 1. Jahresbericht über die Tätigkeit der Abteilung Kultur und Erziehung des Zentralsekretariats der SED für die Zeit vom Mai 1946 bis August 1947*, p. 14.

[70]Protokoll Nr. 10 (II) der Sitzung des Zentralsekretariats am 20. 10. 1947. Zentrales Parteiarchiv, IV 2/2.1/141/6. Much later, working plans for summer 1949, drawn up by Kultur und Erziehung, also included "preparing the repertories for the coming season" (Zentrales Parteiarchiv, IV 2/5/199/20-21). The same office also had a specific "desk chief" or Referent in charge of "theaters and the Volksbühne movement" (Protokoll Nr. 5 [II] der Sitzung des Zentralsekretariats am 6. 10. 47 [Anlage Nr. 4. Aufbau der Parteischulung, Kultur und Erziehung]. IV 2/2.1/ 137/18-19).

tions to budgeting for them. Finally, Volkmann indicated that problems associated with the Volksbühne, as well as the matter of reorganizing the theater system, would be high on the agenda of the ministers' conference in January 1948; and the first mention was also made of an upcoming theater managers' conference. These plans were soon pursued, leading eventually to an "Eastern-zone stage managers' conference" in July 1948 that ushered in an entirely new development in the design of stage censorship.[71] But when the ministers met on 27 and 28 January 1948, the subject of the conference never came up. Discussions were dominated by two other proposals. The first affected the Volksbühne, the second called for the establishment of artistic boards or councils, *Beiräte*, to oversee the entire system of Soviet-zone theaters. The proposal pertaining to the Volksbühne, discussed with the SMAD beforehand, banned use of the name by any other theater, called for recognition of those Volksbühne organizations with their own houses as high-priority theaters (an internal designation that apparently allowed for a more generous allocation of increasingly scarce financial resources), and enjoined the state ministries of culture and education to ask their local finance ministries for a tax-free exemption for Volksbühnen because they fit the designation as "public utilities." The second of the three provisions was accompanied by an elaborate justification. After an overly hasty formation, the Volksbühne was now set to begin a new period of consolidation leading to the elimination of "initial defects" and "purge of unartistic elements." This "reorganization" presupposed clear recognition of the importance of the Volksbühne; those organizations with their own ensembles and houses had cultural-political responsibilities that vastly exceeded the importance of private stages; in particular, the intervention of "art advisory boards" in the activities of all Volksbühnen now guaranteed an improvement in the artistic development of the theaters.[72] This reference to "art advisory boards," or *Kunstbeiräte*, established the link in the second proposal to what was apparently envisioned as a more elaborate system of stage supervision. In fact, this other proposal, which called for the creation of an "artistic council" attached to the DVV, as well as subordinate "artistic advisory boards" within the state ministries of culture and education, may have been recast from the SMAD's "theater order" withdrawn a year earlier, reformulated now in connection with the establishment of other offices of cultural "coordination" within the DVV after issuance of SMAD order 234.[73]

The proposal itself, dated 24 January 1948, stipulated that the artistic boards would be activated by an SMAD order; and this makes it perfectly

---

[71]Protokoll der Abteilungsleiterkonferenz am 27. und 28. 10. 1947, Bundesarchiv, Abt. Potsdam, R-2/1035/28-31. See Chapter Fourteen for further detail.

[72]Abteilung Kunst und Literatur. Referat Theater. Betr.: Volksbühne, 24 January 1948, ibid., R-2/72/43.

[73]For discussion of order 234, and its many cultural corollaries, see Chapter Fourteen.

clear that the latest initiative had been undertaken after discussions with the Russians—perhaps the same top-level talks alluded to in the party secretariat decision taken on 20 October. The proposal in January then said outrightly that the plan for artistic boards had resulted from "intensive consultations" with the cultural division of the SMAD.[74] The plan itself described four areas of activity, though it stopped short of characterizing the "artistic board" as an office of repertory censorship. The euphemism in all discussions pertaining to the theater remained the artistic "improvement" of the stage. The proposed new office was thus said to have developed out of the need to "enhance the system of theaters" in Soviet-occupied Germany, with state agencies both "advising" the "central artistic board" and relieving it of some of the work. The main board, based in the DVV, was then charged with *"enhancing the artistic niveau of the theaters in the sense of making them progressive in a way appropriate to the times and of putting them more directly into the service of democratic renewal."* As part of that responsibility, the office was expected to further the development of "all newly emerging positive artistic elements" in the areas of day-to-day stage operations, the study of theatrical affairs, and training. Most importantly, the board would function, on the one hand, as an "advisory and regulatory institution in all matters pertaining to repertorial issues and, on the other hand, pay close attention to the development of "artistically and ideologically usable young talent." Finally, the board would screen performances with potentially "militaristic or Nazistic tendencies." Descriptions of the three other areas of activity followed. The second called for a subcommittee responsible for evaluating both "foreign and domestic and amateur theater productions"; these evaluations were to be given to the SMAD "censors" and, upon request, to the state governments. The third area provided for an "approval commission," an *Abnahmekommission*, governing all Berlin road companies touring the zone. In the future, such companies would receive certificates of acceptability, *Unbedenklichkeitsbescheinigungen*, only after a positive evaluation had been made. Along with the opinion of the "central office of military censorship," these evaluations were to be regarded as final; that is, once the SMAD order activated the entire plan of establishing artistic boards, neither lower-level Soviet offices of censorship nor any German agency had the right to insist upon another evaluation. However, this provision did not impinge upon the right of the states and local communities to raise the question of "need" as defined in the recently enacted theater law. The final area of responsibility stipulated that state "advisory boards" also be set up and noted that these agencies were primarily responsible for the approval of performances in the

---

[74]Abteilung Kunst und Literatur. Referat Theater. Vorlage für die Ministerkonferenz. Betrifft: Künstlerischen Rat für das Theaterwesen, 24 January 1948, ibid., R-2/72/44. The proposal developed out of a separate report on the "formation of the artistic board"; this report is not among DVV files.

states themselves and for providing the central board with information related to "theater affairs" in the states.[75]

There is no record of an SMAD order that would have enacted this provision; nor is there any indication that a system of "advisory" agencies ever developed. In fact, neither this proposal, nor the one concerning the Volksbühne, appear to have been discussed at the ministers' conference in January 1948. Wandel suggested there that they be aired at the state level first before being passed upon at the next meeting of department heads—unless the ministers had any essential objectives.[76] None are recorded, and the last specific reference to formation of "artistic boards" indicates that the two issues came up again at the ministers' conference on 12 and 13 April 1948. The minutes of this meeting are incomplete, but Volksbühne "guidelines and directives" apparently went out to the state governments; and the subject of both central and state "advisory boards" was talked about. Still, no record of action exists; and considering that concurrent plans being developed separately now anticipated a "theater congress" in April or May,[77] it is possible that the notion of artistic boards was slated for introduction there. If so, any action on it was probably delayed further pending the announcement in July of an economic two-year plan worked out by the SMAD and introduced by the SED.

Literary Censorship

The agency established in spring 1946 in order to censor printed material, the Kultureller Beirat or KB, had developed slowly, too, and was actually in substantial disarray by late 1946. On 1 January 1947, Anton Kippenberger, the head of the Insel Verlag in Leipzig, complained that he had thus far managed to publish only a few slim volumes; and another publisher concluded a week later that the very existence of Soviet-zone publishers was at stake.[78] These complaints reflected twin frustrations. Firms whose efforts to obtain a license to operate had been subject to interminable delays faced complete bankruptcy; and even those licensed were stymied by the second hurdle of wresting a recommendation from the Kultureller Beirat for every single project and then having to await yet another decision by the SMAD. Ironically, when the Russians began licensing more businesses in early 1946, the sec-

[75]Ibid.

[76]Beschlußprotokoll der Ministerkonferenz vom 27. und 28. Januar 1948. 6 February 1948, ibid., R-2/72/49.

[77]Chef der Abteilung Kunst und Literatur. An die Präsidialabteilung. Betrifft: Arbeitsplan für das Vierteljahr des Haushaltsjahres 1947/48, 23 December 1947, ibid., R-2/1155/76.

[78]Kippenberg to J. R. Becher, 1 January 1947, ibid., R-2/1091/10; and Rudolf Marx to Erich Weinert, 8 January 1947, R-2/1090/103-4.

ond problem actually worsened. The Russians had been skeptical about private publishing from the outset, but when persuaded of the need to license certain firms anyway because of the consequences of refusing to do so, the agency formed to "assist the publishers in serving the cultural-political interests and the ideological reeducation of the people," as Weinert described the Kultureller Beirat,[79] was overwhelmed by the sheer quantity of manuscripts submitted by newly licensed presses. Submissions to the KB doubled between December 1946 and the first half of 1947;[80] and its inability to act quickly on them angered publishers and writers alike. Nor had the problem of licensing resolved itself either; of the 71 publishers approved by the SMAD as of 29 January 1947, forty were located in Berlin, but a scant seventeen specialized in books or music (the rest brought out periodicals and newspapers). Nineteen more based their operations in Saxony, and the remainder was scattered throughout the other states or provinces.[81] Any number of others had had license applications recommended by the DVV's office of publishing or Verlagswesen, some long ago, but "Karlshorst" had failed to act upon them yet.[82] During the second quarter of 1947, Verlagswesen screened 200—additional?—applications and recommended that the SMAD approve 70. By June 1947, the SMAD had issued a total of 9.[83] The situation was so bad that one group of Leipzig publishers, representing both licensed firms and businesses whose licensing was "expected," complained to Wandel that the loss of rights, authors, and entire houses to the West had created virtually unsolvable economic difficulties.[84]

Hoping to find a better way of dealing with the problem, plans for a reorganization of the Kultureller Beirat were developed in early 1947, but the KB still finished the year in a state of crisis created largely by the Russians themselves. Many of the difficulties derived from the inescapable fact that the Kultureller Beirat censored,[85] and none of the "restructuring," much of

[79]Protokoll der 27. Sitzung des Kulturellen Beirats für das Verlagswesen, 27 January 1947. Bundesarchiv, Abt. Potsdam, R-2/1132/224.
[80]See Frommhold (Verlagswesen) to Wandel, 29 January 1947, ibid., R-2/1149/125.
[80]Verlagswesen. Tätigkeitsbericht über das 2. Vierteljahr 1947, 27 June 1947, gez. Frommhold, ibid., R-2/1090/258.
[81]Only 1,308 books were published in 1947 (some of which were maps, others translations, and over a hundred unrevised reissues). Only 361 books were classified as creative literature (Buchproduktion 1947 der sowjetischen Besatzungszone, 14 April 1948, ibid., R-2/1149/57).
[82]Frommhold (Verlagswesen) to Wandel, 29 January 1947, ibid., R-2/1149/125.
[83]Verlagswesen. Tätigkeitsbericht über das 2. Vierteljahr 1947, 27 June 1947, gez. Frommhold, ibid., R-2/1090/258-9.
[84]The letter, addressed to Wandel and dated 10 January 1947, was signed by the representatives (ibid., R-2/1149/129). See also the travails of the Leipzig publisher Helmut Koehler (Koehler to Wandel, 5 December 1947, R-2/1149/60-1).
[85]One of the few sets of overall statistics available reveal that, from 1 October 1947 to 31 March 1950, the Kultureller Beirat reviewed 12,125 manuscripts, rejecting 3,373 and "approving" 8,752. See Der Kultureller Beirat für das Verlagswesen, 13 September 1950, ibid., R-2/689/7.

which continued through the early fifties in fruitless attempts to make censorship less odious, nor the hollow talk of the KB's commitment to democratic principles, lessened the resentment caused by that fact. But the KB's own institutional inadequacies made matters worse. The problem was that the KB belonged to the DVV and had no staff of its own. Worse, though the DVV's office of Verlagswesen submitted requests for more personnel in October 1946, which would have benefited the Kultureller Beirat as well, the SMAD's inadequate funding of the DVV led instead to the dismissal of experienced workers or their transfer to other divisions within the administration. In fact, by late December 1946, doubt about the continuing existence of the KB in its "current form" led to a complete suspension of ongoing activity.[86] The SMAD then tried to retrieve the situation through an expansion of the organization's responsibilities, only to withhold the resources necessary and procrastinate in approving an adequate staff of personnel. The Kultureller Beirat had no choice but to continue sharing employees with Verlagswesen and actually went its own way no earlier than 1 August 1947.[87]

Things were supposed to work out much differently. The reorganization of the Kultureller Beirat in early 1947 was thought to be a step in the right direction because the regulation of all publishing activity save the granting of licenses to individual firms would be assigned to a German agency. This had not been the case before. When the KB ended its first meeting ever on 3 June 1946, it reported that the SMAD had acted on its "proposal" to permit the publication of a "large number of works" by licensed presses.[88] The remark was simply an indication that the Kultureller Beirat had not replaced military censorship at all; the KB merely assisted the Russians by screening manuscripts first and passing positive recommendations on to the SMAD for final dispensation. The process remained cumbersome, and the complications associated with it, the lengthy delays especially, were the cause of considerable unhappiness. "Advance censorship," *Vorzensur*, the misnomer applied to the SMAD's control over printed material *prior* to its publication (rather than the confiscation of objectionable material *afterwards*) was now scheduled to be assigned to the Kultureller Beirat entirely in early 1947. The KB would then make such decisions on behalf of the SMAD. Thus it was that the Kultureller Beirat, in accordance with SMAD order 25 dated 25 January 1947, though never published, turned into a "council for ideological questions connected with publishing in the Soviet occupation zone of Germany." Compared with the earlier "form" of the KB, order 25 provided for a larger office of 40 salaried employees, a budget that was adequate to the

---

[86]Aktenvermerk. Betr.: Arbeitsbedingungen, 27 June 1947, gez. Unger, ibid., R-2/1132/109.
[87]See Weinert's remarks in Protokoll der 27. Sitzung des Kulturellen Beirats für das Verlagswesen, 27 January 1947; and Verlagswesen. Arbeitsplan für das 3. Vierteljahr 1947. Gez. Frommhold, ibid., R-2/1132/224 and R-2/1090/237.
[88]Verlagswesen. Aktennotiz, 28 June 1946, gez. Balluseck and Girnus, ibid., R-2/896/1.

task, and, in conjunction with the actual elimination of "advance censorship" authorized by SMAD order 90, issued internally on 17 April 1947, indeed put censorship primarily into the hands of Germans.[89] But the SMAD's failure to act on the staffing plan attached to order 25 until fall 1947, and then only in a scaled-down version,[90] created additional problems. Some of the delays in reorganizing the operations of the Kultureller Beirat may also have been caused by Weinert's illness; in early March 1947, he reported that the "definitive form of the reorganization," namely, the passage of statutes, the administration of the "technical apparatus," and such, had to be postponed for two months while he was away. Weinert asked Herbert Volkmann to chair KB meetings during his absence and expected that the agency's simple increase in size, "emphatically reconfirmed by the SMAD once again," would by itself enable the KB to keep up with the submission of manuscripts. After Weinert's return, the KB could begin the actual "reorganization" of its operations based on new statutes and regulations.[91] In the interim, the "torso" of the original board would continue working on submitted and incoming manuscripts in an attempt to keep their number from billowing.[92]

More delays ensued, though some may have resulted from Balluseck's defection to the West. Heinrich Becker, who worked both for the DVV and the Börsenverein des deutschen Buchhandels, the booktrade association based in Leipzig, suggested later that the emerging form of the Kultureller Beirat had been "torpedoed" by a man, "happily no longer among us," who managed to throw its work back by two years by obstructing its develop-

[89]The decision not to publish order 25 was conveyed by the SMAD's Major Mischin to the head of the Kultureller Beirat, Lothar von Balluseck. See Kultureller Beirat für das Verlagswesen. Betrifft: Etat des Kulturellen Beirats—Besprechung mit Major Mischin, 31 January 1947, gez. Balluseck, ibid., R-2/1132/230. See Befehl des Obersten Chefs der sowjetischen Militäradministration in Deutschland. Nr. 25. Z 164/47. Inhalt: Über die Einrichtung eines "Rates für ideologischen Fragen des Verlagswesens in der sowjetischen Besatzungszone Deutschlands. Zur Sicherung der Kontrolle über den ideologischen Inhalt der in der sowjetischen Besatzungszone Deutschlands erscheinenden Literatur, sowie über die gesamte Verlagstätigkeit," 25 January 1947 (ibid., R-2/1055/35); Anlage zum Befehl des Obersten Chefs der SMAD. Nr. 25. Struktur- und Stellenplan des Sekretariats des "Rates für ideologischen Fragen des Verlagswesens," 25 January 1947 (R-2/1055/36).
[90]See An die Sowjetische Militäradministration. Finanzabteilung. Z. Hd. Herrn Oberleutnant Rukowski, 18 April 1946 (ibid., R-2/2950/237), concerning the application for formal approval of staff positions one day after the passage of order no. 90; and the reference to final SMAD approval in fall 1947, Kielmeyer (Geschäftsführer) an die Personalabteilung und Abteilung Z. Betrifft: Planstellen des Kulturellen Beirats. Pr. d. ZFV. Tgb. Nr. I/1200-74 Vo v. 18. 8. 47, 9 September 1947, ibid., R-2/804/55.
[91]See Protokoll der 32. Sitzung des Kulturellen Beirats für das Verlagswesen, 3 March 1947, ibid., R-2/1132/201-2.
[92]Arbeitsplan für die Konstituierung des Kulturellen Beirats, 26 February 1947, ibid., R-2/1055/11. Some of the records kept of meetings held during the first half of 1947 by the agency's "main committee" or Hauptausschuß, comprised of 200 to 225 members, still exist (see R-2/1132).

ment.[93] But Becker was probably looking for someone to blame for a range of problems that had nothing to do with Balluseck. SMAD order 25 said nothing about an effective date of 1 April 1947; but when the Russians "approved" the budget shortly after the internal release of the decree, at least in principle, Major Mischin told Balluseck that the approval applied to the second quarter of 1947. True, Mischin pledged that enough money would be released by the SMAD to allow Balluseck to hire his staff of employees and to begin paying outside readers for manuscript evaluations right away. But there is no indication that Mischin delivered on either of those promises. In addition, the Russians insisted that the personal papers of all prospective employees, most of whom worked for the DVV already and had long since been screened by the SMAD, be resubmitted.[94] That process wasted more time and allowed the older problems to continue festering. Nor did the promise of 40 employees materialize; the Russians reduced the number to 29 in spring; and for one reason or another, the DVV had a difficult time filling even those spots.[95] These budgetary and staffing delays were still serious enough in June 1947 to keep the KB from making a dent in the backlog of manuscripts that had developed when it suspended work the previous December in anticipation of the very reorganization designed to solve problems now getting entirely out of hand. Worse, the backlog was unrelated to the additional problem of dealing with new projects submitted for approval; and officials complained generally that the volume of work had increased sixfold in comparison with fall 1946. Planning for the third quarter of 1947 would soon be due, new publishing houses had been licensed in the meantime, and the KB anticipated the submission of over 5,000 separate proposals in need of quick action.[96]

These problems appear to have resulted primarily from the SMAD's inadequate or belated funding of the agency, though the Russians may have had political reasons for dragging their feet. In early 1947, the SMAD was anxious to avoid any action that might be interpreted by the allies as a furtherance of administrative centralization; and avoiding that appearance, especially during the Moscow foreign ministers' conference in spring 1947, probably had an effect upon the development of the Kultureller Beirat as well. After all, there was no particular *non-political* rationale for subjecting publishing houses throughout Soviet-occupied Germany to centralized authority; and, much like "repertory management" under discussion at precisely the same time, the centralization or coordination of censorship was doubt-

---

93Ausschuß für Kulturpolitik. 20. Sitzung. 25 June 1949. Berichterstattung: Heinrich Becker, ibid., A-1/61/15.
94Kultureller Beirat für das Verlagswesen. Betrifft: Etat des Kulturellen Beirats—Besprechung mit Major Mischin, 31 January 1947, gez. Balluseck, ibid., R-2/1132/230.
95Tätigkeitsbericht über das 2. Vierteljahr 1947, ibid., R-2/1090/258-9.
96See Kultureller Beirat. Aktenvermerk, 27 June 1947, gez. Unger, ibid., R-2/1132/109.

less one of the primary objectives behind formation of the KB in the first place. At the opening meeting of the heads of personnel divisions within state and provincial administrations in early December 1946, the man in charge of the DVV's personnel office, Lehmann, informed his regional counterparts of plans for the creation of a division of publishing intended, as he put it, to "screen all manuscripts centrally[97]—the earliest reference to an impending reorganization of the Kultureller Beirat. These issues had become especially acute following the formation of state and provincial governments in late 1946. In order to foster the impression of decentralization, the outlying administrations required a degree of independence that, paradoxically, needed to be offset by new mechanisms designed to limit their capacity to act upon it. Efforts to set some of these up, however, apparently encountered some resistance. Questions pertaining to licensed and unlicensed publishing houses were on the agenda of the ministers' conference in early June 1947;[98] but discussion was postponed because the needed statistical material requested from the state governments was still incomplete. The ministers had evidently been asked to provide their assessments of licensed publishers (as well as "proposals for publishers who ought not to be furthered any longer"); to make suggestions for additional licensing in the provinces and states; and to supply lists of rights owned by licensed and unlicensed presses.[99] Licensing then came up again at the conference that met in mid-July 1947; it was agreed that the DVV would ask the Deutsche Bücherei in Leipzig for information concerning "licensed and unlicensed publishing houses throughout the zone"; and mention was made of the desire to transfer the licensing of publishers itself to "German agencies." (Order 25 had nothing to do with the approval of publishing houses themselves; it governed only the operations of licensed firms.) In the event that the SMAD agreed to allow the DVV to screen *and* approve license applications, the ministers felt that it would be best if permission to run a business was issued by the DVV based upon applications passed along to it by them.[100] This suggestion presumably meant that applications would be screened first in the states and provinces.

These discussions reflected the range of efforts to implement orders 25 and 90 throughout Soviet-occupied Germany. Interestingly enough, order 25 itself referred to the Kultureller Beirat by a name that was never once used in public—"council for ideological questions connected with publishing in

[97]Protokoll der ersten Tagung der Leiter der Personalabteilung in den Abteilungen Volksbildung der Provinzial- und Landesverwaltungen am 4. und 5. 12. 1946 in der DVfV, 12 December 1946, ibid., R-2/993/2.
[98]Präsidialabteilung. Tagesordnung für die Ministerkonferenz am 3. und 4. Juni 1947, 14 May 1947, ibid., R-2/55/1.
[99]Präsidialabteilung. Beschlußprotokoll der Ministerkonferenz am 3. und 4. Juni 1947, 9 June 1947, ibid., R-2/55/10.
[100]Vorläufiges Beschlußprotokoll der Ministerkonferenz vom 16. bis 19. Juli 1947, 19 July 1947, ibid., R-2/57/10-12.

the Soviet occupation zone of Germany." Like its forerunner, the new agency would be headed by Erich Weinert and operate on the basis of consultation with representatives from Soviet-zone "mass organizations" and other administrative agencies. But more specifically, order 25 entrusted the KB with "the regulation of the ideological content" of all literature published in Soviet-occupied Germany, as well as with "scrutinizing and confirming the publication plans of all licensed publishing firms in the zone, scrutinizing and reviewing the editorial and technical personnel employed by each firm, processing plans and proposals connected with the activities of publishing houses, and cultivating the development of new groups of writers."[101] A later assessment disclosed that the "council," referred to otherwise only as the Kultureller Beirat, had nothing to do with personnel matters and never concerned itself with developing "new groups of writers" either.[102] Following the internal announcement of order 25, then, the first public indication that changes were imminent came at a ceremony held on 27 February 1947 to license the operations of forty-one publishing houses and approve the publication of fifty-two new journals. At the ceremony, Weinert explained that the production of books had been utterly "chaotic" in 1945 and 1946 and that, though created to deal with the problem, the exact form of the Kultureller Beirat had not yet been definitively established. Now, the flow of work could be improved by expanding the organization's administrative structure. Moreover, he said, the SMAD had eliminated its "advance censorship" of book manuscripts scheduled for release by licensed publishers, as a result of which full responsibility for the approval of each publisher's specific plans devolved upon the KB. Weinert made no mention of order 25.[103]

The SMAD's representative, Major Mischin, echoed Weinert in adding that the elimination of advance censorship was a step taken because of the SMAD's confidence in the reliability of the Kultureller Beirat; but Mischin, like Weinert, said nothing about order 25 and failed to indicate that order 90 had not yet been released either.[104] Some of the publishers present then wondered whether they, as publishers, would be allowed to attend meetings of the Kultureller Beirat now that censorship no longer existed. Weinert quashed the idea and tried to divert attention away from the embarrassing fact that lifting Soviet censorship merely reassigned the dirty work to a German

[101]Befehl des Obersten Chefs der sowjetischen Militäradministration in Deutschland. Nr. 25. Z 164/ 47. Inhalt: Über die Einrichtung eines "Rates für ideologischen Fragen des Verlagswesens in der sowjetischen Besatzungszone Deutschlands. Zur Sicherung der Kontrolle über den ideologischen Inhalt der in der sowjetischen Besatzungszone Deutschlands erscheinenden Literatur, sowie über die gesamte Verlagstätigkeit," 25 January 1947, ibid., R-2/1055/35.
[102]See Der Kulturelle Beirat für das Verlagswesen, 13 September 1950, ibid., R-2/689/7.
[103]"Lizenzierung neuer Verlage und Zeitschriften," *Börsenblatt für den deutschen Buchhandel* 6 (1947): 77-78.
[104]Ibid.

agency.[105] He then claimed that publishers now shouldered more responsibility than ever before, though he must have considered it necessary to reassure them by saying that they should not be afraid to submit a manuscript to the Kultureller Beirat if they were uncertain about its usefulness in the context of democratic renewal. If in doubt, they should leave the decision up to the KB. Mischin, speaking on behalf of the SMAD's press chief, Koltypin, indicated similarly that the Kultureller Beirat, not the publishers, was responsible for the approval of manuscripts. Like Weinert, Mischin tried to make the argument sound as if the elimination of SMAD censorship reflected well upon local publishers, but many surely asked themselves why the KB continued to exist and understood that censorship had simply passed into the hands of a German bureaucracy notorious for its past inefficiencies.[106]

In the meantime, efforts were underway to formalize the structure of the Kultureller Beirat through "statutes" and operating procedures. These documents, most of which were dated 26 February 1947, stressed the "democratic tenets" of the agency's activity and said nothing about censorship. Broken down into five divisions (secretariat, executive board, plenum, specialized commissions, and a committee responsible for the allocation of paper supplies), these bodies were to be comprised of representatives from the central administrations, regional governments, "democratic parties," FDJ, Kulturbund, FDGB, the stage, radio, Schutzverband Deutscher Autoren, and so on. The general idea was that the KB would examine all printed matter and evaluate it with the "systematic regulation of need" in mind and in terms of the economic use of paper supplies. Further provisions concerned the operations and responsibilities of its various bodies. The plenum was obliged to meet only twice yearly and probably served only as a democratic alibi. Real power resided in the twelve-member board, which expected to act upon recommendations made by the sixteen commissions. These groups were responsible for evaluating manuscripts, or having them evaluated by outside readers, and ran the gamut from mathematics, linguistics, religion, music, medicine, trade, agriculture, and law to creative literature. Last, but by no means least, the "paper commission" played a pivotal role because even accepted manuscripts would be ranked according to "need," and not every approved project or set of publishing plans resulted in an appropriate allocation of paper.[107] Roughly speaking, these were the organizational plans held in

[105]Publishers were never permitted to sit on the Kultureller Beirat, though there was later talk of establishing a commission, comprised of publishers, that would make its "wishes" known to the agency. See Protokoll der 7. Sitzung der Planungskommission des Kulturellen Beirats, 4 December 1947. Bundesarchiv, Abt. Potsdam, R-2/1091/140.

[106]Protokoll der Sitzung am 27. February 1947 der Zentralverwaltung für Volksbildung, Verlagswesen, anläßlich der Lizensierung von Verlagen und Zeitschriften, ibid., R-2/1132/ 192-6.

[107]Entwurf Nr. 1. Der Kulturelle Beirat bei der deutschen Verwaltung für Volksbildung. [In hand: Satzung.] 27 February 1947; Entwurf Nr. 1. Geschäftsordnung für die Organe des Kulturellen Beirats; and Geschäftsordnung für die Geschäftsstelle des Kulturellen Beirats, ibid., R-2/

abeyance until the SMAD finally approved the KB's budget and staffing plans much later. In the interim, a few "working committees" were set up to assist the old "main committee" in taking care of incoming manuscripts.[108] By June 1947, only seven such "subcommittees" existed (including creative literature). But by now there were indications of a new crisis brewing that threatened to reduce the work of the Kultureller Beirat to an absurdity. During the second quarter of 1947, the agency screened some 900 publishers' "proposals" and distributed 300 tons of paper. Unfortunately, 300 tons satisfied only 30 percent of the amount needed to cover *approved* projects.[109]

That problem worsened dramatically a few months later, though a number of others had surfaced earlier in connection with the SMAD order, no. 90, that served as the basis for the reorganization of the Kultureller Beirat. Order 90, "Concerning the Activities of Publishing Houses and Printing Presses," was passed on 17 April 1947, but not released until November.[110] No. 90 replaced no. 19, dated 2 August 1945, which had established the earlier restrictions on publishing activity under Soviet occupation law in accordance with "provisional regulations for the work of presses." Order 19, allowed both for the immediate confiscation of the printing presses as well as the court-martialling of the owner in the event that materials were published without the SMAD's permission.[111] Order 90 stated drily that books, journals, newspapers, brochures, and the like could only be published by firms in possession of an SMAD license, that these firms were allowed to publish only those editions provided for under individual licenses and listed in each firm's approved overall plan, but that the censorship of printed matter falling into the above categories had been eliminated. Before order 90, the process seems to have worked in somewhat the same fashion, with the exception that the original KB reviewed each firm's listing of planned books, set its own priorities for the publication of manuscripts once they had been approved by the SMAD, but was nonetheless limited to recommending to the occupation administration that specific books be licensed. Though no book manuscript could be submitted to the SMAD for approval without having passed muster with the Kultureller Beirat, final dispensation thus remained in the hands of the Soviet authorities, both in Karlshorst and locally, until this final stage, called advance censorship, was officially eliminated through

---

1055/2-7, 8-9, and 10. See also the list of proposed members of the plenum (Der Kulturelle Beirat bei der Zentralverwaltung für Volksbildung [R-2/1055/19-21]). All documents dated 26 February 1947.
[108]See Der Kult. Beirat. Vorschläge und Feststellungen des Herrn von Balluseck, 29 February 1947; and Balluseck to Marquardt, 17 March 1947, ibid., R-2/1090/207 and R-2/1055/27-28.
[109]Tätigkeitsbericht über das 2. Vierteljahr 1947, 27 June 1947, ibid., R-2/1090/ 258.
[110]"Über die Tätigkeit von Verlagen und Druckereien / Befehl 90," *Börsenblatt für den Deutschen Buchhandel* 30 (1947): 306-7.
[111]"Maßnahmen zur Verbesserung der Verlage und Druckereien und zur Regelung der Kontrolle ihrer Arbeit," *Befehle des Obersten Chefs der Sowjetischen Militäradministration*, pp. 16-17.

order 90. Thereafter, "scientific literature and *belles-lettres*, which has been approved by the Kultureller Beirat attached to the German Zentralverwaltung für Volksbildung in the Soviet occupation zone of Germany," could be published without advance censorship. Even then, each edition still required that an application be filed with the SMAD and list the number of the SMAD license, the name of the licensee, the title, print run, and so on. In accordance with two other related orders (no. 262, dated 2 September 1946 and 356, 24 December 1946), copies of every publication had to be sent to any number of agencies and organizations listed in this order.[112] Failure to comply with the provisions of order 90 was punishable by fine, confiscation of the edition, in whole or in part, loss of publishing license, or actual prosecution. Order 90 also controlled the activities of printing presses; these were allowed to print any materials by licensed publishers that had been approved by the Kultureller Beirat as well as any material not subject to the authority of that agency, provided that it had passed the SMAD's censor and carried the censor's stamp and signature.[113] Either way, printing presses were allowed to proceed only if the materials presented to them for publication came with a document containing the SMAD's license for the book, name of the licensee, title, print-run, and so on. These could not be tampered with under penalty of law.

Though the provisions of SMAD orders 25 and 90 remained secret at the time, and order 25 was never published, a discussion of the implications suggested by the restructuring of the Kultureller Beirat found its way into print in April 1947 and produced an unusually blunt exchange of opinions. In the 25 April 1947 issue of the *Börsenblatt für den deutschen Buchhandel*, Heinrich Becker, the head of the organization, volunteered an opinion about the work of the restructured KB that bore all the earmarks of an attempt to counter criticism of the organization as a poorly disguised office of censorship. Becker admitted to having traveled to Berlin for "consultations" on this subject just prior to reporting on those discussions in a meeting of the Börsenverein's executive board on 2 April, one day after the apparent effective date of order 25, and writing the editorial published in the *Börsenblatt* a few weeks later.[114] Besides, as a member of the KB's "plenum," which included key Communists like Ackermann, Wandel, Becher, Erpenbeck, Vallentin, Kuczynski, Bredel, Renn, Nagel, Wolf, and Langhoff, together with several

---

[112]See "Bekanntmachung der Deutschen Zentralverwaltung für Volksbildung in der sowjetischen Besatzungszone," *Börsenblatt für den deutschen Buchhandel* 11 (1948): 88.

[113]"Social and political literature: brochures encompassing up to 16 pages, leaflets and posters associated with the political parties, the unions, and public organizations, as well as advertisements for these materials and for theater performances" were still subject to censorship by the SMAD.

[114]See "Sitzung des Vorstandes und Hauptauschusses des Börsenvereins am 2. April 1947," *Börsenblatt des deutschen Buchhandels* 8 (1947): 110.

non-Communists,[115] Becker certainly knew about the order. Not that he mentioned it outrightly or even alluded to its existence; he spoke only of the fact that the elimination of SMAD advance censorship, which, he said, had been announced at the Leipzig book fair on 5 March by Lieutenant Colonel Koltypin, would have a "certain impact" upon the process of considering works for publication generally and would specifically alter the "function of the Kultureller Beirat." Becker then went on to explain in generalities that the tasks of the agency were linked to the peculiarities of the Soviet-zone publishing trade. The plans of licensed publishers, he explained, had to be balanced against the production capacity of typesetters, printers, binders, on the one hand, and simple paper availability on the other hand. There was no way of getting around the necessity of setting priorities based on "urgency," and "urgency" rested on "need."[116]

But "need" was an eminently political consideration. Because the men and women selected to make that determination on behalf of the Kultureller Beirat had to possess a proven "ability to make political judgments," said Becker, the job of establishing the "urgency" of specific manuscripts would exercise a kind of concurrent control over whether the "planned works serve the construction of a progressive democracy." From there Becker launched into an invidious attack upon advocates of "liberal thinking" among the licensed publishers sure to voice their objections to control of any kind because they regarded democracy as being synonymous with the "complete freedom of each individual publisher to produce whatever he wants"; whereas those who truly understood the "errant way of the German people" and took seriously the responsibility incumbent upon German publishing houses because of it thought differently. In any case, such was the justification offered by Becker in support of the "impartial review of publishing-house plans" to be strengthened further "by the examination of manuscripts selected for publication by publishers" whose ability to judge politically, "subjective honesty" notwithstanding, was likely to have been influenced by the spirit of "bourgeois liberalism and nationalism." Not even the "antifascism" of certain publishers necessarily protected them from their upbringing. Thus, those who recognized the necessity of developing a "reliable sense of political judgment in terms of genuine democracy" argued in favor of screening the content of manuscripts because of the preeminent role played by books in molding public opinion. None of this, Becker hastened to add, had anything remotely to do with "petty censorship and its disadvantageous consequences."[117] Such was the public rationale behind the "reorganized" Kultu-

[115]See the list in Der Kulturelle Beirat bei der Zentralverwaltung für Volksbildung, 26 February 1947 [?]. Bundesarchiv, Abt. Potsdam, R-2/1055/19-21.
[116]Becker, "Planmäßige Buchproduktion," *Börsenblatt für den deutschen Buchhandel* 8 (1947): 109.
[117]Ibid.

reller Beirat. With proposed branch offices throughout the zone, wherever a concentration of publishing houses was located, the KB would be provided with a list of each publisher's plans for the immediate future, though Becker stressed that the routine submission and review of each individual book manuscript listed in the plans was not anticipated. Instead, "in the over-whelming majority of cases," the agency could use its knowledge of pub-lisher, author, and topic to formulate an opinion on the overall planning of each individual publisher. If the opinion was favorable, the publisher could proceed with his preliminary work and also count on receiving the necessary supply of paper at the appropriate time. Only rarely would the Kultureller Beirat, or also the publisher, wish to have the definitive text reviewed one last time before its publication. Finally, Becker concluded that the KB could only succeed if it truly limited itself to the approval of overall publication plans, avoided exercising any kind of "censorship function," and worked on a decentralized basis.[118]

It is hard to imagine that Becker and others were naive enough to believe in the possibility of any semi-secret agency passing political judgment on creative and other kinds of literature without slipping automatically into the role of censor; and it is altogether inconceivable that Wandel or Weinert, to say nothing of cultural-political officers from Tjulpanov's bureau, had any illusions about the ultimate intent of restructuring the Kultureller Beirat. The SMAD, whose officers regarded every question related to the book trade as having instantaneous ideological implications, certainly had good reason to characterize the agency privately as a "council for ideological questions" as-sociated with the publishing business." Nor can there be any illusions about the role that it was destined to play in connection with the advancement of Zhdanovist norms of art and literature and within the context of the SED's two-year plan passed in summer 1948. Insiders were hardly the only ones to spot the implications of these developments. Three months after Becker voiced his criticism of "liberal thinkers" among the publishers who took complete freedom to mean that they could print whatever they pleased, he was answered by a man named Johannes Hohlfeld. Hohlfeld took it upon himself to distinguish clearly between the two sets of circumstances used to justify the need for centralized or even state planning in the area of publish-ing. These were, first, temporary difficulties associated with the technical as-pects of publishing, such as the availability of paper and printing presses; and, second, a long-term transformation of basic economic structures. Even if Hohlfeld stopped short of saying so outrightly, he intimated that the latter was occurring under cover of the former. If interfering with the decisions of individual publishers involved more than a temporarily necessary evil caus-ed by paper shortages and the like; if indeed the intention was to effect a

[118]Ibid., p. 110.

fundamental change in the economy, then it was clear to Hohlfeld that any such alterations had to take account of the larger pattern of economic structures and could be accomplished only within the context of economic unity. Baring those kinds of considerations, "if the demand for the cultural and economic unity of Germany is intended as more than a nice phrase," then the priority had to be the creation of a system of publishing valid nationwide.[119]

Hohlfeld then challenged Becker on a number of critical points. First of all, he said, the licensing of publishers was already a measure that provided for a considerable degree of control over the production of books in the zone. Going much beyond that ran the risk of turning the "planned production of books" into their "planned prohibition." Moreover, Hohlfeld went on, whereas Becker had contorted the liberal desire of each individual publisher to bring out whatever he wished into an example of the type of thinking responsible for Germany's "errant path" into fascism, he saw the similarities elsewhere—under Hitler no publisher could publish in accordance with his own desires, but was forced instead to submit to National Socialist "planning" if he wished his business to prosper. Given the experience of the recent past, it was perfectly understandable that publishers had misgivings about notions of a planned economy. Hohlfeld then focused his attention on the political-ideological rationale behind Becker's discussion of the Kultureller Beirat: "When Becker rolls out the heavy artillery of a deficient ability to make political judgments for use against such misgivings, it should be clearly understood that he has hopelessly confused concepts. A liberal view of the economy may be lacking in understanding for socialist ideas, but to deny it the ability to make a democratic judgment is going just a bit too far." The point, said Hohlfeld, was that Becker had first linked liberalism with the nationalism of recent vintage and then proceeded to argue in favor of using democracy to protect socialist opinions *against* liberal opinions—as if the German people had already decided in favor of the one against the other. Moreover, Hohlfeld went on, Becker had indulged in use of the terms "progressive" and "genuine" while speaking of socialist democracy, which was the same as suggesting that "regressive" or "spurious" were apt descriptions of a liberal democracy. Finally, Becker had argued that a "planned production of books" would represent a way of checking whether the anticipated works served the construction of "progressive" democracy and, no less, went a step beyond that in calling for screening each book in terms of its actual contents. Thus, as Hohlfeld explained it, Becker advocated much more than developing a defense against writing hostile to democracy generally; rather, he demanded nothing less than a positive attitude toward a socialist democracy specifically. That political decision, however, which democratic

---

[119]Hohlfeld, "Zur Frage einer planmäßigen Buchproduktion," *Börsenblatt für den deutschen Buchhandel* 16 (1947): 201.

road a united Germany wished to travel, had yet to be taken; and Hohlfeld suggested that the choice was ultimately up to the German people if the word democracy had any meaning at all. Planning the production of books to favor one or the other direction prejudiced that decision entirely, and that choice, after all, would establish the basis of German unity in the future. Indeed, using Becker's own reasoning and under the circumstances existing in Soviet-occupied Germany, controlling the work of the publishers as a means of what he had called both preventing "the contamination of the mind" and "molding public opinion" amounted to little more than a deliberate attempt to withhold from ordinary Germans all the information that they needed to make a responsible decision. Hohlfeld went on to suggest that the matter of whether writing ought to be obliged to adopt a position with respect to one form of democracy would by no means be a settled question even after the German people had rendered their political decision. In any case, only the future would tell whether the practices of a restructured Kultureller Beirat conspired to retard or stimulate the production of good books of creative literature; if it opened the way to valuable and original works of literature, Hohlfeld finished, it deserved every imaginable accolade; if it proved unequal to that important task, it would shovel its own grave.[120]

Hohlfeld's elaborations are probably a fair indication of the amount of resentment toward the Kultureller Beirat in Soviet-occupied Germany. They were then followed by additional commentary in the same periodical, the first, obviously planned that way, was written by Werner Wilk and came immediately after Hohlfeld's article in the identical issue of the journal; the other two, by Felix Meiner and Ernst Adler, followed a month later; and Becker had the last word four weeks after that.[121] These added little to the exchange between Hohlfeld and Becker. Wilk, for instance, a publisher and writer, appeared far too naive in his remarks to have understood the full implications of Becker's original article and took comfort in his own distinction that the Kultureller Beirat was not intended as a "political," but a "cultural-political" regulatory agency—a differentiation that, if it ever made any sense in Soviet-occupied Germany, made none now. Then there was Hohlfeld's question of whether writing should be expected to have a "positive attitude toward a certain form of democracy"; Wilk had no doubt about it and failed to understand why the question had even been asked. Political and politico-economic writing should be clear about its favorization of liberalism or socialism, Marxism or Christian socialism, Wilk said, missing the substance of Becker's comments, and Hohlfeld's objections, to the effect that the Kultureller Beirat existed to establish the top priority in the publication

---

[120]Ibid., p. 202.
[121]The title of the articles was the same, "Zur Frage einer planmäßigen Buchproduktion," *Börsenblatt für den deutschen Buchhandel* 16 (1947): 202-3; 21 (1947): 225-27; and 22 (1947): 233.

of writing congenial only to "progressive democracy." Wilk added only that works of poetry and creative literature would be judged according to artistic criteria anyway, as if by mid-1947 any such thing still existed independent of a rapidly narrowing Zhdanovist definition of aesthetics; and that political considerations entered in only when works of creative literature contained "political elements" that were not "incontrovertibly democratic."

Felix Meiner likewise tended to side in favor of Becker, though he conceded that the previous work of the Kultureller Beirat had been unproductive and suggested that Becker had perhaps been too simplistic in the "polemical portion" of his article. Otherwise, Meiner drew encouragement from Becker's own assurance that the Kultureller Beirat would not be charged with examining every single manuscript, but rather limit its activities to the advance scrutiny and approval of each publisher's quarterly listing of books intended for publication (a practice, incidentally, that was not adhered to). Even then, however, it was understandable that the question of each book's "urgency" still needed to be resolved in light of the problems caused by the shortage of paper and by the limited production capacity of the presses. These were issues that Meiner went on to discuss, but without burdening his suggestions with the hint of an awareness either of the abundant opportunities for the manipulation of the Soviet-zone publishing trade or the rapid deterioration of the political and cultural-political situation. He appeared concerned only with the need to accelerate the decision-making process, for those in positions of responsibility had to be clear that the "further continuation of the already all too distinct departure of authors, and not just those living in the West, would inflict wounds on the local presses virtually impossible to heal." The last commentator, Ernst Adler, rounded out the discussion by raising a number of the same issues, but he managed to ignore all of those related to the long-range political implications of a central coordinating and control agency. Finally, Becker summed up the results of the discussion. He made it clear that he regarded Hohlfeld's response as a "perfect example of the attitude rejected by us" and denied categorically that he himself had in any way contrasted a "Western-liberalist" with an "Eastern-socialist" democracy—precisely what he had done.

The subject then rested for a few months, at least publicly, until Balluseck's replacement, Kielmeyer, discussed procedures in detail in November 1947. In fact, this may have been the only information then available concerning the modalities of the review process to which writers and publishers were expected to adhere, and it was restated several months later because of continuing confusion about proper procedures.[122] By then, however, the Kultureller Beirat appears to have been reeling from two blows to its basic ope-

[122]See "Kultureller Beirat. Mitteilungen. Das Manuskript," *Börsenblatt für den deutschen Buchhandel* 20 (1948): 193.

rations. Difficulties with regional governments were probably less of a threat, but still needed to be dealt with. For some reason, the Mecklenburg branch of the SMAD lifted advance censorship in that state one month before the issuance of order 90, on 15 March, rather than 17 April 1947, and placed the Mecklenburg ministry of culture and education in charge of overseeing the publishing business. Gottfried Grünberg then circulated an announcement locally that his ministry planned on setting up its own Kultureller Beirat to screen manuscripts.[123] Apparently, the state and provincial offices of the SMAD had failed to understand that orders 25 and 90, applied throughout the entire zone and that manuscripts licensed by the Russians in Berlin following examination by the KB there no longer required additional approval by regional offices of the occupation administration. More than likely, the regional commander assumed that the elimination of advance censorship obligated him to replace it with a local German agency and had not been told that the KB in Berlin existed to censor on behalf of the Russians centrally. Balluseck was correct to consider the formation of a "state-based Kultureller Beirat as an office of censorship" as a contradiction of the instructions issued by the SMAD in Berlin;[124] and there is no indication that the Russians allowed the problem to persist. Toward the end of the year, however, officials in Saxony-Anhalt came up with the idea of establishing "preparatory committees" for the Kultureller Beirat attached to each of the state governments. Kielmeyer opposed the notion by insisting, among other things, that such committees would also violate order 25. The SMAD had set up the Kultureller Beirat as an organization independent of the DVV and responsible for the book trade in all of Soviet-occupied Germany. The creation of "preparatory committees" would impinge upon this independence by tying its operations to offices of state government.[125]

These problems must have been minor irritants compared with the crippling shortage of paper. Raw material had always been in short supply,[126] and in fall 1947, Weinert appealed to Sergej Tjulpanov for help because the Kultureller Beirat would be unable to continue its work without sufficient quantities of paper. The statistics cited by Weinert were stark: the Kultureller Beirat had been promised quarterly 300 tons for books and 250 for periodicals. That amount was never actually supplied, the KB was 290 tons be-

[123]Landesregierung Mecklenburg. Ministerium für Volksbildung. Abteilung: Allgemeine Volkskultur. Rundschreiben Nr. 59/47. An alle Kultur- und Volksbildungsämter. An alle Verlagsanstalten und Druckereien. Betr. Zensur, 12 March 1947. Bundesarchiv, Abt. Potsdam, R-2/1149/111.
[124]See Balluseck to Major Mischin, 16 May 1947; Balluseck to Wandel (Betrifft: Landesregierung Mecklenburg - Ministerium für Volksbildung), 17 May 1947, ibid., R-2/1149/119-10.
[125]Aktennotiz. Betr.: Vorbereitende Ausschüsse des Kulturellen Beirates bei den Landesregierungen, 26 November 1947, gez. Kielmeyer, ibid., R-2/1132/103-4.
[126]See Balluseck's letter to a member of the Leipzig city council, Ott, explaining the nature of the problem on 21 January 1947, ibid., R-2/1132/234-6.

hind for the second quarter alone, and the SMAD's representative just told Weinert that the entire third-quarter allotment for books had been canceled along with a previously approved allocation of 162 additional tons. As of 1 October 1947, the KB needed 3,000 just to publish books and periodicals already in possession of a license issued by the SMAD. Weinert told Tjulpanov that the situation threatened to cast doubt upon the "democratic seriousness of our institution," making it vulnerable to attacks by the "enemy press" and "ridiculous" in the eyes of both publishers and the general public.[127]

Nothing happened, and one month later Weinert complained once more about the senselessness of approving manuscripts without being able to give the publisher the paper needed to publish. Weinert had stopped granting such acceptances and warned Tjulpanov that firms would soon have to shut down completely or go into business in other zones.[128] The SED must have broached the subject with the SMAD, too,[129] but the outcome of it all is unclear. Not that the party and its cultural functionaries bemoaned the shortage of paper in every respect. In November 1947, a private meeting took place among a variety of the party's administrative personalities active in cultural organizations and agencies and in the presence of several Russians. Frommhold, who headed the DVV's office of publishing, stressed the importance of bringing out books and journals "as a means of ideologically influencing the people"; and spoke of the continuing existence of licensed private publishing houses, operating in accordance with capitalist principles, alongside "new forms" of presses. Even the private businesses, however, were limited in their capacity to produce as they saw fit, and the work of the Kultureller Beirat was the reason why. The KB rendered its decision based in part upon the availability of paper; and "making a virtue out of the vice of insufficient raw materials," the agency undertook to subject all Soviet-zone publishing projects to "sensible planning." The DVV intended to operate much the same way by using its "licensing policies" in order to reestablish a system of publishing houses on the basis of "sensible planning that takes our special circumstances into account." In due course, Frommhold remarked, "we will overcome publishers who think mostly along mercantile lines and . . . are out of touch with the times." He also warned those in attendance that the meeting was strictly confidential; no one was to know that the talks took place, much less the nature of the subjects discussed.[130]

In spite of the problems, the KB continued operating, and several weeks after Weinert's second letter to Tjulpanov, Kielmeyer outlined the following

[127]Weinert to Tjulpanov, 15 September 1947, ibid., R-2/1091/144.

[128]Weinert to Tjulpanov, 16 October 1947, ibid., R-2/1091/143.

[129]See Protokoll Nr. 126 der Sitzung des Zentralsekretariats am 5. 8. 1947. Zentrales Parteiarchiv, IV 2/2.1/114.

[130]Protokoll der internen Besprechung über Verlags- und Buchhandelsfragen, 13 November 1947. Bundesarchiv, Abt. Potsdam, R-2/1149/67-9.

procedures intended, as he put it, to transform the "chaotic conditions of the publishing trade" into a process of "orderly planning adapted to the needs of the times." Kielmeyer tried to convey the impression that restructuring the Kultureller Beirat resulted from the initiative of the DVV, whereas order 25, which he referred to as the decree providing for a "Kultureller Beirat for the publishing trade," with no mention of the phrase "council for ideological questions," came across as nothing more than the SMAD's formalization of a *German* remedy to the "chaotic conditions" of the trade. Though any number of objections were to be expected from publishers interested chiefly in financial gain and prepared to tolerate no agency with the power to interfere with their plans, said Kielmeyer, order 25 guaranteed an absolutely democratic composition of the organization; and he went on to define its duties. These had changed little since early 1947 and reflected the continuing shortage of personnel. The Kultureller Beirat, wrote Kielmeyer, undertook to review the plans of licensed publishers and determine the "urgency" of these proposals before assigning the quantities of paper available quarterly in line with that determination. The major controlling body of the organization was supposed to be the "plenum"; but now as before, the more important "main committee" or Hauptausschuß met roughly once a week to review the specific recommendations of the specialized commissions. For their part, these Fachkommissionen, which at the time of Kielmeyer's writing still numbered only six, rather than the sixteen first envisaged in February 1947, were to be comprised of persons expert in the areas covered by each of the six commissions.[131] By spring 1948, two more had been added to make eight—science, *belles-lettres*, reference books, music, books for young people, art, and anthologies.[132] There was also a group referred to as the "planning commission," whose official job it was to prevent possible duplication and to rule out the unjustified favorization of one area over the other. More importantly, that body looked to encourage or further the publication of books on certain subjects of cultural-political importance.

Otherwise, the commissions were charged with formulating an opinion on each publisher's plans and project listings based on that commission's relevant collective expertise; on the evaluations of each manuscript prepared by or for the publisher; and, if a review of a specific manuscript by the Kultureller Beirat was considered necessary, on the evaluation prepared by the agency's own readers. These persons were not to be approached directly by the publishers, and their identity was officially concealed from them anyway. The readers numbered 300 as of May 1948.[133] Who they all were, how

[131]Kielmeyer, "Der kulturelle Beirat und das Verlagswesen," *Börsenblatt für den deutschen Buchhandel* 34 (1947): 330.
[132]"Kultureller Beirat. Mitteilungen. Das Manuskript," *Börsenblatt für den deutschen Buchhandel* 20 (1948): 193.
[133]Ibid.

374 · *Censorship and Controversy*

they were chosen, what specific kinds of recommendations they made, the nature of their political or specialized qualifications—little of this is known. But their reports were, in any case, part of the materials then made available to the main committee, which made the final decision on plans and manuscripts in the presence of representatives of the specialized commissions and ranked their recommendations according to three levels of "urgency": 1) most urgent, paper recommended; 2) urgent, paper not recommended; and 3) not urgent, paper not recommended. The actual review process thus began with the submission of each publisher's plans for the upcoming quarter, though, contrary to the claim made in the *Börsenblatt*, this practice of quarterly submission had not been a specific provision of SMAD order 90. Be that as it may, the *Börsenblatt* for March 1948 mentioned that the review of publishers' proposals covering the second quarter of 1948 was nearing completion (though it was also indicated that numerous publishing firms had yet to send in copies of requested manuscripts in spite of repeated entreaties by the Kultureller Beirat and needed to do so within a few weeks if the planning process for 1948 were to be completed). The deadline for submission of plans covering the third quarter of 1948 was set at 30 April 1948, and the *Börsenblatt* also disclosed that the main committee had met twelve times in January and February 1948, rendering decisions on 1,018 proposals.[134] The published statistics for the year 1947 claimed that the central commission had passed on a total of 3,700 titles, going from 400 covering the first quarter of the year to 1,300 during the last. Of these 3,700, 65 percent had been rated "very urgent" or "urgent" and broke down into the following categories: *belles-lettres*, 35 percent; scientific books, 20 percent; reference books, 19 percent; art and music, 17 percent; young people's literature, 9 percent.[135] Possibly the most revealing statistic, what percentage of the 35 percent of rejected books fit the rubric *belles-lettres*, is impossible to determine from the above figures; and the reasons behind rejections are generally just as oblique. Nor do the statistics say anything about the specific criteria used in determining the various levels of "urgency." In his article published in November, however, Kielmeyer mentioned that textbooks, reference books, and "*belles-lettres* dealing with topical subjects" fit the first priority. But what was meant by the phrase "topical subjects"? He answered:

[134]"Kultureller Beirat. Mitteilungen," B*örsenblatt für den deutschen Buchhandel* 13 (1948): 110.
[135]"Kultureller Beirat. Mitteilungen. Jahresbericht 1947," *Börsenblatt für den deutschen Buchhandel* 6 (1948): 51. According to internal statistics, a grand total of 1,308 books were published in Soviet-occupied Germany in 1947; 1,155 were entirely new, the rest revised or unrevised issues (and some maps were apparently counted as book publications). Of the 1,155 books, 361 qualified as creative literature. See Buchproduktion 1947 in der sowjetischen Besatzungszone. Bundesarchiv, Abt. Potsdam, R-2/1149/57.

Well, a literature able to penetrate the broadest possible circles, both dealing with and clarifying the complexes of issues associated with our times in a fashion designed to extricate the reader, consciously and, far better, subconsciously from the circle of ideas related to the past—ideas so dangerous to our development. In other words, a literature that participates in the intellectual reconstruction of Germany. It does not suffice merely to reprint the "same old stuff" from the years prior to 1933 or to plan for a book just because its author had been banned during the Hitler years. In every instance a publisher must review thoroughly whether the work is really highly topical or solely a matter of past—literature. We must not forget that a great deal of work that is absolutely non-Nazi is by no means suitable for fashioning the new German, who is to be braced against a relapse into the mistakes of the past. We cannot help noting nowadays with real alarm how often, and with what partiality, works of bourgeois decadence and narrowly exclusive aestheticism, for instance, are being submitted to us. Twice in one-half a century, these very circles, through resigned disinterest or aloofness, have allowed developments in the direction of a catastrophe to take their course. They will be no less suitable for restructuring our people the third time around.[136]

The First German Writers' Congress

The party's cultural politics continued to harden in fall 1947 in connection with the SMAD's approval of a rigid political line presumably encouraged by Stalin in anticipation of the changes expected to follow the organization of the Cominform in late September 1947.[137] Pieck told the party congress barely a week before, for instance, that the SED required the support of the intellectuals to win the backing of the masses "against reaction and for the new Germany"; but he went a step further than usual by adding that the party's cultural policy had to build upon the foundation of Marxism-Leninism, rather than practice "self-restraint" or make "rotten compromises."[138] Even then, Dymschitz still tried to deny that the SMAD "controlled" stage, film, and literature; the only control exercised in Soviet-occupied Germany was designed to "filter out" Nazi ideology, whereas imposing the American way of life in the Western zones was real totalitarianism and the equivalent of

---

[136]Kielmeyer, "Der kulturelle Beirat und das Verlagswesen," *Börsenblatt für den deutschen Buchhandel* 34 (1947): 335.
[137]See Chapter Six.
[138]Pieck, "Bericht des Parteivorstandes," *Protokoll der Verhandlungen des 2. Parteitages* [20-24 September], p. 93.

fascism. Dymschitz went on to charge that those who ran cultural politics in the other zones popularized the "asocial and amoral" writings of Anouilh and Gide, "that literary Petain,"[139] Sartre and Giraudoux, even as they allowed an iron curtain to descend in an effort to keep Soviet culture out. While stories about the curtailment of creative freedom in the USSR were circulated, every imaginable existentialist pamphlet appeared in the West; and behind it all was an attempt by reaction to prevent Soviet culture from making friends around the world, especially among "German democrats."[140] Erich Weinert also worried that the so-called prejudices of German intellectuals, which grew out of an unwarranted concern with whether the Soviet Union was totalitarian and dictatorial, rather than socialist, played into the hands of the war-mongers. According to Weinert, the intellectuals failed to realize that the doctrine created by Marx and Engels, further developed by Lenin and Stalin, served the national interests of all peoples. They thus rendered themselves susceptible to the suggestion that German friends of the Soviet Union advocated a form of government patterned after a foreign power. But it was imperative now that intellectuals grasp the significance of the October revolution if they wished to avoid being misused by those out to "darken the light shining from the East with the smoke of war."[141]

This was the atmosphere in which the German writers' congress, originally scheduled for July, then postponed till October due to "inadequate preparations," convened in Berlin for the ostensible purpose of celebrating the reconciliation of exiles with inner émigrés.[142] The SMAD order sanctioning the event, with funding by the DVV and overruns covered by the Russians, had been drawn up four weeks earlier,[143] and the most intriguing question is whether the postponement until after the party conference and organization of the Cominform was sheer coincidence. If so, the belligerence of several Soviet writers who descended upon the congress was not; and the tenor of remarks made there both by the Russians and the German Communists certainly suited the hardline policies developing in connection with the SED conference in late September. The writers' congress had all the earmarks of a provocation, then, the irony being that it supposedly met, as Alexander Abusch argued, to effect a reconciliation between the two strands of German literature; whereas the planners promptly manipulated the concept of "unity" in order to prod writers into choosing sides politically. Abusch, for instance,

139"Petain der Literatur," *Tägliche Rundschau*, 19 November 1947.
140Dymschitz, "Totalitäre Kulturpolitik im Westen," *Tägliche Rundschau*, 28 September 1947.
141Weinert, "Die deutsche Intelligenz und die Sowjetunion," *Tägliche Rundschau*, 5 November 1947.
142See "Tagung der Schriftsteller" and "Kulturnachrichten," *Sonntag*, 4 and 18 May 1947. See also Schulmeister, *Auf dem Wege zu einer neuen Kultur*, pp. 164-65; and "Zum 1. Deutschen Schriftstellerkongress," *Neues Deutschland*, 3 October 1947.
143See Auszug aus dem Befehl des Obersten Chefs der Sowjetischen Militäradministration. Nr. 0314, 9 September 1947. Bundesarchiv, Abt. Potsdam, R-2/1091/110.

implored those in attendance to join forces against elements responsible for yesterday's fascism and intent upon using the atomic bomb to wage a new blitzkrieg.[144] Far better evidence of the provocation, however, was the "appeal" to intellectuals in the United States, signed by several Soviet literati, that materialized in Soviet-zone newspapers on 5 October. The timing was hardly accidental. The congress opened the evening before in the Hebbel Theater, then moved to the Soviet sector; and over the next few days there were recurrent allusions to the congress in Paris that met to "defend" culture against fascism in 1935. The analogy was impossible to overlook when the Soviet writers inquired of their American counterparts:

> Is it not reminiscent of fascism when one refuses to tolerate ideals and systems, different from those in the USA, in other countries? Is it not reminiscent of fascism when cries for a new war reach us from your country . . . ? What is it other than a repetition of fascism when claims for world rule are insisted upon, the beginning of the so-called "American" age proclaimed, and demands made for the introduction of a "new order" in the world—claims enforced by threats and in many instances even through the use of the most brutal violence against other peoples?

When the American system of government was foisted upon the world, fascism came to mind, much as it did when American politicians called for use of the atomic bomb upon countries with other social systems. Much more followed along these lines before the Russians ended by demanding that American "masters of culture" condemn the "new threat of fascism."[145] This invective set the tone for the congress, whose planners surely sensed the need to go on the offensive because of growing concern over cultural developments in the Soviet Union. For instance, one of the prominent writers scheduled to address the congress, Theodor Plievier, had just defected to the West and now claimed to have saved his skin in Soviet exile by keeping his mouth shut.[146] But the sponsors of the congress, every one of whom knew perfectly well what happened in the thirties, pretended that the subject did not exist and tried to deflect attention back to fascism past and, ostensibly, present. A plaque displaying the names of German writers and intellectuals who died between 1933 and 1945 served as the backdrop for the opening ceremony, but, not surprisingly, included none of the Germans murdered by Stalin. In return, the American Melvin Lasky hit a raw nerve when he stepped to the rostrum a few days after the opening and remarked upon the plight of Soviet writers. Lasky's speech split the congress right down the

[144]Abusch, "Die Schriftsteller und der Frieden," *Sonntag*, 5 October 1947.
[145]"Mit wem geht Ihr, amerikanische Meister der Kultur? Offener Brief sowjetischer Schriftsteller," *Sonntag*, 5 October 1947.
[146]See *Hamburger Allgemeine Zeitung*, 10 October 1947.

middle, though many in attendance had already reacted by then with resentment to the incessant demand that they make a partisan political decision. Even if the Communists denied having any interest in maintaining themselves in the "majority" or in focusing upon divisions among writers with "differing democratic outlooks,"[147] they appear to have been motivated by few other considerations. Paul Rilla argued that too little an awareness of the developing threat prior to 1933 delivered writers into the hands of the enemy back then; and this fact made it even more imperative that the "spirit of resistance" produce a front of German writers this time around who recognized the need for "a political decision," though not one, Rilla hastened to add, favoring a single political party.[148]

Not that any speaker was so improvident as to echo Pieck's recent remarks about Marxism-Leninism; nor did the principle of political or politicized literature appear inveterately cynical when presented, as the argument routinely was, in terms of Germany's past. Becher warned abstractly that "politics devour literature if literature, in its own way, on its own, fails to become political."[149] But every one of these calls for the politicization of literature met the needs of two-camps thinking. Dymschitz opened the congress by noting that the battle between democracy and reaction was being waged with uncommon intensity in Germany; and then lamented the fact that "literature" had failed to keep pace.[150] Shortly thereafter, the Soviet writer Vsevolod Vishnevskij inveighed against "reactionary forces in Washington and London" that sought to intimidate the USSR with atomic bombs; and went on to add that the world was split into two sides. One fought for "black reaction and signaled the threat of war," the other for freedom and peace; and Vishnevskij concluded by parroting the language of the Cominform in urging the congress to speak out in favor of "a united Germany, a fortified world democracy, and a lasting world peace."[151] The German Communists toned down their rhetoric, but still got their points across. When Alfred Kantorowicz extolled the oneness of German literature, Alexander Abusch interjected that the idea of inner emigration did not condone apolitical "inwardness."[152] The Soviet-zone press then tried to put the best face on the proceedings, celebrating the end of antagonism between the external and inner emi-

[147]Abusch, "Schriftsteller suchen den gemeinsamen Weg," *Neues Deutschland*, 12 October 1947.

[148]Rilla, "Schriftstellerkongreß in Berlin," *Sonntag*, 5 October 1947.

[149]Becher, *Vom Willen zum Frieden*, p. 94.

[150]Dymschitz, "Die Literatur—Seele des Volkes," *Tägliche Rundschau*, 5 October 1947.

[151]Vishnevsky's speech was not published in its entirety in the zone; See Boris Shub, *The Choice*, pp. 75-76; "Grüße der Sowjetunion und aus England," *Neues Deutschland*, 7 October 1947; and "Im Brennpunkt deutscher Kulturprobleme," *Tägliche Rundschau*, 8 October 1947.

[152]Kantorowicz, "Deutsche Schriftsteller im Exil," *Ost und West* 4 (1947): 42-51; "Die erste nationale Tagung der deutschen Schriftsteller. Die Gedenkfeier 'Tod und Hoffnung.' / Der erste Arbeitstag," *Neues Deutschland*, 8 October 1947.

gration while claiming that other subjects of discussion, Literature and Political Power, Is Nazism still Virulent in Literature, and Topical Writing, generated a "purifying rain storm."[153] But there was nothing the least bit purifying about the discussions. Abusch may have considered democratic unity to be the "intellectual thread" that ran through the congress and applauded the passionate desire for peace; but he blustered as well that "international tensions between the new war mongers and the defenders of peace" were reflected during the proceedings.[154] A later commentary acknowledged similarly that one topic, Literature and Political Power, came close to dividing "minds at the congress."[155]

This was hardly surprising, considering that Friedrich Wolf insisted upon "clear decisions" or that Wolfgang Langhoff, objecting to "indifferent views of partisanship," urged writers to "take sides."[156] Wolfgang Harich went off on a more radical tangent, endorsing the use of violence because violence led to "liberation" in the French and Russian revolutions.[157] One editorial published in the Soviet zone, in the CDU's *Neue Zeit*, then got away with stating publicly that Harich's comments were the logical continuation of demands for intermixing literature and politics, criticizing Weinert, Wolf, Langhoff (one of the "most unpleasant contributions to the discussion"), and others who supported the categorical idea of the writer's "political obligations." Nothing demonstrated their "detachment from reality" better, however, than that they were seconded by a "smug, precocious shyster [Harich] who substitutes refined demagogy for what he lacks in profundity."[158] Axel Eggebrecht later put Harich's advocacy of violence in a more ominous light when he spoke extemporaneously on the last day of the congress. There was nothing logically or ethically incongruent about the argument in favor of violence under certain circumstances, said Eggebrecht, only it lost its persuasiveness in the age of the atomic bomb.[159] But the real irony of Harich's remarks was that he delivered them at a congress organized to manifest the desire for what a Soviet writer called "lasting world peace"; and Becher punctuated his address similarly with the cry, "let there be peace."[160] The demand that a sides be chosen nonetheless sufficed to convince both Eggebrecht and

[153]"Der Wille zum Frieden," *Neues Deutschland*, 8 October 1947.

[154]Abusch, "Schriftsteller suchen den gemeinsamen Weg," *Neues Deutschland*, 12 October 1947.

[155]Joho, "Diskussion und Synthese. Bericht über den ersten deutschen Schriftstellerkongress," *Sonntag*, 12 October 1947.

[156]See "Der Dichter und seine Verantwortung. Weitere Vorträge und Diskussionen auf dem Schriftstellerkongress," *Tägliche Rundschau*, 9 October 1947; "Wo bleibt die junge Dichtung? Arbeitstagung des ersten Deutschen Schriftsteller-Kongresses," *Neues Deutschland*, 8 October 1947.

[157]See "Der Dichter und seine Verantwortung," *Tägliche Rundschau*, 9 October 1947.

[158]—ert. "Maß—nicht Maßlosigkeit," *Neue Zeit*, 10 October 1947.

[159]Eggebrecht, "Kritik und Verbindlichkeit," *Ost und West* 4 (1947): 56-57.

[160]Becher, *Vom Willen zum Frieden*, p. 111.

Neue Zeit of the need to expand upon their criticism of Harich. Eggebrecht considered the issue of violence entirely out of place in discussions among writers, and he went on to explain that he himself regarded intolerance as just as "profound a sin" against the intellect as the "disobliging spirit" upon whose ruinous role in Germany's recent past everyone agreed.[161] *Neue Zeit* was even more to the point. The paper quoted Elisabeth Langgässer, who asked in desperation about the place of a writer who declined to recognize the validity of "political activity"; and added that true humanism should emphasize the moderation and tolerance "advocated with such congenial emphasis at the congress, but whose blatant sabotage by large numbers of the audience was displayed at the expression of opinions that failed to accord with their orientation."[162]

Some time later, Dymschitz claimed falsely that the congress had actually agreed upon an interpretation of the role of the writer in accord with Lenin's "only scientific Marxist view of the problem"; and the "progressive" writers at the congress supposedly expressed themselves in a manner that Dymschitz said was a variation of Lenin's words to the effect that "'absolute freedom was a bourgeois or anarchistic phrase.'"[163] Dymschitz was especially pleased that the "auditorium, in concert, drove . . . from the podium a certain aesthetisizing poetess, Frau Richter-Schacht, who tried to protest from the standpoint of 'pure art' against the 'politicization of literature.'" Further, the delegates expressed their amazement at the remarks of Erwin Redslob, who joined the presidium of the congress, but, as an editor of the West Berlin daily *Tagesspiegel* allowed the paper to "slander" it; whereas Ernst Niekisch rightfully attacked "decadent-minded intellectuals" who defended the "profascist" writer José Ortega y Gasset. In a related vein, Dymschitz continued, Albin Stübs made comments rife with decadent individualism; in fact, Stübs' comments served as a graphic illustration of the fact that "nazism is still virulent" because they deprived fascism of its social and historical content. The remarks of Eva Maria Brailsford, speaking on behalf of her husband Noel, a well-known English publicist, also rubbed Dymschitz the wrong way. Dymschitz said that Brailsford, "propagated a typical bourgeois, distorted view of humanism" and "rejected the principle of violence." Dymschitz claimed as well that most delegates were quick to realize "the dangerous essence of the pacifistic-social confessions" of the Brailsfords and said that Wolf and Harich both spotted the "snake in the bouquet" proffered by the British couple. Wolf contrasted the "reactionary pseudohumanism that tries to disarm democracy in its struggle against reaction" with true democratic humanism; whereas Harich proved that violence was necessary for the

---

[161]Eggebrecht, "Kritik und Verbindlichkeit," pp. 57-58.

[162]—ert. "Maß—nicht Maßlosigkeit," *Neue Zeit*, 10 October, 1947.

[163]Dymschitz, "Der Erste Deutsche Schriftstellerkongress. Aufzeichnungen eines sowjetischen Gastes," *Neue Welt* 20 (1947): 99.

triumph of democracy.[164]

The treatment accorded the Brailsfords was one of the many incidents that bothered Eggebrecht. He resented the accusation that the Brailsfords' call for "absolute justice in all zones" was a "prearranged maneuver carried out in response to orders";[165] whereas Dymschitz voiced his confidence that democratic writers would not be blinded by the Brailsfords' kind of morality, having grasped the "new humanism of Gorky, expressed in the concise remark, 'If the enemy refuses to surrender, he will be destroyed.'"[166] It was small wonder, then, that many of the delegates who disagreed with the tone of a congress held in the Soviet sector of Berlin kept silent; and Harich's expression of hope afterwards that people would continue "talking with each other" was hardly enough to make those who had been chastised when they voiced an opinion forget the bitter experience. But Harich was correct in saying that the problem derived from differing views of fascism and that these in turn resided in the fundamental conflict between "bourgeois" and "socialist" ideology. The essence of fascism had to be recognized in order to "be opportune in dealing with the beginnings of the same or a similar kind of disgrace." Harich complained further that the "bourgeois camp" applauded "anonymously and zealously" whenever camouflaged concepts like "totalitarianism" were raised at the congress, but declined to present their own counter arguments. The poet Rudolf Hagelstange hid behind "nebulous allusions and ambiguous metaphors." Or, another example, when Niekisch established parallels between Ortega y Gasset and fascism, the wife of the writer Birkenfeld protested to loud applause. Unfortunately, no discussion followed, and the responsibility for the silence resided with those who, for unfathomable reasons, avoided an "open, courageous exchange of opinions" and ignored the "polite entreaties" of the other side to engage in a discussion. The suggestion that invitations to trade ideas were a "trap" only acquired an element of truth, said Harich, if the ideas of the other side were "too weak" to prevail.[167]

These confrontations paled in comparison with the reaction, during and after the congress, to remarks made by Melvin Lasky. Following Vishnevskij's bellicose speech, Lasky decided to raised the subject of the sanctions imposed upon Akhmatova and Zoshchenko in the aftermath of the central-committee decrees; and, in connection with the debates over the role of the writer and politics, said that Soviet writers were equally familiar with political pressure and censorship. They struggled for cultural freedom, too, working in awareness of the existence of political censorship and the police behind it. What must it be like, he asked, for a Russian writer to worry con-

---

[164]Ibid., p. 100.
[165]Eggebrecht, "Kritik und Verbindlichkeit," p. 56.
[166]Dymschitz, "Der Erste Deutsche Schriftstellerkongress," p. 100.
[167]Harich, "Im Gespräch bleiben!" *Die Weltbühne* 20 (1947): 887-92.

tinually whether "the new party doctrine, the revised state form of social realism or formalism or objectivism, or whatever it might be, was not already superseded and they might not have been branded overnight as "decadent counterrevolutionary tools of reaction"?[168] According to the transcript of the proceedings, Lasky's comments resulted in "outrage" on the part of some in the audience, but strong approval by the others. The moderator, Birkenfeld, who had arranged with Lasky the evening before to put him on the list of speakers, then requested that Lasky be accorded the same attention given "other colleagues from abroad," that is, the Soviet literati, to which, apart from continuing "vigorous approval," others cried out, "Lie less! Talk about Hanns Eisler! That's a violation of the rules of hospitality! A guest from abroad can't talk like that!" Despite the commotion, Lasky went on to speak of Soviet philosophers who were afraid to mention names in their work out of fear of committing an unpardonable ideological sin; and of the fate that had befallen Akhmatova and Zoshchenko, "excommunicated as poisonous scum" mainly because they refused to sing hymns to the new five-year plan. Lasky concluded by telling the audience that "our colleagues in Russia have their problems, too, and perhaps your experiences will help clarify, for them and for us, the basic principles of cultural freedom." Lasky ended, to "tumultuous applause," with a quotation by Gide.

The response followed that afternoon in the form of remarks by one of the Soviet writers in attendance. Valentin Katajev considered Lasky to be an unadorned "war-monger," the kind that he, Katajev, had never met because there were none in the USSR. What Lasky had to say was a lie from start to finish, but nothing new; "the deceased Dr. Goebbels used identical methods in his smear campaign against the Soviet Union, and everyone surely knows how that ended." Katajev added the familiar refrain that the decency and honesty of people was determined by their attitude toward democracy generally and specifically to the Soviet Union. Over the next several days, Soviet-zone newspapers then vied with each other in expressing their indignation at Lasky. Particularly upset that he had forced an "unplanned" talk upon the congress, most of the commentary claimed that his pronouncements were greeted with "roaring laughter" by the delegates because they spotted his "maneuver"; and they all challenged his credentials as a writer and as an independent journalist.[169] Others used his association with the periodicals *New Leader* and *Partisan Review* to charge that he and his circle had opposed Roosevelt's policy of alliance with the Soviet Union and that the journals employed people of the ilk of Gustav Regler, a Communist who broke with the party after the Spanish civil war and in connection with Stalin's show trials.[170]

[168]I quote here from the unpublished transcript of the congress in the Friedrich-Wolf-Archiv.
[169]See "Der Dichter und seine Verantwortung," *Tägliche Rundschau*, 9 October 1947.
[170]See Feistmann, "Lasky und andere. Ein Schlußwort," *Neues Deutschland*, 9 October 1947.

Some of the worst abuse came from Dymschitz, who objected to Lasky's "repulsive external appearance" (he sported a goatee that reminded Dymschitz of Trotsky); and much of the other commentary denounced Lasky outrightly as a Trotskyist. Dymschitz called him a "creature" of the group concected with Ruth Fischer, who had handed her two brothers, the "German antifascists" Hanns and Gerhart Eisler, over to American jailers; and further characterized Lasky as one of the "most dangerous subjects of the present day, an instigator of a new war" before rejecting the charges of persecution of Soviet intellectuals and writers. What was involved was no more than the process of "criticism and self-criticism," he said, and none of those singled out felt like "victims of a totalitarian dictatorship."[171] When Becher's turn to address the congress came, he made a concerted effort to sound accommodating. Though he also insisted upon the politicization of literature, Becher's tones were softer, so much so that even *Neue Zeit* commented favorably; and Eggebrecht was similarly impressed. Still, Becher's plea for peace spelled out prerequisites, behind which hid the standard doctrinal and political premises. He said that being in favor of peace meant depriving war of its mysterious character by spotting its "social manifestations"; insisted that those who thought war was inevitable be regarded as enemies of peace; and urged Germans to "demand" national unity by opposing a "cut-up, quartered, or halved Germany." Becher called upon Germans to proclaim this unity in fighting for the unity of German literature (which, he said, had nothing in common with "regulation" or "management").[172] These sentiments squared poorly, however, with utterances that otherwise dominated the congress. The last speaker from abroad was Boris Gorbatov, one of the signers of the appeal to American writers. He reminded his listeners of the fact that the world was split into two camps, progressive-thinking, democratically minded people, and a band of reactionaries; and each writer had to choose which side to join.[173] A few days later, he added that he himself chose the "rule of democracy" because democracy meant peace, whereas fascism, imperialism, and "Trotskyism" meant war. Gorbatov, concluded by expressing his willingness to demonstrate infinite patience with "friends of democracy and peace," but he recommended hatred for "the enemies of peace" and voiced sympathy for the victims, not the executioners.[174]

Gorbatov's call to arms ended the congress; there was no discussion afterwards because the presidium decided "a bit late," as *Neue Zeit* wrote, that the remarks of guests from abroad would not be commented upon.[175]

[171]Dymschitz, "Ein Provokateur ohne Maske," *Tägliche Rundschau*, 11 October 1947.
[172]Becher, *Vom Willen zu Frieden*, pp. 91-111.
[173]"Ausklang des Kongresses," *Neues Deutschland*, 10 October 1947.
[174]Gorbatov, "'Ich glaube an den Menschen.' Abschiedsworte Boris Gorbatows an den Schriftstellerkongress," *Tägliche Rundschau*, 14 October 1947.
[175]—ert. "Maß—nicht Maßlosigkeit," *Neue Zeit*, 10 October 1947. Discussion of Becher's

Dymschitz then summed things up a short time later by describing the congress as an "ideological review" of the "democratic elements of German literature"[176]—a characterization that corresponded with the proclamation of the two camps theory just a few weeks before. Abusch's retrospective did likewise; in his mind, the congress proved just who was interested in a "provocative division of German writers" and who desired accommodation. The socialist group supported understanding among democrats as the indispensable precondition for German unity and peace; whereas division fulfilled the desires of those opposed to it—"allies of foreign war-mongers."[177]

The Kulturbund Banned

Just a few weeks later, on 1 November 1947, the American military government banned the Kulturbund in the American sector of Berlin for refusing to reapply for a license; besides, the Americans supposedly said, its leading members had been schooled in "Moscow."[178] The prohibition came on the heels of an announcement by General Clay that military government would no longer be silent in the face of the strident anti-American attacks now commonplace in the Soviet zone. But the Kulturbund's problems with the allies began earlier and were directly connected with its increasingly obvious, though still vigorously denied, fidelity to the political objectives of the SED. Following the communal elections in September 1946, and on the eve of the SED's disastrous showing in Berlin, the SPD had started to insist that the Kulturbund restructure its Berlin leadership in line with the outcome of the elections. Following the Berlin elections, and just prior to the selection of the Kulturbund's new leadership there, the SPD then threatened to form its own cultural organization if its demands were not met.[179] The Kulturbund re-

---

speech was apparently also cut off (see Joho, "Ausblick und Hoffnung," *Sonntag*, 12 October 1947). Gorbatov had more to say on the subject of Soviet literature at a reception of congressional delegates held in the "Soviet press club." Evidentally, questions about aesthetic and political issues related to Soviet writers "rained down" on Gorbatov, demonstrating just how many "wrong ideas" about Soviet literature existed today in Germany. Akhmatova's "overly aesthetic verses" were rejected, he said, because they offended "popular feelings"; but because she continued to draw her pension, Akhmatova's stomach never felt "the sting of the criticism." Gorbatov also noted that Sartre and his style of writing went "unloved" in the Soviet Union, adding that there was "no pornography" in the USSR. Not that surrealism was "banned," it just met with no response because it contradicted the national character of the Russian people; "it's alien to us" ("Gorbatow antwortete deutschen Schriftstellern," *Tägliche Rundschau*, 10 October 1947).

[176]Dymschitz, "Der Erste Deutsche Schriftstellerkongress," p. 100.

[177]Abusch, "Schriftsteller suchen den gemeinsamen Weg," *Neues Deutschland*, 12 October 1947.

[178]See Schulmeister, *Auf dem Wege zu einer neuen Kultur*, p. 173.

[179]See ibid., p. 171.

sponded by issuing denunciations of efforts to disrupt the organization with "party squabbling" and, as Becher phrased it, to use the Kulturbund to "play off the occupation authorities" against each other.[180] The situation had deteriorated further during the weeks leading up to the Kulturbund's conference in May, and later complaints about the disruption of its meetings held in the American sector of Berlin date these difficulties back to May.[181] Apparently, the prime cause of the problems were comments like Tjulpanov's at the conference and the anti-Americanism already evident in many of the public remarks delivered by Kulturbund Germans who belonged to the SED. Becher's constant assurances that the organization favored neither the East nor the West probably convinced no one; and had there been any lingering doubt about the organization's bias, the performance of various cultural personalities linked to the SED at the congress in October, along with the anti-Americanism of the Soviet writers in attendance, must have dispelled it. The American press agency DENA reported as early as 7 October that the Kulturbund had actually been banned in the American sector, provoking various expressions of dismay by writers present at the congress. The news came at a convenient time for the sponsors, and they made the most of it in the Soviet-zone press, even though the American military government called the story false; authorities were merely reviewing the situation and, evidently, intended to ask the organization to reapply for a license valid for all of Berlin. The Kulturbund's response was that reapplication was unnecessary because the SMAD had granted permission on 25 June 1945, and order no. 1 issued by the allied Kommandantura on 11 July accepted the validity of licenses granted parties and "public organizations" by the SMAD.[182]

This remained the official position of both the Kulturbund and the Soviet occupation administration. Any interference with Kulturbund operations in West Berlin violated the orders of an allied agency, and the SMAD requested that the Berlin Magistrat put an end to such "antidemocratic activity."[183] But to no avail; some leading SPD officials provided the Americans with a list of objections to the Kulturbund (an act that *Neues Deutschland* called a "party-political offensive" designed to acquire the assistance of the occupation authorities in pursuit of their pro-American objectives);[184] and whether or not the SPD's involvement tipped the scales, the Americans insisted that

[180]"Notizen," "Erneuerung des Kulturbundes," and "Wahlen im Kulturbund," *Sonntag*, 2 and 7 February, 23 March 1947; and Becher's remarks in "Tatsachen gegen Polemik," *Sonntag*, 9 November 1947.
[181]The SMAD, for instance, noted that permission for Kulturbund events in Schöneberg and Kreuzberg had been withheld "as early as May." See the SMAD's communique in "Zur Stellung des Kulturbundes in Berlin," *Sonntag*, 2 November 1947.
[182]See "Kein Verbot des Kulturbundes," *Tägliche Rundschau*, 11 October 1947.
[183]"Zur Stellung des Kulturbundes in Berlin," *Sonntag*, 2 November 1947.
[184]"SPD-Denunziantentum. Neues Licht auf das Kulturbund-Verbot," *Neues Deutschland*, 15 November 1947; see also Schulmeister, *Auf dem Wege zu einer neuen Kultur*, pp. 174-75.

the Kulturbund submit an application for a new license. It was banned when it refused, and the British followed suit on 12 November. Why the Kulturbund refused to reapply, a decision most likely made for it by the SMAD anyway, is unclear. Doing so would have embarrassed the allies had they then outlawed it regardless, suggesting that there must have been a certain usefulness to the ban. It surely helped make a case against what Dymschitz called cultural totalitarianism in the Western zones; and it might also have been considered helpful in driving a wedge between the intellectuals living in West Berlin and allied authorities, thereby encouraging the proper selection of "sides." The Kulturbund's excuse for not reapplying, however, was that it lacked the legal basis to act in such a way. As Becher explained it, the SMAD could then object because the Russians insisted upon the validity of the allied order no. 1.[185] This explanation served as the basis for the argument that the Kulturbund in Berlin had become the "object of a difference of opinion between the occupying powers" and that attempts were underway to play one occupation authority off against the other.[186]

But there was more to the Kulturbund's response. Even though the presidium's initial statement insisted that the ban gave heart to the "enemies of democracy and peace,"[187] the rhetoric remained comparatively mild for the time being. First, there were expressions of bewilderment; because the accusation that the Kulturbund was "politically one-sided" had been so convincingly refuted, what could conceivably have motivated the prohibition?[188] Apart from its references to the organization's political bias, however, the Western press also claimed that the Kulturbund's rank-and-file had lost confidence in its leadership and that a rift in the organization had developed. The Kulturbund responded that any such rift could only have occurred legitimately as a result of "internal disputes," and none existed. Any disharmony must have been caused, then, by outside interference of the kind engaged in by the Western powers.[189] This argument served to justify the very Kulturbund partisanship that had existed from the beginning. But such partisanship now acquired a different rationalization; in fact, by allowing the Kulturbund to be banned, the SMAD supplied the organization with a perfect excuse for becoming more publicly anti-Western. The logic, a derivation of two-camps thinking, was that the Western allies had altered their behavior, not the Kulturbund,[190] and the Soviet-zone press said as much a bit later; "the Kulturbund has not changed. . . . What has changed is a part of the world."[191]

[185]Becher, "Kulturbund dient dem Weltfrieden," *Tägliche Rundschau*, 31 October 1947.
[186]"Das rätselhafte Verbot," *Neues Deutschland*, 6 November 1947.
[187]Ibid.
[188]"Tatsachen gegen Polemik," *Sonntag*, 9 November 1947.
[189]See "Spiel mit offenen Karten," *Sonntag*, 16 November 1947.
[190]See "Kein Verbot des Kulturbundes," *Tägliche Rundschau*, 11 October 1947.
[191]"Klärende Sprache," *Sonntag*, 30 November 1947.

Remaining true to its original principles thus required that the organization side with the forces of peace and democracy and break with the Western allies once they started down the road to reaction; and there was nothing partisan about the decision to opt for peace rather than war. The Kulturbund was banned, wrote Abusch, not as a consequence of its affiliation with a political party but because of its *nonpartisanship*; or put somewhat differently, it had declined to participate in the "anti-Communist propaganda offensive" and was outlawed—not for being Communist, but for considering Marxism to be just as valid as Christian or liberal humanism.[192]

Still, the question of a rift within the organization was legitimate. Herbert Ihering may have meant it sincerely when he wrote about the beneficial consequences of "impassioned" disputes as a means of clarifying questions through "fruitful but creative rivalry";[193] but the writers' congress was a test that the Communists failed because certain issues were essentially prohibited; when some came up anyway, raised by Lasky for instance, it was suggested that he had "usurped the podium" and tried to turn "intellectual discourse" into a hall riot.[194] The latitude for cultural-political discussions had never been more clearly circumscribed in Soviet-occupied Germany than at this forum; and the rift within the Kulturbund widened afterwards as the margins for open discussion narrowed further. In Mecklenburg, organizational changes were made following the congress that brought the Kulturbund's branches under greater control by the statewide board (which reported directly to Berlin);[195] and at the state delegates' conference in mid-October, differences of opinion were fought out, and "battle-line votes" taken, that Karl Kleinschmidt considered proof of a "truly vigorous democracy" in the Kulturbund. Apparently, there had been something of a revolt against the politicization of the organization's activities and against efforts to politicize it further still. But those within the Mecklenburg branch of the Kulturbund known to oppose what Kleinschmidt called the "politically militant concept of culture" went down to defeat. After the votes were counted, Kleinschmidt concluded that there was no longer any room in the organization for the "apostles of political abstinence"; and the conference ended with two resolutions, one pertaining to German unity, the other related to "honest, real, and persuasive democracy." These concerns were intertwined because "Germany will only become one if it is democratic, and it will only become democratic if it is one."[196]

---

[192]Abusch, "Die unliebsame Toleranz," *Tägliche Rundschau*, 25 November 1947.
[193]Ihering, "Der mißverstandene Kulturbund," *Sonntag*, 23 November 1947.
[194]Harich, "Im Gespräch bleiben!" *Die Weltbühne* 20 (1947): 890.
[195]See Tolzien, "Organisatorischer Aufbau des Landesverbandes Mecklenburg," *Demokratische Erneuerung* 7/8 (1947): 4-7.
[196]Kleinschmidt, "Die Landes-Delgiertenkonferenz in Schwerin, am 18. und 19. Oktober 1947," *Demokratische Erneuerung* 9/10 (1947): 3-5.

After a few days of relative restraint, the Soviet-zone press then raised the pitch of its invective. American fanfares of freedom, read one commentary, were in reality the familiar tunes of nazism. Moreover, the ban showed clearly that the fight against communism was not directed at Communists at all but at "freedom-loving, democratic elements." After the experience of Hitler's antidemocratic crusades, ordinary Germans knew how to spot the face of reaction; and all intellectuals interested in democratic renewal now needed to raise their voices promptly against "such brutal, totalitarian acts of repression."[197] When the Kulturbund was evicted from its offices in the American sector of Berlin, *Neues Deutschland* listed the ejection as the last in a series of historical events. These began with the burning of the Reichstag, proceeded to the book-burnings of 10 May 1933 (along with the dissolution of cultural organizations), went on from there to Clay's announcement of a large-scale anti-Communist offensive, and culminated in the banning of the Kulturbund. Upon the Kulturbund's removal from its headquarters in the Western sector, which earlier housed the Nazi Reichskulturkammer, the building was returned to "the false gods of a propaganda offensive" that had been a speciality of the house's last owner.[198] But before moving to "a better sector," the Kulturbund held one last press conference in the old, and three of the organization's top SED officials, Gysi, Abusch, and Willmann, were there to represent it.[199] Nor can there be much doubt about the orchestration of the campaign to defend the Kulturbund. The DVV drew up plans internally to organize intellectuals prominent in cultural life in opposition to the ban, one of the major considerations being that "the entire operation avoid at all costs the impression of orchestration or planning, much less its appearance as an undertaking sponsored by the SED."[200] The party secretariat also picked Anton Ackermann for the job of editing a "resolution" protesting the ban to be presented for acceptance by the committee running the bloc of antifascist-democratic parties.[201]

Becher's, however, was the leading voice in the campaign. He authored an open letter to UNESCO and complained, though this may have been the real reason why the Kulturbund refused to reapply, that the insistence on a new license forced the organization "to choose sides between the occupation powers."[202] At a "mass demonstration" meeting under the slogan "Freedom

---

[197]"Ein Axthieb gegen die Demokratie," *Tägliche Rundschau*, 12 November 1947.

[198]"Betrachtungen vor einem Haus," *Neues Deutschland*, 12 November 1947.

[199]"Umzug in einen besseren Sektor," *Neues Deutschland*, 26 November 1947.

[200]Verlagswesen. Aktennotiz. Betrifft: Verbot des Kulturbundes im amerikanischen und englischen Sektor Berlins, 17 November 1947, gez. Bartels. Bundesarchiv, Abt. Potsdam, R-2/1130/51.

[201]Protokoll Nr. 17 (II) der Sitzung des Zentralsekretariats am 24. 11. 1947. Zentrales Parteiarchiv, IV 2/2.1/147.

[202]"Offener Brief von Johannes R. Becher an die UNESCO und den Internationalen Pen-Club," *Aufbau* 12 (1947): 373-74.

for the Kulturbund! Freedom for a United Germany," Becher then broke his habit of rhetorical temperance by charging that the Kulturbund, committed to reconciliation and nonpartisanship, interfered with those "wire-pullers whose anticommunism surpasses even Hitler's insanity." The prohibition showed who really desired a united Germany and who pretended; and Becher ended by calling upon the Kulturbund members to "make use of their democratic right" to protest the action.[203] Elsewhere, he denied angrily that he had been "schooled" in Moscow any more so than Thomas Mann had been schooled in Washington or New York and that the Kulturbund was "affiliated with a political party."[204] Those who questioned his political motivation, he charged, were too busy throwing stink bombs taken from the arsenal of Goebbels.[205] Indeed, he said, certain circles were bent upon forcing personalities upon the Kulturbund who answered to them in order to bind the organization politically and misuse it for party-political purposes; but the Kulturbund refused to grant any party the "uncontested prerogative of leadership." Finally, he could not help but conclude that the ban reflected fears in the West that a "unified German cultural movement" might become too powerful a factor in the fight for German unity and that it had been barred from a centralized organization in the Western zones by those scheming to divide Germany for that very reason.[206] The weekly *Sonntag* summed up the controversy by suggesting that the "tendency to destroy what has been created" corresponded to the principles responsible for the destruction and misery of the present day.[207] The year closed on a similar note; any attempt to set back efforts designed to create a "new foundation" constituted an act of cultural sabotage because, if the nation were torn asunder, German culture would suffer a blow from which recovery was virtually impossible.[208]

[203]"Einmütiges Bekenntnis. Massendemonstration für die Freiheit des demokratischen Kulturbundes," *Neues Deutschland*, 28 November 1947.

[204]Becher, "Unsere Arbeit geht weiter" *Sonntag*, 9 November 1947.

[205]Becher, "Nur wer sich wandelt. Antwort an den 'Sozialdemokrat,'" *Aufbau* 12 (1947): 418.

[206]See ibid., p. 420; and "Klärende Sprache," *Sonntag*, 30 November 1947.

[207]"Klärende Sprache," *Sonntag*, 30 November 1947.

[208]"Chaos oder Ordnung," *Sonntag*, 14 December 1947.

PART THREE:

IDEOLOGICAL REVERSION AND CULTURAL CONFORMITY (1948)

CHAPTER NINE

Nationalist Deviations

Upon their return to Germany in spring 1945, the Communists were confronted with the challenge of developing a programmatic justification for policies that supposedly modified the party's commitment to violent revolution and dictatorship. The new agenda embraced peaceful development that led in a more leisurely direction toward socialism and considered it "wrong," under current circumstances, to force the Soviet system upon Germany. Initially, these arguments tended to be more pragmatic than ideological; but even then, ideology ran just below the surface, and theoretical discussions never ceased entirely. They went on in the background and hinted that the abandonment of cherished principles was a doctrinally coherent rectification of errant policies of the past. Moreover, because such discussions were generally part of confessions of prior mistakes and miscalculations, the new program typically presented itself as a more "creative" way of achieving socialism than the pattern of party conduct prior to 1933 or 1935. Revisionism thus came across as the paradoxical return to a supple orthodoxy—Marxism-Leninism, in the words of Stalin, was "no dogma." Overall, this remained a daunting rhetorical challenge in light of the fact that "questions of Leninism" had always been so rigidly defined, but then the success of the party's program now was hardly the result of its rhetorical appeals anyway. Preeminence derived from what came to be called in 1948 a "socialist occupation" by the Soviet Union;[1] and once Stalin chose to abandon the hope of influencing developments in the Western regions of the country, this "socialist occupation" was primarily responsible for the far-reaching political changes that then took place in Soviet-occupied Germany.

The Solid Footing of Marxism-Leninism

After spending the first few years working out details of a programmatic validation for the democratic promises delivered in their proclamation of 13 June 1945, however, the Communists had to reverse themselves yet again

[1]See Ende, "Antisowjethetze ist Kriegshetze," *Neues Deutschland*, 22 June 1948.

and develop an explanation for the party's return to the very political objectives from which it struggled to disassociate itself prior to 1948. Because these new goals were substantially identical to the party's pre-1935 program, the rhetorical obstacles this time around were easier to overcome; the SED's retrogression required little more than reerecting much of the old ideological scaffolding, with a few added explanations to refute the suggestion that the new program in 1945 had been designed from the outset to pave the way for the reintroduction of the old. But the greatest irony is that the rationale for the renovated program in 1945—a special German road to socialism—could no longer be considered the consummate expression of Marxism-Leninism; just the opposite, that idea was said to have led to "nationalist" deviations hostile to the Soviet Union. Few of these sweeping changes occurred immediately; the process actually stretched over the entire twelve months, though it unfolded at a much more relentless clip than previous developments and had far more profound consequences. But unlike the events of 1947, definitive decisions appear to have been taken early on, at the instigation of the Russians, and there was little if any hedging thereafter. Indeed, political and ideological evidence of these decisions dates back to late 1947. The principal issues were the complete abandonment of thinking along the lines of a German road to socialism, together with the ultimate redefinition of the SED as a Marxist-Leninist party fashioned after its Soviet counterpart. These events culminated in discussions that took place during the latter part of 1948, but actually capped developments underway since fall 1947.

What makes the year interesting in doctrinal terms is the manner in which the party's rhetoricians endeavored to reconcile the public reversion to radical thinking with their makeshift interpretations of events that lay in the fairly distant past. Needless to say, the significance now attributed to these happenings had a way of changing along with the party's political swings, and the new year marked the centennial of three historical occurrences that were now given readings appropriate to the party's current transformation. Two of them, commemorations of the revolution of 1848 and the publication of the *Communist Manifesto*, took place early in the year; the lessons to be learned from the third, the November revolution of 1918 in Germany, were discussed in the fall; and in each instance the Communists redefined the importance of these events, or stressed them for the first time, to justify the hardening of policy currently underway. For example, from 1945 to 1948 the Communists had rarely referred to the *Communist Manifesto* (though they had republished it in 1945); it contained too many references to postulates, class warfare especially, that undercut the party's democratic and national-unity rhetoric. But in 1948, it suddenly transpired that the Soviet zone was wracked by class warfare after all;[2] indeed, the notion

[2]See especially Dr. Z., "Gibt es in der sowjetischen Besatzungszone Klassenkampf?" *Neues*

served as one of the chief justifications for the demand that the SED transform itself into a "militant party," a Marxist-Leninist party of a new type, in order to counter the threat; and even though many of these discussions cropped up late in 1948, it was scarcely accidental that Alexander Dymschitz had opened the new year with an article celebrating the "specter of communism" first referred to in the manifesto one hundred years before. He used it to warn now about the appearance of a "new anti-Communist crusade."[3]

The discussions of the revolution of 1848 were no less tailored to stress points applicable to the current situation. Paradoxically, the "cause of democratizing Germany" and its "bourgeois-democratic restructuring" begun in 1848 first figured as a preamble to the KPD's disavowal of the Soviet system for Germany; whereas going forward with those changes in 1948 pointed back in the direction of what the identical phrases were earlier intended to repudiate. Completing the process of democratization or, to quote Alexander Abusch, putting the final touches on the "incomplete democratic revolution" undertaken one hundred years earlier, but halted because of its betrayal by the bourgeoisie, would lend the centennial year its true meaning. Abusch went on to explain that the failures of 1848 marked the beginning of the "nationalist degeneration" of the German bourgeoisie, which ended with Hitler. Combining his historical excursion with contemporary two-camps thinking, Abusch added that home-grown and international reactionaries now conspired to obstruct the completion of the democratic revolution of 1848 and, in the process, jeopardized Germany's national unity.[4] The subject was important enough for the SED to devote one of its evening courses for party members to a treatment of the "bourgeois revolution of 1848," and the occasion was used to liken the struggle for German unity and democratization one hundred years earlier to the conflict going on now. But unlike its role in the events of 1848, the bourgeoisie had since become irremediably reactionary, so that the task of completing the "bourgeois revolution" now devolved, oxymoronically, upon the German labor movement.[5] There was an additional attempt to establish a parallel designed to situate a discussion of German history within a proper international context, resulting in a vintage two-camps argument. Just as in 1848, the struggle for German democracy and unity was part of the broader worldwide struggle for peace and democracy, a struggle in which the Germans did not "stand alone."[6] Dymschitz rounded

Deutschland, 7 October 1948.

[3]Dymschitz, "Gedanken zum neuen Jahr," *Tägliche Rundschau*, 1 January 1948.

[4]Abusch, "Das Erinnerungsjahr der unvollendeten Revolution," *Tägliche Rundschau*, 1 January 1948.

[5]"Zum 100. Jahrestag der bürgerlichen Revolution von 1848 in Deutschland," *Sozialistische Bildungshefte* 3 (1948): 12-14.

[6]Ibid. See also "Heute Hundertjahrfeier der Revolution von 1848" and, "Zweite Tagung des

out this particular argument by discussing the Russian involvement in the European revolutions of 1848. Though Western historiographers had fabricated the "reactionary legend" that Russia herself helped strangle the democratic revolutions, the fact of the matter was that her army marched into Europe because of the "malicious intentions of a reactionary monarch," whereas the Soviet army arrived as an "army of revolution, the savior of civilization, the liberator of the peoples of Europe from the fascist yoke."[7]

By early 1948, the two-camps view of the world officialized during creation of the Cominform the preceding fall had become an inseparable part of the SED's political and ideological posture; it was discussed from every conceivable angle and projected back into the past to lend added significance to the historical meaning of the events now being discussed by the party's rhetoricians. Two-camps reasoning served as the ultimate excuse for every political and ideological reversion carried out in 1948, from the abandonment of the German road to socialism to the related demand for turning the SED (back) into a Marxist-Leninist "fighting party." These discussions repeated the main international postulates of the conference held in September 1947, whether in the evening courses devoted to the "main characteristics of the international situation after the second world war" or in further treatments published in the party press.[8] But there was one understandable difference; when the local Communists embraced the idea of "two camps," they applied it directly to Germany and to German unity, using the notion to link political developments in the Soviet zone to those in the emerging people's democracies, to couple Soviet-occupied Germany politically and ideologically to the Soviet Union, and to explain the burgeoning rift between East and West Germany as an unavoidable act of national self-defense. The resulting argument was that the battle between the two main international powers, the United States and the USSR, was being fought out between the two parts of Germany because the Soviet zone had been torn from the "claws of capitalists and large landowners."[9] This argument suggested that the East was reacting to the offensive of the Western imperialists, who struggled to block national unification because it threatened their political and economic supremacy. The cause of the problem thus lay in the West, and the SED emerged as the champion of national unity even as its policies were grounded in doctrinal thinking based on set dichotomies.

Fred Oelßner restated the international premises of two-camps thinking in another discussion. American imperialism blended its pursuit of economic expansion with unbridled anti-Soviet propaganda identical to the methods

---

Deutschen Volkskongresses," *Tägliche Rundschau*, 18 March 1948.

[7]Dymschitz, "Das Jahr 1848 und Rußland," *Tägliche Rundschau*, 18 March 1948.

[8]See "Die Grundzüge der internationalen Lage nach dem zweiten Weltkrieg," *Sozialistische Bildungshefte* 2 (1948).

[9]See ibid., p. 13.

used by the fascists in preparing for the Second World War.[10] Indeed, the idea that the American imperialists not only vied with the German fascists in their pursuit of war against the Soviet Union, but actually outdid them, became commonplace in Soviet-zone rhetoric;[11] moreover, the substitution of American imperialism for German fascism was the major component of two-camps thinking because the dichotomous view of the world, used to legitimize a radicalization of the "democratic and antiimperialist camp," required an adversary worthy of such a response. None was more deserving than fascism in its post-war manifestation as American imperialism. But applying the two-camps theory to occupied Germany raised an interesting question with both international and national implications. If imperialism was the "enemy of the peoples,"[12] there had to be room in the theory for two-camps thinking within the imperialist countries themselves. Applied to the leading imperialist nation, the United States, this meant that there must be a "powerful popular movement" there in favor of peaceful cooperation with the Soviet Union, and this notion served as the rationale behind the international peace crusades of the late forties and fifties. But a similar situation was said to exist as well in both sides of occupied Germany. The differences between the zones mirrored "the battle between the two world camps," Oelßner explained; but because this assessment verged on a declaration of civil war against West Germany, or could turn into one, the contention was attenuated with a new argument. With the help of American imperialism, said Oelßner, the old elements of German reaction were well on their way to reacquiring their preeminence in West Germany, but only by overpowering the "resistance of the popular masses."[13] Shining through Oelßner's remarks was a refurbished theory of two Germanies not unlike the Marxist-Leninist view of fascism in the thirties.

That theory had been abandoned swiftly in 1945 and replaced with the idea of collective guilt. But now, as the Communists reverted to older outlooks, they insisted that the masses in West Germany essentially echoed the SED in opposing what it called the restoration of German imperialism and plans for a new war, except that ordinary Germans in the West were intimidated and terrorized into submission.[14] Or were they? Even as the Communists spoke of mass resistance in allied-occupied Germany, a necessary part of any argument that denied democratic legitimacy to the Western zones, echoes of collective guilt were still audible in the background. Sergej Tjul-

---

[10]Oelßner, "Die Grundzüge der internationalen Lage nach dem zweiten Weltkrieg," *Neues Deutschland*, 3 February 1948.
[11]See "Offene Kriegshetze," *Tägliche Rundschau*, 19 February 1948.
[12]Ibid.
[13]See note 10.
[14]See Tjulpanov, "Die Demokratie in Deutschland wird siegen," *Tägliche Rundschau*, 1 May 1948.

panov said that the Western imperialists undertook to make German reactionary circles even more pliable than they had been under Hitler and incited these "fascist elements" against the Soviet Union, turning Germans into "mercenaries of American imperialism against the forces of democracy." But Tjulpanov added that such nefariousness was incapable of stopping the "movement of the German people" favoring national unity in a struggle against the "agents of Anglo-American imperialism." Indeed, this was the basis for a "German national resistance movement" against Anglo-American reaction, and the German people had begun to understand that the struggle for national unity represented the only road to independence.[15] Whether or not anyone was persuaded by the argument, Tjulpanov hit upon the rhetorical solution for turning the two-camps theory, which coupled not only the Eastern-European popular democracies to the Soviet Union, but did likewise with Soviet-occupied Germany, into a policy that championed the independence of countries under threat of "colonization" by American imperialism. Lex Ende also tried balancing the concepts of popular resistance in the Western zones with evocations of collective guilt. With the support of the "socialist occupation regime," the old face of Germany had been thoroughly changed in the East; whereas the Western zones, under "imperialist occupation" and just like the Papen era that paved the way for Hitler's accession to power, were again "on the way to the crassest class dictatorship of monopoly capital." Among ordinary Germans in allied-occupied zones, he went on, no one wanted a new war; but there was nonetheless a residual tendency toward the old thinking of the Hitler years, and it was time for the masses, including the Social-Democratic rank-and-file, to take an unjaundiced look at the situation in East and West. After all, he said, "the light shines from the East!"[16]

The brighter that that light shown, the more complex the arguments necessary to reconcile past assurances of "no sovietization" with the incorporation of popular democracies and Soviet-occupied Germany into a camp controlled by a country that took pride in its nature as a dictatorship. Not that the next step of renouncing the "German road to socialism" altogether was promptly taken; official repudiation was delayed until fall and occurred in the broader context of Stalin's break with Tito; and even if Tjulpanov is said to have forecast the abandonment of the idea a year before,[17] sporadic efforts were still made to defend it in early 1948.[18] Even then, however, an idea originally designed to lessen fears of a new dictatorship and to reconcile the single-minded pursuit of socialism in one zone with a commitment to national unity was obviously being tailored to two-camps thinking. The question

[15]Ibid.

[16]Ende, "Aus dem Osten kommt das Licht," *Neues Deutschland*, 1 May 1948.

[17]According to Mischa Wolf. See Leonhard, *Die Revolution entläßt ihre Kinder*, p. 399.

[18]See Stößel, *Positionen und Strömungen in der KPD/SED 1945-1954*, pp. 302-3.

was not whether the Soviet zone, feigning democracy, had been changed "socially, economically, and culturally" in a way that complicated reunification, but rather that the "independent German road" to reconstruction renounced the "American path" of restoration.[19] Still, a commitment to policies characterized as "independent" because they differed from "American" solutions fell short of a reaffirmation of the disavowal of the Soviet system for Germany; quite the contrary, in the context of two-camps thinking, any disavowal of "American" or allied approaches to the German problem was synonymous with an endorsement of the Soviet position in *all* matters pertaining to Germany's future as a nation and, in effect, incompatible with any specifically "German" road to socialism. Any such endorsement was thus part and parcel of an acceptance of Soviet political and ideological practices in German or Soviet-zone affairs—"socially, economically, and culturally."

In April 1948, the SED sponsored its last organized discussion in support of the German road to socialism.[20] By now, the signs of "transitional" rhetoric in what had, in a different sense of the word, always been a debate over *transitions* to socialism and, equivalently, proletarian dictatorship were unmistakable. There was an increased emphasis on the possibility that the manner in which the "working class" took over power might just as well be violent as democratic, and Tjulpanov himself soon stressed that all transitions to socialism were revolutionary. By the time the SED finished its own "transition" to a new theory of transition, then, or rather back to the old axioms of Marxism-Leninism, the party's doctrinal position exhibited all the features of a commitment to "sovietization" by force—just what the KPD forswore in summer 1945. The dialectical synthesis was then consummated in an array of arguments that assailed the earlier contrast between the "special *democratic* road" and what was now called the "only possible revolutionary road to socialism" because all such views rested on the "undialectical distinction between democracy and dictatorship." There was nothing "more democratic than the revolutionary action of the popular masses"; the "revolutionary road to socialism is the democratic road, and the dictatorship of the proletariat, the essence of the revolutionary road, signifies at the same time a higher form of democracy"—as Lenin argued, "a million times more democratic than any bourgeois dictatorship."[21] This kind of assessment, published by Fred Oelßner in late 1948, makes it easier to detect the "transitional" nature of rhetoric earlier in the year because these were the positions toward which all treatments of the subject were moving. In the April discussion referred to above, the possibility of a "democratic road to socialism" was still considered worthy of mention;[22] but that possibility, as Ackermann had ex-

---

[19]Schwab, "Der deutsche Weg und seine Gegner," *Neues Deutschland*, 2 February 1948.
[20]See "Die Staatslehre des Marxismus-Leninismus," *Sozialistische Bildungshefte* 4 (1948).
[21]Oelßner, *Der Marxismus der Gegenwart und ihre Kritiker*, p. 180.
[22]"Die Staatslehre des Marxismus-Leninismus," *Sozialistische Bildungshefte* 4 (1948): 13. Ad-

plained in his article two years earlier, depended upon whether the "reactionary state bureaucracy" could be broken first. This caveat had always represented a form of rhetorical blackmail that promised violence in the event of resistance to what could already be seen as a violent act itself—doing away with the remnants of past "bourgeois-democratic" republics that amounted to no more than the "classical form of rule by capitalism" anyway (6). In other words, however sensible it may have sounded to talk in Germany of eradicating the "state apparatus" a few short years after the war's end, the Communists never outgrew the concept of an "open terroristic dictatorship of monopoly capital" (9); crushing the "reactionary state apparatus" thus connoted something more radical than dismantling the political and governmental infrastructure of prostrate nazism.

But this line of reasoning produced the following doctrinal conclusion: whatever the form of transition, violent or nonviolent, "breaking the old state apparatus and establishing the political rule of the working class (dictatorship of the proletariat)" remained the prerequisite to construction of a societal order (10). Now, because a number of "democracies of a new kind" had emerged in Eastern Europe as a consequence of the antifascist struggle of liberation, the "*old state apparatus*" in those countries had been destroyed, proving that it was indeed possible to travel a democratic road to socialism. Even so, the argument ran, no one ought to confuse this "special road to socialism" with the idea of "peaceful growth into socialism" because, under the best of conditions, the transition took place within the context of embittered class warfare. Still, the same possibilities for a "democratic road to socialism" existed in Germany, for in the Soviet zone the fascist state apparatus had also been destroyed and political-economic measures taken to ensure the preconditions of a democratic development. Moreover, this road was just as distinct a possibility in all of Germany, provided that a similar development unfolded in the Western zones (12-14). This discussion nonetheless stopped short of characterizing the transition to socialism as "revolutionary"; in spring 1948, the reemergence of the notion of class warfare functioned as a transitional euphemism instead; and being as yet unwilling to speak of the "only possible revolutionary road to socialism," it was not possible either for the Communists to call proletarian dictatorship the essence of the revolutionary *road*, as opposed to what Ackermann had considered its final destination.

Thus, none of these remarks altered the substance of Ackermann's original article, published in February 1946, though the shifts in emphasis were certainly significant. Ackermann had not gone on to say, for instance, as the April discussion did, that the "'dictatorship of the proletariat' is the supreme form of democracy"; nor had he talked about the implications of Soviet his-

ditional citations from this brochure are provided in the text.

tory, much less noted that "*in the Soviet Union the state will continue to exist as long as the capitalist world around it exists*" (12-13)—an apparent off-hand remark that could nonetheless be taken as an indirect rationale for the consolidation of a separate German socialist state to counterbalance the threat posed by its capitalist correlate in the West. Not surprisingly, then, promises of peaceful and democratic transitions such as this last convoluted discussion dispelled few of the fears of a new dictatorship, and the concerns intensified as the Communist or unity parties throughout Eastern Europe reverted to far more radical policies and radical actions. It may have been hoped that the reference to proletarian dictatorship as the "supreme form of democracy" would soften the impact of the preceding mention of violent monopoly-capitalist class dictatorship—a shrill characterization that had itself been meant to suggest the necessity of a stern dictatorial response. But the fact remains that the SED was getting used to defending the merits of one kind of dictatorship as the only means of confronting the implied dangers of another.

Within a few months, Walter Ulbricht said as much in a speech that explained the reasons behind a new two-year "economic plan" for Soviet-occupied Germany. Bourgeois states were bourgeois dictatorships, he said, whereas "our democracy is a higher form of democracy; it uses force in the interest of the majority against the minority." True, Ulbricht shied away from using the word "dictatorship," but the substance of his remarks was tantamount to the same thing. Reconstruction and the consolidation of democracy unfolded in Soviet-occupied Germany within the context of intensified class warfare and a growing struggle with "dispossessed fascist big capitalists and elements who want to restore monopolistic or formal-democratic conditions." The state existed to "repress these forces."[23] Still, the Communists preferred to avoid the word "dictatorship," at least in public and until the end of the year; and they usually did it through careful definitions of popular democracy that managed to dodge the concept even as the new rhetoric was rife with references to sharpening class warfare. The abandonment of the German road to socialism and its replacement with a theory of revolution, radicalization of the Unity party, and tacit concurrence with the need for dictatorship—these were all adumbrated in a programmatic article written by Tjulpanov, published in May, that may actually have caught the local Communists off guard. In late March 1948, Pieck and Grotewohl traveled to Moscow to report on a variety of developments. During discussions with Mikojan, Merkulos, Suslov, and Semjonov, Pieck complained of the vilification to which the SED was subjected back home and acknowledged that certain accusations, such as the party's ostensible "totalitarian aspirations"

---

[23]Ulbricht, "Die gegenwärtigen Aufgaben der demokratischen Verwaltung [23-24 July 1948]," *Lehrbuch für den demokratischen Staats- und Wirtschaftsaufbau*, pp. 24-25 and 41.

and putative nature as a "Russ.[ian] state party," hampered its activities.[24] But the Germans did not meet with Stalin, and nothing in Pieck's notes suggests that he and Grotewohl left Moscow having been told to anticipate major changes. Tjulpanov's article, however, published a few weeks later, ushered in a qualitatively new period of development in which the SED's ideological and organizational transformation into a "new type of party" coincided with the assumption of what it soon called practical "state" responsibilities associated with the implementation of the two-year plan. Published in the May issue of *Neue Welt* under the pseudonym E. Perling, Tjulpanov delivered his speech first before an audience at the SED's school of advanced study (and perhaps elsewhere as well).[25] Though his remarks concentrated on the popular democracies, Tjulpanov made it clear that these lessons applied to Germany as well and that the possibility existed for the entire nation to take the same popular-democratic route.[26]

That route, however, originally defined more as non-revolutionary, non-violent transformation representing roads to socialism different from the one taken by the USSR, now turned out to be revolutionary after all; but these were nonetheless "revolutions of national popular democracy." Tjulpanov simply meant to imply that, revolutionary or not, these roads still derived from the national needs of each country and were no threat to national independence. Tjulpanov then began making narrow distinctions designed to convey the sense that the *shared* characteristics of "national roads to socialism" were nothing to worry about and certainly not suggestive of Soviet domination of the region. He went to considerable lengths to reconcile suggestions that there would not be major national peculiarities in the Eastern European road to socialism, either between the individual nations or with the Soviet Union, with non-interference in the affairs of countries occupied by the Red Army. The revolutions remained democratic, he said, because their job had been to "liquidate the open terroristic dictatorship of the reactionaries, the chauvinistic elements of finance capital, and to reestablish fundamental democratic rights"—just not on the basis of bourgeois democracy (45). In fact, he added, these revolutions would evolve automatically into a "socialist revolution" if left to their own devices. True, Tjulpanov conceded, they differed in some ways from the Russian revolution, but mostly only in the sense that class warfare began during the struggle against fascism; whereas normally the revolutionary process started with a popular uprising against intolerable conditions that toppled the government and set up "the dictatorship of the victorious class" (47).

---

[24]Interner Bericht Wilhelm Piecks in Moskau am 26. 3. 1948. Zentrales Parteiarchiv, NL 36/695/2-19.
[25]See Leonhard, *Die Revolution entläßt ihre Kinder*, pp. 396-400.
[26]Perling, "Die Entstehung der Volksdemokratie," *Neue Welt* 9 (1948): 40. Further references are supplied in the text.

In the popular democracies, the revolutionary struggle took the form of a "national liberation movement" against fascism, a revolt designed to expel the intruders, not an insurrection provoked internally by repressive local governments. Nevertheless, the task of defeating the enemy still went hand in hand with the battle against "national quislings, against national imperialist cliques, and against internal counterrevolution." Tjulpanov argued that these national democratic revolutions occurred because the job of smashing fascism had been done by "an external force," the Red Army; the popular masses then took it from there (48). The Soviet Union had not brought popular democracy to these countries on the tip of a bayonet, and the USSR did not interfere. Indeed, if the USSR had not provided these countries with considerable moral, organizational, political, diplomatic, and material assistance on their road to popular democracy, the masses, as Tjulpanov called them, would have been compelled *"to apply much harsher forms and methods in the struggle for the establishment of rule by the people."* But the point remained that the popular democracies were well on their way to socialist revolution, proving the truth of Marxism-Leninism that the transition from capitalism to socialism occurred through revolution. Peaceful growth into socialism was an illusion, and Bulgarian, Yugoslavian, Polish, Hungarian, or Czech roads to socialism did not exist (50).

Though the implications for Soviet-occupied Germany were clear, Tjulpanov said nothing at all about the SED. In private, he was more prolix, talking for a solid six hours, often extemporaneously,[27] and some of what went beyond the version later published can be pieced together using two manuscripts based on the same speech. In addition, there exist two sets of notes taken by Anton Ackermann in response to Tjulpanov's remarks; these notes focused upon utterances pertaining to Soviet-occupied Germany that Tjulpanov never committed to paper. The first manuscript, dated 21 April 1948, is revealing because it addressed the question of dictatorship. Though he claimed at the beginning of his speech that his remarks did not represent "in all questions the official opinion of [your] Soviet friends and the Soviet Union," Tjulpanov would never have dared to speak off the cuff about a matter of such importance; in all likelihood, the disclaimer was intended to convey the message that his distinctions were still not ready for public dissemination. Nor is it difficult to see why; Tjulpanov took issue with the official assumption in the popular-democratic countries that socialism there would be attained "without the establishment of Soviet power and without the dictatorship of the proletariat." This was now an incendiary issue, both for those countries and for Soviet-occupied Germany. Though "comrades" like Dimitrov in Bulgaria and Gomulka in Poland had defined popular democracy in terms of a disavowal of dictatorship, Tjulpanov now dissented. There had

[27]See Leonhard, *Die Revolution entläßt ihre Kinder*, p. 398.

never been nor ever would be a state without a dictatorship, he said; Yugoslavia and Bulgaria had one already, whereas Czechoslovakia, Poland, Romania, and Hungary were characterized by a "democratic dictatorship of the working class and peasants" that would "sooner or later change into a dictatorship of the proletariat." Tjulpanov went on to explain how. The difference between the popular-democratic and Soviet dictatorships consisted of the fact that the former was exercised by way of a "bloc government" comprised of multiple parties—a circumstance that could not endure. True, the bourgeoisie was capable of wielding dictatorship through coalition government, but the dictatorship of the proletariat could not. In the end, "bourgeois parties" would have to be eliminated and the bourgeoisie "liquidated" as a class. At the moment, three classes existed in the popular democratic countries, the working class, the peasants, and the bourgeoisie; and there were from three to five political parties. But their fate was sealed:

> Will these parties continue to exist in the future? No. Further historical development will unfold by way of the consolidation of democratic forces, by way of the unification of the parties. . . . Many variations may appear in the process, but in the final analysis there will only be one party. For countries like Yugoslavia and Bulgaria, this is no longer an issue, and in other countries it is on the agenda. This is how the question of the dictatorship of the proletariat will be solved.[28]

The second of Tjulpanov's manuscripts contains additional thoughts about Soviet-occupied Germany in connection with the above elaborations. Most importantly, Tjulpanov concluded that the Eastern zone was developing after the fashion of the popular democracies; the bourgeois parties remained relatively strong and had yet to be discredited in the eyes of the people. But all necessary preconditions for the consolidation of the positions of the working class existed in Soviet-occupied Germany. As for the division of the country, Tjulpanov insisted that it could not last because the German people would not stand for it or the "colonization" of West Germany. Nonetheless, a period of struggle for national unity lay in store, and the mightiest force in the battle would be the Eastern zone. Either the bourgeoisie would follow the working class in that struggle or its own "antinational politics" would leave it discredited in the eyes of ordinary Germans. Even so, Tjulpanov advised against proceeding with the "exclusion" of the bourgeois parties; because of their lingering influence, doing so might provoke the wrong reaction, and it was better to offer them a platform for cooperation that they could reject only at the risk of losing the confidence of the people.[29]

[28]Die Volksdemokratie, 21 April 1948. Zentrales Parteiarchiv, NL 109/20/114-53.
[29]Die Volksdemokratie, undated, ibid., NL 109/22/107-38.

Judging by Ackermann's notes, Tjulpanov must have gone into further detail in discussing the nature of Soviet-occupied Germany and the "essence of soc.[ialist] occ.[upation] policies." In line with his plans to eliminate parties in popular-democratic countries through the consolidation of "democratic elements," Tjulpanov apparently pointed out that, the more antifascist forces came together, "the more they exercise a dictatorship"; and that circumstances would then change into the "rule of the working class." In fact, Tjulpanov seems to have made the point that developments in Soviet-occupied Germany were actually more peaceful than in the popular democracies due precisely to the presence of the SMAD, though the "revol.[utionary] influence of the working cl.[ass]" was correspondingly less developed because the situation came as a "gift." Tjulpanov then went on to characterize Soviet-occupied Germany as a "unique form of antifascist popular democracy," concluding that the "inner regularity of the popular democracies" distinguished the Eastern zone as well; evidently likened the functions of German administrative and quasi-governmental agencies to the offices or divisions of the SMAD, which he seems to have compared further with "the beginnings of proletarian dictatorship" in the Soviet Union; and indicated that reconstruction progressed automatically toward socialism. Indeed, in a very specific sense, he said, a revolution had actually occurred. In Soviet-occupied Germany there existed a "specific form of a transitional period to socialism" that, admittedly, enjoyed the support of a mere minority. Nonetheless, development toward socialism was "guaranteed today by the SMAD," and Ackermann's notes suggest that Tjulpanov had no intention of allowing considerations related to the "rest of Germany" to lead to an "abandonment of rapid progress toward socialism." He said that backing away from a consolidation of the position of the working class out of deference to bourgeois notions of national unity constituted "class betrayal."[30] The other set of Ackermann's notes indicates similarly that Tjulpanov talked at length about the nature of developments in Soviet-occupied Germany. He apparently called the popular democracies "new organs of power, a form of Soviets," which prompted Ackermann to jot down the question, "What do we have?" In response, he, Ackermann, listed various agencies of German administration, concluding that these were only the "beginning" before penciling in additional fragments of definitions, concepts, and understandings. Though Ackermann apparently spotted some of the contradictions in Tjulpanov's characterizations of popular democracy, he marked at least one as being synonymous with "the dictatorship of the proletariat"; and there was no doubt about the preeminence of the "working class" in the advance toward socialism. Ackermann's notes ended with this telling conclusion:

[30]Archival notation: "April 1948. Vortrag vom (S. Tulpanov), SMAD. Hs. Notizen A.A. dazu," ibid., NL 109/20/100-12.

dictatorship + pol. power of the working cl.[ass]
(Stalin)[31]

These remarks show Stalin's policies toward Soviet-occupied Germany evolving rapidly toward the establishment of a local dictatorship completely unencumbered by concern over prospects for national unity; and the German Communists clearly understood the message. The transformation of the SED into a "party of a new type" was the key, and Tjulpanov had opinions on that subject, too. In early May, he evidently delivered another important speech that focused on the need for a "drastic improvement in the quality of the party's organizational and ideological work"; and he discussed those matters in connection with what he called changes in the political and, "one could also say, state situation" in Soviet-occupied Germany. Germany was, in effect, divided; and Soviet-zone development unfolded now according to the manner of the "new democracies." Tjulpanov further indicated that the role of the party as the "decisive power in the zone," ready to do battle to "conquer all of Germany," dictated its organizational consolidation, which he defined by emphasizing the necessity of reconciling its nature as a mass party with a far greater degree of internal discipline. He spoke especially of the requirement for what he called an "unbending, disciplined party *aktiv*," utterly submissive to the party; and these considerations all evolved out of the SED's "ruling state position." Tjulpanov went on to discuss a range of organizational problems, one of which was caused by disturbing numbers of resignations from the party; and he had much to say about theoretical or ideological insufficiencies as well. He complained, for instance, about reactionary activities that had a seditious effect upon the party internally, such as "every conceivable kind of eccentricity in art"; but also assailed tendencies within the party to contrast democracy with the dictatorship of the proletariat and insisted upon the understanding that the "center of world reaction" had shifted from Hitler Germany to the United States.[32]

At a meeting of the SED's board four days later, Max Fechner repeated Tjulpanov's calls for an examination of the party "in ideological and organizational terms"; and Pieck echoed more of his rhetoric. Much like Tjulpanov, Pieck called for an "unbending party *aktiv*, conscious of its responsibilities" and unfailingly reliable. But he also spoke in extraordinary terms of a "strategic change in our struggle" that developed out of shifts in Germany's "political and state situation." He charged that formation of a Western state would split Germany into two parts, each of which developed in different directions set by their own dynamic. Whereas the Western zones suf-

---

[31]Ibid., NL 109/22/139-48.
[32]Written in hand: "8/5 48 Tülpanow," ibid., NL 36/735/54-79.

fered under a permanent "military dictatorship," Soviet-occupied Germany
would evolve as "an independent state entity" whose economy, administration, and political life were permeated by "democratic principles." The division of Germany, Pieck explained, opened up local "perspectives" that necessitated a change in the party's strategy; the SED, the party of workers,
peasants, and progressive intellectuals, was poised to take over full responsibility for the "development of the political, economic, and cultural situation"; and it was now apparent that the SED would actually accede to power,
assuming a "ruling position in the state." There then followed something
akin to a restatement of the fundamental contradiction embedded in Stalin's
earliest postwar prognosis: "The SED must wage the battle for all of Germany and, in the process, work toward the necessity of developing democracy
and realizing socialism." Nonetheless, the party's position in Soviet-occupied Germany did not qualify as "exclusive rule"; other parties existed as
well, though by expanding its influence over the working population, the
SED could manage to compel the others to "support our policies."[33] Further
echoes of Tjulpanov's admonitions resonate throughout Pieck's remarks, but
the above suffice to suggest that critical decisions had just been made about
the separate "political, economic, and cultural" development of Soviet-occupied Germany and imparted to the local Communists.

Practical measures followed. In late June, the party announced a formal
economic policy that endorsed the separate development of the zone, quick-
ening its pace; and the success of this so-called two-year plan for Soviet-occupied Germany was said to hinge upon a major transformation of the SED
that reflected Tjulpanov's call for an acceleration of its organizational and
ideological consolidation. Radicalization was necessary, the official argument ran, because of a combination of threats posed by Western imperialism
and by nationalist deviations within the camp of democracy—Tito had broken with Stalin. Ironically, though Pieck referred generally to economic
planning at the party's board meeting in mid-May, and to the SED's corresponding obligations, the SMAD may have drawn up the two-year plan
largely on its own. In fact, it is conceivable that party leaders knew nothing
about it concretely until Semjonov mentioned the plan privately on 5 June
1948.[34] Evidently, the actual document was then discussed for the first time
at extended meetings of the party secretariat on 10 and 12 June before being
presented formally at the next executive board meeting on 29 and 30 June
1948 as, using Semjonov's characterization, the "party's plan." The discussion on 12 June, a rare stenographic record of which was kept, is especially
important because of utterances that reveal the connection with Tjulpanov's
heavy emphasis upon the SED as a "state party"; but also because of the lin-

[33]Stenographische Niederschrift über die 10. (24.) Tagung des Parteivorstandes der SED . . . am 12. und 13. Mai 1948, ibid., IV 2/1/23/4, 61-62.
[34]Besprechung bei Semjonow - 5. 6. 1948 - 1 Uhr, ibid., NL 36/735/101.

gering sensitivity toward unclarified questions about the nature of democracy in Soviet-occupied Germany.

A dispute quickly broke out over a complaint voiced by one member of the secretariat, August Karstens, that the "occupation regime" continued to interfere in the economy. Karstens wondered whether the SED existed merely to serve as the "recipient of documents." Ulbricht rushed to the defense of the SMAD and pointed out that the plan reflected the party's own economic aims and political aspirations; in particular, the rank and file now needed to grasp the fact that "we are the responsible state party without our saying so openly in quite this way." The higher the quality of work done by German administrative agencies, and the more cognizant they were of their responsibility, "the less the occupation power has to exercise control." In any case, "the plan is going to be implemented," and attitudes exhibited toward it would reveal "who is an honest democrat and who is not." After all, he went on to say, "we are not demanding socialism," to which Helmut Lehmann responded, "nor dictatorship." Ulbricht concurred; "we have yet to achieve the rule of the working class in the Eastern zone, as they have in the popular democracies, and those are a form of the dictatorship of the proletariat." Soviet-occupied Germany was not a popular democracy "yet," said Ulbricht, though he felt "personally" that things would evolve further. In any case, "our goal is socialism," whether or not some mistakenly believed that the final objective was "what we have achieved already."

Grotewohl, too, objected to Karsten's characterization of the SED as a recipient of Russian documents; the plan, as Pieck quickly interjected, had been given to the party so that it could be discussed. But it was understood by all that the economic objectives obliged the party to divert its attention away from "purely organizational endeavors and purely ideological discussions, which proved themselves magnificently during the last few years in the matter of unity, to a stage of implementing practical economic policy in our zone." Doing so promised tremendous advantages, said Pieck, but these depended upon "an ideological and political realignment based on an orientation toward the East." There was no other road to prosperity, and that fact had to be communicated to those who sewed the seeds of mistrust about the Soviet Union. "We can no longer expect anything from the West."[35] Roughly two weeks later, Ulbricht presented the plan at the party's board meeting by blaming the need for such measures on a shift in allied aims in West Germany.[36] In other words, the SED's open endorsement of a planned economy was neither unilateral nor nationally divisive, but reactive. Indeed, lest the

[35]Protokoll Nr. 83 (II) der Sitzung des Zentralsekretariats am 10. 6. 1948. Stenographische Niederschrift über die Beratung des Wirtschaftsplanes 1949/50 im Zentralsekretariat am . . . 12. Juni 1948, ibid., IV 2/2.1/206/26-37, 55-57.
[36]Ulbricht, "Planmäßige Wirtschaft sichert die Zukunft des deutschen Volkes," *Der deutsche Zweijahrplan für 1949-1950*, p. 12.

Communists be accused of embarking first upon policies conducive to a split with the Western zones, the two-year plan began by referring to acts of division committed in connection with the Marshall Plan, which "robs us of the opportunity to acquire our own national German government and a peace treaty for Germany." Far from acting rashly, the SED responded to Western imperialism by announcing its intention of proceeding with peaceful reconstruction free of "slavish dependence on foreign capital."[37]

The "leading democratic force in our country," Ulbricht pointed out, the SED, had been constrained to grasp the initiative and provide a "*dynamic example for the whole of Germany.*"[38] The battle to implement the plan was hence tantamount to a struggle between the forces of progress against reaction—"for democracy, peace, and socialism"; and because it was now freely acknowledged that there was no such thing as "*nonviolent growth into socialism,*" creation of a democratic order signaled not a lessening of class warfare but its intensification. Additionally, waging "conscious, planned class warfare under current conditions and aimed at attaining the socialist ultimate objective" required implementation of the key provisions of the plan as the only means of winning "*final victory over the class enemy.*"[39] Thus, said Ulbricht, the SED could only fulfill the two-year plan and meet future obligations if it took the steps necessary to transform itself into a party of a new type, a fighting party for democracy and for socialism.[40] A few days later, the SED added that the mistakes of the Yugoslav Communist party illustrated the danger of departing the "solid footing of Marxism-Leninism," turning a blind eye to the "intensification of class warfare," and giving up its "fraternal association with the socialist Soviet Union and the party of Lenin and Stalin." The lesson in dialectics was clear; the SED must be turned into a party rooted in Marxism-Leninism, a party of a new type.[41]

Stalinist Occupation Policies

But the problem remained that "the party of Lenin and Stalin" was an acknowledged dictatorship that by definition brooked no rival organization,[42]

[37]"Der Zweijahrplan für 1949/50," *Dokumente der Sozialistischen Einheitspartei Deutschlands* [30 June 1948], vol. II, p. 22.

[38]Ulbricht, "Planmäßige Wirtschaft sichert die Zukunft des deutschen Volkes," p. 7; and "Der Kampf um die Erfüllung des Planes für das zweite Halbjahr 1948 und des Zweijahrplanes 1949/50," *Sozialistische Bildungshefte* 8 (1948): 5.

[39]"Der Kampf um die Erfüllung des Planes für das zweite Halbjahr 1948 und des Zweijahrplanes 1949/50," pp. 22-24.

[40]Ulbricht, "Planmäßige Wirtschaft sichert die Zukunft des deutschen Volkes," pp. 36-37.

[41]"Zur jugoslawischen Frage [3 July 1948]," *Dokumente der Sozialistischen Einheitspartei*, vol. II, p. 81.

[42]The thorny issue of single-party systems had also resurfaced in the SED's theoretical monthly

and the Communists were now on the verge of insisting that the SED must emulate the Soviet party, as "master and guide,"[43] while still denying that it had dictatorial aspirations of its own. Nevertheless, hints of such aspirations cropped up in all redefinitions of the SED. One of the first Stalinist features to appear was an abstract idea with both international and national implications. This was the self-fulfilling prophecy that the "class enemy," whether in the form of international reaction or through "agents" operating within Soviet-occupied Germany, responded to democratic policies with fiercer resistance. Resorting to this argument, the Communists resurrected the paradox of the thirties that class warfare in the Soviet Union intensified as the country approached socialism. This argument replaced the notion that the state withered away with Stalin's ideological rationale for the terror of the thirties. Internationally, the notion of capitalist encirclement sustained the idea, whereas domestically it produced the mentality that supported the call for class vigilance against external and internal enemies of the people.

A comparable atmosphere was settling over Soviet-occupied Germany, along with calls for "greater class vigilance,"[44] though the notion squared poorly with the idea that the East merely reacted to changes in Western foreign policy. In spite of the public suggestion that the SED and its new two-year plan responded to menacing gestures in the West, the Communists also advanced arguments predicated on the contrary. Ulbricht noted that the announcement of economic planning designed to fortify democracy brought with it a sharpening of class warfare, not its lessening, because the "defeated forces of the enemy" then resorted to much stronger means in battling the new order;[45] and a later SED resolution mandating meticulous study of the short-course history of the Soviet Communist party likewise adjusted the idea that the SED reacted to menacing changes in Western foreign policy, if not reversing it completely.[46] True, neither concept wholly excluded the other; the dialectical synthesis of which the party's rhetoricians were always capable remained possible; but advanced singly in different contexts, each

---

(Abramenkov, "Warum gibt es in der UdSSR nur eine einzige politische Partei," *Einheit* 12 [1948]: 1162), paradoxically even as the SED choreographed the creation of two new political parties run clandestinely by the Communists. The National-Demokratische Partei (NDP) was formed on 21 April and licensed by the SMAD on 16 June 1948; the Demokratische Bauernpartei (DBD) came into being a week later, on 29 April, but was also licensed on 16 June 1948.

[43]"Lehrmeister und Wegweiser [6 November 1948]," *Dokumente der Sozialistischen Einheitspartei Deutschlands*, vol. II, p. 152.

[44]See "Der Kampf um die Erfüllung des Planes für das zweite Halbjahr 1948 and des Zweijahrplanes 1949/1950," *Sozialistische Bildungshefte* 8 (1948): 22.

[45]Ulbricht, "Die gegenwärtigen Aufgaben der demokratischen Verwaltung [23. und 24. Juli 1948]," *Die Entwicklung des deutschen volksdemokratischen Staates*, pp. 127-28.

[46]See "Über die Verstärkung des Studiums der 'Geschichte der Kommunistischen Partei der Sowjetunion (Bolschewiki)—Kurzer Lehrgang [20 September 1948],'" *Dokumente der Sozialistischen Einheitspartei Deutschlands*, vol. II, p. 128.

argument promised different benefits. Besides, privately the Communists knew exactly who started the latest round of escalation. Ulbricht admitted behind closed doors that, "when we say that the enemy intensified class warfare, we obviously intensified it as well with the two-year plan." But in public, the party chose to hold the enemy responsible and used the opportunity to acquaint workers and peasants with the "methods of sharpened class warfare." Once their class consciousness had improved, "then we will decide what to do next."[47] Either way, the official conclusion remained that transforming the SED into a party of a new type was imperative; and this transformation was impossible in the absence of intense study of the history of the German and the international labor movement. Discussions of both objectives revolved around the November revolution of 1918, whose thirtieth anniversary was approaching, the importance of the experience of the Soviet Communist party, and its lessons for the SED.[48]

These ideas, along with their practical consequences, were all based on the assumption of class warfare. Prior to 1948, the idea of a nonviolent, nonrevolutionary transition to socialism and the rejection of the Soviet system had glossed over this old postulate, though it persisted in the shape of diluted concepts like progress and reaction and always promised a forceful, even bloody response to what was surely expected to be forceful opposition. But the specific concept of class warfare emerged with renewed vigor; and the careful wording of such earlier documents as the SED's "principles and goals," first published in April 1946, now paid off because the discussions only needed to quote from them to prove that the new policies were no deviation from earlier assurances. The key passage lifted from the SED's statement of principles was that it wished to travel the "democratic road to socialism" but would resort to "revolutionary means" if the capitalists failed to behave like democrats.[49] Not unexpectedly, the "capitalists" behaved true to nature; and in international or interzonal terms, the SED quickly contended that opposition to local democracy occurred in the form of agents sent in from or hired by the outside, with the idea of West Berlin serving as a spy and saboteur center against the East following along with the blockade of the city's Western sectors.[50] In the SED's own internal politics, these assumptions merged with renewed calls for changing it into a party of a new type. The SED needed to be purged of "hostile and degenerate elements,"[51]

[47]Zentrales Parteiarchiv, IV 2/1/100/8. Quoted from Staritz, "Die SED, Stalin und der 'Aufbau des Sozialismus' in der DDR," *Deutschland Archiv* 7 (1991): 691.

[48]See the articles published on 1 October 1948 in the *Tägliche Rundschau*.

[49]"Gibt es in der sowjetischen Besatzungszone Klassenkampf?" *Neues Deutschland*, 7 October 1948.

[50]See "Die theoretische und praktische Bedeutung der Entschließung des Informationsbüros über die Lage in der KPD Jugoslawiens und die Lehren für die SED [16 September 1948], *Dokumente der Sozialistischen Einheitspartei Deutschlands,* vol. II, p. 102.

[51]See "Für die organisatorische Festigung der Partei und für ihre Säuberung von feindlichen und

most of whom happened to be former members of the SPD.[52]

The Yugoslav situation also entered into these discussions. The latest pronouncement on that subject now combined the disparate elements—the dangers of antisovietism within parties professing to be Marxist-Leninist, the related threat of "nationalist" or anti-Soviet deviations galvanized by "enemy ideologies" and "false theories" (principally the "'special German road' to socialism"), the intensification of class warfare in the popular-democratic countries as well as in Soviet-occupied Germany, the necessity of studying questions related to "classes and class warfare in the period of transition," and the lessons to be learned from scrutinizing the short-course history of the Soviet Communist party.[53] Equally portentous in these official party documents was one of the first devote expressions of affection for Stalin; the SED now thanked not only the Soviet Communist party, but "Comrade Stalin" as well for exposing the mistakes of the Yugoslav party and coming to the aid of the working class in other countries.[54] The important lessons taught by the Germans' own November revolution of 1918 were imparted in a resolution passed the same day—the uprising of 1918 remained an unfinished bourgeois revolution due to the absence of a revolutionary working-class party and to the counterrevolutionary role of the right-wing leaders of Social Democracy.[55] The first point differed little from Pieck's pronouncements two years earlier, except that in 1946 discretion still dictated that he temper his recriminations.[56] The adjustment lay in Pieck's earlier definition of the party. Every effort to direct the revolution of 1918 toward a socialist outcome had been confounded, said Pieck in 1946, because the German proletariat lacked a "united, revolutionary, Marxist, mass party," whereas, in the SED's November resolution of 1948, the discussions of a party of a new type called it a tightly organized, highly disciplined, Marxist-Leninist *cadre* party. This document insisted upon the need for "strict discipline," based on democratic centralism, as well as for inner-party criticism and self-criticism as the only means of eradicating "all hostile and pernicious elements." Still, the Communists made their usual bid to reconcile avant-garde rhetoric both

---

entarteten Elementen [29 July 1948]," ibid., p. 83.

[52]Fechner, "Die Rolle der Sozialdemokratie im Jahre 1933," *Neues Deutschland*, 5 September 1948.

[53]See "Die theoretische und praktische Bedeutung der Entschließung des Informationsbüros über die Lage in der KPD Jugoslawiens und die Lehren für die SED," pp. 100-106; and "Über die Entartung der Führung der Kommunistischen Partei Jugoslawiens," *Sozialistische Bildungshefte* 11 (1948).

[54]"Die theoretische und praktische Bedeutung der Entschließung des Informationsbüros über die Lage in der KPD Jugoslawiens und die Lehren für die SED," p. 100.

[55]See "Die Novemberrevolution und ihre Lehren für die deutsche Arbeiterbewegung [16 September 1948]," *Dokumente der Sozialistischen Einheitspartei Deutschlands*, vol. II, pp. 107-24.

[56]See Pieck, "Zwei Revolutionen—zwei Ergebnisse. Der 7. und der 9. November," *Einheit* 6 (1946): 327.

with the discourse of mass movement and, despite the eastward orientation, with further talk of the national interest.[57]

Discussions of the "new type of party" went on right up to and during the SED's party conference in January 1949; but by then, little more than extraneous detail and topical application could be added to what had already been said, for instance, by Fred Oelßner in August 1948. His points were that the doctrine of the new type of party, developed by Lenin and Stalin, was inseparable from the teaching of Marxism-Leninism; that the new type of party was the "agency" of proletarian dictatorship (though he stopped short of saying that the SED aspired to dictatorship); and that the party could only wage class warfare successfully when purged of "hostile, opportunistic, corrupt elements." As part of that process, party members had to be clear in their minds that socialism could only be achieved in alliance with the USSR because "enemies of the Soviet Union are enemies of socialism, period."[58] Now the very notion of turning the SED into a new kind of party, or a "party of a new type," implied strongly that a departure from promises made and assurances given during the process of unification in spring 1946 was imminent; and the concept likewise suggested that the SED willingly relinquished its independence by linking its affairs and policies to a doctrine developed by Lenin and Stalin. But the Communists twice denied the logic of their own reasoning. Oelßner argued against the first conclusion; he told the party to expect a repetition of the groundless assertion that, as the "Russians' party," the SED answered to Moscow;[59] and Ulbricht defended it against the second count—unification had never been meant to countenance merger of the KPD and SPD on the basis of some "middle ground." In making these remarks, Ulbricht echoed one of the twenty-five lessons listed in the SED's resolution on the November revolution: working-class unity was achieved on the basis of the "class struggle."[60] Argued like this, the events of late 1948 did not mark any kind of logical departure from the original principles of party unification; and there was nothing "new" about the new party at all. Ulbricht's remarks made it difficult to see things any other way; he insisted that the ideological foundation of the SED, and the point of the original merger, could only be the teaching of "*Marx, Engels, and Stalin.*" He then took the idea one step further when he called Stalin the "Lenin of our day," insisting that success in the struggle in Germany hinged upon mastering the teachings of both.[61]

[57]See "Die Novemberrevolution und ihre Lehren für die deutsche Arbeiterbewegung," pp. 123-24.

[58]Oelßner, "Für eine Partei neuen Typus," *Neues Deutschland*, 29 August 1948.

[59]Ibid.

[60]"Die Novemberrevolution und ihre Lehren für die deutsche Arbeiterbewegung," p. 122. In the West, by contrast, the reestablishment of the rule of reaction meant that democracy and socialism could be achieved only by means of a "revolutionary mass struggle," (p. 121).

[61]Ulbricht, "Die Partei neuen Typus," *Einheit* 9 (September 1948): 771, 774, and 777.

The way was now clear for the SED to endorse arguments advanced in Tjulpanov's talks the preceding spring for use in Soviet-occupied Germany. In its single greatest retraction, the party denied the existence of a "special German road to socialism"—the very notion that once symbolized the party's preference for democracy over "sovietization." By fall 1948, however, the SED wanted dictatorship as well as democracy; and, like many of its other complete or partial reversions, attempts were undertaken to harmonize conflicting elements by denying that any reversal of previous policies had occurred. Considering the nature of the earlier rhetoric, which never promised more than the possibility of a democratic transition to socialism and pledged violence if attempts were made to thwart it, there was some basis for the party's refusal to concede that it had broken old assurances. But however artfully the "German road" was first defined in spring 1946, Anton Ackermann concluded back then that such a road existed, and he spoke for the KPD. In order to retract now what had been the essence of the party's public commitment to democracy, the SED used its resolution on the November revolution of 1918 to reject the idea that there was anything specifically "German" about the nature of political developments in the Soviet zone;[62] and the party then prevailed upon Ackermann to accept the blame for suggesting it in the first place. But his recantation was preceded by a protracted discussion of all ideologically or programmatically related issues at a meeting of the SED's executive board in mid-September 1948. Ulbricht addressed the body first, talking about the lessons of the Cominform's condemnation of Yugoslavia; and, in the process, referred cryptically to his own "errant evaluation" of events there.[63]

Fred Oelßner spoke next, commenting upon the November resolution, of which he was the primary author, and setting the stage for Ackermann's recantation. Oelßner insisted that "our road, even allowing for the consideration of particularities, is principally the same revolutionary road of Marxism Leninism—a road that can only lead via the political rule of the working class, that is, the dictatorship of the proletariat, to socialism" (184). When Ackermann's turn came, he pointed out what everyone knew already, but was understandably reluctant to admit. He had been far from alone in adopting the mistaken standpoint; he wrote the article entitled "Is there a special German road to socialism?" following discussions within the secretariat and at its request, he said; a positive answer to the question was clearly expected of him; and the offending opinion actually served as a commentary on the party's own "principles and goals." These likewise affirmed the possibility

[62]See "Die Novemberrevolution und ihre Lehren für die deutsche Arbeiterbewegung," pp. 121-23.
[63]Stenographische Niederschrift über die 13. (27.) Tagung der SED am 15./16. September 1948. Zentrales Parteiarchiv, IV 2/1/26/53. Details of Ulbricht's apparent self-criticism appear to have been excised from the record. Further citations are provided in the text.

of a democratic road, besides which virtually everyone present had, at one time or another, either spoken similarly or neglected to take issue with the concept. Only "Comrade Colonel Tjulpanov," some two years earlier, had uttered comments critical of the special German road, though no one drew any conclusions from his remark. But times had changed since 1945, said Ackermann, and reality proved that the theory was "false and pernicious." In particular, the concept "retreated" in the face of anti-Soviet sentiments and, though this was never the intention, effectively set itself apart from the "route taken by the Bolshevist party." Ackermann nevertheless confessed his bewilderment over a different complication arising out of the general problem and, by implication, having to do with dictatorship. Referring to the roads to socialism taken by other Eastern European countries, Ackermann wanted to know if these were "revolutionary-democratic" (the definition proffered by Tjulpanov just a few months earlier); and, a related question, whether the issue of a possible democratic road to socialism was just as pernicious as the theory of a special *German* road.

Ackermann understood the intricacies of the dialectic perfectly well; the issue was not "democracy" at all because, in doctrinal terms, real democracy was dictatorship and dictatorship, democracy. With his political survival at stake, Ackermann's inquiry may thus have been calculated to confront his critics with the theoretical contradictions of their own shifting standpoint and salvage something from "his" position. He ultimately won the point, too, though in practical terms the distinction was inconsequential; the real issue was and always had been the potential for nationalism, vividly demonstrated by Stalin's conflict with Tito, inherent in any emphasis upon roads to socialism that departed meaningfully from the Soviet experience. Still, Ackermann was acutely aware of the rhetorical or ideological hazards in a divided Germany of accentuating revolutionary over democratic development. Of course, Ackermann admitted freely, all current roads to socialism were "revolutionary-democratic" in the sense that class warfare remained unavoidable. Indeed, the discussion excised the word "peaceful," once considered a virtual synonym for "democratic" and an antonym for "sovietization," from the new locutions; and, accordingly, Ackermann went on to conclude that the reactionary "state apparatus" had to be destroyed through the use of violence. But it still seemed to him, with Tjulpanov's words of the previous spring ringing in his ears, that the possibility of a democratic road to socialism continued to exist precisely because of the Red Army and the Soviet Union. Thus, undercutting Oelßner's position, Ackermann brought up passages from the November resolution that characterized the road to socialism as "revolutionary" and wondered, again, whether the path might be labeled "democratic" as well (187-98). The point was ideologically sound, as everyone knew; but, as Ackermann surely understood, largely irrelevant to the political reality behind the debate. Nonetheless, the doctrinal importance of the distinction in a divided Germany may have retrieved his career. It could also have been that Ackermann was simply permitted to confess the error of his way without the abject groveling characteristic of these rituals because the party's brazen reversal enabled him to split a few extra doctrinal hairs in jettisoning a concept on which virtually every other plank of the party's original democratic platform had rested.

The continuation of the debate revealed just how interconnected these issues were and how hard it was to acknowledge that, worse than broken, the party's promises had never been more than tactical expedients. Paul Wandel rejected Ackermann's contention that the matter of a German road to socialism had not been discussed before and reminded him of his attempt to deny at the board meeting back in October 1946 that "the rule of the working class" was a synonym for the dictatorship of the proletariat. Wandel contended that the concept of a German and a democratic road to socialism were equivalents because both contrasted with the Soviet way; whereas the essence of Soviet development had been utterly democratic. Not that he or Ackermann or anyone else who ever spoke in terms of a democratic road ever imagined it free of "bitter class warfare," but others had wrongly supposed that the use of violence was indeed avoidable. The situation was naturally influenced by the defeat of fascism at the hands of the Soviet army, which crushed the state apparatus of the ruling class just as "we could and would have done in a revolution." What followed, however, was something else again. The road to socialism that came after the fall of fascism began with a transitional stage characterized by the creation of genuine democratic conditions after the fashion of the popular democracies. But the further course of development would, Wandel added, require new economic forms and more changes in the state apparatus "at the end of which stood, without a doubt, the rule of the working class"—dictatorship, as Marx and Lenin understood it. Without this dictatorship of the proletariat, socialism could not be achieved, though Wandel agreed with Ackermann that, "on the outside, in our agitation," there was no sense in imitating the old KPD and calling incessantly for dictatorship. Nonetheless, Wandel added, there should be no more concessions to "certain opportunistic notions that fail to recognize Marxism-Leninism as the basis of unity in Germany"; and he added that similar "concessions toward non-Leninist notions" had also resulted from the yearning for working-class unity in 1945. That desire motivated "many of us," as Wandel put it, to search for phrases and conceptions pertaining to political development acceptable to all concerned. At the time, Wandel admitted, there had been firm ideas about a special German road to socialism, by no means regarded as concessions, that derived from an analysis of the situation in Germany and "perspectives" for its future development. Just possibly, Wandel conceded, this view of things had been "illusory" from the beginning and, in any case, was now fundamentally different (206-14).

This was a striking acknowledgment with scores of implications, not the least of them being whether leading Communists, or Stalin, ever actually believed promises that so routinely flew in the face of doctrine. As it was, most of the party's major programmatic statements, not just Ackermann's seminal article, but the corresponding "principles and goals," were teeming with clauses that allowed for contradictory interpretations; and they scarcely found their way into these documents by accident. Helmut Lehmann was absolutely correct in pointing out that talk of a special road always connoted a revolutionary way and could have meant nothing else; "after all," he explained, "we stand on the ground of consequent class warfare; every other conclusion follows logically" (216). But the fact remains that many of the party's programmatic declarations were intended, quoting Lehmann, "to soothe certain worried minds" or, more accurately put, to convey a misleading impression about the party's actual ambitions. Pieck knew it and soon referred to an early assessment that was probably the most embarrassing of them all. Ackermann had already shifted the discussion somewhat away from his old article and onto the SED's "principles and goals"; and Pieck, too, spoke of the "formulation regarding a democratic road to socialism" contained in them. But he also cited the corresponding assurance given in the KPD's original proclamation that the "way of forcing the Soviet system" upon Germany was false because it failed to match current conditions. As Pieck pointed out, this passage was further incorporated into the party's "principles and goals," even if the identical words were not used. Moreover, such formulations did not originate at the top levels of the KPD alone; rather, they had been regarded as expedient "elsewhere," too; no one from the Soviet Communist party, he pointed out, ever objected to them. True, nothing of that nature would possibly be repeated today, but, at the time, it was necessary to overcome Social-Democratic shyness about revolution and violence. Even so, Pieck, like Lehmann, indicated that the "principles and goals" had provided for the use of revolutionary measures in the event that "the others" resorted to violence; and this formulation established the fact that "we ourselves never really expected reaction to capitulate and allow us thereafter to achieve socialism in a democratic, peaceful manner" (219-21). Others, too, like Oelßner, stressed that times had changed and that those changes compelled the party to answer earlier questions regarding the road to socialism differently. For Oelßner, the issue was clear; the special German road to socialism suggested that there might be a way "for us to dodge the dictatorship of the proletariat"; whereas it was now important to understand, at all levels of the party, exactly what was meant in the "principles and goals" by the phrase "political power of the working class." The answer, according to Oelßner, was dictatorship (225-26).

Finally, Otto Grotewohl divulged his thoughts on the subject and, echoing the other speakers, justified the abandonment of previous pledges and promises by reciting the nature of change since 1945. He, too, understood that earlier rhetoric had been heavily influenced by the need to lessen Social-Democratic apprehension about a merger with the KPD; but, while conceding that the notion of a German road to socialism had no "validity whatsoever" in 1948, he rejected attempts to consider it Ackermann's "own private business." The question came up largely because a similar or identical problem developed in connection with the events in Yugoslavia. Still, these matters ultimately boiled down to a question of tactics. Grotewohl rejected the idea that the party's "principles and goals" were now superseded or "antiquated"; and concentrated specifically on the passage that expressed the party's preference for a democratic road *and* its pledge of violence if the "capitalist class" conducted itself undemocratically. Exactly that was now beginning to happen; nonetheless, he cautioned against the use of phrases, like one just published, that enjoined the party to "prepare now for the revolution."[64] Such language struck Grotewohl as detrimental, besides which those subjects could scarcely be captured in programmatic formulations anyway. Grotewohl stressed the importance of instead finding ways of designing political activity that were "elastic"; what was at issue, he said, better fit the description of "education in favor of transformation" that would not come of its own accord, but originate from within a party bent upon taking over power. It made little sense to commit something of that sort to paper, however; and Grotewohl advised against the use of any formulations, "unnecessary at the moment," that damaged the party by complicating its objectives. The phrase, "Our road to socialism is a revolutionary road," taken from Oelßner's draft resolution pertaining to the November revolution, was gratuitous because it shot ahead of developments (237-47).

Grotewohl's admonitions ended the board meeting, and, one week later, Ackermann published his recantation. In it, he generally paralleled Tjulpanov's arguments of several months earlier, except that Tjulpanov had not been compelled to couple his reassessment of conditions in Eastern Europe to an open disavowal of an earlier theory. Ackermann began by quoting from the resolution on the November revolution, citing those passages stating that developments in Soviet-occupied Germany did not represent an indigenous road to socialism or guarantee a peaceful transition; the road was not national, but Marxist-Leninist and thus revolutionary, one that made it possible to go beyond the completion of Germany's democratic renewal to establish the "political rule of the working class as the prerequisite to socialism." That phrase, of course, had always been a synonym for the dictatorship of the proletariat; and, though Ackermann had made this clear in February 1946, in his retraction he still shied away from the word "dictatorship."

---

[64]See also "Die Novemberrevolution und die Lehren aus der Geschichte der deutschen Arbeiterbewegung," *Sozialistische Bildungshefte* 10 (1948): 14.

But the salient point is that the time for third-road ideas or for national orientations even marginally inharmonious with the view of the Soviet Union as the worldwide shield of national sovereignty, against the threat of Western "colonization," had come and gone. The idea of a German road to socialism was misbegotten and dangerous, Ackermann said, because conditions in Eastern Europe following the war resulted not from "specifically German, Polish, or Romanian political, economic, and cultural development"; they sprang from the emergence of the Soviet Union as an international champion of socialism and from the weakened condition of world imperialism. In reality, the notion of a German road actually catered to "strong anti-Soviet attitudes" among segments of the population"; it signaled a retreat in the face of a "wild anti-Communist smear campaign" and erected a barrier in front of the Bolshevist party—this in spite of the fact that all revolutionary parties drew on the teachings not just of Marx and Engels, but especially of Lenin and Stalin. The contention that the German road to socialism differed from the Soviet experience impeded the education of wavering party members in the spirit of Marxism-Leninism and hindered the struggle for the party of a new type. For these reasons, this "serious 'theoretical' blunder" had to be liquidated and "every last trace of it eradicated."[65]

Before the end of the year, there were a few more doctrinal additions to the new thinking that attempted to resolve lingering theoretical ambiguities and inconsistencies caused by the wholesale abandonment of the party's earlier program. The old idea of proletarian dictatorship, mention of which Ackermann had still managed to avoid, was now publicly endorsed along with a new concept of the bloodless revolution. Having determined that the road to socialism was not peaceful, party spokesman hastened to assure Germans that "revolution" did not necessarily denote bloodshed either. This was the sense in which Ackermann's plea in favor of the attribute "democratic" won out. Rudolf Herrnstadt, editor of *Neues Deutschland*, explained that a "relatively bloodless transition to socialism" was now possible because of the October revolution and the recent victories of the Red Army. This was not the same, however, as a peaceful transition; nor was there anything specifically "German" about it; and besides, the class struggle not only continued, it intensified.[66] Oelßner then developed the idea further still. Political power was the fundamental question of every revolution, he said; consequently, the core of revolution was dictatorship, and the doctrine of dictatorship was an indivisible component of Marxism-Leninism. There followed a detailed discussion of the historical origins of the idea in the writings of Marx and Engels (the "class struggle necessarily leads to the dictatorship of

---

[65]Ackermann, "Über den einzig möglichen Weg zum Sozialismus," *Neues Deutschland*, 24 September 1948.
[66]Herrnstadt, "Einige Lehren aus den Fehlern der Kommunistischen Partei Jugoslawiens," *Einheit* 9 (1948): 788.

the proletariat"), its modern German application (by renouncing proletarian dictatorship, Social Democracy helped cause the defeat in the revolution of 1918), the differences in the Soviet experience (where a different route was taken), and the critical question of 1948: Is a peaceful revolution possible? Oelßner answered it in the affirmative and allowed the party to jettison much of its earlier ideological baggage while still clinging rhetorically to concepts like peace and democracy. Under certain circumstances, he explained, it was possible to "disarm" the bourgeoisie without a dictatorship of the proletariat, which could then be "fought for and won" without armed insurrection. But breaking the final resistance of the bourgeoisie and establishing socialism, the stage that Soviet-occupied Germany was rapidly nearing, hinged on the establishment of dictatorship. This had already been outlined in the SED's "principles and goals," Oelßner explained, which stated that the prerequisite of socialism was the acquisition of political power by the working class; and because this phrase connoted dictatorship, it was clear to him that the KPD and SPD had merged based on a "clear acknowledgment of proletarian dictatorship"—regardless of whether the theory of a German road falsely postulated that socialism was possible without dictatorship.[67]

There was an immense difference in party rhetoric between denotations and connotations, however; the SED's "principles and goals" connoted dictatorship. The party's statement of principles had not added the parenthetical expression "dictatorship of the proletariat" to the phrase "acquisition of political power by the working class"; but then neither had Ackermann said that socialism was "possible without dictatorship." Oelßner's basic contention was only partially correct, and he knowingly accused Ackermann of at least one sin that he had not committed. Unlike the "principles and goals," published in April 1946 without mention of dictatorship, Ackermann's article stated clearly that the objective of any road to socialism, including a specifically German transition, lay in the acquisition of the "complete power of the workers (as Marx writes: 'the revolutionary dictatorship of the proletariat')."[68] But what was at issue with these latest analyses was not the need to clarify the doctrine; ways were being sought to reconcile the party's radical reversion to an old revolutionary posture with half-hearted assurances of moderation. Oelßner indicated that the state apparatus in West Germany had to be "smashed"; whereas solving the basic question of revolution in Soviet-occupied Germany, the transition to a dictatorship of the proletariat, could occur without an insurrection and not contradict the principles of Marxism-Leninism. After making the point again that dictatorship was inseparable from Marxism-Leninism, he noted that the party's agitation did not require ceaseless talk of dictatorship; it would be better to use the phrase "rule of the

---

[67] Oelßner, "Die Grundfrage der Revolution," *Tägliche Rundschau*, 7 November 1948.
[68]Ackermann, "Gibt es einen besonderen deutschen Weg zum Sozialismus?" *Einheit* 2 (1946): 23.

working class," though the party needed to comprehend that this meant dictatorship as taught by Marx, Engels, Lenin, and Stalin. Accordingly, there was no such thing as a peaceful transition from capitalism to socialism without class struggle and in the absence of dictatorship. But circumstances in Soviet-occupied Germany made it possible, "thanks to the SMAD," to arrive at the rule of the working class without a violent uprising. It was thus wrong to contrast the revolutionary road to socialism with a democratic transition, as if the former led through an ocean of blood; the revolutionary way was the most democratic, and proletarian dictatorship represented the supreme embodiment of democracy; pursuing these goals, the SED continued work started in 1945, the only difference being that the class enemy had reared its ugly head.[69]

This ideological and political reversion was naturally part of the complete breakdown of East-West relations; in June 1948 the Soviet Union had claimed that all of Berlin lay in Soviet-occupied Germany and began blockading Western access to the city; and as the Eastern-European countries joined the camp of "peace and democracy," two-and-a-half-year-old theories were desperately in need of revision there as well. The change was just as sensational as in Soviet-occupied Germany, even if it merely officialized a process already further advanced, because the national roads to socialism in Eastern Europe had been given the much more formal designation of popular democracy; and by its very definition popular democracy supposedly differed from proletarian dictatorship. This now changed definitively, public; and the prime spokesman of the Communist International's original espousal of democracy in the form of a popular front, the Bulgarian Georgij Dimitrov, was chosen to write the redefinition that took Tjulpanov's article of May 1948 the final step of the way. Like Tjulpanov, Dimitrov did not couch his retraction in the form of self-criticism (much less concede that a retraction had taken place). He merely explained that the popular-democratic regime needed to fulfill the function of a dictatorship of the proletariat in order to "liquidate the capitalist elements and build a socialist economy" and that it had done so. Calling for the popular democracies to form a "united front" with the USSR, he argued that these democracies were incompatible with nationalism and that, "in internationalism and international cooperation under the leadership of the great Stalin, our party sees the guarantee for an independent existence and for the growing success and progress of our country on the road to socialism." Thus, proletarian internationalism and true patriotism were closely intertwined; and it was equally imperative to understand the role of the Communist party of the Soviet Union, the party of Lenin and Stalin, as the leading party of the international labor movement. Finally, Dimitrov concluded that the Soviet regime and the popular-democratic regimes

[69]Oelßner, "Die Grundfrage der Revolution," *Tägliche Rundschau*, 7 November 1948.

actually stood for two forms of "one and the same kind of power"; both were necessarily proletarian dictatorships, for the transition to socialism could not occur without them.[70]

Thus ended one era just as another began. At the board meeting in September, Paul Wandel had argued in favor of "ridding ourselves of all nationalism" and, as revolutionaries, finding the proper relationship to the Soviet Communist party and to Stalin—not as some kind of "idolatry," but because for half a century that party and its rulers had been the international torch-bearer.[71] Three months later, on 21 December 1948, Stalin celebrated his sixty-ninth birthday, and Anton Ackermann was accorded the honor of performing the SED's first annual act of adulation. Every celebration that followed over the next five years tried to outdo the preceding ritual, usually successfully, and all of them centered on Stalin as the "best friend of the German people." Not that Ackermann was the first to coin this particular phrase or that his article genuflected before Stalin as servilely as most of those to come; but he used Stalin's words about the Hitlers who come and go to explain that Stalin had always opposed the "colonization and division of Germany." The imperialist occupation regimes caused the rift by working toward a separate German state and its transformation into a slave "colony of dollar imperialism," whereas, thanks to "Stalin's occupation policies," Soviet-occupied Germany had been turned into a strongpoint for the struggle for democracy nationwide and for national unity.[72]

---

[70]Dimitrov, "Wesen und Aufgaben der Volksdemokratien," *Tägliche Rundschau*, 29 December 1948.

[71]Stenographische Niederschrift über die 13. (27.) Tagung der SED am 15./16. September 1948. Zentrales Parteiarchiv, IV 2/1/26/214.

[72]Ackermann, "Stalin, Führer des Weltproletariats. Zu seinem 69. Geburtstag," *Neues Deutschland*, 21 December 1948.

CHAPTER TEN

Cultural Coordination

No such dramatic shift back to positions that the party had earlier disavowed took place in cultural politics in 1948 because the accelerated pursuit of rigid policies was not dependent upon a reversal quite like the SED's broken political promises. But the atmosphere was every bit as tense, it deteriorated just as steadily, and the year closed with few gaps remaining between the party's consolidation of political power and its coordination of cultural processes. The situation had already taken a turn for the worse when the SED used the congress in September 1947 to launch its "ideological offensive," though, if they existed, there was scant evidence there of plans for an impending cultural crackdown. Pieck argued forcefully that the party's cultural policy be based upon Marxism-Leninism, not upon "self-restraint" or "rotten compromises"; but there were no proposals outlined, and the official resolution stuck to the customary generalities. The party guaranteed artistic freedom and vowed that "mass organizations" would stay nonpartisan.[1] Those random allusions to culture were an acute disappointment to party intellectuals, however, whose individual and collective ambitions were burgeoning and who now clamored for more attention. When Otto Grotewohl expressed general satisfaction at the success of the congress in remarks to the board a few days after, there were unmistakable signs of unhappiness over what some believed was the party's inadequate appreciation of cultural issues. But Grotewohl shrugged off the suggestion that the congress had been "hostile to culture," said that the urgency of political matters explained the need to set "collateral questions" aside, and put an end to discussion of the subject with the lame excuse that, in effect, the entire congress staged a "cultural display" of immense significance.

The humiliation suffered at the writers' congress just a few weeks later then altered the complexion of things and emphasized the urgency of developing new initiatives. On 31 October 1947, three weeks after the debacle, the Zentraler Kulturausschuß met to review the party's cultural work, and regret was expressed, again, that the congress in September overlooked cultur-

---

[1]Pieck, "Bericht des Parteivorstandes," and "Entschließung zur politischen Lage," *Protokoll der Verhandlungen des 2. Parteitages* [20-24 September], pp. 93, 535, and 543.

al issues. But plans now being drawn up were supposed to remedy the situation. These proposals focused mostly on intellectuals who belonged to the party, the reason being that "unsatisfactory factional work" within the organization placed in charge of the congress in October, the Schutzverband deutscher Autoren or SDA, was blamed for its subsequent failure. As Alexander Abusch told the story, the congress had been slated to meet much earlier. But the "crisis" in spring 1947, by which he must have meant the displeasure of the allies over the anti-Western tenor of the Kulturbund conference in May, not least of all Tjulpanov's remarks there, caused delays when its leading personalities considered it better to limit their involvement in preparations for the writers' congress. SDA officials who took over instead then went about things their own way. According to Abusch, only five "soc.[ialists]" sat on the SDA's board of twenty, as a consequence of which preparations for the congress fell into the hands of "our enemies"; and they sponsored "provocations" that ended in its near collapse. Abusch made no mention of the sudden appearance of the Soviet writers, however, whose names were not listed on the program put out by the SDA just in advance of the congress;[2] nor did he account for their "open letter" to American intellectuals on the eve of the congress; and he never acknowledged that their politicization of the event led to "provocations" by others now blamed for the ensuing bedlam. Even so, Anton Ackermann, who conducted the post-mortem on 31 October, called for measures to prevent "our comrades" from being "run over" again by the SDA; the party needed to expand its influence over the organization because, given the increasing gravity of the general situation, doing nothing was potentially dangerous. He proposed that a list of writers who belonged to the party be drawn up as the first step toward their organization; and Richard Weimann declared that they should be organized in "a front of SED writers." He scheduled a meeting for December and said that "steps to register our writers," as well as prepare for what was called a "soc.[ialist] cultural congress," would be decided upon there.[3]

Weimann then delved into the related subject of "working groups" of party intellectuals. This idea had been around for awhile, having first germinated in discussions as far back as mid-1946 in connection with the aspirations of "SED artists." But it must have gone dormant when their overweening ambitions clashed with the party's better sense of tactical forbearance. Just before, however, on 24 January 1947, the SED's division of Kultur und Erziehung drew up instructions on the subject that met with the approval of the party leadership five weeks later.[4] These instructions provided for the

---

[2]See "Erster Deutscher Schriftstellerkongreß. Plan der Tagung," *Der Autor* 6-7 (1947): 1.
[3]Protokoll der Sitzung des Zentralen Kulturausschusses am 31. Oktober 1947; and Zentraler Kulturausschuß. Sitzung am 31. 10. 1947. Kurze Zusammenfassung des Sitzungsergebnisses. Zentrales Parteiarchiv, IV 2/906/4/102-6.
[4]Protokoll Nr. 79 der Sitzung des Zentralsekretariats am 3. 3. 1947, ibid., IV 2/2.1/70/3.

creation of "working groups" of SED intellectuals under the umbrella of the party's local branches, but accountable to Kultur und Erziehung in Berlin. The groups were supposed to improve relations between the party's regular members and its intellectuals, which had apparently been in a state of disarray for quite some time; provide the latter with lessons in scientific socialism; encourage their involvement in the "life of the party"; and work to convert politically unaffiliated intellectuals.[5] There is no evidence that the idea came back to life prior to late 1947, however; and even then, the guidelines may have been withheld internally until March 1948.[6] In the meantime, Kultur und Erziehung had prepared a second set of instructions that may also date as far back as fall 1947.[7] This document had an additional theoretical or aesthetic slant, the practical application of which hinged upon the prior establishment of an effective organizational or administrative apparatus. These guidelines guaranteed creative freedom, but added that such freedom served as an assurance of cultural activity conducted in the interests of the people only when borne of a sense of responsibility for the nation. The SED expected that "progressive art," by which artists themselves were meant, whether party members or not, would gladly devote their attention to the emerging new society; artistic tendencies that depicted a superseded order or opposed to progress would not, however, and were unacceptable.[8]

Such remarks broke no new ground; but they were important because the articulation of these positions had previously been the prerogative of the party's cultural functionaries speaking in their public capacity as "nonpartisan" officials of cultural organizations. With occasional exceptions, the party issued no such injunctions of its own. But this "self-restraint," to use Pieck's characterization at the congress in September, began changing and brought far harsher descriptions of artistic currents "opposed to progress." The shift in emphasis was further evident in remarks calling upon the SED to spare no effort in support of the artists, for the party could not hope to win their backing otherwise and "employ the results of art in our struggle."[9] The embarrassment of the writers' congress shortly after the party meeting in September then provided an additional impetus behind the attention now paid the organizational inadequacies of the party's local and regional cultural appara-

---

[5]"Bildung von Arbeitsgruppen (Arbeitsgemeinschaften) der Geistesarbeiter und Kulturschaffenden der SED). Richtlinien des Zentralsekretariats der SED," *Um die Erneuerung der deutschen Kultur. Dokumente*, pp. 214-15.
[6]See Richtlinien zur Bildung von Arbeitsgruppen der Kulturschaffenden und Geistesarbeiter der SED, 24 January 1947, and later drafts. Zentrales Parteiarchiv, IV 2/906/172/4-5, 6-7; 8-9.
[7]A third, (Künstlerische Gestaltung des Parteilebens. Leitsätze zum Referat des Genossen Kaufmann auf der Kulturtagung in Liebenswalde, Okt. 47. Zentrales Parteiarchiv, IV 2/906/172/17-19), developed out of the same general concerns and clearly existed as early as October 1947.
[8]"Das Verhältnis der Partei zur Kunst und zu den Künstlern," *Um die Erneuerung der deutschen Kultur. Dokumente*, pp. 310-13.
[9]Ibid., p. 311.

tus. This issue was directly related to the realization that the SED's own writers, seen as the key to influencing "sympathetic" intellectuals, needed to be more tightly coupled to the party. Making believers in the politics of Soviet-occupied Germany out of politically uncommitted intellectuals was by no means a recent objective, but the SED's rapid consolidation of power and the problems of a worsening economy increased the practical importance of mobilizing scientists, lawyers, doctors, engineers, teachers, artists, and so on in support of the "political, economic, and cultural reconstruction of Germany."[10] SMAD order 234, which the papers published on 9 October 1947 and which stimulated an assortment of new cultural initiatives,[11] was further evidence of a move to consolidate power in Soviet-occupied Germany that crested logically in the two-year plan announced several months later. The problem in fall 1947 was that the party's failure to appreciate the value of intellectuals had allowed a certain resentment toward them to breed within the rank and file, though it must be understood that, objectively speaking, the party's cultural-political policies had been a "failure" only in comparison with the magnitude of politicization now in store for Soviet-zone intellectuals. The resolution passed at the congress in September referred clearly to "backward attitudes" within the party that resulted from the erroneous sense of an existing "conflict between workers and intellectuals."[12]

In fall 1947, the answer to the problem was thought to reside in an improvement of the party's internal apparatus, right down to the "smallest and lowest-level cell," that would allow the SED to communicate its cultural-political priorities more effectively throughout the entire country. Divisions of Kultur und Erziehung, now combined with Parteischulung, were scheduled to be set up accordingly within all state, regional, county, and local party organizations, each of which would be further broken down into specialized offices that included art, theater, film, and literature. These divisions were subordinate to the department attached to the central party secretariat in Berlin, renamed PKE (for Parteischulung, Kultur und Erziehung), and obliged to file quarterly reports. PKE also mandated the formation of "cultural committees" at each matching level of organization—a possible permutation of the idea first developed by the Gewerkschaft 17, perhaps the equivalent of the Zentraler Kulturausschuß, or maybe even a combination of the two. Intended to serve as "advisory organs" to local and regional PKE's, the committees were to "coordinate cultural work and organize all comrades active in various areas of culture." In the states, these bodies would be comprised of representatives from the appropriate divisions of PKE, the ministry of cul-

---

[10]See Bericht der Abteilung Kultur und Erziehung [ca. fall 1947]. Zentrales Parteiarchiv, IV 2/906/9/1-2.

[11]See below for discussion of SMAD order 234.

[12]"Entschließung zur politischen Lage," *Protokoll der Verhandlungen des 2. Parteitages,* p. 544.

ture and education (that is, Volksbildung), SED teachers, students, scientists, and artists, the cultural editor of the regional party newspaper, as well as the cultural chiefs of the state branches of the FDGB, the Kulturbund, the people's theater, the FDJ, and so on. Every one of the committee members had to belong to the SED. Additional provisions were drawn up in an attempt to raise the "insufficient interest" in cultural issues said to exist among party functionaries; and the greater involvement of the SED's own intellectuals in "party life" was foremost among them. Specifically, they were all strongly encouraged to join the Kulturbund because their membership in this "nonpartisan" organization would enhance opportunities for influencing intellectuals "of all directions."[13]

At roughly the same time, on 31 October 1947, Kultur und Erziehung informed its state branches of a meeting between Ackermann, Becher, Weinert, Wangenheim, Abusch, Kantorowicz, Harich, and others that had taken place on the 23rd. Alexander Dymschitz and Leonid Auslender attended as well,[14] proving that these developments now unfolded with the knowledge and approval of the SMAD. Well before the Kulturausschuß met on 31 October to make the same decision, the more elite group that met on the 23rd had already decided that the SED needed to increase the participation of its writers in the SDA in order to influence its activities and to guarantee a better showing at future congresses. A meeting of writers who either belonged to the SED or sympathized with it, scheduled for January 1948, though later postponed until April,[15] was also arranged now along with the agenda for the discussion already set for 5 December 1947. Several "writer comrades" from each of the Soviet-zone states and from Berlin were asked to attend that session.[16] When it met a week later than planned, on 12 December,[17] the importance of organizing writers who belonged to the party was talked about in detail; but no immediate action was taken other than to ponder the idea of a congress especially for "SED writers" in May 1948.[18] The idea of a far more broadly conceived "large general party cultural congress," the so-called first cultural congress of the Socialist Unity party that met from 7 to 9 May, was then agreed upon at a party board meeting in February 1948 instead; and "SED writers," leaving aside the informal discussion in April, did not gather

[13]Bericht der Abteilung Kultur und Erziehung. Zentrales Parteiarchiv, IV 2/906/9/1-12.
[14]Anwesenheitsliste. Schriftsteller-Sitzung, 23 October 1947, ibid., IV 2/906/254/2.
[15]The date was set for 8 and 9 April 1948 by a "working committee" charged with planning the conference during a meeting on 26 February (see Kurzer Sitzungsbericht, ibid., IV 2/906/254/59).
[16]See the letter itself, dated 31 October 1947, and the responses sent in by the party's state branches and other organizations invited to send delegates (ibid., IV 2/906/1, 7-16).
[17]It was postponed for a week due to the Volkskongreß (See Protokoll Nr. 22 [II] der Sitzung des Zentralsekretariats am 1. 12. 1947, ibid., IV 2/2.1/151/2).
[18]See Protokoll der Tagung der parteigenössischen Schriftsteller am 12. 12. [1947]; and Anwesenheitsliste. Schriftstellertagung am 12. Dezember 1947, ibid., IV 2/906/254/19-23, 25.

until these writers found out in September 1948 from no less an authority than Walter Ulbricht what the party had in store for them.[19]

Food First, Then Morality

The change in plans probably came about because things had begun happening at breakneck speed in fall 1947, creating the need for organizational and administrative improvisation; that pace lasted through late June 1948, when the party announced its two-year plan; and, in turn, the two-year plan stimulated still other initiatives that carried up to the formation of the German Democratic Republic in October 1949 and beyond. These processes unfolded in conjunction with each other, but they often exhibited individual attributes that also require separate examination. The party's growing sense of the importance of its own cultural apparatus and its own intellectuals, for instance, was paralleled by major organizational initiatives developed by the Deutsche Verwaltung für Volksbildung in response to the issuance of order 234 on 9 October 1947. Just two days later, on the 11th, and a scant three after the first German writers' congress ended in disarray, the subject of the DVV and its "weakness" came up in talks between Pieck and Volkov; and one or the other of the two men suggested a division of the administration into separate components, "art" being one of them. Its responsibilities were considered too large for one agency.[20] Nothing quite so radical happened until 1954, when a single ministry of culture was carved out of culture and education, or Volksbildung, the ministry that had continued the work of the DVV after creation of the GDR in October 1949. Instead, proposals for a "reorganization" of the DVV surfaced in connection with order 234 and its general provisions for greater operating efficiency—general because order 234, in spite of its considerable impact upon it, never mentioned culture. The order itself reflected the urgency of measures designed to deal with the chronic inefficiency and low productivity of the crumbling economy. The need to "raise production by increasing performance a.[nd] improving discipline in the workplace" was discussed by Pieck and Marshal Sokolovskij as early as August 1947;[21] and the same concern was reflected in the secretariat's letter to Stalin just prior to the party conference in September. In fact, the letter confirmed that an actual "document" was in preparation, enclosed supporting materials (apparently not extant), and indicated that the subject would be aired at the upcoming congress.[22] It was, too, but not in terms of a concrete proposal, much less an order, and it is not entirely clear who formulated the

[19]See Chapter Eleven.
[20]Besprechung am 11. 10. 1947 im Hause mit Wolkow. Zentrales Parteiarchiv, NL 36/734/386.
[21]Besprechung beim Marschall am 28. 8. 1947, ibid., NL 36/734/ 328.
[22]See ibid., NL 36/734/332-35.

actual decree. The central secretariat appears to have received a copy from the SMAD for discussion on 1 October.[23]

The provisions of the published version were fairly straightforward; entitled "measures for raising worker productivity and for the further improvement in the material condition of workers and employees in industry and transportation,"[24] order 234 raved about the "successes achieved by working people in the reconstruction of a peace economy," only to announce action taken in response to the "low level of worker discipline," insufficient initiative, and "sinking worker productivity." These problems were to be alleviated through a system of inducements, bonuses, better ration cards, paid vacations, and assorted other perquisites calculated to provide workers who increased productivity by meeting or exceeding production norms with tangible benefits.[25] Order 234 resulted in banner headlines; and it must have been trumpeted so widely because other provisions, like piecework wages, were unpopular with the work force in spite of the promise of immediate material rewards. It was important for working Germans to understand, then, that the new requirements had been mandated by order of the SMAD. Publishing it as such certainly accomplished that purpose, and doing so may have been that much more important because the attempt to popularize the measures by pledging a higher standard of living for those who worked harder appears to have had the opposite effect. Many of the highest rewards were reserved for skilled "workers" like engineers or managers, the so-called technical intelligentsia, whose cooperation was such a vital part of improving the efficiency of production; and this fact lowered the morale of ordinary workers whose attitudes order 234 had supposedly been designed to raise. They got a hot meal on the job and little else—but only in return for more work. Ironically, the entire undertaking had an amusing distant echo of the controversy that arose over the staging of Brecht's *Dreigroschenoper* in summer 1945 and objections to the line, considered inappropriate back then, "Feed them first, then talk morality." The party, which had struggled to reverse Brecht's order of priority back then, now proposed to revert to the original—food first, with higher morale in the factories expected to follow. "Give us more to eat, then we'll work more" or "Feed them first, then talk morality" was how *Neues Deutschland* summed up the worker response to criticism of low productivity (though without identifying the quotation from the *Dreigroschenoper*). The paper now agreed with the sequence. It quoted one factory official who wondered how hungry workers could possibly ac-

[23]Protokoll Nr. 3 (II) der Sitzung des Zentralsekretariats am 1. 10. 47, ibid., IV 2/2.1/135/1-2.
[24]"Befehl des Obersten Chefs der Sowjetischen Militärverwaltung—Oberkommandierenden der sowjetischen Besatzungsgruppen in Deutschland. Nr. 234. Über Maßnahmen zur Steigerung der Arbeitsproduktivität und zur weiteren Verbesserung der materiellen Lage der Arbeiter und Angestellten in der Industrie und im Verkehrswesen," *Tägliche Rundschau*, 10 October 1949.
[25]See the accompanying editorial "Ein Schlüßel zur Lösung aller Wirtschaftsprobleme," ibid.

complish the same work as before the war and who, for that reason, "warmly welcomed order 234." Through special food allotments, it relieved workers of the necessity of skipping work to forage for food themselves; if there was any way of establishing the cycle of "more food, more work, more production," order 234 did it.[26]

Though the order said nothing about culture, it was apparently taken for granted that the new policy would benefit intellectuals, too, but in ways resented by the general population. The dissemination of food parcels among the privileged, packages known by their Russian name pajoks, was one such practice; and in keeping with the spirit of order 234, the Russians passed them out selectively. According to Brecht, the stage producer Walter Felsenstein once flaunted the proper procedure with unexpected consequences. He tried to divide his theater's allotment of pajoks equally, whereupon the Russians reduced it to none for two months.[27] Then there was the matter of ration cards. Not that a higher classification for intellectuals came into existence only after order 234; the favored treatment of certain notable personalities seems to have been fairly common from the outset, and the judgment behind the designation was or quickly became political. Herbert Volkmann working within art and literature, told his counterparts in the state and provincial governments in May 1947 that new guidelines governing ration-card classifications for artists had just been worked out by the DVV in conjunction with the Zentralverwaltung für Handel und Versorgung. Assignment to the lowest level IV was left up to local communities; the state ministries of cultural and education grouped the work or activity of "above average" artists, classified as "artistically valuable," at level III; and those whose work or activity was particularly outstanding benefited from the highest designation as "artistically especially valuable." Upon nomination by the state ministries, these favored few were grouped at level II by the DVV. The upper levels, said Volkmann, could be awarded to young artists also if they were thought capable of future achievement. But the higher classification was contingent, he added, upon the "antifascist attitude of the artist."[28] Assuming that ordinary Germans knew about such privileges for artists whose "antifascist attitude" mattered as much as the quality of their work, or was considered to be the same thing, such favoritism explains why opposition to order 234 arose immediately and increased the general resentment toward intellectuals already alluded to in the resolution passed at the party conference in

[26]"Erst kommt das Fressen . . . Arbeitsmoral gegen Hunger—oder umgekehrt?" *Neues Deutschland*, 26 October 1947.
[27]Brecht, *Arbeitsjournal* [9 December 1948], pp. 864-65.
[28]Protokoll über die Besprechung der Leiter der Abteilung Kunst und Literatur bei den Volksbildungsministerien der Länder und Provinzen am 15. und 17. Mai 1947 in Berlin (Punkt 15 der T.O.: Lebensmittelkarte—Einstufung der Künstler). Bundesarchiv. Abt. Potsdam, R-2/1035/11. See also "Um die Einstufung der künstlerisch und geistig Schaffenden in die Lebensmittelkartengruppen," *Kunst und Schrifttum* 2 (1948): 7.

September 1947. Nor was worker suspicion that the SED valued "intellectuals" more highly at all misplaced; the role of the "technical intelligentsia" in raising productivity was clear when order 234 came out. Ulbricht mentioned the subject a few weeks later, for instance, and referred repeatedly to the decree.[29]

But higher ration cards for intellectuals by no means exhausted the cultural applications of order 234, though its further usages required considerable improvisation in the months to come. Discussion of order 234 within the Gewerkschaft 17 defined responsibilities, rather than merely allocating privileges. Artists were expected to help out with cultural programs put on for workers and designed to make work more "enjoyable,"[30] thereby contributing to an increase in production. The assumption that creative intellectuals could stimulate grass-roots enthusiasm for Soviet-zone reconstruction developed later into the chief premise of the cultural provisions associated with the two-year plan. But order 234 set the precedent. The second central delegates' conference in late November 1947, convened by the Gewerkschaft 17 and addressed by the likes of Alexander Dymschitz, Erich Weinert, and Herbert Volkmann, approved a resolution that spoke of the obligation of creative intellectuals to assist working Germans in the implementation of order 234.[31] Even so, no detailed plan of action was outlined there.

Such was not the case in internal discussions taking place within the offices of the DVV; a number of administrative measures were developed immediately after the announcement of order 234; and it is hard to avoid the feeling that the new economic policy was used by the party as a handy excuse to expand central authority over state and provincial government. Whether order 234 was originally intended to justify the initiation of cultural-political measures only loosely connected with the stated intention of the decree, or whether unplanned opportunities created by the order were simply seized upon because there had been no easy way before of effectively "coordinating" cultural policy throughout the zone is a question that cannot be answered for certain. But the measures that the DVV eventually submitted to the SMAD for its approval were worked out in close consultation with its various liaison officers. What followed, therefore, even when the SMAD chose to delay its approval of certain projects or proposals for many months, usually because they cost money, was anything but happenstance. In fact, taken together, the related initiatives undertaken by the DVV in late 1947 or early 1948 may have been regarded as the "reorganization" of the administration that came up during Pieck's talk with Volkov on 11 October 1947.

[29]See Ulbricht, "Die Rolle der technischen Intelligenz bei der Steigerung der Produktion [28 October 1947]," in *Zur Geschichte der deutschen Arbeiterbewegung*, vol. III: 1946-1950, Zusatzband, pp. 348-57.
[30]Pr., "Unsere Landes-Delegiertenkonferenz," *Kunst und Schrifttum* 11 (1947): 1.
[31]"Zweite Zentral-Delegiertenkonferenz. Zum Befehl 234," *Kunst und Schrifttum* 12 (1947): 3.

A few weeks later the secretariat agreed that "special divisions" should be set up within the DVV and the state ministries of culture and education, responsible for "explaining democratic measures" to the population and working to counteract "enemy propaganda."[32] Two of the secretariat's divisions, press generally and regional politics (Werbung, Presse, Rundfunk and Landespolitik) were to draw up tentative proposals. "Reorganizing" the DVV then surfaced again at a secretariat meeting on 8 January 1948 in connection, apparently, with suggestions for the transformation of the DVV's division of cultural enlightenment into something akin to an immense administration of propaganda.[33]

Most of the earliest measures were unrelated, then, to those provisions of order 234 that merely provided for special benefits; but they had everything to do with its underlying premise that poor attitudes affected labor throughout Soviet-occupied Germany and that the system was riddled with "inefficiency." The party thus set out to improve production by "enlightening" the public about the future benefits of social transformation and, in connection with its general "ideological offensive," accelerated the pace. The notion of greater "efficiency" then became an integral part of that acceleration and served as the rationale behind the further centralization and coordination of administrative processes—including those of the DVV. These developments unfolded over a period of many months, but it was first necessary to establish the fact that order 234 had administrative and organizational implications for cultural politics. At a meeting on 27 and 28 October 1947, Herbert Volkmann told the heads of art and literature working within the state ministries of culture and education that order 234 had "tremendous significance" for them and that they needed to devise "positive measures" to comply with it. Volkmann's suggestions included better training for desk chiefs within the divisions, the *Referenten*, along with the swift dismissal of "unsuitable employees"; as well as the possibility of "synchronizing" the organizational structure of all local offices of education with their corresponding departments in both the state administrations and within the DVV itself. He revealed that the DVV planned to "implement" order 234 by setting up a special office responsible for "coordinating the work" of the state governments and "advising" them in the exercise of their responsibilities. "If need be," he said, this office would be equipped with the authority to pursue certain tasks, but no date had been set yet for its actual creation. The department heads approved the idea with no further discussion.[34] One day later, another meeting

[32]Protokoll Nr. 11 (II) der Sitzung des Zentralsekretariats am 27. 10. 1947; Anlage Nr. 1. Zentrales Parteiarchiv, IV 2/2.1/142.
[33]See Protokoll Nr. 34 (II) der Sitzung des Zentralsekretariats am 8. 1. 48, ibid., IV 2/2.1/162. A decision was delayed until a meeting on the 19th.
[34]Abteilung Kunst und Literatur. Protokoll der Abteilungsleiterkonferenz am 27. und 28. 10. 1947 in Berlin. Bundesarchiv. Abt. Potsdam, R-2/1035/ 36.

took place within art and literature that focused more on technical alterations designed to improve the operation of the division.[35]

The subject of order 234 came up again at the December conference of the state ministers of culture and education. They, too, were confronted with resolutions drawn up in advance of the conference. One of these made it clear that order 234 applied to all administrative agencies, not just factories and such; the ministries of culture and education were bound by the order to utilize all the means at their disposal—press, radio, film, schools—to convince the public that implementation of the decree required a change in attitudes. Individual initiative needed to be supplanted by the "people's initiative" because true democracy would come about only when the people recognized when to act without waiting for orders "from above."[36] Further details emerged during the ensuing discussion, but it also began with generalities. The vice president of the DVV, Erwin Marquardt, told the ministers that order 234 had been considered by many to be an exclusively economic matter before the question of cultural and educational involvement in its implementation arose unexpectedly at what he called the "Potsdam consultations" convened by the SED.[37] Marquardt's reference was to a meeting of party functionaries who held key economic and administrative posts convened in Potsdam on 22 October; and some of the remarks made there hinted at what the SED had in mind for this particular campaign to increase production. Economic targets set at the party congress in September 1947, said Walter Ulbricht, were not narrow concerns of the SED; rather, all political parties and, significantly, all mass organizations needed to be involved in the struggle to increase production. Ulbricht, went on to speak of the special need for employees "in administration" to improve their work habits; and the ensuing discussion focused on the related issue of "cooperation" between the central administrations and state governments.[38] The basic point was that anything less than total coordination lowered efficiency—the same issue discussed within the DVV soon after. The centralization of Soviet-zone administrative processes came at the expense of state and local autonomy, however; and at the ministers' conference in early December, Marquardt spoke in a related vein of the difficulty of reconciling "SMAD orders" with the pressure for self-government that reflected itself in strong impulses present in state parliaments. These issues led later to the SED's "state-political conference" the following summer; it met in July 1948, three weeks after the introduction of the two-year plan, to work out the "new tasks of the democratic administrations."[39] But it had already been firmly established by December 1947 that

[35]Abteilung Kunst und Literatur. Bericht, Herrn Weinert, 29 October 1947, ibid., R-2/1091/29.
[36]Entwurf für die Ministerkonferenz im November 1947. Betr. Befehl 234, ibid., R-2/52/30.
[37]Protokoll der Ministerkonferenz vom 2. und 3. Dezember 1947 in Berlin, ibid., R-2/58/3-5.
[38]"Steigerung der Produktion durch Volkskontrolle," *Neues Deutschland*, 25 October 1947.
[39]See below for further discussion.

order 234 required an intensification of the DVV's efforts in the area of "Volksaufklärung"; that such public relations work, referred to as cultural enlightenment, meant winning the support of the people for the implementation of order 234; and that the internal operations of the DVV themselves needed to be reexamined for the sake of improving overall efficiency.[40]

Centralized Enlightenment and Mass Propaganda

At the ministers' conference in December 1947, three general areas of compliance with order 234 were mentioned. The first suggestion, which was not to be voted upon, concerned the matter of better "coordination"; what took place within the DVV ought to generate "roughly identical outlooks" within the state ministries. A commission had already been appointed by the DVV to study the matter further and intended to consult with representatives of the state governments for the purpose of establishing such "coordination." The second suggestion echoed the charge of "bureaucratic formalism" raised at the SED's Potsdam meeting, except that within the DVV "too much bureaucracy" had evidently been a complaint also voiced by the SMAD. Finally, the third suggestion called for the systematic use of culture and education for the purpose of public enlightenment.[41] There were also other measures prepared by the DVV's office of the president and presented to the December ministers' conference for approval as a means of increasing "efficiency." For instance, zone-wide "statistics" on cultural undertakings were to be kept and used for "control." Otherwise, the ministers were presented with the suggestion that "offices of coordination" be set up within the DVV to improve specific cooperation with the mass organizations, a proposal that also echoed the SED's "consultations" in Potsdam; and mention was made of a new "press department."[42]

Press matters were then covered in a specific proposal drawn up by Hans Mahle, who headed the DVV's original division of cultural enlightenment, that advocated the radical "reorganization" and expansion of his entire division. In the draft presented to the ministers for their approval, Mahle argued that cultural enlightenment only made sense if the office in charge of it was fully capable of "organizing and developing large-scale nonpartisan democratic educational work among broad segments of the population in city and countryside," directing the fight against "militaristic and fascist ideologies," and advancing the democratic process of transformation of the masses." The

[40]See Präsidialabteilung. Betr.: Befehl Nr. 234. Gez. Freund. Bundesarchiv. Abt. Potsdam, R-2/809/46-7.
[41]Protokoll der Ministerkonferenz vom 2. und 3. Dezember 1947 in Berlin, ibid., R-2/58/39-40.
[42]Präsidialabteilung. Vorlage für die Ministerkonferenz. Betrifft: Befehl Nr. 234, 18 November 1947, ibid., R-2/58/126-28.

draft resolution ended by pointing out that the DVV's original department, by dint of structural and personnel limitations, had never been equipped to meet such challenges. Those responsible for setting it up probably had no clear idea of the purpose behind it.[43] Now it may be that Mahle intended his last comment as a criticism of the SMAD, the reason being that the DVV's division of cultural enlightenment had never been staffed to the satisfaction of top administrators. One early plan listed thirty-one employees out of a total of 210 for the entire DVV.[44] It was still the largest division of the DVV, growing to forty-six in April 1946,[45] and later in the same year, Mahle had undertaken to expand it dramatically, from 46 employees to 121. This proposal was presented to the SMAD's cadres division on 18 December 1946, where it was scaled back to 31 out of 205.

Considering the nature of Mahle's resolution introduced in December 1947, it may be that party and administration officials had visions early on of a huge department of propaganda—well before the SMAD was inclined to approve an undertaking with so clear an appearance of centralized government or prepared to finance it. In his proposal to the ministers in December 1947, Mahle called "democratic enlightenment" the answer to an American "campaign against communism" geared toward winning the support of the German people for the Marshall Plan. Counter methods of "mass enlightenment" were to include the press, radio, picture propaganda (posters, etc.), and adult education; and Mahle proposed a corresponding breakdown of a coordinated system of controlled information into four divisions. "We are in urgent need of a certain press control," he said; from time to time press conferences should be held at the level of state government to discuss problems of the day, and Mahle concluded that the press was bound to benefit if there were better cooperation between it and the state ministries. The ministries of culture and education should be particularly careful about leaving the press "to its own devices" and supply it instead with suitable material. Much the same was true of radio stations; they needed to work with the ministries, too, and the radio programs should be put together on the basis of prior consultation with their division heads. After all, Mahle concluded, radio played an important role in the education of the people and was highly significant for "propaganda" as well. He also outlined his ideas for picture propaganda and adult education before finishing his presentation by noting that cultural enlightenment within the DVV urgently required reorganization; corresponding divisions needed to be set up in all ministries of culture and education if "we wish to engage in the work of enlightenment on a democratic basis."

[43]Abtl. Kulturelle Aufklärung. Abteilungschef Mahle. Vorlage für die Ministerkonferenz im November 1947, 14 November 1947, ibid., R-2/58/129-33.
[44]Stellenplan der Deutschen Verwaltung für Volksbildung, ibid., R-2/2950/207-219.
[45]Organisations- und Stellenplan der Deutschen Zentralverwaltung für Volksbildung . . . gemäß Schreiben der Deutschen Zentralfinanzverwaltung vom 17. 4. 46, ibid., R-2/1007/77-84.

Further ideas for systematic activity geared to "successful mass propaganda" followed. Major restructuring, refinancing, and restaffing of the division was essential; and the proposal would only work if activity zonewide received the support of the state governments; because these had failed to engage in systematic programs of mass enlightenment themselves, the interests of a unified consolidation of all such work required the prior establishment of main divisions of "cultural enlightenment" there as well.[46] Though they all belonged to the party, the ministers, who apparently heard about the project for the first time, were somewhat reluctant to endorse it on the spot. Otto Halle (province of Saxony) thought the issue too important to be discussed hastily and suggested calling a special ministers' conference; Gottfried Grünberg (Mecklenburg) agreed, whereupon Erich Weinert, who led the discussion, asked testily whether the ministers accepted the necessity of such divisions of cultural enlightenment or not. Paul Reichwaldt, head of general administration, apparently referred back to the DVV's intention of creating offices to improve "coordination" and interjected that culture and education in the state ministries was slated to be organized along the same lines as the DVV. Herbert Gute (Saxony), who may have had a vested interest in Mahle's proposal, then added that "propaganda" cost money and ought to be done right, with adequate financing and a "gigantic staff of experts," or not at all. Weinert took Gute's comment as approval, concluded that the "commission" agreed with the necessity of creating departments of cultural enlightenment in the ministries of culture and education, and added that the SMAD's approval, and willingness to fund the project, now had to be secured. Gute ended the discussion by predicting that provincial and state presidents were certain to object to the idea.[47] Strangely enough, the ministers never voted on the resolution, postponing a decision until the next meeting scheduled for early 1948.[48] But no vote was taken then either; instead, the minutes of the December conference were altered on 10 January 1948 to reflect passage of the resolution to establish state-level divisions of cultural enlightenment.[49] The extant files of the ministers' conferences reveal that no such alteration had ever happened before; but even then, and as late as March 1948, the staffing plan for the DVV's division of cultural enlightenment still provided for only 24 employees.[50]

[46]Protokoll der Ministerkonferenz vom 2. und 3. Dezember 1947, ibid., R-2/58/31-32.
[47]Ibid., R-2/58/33-35,
[48]Beschlußprotokoll der Ministerkonferenz am 2. und 3. Dezember 1947, 17 December 1947, ibid., R-2/58/97-98.
[49]Abänderung des Beschlußprotokolls der Ministerkonferenz am 2. und 3. Dezember 1947, 10 January 1948, ibid., R-2/72/2.
[50]Struktur- und Stellenplan . . . für das Rechnungsjahr 1948, 22 March 1948, ibid., R-2/918/35; the lower figure probably reflected the fact that two sections, publishing (Verlagswesen) and folk art (Volkskunst) had been shifted to the department of art and literature because they were thought to be unrelated to "mass enlightenment." See Präsidialabteilung an die Abteilung Kunst

Simultaneously, related decisions were being made by other bodies. The general proposal to "reorganize" the DVV, which first surfaced at a secretariat meeting on 8 January, just two days before the alteration of the minutes referred to above, was formally voted upon and approved at a session on 19 January attended by Wandel, Mahle, and Volkmann. Pieck and Grotewohl were instructed to enter into the necessary negotiations with the SMAD.[51] Shortly thereafter, as he had clearly been asked to do by the secretariat, Wandel wrote Marshal Sokolovskij by way of Tjulpanov and asked for permission to "expand the Deutsche Verwaltung für Volksbildung and the ministries." He provided the secretariat with a copy, but also requested final approval from that body.[52] The letter itself informed Sokolovskij, perhaps misleadingly, that the ministers' conference in January 1948 agreed unanimously upon the need for an essential strengthening of "state, antiimperialist, and democratic educational work"; and he asked for SMAD approval of appropriate measures that would, he said, conform with the "popular movement for unity and a just peace" as well as provide for the support of "your important order no. 234." Wandel asked Sokolovskij, to issue a formal order, and enclosed a draft for his signature, that would permit the DVV to build a "strong, independent division of cultural enlightenment," sanction the establishment of corresponding divisions attached to the state ministries of culture and education, permit the expansion of art and literature within the DVV, and place cultural enlightenment and art and literature under the direct jurisdiction of the SMAD's office of information.[53] The point behind the last request is unclear; but it must have been related to the search for an arrangement that would enable the two expanded agencies to act, as executive arms of the SMAD, unencumbered by irritating jurisdictional disputes with state government.

No further action was taken until the end of May 1948, at which time the SED received detailed plans for a "main division of cultural enlightenment" from the DVV, agreed that such an agency, operating under the new name "central for reconstruction and enlightenment," was a necessary way of engaging in "state propaganda," and appointed a commission to approach the SMAD with a new draft order based on more finalized plans.[54] Though the subject may have been discussed in the interim, the next mention of it came on 7 July 1948, after announcement of the two-year plan, in a letter sent by

---

und Literatur, Herrn Volkmann. An die Abteilung Kulturelle Aufklärung, Herrn Mahle. Betr.: Strukturänderung beider Abteilungen, ibid., R-2/807/159.

[51]Protokoll Nr. 39 (II) der Sitzung des Zentralsekretariats am 19. 1. 1948. Zentrales Parteiarchiv, IV 2/2.1/166.

[52]An das Zentralsekretariat der SED, Gen. Pieck and Grotewohl, 3 February 1948, gez. Wandel, ibid., NL 36/735/24.

[53]An den Oberbefehlshaber der SMA, 3 February 1948, gez. Wandel, ibid., NL 36/735/25-6.

[54]Protokoll Nr. 80 (II) der Sitzung des Zentralsekretariats am 31. 5. 48, ibid., IV 2/2.1/ 203/2.

Walter Ulbricht over Richard Gyptner's signature to Paul Wandel. Gyptner "suggested" that the board of the "central for enlightenment and reconstruction," or Zentrale für Aufbau und Aufklärung, be chaired by Rudolf Engel, who replaced Weinert as third vice-president of the DVV one month later. Gyptner proposed Herbert Gute as Engel's deputy; and named five board members: Lorenz (listed as head of the SED's "press service"), Edith Baumann, Hans Mahle, Rudolf Herrnstadt, and one unspecified member.[55] The secretariat passed on the matter on 12 July, approving both a more precise definition of the agency's responsibilities and the apparently new draft of an SMAD order. The order itself justified the enterprise by explaining that it was a necessary way of providing the public with "sufficient information with respect to all questions pertaining to economic, cultural, and state life" and, importantly, for the support of the "economic, political, and cultural construction of the German state." Finally, the order enjoined the Deutsche Wirtschaftskommission to provide for the appropriate "material" support of the project and to recognize its importance in the context of the two-year plan.[56] Further details were provided in the accompanying justification that defined the operations of the proposed "central" in terms of popularizing all plans and measures pertaining to the economy, politics, and culture. Apart from internal administration, the "central" was to operate in the areas of information gathering, information evaluation, and state inspection, the latter division working in conjunction with the agency's "external offices."[57]

Three more weeks then passed before the Deutsche Wirtschaftskommission, now involved in the discussions, acted on the DVV's written request of 20 July 1948 for approval of the "central" and agreed to initiate further action leading to the issuance of an "appropriate order."[58] Whether the subject had been discussed in detail with the SMAD following Wandel's original letter to Sokolovskij on 3 February 1948 is unclear, as are the reasons for continuing delays. The first staffing proposal for the "central," dated 1 September 1948, then listed no fewer than 255 positions and had obviously been conceived in the interim as a huge "main administration" existing as a branch of the Deutsche Wirtschaftskommission."[59] to be run by the five-member information council, or *Informationsrat*, suggested by the SED.[60]

---

[55]Ulbricht (i.A. Gyptner) to Wandel, 7 July 1948. Bundesarchiv. Abt. Potsdam, R-2/ 1007/2. Wandel must have approved the "suggestions" quickly because they served a few days later as part of the proposal, or "Anlage," to the secretariat. See Zentrale für Aufklärung und Aufbau. Anlage Nr. 2 zum Protokoll Nr. 94 (II) vom 12. 7. 1948. Zentrales Parteiarchiv, IV 2/2.1/216/15.

[56]Befehlsentwurf, ibid., IV 2/2.1/216/16.

[57]Entwurf. Zentrale für Aufklärung und Aufbau, ibid., IV 2/2.1/216/17-19.

[58]Voretat und Stellenplan der Zentrale für Aufklärung und Aufbau in der DVV," 31 July 1948. Bundesarchiv, Abt. Potsdam, R-2/804/165.

[59]Voretat und Stellenplan der Zentrale für Aufklärung und Aufbau in der DVV," 31 July 1948. Bundesarchiv, Abt. Potsdam, R-2/804/165.

[60]Hauptverwaltung "Zentrale Aufklärung und Aufbau," 1 September 1948, ibid., R-2/1007/227.

The plans drawn up in early September corresponded roughly to those approved by the secretariat on 12 July, but contained additional information. There were three "main departments"; the first included four individual divisions (secretariat/information council; ties with foreign countries; office of cadres; and an office of "control, statistics, and state [affairs]"); the second department included press, radio, and "mass-propaganda" divisions; and the third was broken down into divisions of art (music, theater), literature, and cultural undertakings (cultural work in the factories, in the countryside, and cultural [mass] organizations). This particular plan designated the second of the four main departments as "direct propaganda," a name crossed out by hand in the document and replaced with the word "information"; and the third department was first called "indirect propaganda." "Indirect propaganda" was similarly marked through and "art and literature" penciled in.[61] The plan, which proposed a staff of 243 employees and an annual budget of over seventeen million marks, was accompanied by a summation of the need for such an information agency. Its task would be to "educate the German people toward democracy," provide the public with information about the "economic and political construction of the new state," explain the nature of economic, political, and cultural measures, and "mobilize the masses" in support of their implementation. The connection with order 234 was reestablished in the definition of that branch of the proposed agency responsible for coordinating the activities in the state capitals and "supporting the propagandistic intentions of the government."[62]

Even then, final action was delayed for months. Rudolf Engel spoke to the seventeenth ministers' conference in December 1948 about "coordinating the structure and work of the departments of cultural enlightenment at the state level" as well as organizing a committee to "coordinate and control propaganda and cultural enlightenment in the states and throughout the zone"; and a few days later, Wandel asked Engel to report to him on the matter in writing.[63] But the ideas behind formation of an "information" agency had apparently already shifted. An undated draft of a "minimal program" for the DVV's division of cultural enlightenment suggests that the entire project had again been scaled back to far more modest proportions. Drawn up sometime after announcement of the two-year plan in June 1948 and probably in connection with the ongoing development of the SED's first formal "cultural measures" introduced in January 1949,[64] this "minimal pro-

---

[61]Strukturplan. Zentrale für Aufklärung und Aufbau, 6 September 1948, ibid., R-2/1007/226-36.
[62]Einrichtung einer: Zentrale für Aufklärung und Aufbau, 6 September 1948, ibid., R-2/1007/234-36.
[63]Tagesordnung der 17. Ministerkonferenz am 19. Dezember 1948, ibid., R-2/4009; Ergebnisse der Abteilungsleitersitzung vom 22. Dezember 1948. Tagesordnung: Realisierung der Beschlüsse der 17. Ministerkonferenz, ibid., R-2/2146/5
[64]See Chapter Thirteen.

gram" broke all activity into three main categories: 1) cultural work in the factories (along with the FDGB); 2) cultural work in the countryside (working with the farmers' league, the VdgB, and with the administration of the farm-machine lending stations, the MAS); and 3) the coordination of plans and activities with other cultural organizations like the Kulturbund and the Volksbühne.[65] The many references to the mass organizations here and elsewhere—in all DVV plans for offices of "coordination," at the SED's "Potsdam consultations" on 22 October 1947, at the party's "state-political" conference in Werder in late July 1948, and then again in the SED's cultural plan introduced in January 1949—point to the broader context outside of which major political and cultural-political processes underway since order 234 cannot be fully understood. There had clearly been a shift in emphasis on the role to be played by all mass organizations following order 234; their new obligations within the framework of a national or half-national *governmental* apparatus now figured centrally in all discussions. But this new role presupposed an expansion of oversight. The SED itself needed to secure its domination of the mass organizations; and that was surely one of the reasons behind actions taken by the party leadership with respect to the Kulturbund (see below).

But these measures also went hand in hand with a similar consolidation of party power within central agencies of administration like the DVV; and the entire chain of events, especially apparent in the overall synchronization of diverse developments, reveals much about party strategy during the two years leading up to formation of the German Democratic Republic. It is important to understand, for instance, that on 12 February 1948 the SMAD issued order 32 governing the new composition and authority of the Deutsche Wirtschaftskommission; that this order put the DWK in charge of "coordinating" the activities of the individual central administrations; and that, most importantly, the order invested the DWK with the legal authority to issue ordinances and instructions binding upon "all German organs within the territory of the Soviet occupation zone."[66] It turned the party-dominated DWK into a centralized pre-governmental agency answerable only to the SMAD. Prior to order 32, there had been no such German central administration legally empowered to impose its will on state government; rather, the central administrations had to work primarily on the basis of SMAD orders or instructions and could influence the actions of state ministries mostly on the strength of "suggestions." Shortly after the issuance of order 32, the decision was then taken to incorporate all central administrations with the exception

[65]Entwurf für die Durchführung eines Minimalprogramms für die Abteilung Kulturelle Aufklärung, ibid., R-2/1007/40-41.
[66]See "Befehl Nr. 32 der SMAD über die Zusammensetzung und Vollmachten der Deutschen Wirtschaftskommission [12 February 1948]," *Geschichte des Staates und des Rechts der DDR*, p. 149.

of Volksbildung, Justice, and Internal affairs into the DWK as individual departments; and the following June, the DWK passed a binding resolution calling for the establishment of "uniform" administrative structures in state government set up to match the corresponding departments of the DWK.[67]

At the SED's state-political conference in July 1948, then, Walter Ulbricht raised the issue of the mass organizations again, but in conjunction with the central administrative agencies. He began by attacking administrative "bureaucracy" before echoing the Potsdam consultations of 22 October 1947 with a call for "new work methods" to be developed in the closest possible cooperation with the representatives of the mass organizations; in particular, administrative employees needed to participate in the "political life of the mass organizations" and consider themselves, in fact, as functionaries of these organizations. Such "cooperation" between administrative agencies and the mass organizations, Ulbricht said, would help prevent the emergence of "bureaucratic methods"; but it was equally important, he went on, that "a solid SED party organization with iron party discipline be created within administration; solid party groups with SED party leadership must be formed in the state administrative apparatus."[68] The second part of Ulbricht's remark was, however, a slip of the tongue corrected in the first republication of the original comment;[69] though both publications carried the identical SMAD license number, the phrase was cut out entirely because the reference to a "state administrative apparatus" well over a year prior to formation of the German Democratic Republic and before creation of the Federal Republic hinted at intentions vehemently denied by the SED. Otherwise, Ulbricht explained that the precondition of any change in administrative working methods was a "change in the ideology of employees in administration," and this change applied equally to members of the SED, unaffiliated employees, and those workers belonging to other parties. Even among "conscious socialists" with jobs in administration, there were sure to be "enemies of our party" who needed to be removed.[70]

The constant references in internal DVV plans and memoranda to "coordinating" work both with state governments and the mass organizations fit into this larger context; and more needs to be said later about the SED's "state-political conference" in July 1948 in order to trace its specific repercussions within the administrative apparatus of the DVV. For now it suffices to point out that the SED's cultural plan, introduced in January 1949, in

[67]See "Richtlinien des Sekretariats der DWK über die Tätigkeit der DWK für die sowjetische Besatzungszone [4 May 1948]," and "Beschluß des Sekretariats der DWK über die Vereinheitlichung zur Verbesserung der Zusammenarbeit zwischen der DWK und den Wirtschaftsverwaltungsorganen der Ländern [9 June 1948]," ibid., pp. 154-58.

[68]Ulbricht, "Die gegenwärtigen Aufgaben unserer demokratischen Verwaltung," *Die neuen Aufgaben unserer demokratischen Verwaltung*, p. 32

[69]See Ulbricht, *Lehrbuch für den demokratischen Staats- und Wirtschaftsaufbau*, p. 35

[70]Ulbricht, "Die gegenwärtigen Aufgaben unserer demokratischen Verwaltung," p. 32.

comparison with the "minimal plan" for a restructuring of the DVV's department of cultural enlightenment dating from fall 1948, spoke similarly of the need to involve a variety of "mass organizations" in work related to the two-year plan (mentioning the Kulturbund, branches of the Gewerkschaft 17, people's theaters, the FDJ, and the society for the study of Soviet culture); it contained a comparable section devoted exclusively to "cultural work among the masses," dividing it into the two subsections of factory and farm work and calling for close cooperation with the FDGB; and the plan's third category called for greater support of the "cultural work" of the press and radio.[71] These similarities suggest that the earlier proposal for a central propaganda agency, which must have failed to win the support of the SMAD at that time, was then integrated into the SED's later ideas for a cultural dimension to the two-year plan; and there is some reason to believe that the party, faced with the reluctance of the SMAD to approve such a huge new centralized propaganda apparatus, just as the Berlin blockade got underway, and quite possibly hesitant about fostering any stronger a public impression of state separatism, then looked to established mass organizations like the FDGB to accomplish much the same mass "educational" purpose.

Three other DVV memoranda, one dated 20 May, the other two 25 May 1949, shed additional light on developments pertaining to cultural enlightenment. In the first, Herbert Volkmann complained to Paul Wandel that the new structural plans for both his and Mahle's departments, to be voted upon the next day by the Deutsche Wirtschaftskommission, had not been presented to the two affected departments for discussion there first. He made particular note of his "grave reservations" about the structural plan for the department of cultural enlightenment; its "reorganization," he said, was supposed to eliminate the entirely unsatisfactory situation that existed before; but the area that Volkmann now called "Volkskultur," apparently the heart of the entire reorganized department, had been dealt with so "shabbily" in the structural plan now before the DWK that he seriously doubted its capacity to function at all; and complete ineffectiveness in this division meant the same ineffectiveness for the entire department. Volkmann added a few more details, from which the following may be inferred. The new office called "Volkskultur," within the division of cultural enlightenment, was supposed to rise "from the ruins of the old department." But in the meantime, cultural work in the factories and farms had acquired such proportions, and the "democratic organizations" had fallen so short of meeting the challenge, that one could only hope for "initiative from below to replace the work of the ineffective centrals." Volkmann then suggested that Volkskultur be split in two, cultural work in the factories and the same in the farms.[72]

[71]"Maßnahmen zur Durchführung der kulturellen Aufgaben im Rahmen des Zweijahrplans," *Protokoll der Ersten Parteikonferenz*, pp. 540-44.
[72]Volkmann to Wandel, 20 May 1949. Bundesarchiv. Abt. Potsdam, R-2/1007/47.

Magda Sendhoff, who appears to have been running what was left of the division of cultural enlightenment, backed Volkmann's suggestion and summed up the state of work in the factories and farms. "Central control by the FDGB and the main administration of the MAS cannot be assured either because of a shortage of personnel. Close cooperation with the states (state cultural committees, FDGB, and MAS administration) does not exist as yet." Sendhoff then closed with a request for strengthening cultural enlightenment within the DVV to help compensate for inadequacies elsewhere.[73] This is the extent of what DVV files reveal; on 6 September, with formation of the German Democratic Republic just around the corner, the party secretariat endorsed elaborate plans just approved by the Deutsche Wirtschaftskommission to set up an "information administration." This agency, operating under the aegis of the DWK, was charged with making laws and resolutions passed by the DWK and other administrations "intelligible" to the general population; and provisions were made for a total of 211 employees working under five main departments: press, "peace propaganda," information, broadcasting, and film. Its budget, based on the monthly figures provided for September through December, came to over three million marks annually.[74] The information administration was not headed by Rudolf Engel, however, but by Gerhart Eisler, who had just arrived in Soviet-occupied Germany after fleeing prosecution in the United States on charges of espionage. After creation of the GDR on 7 October 1949, the information office became the government's official press office or Amt für Information.

SMAD Order No. 6

These developments show how order 234 set processes in motion that later culminated in the final stage of political, economic, and cultural consolidation in Soviet-occupied Germany and extended into the early years of the GDR. But there were other developments related to the same order; some can be linked directly to it, whereas others emerged at roughly the same time and can be connected to order 234 solely on the basis of a rationale that included the same quest for improved "efficiency" through centralized coordination or control. Soon after order 234 came out, there was another DVV initiative much like the proposal to restructure cultural enlightenment; except that this one quickly led to an SMAD decree. For some reason, the initiative seems to have been handled even more discreetly than the other proposal; though the subject arose at the same time, plans for an office to

[73]Sendhoff to Wandel, both memoranda dated 25 May 1949, ibid., R-2-1007/45-6.
[74]Protokoll Nr. 42 der Sitzung des Politbüros am 6. September 1949 [Item 5: Schaffung der Verwaltung Information bei der DWK. Berichterstatter: Ulbricht]; Anlage Nr. 1. Schaffung der Verwaltung Information bei der DWK. Zentrales Parteiarchiv, IV 2/2/42/1 and 14-19.

"coordinate" matters of art and literature with the state ministries were apparently never introduced at any of the ministers' conferences, not in early December 1947, in late January, nor mid-April 1948. By then, the outlying ministries would have been in no position to balk anyway because the undertaking had already received the approval of the SMAD in January. In this instance, the circumstances surrounding the new office of coordination were not nearly as convoluted as related developments in cultural enlightenment. On 2 December 1947, even as the ministers met for the first day of their conference, Herbert Volkmann sent copies of DVV communications with the SMAD concerning creation of a new "office [or *Referat*] for coordinating the work of the division of art and literature" to general administration. Volkmann requested that the DVV's office of general administration establish contact with the administration of revenue and, via this office, with the SMAD's corresponding department of finance.[75] The supporting materials included a letter from Erich Weinert to Marshal Sokolovskij; a draft SMAD order drawn up by Weinert for approval, signature, and promulgation; and a letter from Volkmann to Dymschitz. In this letter, dated 8 January 1948, Volkmann asked Dymschitz to have Weinert's letter and draft order passed on to Sokolovskij by way of Tjulpanov and included a request that Tjulpanov intervene personally "wherever appropriate" in support of formal issuance of the decree. Volkmann also told Dymschitz that the DVV's office of personnel would discuss the matter with the SMAD's corresponding cadres division; in addition, the DVV's office of revenue would contact the central revenue administration, which, in turn, was responsible for informing the SMAD office of finance. Otherwise, Volkmann told Dymschitz that the division of art and literature would require some expansion, though there was nothing to compare with the proposed reorganization of cultural enlightenment; and Volkmann added that the order was important as a means of "creating an instrument able to eliminate inadequacies in the state governments and significantly strengthening the cadres" of the DVV.[76]

In a later document, Volkmann added a few more details. The "office for coordination of work" was to be run by the deputy head of art and literature, and the new office would be broken down into two main "desks." The first oversaw cooperation with state governmental authorities, the second, work with the cultural mass organizations. Together, these desks would be responsible for supporting the "weak cadres in the state governments" and backing them up in word and deed; if the difficulties were of an "organizational nature," the new division should be ready to oversee the implementation of

---

[75]Chef der Abteilung Kunst und Literatur an die Abteilung Allgemeine Verwaltung. Betrifft: Einrichtung eines Referats für Koordinierung der Arbeit in der Abteilung Kunst und Literatur, 2 December 1947. Bundesarchiv. Abt. Potsdam, R-2/805/15.
[76]Volkmann to Dymschitz, Informationsverwaltung—Abteilung Kultur—z.Hd. von Oberstleutnant Dymschitz (1 December 1947), ibid.

SMAD orders and the "directions of the central administration"; and it would likewise be responsible for ensuring the cultural political work of the mass organizations as well as carrying out "special tasks" at the state level. It was foreseen that the two office chiefs would spend roughly two weeks out of every month traveling and two weeks in the DVV.[77] In none of his remarks did Volkmann mention order 234, though in his letter to Sokolovskij, Weinert had worked it into his first sentence. The proposal, Weinert said, was designed to "secure compliance with order 234 in all propagandistically effective areas of art and literature." In fact, Weinert seemed at pains to tailor his request to known SMAD concerns by explaining that the offices of art and literature in the state governments were often inadequately staffed due to a shortage of "good cadres"; as a consequence, difficulties were frequently encountered in the "rapid and unified compliance with orders of the Soviet military administration and the resolutions of the conferences of state education and culture ministers." There was, additionally, insufficient state-level cooperation with those mass organizations with cultural responsibilities (Kulturbund, FDGB, Volksbühne); and many of these deficiencies could be remedied through better staffing. Weinert went on to explain that, due to the "propagandistic importance of these tasks," it was necessary to strengthen work in the states by creating a division responsible for "ensuring cooperation" on the spot, "eliminating difficulties," "dispensing advise," and thus supporting the weak cadres in the states. Weinert proposed Herbert Gute as the head of such a division.[78] Weinert's draft order repeated the call for creation of a division designed to further "cooperation with the state governments and the large cultural organizations and to ensure compliance with propagandistic and organizational tasks in the area of art and literature in connection with order 234."[79] By 16 January 1948, the order was in hand, though the SMAD had altered Weinert's language somewhat. The document made no mention of order 234, but otherwise summed up its purpose less euphemistically as contributing to the "further consolidation of control by the Verwaltung für Volksbildung over the activity of corresponding state ministries in the Soviet occupation zone, the coordination of the [DVV's] work with the large German cultural organizations of the entire zone . . . , and the guarantee of systematic local control."[80]

[77]Erlauterungen zum Stellenplan in der Abteilung Kunst und Literatur vom 8. 1. 48, ibid., R-2/1007/164-68.

[78]Weinert to Marshal Sokolovskij, 1 December 1947, ibid., R-2/805/16.

[79]Vorschlag für einen Befehl zur Errichtung eines Referats für Koordinierung der Arbeit bei der Deutschen Verwaltung für Volksbildung, Abteilung Kunst und Literatur, ibid., R-2/ 805/17.

[80]Befehl des Oberbefehlshabers der Sowjetischen Militäradministration in Deutschland. No. 6. [16] Januar 1948. Betrifft: Schaffung einer Koordinierungsstelle für die Länder der Sowjetischen Besatzungszone in der Abteilung für Kunst und Volksbildung [sic] der DVV, ibid., R-2/ 804/76.

The Ideological Power of Marxism

These developments unfolded in lock step with the organizational and administrative changes undertaken in connection with complaints about the party's ostensible inattentiveness toward cultural issues voiced at and after the conference in September 1947. These internal discussions must have provided at least some of the further impulses driving the "reorganization" of the DVV even as, in turn, those changes reflected adjustments considered necessary within the party's own cultural apparatus. On 8 December 1947, a bitter dispute erupted at a board meeting that shifted attention temporarily away from the objective of organizing "SED writers" and led to the replacement of the more narrowly understood gathering of party literati by a broadly conceived cultural congress. As he told the story to the board, Wilhelm Pieck took it for granted that J. R. Becher would speak to the Volkskongreß, which met on 6 and 7 December, on behalf of the Kulturbund. Becher declined, suggested Paul Wiegler instead, and failed to coach him properly. When the Volkskongreß excluded Kulturbund representatives from the delegation picked to lobby the foreign ministers meeting in London, Becher was insolent enough, said Pieck, to protest the omission and accuse the party, again, of being "hostile toward culture." Pieck told Becher on the spot that "comrades" active in the Kulturbund were "political ignoramuses" who took no interest in the work of the party and, at the congress in September and again in connection with the people's congress, had the brass to talk about an "attitude hostile to culture." Pieck told the board that the party intended to talk with the Kulturbund about interest in "political life."[81] Otto Meier rushed to Becher's defense; he criticized Pieck for waiting until the night before the Volkskongreß to ask the Kulturbund to name a speaker, suggested that Becher, a "well-known SED man," was wise not to speak himself, expressed understanding for the anger felt by Kulturbund officials at having been left off the delegation (Becher was added a few days later),[82] and objected to the characterization of them all as "political ignoramuses." Pieck retorted that his remarks applied to Becher only, whom he reviled for his year long absence at board meetings, and lost his temper entirely over Meier's accusation that he, Pieck, had attacked the Kulturbund itself.

The heated exchange that followed between Pieck and Meier, with interjections by Ackermann, brought the meeting to a standstill. When Pieck took the floor later on, he again vented his spleen over Becher's accusation, first

[81]Stenographische Niederschrift über die 5. (19.) Tagung des Parteivorstandes der SED. Zentrales Parteiarchiv, IV 2/1/18/8-12.
[82]See Protokoll Nr. 29 (II) der Sitzung des Zentralsekretariats am 11. 12. 47, ibid., IV 2/2.1/157.

raised at the congress in September, that the party leadership was "hostile" toward culture, intellectuals, and the Kulturbund. Pieck upbraided Becher on the telephone; Becher hung up on him; and Pieck now insisted that "political ignorance" was a proper characterization for such behavior. Finally, calling Meier's insinuation that he had expressed hostility toward the Kulturbund "shameless," Pieck denied having used the phrase "political ignoramasus." The discussion ended in Weimann's conclusion, an opinion widely shared, that the Kulturbund needed to be more systematically included in the party's work as the best way of influencing other intellectuals.[83] Shortly thereafter, the secretariat made plans for a major discussion of the party's cultural politics at a future board meeting and, in preparation for the event, talked things over with representatives of the Kulturbund on 5 January 1948.[84] Kulturbund proposals that also placed cultural policy on the agenda of the board meeting in February, conferred membership in it to four eminent intellectuals, and pushed for a "representative conference" in May for the purpose of airing cultural issues were tentatively accepted.[85] The secretariat endorsed the suggestions three days later, named Paul Wandel to present the report to the board in February, and listed Becher as the main speaker at the cultural conference in May.[86] (This was the same meeting, by the way, that first discussed the "reorganization" of the DVV.) Becher still figured as the featured speaker as late as 22 March 1948 (in the conference program approved by the secretariat),[87] but he had not actually consented to deliver a speech on the subject of "Germany's Cultural Unity and the Intellectuals." Nor did he; that talk was given by a fairly obscure professor by the name of Heinrich Deiters. Moreover, though he was supposed to sit on the presidium,[88] and later did so, Becher never uttered a word at the congress itself, the same stunt that, according to Pieck, he pulled at the Volkskongreß; and it may be that his silence was Becher's peeved reaction to what seems to have been Tjulpanov's private criticism of his remarks to the Kulturbund conference in May 1947 as "bourg.(eois) nationalism."[89]

At the board meeting on 11 February 1948, Wandel summed up the party's cultural accomplishments and charted its path for the near future. His

---

[83]Ibid., IV 2/1/18/36-38, 47-8, 63.
[84]See Protokoll Nr. 30 (II) der Sitzung des Zentralsekretariats am 18. 12. 47; and Protokoll Nr. 32 (II) der Sitzung des Zentralsekretariats am 29. 12. 1947, ibid., IV 2/2.1/158/2 and 160/4.
[85]Protokoll Nr. 33 (II) der Sitzung des Zentralsekretariats am 5. 1. 48; and Anlage Nr. 1 zum Protokoll Nr. 33 (II), ibid., IV 2/2.1/161/1111-2, 4. The four Kulturbund officials "coopted" were Becher, Abusch, Heinrich Deiters, and Werner Krauss. (See Protokoll Nr. 44 (II) der Sitzung des Zentralsekretariats am 9. 2. 1948, ibid., IV 2/2.1/171.)
[86]Protokoll Nr. 34 (II) der Sitzung des Zentralsekretariats am 8. 1. 48, ibid., IV 2/2.1/162/3.
[87]Protokoll Nr. 60 (II) der Sitzung des Zentralsekretariats am 22. 3. 1948, ibid., IV 2/2.1/185/25.
[88]Protokoll Nr. 72 (II) der Sitzung des Zentralsekretariats am 5. 5. 1948; Anlage Nr. 1, ibid., IV 2/2.1/195/3-5.
[89]See Tulpanow Bericht. 11. 7. 1947. Bericht über innerparteiliche Lage im letzten Halbjahr I u. II 47, ibid., NL 36/734/300.

comments centered around much of the usual rhetoric—the party desired to win the intellectuals for the "democratic people's movement," not for socialism itself, and this movement was distinguished by its nonpartisanship. But Wandel acknowledged that the subject of cultural policy arose in the first place only because of protests about what some of its own intellectuals considered the party's neglect of this area; and he went on to emphasize the importance of acquiring the backing of intellectuals for goals connected with the reconstruction of the country. After all, said Wandel, the effect of a single book was potentially enormous; and the same was true of contributions made by scholars, engineers, doctors, and the like. The intelligentsia, creative and technical, had the capacity to influence millions. But the picture that he painted of attitudes prevalent among intellectuals was somewhat discouraging, and Wandel believed that their many reservations could only be overcome once they lost their fear of socialism. Unfortunately, he went on, too many intellectuals cared little about social and political life in Soviet-occupied Germany; few took the prohibition of the Kulturbund personally, for instance, and not very many of the protests against the ban resulted from "independent initiative." The smear campaign against the SED and the Soviet Union had also fostered the impression that the party pursued "totalitarian tendencies," committed itself to an elimination of freedom of speech, to doctrine, dogma, and intellectual impoverishment, and threatened "elemental human rights." In the meantime, Wandel continued, essential changes since 1945 had caused "new fronts" to form that made it difficult to avoid political issues. Besides, the situation was by no means entirely disheartening; nearly 80,000 party members were intellectuals who worked actively at developing their individual capabilities while improving their comprehension of Marxism. Still, Wandel worried about the danger to the party caused by the assumption that, "today or tomorrow," it intended to curtail human rights. Responding to the accusation, he stated that the party's commitment to the freedom of art and science was, to the contrary, solidly anchored in its official statements; and these principles had nothing to do with "tactical issues." Even so, Wandel contended that "complete freedom" was an illusion; intellectuals needed to realize that there was nothing inherently worthwhile about the absence of a consensus in "fundamental questions" and that the existence of conflicting opinions was not proof of democracy. Intellectual dispute and intellectual inquiry could occur, but social progress hinged upon the articulation of a "unified, correct view."[90]

Wandel had more to say on the subject of Marxism because, in his own words, so many intellectuals balked at its monopolistic demands. Apparently, large numbers of Soviet-zone intellectuals were clueless when it came to

[90]Stenographische Niederschrift über die 7. (21.) Tagung des Parteivorstandes der SED am 11./ 12 Februar 1948, ibid., IV 2/1/20/62-99.

the relationship between doctrine and nonpartisanship. Trying to explain it, Wandel said that Marxism was a science; as science, its advocates could not reasonably be expected to slacken their efforts to promote its teachings as the "only correct scientific understanding." But intellectuals had no grounds for believing that the "exclusivity" of Marxism resembled anything from the recent past, that is, fascism; indeed, the revolutionary power of Marxism could serve to rally intellectuals around it once they understood that "our movement," as Wandel called it, would make history and that attempts to avoid it were pointless. Besides, the SED had direct responsibility for cultural affairs throughout Soviet-occupied Germany and was thus accountable for guaranteeing the "material existence" of intellectuals. Once they realized that "our party and our democratic order" assured them of a secure existence, winning their support would be easy. These tasks, connected with what Wandel called the "ideological offensive of Marxism" and focused on the development of a "democratic intelligentsia," needed to dominate the work of the party. Finally, Wandel broached the subject of the Kulturbund. No less than the party itself, the organization had fallen short in its efforts to mobilize intellectuals. But in some instances, it was the party's fault for forcing the Kulturbund to tamper with its nonpartisanship and misusing it as an "auxiliary"; the mere presence of party members in positions of leadership occasionally complicated matters because it eliminated the need to work hard at persuading "our partners." It was simpler, Wandel said, to "let the machinery of the apparatus" produce decisions, resolutions, participation in congresses, and the like. But those difficulties and others specifically related to the Kulturbund did not diminish the fact that it was the "most important organization for our cultural work."[91]

The Kulturbund acted accordingly over the remainder of the year, pointing fingers at the West to divert attention from its own political and ideological commitments. After all, prohibited, the organization offered powerful evidence of Western "totalitarianism"[92]—proof needed at a time when the SED and SMAD were themselves cracking down. Bemoaning the ban on "democratic literature" and book bonfires in the Western zones, Alexander Abusch called for all "intellectual, political, and economic" zonal borders to be torn down.[93] But he did so just before the Russians began their blockade of Berlin, whereupon Abusch characterized the prohibition of the Kulturbund as the start of the "American blockade against democratic culture in Berlin" and as the onset of a "chain of similar acts of violence against other progressive organizations."[94] These acts included the formation of rival

[91]Ibid.
[92]See "Im Koordinierungsausschuß. Das Kulturbundverbot," *Tägliche Rundschau*, 8 February 1948; "Kulturbund im Kontrollrat," *Neues Deutschland*, 7 February 1948.
[93]Abusch, "An die deutschen Kulturschaffenden," *Sonntag*, 21 March 1948.
[94]Abusch, "Der Kulturbund und die geistige Blockade," *Tägliche Rundschau*, 7 August 1948.

projects in the Western sectors of Berlin such as the "free" Volksbühne and the "free" university.[95] There was also a "free" Kulturbund, which must have been a monumental failure, though one would never know it to judge by the abuse heaped upon the organization in the Soviet-zone press. Its organizers, "acolytes of Goebbels," puppet Germans who followed orders issued by their military governments, were execrated for dividing German culture.[96]

Otherwise, the real Kulturbund continued to make forceful denials that it aimed for a "monopoly"; the organization merely wished to "coordinate" things; moreover, anyone who charged that the Kulturbund was "Communist" behaved like a fascist in a campaign destined to end in freedom for "all enemies of democracy" and "bonfires for Marxists or Communists."[97] Such threats to its integrity notwithstanding, the Kulturbund insisted that it would remain true to its principles, easy enough considering that the organization's obligations had not changed "one iota" since its formation and had only become more urgent due to the "refascistization" of the rest of the country. In any case, the Kulturbund never aimed to endorse "tendencies" advanced by any particular side, but it fully intended to embrace undertakings that coincided with its original principles; and because the Kulturbund had not been the one to jettison them, the "decisions made over the last three years" came easy.[98] Indeed, banning cultural organizations like the Kulturbund marked the allies, the Americans especially, as true totalitarians who talked of freedom while refascistizing Germany; whereas the only "freedom" for Western intellectuals minus the quotation marks consisted of the right freely granted them to wallow in existentialist pessimism, the better to render them defenseless when confronted with the invidious actions of the neofascists.[99] The real reason why the allies banned the Kulturbund was because its members promoted the democratic renewal of the nation and opposed Germany's "colonization" by the Americans.[100]

It was typical of early 1948 that the SED's cultural functionaries spoke most about nonpartisan just as the party announced a "change" in its approach to intellectuals involving anything but impartiality. Wandel's report to the party's executive board was an exemplary blend of unalloyed dogma with empty assurances of open-mindedness. According to the resolution passed there, the party needed to rededicate its efforts to win the support of

[95]See "Gelenkte Illusion," *Sonntag*, 1 August 1948.
[96]See Abusch, "Der Kulturbund und die geistige Blockade," *Tägliche Rundschau*, 7 August 1948; Gysi, "Und nun—die Kulturspalter," *Tägliche Rundschau*, 29 July 1948; Hammer, "Scheidung der Geister," *Neues Deutschland*, 23 July 1948.
[97]"Der Kulturbund und seine Gegner," *Neues Deutschland*, 14 April 1948.
[98]See "Sauberkeit," *Sonntag*, 11 July 1948.
[99]See Abusch, "Der Kulturbund und die geistige Blockade," *Tägliche Rundschau*, 7 August 1948.
[100]Hammer, "Die Freiheit der Kultur und ihre Feinde," *Tägliche Rundschau*, 1 August 1948.

progressive intellectuals because they were still insufficiently involved in the "nationwide democratic movement."[101] Though this particular statement also expressed "gratification" at the fact that so many "scholars, artists, writers, and other cultural figures" had joined the movement for unity and a just peace (the fictional "mass movement" behind the Volkskongreß), and were helping build a new democratic order, the resolution alluded to much dissatisfaction. The party had been remiss in its responsibility to help the scientists and artists overcome "obstacles" to their creative endeavors; but many ordinary intellectuals, even those who understood the necessity of restructuring Germany democratically, still cringed at the thought of a "resolute fight" to crush reaction and imperialism. The resolution spoke once again of the party's own "considerable underestimation" of the importance of intellectuals, as well as of its "extreme neglect" of efforts to win them over, before listing specific objectives that summarized developments underway since the party conference the previous fall. Much like Wandel, however, who may well have drafted the resolution anyway, the document attempted to balance the SED's vigorous pursuit of cultural objectives with declarations of respect for nonpartisanship. There was a word of caution about endangering the confidence of the intellectuals in "the sincerity of our nationwide, democratic aspirations" by infringing upon the nonpartisanship of the popular movement for unity and a just peace; and a comparable warning was conveyed about the party's intention of "furthering" the work of the Kulturbund. Without relinquishing the right to stand up for their "consistent democratic viewpoint," party members active in the organization were told to respect the integrity of its nonpartisanship and to oppose any attempt to turn it into a "party appendage." Otherwise, the resolution called for a well-conceived ideological dispute with "bourgeois views," emphasized the significance of instilling a better sense of the party's ideological obligations in its own intellectuals, and talked of expanding its offices of culture according to central guidelines. Finally, as proof of a "tangible change" in the party's cultural work, preparations for a "party cultural conference" would proceed.[102]

The private meeting of "SED writers," first talked about the previous fall, took place one month before. On 8 and 9 April 1948, fifty-six writers and assorted functionaries heard Klaus Gysi tell them that the party resolution passed at the board meeting in mid-February had addressed many of the concerns raised during their meeting on 12 December 1947.[103] But that criticism had to reflect itself now in a greater sense of obligation toward the party; and the writers needed to "confront ideological problems head-on." Gysi's advice culminated in the following exhortation:

---

[101]"Intellektuelle und Partei. Entschließung des Parteivorstandes [11 February 1948]," *Dokumente der Sozialistischen Einheitspartei Deutschlands*, p. 262.
[102]Ibid., p. 265.
[103]See Anwesenheitsliste am 8./9. April 1948. Zentrales Parteiarchiv, IV 2/906/254.

The best writers are among us; and it is our superiority that gives us the right to attack. We must wage our struggle elastically, but not be defensive about it. It is wrong to avoid a critical discussion of recent events in the Soviet Union. When the C. P. of the USSR criticizes writers and musicians publicly, some of whom emerge as winners of the Stalin prize, this goes to show that such a vibrant democratic process has nothing to do with any kind of measure taken by the NKVD.

Gysi went on to conclude that "our previously defensive ideological posture" resulted from a lack of ideological clarity; but the resolution adopted at the board meeting in February had produced major change.[104] The writers were also addressed by Otto Kielmeyer, who defended the work of the Kultureller Beirat and provoked an outburst of anger at that agency. In fact, the gathering of SED writers ended with the acceptance of resolutions that pleaded for something to be done about the "catastrophic paper shortage" and that requested either "reorganization" of the Kultureller Beirat or consideration of some other "organizational" solution.[105]

The cultural conference that gathered one month later focused on more substantive issues of politics. On the eve of the conference, for instance, Alexander Abusch contrasted cultural-political conditions in the East with those in the West while delivering himself of an assessment that repeated the contentions of the February resolution. Though some of the intellectuals had yet to grasp the historical significance of the changes made in Soviet-occupied Germany, many others had begun to overcome their "inner vacillation" and realize the creative possibilities that democratic reconstruction made available to them. This also explained why the Western press slandered the cultural changes in the Soviet zone as a form of regulation and regimentation akin to a fascistic *Gleichschaltung*, even as the Western zones carried out the orders of Wall Street by waging a "cold war against the intellect." Thus it was that "Marshall-plan politicians" tried to gag Western intellectuals engaged in an honest quest of a shared democratic road to national unity. The struggle to "renew" the German people and safeguard the unity of German culture was thus an on-going battle waged by intellectuals in East *and* West.[106] Even while reiterating its support of cultural unity in spring 1948, however, the SED also intensified efforts to bring Soviet-zone culture into substantial conformity with Soviet norms and announced that the future na-

[104]Tagung parteigenössischer Schriftsteller der Ostzone am 8. und 9. April 1948, ibid., IV 2/906/254/66-8.
[105]Entschließung der SED-Schriftstellertagung vom 8. und 9. April 48 (der Kulturabteilung zur Bearbeitung überwiesen). Zentrales Parteiarchiv, IV 2/906/254/76-7.
[106]Abusch, "Das Ringen der deutschen Intellektuellen um die Demokratie," *Tägliche Rundschau*, 1 May 1948.

tional German culture would "bear the name of socialism."[107]

Taken literally, the party's rhetoric suggests that the SED had lost interest in any kind of moderate cultural-political position adopted for the sake of national unity, just as the party's hardening ideological stance effectively dashed the few remaining possibilities for political and economic reunification with the rest of Germany. As Tjulpanov said in late April, failure to consolidate the position of the working class out of deference to bourgeois concepts of national unity constituted "class betrayal."[108] Abusch summed up the new rigidity during the conference in May by noting that "the struggle for Germany's cultural unity can only be waged as part of the fight for the democratization of all Germany."[109] But if the party leadership ever sensed that local permutations of Zhdanovist cultural ideals had no realistic chance of acceptance in West Germany, then their calls for cultural unity were hollow; at best the party's national posture might lessen the adverse impression made by the worsening cultural climate in Soviet-occupied Germany and hide what had probably been a conscious decision to accept the cultural division of Germany as part of the price of controlling half the country politically. After all, the new discourse made it clear that cultural unity hinged on political change in West Germany capable of guaranteeing a healthy climate for a "socialist" national culture. Much of this thinking is reflected in the "resolution on cultural politics" passed at the May conference. The Communists never hid their determination to work toward socialism; but never before had they insisted openly that the "intellectual power" of Marxism be brought to bear in order to change "our social structure" *and* renew German culture.[110]

True, changes occurring all along in cultural politics had increased limitations on creative activity considerably through the imposition of socialist-realist principles, though these were defined in the language of democracy rather than called by their proper name. But the Communists now coupled Marxism with the future of German culture in ways that they had thus far avoided. The current intellectual age, the resolution stated, was distinguished by the contradiction between the inescapable crisis of bourgeois thought, expressed in fashionable philosophies that transfigured the decline of capitalism into existential fear, and the intellectual power of Marxism. This remark sharpened the cultural equivalent of the two-camps theory by substituting the far more narrowly defined concept of Marxism for generalities like peace and democracy. Into this dichotomy the Communists then fit not

---

[107]See "Wende der Kultur," *Neues Deutschland*, 5 May 1948.
[108]April 1948. Vortrag vom (S. Tulpanov), SMAD. Hs. Notizen A.A. dazu, Zentrales Parteiarchiv, NL 109/20/100-12.
[109]*Protokoll der Verhandlungen des Ersten Kulturtages der Sozialistischen Einheitspartei Deutschlands* [5-7 May 1948], p. 115.
[110]"Entschließung zur Kulturpolitik," ibid., p. 265. Subsequent citations are provided in the text.

only the hardening cultural policy designed specifically for Soviet-occupied Germany, but, with no modifications worthy of mention, declared that this same program committed them to a "nationwide democratic cultural program" (264). The fact of the matter was that by 1948 the Communists hoped to use intellectuals in East *and* West to help win the cold war. But this required a different set of tactics based on a more open profession of their ideological beliefs and political intentions—at the very moment that the combined effects of cultural zhdanovism and the transformation of the SED into a Stalinist party complicated the task of winning supporters immeasurably.

The resolution passed in May suggests the extent of the problem caused by linkages that the party now freely acknowledged: *"The new epoch of culture will be the culture of socialism! Everything for the unity of Germany! Everything for the democratic renewal of Germany! The future belongs to socialism! (270)."* Nor did Wilhelm Pieck try to hide the fact that the party planned major changes; he opened the conference by noting that the SED had organized the gathering for the express purpose of making a "tangible change" in the party's cultural work and for proclaiming its cultural program (9). But Pieck also alluded to challenges that later speakers explained more fully. He began by dredging up the subject of collective guilt, less so generally than as he thought that it applied to the majority of intellectuals. The party hoped to use these intellectuals to popularize its developing plans for reconstruction, but could not hope to do so without their enthusiastic backing. In response to their apathy, the party reminded them of their collective behavior under the Nazis in order to suggest that their present political abstinence, or obstinacy, matched their earlier conduct. But Pieck also insisted upon making certain clumsy assurances that hinted at the real problem. The SED recognized the full equality of all other parties, he said, but it had the "greater responsibility" to see that Germany not be dismembered and the people reduced to colonial subjects, driven into a new war against the Soviet Union. Even so, he added, this should not be twisted into meaning that the SED laid claim to exclusivity, besides which the party had no stomach for a party dictatorship anyway; rather, the Communists wanted the broadest possible democracy (12-13). Other speakers returned to the same subject, or circled around it; but either way, the conference indicated that the specter of "sovietization" still hobbled the party in its efforts to win supporters.

Otto Grotewohl, for instance, contrasted the party's vision of a future German culture and the scientific world view of Marxism with the nihilism, neofascism, and "democratically camouflaged big-capitalist totalitarianism" of the West. True, he went on to say that the German Communists would not be Marxists if they sought to transfer the Soviet experience to Germany (58), but also indicated that "we cannot yet set ourselves the task today of creating in Germany a socialist culture because the necessary prerequisites are still lacking." Not only did his comment equate "socialist culture" with the general characteristics of Soviet culture, it clearly revealed the nature of the SED's ultimate objective. More worrisome than Grotewohl's "cannot yet" were his detailed remarks about the party's cultural preferences and aversions. He linked the latter to those cultural tendencies of the past that had caused so many intellectuals to succumb to the allures of fascism, asking which historical currents "can we accept because they correspond with the trends that we represent and which must we reject because they preceded and prepared the way for an attitude of mind that ultimately led to fascist dictatorship" (32). Grotewohl answered that the sole determinant of the truth and value of a cultural trend resided in its relationship to historical and social development. Hence, any intellectual movement not anchored in the masses remained "rootless" and necessarily decadent—the mere semblance of culture because it did not express historical movement. Art for art's sake was a mark of "decadence, alienation from life," and as such was "inimical to the people"; whereas true culture dealt with the real issues of the day. It thus needed to take a stand on the question, "for or against the people's struggle for liberation—for the restructuring of existing conditions in the interest of human liberation or for the retention of these circumstances with all their contradictions." There was no alternative (33-34).

Grotewohl would have been hard-pressed to come up with a better cultural equivalent of the two-camps theory in his bid to nudge intellectuals in the proper direction, and it seems perfectly clear that they could avoid being relegated to the wrong side only if they stopped vacillating. This naturally raised the question of the party's plans for intellectuals too stubborn or too naive to grasp the signs of the times and who persisted in creating art that Grotewohl called "inimical to the people."[111] Nonetheless, while he admitted that intellectuals often shuddered when they heard talk of the "science" of Marxism-Leninism, Grotewohl felt justified in promising that the party had no plans to force its views on anyone; "we put our entire trust in the power of persuasion inherent in our world view; we know that Marxism is all-powerful because it is true" (62-63). One of the party's rising cultural functionaries, Stefan Heymann, argued similarly that party members needed to discuss matters with the intellectuals more frequently, using these talks to express their Marxist principles clearly because the past had shown that the discussions would end with the Communists "the winners" (240-42).

But "Marxism-Leninism" was losing its powers of persuasion to a considerable degree because events in the Soviet Union, principally the central committee's announcement of its various decrees and Zhdanov's vicious speech, spoke more eloquently to the nature of socialist culture than all the other rhetoric combined. Doubts caused by these events had to be dispelled, and in spring 1948 ten Soviet-zone intellectuals, including the poet Stephan

---

[111]Ibid., p. 34. The phrase was "Volksfeindlichkeit."

Hermlin, writers Bernhard Kellermann, Eduard Claudius, and Anna Seghers, the stage producer Wolfgang Langhoff, Wolfgang Harich, and Jürgen Kuczynski went on a tour of the Soviet Union conducted by Alexander Dymschitz. They returned to regale the Soviet-zone press with reports of their personal experiences, full of wonder and amazement and just in time for the May conference. No less than four of them, Hermlin, Claudius, Seghers, and Kellermann, wrote travelogues in which they lavished praise on the USSR,[112] whereas Langhoff rushed to the podium at the May conference to testify in a particularly auspicious setting. Langhoff had never visited the USSR, he admitted, and wondered whether his previous assumptions would withstand the "confrontation with reality"; they did, he said, and the rest of the world could sleep easy (152). But those generalities were less important in the context of the conference than Langhoff's remarks on the subject of the central-committee edicts, the fourth of which had just been passed excoriating Soviet composers. For understandable reasons, artists and intellectuals skeptical about the SED's cultural-political intentions took the decrees as an ill augury, rather than as evidence of cultural policies that guaranteed a bright future. For the Communists, it was a simple matter of providing verbal assurances that resolved the apparent contradictions. Langhoff related how he had asked Ilja Ehrenburg whether there was anything to the charge of state coercion and regimentation in the USSR and how it affected creative freedom. Ehrenburg assured him that no country in the world enjoyed such a variety of styles and artistic means of expression as Soviet writers, and that assurance was apparently enough for Langhoff. Even so, he also discussed the subject with no less an authority than Mikhail Zoshchenko, one of the targets of the central-committee decrees; and Zoshchenko uttered his indignation at the Western press for publishing misleading reports about his situation. As Langhoff put it, the objections to Zoshchenko's writing had been voiced by the Soviet general public and had nothing to do with a "ruling from above, an act of coercion, a ban" (153).[113]

Langhoff's report of his personal experience was meant to put the matter to rest at the conference in May, but cultural-political events in the USSR remained a source of concern; and it seems unlikely that Heinrich Deiters' remarks on the subject helped either. He, too, alluded to questions associated with "art-political events" in the Soviet Union, adding that the public there was fully justified in using its "agencies to involve itself in helping work out artistic standards"; the public had a perfect right, he went on, to evaluate artistic accomplishments according to their value or lack of value to the life of society. This had nothing to do with control over the production of art; it

[112]See Claudius, *Notizen nebenbei;* Bernhard und Ellen Kellermann, *Wir kommen aus Sowjetrußland*; Hermlin, *Russische Eindrücke*; Seghers, *Sowjetmenschen. Lebensbeschreibungen nach ihren Berichten.*
[113]See also Langhoff, "Moskauer Impressionen," *Die neue Gesellschaft* 8 (1948): 29-32.

was a matter of cooperation between the artists and society's "political appointees." Anyway, there was no such thing as a region free of politics; the intellectuals had to "recognize that their abilities always serve a political cause; the only choice available to them is the pick of which one" (74).

But what "agencies" did Deiters have in mind and what kinds of artistic standards were emerging in Soviet-occupied Germany? Many of these agencies already existed, the main one being the SED itself; as Pieck put it at the board meeting in December 1947, the SED was actually the best Kulturbund or cultural association around;[114] and in the course of 1948, the artistic standards acceptable to the party became clearer then ever before. At the May conference, Anton Ackermann delivered the major address, entitled "Marxist Cultural Politics," and fleshed out Deiters' argument. He repeated the general contention that the "party of Marxism-Leninism" differed from all other parties because scientific points of view guided it, whether the questions involved politics, economics, or cultural issues and whether day-to-day problems or the ultimate objectives of the "movement" were involved (73). But having just pronounced a theory of single-party exclusivity, Ackermann went on to explain that socialism did not bring the national culture of any people "into line"; it was not a *Gleichschaltung*, and the proof of that assertion resided in the words of none other than Stalin—the multi-national culture of the USSR was "national in form, socialist in content." Correspondingly, a future socialist culture in other countries would never "liquidate" national cultures, nor would the cultural forms of one nation ever be exported to another. The culture of a socialist Germany would not be a "copy of the culture of other peoples" (192-93). As a matter of fact, Ackermann went on to say, cultural-political events in the Soviet Union offered evidence favoring, not refuting this contention. Certain Soviet composers had just been taken to task because they hid their renunciation of the cultural heritage behind a cloak of experimentation, whereas "Marxist critics" in the USSR insisted upon the continuation of that heritage along with truthfulness and "masterly ability." In like manner, "German Marxists" demanded that art respect the achievements of the classics, demonstrate real ability, and do battle against "artificial, false experimentation." Those who chose to resist these demands only proved their own "maliciousness and decadence" because decadence in art consisted of the empty abstraction, the destructive pursuit of ill-conceived originality in total disregard of the classical heritage, and the lack of professional ability. Ackermann called the result "pseudo-art," divorced from reality and alien to the people—*volksfremd* (195-96).

Ackermann's remarks were a categorical endorsement of the artistic and cultural-political standards that the central-committee decrees reaffirmed in

---

[114]Stenographische Niederschrift über die 5. (19.) Tagung des Parteivorstandes, 8 December 1947. Zentrales Parteiarchiv, IV 2/1/18/12.

the USSR, and this endorsement made it plain that only art conceived along those lines would be acceptable to the SED. As a natural consequence, the SED's hopes of using the intellectuals to hasten the pace of "Germany's economic, political, and cultural reconstruction," as Ackermann put it, were bound to fade if the party failed to gain their public acceptance of the basic principles embodied in those edicts. But the virtual collapse of the writers' congress in October 1947 over this very issue proved just how difficult the task would be, and the appearance of the last edict in February 1948, which condemned Muradeli's opera *The Great Friendship* for its dissonance and atonality, only made matters worse. Nevertheless, in an attempted display of conciliation, Ackermann called upon the party membership to divest itself of any lingering prejudice toward intellectuals and judge them entirely on their actions and accomplishments; but he finished his sentence by appending the additional remark that they be evaluated on "the position adopted by them with respect to the new democratic order" (198). Under those circumstances, Ackermann's further comment that the SED had no interest in "coercion" was less than persuasive. Of course, the Communists preferred that the intellectuals adopt the positions voluntarily, and Ackermann promised the party's sympathetic support to those who proved themselves to be "friends of democracy and peace" (198). But in 1948, the party expanded considerably the responsibilities incumbent upon such "friends" or, put differently, curtailed severely the kinds of cultural activities capable of passing muster. For despite the contention that the conference had not been marked by "narrow-minded dogmatism" or "totalitarian cultural tendencies," the party used it to confront German intellectuals with an "ideological choice"; the SED called upon them to reject "decadence" while advocating the use of the "intellectual power of Marxism" to renew culture because, as Pieck put it, without Marxism there could be no change in Germany's intellectual development (271). Pieck also urged that the party's demands be put into action in order to bring about the culture of socialism and that these demands be "hammered into the consciousness" of working Germans. In that vein, and with a promise to do everything necessary to ensure the victory of the "democratic movement," Pieck closed the conference.[115]

A few days later, Ackermann told a board meeting that the congress had been a "planned manifestation of the superiority of Marxism over its enemies, the intellectual vigor of our movement, and the noble ethical desire for culture inherent in our struggle." But this "spirit" needed to permeate every branch of the party; and to emphasize his point, Ackermann repeated criticism voiced a few days earlier by Sergej Tjulpanov. Speaking of the SED's "dominant state position," Tjulpanov had chastised the leadership for its

[115]"Kultur aus dem Volke," *Sonntag*, 16 May 1948; Pieck, "Schlußansprache," *Protokoll der Verhandlungen des Ersten Kulturtages der SED*, pp. 272 and 274.

failure to exercise adequate control over the "implementation of resolutions" passed at the uppermost levels of the party.[116] Ackermann used identical criticism, without attribution, to warn that the party's state boards needed to follow through with the cultural objectives just set. He recommended that conferences be scheduled at the state level for the purpose of effecting a "genuine change" in the party's attitude toward the intelligentsia and focusing attention on the resolution passed in February, which had been largely ignored. These state conferences also needed to work out "the significance and meaning" of order 234 in the area of culture and education much more emphatically than happened at the party's cultural congress in Berlin. That meeting had been "gesamtdeutsch," or nationally oriented, he said, implying that it would have been foolish to place an SMAD order at the center of a public discussion intended to popularize the national attraction of the SED's cultural policies. Otherwise, Ackermann went on to call for sharp criticism of "sectarian mistakes in our attitude toward the intellectuals," but also underscored the importance of differentiating properly between progressive, reactionary, and vacillating intellectuals.[117]

Copies of Ackermann's remarks were then sent to the party's state and regional boards, divisions of PKE, along with recommendations intended to deal with the "indifference of party functionaries and party members toward cultural matters." The entire party needed to be infused with a "robust socialist cultural consciousness"; and the circular listed organizational initiatives designed to accomplish the objective. Apart from state conferences, the circular proposed regional meetings as well and called again for the creation of viable cultural divisions at all levels of party organization. A pamphlet devoted to cultural politics had just been published for use in evening courses;[118] and other instructions repeated many of the recommendations issued and reissued periodically ever since the party conference in September 1947. The party's local, regional, and state organizations were reminded of their responsibility to file quarterly reports with Kultur und Erziehung; prodded, "yet again," to prepare files on "SED intellectuals" and "SED cultural functionaries"; told to oversee the formation of "working groups of SED intellectuals"; and given to understand that the "construction of a new democratic state" hinged upon an alliance of intellectuals and workers.[119] Erich Gniffke, who fled the zone soon after, made the same point at the next board meeting and stressed the character of the SED as "a cultural party in the

---

[116]See the untitled manuscript with "8/5 48 Tülpanow" hand-written at the top. Zentrales Parteiarchiv, NL 36/735/57-9.

[117]Stenographische Niederschrift über die 10. (24.) Tagung des Parteivorstandes der SED am 12. und 13. May 1948, ibid., IV 2/1/23/36-42.

[118]See "Die Kulturpolitik der SED," *Sozialistische Bildungshefte* 7 (1948).

[119]An alle Landesabteilungen / Partischulung, Kultur u. Erziehung. Ende Mai 1948; Rundschreiben an die Landes- und Kreisvorstände der SED, Abt. für Parteischulung / Kultur und Erziehung. Im Mai 1948, ibid., IV 2/906/60/359-665.

broadest sense of the word"—the leading intellectual power in the democratic reconstruction of the nation.[120]

Enemies of the People

In spring 1948, Ackermann still considered it wise to practice restraint in disputes over directions and tendencies in art due to the grotesque fact, as he called it, that "our own artists" stood for something much different from "a healthy realism" in their artistic predilections; whereas other artists, politically distant, endorsed outlooks "closer to ours than our own comrades." Confusion surely reigned in these matters, he said, but "we do not consider the time right to engage in major disputes over different directions and isms in art."[121] This was true only for tactical reasons, however, and then merely in comparison with the devastation that occurred later in the year. Otherwise, the delegation of intellectuals sent to tour the USSR and report on its findings, numerous articles in defense of the central-committee decrees,[122] detailed treatments of the perquisites available to Soviet writers, stark contrasts with the mindlessness of reactionary Western intellectuals, heartrending stories about the plight of progressive colleagues in the West struggling to be heard in a neofascist "totalitarian" environment—these were the subjects hashed and rehashed during the year. They paralleled every one of the organizational changes underway and fell into place within the two-camps view of the world that culminated in the international peace crusade launched in Wroclaw in late summer.

The SED seems to have believed that it could gain wider acceptance of its own cultural-political positions if it managed to blacken the image of America and the West while altering popular perceptions of the USSR.[123] The society for the study of Soviet culture had been organized for that latter purpose in 1947, and the organization met just two weeks after the cultural conference in May for its first annual convention. During the meeting, Jürgen Kuczynski tried to explain how an organization designed to promote the idea of a new Germany patterned increasingly after the Soviet Union pur-

[120]Stenographische Niederschrift über die 11. (25.) Tagung des Parteivorstandes der SED am 29. und 30. Juni 1948, ibid., IV 2/1/24/202-3.

[121]Stenographische Niederschrift über die 10. (24.) Tagung der SED am 12. und 13. Mai 1948, ibid., IV 2/1/23/41-2.

[122]See, for instance, the complete version of Gorbatov's press conference in October 1947 published shortly after the cultural conference the following May, in *Die neue Gesellschaft* 7 (1948): 18-23; it contained his impassioned defense of the treatment accorded Zoshchenko and discussion of the tremendous material and financial benefits showered upon Soviet writers.

[123]See, for instance, Alfred Kurella's two books, *Ich lebe in Moskau* and *Ost und oder West*. See also the book by the dean of Canterbury, Hewlett Johnson, *Ein Sechstel der Erde*. Ehrenburg's *In Amerika* also fits into this category.

sued quintessentially nationalist objectives; and one of the ways of arguing this point was to use notions suggestive of collective guilt to prod ordinary Germans into support of the two-camps principles that governed the organization. "We," he said, meaning the organization over which he presided, "take a clear and unequivocal stand for peace and prosperity, for Germany, for the Soviet Union; against war and misery, against the Germans who destroy our nation, against the forces of world reaction";[124] and Tjulpanov, speaking to the same audience, charged that no nation and no people had inflicted as much damage upon the culture of the Soviet Union as Germany and German fascism. The society therefore had a moral obligation to promote greater understanding of Soviet culture as a way of combating the slanders injected daily into the German people by "foreign, Anglo-American imperialist circles and by German reaction."[125] Like Tjulpanov, Kuczyinski also acknowledged the difficulty of the task because, as he freely admitted, so many people had yet to change their minds about the Soviet Union. But unlike Tjulpanov, after attributing the hardened attitudes toward the USSR mostly to anti-Soviet crusades of the most recent vintage, Kuczynski alluded to other reasons for their existence. He hinted that Germans living under Soviet occupation tended to regard the Russians as hostile intruders, perhaps even understandably in the sense that any occupation met with a "certain rejection, antagonistic attitudes, antipathy." He did not isolate the cause of at least some of that hostility.

These were just some of the odds stacked against the SED in 1948, and they only worsened in 1949 when reports and rumors of Soviet concentration camps surfaced regularly. In fact, the enormity of the task may have lent the party's attacks upon the West their rabid quality, reflecting the SED's belief that it must make a major effort to vilify Western culture as latently or blatantly fascist for there to be any hope of gaining widespread acceptance of its own tainted positions. The discussions that filled the pages of the Soviet-zone press in 1948 thus alternated between harsh attacks upon the decadence of Western culture and praise of the achievements of the Soviet Union before reemerging, with the proper consequences drawn, in the form of an agenda tailored to Soviet-occupied Germany; and each of these general topics split into a variety of their own interrelated dichotomies, subcategories, and topical applications. The denunciations of Western culture, for instance, always included mention of the progressive intellectuals who labored under the adverse conditions of capitalism, whereas the discussions of Soviet culture used the central-committee edicts both to illustrate the absence of similar correctives in the West and to demonstrate the superiority of

---

[124]"Unsere nationale Aufgabe. Ansprache von Prof. Jürgen Kuczynski auf der Jahresversammlung der Gesellschaft zum Studium der Kultur der Sowjetunion [22 May 1948]," *Die neue Gesellschaft* 5/6 (1948): 1-3.
[125]"Rede von Oberst Tjulpanow," ibid., p. 12.

Soviet democracy—the edicts were conclusive evidence that the voice of the Soviet people had been heard. The decay in all areas of bourgeois literature, by contrast, paralleled the general crisis of capitalism, and the names mentioned in one particular commentary included George Orwell, author of an "anti-Soviet pasquinade," the title of which this analyst could not bring himself to utter; and Arthur Koestler, around whom wafted a "foul odor." But others who had not written such "anti-Soviet" tracts were just as summarily dismissed; they ran the gamut from W. H. Auden, Graham Greene, Henry Miller (a "pornographer"), Thornton Wilder, Eugene O'Neill, to a host of others. Still, this particular article hastened to add that there were "two Americas, two Englands, two Frances"; George Bernard Shaw, John Priestly, Louis Aragon, Upton Sinclair, and others like them would continue to speak in the voice of their people, and all the while Soviet literature, "shining in the light shed by the Communist idea," would lead progressive writers laboring under the conditions of capitalism down the right path.[126]

There was little variation in these kinds of discussions; all of them undertook to explain the significance of Soviet culture for "all mankind,"[127] even as the pattern of party interference established by the central-committee decrees detracted from the message by suggesting that an analogous administrative regulation of Western art and literature would occur if the right opportunity ever presented itself. The Communists were outraged, for instance, that the Hebbel Theater performed a play by Jean-Paul Sartre, *The Flies*, and many a suggestion was made that it ought properly to have been banned. Sartre's prominent commentaries on a range of other artistic, philosophical, and political matters made him a prime target of Soviet-zone commentators, who hated him all the more because of his unorthodox leftist leanings. The reaction to *The Flies* nevertheless added little to the pattern of earlier disputes; the commentators merely interpreted the play as a classic illustration of what Ackermann called Sartre's "wanton contra-humanism."[128] Phrases like "coffee-house art of Parisian boulevards with a decadent aftertaste," "foul justification of the capitalist system," "apology with the penetrating stench of blood," "expression of profound decay of social conditions," "intellectual enslavement of the people," "decadence of bourgeois culture" capture the essence of the criticism completely.[129] What most incensed the Communists were Sartre's utterances about "committed" writing, published in *What is Literature?*, because these pronouncements scorned the

126Anisimov, "Der Verfall der modernen Literatur," *Neue Welt* 1 (1948): 80-98.

127Marianov, "Zwei Welten—zwei Literaturen," *Tägliche Rundschau*, 21 January 1948.

128Ackermann, "Die existentialistischen 'Fliegen' Jean-Paul Sartres," *Neues Deutschland*, 4 January 1948.

129Zeisberg, "Kaffeehauskunst oder Dekadenten," *Tägliche Rundschau*, 31 January 1948; Ackermann, "Die existentialistischen 'Fliegen' Jean-Paul Sartres," *Neues Deutschland*, 4 January 1948; Tschernjak, "Der Sartrismus, ein Zeichen des Verfalls der bürgerlichen Kultur," *Neue Welt* 9 (1948): 103.

party's arguments about politicized art. At a time when the Communists insisted that writers make an ideological choice, Sartre argued that a writer need not offer his services to a political organization to reach the masses. He said that "Stalinist Communism" was "incompatible in France with the honest practice of the literary craft" and he went on to discuss the psychological deformation in Communist writers that even "corpselike obedience" was powerless to prevent. When one Communist called him a grave-digger, he pled guilty, but answered that he preferred to bury literature with his own hands rather than make it "serve ends which utilize it." Anyway, grave-diggers were honest people, "certainly unionized, perhaps Communists," and he would rather be a grave-digger than a lackey.[130]

What complicated the issue for the Communists was Sartre's concurrent criticism of the bourgeoisie; and in any case he rejected the very argument upon which the Communists rested all others. Sartre did not regard the bourgeoisie and the Communist party as the only two alternatives or believe that a decision in general favor of the party remained "ineffectual and abstract" unless accompanied by formal membership in it. "In so far as a scurvy, opportunistic, conservative, and deterministic ideology is in contradiction with the very essence of literature," he opposed both the party and the bourgeoisie. This meant that he wrote "against everybody."[131] The Communists responded by asking the only question that mattered, which camp did his ideals serve?, and answered that he played into the hands of "the enemies of democracy."[132] Otherwise, the discussions degenerated after the first sentence into ad hominem attacks that rendered Sartre's positions virtually unrecognizable. Baffled by his arguments and indifferent to the subtleties of his actual position, they garbled his message beyond recognition in order to draw the simple conclusion that Sartre favored reaction despite his "revolutionary professions"; he was simply the latest recruit to the "camp of anticommunism."[133] Dymschitz summed things up with a denunciation that characterized Sartre as a "profoundly anti-democratic phenomenon, a decadent, individualistic, reactionary writer who is particularly dangerous and injurious (*schädlich*) because of his flirtations with the revolution"; he was, to put it succinctly, a scribbler, a "Pasquillant." Dymschitz drove home his point by using Sartre and the Communist writer Aragon to illustrate the two-camps dichotomy that ran through all of French literature. These two men typified "two worlds and two intellectual outlooks: a new world of noble emotions and grand ideas, and a putrefying, dying world that does not shun the most unworthy means in its struggle against the triumphant new."[134]

[130]Sartre, *What is Literature?* pp. 256, 259, and 264.
[131]Ibid., pp. 264-65.
[132]Tschernjak, "Der Sartrismus," *Neue Welt* 9 (1948): 101.
[133]Cavallo, "Aus der Geschichte herausgefallen," *Neues Deutschland*, 8 January 1948.
[134]Dymschitz, "Zwei Franzosen," *Tägliche Rundschau*, 19 February 1948.

Dymschitz' comment never went beyond variations on familiar themes, all of which are best summed up in Sartre's own dismissal of the party's customary brand of polemics: "Persuasion by repetition, by intimidation, by veiled threats, by forceful and scornful assertion, by cryptic allusions to demonstrations that are not forthcoming, by exhibiting so complete and superb a conviction that, from the very start, it places itself above all debate. . . . The opponent is never answered; he is discredited; he belongs to the police, to the Intelligence Service; he's a fascist."[135] These rabid denunciations of intellectual positions that clashed with the party's superb convictions obviously heightened concern about the SED's ulterior motives; and they renewed fears that the Communists aimed to regulate competing viewpoints as a simple matter of political and ideological principle.

Related developments in the Soviet Union did nothing to alter the impression that cultural politics in Soviet-occupied Germany had settled into a fixed routine of doctrinal intimidation and were well on the way to full enforcement; in fact, implausible assertions that the central-committee edicts neither "sanctioned" nor "violated" anyone probably heightened concern,[136] rather than lessening it. It was equally far-fetched to maintain that none of the criticized artists lost their jobs or were hindered in their activities, much less, in the case of the composers, that their work was still performed in Soviet concert halls.[137] Those kinds of stories were spread by local propagandists like Stephan Hermlin, who had returned from his spring visit to the Soviet Union to insist, with impeccable timing, that Zoshchenko's writings had never been "banned."[138] The name of Akhmatova, who went unpublished for years, apparently slipped his mind; and Hermlin did not bother to point out either that both writers had been expelled from the Soviet writers' union or that its president, Nikolai Tikhonov, had been demoted. When Zoshchenko himself was trotted out to meet the delegation of Soviet-zone intellectuals in April, his sanguine appearance merely demonstrated the worthlessness of "anti-Soviet fairy tales disseminated in other countries."[139] Hermlin did concede that Boris Pasternak had been roundly "criticized," though it was more important to Hermlin that Pasternak remained widely venerated anyway; and in general, Hermlin continued to suggest that the atmosphere for Soviet artists was uncommonly conducive to creativity. Besides, read one commentary, the Western accusation that the Soviet Union had just launched an assault against modern music when it issued its edict in February was merely in-

---

[135]Sartre, *What is Literature?* p. 257.
[136]See Peresvetov, "Von wo kommt die Gefahr? Zu den Auseinandersetzungen um die 'bedrohte' Musik," *Tägliche Rundschau*, 24 March 1948. See also "Förderung volksnahen Musikschaffens," *Tägliche Rundschau*, 29 April 1948, and "Recht der Kritik," *Sonntag*, 11 April 1948.
[137]"Recht der Kritik," *Sonntag*, 11 April 1948.
[138]Hermlin, *Russische Eindrücke*, p. 55.
[139]"Begegnungen und Bekanntschaften," *Tägliche Rundschau*, 25 April 1948.

tended to divert attention from the intimidation of progressive composers in the West for their involvement in "un-American activities."[140]

But this last edict was even more savage in tone than the others, and, though the decree itself did not appear in Soviet-zone newspapers, the party press devoted a considerable amount of space to discussions of the indictment of Muradelli's opera and to the stinging criticism of Prokoviev, Khachaturian, and Shostakovich. Like the discussions of earlier decrees, the commentary on the last also sanitized its content through selective citations; but there was a clearer willingness to engage the controversial issues, and the discussions made it plain that certain principles were considered applicable to Soviet-occupied Germany. The attention focused on the matter reflected the SED's hope of trying to persuade German intellectuals in East and West of the actual merits of the cultural-political and artistic positions staked out by the decrees. The trouble was that doing so required the commentators to characterize the resolutions as appealing instances of cultural democracy entirely worth emulating. Hermlin devoted an entire section of his tract to the subject of "Freedom and Responsibility of the Soviet Writer." True, he did not mention the edicts specifically; instead, he began by directing his gaze westward, at the "immoralist" André Gide. Ridiculing the idea that Gide's "intellectual betrayal" had anything in common with a quest for truth, and after pillorying Melvin Lasky for suggesting that Soviet literature was in any way "controlled," Hermlin turned his attention to the freedoms enjoyed by Soviet writers. He had first-hand experience, he said, of the atmosphere in which Soviet writers lived, one in which the control over Western writers exerted by "professional critics" contrasted with the "supervision" of Soviet writers practiced above all by "millions of working people." Nowhere else had Hermlin experienced such "clean, serious, and matter-of-fact criticism" that only sought to "help," never "destroy."[141] Indeed, the party's desire to assist Soviet artists in the creation of politically acceptable art had some general points in common with the SED's February plan to offer the intellectuals greater "support," a resolution that followed the publication of the fourth central-committee edict by a single day. In any case, Zhdanov's disparagement of Akhmatova as a cross between a nun and a harlot made it appear that Hermlin had visited a different country when he referred to "clean, serious, and matter-of-fact criticism"; and the fourth edict failed to fit Hermlin's description any better. It condemned the "formalist direction in Soviet music as one inimical to the people that, in practical terms, is destined to end in the liquidation of music." The rest of the edict juggled concepts like "non-artistic," "confused noise," "alien to the normal human ear," "obsession with disingenuous 'originality,'" "formalistic distortions inimical to

---

[140]See Peresvetov, "Von wo kommt die Gefahr?" *Tägliche Rundschau*, 24 March 1948.
[141]Hermlin, *Russische Eindrücke*, pp. 46-56.

the people," "atonality," "antidemocratic," "dissonance," and so on.[142]

Though they may not have troubled Hermlin, these principles were far more menacing than any yet put forward in the post-war Soviet Union; they not only tightened up older arguments considerably, they established the various counts of a new criminal indictment. These charges were then hurled at writers, artists, and composers in a tense atmosphere that resembled the mood of the nineteen-thirties blood purges more with every passing day. The frequent use of idioms derived from the phrase "enemy of the people," which had not been employed in the first three edicts, is just one indication of the worsening climate. Indeed, the fourth edict mentioned a denunciation of Shostakovich's opera *Lady Macbeth of Mzensk*, published in *Pravda* in 1936, that had helped launch the last crusade against formalism in an era of unbridled terror. Now, as the Soviet Union was about to embark upon the next round of wanton violence, the term "enemy of the people" resurfaced in cultural politics; and suddenly the criticism of specific artistic practices voiced in the first three edicts became far more malevolent. Moreover, the phrase had been picked up by the German Communists when Otto Grotewohl employed it in his speech to the SED's cultural conference in May. The preferences of certain individual artists now fell into the category of criminal offenses, and general artistic trends unacceptable to the party became political conspiracies entered into by artists unduly influenced by the seditious West. The *Tägliche Rundschau* had already published commentary in January 1948 that foreshadowed those developments and placed them in a Western context. Several weeks before the fourth edict appeared, this article had applied many of the lessons of the forthcoming Soviet decree to French "modern" music and used the central committee's arguments to generate a new political and ideological transgression—cosmopolitanism. The *Tägliche Rundschau* began by lashing out at four "notorious" French composers whose music had nothing in common with the French people or the French nation. But the usual pejoratives, "expressionistic," "Schönbergian contortions," "naturalistic sound imitations," were less important than the principal point that the *Tägliche Rundschau* applied to every form of artistic expression in nations all around the world. Modern bourgeois decadent art refused to sink the roots of its artistic creativity into its national soil. Such artists thus revealed the "spuriousness of the bourgeoisie's nationalistic slogans by exposing their cosmopolitanism and hostility with respect to their nation's vital interests." Indeed, no one would be sorry if the music of Igor Stravinsky ("pathetic clownery") or Benjamin Britten, with all its amorality, pathological sexuality, and sick obsessions, fell silent.[143]

[142]"Über die Oper 'Die große Freundschaft'" (10 February 1948), *Beschlüsse des Zentralkomitees der KPdSU (B) zu Fragen der Literatur und Kunst (1946-1948)*, pp. 25-32.
[143]Gorodinskij, "Jenseits des Schönen. Die Musik der dekadenten Bourgeoisie," *Tägliche Rundschau*, 17 January 1948.

Forms of artistic expression outlawed in the Soviet Union thus became vivid manifestations of treason and national betrayal—not just in the Soviet Union, where the charge of cosmopolitanism quickly became a euphemism for Jewishness and a sign of the ideological contamination of Soviet artists by outside influences, but in other countries as well. For the Soviet spokesmen of cultural Zhdanovism had claimed for themselves the right to determine which forms of artistic creativity were truly representative of other nations and which ones betrayed their national interests, thereby transforming the central-committee edicts into a great deal more than an internal Soviet affair. Once the actual edict had been issued, the *Tägliche Rundschau* rushed to publish additional commentary. The first article out noted that the formalistic faults identified by the edict, involving iniquities like the "quest for a false originality," cut off the work of various Soviet composers from the "demands and artistic taste of the Soviet people." The advocacy of atonality violated the principles of melodious Russian folk music, though Soviet music critics had nevertheless preferred to coddle composers whose formalistic indulgences were "inimical to the people." But the most serious charge politically was the conclusion that composers like Prokoviev, Khachaturian, and Shostakovich wrote music characteristic of the decadent modern art of the "bourgeois West"—music that had lost all contact with the people and was destined to "liquidate" art. The logical conclusion about this kind of artistic activity was that the people, "through the voice of their avant-garde," had every right to make certain demands of the composers designed to help them find the way back to the people and to create the "most democratic art in the world." Anyway, the stigmatized composers had participated personally in the formulation of the decree that condemned them.[144] Other articles on the subject soon appeared, and one of them, by a certain Karl Schönewolf, revealed the extent to which commentators were now prepared to go to stigmatize unacceptable forms of art. Schönewolf's charge that Soviet composers suffered from the "ruinous influence of certain Western individualists" merely echoed the decree; but what followed injected a more ominous note into the discussion. Schönewolf spoke of "individualistic experiments" in all areas of artistic activity and then noted that the Third Reich was the worst experiment to which Germany had ever been subjected—a terrible illustration of the "nefarious German predilection" for extreme experiments no doubt in need of regulation.[145]

As twisted as his reasoning was, it probably reflected Schönewolf's strained effort to tailor one of the charges leveled at Zoshchenko, that his wartime writings had given "no aid to the Soviet people in their struggle against the German robbers,"[146] to Soviet-zone circumstances by linking un-

[144]Barskij, "Für eine volksverbundene Kunst," *Tägliche Rundschau*, 13 February 1948.
[145]Schönewolf, "Experiment, Wirrwarr und Klärung," *Sonntag*, 29 February 1948.
[146]See Swayze, *Political Control of Literature in the USSR, 1946-1959*, p. 41.

acceptable forms of art to a deficient commitment to antifascism. Similar insinuations, that Sartre's wartime writings were insufficiently antifascist had become a salient feature of the attacks upon him.[147] What lent these accusations their particular quality was that they went far beyond philosophical abstractions and, both in the USSR and in the newly created Eastern-European popular democracies, were staked out in a political atmosphere in which the articulation of a counter argument automatically marked its representative as an "enemy of the people."

Late in the year, Alexander Dymschitz leveled a similar attack upon the German composer Hindemith, even if he stopped short of the final slur. Dymschitz based his argument on the contention that Hindemith's opposition to fascism was "not revolutionary" and that the hero of his opera *Mathis der Maler*, the sixteenth-century artist Grunewald, embodied the kind of opposition to the forces of reaction destined to fail because of its "individualism." Dymschitz concluded that Hindemith's artist-hero advocated a brand of politically impotent art, "pseudo-art," isolated from the people. Though Dymschitz stopped short of calling Hindemith an "enemy of the people," he did employ a term, "pernicious," that was no less a product of the purges than the other smear.[148] But Dymschitz had already set the parameters for these kinds of discussions much earlier in the year when he defined the war waged by Hitler against the Soviet Union as a battle of two cultures, an "armed struggle of socialist culture against a decadent, imperialist 'culture,'" and used it to explain why the Russians were "against decadence." In his mind, all forms of artistic creativity became manifestations of ideology; and because ideology mirrored basis-superstructure interdependencies, its manifestations fell into one category or the other. An ideological or cultural "third-road" was no more conceivable than a political compromise. This is how Dymschitz placed cultural discussions not only in the Soviet Union, but everywhere else within a quintessentially political-ideological context. "Two worlds stand opposite each other," he wrote, "the world of flourishing socialism and that of putrefying capitalism, condemned to an inevitable death"; and these worlds likewise expressed themselves ideologically in the form of "bourgeois-decadent 'creativity'" and "democratic creativity." Dymschitz then expressed his undying hatred of the former precisely because, being anti-democratic and individualistic, it was divorced from the life of the people, whereas "we are humanists"; and that was why they recoiled at music incapable of expressing the soul of the people, sensed "no love" for a philosophy of fear, and disliked art, like Chagall's, that had lost a sense of space; that was why they derived no pleasure from decadent theories about the intellectual freedom of the artist and despised the "crafty

---

[147]See Tschernjak, "Der Sartrismus, ein Zeichen des Verfalls der bürgerlichen Kultur," *Neue Welt* 9 (1948): 97-99.

[148]Dymschitz, "Künstler und Volk," *Tägliche Rundschau*, 26 September 1948.

mendacity" of bourgeois decadents who spoke of such freedom in a world in which the capitalists subjugated art and in which "the honest democratic artist is condemned to thousands of torments." Worst of all, this culture was rapidly appropriating the experiences of Hitler's cultural politics, for the "culture" of bourgeois decadence was quickly fascistizing itself, lulling the vigilance of the masses to sleep by hiding the truth about the USSR.[149]

In June 1948, Zhdanov's commentary on the fourth edict came out in Soviet-occupied Germany. This was the first time that any of his unabridged utterances on cultural affairs had appeared there, and his remarks capped the discussions with an assortment of sinister innuendoes the likes of which had never before graced the pages of the local press. Zhdanov's lurid disclosures, revelations of artistic conspiracies both national and foreign, the determination that Russia was besieged by outsiders *in the area of art*, and the kinds of responses alluded to if the miscreants again failed to heed the warning first issued in 1936 over Shostakovich's opera—all this was uttered in an unctuous tone of Great-Russian and Soviet chauvinism that must have dismayed Soviet-zone readers even by the plummeting standards of 1948. "Abnormality," "ideological confusion," "naturalistic failings," "vulgarity," "violation of healthy norms," "pathology" were just some of the characteristics that Zhdanov chose to rebuke in discussing music. It was not merely that Soviet composers lagged behind achievements in other "areas of ideology" generally and had no one to blame but themselves; rather, Zhdanov attributed these deficiencies to the intrusion of alien ideologies into the Soviet Union from the West. He made it clear that "our party," which expressed the interests of "our state and our people," would lend its support only to a healthy direction in music; and he insisted that a "masked" battle was being waged against this music by revisionists who willfully disguised their formalist predilections with a public display of concurrence with the principles of socialist realism, the better to "smuggle" in their revisionist contraband. The essential point remained that a kind of ideological war was on. Confronted with this menace, there was an urgent need for other composers to defend Soviet music against the intrusion of elements of bourgeois decay and never forget that the USSR was "now the true protector of the musical culture of the entire world, just as it stands in all other areas as a bulwark of human civilization and culture against bourgeois decline and the fall of culture." Precisely because "alien bourgeois influences" would find fertile soil among the "vestiges of capitalism in the consciousness of several representatives of the Soviet intelligentsia," Soviet composers needed to sharpen not only their musical but their political ear.[150]

---

[149]Dymschitz, "Warum wir gegen Dekadenz sind," *Tägliche Rundschau*, 21 March 1948.
[150]Zhdanov, "Fragen der sowjetischen Musikkultur," *Neue Welt* 11 (1948): 3-18.

This war mentality was a direct application of two-camps thinking to internal Soviet politics, in this case cultural politics; and Dymschitz had spoken in much the same vein in his remarks concerning the war between the two worlds in the area of ideology and culture. But Zhdanov brought up another pejorative widely used in the USSR since summer 1947, but new to discussions in Soviet-occupied Germany—"kowtowing to the West," in this instance, to "rotting bourgeois music." Nor did he neglect to brand the formalist direction in Soviet music as an "enemy of the people"; and, finally, he took the opportunity to clear up one other misunderstanding related to ill-conceived notions of nationalism and internationalism. Because Zhdanovism mingled Soviet and Great-Russian chauvinism with anti-Western xenophobia, Zhdanov himself needed an epithet, "cosmopolitanism," that legitimized cultural isolationism by outlawing foreign influence as decadence—a menace to true internationalism. But the epithet also had to transform the imposition of Soviet cultural-political norms throughout Eastern Europe into an international act of self-defense against the real threat to world civilization. Many of these points were pursued within the context of the Wroclaw conference that met in August under the pretext of defending world peace and culture; but for now Zhdanov spoke mostly of Soviet affairs. He suggested that composers whose music kowtowed to the West simply did not realize how strict adherence to the principles of Russian and Soviet national music respected the spirit of internationalism because true internationalism flourished only when national art prospered. Those who ignored this simple principle by allowing themselves to be influenced by the modern artistic innovations or experiments of the West were therefore not internationalists at all; they were "homeless cosmopolitans" whose patriotism (and race) was as suspect as their politics. Within a few months, the intellectual malignancy of "cosmopolitanism" was diagnosed in Soviet-occupied Germany, too, and the debates that raged all drew their inferences from Zhdanov's reasoning. As he explained it, the veneration of Russian and Soviet music, whose norms and forms Zhdanov regarded as uniquely qualified to express the national interests of other countries as well, expressed the strongest commitment to internationalism. For it enabled the Soviet Union to "give something to other peoples," though this was best accomplished by avoiding the impoverishment of Russian national art caused by the obliteration of its own national characteristics through the blind imitation of foreign examples.[151]

It is hard to imagine that Zhdanov's logic lessened concerns about the political or cultural "sovietization" of Eastern Germany; after all, Zhdanovism there developed as part of the effort to transfer the Soviet system to Germany that the SED once so strongly repudiated, though for that reason it was now defined as a national obligation inextricably linked to Germany's

[151]Ibid., p. 18.

atonement for her fascist past. Many of these cultural-political ideas corresponded likewise to the SED's related attempt to define its Eastern orientation in national terms that permitted the party rhetorically to predicate the nation's future, political and cultural, upon its implementation of solutions imported from the Soviet Union. Even so, the success of the rhetoric, if there was any, always hinged on the definition of these new cultural norms as intrinsically democratic, inherently national, and utterly opposed to the real threat of foreign intervention—the intrusion of alien ideologies, with all their decadent side effects, from the West. Cultural Zhdanovism thus served definite political ends, whether these embraced Soviet domestic politics or foreign-policy objectives throughout Eastern Europe, in Soviet-occupied Germany, or internationally as part of the peace crusade in defense of culture. By arguing that the most democratic country in the world produced the most democratic art, the successes of Soviet culture could logically be attributed to the political system; and because the miserable shape of Western culture was blamed on the hopeless situation of the bourgeoisie, Zhdanovism followed a simple routine of two-camps polarization. It popularized "Soviet culture" while denigrating "Western 'culture'"; and both facets of the campaign reflected the broader effort to gain widespread approval of Soviet conduct generally, foreign and domestic. But Soviet cultural politics still had to be tailored to fit specific applications; in Soviet-occupied Germany, for instance, expedience originally dictated that caution be exercised in discussions of the central-committee edicts; and later on the anti-Semitic component of the Soviet assault on cosmopolitanism needed to be ignored when that particular crusade found its way into the Soviet zone.

But otherwise, local Zhdanovists were equal to the rhetorical tasks confronting them. Hermlin defined the "'acknowledgment of the necessity' of the dawning Communist society" as the zenith of artistic freedom,[152] when he was really advocating the kind of voluntary intellectual surrender to a particular orthodoxy that he personally embraced along with the coercion of those who refused to go along with it. As part of their effort to persuade hesitant intellectuals, the party's spokesmen tried to simplify their task somewhat through arguments that equated defense of the German cultural heritage with the implementation of principles inherent in the edicts. In 1948, the SED, or rather "the democratic organizations, agencies of the Soviet occupation zone, and all those who support German unity" began gearing up for a "worthy" celebration of Goethe's two hundredth birthday. Not surprisingly, Anton Ackermann contended that the "destiny of the nation" and Germany's cultural legacy generally, as well as Goethe's "immortal work" specifically, were best preserved by placing them in the hands of the working class. Naturally, Goethe also emerged as an unswerving opponent of "chau-

[152]Hermlin, *Russische Eindrücke*, p. 56.

vinism" who worked toward the preservation and cultivation of national characteristics, not for the purpose of setting one nation apart from the other but for the "most intimate association of national cultures."[153]

There was a topical side to the preservation of Goethe's heritage that involved the treatment of intellectuals who failed to conduct themselves in accordance with the developing standards of Zhdanovism. Hermlin told the interesting story of an unpublished biography of Goethe written in 1932 to mark the hundredth anniversary of his death. This manuscript had somehow fallen into Hermlin's hands, and he quickly discovered that the back of each page was full of quintessentially fascist writing. Hermlin did the natural thing; he contrasted these abhorrent comments with the discussion of Goethe written by the same author on the front side; and to clear up any confusion about the broader relevance of his discovery, an editorial comment following Hermlin's article had this to say. Just as the biographer had lauded Goethe's humanism on one side of the paper while venting his fascist spleen on the other, so too did the various false prophets of a "free" culture living in West Berlin battle "against humanity and against culture, for fascism and the resurrection of barbarity." Hermlin recommended that the pen be "knocked out of their hands, once and for all."[154]

In Defense of Peace

Zhdanovism challenged intellectuals around the world to make a narrow political choice, and those who decided against "peace and democracy" became the targets of extraordinary abuse. None was worse than Alexander Fadejev's in his blistering address to the "world congress for the defense of peace" in Wroclaw, Poland, in summer 1948: "If jackals could learn to type, or if hyenas could hold a fountain pen, they would probably write works similar to those by Henry Miller, Eliot, Malraux and the rest of the Sartre types."[155] Even so, in speaking of intellectuals around the world whose styles of writing and habits of mind displeased the Stalinists, Fadejev added little to the harsh sentiments first expressed by Zhdanov in 1946. The difference was that Zhdanov had vilified *Soviet* writers and artists, even if he blamed their deficiencies on the influence of Western decadence; whereas the complete tenets of Zhdanovism were now ready for export to the popular democracies and to Soviet-occupied Germany minus the earlier barriers. True, the first tentative effort to stake out a systematic Stalinist position in literary matters occurred at the writers' congress in Berlin in October 1947 in con-

[153]Ackermann, "Sinn und Bedeutung des Goethe-Jahres 1948," *Tägliche Rundschau*, 29 August 1948.
[154]Hermlin, "Die Goethe-Fassade," *Tägliche Rundschau*, 8 August 1948.
[155]Fadejev, "Kultur, die für den Frieden kämpft," *Tägliche Rundschau*, 5 September 1948.

nection with the general "ideological offensive" launched at the party conference a few weeks earlier; and the letter penned to American "masters of culture" by various Soviet writers, followed by the incendiary remarks of Vishnevskij at the congress itself, were the events that precipitated Lasky's speech. Nor was it Lasky's idea entirely; he prepared his remarks, the night before, at the behest of Günter Birkenfeld, who served as moderator the next day and got him on the podium to begin with.[156] During Lasky's speech, as Hans Mayer tells it, Alexander Dymschitz actually thought about having him ejected from the stage,[157] though his remarks were positively temperate in comparison with Vishnevskij's vituperations.

Every one of Lasky's remarks about cultural Zhdanovism was fully justified under the circumstances. Tjulpanov, Dymschitz, the Soviet writers in attendance themselves, and the local Communists present, the lucky ones who survived Stalin's purges, knew exactly what Lasky meant when he referred to "the Russian apparatus of political concentration camps and slave labor"; and not one of them could have missed the point when Lasky noted that Soviet writers, too, "are having their struggle for cultural freedom. To their difficulties, I think, all of us must bring a certain measure of open-hearted sympathy." Following that remark, Lasky looked at Katajev, Gorbatov, and Vishnevskij, and stated emphatically, "We know how soul-crushing it is to work and write when behind us stands a political censor and behind him stands the police."[158]

Remarks of that sort are conveniently forgotten in the contention that "the Americans," in the person of Lasky, were responsible for ending the open exchange of ideas begun at this bridge-building congress.[159] Lasky did little more than answer the Soviet charges of American war-mongering that were just as overbearing as anything uttered by Fadejev two years later in Wroclaw; and responded to the sanctimonious Soviet concern with creative freedom in the West by bringing up the sore subject of Zoshchenko, Akhmatova, Eisenstein, and others. On this subject, the Russians were vulnerable and responded in Berlin accordingly. In fact, they had no other choice; apart from various retorts from the audience, there was much encouragement; when Lasky finished, the applause lasted for several minutes. Ricarda Huch, the octogenarian honorary president of the congress whose flight from the zone had already been planned (she left and died five weeks later), told Lasky at the banquet that evening that she shared his sentiments.[160] When the Wroclaw congress met in mid-1948, then, the situation was much different. The consolidation of political power in Eastern Europe was much fur-

[156]See Shub, *The Choice*, pp. 76-77.
[157]Mayer, *Ein Deutscher auf Widerruf*, p. 391.
[158]Shub, *The Choice*, p. 80.
[159]Mayer, *Ein Deutscher auf Widerruf*, p. 390.
[160]According to what Lasky told me; Shub, *The Choice*, p. 83, has it slightly differently.

ther advanced, and Zhdanovism could be shipped abroad. Indeed, Zhdanov himself seems to have designated Fadejev, who had replaced Tikhonov as president of the Soviet writers' union, as the man to deliver the message.[161] In his speech, Fadejev (and others) began making the fundamentals of socialist realism intellectually, morally, and politically compulsory *outside* of the Soviet Union. But the process itself acquired certain complexities due to its internationalism. Local party intellectuals and cultural functionaries throughout Eastern Europe focused their attention on three different groups. The first category was the bevy of prominent intellectuals in Western Europe and around the world who already sympathized with the Soviet Union and had been doing so for some time; if their general endorsement of Stalinist politics could be broadened to include Zhdanovist aesthetics, rather than just "peace," these personalities could be used to proselytize in their own countries at two interlocking levels of intellectual activity, politics and culture, with each commitment reinforcing the other. The second group was comprised of generally sympathetic intellectuals and artists in the popular democracies themselves, non-Communists, whose support for these new regimes, especially if enhanced by their acceptance of Zhdanovist cultural values, could make it easier for the ruling parties to win the backing of the masses. The third category was comprised of party intellectuals and artists themselves in Eastern Europe and Soviet-occupied Germany, not all of whom were open to every tenet of socialist realism but who, if they had not yet learned to conform entirely, needed to develop a better appreciation of the fact that the acceptance of these principles was not up to them.

Within the Soviet Union, then, Zhdanovism ended the period of ideological relaxation that had existed during the war and began a phase of repression lasting until the post-Stalinist "thaw"; in the popular democracies, the process tried to make centuries-old cultures square with the patterns of Soviet culture under Stalin; in the West, the ripples of Zhdanovism engendered an "international peace movement" in support of Soviet foreign policy and comprised of intellectuals, in the mold of the fellow travelers of the twenties and thirties, from both sides of the iron curtain; and finally, in Soviet-occupied Germany, coupling cultural processes to Zhdanovist norms of artistic creativity redounded to the direct political benefit of the SED, even as it sealed the cultural division of the nation behind a billowing cloud of nationalist rhetoric. Thus, Wroclaw had implications that went well beyond the narrower needs of Soviet-zone cultural politics, though the national implications of Zhdanovism were greatest in Germany because of its division. A greater effort was necessary there to reconcile two-camps thinking with the idea of an international consensus—a "worldwide movement,"[162] as Abusch

[161] Toranska, *"Them," Stalin's Polish Puppets*, p. 290.
[162] Abusch, "Wroclaw wird weiterwirken," *Tägliche Rundschau*, 12 September 1948.

called it—that all German intellectuals could play a role in forming and that could also be seen to unite the two Germanies culturally. Indeed, if this strategy worked, the "spirit of Wroclaw" might soften the shock of a cultural division of the nation and distract attention from the fact that the SED's endorsement of Zhdanovism caused it. The stakes were especially high in Germany, but the rewards plenty if the peace rhetoric ever made inroads among West German intellectuals. Indeed, much of the local discussion of Wroclaw undertook to reduce problems generally to the simplest issue—war and peace. J. R. Becher claimed that the world consisted of two camps, though he tried to back out of the dichotomy by insisting that "East-West antinomies" were not the real issue and that "ideological and religious differences of opinion" were ultimately of little consequence.[163] This was nonsense, and Becher knew it; his rhetoric directly contradicted the essence of Zhdanov's two-camps address one year earlier; and Becher conceded as much when he added that one side indisputably wanted war, the other peace, and even if there were occasional tiffs among friends in the latter camp, compared with the shared desire for "peace, peace, and nothing but peace" these differences dissolved into insignificance.[164]

The congress for world peace thus met on 25 August 1948 for the purpose of identifying those "social forces," as Abusch put it, who were again threatening peace.[165] By now, however, especially after creation of the Cominform, there was no longer any doubt about the identity of the war-monger—it was the United States. The main objective of the congress was to secure agreement on that point and, accordingly, to forge the broadest possible consensus on the basis of the doctrinally narrowest workable platform. Wroclaw was actually fairly successful, too, certainly more so than the German writers' congress ten months earlier;[166] and what disharmony surfaced

---

[163]Becher, "Die zwei Partien," *Sonntag*, 19 September 1948. See also Kurella, *Ost und oder West*, passim, especially pp. 186 ff.

[164]Becher, "Die zwei Parteien," *Sonntag*, 19 September 1948.

[165]Abusch, "Der neue Weltbund des Geistes," *Neues Deutschland*, 21 August 1948.

[166]Hans Mayer, who attended the Wroclaw conference (and who, by his own admission, defended Fadejev's speech), later called the Wroclaw conference a "disaster" as a consequence of Fadejev's remarks. This is not true; the relative success of the enterprise was not just a function of the proceedings themselves, but had a great deal to do with the subsequent mythologization of the event in the Communist press. In this regard, it is worth comparing Mayer's remarks in his "Tagebuch vom Breslauer Kongreß" (*Sonntag*, 19 September 1948) with his discussion of the congress thirty-three years later. See Mayer, *Ein Deutscher auf Widerruf*, pp. 386-96, 397-411. See also Max Frisch's diary entry of 25 August 1948, in which he records some of Mayer's private remarks to him in Wroclaw (such as the distinction between "bad terror" and "good terror" and Mayer's scorn for André Gide). Frisch, *Tagebuch 1946-1949*, p. 603. Indeed, Mayer, in a speech given in Frankfurt in early summer 1948, had already pronounced a definitive verdict against writers and intellectuals like Camus, Sartre, Gide, Koestler, and others, preferring the love for humanity expressed by Gorbatov the preceding fall at the Berlin writers' congress. See Mayer, "Der Schriftsteller und die Krise des Humanismus," *Sonntag*, 6 June 1948.

was either ignored in the Communist press altogether or attributed to the odd delegate of ill will. When it came time to vote, there were 371 ballots cast in favor of the final manifesto, only twelve against and a few scattered abstentions.[167] True, even the Communists called the document a "minimal program,"[168] and its careful rhetoric paled in comparison with the cold-war paroxysms of the Soviet writers who spoke up at the congress. It was not the case, however, that the audience was completely dominated by Soviet delegates or by intellectuals from the Eastern European popular democracies. In fact, there were actually a few moderately critical voices at the congress, but certainly none to compare with Lasky's performance in Berlin. Otherwise, some forty-five nationalities were represented, including many from underdeveloped nations who added to the flair of the congress by appearing in native costume and who, presumably, represented national cultures in danger of being eradicated by the cultural nihilism of Western imperialism. In addition, many of the other delegates were the same Western fellow travelers of years gone by, except that by now most had shifted from the pro-Soviet and antifascist positions of the thirties to the new combination of unflinching support for the post-war Soviet Union and a staunchly anti-American posture passed off as latter-day antifascism. Nonetheless, the usual effort was made to deny that the congress was a "propaganda trick," that the German delegates carried "the party card of the SED," and that the entire production was anything but a voluntary gathering of free spirits.[169] But, for whatever it is worth, each member of the German delegation, including those from the Western zones, like Hans Mayer, was approved beforehand by the party secretariat, which put Alexander Abusch "in charge" of the delegation. Before its departure, Otto Winzer also drew up "guidelines" governing the activity of the delegation while in Wroclaw; and, following a discussion of their content, Winzer, Franz Dahlem, and Anton Ackermann made final adjustments to the document.[170]

The pitch of the rhetoric at Wroclaw then matched the antifascist sentiment of the Paris congress in defense of culture in 1935, with which it was compared;[171] and it is interesting to note that, much like the popular-front era

---

[167]The "peace manifesto," containing much talk of a new fascism, was reprinted in *Aufbau* 9 (1948): 737. See also the collection of speeches, *Der Weltfriedenskongreß*, published privately by the Kulturbund as material for their own officials (Material für Referenten). It included the manifesto, Mayer's "Tagebuch vom Breslauer Kongreß," most of the major speeches, and the Kulturbund's official "resolution against war-mongering and anti-Soviet crusading."

[168]Abusch, "Wroclaw wird weiterwirken," *Tägliche Rundschau*, 5 September 1948.

[169]See "Kultur und Frieden," *Sonntag*, 22 August 1948; and "Bilanz von Breslau," *Aufbau* 9 (1948): 735.

[170]Protokoll Nr. 102 (II) der Sitzung des Zentralsekretariats am 16. 8. 48; and Protokoll Nr. 104 (II) der Sitzung des Zentralsekretariats am 23. 8. 48. Zentrales Parteiarchiv, IV 2/2.1/223 and 225.

[171]See Abusch, "Der neue Weltbund des Geistes," *Neues Deutschland*, 21 August 1948.

following the Paris congress, the post-war peace crusades also unfolded during a period of vicious repression in the Soviet Union. For that reason, much of what was said at Wroclaw served prophylactic purposes; every conceivable effort was made to isolate American imperialism as the global threat to national cultures, and the reason given for the Wroclaw congress in the first place was to rally intellectuals of "varying political persuasions" for the sake of forming an international front in defense of peace, intellectual freedom, and the uninhibited national cultural development of all peoples.[172] The manifesto, though it never mentioned the United States by name, called similarly upon the "intellectuals of the world" to protect world culture and civilization against the onslaught of a new fascism.[173] The manifesto also insisted that intellectuals back "free cultural development" as well as work toward the close cooperation of people around the world. But in the context of the times, statements favoring both national "freedom" and international "cooperation" amounted to a reformulation of the principal tenet of vintage Zhdanovism that transformed Soviet cultural expansionism into an act of international solidarity against the cosmopolitan threat to national cultures. A number of bewildering and conflicting currents thus converged at Wroclaw. When the Paris congress convened in 1935, the popular front generally and socialist realism specifically were still in their infancy; in the interest of building a broad consensus and because there was not yet a sufficient basis for any discussion of socialist realism, controversial issues with the potential of ruining the congress were simpler to disregard. The defense of culture, under the universally acknowledged threat of fascism, remained a preeminently political consideration summed up as antifascism. Certainly the antifascist spirit of Paris was inseparable from unqualified support for the Soviet Union, but Stalinism was not quite mature enough ideologically, politically, or culturally to make the building of a consensus as problematical in 1935 as it soon became. Things changed quickly after the congress; within a matter of months, all these issues broke into the open with the staging of the first show trial in Moscow and the first socialist-realist campaigns against "formalism." Nor was it long before these disputes found their way into the German emigration, politically over the trials and culturally because of Lukács' denunciation of "antirealistic" styles of writing as decadent harbingers of intellectual and ideological fascism.

In contrast to circumstances that existed in 1935, in 1948 Stalinism was well on the way to becoming as fully developed, in its every political and cultural-political manifestation, as it had been in 1937 or 1938—with the added dimension of antisemitism. By 1948, socialist realism was anything but the comparatively vague assortment of political and formal requirements

---

[172]Abusch, "Wroclaw wird weiterwirken," *Tägliche Rundschau*, 12 September 1948.
[173]"Das Friedensmanifest des Weltkongresses," *Aufbau* 9 (1948): 737.

that it had been at the time of the Paris congress thirteen years earlier; and even if the ideological and artistic standards had been relaxed during the war, the patterns established between 1936 and 1939 were strongly reasserting themselves. It had been a simple matter for Zhdanov to dredge up the *Pravda* article of 1936 condemning Shostakovich for composing "confusion" in place of melodies while making his point about Soviet or decadent Western music in 1948. In any case, the edicts of 1946 and 1948 marked the return of Soviet art and literature to the strict regimen of the thirties, soon expanding it to include a strong anti-Semitic component; and the question related to Soviet foreign policy is how the USSR set out to standardize these principles not just throughout Eastern Europe and Soviet-occupied Germany, but among Western intellectuals as well. The strategies naturally differed; the "socialist occupation" of Eastern Europe presented prime opportunities for spreading the gospel according to Zhdanov that were unavailable in the West. With mostly minor tactical modifications, the political and cultural content of exported Zhdanovism was nevertheless largely the same. During the discussions at Wroclaw, for instance, given the congress' predominantly westward orientation, using the notion of an imperialist threat to national cultures as a means of establishing the broadest possible political consensus was likely considered to be a more successful way of appealing to Western intellectuals than any outright, and obviously unenforceable, ban on specific artistic forms. It was surely assumed that the desired consensus was more likely to emerge based on issues of war and peace than on discussions of decadent practices in the area of art leading to certain guidelines mandatory for all writers interested in preserving peace. Those questions certainly came up, and not just in Fadejev's remarks; but the fairly vague discussions of "formalism" never got down to the essence of the central committee's cultural edicts, at least not in the major speeches; and the entire issue appears to have been subordinated substantially to broader issues related to threats of a new war.

None of this implies that diverting attention away from the decrees was not an integral part of the strategy behind the Wroclaw congress; and, surely to soften their impact, Abusch made a point later of arguing that real cultural repression occurred elsewhere. He referred to the desperate plight of "free intellects" in America and to the intellectual witch hunts there, as well as to the cold war waged against progressive intellectuals in allied occupied Germany, pressured and gagged by Marshall-plan politicians into what he called *Gleichschaltung* or conformity.[174] The beginnings of congressional hearings on un-American activities certainly suggested that there was something to the argument. But at the congress itself Abusch clearly established the political priorities of the German intellectuals in attendance with a rabid two-

[174]Abusch, "Wroclaw wird weiterwirken!" *Tägliche Rundschau*, 12 September 1948.

camps speech applied to German circumstances. He wished to call the attention of the delegates to the fact that "the American policy of splitting up Germany" had rejuvenated "dangerous intellectual currents" with the hope of using them "as a weapon in the so-called occidental crusade against the Eastern European people's democracies and against the Soviet Union."[175] But the more important point is that the general absence of any protracted public discussion in Wroclaw concerning the plight of Soviet writers and artists suggests either that no one was there to bring it up, that by manipulating the list of speakers the organizers of the congress managed to prevent it from being raised in the first place, at least from the podium, and (or) that Soviet delegates had themselves been instructed to avoid any particular mention of the decrees with the hope of forestalling any specific discussion of them and their repercussions within the Soviet Union. Nor are these suggestions incompatible with the nature of the choleric pronouncements of Fadejev or Ehrenburg or Lukács or Ernst Fischer. It was probably easier to get away with hurling insults at various Western pornographers, mystics, and cultural fascists as long as the focus was kept upon them. These were, after all, assessments with which the majority of delegates tended to agreed.[176] But it was something else again to make the same kind of slur stick in reference to wayward Soviet writers, artists, and composers, much less suggest that any of those attending the congress might themselves fit the same description. If it was indeed the intent of the planners to avoid the provocative subject of the central-committee decrees, the strategy certainly points to an awareness of the fact that those issues could interfere with the formation of a political consensus on a broader issue among intellectuals from both sides of the iron curtain.

None of this is exactly borne out by the comments of Jakob Berman, whose story of the Wroclaw congress may have some elements of truth to it. Berman was certainly in a position to know at the time, though his capacity to remember and retell the story truthfully three decades later is as questionable as his original perceptions. According to Berman, the idea for the congress came from another Polish Communist, Jerzy Borejsza, who had spent the war years in the USSR and whose brother headed the interrogation department of the Polish ministry of public security. Borejsza told Berman a few weeks before the event: "If they don't make us call everything off the day before the Congress, and if the USSR sends a delegation of sufficient stature, then this Congress could become a major event; and if we play it right in the internal market, it could serve as an excellent *intermezzo* between one symphony *furioso* and the next symphony *furioso* which we shall shortly begin to play out."[177] What happened, then, according to Berman,

---

[175]Abusch, "Der deutsche Beitrag," *Der Weltfriedenskongreß*, p. 39.
[176]See Mayer, "Der Schriftsteller und die Krise des Humanismus," *Sonntag*, 6 June 1948.
[177]Toranska, *"Them," Stalin's Polish Puppets*, pp. 290-91.

was that the Soviet delegation to the congress was received by Zhdanov just prior to its departure and presumably given marching orders. Because of the nature of Fadejev's remarks to the congress, Berman then concluded that these were something akin to an order to break up the event. Following Fadejev's speech, Borejsza immediately called Berman to express this concern, Berman phoned Molotov, telling him that there was nothing to be gained by breaking up the congress; and Berman concluded that Molotov issued "new directives" because "Ilja Ehrenburg made a beautiful speech which entirely changed the atmosphere of the Congress."[178] The only problem with Berman's account is that the nature of Ehrenburg's remarks fail to fit this description. Ehrenburg spoke for forty minutes, even though the normal limit was ten, and he may well have tried to take some of the sting out of Fadejev's pronouncements without affecting their substance. Ehrenburg's personal demeanor seems to have been less arrogant and abrasive than Fadejev's, and his speech lacked any abuse of Western intellectuals to compare with his countryman's. But politically there was little difference. Not that there was no risk involved in trying to turn a "cultural conference" whose critics were denounced as "enemies of culture" and as "war-mongers," like Hitler,[179] into a gathering devoted to political issues. But the risk was considered worth taking in the interests of potential political gain; besides, the most highly publicized speeches welded culture so tightly to politics that no political inferences could be drawn other than the ones intended by those who scripted the congress. The arguments associated with Wroclaw all came down to something like this: the efforts of peace advocates would be futile if it proved impossible to go beyond broad "cultural understandings" toward "political cooperation among the peoples of the world"; and the fact that keeping the peace remained the top priority, whatever the importance of certain other cultural aspects and values, only meant in other contexts that some art forms prevented war and some facilitated it.[180]

However one looks at Wroclaw, then, it was just as much a manifestation of two-camps thinking as cultural Zhdanovism, even if the public discussions largely excluded talk of dissonance and atonality in music. But, ironically, much as Zhdanovism defined itself as the protector of national cultural values when its prime purpose was to bring culture internationally into conformity with "national" Soviet norms, the divisions inherent in all two-camps arguments were similarly turned into their opposite. That is, the Soviet-zone press, in commenting upon Wroclaw, roundly condemned the division of Europe into "hostile camps," one for and the other against socialism; such a division risked the annihilation of European culture, and for that reason the struggle for socialism in Europe was equally a battle to save the

[178]Ibid.
[179]"Kultur und Frieden," *Sonntag*, 22 August 1948.
[180]Ibid.

highest values of European culture. The basic principle of the equality of peoples and respect for their national characteristics, along with the greatest possible international economic, political, and cultural cooperation, was therefore "an historical necessity for all of Europe."[181] But if one single theme other than the imperialist threat to national cultures dominated the congress, it was the virtual ultimatum that intellectuals around the world plant their feet firmly in one camp or the other. This was the keynote of Fadejev's remarks, who delivered a speech that did exactly what *Sonntag* decried; he split the world neatly into two hostile camps—the democratic camp bent on consolidating the victory over fascism and determined to maintain the national independence of various peoples; and the imperialist camp, out to suppress the popular movement in favor of the rule of reaction. Indeed, said Fadejev, the reactionary crusade against "the progressive ideology" made considerable use of such literary "agents of reaction" as Eugene O'Neil, the pornographer Henry Miller, the renegade Dos Passos, and the decadent mystic T. S. Eliot, whose profascist sympathies Fadejev considered an established fact. Fadejev said nothing about the treatment accorded the likes of Zoshchenko and Akhmatova and concentrated his message on the contention that creative intellectuals worldwide were obligated to act politically. Intellectuals around the world needed to be "mobilized," and progressive elements in every capitalist country had to join in resisting the attempts by reaction to suppress the culture of the peoples.[182]

Ehrenburg made many of the same points, but deviated on others. Unlike Fadejev, for instance, he tried to deny that the cultural issues at stake or the threat to peace came down to differences between East and West. The principal task of progressive intellectuals everywhere, he said, was to expose those who imitated the fascists in talking about the defense of "Western culture" while preparing for war. He then went on to speak about the "Yankee" attempt to use America's standardized "culture" to benumb Europe prior to its enslavement in an all-out assault on the national singularity and essential differences of the peoples of Europe; whereas the Russians, by contrast, countered the "nationalist-cosmopolitan delirium of the imperialists" with "our patriotism and our internationalism," which called for the profound respect and love for the genius of other peoples. Ehrenburg concluded by pointing out that for thirty years the Soviet Union had been accused of interfering in the affairs of other countries; none other than Hitler himself had made such a claim, and the "new marauders" now repeated it. But Ehrenburg insisted that "we are far removed from the desire to impose our institutions, our customs, and our culture upon other peoples," only to suggest in the same breath that accusing the USSR of harboring such sinister intentions

---

181"Wroclaw gegen die Kriegshetzer," *Neues Deutschland*, 28 August 1948.
182Fadejev, "Kultur, die für den Frieden kämpft," *Tägliche Rundschau*, 5 September 1948.

made about as much sense as faulting the gulf stream for influencing Danish or Norwegian agriculture.[183] There was nothing new about this argument; it was merely Ehrenburg's way of "naturalizing" Soviet cultural or political expansionism and restated the essence of Stalin's article on the "international character of the October revolution."[184] If there was any real difference between the two speeches, Fadejev's and Ehrenburg's, it was little more than one of perceptions; either talk was sufficient to capture the two-camps tenor of the Wroclaw congress.

Even so, two others, by the Austrian Communist Ernst Fischer and by Georg Lukács, are worth mentioning because they further illustrate the treatment accorded intellectuals who declined to join what Abusch called the new "world league of intellects."[185] Fischer noted that all decent intellectuals desired peace; but peace hinged upon a decisive battle against imperialism, and not all intellectuals realized it. The vast majority of intellectuals backed imperialism unwittingly, turning themselves into "intellectual eunuchs"; and this political and social self-emasculation was one of the most discomfiting manifestations of the present day. Fischer considered it the goal of progressive intellectuals to "persuade" the masses of otherwise decent intellectuals of their untenable position as political and social eunuchs.[186]

Jürgen Kuczynski, writing in the SED's monthly *Einheit*, singled out Fischer's article for particular praise. Kuczynski was smitten by Fischer's phrase "decent and honest eunuchs" in reference to those intellectuals who, as Kuczynski put it, "believe that they can adopt a position between both camps, the camp of peace and the camp of war, concentrating on cultivating their 'individual personalities'"; and who had no desire "to join any party or any organization" out of a fear that such attachments would "retard their 'moral and cultural development.'"[187] Lukács argued along somewhat different lines, but made the same basic point. He had always maintained that subjective intentions were irrelevant, either in political or literary-theoretical terms, and he probably regarded Fischer's concept of individual "decency" as utterly immaterial; what mattered to him was the historical content and the objective consequences of a given intellectual or philosophical posture. In his address to the congress, Lukács dealt generally with these kinds of issues, but his main point contained a slightly different inflection. He suggested that modern-day reaction would not necessarily travel the same road as German fascism, nor employ the exact same intellectual means, though the military result would surely be the same. If anything, Lukács' was only a slightly more creative philosophical rationale for suggesting that no mean-

[183]Ehrenburg, "Friede den Völkern," *Tägliche Rundschau*, 19 September 1948.
[184]Republished by *Die neue Gesellschaft* 10 (1948): 1, shortly after the Wroclaw congress.
[185]Abusch, "Der neue Weltbund des Geistes," *Neues Deutschland*, 21 August 1948
[186]Fischer, "Das intellektuelle Eunuchentum," *Tägliche Rundschau*, 18 September 1948.
[187]Kuczynski, "Der Kongreß von Wroclaw," *Einheit* 11 (1948): 1111.

ingful political or cultural changes had taken place in the imperialist camp. Now as before, the essence of reaction remained the monopoly-capitalist urge to rule; and this was the source of the constant threat of new world wars. It was just that the "new fascism" would employ different ideological methods than Hitler, and nowadays these revolved around "fetishized" concepts of democracy. This was Lukács' key point, for in his mind many intellectuals remained defenseless in the face of imperialism because they failed to inquire into the real content of democracy. It was a disgrace, therefore, that broad segments of the best intellectuals failed to comprehend these matters, clear as they were; though many turned away from imperialism and the preparations for a new war, it was still incumbent upon all intellectuals to transform these emotions into knowledge; and this could only occur, he said, on the basis of Marxism-Leninism.[188]

[188]Lukács, "Verantwortlichkeit der Intellektuellen," *Tägliche Rundschau*, 10 October 1948.

CHAPTER ELEVEN

According to Plan

By late 1948, every important cultural-political process set in motion during the preceding three-and-a-half years converged in the demand that Soviet-zone writers and artists, party members or not, focus their efforts on tasks linked to the SED's two-year plan of economic development. True, the party's plan, or the SMAD's, had been presented to the Deutsche Wirtschaftskommission (DWK) for dispensation and implementation,[1] but there was never any question about its ratification. The DWK, which coordinated the activities of what used to be separate administrations, amounted to little more than an appendage of the SED;[2] and at the party board meeting convened to rubber-stamp the plan, Ulbricht buttressed his remarks on economic issues by advocating corresponding steps to ensure the transformation of the SED into a party of a new type.[3] One month later, these arguments crested in the call to strengthen the party by purging it of "hostile and degenerate elements," a resolution that reemphasized the "leading role" of the SED in every aspect of "state, economic, and cultural life."[4] Fred Oelßner, speaking after Ulbricht at the board meeting in late June, had made it clear already that the provisions of the two-year plan were just the same as the "party's program" and that transforming the SED into a "party of a new type" was the key to implementation of the plan. Anton Ackermann also talked of the "leading role" of the SED, but went on to predict that fulfilling the plan would dramatically escalate class warfare because Western imperialism was bound to send its agents into the zone to disrupt the economy.[5]

---

[1]See *Der deutsche Zweijahrplan für 1949-1950*, p. 4.

[2]See, e.g. the discussions and decisions made at the following secretariat meetings on 2 April (Protokoll Nr. 64), 19 April (Nr. 68), and 29 November 1948 (Nr. 134). Zentrales Parteiarchiv, IV 2/2.1/189, 192, and 252.

[3]Ulbricht, "Planmäßige Wirtschaft sichert die Zukunft des deutschen Volkes," *Der deutsche Zweijahrplan für 1949-1950*, pp. 36-37.

[4]"Für die organisatorische Festigung der Partei und für ihre Säuberung von feindlichen und entarteten Elementen [29 July 1948]," *Dokumente der Sozialistischen Einheitspartei Deutschlands*, vol. II, p. 83

[5]Oelßner, "Hebung des politischen ideologischen Niveaus unserer Partei"; and Ackermann, "Die führende Rolle der Partei," *Der deutsche Zweijahrplan für 1949-1950*, pp. 96-98 and 62-66.

Finally, Otto Grotewohl added later that the SED alone possessed the ability to carry out the provisions of the two-year plan due its plenitude of singular characteristics. Unconvinced, the CDU's daily newspaper scoffed at Grotewohl's declaration that the SED was nonetheless not a "totalitarian party"; his standpoint, the paper said, "sweats exclusive rule from every pore."[6]

It was true enough, and by fall the SED had never been closer to establishing exactly what it forswore a few years before, a "single-party system." But the participation of the intellectuals in the plan remained an unanswered question. For unknown reasons, the SED had neglected to develop a cultural component ahead of time, possibly because the SMAD gave the party such short notice that a plan of Soviet-zone reconstruction was imminent. There were no provisions for cultural affairs whatsoever attached to the actual document, but then none had shown up originally in order 234 either. Cultural usages were fashioned subsequently, and the same sort of thing happened following publication of the two-year plan. The general thinking was absolutely identical. A rise in productivity hinged on a fundamental alteration of the poor attitudes of working Germans toward the Soviet zone; and because cultural figures were thought to possess the capacity for influencing ordinary Germans, it was assumed that the enthusiastic support of the party's two-year plan by the intellectual elite would rub off on the country's work force. It was taken for granted that the personal prestige of prominent artists would serve to burnish political and economic policies endorsed by them and that the effectiveness of the two-year plan could be enhanced through a combination of their personal exhortations on site, in the workplace, and the creation of topical art tailored to the plan's provisions.

These issues, the real beginning of art commissioned by the authorities to fit needs defined by the SED, dominated discussions from early summer through the end of the year and, in various permutations, well beyond. But Soviet-zone intellectuals could only be used to help mold the political outlook and associated work ethic of ordinary people if they themselves believed in the party's principles and priorities. This meant, as Paul Wandel said in September 1948, that the SED's cultural politics had to "fortify Marxism-Leninism among the intelligentsia"; and he made it just as clear that a portion of the intellectuals persisted in being politically "passive."[7] That lament still reverberated months later,[8] and it is hard to escape the impression that passivity, or "political abstinence," became a major irritant to the implemen-

---

[6]"Falscher Zungenschlag," *Der Morgen*, 4 July 1948. Quoted from Suckut, *Blockpolitik in der SBZ/DDR 1945-1949*, pp. 251-52. Two days later Pieck protested that Grotewohl had been misunderstood and that the SED had no interest in ruling or running the country by itself (Pieck, "Der Ausweg aus der Not," *Neues Deutschland*, 6 July 1948).

[7]"Aufgaben für unsere Kulturschaffenden," *Neues Deutschland*, 26 September 1948.

[8]See Dornberger, "Den politischen Abstinenzlern ins Gewissen," *Schöpferische Gegenwart* 1/2 (1949): 1-2.

tation of the two-year plan. In view of the supreme national and international importance of "antifascist-democratic" reconstruction in Soviet-occupied Germany, as defined by the SED, passivity in the face of those vital tasks was thought to conceal either criminal negligence or even latent opposition. In any case, in order to involve creative intellectuals in the two-year plan, it was imperative that they be brought, first, to the point of endorsing the general thinking behind the two-camps view of the world woven into the fabric of the plan; and, second, these same intellectuals had to be prepared to go beyond politics, often expressed as a simple matter of war and peace, by subscribing to the formal prescriptions of aesthetic zhdanovism. As the party's resolution passed in January 1949 later put it, "the cultural task of educating people in the direction of a new social awareness and a new attitude toward work can only be accomplished if all writers and artists direct their full energy and enthusiasm to the job. The contribution of artists and writers to the two-year plan consists of their developing a *realistic* art."[9]

Art commissioned by the party in support of its current objectives thus presupposed this dual endorsement of politics *and* politically defined aesthetics; without both, artists would be ill-equipped to play the role reserved for them by the party in implementation of its two-year plan. Worse, the lack of compliance in both areas, political and formal or aesthetic, would have suggested that the remittent potential for resistance to these objectives might linger on or actually break out. Of course, this never happened, at least not until the early fifties, and then hardly as an expression of fundamental opposition to the GDR. In the forties, intellectuals were brought to the point of compliance through the force exerted by two key ideas—antifascism and democracy, but also Marxism-Leninism in its first subtle and then not-so-subtle indications. The seeming coherence of it all, particularly after years of fascism, developed into an allure that proved difficult for certain kinds of intellectuals to resist, both for those whose ambitions outweighed their talents, but who sensed that they could bridge the gap by ideological rote; but also for young German artists and writers rendered politically compliant by a conscience burdened with an awareness of the havoc wrought by their own country; and the entire bandwagon atmosphere of the zone, with its subliminal hints and sharp accusations about the fascist past, carried along many of the rest. There were simply few writers and artists still in the zone prepared to buck the trend and even fewer opportunities, other than leaving, for those who might have contemplated it for any organized opposition.

[9]"Maßnahmen zur Durchführung der kulturellen Aufgaben der SED," *Protokoll der Ersten Parteikonferenz*, p. 538.

Planned Culture

Developing a cultural policy closely "coordinated" both with the two-year plan and with its own individual components was not easy on such short notice; and, though efforts benefited from three-and-a-half years of administrative, ideological, and "aesthetic" preparations, what was known internally as the "cultural plan" took several months to develop before eventually culminating in a cultural "ordinance" passed by the Deutsche Wirtschaftkommission on 31 March 1949.[10] The process commenced immediately after the announcement of the two-year plan on 31 June 1948, however; and in the beginning, it was a joint effort undertaken by the party's cultural division, or PKE, and by the DVV. All mass organizations joined in soon enough. But early efforts focused on development of an overall strategy that must have started with the secretariat's endorsement on 12 July 1948 of a comprehensive "working plan for the campaign" in support of economic reconstruction. (Incidentally, the secretariat approved the DVV's design of a "central for enlightenment and reconstruction" at the same meeting.) The working plan called generally for a shift in the work of the party, the mass organizations, and "administration" directed at guaranteeing the success of the two-year plan "in every respect." One subsection of the plan, entitled "administration," spoke outrightly of "state administration" and looked for discussions of the plan to take place at all divisional levels.[11] Cultural work warranted its own subsection; it focused preeminently upon the "organization" of artistic presentations by the "best actors, singers, musicians, and authors" in the factories themselves; and recommended that "SED writers and authors" study the new work habits there in order to write books capable of improving morale in the factories. Artists and sculptors were similarly expected to place their creative activity at the disposal of what was called "new," rather than "re"-construction.[12] A few days later, on 19 July, the secretariat discussed the "campaign" further and requested each of its divisions, of which PKE was merely one, to submit their "plans and instructions" to the party leadership for "coordination." PKE was told to work with the DVV to draw "groups of writers and artists" into the campaign.[13]

---

[10]See Chapter Thirteen.

[11]Protokoll Nr. 94 der Sitzung des Zentralsekretariats am 12. 7. 1948; Anlage Nr. 1. Arbeitsplan für die Kampagne über den Zweijahrplan 1949/50. Zentrales Parteiarchiv, IV 2/2.1/216/5-10.

[12]Auszug aus: Arbeitsplan für die Kampagne über den Zweijahrplan 1949/50. Text vom Zentralsekretariat am 12. Juli bestätigt, ibid., IV 2/906/169. This passage, listed as subsection VIII, is not included in the attachment to the secretariat's protocol of 12 July 1948 cited in the preceding footnote. That attachment, or Anlage, ends with subsection IV and must be incomplete.

[13]Protokoll Nr. 95 (II) der Sitzung des Zentralsekretariats am 19. 7. 1948, ibid., IV 2/2.1/217.

Both bodies then swung into action. On 16 July, Richard Weimann, head of PKE, asked members of its cultural committee, the Zentraler Kulturausschuß, to attend a meeting on the 23rd for discussion of an enclosed "cultural plan." Additional invitations went out to the DVV's top administrators, Otto Kielmeyer, Alexander Abusch, and Walter Maschke representing the Kultureller Beirat, the Kulturbund, and the FDGB.[14] Weimann opened the meeting by explaining that the secretariat had approved certain guidelines already; and these, following discussion and possible augmentation, needed to be developed over the next two weeks into a final draft that could be submitted to the secretariat for final approval. Weimann then asked the representatives present on behalf of "organizations," as well as "state and public offices," for comment. Volkmann spoke of plans to set up a "cultural endowment" that would make it possible to commission works from artists and writers on themes related to the two-year plan; Maschke focused on problems of cultural work in the factories; and Gysi, referring to culture in terms of "increasing general worker productivity," said that the Kulturbund had just begun to discuss such issues. Both writers and artists, he said, now faced "pressing responsibilities."[15] This discussion of a tentative "cultural plan" or program culminated in a resolution, "Measures in Support of Cultural Tasks in Connection with the Two-Year Plan," that was circulated at the party conference in January 1949;[16] and that document reappeared, reworked, as the ordinance passed on 31 March 1949 by the Wirtschaftskommission. But in the meantime, the party's tentative "cultural program" served in part as the basis for the development of a corresponding plan passed at the DVV's conference of ministers on 12 August 1948; and PKE defined its next steps accordingly in terms of close cooperation with that administration, the state ministries of culture and education, and "democratic organizations" such as the Kulturbund and FDGB. Specific provisions were made for the creation of "cultural planning and working commissions" within the DVV and the state ministries. These commissions, consisting of representatives of administrative agencies and of the so-called democratic organizations, "under the leadership of the party," would "coordinate cultural work in its entirety, investigating and controlling all important issues and undertakings."[17]

The DVV plan, all eighteen pages of it, developed out of separate proposals drawn up first by the administration's individual divisions. Two of them, cultural enlightenment and art and literature, are the most relevant

[14]See ibid., IV 2/906/4/132.
[15]Protokoll der Sitzung des Zentralen Kulturausschusses vom 23. July 1948, ibid., IV 2/906/4/133-37.
[16]The two almost identical drafts that survive in the private papers of both Ackermann and Ulbricht (Entwurf zum kulturellen Plan, ibid., NL 182/931/174-95 and NL 109/89/29-63) must be an intermediate version of the final document available at the party conference in January 1949.
[17]Arbeitsplan der Abteilung Parteischulung, Kultur und Erziehung für das Gebiet Kultur und Erziehung, ca. late August 1948, ibid., NL 109/89/61-2.

here. Magda Sendhoff, speaking on behalf of cultural enlightenment at a meeting on 14 July, said that her division wished to examine the issue in connection with its planned expansion; and Herbert Volkmann remarked that literature, art, and film could play a pivotal role in "propagandistic" support of the program of economic reconstruction; "the artists of the Soviet zone should be harnessed to this objective," he said, "and steered toward topics important for propagandizing the plan." To encourage their support, Volkmann suggested a "cultural fund" or endowment, indicating that the idea had already won the approval of Wandel and the SMAD; and Wandel himself noted, though less specifically, that the DVV could contribute greatly to the fulfillment of the two-year plan.[18] Shortly afterwards, more detailed plans were drawn up by the division of art and literature and by its art office. The divisional plan indicated that initial preparations for the commencement of the "cultural two-year plan" needed to be complete by 31 December 1948 and listed a number of its top priorities. These included improving the "quality of cultural performances along with the repression of decadent directions in art"; making performances much more widely available to working Germans; "propagating the economic two-year plan" by way of art and literature; participating directly in its implementation through film and publishing; popularization of economic and cultural constructions in the Soviet Union; and establishing a secure financial basis for free-lance writers and artists built around a cultural endowment. A variety of internal administrative improvements and measures followed, such as the completion of the card file on all artists and an evaluation of corresponding state-level divisions in terms of competency and ideology. The separate offices had their own individual priorities. Performing arts intended to evaluate all Soviet-zone theaters, for instance; whereas literature planned on completing the job of relicensing the operations, or revoking the licenses, of all publishing houses and carrying out a "reorganization of the Kultureller Beirat" (see below). Other objectives included improvements in the "people's theater movement" designed to make it, by 1950, the dominant factor in theater life; systematic evaluations of the "repertories of all theaters"; consultations with directors and producers; and a host of other initiatives related to each of the divisions other offices (film, amateur art, museums, etc.).[19]

A few weeks later, on 17 August 1948, the commission on pictorial arts within the party's division of PKE met to discuss the implications of the two-year plan for its own special area of jurisdiction. Max Grabowski stressed the importance of supporting the plan by using art in a "propagandistic"

---

[18]See Sitzung der Abteilungsleiter am 14. Juli 1948. Thema: Die Arbeit der Deutschen Verwaltung für Volksbildung in Verbindung mit dem Zweijahrplan. Bundesarchiv, Abt. Potsdam, R-2/465/35-39.

[19]Abteilung Kunst und Literatur. Zweijahresplan, 3 August 1948. Zentrales Parteiarchiv, IV 2/906/169/1-14.

way, but pointed out that influencing the consciousness of the people hinged upon an abandonment of "bourgeois ideologies" in favor of depictions of the emerging new society. This meeting was also attended by Gerhart Strauß, head of the DVV's office of pictorial arts, who revealed that his administration had already prepared plans for a "central commission" conceived for the purpose of overseeing developments throughout the zone.[20] That idea then reappeared in a set of "guidelines," prepared shortly thereafter by PKE, that rejected "individual means of expression" in favor of "realistic" art. "Productivity and qualification" were special concerns, each being a function of art's capacity to effect changes in the consciousness of working Germans; and individual artists would be expected to depict in their works the "new content of our age, the emergence of a new order and society," in a manner accessible to ordinary people. This plan also mentioned a "central commission," comprised of representatives from the Wirtschaftskommission, the Kulturbund, the party, and the FDGB, for the purpose of "regulating and controlling the activity of artists"; and the remainder of the exposé outlined plans for its operations.[21] These discussions coincided roughly with the preparation of the DVV's own set of proposals and plans and their presentation to the state ministers for approval on 12 August 1948. This plan surpassed the others in lofty rhetoric about the "inestimable political significance" of the two-year plan. It inaugurated a "higher phase" in the struggle for "Germany's genuine national greatness," reinforced the "victory of the people over imperialist reaction," and, by way of further democratic transformation, led to the "consolidation of state power." For the DVV, the two-year plan heralded the corresponding development of an "non-bureaucratic state administration" that served the interests of working Germans. The two-year plan was therefore a "*cultural accomplishment*" of the highest magnitude.[22]

The DVV's most important tasks, which involved each of its individual divisions and all their own internal branches, included the general objective of encouraging the personal initiative of "millions of people in factories, administrations, institutes, schools, and in the cities and countryside." More specifically, the DVV set itself the priority of providing for a "fundamental theoretical examination" of all problems related to the two-year plan and, at the same time, opposing "errant and unscientific economic and state theories at variance" with the interests of the people. But these objectives presupposed the transformation of the DVV into an instrument of "state administra-

---

[20]Protokoll der Sitzung der Fachkommission für Bildende Kunst am 17. 8. 1948, 21 August 1948, ibid., IV 2/906/4/192-96.
[21]Richtlinien für die Arbeit auf dem Gebiet der bildenden Kunst im Zweijahrplan, ibid., IV 2/906/169/1-4.
[22]Beschluß der Konferenz der Volksbildungsminister vom 12. August 1948 über die Beteiligung der Volksbildung an der Durchführung des Zweijahresplanes, 21 August 1948. Bundesarchiv, Abt. Potsdam, R-2/76/1.

tion" and required that its work be "politicized." The resolution then outlined a multitude of goals arranged around the administration's six divisions. Some of these, devised by cultural enlightenment or by art and literature, are familiar already from earlier discussions. Otherwise, the DVV's own administrative strategies reveal how little the two-year plan had to do with straight economics. The resolution declared that the entire structure of the DVV, and its internal operation, were to be reexamined from "top to bottom" and made to conform with new responsibilities developing out of the two-year plan. Corresponding reappraisals of state and local administrations were also anticipated. Closely akin to such reexaminations was the "thorough evaluation" of all employees in terms of their abilities and "devotion to the people." Moreover, "strengthening the administrative apparatus" required the centralization of personnel policies in collaboration with the interior administration.[23]

Much of this rhetoric, especially the recurrent complaints about "bureaucratism," derived from previous exhortations and admonitions. "Bureaucratism," for instance, was a concept developed by Stalin in 1934 to describe the slothful or lethargic implementation of decisions reached at the upper levels of the party or administrative bureaucracy. This is especially relevant to the situation in Soviet-occupied Germany because these concepts molded the outlooks that translated into direct action. In his address to the seventeenth congress of the Soviet Communist party, Stalin assailed bureaucrats and office dwellers who ignored party resolutions; and he demanded that such "unreliable, vacillating, degenerate elements" be purged from the party. Otherwise, the decisions of administrative agencies would continue to be undercut or sabotaged. "Will the decisions of leading organizations be carried out," Stalin asked, "or filed away by bureaucrats and pencil pushers?" Would the apparatus function "in a Bolshevist fashion" or continue spinning its wheels?[24] These questions were germane to local discussions even if "bureaucratism" was supposedly the opposite of democratic, rather than "Bolshevist" administration. But by mid-1948, a thin wedge of rhetoric was all that separated those two attributes. In Soviet-occupied Germany, "bureaucratism" surfaced first in connection with order 234; but it had manifested itself more recently in Tjulpanov's internal criticism of the SED in May 1948 for its ostensibly ineffective oversight of action taken in response to the centralized issuance of instructions;[25] and, in accordance with Stalin's rhetoric, the party was on the threshold of a major purge. The administrative application for the DVV derived from the injunction that "fundamental deviations" from decisions made at the ministers' conferences were not to be

[23]Ibid.

[24]Stalin, "Rechenschaftsbericht an den XVII. Parteitag über die Arbeit des ZK der KPdSU (B) [26 January 1934]," *Fragen des Leninismus*, p. 583.

[25]See "8/5 48 Tülpanow." Zentrales Parteiarchiv, NL 36/735/54-79.

undertaken without the permission of the DVV because such departures would lead to a "strong divergence of development in the zone."[26]

Issues of centralized jurisdiction versus state autonomy remained as hotly contested as ever; and by their very nature, these questions were scarcely extraneous to matters of cultural "coordination" and organization. But they need to be understood within a political or administrative context. At the SED's "state-political" conference on 23 and 24 July, Walter Ulbricht insisted that the two-year plan was indeed a "matter of state"; it acquired such importance because the DWK, "the highest economic executive body responsible for central management and control in implementing the plan," rendered it valid "for the entire zone" once it chose to ratify the program. After all, Ulbricht explained, SMAD order 32, issued on 12 February 1948, assigned political, legislative, and administrative responsibility for all economic measures to the DWK as the "central German authority"; DWK laws, ordinances, regulations, and resolutions were legally binding upon all governmental and administrative bodies. The two-year plan required no additional approval at the level of state government because it was law already; as such, it limited the state parliaments to the passage of legislation and resolutions associated merely with the implementation of a plan that was legally binding for all of Soviet-occupied Germany. "Until the reestablishment of German unity," Ulbricht continued, the laws and ordinances passed by the DWK took precedence over the "laws and ordinances of the states"; and the DWK required this authority because, "in the absence of a central institution, there had developed a certain particularism in the course of constructing our democratic order from bottom to top." No further rational basis existed for the continuing presence of "particularist interests"; the state governments, counties, and communities were all obliged to engage in their activities "within the framework of DWK decisions regarding the economic plan." Ulbricht ended his argument with the reassurance that there was no intention of "pushing the state parliaments aside or doing away with them."[27]

Ulbricht's pronouncements hinted at the depth of the conflict between state and central authority, suggesting that the DWK was an agency first created and then outfitted with the additional powers needed to overcome resistance to centralization. SMAD order 32 invested the DWK with the authority to "coordinate" the operations of the Soviet-zone central administrations; the reorganization of those agencies under the aegis of the DWK came a month or so later (the formal guidelines were dated 4 May 1948); and the important establishment of DWK "central control commissions" for the en-

---

[26]Beschlußprotokoll Nr. 14 der Ministerkonferenz vom 10. bis 13. August 1948. Zu 4 g. Verbesserung der Zusammenarbeit mit den Ländern, 23 August 1948. Bundesarchiv, Abt. Potsdam, R-2/77/1-4.

[27]Ulbricht, "Die gegenwärtigen Aufgaben der demokratischen Verwaltung," *Die neuen Aufgaben der demokratischen Verwaltung*, pp. 26-28.

forcement of policy followed on 15 June—all major steps in its development into an unrivalled central governmental agency.[28] By mid-1948, it numbered 5,000 employees; by early 1949, 10,000;[29] and with the creation of the German Democratic Republic in October 1949, most of the DWK's offices were transformed into governmental agencies, administrations, and ministries. But in mid-1948, once the powers of the DWK had been expanded, the SED wasted little time in announcing its two-year plan; and the party met for its "state-political" conference soon thereafter. These events were all relevant to the activities of the DVV because, in spite of its name, the Wirtschaftskommission was never limited to setting economic policy. Though the DVV itself had not been incorporated into the DWK, all important measures developed by it apparently required confirmation by that commission or were developed more or less jointly. This may have been the case, at least in part, because the DVV still lacked the comprehensive powers with which the DWK had been invested. By working with or through the DWK, measures developed by the DVV acquired the same force of law throughout the zone as earlier actions openly sanctioned by SMAD orders, only without the perceived stigma of operating on the basis of those decrees. Indeed, the cultural ordinance passed by the DWK on 31 March 1949 was the first major *cultural* initiative presented to the public as the ostensible result of the DWK's deliberations; and it was also signed by Paul Wandel on behalf of the DVV. It was later revealed, however, that the ordinance only took effect formally upon the issuance of an SMAD order. Indeed, the local Communists confirmed the existence of the order rather reluctantly. That the specific clauses attached to the ordinance otherwise derived from the SED's cultural plan, which was developed in conjunction with the DVV's proposed participation in cultural activities tied to the two-year plan, merely discloses the full extent of the internal administrative coordination involved in the formulation of political and cultural-political policy.[30]

Further aspects of the party's "state-political" conference in July 1948 affected the formulation of priorities within the DVV. The resolution passed there on 12 August 1948, for instance, indicated that the "administrative apparatus" should be improved through the centralization of personnel policies in collaboration with the interior administration. This bright idea, seen as a solution to the problem of "bureaucratism," scarcely originated within the DVV; rather, by mid-1948 the party itself had decided to coordinate the work of all personnel departments; and it was no coincidence that the subject was explained at the state-political conference by none other than Erich Mielke, then vice president of the interior administration, but soon to begin

[28]See the relevant documents in *Geschichte des Staates und des Rechts*, pp. 148-59.
[29]See Zank, "Wirtschaftliche Zentralverwaltungen und Deutsche Wirtschaftskommission," *SBZ-Handbuch*, p. 266.
[30]See Chapter Thirteen and Fourteen.

his life-long career in the secret police. Mielke's elaborations are important for many reasons, but, for our purposes here, pertain mostly to their repercussions within the DVV's office of personnel. Still, Mielke's line of reasoning is significant in its own right as a classic example of how the thinking of German Communists was affected by slogans and propositions formulated by Stalin himself. Mielke began by explaining that the implementation of the two-year plan required the "mobilization" of all segments of society and that, as the SED's plan, the new policy was far more than a general blueprint for the reconstruction of Germany; it was nothing less than the "political and economic program of the new democratic order with the goal of its further development"; and, in particular, "personnel management," *Personalpolitik*, needed to transform the "state apparatus" into an instrument capable of guaranteeing the mobilization of all elements of society toward the implementation of the plan.[31] Ulbricht had already spoken in much the same vein while introducing the two-year plan; "the power of the state serves working people, reconstruction of the economy, and culture; it serves to repress the old fascist, reactionary forces and to deprive saboteurs of their ability to cause damage."[32] At the state-political conference a month later, Ulbricht developed his ideas further. "Our democracy is a higher form of democracy," he said, "it utilizes force in the interests of the majority against the minority. The supreme form of democracy and its complete development is only possible under socialism. This is the Marxist-Leninist understanding of the essence of democracy."[33] Ulbricht did not point out that, in his mind, democracy on the road to socialism merged into dictatorship because, the closer the approach to socialism, the greater the intensification of class warfare; but his comments hinted at the same thing: "Administration is the exercise and application of state power."[34]

Mielke, having quoted Ulbricht's definition of state power, then tailored the idea of effective administration through meticulous personnel management to the requirements of the two-year plan and buttressed his remarks with references to key passages from Stalin's address to his party's seventeenth congress in 1934. These passages made it perfectly clear that the notion of "new work methods" and an elimination of "bureaucratism" were transplanted from Stalin's speech to Soviet-occupied Germany. The substance of his remarks, and Mielke's entire elaborations, was the idea that a correct party line was insufficient in the absence of effective organizational

---

[31]Mielke, "Die Personalpolitik in der Verwaltung," *Die neuen Aufgaben der demokratischen Verwaltung*, p. 60.
[32]Ulbricht, "Planmäßige Wirtschaft sichert die Zukunft des deutschen Volkes," *Der deutsche Zweijahrplan*, p. 14. The latter phrase was, "Unschädlichmachung."
[33]Ulbricht, "Die gegenwärtigen Aufgaben der demokratischen Verwaltung," *Die neuen Aufgaben der demokratischen Verwaltung*, p. 17.
[34]Ibid.

work—mostly *Personalpolitik*. The passage cited by Mielke read: "Victory never comes by itself; it is normally hard-fought. Good resolutions and declarations concerning the party's general line only represent the beginning because they point solely to the desire to triumph, not to victory itself."[35] In those sections not quoted directly by Mielke, but surely dominant in his thinking, Stalin went on to explain that, "once the correct line is established, . . . further success depends upon organizational work, on organizing the struggle for the implementation of the party line, on the correct selection of people, on supervising adherence to the resolutions of the regulatory organs." Stalin summed things up in one pithy remark: "Given a correct political line, organizational work decides everything."[36] He then proceeded to rail against "bureaucratism," and it is hard to escape the impression that both the SED and the SMAD hit upon the same idea not because they attached any meaning to "bureaucratism" as such; the characterization, the same as the related charge of using "old work methods," simply applied to attitudes opposed to transforming governmental administrations into the state executive organs of a single party; and turning administrative employees into "a new type of worker."[37] Later in the year, Franz Dahlem called for an improvement in the "working methods" of party leadership at the level of every conceivable Soviet-zone administrative agency, factory, mass organization, and union; and reduced the general idea to its barest essentials when he again cited Stalin: "cadres make the decisive difference."[38]

But Mielke had already said the same thing when he spoke at length about the need for "new working methods" in administration and a struggle against the "outgrowth of bureaucratism." Like Stalin, Mielke also argued in favor of criticism and self-criticism as a prerequisite to the success of new methods; in particular, "schooling" of administrative employees needed to be intensified as part of the "consolidation of the influence of progressive democratic elements in administration"; and the basis for the correct understanding of each employee's specialized job resided in "mastery of the modern scientific state doctrine" contained in the teachings of Marx, Engels, Lenin, and Stalin. Mielke then called for a "purge of the administrative apparatus" because the two-year plan could not succeed until that apparatus had been "aired out"; and he then brought up the specific issue of *Personalpolitik*. Personnel departments, he said, needed to function exactly as Stalin had said in his speech to the seventeenth congress because the "main issue in

[35]Mielke, "Die Personalpolitik in der Verwaltung," *Die neuen Aufgaben der demokratischen Verwaltung*, p. 60.
[36]Stalin, "Rechenschaftsbericht an den XVII. Parteitag über die Arbeit des ZK der KPdSU (B)," *Fragen des Leninismus*, pp. 577-79.
[37]"Stellung der SED zur Personalpolitik in der Verwaltung," *Die neuen Aufgaben der demokratischen Verwaltung*, p. 95.
[38]Dahlem, "Zur Verbesserung der Arbeitsmethoden aller Parteileitungen," *Neues Deutschland,* 2 December 1948.

organizational work is the selection of people and supervision of the implementation of resolutions." One of Mielke's more specific proposals was for
keeping "precise, clearly comprehensible personnel files and exact personnel
statistics"; if this were done correctly, it would mean that "we are informed
about a person at all times, and we can judge him before he enters the administration." Those files would facilitate the location of "usable" people.
Mielke concluded that "a correct *Personalpolitik* in administration makes a
decisive contribution to the realization of the two-year plan"; this kind of
personnel management complicated the job of the "class enemy" in his bid
to sabotage reconstruction and trained administrative employees in "class
vigilance." Finally, every worker in administrative agencies was required to
have a "conscious, friendly attitude toward the Soviet Union" because such
was the litmus test of his or her democratic consciousness.[39]

Mielke's utterances cast additional light on the DVV's plans for improving the "coordination" of cultural work with the offices of local government.
This issue was important in a variety of contexts and probably explains the
delays and difficulties that plagued the DVV for some time to come. Internal
discussions throughout the remainder of the summer and into the fall focused on "concretized" two-year plans that the state ministries had been asked to submit in multiple copies for further examination at the next ministers'
conference set for 8 and 9 October. The DVV intended to reviewed these
plans, along with the proposals of its own divisions, before the conference;
and the divisions were also asked to report on the degree of state compliance
with the provisions of the main two-year-plan proposal passed at the conference in August.[40] But the ministries were tardy with their submissions; in the
case of both cultural enlightenment and art and literature, neither Saxony nor
Saxony-Anhalt had responded by 25 September. Two days before the scheduled ministers' conference, there had still been no response from the Saxon
state ministry, and Volkmann criticized the other submissions for their
"complete lack of concretization." Moreover, plans had been conceived, he
said, with no thought given to "zonewide coordination" and with no realistic
basis.[41] Most likely due to the inadequacy of the submitted proposals, discussion at the conference on 9 October appears to have been confined to generalities.[42]

[39]"Stellung der SED zur Personalpolitik in der Verwaltung," pp. 62-69.
[40]Rundschreiben and alle Abteilungen des Hauses, 21 September 1948, Bundesarchiv, Abt.
Potsdam, R-2/76/47; Rundschreiben, 25 September 1948, ibid., R-2/76/54.
[41]Abteilung Kunst und Literatur and die Präsidialabteilung. Betrifft: Zweijahresplan der Länder, 7 October 1948, ibid., R-2/4009/120.
[42]Beschlußprotokoll Nr. 16 der Ministerkonferenz vom 9. Oktober 1948, 13 October 1948, ibid.,
R-2/76/2.

The Gewerkschaft 17

By summer 1948, the SED was adamant about finding a way of placing creative intellectuals in the direct service of the party's political, ideological, and cultural policies. Persuading the writers and artists to devote themselves to creative "renditions" of those connections, while steering clear of unacceptable "forms," was considered as central to success as the tightening of organizational constraints. Whereas the latter strategy remained largely hidden from view, the former became more than ever a subject of public debate. The SED's cultural "measures," which were released in January 1949, but must have existed as a draft in summer 1948, stated unequivocally that success in the pursuit of cultural-political tasks connected with the two-year plan hinged upon a resolute struggle against "manifestations of neofascism, decadence, and formalist and naturalist distortions of art, which only reflect the degeneration of the monopoly-capitalist system."[43] Going into fall 1948, then, cultural politics in Soviet-occupied Germany blended Zhdanovist "theoretical" tenets with the organizational strategies designed to implement them in the context of the two-year plan. For instance, the resolution just referred to stipulated that the "democratic mass organizations," such as the Kulturbund, the Gewerkschaft 17, the people's theaters, the society for the study of the culture of the Soviet Union, and others, had to stimulate social initiative and secure the "universal cooperation" of both intellectuals and ordinary workers and peasants.[44] Unfortunately, the Gewerkschaft 17 was still stuck in the doldrums; in fact, the situation was so bad that, on 5 July 1948, the party's central secretariat recommended that "comrades in the leadership of the FDGB" form "independent associations" out of the union's six divisions, though their independence would have been relative because they still remained subordinate to the FDGB.[45] One week later, at the same session that met to consider the SED's two-year-plan "campaign" and the proposal for a propaganda "central," the secretariat accepted a modified solution developed by the union leadership in talks with Ackermann and Paul Merker (who oversaw union affairs for the party). In the future, the Gewerkschaft 17 would consist only of theater personnel—stage hands, technicians, and the like. The other divisions were to form a "cartel," represented on the board of the FDGB, but free of the old union.[46]

---

[43]"Maßnahmen zur Durchführung der kulturellen Aufgaben im Rahmen des Zweijahrplanes," p. 201.

[44]Ibid., p. 208.

[45]Protokoll Nr. 93 (II) der Sitzung des Zentralsekretariats am 5. 7. 1948. Zentrales Parteiarchiv, IV 2/2.1/215/2.

[46]Protokoll Nr. 94 (II) der Sitzung des Zentralsekretariats am 12. 7. 1948; Anlage Nr. 3, ibid., IV

The Gewerkschaft 17 was rapidly approaching the end of its usefulness. By 1948, the notion of "union" representation for intellectuals made little sense anyway, and the cultural-political aspirations of the Gewerkschaft 17, based on outmoded concepts of "Mitbestimmung," conflicted with the prerogatives of more prominent organizations. Cultural work in the factories was, after all, said to be the preserve of the FDGB; and cultural or artistic events there were to be sponsored by the offices of the people's theater charged with that responsibility.[47] Besides, the formulation of cultural policy, at least in its "nonpartisan" form, had always been looked upon by the Kulturbund as its own preserve; that the Gewerkschaft 17 still perceived itself to be an "important cultural-political force in the struggle for the ideological reeducation of the German people in the spirit of progress and democracy,"[48] points to the presence of a rival ambition unappreciated by the Kulturbund. The union's insistence upon exercising the right of "codetermination," for instance, had it ever been granted, might have enabled it to wield power and influence in ways unavailable to the Kulturbund; and in October 1947, the Gewerkschaft 17 reaffirmed its sense of this prerogative. There could be no doubt, Prietzel said, "that the elected representatives of our membership will not allow the right to play a major role in all organs of public administration in influencing the direction of our artistic and cultural life to be curtailed." The same was true of codetermination in cultural establishments, he said; even if the question remained "controversial," the union intended to persist in its efforts to influence art and cultural policy within cultural agencies under public administration; and Prietzel called for the formulation of a specific cultural program. "If our union wishes to be a leader in all questions pertaining to art and cultural politics," he added, "its members and functionaries needed to be aware of their obligation to be the "intellectual leaders" of all working Germans.[49]

The union's second delegates' conference in December 1947 then passed just such a "cultural-political manifesto" based upon a concept, codetermination, that had already lost its usefulness. But that fact impressed itself slowly upon the minds of the union leadership. In April 1948, the board met to discuss cultural-political issues and, accordingly, codetermination. One of the main speakers happened to have been Fritz Erpenbeck, who had nothing whatever to do with the union and made pronouncements that are difficult to regard as an expression of his own private thoughts on the subject. Soviet-occupied Germany had a special cultural-political "mission," he said, which

2/2.1/216/1 and 22.
[47]"Maßnahmen zur Durchführung der kulturellen Aufgaben im Rahmen des Zweijahrplanes," p. 209.
[48]"Was ist und was will die Gewerkschaft für Kunst und Schrifttum," *Kunst und Schrifttum* 1 (1947): 1.
[49]Prietzel, "Zu unserer Delegiertenkonferenz," *Kunst und Schrifttum* 10 (1947): 2.

developed out of the advanced stage of the democratization of its economy and administration. Reading between the lines, Erpenbeck must have intended his assessment of local democracy to lead to a specific conclusion because he then flatly rejected the idea of codetermination in Soviet-zone cultural establishments—a reasonable argument to make when linked with such praise of economic and administrative democratization. The union officials missed the point, however; Prietzel noted that Erpenbeck's rejection of codetermination contradicted his view of the progressiveness of local government.[50]

But because the union regarded codetermination as the primary means by which it would influence the direction of cultural politics in the zone, the elimination of that prerogative cast considerable doubt upon the need for a "union" at all beyond a redefined role as an auxiliary of the party; it certainly raised questions about the need for the union's own cultural-political program. After all, the Gewerkschaft 17 had undertaken from the very beginning to define its cultural politics as the particular "message" spread by its right to have a guaranteed say in the articulation of all policies associated with cultural matters; and had sought early on to work out the various particulars of this role, quickly encountering, however, resistance from both the FDGB's division of Schulung und Bildung and from the Kulturbund. The very first delegates' conference of the Gewerkschaft 17, which met on 17-18 July 1946, had elected a cultural-political committee to "develop the scientific basis for the union's cultural policy," but as of late 1946 had "unfortunately" not managed to do so.[51] Evidently, complaints were then voiced at the Berlin delegates' conference on 26 March 1947 about the "inactivity" of the Gewerkschaft 17 in the area of cultural politics, even as the union's representative to the second delegates' conference of the Berlin FDGB on 29 and 30 March, Edmund Sabath, criticized the FDGB for its own lack of cultural-political initiative.[52] Indications are that the Gewerkschaft 17 had been stymied in its efforts to establish its general jurisdiction in cultural-political affairs by the FDGB's division of Schulung und Bildung, which neither delegated authority nor assumed it.[53]

These growing complaints led to three cultural-political resolutions that were passed by the Soviet-zone FDGB at its second congress a few weeks later. The first two were introduced by Schulung und Bildung and made a variety of general points about the role of the FDGB in raising the cultural level of the German people; and the third, presented by the Gewerkschaft 17,

[50]See "Theorie und Praxis. Kulturpolitische Tagung des Zentralvorstandes," *Kunst und Schrifttum* 6 (1948): 24.
[51]*Geschäftsbericht des Freien Deutschen Gewerkschaftsbundes 1946*, p. 375
[52]"Delegiertentagung der Gewerkschaft 17, Groß-Berlin" and, "Zweite Delegiertentagung des FDGB Groß-Berlin," *Kunst und Schrifttum* 4 (1947): 1-2.
[53]Schlichting, "Die Delegierten-Konferenzen," *Kunst und Schrifttum* (Groß-Berlin) 4 (1947): 1.

basically repeated those points.[54] Later in the year, the Gewerkschaft 17 then reiterated its claim to be the preeminent cultural-political organization in Soviet-occupied Germany;[55] and at the union's state-level delegates' conferences held in fall 1947, the Gewerkschaft 17 focused yet again on the relationship between "codetermination" not only in its economic and social application, but with particular emphasis on the principle as a "cultural political necessity."[56] Finally, at the second zone-wide delegates' conference in November 1947, the organization finally passed its own formal resolution on cultural politics, though not unanimously, and drew up a "cultural-political manifesto." This resolution subscribed to the proposition that creative intellectuals needed to play a preeminent role in "helping to mold the democratic man" by means of their own areas of activity; and emphasized the objective of raising the cultural level of working people by spreading German and international culture, thereby helping to make them "valuable fighters for the idea of socialism."[57] But the irony of the manifesto is that it anticipated the functional changes now pending in the zone and ultimately responsible for transforming all union branches into executive arms of the SED's new political, economic, and cultural policy. Thus, even as the Gewerkschaft 17 undertook to establish its importance as an agency of cultural politics, the SED was just a few months away from doing away with the need for any such organization altogether.

The unnamed authors of the cultural-political manifesto began the document by reformulating some of the original thinking behind the union. This meant that they emphasized the conceptual difference between the Gewerkschaft 17 and all previous professional associations or guilds. Built around the defense of parochial interests, these organizations had lacked any guiding idea. By contrast, the manifesto tried to turn what might otherwise have come across as a potentially irreconcilable bipolarity into a synthesis; and it was this synthesis, called a "militant unity," that supposedly distinguished the FDGB and the Gewerkschaft 17 as unique organizations. For both were engaged in traditional union pursuits connected with the militant advocacy of their members economic and social rights; but also realigned this basic objective and redefined "battle strategy" in answer to the "transformed political and economic circumstances" existing in the Soviet zone. Both the FDGB and the Gewerkschaft 17 fought for more than the mere defense of workers' rights; they engaged directly in the struggle for a "democratic Germany."[58] The manifesto went on to insist that the act of transforming the Ge-

[54]"Zweiter Zonen-FDGB-Kongreß," *Kunst und Schrifttum* 5 (1947): 1-2.
[55]Prietzel, "Die gewerkschaftliche Erfassung der 'geistig Schaffenden,'" *Kunst und Schrifttum* 9 (1947): 3.
[56]Pr., "Unsere Landes-Delegiertenkonferenzen," *Kunst und Schrifttum* 11 (1947): 1.
[57]"Zur Kulturpolitik," *Kunst und Schrifttum* 12 (1947): 2.
[58]"Kulturpolitisches Manifest," *Kunst und Schrifttum* 2 (1948): 2-3. Further references are to

werkschaft 17 into a "progressive cultural union" could succeed only if its members, in touch with the nature of "changes in social structures resulting from the situation existing today," applied these principles to their personal lives and outlooks. Accordingly, intellectuals needed to view union membership not just as an opportunity for the establishment of their own rights as professionals, but as an acknowledgment of profound cultural-political responsibility toward all working people.

The manifesto then listed the union's "present obligations," virtually all of which were built around the idea of wielding cultural-political influence based on codetermination. This detailed register of union prerogatives and privileges, one of them even going so far as to assert the rest in connection with "political parties," makes the organization's broader understanding of "codetermination" and its inseparability from the union's concept of cultural politics fairly evident. But the universality of these pretensions makes it equally apparent that any such overarching principle, once established, had some capacity to transform the union, or rather its seven divisions, into a potential source of opposition. In the event that the union itself, or, more accurately, factions of it, should ever shy away from the advocacy of policies not absolutely identical with those of the SED, the Gewerkschaft 17 might have been turned into the very *organized* locus of opposition that otherwise had no hope of forming in Soviet-occupied Germany. Of course, that potential resided not in the union leadership, which did its best to control the divisions on behalf of the party, but within the organization's discontented "divisions." The situation was definitely volatile and helps explain why, having recreated any number of once independent professional associations, the FDGB was so loath to grant them autonomy either from the union itself or, initially, from its own creation—the Gewerkschaft 17. These considerations also explain how, by insisting that union membership required intellectuals and artists to be enthusiastic advocates of a collective political idea, rather than merely selfish supporters of their own professional interests, the manifesto advanced an argument that destroyed itself by anticipating the end of unions in Soviet-occupied Germany as anything other than subsidiaries of the SED. The union framers of the cultural-political manifesto set out to make their organization indispensable, but only helped put themselves out of business. For with the party's consolidation of power, the union's "central idea," the cultural-political principle of codetermination, dissolved, leaving a program that merely duplicated the Kulturbund's.

But this process took some time; and in the months following publication of the manifesto, indications are that the document resolved none of the controversial issues pertaining to the union's pursuit of its cultural-political prerogatives. In mid-April 1948, the board held a conference to discuss matters

this same source.

associated with questions of cultural politics and codetermination and tentatively scheduled a major conference for later in the year. These plans were to be arranged with Schulung und Bildung; but because of repeated complaints about poor cooperation with its outlying branches, the Gewerkschaft 17 expected to approach the FDGB's own executive board with the request that it urge the Schulung und Bildung to cooperate with the Gewerkschaft 17 on all cultural-political matters.[59] A month later, the Berlin branch of the Gewerkschaft 17 insisted formally that the organization *was* the FDGB's cultural union; but in order to meet its obligations, a committee needed to be created "within" or "along side" Schulung und Bildung and be comprised of delegates from each of the separate divisions of the Gewerkschaft 17. This cultural committee should then have the final say with the FDGB in all matters pertaining to art; especially with respect to artistic and educational events, Schulung und Bildung ought not to exercise sole responsibility.[60] Several more weeks passed before the Gewerkschaft 17 returned to the subject of its upcoming cultural-political conference and announced in August 1948 that the gathering, now sponsored jointly by the Gewerkschaft 17, Schulung und Bildung, and, all of a sudden, the Kulturbund, would meet in late September. The announcement added that this conference would formalize the cultural-political tasks of the Gewerkschaft 17 in connection with the two-year plan. The presence of Kulturbund representatives at the conference, like Alexander Abusch, was not explained.[61] Indeed, when the conference convened in late October, the proceedings were opened by the Kulturbund's Klaus Gysi "in the name of the Kulturbund"; and Gysi noted that this "joint meeting" of the Kulturbund, the FDGB, and the Gewerkschaft 17, which he mentioned here and elsewhere in that order, was "part of the Kulturbund's week" of events sponsored in association with the motto "peace."[62]

This conference is discussed in detail in the broader context of its relationship to the Wroclaw peace conference, the Kulturbund's endorsement of it, and the relationship of both to the SED's two-year plan. For now it suffices to establish the fact that the Gewerkschaft 17 had, in effect, been elbowed aside. High-level union officials certainly had that impression even before the conference convened. In September 1948, Prietzel wrote that the union's cultural-political discussions scheduled for August had "unfortunately" not been able to take place as planned. "Other organizations" wanted to hold cultural-political events at the same time; and, "along with the fact

[59]Pr., "Theorie und Praxis. Kulturpolitische Tagung des Zentralvorstandes," *Kunst und Schrifttum* 6 (1948): 23.
[60]"Zweite Delegiertenkonferenz der Gewerkschaft Kunst und Schrifttum Groß-Berlin," ibid., p. 24.
[61]"Zwei wichtige Veranstaltungen unserer Gewerkschaft," *Kunst und Schrifttum* 8 (1948): 31.
[62]See *Der Zweijahrplan und die Kulturschaffenden. Protokoll der gemeinsamen Tagung des Kulturbundes, des FDGB und der Gewerkschaft Kunst und Schrifttum am 28. und 29. Oktober 1948*, p. 7.

that our cultural-political working conference could have been undertaken anyway" only in collaboration with Schulung und Bildung, the overlapping of events created problems. Prietzel then explained that the FDGB's executive board had been responsible for initiating a "change in our plans." A "joint cultural-political conference of the FDGB, the Gewerkschaft 17, and the Kulturbund," he said, mentioning the organizations in a sequence different from Gysi's, would gather in late October 1948; the Gewerkschaft 17 itself would convene "our own cultural-political working conference" later to discuss the practical implementation of the results of the larger gathering.[63] The union's meeting never occurred, and the leadership was not exactly happy about the situation when it told its members that their meeting could not take place because Schulung und Bildung, the Kulturbund, and the SED all intended to convene on their own.[64] That conference, with an agenda built around the two-year plan, met in late October; and just before, Prietzel again spoke of a meeting sponsored, as he put it, by the Gewerkschaft 17, Schulung und Bildung, and the Kulturbund. He ended his report with the declaration that the union ought to be regarded as the exclusive representative of creative artists because all other mass organizations were associations for "consumers" of art. The board also insisted that the union play the leading role in all cultural-political events and that there be a clearer demarcation between its responsibilities and the Kulturbund's.[65] At its next meeting, the board then protested the fact that Walter Maschke, and not one of its own officials, was set to deliver the main speech to the conference the next day.[66]

Not that union men like Prietzel or Kurt Liebmann were muzzled there; but neither gave a talk to compare with the ones delivered by Abusch or Maschke. The party leadership, it seems, was simply fed up with the union's insistence upon an organizational structure bitterly resented by creative intellectuals and with its refusal to curb ambitions that had long since outlived their usefulness. Still misunderstanding the direction of developments, however, some of the union leaders may have felt mollified by the inaccurate impression that the union was now going to be taken more seriously. As Prietzel put it in his remarks to the conference in October, the Gewerkschaft 17 hoped in the future for better cooperation from the Deutsche Wirtschaftskommission and all other administrative agencies. "Time and again we have had to conclude that decisions involving culturally important matters are made without listening to our union beforehand." This could not continue if the union were to fulfill the tasks specifically assigned to it at the

---

[63]Pr., "Kulturpolitische Arbeitstagung," *Kunst und Schrifttum* 9 (1948): 38.

[64]An die Kollegen Vorstandsmitglieder der Gewerkschaft Kunst und Schrifttum, 9 September 1948. Archiv der Gewerkschaftsbewegung, Sig. 3.

[65]Pr., "Sitzung des Zentralvorstandes," *Kunst und Schrifttum* 10 (1948): 41.

[66]Beschlußprotokoll der am 27. Oktober stattgefundenen Zentralvorstandssitzung. Archiv der Gewerkschaftsbewegung, Sig. 3.

conference. In fact, in connection with these two-year-plan tasks, Prietzel noted that the union's own cultural-political conference, plans for which were dropped in favor of the joint conference, now needed to be rescheduled.[67] Like Prietzel, Liebmann also misread the situation. He believed that the FDGB, via its factory organization, and the Gewerkschaft 17, "on the strength of its clearly acknowledged cultural right of codetermination," would be the "central agency capable of systematically coordinating and managing the initiative of all relevant organizations."[68] Nothing of the sort ever happened; in Sachsen-Anhalt there were acrid complaints about the "old problem" of which organization would move things forward in cultural-political matters; this particular commentary added that the central management of the Gewerkschaft 17 had passed a resolution designed to put an end to such debates and that the joint conference held in late October passed on it. The Gewerkschaft 17 was to be regarded as an organization of creative artists, the Kulturbund as an association comprised of consumers of art. With this resolution, the fundamental provisions of Liebmann's cultural-political manifesto appeared to have "prevailed."[69] The trouble was that the union's manifesto, which may or may not have been discussed privately at the conference, was certainly *not* passed there. Nor had local offices of the FDGB's Schulung und Bildung altered their conduct. In Magdeburg, Schulung und Bildung engaged in cultural-political work without paying any attention to the cultural-political manifesto or giving any of the union's seven divisions the chance to take the lead in cultural events.[70]

These difficulties pale in comparison with the headaches caused by the union's final unraveling, though the two processes were closely intertwined. The many efforts made to justify the concept of a single union like the Gewerkschaft 17, such as one undertaken by Prietzel in fall 1947,[71] never made the divisions' loss of independence as autonomous associations easier for them to swallow; and the entire issue reached the crisis stage a few months later in Berlin. Needless to say, the Soviet blockade of the city in June 1948 helped bring matters to a head, though trouble had been brewing there for many months. On 25 October 1947, high-level talks took place that focused on ways of providing the seven divisions of the Gewerkschaft 17, especially the association of theater workers or GDBA, more independence; but the organizational structure of the central union, to say nothing of involuntary membership in the FDGB, remained intact; and another proposal, moving

---

[67]"Gewerkschaft 17. Bericht durch Herrn Amandus Prietzel," *Der Zweijahrplan und die Kulturschaffenden*, pp. 127-28.
[68]Ibid., p. 54.
[69]Reinhardt, "Kulturschaffende nicht genügend aktiv," *Kunst und Schrifttum* 12 (1948): 49.
[70]Ibid.
[71]Prietzel, "Die gewerkschaftliche Erfassung der 'geistig Schaffenden,'" *Kunst und Schrifttum* 9 (1947): 3.

the office of the GDBA's central management to the Soviet-sector of Berlin, scarcely lent itself to a mediation of the dispute either.[72] The meeting was attended by Karl Raab (who stood in for Ackermann); Paul Merker and Rudolf Belke for the SED's secretariat; Göring and Jendretzky as FDGB chairmen; Inge Wangenheim for the GDBA; and Herbert Volkmann for the DVV. It was agreed that Wangenheim should become head of the Soviet-zone GDBA and Erich Otto her deputy. On 8 November 1947, the administrative board of the GDBA rejected the idea of switching its operations to "another zone" and threatened to pull out of the FDGB altogether.[73] (Incidentally, according to Wangenheim, Otto had declined to set foot in Soviet-occupied Germany ever since an SMAD officer said that Otto should be arrested for remarks made in Weimar.)[74]

The situation went steadily downhill then, and oratory did nothing to stop the slide. In December 1947, Jendretzky reaffirmed the FDGB's commitment to the establishment of one union organization in all of Germany, added that prospects for national unification were poor in the absence of it, warned that "not everyone whose lips utter the word 'unity' favors its immediate realization," and concluded that persons who opposed union unity by helping to delay it aided and abetted the enemies of democracy in Germany.[75] But by now, the Berlin chapter of the FDGB had to contend with an ostensibly disunifying splinter group calling itself the Unabhängige Gewerkschaftsopposition (UGO), the independent union opposition present within the FDGB, and comprised mostly of Social and Christian Democrats who undertook to influence the direction of the union.[76] With another round of elections scheduled, UGO organizers tried to "split" the FDGB by insisting, among other things, upon an electoral provision calling for the identification of candidates according to their party membership.[77] The idea would have enabled the rank-and-file to spot union leaders, functionaries, and delegates whose membership in the SED was kept mostly private. The FDGB said that the provision was an underhanded attempt to inject "party-political quarrels" into the nonpartisan FDGB and opposed it.

These differences quickly found their way into the Gewerkschaft 17 and its seven divisions, influencing discussions both at the zonal level, but especially within the Greater-Berlin branch of the union, and further encouraging

[72]Sitzung am 25. Oktober 1947. Betr.: Maßnahmen zur Sicherung einer grösseren Selbständigkeit der Sparten in der Gewerkschaft 17, insbesondere der Genossenschaft deutscher Bühnenangehöriger." Archiv der Gewerkschaftsbewegung, Sig. 278.

[73]Verrwaltungsrat der Genossenschaft Deutscher Bühnenangehöriger, 8 November 1947, ibid., Sig. 1480.

[74]Besprechung im Landesvorstand über die Neuorganisation der Bühnengenossenschaft, ca. June 1948, ibid. The reference is to the meeting held in Weimar back in August 1946.

[75]"Gewerkschaftseinheit ist möglich," *Kunst und Schrifttum* (Groß-Berlin) 2 (1948): 5.

[76]"Keine Spaltung—Einheit," *Kunst und Schrifttum* (Groß-Berlin) 3 (1948): 9.

[77]"Gewerkschaftseinheit ist möglich," *Kunst und Schrifttum* 2 (1948): 5.

"divisional egotism." Prietzel said in April 1948 that efforts were underway among artists living in Berlin aimed at breaking up the Gewerkschaft 17; worse, he said, there was open talk of severing the union from the FDGB entirely and establishing an organization with a Western license.[78] At the time, separatist sentiments were strongest among stage artists organized within the Genossenschaft deutscher Bühnenangehöriger (GDBA); but Prietzel acknowledged that similar sentiments were prevalent elsewhere. "Forces" were at work, he said, acting on "orders from the outside" or possibly on the basis of inner conviction, who opposed all of the progressive insights related to the new union structure and made necessary by unprecedented political, economic, and social conditions. These forces refused to believe that a "new way" was called for, and in the area of union organization this "new way" hinged upon the closest possible linkage between workers, employees, and creative intellectuals.[79] In Berlin, the discussions all focused on the upcoming "Verbandstag," a delegates' meeting of the Greater-Berlin branch of the Gewerkschaft 17 scheduled for 11 and 12 May 1948.[80]

As Prietzel described the meeting, there were repeated clashes of opinions—small wonder, he said, considering the nature of conditions in Berlin; and these differences manifested themselves in the vote taken on an official resolution concerning the unity of the FDGB. The final paragraph of this resolution expressed the feeling that every progressive artist and creative intellectual belonged in a "unified free union movement" whose activities and goals were "independent of the parties or any other influences." Many of those who cast their vote on the resolution failed to take that stipulation seriously; it passed by only 50 for, 23 against, with six abstentions—an outcome not nearly sufficient as an expression of unbridled enthusiasm for the FDGB;[81] and matters only deteriorated in Berlin thereafter. In late May, the UGO began calling itself the "provisional directorate of the FDGB Groß-Berlin. The persons behind this declaration were declared to be in violation of the FDGB's statutes and dismissed as members of the union. The FDGB undertook one last attempt at a "settlement." It offered to accept penitent members of the UGO back into the fold if they contented themselves with a third of the seats on the FDGB's executive board (a "reflection" of their actual strength), recognize the FDGB's statutes, promise to abide by any resolution

[78]Prietzel, "Der neue Weg," *Kunst und Schrifttum* 4 (1948): 13-14.
[79]Ibid.
[80]See Schlichting, "Gruß an unsere Delegierten," *Kunst und Schrifttum* (Groß-Berlin) 5 (1948): 19; see also the concerns of the FDGB-loyal faction of the Genossenschaft Deutscher Bühnenangehöriger on the eve of the Berlin meeting ("Bedeutung des Verbandes der Gewerkschaft für die GDBA," *Kunst und Schrifttum* [Groß-Berlin] 5 [1948]: 20), as well as the official positions of the union-loyal leadership of the other divisions published in the same May edition of *Kunst und Schrifttum* (Groß-Berlin).
[81]See Pr., "Zweite Delegiertenkonferenz der Gewerkschaft Kunst und Schrifttum Groß-Berlin," *Kunst und Schrifttum* 6 (1948): 24.

passed by a "democratic majority," close down its two independent newspapers, and so on.[82] That never happened, and the UGO split from the FDGB. The corresponding rift within the Greater-Berlin chapter of the Gewerkschaft 17 was more complex, owing to the existence of seven divisions with their diverse constituencies and different sets of opinion. To make a long story short, the FDGB's attempt to "resolve" the general crisis by presenting the UGO with the list of virtual ultimatums referred to above called upon every union functionary to accept the FDGB's statutes and, by extension, the statutes of the Gewerkschaft 17. The equivalent of a loyalty oath, the FDGB insisted that these declarations would reflect support "for the unity of the union movement" in the face of a rift created by the "foreign procapitalist powers."

The administrative board of the Genossenschaft Deutscher Bühnenangehöriger rejected the ultimatum and declared itself an "independent, autonomous organization."[83] Union officials responded by insisting that the administrative board of the GDBA ran the affairs of the Berlin chapter of the organization and had no jurisdiction over its Soviet zone branches. Moreover, because the decision to become independent meant a break with the FDGB, the board had effectively passed a measure that ignored the prerogative of each individual member of the GDBA to decide upon his or her affiliation with the FDGB. Finally, the members of the administrative board themselves belonged to the FDGB and the Gewerkschaft 17; the statutes of those two outfits were not only binding upon all members, but had been originally voted on by the same persons in the Berlin GDBA who now violated the very statutes approved by them. They were thus automatically expelled from the FDGB.[84] This crisis must have led, then, to discussions by the party secretariat on 5 and 12 July 1948 that attempted to prevent the inevitable by allowing six of the union's divisions to form ostensibly "independent associations," but still under the umbrella of the FDGB.[85]

Such a solution obviously failed to address the problem of real independence. Besides, the secretariat's decision to reduce the Gewerkschaft 17 to theater workers (stage hands, technicians, and the like), while allowing the other six divisions to set up a "cartel" free of the old Gewerkschaft 17, but still linked to the FDGB,[86] was never implemented. Just a few days later,

[82]See "An alle Funktionäre und Mitglieder des FDGB Groß-Berlin" and, "Der Vermittlungsvorschlag," *Kunst und Schrifttum* (Groß-Berlin) 7 (1948): 29.
[83]See Der Präsident [der GDBA] an den Bundesvorstand des FDGB, 28 June 1948. Archiv der Gewerkschaftbewegung, Sig. 1480.
[84]"Mit—ohne—oder gegen den FDGB," *Kunst und Schrifttum* 7 (1948): 30. See also "Gewerkschaft 17 und UGO," *Kunst und Schrifttum* (Groß-Berlin) 8/9 (1948): 39, for additional details concerning the later resignation of the former head of the GDBA in Berlin, Erich Otto.
[85]Protokoll Nr. 93 (II) der Sitzung des Zentralsekretariats am 5. 7. 1948. Zentrales Parteiarchiv, IV 2/2.1/215/2.
[86]Protokoll Nr. 94 (II) der Sitzung des Zentralsekretariats am 12. 7. 1948. Anlage Nr. 3, ibid., IV

another attempt was made to persuade Erich Otto and the GDBA not to break away, the result being an announcement that the *Berlin* branch of the Gewerkschaft 17 had reorganized. Its seven divisions would form a "cartel" of independent associations with complete financial and administrative autonomy represented by its own people on the executive board of the FDGB.[87] It was none too soon, either; in fall 1948, the Presseverband conceded that certain members were still guided by either prejudice or false information into believing that the FDGB was "somehow influenced by party politics or had lent itself to being the mouthpiece or executive organ of a single occupying power";[88] and it later transpired that rifts had split not only the Berlin Presseverband (losing 200 members), but the Deutscher Musiker-Verband as well (300 members defected to the UGO). The Schutzverband Bildender Künstler (SBK) and Deutscher Autoren narrowly avoided splintering when the organizational restructuring referred to above staved off the rift. The Internationale Artisten-Loge and the Verband Technik und Verwaltung were said to have been more immune to the allures of the UGO,[89] but with formation of the "cartel," the Gewerkschaft 17 had effectively ceased to exist in Berlin. By early September 1948, the management of the Gewerkschaft 17 finally admitted that the organizational idea behind the union and its seven divisions had failed there. The union's Verbandstag the previous May, wrote Max Schlichting, had demonstrated that a large portion of the artists who belonged to the union did not approve of its specific structure. The board of the FDGB had thereupon appointed a special commission to investigate the possibilities of a reorganization with an eye to turning the seven divisions into "autonomous associations with responsibility for their own finances and administration." These seven "autonomous" associations were to be consolidated within a "cartel of associations for art and writing" (Kartell der Verbände für Kunst und Schrifttum Groß-Berlin). Even then, however, the cartel remained part of the FDGB.[90] This underlying administrative and programmatic subordination had always been the source of the problem and remained unresolved by the formation of the "cartel," officialized by a decision of the Soviet-zone FDGB on 4 October 1948. Still, union officials tried to put on the best face. The conversion of the Berlin Gewerkschaft 17 into a cartel did not constitute a "new creation" at all; rather, the measure merely took the step of legalizing conditions that had existed since

---

2/2.1/216/1 and 22.

[87]Aktennotiz über die Sitzung vom 16. 7. 48 zwischen den Vertretern der Reorganisations-Kommission und der Genossenschaft Deutscher Bühnen-Angehörigen; and Presseverlautbarung des Vorstandes der Gewerkschaft Kunst und Schrifttum Groß-Berlin. Archiv der Gewerkschaftsbewegung, Sig. 1480.

[88]"Der Presseverband im FDGB," *Kunst und Schrifttum* (Groß-Berlin) 8/9 (1948): 38.

[89]Schlichting, "Bilanz und Prognose," *Kunst und Schrifttum* (Groß-Berlin) 1 (1949): 1.

[90]Schlichting, "Aussprechen was ist!" *Kunst und Schrifttum* (Groß-Berlin) 8/9 (1948): 33-34.

the formation of the organization. The idea now was to unleash the "creative organizational forces" that had been pent up by "petty organizational squabbles," even though it was admitted that the rules and statutes of the associations still conformed substantially to those of the FDGB.[91] The deepening crisis in Berlin then rendered the entire question moot.

Union officials struggled that much harder to justify their continuing existence throughout Soviet-occupied Germany. In mid-October 1948, the board defied the FDGB's request to hold off with "obligatory resolutions" in matters of reorganization and made a new series of proposals. The board rejected beforehand the notion that the Soviet-zone Gewerkschaft 17 should follow the example just set in Berlin; and suggested still another scheme designed to create the appearance of independence for its seven divisions while retaining the union's old structure. The plan foresaw the creation of new central boards for each of the seven Soviet-zone divisions, but now based in Berlin, integrated into the executive board of the Gewerkschaft 17, and subject to "coordination" of their work by a "cultural secretary." Prietzel suggested Kurt Liebmann for that position, who, as head of the proposed cultural secretariat, would have to be approved by both the SED and the SMAD.[92] That thinking apparently changed, however, because the prediction was made a few months later that the Soviet-zone Gewerkschaft 17 would indeed adapt itself to the Berlin solution;[93] and as a matter of fact, a reorganization of that sort was considered for several weeks before the Gewerkschaft 17 finally made or was forced to make changes that gutted it. On 6 January 1949, just prior to a gathering of its full board, a meeting of the union's party "faction" met in the presence of a representative from the central secretariat by the name of Paffrath. Speaking on behalf of Anton Ackermann and Paul Merker, Paffrath told the "faction" that the party had altered the resolution passed, evidently, back on 12 July 1948. The solution now proposed was that the three divisions comprised of "productive artists," essentially writers, artists, and journalists, be removed from the Gewerkschaft 17; the other divisions, representing mostly technical and administrative employees, would remain, but organize and operate within cultural enterprises separately from artists and such who had always dreaded the idea of being outvoted in matters pertaining to creative decisions.

To judge by the minutes, the remainder of Paffrath's proposal left more questions open than answered, but the important point remains that the union leadership, even though those present belonged to its "party faction," reacted

[91]See "Das Kartell steht," *Kunst und Schrifttum* (Groß-Berlin) 10 (1948): 41.
[92]Prietzel an den Bundesvorstand des FDGB. Z. Hd. d. Kollegen Jendretzky, Göring, Kaufmann, Warnke, Maschke. 14 October 1948; and Beschlußprotokoll der am 27. Oktober 1948 stattgefundenen Zentralvorstandssitzung, ibid. See also "Sitzung des Zentral-Vorstandes. Wichtige Vorstandsbeschlüsse," *Kunst und Schrifttum* 10/11 (1948): 40.
[93] Schlichting, "Bilanz und Prognose," *Kunst und Schrifttum* (Groß-Berlin) 1 (1949): 1.

angrily and opposed the idea. Nor were they happy at the repeated suggestion that the Gewerkschaft 17 had failed in its cultural-political responsibilities—criticism most likely caused by anger at the union for its heavy-handed insistence upon an organizational form that consistently alienated the intellectuals. The "party faction" requested that the matter be further discussed on the basis of the union's own resolution passed on 13 October 1948. Paffrath then reminded them all that they were present at a party, not a union meeting, and held them responsible for their actions. When the party passed a resolution, he said, it ought not to be considered from the vantage point of the Gewerkschaft 17, but from the position of the party. Otherwise, Paffrath stressed the importance of winning the support of creative intellectuals for undertakings connected with the two-year plan and indicated that the most recent resolution might actually be revised yet again.[94]

Though Prietzel made further entreaties later in the month,[95] time had run out. On 15 February, Prietzel informed the FDGB that the union intended to meet on 22 February to make a final decision about its reorganization and requested that both the FDGB and the party secretariat send representatives.[96] The meeting occurred as scheduled and split the Gewerkschaft 17 roughly according to the terms of the "resolution" given its party faction at the meeting on 6 January.[97] The decision was characterized as an attempt to improve the union's ability to respond more effectively to "particular practical tasks" that had arisen in connection with the FDGB's Bitterfeld resolutions and the two-year plan. The Gewerkschaft 17 was to be divided into two unions, a Gewerkschaft "Bühne, Film, Artistik, Musik," encompassing the previous corresponding divisions and "Technik und Verwaltung"; and a Gewerkschaft "Kunst und Schrifttum," to include the associations of writers, artists, and journalists.[98] Prietzel was left in charge of the latter, but the union had been reduced to meaninglessness.[99] Scarcely a year passed before the second of the two unions was dissolved altogether; the writers' and artists' associations were incorporated into the Kulturbund and soon reappeared as the East-German Schriftstellerverband (DSV) and the Verband bildender Künstler (VdK).

[94]Aus der Diskussion der am 6. 1. 1949 stattgefundenen Fraktionsbesprechung im SED-Haus. See also Bericht über die am 6. und 7. Januar 1949 abgehaltene Tagung des Zentralvorstandes. Archiv der Gewerkschaftsbewegung, Sig. 3.
[95]Prietzel an den Bundesvorstand des FDGB, 28 January 1949, ibid., Sig. 1480.
[96]See Prietzel an den Bundesvorstand des FDGB, 15 February 1949, ibid.
[97]Betr.: Reorganisation der Gewerkschaft 17 - Kunst und Schrifttum, 22 February 1949, gez. Göring, ibid.
[98]Pr., "Entscheidung in der Organisationsfrage," *Kunst und Schrifttum* 3/4 (1949): 13.
[99]See Prietzel's bitter complaint to the FDGB about the behavior of the Deutsche Wirtschaftskommission, which simply ignored the union. Prietzel an den Bundesvorstand des FDGB, 29 April 1949. Archiv der Gewerkschaftsbewegung, Sig. 1480.

In the meantime, however, the FDGB had continued along its inexorable path to complete subservience. Even before the FDGB met in Bitterfeld in late November to begin its final transformation into a Leninist "mass organization," geared now toward implementing the provisions of the two-year plan, its Berlin branch had already passed a resolution that drew a variety of uncompromisingly harsh conclusions from its recent experience with the UGO's determination to split the union. The Marshall Plan and its need of a West German "colonial state"; the "intensification of class contradictions"; the presence of class enemies; the intention of "united foreign and German imperialism" to put the West German economy on a war footing, and to turn Berlin into a forward outpost, all for the sake of fighting the advances of democratic forces; the UGO as an "agent of American monopoly capital" directed and supported by the American Federation of Labor; the "battle against conscious agents of monopoly capital," anti-Soviet crusading in the West; the demand that the Berlin unions declare their commitment to the Soviet Union, to the countries of popular democracy, and to Soviet-occupied Germany; the "encroachment of reactionary and seditious views" into Soviet-zone factories; the necessity of linking Berlin's economy to that of the Soviet-zone and of using the two-year plan to render both independent of all crises spawned by Western capitalism—this is just a sampling of union rhetoric; and the afterthought that none of these positions in any way affected the "FDGB's nonpartisanship and its position with respect to the political parties" merely illustrated how advanced the Soviet-zone corruption of the term had become.[100] Finally, this resolution demanded that all union officials take a position on the matters raised in the document and look closely at conditions within their own area of responsibility.

This demand led to an embarrassing act of contrition by Max Schlichting, "provisional head of the cartel Kunst und Schrifttum Groß-Berlin." Schlichting called upon the leadership of each district board and each union division to convene meetings for the purpose of "discussing" the FDGB's resolution; and from there he proceeded to touch upon that section of the same document which spoke of the "class enemy organizing itself" within the FDGB and which chastised union functionaries for their supposed laxity in compromising with union-splitters. They should have been unceremoniously kicked out. In this context, Schlichting duly noted that there had been such a tendency within the Gewerkschaft 17 to make compromises and concessions; and he himself had often been guilty of the same, even to the point of giving up on the idea of a union. Indeed, he added, his entire policy as head of the Berlin Gewerkschaft 17 was geared toward "mediation, compromise, and concession," the result of which had been the attempt to solve the

---

[100]"Entschließung des FDGB Groß-Berlin vom 1. November 1948," *Kunst und Schrifttum.* Sonderausgabe (November 1948): 2-6.

impending rift in the union through formation of the cartel. Nonetheless, Schlichting stopped short of groveling; it was up to union members, he said, to decide whether an "uncompromising, strictly centralized policy" of sticking to the previous structure in Berlin would have achieved better results, especially in view of the fact that the creation of the cartel had not prevented the rupture within the GDBA and the Verband der Deutschen Presse. Besides, the board of the Berlin Gewerkschaft 17, as well as the city district heads, had at the time almost unanimously favored the idea of a cartel as the sole means of responding to the uniqueness of circumstances in Berlin.[101] What Schlichting failed to reveal was that, in forming the cartel, he had acted at the behest of the party anyway.[102]

The Kultureller Beirat

The early draft versions of the SED's two-year cultural plan that survive in the papers of Ulbricht and Ackermann, which served as the basis for the document circulated at the party conference in January 1949, are virtually identical except for a sentence added in Ulbricht's. In both drafts, authors are enjoined to use their writing to explain the meaning and significance of the two-year plan to the entire people" and the point made that "coordination and planning of this work shall be undertaken by the German publishing commission."[103] This "publishing commission," or Deutsche Kommission für das Verlagswesen, was to be nothing more than the old Kultureller Beirat following another reorganization of its operations. The development of the KB, as well as the DVV's office of publishing, had already been affected by the issuance of order 234 and by plans to improve the "coordination" of cultural-political activities in all of Soviet-occupied Germany. In fact, there was a later reference made to publishing firms that would be "restructured" in connection with the "necessities arising out of order 234 and the two-year plan";[104] and Ulbricht's draft of the cultural plan made it clear that restructuring was the same as shutting down a "number of publishing houses" (that passage was excised in the version of the cultural plan circulated at the party conference in January 1949).

Ironically, just as the Kultureller Beirat first began gearing up for the latest change in its operation in early spring 1948, it was hit with the prospect of a significant reduction in staff that would have further hampered its

[101]Schlichting, "Grundlegende Entschließung und eine Erklärung," ibid., p. 1.

[102]See Schlichting's off-the-cuff remark at the meeting of the party faction on 6 January 1949. Archiv der Gewerkschaftsbewegung, Sig. 3.

[103]Entwurf zum kulturellen Plan, no date. Zentrales Parteiarchiv, NL 182/931/195.

[104]Abteilung Kunst und Literatur. Planung für das II. Vierteljahr 1948/1949, 20 July 1948. Bundesarchiv. Abt. Potsdam, R-2/1155/62.

work—the KB learned in March 1948 that the size of its secretariat had to be decreased. This measure was out of all proportion to the importance of the organization and probably reflected nothing more than the economic exigencies then affecting administrative agencies and cultural undertakings in Soviet-occupied Germany.[105] Herbert Volkmann petitioned the office of finance for retention of an adequately staffed secretariat and, in the process, provided relevant information about its daily routine. He began with a reference to SMAD order 25 as a way of making the point that, behind what he called the modest title of council for ideological questions in matters related to publishing, hid the "most important democratic instrument for purposeful and effective economic planning directed at the entire system of publishing in the Soviet zone of occupation and the Soviet sector of Berlin." Its responsibilities included the "specialized and ideological screening" of all nonpolitical publications in Soviet-occupied Germany and Berlin (political literature, Volkmann said, remained subject to "precensorship" by the SMAD). In pursuit of those responsibilities, the KB relied on its main committee, which consulted with a dozen specialized commissions comprised of 8 to 15 unpaid experts each. To judge by its title, one of the commissions, the "Lektorenüberwachungskommission," must have watched over the agency's staff of no less than four hundred "readers and evaluators."

The trouble was that the KB could only do its job with the support of its own fully sized secretariat; earlier attempts to have the work done "on the side" by some division of the DVV had failed miserably. Some 400 to 500 individual publishing projects now reached the secretariat monthly and had to be dealt with from their arrival to the issuance of permission to print; the secretariat also gathered, evaluated, and reported further upon 600 to 800 appraisals a month; calculated and supervised both paper requests submitted by publishers for individual titles as well as the edition size applied for by the publisher (then either accepted or altered by the KB); arranged for final approval of the paper supply through the SMAD's office of information; represented the KB in the offices of the occupation administration as well as dealing with all German administrative agencies; worked additionally with local political and cultural authorities; and negotiated with publishers and authors. The secretariat received forty visitors, took care of 80 to 100 incoming and outgoing letters, arranged for 20 to 30 deliveries by messenger, received and sent off 60 manuscript evaluations, and made 650 to 700 phone calls—all in a day's work.[106] Volkmann argued accordingly against any reduction in

[105]The DVV's art and literature noted in mid-April 1948, for instance, that it was unable to pursue plans for an academy of arts, nor a variety of other anticipated projects, because the division of visual arts had had its budget cut. See Referat Bildende Kunst. Gez. Strauß. Betrifft: Arbeitsplan April-Juni 1948, 14 April 1948, ibid., R-2/1155/67.
[106]Volkmann an die Personalbestands-Kommission bei der Deutschen Zentralfinanzverwaltung. Antrag auf Erhaltung des Sekretariats des Kulturellen Beirats für das Verlagswesen," 3 March

staff, especially considering that the secretariat had never been given the forty employees authorized by order 25; in the process of "implementing" the order in June 1947, Volkmann said, the DVV and the SMAD had settled on twenty-nine instead. This figure was "accepted," retroactive to 1 July 1947, by the president of the office of finance on 18 August 1947. But twenty-nine staff members was the absolute minimum necessary to comply with orders 25 and 90, Volkmann said and warned against transferring the secretariat's work back to a division of the DVV or some other agency. This route had been taken before and failed.[107] Whether the finance office suggested such a course of action or advocated it indirectly through a radical reduction in the size of the secretariat is unclear, but the compromise reached fell short of the KB's expectations. On 5 March 1948, finance agreed to twenty staff members and then, ten days later, raised the number to twenty-three. This figure represented the "maximum," however, and the additional three positions, as well as the original twenty, still had to come from the DVV's own personnel.[108]

These difficulties overlapped with the start of a new round of discussions about the authority of the Kultureller Beirat and the nature of its operations. In late March, working in conjunction with the DVV's office of publishing, the SMAD's information office prepared new guidelines governing the activities of publishers and presses. These provisions did not depart dramatically from the ones established by orders 356 and 90 (issued on 24 December 1946 and 17 April 1947 respectively); but most of the regulatory responsibility was shifted from the SMAD to the DVV; and, according to what Major Mischin told Alfred Frommhold, the SMAD intended to issue an order to that effect. In fact, the first draft of the order already existed, and Frommhold sent a copy of it, the revised guidelines, and the rest of the above information to Paul Wandel.[109] For reasons unknown, there was no immediate action taken, though the subject of the Kultureller Beirat and its "reorganization" then came up intermittently from spring 1948 through December 1949 and beyond. In May 1948, at the third session of the cultural-political committee working under the aegis of the Deutscher Volksrat,[110] Heinrich Deiters expressed his interest in having a discussion of the "management and

---

1948, ibid., R-2/1007/147-56.
[107]Ibid.
[108]Personalbestandskommission bei der Deutschen Zentralfinanzverwaltung in der sowjetischen Besatzungszone an die Deutsche Verwaltung für Volksbildung. Betrifft: Neufestsetzung der Planstellen für die Rundfunksender und den Kulturellen Beirat, 15 March 1948, ibid., R-2/1007/202.
[109]See Verlagswesen. Herrn Präsident Wandel. Betrifft: Tätigkeit von Verlagen und Druckereien. Gez. Frommhold, 3 April 1948; Entwurf. Befehl des Obersten Chefs der Sowjetischen Militär-Administration, 31 March 1948; Richtlinien für die Tätigkeit der Verlage und die Herausgabe von Druckerzeugnisse, 30 March 1948, ibid., R-2/1149/2-16.
[110]See Chapter Thirteen for discussion of this particular "cultural-political" committee.

consolidation of book publishing" to follow a future talk by some representative of the Kultureller Beirat. The critical issue was how to "avoid the establishment of a censorship agency; the authors are vehement in their objections to it."[111] As things developed, no one spoke to the committee on that subject until Heinrich Becker addressed the group almost a year later and undertook to explain the rationale behind what was passed off innocuously as "economic planning" in the publication of books. Becker did not focus directly upon the Kultureller Beirat, however, and noted cryptically that that situation was "not ideal." Since early 1946, he said, and repeatedly thereafter, attempts had been made through "requests, submissions, threats, scoldings, complaints, good advice, and every possibility of psychological influence" to persuade authoritative offices to consider ways of including the publishers in discussions of their own plans and programs. He himself had proposed the inclusion of three groups in the process—authors, publishers, and the "politically and cultural-politically responsible persons in the authoritative offices of administration." But efforts to make the publishers members of "the decisive agency," the Kultureller Beirat, had never been approved; neither as "real authorities," nor on a mostly informal basis had they been allowed to participate. Apparently, Becker said, the prevalent feeling among those with the power to make such a decision was that an eye had to be kept on "these guys, who naturally work primarily on the basis of mercantile considerations." This was the reason why publishers had been excluded, though Becker felt that resolving problems connected with "planned publishing" hinged upon their participation; and he added that he had renewed his proposal to build the "publishing commission now being considered" around the three pillars of author, publisher, and authorities.[112]

The "publishing commission," the formation of which Becker still considered imminent as late as June 1949, was the identical organization referred to in the earliest drafts of the two-year cultural plan—the "restructured" Kultureller Beirat under active consideration since the beginning of 1948. Exactly why this reorganization never took place is uncertain; the problems with the KB in early 1948 were just as grievous in early 1948 as they had been in late 1946 or, following the issuance of order 25 in spring 1947, throughout the remainder of that year; and the reason why negotiations with the SMAD never led to an agreement, at least not by December 1949, may have been due to the fact that "reorganization" hinged upon the SMAD's readiness to relinquish its right to censor. What went on in private deliberations is unknown; but the Kultureller Beirat and its reorganization was a subject touchy enough to be avoided as a topic of discussion on the agenda of the cultural-political committee working under the aegis of the Deutscher

[111]Ausschuß für Kulturpolitik. 3. Sitzung, 8 May 1948, ibid., A-1/45/25.
[112]Ausschuß für Kulturpolitik. 20. Sitzung. 25 June 1949. Das Verlagswesen. Berichterstattung: Heinrich Becker, ibid., A-1/61/18 and 40.

Volksrat after Deiters first brought it up in April 1948. It was never mentioned again in that forum until Deiters listed creation of a "Deutsche Kommission für das Verlagswesen," which he still characterized as being in the process of formation and intended to assume "certain functions" of the Kultureller Beirat, while presenting his proposal for a nationwide cultural plan on 17 March 1949.[113] Deiters' ideas for a cultural program suited to all of Germany thus included the Soviet-zone office of censorship. The irony escaped him.

The allusion to the Deutsche Kommission für das Verlagswesen contained in the party's "cultural plan" introduced at the conference in late January 1949 was the first and last public reference to it, though by then the proposal had been under advisement for a year. Again, action seemed imminent at the time, the party secretariat having just voted in favor of a draft SMAD order concerning the establishment of a "Verlagskommission" at a meeting on 10 January 1949.[114] But the subject still remained under wraps; Deiters planned on discussing the KB at a session of the cultural-political committee of the Deutscher Volksrat that same month until Ludolf Koven, deputy head of the KB, advised against it; the topic should not be raised because the organization was scheduled to be "rearranged very soon through an SMAD order."[115] But then the KB disappeared from the cultural ordinance passed by the Wirtschaftskommission on 31 March 1949, which was itself based on the party's plan. Whether reorganization of the KB failed to occur then or even later because the SMAD could not overcome its hesitation about giving up the right to censor cannot be resolved on the basis of available information; but it is certainly possible because the references to an order setting up new guidelines on publishing and printing, which go back to March and April 1948, all had the reassignment of censorship to the DVV, and the Kultureller Beirat as a main division of it, in common. In early April 1948, Frommhold outlined plans for the coming quarter and noted that the duties of his office of publishing were expected to increase considerably "after enactment of the new order planned by the SMAD." Frommhold added that several questions associated with the new regulations still needed to be clarified following a meeting with the SMAD's office of information on 7 April 1948 and that the DVV could not resolve these questions alone. Nonetheless, Frommhold proceeded from the assumption that the regulations would be completed within the month. Further details followed; the SMAD's office of information in-

[113]See Ausschuß für Kulturpolitik. 17. Sitzung, 17 March 1949, ibid., A-1/58/35; and Deiters' "Gesamtdeutsches Kulturprogramm." Bundesarchiv, Abt. Potsdam, A-1/76/173-76.
[114]See Protokoll Nr. 142 (II) der Sitzung des Zentralsekretariats am 10. 1. 1949; Anlage Nr. 3. Befehl des Obersten Chefs der Sowjetischen Militärverwaltung in Deutschland. Nr. ____. Errichtung und Aufgabenbereich der Deutschen Verlagskommission. Zentrales Parteiarchiv, IV 2/2.1/260/4, 12-13.
[115]Vertraulich! Aktenvermerk. Signed Lorf [?]. Betr.: Unterausschuß Kunst und Literatur, 12 January 1949. Bundesarchiv, Abt. Potsdam, A-1/73/63.

tended to issue an order that would shift the authority to regulate the activities of licensed firms to the president of the DVV, but Frommhold did not know when it would come out. The DVV was supposed to receive additional authorization to grant and suspend the licenses of publishing houses altogether, rather than just making recommendations for the SMAD to act on.[116]

A DVV plan for the "second quarter" of 1948-49 prepared three months later, dated 20 July 1948, then mentioned the "continuation of negotiations about the order, in preparation, related to the regulation of publishing firms, printing presses, etc.," establishment of a plan "for the future licensing of publishers," a report on the activity of previously licensed publishers, and proposals "for the elimination of publishing houses whose activity is unsatisfactory;[117] and all the while, complaints about the KB continued to mount. "SED writers" had vented their anger at the gathering in early April 1948; and their bitterness probably led to a PKE meeting on 21 July 1948 to discuss the problems. Richard Weimann confirmed there that the SMAD wished to shift the "political evaluation and censorship" of printed matter to the DVV; and Otto Kielmeyer, the man in charge of the Kultureller Beirat, admitted, for the first time, that order 25 provided specifically for the "ideological regulation" of publishing activities. The ensuing discussion then focused on guidelines that could be presented to the party secretariat and the DVV for their approval. Some of the individual points brought up included placing political considerations in the forefront of the KB's work because the pending SMAD order authorized the DVV to censor political literature. In the order as well, said one participant in the discussion, were further provisions that created an excellent opportunity either to reissue publishing licenses or revoke them as part of a "purge action"; and the party representative present, Holms, asked for a list of "readers" with whom the SED could deal directly—such as Paul Rilla, Stephan Hermlin, and Alfred Kantorowicz.[118] These suggestions, especially the idea of turning the Kultureller Beirat into a "main division" of the DVV, then came before the secretariat for approval on 23 August 1948. In addition, the secretariat expressed its "gratification" at the fact that the SMAD intended to allow the KB to regulate non-periodical political literature, license publishing houses directly, and disseminate all necessary raw materials with the exception of paper.[119]

But, as we have seen, still no decision had been reached by the end of 1948 or early 1949; and, apart from the apparent reluctance of the Russians

[116]Verlagswesen. Frommhold. Arbeitsplan April-Juni 1948, 9 April 1948, ibid., R-2/1155/72.
[117]Abteilung Kunst und Literatur. Volkmann. Planung für das II. Vierteljahr 1948/1949, 20 July 1948, ibid., R-2/1155/62.
[118]Protokoll der Besprechung über die Arbeit des kulturellen Beirats, 21 July 1948. Zentrales Parteiarchiv, IV 2/906/150/1-5.
[119]Protokoll Nr. 104 der Sitzung des Zentralsekretariats am 23. 8. 48; Anlage Nr. 2. Reorganisierung und Erweiterung der Vollmachten des Kulturellen Beirats, bid., IV 2/2.1/225/3 and 7.

to get out of the business of censoring themselves, one of the other reasons for the delay may have been problems with state government. Plans mentioned above called for a "conference with division heads of the state governments" to discuss the reorganization of publishing in terms of "the coming order"—even as complaints about the Kultureller Beirat steadily increased. In October 1948, the Saxon minister of culture and education, Helmut Holtzhauer, requested that policies in the "area of publishing (licensing, censorship, printing)" be placed on the agenda of the ministers' conference scheduled for 26 and 27 November 1948; and individual authors vented their own frustrations at the Kultureller Beirat.[120] Unfortunately, few of the KB's internal discussions can be documented because its files are so fragmentary; but one session, which met on 3 December 1948, provides some indication of the thinking of those who ran it and their inability to fathom the nature of their activities. The KB invited a number of journal editors to a discussion of Soviet-zone politics centering on the work of the Deutscher Volksrat; and a man by the name of J. M. Lange, who worked for the KB, talked about the "responsibilities of the journals." The Kultureller Beirat, Lange told his audience, would "in the future" be in a position to provide the journals with the "material basis" for their work because responsibility for apportioning paper allotments to them was soon to be reassigned to it. Lange went on to insist that the KB was "no institution of censorship," regardless of what some people said; it admittedly exercised an "ideological function" to the extent that paper allotments rested upon the determination of whether a particular journal truly met its responsibilities within the context of "the reconstruction of our people"; in this respect, the agency carried out a "certain ideological function" without, he claimed, "regulating" any journal's scientific, technical, or intellectual activity. "This is not our job; but we certainly see to it that the material appearing in your journals does not obstruct the general work of reconstruction."

Lange provided two examples of how the KB declined to censor journals. One particular periodical, he said, obtained all its information from the Western zones and—through its failure to understand that the Soviet Union had achieved significant scientific accomplishments—ignored the "difficult struggle to reestablish and reorganize production" in Soviet-occupied Germany. Regrettably, "we were constrained to withhold the license for a paper allotment for this journal, which once possessed an international reputation; this was a measure absolutely necessary for our protection." Lange told of yet another scientific journal that reprinted an editorial from an American paper containing the usual demands of a monopoly-capitalist society and the Marshall Plan—that is, "enslaving Germany to American monopoly capi-

120See the letters by Karl Grünberg (15 November 1948) and Maria Langner (2 December 1948), ibid., R-2/1094/6-7a and 10.

tal." In this case, too, "we were constrained to take a very close look at the paper allotment assigned to this publication and ascertain whether it really fulfilled its purpose in the context of the two-year plan, in the context of the reconstruction of our economy." Lange added that numerous other journals fell short of expectations; he particularly lamented their failure to report on the Lyssenko discussion in the USSR; and he listed the titles of numerous journals that similarly ignored the "question" of the Soviet Union.[121]

In response to his elaborations, at least one editor commented that he personally did not regard the KB as "a censoring agency or an operation that enforced political guidelines by way of paper allotment." Here things stood just weeks before the SED's first conference in late January 1949; and the regulation of the publishing trade certainly figured into the two-year "cultural plan" circulated there. By then, the KB's deputy head Ludolf Koven had already written that books in Soviet-occupied Germany acquired a "new task" on account of the two-year plan, which made demands on all elements of society, and that Soviet-zone publishers needed to decide how they could help fulfill it through the "sensible" production of books. Koven then expressed his vexation at receiving a report from one publisher who knew virtually nothing of the two-year plan; and followed up with a threat. Paper, he said, had to be allocated to those publishers who served the interests of the people by publishing in accordance with the needs of the plan. In the process, certain firms accustomed to bringing out large numbers of books would be unable to publish as actively as in the past because their programs were too loosely connected with present needs. Koven argued that "our" publishers needed to be in a position to make specific recommendations to their authors and to commission works, independent of the "wishes of certain authors." Under those conditions, publishers could be confident that military government, the DWK, and the Kultureller Beirat would do everything to provide cooperative firms with raw materials. But no one need fear that the objectives outlined in the two-year plan placed any "limitation on the activities" of the publishers.[122]

The thinking behind the growing linkage between the two-year plan and creative writers emerged more clearly in Koven's further remarks. The publication of technical literature was insufficient in itself to achieve one of the other goals of the two-year plan, "increasing worker productivity" by 30 percent; indeed, this problem was not preeminently a matter of technology at all; it was a question of the workers' attitude toward their job. In accordance with the Marxist concept that "being determines consciousness," Koven ex-

[121]Sitzung des Kulturellen Beirats der Deutschen Verwaltung für Volksbildung am 3. Dezember 1948 (im Hause des Deutschen Volksrates), ibid., A-1/64/1a-51.
[122]l.k., "Vor welchen Aufgaben steht der Buchhandel? Die Verlagsproduktion und der Zweijahrplan in der sowjetischen Besatzungszone," *Börsenblatt für den deutschen Buchhandel* 35 (1948): 330.

plained that ways had to be found to influence the broadest possible strata of the working population with an eye to winning their participation in achieving the goals of the two-year plan. The working population could scarcely be infused with a "new working ethos" by reading works written by "bourgeois authors for an insatiated bourgeoisie." Much the same was true, Koven said, of psychological novels and tawdry books written for the sole purpose of diversion. But nor did literature written against war and fascism, whose subject matter ended during the war or right after it and generally left the question of "what next?" unanswered, suffice any longer. It was time for "young authors to visit the factories and the mines, to climb on top of locomotives or to go out into the low lands to get a sense of how the majority of the population is living and working, what kinds of hopes and worries they have, in order to create a literature that fortifies their courage to go on living, as well as their delight in creativity, and that thus contributes to a greater happiness at being alive and, with it, to an improvement of the material side of life."[123]

The Pursuit of Peace

The Wroclaw congress in August 1948 closed with a resolution that called for the establishment of an international liaison office in Paris, formation of a peace committee in every country, and national conferences "in defense of peace."[124] The Kulturbund drew the appropriate "German conclusions," issued a resolution that equated "war mongering" with "anti-Soviet crusading," and expelled the deputy mayor of Berlin, Friedensburg, for conduct unbecoming a member of the organization.[125] Internally, the party welcomed what Ackermann claimed was the Kulturbund's first declaration in favor of "the camp of peace, democracy, and progress, against the camp of reaction and war"; and reemphasized the need to purge members "infected" by antibolshevism. But the policy required that the SED assign "competent comrades" to work within the Kulturbund. Action was necessary in the organization's state branches especially; their boards currently offered no assurance that they would be able to live up to their responsibilities during the "sharp battle" approaching.[126] But the paradox of the "battle" that followed was its militant obsession with keeping the peace; and before long, the Kulturbund moved to convene a "congress of German creative intellectuals" patterned after Wroclaw.[127] First, however, Alexander Abusch asked for the party's

[123]Ibid.
[124]See "Das Friedensmanifest des Weltkongresses," Aufbau 9 (1948): 737.
[125]See "Kulturbund-Mitglieder gegen Friedensburg," Neues Deutschland, 11 September 1948.
[126]Stenographische Niederschrift über die Arbeitstagung der Abt. Parteischulung, Kultur u. Erziehung vom 7. bis 8. September 1948. Zentrales Parteiarchiv, IV 2/1.01/97/46.
[127]See Abusch, "Wroclaw wird weiterwirken," Tägliche Rundschau, 12 September 1948.

blessing, the secretariat consented,[128] and from that point onward the struggle for peace was inseparable from the party's two-year plan of economic development. That same plan, or rather its cultural corollary, then confronted intellectuals with related demands worked out in conjunction with the narrowest definitions yet of permissible "forms" of creative activity and new sets of political and cultural-political linkages. Accordingly, no Kulturbund conference devoted just to peace convened that fall; rather, the meeting held on 28 and 29 October, the same one officially sponsored by the Kulturbund, the FDGB, and the Gewerkschaft 17, discussed the broader ramifications of the congress in Wroclaw in terms of the practical cultural applications of the two-year plan.

These events also coincided with the final phase of the SED's transformation into a Stalinist "party of a new type"; and in that connection, Walter Ulbricht stressed the need for an "ideologically tough, disciplined core of functionaries" capable of overcoming the paralysis caused by members under the influence of "enemy ideologies."[129] Ulbricht made the same demand with respect to mass organizations; the party had to improve its oversight of "SED functionaries" within them;[130] and as part of the burgeoning purge of "hostile and degenerate elements" in the wake of Tito's break with Stalin, it was solidly established that members who held positions of leadership in mass organizations and cultural institutions belonged to the SED's "core staff of functionaries." They were, accordingly, expected to "represent the party line" within these agencies,[131] and doing so translated into unswerving allegiance to the "teachings of Marx, Engels, Lenin, and Stalin."[132] The secretariat then requested privately that "SED comrades in the leadership of the Kulturbund" prepare concrete proposals with respect to the conference of intellectuals set for the end of October to discuss the two-year plan;[133] and at roughly the same time, the Kulturbund reported publicly on the initial results of its campaign to "activate" the intelligentsia. Conferences had been staged in its regional branches that worked out the link between the congress in Wroclaw and the "peace obligations" of Soviet-zone intellectuals in connection with the two-year plan.[134]

---

[128]Protokoll Nr. 108 (II) der Sitzung des Zentralsekretariats am 13. 9. 1948. Zentrales Parteiarchiv, IV 2/2.1/229/1.

[129]See Ulbricht, "Planmäßige Wirtschaft sichert die Zukunft des deutschen Volkes," *Der deutsche Zweijahrplan für 1949-1950*, pp. 39-41.

[130]Ibid., p. 41.

[131]"Für die organisatorische Festigung der Partei und für ihre Säuberung von feindlichen und entarteten Elementen," *Dokumente der Sozialistischen Einheitspartei Deutschlands* (29 July 1948), vol. II, pp. 83-87.

[132]See "Der Kampf um die Erfüllung des Planes," *Sozialistische Bildungshefte* 8 (1948): 28.

[133]Protokoll Nr. 117 (II) der Sitzung des Zentralsekretariats am 4. 10. 48. Zentrales Parteiarchiv, IV 2/2.1/238/2.

[134]See "Kulturbund und Zweijahrplan," *Neues Deutschland*, 2 October 1948.

At one of these meetings, Abusch explained that the program of reconstruction ended the agonizing "uncertainty of the transitional period between war and peace" that had proved so confusing to the intellectuals. Their participation in an undertaking swept along by the "initiative of the people" would now bring them closer to the people; and Abusch expressed his feeling that "outstanding writers" could support factory and farm "activists" by devoting themselves to literary reportage about "these new people and their endeavors." He denied advocating literature concerned only with issues of the day, however, and merely wished to emphasize, he said, that visits to factories and farms provided writers with a much better understanding of contemporary life. Such insights would find their way into "higher" forms of art later.[135] Abusch also saw a specific role for Soviet-zone artists, though he failed to discuss it in any detail. Max Grabowski had no such hesitations and argued that art was a decisive means of "forming and changing the consciousness of the people." But "regressive bourgeois and petty bourgeois ideas" first needed to be eliminated; and he went on to explain that it was incumbent upon art to "increase its productivity," just as raising productivity was a top priority in other Soviet-zone areas of production. Higher "productivity" in art meant that it must prove its capacity to affect the consciousness of the people for whom it was created. This was not yet the case because contemporary art remained predominantly the expression of a "bourgeois ideology hostile to the people."[136]

Even the SED's resolution on the lessons of Yugoslavia called for the formulation of a "cultural plan" for the obvious reason that economic strides would encounter tremendous difficulties if "*the cultural niveau of the working population*" were not improved;[137] and to that end, the party held two especially significant meetings the beginning of September. The first, on the 2nd and 3rd, was tailored mostly to writers and artists who belonged to the SED; and the second meeting from the 7th to the 9th, addressed itself to the SED's state-level "cultural divisions." Both were treated to talks by Ulbricht and Ackermann that included some of the harshest rhetoric ever uttered in Soviet-occupied Germany in cultural-political affairs. Though much of the language was familiar from other discussions of cultural issues that developed out of order 234 and the two-year plan, the party's insistence that Soviet-zone intellectuals throw themselves behind reconstruction had become entirely uncompromising. Literary or artistic activity affected the life of the new society in one of two ways, said Ackermann, supportive or "hostile." The issue was not party membership at all, but creative intellectuals had an

[135]Abusch, "Der Zweijahresplan und die Kulturschaffenden," *Sonntag*, 29 August 1948.
[136]Grabowski, "Kunstschaffende und Wirtschaftsplan," *Neues Deutschland*, 20 August 1948.
[137]"Die theoretische und praktische Bedeutung der Entschließung des Informationsbüros über die Lage in der KP Jugoslawiens und die Lehren für die SED" [16 September 1948], *Dokumente der Sozialistischen Einheitspartei Deutschlands*, vol. II, p. 104.

obligation to "join the ranks in the battle front fighting for a cause synonymous with the cause of the people and the entire nation." Ackermann then addressed himself to the related responsibilities of theaters, administrative agencies, unions, authors' associations, musicians, the Kulturbund, and so on, before coming to the matter of "form and content." The intensification of class warfare would lead unavoidably to a much "sharper dispute over literature and art," said Ackermann; and that meant realism, which he considered attainable only if writers and artists were well-grounded in the world view of the proletariat. Art and literature now needed to move away from "lifeless abstractions alien to the people" and "away from formalism." Where, asked Ackermann, was the novel to compare with Gladkov's *Cement*? The repertories of Soviet-zone theaters also left much to be desired, even if the most important stages were in the hands of "reliable comrades." Not that the party intended to draw up "service regulations" for art and literature; it merely wished to provide "suggestions" and "pointers." Finally, Ackermann announced that the party proposed to take the ideological offensive, and the same was true with respect to art and literature. In particular, there would be no further reluctance to talk about the discussions of literature, art, music, and philosophy occurring in the Soviet Union.[138]

Ulbricht's speech followed, though neither these remarks, nor the ones that he made a few days later, were published at the time.[139] *Neues Deutschland* said something about Ulbricht's "refreshing plain-spokenness," but in actual fact, the belligerence of his remarks angered his audience. What upset party writers and artists most must have been Ulbricht's acerbic criticism of them for writing "novels about the emigration" and concentration-camp accounts, when they ought to be depicting land reform or the rebuilding of a factory in Soviet-occupied Germany. "You have lagged behind, far behind," he said. Nor was the absence of a few tons of paper any excuse, he said, alluding to the constant complaints about the Kultureller Beirat, but rather "what's done with the paper." Subject matter existed in abundance, he went on; a battle had been waged for a new social order, and "you show up three years later and start portraying problems that ought to have been settled long ago." Why, he asked, had it not been possible to go public with a program of special responsibilities for artists in connection with the two-year plan? "You speak eloquently about formalism here," he said, "but why don't we get started with a discussion in this area?" Was it really necessary for the "progressive democratic movement" to be publicly associated with "pictures of crippled women" painted by artists who regarded such paintings as art in touch with the times, instead of being represented by progressive artists re-

[138]Stenographische Niederschrift über Referat Anton Ackermann und Diskussion in der Parteihochschule "Karl Marx" in Klein-Machnow, 2 September 1948. Zentrales Parteiarchiv, IV 2/1.01/96/1-25. See also "Bekenntnis und Verpflichtung," *Neues Deutschland*, 5 September 1948.
[139]They were briefly summarized in the above article in *Neues Deutschland*.

sponsible for a "genuine, realist art that speaks to the people?" Ulbricht insisted that it was the SED's prerogative to oppose "expressionist and other views." Not that "we want such artists to be included in the purge and excluded from the party"; they could belong to a variety of different artistic directions; but "as a party, we have a specific standpoint, realism, and with the help of our journals and in every other way this standpoint is going to be implemented."[140]

Just a few days passed before Ulbricht spoke out again, this time at the PKE meeting from 7 to 9 September; and again Ulbricht railed at writers and artists who failed to grasp the fact that the two-year plan was also a plan of cultural reconstruction. Ulbricht assailed them for not heeding the admonition to visit factories; "we cannot successfully implement the two-year plan if the cultural and ideological niveau of the population is not raised more quickly—if the battle on the cultural front is not waged energetically and with a clear sense of purpose." It was particularly important, he explained, to find out who was concerned with solving problems and who shied away from participation or even "openly sabotaged." Ulbricht then warned about the continuing existence of "enemy ideologies" and complained that the Kulturbund, for one, had not done enough to combat them. As for the preoccupation that "our writers" still had with the years of emigration, Ulbricht reiterated that their private concern with such issues would not be interfered with; but nor should they expect the party to "give them the paper to do it with." Again he lamented the absence of works dealing with land reform, and again he grumbled that writers were not visiting the factories to study "the new men, the activists." He was particularly irritated that these very factory activists held meetings in rooms whose walls stayed undecorated while too many artists spent valuable time painting "crippled woman and children"; and yet again he maligned "our journals" for glorifying expressionism, rather than exerting an influence favorable to realism. He added:

> We have among us such a degree of tolerance that, in the name of artistic freedom, everyone has the right to engage in all sorts of foolishness. But we have the right, once and for all, to work out our line in the area of artistic creativity. Must we really accept such things? Right now, we do accept them. The most monumental expressionistic nonsense appears in our newspapers, and we patiently take note of it. We are not opposed to artistic creativity; there are members among us who have widely differing views on art; that's their business. But as a party we must

[140]See Stenographische Niederschrift über Referat Anton Ackermann und Diskussion, 2 September 1948. Zentrales Parteiarchiv, IV 2/1.01/96/63-71. Ulbricht's remarks were not published until years later. See "Der Künstler im Zweijahrplan. Diskussionsrede auf der Arbeitstagung der SED-Schriftsteller und Künstler," Ulbricht, *Zur Geschichte der deutschen Arbeiterbewegung*, vol. III, 1946-1950, pp. 312-16. I quote from the stenographic record.

develop a progressive view of things and proceed from the position of *socialist realism*, not from this or that art trend and expression of bourgeois decadence that has succeeded in penetrating our ranks. What necessary purpose does all this serve? To keep from losing party members? That's not it at all; we leave things up to those involved and do not impose guidelines on individual party members who create art. But the public must know where the party stands and what we promote.[141]

Ulbricht demanded that the party expand its ranks by aiding in the development of "democratic elements among the intellectuals." The way to do so, he thought, was to discuss ideological matters with the intelligentsia as a means of identifying friends and isolating foes—by bringing the erroneous ideas of hostile intellectuals into the open and showing just how they hampered and sabotaged progress. Everyone benefited when the party discussed matters with a reactionary because those intellectuals who had previously vacillated were then won over. This was Ulbricht's notion of the "ideological struggle," a necessary part of the process of determining who was progressive and who, presumably, was a saboteur. His whole argument came down to the desire to see that these questions be "resolved more democratically than has thus far been the case and that there be a free exchange of opinions"; and he concluded his remarks with an elaborate discussion of the principal ideological issues into which the party intended to weave its cultural policy. By fall 1948, these questions all pertained to definitions of socialism, popular democracy, the role of the party, and the right attitude toward the Soviet Union. The essence of socialism as the Soviet Union had built it, he concluded, was the same for Germany and other nations; and a clear understanding of this issue would assist the SED along the road to becoming a party of a new type.[142] One other party gathering took place on 24 and 25 September; and again the hall reverberated with suggestions that writers and artists "go into the factories." Even as the SED waged a bitter struggle against "alien" intellectual influences, Paul Wandel welcomed adherents of doctrines "other than Marxism-Leninism"—as long as such people fit the description of genuine democrats. But he also said that the SED's cultural politics needed to "fortify Marxism-Leninism among the intelligentsia."[143] This was especially the case because, as he put it, a portion remained passive in spite of the fact that the division of Germany required a stepped-up struggle for national unity to be waged in the area of culture.[144]

---

[141]Stenographische Niederschrift über die Arbeitstagung der Abt. Parteischulung, Kultur und Erziehung vom 7. bis 9. September 1948. Zentrales Parteiarchiv, IV 2/906/61/9-31. My italics.
[142]Ibid.
[143]"Aufgaben für unsere Kulturschaffenden," *Neues Deutschland*, 26 September 1948.
[144]Leuteritz, "Die Kulturschaffenden dürfen nicht nachstehen—kulturpolitische Arbeitstagung der SED in Berlin," *Tägliche Rundschau*, 26 September 1948.

One month after Ulbricht and Ackermann lectured on the inadequacies of Soviet-zone art and literature, the Kulturbund kicked off a "peace week" that started with a rally in the spirit of Wroclaw and ended with the conference cosponsored by the Kulturbund, the FDGB, and the Gewerkschaft 17 on 28 and 29 October 1948. Compared with the party's private discussions in early September, there was little of overarching significance said at any of the events leading up to that particular gathering. In fact, the most noteworthy occurrence had nothing to do with the "peace week." Bertolt Brecht returned to Germany just in time to attend the rally and see a performance of Julius Hay's play *Haben* that he considered "entirely unrealistic."[145] But these were Brecht's private thoughts at the time, and the dispute over his own kind of "realism" broke out only after the premiere of *Mutter Courage* early the next year. Otherwise, the Kulturbund's peace rally went off without a hitch, unmarred by any of the embarrassing incidents that tarnished some of the earlier congresses and conferences. Becher, speaking again, regaled the audience with his usual eloquence. He opened by mentioning the end of the thirty-year war on 24 October 1648 and, in the spirit of Wroclaw, insisted that no single nation, party, sector, zone, or confession of faith could speak justifiably on behalf of all peace-loving people. But he followed up this concession with much talk of the other side's lies, slanders, malicious rumors, acts of violence and sabotage, rampant spying, preparations for a German civil and new world war, and to efforts to subjugate the world to a new "totalitarianism of fascist vintage."[146]

Abusch tried similarly to reconcile what amounted to two-camps thinking with German nationalism by contriving a nationwide dimension to the SED's two-year plan of economic and cultural development. He explained that the participation of the intellectuals in building a democratic Germany independent of foreign countries and a model for the entire nation should focus on creation of a cultural life worthy of emulation by all other zones. He then summed up the situation by explaining again that efforts to rebuild the Soviet zone remained staunchly opposed to any division of the nation. In particular, Abusch assailed American imperialism for planning to use the "separate West-German state" as a forward bastion of expansionism, whereas the world congress of intellectuals in Wroclaw had recognized the Soviet Union as the strongest force favoring peace. Open-minded Germans needed to understand who struggled with them for the "reunification of our fatherland" and pick sides accordingly.[147] The Kulturbund leadership organized its

---

[145]Brecht, *Arbeitsjournal* [23 October 1948], p. 848. That Brecht's diary during these first few weeks is punctuated by entries concerning the Soviet antiformalism campaign against music is also an indication of how pervasive that issue was in Soviet-occupied Germany. See ibid [18 October and 26 November 1948], pp. 842 and 863.

[146]Becher, "Mahnung an die Menschen guten Willens," *Tägliche Rundschau*, 26 October 1948.

[147]Abusch, "Der Geist der Kulturbundwoche," *Tägliche Rundschau*, 23 October 1948.

peace week to make the related point that the successful defense of culture hinged on emphatic action in support of peace;[148] and there was nothing illogical about it when the Kulturbund then concluded the campaign with the conference organized in conjunction with the FDGB and the Gewerkschaft 17. This gathering met to work out the more precise patterns of cultural activity within the framework of the two-year plan and, accordingly, appropriate for the defense of peace. But every effort was made to coordinate the conflicting elements of a separatist outlook with national definitions of these same policies. Though there was little apprehension about referring to "our zone" while discussing the putative benefits of the plan, the speakers made sure that they defined it both as an independent German undertaking geared toward solving local problems without "foreign capital," that is, the Marshall plan; and as a program of critical importance nationwide. It could, after all, be implemented in other regions of Germany, too, if only "political preconditions identical to those here in our zone" were created.[149] Abusch spoke in the same vein when he called the plan "national" and "German" because it aspired to build up a German economy free of American monopoly capital and exemplary for all zones. But he also made his nationalism an integral part of two-camps thinking when he added that the plan for peace was inextricably bound up with the fight against the "Marshallization of Germany" (27-29).

Otherwise, said Abusch, the main issue was cementing the relationship between "a broad cross-section of our people and the creative intellectuals" (13). This had been true since 1945, but the two-year plan, said Abusch, now made it possible to do a much better job of overcoming the "rift" between worker and intellectual than earlier "abstract discussions" had accomplished (32). There was certainly nothing theoretical about Abusch's insistence that the cultural intelligentsia use art to raise the workers' productivity by creating a new work ethos (31); and he also stressed the importance of waging a "resolute battle against the importation of elements of neofascism, pessimism, decadence, and other products of the so-called 'Atlantic culture' of North-American monopoly capital (29)." Abusch then set out to define some of the specific duties of the writers. Ulbricht and Ackermann had recently done likewise, and Abusch's remarks leave the distinct impression that he wished to restate many of their positions. But he may also have hoped to resolve the inherent contradictions between propaganda and art without being quite as abrasive. Abusch actually disputed Ulbricht's most offensive statement, though without mentioning his name. The demand that the party's writers deal with current problems, Abusch said, should not be taken too

[148]See Leuteritz, "Manifestation des Friedenswillens. Woche des Kulturbundes vom 24. bis 30. Oktober 1948," *Tägliche Rundschau*, 20 October 1948.
[149]See *Der Zweijahrplan und die Kulturschaffenden*, pp. 9 and 12-13. Subsequent page references are supplied in the text.

literally and by no means meant that they could not write about the past (32). He then answered one of Ulbricht's inquiries by asking whether it was possible to draw up tasks for writers, artists, and filmmakers—whether "artistic creativity" could be planned at all (36)—before avowing that "none of us intends to constrict the tasks of writers and artists or reduce these to the obligation of rendering direct propagandistic assistance for the two-year plan." This was not the response that it appeared to be, however, because Abusch noted that writers particularly had a special facility for intervening directly in the publicistic struggle for the two-year plan using certain kinds of less formal writing. There had been comparable instances of this in the Soviet Union prior to the completion of the more substantial works of literature that emerged in the course of the five-year plan there (37). Still, unlike Ulbricht, Abusch chose not to utter the fateful words "socialist realism." He clung to the usual tactical equivalent by advocating publicly a "realistic literature and art close to the people," and he also predicated the success of this writing on the concomitant need to overcome "the pessimistic currents in art that exhaust themselves in sterile abstractions and formalistic experiments" (38).

Abusch's comments were no less an indication of things to come than Ulbricht's; but Abusch was more solicitous outwardly of the party's own writers, and he made more of a rhetorical gesture toward the unaffiliated. Abusch insisted once again that propaganda would not be substituted for art; and he also denied any interest in "regulated art"; that was definitely something "we do not want." But he stated clearly that "we do not favor a so-called autonomous art isolated from society—lifeless, sterile, and consigned to decay." Neither a "mediocre utilitarian art" nor "production-line utilitarian literature" fit the bill, though Abusch insisted emphatically upon the role that "high-quality" utilitarian art could play and concluded by explaining that the Soviet zone could use its cultural achievements as a way of becoming the model for cultural renewal throughout Germany, just as the two-year plan provided an example of an economic policy appropriate for the entire nation.[150] But the real milepost in the speeches given by Ulbricht, Ackermann, and now Abusch was the assumption that writers could reasonably and feasibly be assigned topics dealing with current Soviet-zone problems. But there were certain creative problems involved. In years past, the party's writers were compelled to deal with what they considered to be the bourgeois dictatorship of the Weimar Republic and then with fascism. This was a challenge that they welcomed; they thought that they knew how these worlds worked and for years wrote novels about little else. Ulbricht, however, had just scorned this literature in his two speeches and virtually mandated topical writing that took all its cues from political developments in the

[150]Ibid., pp. 42 and 44.

Soviet zone. An educational literature geared toward inspiring Germans into greater efforts in the workplace and into unqualified backing of the party's two-year "peace" plan of economic construction was the principal priority now. But the transition from "destructive" writing critical of class society during the Weimar years or under fascism to a "constructive" literature of affirmation proved to be a difficult task. Though Ulbricht ignored the difficulties, others perceived them clearly. The FDGB representative to the conference in late October, Walter Maschke, said that artists must inspire their fellow citizens to work harder in favor of his country, to participate "actively and positively," and to be conscious of the fact that the change in the nature of class warfare dictated a new attitude toward work. In the past, by contrast, artists who had sided with the proletariat sought to influence the worker in the opposite direction of resisting repression and exploitation.[151] Abusch tried to get around the problem by suggesting that it did not exist; writers merely needed to create "high-quality" rather than "mediocre" utilitarian art associated with the two-year plan, while reserving the right to take more time in turning these issues into panoramic novels later. In the meantime, Abusch tried to allay the writers' concern by adding that "we want no art-ersatz" and that "we understand the special laws of artistic creativity"; "we want works of the highest artistic quality that, in a deeper sense, express our new social reality and its lofty goals; we want a realistic art."[152]

Several weeks after the conference in October, there was a bizarre incident involving an article written by a certain Martin Boettcher, published in *Neues Deutschland*, that echoed the substance of what had already been said both by Ulbricht and Abusch about the party's own writers; and *Neues Deutschland* chose to characterize it as representing a position midway between the two "extreme sets of views" sent in to the paper following the appearance of an unsigned article just a few weeks after Ulbricht's second speech. Referring to discussions at the SED's recent cultural meetings, this earlier article insisted upon writing that closely accompanied "our political tasks" and mimicked Ulbricht in asking why there had been no "grandiose poetic depiction . . . of our age"—an epic about factories owned by the people, or a novel about land reform and resettlement.[153] But Boettcher berated the party's most prominent writers by name—Erpenbeck, Becher, Friedrich Wolf, Anna Seghers, Hans Marchwitza, and Willi Bredel. Judging by their works, he said, "our writers and poets" had neglected current events entirely; Boettcher expected of them something akin to Upton Sinclair's novel about Sacco and Vanzetti, written shortly after their execution.[154] His point was

[151]*Der Zweijahrplan und die Kulturschaffenden,* pp. 19 and 25.
[152]Ibid., p. 38.
[153]"Zeitliteratur oder Literatur für unsere Zeit," *Neues Deutschland,* 1 October 1948.
[154]As it turned out, this was not the best example because Rein, who himself fled the zone a few years later when his writings came under fire, denounced Sinclair several months later as a rene-

simply that the SED's writers ought to react to breaking events, instead of contenting themselves with what he called the Kulturbund's sporadic condemnations of war-mongers. He went on to suggest that the party's best writers must have convinced themselves that they could "wander around a thin strip of no man's land" even as the class struggle intensified; just as deplorably, the "progressive press" let them get away with it.[155]

The basic affinity with Ulbricht's views is impossible to overlook; Ulbricht himself had accused the party's writers of having "lagged behind, far behind," though he failed to name names and never referred to no man's land. Nonetheless, there was an air of authority about Boettcher's remarks, and J. R. Becher reacted by informing Pieck and Grotewohl that he intended to resign his party responsibilities until the matter had been investigated. Becher was beside himself at the suggestion of "class betrayal" and at the newspaper's characterization of the article as "moderate."[156] The next day, the editors of *Neues Deutschland* met with unnamed writers to discuss Boettcher's article. The writers complained that the "attack" strengthened the hostility toward intellectuals present within the party already and illustrated the paper's tendency to go after progressive "elements" while praising "formalistic artists." The editors denied having any such intention and blamed the writers for reading too much into the piece. But it was agreed that Abusch would publish a response, along with an "appropriate explanation" by the paper. If that proved insufficient, Ackermann was expected to publish a second article.[157] On the 19th, then, Abusch refuted Boettcher's article by calling it a "political mistake," though his own remarks did not diverge all that significantly from comments made by Ulbricht or Boettcher. The tone was different, however; Abusch lavished praise on the party's excellent poets and "realistic" writers. But he repeated the substance of his speech at the conference in late October, distinguishing between the artists' propagandistic and their creative activity in order to contend that a happy balance could be struck. This distinction allowed Abusch to make another point that favored Ulbricht's style of instantaneous utilitarianism. He again pleaded for a "publicistic" response to the two-year plan while conceding that the "great work of art" required a longer period of gestation. During times of change and the accelerating pace of class warfare, he explained, developments could not always find their way into literature immediately. In this sense, Boett-

---

gade and a "traitor to his own work" for committing the unpardonable sin of uttering comments critical of the USSR. Rein himself was then taken to task for not having gone far enough in his criticism of Sinclair. See Rein, "Der Renegat Upton Sinclair," *Einheit* 7 (1949): 669.

[155]Boettcher, "Dichter im Niemandsland," *Neues Deutschland*, 12 December 1948.

[156]Becher to Pieck and Grotewohl, 14 December 1948. Zentrales Parteiarchiv, NL 36/661/23.

[157]Aktennotiz über die Diskussion zwischen Schriftstellern und Redaktionen des "Neuen Deutschland" am 15. 12. 48, veranlaßt durch den Artikel des Genossen Böttcher über die Lage bei den fortschrittlichen Schriftstellern, ibid., IV 2/9.06/254.

cher's comments were ill-founded; but his criticism retained a certain validity, Abusch intimated, because there remained a dearth of writing useful to the two-year plan—"reportage, sketches, short stories, songs, plays for amateur theater productions," and the like. Nothing stood in the way of remedying such deficiencies, he hinted, because a "quick publicistic response" did not curtail the writers' freedom to take time in developing preliminary insights in more challenging forms of writing.[158] *Neues Deutschland* concurred with "most of these points," Ackermann never wrote a second article, and he also persuaded Becher not to resign his party posts.[159]

Degenerate Art

As late as spring 1948, Ackermann had still considered it wiser to avoid bitter disputes over what he called "different directions and isms in art" because the time for such debates was not "right."[160] But he changed his mind soon enough. At the PKE conference from 7 to 9 September 1948, he said that the party leadership planned on speaking openly in the matter of "realism" versus "abstract art"; and "we want a sharp, clear-cut exchange of views." He assured his listeners that the party had no intention of kicking writers and artists out of the party for refusing to comply, but they needed to understand the seriousness of the question. A party of a new type, he added, could not stand for internal confusion over a subject such as "the state"; and the party insisted similarly upon clear-cut distinctions in matters pertaining to "artistic forms that correspond to our world view and the goals of our struggle," as opposed to forms that express "bourgeois decadence and the subversion of the rotting capitalist system."[161] Given remarks of that sort, it is not unreasonable to conclude that insiders like Ackermann, and certainly Ulbricht, sensed what was coming or knew about it well in advance. In November 1948, Alexander Dymschitz began the campaign against formalism. True, both Dymschitz and Tjulpanov had written for the local press before; but Tjulpanov usually spoke about cultural politics in more general terms, and Dymschitz either did the same or focused more of his attention on popularizing Soviet art, rather than setting new trends. They both broke that pattern when they commented on Soviet-zone culture at the Dresden art exhibit in fall 1946, though this remained more of an isolated occurrence. The two articles published by Dymschitz in November 1948, however, both entitled

[158]Abusch, "Über das Schaffen unserer Schriftsteller," *Neues Deutschland*, 19 December 1948.
[159]Pieck to Becher, 31 December 1948, ibid., NL 36/661/28.
[160]Stenographische Niederschrift über die 10. (24.) Tagung der SED am 12. und 13. Mai 1948. Zentrales Parteiarchiv, IV 2/1/23/41-2.
[161]Stenographische Niederschrift über die Arbeitstagung der Abt. Parteischulung, Kultur u. Erziehung vom 7. bis 9. September 1948, ibid., IV 2/1.01/97/2, 36-37.

"The Formalist Direction in German Art," constituted the first such open intervention by a Soviet cultural officer. As such, his comments sparked a protracted discussion in the Soviet-zone press that continued throughout the next year and became hopelessly one-sided when one of the few remaining voices of opposition in the zone, the monthly *Bildende Kunst*, ceased publication "temporarily" in late 1949. With its demise, the only forum for modern art disappeared. The loss is especially evident when compared with the journal's self-characterization upon its reappearance in 1953; it began publishing again as a "militant organ for socialist realism" that raised its voice against all "decadent currents hostile to art and the people—formalism, naturalism, and kitsch." Ironically, the last issue of the old *Bildende Kunst* printed reproductions of paintings hung at the second German art exhibition in Dresden that afforded one of the last contrasts, however slight, between politically uninfluenced or independent art and programmed illustrations of an emerging East German society.[162] The art displayed at the exhibition four years later revealed busts of Karl Marx, Wilhelm Pieck, and Ernst Thälmann, together with innumerable portraits of people's policemen, people's judges, SED politicians, workers in every imaginable pose, smiling Soviet soldiers, peaceful reconstruction, and plaster casts of female tractor drivers.[163]

Not that there was no advanced warning about Dymschitz' articles. Criticism of expressionism and modern art had always dominated discussions in the zone, and those debates continued, largely in the pages of *Bildende Kunst*, up to the day that the *Tägliche Rundschau* set the authoritative parameters for all future arguments by publishing Dymschitz' two articles. The editors of *Bildende Kunst* actually began the year with Aesopian allusions to the difficulties confronting the journal. The editors asked their readers to bear in mind that the editorial board and the publisher often encountered "tremendous difficulties" and that they could not always accomplish what they deemed "desirable." But the editors also suggested that they remained committed to the exchange of differing ideas and wanted the journal to stay open to any "honest and well-reasoned opinion."[164] This commentary followed the full-page illustration of a Picasso oil, a wildly contorted or, to use Ulbricht's later language, "crippled" woman of the kind denounced by now as irredeemably decadent; and certain editors were apparently deft enough as well to buttress their tacit endorsement of modern art by printing an assortment of letters to the editor that either supported a sensible approach to modern art or opposed it with arguments like this one: "I refuse to be molested anymore by

---

[162]See Pommeranz-Liedke, "Die Frage nach dem Bild des Menschen. Betrachtungen zu Bildern der 2. Deutschen Kunstausstellung Dresden," *Bildende Kunst* 10 (1949): 316-29.
[163]See *Dritte Deutsche Kunstausstellung*.
[164]"Ins zweite Jahr," *Bildende Kunst* 1 (1948). See the overleaf.

the filth of your intellectual cesspool."[165]

The quasi-official critics of modern art in Soviet-occupied Germany rose slightly above that level of discourse, but the rejection was just as firm. One of them, Heinz Lüdecke, tried to be a touch more sophisticated by noting that Marxist criticism in the Soviet Union characterized modern art rightfully as "decadent" but that "decadent" was a sociological concept, not a form of vilification.[166] The discussion in *Bildende Kunst* then went back and forth until it crested in an article by Karl Hofer that he titled "Art and Politics." Evidently, Hofer wrote this essay earlier in the year because it was the subject of a private discussion, attended by the SMAD's Barski, Ackermann, Grabowski, Lüdecke, Nerlinger, Keilson, and Weimann on 12 March 1948. Keilson suggested there that Hofer be removed as editor in order to guarantee a "unified line," whereas Ackermann remained willing to accept the occasional appearance in the journal of "abstract and modern art." But in every instance, there needed to be a clear-cut "antiposition." The immediate problem was that Hofer had written an article containing the sentence, "Politicians use art like a whore." Ackermann viewed it as an attack on the SED and the SMAD; Weimann considered Hofer's resignation unavoidable; Nerlinger indicated that several other persons would have to leave the editorial board; and Barski warned that the SMAD would ban the issue if Hofer's article appeared in its present form. Nerlinger was then asked to write a "sharp counter article. Either both essays would be published or none.[167] Both did come out, though months later, and probably then only after more discussion at the level of the secretariat.[168]

The published version of Hofer's article bore no further trace of the offending sentence, though his other points were scarcely any more acceptable. He began by admitting that the Western religious art of times past had been pure propaganda, created to serve the needs of the all-powerful Catholic church; and still, many of the greatest masterpieces of all time dated back to this period of faith. But Hofer refused to infer that the same thing could occur nowadays in the service of what he called transparently a new kind of faith or *Weltanschauung*. Further political impieties and improprieties followed, for instance, Hofer's rejection of oversimplified views concerning the relationship between art and the people. Hofer claimed that the work of Käthe Kollwitz left ordinary people unaffected—not because her art was in any way faulty but because of the normal and natural way that any great art functioned. Hofer's contention that the art of a given age was never under-

---

[165]See "Das Publikum sagt seine Meinung," *Bildende Kunst* 1 (1948): 27-29.
[166]Lüdecke, "Die Entwirklichung der bürgerlichen Kunst," *Bildende Kunst* 5 (1948): 10-13.
[167]Besprechung bei dem Genossen Ackermann am 12. 3. 1948, 20 March 1948. Zentrales Parteiarchiv, IV 2/9.06/171.
[168]See Protokoll Nr. 125 (II) der Sitzung des Zentralsekretariats am 25. 10. 1948, ibid., IV 2/2.1/244/5.

stood by its contemporaries was another of his objectionable opinions, and so was his insistence that the result of demands made upon art was the rapid emergence of charlatans. Hofer's conclusion that the Hitler years best illustrated the consequences of insisting that art respond to non-artistic demands was equally blunt, and he added provocatively that it made no difference whether these demands served good or evil causes. Ironically, in explaining why this was so, Hofer touched upon a problem that had already come up at the cultural conference in late October when Maschke discussed the difficulties of being politically positive and socially constructive in art. Hofer concluded that the successful use of art to treat political and social circumstances appeared to permit only "negative" depictions, not positive affirmations. He then finished his essay on one final note of anathema; he rejected the "mindless" cliché that split art into the two categories of "bourgeois monopoly-capitalistic" and "socialist." All art, he said, belonged to a future society; and, as always, art was ahead of its time. This was so not because of the isolation of art or its incomprehensibility but because of the "hopelessly ruined taste of the masses."[169]

Nerlinger then published his commissioned response, any discussion of which can be dispensed with; it served its purpose, and, in all likelihood, so had Hofer's because Dymschitz used him as an excuse to write his own two articles. Not that Dymschitz' essays concentrated heavily on Hofer's arguments; much of what Dymschitz had to say rehashed familiar clichés. There was the same stale talk of formalism and decadence to go with mention of the relation of each to the camps of "international democracy" and "imperialist repression." But Dymschitz added a slightly new note by developing Zhdanov's suggestion that decadent forms of art represented something of a premeditated attempt to "liquidate" true art. In pursuing this line of reasoning, Dymschitz employed concepts embarrassingly redolent of Nazi jargon, and it stretches the limits of credibility to believe that these terms cropped up accidentally. It seems more reasonable to suggest that Dymschitz knowingly used fascist terminology to denounce modern art in hopes of pandering to currents of public opinion that shared his revulsion, however different the reasons may have been. Dymschitz referred contemptuously to "influences alien to the essence" of art (*wesensfremde Einflüsse*) and extolled the struggle for its deliverance from the perils of capitalism, which endangered art's supposed "innermost essence." He then suggested that the formalist direction in art risked causing artistic creativity to "degenerate" (*entarten*) and represented a "direct attack upon the essence of art."[170] In making this argument, Dymschitz knowingly appealed to the prurient taste of Germans whose predilections in art, due in no small measure to the last twelve years,

169Hofer, "Kunst und Politik," *Bildende Kunst* 10 (1948): 20-22.
170Dymschitz, "Über die formalistische Richtung in der deutschen Malerei," *Tägliche Rundschau*, 19 November 1948.

now seemed to hint at the possibility of popular support for occupation policy. But by the same token, this approach risked the definitive alienation of
unaffiliated artists who had become the targets of the party's affections in
the context of the two-year plan; and compounding the problem was the fact
that the earlier work of some of the most reputable artists, Hofer especially,
had been confiscated by the Nazis because they were "degenerate."

Dymschitz attempted to redress this particular imbalance by distinguishing between "formalistic" artists who belonged "organically" to bourgeois
decadence and whose decadent work resulted naturally from a reactionary
view of the world; and artists who belonged to the camp of democracy, even
if their work had been subject to the influence of reaction. Dymschitz knew
how to tell the difference, he said, between the surrealist Salvador Dali, who
had sung the praises of Hitler and Franco; and Pablo Picasso, a "militant antifascist" who had nonetheless indulged for years in unbridled formalism.
Dymschitz also distinguished between a writer like André Gide, a "fascist
collaborator" whom Dymschitz called the "Petain of art," and Franz Mase-
reel. With the likes of Sartre, Gide, Malraux, Eliot (who won the Nobel prize
a few months later), Maughman, or Dali, said Dymschitz, expanding the register of artist-pariahs established by Fadejev in Wroclaw, there was no point
in discussing matters of any kind; whereas the others needed to be brought
back to the path of truth that led to a "democratic and realistic art." Dymschitz then turned his attention to German "formalist painters" who, he acknowledged, rejected poltically not only Hitler fascism but, presumably,
what Dymschitz called the "countless new post-war varieties of fascist ideology." However, Dymschitz went on to draw a clear distinction between a
political disaffection for all things fascist or reactionary and certain kinds of
subjective artistic indulgences that, by ignoring the principles of realism, actually nurtured political and ideological malignancies. Dymschitz then named the names of prominent artists whose work had been impoverished by
their renunciation of "realism." Hofer came first. Dymschitz suggested that a
type of "masked theater" had replaced the depiction of vibrant life in his
work. Who was able to recognize himself in Hofer's tragic masks while
looking at his "carnival of monstrosities"? There followed any number of
other characterizations of Hofer's work in the same vein, ending with Dymschitz' determination that such subjective and antirealistic practices constituted a direct threat to life and to art.[171]

Dymschitz' second article continued his polemic with a somewhat leng-
thier discussion of Picasso. It included Dymschitz' contemptuous dismissal
of his Cubist masterpieces as "perverse and schematic" and a strained effort
to show how he had been enticed down the road of formalism until Picasso,
the artist, stood in direct contradiction to Picasso, the member of the French

---

[171]Ibid. The phrases were "lebensfeindlich" and "kunstfeindlich."

Communist party. In Dymschitz' estimation, Picasso's art had become irrelevant to his artistic mastery; Picasso was apparently a great artist not because of his work, but despite it, and by dint of his political convictions. Not surprisingly, Dymschitz mustered no admiration at all for a decadent artist who lacked the political credentials. He referred to Chagall's "sick" creativity—his neglect of a sense of space and the "alogical combinations of monstrous oddities and horrible naturalisms." Finally, Dymschitz made one last feeble attempt to resolve the lingering contradiction caused by a cultural policy that uttered its pronouncements in the name of ordinary Germans whose taste in art, though for other reasons, was as narrow as that of the Communists. Whenever questions concerning popular attitudes toward works of art came up, said Dymschitz, the artists criticized defended themselves by insisting that the taste of these Germans had been hopelessly corrupted by the "aesthetics" of fascism. This was no doubt true, but it did not relieve "decadent-formalist art" of the obligation of heeding popular criticism. The people still benefited from basically "healthy attitudes" about art, whereas the works of the formalists were sick and anemic. Besides, Dymschitz concluded, the German people were well on the way to "liberating themselves from the influence of fascist 'aesthetics'" and doing so much faster than the formalists could ever imagined.[172]

[172]Dymschitz, "Über die formalistische Richtung in der deutschen Malerei," *Tägliche Rundschau*, 24 November 1948.

PART FOUR:

STALIN AND THE FATE OF THE NATION (1949)

CHAPTER TWELVE

Theories of Dictatorship

In March 1948, Sergej Tjulpanov spoke to leading German Communists on the occasion of the centenary of the *Communist Manifesto* and used the opportunity to discuss variant roads to socialism. Quoting Lenin, Tjulpanov told his audience that all "nations will achieve socialism," but that the path to it would not always be identical. Each nation would develop its own characteristics instead, some adhering to this or that form of democracy, others to one or the other kind of proletarian dictatorship. The Soviet Union, for instance, exhibited to the world a democracy "of the most advanced type;" certain other countries progressed toward socialism by way of popular democracy; and all such variations merely confirmed the validity of Marxism-Leninism.[1] Tjulpanov declined to share his feelings publicly on the subject of which path Germany would take, however, and also passed up the chance to restate his support for a "special German road to socialism." But by describing only two broad paths, Tjulpanov implied that Germany would follow only one or the other, neither of which was "German." The first was the Soviet approach; and Tjulpanov's characterization of the USSR as the most advanced form of democracy hardly concealed the fact that the Soviet Union considered itself a dictatorship, which the SED denied having an immediate interest in establishing; whereas the second, the popular-democratic road to socialism, differed from the first precisely because these regimes had never been officially designated as dictatorships. The reasoning inherent to the argument suggested, then, that Soviet-occupied Germany would take the road of popular democracy; and in any event, as the "party cell" of the SMAD told the Germans while celebrating the *Communist Manifesto*, outfitted with the "unvanquishable teaching of Marx, Engels, Lenin and Stalin," the SED would lead the working class to socialism as part of the defense of the national interests of all democratic Germans.[2]

These kinds of comments were heavily influenced by the need to reconcile what was tantamount to "sovietization" with the pursuit of national uni-

---

[1]"Demokratie und Vorwärtsbewegung zum Sozialismus. Eine Rede Oberst Tjulpanows zum Jahrhundertfeier des Kommunistischen Manifests," *Tägliche Rundschau*, 2 March 1948.
[2]"Gruß an die SED. Adresse des Parteiaktivs der KPdSU des Stabes der SMV," *Tägliche Rundschau*, 2 March 1948.

ty, and popular democracy served those ends best because it dodged the issue of dictatorship without requiring an excessive number of other alterations to the fundamentals of Marxism-Leninism. Not that the party relied on popular democracy alone to deny its commitment to dictatorship; there were other ways of pretending, though the nature of the party's own ideology rendered them inherently deceitful and easily discernible as such. For instance, in early 1949, Pieck declared again that the party did not aspire to dictatorship; but, as the only argument against it, he explained that it would play into the hands of those forces bent upon dividing Germany for the party to act, by pursuing dictatorship, as if it had accepted the inevitability of national division.[3] Pieck's disavowal was just as problematical as an endorsement of dictatorship because of his tacit admission that national unity was, at best, a short-range objective; the ideological and practical goal afterwards had not changed in the least, and the party's emphasis on the "international significance" of the October revolution, the need to learn from the "experience" of the Soviet Communist party,[4] suggested nothing less. Figuring out how to reconcile its devotion to a foreign dictatorship with the party's pursuit of a united Germany then required resourceful solutions to increasingly complex rhetorical challenges. No top Communist really took the notion of an uncontested transition to socialism seriously, for instance, which would have hinged upon a renunciation of class warfare; and contested transitions meant bloodshed. By late 1948, repudiating the notion of a peaceful road to socialism forced the party to admit it, resulting in correspondingly feeble attempts to avoid the impression of ruthlessness. Rudolf Herrnstadt said that the possibility of a "*relatively* bloodless transition to socialism" existed in some countries; but, he added, those were prospects created by the October revolution and the victories of the Soviet army. There was nothing "German" about the situation. Besides, neither in those countries, nor in "parts of a country," would the bourgeoisie decline to avail itself of its remaining opportunities to wage class warfare. Accordingly, there could be no talk of a "special road to socialism," none of a "peaceful" path either, and least of all any about the matter of a "special, peaceful, 'German' road to socialism."[5]

More discussions concerning the circumstances under which class warfare intensified followed in late 1948 and throughout 1949 in connection with the Leninist precept that "the dictatorship of the proletariat represents a continuation of the class struggle";[6] and, in any case, there was only one

---

[3]Pieck, "Lehren der Parteikonferenz," *Einheit* 3 (1949): 198-99.
[4]See, e.g., "Über die internationale Bedeutung der Oktoberrevolution," *Sozialistische Bildungshefte* 8 (1949), especially p. 10; "Lernen aus den Erfahrungen der siegreichen Partei. Beschluß des Parteivorstandes der SED vom 4. Mai 1949," *Einheit* 6 (1949): 481-83.
[5]Herrnstadt, "Einige Lehren aus den Fehlern der Kommunistischen Partei Jugoslawiens," *Einheit* 9 (1948): 800-801. My emphasis.
[6]Steinberg, "Die Lehre Lenins-Stalins vom Klassenkampf in der Übergangsperiode," *Neue Welt* 2 (1949): 23.

road to socialism, Marxist-Leninist, and no German, Russian, or "Yugoslavian way."[7] But if there was no such thing as a "special German road," did the promise of no "Soviet system" still bind the party? If so, how, considering that all roads to socialism led in an identical direction? In spite of his talk of differences, the critical distinctions established in Tjulpanov's seminal article published in May 1948 ruled out the idea of national roads to socialism by establishing the clearest linkage thus far between popular democracy and the Soviet Union, but without taking the final step of calling the popular democracies dictatorships. By emphasizing that all of Germany could travel the path of popular democracy, Tjulpanov set the stage for Ackermann's renunciation of a German road without forcing the SED to rescind, yet, its associated promise of no Soviet system—no dictatorship. But a complication developed late in the year. In summer 1948, the SED announced its two-year plan; and in commenting upon it, as well as in remarks made later that fall, Otto Grotewohl drew different conclusions about the nature of what the SED now called "a new period" in its development. This period revolved around four interrelated issues and created the need to coordinate the doctrinal as well as practical processes associated with each one individually. These processes lasted through the remainder of the year and, with a major alteration to one of them, on into the next. The first was the transformation of the SED into a "party of a new type"; barring that, none of the other pursuits had much of a practical chance of being realized as the party envisaged them because each hinged upon the establishment of the SED's dominance; and one of them, national unity, had no chance of realization given the attainment of the remaining two: 1) Soviet-zone emulation of the popular democracies in conformity with the earlier utterances of Tjulpanov ("the only course of development," as Grotewohl concluded in June 1948, "that is open to us . . . and that we, as a Marxist-Leninist party, must recognize clearly"); and 2), because of the division of Germany caused by the Western allies, orienting "the direction of our party in the implementation of the economic plan unambiguously and with no restraint whatsoever toward the East." According to Grotewohl, the party's commitment to German unity was unaffected by either of these latter two commitments.[8]

This Eastern orientation, which went with the party's determination to pattern the Soviet-zone after popular democracy as well as to align itself and the zone with the Soviet Union, served as one of the chief items of discussion through December 1948. The subject briefly filled the void left by the party's disavowal of a "German road to socialism" while still allowing the SED to suggest that dictatorship was a distant prospect not worth worrying about. Fred Oelßner's remarks in late July 1948 echoed Tjulpanov's pro-

[7]Herrnstadt, "Einige Lehren aus den Fehlern der Kommunistischen Partei Jugoslawiens," p. 800.
[8]See Grotewohl, "Unsere Partei die führende Kraft. Das Ziel des Zweijahrplanes," *Neues Deutschland*, 1 July 1948.

nouncements the previous spring. "We are in a transitional stage in which state authority must develop first in the direction of a popular-democratic and then a socialist state."[9] Karl Schirdewan considered the SED the "leading party in popular-democratic development"; Paul Merker spoke of the contingencies upon which the progression of Soviet-occupied Germany toward a popular democracy hinged; and Edwin Hoernle, calling land reform the first major "popular-democratic" measure, noted that this had been a policy which revealed the "popular-democratic way."[10]

But it was given to Grotewohl to develop his thoughts on the subject. His comments were important because Grotewohl committed the Soviet zone to popular-democratic development even more explicitly than others before him while developing the idea out of a Stalinist obsession with the intensification of class warfare. The incongruity that resulted again pointed to the underlying artificiality of the rhetoric. Not that linking concepts associated with these sets of ideas was unprecedented; since spring 1945 the party had always attributed its progressively more radical measures not to the single-minded pursuit of objectives that it had set for itself but to the nationally disunifying actions of the Western allies. Once the party began interpreting all such actions as expressions of class warfare, on an international as well as national scale, it could use them as an excuse to radicalize its own policies in conformity with the two-camps approach to international affairs articulated by Zhdanov in fall 1947. The incongruity was that the SED blamed the Western allies for intensifying class warfare and then used it to justify the party's eastern "orientation" toward countries officially regarded as something other than dictatorships. The SED's eastern orientation included the decision to replace the German road to socialism with what Grotewohl now called the "basic strategic line" to be followed by the party in reaction to the imperialist policies of the Western powers. Thus, he said, in accordance with the tenets of Marxism-Leninism, the Soviet zone would realize those principles of development which established the preconditions for the transition from a popular democracy to a socialist societal order; and this popular-democratic solution represented the "only possible" route for the Soviet zone.[11] Grotewohl then went on to explain the nature of class warfare in the Soviet zone; it began to intensify, he said, when the foreign and domestic enemies of democratic renewal undertook to sabotage the two-year plan. The party now needed to rid itself of the "non-Marxist" notion that class warfare subsided in the Soviet zone as a consequence of democratic change and that there was a "peaceful, uncontested road to socialism." Grotewohl followed

[9]See Stößel, *Positionen und Strömungen in der KPD/SED 1945-1954*, p. 294.
[10]See Schirdewan, "Der Funktionär der sozialistischen Partei"; Merker, "Der Klassenkampf im Dorfe"; and Hoernle, "Probleme der Agrarpolitik im neuen Deutschland," in *Einheit* 9 (1948): 787, and 11 (1948): 1022 and 1030.
[11]Grotewohl, "Die Partei muß führen," *Einheit* 11 (1948), pp. 1003-4.

up with an additional Stalinist inference that the class enemy always reacted to the loss of power by redoubling its efforts to win back past influence. The enemy never gave up "without a fight," he added, citing an appropriate quotation from the writings of Stalin.[12]

This linkage, between the party's endorsement of popular democracy as the "only possible" route for the Soviet zone and the determination that the class enemy never surrendered "without a fight," created the doctrinal disparity referred to above; and it had implications that went well beyond its incompatibility with the SED's earlier talk of a peaceful road to socialism. In ideological terms, meeting the challenge of class warfare *always* required the establishment of a proletarian dictatorship, making it doctrinally illogical to speak of sharpening class warfare while proposing to meet the challenge with a "transitional form" of state power distinct from and, by definition, weaker than proletarian dictatorship—either in the popular democracies or in Soviet-occupied Germany. As a result, even though they had repudiated the notion of a peaceful road to socialism, the German Communists were still plagued by the ideological inconsistency of having to endorse a non-Soviet "transitional form," popular democracy, that distinguished itself from the Soviet system by the absence of dictatorship. But by the same token, resolving those doctrinal anomalies by redefining popular democracy as a dictatorship, which happened in December 1948, only replaced one ideological dilemma with a programmatic obstacle of a different kind. National unity could hardly be persuasively pursued on the basis of the SED's open commitment to the formation of a dictatorship. What followed the end of 1948 and in 1949 was therefore theoretically convoluted and even more riddled with internal contradictions than the policies that preceded it. On 15 December 1948, not long after the publication of Grotewohl's reference to popular democracy as the "only possible route" for Soviet-occupied Germany, Pieck, Oelßner, and Grotewohl arrived in Moscow, met with Stalin, and, following Dimitrov's redefinition of popular democracy as just another "form" of proletarian dictatorship, returned to the Soviet zone on 24 December to spread the word.

The discussion with Stalin had been in the planning since mid-October 1948.[13] First set for the end of November, it was delayed until 18 December for reasons that the Russians said were "*sekret*,"[14] but that just happened to coincide with Dimitrov's speech in Sofia on the 19th. In preparation for the meeting, party leaders were asked to draw up a "document" that provided their answers to questions apparently given to them beforehand by the Rus-

[12]Ibid., pp. 1000-1.
[13]Besprechung am 16. 10. 1948 mit: G. L. Ruskich, G. M. Russow, Semjonow, Tulpanow. Zentrales Parteiarchiv, NL 36/735/150-2.
[14]W. Pieck: in der Sekretariatssitzung am 27. 12. 1948. Bericht über Besprechung am 18. 12. 1948, ibid., NL 36 /735/64-74.

sians. This document, written by Pieck, Ulbricht, and Grotewohl, said little that could not have been inferred from the party's public rhetoric;[15] but during the talks themselves, more was revealed. There are two records of the four-hour discussion; Pieck either took notes on the spot or did so shortly thereafter; and used them again to prepare his oral report to the secretariat on 27 December 1948. The most important of Stalin's determinations was that Soviet-occupied Germany could "not yet" be regarded as a popular democracy and that a "cautious" or "zig-zag" road to socialism was necessary, rather than an open struggle with "breast bared." These kinds of tactics also caused Stalin to reject the SED's request to join the Communist Information Bureau (the issue had not yet "matured sufficiently"); but did not prevent him from encouraging the SED to abolish the practice of "parity," which had dictated that Communists and former Social Democrats be equally represented in important party posts. Nor did the need for caution stand in the way of Stalin's further encouragement of the party's purge of "hostile" or "vacillating elements" in positions of leadership. In fact, in Stalin's mind, the purge was at least partially related to the continuing development of the SED into the "leading state power" because of its growing attraction to "insufficiently schooled" people out to gain personal advantage. Stalin also considered improvement in the party's "operative leadership" to be important and recommended the formation of a seven-member politburo and five-member "small secretariat." Finally, tentative plans were discussed for the establishment of a "prov.[isional] German government," possibly as soon as February or March 1949, if the allies proceeded with formation of a Western government. This meant that a parliament or "Volkskammer" would be created by expanding the plenum of the Deutsche Wirtschaftskommission and having that new body "elect" a government.[16]

The results of these talks had an immediate impact upon the SED's efforts to define the nature of Soviet-occupied Germany.[17] On 28 December 1948, Ulbricht charged that Western newspapers lied when they wrote about a "transition to popular democracy in the Eastern zone;[18] and two days later Wilhelm Pieck gave the same paper an interview in which he rejected the notion that popular democracy either existed in the Soviet zone already or that the SED thought in terms of an imminent transition to one.[19] In accordance with past practices, however, Pieck ushered in the party's latest reversal without acknowledging that one had occurred. But the nature of the

[15]Antwort auf die Frage zur Besprechung [in hand: am 18. 12. 48], ibid., NL 36 /695/48-58.

[16]See note 15 and Ergebnis der 4stündigen Besprechung am 18. 12. 48, ibid., NL 36/735/42-45.

[17]This was, in fact, one of the questions that Pieck intended to ask Stalin, and the preliminary suggestion was "higher demo.[cratic] order." See Notizen für die Besprechung in Moskau, ibid., NL 36/735/31-35. The party leaders also referred to formation of a "German government for the Soviet occupation zone." See Note 16.

[18]"Walter Ulbricht über Presselügen," *Neues Deutschland*, 28 December 1948.

[19]Pieck, "Über die Politik der SED," *Neues Deutschland*, 30 December 1948.

questions put to him and his choice of words in answering them made it apparent that the SED, having recently endorsed popular democracy as the "only possible" route locally, had been placed in an untenable position by Stalin's private determination that Soviet-occupied Germany did not "yet" classify as one. Dimitrov's characterization of popular democracy as dictatorship certainly influenced Stalin, and may well have been the determining factor, because of the lingering need to pretend that the Soviet zone set an example politically, economically, and culturally for a reunited Germany.

Indeed, Pieck referred to Dimitrov's speech on "the character of popular democracy" and now used that reference to *contrast* conditions in those countries with the "political situation" in Soviet-occupied Germany. He refrained from making the point explicit, however, that the issue was dictatorship. Pieck's interviewer failed to mention it either, though both knew what the substitute phrases stood for. Pieck was asked whether the SED desired to "rule alone" in Soviet-occupied Germany, not whether it aspired to dictatorship; and Pieck answered obligingly that the party did not. The SED retained its commitment to coalition politics, he added, and it was just as incorrect to say that "the rule of the working class and thus popular democracy" had been established in the zone.[20] But the premise of that artless statement best conveyed the thinking behind the party's reversal. The "rule of the working class" was a phrase synonymous with dictatorship, and the ostensible absence of such exclusive rule had previously been the reason why the popular democracies did not characterize themselves as dictatorships. Now, all of a sudden, the "rule of the working class" and popular democracy had become identical concepts, instantly transforming them all into dictatorships. Now at the height of the Berlin blockade, a dictatorship for Germany was not a policy that the SED could endorse and retain its national credibility, besides which there may have been some fear of provoking the Western allies into something more dramatic than an airlift. But if Soviet-occupied Germany was considered to be neither a Soviet system nor a popular democracy, both of them being dictatorships; and if no German road to socialism could possibly existed, what exactly was the zone? The German Communists spent the coming months trying to answer the question and developed little more than an additional set of doctrinal incongruities to accompany the earlier contradictions.

Reinforcing the Antifascist-Democratic Order

For instance, scarcely had the SED outlawed the notion of a German road to socialism than an acrid debate broke out in the pages of *Neues Deutschland*

[20]Ibid.

over a closely related issue. A variety of intricate arguments then ensued due to the need to find a way of reconciling the SED's public commitment to German unity with its "Eastern orientation" toward countries that, as of 19 December 1948, were all dictatorships. The SED was understandably wary about putting the question in those terms, and this concern helps explain the exchange that took place between the party's original authority on the subject of a German road to socialism, Ackermann, and Rudolf Herrnstadt; as well as of important party discussions that occurred during the first months of 1949. These theoretical debates had little effect upon the actual course of developments leading to a divided Germany in 1949; but because they attempted to get around the implications of policies and objectives that served poorly as a realistic basis for national unity, the nature of these discussions suggest that the party leadership understood the implications fully, pursued the policies in spite of them, and accepted the consequences. After his bitter experience a few months before, Ackermann probably felt the need to shift to the opposite extreme and wrote on 21 December 1948, in celebration of Stalin's birthday, that "Marxism-Leninism knows no special national forms. In content and form, it spans the globe and possesses international validity."[21] This determination appeared to conform with the renunciation of any national road to socialism. But just a few weeks later, Herrnstadt published a meticulous refutation of the first half of Ackermann's remark. Even though national roads to socialism had been discredited, Herrnstadt nonetheless insisted that Marxism-Leninism "realized itself in national forms"; and he did so out of a need to develop an argument that retained an element of credibility for the party's national politics in spite of the abandonment of a German road to socialism. The key idea, and surely the major reason for the article in the first place, tied in with the SED's recent repudiation of what had just previously been considered the "only possible route" to socialism in Soviet-occupied Germany. The party's endorsement of popular democracy in fall 1948 had, after all, reflected its acceptance of the understanding that there was no national or German road to socialism. But in order to distance the SED's objectives from countries that had been declared dictatorships, someone had to improvise a new theory of "national forms" to replace the old. Herrnstadt, who may or may not have been acting on his own, began by dismissing the idea of "forms valid elsewhere," such as popular democracy, and then stressed the need to inquire into the nature of the "specific German situation." This could not be done, he said, based on the assumption that Marxism-Leninism "knows no special national forms."

A painstaking analysis followed, the principal points being Herrnstadt's criticism of a tendency within the party to "skip over developmental stages" and his endorsement of a "progressive democratic order that accords with

[21]Ackermann, "Stalin, Führer des Weltproletariats," *Neues Deutschland*, 21 December 1948.

our stage of development." Such a policy, he added, depended upon the backing of the antifascist bloc of parties and mass organizations led by the working class.[22] Herrnstadt's reaffirmation of bloc politics, which within the framework of an argument entitled "On the Way to a Party of a New Type" nonetheless proved somehow that Soviet-occupied Germany was no dictatorship, stressed the national forms of Marxism-Leninism as a way of appearing more moderate than Ackermann's disavowal of any German particularities whatsoever. Herrnstadt's remarks infused a little more life into the idea of special German circumstances both sanctioned by Marxism-Leninism and perfectly compatible with the further evolution of the twin "isms." But then Herrnstadt's reference to a "progressive democratic order" merely restated Pieck's preference, expressed a few weeks earlier, for the "strengthening of the existing new democratic order" as a policy meant to contrast with the one previously geared toward popular democracy.[23] If Soviet-occupied Germany now traveled neither a Soviet nor a popular-democratic route, however; and considering that no notion of national peculiarities had ever altered the party's final objective, it is difficult to take the new policy of "strengthening the antifascist-democratic order" as anything other than a tactical rejuvenation of a German road to socialism that, now as before, was fated to end in dictatorship. Nonetheless, because the idea of a special road turned originally on the SED's public commitment to democracy, it came as no surprise that this commitment to cooperation with antifascist-democratic parties and mass organizations was now reaffirmed; and this reaffirmation occurred in the form of the earlier promise that the SED did not aspire to "any kind of preferential position" in cooperating with other parties; the SED wished to share responsibility equally.[24] In fact, Pieck associated the act of "strengthening the antifascist-democratic order" with a rejection of "rumors about the . . . SED's plans for dictatorship" spread by persons who wished only to disrupt cooperation with the other local parties.[25]

Without reestablishing the point that Marxism-Leninism realized itself "in national forms," then, the force of logic would have constrained the party to define Soviet-occupied Germany now either as a Soviet system or as a popular democracy and, in either case, as a dictatorship. Out of concern over its national credibility, the SED was able to do neither in early 1949. Nonetheless, the basic idea of "national forms" and a "specific German situation" still lent itself to misinterpretation, and for this likely reason, Ackermann tipped the scales back toward the doctrinal mainstream in his response to Herrnstadt, who then answered Ackermann yet again before Pieck put an end to the discussion by coming down on both sides of the issue. Acker-

[22]Herrnstadt, "Auf dem Wege zur Partei neuen Typus," *Neues Deutschland*, 9 January 1949.
[23]Pieck, "Über die Politik der SED," *Neues Deutschland*, 30 December 1948.
[24]Pieck, "Gegen die Kriegshetzer—für den Frieden," *Neues Deutschland*, 8 March 1949.
[25]Pieck, "Lehren der Parteikonferenz," *Einheit* 3 (1949): 198.

mann went for the jugular with a vicious challenge to Herrnstadt's ideological integrity, charging that his belief in national forms was incompatible with the internationalism of the labor movement, shaded over into "bourgeois nationalism" (the same accusation that Stalin leveled at Tito), and could not be reconciled with Marxism-Leninism. Worse, Ackermann likened the issues involved in his dispute with Herrnstadt to the arguments used by Stalin to destroy the "Trotskyist-Menshevist 'theory' of Zinoviev" years earlier. Finally, he concluded that Herrnstadt's theory damaged the party by allowing "those opportunistic elements who view Leninism with hostility to base themselves gleefully on the ostensible necessity of a 'special national German form' of Marxism-Leninism."[26] Curiously, just a few days later (and a week before Herrnstadt's second response was published), Ackermann seemed to contradict himself when he spoke of "the application of Leninism in accord with special German circumstances." By referring to the need to apply "Marxist-Leninist theory at any given time in accord with special circumstances in our country," Ackermann retracted the offending argument before Herrnstadt had a chance to act.[27]

He did not admit to having done so, however, and Herrnstadt still had the last word. Not surprisingly, Herrnstadt defended himself against Ackermann's insinuations, but otherwise undertook to prove the correctness of his position regarding "national forms" by distinguishing clearly between Soviet-occupied Germany and the popular democracies. In so doing, he fit his disagreement with Ackermann even more clearly into the context of the party's ongoing discussions concerning the nature of the Soviet zone and addressed the very issue that, whether Ackermann realized it or not, led to the controversy in the first place. After all, Ackermann denied the existence of national forms in an article published on 21 December 1948, a scant two days after Dimitrov's speech in Bulgaria and a week or so before Ulbricht and Pieck, having returned from Moscow, made the first official determination that the Soviet zone was, in fact, not a popular democracy; and the entire discussion, not definitively settled until the SED met for its first party conference from 25 to 29 January 1949, broke out at a time in which few top Communists knew what programmatic developments the next day might bring. Not that Herrnstadt focused directly on the question of dictatorship raised by Dimitrov's redefinition of popular democracy and related it to conditions in the Soviet zone. Now as before, the SED treated the subject of dictatorship as it applied to Soviet-occupied Germany as gingerly as circumstances permitted,[28] though considering the implications of the party's posi-

---

[26]Ackermann, "Eine notwendige Antwort," *Neues Deutschland*, 16 January 1949.

[27]Ackermann, "Lenin und die deutsche Arbeiterbewegung," *Neues Deutschland*, 21 January 1949.

[28]Indeed, several months later Dimitrov died suddenly while visiting Moscow, and in commemoration the SED republished his speech in *Einheit* (8 [1949]: 676-79)—minus the most impor-

tion on the subject of "Leninism,"[29] skirting the issue of dictatorship requir-ed a considerable degree of rhetorical agility. Herrnstadt paraphrased Dimi-trov's comments to the effect that the dictatorship of the proletariat took the form of a Soviet regime in the USSR, whereas in Bulgaria and "several other countries" the dictatorship of the proletariat was exercised by a "popular de-mocratic regime." Unless one wished to suggest that Dimitrov was no Marx-ist-Leninist, said Herrnstadt, how could his analysis be anything but a deter-mination that "special national forms" existed and derived from a Marxist-Leninist assessment of differing circumstances? Herrnstadt also quoted pas-sages from Pieck's interview with *Neues Deutschland* on 30 December 1948, referred to the same remarks by Lenin concerning different "forms" of democracy and dictatorship most recently cited by Tjulpanov, in May 1948, and explained that "recognizing the possibility and the presence of special national forms leads to a study of nationally conditioned circumstances, to differentiations, to working out the correct political line and the correct methods in the class struggle."[30]

Herrnstadt then alluded to the real issue when he suggested that Acker-mann's dismissal of the idea of "special national forms" had occurred at the precise moment in which the party needed to take up its analysis of "our es-pecially complicated *nationally* determined circumstances."[31] What Herrn-stadt meant to convey was a distinction with important implications for the SED's support of national unity. Neither Ackermann nor anyone else could persist in arguing that Marxism-Leninism knew no national forms without conceding that the Soviet zone was a dictatorship already or well on the way to becoming one; whereas the Communists were in need of a theoretical context that would allow them to argue both sides of key issues as the only means of retaining any credibility on the subject of German unity. They had to continue their transformation of the SED into a Marxist-Leninist party of a new type, modeling it after "the first party of a new type," "the party of Lenin and Stalin, the Bolshevist party of the Soviet Union"[32]; define further their staunch commitment to "Leninism," which Oelßner said was synony-mous with "the theory and tactics of the dictatorship of the proletariat";[33]

---

tant passages from his closing remarks in which he had concluded that, "in accordance with the teaching of Marxism-Leninism, the Soviet regime and the popular democratic regime are two forms of one and the same power . . . , the dictatorship of the proletariat." (See "Auf dem Boden des Marxismus-Leninismus," *Neues Deutschland* 28 December 1948.)

[29]See "Lenin und der Leninismus," *Sozialistische Bildungshefte* 3 (1949), passim.

[30]Herrnstadt, "Antwort auf eine Polemik," *Neues Deutschland*, 23 January 1949.

[31]Ibid. My italics.

[32]See Burdschalov, "Über die internationale Bedeutung der historischen Erfahrung der Partei der Bolschewiki," *Neue Welt* 23 (1949): 50. Ackermann made his remarks at the conference in January 1949 (*Protokoll der Ersten Parteikonferenz der Sozialistischen Einheitspartei Deutsch-lands*, p. 470).

[33]See Oelßner, "Die Diktatur des Proletariats—die Hauptfrage des Leninismus," *Einheit* 8

orient the Soviet zone toward the East based on graphic contrasts between the peace policies of the Soviet Union, a "friend of the German people," and the colonial intentions of the Western "imperialist camp of war mongers";[34] and present themselves as champions of national unity who favored antifascist democracy over that very institution, dictatorship, toward which all of the above policies were geared. Denying that there was any such thing as a "special German road to socialism" while still providing for "special national forms" was apparently the best theoretical bridge that they were capable of constructing between incompatible sets of outlooks.

This discussion of popular democracy, dictatorship, and national forms suggests that the price paid by the SED for the latest of its many reversals was programmatic incoherence and the further diminishment of what these distinctions were supposed to enhance—the party's public commitment to national unity. Nor did Pieck succeed in clearing up much of the confusion left over from Ackermann's exchange with Herrnstadt and caused by the fact that the party had reversed itself on the subject of popular democracy. Pieck criticized Herrnstadt *and* Ackermann, but in the end also sided with both because, in their own way, each had stressed certain positions important to the party. Pieck favored Herrnstadt's argument when he said that Marxism-Leninism would be realized in individual countries in accordance with the local conditions under which the proletariat waged the class struggle;[35] and this meant that the need to champion German unity required the SED to "wage the class struggle" differently than it would have done otherwise. Herrnstadt had said much the same thing; and, indeed, at the party conference a few days later, it was resolved that "reinforcing the antifascist-democratic order as the basis of the struggle for reestablishing Germany's unity" was the SED's primary objective.[36] But Pieck sided with Ackermann as well when he insisted that there were "no roads to socialism distinct from Marxism-Leninism"; that being so, what was the point of a debate about "special national forms"?[37] Much the same thing was said in private; at a meeting on 21 January 1949, the central secretariat passed a resolution that directed *Neues Deutschland* in the future to inform the secretariat if an article intended for publication contained an attack upon a member of that body (though there is no compelling reason to think that Herrnstadt had acted on his own).[38] A day later, Ackermann pleaded his case before the larger board.

(1949): 723.

[34]Pieck, "Der Kampf um den Frieden und gegen die Kriegshetze," *Protokoll der Ersten Parteikonferenz*, p. 79.

[35]Pieck, "Kurzes Nachwort," *Neues Deutschland*, 23 January 1949.

[36]See "Entschließung der Ersten Parteikonferenz der SED," *Protokoll der Ersten Parteikonferenz*, p. 524.

[37]Pieck, "Kurzes Nachwort," *Neues Deutschland*, 23 January 1949.

[38]Protokoll Nr. 145 (II) der Sitzung des Zentralsekretariats am 23. 1. 1949. Zentrales Parteiar-

The personal debate between himself and Herrnstadt should be discontinued, he said, not because all issues had been resolved, but because "philosophical questions concerning the form and content of Marxism-Leninism as a science" ran the risk of complicating its practical application to the "current, special, concrete circumstances in our country."[39] But Ackermann worried, too, about the potential for confusion among the rank and file over the meaning of another critical concept. The designation "party of a new type" might be taken to imply that some kind of "special, national, German kind" of party existed, he said; whereas the point of the concept was to create one "party modeled after the Bolshevist party of the Soviet Union."[40]

When it met from 25 to 29 January 1949, the party conference took a stand on many of these issues that resolved the lingering ambiguity associated with each individually, but only when they were discussed in curtailed contexts and obvious implications and interconnections ignored. The conference resolution established categorically that "the present system in the Soviet zone of occupation is an antifascist-democratic order in which the working class holds decisive positions; it is not a popular democratic order because circumstances in the zone differ markedly from those in the popular democratic countries."[41] Pieck and Grotewohl argued similarly, but provided additional commentary from which important inferences can be drawn about the tactical thinking behind the disavowal of popular democracy and the party's short- and long-range objectives. For neither managed to hide the fact that the party considered popular democracy, referred to elsewhere as a "state form of proletarian dictatorship,"[42] or any other form of proletarian dictatorship,[43] as only temporarily and tactically unsuitable for Soviet-zone circumstances. The disavowal of popular democracy as dictatorship beginning in late 1948 and early 1949 therefore fits the same category of expedience as the KPD's earliest repudiation of a "Soviet system" because it did not accord with "current conditions" in Germany. These various systems of dictatorship were only inappropriate at the moment; whereas even now, though mostly in other contexts, the Communists were perfectly clear about their vision of the future. Much as Tjulpanov had said the previous May, it was merely a matter of the pace of transition. Nonetheless, the Communists

---

chiv, IV 2/2.1/263.

[39]Stenographische Niederschrift über die 16. (30.) Tagung des Parteivorstandes der SED am 24. Januar 1949, ibid., IV 2/1/30/29-35.

[40]Ibid.

[41]"Entschließung der Ersten Parteikonferenz der SED," *Protokoll der Ersten Parteikonferenz*, p. 524.

[42]See "Was ist Volksdemokratie?" *Sozialistische Bildungshefte* 2 (1949): 12.

[43]Ackermann had already thought to ask whether the popular-democratic "form" of dictatorship would not develop in the direction of the "classical form" that existed in the Soviet Union. After all, he said, Lenin established in *Childhood Diseases* that Soviets or councils constituted the "real form of the dictatorship of the proletariat" (see note 41).

still pretended otherwise. Pieck complained that "enemies" spread rumors about "our assessment of the present stage reached by us in the Soviet occupation zone and about further development," hoping to disrupt cooperation with the other antifascist-democratic parties.[44] This was Pieck's way of indicating that critics of the SED continued to warn of its conspiratorial commitment to dictatorship and that these critics were malicious in telling other parties to be wary of its hollow promises of democratic cooperation.

But Pieck was also concerned about confusion in the lower ranks of the SED caused by the party's sudden repudiation of popular democracy; and to better understand this confusion, some of the broader implications of that disavowal need to be considered from the standpoint of ordinary party members committed to the same principles of "Leninism," foremost among them dictatorship, discussed by the party in all other contexts in 1949. They had been entirely justified in concluding that the renunciation of any German road to socialism the previous fall cleared the way for the rapid establishment of dictatorship because the promise of democratic development had been nothing more than the tactical and temporary assurance of "no sovietization"; and no sovietization meant no dictatorship. By renouncing the democratic road to socialism, the party indirectly endorsed what the previous theory had disavowed—a Soviet system for Germany sooner, rather than later, and a form of transition to it patterned after the Soviet experience. For national reasons, however, the Communists had still considered it unwise to endorse publicly the use of Soviet methods and Soviet solutions. These same considerations also led the party briefly to embrace the popular-democratic way to socialism instead because, as they argued, dictatorship was not involved. These were all artful distinctions most likely understood as such by lower-echelon party members; and they probably welcomed Dimitrov's redefinition of popular democracy as dictatorship because it appeared to eliminate the last hindrance to the SED's swift development into the same kind of system. But the sudden transformation of popular democracy into dictatorship left the SED momentarily with no sound way of proscribing a German road to socialism without favoring dictatorship and thus, in the absence of a new theory, unable to establish a credible program of national politics. The idea of "reinforcing the antifascist-democratic order" joined with formation of a "national front" later in the year to fill the gap.

But by early 1949, the rhetorical dilemmas defied solutions more stubbornly than ever before. Not that the party's spokesmen lacked the imagination to devise answers designed to obscure the real issues; but their answers had never been less persuasive because the attempt to reconcile obvious opposites generated such a steady stream of doctrinal contrivances. Grotewohl

[44]Pieck, "Der Kampf um den Frieden und gegen die Kriegshetze," *Protokoll der Ersten Partei-konferenz*, p. 69.

spoke of the iniquities associated with the "theory of a special German road to socialism"; it fostered both anti-Soviet and nationalistic tendencies, interfered with party discussions concerning the importance of Leninism as the only form of "undistorted Marxism," and complicated full acceptance of the fact that, "in our party, no one can be a Marxist without being a Leninist."[45] Grotewohl was not, however, foolish enough to add that, according to Lenin, one became a Marxist only by extending one's acknowledgment of the class struggle to an acknowledgment of the *"dictatorship of the proletariat"* and that this recognition was the touchstone of a real understanding of Marxism.[46] This particular determination was reserved for other contexts, but Grotewohl made additional remarks that contained many of the same implications. He spoke of the party's renunciation of a German road to socialism while discussing "the leading role of the Soviet Union in the antiimperialist struggle and the leading role of the Communist Party of the Soviet Union, the party of Lenin and Stalin, in the international labor movement"; and he used these comments to insist that a democratic development in Germany could occur only in "the closest possible association with the Soviet Union," adding that the SED viewed Leninism as "undistorted Marxism, which Lenin and Stalin developed further in the age of imperialism."[47] But by the time Grotewohl got around to these comments, he had already spoken fondly of the antifascist cooperation with other parties and the basis for formation of the SED made possible by the KPD's original favorization of an "antifascist-democratic regime" in place of "a Soviet system" imposed on Germany.[48]

The trouble was that the SED could not cling to its promise of no Soviet system for Germany after having outlawed the notion of a German road to socialism grounded in democracy; neither concept made any sense in the absence of the other. But Grotewohl had more to say that helps in understanding the theoretical impasse, the political reasons that created it, and the insurmountable contradictions built into rhetoric designed to rationalize both the SED's continuing transformation into a Stalinist party committed to dictatorship *and* to suggest that the SED willingly relinquished or postponed its prerogatives for the greater good of the nation. Grotewohl spoke first of the need to learn from the history of Lenin's development of a party of a new type as the best means of establishing one in Germany; and he added that turning the SED into a similar revolutionary party assured "the road to completion of democratic development in all of Germany and its transition to the

---

[45]Grotewohl, "Die Politik der Partei und die Entwicklung der SED zu einer Partei neuen Typus," *Protokoll der Ersten Parteikonferenz*, p. 374.

[46]See "Lenin und der Leninismus," *Sozialistische Bildungshefte* 3 (1949): 4.

[47]Grotewohl, "Die Politik der Partei und die Entwicklung der SED zu einer Partei neuen Typus," *Protokoll der Ersten Parteikonferenz der SED*, pp. 373-74; and Grotewohl, "Die Parteikonferenz als Schritt auf dem Wege zur Partei neuen Typus," *Einheit* 3 (1949): 203.

[48]Grotewohl, "Die Politik der Partei und die Entwicklung der SED zu einer Partei neuen Typus," *Protokoll der Ersten Parteikonferenz*, p. 331.

period of the rule of the working class."[49] But he did not point out that the phrase "rule of the working class" was just another way of saying "dictatorship"; doing so would have been as imprudent as expanding upon his remarks to establish the party's priorities even more clearly; and these priorities began with the complete transformation of the SED into a Leninist-Stalinist party of a new type as the first step toward democracy in all of Germany. As the only basis for unity, such a democracy nationwide would then shade into "the period of the rule of the working class," dictatorship, and not one single aspect of the SED's vision of national unity in 1949 pointed in any other direction. Rather then admit it, Grotewohl dodged the issue by distinguishing between Soviet-occupied Germany and the popular democratic countries and added that, "at the present time, we must concentrate the attention of the party and the people as our top priority on questions that are acute for all of Germany."[50] Even so, he stated that the establishment of popular democracy in all of Germany could occur only after the "national struggle has been successfully waged and a united Marxist-Leninist party is present."[51] This additional inference came closer still to an admission that the SED could not conceive of a united Germany independent of a dictatorship over all of it. Just a few months later one of the party's *Sozialistische Bildungshefte* voiced the same sentiments with a bit more clarity. The SED needed to set itself the task locally of "further strengthening and expanding the democratic order"; this included battling "for the reestablishment of German unity." Not that the achievement of this and other objectives meant the prompt "realization of the political rule of the working class," but the success of the struggle for that latter goal, the standard euphemism for dictatorship, was clearly predicated upon preconditions such as the establishment of national unity.[52]

Grotewohl also intimated in other ways that "reinforcing the antifascist-democratic order" was at most a transitional objective. Talking about an imminent shift to popular democracy now was a mistake, Grotewohl warned, because it "disorganizes the party and blocks the possibilities for the resolution of the practical tasks of the immediate future." At the "present moment," he said, the party needed to concentrate its attention less on issues relevant to the countries of popular democracy than on matters that are "currently" urgent for us. Thus, conversations relating the Soviet-zone to popular democracy "currently" disrupted the consolidation of the working public within the mass organizations and retarded the mobilization of these organi-

---

[49]See Grotewohl, "Die Parteikonferenz als Schritt auf dem Wege zur Partei neuen Typus," *Einheit* 3 (1949): 203.

[50]Grotewohl, "Die Politik der Partei und die Entwicklung der SED zu einer Partei neuen Typus," *Protokoll der Ersten Parteikonferenz*, p. 333.

[51]Ibid., p. 334.

[52]See "Lenin und der Leninismus," *Sozialistische Bildungshefte* 3 (1949), pp. 7-8.

zations behind the leadership of the party. Nonetheless, Grotewohl added that the SED still acted in conformity with its "principles and goals" because it was unwaveringly committed to a socialist society that could only be achieved following the establishment of the "rule of the working class."[53] In his address to the conference, Wilhelm Pieck also made use of the phrase "rule of the working class" as the blandest substitute for dictatorship, but hinted just as strongly that the party's ultimate objective remained unchanged. His interview with *Neues Deutschland* in December 1948, Pieck said, had produced a certain amount of consternation among some comrades; this concern was unwarranted, however, because he had merely stressed that the party needed to strengthen the existing democratic order in Soviet-occupied Germany so as to prevent reactionary elements from reacquiring their old positions of power and influence. If the party did so successfully, he indicated, it would have accomplished "a great deal for the further development of Germany." His comments the previous December could only have upset comrades who were unclear about the situation in Soviet-occupied Germany and inclined to "exaggerate" it by drawing conclusions that failed to mesh with the facts.[54] The underlying message was clear: characterizing Soviet-occupied Germany as a popular democracy or advocating its rapid transformation into one "exaggerated" the situation because such rhetoric spelled dictatorship—either right away or imminently. Drawing improper "conclusions" about Soviet-zone circumstances, Pieck warned, perhaps with the volatility of the Berlin crisis in the back of his mind, was "very dangerous and could lead to measures that would be disadvantageous to the fulfillment of the tasks before us." The party needed to focus its attention instead upon "the tasks confronting us today in the Soviet occupation zone and throughout all of Germany," rather than complicating matters by engaging in discussions of "what will happen later in Germany and in the Soviet zone of occupation once we have achieved the necessary assurances and preconditions for the fulfillment of our democratic demands." In order to "calm worried minds," Pieck made a final point of stating that the party's "principles and goals" were as valid now as they had been before and committed the party to the struggle for socialism.[55]

What is Leninism?

These kinds of arguments fostered the impression that "reinforcing the antifascist-democratic order" meant the elimination of proletarian dictatorship

[53]Grotewohl, "Die Politik der Partei und die Entwicklung der SED zu einer Partei neuen Typus," *Protokoll der Ersten Parteikonferenz*, p. 335.
[54]Pieck, "Der Kampf um den Frieden und gegen die Kriegshetze," ibid., pp. 69-70.
[55]Ibid.

altogether. They did not, and in this sense the rhetoric differed little from that used to create the earlier impression, just as misleading, that a German road to socialism removed dictatorship from the party's agenda entirely. No sooner had the latest arguments favoring the development of an antifascist democracy emerged in early 1949 than it was already defined in Marxist-Leninist concepts synonymous with dictatorship and in substantial harmony with the realities of life under a "socialist occupation regime."[56] But the party nonetheless acted as if its devotion to national unity led to a voluntary suspension of the SED's pursuit of its preferred objectives. Kurt Hager explained that the "essence of the antifascist-democratic order" could be fully comprehended only when the "struggle for the national existence of our people" in all of Germany was kept in mind. He came out strongly against two notions that he said were prevalent within his own party—the "radical" idea that a proletarian dictatorship existed in Soviet-occupied Germany already; and the "pessimistic" view that strengthening the antifascist-democratic order actually opened the "scissors" of a split between both parts of Germany, rather than closed it. Though Hager could not say so openly, he may have been referring to disparate attitudes held by the Communist and Social-Democratic factions of a still disunited SED. If so, the pessimistic view would have soon merged with the radical attitude anyway in the common belief that Soviet-occupied Germany was a dictatorship now. Then again, the two outlooks may at times have emanated from a single source opposed to the SED's development into a "party of a new type."[57] For any view of strengthening the antifascist-democratic order that "pessimistically" took it to be an *impediment* to national unity would likely have adopted the related position that the entire idea dovetailed with dictatorship and for that reason was not a serious basis for the reestablishment of German unity. As it was, Hager contented himself with claiming that both "fallacious and pernicious theories" sprang from the desire to skip over necessary stages of development; but he stopped far short of capping his argument with the conclusion that strengthening the antifascist-democratic order was a necessary stage in development *toward dictatorship*. He continued to act instead as if the issues were unrelated and considered it self-evident that an antifascist-democratic order, "not a Soviet state," had been created in Soviet-occupied Germany; a "democratic transformation," not a "proletarian revolution" had occurred. Suggestions to the contrary complicated "our present objectives."[58]

---

[56]See Timofejev, "Das imperialistische und das sowjetische Besatzungsregime," *Tägliche Rundschau*, 23 February 1949.

[57]Internally, there was considerable concern over the number of party resignations during the year and the reasons why, a goodly number of which had to do with this very issue. See Die Erfüllung der Beschlüsse der ersten Parteikonferenz (an analysis of internal party affairs prepared by the SMAD and given to Pieck). Zentrales Parteiarchiv, NL 36/735/248-77.

[58]Hager, "Antifaschistisch-demokratische Ordnung," *Einheit* 4 (1949): 299-301.

But the fact remained that the party's official "present objectives" concentrated on the reestablishment of German unity through the spread of the Soviet-zone model to the Western regions of the country, whereas by 1949 there was little to distinguish the "antifascist-democratic order" theoretically or practically from dictatorship. Hager had gone on to explain that the work of building up the Soviet zone, both on its own merits and in its relation to the struggle for German unity, turned on the success of steps taken to transform the SED into a "party of a new type"; that act alone created the preconditions for a "transition to socialism."[59] By now, however, every discussion devoted to the nature of the party centered on "Leninism"; and there was no way of reasserting the preeminence of "Leninism" while still avoiding the allied issue of dictatorship. Nothing indicated that the SED ever advocated antifascist democracy as an end in itself, either in the Soviet zone alone or in a reunited Germany; and the re-inclusion of "Leninism" in 1949, usually omitted in 1945 and 1946 because it sounded too much like "sovietization," serves to confirm it. This point explains why Stalin's insistence that Leninism was not a "purely Russian and exclusively Russian" but rather an international phenomenon was so often quoted;[60] and the contention figured prominently in a variety of other arguments to the effect that Leninism had "international validity." Moreover, because Marxism and Leninism formed an "indivisible unity," they had to be embraced together or rejected in common; there was no such thing as Marxism without Leninism. The revolutionary spirit that infused the teachings of Marx and Engels, Lenin *and* Stalin, said Anton Ackermann, was one and the same; and the teachings of Lenin *and* Stalin formed the quintessence of the struggle of the entire international labor movement. The revolutionary working-class parties of all countries were thus certain to have the "same experiences as the Bolshevist party."[61] This applied to the SED as well, which in May 1949 passed another resolution calling for study of the *Short Course* history of the Soviet Communist party;[62] and these kinds of statements came down to the acknowledgment that becoming a party of a new type meant "developing into a party modeled after that of Lenin and Stalin."[63] Not only did the SED claim to have its own historical reasons to "learn from the Bolsheviki,"[64] by the end of the year the "bolshevization of Communist parties" under the leadership of Lenin and Stalin came in for praise; and the "general principles of bolshe-

---

[59]Ibid., p. 307.

[60]See "Was ist Leninismus?" *Neuer Weg* 5 (1949): 21.

[61]Ackermann, "Der Marxismus-Leninismus, die theoretische Grundlage unserer Politik," *Neuer Weg* 1 (1949): 8-9.

[62]See "Zur Verbesserung des Studiums des Kurzen Lehrgangs der Geschichte der KPdSU (B) [5 May 1949]," *Dokumente der Sozialistischen Einheitspartei Deutschlands*, vol. II, pp. 246-49.

[63]Ackermann, "Der Marxismus-Leninismus, die theoretische Grundlage unserer Politik," *Neuer Weg* 1 (1949): 8.

[64]"Lenin und der Leninismus," *Sozialistische Bildungshefte* 3 (1949): 12.

vism" were considered "obligatory" for all countries.[65]

Among these principles, then, was dictatorship, and the SED said so in most theoretical arguments save the ones devoted to the reinforcement of an antifascist democracy. In January 1949, the SED used the thirtieth anniversary of the murder of Rosa Luxemburg to criticize her for failing to realize that the proletariat could never prevail in the absence of "a militant Marxist-Leninist party"; and for many of the same reasons existing back then, the SED now needed to transform itself into such a party in order to lead the working class "to the triumph of the dictatorship of the proletariat."[66] Fred Oelßner called dictatorship "the main question of Leninism." Quoting Stalin to the effect that Leninism was Marxism in the age of imperialism and that Leninism represented the "theory and tactics" of revolution and dictatorship, Oelßner developed an argument that equated such a dictatorship with "the supreme expression of democracy, proletarian democracy." This was the theoretical context in which his own party's disavowal of dictatorship in favor of antifascist democracy began to make more theoretical, if not much common sense; and Oelßner applied another of Stalin's key insights to Soviet-occupied Germany. The working class was capable of prevailing over the bourgeoisie without a dictatorship, according to Stalin; but because the bourgeoisie could be counted upon to put up further resistance, "marching toward the final victory of socialism" required the destruction of the old state apparatus and its replacement with a proletarian state apparatus. "This state apparatus," said Oelßner, "is the dictatorship of the proletariat."[67]

The Stalinist idea embedded in this argument was the notion that class warfare intensified along the way to socialism; and Ulbricht had already drawn the proper local inferences in December 1948 when he claimed that the class struggle had intensified recently and that there was no such thing as "peaceful development toward socialism."[68] But, unlike Oelßner, Ulbricht left the subject of dictatorship out of the equation, though it was reinjected the same month in a pamphlet devoted to lessons learned from the history of the Soviet Communist party. From it the SED knew that there could be only one road to socialism—by way of the "revolutionary class struggle and via the dictatorship of the proletariat." There was no "special German road" to socialism, the notion having served only to awaken the "illusion that it was possible to achieve socialism without a class struggle during the transitional period and through the avoidance of the dictatorship of the proletariat."[69]

[65]Burdschalow, "Über die internationale Bedeutung der historischen Erfahrung der Partei der Bolschewiki," *Neue Welt* 23 (1948): 50-51.
[66]"Rosa Luxemburg und Karl Liebknecht," *Sozialistische Bildungshefte* 1 (1949): 6 and 13.
[67]Oelßner, "Die Diktatur des Proletariats—die Hauptfrage des Leninismus," *Einheit* 8 (1949): 723, 726-27, 736-37.
[68]See Ulbricht, "Die SED vor der Parteikonferenz," *Neue Welt* 22 (1948): 70 and 74.
[69]"Was lehrt uns die Geschichte der KPdSU (B)?" *Sozialistische Bildungshefte* 12 (1948): 11-12.

Another pamphlet, quoting Lenin, explained that the bourgeoisie would naturally continue to resist following the initial destruction of the "bourgeois capitalist state apparatus"; and that fact made dictatorship necessary. However diverse the "political forms" of transition from capitalism to communism, said Lenin, dictatorship was the one feature essential to all of them.[70]

Even theoretical discussions that omitted the subject of dictatorship, the better to emphasize the consolidation of the antifascist-democratic order, tried to link the latter idea to the Leninist-Stalinist notion of intensifying class warfare. "Certain working people," read one commentary, felt that the class struggle subsided with the further development of "our new order"; whereas the more that order established itself, and "the greater the successes met with in fulfillment of the two-year plan, the more desperately the class enemy fights to win back his old positions."[71] Reinforcing the antifascist-democratic order was a necessity born of the need to repress the class enemy as the first priority and only then to reestablish national unity; and yet, by definition, crushing the class enemy remained a task that could only be accomplished through dictatorship. Nonetheless, most discussions of reinforcing the antifascist-democratic order still insisted upon linking that process to intensifying class warfare; and this view of things also explains why most accounts of antifascist democracy in 1949 came down to the urgency of transforming the SED into a "party of a new type." Even then, someone like Hager still maintained that Soviet-occupied Germany was not a dictatorship; dictatorship presupposed the "leading role of the Marxist-Leninist party," which shared power with no other party; and the SED had "only just begun to become a party of a new type."[72] In the same vein, Oelßner argued that, when characterizing the status of Germany based on the "current level of Marxist-Leninist state theory, we have to say that . . . we have not yet achieved the dictatorship of the proletariat." But Oelßner stated unequivocally that "we Marxist-Leninists naturally fight . . . for the dictatorship of the proletariat as the indispensable precondition for socialism." They had said so in their "principles and goals," and "we stand solidly by this goal, knowing that we shall someday achieve the dictatorship of the proletariat not just in the Eastern zone, but in all of Germany."[73]

---

[70]"Lenin und der Leninismus," *Sozialistische Bildungshefte* 3 (1949): 8-9.
[71]"Unser Kampf für die Festigung der antifaschistisch-demokratischen Ordnung," *Sozialistische Bildungshefte* 4 (1949): 12.
[72]Hager, "Antifaschistisch-demokratische Ordnung," *Einheit* 4 (1949): 301 and 303.
[73]Oelßner, "Die Diktatur des Proletariats—die Hauptfrage des Leninismus," *Einheit* 8 (1949): 723, 726-27, 736-37.

Rootless Cosmopolitanism

These conclusions suggest why the SED's ringing endorsement of national unity struck such a discordant note by now, the more so when party leaders referred to the corresponding need for an "absolutely positive relationship with the Soviet Union."[74] By 1949, certain doctrinal suppositions, like those connected with "Leninism," had never been harder to ignore; and yet the party still clung to its national pretensions. In fact, the greater the SED's "new orientation,"[75] eastward, the more emphatically it talked of its national commitment westward. But under the circumstances, such rhetoric pointed to German unity on the basis of an eastern alignment; and the synthesis that emerged toward the end of the year shows it most clearly. Stalin was "Germany's best friend" because, as Alexander Abusch put it, he had the answer to questions connected with "the fate of the German nation."[76] The arguments used to tie the SED and, soon, the German Democratic Republic to Stalin and the Soviet Union only added up rhetorically, however, if rapprochement with the West was solidly blocked. Alignment with the Soviet Union meant allegiance to Stalin, and Stalin was unaccustomed to divided loyalties. The Soviet-zone consequences in 1949 lay in a further round of hostility toward all things politically, economically, and culturally "Western"; along with dire warnings of the threat to the nation residing in such influences. The SED charged that imperialism took shape as "bourgeois nationalism" and "cosmopolitanism," which menaced West Germany especially through American "colonization"; and praised internationalism because the "national fate of Germany" hinged upon "friendship with the Soviet Union."[77]

Most of these arguments were local adaptations of positions originally developed, or being established now, in Soviet theoretical debates that hid various aspects of Soviet foreign and domestic policy. As a consequence, the SED's full endorsement of propositions tied to Soviet interests, whatever the doctrinal pretext in Soviet-occupied Germany, vastly exceeded the dictates of "friendship"; and the SED's unqualified acceptance of these ideas meant that its policies were fated to play a role substantially divorced from national politics. Stripped of its ideology, the SED's emphasis on East-West dichotomies was nothing more than the party's latest version of the Zhdanovist two-

[74]Grotewohl, "Die Politik der Partei und die Entwicklung der SED zu einer Partei neuen Typus," *Protokoll der Ersten Parteikonferenz*, p. 332.
[75]See Grotewohl's comment in *Protokoll der Ersten Parteikonferenz*, p. 148.
[76]See Hauser, "Deutschlands bester Freund," *Die neue Gesellschaft. Stalin-Sonderheft* 12 (1949): 881-86; Abusch, *Stalin und die Schicksalsfragen der deutschen Nation*, passim.
[77]Dahlem, "Lebendiger proletarischer Internationalismus," *Einheit* 4 (1949): 294.

camps argument; the two-camps argument rationalized the incorporation of Eastern Europe into the sphere of Soviet influence; and the SED's opinions on all such subjects led virtually no national or half-national existence independent of their niche within this broader context. That the German Communists prospered under those conditions made them neither "creative" Marxist-Leninists nor national politicians. Their political prominence remained inherently artificial—a benefit available to them for playing their witting or unwitting part in the larger scheme of Soviet foreign policy and an advantage always at risk of being lost, as some of them sensed, to any Soviet reassessment of the worth of the territory entrusted to them. Ideologically there was scarcely a single idea developed in these years with a trace of non-Stalinist originality; however capable the party's spokesmen were of developing eloquent arguments in support of any political proposition handed to them, the fact remains that every key idea was derivative. In its practical political and ideological consequences, the SED's blend of bitter hostility toward the West and obsequious imitation of the Soviet Union reinforced Soviet policies devised to meet Soviet interests; and it ignored or departed from certain implications and applications of that policy only when complying either made no sense locally or would have directly conflicted with Soviet-zone objectives. The fact is that anticosmopolitanism evolved in Soviet-occupied Germany as the latest manifestation of two-camps thinking associated with Zhdanov's name, whereas one of the different purposes served in the Soviet Union by the crusade against "cosmopolitans" after Zhdanov's death in August 1948, and accelerated in January 1949, was to purge his followers from the ruling apparatus.[78] Whether this internal struggle between politicians first associated with Zhdanov and those who allied themselves with Malenkov and Beria extended into the Soviet military administration or into the SED, however, or whether such disputes actually influenced policy in Soviet-occupied Germany, remains mostly a matter of speculation.

Then there was the issue of antisemitism. What took place in the Soviet Union beginning in late 1948 and in 1949 classified as a pogrom; and the SMAD, many of whose officers were Jewish themselves, had the job of coordinating local discussions of "cosmopolitanism" without allowing its anti-Semitic component to confuse the issue of the SED's hostility toward American imperialism. The elimination of so-called cosmopolitans in Soviet intellectual life, however, quickly became an important part of a wave of Stalinist terror that probably rivaled the worst of the thirties, except that it so often focused on Jews; and in this respect, it surpassed anything preceding it. Nor did the "Zhdanovshchina" from 1946 through early 1948 come close to comparing; many of the terms of abuse used during the terror of the "Black

[78]See Hahn, *Postwar Soviet Politics. The Fall of Zhdanov and the Defeat of Moderation 1946-1953.*

Years," beginning in late 1948 and ending in 1953, may have been developed during the earlier years of the Zhdanovshchina, but the central-committee edicts, along with Zhdanov's commentaries, did not function originally as the public justification for bloodshed. The abuse remained mostly verbal; and apart from ominous exceptions,[79] it was not anti-Semitic. But the events prefigured by the murder of the actor Shlomo Mikhoels in January 1948 were altogether different. The "physical assaults against Jewish culture and Jewish lives," which reached a crescendo in 1948 and 1949,[80] and broke out again in the early fifties, began in earnest with the final destruction of the Jewish Antifascist Committee in late 1948; continued with the eradication of Jewish and Yiddish theaters in Moscow and throughout the Soviet Union, the abolition of Jewish and Yiddish publishing houses, schools, newspapers, and libraries; proceeded to the discovery of a Jewish "doctors' plot" against Stalin a few years later; and culminated shortly before his death in the preparation of plans to resettle Soviet Jews in remote regions of the country. These facts hint at the scale of a tragedy that coincided with the SED's linkage of friendship with the Soviet Union to the "national fate" of Germany. Moreover, the Black Years, the eradication of organized Jewish culture in the Soviet Union and another round of mass murder, was now the second major period of Soviet terror that, in one way or another, molded the thinking of German Communists who had spent time in the Soviet Union and corrupted the minds of the rest. This was not an entirely novel development to many Communists in top positions of leadership; they had already experienced something like it before. But assuming that some of them grasped the inherent senselessness of what had happened during the thirties, and that their ambitions after 1945 did not include sponsoring anything quite like it in Germany, then many must have labored under the illusion that a new Germany could be built upon the basic principles of Marxism-Leninism, be inextricably linked to the Soviet Union, bow down to Stalin, and never engage in patterns of repression even remotely comparable with their experience in Soviet exile.

Besides, many who had watched it unfold likely persuaded themselves after 1945 that the terror of the thirties would not be repeated; at least not in Germany; and after the war, those Communists who, as J. R. Becher said, "spent thirteen years sitting on a suitcase waiting for them to pick you up,"[81] tried to put the experience out of their mind. The challenge of rebuilding, along with the enthusiasm generated when things went their way, helped them repress bad memories until their own party turned on some of them in the fifties. Many of the old reflexes, fear and cowardice among them, then

[79]See Levin, *The Jews in the Soviet Union since 1917*, vol. 1, pp. 468-69.
[80]Ibid., p. 500 and passim.
[81]According to what Becher told Gustav Just in 1956, following the arrest of Wolfgang Harich and in response to Just's entreaties that Becher protest. Just told the story to me in 1984.

returned. Prior to that, however, few of the Germans who survived Soviet exile had much to say about their experiences privately, and nothing publicly, to Communists who stayed behind or returned to Germany from Western exile. But those Communists who may have clung to the notion that they could build upon what they regarded as the ideals inherent in the Soviet experience and somehow remain immune to the ugly side of the reality either ought to have had second thoughts by 1949; or they honestly could not bring themselves to understand that certain doctrinal tenets had often produced terror as part of the pursuit of noble ends; and that if these tenets once again encouraged violence in the Soviet Union, a similar situation might well emerge in connection with the prevalence of related language elsewhere. As it happened, the signs of trouble developing in the Soviet Union, most of them reflected in the rhetoric, were either noticed and ignored or recognized for their similarity with earlier public campaigns associated with waves of terror and endorsed anyway. The Soviet campaign against cosmopolitanism was thus closely related to developments in Soviet-occupied Germany; and this remains true even if leading Communists there did not always have detailed information available to them. The occupation officers definitely knew what was going on at home and likely steered discussions now much like they had managed earlier commentary dealing with the sensitive subject of the central-committee edicts on art and literature. What emerged under these conditions mostly fit the description, then, of broad assessments of international developments useful in justifying the SED's hostility toward the West, rather than anticosmopolitanism in its Soviet domestic manifestations. This was easy enough to accomplish; in the Soviet Union, offenses such as "kowtowing to the West" were not originally anti-Jewish; they grew out of ideological determinations based on two-camps thinking that only later, in early 1949, acquired anti-Semitic overtones; and even then the arguments could be scaled back to generalities that tended to hide the anti-Semitic inferences drawn only when appropriate to Soviet domestic considerations. Elsewhere, anticosmopolitanism manifested itself mostly as antiamericanism.

This more than sufficed to affect the political, intellectual, and cultural climate in Soviet-occupied Germany for years to come, though reflections of Soviet foreign and domestic affairs were not always immediately recognizable as such and the anti-Jewish angles absent in the German Democratic Republic until the Slánsky trial in Czechoslovakia in late 1952. It was still disturbing, though, when Wolfgang Harich wrote that "the struggle of the German people against American imperialism and its German lackeys, the fight for the establishment and constant strengthening of the national front of all patriotic Germans, the struggle against the high treason of homeless cosmopolitans are the only means of saving Germany from ruin."[82] For in its

[82]Harich, "'Abend' oder nationale Souveränität? Der Kosmopolitanismus—eine tödliche Gefahr

Soviet context, the phrase "homeless cosmopolitans" had been from the beginning the prime euphemism for all Jewish intellectuals attacked for "unpatriotic" attitudes. In its Soviet context, Harich's comments could have been taken to mean that German "patriots" should defend their country against foreign and domestic Jews. It is inconceivable that Harich understood the implications of his remarks at the time and not hard to believe that he, like others, saw the concept as a way of reconciling "left-wing nationalism" with what he looked back upon much later as his "Russophilia."[83] Cosmopolitanism, "homeless" or otherwise, just meant different things in different contexts; as part of two-camps rhetoric in 1949, cosmopolitanism was identical with American imperialism around the world and with the betrayal of Germany's national interests by local "quislings," ready to sell out "our people" to foreign monopoly capital.[84] Nor is it safe to assume that Fritz Erpenbeck knew exactly what he was saying when he mentioned the Academic Jewish Theater in Moscow in order to explain that Soviet art was not Russian, White Russian, Ukrainian, Georgian, Tatar, Usbek, Jewish, Gypsy, Latvian, or Azerbaidzhan, but socialist realist. By the time Erpenbeck uttered those remarks in August 1949, the Tatars were only one of several national minorities expelled from their homeland; and there were few Jewish theaters remaining with doors still open.[85] After months of terror, the Moscow Jewish State Theater was shut down sometime after November 1949, its director Mikhoels having been murdered two years earlier. Erpenbeck had simply wanted to say that the Soviet stage was the "most highly developed in the world," the Jewish stage included; and that Germans in Soviet-occupied Germany should be grateful recipients of the experience so willingly passed on to them by Soviet artists.[86] That experience did not extend to producers like Tairov and Meyerhold, however; Erpenbeck spoke disapprovingly of their "mechanically experimental failures" (he preferred Stanislavskij), even though he must have known that Tairov's theater was closed by the authorities in the thirties and Meyerhold murdered.

Still, when the subject of "cosmopolitanism" came up in Soviet-occupied Germany in spring 1949, the concept generally illustrated the SED's defense of German unity against the threat of American imperialism in its ostensibly cosmopolitan manifestations. In a private conversation with Pieck on 10 June 1949, Semjonov defined cosmopolitanism, the source of "the danger," in terms of its desire to "eliminate" other nations and the "national arrogance" of its own concern with the "repression of other peoples." True na-

---

für das deutsche Volk," *Neue Welt* 11 (1949): 68.

[83]This is Harich's explanation to me in 1991.

[84]"Tag der Geburt der Deutschen Demokratischen Republik," *Neues Deutschland*, 7 October 1949.

[85]See Levin, *The Jews in the Soviet Union since 1917*, p. 504.

[86]Erpenbeck, "Freundschaft," *Theater der Zeit* 8 (1949): 1-3.

tionalism, he added, was the new way.[87] The threat of cosmopolitanism served additionally as a contrast to the putative benefits of true international-ism and, accordingly, eliminated any possible ambiguity in theories based on two-camps dichotomies. The Ways were then found to brand American imperial-ists as "worthy successors of the German fascists" and arguments developed that depicted the Soviet Union, by comparison, as "a citadel of the culture of progress, a citadel of civilization."[88] The propositions inherent to "proletari-an internationalism" versus "homeless cosmopolitanism," or "bourgeois na-tionalism," prospered in Soviet-occupied Germany well within the realm of such generalities. At its conference in January 1949, the SED said that the party's "basic political task" called for strengthening the antifascist-demo-cratic order as the "basis for the struggle to reestablish German unity on a democratic foundation and to develop Germany in the direction of a progres-sive societal order."[89] This was the "national" side of the party's official re-solution; dictatorship, the ultimate outcome of all such developments, was missing, and the word itself gave way to a string of euphemisms in the SED's listing of characteristics otherwise associated with the party of a new type.[90] But the international side of the resolution avoided the subject of dictatorship, too; a Marxist-Leninist party was informed with the "spirit of internationalism," and this internationalism determined the party's place in the global struggle between "war mongers and the forces of peace." In this struggle, the document continued, the Marxist-Leninist party stood solidly in the camp of democracy and peace, on the side of the popular democracies and the revolutionary working-class parties of the entire world. The SED thus acknowledged the "leading role" of the Soviet Union and its Commu-nist party in the battle against imperialism.[91]

There was no talk here of patterning Germany after any of the "forms" of dictatorship characteristic of the popular democracies or the USSR. To the contrary; Grotewohl explained that an "absolutely positive attitude toward the Soviet Union" was the decisive prerequisite to successful *democratiza-tion* of the Soviet zone and played a critical role in Germany's road to a de-mocratic order and to national unity.[92] These considerations explained how the party's spirit of internationalism transformed it into such an inveterate

[87]Besprechung am 10. 6. 1949 mit Semjonow. Zentrales Parteiarchiv, NL 36 /735/106-7. The ar-chive dates this conversation, almost certainly mistakenly, 10 June 1948.
[88]"Gegen Nationalismus—für proletarischen Internationalismus," *Neues Deutschland*, 28 May 1949; Pavlov, "Kosmopolitismus—eine ideologische Waffe der amerikanischen Reaktion," *Neue Welt* 7 (1949): 34.
[89]"Entschließung der Ersten Parteikonferenz: Die nächsten Aufgaben der Sozialistischen Ein-heitspartei Deutschlands," *Protokoll der Ersten Parteikonferenz*, p. 524.
[90]Ibid., pp. 524-31.
[91]Ibid., p. 528.
[92]Grotewohl, "Die Politik der Partei und die Entwicklung der SED zur einer Partei neuen Ty-pus," ibid., pp. 332-33.

enemy of nationalism,[93] even as other personalities, like Pieck, talked of the importance of stressing the "national character" of the party's policies. The SED was the only party that worked toward Germany's "national deliverance," Pieck said, but this commitment had nothing to do with the nationalistic policies of war mongers; and the party's advocacy of understanding with other peoples, "especially with the Soviet Union," made the difference apparent. Besides, given the strength of the Soviet commitment to peace, the German people could count themselves lucky that they had their "best friend in the Soviet government, with Comrade Stalin at the top."[94] The "spirit of internationalism" was thus discussed from every imaginable angle with the exception of any specific linkage to a dictatorship infused with the life of the same spirit; and in the final analysis, the subject of cosmopolitanism versus internationalism came down to two-camps banalities. Attempting to eliminate all national obstacles in the way of worldwide expansion, American monopolists relied upon the ideology of cosmopolitanism—the "obverse" of bourgeois nationalism. Deathly afraid of socialism, the imperialists hoped to use cosmopolitanism to undermine "sacred feelings of patriotism" and weaken the will of the people in their fight for freedom and independence. Thus it was that both nationalism and cosmopolitanism were used to sap the energy of the "camp of socialism." In the popular democratic countries, nationalists gave themselves away by taking a hostile attitude toward the Soviet Union (Tito was the classic example); whereas the USSR alone assured these countries of both their national existence and the victory of socialism. Their attitude toward the Soviet Union, the "litmus test of real proletarian internationalism," was the mark that distinguished all Communists and patriots.[95]

The additional articles devoted to cosmopolitanism contributed little to the substance of the argument. Some concentrated upon cosmopolitanism as the ideological underpinning to the American drive for world domination and the means by which the European continent would be colonized (cosmopolitanism preached a "repugnant fawning over the United States");[96] others focused more upon the antidote—the proletarian internationalism of the Soviet Union and its ideological wellspring. The very notion of cosmopolitanism was alien to Marxism-Leninism, read one, because the proletariat knew no "national nihilism"; workers were as concerned with the fate of other peoples as with the destiny of their own fatherland, and this attitude explained why Communists, internationalists, were genuine patriots.[97] Socialism

[93]See ibid., p. 385.
[94]These remarks are Pieck's ("Lehren der Parteikonferenz," *Einheit* 3 [1949]: 195-97).
[95]"Gegen Nationalismus—für proletarischen Internationalismus," *Neues Deutschland*, 28 May 1949.
[96]Pavlov, "Kosmopolitismus—eine ideologische Waffe der amerikanischen Reaktion," *Neue Welt* 7 (1949): 31-32.
[97]Titarenko, "Kosmopolitismus als Waffe der imperialistischen Reaktion," *Neues Deutschland*, 25 March 1949.

alone realized the complete national liberation of all peoples; and the Soviet Union proved it, having allowed the various minorities suppressed under czarism to develop along their own national lines. Nor did the Soviet Union ever pursue a policy of national repression on an international scale. The Soviet Union, the guardian of the freedom of all people, stood ready to assist those threatened by "imperialist repression."[98] The proletarian internationalism practiced by the Soviet Union was especially noteworthy in the case of Germany, considering the horrors of the war just waged against the USSR; for in spite of it, the Soviet Union supported the German people in their struggle for national unity, national independence, and a just peace.[99] Precisely because the Soviet Union guarded the "national interests of *all* people," the true test of a genuinely democratic outlook, "for internationalism *and* patriotism," came down to one's attitude toward the Soviet Union.[100]

Most of these commentaries discussed the political importance of battling cosmopolitanism in just such general East-West terms. Though few made specific references to events within the Soviet Union itself, two articles published by the SED's monthly *Einheit* in fall 1949 chose to focus on the "ideological offensive" in the Soviet Union, relate it to international developments, and tailor certain conclusions to the situation in Germany. The "ideological offensive," Ernst Hoffmann explained, was part of the construction of Communist societies under conditions of intensified class warfare brought about by an international shift in favor of the forces of progress. After hinting at the notion that the class enemy never surrendered without a fight, Hoffmann then explained that international reaction, led by American imperialism, fully intended to recover its lost positions by starting a third world war; and as part of their actions the imperialists employed the weapon of "ideological subversion" to destroy proletarian positions from within. "Thousands of canals," he said, were used to pump the products of decadent bourgeois ideology into the minds of the masses; and meeting this challenge required a higher level of class consciousness, greater ideological maturity within different working-class parties, as well as the mastery of Marxism-Leninism by each party's leadership—however unique the "concrete historical challenges" faced in various countries. These parties, everywhere, needed to redouble their resolve to "travel the road of the Bolsheviki."[101]

The Soviet Union figured in because the "party of Stalin" had been the first to spot the threat and begin an ideological offensive against its own internal subversion occurring over a range of scientific and artistic activity.

---

[98]Korb, "Was ist Kosmopolitismus?" *Neues Deutschland*, 13 April 1949
[99]Hoffmann, "Die Stellung des Marxismus zum bürgerlichen Kosmopolitismus," *Einheit* 7 (1949): 608.
[100]Harich, "Kosmopolitismus und Internationalismus," *Tägliche Rundschau*, 1 April 1949.
[101]Hoffmann, "Über die internationale Bedeutung der ideologischen Offensive in der Sowjetunion," *Einheit* 8 (1949): 680-82.

The party resolutions designed to deal with such subversion, carried out by "bourgeois cosmopolitans" who smuggled their ideology into the Soviet Union as a way of weakening patriotism and undermining national culture, were all geared toward eliminating the "vestiges of capitalism in the consciousness of the people." In support of this point, Hoffmann quoted an appropriate selection from Stalin's remarks to the party congress in 1934. Stalin had also spoken of backward "vestiges" in the consciousness of the Soviet people, explaining that consciousness lagged behind economic progress; and from outside the USSR, the encircling capitalist countries took advantage of regressive residues in people's outlooks and attitudes.[102] Hoffmann then used the idea of hostile encirclement to apply assumptions associated with the "ideological offensive" in the Soviet Union to other countries in Eastern Europe; and throughout the "antiimperialist democratic camp" and in Soviet-occupied Germany, this thinking deepened the obsession with local and infiltrated enemies. The politburo had already passed a resolution that called for an "ideological dispute" with Trotskyism based on Stalin's letter to *Proletarian Revolution* back in 1931, which illegalized any view of Trotskyism that took its Marxist pretensions seriously.[103]

The show trials of American-Titoist agents set to begin in Hungary and Bulgaria, principally Rajk and Kostov, with repercussions in Czechoslovakia and the German Democratic Republic, as well as the hunt for agents and saboteurs, all had their roots in this "ideological offensive." But in Soviet-occupied Germany, related discussions also had a bearing on the subject of national unity. The notion of capitalist encirclement, raised by Hoffmann, along with the feeling that wrong ideas still polluted the minds of the masses, produced unimaginable hostility toward West Germany as the principal external threat; and politically and culturally, the same notion led to the complete isolation of Soviet-occupied Germany and the German Democratic Republic as the only means of shielding it from Western influences. One of the worst practices was the development of an internal Soviet-zone mistrust of party and state personnel with ties, past or present, to the West. A secret "Soviet order no. 2" was issued in January 1949 that called for the elimination of persons with Western connections of any kind, including imprisonment after the war as POW's, from party positions, administrative agencies, and mass organizations; the services of such persons were too likely to be solicited, or had already been, by enemy agents.[104] The police force was screened and purged, as were employees who worked for the DWK and the Interior Administration.[105] Antifascists who fled to the West during the Hit-

---

[102]Ibid., pp. 683, 686, and 688.
[103]Protokoll Nr. 35 der Sitzung des Politbüros am 26. Juli 1949; Anlage Nr. 3. Beschluß des Kleinen Sekretariats vom 23. Juli 1949. Zentrales Parteiarchiv, IV 2/2/35/1 and 15.
[104]See Stern, *Porträt einer bolschewistischen Partei*, p. 118.
[105]See Betr.: Angestellte der DWK, der Innenministerien und der Polizei, die in den Jahren 1947

ler years suffered as well, leading Communists among them, and repercussions lasted well into the fifties. But the discrimination started sooner; in summer 1948, Wilhelm Koenen, who had fled to England, demanded an end to the treatment of people as "second-class comrades just because of the misfortune of their having been in English or American emigration, rather than Soviet."[106] Following a politburo resolution that focused on the effectiveness of the society for the study of Soviet culture,[107] the organization was found suffering from serious deficiencies. "Antidemocratic agents" had snuck into the society;[108] and this finding was followed by an investigation of its leadership carried out by the party's new central control commission or ZPKK. That agency acted on reports that top officials in the society were bent upon accepting as members the largest possible number of "comrades who were in Western emigration" and rejecting those who had been in the Soviet Union. The ZPKK made several recommendations designed to remedy the society's "ideological and organizational weaknesses."[109]

These events, roughly parallel, should be kept in mind when examining the implications of Hoffmann's two articles. In his second, he had more to say about the relationship of the ideological offensive in the Soviet Union to the struggle for German unity. The Anglo-American imperialists were especially concerned, he said, with destroying the national existence of the German people; apart from the degradation of the local economy, they "force imported state and cultural institutions on West Germany and drown Germany's progressive national culture in a mudslide of American pseudoculture." Indeed, a gigantic apparatus had been mobilized for the purpose of poisoning the minds of the German people, Hoffmann continued, charging that the apparatus enjoyed the unequivocal support of the "colonial occupation regime." West Germany and West Berlin had been transformed into a training field for Anglo-American cosmopolitans and their German agents valuable for testing methods of eradicating the national singularity of a people by degrading them into "foreign legionnaires of Wall-Street millionaires."[110] Hoffmann's denunciation of the threat to Germany's "national

---

und 1948 aus Kriegsgefangenschaft westlicher Gewahrsamstaaten entlassen wurden. 7 January 1949; and Entlassungen nach Befehl II/49 in den VP-Ämtern 1-8 [undated; late 1949]. Bundesarchiv, Abt. Potsdam, O-1/7/47 and 151.

[106]Koenen complained that two of his nominees for positions on the party's "control commission" in Saxony, men named Scharze and Lang, had been rejected by the central control commission, apparently for that reason. See Betr.: LKK Sachsen. 30 August 1948, ibid., 0-1/38/27.

[107]Protokoll Nr. 7 der Sitzung des Politbüros am 1. März 1949; Anlage Nr. 1. Betrifft: Gesellschaft zum Studium der Sowjetkultur. Zentrales Parteiarchiv, IV 2/2/7.

[108]Stefan Heymann an das Kleine Sekretariat, 29 March 1949, ibid., NL 182/931/61-3.

[109]See Gen. Ulbricht zur Kenntnis. Betr.: Gesellschaft zum Studium der Kultur der Sowjetunion. Zonenleitung Berlin, 10 July 1949; Betr.: Gesellschaft zum Studium der Kultur der Sowjetunion, ibid., NL 182/931/102-4.

[110]Hoffmann, "Die Bedeutung der ideologischen Offensive in der Sowjetunion für Deutsch-

existence" mounted by foreign cosmopolitans and their local German agents then led to a plea for the reestablishment of German unity that rationalized a Soviet-zone form of entrenchment comparable to the Soviet intellectual and cultural isolationism of these years. Both countries, having sealed themselves off from the Western world, had their intellectuals develop xenophobic and chauvinist arguments in support of their own seclusion. Within the context of debates over German unity, Hoffmann's talk of the threat of "imperialist ideological subversion" produced an argument favoring just such seclusion; it came in the form of unity under the precise political, economic, and cultural conditions that existed in Soviet-occupied Germany and thus, given the times, none at all. As Hoffmann put it, "our zone" served as the basis of the struggle for national unity and the defeat of the "imperialist ideological attack on the national existence of the German people." Shielded by the Soviet occupation regime, the antifascist-democratic order protected against dismemberment of the country and represented the most important precondition for preventing the "ideological demoralization of the German nation by agents of aggressive imperialism."[111]

Hoffmann then turned his attention toward the consciousness of Germans living in Soviet-occupied Germany; and what resulted was akin to Stalin's conclusion that class consciousness always lagged behind social progress. Hoffmann spoke of the "backward ideological condition of large segments of the population"; "the consciousness of the people," he said, "lags behind their new social existence." The same idea played a role in all discussions devoted to the SED's two-year plan, except that here Hoffmann developed the argument out of Stalin's remarks to the seventeenth party congress and discussed the problem within the context of Soviet unhappiness with the sedition of "unpatriotic" cosmopolitans. Unlike Harich, Hoffmann never characterized cosmopolitans as "homeless"; but he spoke of the need for a new German "patriotism," a higher level of national consciousness that represented the Soviet-zone antidote to "cosmopolitanism" and dovetailed with demands associated with the party's two-year plan to raise productivity by elevating the consciousness of the people. That underdeveloped consciousness, Hoffmann said, hindered both local reconstruction and the formation of a broad national people's movement for German unity; for the role of Soviet-occupied Germany in reestablishing national unity would increase dramatically as soon the "overwhelming majority of our workers, farmers, and intellectuals" had been infused with the spirit of reconstruction. Therein lay the inexhaustible source of the "new patriotism" and love of working people for their "true fatherland"; such patriotism rendered "Wall-Street's cosmopolitan-nationalist poison" harmless. Hoffmann finished by charging

---

land," *Einheit* 9 (1949): 793-94.
[111]Ibid., pp. 796-97.

that the party had done far too little to "popularize and exploit the ideological offensive in the Soviet Union." There it had already reigned devastating blows upon "the enemies"; and if the SED followed this example, it would doubtless succeed in Germany as well at inflicting heavy blows upon the "Anglo-American war-mongers and purveyors of poison."[112]

Hoffmann's final paragraph was one of those comments with such terrible implications had they been taken in the vein of Soviet domestic politics. Not that these utterances were intended to further the purpose served in the Soviet Union, but "cosmopolitanism" then comes across, like so many other party slogans, as little more than a demagogic expedient; these ideas meant whatever they needed to mean in any specific context; and in 1949 they focused on American imperialism and the prevalence of its "agents" throughout Eastern Europe. Antiamericanism and antisemitism coincided later, for instance, in the SED's first resolution on the subject of Rudolf Slánsky in late 1952 and its many hints of connections between Jewish and American capital.[113] But by then, Soviet hostility to the state of Israel probably explained much of it. The antisemitism of the Soviet leadership, while present in other Eastern-European parties, was not endemic to the SED despite the fact that the party's Slánsky resolution concocted links between top German Communists in Mexican exile and Zionist agents of American imperialism. The journal *Freies Deutschland*, which in summer 1942 published an appeal to "Jews around the world" signed by fifty Soviet Jewish intellectuals associated with the Jewish Antifascist Committee (most of whom perished after 1948),[114] had supposedly begun "defending the interests of Zionist monopoly capitalists" soon after Paul Merker joined the group of émigrés in Mexico.[115] In the trial itself, in late 1952, eleven of the defendants executed were Jewish, including Slánsky and André Simone, whose ties with German Communists in Mexico and elsewhere had been legion.

Indeed, though these events happened a few years later, the Slánsky show trial and the SED's arrest of its own designated "Slánsky," the non-Jew Merker, who was first "implicated" in the Hungarian trial of László Rajk, make far less sense outside the context of the campaign against cos-

[112]Ibid., pp. 797-99.
[113]See "Lehren aus dem Prozeß gegen das Verschwörerzentrum Slansky [20 December 1952]" and "Über die Auswertung des Beschlusses des Zentralkomitees zu den 'Lehren aus dem Prozeß gegen das Verschwörerzentrum Slansky' [14 May 1953]," *Dokumente der Sozialistischen Einheitspartei Deutschlands*, vol. IV, pp. 199-219 and 394-409. These resolutions, and actions taken by the SED, followed up on the party's investigation of members said to have had dealings with Noel Field; Field had been "implicated" during the Hungarian trial of László Rajk in late 1949. See "Erklärung des Zentralkomitees und der Zentralen Parteikommission zu den Verbindungen ehemaliger deutscher politischer Emigranten zu dem Leiter des Unitarian Service Committee Noel H. Field," *Dokumente der Sozialistischen Einheitspartei Deutschlands* [24 August 1950], vol. III, pp. 197-213.
[114]"An die Juden der ganzen Welt!" *Freies Deutschland* 8 (1942): 1-2.
[115]"Lehren aus dem Prozeß gegen das Verschwörerzentrum Slansky," p. 205.

mopolitanism launched in early 1949; and in the German Democratic Republic, that campaign continued well into the fifties with its predominant inner-party consequences coming in the form of a rift between Communists who had fled to the West after 1933 and those who found a haven, of sorts, in the Soviet Union. Jürgen Kuczynski was "brutally" relieved of his post as president of the society for the study of Soviet culture when "representatives of the Soviet occupation regime" requested it.[116] Kuczynski was Jewish and had returned from British exile. Gerhard Eisler, who ran the Amt für Information formed out of the DVV's division of cultural enlightenment, probably lost his job for similar reasons, though the Amt itself was dissolved altogether before being replaced by a new government press office. Eisler also figured as one of the leading candidates in plans for an East German show trial.[117] Later, following his return from Soviet exile, Alfred Kurella berated Wieland Herzfelde for having fled to the West; Herzfelde and his brother John Heartfield were both kicked out of the party, and Herzfelde feared "arrest and execution" at any time."[118] These were also the years when German-Czech writers like F. C. Weiskopf and Louis Fürnberg burned their diaries for fear that their associations with André Simone might cost them their lives.[119] Still later, Merker, sentenced to eight years in prison following the Slánsky trial and half-heartedly rehabilitated after Stalin's death, made a cameo appearance in the show trial of Walter Janka in 1957 as a witness against a "group" that had supposedly groomed Merker as a "German Gomulka" able to replace the "Stalinist" Ulbricht. Though no effort was made to locate the source of Janka's alleged offenses in associations with Merker dating back to their years in Mexican exile, and there were no specifically anti-Semitic elements to the trial, at the very least Merker was useful for establishing a sense of guilt by association.[120] It was also ironic that Harich, who had written so copiously on the subject of cosmopolitanism in 1949 and later played the role of star witness against both Janka and himself, became one of its last victims when he was sentenced in 1957 to ten years in prison.

In one way or another, these events all evolved out of the Soviet "ideological offensive" that began in early 1949. By fall, the party press was full

---

[116]Kuczynski, *Dialog mit meinem Urenkel*, pp. 51-52.

[117]Hermann Axen to Otto Grotewohl. Betr.: Auflösung des Amtes für Information. 23. 12. 52. Zentrales Parteiarchiv, NL 90/296/209. See Weber, "Schauprozeß-Vorbereitungen in der DDR," Semjonov had complained to Pieck in the context of the Rajk trial about the possible existence of "agents in the apparatus, under Eisler, people from the Western powers," as early as 24 December 1949; and in connection with the trial of Slánsky, the politburo concluded on 25 November 1952, just one month before the dissolution of the Amt für Information, that Eisler had had "connections."

[118]According to what Herzfelde told me in 1979.

[119]See Uhse, *Reise- und Tagebücher*, vol. II, pp. 242-43.

[120]According to what he told Janka, however (and Janka told me), Merker was regularly abused while still in prison as the "king of the Jews."

of calls for greater "revolutionary vigilance." Hans Teubner, whose own "links" to Noel Field were soon discovered, ranted about Trotskyist agents and right-wing socialist leaders; and Hanna Wolf raved about "ideological" vigilance; "enemies of the German people, of German unity and peace, USA imperialism and its agents in the ranks of the Schumacher SPD," were determined to subvert the SED through the use of espionage, rumor-mongering, sabotage, anti-Soviet crusades and such.[121] The least of the lessons to be learned by the SED in connection with the trial of László Rajk, said Kurt Hager, was that "the American imperialists and their swarm of German lackeys, from the Bonn government of marionettes to the SPD's Ostbüro," would do everything in their power to prevent the consolidation of the German Democratic Republic and to hamper the struggle for a unified Germany.[122] Matters only worsened as the year ended with revelations that the Yugoslav Communist party had degenerated into an "antidemocratic regime of a fascist type.[123] By the end of September, Rajk and others, having confessed to acts of espionage and subversion in their own country, but directed by the "Tito clique,"[124] were executed. Another trial, with similar disclosures about the activities of "Anglo-American imperialists and their agent Tito," and with an identical outcome, followed in Bulgaria.[125] The repercussions in Soviet-occupied Germany were felt immediately. For instance, during a conversation between Pieck, Ulbricht, Dahlem, and the West German Communist Max Reimann, "doubts" were voiced by the three Russians present about Kurt Müller, Reimann's deputy, and, going back to 1934, about Müller's wife. The NKDV had arrested Wilhelmina Müller in 1936 in Moscow; when she tried to defend herself under interrogation by explaining that her husband had been imprisoned and tortured beyond recognition by the Gestapo in 1934, her interrogator responded that his treatment in Nazi Germany had been staged "for the sake of appearance."[126] Now, in November 1949, the Russians spoke of "connections with Trotskyist groups," with "terrorist tendencies" directed at the central committee, either his or hers, and demanded Müller's "removal" (his wife was still in a Soviet concentration camp, where she remained until after Stalin's death). Pieck wondered if Müller ought to be sent "to Moscow," but he was arrested instead during a

---

[121]Teubner, "Wachsamkeit und politische Weitsicht," *Einheit* 7 (1949): 597; Wolf, "Ideologische Wachsamkeit tut not!" *Neues Deutschland*, 7 August 1949.
[122]In *László Rajk und Komplicen vor dem Volksgericht*, p. 10.
[123]"Die KP Jugoslawiens in der Gewalt von Mördern und Spionen. Resolution des Informationsbüros der Kommunistischen und Arbeiterparteien. Die revolutionäre Wachsamkeit muß erhöht werden"; "Niederlage der Tito-Faschisten"; *Neues Deutschland*, 1 and 14 December 1949.
[124]See Eildermann, "Die Entartung der Tito-Clique," *Einheit* 11 (1949): 1013-14.
[125]"Die verbrecherischen Pläne der anglo-amerikanischen Imperialisten und ihres Agenten Tito gegen Bulgarien. Die Anklageschrift gegen den Verräter Kostoff und seine Komplicen," *Neues Deutschland*, 9 December 1949.
[126]From my conversations with Wilhelmina Slavutskaja in 1977 in Moscow.

visit to Berlin in March 1950. The names of Fritz Sperling, another West German Communist, and Leo Bauer, came up during the same conversation, and Pieck considered it wise at the time not to tell Sperling of the doubts that had arisen about Müller.[127] Bauer was arrested in August 1950, Sperling in February 1951. Müller and Bauer were freed from Soviet prison camps in 1956.

One Nation, One People, One State

These were the kinds of developments that took place during the months leading up to the establishment of the German Democratic Republic in October 1949; and still the party kept the idea of national unity at the center of its propaganda. But Stalin himself, working through men like Tjulpanov and Semjonov, provided for a new twist intended to revitalize the SED's commitment to a united Germany even as final steps were taken toward formation of the GDR. The latest stunt, proclamation of a "national front" at the third German people's congress in May 1949, was depicted as a political "compromise."[128] But this manifestation of an "awakening national consciousness among the German people" did nothing to stop the inevitable division of the country and was, in fact, intended to accompany it.[129] Tentative plans had already been made during the talks with Stalin in December 1948 to form a "prov.[isional] German government," "maybe" as early as February or March 1949, if the West had already set up one of its own;[130] and there is every reason to believe that the "national front," which party leaders said resulted from "Comrade Stalin's initiative,"[131] conformed with his notion of a "zig-zag road to socialism." The events surrounding its proclamation, however, were inseparable from the final maneuvering connected with the establishment of the new government. The subject of a "national front" came up, perhaps for the very first time, on 6 May 1949 during a conversation between Semjonov and Grotewohl. Semjonov was just back from "home (St.[alin])" and reported that Stalin considered it necessary to take a step "further" than the people's congress. A "national front for unity" apparently was his idea of such a step. Grotewohl then raised the matter when the presidium of the pre-parliamentary Volksrat, the executive body of the people's

---

[127]Besprechung mit Ulbricht, Dahlem, Reimann, Gregorian, Smirnow, Borissoglebski, 13 November 1949. Zentrales Parteiarchiv, NL 36 /656/240.
[128]"Die nationale Front des demokratischen Deutschland und die SED [4 October 1949]," *Dokumente der Sozialistischen Einheitspartei Deutschlands*, vol. II, p. 379.
[129]"An alle vaterlandsliebenden Deutschen," *Neues Deutschland*, 31 May 1949.
[130]W. Pieck: in der Sekretariatssitzung am 27. 12. 1948. Bericht über Besprechung am 18. 12. 1948, ibid., NL 36 /695/68.
[131]Zur Einleitung der Besprechung [with Stalin]. 19 September 1949, ibid., NL 36/695/109.

congress, met on the 9th; a top-level discussion between Grotewohl, Ulbricht, Sokolowskij, Chuikov, and Semjonov took place in the evening; and the third people's congress was set for 11 and 12 June. One day later, on the 10th, Pieck, on vacation in the Soviet Union, wrote Molotov to request an appointment for the purpose of discussing that meeting "in connection with formation of a Ger.[man] government." The idea then and later was to use the congress itself to set up a government or to have the Volksrat do it.[132] Molotov never responded. On 18 May, Grotewohl and Ulbricht met again with the Russians, this time with Chuikov, Koval, Semjonov, and Tjulpanov; agreement of some kind was reached about the national front; and the dates for the congress were moved up to 29 and 30 May, though the idea of a national front had not been placed on the agenda as of 19 May. On the 20th, then, came the "suggestion from home—(M[oscow])" to include "creation of a national front" on the program, and Semjonov delivered the news to party headquarters.[133]

In the meantime, on the 15th and 16th, the zonewide vote on a single list of delegates to the people's congress had been counted, based on a ballot that read, "I favor calling the 3rd German people's congress to fight for the unity of Germany and a just peace and vote, accordingly, for the following list of candidates." The names followed, along with a box to be checked "yes" or "no."[134] Fully one-third of the population voted "no," which only heightened the sense of urgency about the upcoming congress. In fact, the election outcome may help explain why so much attention was being paid to the national front. One of the ideas behind it, allowing former Nazis to vote in future elections and appealing to their patriotism, reflected a sense of the need to increase the party's base of support. But for a combination of reasons, the idea of a national front met with the opposition of the "bourgeois parties" present in the bloc of antifascist democratic parties and the Volksrat, who considered the people's congress "movement" to represent such a national front already. That opposition was overcome and the idea accepted.[135] Just days before it met, there had still been some expectation that the people's congress would actually pass a constitution and form a government with the Volksrat as the new parliament;[136] but late spring and early summer were used instead to work out the details of the party's own public attitude toward the national front. Several conversations took place in June and July between Pieck, Ulbricht, Oelßner, Semjonov, and Tjulpanov; and the subject

[132]Notizen zum Brief Wilhelm Piecks an Genossen Molotow sowie Disposition zur vorgesehenen Besprechung beim Genossen Molotow, ibid., NL 36 /695/81-85.
[133]Notizen zur National Front 1949, ibid., NL 36/695/86-92.
[134]See Protokoll Nr. 17 der Sitzung des Politbüros am 20. April 1949; Anlage Nr. 1. Stimmzettel, ibid., IV 2/2/17/2 and 8.
[135]Zur Einleitung der Besprechung [with Stalin], 19 September 1949, ibid., NL 36/695/109.
[136]See Angelegenheit Volkskongreß, ibid., NL 36/695/90.

of the discussions was the language and timing of the SED's own national-front manifesto.[137] On 21 July, the party board issued a curt statement; and an elaborate platform followed on 4 October, just a few days before formation of the German Democratic Republic.

The party's support of a national front could not be distinguished from its crusade against cosmopolitanism as the chief threat to a form of German nationalism that benefited from "proletarian internationalism." But by mid-1949, the gap between national rhetoric and local reality was unbridgeable; and considering that the SED had always used national unity as its reason for backing antifascist-democratic coalitions broader than Marxism-Leninism, the idea behind a program broader still made no sense. The suggestion that a party now sworn to "Leninism" had become a staunch advocate of a political program open to every German citizen, "democrat or not,"[138] taxed the imagination; and when looked at a bit more closely, the "national front" revealed a familiar pattern. The party feigned ideological and political moderation where none was present. First of all, the national front depended upon standard two-camps thinking; this was readily apparent in the SED's call for creation of a national front aligned against "American imperialism and in support of the incorporation of the German people into the antiimperialist camp, whose most powerful element is the Soviet Union."[139] Even so, the program also claimed that its focus on national unity and "reestablishment of the national independence of our German fatherland" opened the national front to all sorts of people with no prior endorsement of a "democratic or economic platform" such as those advanced by the people's congress and its elected Volksrat.[140]

The national front was thus intended to include elements to the right of the very coalition said to comprise earlier broad initiatives; and Ulbricht explained just how far to the right when he said that peace-loving people who supported German unity were not to be judged by their earlier membership in the Nazi party but by their opposition to a "forty-year occupation and colonization" of West Germany and its use as a staging ground for war. It was critically important for all democratic elements to realize that many Germans throughout the country desired a "peaceful development and German unity" without, as yet, being democrats.[141] Nonetheless, neither in theory nor in practice did any such characterization of the national front as "much broader" begin to alter the nature of political circumstances in Soviet-occupied

---

[137]Notizen zur Nationalen Front, ibid., NL 36/695/87.
[138]"Die Nationale Front des demokratischen Deutschland und die Sozialistische Einheitspartei Deutschlands," *Dokumente der Sozialistischen Einheitspartei Deutschlands*, vol. II, p. 351.
[139]"Schaffung der Nationalen Front des demokratischen Deutschland. Beschluß des Parteivorstandes [21 July 1949]," *Dokumente der Sozialistischen Einheitspartei Deutschlands*, p. 287.
[140]Ulbricht, *Warum Nationale Front? Rede auf der Parteiarbeiterkonferenz der SED Groß-Berlin am 17. Mai 1949*, p. 9.
[141]Ibid., pp. 5-6, 10-11.

Germany; it closed the opening "scissors" of development between both parts of the country no more than the narrower call to reinforce antifascism and democracy; and the SED made it equally clear that "nationalism" itself, which in party rhetoric rhymed with antisovietism, had no place in the minds of party members. The leading role of the Soviet Union in the battle for freedom and democracy needed to be as much a part of their fundamental outlook as an "intimate friendship with the comrades of the Soviet occupation force."[142]

In much the same vein, Ulbricht underscored the fact that formation of a national front by no means heralded the "renunciation of an antifascist-democratic order"; no German who desired German unity and peace would expect such a thing because antifascism and democracy formed the strongest pillar in support of those objectives. Besides, neither the party's adherence to basic principles of Marxism-Leninism nor its essential "internationalism," the party's "intimate ties to the Soviet Union," were in any way affected; and Ulbricht went on to warn of cosmopolitanism, the "ideology behind preparations for military aggression," as part of his argument in favor of a national front.[143] Other definitions followed, but most touched upon the same themes. A party resolution in July 1949 spoke of the need to give Germany's national defense against American and British imperialism a "broad mass character"; but the resolution also insisted that "consolidating previous progressive accomplishments" remained the focus of democratic objectives in the Soviet zone and also retained its importance for developments throughout all of Germany;[144] whereas Fred Oelßner explained why the SED decided to make "the national question the axis of our politics" by warning of the threat to the existence of the German nation posed by American imperialism. With that explanation, Oelßner yoked the proposition that class warfare was intensifying in Soviet-occupied Germany, and elsewhere, to what he and others still tried to pass off as a softening of the party's attitude toward other political viewpoints. The national movement had gone well beyond the parameters of an antifascist-democratic movement, he said; portions of the bourgeoisie, including "non-democrats," former Nazis and military men, opposed the colonization of West Germany. Under those circumstances, the SED had no right to refuse to cooperate with national elements just because of their objections to "antifascist democracy" or "our two-year plan." Participation in the national front was therefore not contingent upon the renunciation of anyone's political principles, but then neither did the SED dream of giving up its struggle to "reinforce the antifascist-democratic order and our ultimate

[142]"Über die Gefahr nationalistischer Abweichungen [5 May 1949]," *Dokumente der Sozialistischen Einheitspartei Deutschlands*, vol. II, p. 245.
[143]Ulbricht, *Warum Nationale Front?* pp. 9. 15, 17-18, 40.
[144]"Die nächsten Aufgaben der Partei [24 August 1949]," *Dokumente der Sozialistischen Einheitspartei Deutschlands*, vol. II, p. 294

objective, socialism."[145] Another statement used the party's indulgence toward all nationally minded Germans who had "German feelings" as the reason why none of them had any right to demand "of us that we dispense with the democratic order."[146]

Such was the nature of what the party considered its "compromise" for the sake of a national struggle.[147] As Anton Ackermann put it, rejecting the idea that the policy smacked of "tactics with a wink," the SED acquired the "necessary elasticity, combined with a commitment to principle and firm resolve," only by appropriating the full richness of Marxist-Leninist theory and benefiting from the experience of the Soviet Communist party.[148] With formation of the German Democratic Republic only days away, the party expressed its hope that the national front would serve as the basis for uniting "all German patriots" regardless of whether "this or that German considers himself a supporter of the democratic camp."[149] At about the same time, however, the SED also insisted that "enlightenment" on the subject of the Soviet Union would not be relaxed in the interest of such a national front and added that those who failed to "take an unqualified stand in support of the USSR ended up unavoidably in the camp of imperialist warmongers."[150] Just prior to formation of the German Democratic Republic, Stalin again beckoned party leaders to Moscow for final talks about formation of the government. They apparently stayed from 16 through 28 September and talked about a range of issues that included Stalin's reaction to the party's official position on the national front, that is, the document published on 4 October, and his "advice" on how to go about setting up "a provisional German government in the Soviet zone of occupation"—rapidly, over a period of six days, to avoid disruption from the West or by the "reactionary wing" of the local bourgeois parties.[151] Things then went according to plan. On 4 October 1949, the party released its statement on the national front, its provisions apparently having been approved by "Comrade Stalin"; and the day after formation of the government, the Volksrat published its own manifesto that called for "every conceivable form of cooperation among patriotic elements—workers, employees, scientists, artists, young people, nationally conscious entrepreneurs, every German women, every German man inde-

[145]Oelßner, "Nationale Front und SED," *Neuer Weg* 8 (August): 1-2.
[146]"Warum Nationale Front?" *Neuer Weg* 7 (1949): 10.
[147]"Die Nationale Front des demokratischen Deutschland und die SED," *Dokumente der Sozialistischen Einheitspartei Deutschlands*, vol. II, p. 379.
[148]Ackermann, "Das Bündnis aller patriotischen Kräfte," *Tägliche Rundschau*, 10 September 1949.
[149]"Die Nationale Front des demokratischen Deutschland und die SED," *Dokumente der Sozialistischen Einheitspartei Deutschlands*, vol. II, p. 369.
[150]"Sollten wir schweigen über die UdSSR?" *Neues Deutschland*, 25 September 1949.
[151]Zur Einleitung der Besprechung, 19 September 1949. Zentrales Parteiarchiv, NL 36/695/108-21.

pendent of party affiliation or political conviction.[152]

These last two endorsements of the national front, the latter just before the Volksrat became the provisional people's chamber or Volkskammer of the GDR, were designed to reinforce the sense of public identity between the German people, their nationality, and the new German state. The same idea went into the phrase contained in the party's statement, "one nation, one people, one state,"[153] though the SED presumably passed up the opportunity to add "one party" to it because any such hint of dictatorship right now conflicted with the national-front ambiance surrounding formation of the government; and that government was identical with the party anyway. But the SED hit upon another way of representing the new consensus that achieved much the same purpose. In fall 1949, it sponsored two torch-light processions, the first honoring Wilhelm Pieck, the new president of the republic, the second in celebration of Stalin's seventieth birthday.[154] Both flag-waving "mass demonstrations" had an air of spontaneity about them, and both were meant to reflect well upon the political maturity of the German people after thirteen years of fascism, though the party chose to make its point by resorting to a ritual used recently to appeal to political instincts of a much different kind. Whether the SED hoped to increase support for the new country by speaking a language familiar to Germans whose consciousness was still thought to "lag behind social progress"; or hoped to relive fond memories of Soviet exile by putting on corresponding demonstrations of the moral-political unity of the *German* people is hard to say. Personality cults were common to both political cultures, however, and Pieck's figured prominently. There was, after all, "no man more popular in Germany" than Pieck; and his presidency was said to derive from the fact that the German people had "risen up" after three years of provocation by foreign and domestic reaction bent upon preventing a "matured German people" from traveling the road to progress.[155] Though the rhetoric was not absolutely identical, the echoes of earlier descriptions of Pieck as the "leader" or *Führer* of the German people were clear; and the various references to "incorruptible Germans" served as a reminder that the "entire people" had once before taken to the streets to rejoice over the formation of the SED in 1946.

These events were reflections of the SED's turn away from disagreeable talk of past inadequacies and collective guilt; and toward the more welcome vision of the new national destiny that arose out of public contrition. In his

[152]"Die Nationale Front des demokratischen Deutschland," *Neues Deutschland*, 8 October 1949.
[153]"Die Nationale Front des demokratischen Deutschland und die SED," *Dokumente der Sozialistischen Einheitspartei Deutschlands*, vol. II, p. 367.
[154]See *Die ersten Jahre*, p. 273; and "Hunderttausende in der Stalinallee. Gewaltige Massendemonstrationen zu Stalins Geburtstag / Grundsteinlegung eines neuen Wohnblocks," *Neues Deutschland*, 22 December 1949.
[155]Herrnstadt, "Wilhelm Pieck, Präsident der Deutschen Demokratischen Republik," *Neues Deutschland*, 12 October 1949.

telegram of congratulations to "the German people" upon the creation of the republic, Stalin played upon just such feelings of national destiny when he said that the German and Soviet people, having made the "greatest sacrifices" during the last war, possessed the most potential in Europe for the "accomplishment of great acts of global significance."[156] Given such promises of national glory, it was only natural that political priorities for a new Germany crested in 1949 in the adulation of the other political personality who had made it possible. Lavish celebrations of Stalin's seventieth birthday on 21 December 1949 were the result.[157] Indeed, the party began preparing the festivities just weeks after the formation of the German Democratic Republic on 7 October; and both of these events, the emergence of a new Germany and the observance of Stalin's birthday, celebrated the rehabilitation of the German people that resulted from Stalin's special feelings of affection for them; evidenced in selfless acts of friendship going back more than thirty years, "no foreign statesman had discerned and defended the interests of the German people in the past and present like Generalissimus Stalin."[158] Just how justified his confidence had been all along was apparent when the German people displayed their political maturity in the expectation that the Volksrat, meeting on 7 October, would carry out the "will of the nation"; and that will called for the establishment of the German Democratic Republic.[159] In their support of the new democracy, the German people proved themselves and were given the chance to do so only because Stalin had refrained from retaliating against them after the war.[160] There was no better proof of the fact that Stalin was the "best friend of the German people";[161] and his solemn promise that the Hitlers came and went, but that Germans and the German nation remained, now soared to new heights of popularity. The phrase was woven into countless statements made in connection with the new nation, and Stephan Hermlin, altering the usual translation for the sake of a better rhyme, immortalized it in an epic poem.[162]

---

[156]"Telegramm des Vorsitzenden des Ministerrates der UdSSR, J. W. Stalin," *Neues Deutschland*, 14 October 1949

[157]See "Gruß und Glückwunsch J. W. Stalin—dem Genius der Epoche," *Dokumente der Sozialistischen Einheitspartei Deutschlands*, vol. II, pp. 403-6.

[158]Ibid., p. 404; "Die folgerichtige Deutschland-Politik der Sowjetregierung," *Neues Deutschland*, 12 October 1949.

[159]"Tag der Geburt der Deutschen Demokratischen Republik," *Neues Deutschland*, 7 October 1949.

[160]Abusch, *Stalin und die Schicksalsfragen der deutschen Nation*, p. 160; "Teurer Freund Josef Wissarioniwitsch," *Dokumente der Sozialistischen Einheitspartei Deutschlands*, vol. II, p. 408.

[161]See "Stalin—der beste Freund des deutschen Volkes," *Sozialistische Bildungshefte* 9 (1949). See also Wolf (Hanna), "Stalin—der beste Freund des deutschen Volkes"; Pieck, "Stalin—für das deutsche Volk"; Grotewohl, "Stalin, Freund und Helfer des deutschen Volkes"; Maron, "Der zuverläßigste Freund des deutschen Volkes"; *Neues Deutschland*, 15 and 21 December 1949.

[162]Hermlin, "Stalin," *Aufbau* 12 (1949): 1063-69. "Die Hitler kommen und gehen," he wrote,

On 10 October 1949, the Soviet zone of occupation ceased to exist when the SMAD transferred administrative functions to the new government; following the formation of the Federal Republic of Germany several weeks earlier, the division of Germany was complete, though the Soviet government hastened to add that this division could not last long "because such circumstances conflict with the deepest longings of the German people." For now, however, German "sovereignty" existed in the form of the German Democratic Republic and as a direct result of Stalin's confidence in the people.[163] Only rarely did such discussions revert to comments reminiscent of the theory of collective guilt or allude directly to "vestiges" of the past. In the government's response to Stalin's telegram of congratulations, Pieck and Grotewohl assured Stalin that his noble words had reminded the German people of their historical guilt and deepened their determination to fulfill the obligations that grew out of the Potsdam accords.[164] Alexander Abusch noted similarly that Stalin's telegram obliged the German people to "prove" their intention of traveling a new road;[165] and yet another statement expressed the hope that the German people would finally understand what "friendship with Stalin" really meant after so many mistakes paid for in blood. Friendship with Stalin meant friendship with the Soviet Union, but also with the European popular democratic republics and the entire camp of peace and progress; and in order to build up a "large, powerful, and peaceful Germany," Germans needed to be infused with the same kind of respect for other peoples taught by Stalin. Working hard toward this kind of Germany was one way of honoring Stalin himself.[166] It was entirely fitting, then, for "immense crowds" of Berliners to congregate in the Stalin-Allee, formerly Frankfurter Allee, to pour the foundation for a new complex of apartments; and to celebrate Stalin's birthday. The main speaker cheered Stalin repeatedly to the enthusiastic response of the crowd; and the event culminated when Berliners spotted the "person of the president," Pieck, while making their way past the tribunal. Young people unfurled flags, men tossed hats, and women waved. The evening was then capped by a "gigantic" display of fireworks that put a hammer and sickle up against the horizon together with a portrait of Stalin. Above his head, the number "70" lit up in flames, and so did the letters beneath it, wishing Stalin a "happy birthday from the workers of the world."[167]

"/Aber das deutsche Volk, der / Deutsche Staat bleibt *bestehen.*" My italics.

[163]"Die folgerichtige Deutschland-Politik der Sowjetregierung," *Neues Deutschland*, 12 October 1949.

[164]"Telegramm an J. W. Stalin," *Neues Deutschland*, 15 October 1949.

[165]Abusch, *Stalin und die Schicksalsfragen der deutschen Nation*, p. 159.

[166]"Freundschaft für immer mit Stalin," *Neues Deutschland*, 1 December 1949.

[167]"Hunderttausende in der Stalinallee," *Neues Deutschland*, 22 December 1949.

CHAPTER THIRTEEN

Privileges and Perquisites

Cultural politics in Soviet-occupied Germany consisted of a never-ending search for ways of using creative intellectuals to further the cause of one party's policies while fostering the impression of a consensus. Just as the Berlin blockade ended, for instance, an article in the *Tägliche Rundschau* blamed the interruption of a "cultural dialogue" on those in the West who had allowed an iron curtain to descend, persisted in characterizing the Kulturbund as a "nonpartisan organization" that offered the best platform for dialogue capable of bypassing all philosophical and other kinds of "border markers," and demanded that its prohibition in West Berlin be lifted.[1] Behind the scenes, however, the party itself had just set new guidelines for the organization. The underlying tasks of the Kulturbund were unchanged, these read, but they needed to be adapted to the "new conditions of the class struggle." The Kulturbund was now expected to stress the fight for cultural unity *and* the involvement of all intellectuals in reinforcing the "new democratic order in our zone." The party looked for the Kulturbund to emphasize that the battle against "ideological preparations for war" was now its top priority; that no intellectual could be considered progressive without a "positive attitude" toward the USSR; and that the two-year plan contributed to the development of a democratic culture. Kulturbund branches at the lowest level were criticized specifically for programs said to reflect "old bourgeois traditions." The organization's state and regional secretariats needed to bring them into conformity with the new guidelines and then exert better "control" over their implementation. Local party organizations were also advised to intervene and work to changing the branches from "bourgeois" outfits to "genuine militant organizations." Finally, "sectarian tendencies" in some of the branches had to be dealt with severely to avoid endangering the "alliance between workers and intellectuals"; whereas stronger "ideological control" over reactionary elements who persisted in voicing their "antidemocratic" ideas in public discussions was the higher priority in others.[2] Under the watchful eye of the party, then, which recommended an expanded emphasis

---

[1]Ltz., "Unterbrochenes Kulturgespräch," *Tägliche Rundschau*, 12 May 1949.
[2]Vorlage an das kleine Sekretariat. 19 April 1949. Zentrales Parteiarchiv, IV 2/906/140.

upon the "role of the Soviet Union as a bastion of peace," work on an up-dated statement of Kulturbund principles went forward, though it was not re-leased until the Kulturbund conference in November 1949.[3]

The SED and the Intellectuals

On New Year's Day, 1949, Wolfgang Harich issued another word of warn-ing about apoliticality; notions of "independence," "strict objectivity," the disdain for "ideology"—these attitudes masked the fact that intellectuals his-torically served the interests of despotism. Nowadays, the "masters" were billionaires out to exploit entire continents, financial magnates involved in every conflict on earth, and mammoth trusts with no scruples about sacrific-ing entire peoples and countries to higher profits. To disguise its intentions, imperialism resorted to "lies, misconceptions, delusions, illusions, and preju-dices" to corrupt the minds of the people; and writers of "bourgeois deca-dence," who fancied themselves free thinkers, were the source of the "ideo-logical opium" used to numb the awareness of the masses. But Soviet-zone intellectuals, Harich said, stood on the threshold of marvelous opportunities as part of Germany "moved relentlessly toward a socialist future"; because the "revolutionization of society" went hand in hand with a "revolutioniza-tion of the intellect," calls for an alliance between workers and intellectuals acquired a specific meaning. For the first time ever, the social dependence of the intelligentsia no longer hid behind an illusion of independence. Needless to say, Harich finished, the "masters of Wall Street" had other ideas; they preferred politically apathetic, individualistic, and pessimistic intellectuals who trembled in fear of communism. These same intellectuals could choose accordingly, between joining forces with the German working class in the construction of a new society or bowing to foreign reactionaries.[4]

Harich made no mention of the SED, but two other commentaries pub-lished just a few weeks before the party conference in late January, were more forthcoming about its intentions. Both articles, one by Otto Grotewohl, the other by Gottfried Grünberg, called attention to issues that had acquired considerable urgency since the introduction of the two-year plan the previ-ous summer and alluded to cultural-political initiatives about to be taken as part of the "antifascist-democratic" reinforcement of the Soviet zone.[5] These initiatives were all part of the cultural plan, now called internally "proposals for the implementation of cultural tasks in the context of the two-year plan,"

[3]Stefan Heymann to Alexander Abusch, 30 June 1949, ibid., IV 2/906/140/4; "Grundaufgaben des Kulturbundes," *Aufbau* 12 (1949): 1134-35.
[4]Harich, "Die Intelligenz am Scheideweg," *Tägliche Rundschau*, 1 January 1949.
[5]See Grotewohl, "Die SED und die Intellektuellen"; and Grünberg, "Partei und Intellektuelle. Diskussionsbeitrag zur Parteikonferenz," *Neues Deutschland*, 9 January 1949.

that entered its final stages of preparation after a top-level commission headed by Ackermann had been assigned the task of preparing a penultimate draft a few months earlier. The "plan" was ready just a few days before the opening of the conference on 25 January and a decision made to disseminate it informally there. Afterwards, it would go to the DWK for final action.[6] This is how it happened, too; but strangely enough, the subject of culture was scarcely mentioned at the conference itself. Pieck spoke of the struggle for peace and against war-mongering; and Grotewohl spent so much additional time explaining the difference between popular democracy and anti-fascist-democratic reinforcement, as well as discussing the nature of a "party of a new type," that little was left for more than a cursory mention of the cultural plan presented to conference delegates "for discussion." Nor did Ulbricht have much to say; he limited himself to an announcement that the SED had already asked the DWK to provide for higher salaries and better support for members of the "technical intelligentsia," engineers, technicians, professors, foremen, scientists, etc., and complained that too many workers and employees, party members included, remained biased against the technical intelligentsia.[7] Otherwise, Ulbricht passed over the SED's cultural "proposals," now called "measures," in silence, though the plan served as the basis for actions affecting both technical and creative intellectuals.

Judging by the published proceedings, there was no discussion of the plan either; nor were the "measures" introduced to the public right away, though practically every other word uttered at the conference appeared a day or so later in the newspapers. The party's cultural "measures," however, were not included in conference coverage by *Neues Deutschland*; and the *Tägliche Rundschau* found space for no more than a fleeting reference to "improvement in cultural work."[8] The strange thing was that both Grotewohl and Grünberg had mentioned the plan in their articles a few weeks earlier. But it may be that party leaders kept a lid on discussion during the conference itself in order to avoid a dispute caused by the presence of considerable opposition to the idea of special treatment for intellectuals. The conference resolution, for instance, called for a decisive struggle against the "pernicious sectarian attitudes toward intellectuals" that had penetrated the party's own ranks;[9] and those attitudes, criticized at least as far back as the party confer-

[6]Protokoll Nr. 119 (II) der Sitzung des Zentralsekretariats am 11. 10. 48. Zentrales Parteiarchiv, IV 2/2.1/239/3. Commission members included Wandel, Rudolf Engel ("Amt für Aufbau u. Aufklärung"), Stefan Heymann (PKE), Käthe Selbmann (representing the office of Walter Ulbricht), and Grete Witkowski (DWK). See also Protokoll Nr. 140 (II), 30 December 1948, Protokoll Nr. 142 (II), 10 January 1949, and Protokoll Nr. 44 (II), 17 January 1949, ibid., IV 2/2.1/258/2, 260/2, and 262/2.
[7]Ulbricht, "Die Erfahrungen auf dem Gebiet der Staats- und Wirtschaftspolitik und die Durchführung des Zweijahrplanes," *Protokoll der Ersten Parteikonferenz*, pp. 205-6.
[8]"Zu den Ereignissen der Parteikonferenz der SED," *Tägliche Rundschau*, 29 January 1949.
[9]"Entschließung der Ersten Parteikonferenz," *Protokoll der Ersten Parteikonferenz*, p. 522.

ence in September 1947, appear to have worsened. Grünberg referred to the problem in his article on 9 January; and, though Grotewohl failed to divulge his own thoughts on the subject the same day, saying nothing about it either at the conference a few weeks later, he still touched upon the cause of the problem. In fact, Grotewohl was among the first to reveal publicly that the party planned on taking steps to improve the "living conditions" of both older and younger Soviet-zone intellectuals, artists, writers, and theater people in order to further formation of a "new intelligentsia." The DWK, Grotewohl said, was contemplating the enactment of tax benefits for writers and artists, in addition to which the SED also backed creation of a "cultural fund" for use in stimulating the productivity of creative intellectuals; and the party's cultural plan itself, to be announced at the upcoming conference, would serve as the basis for further action by the DWK in support of intellectuals in Berlin and throughout the Soviet zone.[10]

As it was, three months elapsed from the date of Grotewohl's comments, two after the conference, before the DWK finally met on 31 March to pass what it chose to call an "ordinance governing the preservation and development of German science and culture, the further improvement in the condition of the intelligentsia, and the enhancement of its role in production and in public life."[11] The long delay raises questions, especially considering that most of the measures had been under private advisement by the Kulturbund, the DVV, the SED, and the SMAD for many months. Indeed, both the party's cultural plan and the DWK's ordinance, drawn up by the same people anyway, were comprised of measures that rounded out a variety of mostly unpublicized initiatives under consideration or actual development since late 1947 and the issuance of order 234. Each one of these fits into the accelerated program of Soviet-zone consolidation begun with the introduction of the party's two-year plan in June 1948; and they all bore upon other important decisions taken in 1949 in connection with the "antifascist-democratic" consolidation of Soviet-occupied Germany in a separate state. The reason why so many of the cultural policies born of order 234 had been kept partially or entirely secret was probably two-fold. First, these behind-the-scenes administrative initiatives pointed in almost every instance to conspicuous state or party or party-state management of culture. Together with the further hardening of "theoretical" standards for art and literature in 1949, public discussion of these initiatives would have made it clearer still that the SED had established both the norms and the forms of cultural regimentation in Soviet-occupied Germany; that such regimentation squared poorly with the party's insistence on Soviet-zone achievements as the only conceivable basis for na-

[10]Grotewohl, "Die SED und die Intellektuellen," *Neues Deutschland,* 9 January 1949.
[11]See *Der Kulturplan. Verordnung über die Erhaltung und die Entwicklung der deutschen Wissenschaft und Kultur, die weitere Verbesserung der Lage der Intelligenz und die Steigerung ihrer Rolle in der Produktion und im öffentlichen Leben.*

tional unity; and might actually have been thought capable of provoking the allies into a more powerful response to the Berlin blockade. The second reason for the secrecy could already be inferred from Grünberg's article. The SED could not resort to coercion as a means of making Soviet-zone intellectuals compliant, at least not in 1948 or 1949; and all indications are that pure persuasion had fallen woefully short of expectations. In connection with the flagging economy, the low productivity of Soviet-zone factories, and deteriorating morale, the SED had drawn two closely related conclusions. The two-year plan was considered unlikely to produce an "economic upswing," first, in the absence of full integration of the technical "intelligentsia" into the new economic structure; and, second, without a analogous integration of creative intellectuals whose personal authority, it was hoped, could help change the bad attitudes of working Germans toward Soviet-zone reconstruction.

The more that process accelerated, the more urgent the need to acquire the backing of all intellectuals—technicians, engineers, teachers, professors, biologists, agronomists, physicists, artists, writers, and so on. The solution to the problem of full integration, as well as the cause of so many objections to the proposed solution, was thus thought to reside in a system of special benefits. Not that Grünberg had spoken so bluntly; but the inferences are hard to overlook. He complained that cultural affairs had often been regarded within the party as a "fifth wagon wheel," adding that the SED tended to drift between declarations concerning the necessity of cultural work and periodic grumbling about the reactionary attitudes of intellectuals.[12] Grünberg then proceeded to draw an unflattering comparison between the attention paid Soviet-zone intellectuals by the SMAD and the disinterest characteristic, he said, of his own party. But this particular point almost surely had less to do with the facts than with the pressing need to make it clear that meeting what Grünberg called the "material needs" of the intellectuals followed an example set by the Russians. If for no other reason than this, the opposition simply had to cease. Like it or not, those who were discontent with the idea of favoritism toward intellectuals had to grasp the fact that they were obstructing *Soviet* occupation policy. Grünberg concluded his argument by charging that the party erred in "simply ignoring" progressive scientists, teachers, and artists; it should place such intellectuals in the forefront and provide them with much needed assistance.[13] This criticism reflected the realization that persuasion alone had failed to garner sufficient support for the two-year plan and the consolidation of the "antifascist-democratic order"; and that measures designed to meet "material needs" were now considered an unavoidable part of forging a "new intelligentsia."

[12]Grünberg, "Partei und Intellektuelle," *Neues Deutschland*, 9 January 1949.
[13]Ibid.

Once formalized on 31 March 1949, the new provisions created a cultural counterpart to the earlier SMAD order 234 entitled "measures for raising worker productivity and for the further improvement in the material condition of workers and employees in industry and transportation." Even the wooden language used in the DWK's ordinance, especially the phrase "further improvement in the condition of the intelligentsia," resembled the awkward phrasing of order 234, and both, given the endless succession of genitives, might have been translated from the Russian. Regardless, each was an admission of failure in the form of the realization that individual initiative hinged on the promise of personal benefit. Order 234 had raved about the "successes achieved by working people in the reconstruction of a peace economy," only to announce measures taken in response to the "low level of worker discipline," insufficient initiative, and "sinking worker productivity." These problems were to be solved on the basis of a system of inducements, bonuses, better ration cards, paid vacations, and assorted other perquisites calculated to provide workers who increased productivity by meeting or exceeding production norms with tangible benefits. The later DWK ordinance, some provisions of which derived their authority directly from order 234, was drawn up with the same goal in mind, but tailored to technical, scientific, and creative intellectuals. The developments set in motion by order 234 were then continued through late 1947 and 1948—in some cases with a vengeance, in others only after considerable delays and difficulties—in the form of actions taken in conformity with the two-year plan. The problems associated with the establishment of a "cultural fund" are especially revealing because they point to a dilemma faced by the SED in its efforts to enlist intellectuals in support of the two-year plan. The first mention in extant DVV files of "establishing and administering a fund for the support of literary work" dates all the way back to the weeks following announcement of order 234 in October 1947; though this and other plans for the next several months had been "discussed beforehand with the SMAD,"[14] the adverse public reaction to order 234 must have shown that favoring the intellectuals was bound to upset working Germans whose support of the two-year plan was even more critical than the related, but more limited objective of increasing production promoted by order 234.

This was the nature of the impasse; without special treatment, the intellectuals were thought likely to ignore the two-year plan; with it, anger at a system of privileges for intellectuals might well cause the workers to do the same. Wandel mentioned the situation generally in his report to the board in February 1948;[15] and the subject of "creation and organization of a stipend

[14]An die Präsidialabteilung. Betrifft: Arbeitsplan der Abteilung K für das IV. Vierteljahr des Haushaltsjahres 1947/48, 23 December 1947. Bundesarchiv, Abt. Potsdam, R-2/1155/76-77.
[15]Stenographische Niederschrift über die 7. (21.) Tagung des Parteivorstandes der SED am 11./ 12. Februar 1948. Zentrales Parteiarchiv, IV 2/1/20/86.

fund for writers" surfaced again in April 1948 in connection with the remark that an SMAD order had not yet been "effected."[16] The delays extended through the announcement of the party's two-year plan the following summer, continued on to the semi-public introduction of the cultural plan in January 1949, before culminating in the ordinance passed by the DWK on 31 March 1949—even though the party secretariat had gone ahead and endorsed the idea of assisting "freelance artists" on 2 August 1948 and drew up concrete plans shortly thereafter. At a DVV meeting a few weeks earlier, Herbert Volkmann indicated that the SMAD had in fact already approved the idea in principle; and barely two weeks later, he prepared a formal proposal for the upcoming ministers' conference set for mid-August. The proposal called upon the ministers to back the idea of a cultural fund financed by a slight rise in the price of tickets to cultural events and designed to "stimulate artists and writers into participating in the democratic construction of Germany, especially the implementation of the two-year plan." Volkmann's proposal explained that mass organizations like the Kulturbund and the FDGB had participated in preliminary discussions and added that the Kulturbund would take the lead in "planning and supervising" the fund.

The idea behind it was simple. Artists, writers, and scientists needed to regard their work as a way of "permeating the consciousness of the masses with the necessity of implementing the [two-year] plan." The intellectuals had to be encouraged to engage these problems themselves in their creative activity, but none of this was possible without a "material basis" for their endeavors impossible to provide through an expansion of any particular administrative budget. In order to "preserve artistic capacity" and "make it usable in building democracy," ways had to be found to expand the activities of creative intellectuals by offering them commissions and prizes. Volkmann concluded by noting that the plan had been discussed with the SMAD's office of information and with the mass organizations. The Kulturbund and the FDGB intended to make 50,000 marks each available for initial financing (the same set-up soon approved by the secretariat).[17] Two weeks later, as part of its discussion of cultural and educational issues in their relation to the two-year plan, the ministers' conference supported the idea with minor alterations;[18] and a few days after, on 18 August, even more concrete plans were agreed upon. The party functionaries responsible, including Herbert Gute, Klaus Gysi, Alexander Abusch, Heinz Willmann, Walter Maschke, and Ri-

[16]Abteilung Kunst und Literatur. Referat Literatur. Arbeitsplan für das 1. Quartal 1948/49. 6 April 1948. Bundesarchiv, Abt. Potsdam, R-2/1155/70.

[17]Vorlage für die Ministerkonferenz. Betrifft: Schaffung eines Kulturfonds, 28 July 1948, ibid., R-2/77/75-76; Protokoll Nr. 99 (II) der Sitzung des Zentralsekretariats am 2. 8. 48 ("Die Lage der Geistesschaffenden nach der Währungsreform"). Zentrales Parteiarchiv, IV 2/2.1/220/2.

[18]Beschlußprotokoll Nr. 14 der Ministerkonferenz vom 10. bis 13. August 1948. 23 August 1948. Bundesarchiv, Abt. Potsdam, R-2/77/4.

chard Weimann, intended to give these to the DWK, which would have them "confirmed" by Sokolovskij.[19]

Though Gysi went on the radio to discuss the fund on 12 August 1948,[20] still nothing was finalized for several more months, perhaps because both SED and SMAD considered it wiser to make any program of privileges for intellectuals part of an overall cultural plan that required more preparation and, by having the DWK do the honors, could be made to appear separate from the SED. The idea of a cultural fund was among the party's "measures" in January 1949;[21] but that document was only disseminated internally before being given to the DWK for final promulgation as a quasi-governmental plan—this in spite of the fact that the same document was referred to several weeks before, within the DVV, as the "cultural plan of the SED" and still characterized later as the "cultural plan (of the two-year plan)."[22] After passage of the DWK ordinance on 31 March 1949, then, the Kulturbund's Heinz Willmann provided a retrospective explanation for the endless succession of delays. The Kulturbund and the DVV began discussing the need for a cultural fund as soon as word of plans for currency reform in the Western sectors of Berlin leaked out in mid-1948, Willmann said;[23] once those plans were complete, a proposal was sent to the DWK and to the "responsible authorities" of the SMAD. Willmann went on to describe a project that differed only slightly from the version presented to the ministers' conference by Herbert Volkmann several months before; and it appears as if this first proposal had actually been sent to both DWK and SMAD in much the same form. Even though Volkmann said earlier that these issues had all been discussed with the SMAD, Willmann noted that both "German as well as Soviet administrative offices" objected; these reservations led to the reformulation of the proposal on 25 November 1948, "expanded" and made more "specific," though most of its provisions remained intact. The concern, said Willmann, was over the nature of the financing—taxing ticket prices at a time when it was important to raise wages. Following discussions with "German authorities," those reservations were allayed; and the SMAD had also

---

[19]Protokoll der Sitzung des Gründungsausschusses des Kultur-Fonds am 18. August 1948. Zentrales Parteiarchiv, IV 2/906/112/1-2.

[20]See Deutscher Volksrat. Ausschuß für Kulturpolitik. Informationsmaterial. Gründung eines Kulturfonds. Vortrag v. Klaus Gysi im Berliner Rundfunk, 12 August 1948, Bundesarchiv, Abt. Potsdam, A-1/76/55.

[21]"Maßnahmen zur Durchführung der kulturellen Aufgaben im Rahmen des Zweijahrplanes," *Protokoll der Ersten Parteikonferenz*, p. 540.

[22]Beschlußprotokoll der Abteilungsleitersitzung am 14. Dezember 1948 and Protokoll der Abteilungsleitersitzung vom 11. Juli 1949. Arbeitsplan der DVfV für das 3. Quartal 1949. Bundesarchiv. Abt. Potsdam, R-2/2146/3 and R-2/2146/18.

[23]Actually, the subject came up as early as 26 July 1948 at a secretariat meeting; and Otto Meier was asked to discuss the matter with Kulturbund and DVV "comrades" attending the next board meeting. Protokoll Nr. 96 (II) der Sitzung des Zentralsekretariats am 26. 7. 1948 ("Die Lage der Geistesschaffenden nach der Währungsreform"). Zentrales Parteiarchiv, IV 2/2.1/218/2.

come forward with counter proposals that were examined in repeated meetings with "the political advisor of the supreme commander of the Soviet military administration as well as with Ambassador Semjonov."[24] Talks also took place with the DWK, and the final outcome then went well beyond the idea of a fund for writers. As Willmann put it, the above chain of events led to nothing less than the DWK's entire ordinance of 31 March 1949; but he closed his remarks by cautioning that, with the regulations now public, there was bound to be resistance from both urban and rural workers to this "generous support of the intellectuals."[25]

Even so, Willmann never explained why several more months elapsed after the original proposal had been reformulated on 25 November 1948 and apparently approved by the SMAD; but the date itself provides some clues. On 2 December 1948, the supreme commander of the SMAD, Sokolovskij, received the mayor of (East) Berlin to discuss the work of the newly constituted Magistrat. His political advisor, Semjonov, also attended the reception; and during the meeting, Sokolovskij suddenly informed the mayor that he had two "wishes." The first pertained to the intelligentsia. Sokolovskij began by blaming Berlin's previous Magistrat, which had been forced to move its operations to the Western sectors of the city when its functions were obstructed in the East, for neglecting the "needs" of the intellectuals. Coming at the height of the Berlin blockade and combined with the Soviet offer to provide for the entire city, Sokolovskij's remarks were an obvious attempt to curry favor with intellectuals living in the Western sectors of the city. Sokolovskij further enhanced his argument by emphasizing the importance of the intellectuals in the construction of a "better life"; and he added that the great minds of German science, technology, culture, and art in Berlin and Soviet-occupied Germany had to be placed in a material position unthinkable under the conditions of a capitalist society. But Sokolovskij then acknowledged the real target of his criticism when he concluded that there had been a "certain underestimation of the important role of intellectuals in political and economic life," even among working Germans; this underestimation occasionally expressed itself in mistrust and even "hostility." Intellectuals in Berlin particularly, Sokolovskij went on to say, were "at a turning point" because a certain number remained "reactionary" and hostile toward "democratic change." But he also made it clear that his ideas applied not only to Berlin, but to the "Soviet occupation zone as well as all of Germany"; and he concluded with general references to the need to provide the intellectuals with an income, food, and other material goods in order to free them of worrying about their "daily bread."[26]

[24]Semjonov *was* the political advisor.
[25]Deutscher Volksrat. Ausschuß für Kulturpolitik. 18. Sitzung. 9 April 1949. Bundesarchiv. Abt. Potsdam, A-2/59/11-36.
[26]"Marschall W. D. Sokolowskij empfing Oberbürgermeister Friedrich Ebert," *Neues Deutsch-*

These latter comments fit with the language and thinking of both the party's cultural plan, a draft of which was then circulating, and with the DWK's later cultural ordinance. Sokolovskij's remarks then figured prominently in Grotewohl's comments published on 9 January 1949, in which he referred specifically to the SED's cultural plan and noted that the party supported the "idea of a cultural fund."[27] Sokolovskij's "wish" marked the beginning of a final resolution of the problem. A few weeks later, the DVV requested that all division heads submit specific lists of "outstanding artists, teachers, scientists, etc." living throughout the zone; the personnel office, in consultation with Paul Wandel, would then make its own on-the-spot determination about the "material circumstances of such persons" before issuing recommendations to the DVV's relevant offices.[28]

Personnel Management

Sokolovskij's second "wish" in December 1948 was that "bureaucratism" be eradicated in the offices of the city's "democratic administration." Though he again fixed the blame for "bureaucratic methods of administration" upon the old Magistrat, Sokolovskij's so-called wish had absolutely nothing to do with the defunct unified government of a now divided city; rather, his remarks echoed those made at the SED's "state-political" conference the previous July and its attack upon "bureaucratism," as well as for improving the position of the party, in what Ulbricht had imprudently called the "state administrative apparatus." These general plans affected the work of all "administrations," including the DVV, and one of the most important objectives was the development of a better system of personnel files and personnel statistics. Not that the DVV had neglected to compile such information prior to 1948; quite the contrary; and most of it tracked the party affiliations of administration employees. The statistics reveal nothing surprising; the SED dominated the DVV from day one and tightened its hold still further with the passage of time. In fact, it may have been easier to "air out" the DVV after July 1948, using Mielke's language,[29] because the administration adhered to higher ideological standards to begin with. One compilation dated 11 March 1948 listed a total of 121 employees out of 206 who belonged to the SED (66 were unaffiliated; 7 belonged to the CDU and 7 to the LDP; and 5 were

---

land, 4 December 1948.

[27]Grotewohl, "Die SED und die Intellektuellen," *Neues Deutschland*, 9 January 1949.

[28]Ergebnisse der Abteilungsleitersitzung vom 22. Dezember 1948. Tagesordnung: Realisierung der Beschlüsse der 17. Ministerkonferenz, 23 December 1948. Bundesarchiv. Abt. Potsdam, R-2/2123/21.

[29]"Stellung der SED zur Personalpolitik in der Verwaltung," *Die neuen Aufgaben der demokratischen Verwaltung*, pp. 62-69.

still members of the West Berlin SPD). Of the 121 SED members, this list-ing indicated that barely half, 64, joined from the KPD; 29 were previously Social Democrats, and 28 joined the SED directly—either with no previous party affiliation or as former Nazis.[30] The percentage of employees who be-longed to the SED went up to 60.5 percent by 31 March 1948 (30.2 percent were unaffiliated, and only a few belonged to the other parties).[31] Even then, the percentages were skewed by the fact that a far greater number of the top positions had always been reserved for members of the SED who, more often than not, came to the party from the KPD.[32] The DVV also compiled statistics that showed the political affiliation of employees who worked in the state ministries of culture and education; two sets from Schwerin showed 64.5 percent of all employees to be SED members as of 1 July 1948, with 30.5 percent unaffiliated, compared with 74.4 percent (and 22.1 percent) by the end of the year.[33] The figures for Brandenburg, however, told a different story; on 1 October 1948, they fell into these categories: SED, 23 percent; LDP, 2 percent; CDU, 1 percent; unaffiliated, 72 percent. By 31 December 1948, the SED had 38.8 percent; LDP, 2.5 percent; unaffiliated, 57.5 per-cent; and by January 1949, SED, 49.6; CDU, 1.4 percent; LDP, 2.9 percent; unaffiliated, 46.1 percent.[34]

These documents indicate the type of activity engaged in by the DVV's personnel office and suggest that much of what Erich Mielke advocated in July 1948 had been happening all along. But the pace could always be pick-ed up or general procedures tightened. Unfortunately, these kinds of devel-opments are especially difficult to document; internal memoranda were con-sidered highly confidential and probably became part of general DVV files that themselves failed to survive intact fairly infrequently. Moreover, much of the confidential material appears to have been compiled at the request of the SMAD's own "cadres' department"; and communications with the occu-pation administration exist in far smaller numbers than do other documents. Accordingly, only a few general conclusions can be suggested. Not surpris-ingly, the DVV's personnel office had its own copy of the SED's "position" in the matter of *Personalpolitik* within governmental administration. In fact, this particular paper served as the general basis for many of Mielke's re-marks in July 1948. It noted that top jobs should go only to "the most politi-cally conscious and progressive personnel most committed to democracy"; and that there was no place in administration for "enemies of democracy,

[30]DVFVO - Personalstand vom 11. 3. 48, Bundesarchiv, Abt. Potsdam, R-2/999/50.
[31]Personalstatistik der DVV nach dem Stande vom 31. 3. 48, ibid., R-2/999/48.
[32]See Namensliste der leitenden Angestellten der DVV. Stand: 10.3.1947, ibid., R-2/918/43-50; see also the statistics dated 12 August 1949, ibid., R-2/911/73-76.
[33]Personalstatistik des Ministeriums für Volksbildung nach dem Stande von 1. 7. 1948; and Per-sonalstatistik Schwerin nach dem Stande vom 31. 12. 48, ibid., R-2/963/21 and 24.
[34]Personalstatistik der Landesregierung Brandenburg / Ministerium für Volksbildung, Wissen-schaft und Kunst, ibid., R-2/963/8-11.

agents, Schumacher types, spies, saboteurs, etc., who have crept into the administrative apparatus." Bureaucrats, those "civil servants" who, in spite of their best intentions, hampered work, failed to implement resolutions, and thus became "saboteurs," were also unwanted; along with "bribable, corrupt elements," such persons needed to be "exposed and fired." The document then discussed the obligations of personnel offices in ridding the administrative apparatus of such persons; fulfilling those obligations required inspections of personnel offices themselves as a means of creating "qualitatively strong, centralized personnel divisions" capable of making the correct selection of workers. Other provisions included instructions for setting up a system of "unified personnel management" in administrative agencies; this objective stipulated that every state establish a main administration of personnel and schooling in its interior ministry; and the document called as well for main administrations of personnel and schooling within the interior administration. Finally, the paper noted that "the common task of all democratic mass organizations is the consolidation of democratic state power and the development of a new economic order"; and outlined a variety of objectives, such as increasing production, developing new discipline, implementing resolutions, and fighting "bureaucratism," that the administrative apparatus and the mass organizations together needed to achieve.[35]

The precise impact of these new policies upon the DVV is, however, difficult to gauge. In early August 1948, the administration redefined its general objectives for personnel management in connection with the implementation of the two-year plan; and these focused preeminently on the ideological qualifications of all employees who worked for the DVV or the corresponding state ministries. In particular, plans were made for the "systematic" and periodic screening of administrative employees, teachers and educational administrators, and the "systematic registration, selection, and support of creative intellectuals who ally themselves with the people and are possessed of the capacity to portray the joys and travails of a new life." Personnel offices needed to be in a position to establish the status of "culture and education" at any given time.[36] But again, the exact implementation of these plans is difficult to document. There are few signs of anything resembling a "purge" within the DVV, and it is entirely possible that none occurred because of the careful selection of employees all along. But there are sporadic indications that the DVV's personnel office began sending the Russians lists of employees more frequently after mid-1948, though the nature of extant documents makes conclusions unreliable. On 29 June 1948, the DVV provided the Russians with a description of employees who left the administration in 1947; of 104, only 9 were listed as having been fired "for reasons connected with se-

[35]Stellung der SED zur Personalpolitik in der Verwaltung, ibid., R-2/1291/61-64.
[36]Die Aufgaben der Personalabteilung in der Zeit der Durchführung des Zweijahresplanes, 6 August 1948, ibid., 941-46/17-17a.

curing the democratic administration politically." As of 30 April 1948, 59 had left the DVV, among them 6 for the above political reasons; and 6 more were expected to be fired.[37]

There were also rosters of "local professors" who had been abroad during the Nazi years; as well as a list sent to the SMAD of professors who had come back to Soviet-occupied Germany after having been named to chairs.[38] Because many of these men had been back in Soviet-occupied Germany for quite some time by now, the late date of this list, 22 November 1948, might suggest a connection with the campaign developing in the Soviet Union against former Western émigrés or "cosmopolitans." Yet another document, as well as its timing, warrants similar suspicion; the apparently quick reduction in DVV personnel from 253 in very late 1948 to 224 beginning in 1949 "after inspection by the Malz commission" raises tantalizing questions that simply cannot be answered on the basis of available evidence, though there was an additional internal reference in mid-December 1948 to an impending "reorganization" of the agency that may have resulted from some kind of "inspection."[39] Still other statistics, undated, characterized the reasons why employees left the DVV in terms of their "own wishes," unspecified "structural changes," or "firing in order to strengthening the administration democratically." But only 19 of 110 fit the latter description.[40] Finally, there were statistics compiled on 31 March 1949 that, in addition to showing who joined the SED from the KPD and the SPD, included columns for "political emigration" broken down into only three categories: the Soviet Union, Britain/USA, and "other countries."[41] This column may have reflected developing mistrust of émigrés in the context of "cosmopolitanism," but no additional information is available to prove it conclusively. A few months later, the DVV's personnel office sent the SMAD statistics of departures and hirings for all of 1948 and the first five months of 1949. As of 1 January 1948, the DVV had a total of 199 employees; in the course of the year, fully 110 left the administration and were replaced by 100 new employees, but no reasons were given for their departure. During the first five months of 1949, 14 employees left and 35 were hired.[42] It is also worth noting that the politburo passed a pair of resolutions, in March and April, aimed at improving the

[37]Personalabteilung an die Abteilung Volksbildung der SMAD der Kaderabteilung. Betr. Ausgeschiedene Mitarbeiter der DVV, 29 June 1948, ibid., R-911/129.
[38]Karlshorst z.d.A. Abteilung W, Berufungen aus dem Ausland, 21 November 1948, ibid., R-2/911/109-111.
[39]Willi Lehmann an die SED. Zentralsekretariat z. Hdn. Gen. Plenekowski. 11 December 1948, ibid., R-2/911/115; and Beschlußprotokoll der Abteilungsleitersitzung am 14. Dezember, ibid., R-2/2146/3.
[40]Entlassungen, ibid., R-2/911/89-95.
[41]Statistik über die Angestellten der DVV, 31 March 1949, ibid., R-2/963/4.
[42]An die SMAD. Abteilung Volksbildung. Kaderabteilung. Betr.: Personelle Zusammenstellungen (Einstellungen und Entlassungen 1948/1949), 4 June 1949, ibid., R-2/911/80.

"development of new staff for top functions in party, state administration, and the mass organizations," as well as "screening all cadres from the standpoint of their reliability." The DWK was targeted specifically for an "investigation" or *Überprüfung* understood in terms of "the question of vigilance and to defend against hostile activity." DWK employees still living in the Western sectors of Berlin, for instance, but also anyone who "might have connections with the West" had to be investigated.[43]

Finally, the DVV's personnel office also got on with its efforts to "register" and "screen" creative intellectuals living in Soviet-occupied Germany. A plan of action drawn up on 5 October 1948 called for the screening of 120 such persons. By January 1949, the office had succeeded in examining information about 383 instead and boasted that its plan had been "overfulfilled" by 319 percent. Persons were scrutinized with respect to their activity prior to 1945, their "attitude toward democratic-progressive tasks *since 1945,*" and also in terms of the "expedience of reaching our socialist goals, based on the guidelines and instructions of the SMAD at any given time!" By 31 December 1948, the DVV's personnel office had "screened" a grand total of 1,834 creative intellectuals (stage directors and producers, actors, dancers, conductors, band leaders, singers, instrumentalists, authors and writers, composers, painters, sculptors, architects, and so on). The personnel office also undertook "political investigations" of individual operations like stage theaters. The theater in Eisenach was said to be a "nest" of agents of American imperialism and had been put under the "control of the ministry of the interior," though not the interior administration. In addition, the DVV's personnel office combined forces with the state ministry of culture and education in Saxony to investigate the staff of the radio station in Leipzig; and conducted a variety of other such examinations of stations throughout the zone. Some 2,500 employees, occupying the most sensitive positions, were screened and a decision made that any future staff changes required the approval of the personnel office. There was a special concern that neither the ministries of interior nor culture and education had paid sufficient attention to radio "program regulation."[44]

These activities continued throughout 1949, with "examinations" and "investigations" of art institutions, libraries, academies of art, music schools, state archives, universities, and so on; and an internal DVV "reexamination of personal questionnaires and their coordination with the requirements of personnel-statistical files to comply with requests made by the SMAD and the DVdI" (or interior administration).[45] The ordinance passed on 31 March

---

[43]Protokoll Nr. 8 der Sitzung des Politbüros am 8. März 1949; Protokoll Nr. 18 der Sitzung des Politbüros am 26. April 1949. Zentrales Parteiarchiv, IV 2/2/8/12-13 and IV 2/2/18/2.

[44]Personalabteilung. Arbeitsbericht des Referenten Fischer. Berichtszeit IV. Arbeitsplan vom 5. 10. 1948, January 1949, ibid., R-2/907/17-21.

[45]Personalabteilung. Willi Fischer, 16 March 1949, Arbeitsplan 2. Quartal 1949; and Arbeits-

1949 then led to another round of examinations of personnel offices at work within local government and within various institutions and agencies.[46] By July 1949, the DVV's personnel office boasted of 2,414 individual listings of creative intellectuals and artists, a number that, after twenty-five months of work, had gone up to 3,023 files by October. Personnel also reported that "all theaters" were being looked at in terms of their staff and their "art.[istic], progress.[ive] development."[47]

"An Historical Hour—An Historical Document"

Whether or not a real shake-up of the DVV took place in the aftermath of the SED's state-political conference in summer 1948, or in connection with the hunt for "agents of American imperialism," the Stalinist philosophy of organization behind the general call for "new work methods" dominated the thinking of the DVV's top leadership regardless. When he took the rostrum at the conference in late January 1949, Paul Wandel characterized the meeting as a "congress that clarified our party's general line." But he added, with a reference to Stalin, that much more was required if the "first preconditions of victory" were to be developed into victory itself and made the further point that the conference should lead to a serious reexamination of cultural work. This area of activity, he concluded, suffered from greater shortcomings than did others.[48] But Wandel made no mention of the SED's cultural plan, a strange omission considering that the document had become the focus of the DVV's own internal planning. Privately, Wandel requested that his division heads provide him with a written response to the "newly revised cultural plan of the SED"; opinions were also solicited from the state ministries of culture and education; and taken together, these materials were supposed to aid the DVV's divisions in preparing new two-year plans for submission to Wandel.[49] But by early 1949, every complaint about the party's cultural work was meant to prepare the way for the very cultural initiative expected to provoke opposition to it; and the anticipated hostility would certainly explain why conference delegates received the SED's cultural plan in the form of a pre-existing document. Wandel spoke at the very end of the

plan für das Arbeitsjahr 1949, 29 March 1949, ibid., R-2/907/14 and 10.
[46]Arbeitsplan der Personalabteilung in der DVV für das III. Quartal (Juli bis September 1949), ibid., R-2/941-46/44-48.
[47]Arbeitsplan II. Quartal 1949. Abschlußbericht, 2 July 1949; and Betr.: Teilbericht zum Arbeitsbericht der Personalabteilung, 22 October 1949, ibid., R-2/907/1-2 and 4.
[48]See *Protokoll der Ersten Parteikonferenz*, pp. 491 and 494.
[49]Beschlußprotokoll der Abteilungsleitersitzung am 14. Dezember 1948; and Ergebnisse der Abteilungsleitersitzung vom 22. Dezember 1948. Bundesarchiv. Abt. Potsdam, R-2/2146/3 and R-2/2123/21.

conference, and his silence on the subject of the plan suggests that the meeting most likely concluded with no formal presentation of the plan (to say nothing of any discussion). The party's main resolution contained only a few vague references to cultural work in the factories and villages and to the importance of cultural mass organizations. Otherwise, that statement confined itself to a shrill call for an end to the "pernicious sectarian attitudes" toward the intellectuals said to exist within the party itself.[50]

The resolution contained no mention of the fact that the party had already worked out a detailed cultural "two-year plan" and that the plan coupled intellectuals, artists, and scientists to its economic and political counterpart with calls for an increase in the cultural niveau of Soviet-zone Germans generally; for support for science, research, and art; and for the development of "a new democratic intelligentsia." These "measures" included three sets of provisions. The first listed activity according to the further categories of culture and education, science and research, art and literature; followed by the second heading of cultural mass work (factories and villages); and the last, which explained the need for greater press and broadcast involvement in the two-year plan and support of cultural work associated with it, concluded the document.[51] Altogether, the plan listed a number of specific actions; but those sections pertaining to art and literature were comprised mostly of general rhetoric that had already been heard in the aftermath of order 234. For instance, the "cultural task" of changing popular attitudes toward work and altering social perceptions could only be accomplished if writers and artists committed their energy and enthusiasm to the job; their contribution to the two-year plan thus consisted of developing a "realistic art" and aspiring to the highest possible artistic achievements. The remarks echoed earlier calls for an improvement in the "quality" of cultural activity; and these turned on the idea behind order 234 that increasing factory production hinged upon bettering the quality of work. But improving morale by promising material rewards had also been part of order 234; and the cultural-political parallel centered on the idea that the enthusiasm of intellectuals, if it could be sparked in response to material incentives, would help promote similar enthusiasm among the working population.

Mention of two related measures geared toward facilitating cultural activism followed, one of which, literary censorship and the formation of a so-called publishing commission or Deutsche Kommission für das Verlagswesen, has already been discussed because the subject dated back to summer 1948.[52] It was not discussed now or later in connection with censorship,

[50]"Entschließung der Ersten Parteikonferenz. Die nächsten Aufgaben der SED," *Protokoll der Ersten Parteikonferenz*, pp. 520-22.
[51]"Maßnahmen zur Durchführung der kulturellen Aufgaben im Rahmen des Zweijahrplanes," ibid., pp. 532-44.
[52]See Chapter Eleven.

however, at least not publicly; nor did the further description of the preeminent role of theaters in developing a "new democratic consciousness," along with a fleeting reference to "progressive program planning," couch the matter in terms suggestive of censorship. Nonetheless, censorship and regulation were now preeminent objectives served, additionally, by the raucous debate about "formalism" and "cosmopolitanism." Accordingly, the SED's cultural plan included the obligatory denunciation of "decadent" or "formalistic and naturalistic distortions of art."[53] But the success of the plan was nonetheless thought to hinge upon the establishment of a "cultural fund" designed to encourage the participation of artists and intellectuals in the goals of the two-year plan without necessarily having to resort to censorship. Over time, the idea worked, too; a "new democratic intelligentsia," a mix of older party stalwarts and "young talent," evolved. Some, representatives of both generations, still needed periodic censoring; but many were perfectly content to police their own writing either because they believed in the necessity of presenting the party's truth as their own, lost the ability to distinguish between the two, or considered their own prosperity and public notoriety worth exchanging for a literary endorsement of the party's politics. All the while, hostility toward the idea of special privileges for intellectuals continued to grow. The conference in January 1949 settled nothing; and it was apparently decided to postpone any internal organized debate of the SED's cultural intentions for several more weeks. The first formal party debate then took place in mid-March at a one-day SED "cultural conference" that met to consider the "implementation of resolutions in the area of culture passed at the party conference."[54]

Statements made there indicate that widespread hostility toward the plan threatened the party's attempt to secure the support of the intellectuals. The risk of something akin to a serious backlash was apparently considerable; and calling the meeting in mid-March to discuss the party's cultural "resolutions" when no resolution as such had been officially passed at the conference in late January, at least not in the form of the cultural "measures," hints at the extent of consternation within the party's inner circles. Nor is it insignificant that the SMAD's *Tägliche Rundschau* weighed into the discussion a few days before the meeting on 14 March with two lengthy articles by Wolfgang Harich. Harich managed to keep his remarks more within the realm of the theoretical; and he most likely did so as a way of avoiding too strong an impression of Soviet interference in such delicate matters. Articles published in the *Tägliche Rundschau* were, in all probability, either commissioned in the first place or definitely dependent upon prior approval by the paper's

53"Maßnahmen zur Durchführung der kulturellen Aufgaben im Rahmen des Zweijahrplanes," pp. 533, 538-39.
54"Aktive deutsche Kulturpolitik. Konferenz der Kulturfunktionäre der SED," *Tägliche Rundschau*, 15 March 1949.

editorial board. But it was perfectly clear that Harich understood the context of his remarks, even if he was smart enough to begin his first article with a lengthy disquisition on the *future* of communism. Doing so allowed him to speak of cultural developments destined to occur "in the period of the dictatorship of the proletariat" without undue emphasis upon the nearness of that coming day.[55] Having made the point that workers and intellectuals needed each other, Harich thus explained both the nature of their future cooperation "in the epoch of the dictatorship of the proletariat" and the beneficial outcome, suggesting, nonetheless, that this bright day had, in essence, already begun to dawn.

Though his article probably changed few minds, it was a slick way of presenting the argument because Harich could then proceed to make two main points in his next essay: first, creating and consolidating an alliance between the working class and intellectuals was already a decisive task now, "in the transitional period leading toward proletarian dictatorship"; but it was incumbent upon both sides to "liquidate thoroughly" old tensions, differences, misunderstandings, and resentment. Harich then took up the subject of conditions in Soviet-occupied Germany specifically; but, having effectively acknowledged the direction of local developments toward dictatorship, he nonetheless coupled his remarks to the principal theoretical and political finding of the party conference in late January. In Harich's words, "there is no dictatorship of the proletariat here, but rather—under the protection of the Soviet occupation force—an antifascist-democratic order."[56] Even though Harich failed to put it in these terms, he argued that the alliance between workers and intellectuals had to be formed during the "transitional period" leading to dictatorship for it to be in place *during* the dictatorship. But what Harich said instead was much simpler; democratic reconstruction would be impossible without the participation of the intellectuals; every responsible office or agency was actively engaged in efforts to win their support; and measures taken to improve the "material" standing of the intellectuals served this purpose. Always preoccupied with theoretical considerations, however, Harich made it clear that winning the intellectuals' "ideologically" was an important task of the class struggle as well; questions of consciousness were involved; and Harich had plenty to say about the subject of "reactionary bourgeois ideologies" (decadence and such). Still, any worker whose "ultraleft radicalism" worked to confirm the intellectuals' predisposition toward mistrust of workers, thereby driving the intellectuals back into the open arms of reaction, waged class warfare incorrectly. Moreover, this "suicidal" ultraleft radicalism was "shockingly full of life in the Soviet occupation zone" in certain localities and in certain factories; and Harich left

[55]Harich, "Arbeiterklasse und Intelligenz. I," *Tägliche Rundschau*, 10 March 1949.
[56]Harich, "Arbeiterklasse und Intelligenz. II," *Tägliche Rundschau*, 11 March 1949.

no doubt about the reason for it. As long as the economy could not fully satisfy the needs of every citizen, certain persons had to be rewarded in relation to their abilities and accomplishments; in order to create the economic preconditions for universal prosperity, tangible differences in the distribution of material goods remained an indispensable stimulus; and Harich concluded his article with talk of "pernicious radicalism" that took shape in hostility toward temporarily necessary social inequalities.

The major speech at the SED's "cultural conference" a few days later was given by Stefan Heymann, who had replaced Richard Weimann as head of the party's division of PKE. Heymann referred directly to the sore subject of "food packages for intellectuals";[57] and, befitting the purpose of the meeting, talking constantly about the natural prerogatives of the party in pursuing cultural objectives. "We have taken the first steps toward assuming the leadership of the state and the economy," he said, "but we have not gone beyond exceptionally modest beginnings in the area of culture. Why not?" Heymann answered his own question in a variety of ways; for instance, every worker understood the principle of linking compensation to level of accomplishment, but could not grasp the fact that the principle applied to intellectuals as well. This misunderstanding had to be "thoroughly eliminated." There were also many intellectuals, including some members of the party, who clung to their own arrogance with regard to the working class and "its party." Many intellectuals generally, said Heymann, had no quarrel with the SED's right to lead in matters pertaining to politics and economics; but considered culture their domain and brooked no interference by the party. These were the two sets of prejudices that obstructed the party's realization of its "leading role" in the area of culture; and Heymann went on to outline most of the provisions originally included in the party's cultural "measures." In fact, Heymann's summation of the plan's main clauses suggests that he was unable to simplify matters by referring the delegates attending this cultural conference to their own copies of the SED's plan, from which Heymann was paraphrasing, because access to the document had been restricted. In any case, Heymann concluded his summary of the "most important problems of our cultural work" by stating that these objectives could not be met in the absence of "a *complete turnabout* of certain party circles in the matter of the previous attitude toward cultural politics." Now more than ever, he concluded, revealing that opposition to the SED's cultural intentions was not limited to the rank-and-file, the party's cultural functionaries needed to apply the SED's rightful claim of leadership to the cultural sphere; they had to stop lagging behind economic and administrative developments and "recognize as binding and obligatory the party's resolutions concerning its cultural responsibilities." Though every party member had long ago come to regard the party's

[57]Heymann, "Der Zweijahrplan und die Kulturaufgaben," *Neues Deutschland*, 13 March 1949.

directives and their implementation in other areas as self-evident, there was a "failure of the party membership" in cultural affairs.[58]

The remarks made by Harich and Heymann convey a sense of the depth of hostility toward the party's cultural-political proposals; this hostility had existed at least since order 234, but most likely surfaced well before then because the practice of issuing better ration cards to intellectuals predated the announcement of order 234; and it is valid to suggest that this anger went well beyond any other internal criticism of central party policies publicized in the Soviet-zone press. Still, for one reason or another, the party leadership and the SMAD finally decided against any further delays in early 1949; and the cultural conference in mid-March served as the bridge that led from the political conference six weeks earlier to the DWK's plenary session meeting fourteen days later to formalize all earlier initiatives, public and private, through passage of a comprehensive new ordinance. But the people behind the session still chose their words carefully; the DWK meeting thus suffered from its own peculiarities; and every one was related to the broad unpopularity of the plan. The "proposal" itself, the *Vorlage*, was presented at the second plenary session of the DWK, the first having met the day before; and it was apparent from the remarks of certain participants that they had not seen the document before receiving it on the day of its passage—31 March 1949.[59] One delegate even complained that the draft had been handed out "at the last moment" and expressed his regret that there was so little time to study it (48). In fact, most delegates may have shown up for the session on 31 March 1949 with no prior indication that the ordinance existed; and even if they knew of it, what followed hardly qualified, to use Heinrich Rau's words, as a "discussion"; the deliberations were dominated by the prepared remarks of four party functionaries—Rau, who headed the DWK; Abusch, representing the Kulturbund; Wandel, in his capacity as head of the DVV; and Grotewohl, who spoke officially for the SED.

It was Grotewohl who made the only references to the party, but otherwise pretended that the ordinance came into existence independent of the SED; and he certainly never acknowledged the connection between it and the party's cultural plan. Though there were a few remarks by the selected representatives of the other political parties and mass organizations attending, most only raved about the ordinance ("an historical hour, an historical document" [45]), and the outcome of the "deliberations" was never in any doubt. The plan passed by a unanimous vote, and the session ended in a standing ovation. Even so, the public commentary was full of derogatory remarks about criticism of the basic idea behind the plan, special privileges; and hinted strongly that certain intellectuals were unhappy with it as well be-

[58]"Aktive deutsche Kulturpolitik. Konferenz der Kulturfunktionäre der SED," *Tägliche Rundschau*, 15 March 1949.
[59]See *Der Kulturplan*, p. 44. All further page references are provided in the text.

cause they disliked the politics behind the ordinance. The hostility also explains why Rau began the session by identifying the Russians as the source of inspiration for the plan; it had been developed by the secretariat of the DWK in collaboration with the DVV, he said, "at the request" of the Soviet military administration; and Rau went on to characterize Soviet assistance as a classic illustration of the teachings of Lenin and Stalin concerning support for the national aspirations of other peoples (6). Indeed, later on in the proceedings, Wandel went out of his way to explain again that the "proposal" resulted from the initiative of the SMAD; the plan's "verve" and "daring" testified eloquently to the involvement of the SMAD, though he added that there was nothing essentially new about this interest in the welfare of German culture because the ordinance represented the direct continuation of SMAD policy in Soviet-occupied Germany since 1945. In fact, throughout German history there had never been a "government" that furthered the development of German culture as much as the SMAD (15-16).

But Wandel's enthusiasm hid ulterior motives; flattering the Russians must have struck him as a necessarily subtle way of making the essential point that the DWK ordinance was the equivalent of occupation law—with a slightly lower risk involved than saying so outrightly and confirming the unpopular fact that the DWK, as well as every other Soviet-zone administration, remained an exponent of a foreign power dictating domestic policy on occupied German territory. Wandel tried to direct the thoughts of his audience away from such notions—unsuccessfully, as it was admitted—by adding that the proposal would become "the law of the land" upon formal passage by the plenum, as if its enactment bore witness to local independence. Besides, this was patently untrue; regardless of its passage at the DWK plenum, the ordinance required an SMAD order two days later before it took effect. But Wandel knew better than to get into the legal and administrative intricacies of occupation law because doing so was tantamount to admitting that nothing happened in Soviet-occupied Germany without the approval of the SMAD. He was clever enough to attempt more flattery instead by hailing the existence of a marvelous synthesis: however beneficial SMAD intentions, in all "modesty" he was proud to point out that these could not have been realized in the absence of segments of the German people who shared the identical view of culture and its progressive development. Surprisingly, Wandel was not referring to the SED. Rather, he said that the present "proposal" was just as direct a continuation of the cultural politics pursued since 1945 by the block of German democratic parties and organizations (17). But this was true only in the sense that the "block" rarely developed any policy not initiated or sanctioned by the SED; and the same thing applied to the present "proposal"—it evolved out of the SED's cultural plan and was apparently presented to the DWK plenum in the form of a fait accompli. Whether Wandel's rhetoric convinced any of the critics is doubtful;

at this particular forum he was probably preaching to an audience consisting mostly of the converted anyway. But his praise of the antifascist-democratic "block" was still a deft way of avoiding the equally sensitive issue of the relationship between the ordinance and the SED's cultural plan.

As it was, Wandel passed over the SED in silence, and Grotewohl also skirted the issue. The SED had to work through an administrative agency anyway because no political party was empowered to pass laws; and the SED's cultural plan could not have been declared legally binding even if the party had passed it in the form of a resolution first; it would have bound only party members and, for whatever such a right was worth by 1949, could have been legally ignored in the various agencies of Soviet-zone administration still capable of resisting manipulation by the party functionaries working in them. But as a DWK ordinance, it was as much a law as the two-year plan, the more so given its backing by the Russians; and for this reason especially, none of the speakers was shy about thanking the SMAD. Abusch even suggested that the original initiative came from Sokolovskij in December 1948 (25), but this was misleading; the idea went back to late 1947, and it cannot be determined who came up with it first. Even after the Russians abandoned the reservations to which Willmann privately referred and threw their support behind the idea of a "cultural fund," none of the expressions of gratitude ever explained the exact nature of the SMAD's backing. Either the military administration put up the money or approved its use for this purpose; in its final form, the ordinance went far beyond the establishment of a modest "cultural fund" financed by a small increase in ticket prices; the bill ran into millions of marks, and the money had to come from somewhere. If the funds came from the Russians, the official gratitude may be understandable; however, the Germans would have been reluctant to admit it for fear of identifying the ordinance even more clearly with Soviet policy and offending overly fastidious intellectuals. After all, critics charged anyway that the ordinance was intended to "buy" or "bribe" the intellectuals.[60] But by the same token, if the Russians merely approved the idea as part of the DWK's overall budget, admitting it would have been an embarrassing acknowledgment that the Germans could not spend their own money without asking the SMAD first; and if the funds indeed came from the local economy, then the SMAD's support of the ordinance must have been confined mostly to rhetoric—simple encouragement worth such a display of gratitude only as a gesture of servility or for the sake of helping quash the expected opposition to the plan. This dramatic a display of abject appreciation was indeed unparalleled even in Soviet-occupied Germany; no previous praise of the SMAD ever characterized the occupation regime, like Wandel, as the best "government" that Germans had ever experienced. But it was critically important

[60]Zweiling, "Intelligenz und Arbeiterklasse," *Einheit* 5 (1949): 394.

that the DWK achieve the appearance of an overwhelming consensus; among other things, the plenary session was broadcast live on the radio; and whatever other questions the delegates may have had about the plan, the remarks about the Russians probably sufficed to dispel any lingering doubts about SMAD support of it and lessened the likelihood of voices being raised in opposition.

Under those circumstances, the unanimous vote was a foregone conclusion, particularly after each of the major speakers so vigorously denounced opposition to the plan. Rau went on at considerable length about the "backward, pernicious view" of working-class Germans that they could rebuild the country without the intellectuals; the "old bourgeois intelligentsia, together with our new intelligentsia and along with workers and farmers, are capable of great, progressive accomplishments" (8-9). For that reason, these persons needed to be given the opportunity to participate, said Rau, and he went on to outline some of the plan's provisions. A few included raising the number of "professors, engineers, and artists" who received an extra hot meal daily in accordance with order 234 from 30,000 to 40,000; and this particular benefit was to be made available to the companies of "leading theaters," the members of large orchestras, and other artistic institutions. Further privileges included the establishment of a fund, a hefty sum of 10 million marks, to finance the construction of private homes for scholars, professors, engineers, artists, doctors, and teachers; these intellectuals were also to receive an extra supply of heating coal; and the plan provided additionally for the opening of two rest centers for scientists and artists (10).

Wandel also combined his remarks about the necessity of developing a "new democratic intelligentsia" quickly through the assistance of the measures outlined in the ordinance with specific references to criticism of the idea. Unlike Rau, Wandel focused on the objections of members of the academy of sciences. The DWK ordinance called for doubling academy membership from 60 to 120; and certain academicians evidently concluded that the dilution in quality through the addition of so many new members was politically motivated. There were objections as well to the formation of new divisions within the academy, including "social sciences" and "languages, literature, and art." Considering that the plan also provided academy members with considerable additional privileges, the opposition suggested that favorable treatment alone was not necessary sufficient to bring about enthusiastic compliance; and a certain measure of browbeating at the DWK plenum then followed. Not that Wandel discussed these problems in detail, but he alluded to most of them. He denied the existence of any "intentions" behind the plan other than the desire to turn the academy into a center of German science; still, the academy needed to perceive the tasks "arising out of our people's most elementary intellectual and material necessities of life." The demands made upon the academy were thus not raised "arbitrarily by any particular state agency;" they represented the interests of the people. Finally, he said, echoing some of the Stalinist utterances made at the party's state-political conference the previous summer, academicians who still hesitated needed to grasp the fact that the academy's "old way of working" no longer met new requirements; he asked that "narrow reservations" be set aside (20-21); and he closed his remarks generally with another expression of gratitude to the SMAD, the Soviet government, and the Soviet people.

Grotewohl failed to mention the Russians at all; but more than any of the other speakers, he devoted his lengthy remarks to the various objections to the ordinance and indirectly demanded compliance by his party's rank-and-file by making it clear that the plan dovetailed with party policy. Like it or not, members of the SED were obliged to support it; and Grotewohl conveyed this message in a number of ways. Having first mentioned the "lack of understanding" among working Germans (29-30), he then read from the party's cultural resolution passed at its conference in September 1947 before asking why both workers and scientists questioned the "intentions" behind the plan when there were none other than those developed to help the German people in their entirety (30). In much the same vein, Grotewohl also brought up the subject of the SED's cultural conference in May 1948 and referred unambiguously to the "binding resolution" passed there. It stated that the SED advocated the "generous support" of culture and education, science, art, and literature; and aspired to living conditions for creative intellectuals that would allow them to concentrate fully on the development of their creative energy. The party felt that the current proposal marked the beginning realization of its own "pledge (39)," said Grotewohl, still pretending as if the ordinance had somehow been drawn up without the participation of the SED. But Grotewohl had more to say. He proceeded to contrast politically "unorganized elements among working Germans who have yet to grasp completely the interconnections and important social objectives outlined by this proposal" with "politically organized workers in our zone" free of such misunderstandings (37). With that distinction, Grotewohl could not have issued a stronger warning; the indisputable fact was that bitterness over the idea of special privileges for intellectuals was widespread among "politically organized workers"—members of the SED. Grotewohl's denial of the obvious now indicated that, as far as the party was concerned, from here on out such "pernicious sectarian attitudes toward intellectuals" were considered unworthy of further acknowledgment. The ordinance was official policy for "politically organized" workers; needed to be fully recognized as such; and the SED had no intention of debating the issue further with its own rank-and-file.

Even so, Grotewohl pleaded for understanding; everything done today in favor of the older generation of scientists and intellectuals would fall into the lap of the "new intelligentsia," the "worker-and-peasant intelligentsia," tomorrow. In the meantime, the party was fully cognizant of inequalities; "a group of our people is to receive assistance that goes vastly beyond the normal level"; and thus far, due to shortages, every measure taken had gone toward the favored treatment of those bearing the brunt of reconstruction—activists and factory workers who benefited from order 234 because of the particular importance of their labor for the general well-being. Unfortunately, Grotewohl explained, these discrepancies would probably exist for some time to come; but "we must see to it that each individual recognizes the need for supporting and adequately compensating those who do the most in accordance with the currently established principle; and that each individual regards this principle as the source of the strongest impulses behind both the two-year plan and the solution of all problems connected with reconstruction" (35). But like Wandel, Grotewohl chose to reserve some of his remarks for those intellectuals skeptical about the ordinance for entirely different reasons; and his comments were equally blunt. He took aim at the suggestion that the plan somehow masked undeclared intentions, demanding that the "gentlemen" of science and art recognize the necessity of structural changes related to a severing of the earlier ties between monopoly capitalism and scientific research institutions; it was incumbent upon them to approve of these "structural changes" before translating approval into active participation. For the day was over when scientific activity took place under the conditions of "Olympian leisure" (32). Much the same was true of art, literature, painting, sculpture, and theater; art "in our time," said Grotewohl, had the responsibility of instilling the spirit of enthusiasm in working Germans and enhancing their contribution to the "overwhelming job of reconstruction." Grotewohl hastened to conclude, however, that "we have no intention of regimenting art, coercing the mind into compliance, or introducing an automatic cadence into art; we haven't the slightest intention of mechanizing intellectual life." But, he ended, "exaggerated individualism" no longer enjoyed a justified existence among the German people (34).

"Orders from Moscow"

Two days after passage of the new ordinance, the SMAD took a step that it and the SED would have preferred to avoid. The *Tägliche Rundschau* published the order that officialized the ordinance and committed all branches and offices of the occupation administration to assist "German democratic organs" in its implementation.[61] With the issuance of SMAD order 36, the

---

[61]"Befehl des Obersten Chefs der Sowjetischen Militärverwaltung und Oberbefehlshabers der sowjetischen Besatzungstruppen in Deutschland. Nr. 36. 2 April 1949," *Tägliche Rundschau*, 3 April 1949. Neues Deutschland also printed the order, but placed it in an inconspicuous corner ot the paper.

cultural program was now doubly binding as legislation passed by a German agency empowered to enact it and as formal Soviet occupation law. But the need for the redundancy went unexplained; the SMAD had long since given the DWK the right to pass laws, in February 1948, and its ordinances ought to have been legally binding just by themselves. SMAD orders that privately authorized or put them into effect probably served no purpose other than to comply with the Soviet administrative bureaucracy. The prominent publication of what should have been a legally gratuitous Soviet order now is probably a further indication that intellectual arguments in support of the plan had been insufficiently persuasive. Ordinary people remained staunchly opposed to it.[62] But using Soviet occupation law to pressure Germans into complying with an ostensibly *German* plan praised, no less, as a national counterbalance to the "Americanism" threatening West German culture entailed certain risks. It emphasized the party's reliance upon Soviet patronage and deepened popular resentment of the Russians—so much so that the German Communists soon hinted at the problem. Klaus Zweiling, the editor of *Einheit*, acknowledged in May 1949 that the ordinance required the legal backing of an SMAD order, but insisted that "this 'order,'" by which he meant the *entire* DWK plan, had been thoroughly discussed beforehand by progressive segments of the very population ostensibly "subjugated" by it. Zweiling's remarks conveyed the message that there was nothing domineering about the Soviet action; it had no effect upon the democratic substance of a German ordinance because there had never been an occupation power "in the history of all mankind," and with the exception of the socialist version was none now, capable of such a display of democracy.[63]

More public commentary followed on the heels of high-level party discussions devoted to implementation of the plan. Stefan Heymann, on behalf of the division of PKE, made several pages of detailed proposals that included his recommendations for "commissions" assigned to oversee the plan's general provisions for the reorganization of the academy of sciences and for the formation of a new academy of arts. Ackermann, Oelßner, Heymann, Wandel, Rompe, and Naas were in charge of drawing up specific plans for the former and submitting them to the politburo for approval; and Ackermann, Heymann, Held, Grabowski, Engel, and Volkmann made up the latter.[64] The politburo met a few days later, on 12 April 1949, to work out further details that illustrate the intricate connections that existed between politburo, "Kleines Sekretariat," DWK, DVV, and so on. Ackermann was put in

[62]See, e.g., the summary of overwhelmingly negative attitudes in Abt. Kultur und Erziehung. [Landesvorstand Sachsen.] Stand der Arbeiten bei der Durchführung der DWK-Verordnung zur Entwicklung der Kultur, 17 May 1949. Zentrales Parteiarchiv, IV 2/906/109/27-34.

[63]Zweiling, "Intelligenz und Arbeiterklasse," *Einheit* 5 (1949): 402.

[64]Vorschläge zur Durchführung der Kultur-Verordnung der DWK lt. Protokoll vom 5. 4. 49. Zentrales Parteiarchiv, IV 2/906/109/93-97.

charge of the entire program, but efforts persisted to hide the fact that the ordinance was a party policy. For instance, the original resolution authorizing formation of a "cultural fund," passed by the secretariat on 2 August 1948, was to be reissued by "comrades" in the DWK as an ordinance prepared by that agency.[65] As a matter of fact, virtually nothing happened until the politburo and the DWK finally passed necessary resolutions late in the year.[66]

In the meantime, the campaign in favor of the overall ordinance was in full swing.[67] Ten days after its passage, the *Tägliche Rundschau* published a lengthy editorial signed by the customarily authoritative pseudonym "Orlov"; and two days later *Neues Deutschland* reprinted the remarks that started out with an audible echo of the Stalinist philosophy of organization. "With the line now set and the tasks worked out concretely, the comprehensive organizational, political, and propagandistic work needs to begin if tangible success is to be achieved."[68] This was just the first of many post-plenum commentaries that fluctuated between simple elaborations of the plan's generous provisions and the complex historical and contemporary dialectics behind it—all part of a concerted effort to talk both workers and intellectuals into accepting the idea. In spite of claims to the contrary, however, every discussion disclosed that the ordinance remained broadly unpopular. Orlov's article likened material incentives for intellectuals to the same basic idea behind order 234; but his approach relied upon the reference to an earlier Soviet order highly controversial in its own right, as well as the conspicuous use of a well-known Soviet pseudonym, to hint at the very fact that provoked more opposition—the cultural plan had the strong backing of the SMAD. Opposition to the ordinance thus violated occupation law, and undercutting its provisions could be legitimately interpreted as a challenge to the authority of the SMAD. The Soviet commentary nonetheless shied away from outright threats, whereas Ackermann exhibited no such hesitation. He insisted upon "complete clarity" when it came to intellectuals and workers, echoing the now familiar Stalinist tenet that the consciousness of the people had not kept pace with progressive developments in Soviet-occupied Germany. The animosity toward intellectuals, for instance, was one such attitude that needed to be "eradicated because it is pernicious and dangerous."[69]

[65]Protokoll Nr. 16 der Sitzung des Politbüros am 12. April 1949; Anlage Nr. 1. Durchführung des Beschlusses der DWK vom 31. März zur Entwicklung der Kultur und zur Verbesserung der Lage der Intellektuellen, ibid., IV 2/2/16.
[66]Stellungnahme zur Durchführung der Kulturverordnung der DWK, undated, gez. Stefan Heymann, ibid., IV 2/906/109/118.
[67]See, for instance, Entwurf eines Rundschreibens. Betr.: Propaganda für die Kulturverordnung der DWK, ibid., IV 2/906/109/22-3.
[68]Orlow, "An die Arbeit!" *Tägliche Rundschau*, 10 April 1949; Orlow, "An die Arbeit! Eine bedeutsame Veröffentlichung in der 'Täglichen Rundschau' über die Verwirklichung des Kulturplanes der DWK," *Neues Deutschland*, 12 April 1949.
[69]Ackermann, "Arbeiterklasse und Intelligenz," *Neues Deutschland*, 13 April 1949.

Ackermann voiced similar complaints when the board met in May; it was imperative that bad attitudes be overcome because improving the "material situation of intellectuals" was the key to winning their participation in democratic reconstruction. He explained further that the DWK ordinance gave the party a "new weapon" capable of "isolating reactionary elements within the intelligentsia who took their cues from Anglo-American imperialism, of winning the large mass of scientists, technicians, artists, and writers who vacillate and hesitate in their attitudes toward us, and of pulling them to our side."[70] But these kinds of arguments confirmed the suspicions of intellectuals critical of the plan. One in particular expressed opinions that the party characterized as "profascist," but considered typical of the "indifferent intelligentsia." This intellectual was skeptical about the sincerity of any overture aimed at the "bourgeois intelligentsia," concluding that both the SED and the DWK acted "on orders from Moscow." Moreover, he said, the Russians had good reason to improve the relationship between intellectuals and workers in Soviet-occupied Germany because of their own bitter experience. After the revolution, tens of thousands of intellectuals were "murdered, hundreds of thousands deported to Siberia, and the rest, robbed of their economic basis, succumbed to misery, poverty, and despair." The Russians had learned from the experience and wanted to make sure that the local economy did not suffer from the absence of qualified intellectuals. But the SED had already spent so much time scorning intellectuals as "servants of capitalism," as "war criminals," that thousands of engineers, scientists, and doctors, deprived of their existence, had fled to the West. As a result:

It will be even more difficult for the SED to come up with plausible arguments capable of answering for and justifying these measures to its own members. Workers look upon the situation mistrustfully, with no understanding; and, for the time being, the intellectuals targeted have also taken a wait-and-see attitude, full of reservations about the situation and as yet uncertain whether they should heed the sound of the sirens from the other camp. Well, the future will tell whether the SED is serious about its offer and whether intellectuals will really ever benefit from all the promises. Personally, for the time being I belong to the hesitant and think that I can wait until the monumental confrontation, coming for sure between East and West, will take care of matters and solve them in ways much different than anyone can dream of.[71]

---

[70]Stenographische Niederschrift über die 18. (32) Tagung des Parteivorstandes der SED am 4./ 5. Mai 1949. Zentrales Parteiarchiv, IV 2/1/32/41-43.

[71]Abt. Kultur und Erziehung. [Landesvorstand Sachsen.] Stand der Arbeiten bei der Durchführung der DWK-Verordnung zur Entwicklung der Kultur. 17 May 1949, ibid., IV 2/906/109/29.

The response to attitudes of this sort was sharp enough. Those who insisted that the ordinance undertook to "buy" or "bribe" intellectuals were considered "Trotskyist and similar agents of Western monopoly capitalists out to obstruct the consolidation of an alliance between the working class and the intelligentsia because they are afraid of it."[72] It is not at all certain, however, that intellectuals were uniformly critical of the ordinance. The report referred to above claimed that many were actually well-disposed toward it; the problem was with workers and other employees, especially within the party, who strongly opposed the plan. Nor is it difficult to see why; ordinary Germans received nothing other than what turned out to be a hollow promise that their circumstances would improve with time because of contributions made by those who were not required to wait patiently; whereas the intellectuals themselves, both the ones whose political principles had previously matched the SED's, or did so now, as well as those who went along for reasons unrelated to political conviction, gained immediately. The material benefits promised them were extraordinary indeed, gladly accepted, it seems,[73] and, too, by no means limited to the privileged few. High-level administrative personnel joined professors, prominent writers, artists, composers, stage producers and directors, editors, doctors, police chiefs, and such in category no. 1; categories no. 2 and no. 3 encompassed a corresponding range of professions, but these were equally dominated, in addition to somewhat less distinguished creative intellectuals, by legions of politicians and administrators at successively lower levels of state and local government.[74]

Theoretical explanations were then expected to satisfy ordinary working Germans either left to fend for themselves or given to understand that they, too, through hard work, could improve upon their standard of living. The DWK ordinance, read Ackermann's account, adhered to the same principle embodied in SMAD order 234, "work more, live better"; and rewarded intellectuals no differently than order 234 profited worker activists.[75] Nonetheless, the idea was wracked by its conflicting objectives. The party wanted to use the intellectuals to improve the apathetic attitudes of working Germans toward their jobs generally and the two-year plan specifically; but this segment of the population remained bitterly opposed to the idea of special privileges for intellectuals and equally unimpressed by the implied warning that,

---

[72]Zweiling, "Intelligenz und Arbeiterklasse," *Einheit* 5 (1949): 394.

[73]See the long list of promises made by Otto Grotewohl following a discussion with unnamed intellectuals on 16 March 1949—well in advance of the DWK's passage of the actual ordinance. Vorschläge des Genossen Grotewohl zur Unterstützung der Intellektuellen, 19 March 1949. Zentrales Parteiarchiv, IV 2/906/109/3.

[74]See DWK an alle Landesregierungen. Betr.: Richtlinien für die Durchführung der Ziffer 3 des Beschlusses Nr. S 32/49 vom 4. 2. 1949 der DWK, 16 March 1949; Musterliste der Angehörigen der schaffenden Intelligenz, an die Ausgabe der Zuweisungen nach Form 1, 2, 3 empfohlen wird. Ibid., IV 2/906/17-21.

[75]Ackermann, "Arbeiterklasse und Intelligenz," *Neues Deutschland*, 13 April 1949.

motivated by greed alone, intellectuals would otherwise spurn Soviet-zone reconstruction. Party spokesmen dealt with these attitudes by relying again upon Stalin's argument that consciousness lagged behind social progress and challenged the intellectuals do something about their outlook. Zweiling, for instance, had quickly shifted his discussion of material incentives to the problem of bad attitudes toward "progress" and thereby admitted, inadvertently, that reason alone had made no greater an impression upon intellectuals than workers. But when the party's appeals to reason failed, and, worse, certain unappreciative intellectuals not only expressed misgivings about the program of special treatment, but dared question the political motives behind it, most attempts at persuasion took on menacing overtones. Zweiling developed his argument out of rhetoric designed to dispel the "illusion"—if an illusion it was, he said pointedly, rather than a diversionary idea spread by "masked agents"—that science and art could ever be unpolitical.[76]

This point echoed earlier debates, but by now the political parameters tightened rapidly, as the sinister allusion to "masked agents" illustrates. Zweiling urged intellectuals to foster a consciousness worthy of the "changed social circumstances" in Soviet-occupied Germany, thereby contributing to a process of self-maturation leading toward greater social consciousness. Only then would they be fully committed to the requisite *conscious* participation in social evolution capable of rendering them truly "free." Zweiling's remarks were a simple restatement of the party's principal argument that political commitment was the absolute prerequisite of creative freedom; whereas political aloofness or abstinence led to the artist's enslavement to someone else's intentions. True, Zweiling admitted, under capitalism the intellectuals enjoyed certain liberties that "we shall not grant them," but this was no more than the freedom to contribute to the political and ideological suppression of the working class and of all progressive elements in the world by monopoly capitalism, as well as to a third world war. Those intellectuals powerless to determine which kind of freedom actually deprived them of their individual personality and which enhanced it merely testified to their own meager intelligence. Besides, cultural politics in Soviet-occupied Germany were said to be broadly inclusive; only intellectuals who acted as "agents of monopoly capitalism" would be pushed out—*verdrängt*—of the antifascist-democratic order. Not that there was any intention of rendering these persons "superfluous," said Zweiling; such intellectuals were that and more already; but as far as the rest were concerned, it was incumbent upon the working class to include all honest intellectuals interested in cooperation even when such persons could not yet be considered "convinced democrats."[77] Another commentary then likened the concept of forming a new

---

[76]Zweiling, "Intelligenz und Arbeiterklasse," *Einheit* 5 (1949): 397.
[77]Ibid., p. 398.

intelligentsia to the "experiences" of the Soviet Communist party in related matters. Considering that the SMAD had done more for German culture than any German government, ever, it could be properly argued that this support of "our national culture and our progressive intelligentsia" sprang from the essence of a socialist societal order. Under the leadership of Lenin and Stalin an immense cultural revolution had led to a "new Soviet intelligentsia"; Soviet intellectuals enjoyed "unrestricted creativity" and support; and in similar ways, the work of the intellectuals had acquired a new meaning in Soviet-occupied Germany as well.[78]

[78]"Arbeiterklasse und Intelligenz," *Sozialistische Bildungshefte* 5 (1949): 8-11.

CHAPTER FOURTEEN

Norms and Forms

The SED was now poised for the fight against "Americanism in the area of culture" and made itself clear about standards and expectations.[1] That provision of the cultural ordinance which established "national" prizes for literature, painting, graphic art, sculpture, music, theater, and film ruled out "formalistic, expressionistic, and other disgusting manifestations." Devoid of content, such products were of no use to the people.[2] The problem was that democratic content could not be captured using forms developed by "the enemy"; and many local artists and writers still indulged themselves in such practices. In fact, the predilection for such forms, apolitical by definition, was now thought to increase the likelihood that those who employed them were or might actually be "masked agents."[3] Realism, in form and content, was "the only possible" aesthetic and the "criterion of all true art." Using these arguments, if Franz Marc, who died long before Hitler came to power, could be branded a forerunner of fascism because his "world view" as an expressionist somehow coincided with fascist outlooks,[4] then it made just as much sense to call Herbert Sandberg a "formal fascist" due to his defense of modern techniques in 1949.[5] The same kind of thinking caused Oskar Nerlinger to conclude that "Paul Klee's lyricism" appealed to no one and would not be missed. Besides, that something happened to be disallowed during the Nazi years was "no good reason for doing it now—just because one 'may.'"[6] Nerlinger had no hesitation about criticizing Picasso either, whose political convictions he praised, for his choice of a "formal language" in *Guernica* that was incapable of expressing socialist content.

---

[1]Beschlußprotokoll der Referentenbesprechung am 31. August 1949. Zentrales Parteiarchiv, IV 2/906/12/43; and also the references to "Americanism" in literature, music and film made by Wilhelm Girnus at a meeting convened, appropriately, by the Kultureller Beirat. "Im Dienste des Fortschritts," *Börsenblatt für den deutschen Buchhandel* 17 (1949): 137.
[2]Orlow, "An die Arbeit!" *Neues Deutschland*, 12 April 1949.
[3]See Zweiling, "Intelligenz und Arbeiterklasse," *Einheit* 5 (1949): 397.
[4]Heymann, "Die Gefahr des Formalismus," *Einheit* 4 (1949): 343.
[5]"Opportunismus, Formalismus, Realismus?" *Neues Deutschland*, 13 March 1949.
[6]Nerlinger, "Überwindung des Formalismus," *Tägliche Rundschau*, 9 January 1949.

These were the kinds of arguments that Dymschitz' pronouncements on formalism emboldened. But there was something odd about his participation in the campaign right now. Even assuming that Dymschitz published his two articles in November 1948 with no knowledge of the impending denunciation of "unpatriotic" and "homeless cosmopolitans" back home, generally Jews, it is inconceivable that he was oblivious to those circumstances as of January or February. Not that Dymschitz, himself Jewish, abused "homeless cosmopolitans" in any of his known remarks about formalism; there was no mention of them in his last word on the subject;[7] and the campaign against formalism wound down, for the time being, in late February. But just as it tapered off with Dymschitz' final article on 27 February, discussions of cosmopolitanism generally and ones that focused specifically on cultural developments in the Soviet Union began picking up. By then, however, Dymschitz was no longer around to write any of them. He returned to Moscow in early March—just days after his last essay came out.[8] Whether his departure was actually tied in with the Soviet campaign against cosmopolitanism is an open question; but it is hard to imagine that these developments had absolutely no affect upon Dymschitz' position within the SMAD, even if there is no way of knowing for sure and no evidence to prove that the obsession with "cosmopolitans" caused what seems to have been an abrupt return to Moscow. There were connections in other cases, however; somewhat later, the editorial board of the *Tägliche Rundschau* met one day for a discussion that took place in spite of several empty chairs around the table. The Jewish officers and editors had been picked up from their apartments the night before and transported to parts unknown.[9]

Though it has never been solidly documented, the outbreak of antisemitism in the Soviet Union must, then, have been felt within the SMAD. Still, deliberately or not, Tjulpanov left out the adjective "homeless" when disputing what he branded as Western suggestions that Goethe was a "cosmopolitan spirit,"[10] even though an article had already appeared in the *Tägliche Rundschau* that mentioned "vagabonds without passports" and "homeless cosmopolitans, as the Soviet people call such persons." After listing names of Soviet theater critics clearly recognizable as Jewish, the author charged that they were members of an "antipatriotic group" responsible for having propagated a type of art "hostile toward the people, formalistic, and devoid of principles." In fact, these "homeless bourgeois cosmopolitans" were "ideological agents of American imperialism." In the absence of their annihilation, now accomplished, there would have been no "upswing" in Soviet literature and art; but the destruction of bourgeois cosmopolitanism retained its

---

[7]Dymschitz, "Ein Nachwort zur Diskussion," *Tägliche Rundschau*, 27 February 1949.
[8]See Brecht to Weigel, no date [the beginning of March 1949], *Briefe*, pp. 559-60.
[9]Reinhardt, *Zeitungen und Zeiten*, pp. 34-35.
[10]Tjulpanov, "Goethe und das Lager der Demokratie," *Neue Welt* 15 (1949): 5.

importance for "progressive democratic elements" around the world.[11] How much of this weighed on Dymschitz' mind in January and February is impossible to tell, but several months after his return home, Dymschitz sent an article back to Soviet-occupied Germany that also narrowly averted the anti-Semitic issue by leaving out the attribute "homeless" in front of cosmopolitan. Otherwise, Dymschitz sounded familiar themes. He disputed "evil and malicious legends" to the effect that Goethe was no patriot; insisted that past attempts to deny "national traits" in Goethe's work, its "national roots" and "patriotic content," had always been tied to efforts aimed at denying the national unity of the German people; and concluded that attempts to prove Goethe's "antipatriotism" nowadays tied in similarly with efforts, hiding behind cosmopolitanism, to "Marshallize Europe intellectually."[12]

The phrase "*rootless* cosmopolitan" did find favor with Otto Grotewohl, however, who used it to discuss Goethe's contrasting contributions to a German national consciousness;[13] and a few months later, the SED's own manifesto referred to the "cosmopolitanism propagated in the West," American-inspired, before likewise praising Goethe's "decisive contribution" to formation of a German national consciousness.[14] In fact, the entire "Goethe celebration of the German nation," which requires no further discussion here, neither of Thomas Mann's visit to Weimar, J. R. Becher's customary pathos there, nor the SMAD's approval of the commemoration,[15] mirrored the par-

[11]Arkaschin, "Kosmopolitismus—reaktionäre Ideologie von heute," *Tägliche Rundschau*, 11 March 1949.

[12]Dymschitz, "Goethe als Künder der nationalen Einheit Deutschlands," *Neues Welt* 16 (1949): 3-7.

[13]See Grotewohl, "Amboß oder Hammer," *Neues Deutschland*, 23 March 1949. My italics. The first draft of Grotewohl's speech was apparently written by Pieck's secretary, Walter Bartel; but the phrase, "Goethe was by no means a rootless cosmopolitan," appeared in successive later drafts in what seems to be Grotewohl's handwriting (Zentrales Parteiarchiv, NL 90/143/6, 40, 62, 196, 247). The party also approved the speech to be given a day before Grotewohl's by Hans Mayer, who was brought to Berlin from Leipzig beforehand to discuss "his materials" with Grotewohl (Grotewohl an den Kreisvorstand der SED, Leipzig. Z. Hd. Gen. Sindermann and Brett-schneider, 23 February 1949, ibid., NL 90/143/1). Mayer made no mention of "cosmopolitanism" and called for the "suppression of any thought that desires to use or misuse Goethe" for any particular purpose. But he focused otherwise upon "tendencies hostile to culture" that he said were characteristic of the concluding bourgeois epoch and had culminated in the "profound barbarism of Auschwitz and Buchenwald." See "Das neue Goethe-Bild der deutschen Jugend," *Tägliche Rundschau*, 22 March 1949.

[14]"Manifest—Zur Goethe-Feier der deutschen Nation [28 August 1949]," *Dokumente der Sozialistischen Einheitspartei*, vol. II, pp. 332-34

[15]See Kulturelle Aufklärung. Betr.: Finanzierung für das Goethe-Jahr, 8 March 1949. Bundesarchiv, Abt. Potsdam, R-2/1096/54-57. SMAD order no. 15, dated 11 February 1949, which had apparently been drawn up by the "Zentraler Goethe-Ausschuß," sent by J. R. Becher to the DWK's secretariat to be forwarded to Sokolovskij for approval in the form of an order, authorized the commemoration. By then, the draft order had already been discussed "in lengthy consultations" with the SMAD's information office. See Becher to Heinrich Rau, no date, ibid., R-2/1096/69.

ty's mix of national propaganda and cultural isolationism. One of the main purposes of the event was to counter suggestions that Soviet-occupied Germany, busy blending Zhdanov's aesthetics with bitter hostility toward the West, had not cut itself off from international influences, but rather acted to meet an American threat bent upon the annihilation of Germany's cultural identity. Celebrating Goethe's two-hundredth birthday was just another way of establishing a national alibi that, nonetheless, came down to the reconciliation of Goethean attitudes with Stalin's obsession with Soviet Jews whose antipatriotism stemmed from their lack of national roots.

In the Soviet Union, these ideas served additional domestic purposes rooted in Stalin's talk of vestiges of backward attitudes in the minds of Soviet people and his obsession with capitalist encirclement; and in Soviet-occupied Germany, mutatis mutandis, they did the same. Needless to say, intellectuals like Dymschitz, as well as some of the Germans who mimicked his arguments, gilded their opinions of formalism with as much sophistication as they were capable of mustering; but unembellished, the remarks still came down to the primitive assumption that "decadent" literature, art, or music was *volksfeindlich*—full of hatred toward the people. All decadents started from this position of hatred and, regardless of the mask that they hid behind, were "enemies of the people."[16] Generally speaking, however, the arguments against formalism were couched in somewhat loftier theoretical terms that fell into two categories: opposition to formalism that ended in less categorical judgments (often rooted in sincere reservations about poor imitations of modern art); and utterly uncompromising denunciations of formalism and decadence based on intimidation and threats. At the opposite end of the spectrum, then, there was also an undercurrent of concern about state-sponsored art that managed to find its way into print.

Judging by the reaction to critics who rejected formalism in principle, but still favored intellectual arguments over innuendo, the sponsors of the debate worried more about internal unorthodoxy than outright opposition. There is no other way to explain the treatment of Horst Strempel and Herbert Sandberg—artists with ties to the party. Strempel argued that democratic artists might have an obligation to continue certain formal innovations, going back to Cezanne, in order to preserve these for the "working class"; once socialism had been realized in Germany, then "we will achieve 'socialist realism.'"[17] Strempel endorsed Dymschitz' rejection of *l'art pour l'art,* but the notion that socialist realism could develop only under the conditions of socialism struck Dymschitz as "un-Marxist."[18] Even so, he soon softened his remarks in order to avoid the impression that the campaign against formalism favored socialist realism right away. No one expected "German artists

[16]Anisimov, "Betrübte Totengräber," *Tägliche Rundschau,* 5 January 1949.
[17]Strempel, "Gestaltung der Gesetzmäßigkeit," *Tägliche Rundschau,* 5 January 1949.
[18]"Formalismus oder Realismus?" *Neues Deutschland,* 18 February 1949.

influenced by formalism" to set out down that road immediately; advocates of "realism" merely urged formalist artists to embark upon the road to realism generally, not necessarily to steer directly toward the "banks of socialist realism." But it was not true that socialist realism in art could only be realized after the attainment of socialism; and the efforts of "truly socialist artists in Germany" to create a revolutionary art in their own country would be thrown off stride if this mistaken assumption were not corrected.[19]

The opponents of formalism all agreed on one issue, however; as Nerlinger argued, "realism is not a style, but an intellectual attitude"; a socialist artist viewed the world differently than a bourgeois artist. The result was a realistic vision of his surroundings and the corresponding necessity of a "realistic formal representation of his artistic message."[20] Dymschitz sharpened the argument by insisting similarly that formalism and realism stood for diametrically opposed perceptions of life. Reaction was the enemy; decadence was part of reaction; and people like Sandberg, who adored the "'quality of form' in decadent art," could not understand that "'perfect' form" represented the consummate means of reactionary deceit and hypnosis. The battle against formalism was part of the struggle against the "rotten 'culture' of bourgeois decadence" because genuinely new art could never emerge under the influence of the "'qualities' of decadent formalism."[21] Art according to Dymschitz was indistinguishable from politics; it fit either a reactionary or progressive description; and, devoid of transcendent value, had to be made aware of its responsibility to "participate in the construction of the new society." Socialist realism was the kind of art that defined itself in terms of just such a "political obligation"; it preferred to depict human beings in their social existence; and social existence was dominated by the need to establish an antifascist-democratic order and by the two-year plan.[22]

Opposing arguments came in response to these ideas. One was critical of "sterile formalism," but leery of Dymschitz' advocacy of "general, uniform principles" in art because of the implied threat of replacing unbridled individualism with "standardized state art"; "for obvious reasons, we are mistrustful in Germany about proposals for 'healthy principles.'"[23] Further objections followed. "You know," Dymschitz was apparently told, "we had to endure a traveling exhibition of 'degenerate art' in Germany during the wretched era of nazism." Whatever the gap between the pseudo-world view of nazism and Marxism, the critic continued, in attitudes toward painting and the pictorial arts both sides utilized the same concepts in support of tighten-

---

[19]Dymschitz, "Ein Nachwort zur Diskussion," *Tägliche Rundschau*, 27 February 1949.
[20]Nerlinger, "Überwindung des Formalismus," *Tägliche Rundschau*, 9 January 1949.
[21]"Formalismus in der Sackgasse," *Neues Deutschland*, 20 February 1949; Dymschitz, "Ein Nachwort zur Diskussion," *Tägliche Rundschau*, 27 February 1949.
[22]Vogt, "Formalismus, Naturalismus, Realismus," *Neues Deutschland*, 15 February 1949.
[23]"Für fortschrittliche Kunst—gegen Dekadenz," *Tägliche Rundschau*, 2 February 1949.

ing the links between artists and the masses. But what exactly was the answer when ordinary people failed to understand an artist's work, asked, "why are we paying you?" and answered their own question by remarking, "not so that you can make fools of us with your degenerate isms." What happened then when the artist, following his own conscience, declined to submit? Were the people's representatives sitting in the responsible "ministry" justified in withholding support? If so, artists who lived and worked in a socialist society could find themselves in straits just as dire as their starving colleagues in capitalist countries. Another commentary reversed the order of priorities entirely; if there was to be an intellectual and artistic upswing, the artists must not descend to the level of the people; the people needed to ascend toward "their artists, their elite." Still others uttered different blasphemies; there was a real danger that "genuine" would be supplanted by "surrogate" experience. Kitsch, a threat to any socialist art, would then result because art insufficiently formed, socialist content notwithstanding, would produce dilettantism, rather than socialist realism. Formalist accomplishments therefore needed to serve socialist-realist purposes.[24]

None of these opinions had a chance of prevailing; and during a discussion organized to debate the merits of Karl Hofer's work, whose article on art and politics a few months earlier hovered in the background, Dymschitz corrected what *Neues Deutschland* called the many "open and hidden misunderstandings." Chief among them was Sandberg's idea that the formal accomplishments of the past fifty years remained important for the development of art; that the greatest danger resided not in formalism, but in the trivialization of artistic taste; and that art would continue to exist only if it utilized achievements, the formal included, arrived at since the turn of the century. Dymschitz countered that German artists merely imitated French modernists; and gave his assessment a patriotic twist by adding that "the national tradition" was important to the development of democratic art in Germany. Sandberg had also ventured to say that the seeds of the future germinated in "decadence." Dymschitz denied it, charging Sandberg and others with "ideological mistakes." He said that Sandberg had defended decadence against "annihilating criticism"; whereas what Dymschitz said about Hofer had nothing to do with annihilation; "we want to help Hofer, not destroy him." Dymschitz also criticized Sandberg for his remark about the "triumph of mediocrity" and dismissed "pretensions of genius." Socialist realism could claim any number of great works of art. Still, Dymschitz repeated, the issue was not "socialist realism or formalism," but development toward realism generally. This could not be achieved through "prohibition," however, and he personally had no right "to condemn other works."[25] A week later, Dym-

<hr>

[24]The above remarks are all from ibid.
[25]See "Formalismus oder Realismus?" *Neues Deutschland*, 18 February 1949; Dt. "Das Schlußwort spricht die Praxis," *Tägliche Rundschau*, 20 February 1949; "Formalismus in der Sack-

schitz summarized his positions and left for home. The "'principles' and practices of formalism" had nothing to do with real art, he said; formalism destroyed it. But criticism of it nonetheless remained free from any intention of "'commanding' a new form." Besides, people, progress, and history had already reached a verdict—formalism was the product of a degenerating, disintegrating bourgeois society and destined to perish with it. However, its continuing influence on "politically progressive, though creatively vacillating artists," had to be criticized in the interest of the correct development of art.[26]

Beckmesserei

One last exchange, between Herbert Sandberg and the SED's Stefan Heymann, followed on the heels of Dymschitz' closing remarks. It began when Sandberg complained in *Neues Deutschland* that his opinions about art were considered more than sufficient by some to disqualify him as a Marxist altogether and pointed out, in defense of his politics, that he had paid for them with ten years in Nazi prisons and camps. Sandberg pleaded now for a fair assessment of "Hofer and Chagall" and insisted upon the right to regard himself as "a realist."[27] Heymann lashed out at Sandberg for refusing to drop the subject and characterized his stubbornness as "pernicious"—*schädlich*. If they wished, Sandberg and his friends could continue to voice their opinions; no one would prevent them, either, from painting what and however they wanted; but Sandberg would have to put up with "our" conclusion that he qualified *"neither as a Marxist, nor as a realist."*[28] In yet another article, Heymann went on to insist that expressionism actually paved the way for fascism, dismissed the fact that the fascists then turned on what he called their pioneers as one of history's "ironic jokes," and proceeded to jeer Hofer more roundly than Dymschitz. Hofer, said Heymann, was guilty of "aristocratic arrogance" for suggesting that popular taste in art was corrupt and that it would correspond with demanding artistry only after the new society had arrived. "Comrade Zhdanov" had already rejected this argument as "separation from the people," said Heymann, who noted also that the central committee objected when "formalist composers" blamed the masses for their inability to appreciate modern music. Hofer's "snobby arrogance" was comparable.[29]

gasse," *Neues Deutschland*, 20 February 1949.
[26]Dymschitz, "Ein Nachwort zur Diskussion," *Tägliche Rundschau*, 27 February 1949.
[27]"Opportunismus, Formalismus, Realismus?" *Neues Deutschland*, 13 March 1949.
[28]Heymann, "Naturalismus, Realismus und—Marxismus," *Neues Deutschland*, 27 March 1949.
[29]Heymann, "Die Gefahr des Formalismus," *Einheit* 4 (1949): 346-48.

Fritz Erpenbeck's criticism of Brecht's *Mutter Courage*, which opened to tumultuous ovations in the Deutsches Theater on 11 January 1949, makes less sense outside this general context. Of course, there had been individual and collective misgivings about Brecht for years within the party, not to speak of bitter rivalries and personal animosities. His known associations and acknowledged affinities with Soviet theater personalities like Meyerhold, Tairov, Okhlopkov, Vachtangov, or even Tretjakov, who violated the norms of socialist realism in the thirties and, in some instances, paid dearly for doing so, hardly improved the situation; and related "theoretical" issues surfaced right after the war when Hans Jendretzky and Erpenbeck objected to the performance of *Die Dreigroschenoper*. Nor did the controversy about to break out now over *Mutter Courage* put the matter to rest. Two years later, another campaign resulted in a stronger condemnation of Brecht dominated by slogans, such as Wandel's, like "Learn from the Soviet Union how to build our own national German culture"; and by criticism of such threats as American boogie-woogie music or "hit-tune cosmopolitanism."[30] This later campaign originated at the highest levels of the party; but whether the same is entirely true of Erpenbeck's criticism of *Mutter Courage* in January 1949 is a more open question. To assume that the controversy witnessed to nothing more than the personal opinions of critics with no political backing, however, would be to misunderstand the context of the debate.

When Brecht crossed over the border into Soviet-occupied Germany in October 1948, he was told by the party functionary present that "the order of priority is now morality first, then food"[31]—not a very encouraging start regardless of whether the man who uttered the words, Otto Buchwitz, happened to be speaking on higher authority. But that frigid reception was the least of the mysteries surrounding Brecht's return and his efforts to form a theater ensemble of his own. According to Max Frisch, Dymschitz had earlier asked him to deliver a letter to Brecht, while Brecht was still in Zürich, that contained a Soviet invitation to settle in Berlin and what amounted to the promise of a theater.[32] If this is true, the problems that soon developed may suggest that attitudes toward Brecht had changed within the SMAD or, at the very least, that his supporters there were less ready to stick their necks out after the formalism campaign got underway. The indecision that then resulted seems to have left Brecht, by mid-January 1949, on the verge of leaving Berlin in a huff. On 6 January, Brecht was called out of rehearsals of *Mutter Courage* for talks with the mayor of Berlin, Friedrich Ebert, that took place in the presence of Wolfgang Langhoff, who headed the Deutsches Theater, Fritz Wisten, who ran the theater that Brecht wanted (on the Schiff-

---

[30]See *Der Kampf gegen den Formalismus in Kunst und Literatur, für eine fortschrittliche deutsche Kultur.*
[31]Brecht, *Arbeitsjournal* [22 October 1948], p. 847.
[32]Mittenzwei, *Das Leben des Bertolt Brecht*, p. 236.

bauerdamm), and from the SED's Anton Ackermann, Hans Jendretzky, and Otto Bork. Dymschitz was not present, though he later claimed to have been and started the legend that Brecht nobly refused to move into the Schiffbauerdammtheater until Wisten received a stage of his own. Brecht left this discussion with dwindling optimism. Ebert had said neither "hello," nor "goodby," declined to address him personally, and made cutting remarks about "uncertain projects that would destroy that which exists already." The party representatives, Ackermann most likely, offered Brecht the undersized and inappropriate Kammerspiele and spoke of the possibility of guest appearances in the Deutsches Theater or on Wisten's stage. But according to Brecht, they complained about the shortage of money and spoke of the priority of establishing a home for the Volksbühne. Indeed, several weeks later the politburo gave the Schiffbauerdammtheater to the Volksbühne.[33] Though there was then some talk in February 1950 of basing the Berliner Ensemble in the Komische Oper, and, the following October, of moving it into the Schiffbauerdammtheater a year later, that building did not become Brecht's until 1954, when the Volksbühne switched to its location on Luxembourg Square.[34]

Brecht held the Volksbühne in utter disdain in early 1949, however; the conversation in Ebert's office all but exhausted his patience; and one of his staunchest admirers, Wolfgang Harich, wrote Anton Ackermann on 17 January to warn that Brecht, due to Ebert's behavior and as a result of his own "stubbornness," might well leave town. Determined to prevent that from happening, Harich arranged for a discussion between Brecht and a number of his prominent supporters (Anna Seghers, Hans Mayer, Peter Huchel, Paul Rilla, Max Schroeder, Herbert Ihering, Langhoff, Ernst Legal, Walter Felsenstein, Erich Engel, Ernst Busch, Slatan Dudow, Hanns Eisler, and Paul Dessau). "As representatives of the party," Stefan Heymann (PKE), Rudi Engel (DVV), and Otto Bork, from the city Magistrat, were to participate as well; and Harich had been instructed by this group to find out beforehand from both Ackermann and Dymschitz exactly what "apparently" stood in the way of the realization of Brecht's plans. According to what Heymann first told Harich, Brecht insisted upon conditions that the city could not meet financially and that were, in addition, an affront to Wisten. Besides, the party wished to merge the Volksbühne with the Schiffbauerdammtheater anyway and put it under the direction of Wisten. That particular building was there-

[33]Protokoll Nr. 3 der Sitzung des Politbüros am 15. Februar 1949. Zentrales Parteiarchiv, IV 2/2/3. Incidentally, there is every indication that Soviet-zone theaters *were* in dire economic straits in early 1949; but it is impossible to determine which of these considerations, economic or political, predominated in Brecht's case at this precise moment.
[34]See Ministerium für Volksbildung. HA Kunst und Literatur. Arbeitsbericht Monat Januar 1950, 18 February 1950; Arbeitsbericht Monat März, 3 April 1950; Arbeitsbericht Monat April, 6 May 1950. Bundesarchiv, Abt. Potsdam, R-2/4775/107, 90, 83-89; and also the letter to Hans Lauter, head of the central-committee's cultural division, 9 October 1950, ibid., IV 2/906/90/99.

fore unavailable, and Brecht's "incomprehensible" disinterest in the Kammerspiele eliminated the only other possibility. On 14 January, Harich had broached the same subject with Dymschitz, who reportedly said that Brecht needed to be more realistic about the situation in Berlin, accept conditions as they were, and start working with other people. "If that does not appeal to him, it is certainly regrettable; but nothing else can be done." Dymschitz added that those remarks represented his own personal opinion and were "by no means the official standpoint of the SMAD." But what exactly that standpoint was, remains unclear; Dymschitz's contention that the SMAD considered the affair to be a "German matter exclusively" was unconvincing because there had never been any such thing. Harich went on to tell Ackermann that Dymschitz had nonetheless not been opposed to his, Harich's, "little conspiracy" on behalf of Brecht and would welcome a solution acceptable to everyone. Harich then informed Ackermann that the discussion with Brecht would take place that evening. In the meantime, he had already discussed matters with Brecht, who remained adamant about staging his plays in the Schiffbauerdammtheater, but did not object to the idea of Wisten staying on as director if he, Brecht, exercised complete artistic control over his own ensemble. In his recommendations to Ackermann, Harich took an even tougher line and suggested that the actors engaged by the Schiffbauerdammtheater, under Wisten, merge with the Volksbühne and continued performing in a theater located in the Kastanienallee until it established its artistic reputation. Harich also proposed that Wisten be put in charge of the Volksbühne, too, as well as manage the Schiffbauerdammtheater, but with no artistic influence over the latter. The artistic director needed to be a "personality suggested by Brecht," and Brecht should have the broadest possible power over its affairs.[35]

Harich's actions seem to have upset Ackermann, who threatened him with a "severe reprimand" for violating party discipline.[36] But a compromise was soon reached when Langhoff evidently suggested that, for the time being, Brecht house his "ensemble" within the Deutsches Theater, though it is obvious that such an offer still required party approval,[37] Soviet, too, and a source of funding. By late February, then, tentative plans had been drawn up by the DVV's division of art and literature for the establishment of a "2nd independent ensemble in the Deutsches Theater in Berlin (direction Bert Brecht, Helene Weigel)" that would play four months out of the year in Ber-

[35]Harich to Ackermann, 17 January 1949. Zentrales Parteiarchiv, NL109/89/113017.

[36]Ackermann's anger subsided soon after, perhaps in connection with other decisions that favored the solution actually agreed upon. Harich could not remember his letter to Ackermann, but it corroborated everything that he told me. (From my conversation with Harich in 1991.)

[37]It must have existed, too; one of the official events scheduled for participants in the party conference from 25 to 28 January 1949 was a performance of *Mutter Courage*. See Protokoll Nr. 145 (II) der Sitzung des Zentralsekretariats am 23. 1. 1949. Zentrales Parteiarchiv, IV 2/2.1/263/ 1-2.

lin and spend five touring throughout the zone.[38] This was also the solution agreed to eventually, except that the plan still had to be submitted to the SED, reviewed and authorized by the SMAD, and passed on to the DWK for its "official" stamp of approval. All this took time, and the fact that the formalism campaign generally and Erpenbeck's criticism of *Mutter Courage* specifically coincided with the final chain of events hints at the presence of other considerations at least partially responsible for the delays.

Not until 23 March 1949, several weeks after the arrangement was first alluded to in DVV files, did the SED's Kleines Sekretariat take action, consenting to the idea and agreeing to discuss financing with the SMAD. Just short of one-and-a-quarter million marks were required annually, as well as $10,000 a year for the fees of guest stars and 340,000 marks in initial outlays.[39] But there was nothing especially "rapid" about what happened then.[40] Four more weeks elapsed before Ulbricht got around to informing Heinrich Rau, as head of the DWK, that the politburo, supposedly upon the recommendation of Pieck and Grotewohl, had authorized Helene Weigel to form a new ensemble and put on "three progressive plays" starting in September 1949. These would be performed on one of the stages of the Deutsches Theater and constitute part of its official repertory for six months. During the other half of the year, as the DVV had already indicated, the troupe would tour Soviet-occupied Germany. Other than the mention of Pieck and Grotewohl, which sounds suspiciously as if Ulbricht himself did not personally endorse the idea or wish to be identified with it, his memorandum to Rau merely repeated the language and terms contained in the resolution passed by the Kleines Sekretariat. By then, however, Ulbricht added that he had already discussed the "political" side of the issue with the SMAD; and instructed Rau to get a corresponding measure passed by the DWK's secretariat.[41] After the members of the Berliner Ensemble had been "screened" by the party, and their personnel papers passed along to the Kleines Sekretariat, a contract was drawn up and signed in late October 1949, retroactive to 1 April, by Paul Wandel on behalf of the DVV and Helene Weigel. That contract also stipulated which three plans were to be performed between 1 September 1949 and 31 August 1950.[42]

---

[38]Abteilung Kunst und Literatur. Übersicht über den Arbeitsplan für 1949, 21 February 1949. Bundesarchiv, Abt. Potsdam, R-2/1155/77h.

[39]Finanzierung des Helene-Weigel-Ensembles. Protokoll Nr. 14 der Sitzung des Kleinen Sekretariats am 23. März 1949. Zentrales Parteiarchiv, IV 2/3/14/2.

[40]See Mittenzwei, *Das Leben des Bertolt Brecht*, pp. 356-58. "Rapid" is Mittenzwei's word, and it is only one of his inaccuracies. The Kleines Sekretariat, headed by Ulbricht, made the decision, not the politbüro. There is no evidence either to document Dymschitz' involvement in it. Mittenzwei writes that Dymschitz "mobilized all available assistance," but neglects to mention that he was long gone by the time the Kleines Sekretariat, and the SMAD, finally took action.

[41]Ibid.; and Ulbricht to Rau, 29 April 1949. Zentrales Parteiarchiv, IV 182/931/79.

[42]Beschlußprotokoll der Referentenbesprechung [PKE], 31 August 1949, ibid., IV 2/906/12/43.

Brecht first heard that his plans had been approved on 18 May 1949. By then, the process had taken almost five months; and it is hard to avoid the impression that the delays had some connection with the controversy over *Mutter Courage*. The uncompromising attacks upon "formalism" and "decadence" provided Brecht's detractors with the best kind of argument for use against him; and the authoritative nature of the campaign, particularly its patent Soviet origins, made it risky to ignore arguments couched in those terms. If Brecht indeed came to Berlin following an invitation by Dymschitz in fall 1948, along with his promise of a theater, what appears to be Dymschitz' detached attitude to the very real prospect of Brecht's departure from Berlin in January 1949 certainly hints at problems. It just may be that Dymschitz, worried about his own future, refused to go out on a limb for Brecht. He was back in Moscow by March 1949 anyway; and it is entirely possible that Brecht got his ensemble, if not yet his own theater, simply because the triumphant premiere of *Mutter Courage* on 11 January 1949 made it impossible for the party or the SMAD to ignore him. But influential critics were not obligated to praise him, and, a week after the discussion with Ackermann in Ebert's office, Brecht was attacked for the "decadence" of the very play that established his postwar reputation. But the nature and timing of the ensuing debate raises tantalizing questions. The day after *Mutter Courage* opened, *Neues Deutschland* ran a story, signed only "M.S.," that gushed with praise of Brecht. "M.S." considered the performance a "sensation," culturally and politically; applauded Brecht's "powerful experimental energy"; said that he was viewed worldwide, "without dispute," as the most significant creative personality of the modern theater; concluded that Brecht was in perfect conformity with the theater responsible for performing his play; and was in equal harmony with the "society" behind the theater.[43]

This article, hardly a review, couched its celebration of Brecht's genius in terms so categorical that they appeared to rule out further discussion. Moreover, this kind of authoritative statement in *Neues Deutschland* would normally have precluded any unless thinking within the party itself was divided enough to permit the publication of an equally categorical countervailing opinion. In fact, this is what happened, though the actual criticism appeared elsewhere. The next day, Max Schroeder, "M.S.," published a second article that was equally adulatory; and ended his remarks with the comment that a discussion of *Mutter Courage* would follow in a future issue of the paper.[44] Evidently none did, and Erpenbeck's article came out five days

The authorized plays were Gorky's *Vassa Shelesnova*, Brecht's *Herr Puntila und sein Knecht Matti*, and Grieg's *Tage der Kommune* in Brecht's version. See Wandel's contract with Weigel in Bundesarchiv, Abt. Potsdam, R-22/4052.
[43]"Bertolt Brecht. Zur deutschen Erstaufführung seiner 'Mutter Courage,'" *Neues Deutschland*, 12 January 1949.
[44]Schroeder, "'Verflucht sei der Krieg!' Deutsche Erstaufführung Bertolt Brechts 'Mutter Cou-

later, in *Die Weltbühne*, possibly suggesting that *Neues Deutschland* was editorially or politically stalemated. The essence of Erpenbeck's argument was simple enough; he never denied that Brecht's work achieved the highest aesthetic and philosophical quality; and there was no point, he added, in confirming what the "daily press" said about the sensational success of the premiere. But then, he went on, neither "quality" nor intention had a thing to do with it; the question was, "at what point does the road, progressive aspirations and the most refined formal ability notwithstanding, lead hopelessly into decadence alienated from the people?"[45]

Coming on the heels of standing ovations and widespread acclaim, there was an inescapable irony to the situation now developing. That irony only intensified when Erpenbeck was humiliated a few weeks later by someone, Wolfgang Harich, who otherwise found formalism, decadence, and cosmopolitanism singularly disgusting, wrote indefatigably about both, had just published, in the same issue of *Die Weltbühne* that carried Erpenbeck's review of *Mutter Courage*, a blistering attack upon Sartre for daring to suggest that Communists were "hostile toward intellectuals";[46] but could not conceive of Brecht being either "decadent" or "alienated from the people." It struck him as so absurd that Harich dismissed Erpenbeck's criticism as "Beckmesserei," after the pedantic figure in Wagner's *Die Meistersänger*. But Harich, who had no trouble dissecting the flimsy logic behind Erpenbeck's reasoning, built his arguments around the assumption that progressive content could be adequately represented in innovative forms. The basic idea was, of course, the very proposition categorically rejected by Dymschitz, Heymann, and others in the ongoing debate over formalism. They argued that experimental forms in the ostensible service of progress and revolution actually constituted left-wing sectarianism. But Harich, luckier than Sandberg, got away with the argument; and it is hard to believe that his own eloquence was the sole reason why. Knowingly or not, Harich must have served here as the mouthpiece for others who supported Brecht for reasons of their own and prevailed, temporarily, in this particular confrontation. Otherwise, though normally more alert to the latest of dialectical discoveries, Harich missed the point that Brecht grasped immediately; Erpenbeck's remarks followed "the 'line,'"[47] even if that "line" suffered a momentary defeat possibly related to the public success of *Mutter Courage* and the sensitivity of the moment. Harich appears to have discerned little of this; and nowhere was his inexperience in these matters more obvious than in his remark that Erpenbeck, during his ten years in the Soviet Union, had failed to notice how

rage' im Deutschen Theater," *Neues Deutschland*, 13 January 1949.

[45]Erpenbeck, "Einige Bemerkungen zu Brechts 'Mutter Courage,'" *Die Weltbühne* 3 (1949): 101-3.

[46]Harich, "Monsieur Sartre wird mißverstanden," ibid., p. 99.

[47]Brecht, *Arbeitsjournal* [28 January 1949], p. 895.

novels there had been rendered into dialogue and put on stage. By way of example, Harich mentioned two directors with innovative interests, Tairov and Okhlopkov, both targets of official harassment.[48]

Erpenbeck, in his response to Harich, seems to have realized that he was now fighting a losing battle, though he certainly never believed, as he suggested, that his exchange with Harich had nothing to do with "Brecht's theater plans."[49] Erpenbeck surely knew of Brecht's interest in his own ensemble; must privately have opposed the idea; and may have accepted the setback now because he had no choice—despite the fact that Dymschitz' attack on formalism and decadence generally, which relied on conceptual arguments just like Erpenbeck's, had seemed to provide a prime opportunity to go after Brecht. Nor is it clear how Dymschitz figured into the discussion. It is hard to imagine that he knew nothing in advance of Erpenbeck's review of *Mutter Courage*; and for reasons connected with the campaign against formalism, which became publicly synonymous with anticosmopolitanism in the Soviet Union in late January, it is possible that Dymschitz was either powerless to stop it or not about to shoulder the risk of intervention himself. These uncertainties add to the difficulty of accounting fully for Harich's refutation of Erpenbeck's arguments based on reasoning that Dymschitz elsewhere categorically rejected. But Harich may have disclosed the real reason why he was allowed to draw upon these arguments when he ended his article with a reference to Brecht's importance for theater in Berlin. Permitting Erpenbeck's kind of criticism to prevail, within days of Brecht's triumph and at the height of the Berlin blockade, would have required a chorus of additional condemnation scarcely capable of enhancing the reputation of cultural politics in Soviet-occupied Germany at a critical time; and the success of *Mutter Courage* may then have contributed directly to the positive outcome of discussions about a new ensemble.

Not that Erpenbeck surrendered without a fight, and he certainly knew how to take care of himself. His remark to Harich, "Let's not exaggerate our importance,"[50] suggests an awareness of opportunities, tactically limited for the moment, yet to come; the events of early 1951 indicate that Brecht's opponents had suffered no more than a temporary defeat; and Erpenbeck quite likely took it as such. Indeed, when the attacks came later, they focused on *Soviet* art and literature as the healthy source of inspiration for East German culture best able to meet the threat of Western formalist and cosmopolitan sedition. Moreover, in the course of the discussion in 1951, Erpenbeck was personally vindicated as one of the few critics whose writing pointed in the proper "direction."[51] By April 1951, he had become the GDR's anointed

[48]Harich, "'Trotz fortschrittlichen Wollens . . . ,'" *Die Weltbühne* 6 (1949): 215-19.
[49]Erpenbeck, "Polemik statt Diskussion," *Die Weltbühne* 9 (1949): 328.
[50]Ibid.
[51]"Entschließung des Zentralkomitees der Sozialistischen Einheitspartei Deutschlands auf der

ymschitz, Heymann, and others insisted that their criticism was neither
ically nor artistically normative. But even the suggestion that persons
aged in creative pursuits succumbed to the influence of "foreign" ideas
of simple ignorance and needed only to elevate their consciousness to
level of the progressive society around them allowed for dangerous in-
nces. The distinction between a consciousness encumbered by notions
demic to capitalist societies and what Zweiling called "*maskiertes Agen-
ntum*" was, under the best of circumstances, a narrow one and, either way,
intessentially Stalinist. In Soviet-occupied Germany, then, the notions of
rmalism and cosmopolitanism assisted the SED in its growing determina-
on to seal off the country culturally and politically from Western Europe
nd, by extension, from America. Heymann delved into the nature of the
new twentieth-century mythos," Americanism or the culture of dying imperialism,[62] and also discussed the subject of formalism and decadence in connection with the second Dresden art exhibition in fall 1949. He used that opportunity to complain about the inconclusive end to the discussion begun by
Dymschitz; it had been too "isolated" from other critical issues associated
with cosmopolitanism and the development of Soviet art. Heymann argued
now that local artists were obliged to familiarize themselves with the "problems of Soviet art and with the countless discussions of these questions in
the Soviet Union"; without an intimate awareness of such issues, along with
an "application of the same principles to the questions of pictorial art here at
home," it would be impossible to develop a truly realistic art. "Our great national struggle for the unity of Germany and for peace is indivisible from the
constant consolidation of our democratic republic"; there was a corresponding need for works of art capable of strengthening and elevating the "moral
and cultural consciousness of our people"; and doing so presupposed the
"total liquidation of cosmopolitanism" in art. Heymann was especially worried because the exhibition in Dresden revealed, "with horrifying clarity,"
that the intellectual content of almost every picture was "cosmopolitan, that
is, devoid of national roots." The situation was so bad that no national prize
could be conferred. No artist met the standards, and those standards, as Heymann admitted, were "ideological," not artistic.[63]

That political purposes were behind the prizes explains why Karl Hofer
never qualified. Privately, the DVV's man in charge of art, Gerhart Strauß,
actually renominated Hofer for the national prize, first category, after Hofer
came out publicly in favor of the Paris peace conference and against the division of Berlin. His first nomination of Hofer, Strauß wrote Paul Wandel,
had been "deferred." But in spite of "certain attacks on him from our side,"
Hofer had now "joined us unequivocally," besides which his rank as a paint-

[62]Heymann, "Ein neuer Mythos des XX. Jahrhunderts. Der 'Amerikanismus'—die 'Kultur' des
sterbenden Imperialismus," *Einheit* 11 (1949): 996-1005.
[63]Heymann, "Kosmopolitismus und Formalismus," *Neues Deutschland*, 1 December 1949.

theater censor;[52] and he was also named to the ten-member state commission
on art, the infamous Staatliche Kommission für Kunstangelegenheiten, created in July 1951. But in 1949, Erpenbeck had already known how best to
refute some of Harich's strongest arguments by coupling his opinions to developments characteristic of Soviet art and literature. After Harich's imprudent mention of Tairov and Okhlopkov, Erpenbeck informed him that the
charge of "decadence alienated from the people" had been leveled in the Soviet Union not just against Tairov, but against Meyerhold, Shostokovich,
and Prokoviev; and added, though he knew better, that these discussions had
taken place in a "democratic and dispassionate" atmosphere. By 1949, of
course, Meyerhold, murdered, had been dead for several years; and Erpenbeck mentioned his name twice, telling Harich that, like Brecht, Meyerhold
had traveled the "descending path, progressive aspirations notwithstanding,
leading to the exclusivity of 'left-wing' sectarianism"; and no one took this
criticism to be "monstrous," as Harich regarded Erpenbeck's suggestion that
Brecht's work was decadent. Erpenbeck then got at the heart of the matter
when he alluded to the fact, though he made no reference to Stalin, that the
struggle against the vestiges of bourgeois consciousness, precisely the lingering influence responsible for the unacceptable blend of revolutionary "aspirations" and decadent bourgeois art forms, was a battle still being fought
in the Soviet Union.

Several weeks more elapsed before Erpenbeck returned to his main theoretical points, but this time he said nothing about Brecht specifically; and
concentrated on an overarching interpretation of "realism" as the depiction
of social-historical truth. There was now a perfect justification for distinguishing between classical, bourgeois, and socialist realism, he said; and
indicated that the latter was the only brand of realism that conformed to "our
reality."[53] This lengthy article lacked a single sentence that conflicted with
the positions of Dymschitz or Heymann; and by addressing the issue of socialist realism, a subject essentially absent in the direct exchange with Harich, Erpenbeck undertook to establish a Soviet cultural-political context for
later discussions of East German formalism and decadence in which he was
unlikely to lose. In so doing, he anticipated the remarks of politicians and
cultural figures at the SED's conference in March 1951, who vied with each
other in unembellished praise of Soviet culture, argued strongly in favor of
"following the example of the Soviet Union," made conspicuous references
to "Comrade Zhdanov," and issued a call to arms in defense of "our national
culture" and against the "advancing ideology of cosmopolitanism." Fred

Tagung vom 15.-17. März 1951," *Der Kampf gegen Formalismus in Kunst und Literatur, für
eine fortschrittliche deutsche Kultur*, p. 161.
[52]See below.
[53]Erpenbeck, "Formalismus und Dekadenz. Einige Gedanken aus Anlaß einer mißglückten Diskussion," *Theater der Zeit* 4 (1949): 1-8.

Oelßner discussed cosmopolitanism in direct connection with Brecht; and asked whether Brecht's *Mutter*, adapted from Gorky's novel, qualified as realistic at all. He himself considered it a synthesis of "Meyerhold and proletcult"; and in connection with Brecht's *Verhör des Lukullus* argued that "we simply cannot allow things to develop as they please." There was an enemy influence at work; Oelßner characterized it as "Americanism"; and development toward a "new progressive art" would be stunted in the absence of a struggle against such "cosmopolitanism, formalism, trash, etc."[54]

Ideological Sabotage

These later events reveal the importance of the issues already present in the exchange between Erpenbeck and Harich. But their debate, despite a few additional contributions to it,[55] ended as suddenly as it began; and at about the same time, the general campaign against formalism shaded into discussions of cosmopolitanism. Most of these, including Harich's, then focused more on the political implications of the concept; and it is hard to know for sure whether the Germans even understood what "cosmopolitanism" meant conceptually, to say nothing of racially, or how to apply it to local circumstances. By the fifties, they did; it was "Americanism," pure and simple; but commentaries published in March and April 1949 already cleared up some of the uncertainty. The first, by a Soviet writer, explained that the newspaper *Pravda* had recently undertaken to expose and destroy an "antipatriotic group of stage critics" who entertained extraordinarily dangerous notions about literature, dramaturgy, and other forms of art. A discussion of those matters followed, with much talk of Soviet patriotism and "homeless cosmopolitanism" as a weapon of Anglo-American reaction out to enslave other peoples through the spread of "modern bourgeois 'culture,' which is depraved and decadent"; and the article went on to excoriate specific critics, virtually everyone Jewish, for masking their "ideology of sabotage" or *Schädlingsideologie* with insincere recantation. The article also explained that these cosmopolitans were, by their very nature, formalists because the "antipatriotic group of critics propagated a formalist art devoid of principle and inimical to the people"—*volksfeindlich*. Moreover, it was important to understand that formalism had nothing to do with the perfection of artistic form. Formalism served the cause of art devoid of either principle or con-

---

tent; created for a gang of snobs and aesthetes with [...] cal aesthetic views," such art had a hostile bent [...] Painters like Chagall or composers like Schoenbe[...] never be regarded as artists who created for the peo[...] was the "fruit of the profound disintegration of mo[...] Hindemith in particular, already attacked by *Neues D*[...] for additional condemnation in the *Tägliche Rundscha*[...] mopolitan from overseas" who had developed the obno[...] lishing his German with American sentence fragments; a[...] as well, the "Hindemith of today, the American Hindemith[...] Hindemith," showed little inspiration in his work, prefer[...] on the technical side of music instead. In fact, "there is n[...] person as the *German* composer Paul Hindemith."[58]

   Neues Deutschland voiced its opinion of cosmopolitani[...] Union in late April in an article that hinted at aspects of the [...] clearly recognizable in local discussions as well. Reasons of [...] viet theater critics were attacked originally because they wo[...] deteriorating artistic quality of stage performances; and th[...] twisted this modest objection to mediocre art into the accusatio[...] tics, antipatriotic and not really "Soviet" or Russian either, insu[...] viet art and the Soviet people by whining about "cheap optimisı[...] agit-prop content," "idyllic limitations," and the "excessive empha[...] itics." What they supposedly wanted instead was *l'art pour l'art*[...] masked their true objective behind a show of concern about better [...] The clearest Soviet-zone manifestation of these arguments agains[...] politan outlooks and artistic practices occurred similarly in the cat[...] rejection of the notion that a heavy emphasis of content over form le[...] "triumph of mediocrity," as Sandberg had suggested; and in the corre[...] ing local demands for the politicization of art. It made perfect sense,[...] for Ernst Held to suggest that Wolfgang Langhoff had "shut" his thea[...] performances of Soviet plays not for political or philosophical reasons[...] because of "artistic" objections;[60] whereas, even had the charge been t[...] the latter offense was indistinguishable from the former and led to identi[...] consequences. The notion of waiting for a "new Shakespeare" to arrive [...] the Soviet-zone theatrical scene, Held insisted, was irresponsible.[61]

---

[54]"Entschließung des Zentralkomitees der Sozialistischen Einheitspartei Deutschlands auf der Tagung vom 15.-17. März 1951," pp. 22, 51-52, 72.

[55]See Altermann, "Wo beginnt die Dekadenz? Bemerkungen zur Polemik um Brecht's 'Mutter Courage,'" *Tägliche Rundschau*, 12 March 1949. Altermann's remarks found fault with both Harich and Erpenbeck and may have signaled publicly that the debate needed to end. According to what Harich told me, the SMAD's Susanne Altermann was no admirer of Brecht.

[56]Arkaschin, "Kosmopolitismus—reaktionäre Ideologie von heute," *Tägliche Rundschau*, 11 March 1949.

[57]"Was hat uns Hindemith zu sagen?" *Neues Deutschland*, 19 February 1949.

[58]Laux, "Musikalischer Kosmopolit aus Übersee," *Tägliche Rundschau*, 24 February 1949.

[59]Kraus, "Kosmopolitismus und Sowjetpatriotismus," *Neues Deutschland*, 27 April 1949.

[60]Held, "Fragen an W. Langhoff. Warum spielen das Deutsche Theater und die Kammerspiele keine Sowjetstücke," *Neues Deutschland*, 21 June 1949.

[61]Held, "Warten bis ein neuer Shakespeare kommt?" *Neues Deutschland*, 26 May 1949.

er justified the award at any time.[64] Hofer was not selected,[65] however; in June 1949, the politburo agreed that the prizes needed to serve the interests of "national German culture" while "energetically fighting against all manifestations and tendencies of cosmopolitanism." "Abstract, formalistic directions in literature, art, and music" had to be beaten back and realism fortified.[66] Hofer never had a chance because his formal inclinations could not pass muster. The same politburo meeting also approved the preliminary list of candidates, which included Brecht on his own merits as well as the actors who performed in the production of *Mutter Courage*. When Brecht found out in June 1949 that he was up for the prize, but only at the second level of distinction, and possibly just as a member of the "collective" that put on the performance of *Mutter Courage*, he found the classification degrading and made it known through Helene Weigel that he would not accept.[67] Several weeks later, evidently still on the list, Brecht used Erich Wendt to get the point across; and Wendt warned Wilhelm Pieck accordingly of the potential for scandal.[68] Weigel herself, who starred in *Mutter Courage*, accepted the second prize along with the other actors.

By late summer 1949, there was mounting concern within the party over the state of art in Soviet-occupied Germany and, it seems, a growing readiness to do still more about it. In connection with the Dresden art exhibition, Heymann wondered how long current circumstances would be permitted to continue "without action" and called for "ideological clarification." But he also tried to argue, paradoxically, that clarification hinged upon a multiplicity of artistic expression, not "standardization."[69] The opposite was true, of course; the titles of articles critical of the exhibition allude to the usual reasons for the dissatisfaction;[70] and internal memoranda illustrate just how impossible it was by now to keep up the appearance of moderation.

The exhibition first received approval at one of the DVV's minister conferences in winter 1949, but the details were left up to the state of Saxony, and, by April, a warning about the lack of a "programmatic" focus had already been sounded within the DVV.[71] There were two problems. One was

[64]Abteilung Kunst. Referat Bildende Kunst. Dr. Strauß. Betrifft: Professor Karl Hofer, 29 April 1949. Bundesarchiv, Abt. Potsdam, R-2/1147/99.
[65]See also the document Durch Boten! An die Sowjetische Militäradministration. Betr.: Nationalpreisträger im Goethe-Jahr 1949, ibid., R-2/911/42-46.
[66]Protokoll Nr. 29 der Sitzung des Politbüros am 28. Juni 1949; Anlage Nr. 3. Beschluß. Betr.: Verleihung der Nationalpreise. Zentrales Parteiarchiv, IV 2/2/29/33-36.
[67]See Brecht, *Arbeitsjournal* [18 June 1949], p. 906.
[68]Wendt to Pieck, 19 August 1949. Zentrales Parteiarchiv, NL 36/661/69.
[69]Heymann, "Kosmopolitismus und Formalismus," *Neues Deutschland*, 1 December 1949.
[70]See also Engels, "Warum die bildende Kunst im Rückstand ist. 2. Deutsche Kunstausstellung in Dresden," *Neues Deutschland*, 11 September 1949; and Lüdecke, "Ausweichen vor der Wirklichkeit," *Neues Deutschland*, 23 and 26 August 1949.
[71]Abteilung Kunst und Literatur. Referat bildende Kunst. Herrn Präsident Wandel über Herrn Volkmann. Betrifft: Zweite deutsche Kunstausstellung Dresden. Gez. Dr. Strauß, 1 April 1949.

that the planners, with the approval of the DVV, asked a group of artists who were members of the SED to prepare murals depicting workers engaged in activities associated with the two-year plan; and these murals themselves ended up being stigmatized as "formalistic." In fact, they might never have been exhibited at the opening on 10 September 1949 if a way had been found to prevent it. In an internal report written just days before the opening, Strauß talked about the murals, but also warned about the other problem developing in connection with the entire show. Some 1,500 works had been submitted, 670 of them from West Germany; and the quality of the latter exceeded that of the East German works. Due to the lack of "suitable submissions," the right impression would be made by no more than 20 percent of the pictures shown. The "formalist character" of the upcoming exhibition was further assured by the fact that the organizers took it upon themselves to give their representatives a free hand in selecting works from West Germany without providing for a jury verdict on the pieces chosen; "our protestations remained ineffectual," introducing an additional "element of uncertainty." Problems with the ten murals, still in preparation by the "collective," then arose when the artists refused, in part, to show the pictures to the jury; and the exhibition planners backed the artists. Strauß responded by having the jury pass a resolution authorizing a special commission to screen the works; its members managed to see two of the ten; but the other studios were "inaccessible." Another commission was subsequently formed, also for the purpose of "screening" the murals before they were hung, and apparently examined some of the paintings on 9 September. The first two seen were adjudged, in part, "insufficient" and, in part, "formalistic." A decision on whether to exhibit them had to await their completion.[72] An attempt to influence these works during the final stages of their preparation may also have occurred. One published report, written by a party artist who was privately blamed for the situation, Gert Caden, contained cryptic allusions to various "difficulties," "obstacles," and "impending catastrophes" avoided just in the nick of time; but indicated that the murals, after examination and approval of preparatory work by the artistic management, "in part" went through another thorough discussion with the collective before work was completed "without any influence exerted" and at the "sole discretion of the group of artists."[73]

But the murals were not the only problem.[74] Even before the opening, an internal memorandum characterized the works scheduled for showing as "predominantly formalistic." Fortunately, there would be no surrealistic pieces because the Western artists had not submitted any; however, such was

Zentrales Parteiarchiv, IV 2/906/183.

[72]Abteilung Kunst und Literatur. Referat bildende Kunst. Betrifft: 2. deutsche Kunstausstellung, Dresden. Gez. Dr. Strauß, 29 August 1949. Bundesarchiv, Abt. Potsdam, R-2/1093/38-39.

[73]Caden, "Zwölf Wandbilder entstehen," *Bildende Kunst* 9 (1949): 269-70.

[74]See Müller, "Über zehn Wandbilder," *Bildende Kunst* 10 (1949): 330-35.

not the case with "abstract and expressionistic works" due to the fact that artists outside of Soviet-occupied Germany, believing that creative freedom was suppressed there in favor of a Nazi-like art judged to be realistic, agreed to participate only when given the firm assurance that their work would be exhibited. This resulted in a promise that certain paintings would be hung with no prior evaluation and in the showing of some works considered by the jury to be "absolutely formalistic." The author of this unsigned memorandum concluded that such an approach seemed justified in terms of the necessity of winning Western creative artists for "our all-German goals in the context of the national front." Moreover, this organizational strategy also helped eliminate "misunderstandings" about the nature of art discussions going on in Soviet-occupied Germany.[75] Functionaries like Strauß or Grabowski or Heymann thought otherwise, though they tended to blame each other for the state of affairs. Grabowski conceded that the "creation of the national front" called for the inclusion of bourgeois artists in planning for the show; this permitted the participation of West German bourgeois artists; but "all those efforts geared toward promoting art that corresponds with our ideological demands" were then shoved to the background. In fact, said Grabowski, the coordinated intrigues of bourgeois artists who could count upon the support of the exhibition planners "successfully sabotaged the efforts" of the DVV and party representatives to give the show an "ideologically positive appearance"; and Grabowski suggested that disciplinary measures would be taken against certain members of the planning group.[76]

Though Rudi Engel, vice president of the DVV, tried to put the best face on things in public,[77] Heymann was incensed. He called the exhibition a "show of formalism" and considered it to be in "screaming contradiction to democratic development in our zone." Even "our artist-comrades" had developed a sense of the degree to which they had stumbled into a dead end; and, alluding to the murals, Heymann concluded that the attempt to help them out of it had failed because "you cannot use formal changes to force new content." The need for an "ideological dispute" in the ranks of the artists was the most important lesson to emerge out of the Dresden exhibition, he said, and bitterly criticized "Comrade Gert Caden," an "unmitigated formalist and poor painter," for a series of actions. But Heymann also pointed the finger of blame at Grabowski for failing to stand up to Caden. A list of details followed in Heymann's report, confidential copies of which he sent to such luminaries as Pieck, Grotewohl, Ackermann, and Wandel. One of the nastiest points was his criticism of favorable comments made by local

[75]Bericht über die Vorbereitung zur zweiten deutschen Kunstausstellung in Dresden, no date, unsigned. Zentrales Parteiarchiv, IV 2/906/183.
[76]Bericht über die zweite deutsche Kunstausstellung, no date, gez. Max Grabowski, ibid., IV 2/906/183.
[77]Engel, "Zur Situation der deutschen Kunst," *Bildende Kunst* 10 (1949): 311-12.

party functionaries, Helmut Holtzhauer and Max Seydewitz, in reference to works painted by the "reactionary and semi-fascist painter Otto Dix." Heymann considered this favoritism to be an insult to a painter by the name of Max Lingner. Lingner, a "realist," enjoyed the patronage of the party; insulting Lingner was therefore a deliberate "affront to the party."[78]

Exercises in Futility

The vigorous denunciations of cosmopolitanism, which the party later characterized as the "root" of formalism,[79] went hand in hand with the further development of regulatory agencies that were considered just as exemplary for a reunited Germany as the norms themselves. Alexander Abusch began his remarks about the DWK's cultural ordinance, for instance, by insisting that the plan was a model "for all of Germany, for a unified, democratic Germany."[80] Other talks devoted to a "cultural program" for all of Germany had commenced a year earlier, however, with the establishment of a cultural committee working under the auspices of the Deutscher Volksrat. Set up in the beginning to help buttress the national parliamentary pretensions of the Deutscher Volksrat, which was itself created on 18 March 1948 by the second Volkskongreß, this "cultural committee" was one of seven such advisory bodies secretly approved by the SED.[81] It was officially comprised of persons who represented the various political parties and mass organizations, though the chairmanship went to the SED by default, and the secretariat reminded all party members of their special "obligations."[82] The committee then spun its wheels once or twice a month from April 1948 through spring 1949, trying to exercise responsibilities that had never been defined, much less ever really assigned, and purporting to speak about issues of vast significance on behalf of the entire nation. The chairman, Heinrich Deiters, indicated that "all cultural activities" falling under the purview of the Volksrat had been entrusted to the committee; but seemed unsure of himself when he added that the group would work out its actual responsibilities as these emerged from specific situations.[83]

[78]Heymann to Pieck, Grotewohl, Ackermann, Wandel. Vetraulich, 13 September 1949. Zentrales Parteiarchiv, IV 2/906/183.

[79]"Die gegenwärtige Lage und die Aufgaben der Sozialistischen Einheitspartei Deutschlands," *Protokoll der Verhandlungen des III. Parteitages der Sozialistischen Einheitspartei Deutschlands* [20-24 July 1950], vol. 2, p. 264.

[80]*Der Kulturplan*, p. 25.

[81]See Protokoll Nr. 82 (II) der Sitzung des Zentralsekretariats am 7. 6. 48; Anlage Nr. 2. Geschäftsordnung des Deutschen Volksrates. Zentrales Parteiarchiv, IV 2/2.1/205/10.

[82]See Protokoll Nr. 57 (II) der Sitzung des Zentralsekretariats am 19. 3. 1948 and Protokoll Nr. 94 (II) am 12. 7. 48, ibid., IV 2/2.1/216/2.

[83]Deutscher Volksrat. Sekretariat - Abteilung III, IV - Fachausschüsse. Kulturausschuß. 5. Sit-

The secretariat of the Volksrat, which supervised and coordinated the work of all seven of its committees, shed additional light on the subject several weeks later when the cultural committee stumbled into areas closed to it. The Volksrat, the secretariat told the group, regarded itself as the "sole national representative of the German people"; but, supposedly, it was not "a zonal parliament."[84] Given the reality of the situation, his distinction implied that the committee's actual assignment was limited to the issuance of hollow proclamations on the subject of German unity; and yet even these failed to meet with the approval of mostly anonymous censors at work within the secretariat of the Volksrat, whose job it was to prevent any of the seven committees from doing much of anything. The cultural-political committee was told that it had no business concerning itself with regional state affairs unless these involved overarching questions related to the reestablishment of German unity. Accordingly, none of the committees were empowered to pass resolutions designed to initiate specific action on the part of any agency in Soviet-occupied Germany, much less exercise authority over the states; the committees could influence regional legislation only through recommendations designed to coordinate state lawmaking "within Germany" as a whole and "on the basis of the current political circumstances inside the Soviet occupation zone." These provisions, the statement said, would ensure that state-level legislation leading in divergent directions could be influenced in the interests of German unity, if only in Soviet-occupied Germany; but it was also "thinkable" that recommendations made by the committees might strike a responsive chord in this or that West German state.[85]

As a consequence of these limitations, the cultural committee was restricted from the outset to activities that never transcended the bounds of a round-table discussion attended by mostly faceless personalities; and they spent their time talking about events over which they had absolutely no influence—not in Soviet-occupied Germany and definitely not in the West. Little notice was taken of the Volksrat there other than as the latest SED stunt; and, especially when compared with the ambitious plan of developing a "cultural program" for all of Germany, the committee labored in even greater obscurity. As one document lamented in early 1949, the group had nothing to show for its efforts; the results were limited to "resolutions accorded insufficient attention either by the press or by the institutions at which they were addressed"; and there was no trace of a resonance in the Western zones either.[86] What little latitude was originally given the commit-

---

zung, 12 June 1948. Bundesarchiv, Abt. Potsdam, A-1/47/23.
[84]Deutscher Volksrat. Sekretariat. Abteilung III. Hauptreferent Ausschüsse. An den Sekretär des Ausschusses für Kulturpolitik. Betrifft: Anfrage des Ausschusses für Kulturpolitik über seine Aufgaben in besonderen Fällen, 2 August 1949, ibid., A-1/49/10.
[85]Ibid.
[86]Entwurf. Vorschläge für eine verbesserte Arbeitsweise des Ausschusses für Kulturpolitik, no

tee, almost nothing to begin with, dwindled even further whenever it undertook to issue "manifestos" and resolutions for publication in the Soviet-zone press. The secretariat first tried rewriting these entirely, to the consternation of committee members who found out about it when they read unrecognizable statements published under their name. Later, the secretariat changed tactics; at the start of any particular meeting, the group was provided with pre-prepared drafts of resolutions that committee members, after "discussion," were expected to pass substantially intact; and in late 1948, the SED took additional steps to control an emasculated committee powerless to accomplish anything anyway. These latter events occurred in connection with the group's discussion of the national cultural program that had been on the committee's agenda from the beginning. In fact, Deiters announced at the first meeting that he would draw up preparatory papers to serve as the basis for the committee's consideration of a "unified German cultural program."[87] But before the discussion took place, the committee found itself caught up in its first controversy over the publication of an official pronouncement. At just its second meeting on 23 April 1948, the group nominated a subcommittee to prepare a "cultural manifesto" intended to introduce the committee to the public.[88] The subcommittee included Anton Ackermann, who attended the first meeting of the general committee, but missed most of the rest without troubling to excuse himself; and J. R. Becher, who missed them all. In fact, Horst Brasch drafted the manifesto all by himself because no one else showed up for the first subcommittee meeting.

The document that Brasch presented on 22 May 1948, purporting to be an "appeal by the German people to all creative intellectuals," possessed no intrinsic importance; it lamented the threat to German culture posed by national disunity and talked about "current efforts to create a West German state."[89] The committee then discussed the draft, and minor emendations were approved. Only two publications printed the manifesto—*Deutschlands Stimme*, put out by the Volksrat; and *Neues Deutschland*. But both versions, to quote angry committee members, had been "mutilated" beyond recognition. The warning about the threat to German unity had been transformed into a blistering denunciation of "narrow-minded particularist elements" in the West; the statement charged further that the division of Germany was destined to do lasting damage to culture throughout all of Germany; and the edited version called accordingly for the establishment of an "indivisible democratic German republic."[90] To make a long story short,[91] a man named

date [probably early 1949], ibid., A-1/70/52-56.
[87]Kulturausschuß. 1. Sitzung, 15 April 1948, ibid., A-1/45/4.
[88]Kulturausschuß. 2. Sitzung, 23 April 1948, ibid., A-1/45/14.
[89]"Aufruf des deutschen Volkes an alle Kulturschaffenden!" Kulturausschuß. 4. Sitzung, 22 May 1948, ibid., A-1/46/10-12.
[90]"An die Kulturschaffenden. Ein Aufruf des Deutschen Volksrates," *Neues Deutschland*, 9

Mutius, who worked in the press office of the secretariat, rewrote the manifesto until it barely had "anything in common" with the original text—or he acted on higher orders. None of the committee members was satisfied with the explanation; the head of the secretariat, Erich Gniffke, replaced by the Wilhelm Koenen when Gniffke fled to the West, insisted that the press office acted correctly; and Deiters recommended that the committee drop the matter; Deiters also advised against publishing the original manifesto.[92]

The subject came up once more at the meeting on 2 August 1948, when the committee decided to request formally that the press office publish committee reports unabridged or not at all.[93] Not long after, however, much the same thing occurred again in connection with the committee's discussion of the cultural-political paragraphs contained in the SED's draft constitution under consideration by the Volksrat generally. Indeed, the committee was "surprised" to discover that the Volksrat intended to discuss the constitution the next day, "cultural-political paragraphs" included; whereas no one bothered to ask the committee for its impressions. Deiters then declared his intention of requesting that the group be given the opportunity to debate the relevant paragraphs, and make recommendations, before final acceptance of the constitution.[94] These talks took place at the next committee meeting on 21 August 1948 following introductory remarks about the draft constitution, an SED document to begin with, by Otto Meier. This was one of the few meetings attended by Ackermann, who spoke more often than any other member, freely offered his authoritative advice on numerous points; and strongly influenced a discussion that occasionally threatened to veer off in undesirable directions.[95] The deliberations continued at the next meeting on 4 September and were expected to go on at yet another on 9 October.[96] Also on the agenda of the October meeting was the "material plight of creative intellectuals"—the usual euphemism for the subject of a cultural plan based on special privileges. But neither the constitution nor the matter of assistance to intellectuals came up for discussion. It also turned out that the committee had entrusted one of its members, Kurt Schwarze, together with the secretariat's representative, with the task of preparing a communiqué regarding the group's opinion of the draft constitution; and the document had been drawn up. But Schwarze, the group's delegate from the Liberal Democratic party,

June 1948.
[91]See also Zur Vorlage Abteilungsleiterbesprechung (signed Georg-Wilhelm Jost), 14 June 1948; Panitz to Jost, 14 June 1948. Deutscher Volksrat. Sekretariat - Abteilung III, IV - Fachausschüsse. Kulturausschuß. Bundesarchiv, Abt. Potsdam, A-1/47/50-55.
[92]Kulturausschuß. 6. Sitzung, 1 July 1948, ibid., A-1/48/13.
[93]Kulturausschuß. 7. und 8. Sitzung, 2 August 1948, ibid., A-1/49/4-5.
[94]Ibid., A-1/49/70.
[95]See Ausschuß für Kulturpolitik. 9. Sitzung, 21 August 1948, ibid., A-1/50/9-55.
[96]See Ausschuß für Kulturpolitik. 10. Sitzung, 4 September 1948, ibid., A-1/51.

now told his colleagues on the committee that the secretariat had again published an "edited" version.

The committee decided to draft another statement, outlining its position on the cultural aspects of the constitution. But before the group could begin work, Walter Maschke, who represented the FDGB (and the SED), told the committee that the draft had already been approved by the group within the Volksrat charged with those responsibilities. Recommendations made by the cultural-political committee could no longer be considered. "Another misfire," Schwarze concluded; "we have yet to accomplish anything positive. I thought that our work on the constitutional provisions would be the first positive outcome worth showing the public, and it, too has apparently been squandered." The CDU representative, Peter Bloch, then wondered why discussion of the draft had been included on the day's agenda in the first place; but, unaware of the real reasons, he concluded that his own party had been to blame.[97] It was not; Maschke had deliberately sabotaged the meeting because neither Otto Meier nor Anton Ackermann desired any inconvenient discussions of constitutional provisions by this particular committee. Right before the scheduled session, Maschke told a man named Lorf, who represented the secretariat of the Volksrat at committee meetings, that he intended to obstruct the session's deliberations; the SED, he said, had no interest in continued discussion. The party also wanted the subject of assistance to intellectuals tabled because work on that proposal had not yet progressed far enough to be talked about by this body. Neither the vice president of the DVV, nor his representative, Herbert Gute, intended to appear at the meeting; and Maschke expressed his displeasure with the secretariat for failing to consult with Meier or Ackermann before calling the committee meeting in the first place. The session then "developed in accordance with Mashke's wishes";[98] and members were left wondering just what had happened.

The group failed to meet again until late November; and in the interim, the SED took steps to ensure that further discussions went more according to plan. Ackermann scheduled a meeting in his office on 25 November 1948 for committee members who belonged to the SED.[99] These talks, which planned the "future duties" of the cultural-political committee, led to the decision to break the committee into "subcommissions" charged with assessing the extent of democratization in the Western zones. In particular, the commissions were to look into the "Bonn project for a constitution," ascertain its "undemocratic spirit," and draw up a formal resolution. These commissions were supposed to be "elected" at the next meeting and be expanded by the

[97] Ausschuß für Kulturpolitik. 11. Sitzung, 9 October 1948, ibid., A-1/52/17.
[98] Deutscher Volksrat - Sekretariat - Abteilung 3. Vorlage an 31. Betr.: 11. Sitzung des kulturpolitischen Ausschusses, ibid., A-1/65/134.
[99] Aktennotiz. Betrifft: Telefongespräch mit Herrn Einig, Haus der Einheit. Signed: Jost and Lorf, no date [mid-November 1948], ibid., A-1/65/89.

addition of "experts" assigned to each.[100] Further details were arranged the next day in consultations between Lorf and Deiters; two courses of action decided upon; and the "results," as Ackermann had requested, sent to him at party headquarters.[101] In line with Ackermann's wishes, Deiters would make a number of points at the next committee meeting, chief among them the importance of the committee's obligation to focus on the "results of the two-year plan and its connection with cultural politics." Specific proposals for eight subcommissions were also to be made; these would be put in charge of schools, institutions of higher education, adult education, literature and publishing houses, youth affairs, press and radio, theater, film and music, and sport. Each of the commissions would then be assigned reliable "experts," most of whom came from the DVV. The commission on theater, film, and music was to be advised by Fritz Erpenbeck and Hermann Matern (then director of DEFA); press and radio would benefit from the sage counsel and wise advice of Rudi Engel and Karl Eduard von Schnitzler.[102] This was the first course of action; the second involved formation of an additional "main commission," comprised of Deiters, Baumann-Schosland (CDU), Ilse Berghaus (LDP), Helga Lange (FDJ), Ackermann, and, as consulting "expert," Paul Wandel. "Basic lectures" would be delivered to the entire cultural-political committee; these presentations would be reworked by the main commission and passed along to the presidium of the Volksrat as resolutions. The first three "lectures" included, "The Tasks of Cultural Politics in the Struggle for a Just Peace" (Wandel), "Cultural Politics as Economic Planning" (Ackermann), and "The Cultural-Political Paragraphs of the Bonn Draft Constitution and their Significance for Germany's Development" (Erich Glücksmann). These two courses of action would guarantee a "rapid involvement of the committee in the propagandistic work of the Volksrat" through the efforts of the main commission; while giving the subcommissions time to work on their jobs at a more relaxed pace.[103]

Following Deiter's presentation of these plans to the committee on 27 November 1948,[104] the group's sessions were restructured accordingly. Just before the subcommissions were formed during the meeting on 8 January 1949, however, Deiters and Lorf met again. Deiters advised the secretariat to refrain from organizing the meetings of the subcommissions "too strongly" because it would paralyze their initiative; but Lorf managed to secure Deiters agreement that the secretariat would engage in "prior discussions" with

[100]Aktennotiz über die Besprechung der Herren Jost und Lorf bei Herrn Ackermann am 25. November 1948, ibid., A-1/70/57.
[101]Lorf to Ackermann, 27 November 1948, ibid., A-1/74/21.
[102]Vorlage zur Besprechung mit dem Vorsitzenden des kulturpolitischen Ausschusses, 26 November 1948, ibid., A-1/65/122-24.
[103]Bericht über die Besprechung mit dem Vorsitzenden des kulturpolitischen Ausschusses am 26. 11. 1948, ibid., A-1/74/22.
[104]Ausschuß für Kulturpolitik. 12. Sitzung, 27 November 1948, ibid., A-1/53.

certain subcommission members or with their consulting experts; and, if necessary, prepare written materials beforehand.[105] As things developed, after consultations with the SED, the secretariat arranged for Stefan Heymann to talk to the cultural-political committee on 8 January about cultural politics and the two-year plan—the SED had agreed that the committee should concern itself more directly with the plan.[106] In addition, it was decided that a "resolution" based on Heymann's report should be drafted beforehand; and also understood that the discussion of Heymann's presentation needed to be "very well prepared" by, again, talking with important members of the subcommissions and the main commission prior to the meeting.[107]

Evidently, the "resolution" was considered to be a bad idea after all; and this maneuvering underscores the sensitivity of the entire subject of a "cultural plan," associated with the two-year plan, during the weeks leading up to the SED conference in late January. Heymann agreed with Lorf that there should be no committee resolution based upon his presentation; moreover, he would limit himself to reporting "on the cultural plan of the Socialist Unity party expected in the next few days." Heymann also promised that committee members would receive copies of the SED's plan just as soon as it was approved by the party's board; and it was decided—on behalf of the group, but without consulting with it beforehand—that the committee would pass Heymann's report on to its subcommissions along with the party plan, but only after the latter had been "definitively passed" by its inner circle.[108] Indeed, the entire subject of a "cultural plan" remained so sensitive that permission to prepare mimeographed copies of the committee's meeting on 8 January 1949, at which Heymann delivered his report,[109] and to disseminate them among the other Volksrat committees, was temporarily denied.[110]

Right after Heymann's report, the secretariat set the agenda for the committee's next meetings. Among other things, the group needed to discuss the matter of cultural politics in West Germany as reflected in the draft proposal for a West German constitution; and the committee, as well as its subcommissions, were expected to "deal with" both Heymann's report and the "cultural plan of the SED."[111] The head of the subcommission on literature and publishing was Peter Bloch, the CDU representative; presentation of the

---

[105]Unterredung zwischen Herrn Prof. Deiters und Herrn Lorf, 22 December 1948, ibid., A-1/65.
[106]Aktennotiz. Betrifft: Kulturausschuß, 5 January 1949, ibid., A-1/65/72.
[107]Aktennotiz für Herrn Lorf, 6 January 1949, ibid., A-1/65/71.
[108]Betrifft: Kulturpolitischer Ausschuß. Unterredung mit Herrn Stefan Heymann, 7 January 1949, ibid., A-1/65/67.
[109]See Unkorrigierte Niederschrift. Ausschuß für Kulturpolitik. 14. Sitzung, 8 January 1949. Stefan Heymann: Aufgaben der Kulturpolitik im Zweijahrplan, ibid., A-1/55/32-45.
[110]Ausschuß für Kulturpolitik. Hausmitteilung. Abteilungsleiter III von Kulturausschuß 12. 1. 49 (Lorf), ibid., A-1/65/68.
[111]Betr. Aufgaben des Kulturpolitischen Ausschusses. Rücksprache zwischen Herrn Jost und Lorf, 12 January 1949, ibid., A-1/65/61.

West German constitution fell into his group's jurisdiction; and he delivered a report of that document's cultural provisions that was critical, but insufficiently so.[112] A problem then arose because Bloch had been asked, by the secretariat itself, to follow up his presentation with a draft resolution; and when he introduced his statement to committee members, it turned out that the secretariat had drawn up a document of its own. A lengthy discussion ensued; Bloch expressed his unhappiness at the waste of his time; and a compromise of sorts was reached to "merge" the two documents into one.[113] Bloch also indicated that his subcommission intended to meet on 19 February 1949 to discuss ideas for a "all German cultural plan"; by then, each member would have a copy of Heymann's report and the SED's cultural program; and other committee members also requested that that "cultural plan as an appendix to the two-year plan" be placed at the top of the agenda for the next meeting. The committee then concentrated most of its energy on its own all-German cultural plan; and the fact that the matter failed to come up earlier, after appearing tentatively in the documents of the committee's first meetings a year before, indicates that the party had not wanted it discussed sooner. Now, it coincided with final plans for the issuance of the DWK's cultural ordinance, though committee members probably had no advanced knowledge of those plans.

Initial thinking called for the development by the committee of "guidelines for an all-German cultural program" to be presented at a session of the Volksrat.[114] By the time the committee met on 19 February, a variety of information was available that included Heymann's report, the SED's cultural plan, FDGB guidelines for cultural-political work, and ideas developed by a man named Ernst Hadermann designed to structure the discussion.[115] Hadermann, no doubt acting on Ackermann's instructions, said that the idea behind an all-German cultural plan was different from a "cultural two-year plan for the Soviet-zone of occupation"; the DVV had taken care of that task working with both the state ministries of culture and education and the DWK; and it was now in the process of "further concretization." Instead, the cultural-political committee needed to develop a cultural program that would be valid throughout all of Germany and not limited to two years. These guidelines should pay particular attention to "organizational forms" and "material preconditions"; and they needed to make the "cultural work already accomplished in the Eastern zone, as well as still aspired to, the basis

[112]Ausschuß für Kulturpolitik. 15. Sitzung, 5 February 1949. Das Bonner Grundgesetz und seine kulturpolitischen Auswirkungen. Berichterstattung: Dr. Peter Bloch, ibid., A-1/56/26-64.
[113]See Bloch's version (ibid., A-1/76/120, complete with remarks unacceptable to the SED that "finalization of the constitution for an indivisible German republic must be the job of a future German national assembly" and "differences in the construction of the state can be bridged"); and the final version (ibid., A-1/56/88-101).
[114]Dem Vorsitzenden zur Vorlage, 5 February 1949, ibid., A-1/74/57-8.
[115]Ausschuß für Kulturpolitik. 16. Sitzung, 19 February 1949, ibid., A-1/57/56.

of an all-German cultural program."[116] What emerged, then, was nothing more than a collection of documents, designed to influence the discussions at the committee's seventeenth session on 17 March 1949, comprised of the interlocking programs for Soviet-zone culture drawn up by the various mass organizations controlled by the SED; and the party's own "measures for the implementation of cultural tasks in connection with the two-year plan."[117]

Deiters then appeared at the meeting on 17 March 1949 with his own or, most likely, the party's prepared guidelines. He introduced them by remarking that an all-German cultural plan was desirable because "we must think about what needs to happen in the cultural sphere throughout all of Germany in the aftermath of the work accomplished in the Soviet zone."[118] Deiters supplied committee members with a document comprised of eight sections (preamble; organization and financing; schools; universities and institutes of higher education; general education; collections and museums; literature and press; art, film, and radio).[119] At Heymann's request, these guidelines had been sent to the SED the day before the meeting.[120] But when the group next met on 9 April 1949, the DWK's cultural ordinance had been passed and essentially rendered the work of the cultural-political committee entirely irrelevant. By then, Heymann had been "coopted" into the committee (in place of Ackermann);[121] and his first action as a committee member was to provide the group with preprepared "draft resolutions" approving the world peace conference in Paris, which continued the work of the Wroclaw congress; and the DWK ordinance that committee members had known nothing about.[122] Heymann's resolution concerning the peace conference, containing references to atomic bomb factories in the United States, a description of the North Atlantic Treaty Organization as a new "anti-Comintern pact," and

[116]Vorschlag für die Gestaltung des gesamtdeutschen Kulturprogramms, 18 February 1949, ibid., A-1/57/105.

[117]See the following documents all characterized as "Informationsmaterial zur Vollausschußsitzung am 17. 3. 49"; "Beschluß der Volksbildungsminister vom 12.8.1948"; "Der Zweijahrplan und die Kulturschaffenden (Abdruck des Kongreßberichtes vom Oktoberkongreß)"; "Referat von Stefan Heymann 'Die Aufgaben der Kulturpolitik im Zweijahrplan,' auf der 14. Sitzung des Kulturpolitischen Ausschusses des Deutschen Volksrates am 8. 1. 1949"; "Maßnahmen zur Durchführung der kulturellen Aufgaben des Zweijahrplanes"; "Berliner Kulturprogramm des Kulturbundes"; "Richtlinien der kulturpolitischen Arbeiten des FDGB"; "Beitrag zum Kulturplan, von der VdgB"; "Beitrag zum Kulturplan der LDP"; "Material zur Kulturpolitik der CDU"; "Entschließung des zentralen Ausschusses für Kulturarbeit in den Betrieben auf seiner Arbeitstagung am 18. November 1948"; "Richtlinien für die Aufgaben und die Tätigkeit der Kulturkommission und Obleute der Betriebe"; "Arbeitsplan für die Kulturarbeit der FDJ bis zum III. Parlament (24 February 1949)," ibid., A-1/76.

[118]Ausschuß für Kulturpolitik. 17. Sitzung, 17 March 1949, ibid., A-1/58/18.

[119]See Informationsmaterial zur Vollausschußsitzung am 17. 3. 49, ibid., A-1/174-76.

[120]See ibid., A-1/76/76.

[121]See concerning Heymann's cooptation, Notiz für Frau Preuß, 23 March 1949 (A-1/65/44); and Deiter's comments at the start of the eighteenth session on 9 April (ibid., A-1/59/8).

[122]See the letter to Deiters dated 8 April 1949 referring to the two draft resolutions (A-1/74/48).

calls for German cultural unity, was approved without a single objection following meaningless stylistic alterations suggested by Heymann himself.[123] After Willmann's discussion of the cultural fund,[124] the committee passed Heymann's resolution in support of the DWK's cultural ordinance.

In connection with the Volkskongreß that met on 29 and 30 May 1949, which selected the "second" Deutscher Volksrat, the activities of the cultural-political committee then tapered off considerably. It met for its nineteenth meeting on 7 May 1949 before convening for the last time on 25 June 1949. On 2 June 1949, the secretariat of the Volksrat seems to have decided that its committees, including the cultural-political committee, would remain intact; and as late as 19 September 1949, when Deiters resigned as chairman, there was still talk of "reconstituting" the committee. But there is no indication that it ever was;[125] nor is there a record of any later meetings. The groups were likely disbanded when the Volksrat turned into the Volkskammer of the German Democratic Republic on 7 October 1949.

Stage Censorship

The first mention of plans for a "theater congress," tentatively scheduled for April or May 1948, appeared in conjunction with the idea of "artistic advisory boards" capable of contributing to the "management" of repertories.[126] In all likelihood, this meeting was intended to be part of a "reorganization" of Soviet-zone theaters that centered on the search for better methods of regulation. Though a later DVV memorandum also referred to the screening of repertories in the same context as some kind of "theater planning office for the procurement of supplies," and reorganization of the Volksbühne,[127] the "stage managers' conference" did not gather until after the party released its two-year plan on 29 June 1948. When the conference convened on 16 July, the assembled sixty or so managers were addressed by Fritz Selbmann, deputy head of the DWK, who briefed them on the two-year plan and the relationship between the "economy and culture." Dymschitz attended, too; and there is good reason to believe that the Russians were just as interested in finding a permanent solution to the regulation of theaters. "Program planning and improving the artistic niveau of theaters in the Eastern zone" then

---

[123]Ausschuß für Kulturpolitik. 18. Sitzung. Stellungnahme zum Verbindungsausschuß der Kulturschaffenden zur Weltfriedenskonferenz, ibid., A-1/59/8-11.

[124]See Chapter Thirteen.

[125]Deiters to Koenen, 19 September 1949, ibid., A-1/74/41.

[126]Betrifft: Arbeitsplan der Abteilung K für das Vierteljahr des Haushaltsjahres 1947/48, 23 December 1947, ibid., R-2/1155/76. See also Chapter Seven.

[127]Abteilung Kunst und Literatur. Referat Theater. Betrifft: Arbeitsplan des Theaterreferats für das I. Quartal des Haushaltsjahres 1947/48, 6 April 1948, ibid., R-2/1155/68.

dominated discussions and must have figured in the decision made at the conference to set up an agency called the Büro für Theaterfragen. In fact, it may be that the earlier idea of an "artistic advisory board" reemerged now in the form of this new "cooperative" venture undertaken by Soviet-zone theaters, the Gewerkschaft 17, the Bund Deutscher Volksbühnen, and the DVV; and depicted as an undertaking designed to assist all Soviet-zone theaters in the acquisition of materials and supplies necessary for the fulfillment of their own "two-year plans."[128]

Many of the office's documents show that it had indeed been created for the purpose of economizing theater operations throughout Soviet-occupied Germany by means of greater cooperation and coordination; but there is no doubt that "coordination" also applied to matters of program planning. The Berlin "working committee," for instance, consisted of six commissions; "repertory and authors' issues" was the first, followed by legal affairs, then financial matters, young talent, editorial board, and supplies.[129] In addition, the question of a "repertory commission" came up for discussion at a later meeting of the same working committee that left no doubt about the thinking behind it. At the suggestion of a certain Wengels, from the SED's division of PKE, it was decided that a commission should be set up within the Büro für Theaterfragen in order to keep the programs of theaters located in the Soviet sector of Berlin in adjustment with each other through the "coordination" of their repertories. The commission intended also to offer its "help and advice" to stage managers in the preparation of their programs.[130] But these intentions appear to have been crossed by the fact that stage censorship remained the prerogative of the SMAD, and the Russians could not overcome their lingering reluctance to put "censorship in German hands" once and for all.[131] In the meantime, regulation apparently continued as before; theater managers in all of Soviet-occupied Germany negotiated directly with the local offices of the SMAD (with the exception of Mecklenburg, which had set up its own unpopular office of "precensorship" within the appropriate ministry).[132]

The Büro für Theaterfragen may also have been seen originally as a way of dampening claims still made by the Gewerkschaft 17 that it exercised the

[128]See Büro für Theaterfragen. Arbeitsgemeinschaft der Bühnen und der Gewerkschaft 17 im FDGB, des Bundes Deutscher Volksbühnen und der Deutschen Verwaltung für Volksbildung. Bundesarchiv, Abt. Potsdam, R-100/900/98; and "Die Bühne und der Zweijahrplan," Neues Deutschland, 21 July 1948.

[129]Geschäftsbericht, 18 January 1949. Bundesarchiv, Abt. Potsdam, R-100/900/98.

[130]Protokoll über die Sitzung des "Berliner Arbeitsausschusses," 9 July 1949, ibid., R-100/900/89.

[131]See the allusions in Protokoll über die Kommissionssitzung des Berliner Arbeitsausschusses, 8 March 1949 and also 26 April 1949, ibid.

[132]See Protokoll der zweiten Tagung des "Büro für Theaterfragen," 13 and 14 November 1948, ibid.

right of "codetermination" in theaters. Several members of the board that ran the union were kept in the dark about plans for the new office dominated, no less, by theater *management*; they reacted testily when they found out about it; and, unpersuaded by the argument that "we can no longer look upon stage managers, like we did before, as employers," consented to attend meetings of the organization only for "informational" purposes.[133] It seems fairly clear, then, that the focus on repertory regulation had shifted from union "codetermination" to the more promising approach of influencing the actions of stage managers and directors themselves. There is surely significance in the fact that a functionary like Fritz Erpenbeck, who shocked union leaders in May 1948 by rejecting wholesale the idea of a contractually guaranteed right of codetermination,[134] also attended the first formal meeting of the Büro für Theaterfragen on 22 January 1949;[135] and was later considered the top candidate to assume control of it.[136] But there is no question that regulation was the key idea behind the undertaking. At the meeting in July 1948, it had already been noted that the assembled stage managers considered an "artistic repertory" and "improved quality" achievable only on the basis of co operation with a variety of "democratic organizations," but desired to see the idea of codetermination in artistic matters reduced to the "right to be consulted." Only then could sufficient latitude be granted to the "personal artistic responsibility" of the manager.[137]

Herbert Volkmann introduced his plans for 1949 with remarks to the effect that there was a need for "constant discussion within the Büro für Theaterfragen with theater directors in matters pertaining to repertory planning," development via the Volksbühne of a new group of theater-goers from the ranks of workers, bringing artists and workers together in the workplace, and, yet again, "reorganizing the system of theaters." This latter goal included plans to reexamine the operations of theaters throughout the zone in hopes of getting the "most important" stages on a solid financial footing while shutting down "theater operations that are artistically deficient and economically unjustifiable." The DVV expected to reduce the number from 105 to 85. There were also plans for improving the Volksbühne "movement," such as expanding the secretariat of the Bund Deutscher Volksbühnen and rebuilding the old Volksbühne theater; and, in addition, provisions for the "ideological schooling" of functionaries who worked both for the Volksbühne and other theaters. The goal of "improving the ideological and

---

[133]Bericht über die am 6. und 7. Januar 1949 abgehaltene Tagung des Zentralvorstandes. Archiv der Gewerkschaftbewegung, Sig. 3.
[134]"Theorie und Praxis," *Kunst und Schrifttum* 6 (1948): 23.
[135]"Das Theater und die Probleme der Zeit," *Neues Deutschland*, 25 January 1949.
[136]Referentenbesprechung am 12. 8. 1949. Beschlußprotokoll. Zentrales Parteiarchiv, IV 2/906/12/37-9.
[137]"Die Bühne und der Zweijahrplan," *Neues Deutschland*, 21 July 1948.

artistic niveau of the theaters" would be aspired to by "working through and criticizing, on a regular basis, theater repertories" at the monthly stage-manager conferences held by the Büro für Theaterfragen.[138] But these plans also listed "creation of a German office of theater censorship (consultations with the information agency of the SMAD)" as one of the DVV's top priorities in 1949,[139] meaning that for one reason or the other the Büro für Theaterfragen was not yet considered as such.

Still no decision had been made as to whether the Volksbühne or the Büro für Theaterfragen would assume responsibility for "repertory management" as late as November 1949.[140] In fact, neither one got the assignment, which hinged on the SMAD's relinquishment of its right to censor anyway; and back when the search for the right agency first got serious, in early 1949, the Russians stalled. In spring, the SMAD may have flirted with the idea of assigning responsibility for "theater censorship" to the Germans because the DVV asked the commission in charge of repertory issues within the Büro für Theaterfragen how it would react to such an event. Herbert Ihering replied that "an office of censorship" should work to remove any need for it by raising the consciousness of theater directors. But in the interim, it ought not to go beyond determining whether a given play exhibited Nazi or militaristic tendencies, anti-Soviet sentiments, or "hurt democratic development."[141] Apparently, the question of "placing censorship in German hands" went to the SMAD for a decision in early May 1949. Though none had been made as of late June, stage censorship finally became a German prerogative in the days following formation of the German Democratic Republic or occurred upon creation of the government.[142] Wolfgang Langhoff said on 15 October 1949 that the government had the right to oversee the repertories of all theaters, approving or prohibiting the performance of plays; and there was talk of setting up a "repertory commission" comprised of representatives of the Ministerium für Volksbildung (MfV), which replaced the DVV, the party, the union, and the Büro für Theaterfragen. The SED was to be apprised of the names of commission members and an accord reached with the party's cultural division. Obtaining copies of theater repertories from stages around the country would be the first step.[143]

[138]Abteilung Kunst und Literatur. Übersicht über den Arbeitsplan für 1949, 21 February 1949. Bundesarchiv, Abt. Potsdam, R-2/1155/77a-77h.

[139]Ibid.

[140]See Zur Situation der Volksbühnen-Organisation, 14 November 1949, ibid., R-2/1095/34-9.

[141]Protokoll der Tagung des "Büro für Theaterfragen," 12 and 13 March 1949, ibid., R-100/900/89.

[142]Protokoll für die Tagung des Arbeitsausschusses der Mitglieder des Büros für Theaterfragen, 7 and 8 May, 25 and 26 June, and 14 and 15 October 1949, ibid.

[143]Protokoll über die Tagung des Arbeitsausschusses der Mitglieder des "Büro für Theaterfragen," 14 and 15 October 1949 (see also the bundles of requests for repertory plans sent out to theaters around the country), ibid., R-100/900/3 and 101.

In December 1949, after the DVV became the MfV and Volkmann's old division turned into the "main division of art and literature" within it, plans for the first quarter of the new year envisioned "taking over control of theater programming with the goal of improving theater programs." The MfV expected to ask the government to set up a "repertory commission" to oversee performances; the proposal was expected to take effect on 15 January 1950 (or a month after action by the government); and the commission would operate as a "regulatory organ for dramatic literature performed on stage.[144] Those discussions went on for months. "Establishment of a repertory commission" appeared again in plans dated 15 March 1950; the government decision was expected by 31 May at the latest; revisions in the proposal were then requested in late March and resubmitted in early May.[145] But no action had been taken as of September 1950. Whether the commission should be "anchored" in the MfV or be independent remained an unsettled question.[146] Though it cannot be pinpointed exactly, the repertory commission formed within the MfV's main division of art and literature then set up operations in November 1950. The MfV sent out a circular on 15 November explaining that the commission was responsible for "advising all theaters in terms of planning a progressive repertory."[147] Fritz Erpenbeck's name showed up on the commission's numbered "instructions" by 2 April;[148] and on the same day, a set of directions went out to every East German theater that may well have marked the beginning of systematic censorship. The requirements were disarmingly simple. All repertories, along with any changes to be made during the season, required the approval of the MfV. No play could be accepted, rehearsed, or performed in the absence of ministerial approval; and, though the "suggested" programs for the new season would be discussed first within the corresponding state ministries, these "suggestions" had to be submitted to the "repertory commission" of the MfV in Berlin by 31 May, along with "analyses" of the proposed programs and the results of local "consultations," for final acceptance. The commission was also authorized to grant contingent approvals and, apparently in the case of specific plays, to require a "test performance" before making a definitive decision.[149]

[144]Hauptabteilung Kunst und Literatur. Arbeitsplan für das 1. Quartal 1950, 15 December 1949; and Ministerium für Volksbildung. Arbeitsplan 1. Quartal 1950. Richtlinien für den Arbeitsplan 1950, ibid., R-2/1155/263-64 and R-2/4775/61.

[145]See Ministerium für Volksbildung. Arbeitsplan 2. Quartal 1950, 15 March 1950; Hauptabteilung Kunst und Literatur. Arbeitsbericht Monat März, 3 April 1950; Hauptabteilung Kunst und Literatur. Arbeitsbericht Monat April 1950, 6 May 1950, ibid., R-2/4775/41, 46, 83, 91.

[146]Sekretariat des Ministers. Protokoll über die Sitzung der Abteilungsleiter am 28. 8. 50, 4 September 1950, ibid., R-2/2146/62.

[147]Ministerium für Volksbildung. HA Kunst und Literatur. Anweisung Nr. 72. Gez. [Maria] Rentmeister, 13 November 1950, ibid., R-2/3994/119.

[148]Ministerium für Volksbildung. Hauptabteilung Kunst. Spielplankommission. Die ideologische Vorarbeit bei Theaterinszenierungen. Anweisung Nr. 98, 2 April 1951, ibid., R-2/3994/57.

[149]MfV. HA Kunst. Spielplankommission. Betr.: Spielpläne. Anweisung Nr. 99, 2 April 1951,

The Freedom of Artistic Creativity

Publishing was equally in need of permanent regulation; and efforts to establish an organization better than the Kultureller Beirat continued throughout the year. In February 1949, Volkmann said that, aside from their obligation to promote "progressive literature" and contribute to "ideological clarity," publishers needed to devise more economic methods of doing things; and firms unable to "point to accomplishments that justify their existence" would be shut down. He added that all such matters were expected to fall under the purview of a "German publishing commission, scheduled to be created, with responsibility for the dissemination of paper as well."[150] A month later, Volkmann again included "formation of a German publishing commission. (Reorganization of the Kultureller Beirat)" among his top priorities for 1949-50;[151] but the restructured organization was left out of the DWK's cultural ordinance released on 31 March 1949. Apparently, this was just the last in a long string of delays; and the subject never came up either at a meeting of all "Soviet-licensed publishers" convened by the Kultureller Beirat on 7 and 8 April 1949. During these discussions, there was much talk about the ordinance, and Stefan Heymann spoke at length about the "responsibilities of the publisher in the two-year plan." He argued that publishing, as "part of the economy," needed to be incorporated into the plan, but, of course, declined to point out that economic planning in the area of publishing spelled censorship. He argued instead that publication projects should "serve the consolidation of our democratic order and the struggle for unity and a just peace" before calling upon publishers to exert an educational influence by awakening the "consciousness" of writers through a deepening of their social awareness. Here again, Heymann declined to explore the implications of his demands; but these were tantamount to the insistence that the publishers themselves should promote appropriate writing by publishing it alone and, correspondingly, rejecting literature considered inappropriate in the context of the times. In both instances, the rationale hinged upon "social" and "economic" considerations and was thus looked upon as a means of raising the consciousness of writers by justifying the censorship of their work with an assortment of lofty sentiments.[152]

---

gez. [Maria] Rentmeister (Hauptabteilungsleiter), ibid., R-2/3994/56-57.
[150]Übersicht über den Arbeitsplan für 1949, 21 February 1949, ibid., R-2/1155/77a-77q.
[151]Wichtigste Vorhaben im Arbeitsplan 1949/50, 21 March 1949, ibid., R-2/1155/231-32.
[152]"Im Dienste des Fortschritts. Arbeitstagung der sowjetisch lizenzierten Verleger," *Börsenblatt für den Deutschen Buchhandel* 17 (1949), pp. 137-40.

Wilhelm Girnus noted further that publishers bore the responsibility for battling "decadent and subversive manifestations of Americanism (Sartre!)" designed to wear down the resistance of "our people." Latter sessions of the conference were then spent in meetings between publishers and "leading representatives of the Kultureller Beirat"; and the talks ended with agreement that similar meetings should be held at periodic intervals.[153] Judging by the published account of the gathering, there was no indication given there that the KB was on the verge of being reorganized. In fact, the meeting may have been scheduled originally to announce formation of a new commission, perhaps in connection with passage of the DWK ordinance, and then shifted its focus when it became apparent that, for the foreseeable future, the KB would continue working more or less as it had before. On 16 August 1949, for instance, the agency's staffing plans were approved by the DWK along with those of other divisions of the DVV and a variety of additional Soviet-zone cultural establishments run by it;[154] and all the while complaints about the Kultureller Beirat mounted. The head of the Schutzverband Deutscher Autoren, Werner Schendell, pleaded for its reorganization in a letter to Paul Wandel in early July; this complaint was still being dealt with in October and November; and on 1 November 1949, the Thuringian branch of the SDA complained to Wandel, now head of the new Ministerium für Volksbildung, about the practices of the Kultureller Beirat. The SDA had suggested improvements to Wandel on numerous occasions and requested inclusion in the "process of publication licensing to be newly created." The letter expressed the hope that the SDA's wishes would be respected in the reorganization undertaken in connection with the formation of a government; and added that, otherwise, "we shall be unable to meet our responsibilities arising out of the necessities of the times." The letter closed with a final plea that Wandel put an end, once and for all, to the "deplorable state of affairs created by the bureaucratic Kultureller Beirat."[155]

By then, final efforts were underway to set up the Deutsche Verlagskommission (DVK). A few days prior to formation of the German Democratic Republic, Wandel sent detailed recommendations to the SED "in compliance with the Politburo assignment regarding the supervision and organization of publishing."[156] He included with his proposal a copy of a corresponding ordinance, prepared "quite a while ago," that would require some updating.

[153]Ibid.

[154]See Personalabteilung an die Allgemeine Verwaltung. Betr. Stellenpläne, 26 August 1949. Bundesarchiv, Abt. Potsdam, R-2/927/1-11.

[155]See Schendell to Wandel, 8 July 1949; Vorschlag für eine Umgestaltung des Kulturellen Beirats; Der Justitiar an Herrn Wandel and Herrn Ludwig. Betr.: Vorschlag des Schutzverbandes Deutscher Autoren zur Umgestaltung des Kulturellen Beirats, 25 October 1949; Sekretariat des Ministers an den Schutzverband Deutscher Autoren. Z. Hd. des Herrn Schendell. Betrifft: Kultureller Beirat, 28 November 1949, ibid., R-2/1132/7, 10, 13-17.

[156]Wandel an die SED, 3 October 1949, ibid., R-2/741/10.

Wandel's proposal began by noting that the SMAD needed to issue an order placing the "licensing of publishing houses" within the DVV and permitting it to create "appropriate institutions in the form of a Deutsche Verlagskommission." This measure would then be enacted following issuance of an ordinance by the DVV and the DWK. The new agency would regulate activities connected with the preparation of literary, artistic, and musical printed matter, including journals and recordings; issue and revoke licenses; and apportion "raw materials." The agency would see to it that all such undertakings "served Germany's peaceful and democratic development, the construction of a peace economy, and a progressive culture. Wandel's proposal included certain other provisions; newspapers, were to be "licensed and regulated" by the newly created main administration of information or, as it was soon called, Amt für Information. Certain other materials, including posters and leaflets with "political, trade-union, cultural, and religious tendencies," would be screened and approved, "in accordance with the proposal of the SMAD," by the interior administration.[157]

The new commission was otherwise structured much like the Kultureller Beirat. Its main office would work with thirteen subcommissions charged with making "political and specialized decisions" about the planning and production of publishing houses. Most of these subcommissions matched those formed by the KB, but two were different. The subcommission for social sciences was responsible for the regulation of "Marxist" writing, though whenever "agitational literature" was involved, it would issue approval only with the agreement of the main administration for information. The other one, called the "subcommission for confirmation (the office of censorship)," would render final decisions on all recommendations made by the remaining subcommissions. Wandel's proposal also called for a special "division of publishing" to be set up within the politburo itself, vested with the authority to oversee publishing operations owned by the party, as well as "organizations close to it"; and to exercise the "ideological regulation of the Deutsche Verlagskommission." Its "subcommission for confirmation," which Wandel again referred to as "the censor," had to be staffed by "very reliable, ideologically well-versed comrades" working in "close touch with the party." Finally, the SMAD still needed to invalidate orders 356 (24 December 1946), 25 (25 January 1947), and 90 (17 April 1947) once the ordinances setting up the new commission replaced them, whereupon the DVK would require a "sufficient number of politically qualified employees who must be confirmed by the appropriate office within the party."[158]

The ordinance that Wandel included in his letter provided additional details about the minute regulation of every aspect of publishing; it indicated

[157]Vorschlag zur Errichtung einer Deutschen Verlagskommission, ibid., R-2/741/11.
[158]Ibid., R-2/741/11-13.

that all previously issued publishing licenses required renewal and that the DVK was fully authorized to issue, reissue, and revoke licenses; mandated both the submission of biannual publishing plans and the DVK's approval of every individual printed work; and so on.[159] There were also provisions that outlined the punishments to be meted out in the event of violations.[160] Related documents provided additional details; one of them, a somewhat earlier proposal for the establishment of the DVK dated 30 September 1949, noted that a commission should be set up within the SED's central secretariat for the purpose of "regulating" the work of the new agency by setting its guidelines; establishing a "political board to evaluate and coordinate publishing plans"; and "appraising the literature in political terms." The cooperation of the DVK with the party's corresponding commission would be secured, first, by naming one person to serve as the "political director" of both commissions; and, second, by including the "political board" or politisches Lektorat in the staffing plan of the main commission.[161] The documents also included a staffing plan for the agency's secretariat, calling for fifty-nine positions; whereas, at the time, the Kultureller Beirat and the DVV's office of publishing worked on the basis of a combined total of thirty-five.[162] Finally, Wandel or his office drafted an SMAD order authorizing the "establishment" and defining the "responsibilities" of the publishing commission. The purpose of the order, according to its own language, was to "include German democratic organs in a more active participation in reconstruction and to promote progressive development in the publishing and booktrade" within Soviet-occupied Germany. The order contained many of the provisions common to the accompanying and all previous documents, but added that "all licenses issued by the SMAD must be renewed by the Deutsche Verlagskommission within three months after promulgation of this order." It called upon the DWK to approve the staffing plan and provide the financial backing; directed the head of the SMAD's office of finance to make the necessary funds available; and indicated that the "censorship organs" of the SMAD retained the right to screen and approve certain material mentioned in earlier documents (posters, leaflets, etc.).[163]

Wandel apparently intended this draft order to reach the SMAD along with another elaborate justification of the overall measure; this justification

[159]See Deutsche Verlagskommission. Verordnung Nr. 1, ibid., R-2/741/14-22.

[160]Entwurf. Strafbestimmung zu dem vorgesehenen Befehl der SMAD über die Errichtung und den Aufgabenbereich der deutschen Verlagskommission, ibid., R-2/741/23-25.

[161]Sec Vorschlag für die Errichtung der Deutschen Verlagskommission, 30 September 1949, ibid., R-2/741/25-26; and Vorschlag für eine Verordnung der Deutschen Wirtschaftskommission über die Errichtung der Deutschen Verlagskommission (R-2/741/2).

[162]Vorschlag für Struktur- und Stellenplan der Deutschen Verlagskommission, ibid., R-2/741/28.

[163]Befehl des Obersten Chefs der Sowjetischen Militärverwaltung in Deutschland. Nr. __ Errichtung und Aufgabenbereich der Deutschen Verlagskommission. Ibid., R-2/741/29-30.

repeated many of the same provisions, utilized much the same language, but also contained a few new details. One of the most important measures necessary to ensure the success of the two-year plan, it read, was the creation of literature that served the needs of economic reconstruction and cultural progress while contributing to political development and ideological consolidation. The precondition, however, was the existence of a "central ideological planning and regulatory apparatus" able to transform the publishing trade "into a usable instrument." The document then summarized the previous system as having been based upon three factors: the SMAD issued licenses to publishing houses and censored political writing; the Kultureller Beirat then screened "non-political and non-periodical literature," granting licenses for individual publications and apportioning paper provided by the SMAD; whereas the DVV supervised the activities of the publishing houses and made licensing recommendations to the SMAD. This fragmentation of responsibility, together with the "limitations imposed upon the authority and the personnel size of the German agencies," had delayed the development of a "homogenous publishing trade" and a "progressive literature." The systematic planning associated with the two-year plan now required more responsibility, not less; the old KB had been too limited in its capacity to promote the contribution of the intelligentsia to the economic, cultural, and political reconstruction of Germany. The document went on to propose a new SMAD order that would supersede earlier decrees governing publishing. The new commission needed to be an "independent institution" whose director would answer to the president of the DVV. Upon acceptance of the proposal, "the entire ideological promotion and supervision of publishers and both periodical and book production, in accord with progressive social development, becomes the responsibility of a German agency. A unified instrument will be created that, constructed properly, can enact all necessary measures in consideration of their interrelation."[164]

Many of these documents, and all of the basic ideas behind them, date back to early 1948; the same is true of the proposed order; and it is entirely possible that the establishment of a new publishing commission had been delayed for close to two full years because the SMAD hung on to its right to censor. Nor were the Russians anxious to do so now either. A week after Wandel submitted his proposal for a new commission to the SED, and two days after creation of the German Democratic Republic, he wrote two more letters. One went to Anton Ackermann and Gerhart Eisler, as head of the main administration of information; the other was addressed to Ulbricht. Wandel sent both Ackermann and Eisler a copy of objections to the "new arrangement" raised "by a representative of the SMAD's office of culture and

---

[164]Begründung für die Notwendigkeit zur Errichtung einer deutschen Verlagskommission, ibid., R-2/741/31-32.

education; and he suggested that the three of them consult once more before passing their "joint proposal" along to the SED's so-called "Small Secretariat." But the proposal, or an adjusted version,[165] then went to that body the same day along with another letter from Wandel. In it, he explained that a certain Danilov, described as the head of the SMAD's office of culture and education, had objected "vigorously" to the proposal. According to Wandel, Danilov was against the idea of attaching the publishing commission to the DVV and wanted "an office of censorship modeled after GLAVLIT," the Soviet arrangement, "to be either independent or set up within the ministry of the interior." Danilov's particular argument, which Wandel left substantially unelaborated, was that the DVV had biases of its own and would be neither "independent" nor "strict enough in its censorship activity." Wandel noted that the Small Secretariat needed to know of Danilov's objections prior to its "passage of the measure."[166] These concerns apparently delayed a decision yet again. On 8 November, Wandel, now with the rank of minister, wrote Volkmann that a resolution of the matter remained "uncertain"; as a consequence, problems caused by the old KB needed to be addressed; and Wandel asked Volkmann to set up a meeting between its functionaries and "some of the most important opponents (writers' union and others)."[167] In mid-November, another Soviet officer, by the name of Danilenko, appeared in the offices of the KB and introduced himself as the successor of the previous officer assigned to the organization. In a discussion with its top officials (Pincus, Frommhold, and possibly Koven), Danilenko listened to a report of the organization's current responsibilities and activity as well as of the "status of publishing in the territory of the GDR." He asked additionally to be kept apprised of all basic decisions, alterations, and important business; and reminded the Germans that "order 90" had yet to be rescinded.[168]

If nothing else, the Kultureller Beirat had received a new name, "Amt für Verlagswesen (Kultureller Beirat),"[169] by 1 December 1949, which compared with the renaming of other agencies like the Amt für Information; and after so many delays, the head of the SMAD, General Chuikov, finally rescinded order 90 on or about 28 February 1950 by granting the Amt für Information the authority to regulate all publishing activity in the German Democratic Republic.[170] In August 1950, the decision was made to incorporate

[165]See also ibid., R-2/741/6-9.

[166]Wandel an Ackermann, Eisler. Betrifft: Kontrollstelle für Literatur und sonstige Drucksachen (Deutsche Verlagskommission), 10 October 1949; Wandel an das kleine Sekretariat der SED. Betrifft: Kontrollstelle für Literatur und sonstige Drucksachen (Deutsche Verlagskommission), 10 October 1949, ibid., R-2/741/4-5.

[167]Wandel to Volkmann, 8 November 1949, ibid., R-2/741/1.

[168]Aktennotiz. Signed Koven [?], 17 November 1949 [?], ibid., R-2/1132/1.

[169]See Protokoll der Besprechung am 1. 12.1949 im Ministerium für Volksbildung. Betr. Aufgaben des Amtes für Verlagswesen (Kultureller Beirat)," ibid., R-2/1055/45-52.

[170]See Hauptabteilung Kunst und Literatur. Arbeitsbericht Monat Februar 1950, 3 March 1950,

what was still referred to as the Kultureller Beirat into the MfV; together with the offices in charge of libraries and literature, a new "main department" called "Books, Libraries, und Publishing" was to be created; but the staff of evaluators, the so-called zentrales Lektorat, would stay attached to the Amt für Information.[171] More important structural changes, the beginning of solutions that then endured for decades, took place the following spring. In May 1951, provisions were made for the formation of a larger Amt für Literatur und Verlagswesen designed to further the cause of "democratization" through an "intensified, better planned, and systematic regulation and promotion of the production of books and newspapers." The main division of literature within the Ministerium für Volksbildung was to be dissolved.[172] Around 25 July, then, according to a file memorandum, the Kultureller Beirat ceased operations.[173] This scrap of paper said that the KB had been incorporated into the MfV's department of literature, but, in fact, that department had already been restructured as the infamous state commission for art affairs or Staatliche Kommission für Kunstangelegenheiten. This organization, run by Helmut Holtzhauer, was comprised of ten members (Girnus and Erpenbeck among them);[174] and emerged after the SED's fifth central-committee conference that met in March 1951 to begin the next offensive against formalism, decadence, and cosmopolitanism. The meeting ended in the "recommendation" for a new state commission because the MfV was thought to be overburdened with other responsibilities.[175]

A few months later, the government of the GDR issued two new ordinances. The first established the new commission, the second defined its responsibilities in terms of the "development of a realistic art." In his extensive commentary, Otto Grotewohl added further details. The "unculture" of cosmopolitanism, kitsch, and gangster literature, he said, poisoned the national consciousness of the German people and destroyed its culture. The state commission on art affairs was called to lead the way in the struggle against these manifestations; and Grotewohl went on to define the menace of "formalism and cosmopolitanism" as the intellectual superstructure of de-

---

ibid., R-2/4775/102.

[171]Sekretariat des Ministers. Protokoll über die Sitzung der Abteilungsleiter am 28. 8. 50, 4 September 1950, ibid., R-2/2146/62.

[172]Entwurf einer Verordnung über die Entwicklung fortschrittlicher Literatur, 16 May 1951, ibid., R-2/1152.

[173]See Aktenvermerk, 25 July 1951, ibid., R-2/1242/24.

[174]They were Hermann Abendroth, Fritz Dähn, Fritz Erpenbeck, Wilhelm Girnus, Otto Lang, Otto Nagel, Maria Rentmeister, Hans Rodenberg, and Hans Sandig. See "Die Kunst im Kampf für Deutschlands Zukunft. Ministerpräsident Grotewohl führte die Staatliche Kommission für Kunstangelegenheiten in ihre Aufgaben ein," *Neues Deutschland*, 1 September 1951.

[175]Lauter, "Der Kampf gegen den Formalismus in Kunst und Literatur, für eine fortschrittliche deutsche Kultur," *Der Kampf gegen den Formalismus in Kunst und Literatur, für eine fortschrittliche deutsche Kultur*, p. 40.

caying capitalism. No one need fear the new art commission, Grotewohl continued, because its task was to encourage, not discourage. But he stated that "literature and the visual arts are subordinate to politics"; ideas in art had to accord with the "direction of the political struggle"; and "what has proven its correctness in politics is equally correct in art." Therefore, he continued, "political criticism in the evaluation of our art is primary; artistic criticism is secondary"; and Grotewohl concluded by defining art in the imperialist world. Its characteristics included the rejection of realism; the renunciation of national traditions through subjugation to an "ideology, cosmopolitanism, inimical to the people"; and the absence of a forward-looking perspective. The only solution lay in a turn to realism in art that would be facilitated if German creative intellectuals learned from their Soviet counterparts. Grotewohl closed his remarks by urging the state commission to define its responsibilities in terms of the development of an "art that, harmonically, realistically, and, in close touch with the people, leads to a complete and profound reflection of real life."[176] The state commission for art affairs and its office of publishing lasted barely eighteen months. Following the uprising on 17 June 1953, meetings with dissatisfied artists were held to discuss the "errors" of the art commission; and its members themselves, called to account, expressed remorse. But, as Brecht described it, pinning them down on any specific error proved to be an impossible task.[177]

New rounds of meetings were then held among party functionaries and artists; and the validity of much of the criticism of the state commission was acknowledged, though in mid-September 1951 the Kulturbund expressed its opposition to any tendency that favored "'absolute' freedom" in the area of art.[178] Grotewohl told a group of artists a short time later that the demands for "general freedom of opinion," the insistence upon complete freedom of the press, teacher independence, and the right to advocate any scientific and artistic view whatsoever constituted "rotten liberalism"; and the party's "new course," enacted after the uprising, made no provision for the abandonment of "regulation and clarity." Not that anyone interested in producing "formalist art" would be hindered, but such artists could not count upon state assistance either. "Though we have no wish to be narrow-minded and issue decrees, we are also disinclined to retreat back down the long road that we have put behind us in the area of cultural politics." The past discussions of realism and formalism, Grotewohl said, were a key part of those proud accomplishments. True, the "mistakes" of the art commission needed to be remedied, and that organization was indeed disbanded. But Grotewohl announced plans for a new ministry to take its place. The MfV, the old DVV,

---

[176]"Die Kunst im Kampf für Deutschlands Zukunft," *Neues Deutschland*, 2 September 1951.

[177]Brecht, "Nicht feststellbare Fehler der Kunstkommission," *Gesammelte Werke 10. Gedichte 3*, p. 1007. Brecht heaped just as much scorn on the commission's Amt für Literatur (ibid.).

[178]See "Die deutschen Kulturschaffenden und ihr Ministerium," *Aufbau* 2 (1954): 112.

would now administer just science and education, leaving cultural issues up to an entirely separate ministry of culture.[179] Formally established on 7 January 1954 and headed by Johannes R. Becher, the new ministry began work with a solemn pledge that the German Democratic Republic would defend the "indivisibility" of German culture and make it a model for the "future, unified, democratic, independent, and peace-loving Germany." The government promised to "protect German culture from decadence and cosmopolitan rootlessness" as it promoted the development of a realistic German art, "rich in forms," pervaded by the ideas of peace, democracy, and socialism. "In this spirit," the German Democratic Republic furthered the freedom of artistic creativity.[180]

[179]"Fragen der Kultur und Kunst im neuen Kurs. Eine Aussprache zwischen Ministerpräsident Otto Grotewohl und führenden Kunst- und Kulturschaffenden der DDR," *Neues Deutschland,* 24 October 1953.

[180]"Für die Blüte und Verteidigung der deutschen Kultur. Die Verordnung über die Bildung eines Ministeriums für Kultur der Deutschen Demokratischen Republik vom 7. Januar 1954," *Neues Deutschland,* 15 January 1954.

REFERENCE MATTER

TRANSLATIONS AND ABBREVIATIONS

Amt für Information	Office of Information
Bund Deutscher Volksbühnen	Association of German People's Theaters
Büro für Theaterfragen	Office of Theater Affairs
Deutsche Verlagskommission (DVK)	German Publishing Commission
Deutsche Verwaltung für Volksbildung (DVV)	German Administration of Culture and Education
Deutsche Wirtschaftskommission (DWK)	German Economic Commission
Deutscher Volksrat	German People's Council
Deutscher Schriftstellerverband (DSV)	German Writers' Union
Deutsches Amt für Wirtschaftsplanung (DAW)	German Office of Economic Planning
Freier Deutscher Gewerkschaftsbund (FDGB)	Free German Federation of Unions
Genossenschaft Deutscher Bühnenangehöriger (GDBA)	Alliance of German Stage Workers
Gesellschaft zum Studium der Kultur der Sowjetunion	Society for the Study of the Culture of the Soviet Union
Gewerkschaft 17 für Kunst und Schrifttum	Union 17 for Art and Writing
Grundsätze und Ziele	Principles and Goals
Kammer der Kulturschaffenden	Board of Creative Intellectuals
Kommunistische Partei Deutschlands (KPD)	German Communist Party
Kulturbund zur demokratischen Erneuerung Deutschlands	Cultural League for the Democratic Renewal of Germany
Kulturelle Aufklärung	Cultural Enlightenment
Kultureller Beirat (KB)	Cultural Advisory Board
Kulturfond	Cultural Foundation

Ministerium für Volksbildung (MfV)	Ministry of Culture and Education
Parteivorstand (PV)	Party Executive Board
Parteischulung, Kultur und Erziehung (PKE)	Party Schooling, Culture, and Education
Personalabteilung (PA)	Office of Personnel
Rat für Kunst und Literatur	Council of Art and Literature
Schutzverband Bildender Künstler (SBK)	Protective Association of Artists
Schutzverband Deutscher Autoren (SDA)	Protective Association of German Authors
Sowjetische Militäradministration (SMAD)	Soviet military administration
Sozialistische Einheitspartei Deutschlands (SED)	Socialist Unity Party
Staatliche Kommission für Kunstangelegenheiten	State Commission for Art Affairs
Unabhängige Gewerkschaftsopposition (UGO)	Independent Union Opposition
Verlagswesen	Office of Publishing Affairs
Volksbühnen	People's Theaters
Zentraler Kulturausschuß	Central Cultural Commission
Zentralverwaltungen (ZV)	Central Administrations
Zentralsekretariat (ZS)	Central Secretariat

Deutschlands
Ost und West. Beiträge zur kulturellen und politischen Fragen der Zeit
Schöpferische Gegenwart. Kulturpolitische Monatszeitschrift Thüringens
Sinn und Form. Beiträge zur Literatur
Sonntag. Eine Wochenzeitung für Kulturpolitik, Kunst und Unterhaltung
Sozialistische Bildungshefte. Hg. vom Zentralsekretariat der Sozialistischen
    Einheitspartei Deutschlands. Abteilung Parteischulung, Kultur und
    Erziehung zum politischen Bildungsabend
Tägliche Rundschau. Zeitung für die deutsche Bevölkerung
Theater der Zeit. Blätter für Bühne, Film und Musik
Das Volk. Tageszeitung der Sozialdemokratischen Partei Deutschlands
Die Weltbühne. Wochenschrift für Politik, Kunst, Wirtschaft

LITERATURE

Abusch, Alexander. *Der Irrweg einer Nation*. Berlin: Aufbau Verlag, 1951.
_____. *Mit offenem Visier. Memoiren.* Berlin: Dietz Verlag, 1986.
_____. *Mit wem seid ihr, Meister der Kultur. Die Rolle der Kulturschaf-*
    fenden im Kampf um den Frieden. Rede, gehalten am 25. November
    1949 in Berlin auf dem Zweiten Bundeskongreß des Kulturbundes zur
    demokratischen Erneuerung Deutschlands. Mit einem Anhang:
    Wroclaw—Paris—Rom. Berlin: Aufbau Verlag, 1950.
_____. *Stalin und die Schicksalsfragen der deutschen Nation*. Berlin: Auf-
    bau Verlag, 1949.
Ackermann, Anton. *Fragen und Antworten*. Berlin: Verlag Neuer Weg
    [1946].
Alexander Dymschitz. Wissenschaftler. Soldat. Internationalist. Berlin:
    Henschelverlag, 1977.
Allgemeine Deutsche Kunstausstellung Dresden 1946 [no place, no date].
Antonov-Ovseenko, Anton. *The Time of Stalin. Portrait of a Tyranny*. New
    York: Harper and Row, 1981.
Aus den Erfahrungen des Sowjet-Theaters. Neudruck einer Aufsatzreihe von
    Julius Hay und Maxim Vallentin. Weimar: Thüringer Volksverlag,
    1945.
Becher, Johannes R. *Auf andere Art so große Hoffnung. Tagebuch 1950.*
    Eintragungen 1951. Berlin: Aufbau-Verlag, 1955.
_____. *Der Aufstand im Menschen*. Berlin: Aufbau-Verlag, 1983.
_____. *Befreiung. Deutsche Kultur und nationale Einheit*. Berlin: Aufbau-
    Verlag, 1950.
_____. *Befreiung. Deutsche Kultur und nationale Einheit. Rede gehalten*
    am 24. November 1949 in Berlin auf dem Zweiten Bundeskongreß des
    Kulturbundes zur demokratischen Erneuerung Deutschlands. Berlin:

BIBLIOGRAPHY

ARCHIVES

Archiv der Gewerkschaftbewegung (Berlin)
Bundesarchiv. Abteilung Potsdam (formerly Zentrales Staatsarchiv)
Zentrales Parteiarchiv (formerly Institut für Marxismus-Leninismus.
   Zentrales Parteiarchiv)

NEWSPAPERS AND PERIODICALS

Aufbau. Kulturpolitische Monatsschrift
Die Aussprache. Mitteilungsblatt für die Mitglieder und Freunde des
   Kulturbundes zur demokratischen Erneuerung Deutschlands
   Mecklenburg-Vorpommern
Der Autor. Zeitschrift des Schutzverbandes deutscher Autoren in der
   Gewerkschaft für Kunst und Schrifttum des FDGB
Berliner Zeitung
Bildende Kunst. Zeitschrift für Malerei, Graphik, Plastik und Architektur
Börsenblatt für den deutschen Buchhandel
Demokratische Erneuerung. Mitteilungsblatt für die Mitglieder und
   Freunde des Kulturbundes, Mecklenburg-Vorpommern
Deutsche Volkszeitung. Zentralorgan der Kommunistischen Partei
   Deutschlands
Einheit. Theoretische Zeitschrift des wissenschaftlichen Sozialismus
Freies Deutschland
Heute und Morgen. Literarische Monatszeitschrift
Kunst und Schrifttum. Mitteilungsblatt der Gewerkschaft Kunst u.
   Schrifttum im FDGB Groß-Berlin
Kunst und Schrifttum. Mitteilungsblatt der Gewerkschaft Kunst u.
   Schrifttum im FDGB sowjet. Besatzungs-Zone
März. Eine literarische Monatsschrift
Die neue Gesellschaft. Monatszeitschrift der Gesellschaft zum Studium der
   Kultur der Sowjetunion
Neue Welt. Halbmonatsschrift
Neue Zeit. Tageszeitung der Christlich-Demokratischen Union
Neuer Weg. Monatsschrift für aktuelle Fragen der Arbeiterbewegung
Neues Deutschland. Zentralorgan der Sozialistischen Einheitspartei

Kulturbund zur demokratischen Erneuerung Deutschlands, 1949.

_____. *Deutsches Bekenntnis. Sieben Reden zu Deutschlands Erneuerung.* Berlin: Aufbau Verlag, 1947.

_____. *Erziehung zur Freiheit. Gedanken und Betrachtungen.* Berlin: Aufbau Verlag, 1946.

_____. "Gedichte." *Sinn und Form* 2 (1990): 341-45.

_____. *Publizistik II. 1939-1945.* Berlin and Weimar: Aufbau Verlag, 1978.

_____. *Publizistik III. 1946-1951.* Berlin: Aufbau-Verlag, 1979.

_____. *Uns ist bange, aber wir verzagen nicht. Ein Beitrag zur Moskauer Friedenskonferenz. Ansprache auf der 2. Landestagung des Kulturbundes zur demokratischen Erneuerung Deutschlands, Landesleitung Brandenburg, am 1. März.* Potsdam: Kulturbund zur demokratischen Erneuerung Deutschlands, 1947.

_____. *Vom Anderswerden.* Berlin: Aufbau-Verlag, 1949. Berlin: Aufbau Verlag, 1947.

_____. *Vom Willen zum Frieden. Zwei Reden.* Berlin: Aufbau Verlag, 1947.

_____. *Wir, Volk der Deutschen. Rede auf der 1. Bundeskonferenz des Kulturbundes zur demokratischen Erneuerung Deutschlands.* Berlin: Aufbau Verlag, 1947.

Befehle des Obersten Chefs der Sowjetischen Militärverwaltung in Deutschland. Sammelheft 1. 1945. Berlin: SWA-Verlag, 1946.

Begegnung mit russischem Kulturgut. Volksbildung und Gesellschaftsordnung in der Sowjetunion. Als Manuskript gedruckt. 3. Folge [1948].

Behrens, Friedrich. *Der geistige Arbeiter im Kampf um ein neues Deutschland. Vortragsreihe der Kulturabteilung der KPD.* Leipzig, 1945.

Bericht über die Verhandlungen des 15. Parteitages der Kommunistischen Partei Deutschlands. Berlin: Verlag Neuer Weg GMBH, 1946.

Beschlüsse des Zentralkomitees der KPdSU (B) zu Fragen der Literatur und Kunst 1946-1948. Berlin: Dietz Verlag, 1952.

Braulich, Heinrich. *Die Volksbühne. Theater und Politik der deutschen Volksbühnenbewegung.* Berlin: Kunst und Gesellschaft, 1976.

Brecht, Bertolt. *Arbeitsjournal.* Frankfurt am Main: Suhrkamp Verlag, 1973.

_____. *Briefe. 1913-1956.* Berlin: Aufbau-Verlag, 1983.

_____. *Gesammelte Werke 10. Gedichte 3.* Frankfurt am Main: Suhrkamp Verlag, 1967.

Bredel, Willi. *Ernst Thälmann. Ein Beitrag zu einem politischen Lebensbild.* Berlin: Dietz Verlag, 1948.

_____. *Ernst Thälmann. Beitrag zu einem politischen Lebensbild.* Berlin: Dietz Verlag, 1950.

The Central Committee Resolutions and Zhdanov's Speech on the Journals Zvezda *and* Leningrad. Royal Oak: Strathcoma Publishing Co., 1978.

Chamberlin, Brewster S. *Kultur auf Trümmern. Berliner Berichte der* amerikanischen Information Control Section Juli-Dezember 1945. Stuttgart: Deutsche Verlags-Anstalt, 1979.

Claudius, Eduard. *Notizen nebenbei.* Berlin: Verlag Kultur und Fortschritt, 1948.

DDR. Dokumente zur Geschichte der Deutschen Demokratischen Republik 1945-1985. Munich: Deutscher Taschenbuchverlag, 1986.

Der deutsche Zweijahrplan für 1949-1950. Der Wirtschaftsplan für 1948 und der Zweijahrplan 1949-1950 zur Wiederherstellung und Entwicklung der Friedenswirtschaft in der sowjetischen Besatzungszone Deutschlands. Berlin: Dietz Verlag, 1948.

Die deutsche Volksbühne. Protokoll des Bundes Deutscher Volksbühnen, Berlin, 16. bis 18. Mai 1947. Berlin: Verlag Bruno Henschel, 1947.

Deutsche Kultur und Arbeiterbewegung. Hg. vom Landesvorstand Thüringen der SED, 1946.

Dokumente der Sozialistischen Einheitspartei Deutschlands. Beschlüsse und Erklärungen des Zentralsekretariats und des Parteivorstandes. Berlin: Dietz Verlag, 1948.

Dokumente der Sozialistischen Einheitspartei Deutschlands. Beschlüsse und Erklärungen des Parteivorstandes des Zentralsekretariats und des politischen Büros. Vol. II. Berlin: Dietz Verlag, 1952.

Dokumente der Sozialistischen Einheitspartei Deutschlands. Beschlüsse und Erklärungen des Parteivorstandes des Zentralkommittees sowie seines Politbüros und seines Sekretariats. Vol. III. Berlin: Dietz Verlag, 1952.

Dornberger, Paul. *2 Jahre Kulturbund zur demokratischen Erneuerung Deutschlands. Land Thüringen. Bericht zur 2. ordentlichen Landes-Delegiertenkonferenz Weimar, 17., 18., 19. März* [no place, no date].

Dritte Deutsche Kunstausstellung. Dresden: VEB Verlag der Kunst, 1953.

Dymschitz, Alexander. *Ein unvergeßlicher Frühling.* Berlin: Dietz Verlag, 1970.

Ehrenburg, Ilja. *In Amerika.* Berlin: SWA-Verlag, 1947.

Ein Interview J.W. Stalins durch den Korrespondenten der "Prawda" anläßlich der Rede Churchills. Berlin: SWA-Verlag, 1946.

. . . einer neuen Zeit Beginn. Erinnerungen an die Anfänge unserer Kulturrevolution 1945-1949. Berlin: Aufbau Verlag, 1980.

Einheit Deutschlands und Gemeindewahlen. Berlin: Dietz Verlag, 1946.

Einheitsfront der antifaschistisch-demokratischen Parteien. Berlin: Dietz Verlag, 1945.

Erinnerungen an Johannes R. Becher. Leipzig: Verlag Philipp Reclam jun., 1974.

Die Erneuerung der deutschen Kultur. Vortragsdisposition Nr. 9 Berlin: Verlag Neuer Weg, 1946.

Erpenbeck, Fritz. *Wilhelm Pieck. Ein Lebensbild.* Berlin: Dietz Verlag,

1951.

Errichtung des Arbeiter- und Bauernstaates der DDR 1945-1949. Berlin: Staatsverlag der Deutschen Demokratischen Republik, 1983.

Der erste Bundeskongreß. Protokoll der ersten Bundeskonferenz des Kulturbundes zur demokratischen Erneuerung Deutschlands am 20. und 21. Mai 1947. Berlin: Aufbau Verlag, 1947.

Die ersten Jahre. Erinnerungen an den Beginn der revolutionären Umgestaltungen. Berlin: Dietz Verlag, 1985.

Friedensburg, Ferdinand. *Es ging um Deutschlands Einheit. Rückschau eines Berliners auf die Jahre nach 1945.* Berlin: Haude & Spenersche Verlagsbuchhandlung, 1971.

Frisch, Max. *Tagebuch 1946-1949. Gesammelte Werke.* Vol. II. Frankfurt: Suhrkamp Verlag, 1976.

Für die kulturelle Einheit Deutschlands. Die Kulturschaffenden Thüringens nehmen Stellung. Weimar: Kulturbund zur demokratischen Erneuerung Deutschlands, 1948.

Für Frieden und Volksdemokratie. Bericht über die Tätigkeit einiger kommunistischer Parteien gehalten auf der Konferenz in Polen Ende September 1947. Berlin: Verlag "Tägliche Rundschau" [no date].

Gaillard, Ottofritz, and Maxim Vallentin. *Das deutsche Stanislawski-Buch. Lehrbuch der Schauspielkunst nach dem Stanislawski-System. Mit einem Geleitwort von Maxim Vallentin und einem Anhang über Laienspiel von Otto Lang.* Berlin: Aufbau-Verlag, 1946.

Gelöbnis zur Einheit. Kundgebungen für die antifaschistisch-demokratische Einheit anläßlich des 70. Geburtstages von Wilhelm Pieck. Berlin: Verlag Neuer Weg, 1946.

Geschichte der Kommunistischen Partei der Sowjetunion (Bolschewiki). Kurzer Lehrgang. Berlin: Verlag der Sowjetischen Militäradministration in Deutschland, 1946.

Geschichte des Staates und des Rechts der DDR. Dokumente 1945-1949. Berlin: Staatsverlag der Deutschen Demokratischen Republik, 1984.

Girnus, Wilhelm. "Gegen den Formalismus in der Kunst—für eine fortschrittliche deutsche Kultur. Referat auf der Kultur-Tagung des demokratischen Rundfunks am 15. April 1951." *Der demokratische Rundfunk im Kampf für eine realistische Kunst* [no place, no date].

Gniffke, Erich. *Jahre mit Ulbricht.* Cologne: Verlag Wissenschaft und Politik, 1966.

Die große Kontroverse. Ein Briefwechsel um Deutschland. Hamburg-Geneva-Paris: Nagel Verlag, 1963.

Hahn, Werner. *Postwar Soviet Politics. The Fall of Zhdanov and the Defeat of Moderation 1946-1953.* Ithaca: Cornell University Press, 1982.

Hammer, Franz. *Zeit der Bewährung. Ein Lebensbericht.* Berlin: Verlag Tribüne, 1984.

Hermlin, Stephan and Hans Mayer. *Ansichten über einige Bücher und Schriftsteller*. Berlin: Verlag Volk und Welt [1947].

Hermlin, Stephan. *Russische Eindrücke*. Berlin: Verlag Kultur und Fortschritt, 1948.

Hiebel, Irmfried. "Weiskopf in Prag." *Die Weltbühne* 11 (1984): 344-47.

Im Zeichen des Roten Sterns. Erinnerungen an die Traditionen der deutschsowjetischen Freundschaft. Berlin: Dietz Verlag, 1975.

Die Intellektuellen kämpfen für den Frieden. Stimmen von der 1. Tagung des Weltfriedensrates in Berlin vom 22. - 24. Februar 1951. Berlin: Kulturbund zur demokratischen Erneuerung Deutschlands, 1951.

Ivanov, N. K. *Der Sowjetstaat—ein Staat von neuem Typus*. Berlin: SWA-Verlag, 1947.

Jäger, Manfred. "Literatur und Kulturpolitik in der Entstehungsphase der DDR (1945-1952)." "Aus Politik und Zeitgeschichte," *Das Parlament*, 5 October 1985.

Johnson, Hewlett. *Ein Sechstel der Erde*. Berlin: Verlag Volk und Welt, 1947.

Josef Stalin. Kurze Lebensbeschreibung. Berlin: Verlag der sowjetischen Militärverwaltung, 1946.

Kamnitzer, Heinz. *Weltbürgertum und Nationalstaat. Die gesellschaftliche Funktion des Kosmopolitismus. Material zur Vorbereitung des III. Bundestages*. Kulturbund zur demokratischen Erneuerung Deutschlands, 1951.

Der Kampf gegen den Formalismus in Kunst und Literatur, für eine fortschrittliche deutsche Kultur. Referat von Hans Lauter, Diskussion und Entschließung von der 5. Tagung des Zentralkomitees der Sozialistischen Einheitspartei Deutschlands vom 15. - 17. März 1951. Berlin: Dietz Verlag, 1951.

Karpinskij, W. A. *Die Gesellschafts- und Staatsordnung der UdSSR*. Berlin: SWA-Verlag, 1947.

Kellermann, Bernhard. *Was sollen wir tun? Mit Diskussionsbeiträgen von Theodor Plievier, Th. Lieser, Adam Scharrer, Bernhard Bechler, Robert Havemann*. Berlin: Aufbau Verlag, 1945.

Kellermann, Bernhard, and Ellen Kellermann. *Wir kommen aus Sowjetrußland*. Berlin: Verlag Kultur und Fortschritt, 1948.

Koselskij, Sergej. *Lügen-Fabrikation. Wesen und Gebräuche der amerikanischen Presse*. Berlin: SWA-Verlag, 1948.

Kraminov, D. *Am Rande des großen Krieges. Die zweite Front*. Berlin: Allgemeiner deutscher Verlag, 1948.

Kuczynski, Jürgen. *Dialog mit meinem Urenkel*. Berlin: Aufbau Verlag, 1984.

_____. *Das Land der frohen Zuversicht. Eine Geschichte der Sowjetunion für Jugendliche, die auch Erwachsene lesen können*. Berlin: Verlag

Kultur und Fortschritt, 1949.

_____. *Über einen Weg des Aufbaus deutscher Kultur.* Berlin: Verlag Kultur und Fortschritt [no date].

Kulturbund zur demokratischen Erneuerung Deutschlands. Hinweise und Richtlinien für die organisatorische Arbeit. Berlin: Kulturbund zur demokratischen Erneuerung Deutschlands, 1948.

Die kulturelle Verantwortung der Arbeiterklasse. Vier Referate von Willi Bredel, Wilhelm Girnus, Stefan Heymann, Walter Maschke aus Anlaß der Weimartage der Aktivisten vom 9. bis 12. Juni 1949. Berlin: Die freie Gewerkschaft, 1949.

Der Kulturplan. Verordnung über die Erhaltung und die Entwicklung der deutschen Wissenschaft und Kultur, die weitere Verbesserung der Lage der Intelligenz und die Steigerung ihrer Rolle in der Produktion und im öffentlichen Leben. Schriftenreihe der Deutschen Wirtschaftskommission. Stenographischer Bericht über die Sitzung der Vollversammlung der DWK am 31. März 1949. Berlin: Deutscher Zentralverlag, 1949.

Kulturwille. Blätter zum Erfurter Kulturschaffen. Hg. vom Rat der Stadt Erfurt und dem Kulturbund zur demokratischen Erneuerung Deutschlands anläßlich der Kulturwoche, 1947.

Kulturwoche der SED vom 5. - 12. Oktober 1947. Erfurt, 1947.

Kurella, Alfred. *Ich lebe in Moskau.* Berlin: Verlag Volk und Welt, 1947.

_____. *Ost und ~~oder~~ West. Unsinn, Sinn und tiefere Bedeutung eines Schlagwortes.* Berlin: Verlag Volk und Welt, 1948.

Kurzer Einführungslehrgang für neue Mitglieder der SED. Berlin: Verlag Einheit, 1948.

László Rajk und Komplicen vor dem Volksgericht. Berlin: Dietz Verlag, 1949.

Lenin, Vladimir. *Zwei Taktiken der Sozialdemokratie in der demokratischen Revolution.* Berlin: Verlag Neuer Weg, 1946.

Leonhard, Wolfgang *Die Revolution entläßt ihre Kinder.* Frankfurt am Main: Ullstein Verlag, 1976.

Lesnik, S. *Die politischen Freiheiten in der Sowjetunion.* Berlin: SWA-Verlag, 1946.

Levin, Nora. *The Jews in the Soviet Union since 1917. Paradox of Survival.* Vol. 1. New York: New York University Press, 1988.

Liste der auszusondernden Literatur. Hg. von der Deutschen Verwaltung für Volksbildung in der sowjetischen Besatzungszone. Erster Nachtrag nach dem Stand vom 1. Januar 1947. Berlin: Deutscher Zentralverlag, 1948.

Liste der auszusondernden Literatur. Hg. von der Deutschen Verwaltung für Volksbildung in der sowjetischen Besatzungszone. Zweiter Nachtrag nach dem Stand vom 1. September 1948. Berlin: Deutscher Zentralverlag, 1948.

Lukács, Georg. *Deutsche Literatur während des Imperialismus*. Berlin: Aufbau Verlag, 1947.

Mayer, Hans. *Ein Deutscher auf Widerruf. Erinnerungen*. Vol. I. Frankfurt am Main: Suhrkamp Verlag, 1981.

Michajlow, N. N. *Die Weiten und Reichtümer des Sowjetlandes*. Berlin: SWA-Verlag, 1947.

Mittenzwei, Werner. *Das Leben des Bertolt Brecht. Oder der Umgang mit den Welträtseln*. Berlin: Aufbau Verlag, 1988.

Molotov, W. M. *Fragen der Außenpolitik. Reden und Erklärungen April 1945-Juni 1948*. Moscow: Verlag für fremdsprachige Literatur, 1949.

Müller, Reinhard, ed. *Die Säuberung. Moskau 1936: Stenogramm einer geschlossenen Parteiversammlung*. Reinbek: Rowohlt Taschenbuch Verlag,1991.

Der nationale Kampf der KPD und die Einheit Deutschlands. Vortragsdisposition. Berlin: Verlag Neuer Weg, 1946.

Die neuen Aufgaben unserer demokratischen Verwaltung. Berlin: Dietz Verlag, 1948.

Oelßner, Fred. *Das Kompromiß von Gotha und seine Lehren*. Berlin: Dietz Verlag, 1950.

_____. *Der Marxismus der Gegenwart und ihre Kritiker*. Berlin: Dietz Verlag, 1948.

_____. *Die Wirtschaftskrisen. Erster Band: Die Krisen im vormonopolistischen Kapitalismus*. Berlin: Dietz Verlag, 1949

Pankratowa, A. M. *Die Vergangenheit des Sowjetlandes*. Berlin: SWA-Verlag, 1947.

Pieck, Wilhelm. *Gesammelte Reden und Schriften*. Vol. 6. Berlin: Dietz Verlag, 1979.

_____. *Der neue Weg zum gemeinsamen Kampfe für den Sturz der Hitlerdiktatur. Referat und Schlußwort auf der Brüsseler Parteikonferenz der KPD*. Berlin: Verlag Neuer Weg, 1947.

_____. *Probleme der Vereinigung von KPD und SPD. Referat gehalten auf der ersten Parteikonferenz der Kommunistischen Partei Deutschlands*. Berlin: Verlag Neuer Weg, 1946.

_____. *Um die Erneuerung der deutschen Kultur. Rede des Vorsitzenden der KPD auf der Kulturtagung*. Berlin: Verlag Neuer Weg, 1946.

_____. *We are fighting for a Soviet Germany*. New York: Workers Publishers, 1934.

_____. *Zur Geschichte der kommunistischen Partei Deutschlands. 30 Jahre Kampf*. Berlin: Dietz Verlag, 1949.

Pike, David. *German Writers in Soviet Exile 1933-1945*. Chapel Hill: University of North Carolina Press, 1982

_____. *Lukács and Brecht*. Chapel Hill: University of North Carolina Press, 1985.

Protokoll der Ersten Parteikonferenz der SED. Berlin: Dietz Verlag, 1949.

Protokoll der Verhandlungen des 2. Parteitages der Sozialistischen Einheitspartei Deutschlands. Berlin: Dietz Verlag, 1948.

Protokoll der Verhandlungen des Ersten Kulturtages der SED. Berlin: Dietz Verlag, 1948.

Protokoll der Verhandlungen des III. Parteitages der Sozialistischen Einheitspartei Deutschlands. Berlin: Dietz Verlag, 1951.

Protokoll des 1. Deutschen Volkskongresses für Einheit und gerechten Frieden am 6. und 7. Dezember 1947. Hg. im Auftrage des Ständigen Ausschüsses des Deutschen Volkskongresses Berlin: Kongreß-Verlag, 1948.

Reinhardt, Rudolf. *Zeitungen und Zeiten. Journalist in Berlin der Nachkriegszeit*. Cologne: Verlag Wissenschaft und Politik, 1988.

Rubenstein, N. *Die Sowjetunion und die öffentliche Meinung im Auslande*. Berlin: Verlag "Tägliche Rundschau" [1948].

Sartre, Jean-Paul. *What is Literature?* New York: Philosophical Library, 1949.

Saslawski, D. *Von der Sowjetdemokratie*. Berlin: SWA-Verlag, 1946.

Satzung der Gewerkschaft Kunst und Schrifttum. Hg. vom Zentralvorstand der Industriegewerkschaft Kunst und Schrifttum im FDGB für die sowjetisch besetzte Zone [no place, no date].

SBZ-Handbuch. Staatliche Verwaltungen, Parteien, gesellschaftliche Organisationen und ihre Führungskräfte in der Sowjetischen Besatzungszone Deutschlands 1945-1949. Munich: R. Oldenbourg Verlag, 1990.

Der Schriftsteller in unserer Zeit. Reden auf der Landeskonferenz der sächsischen Schriftsteller in Dresden am 29. April 1948. Dresden, 1948.

Schulmeister, Karl-Heinz. *Auf dem Wege zu einer neuen Kultur. Der Kulturbund in den Jahren 1945-1949*. Berlin: Dietz Verlag, 1977.

Seghers, Anna. *Sowjetmenschen. Lebensbeschreibungen nach ihren Berichten*. Berlin: Verlag Kultur und Fortschritt, 1948.

Selbmann, Fritz. *Aufbruch des Geistes. Zur Frage der neuen deutschen Volkskultur*. Referat auf der Kulturtagung des Antifaschistischen Blocks [Leipzig, 29 June 1945]. Leipzig: Antifaschistischer Block, 1945.

Shub, Boris. *The Choice*. New York: Duell, Sloan and Pearce, 1950.

Der Sieg des Faschismus in Deutschland und seine Lehren für unseren gegenwärtigen Kampf. Vortragsdisposition. Hg. v. Zentralkomitee der KPD. Berlin: Verlag Neuer Weg, 1945.

Simonov, Konstantin. *Die russische Frage. Schauspiel in drei Auszügen und sieben Bildern*. Berlin: Verlag Bruno Henschel & Sohn, 1947.

Die Sowjetdemokratie und ihre Schöpfer. Berlin: Verlag "Tägliche Rundschau," 1946.

Sozialistische Kulturarbeit. 1. Jahresbericht über die Tätigkeit der Abteilung Kultur und Erziehung des Zentralsekretariats der SED für die

Zeit vom Mai 1946 bis August 1947. Berlin: Dietz Verlag, 1947.

Der Spartakusbund und die Gründung der KPD. Vortragsdisposition Nr. 22. Hg. vom Zentralkomitee der Kommunistischen Partei Deutschlands. Berlin: Verlag Neuer Weg, 1945.

Stalin, Josef. *Fragen des Leninismus*. Berlin: Dietz Verlag, 1951.

_____. *O velikoj otechestvennoj vojne sovjetskogo sojuza*. Moscow: Vojennoe izdatelstvo ministerstva vooruzhennykh sil sojuza SSR, 1949.

_____. *Über die Grundlagen des Leninismus*. Berlin: Verlag Neuer Weg, 1946.

Stalin, der Lenin von heute. Berlin: Verlag "Tägliche Rundschau" [1949].

Staritz, Dieter. *Die Gründung der DDR. Von der sowjetischen Besatzungs-herrschaft zum sozialistischen Staat*. Munich: Deutscher Taschenbuch-verlag, 1984.

_____. "Die SED, Stalin und der 'Aufbau des Sozialismus' in der DDR." *Deutschland Archiv* 7 (1991): 686-700.

Stern, Carola. *Porträt einer bolschewistischen Partei. Entwicklung, Funktion, und Situation der SED*. Cologne: Verlag für Wissenschaft und Politik, 1957.

Stößel, Frank. *Positionen und Strömungen in der KPD/SED 1945-1954*. Cologne: Verlag Wissenschaft und Politik, 1985.

Struck, Peter. "Die Sowjetische Militäradministration in Deutschland (SMAD) und ihr politischer Kontrollapparat." In Hans Lemberg, ed., *Sowjetisches Modell. Kontinuität und Wandel in Ostmitteleuropa nach dem Zweiten Weltkrieg*. Johann-Gottfried-Herder-Institut, Marburg an der Lahn, 1991.

Suckut, Siegfried, ed. *Blockpolitik in der SBZ/DDR. Die Sitzungsprotokolle des zentralen Einheitsfront-Ausschusses*. Cologne: Verlag Wissenschaft und Politik, 1986.

Swayze, Harold. *Political Control of Literature in the USSR, 1946-1959*. Cambridge: Harvard University Press, 1962.

Teschner, Gertraud. "Zum 100. Geburtstag J. W. Stalins." *Neues Deutschland*, 21 December 1979.

Thälmann, Ernst. *Im Kampf gegen die faschistische Diktatur. Rede und Schlußwort des Genossen Ernst Thälmann auf der Parteikonferenz der KPD. im Oktober 1932*. Hg. vom ZK. der KPD., 1932.

Tjulpanov, Sergej. *Deutschland nach dem Kriege 1945-1949. Erinnerungen eines Offiziers der Sowjetarmee*. Berlin: Dietz Verlag, 1987.

Toranska, Teresa. *"Them." Stalin's Polish Puppets*. New York: Harper & Row, 1987.

Über "die Russen" und über uns. Diskussion über ein brennendes Thema. Hg. Verlag Kultur und Fortschritt im Auftrage der GSKS, Groß-Berlin, 1949.

Uhse, Bodo. *Reise- und Tagebücher*. Vol. II. Berlin: Aufbau-Verlag, 1981.

Ulbricht, Walter. *Demokratischer Wirtschaftsaufbau.* Berlin: Verlag Neuer Weg, 1946.

_____. *Die Entwicklung des deutschen volksdemokratischen Staates. 1945-1958.* Berlin: Dietz Verlag, 1958.

_____. *Lehrbuch für den demokratischen Staats- und Wirtschaftsaufbau.* Berlin: Dietz Verlag, 1949.

_____. *Der Plan des demokratischen Neuaufbaus.* Berlin: Verlag Neuer Weg, 1946.

_____. *Warum Nationale Front? Rede auf der Parteiarbeiterkonferenz der SED Groß-Berlin am 17. Mai 1949* [no place, no date].

_____. *Zur Geschichte der deutschen Arbeiterbewegung. Aus Reden und Aufsätzen.* Vol. II: 1933-1946. Berlin: Dietz Verlag, 1953.

_____. *Zur Geschichte der deutschen Arbeiterbewegung. Aus Reden und Aufsätzen.* Vol. II: 1933-1946. Zusatzband. Berlin: Dietz Verlag, 1966.

_____. *Zur Geschichte der deutschen Arbeiterbewegung. Aus Reden und Aufsätzen.* Vol. II: 1933-1946. 2. Zusatzband. Berlin: Dietz Verlag, 1968.

_____. *Zur Geschichte der deutschen Arbeiterbewegung. Aus Reden und Aufsätzen.* Vol. III: 1946-1950. Berlin: Dietz Verlag, 1953.

_____. *Zur Geschichte der deutschen Arbeiterbewegung. Aus Reden und Aufsätzen.* Vol. III: 1946-1950. Zusatzband. Berlin: Dietz Verlag, 1971.

Um Deutschlands neue Kultur, Aufruf und Ansprachen gehalten bei der Gründungs-Kundgebung des Kulturbundes zur demokratischen Erneuerung Deutschlands für die Provinz Sachsen am 14. Oktober 1945 in Halle (Saale). Halle, 1946.

Um die Erneuerung der deutschen Kultur. Dokumente zur Kulturpolitik 1945-1949. Berlin: Dietz Verlag, 1983.

Um die Erneuerung der deutschen Kultur. Erste Zentrale Kulturtagung der Kommunistischen Partei Deutschlands vom 3. bis 5. Februar. Stenographische Niederschrift. Berlin: Verlag Neuer Weg, 1946.

Unser Weg. Veröffentlichung der Landesleitung Brandenburg des Kulturbundes zur demokratischen Erneuerung Deutschlands anläßlich der ersten Wiederkehr des Gründungstages des Kulturbundes. Potsdam, 1946.

Vier Jahre Kulturbund. Aus seiner Arbeit [no place, no date.]

40. Parteitag der Sozialdemokratischen Partei Deutschlands. Berlin: Vorwärts-Verlag, 1946.

Die Wahrheit über Amerika. Als Manuskript gedruckt. Nur für den inneren Gebrauch bestimmt! Potsdam: Kulturbund zur demokratischen Erneuerung Deutschlands, 1950.

Weber, Hermann, ed. *Parteiensystem zwischen Demokratie und Volksdemokratie.* Cologne: Verlag Wissenschaft und Politik, 1982.

Weber, Hermann. *Geschichte der DDR.* Munich: Deutscher Taschenbuchverlag, 1985.

_____. "Schauprozeß-Vorbereitungen in der DDR." Paper presented at the Internationales wissenschaftliches Symposium an der Universität Mannheim: "'Weiße Flecken' in der Geschichte des Weltkommunismus—Stalinistischer Terror und 'Säuberungen' in den kommunistischen Parteien Europas seit den dreißiger Jahren," Mannheim, Germany, 22-25 February 1992.

Weinert, Erich. "Kulturarbeit nach der Befreiung [17 May 1947]," *Neue Deutsche Literatur* 4 (1980): 5-35.

Weiss, Grigorij. *Am Abend nach dem Kriege. Erinnerungen eines sowjetischen Kulturoffiziers.* Berlin: Verlag der Nation, 1981.

Der Weltfriedenskongreß. Ein Material für Referenten. Hg. vom Kulturbund zur demokratischen Erneuerung Deutschlands [1948].

Wilhelm Pieck. Dem Vorkämpfer für ein neues Deutschland zum 70. Geburtstag. Berlin: Verlag Neuer Weg, 1946.

Willmann, Heinz. *Steine klopft man mit dem Kopf. Lebenserinnerungen.* Berlin: Verlag Neues Leben, 1977.

_____. *Zwei Jahre Kulturbund. Tätigkeitsbericht.* Berlin: Aufbau Verlag, 1947.

Winzer, Otto. *Sozialistische Politik? Eine kritische Stellungnahme zu Reden und Aufsätzen von Dr. Kurt Schumacher.* Berlin: Dietz Verlag, 1947.

Wolin, B. M. *Der Kampf um den Sieg des Sozialismus in der UdSSR.* Berlin: SWA-Verlag, 1947.

Zhdanov, Andrej. *Über die internationale Lage.* Berlin: SWA-Verlag, 1947.

Zur Kritik des deutschen Kulturschaffens. Sichtung und Auswahl. Material für Vorträge in den Wirkungsgruppen des Kulturbundes zur demokratischen Erneuerung Deutschlands, Land Thüringen. Weimar, 1948.

Zur Verbesserung unserer Kulturarbeit. Entschließung des 1. Landeskulturtages am 14. und 15. August 1948 in Potsdam. SED. Landesverband Brandenburg, Abt. Parteischulung, Kultur und Erziehung, 1948.

Zwei Jahre Wirkungsgruppe Chemnitz des Kulturbundes zur demokratischen Erneuerung Deutschlands. Chemnitz, 1947.

Der Zweijahresplan ist eine kulturelle Großtat. 1. Sozialistischer Kulturtag. Leipzig, 20. - 21. November 1948 [no place, no date].

Der Zweijahrplan und die Kulturschaffenden. Protokoll der gemeinsamen Tagung des Kulturbundes zur demokratischen Erneuerung Deutschlands, des Freien Deutschen Gewerkschaftsbundes und der Gewerkschaft Kunst und Schrifttum am 28. und 29. Oktober 1948. Hg. vom Kulturbund zur demokratischen Erneuerung Deutschlands und vom Freien Deutschen Gewerkschaftsbund. Berlin: Aufbau-Verlag, 1949.

Index

In this index, an "f" after a number indicates a separate reference on the next page, and an "ff" indicates separate references on the next two pages. A continuous discussion over two or more pages is indicated by a span of page numbers, e.g., "pp. 57-58." *Passim* is used for a cluster of references in close but not consecutive sequence.

Library of Congress Cataloging-in-Publication Data

Pike, David, 1950
    The politics of culture in Soviet-occupied Germany,
1945-1949 / David Pike.
      p.   cm.
    Includes bibliographical references and index.
    ISBN 0-8047-2093-2 (alk. paper) :
    1. Germany, East—Politics and government.   2. Kommunistische
Partei Deutschlands—History.   I. Title
DD285.P55 1992   92-21441
320.9431'09'044—dc20   CIP